Autodesk AutoCAD 2027 Fundamentals

Elise Moss

AUTODESK Certified Instructor
SILVER

AUTODESK
Authorized Developer

SDC PUBLICATIONS

SDC Publications
P.O. Box 1334
Mission, KS 66222
913-262-2664
www.SDCpublications.com
Publisher: Stephen Schroff

ISBN-13: 978-1-63057-801-5
ISBN-10: 1-63057-801-0

Printed and bound in the United States of America.

Preface

No textbook can cover all the features in any software application. This textbook is meant for beginning users who want to gain a familiarity with the tools and interface of AutoCAD before they start exploring on their own. By the end of the text, users should feel comfortable enough to create a basic drawing. This textbook covers the topics users are tested on for proficiency for the AutoCAD certification exam.

The files used in this text are accessible from the Internet from the book's page on the publisher's website: www.SDCpublications.com. They are free and available to students and teachers alike.

We value customer input. Please contact us with any comments, questions, or concerns about this text.

Elise Moss
elise_moss@mossdesigns.com

Acknowledgements from Elise Moss

This book would not have been possible without the support of some key Autodesk employees.

The effort and support of the editorial and production staff of SDC Publications is gratefully acknowledged. I especially thank Stephen Schroff for his helpful suggestions regarding the format of this text.

Finally, truly infinite thanks to Ari for his encouragement and his faith.

- Elise Moss

About the Author

Elise Moss has written articles for Autodesk's Toplines magazine, AUGI's PaperSpace, DigitalCAD.com and Tenlinks.com. She has taught CAD classes at Santa Clara University, Laney College, San Francisco State University, DeAnza College, Silicon Valley College, and for Autodesk resellers. Autodesk has named her as a Faculty of Distinction for the curriculum she has developed for Autodesk products. She holds a baccalaureate of science degree in Mechanical Engineering from San Jose State. She continues to work as a mechanical engineer in Silicon Valley.

Elise is a third-generation engineer. Her father, Robert Moss, was a metallurgical engineer in the aerospace industry. Her grandfather, Solomon Kupperman, was a civil engineer for the City of Chicago. Her son Benjamin is an electrical engineer. Her son Daniel is a structural designer.

She can be contacted via email at elise_moss@mossdesigns.com.

More information about the author and her work can be found on her website at www.mossdesigns.com.

Other books by Elise Moss

Autodesk Revit Architecture 2027 Basics
AutoCAD Architecture 2027 Fundamentals

Table of Contents

Notes:

Lesson 1.0 – The AutoCAD Environment

Objectives

This section introduces the interface available within AutoCAD starting with the Pointing Device. The AutoCAD window includes the Pull-Down (POP) menus, Toolbars, the Drawing Window, Command Prompt, Work Spaces, Ribbon, and Status Bar. In addition, you will learn special Keyboard options and Shortcut (Cursor) menus, how to use the Dialog Boxes, and how to access AutoCAD's on-line Help.

- **Work Space**

  Customize which menus and toolbars are available; modify the appearance of the work environment.

- **Pointing Device**

  Use the mouse for selecting options in the AutoCAD window.

- **Shortcut Menus**

  Right-click your pointing device to display context sensitive Shortcut (Cursor) menus.

- **AutoCAD Window**

  The AutoCAD window consists of the following areas:

- **Title Bar**

  Minimize and maximize the AutoCAD window from the title bar.

- **Pull-Down Menu**

  Select commands from the Pull-Down (POP) menu headings.

- **Toolbars**

  Use AutoCAD toolbars as another method for selecting commands.

- **Drawing Window**

  Create your drawing and drawing layouts in this area.

- **Command Prompt**

  The Command Prompt will prompt you for the next step.

- **Status Bar**

  This area contains handy toggle switches and displays the x,y,z coordinates.

- **Dialog Boxes**

  Create your drawing and drawing layouts in this area.

- **Keyboard Options**

  Use the keyboard to type command options, text, or press Escape to cancel commands.

- **Help Menu**

  Use the AutoCAD Help menu to learn more about the program.

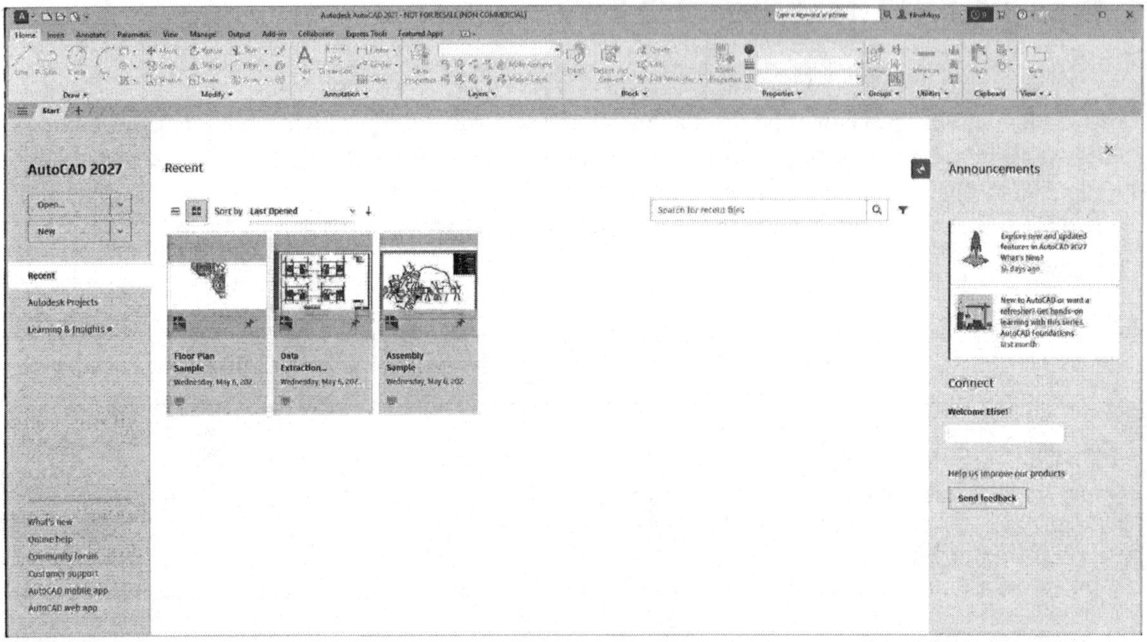

The Start tab acts as a launch pad for users. You can see a list of Recent Documents, open files, get access to files stored on the cloud, and access learning resources.

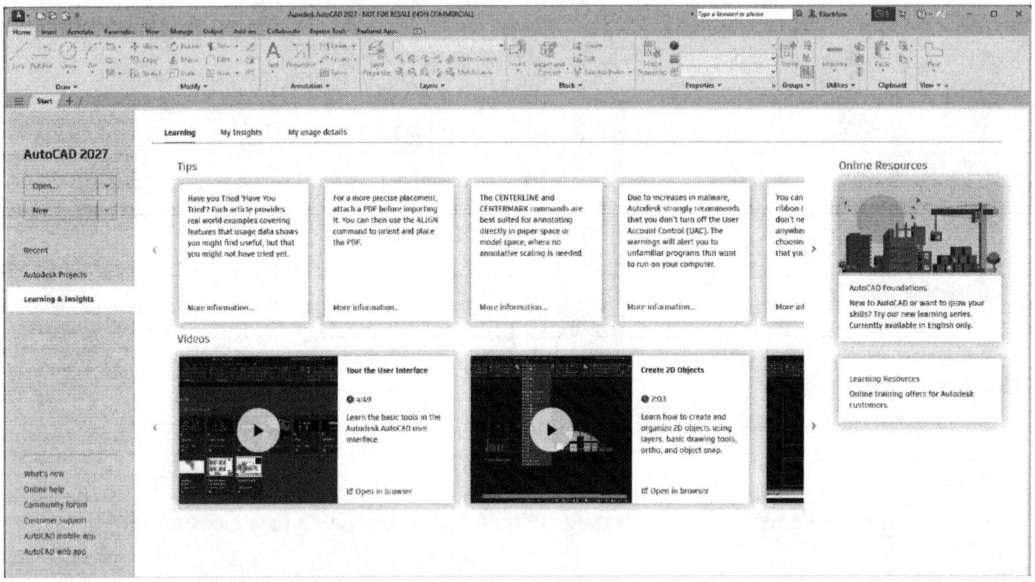

If you click the Learning link on the left bar, you will see a series of tips as well as videos to help you get started.

The Autodesk Projects link connects you to the Desktop Connector service. This is a separate installation. You can download the Desktop Connector software for free from Autodesk's website. In order to use it, you need to have a login account with Autodesk. The service allows you to access files you have stored in Dropbox or other cloud services, but you will need to set up access to each of your cloud accounts.

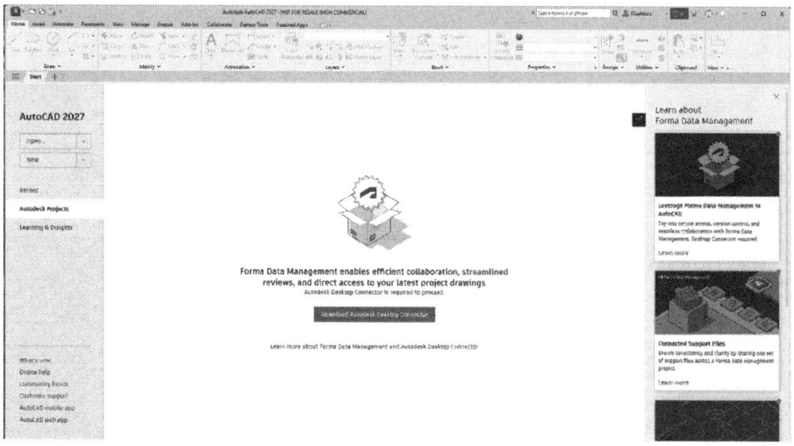

The 2027 release includes Forma Data Management which allows users to share documents between teams.

Forma Data Management replaces Autodesk Docs.

Both are paid services. They basically act as cloud storage and the cost depends on how much storage you need.

Work Space

Command Overview

The Workspace tool allows you to customize the appearance of your work environment.

By default, AutoCAD comes with three defined workspaces:

3D Modeling, Drafting & Annotation, and 3D Basics.

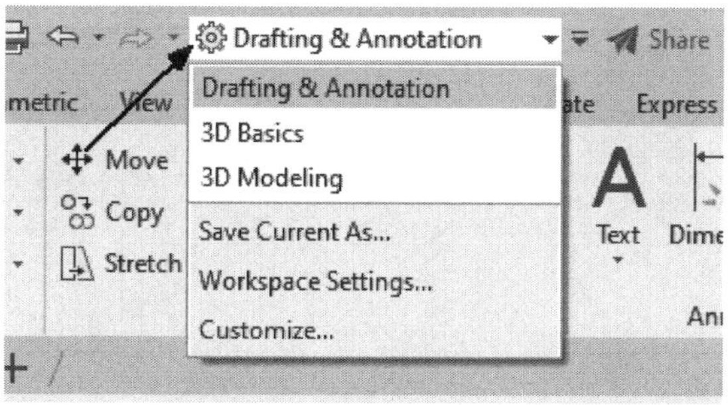

Accessing Workspaces on the Quick Access toolbar

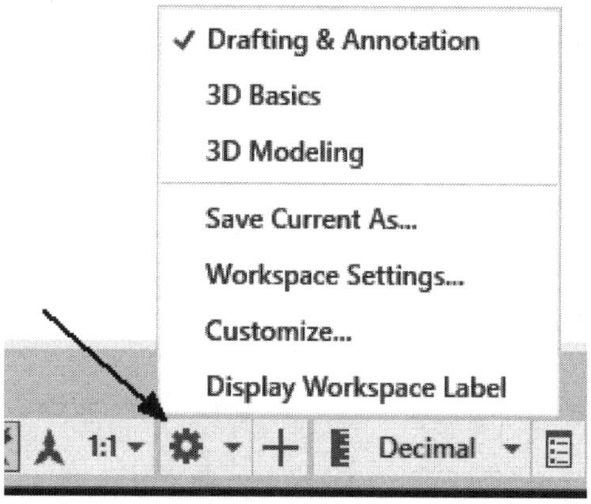

Accessing Workspaces on the Status bar

Workspaces can be accessed in different locations on your screen: the Quick Access Toolbar and in the Status Bar.

If you want to save your current work environment (system settings, active toolbars, and menus) simply select 'Save Current As' to apply the active settings to a new or existing workspace.

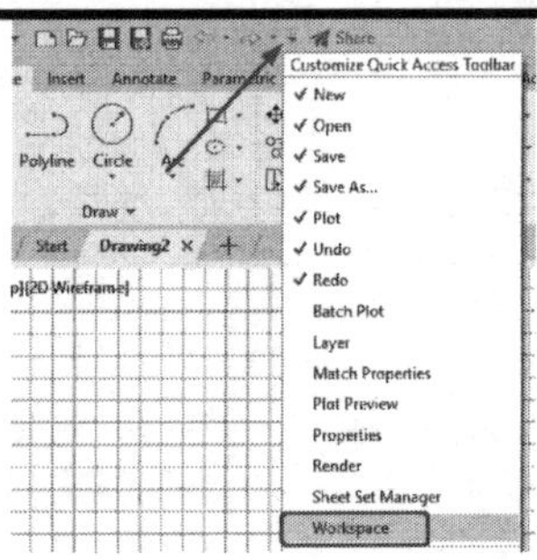

Select the down arrow on the Quick Access Toolbar to add or remove tools from the toolbar.

Place a check by left clicking on the item to add it to the toolbar.

Drawing Tabs

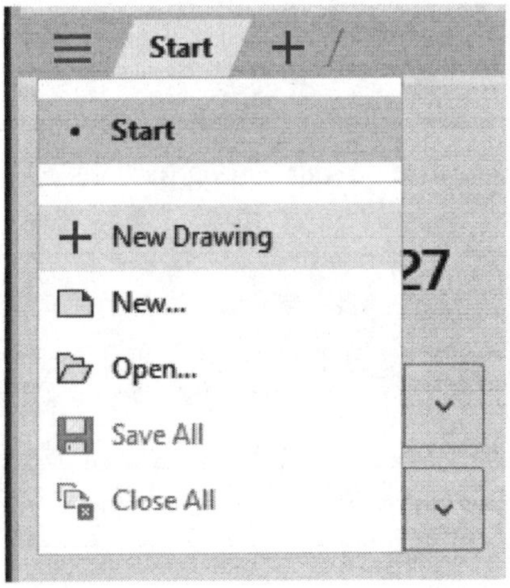

Drawing tabs allow you to quickly switch from one open drawing to another. The three horizontal lines tab provides a drop-down list that allows you to start a new drawing using an assigned template, start a new drawing and search for a desired template, open an existing drawing, save all the active drawings, or close all the active drawings.

The Start tab opens the launch pad area.

The + tab creates a new drawing using an assigned template.

Command Exercise

Exercise 1-1 - Workspace

Drawing Name: **(none, start from scratch)**
Estimated Time to Completion: 5 Minutes

Scope

1. *Create a workspace called My AutoCAD.*
2. *Close the Tool Palettes.*
3. *Locate the My AutoCAD workspace on the toolbar.*
4. *Set the My AutoCAD workspace as Current.*

Solution

1. 

Click the + tab on the Launch window to start a new drawing.

2. 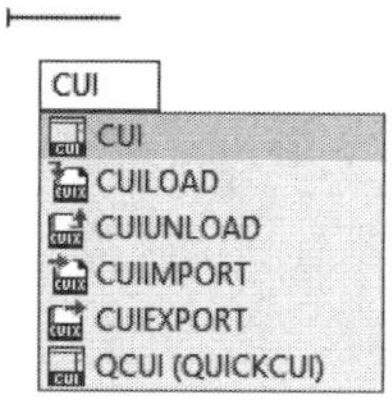

Type **CUI** on the command line or in the drawing window.

3. 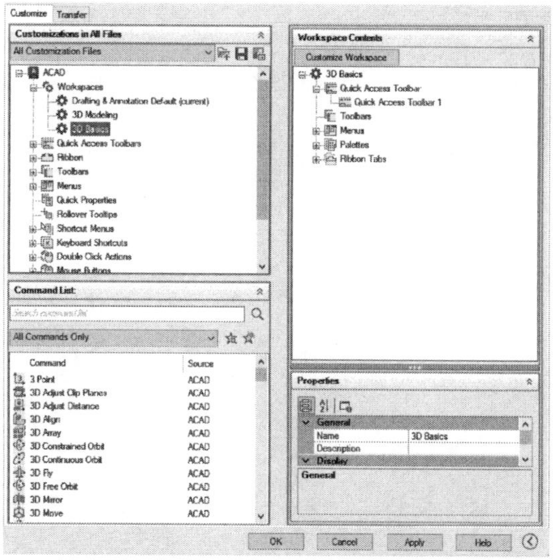

The Customize User Interface dialog appears.

This dialog allows you to customize your work environment.

4. 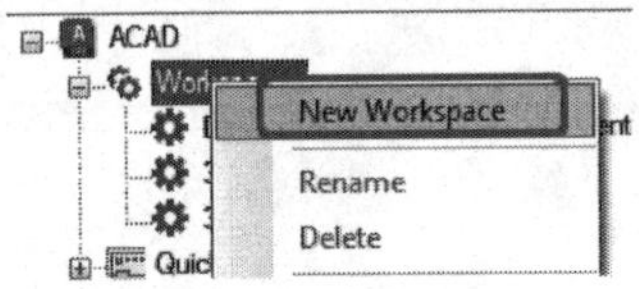

Highlight **Workspaces**.

Right click and select **New Workspace.**

5. 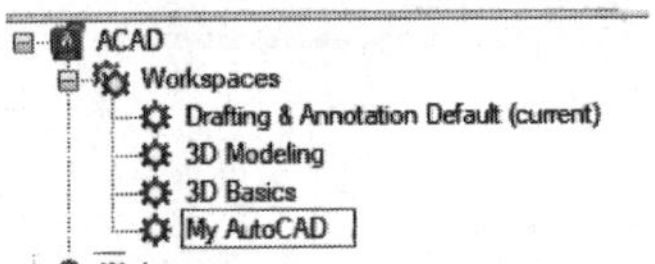

Rename the new workspace **My AutoCAD**.

6. 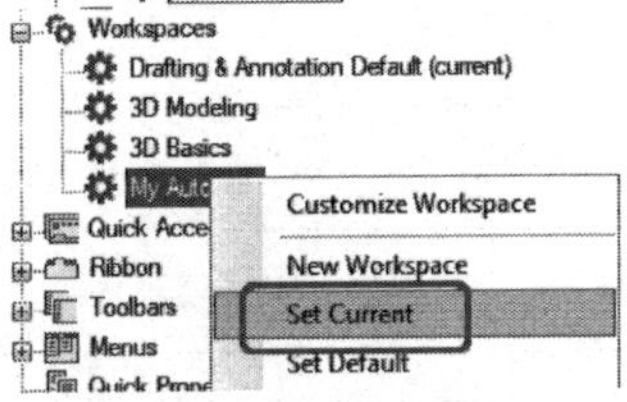

Right click on the new workspace and select **Set Current.**

7. 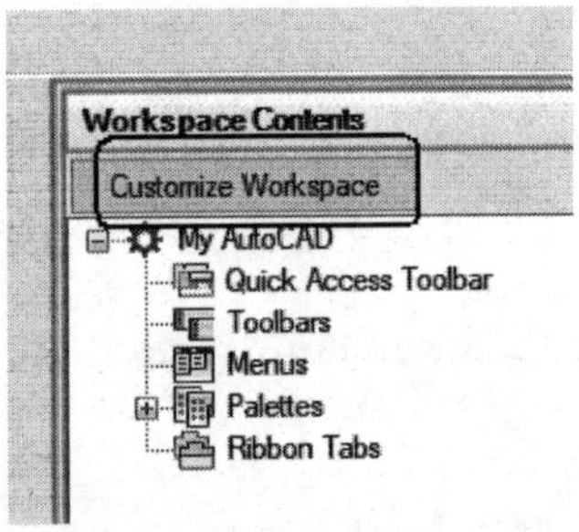

Click on the **Customize Workspace** button in the top right panel.

8. 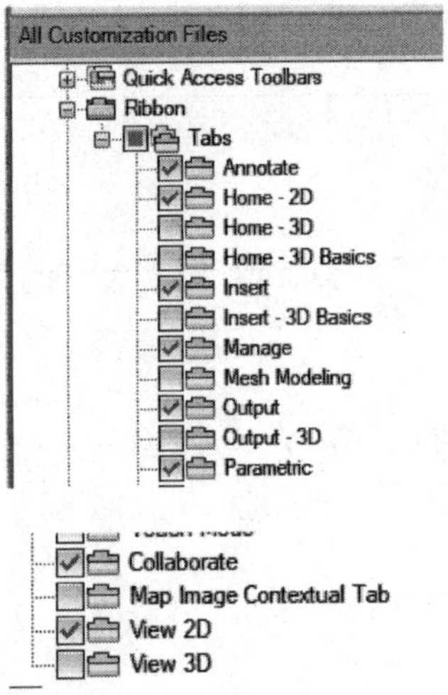

Place a check next to the following under the Ribbon Tabs folder in the left panel:

- Annotate
- Home - 2D
- Insert
- Manage
- Output
- Parametric
- Collaborate
- View 2D

9. 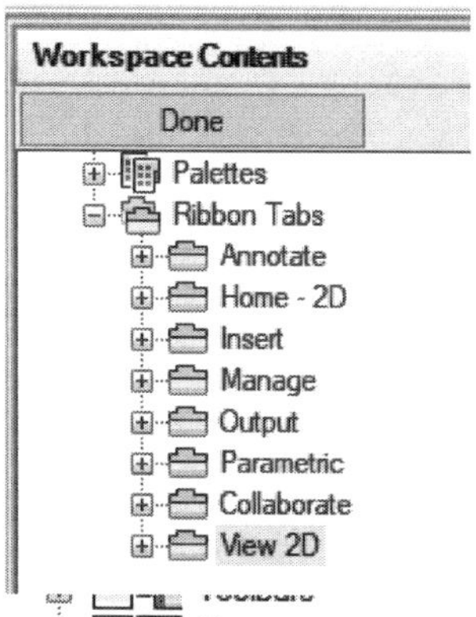

Notice how the tabs are added in the right panel as they are checked.

10. 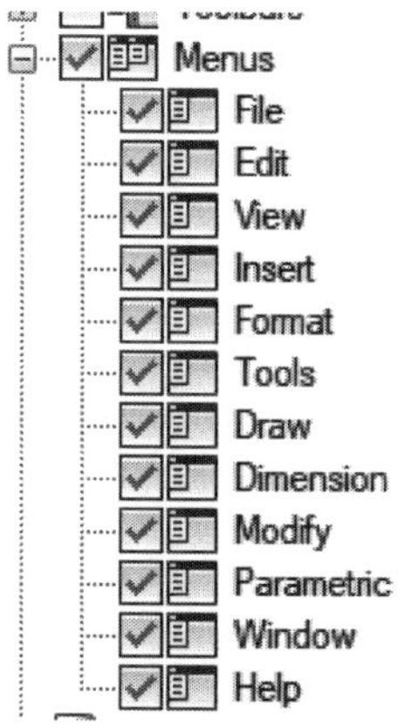

Place a check next to all the Menus to add the Menus to the workspace.

11. 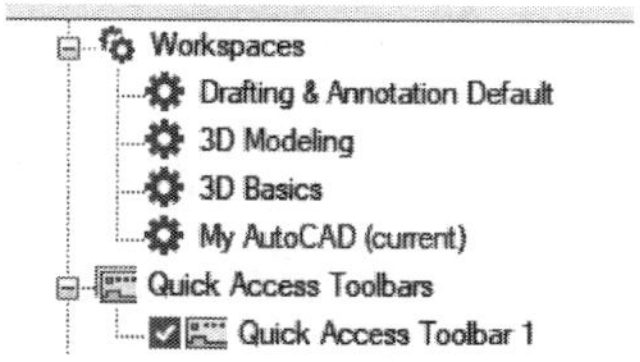

Place a check next to the Quick Access Toolbar 1.

12. 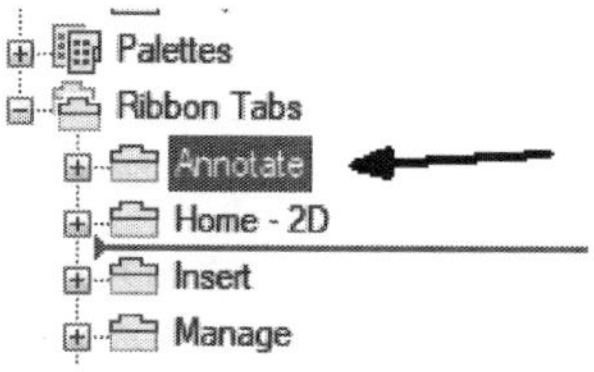

Drag the Annotate ribbon tab below the Home-2D tab.

13. 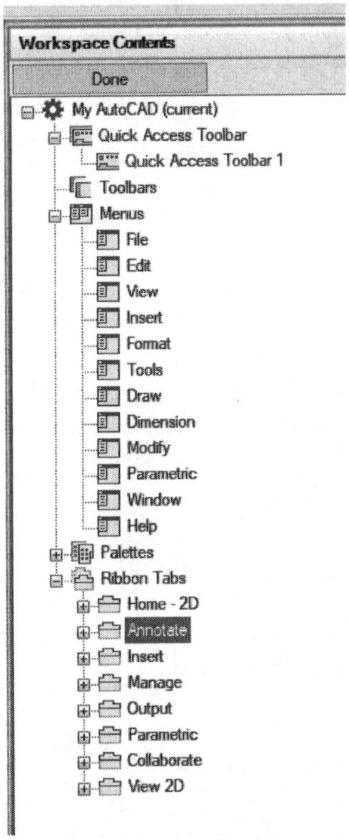

Check in the right side pane.

Verify that the Quick Access Toolbar 1, the menus, and the ribbon tabs are shown.

Click **Done.**

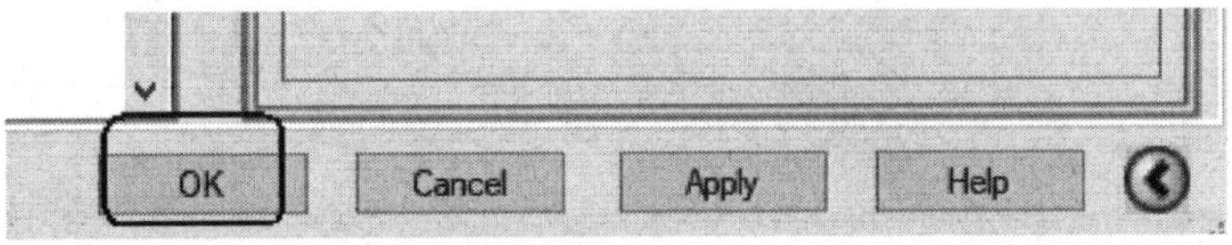

Click **OK** to close the dialog box.

When you click OK, your changes are saved and the dialog box will close.

When you click Apply, your changes are saved and the dialog box remains open. You can then preview any changes before you click OK to close the dialog box.

14. 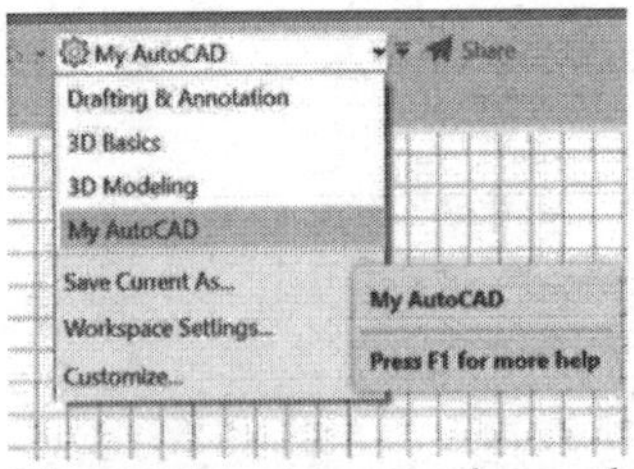

The workspace drop-down list now includes **My AutoCAD.**

Select the **My AutoCAD** workspace.

15. The workspace now shows the ribbon tabs that were selected.

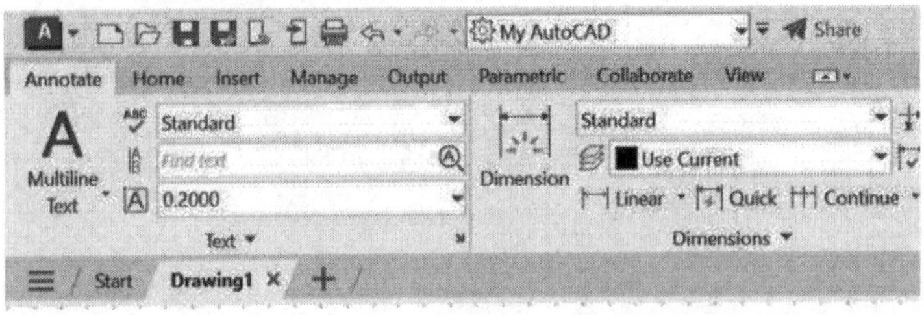

16. Switch to the **Drafting & Annotation** workspace.

Compare the tabs listed.

You can drag and drop to rearrange the menu tabs. See if you can move the Home menu to the first position in the My AutoCAD workspace so it looks like the Drafting & Annotation workspace.

Pointing Device—Mouse

Command Overview

Use the pointing device to select objects and options. This tutorial reviews the functions of a two or three-button mouse, though there are other pointing devices available. The pointing device is configured in the *Systems Tab* in the *Options* dialog box. The default setting is automatically set to the "current system pointing" device; this will typically be a two button mouse, the three button mouse, or the Microsoft IntelliMouse®. The left button (LMB) is typically the Pick button and the right button (RMB) is the <ENTER> button. Pressing the <ENTER> button when the cursor is in the Drawing Window activates a Shortcut Menu with the option to repeat the last command. This feature can be disabled in the *User Preferences* Tab of the *Options* dialog box, by removing the checkmark from "Shortcut menus in drawing area."

If this option is selected, pressing the right button on the mouse (RMB) will either execute a command, proceed with the command (by accepting the default option), or if the Command Prompt is blank, repeat the last command. Using shift + the <ENTER> button activates the Object Snap shortcut menu. These shortcut menus will be covered later.

Two Button Mouse:

Button	Action
Left (LMB)	Use to pick or select objects or options
Right (RMB)	Use to <ENTER> to complete the command, repeat the last command, or access a context sensitive cursor menu
Shift + Right (RMB)	Brings up the Object Snap cursor menu

Three Button Mouse:

Left (LMB)	Use to pick or select objects or options
Right (RMB)	Use to <ENTER> to complete the command, repeat the last command, or access a context sensitive cursor menu
Middle Button	Brings up the Object Snap cursor menu

Microsoft Intellimouse:

Button	Action
Left (LMB)	Use to pick or select objects or options
Right (RMB)	Use to <ENTER> to complete the command, repeat the last command, or access a context sensitive cursor menu
Shift + Right (RMB)	Brings up the Object Snap cursor menu
Middle Button (press + drag)	Use to pan the drawing
Middle Button (roll)	Use to zoom the drawing

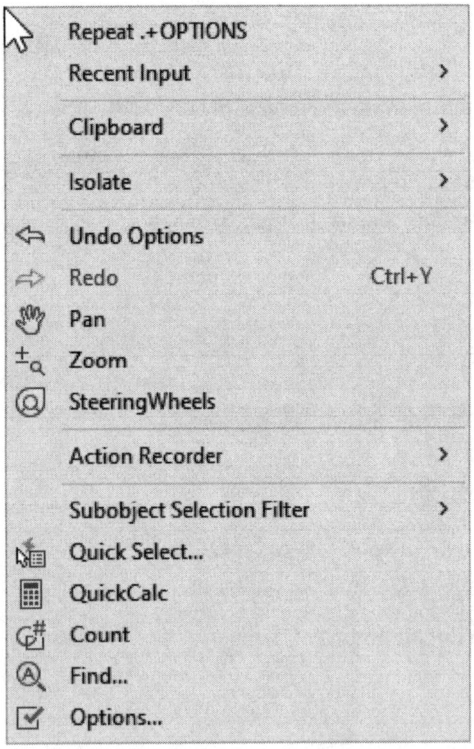

The RMB Shortcut Menu

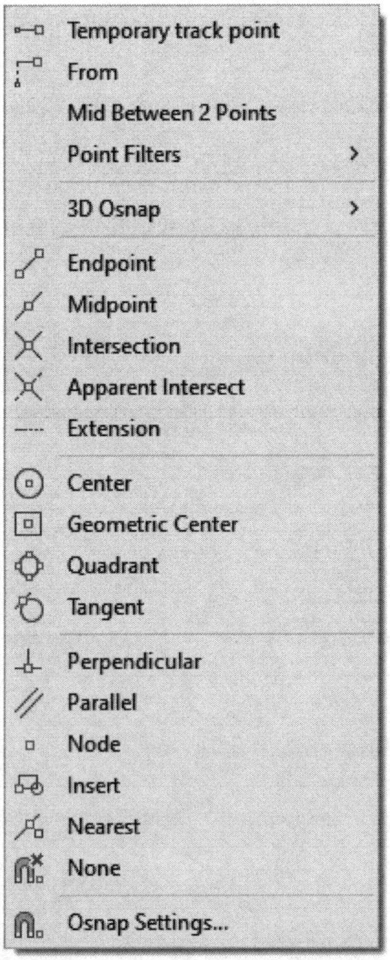

The Shift + RMB Shortcut Menu

General Procedures

1. Pick a command from the toolbar using the left button on the mouse.
2. Follow the Command Prompt prompts.
3. Press <ENTER> to complete the command or continue to the next step. Press <ENTER> again to repeat the command or select a choice from the Shortcut menu.

Tips & Tricks

- Picking in a blank area of the drawing window will create a selection window. Press escape to cancel this selection window, or simply make the other corner.
- Making a selection window from right to left will select all objects the window crosses. Making a selection window from left to right will only select the objects completely within the selection window.
- Picking objects in the drawing window when the Command Prompt is blank will highlight the objects and display the *grips*. Press Escape (**Esc** on the keyboard) two times to cancel the grips and the selection.
- The left and right button functions can be reversed from the Windows Settings menu (from the Start bar). Select "Control Panel" then select "Mouse."

Command Exercise

Exercise 1-2 – Using the Mouse

Drawing Name: **(none, start from scratch)**
Estimated Time to Completion: 5 Minutes

Scope

Practice the Left and Right button mouse functions:

1. *Draw line segments.*
2. *Press the right button on the mouse to repeat the line command.*
3. *Practice selecting a single object.*
4. *Practice making a selection window.*
5. *Activate the object snap shortcut (cursor) menu.*
6. *Activate the toolbar shortcut menu.*
7. *Activate the Command Prompt shortcut menu.*

Solution

1. 

Click the + tab on the Launch page to create a new drawing.

2. 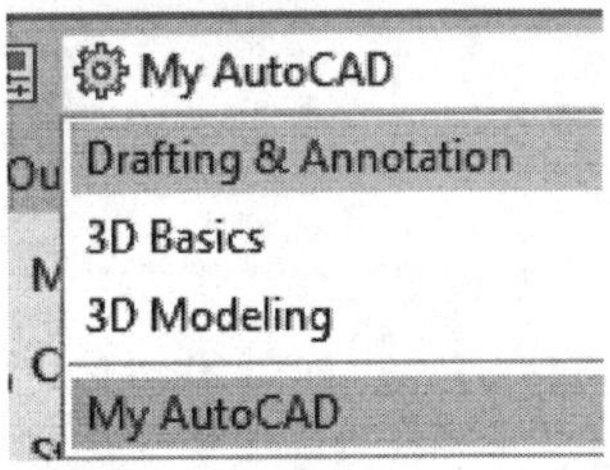

Set the Workspace to **Drafting & Annotation**.

3. 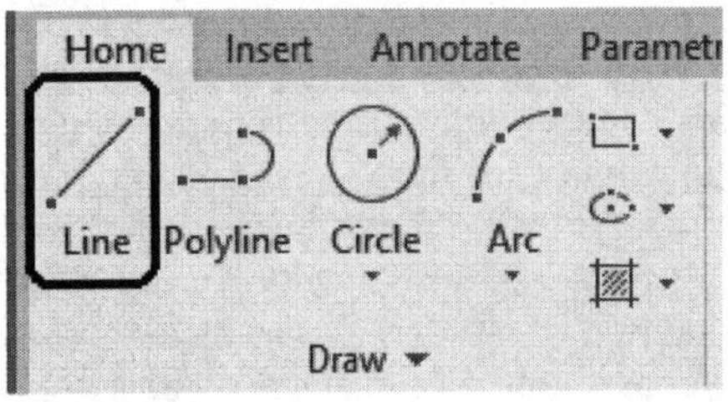

Locate the **line** command on the Home tab of the ribbon and draw some line segments.

Left click to place the points that define a line.

The shortcut for Line is 'L'.

Left click to place a second point for the line.

4. 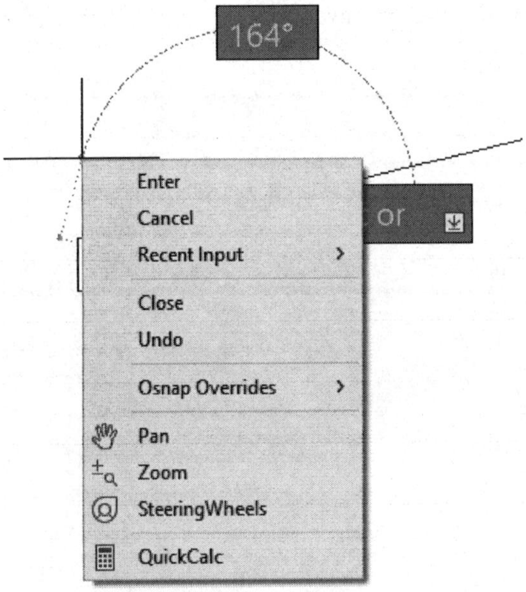

Press the right button on the mouse.

This will bring up a context sensitive cursor menu.

Select '**Enter**' to complete the line command, so that the Command Prompt is blank.

5. 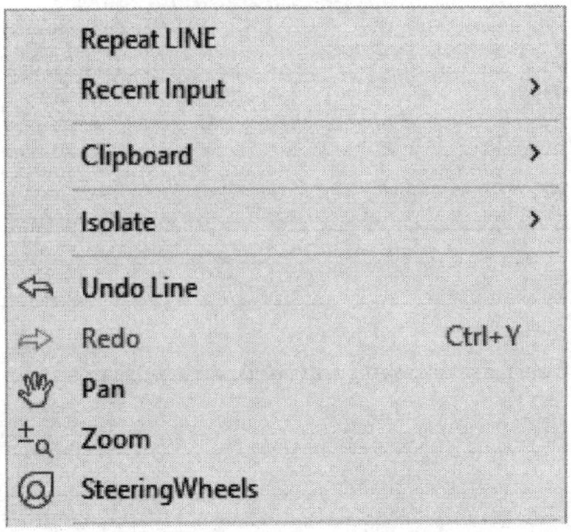

Press the right button on the mouse again.

This will bring up a context sensitive cursor menu.

Select 'Repeat Line' to repeat the line command.

Left click to place some points to define the line.

Complete the line command by clicking ENTER.

The Command Prompt should be blank.

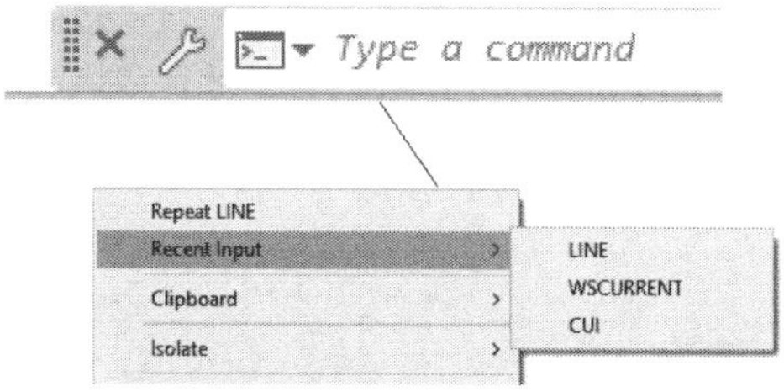

Note that if you right click and expand Recent Input, you can select any of your most recent commands.

6. Select one of the line segments by clicking it with the mouse.

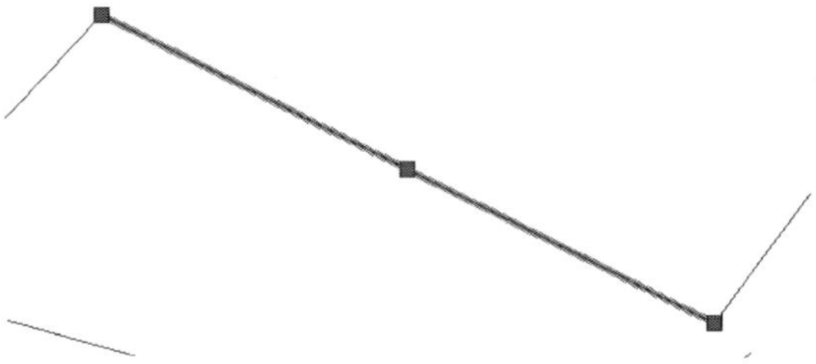

Notice that it is highlighted and notice the grips (these are the blue boxes on the line).

7. Press <ESC> once to cancel and clear the grips.

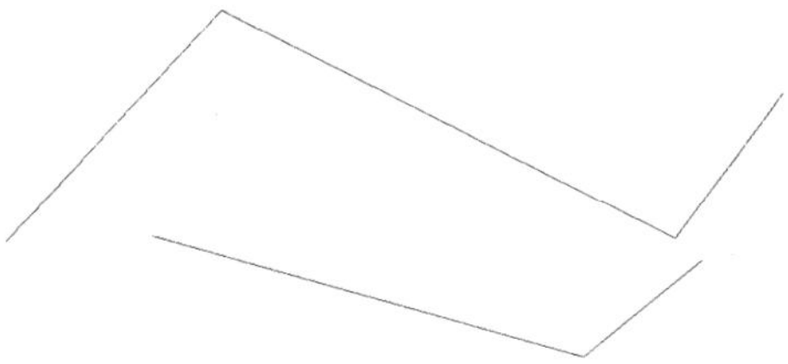

8. Pick in the blank area of the drawing.

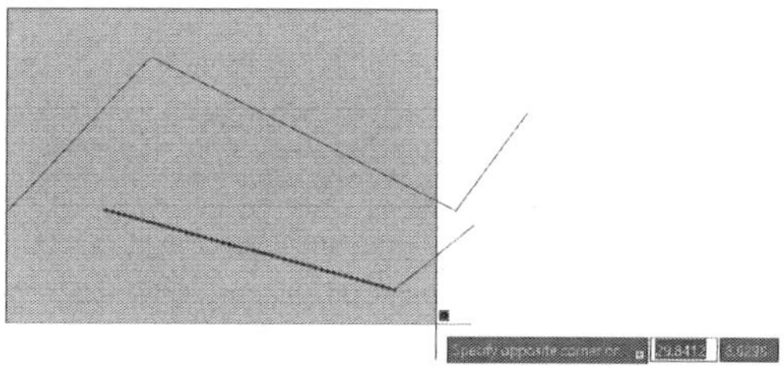

Move the mouse towards the right.

Notice this will create a rectangular selection window. You will be prompted to select the other corner. Make the selection window from Left to Right and notice that only the objects completely within the window will be selected. Press <ESC> to cancel the selection.

Now make the window from right to left and notice that the lines that are crossed by the selection box are now highlighted. Press <ESC> again to exit.

9. 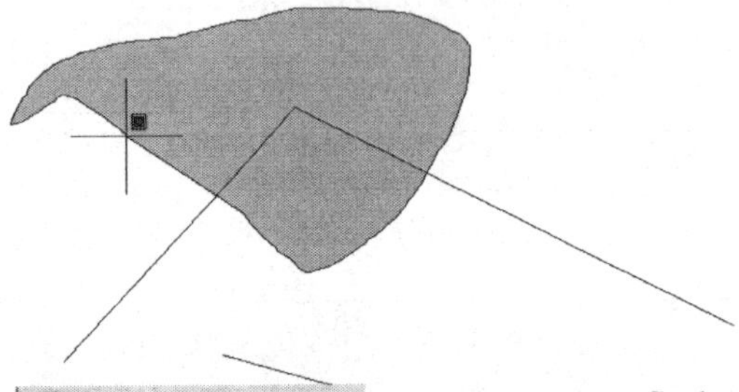

If you hold down the left mouse button, this puts you in LASSO mode to select objects.

10. 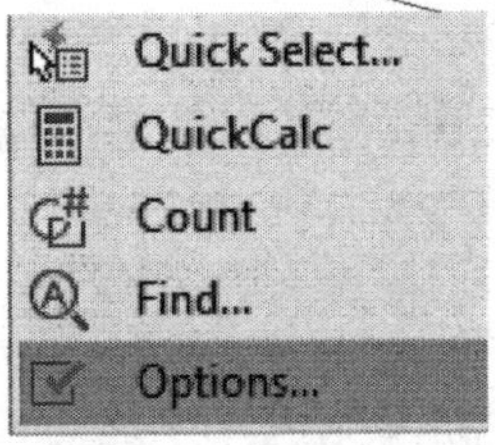

Many users find LASSO mode annoying. To turn it off, right click anywhere in the display window and select OPTIONS from the shortcut menu.

11. 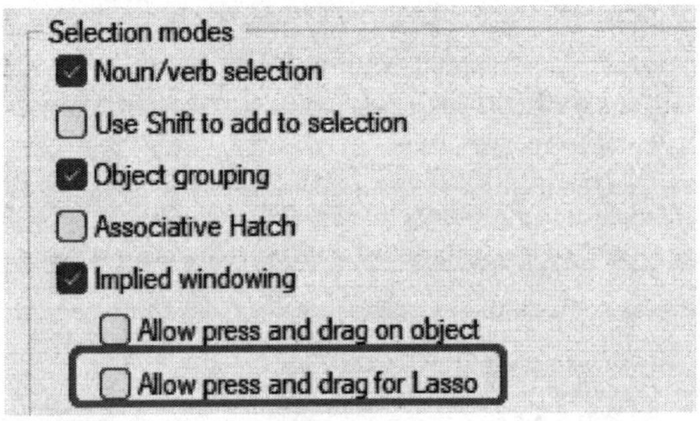

Click the **Selection t**ab.

Disable **Allow press and drag for Lasso**. Click **OK** to close the dialog box.

Extra: *If you have the Microsoft Intellimouse, roll the middle button to zoom the drawing in and out. Press the middle button and drag to pan.*

Tips & Tricks

- *To turn off the rollover help tips, type ROLLOVERTIPS on the Command Prompt and enter 0.*

AutoCAD Window
Overview

The AutoCAD window consists of a Title Bar, Pull-Down Menus, Toolbars, a Drawing Window, the Ribbon, the Command Prompt, and the Status Bar.

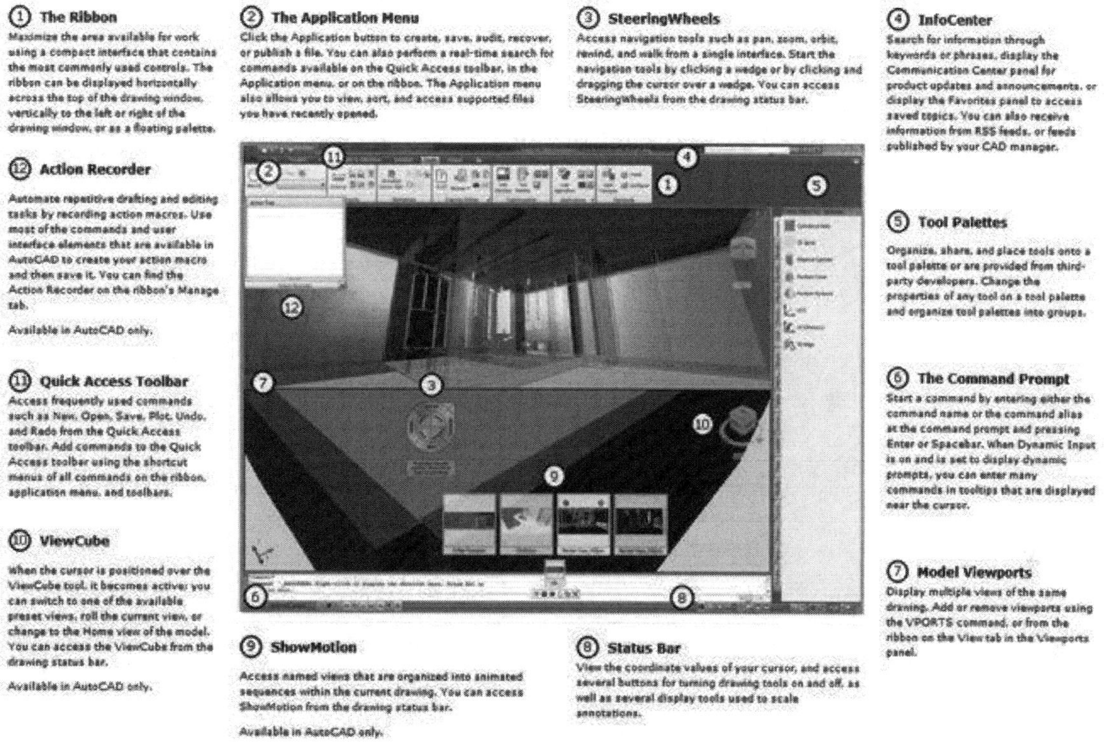

- Remember to press the <ENTER> key after typing a command, a command alias, or a system variable.
- Commands, aliases, or system variables are not case sensitive.
- A *default* is the most common or last option selected and will be shown in parentheses. Press <ENTER> to accept the default. It is not necessary to type the default over again.
- When in doubt about a command location, type it (and remember to press <ENTER>). This will usually begin the desired command.

AutoCAD Window Detail	Location	Function Overview
Title Bar	Top	• Lists the name of the current drawing. • Contains buttons to minimize, maximize or exit AutoCAD. • Contains buttons to minimize, maximize or close the current drawing.
Pull-Down Menu	Beneath the Title Bar	• Lists AutoCAD commands by category. • Also referred to as "POP." • Words followed by a black arrow will display an additional list of related options. • Words followed by an *ellipsis* (…) will open a *dialog box.*
Toolbars	Docked at sides or floating in the drawing window	• Displays commands as icons (buttons) in related toolbar categories. • The toolbar pictured in the top row is the *Standard Toolbar*. • The toolbar beneath it is the *Object Properties Toolbar.* • Accessing a command from a toolbar is usually a faster, more direct approach. • The toolbars contain most of the commands, but not all of them.
Tool Palettes	Floating or Docked	• Displays commands, blocks, or hatches as icons (buttons) in related categories. • The Tool Palette can be set to be transparent, so you can see drawing objects underneath. • You can set the properties of the tools on the Tool Palette. For example, you can set a line tool to always place on a specific layer and/or line type. • You can create a Tool Palette for all your blocks. • You can hide or display Tool Palettes easily.
Drawing Window	Middle area	• Area where the drawing is created. • The Model tab is for creating the drawing or 3-dimensional model. • The Layout tabs are for creating the finished layout for plotting or printing.
Command Prompt	Bottom	• Area where AutoCAD prompts the user for the next step. • The user must press <ENTER> after typing the Command or Command Prompt options. • The escape key (ESC) will cancel any command leaving the Command Prompt blank and ready for the next command. • Ctl+9 displays or hides the Command Prompt window.

Status Bar	Beneath the Command Prompt	• Displays the coordinates of the cursor location. • Displays the ON/OFF status of special toggle switches. • Single-click to toggle these options ON or OFF.
Dynamic Input	At the end of the cursor	• When DYN is enabled, you can close the Command Prompt window and enter prompts at a smaller window located at the end of the cursor.

Title Bar

Overview

The Title Bar will display the name of the drawing. Buttons are displayed in the upper right-hand corner to minimize, maximize, re-size, or close the AutoCAD window or an individual drawing file. Remember that when any program is minimized, it will remain listed in the Start Bar.

General Procedures

To maximize the AutoCAD Window, select the following icon:	
To maximize the Drawing Window, select the following icon:	
To minimize the AutoCAD or Drawing Windows, select the Minimize button.	
To bring the AutoCAD Window to the foreground, select AutoCAD from the Start bar.	
AutoCAD has tabs to allow for easy switching between drawing files.	

- Keep the AutoCAD and Drawing windows maximized for optimum drawing space.
- Use the Alt+Tab keys to alternate between programs, or select the program from the Start bar.
- Practice Minimizing and Maximizing the AutoCAD and Drawing Windows.

Drawing Window

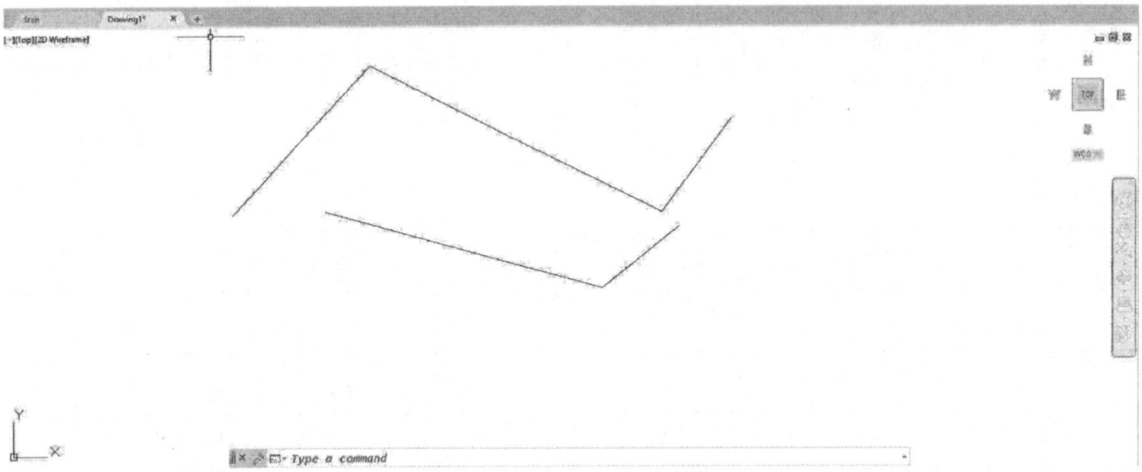

Overview

When working in the Drawing Window, be sure that the Model Tab is selected. Later this text will cover how to create a drawing Layout. The cursor must be in the Drawing window in order to pick points for drawing objects, or select objects to modify. Right-click in the drawing window to execute a command, proceed with the next step of the command, or if the Command Prompt is blank, repeat the last command. Picking (LMB) in a blank area of the drawing window will initiate a selection window or box. You must pick the opposite corner whether you want to select an object or not, or press Escape to cancel the selection window. Multiple drawings may be opened in one AutoCAD session. Minimize a drawing window, or use the options from the **Window** Pull-Down menu to select the current drawing. Close the drawings that are not being used.

Command Prompt

Command Prompt Overview

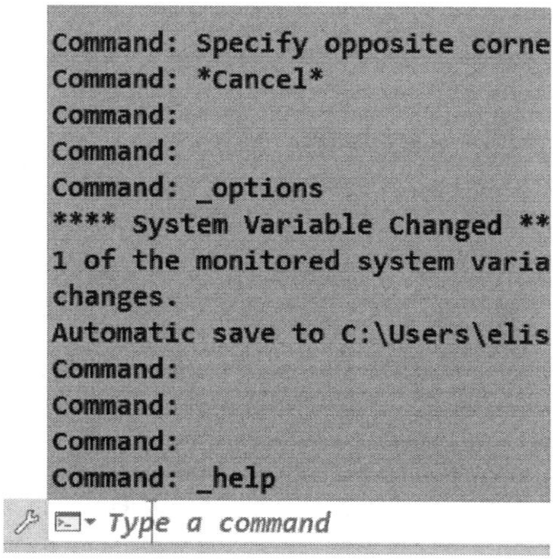

The F2 function key will open the AutoCAD Text Window, which will display all previous Command Prompts. These lines can be viewed and copied, but they cannot be changed. Left click in the drawing window to close the AutoCAD Text Window.

There are two icons on the left of the command prompt window.
The first accesses a shortcut menu as shown.

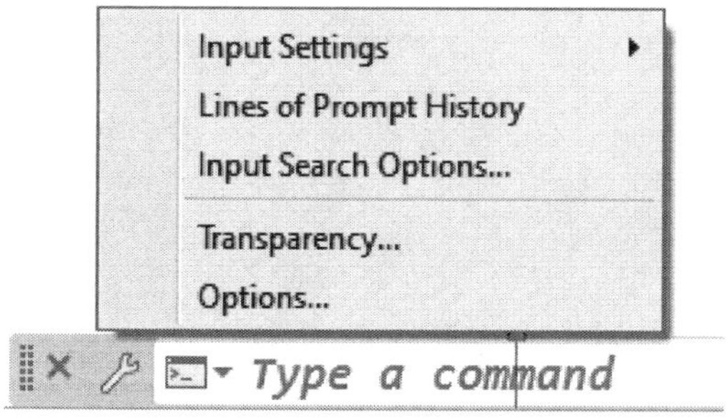

The Input Settings allows the user to determine how the command prompt interacts with user input.

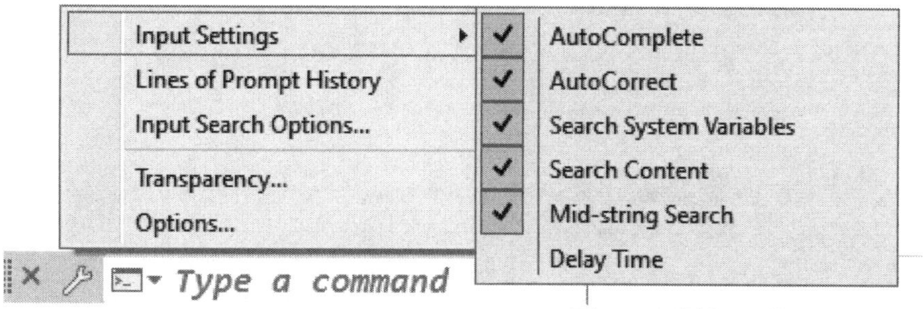

The second icon lists the most recent commands selected by the user.

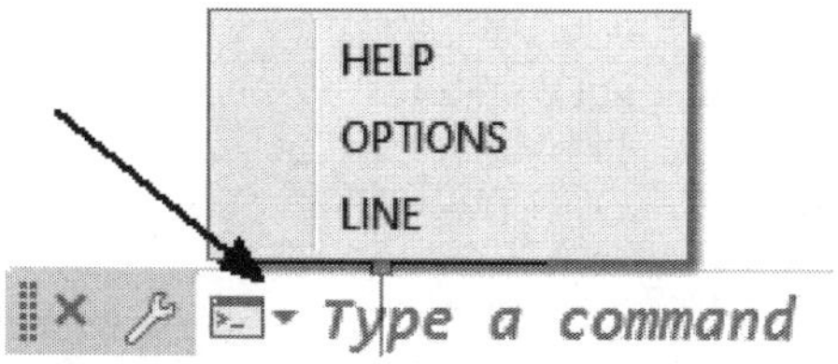

General Procedures

How to follow the Command Window prompts:

1. Type the command, the command alias or the Command Prompt option and Press <ENTER>.
2. Follow the Command Prompt prompts:
    - When prompted to select objects, pick the objects then press <ENTER> to continue.
    - When presented with Command Prompt options, type the capitalized letter of the option and press <ENTER> to continue.
    - When presented with a default choice in parentheses or < > press <ENTER> to accept the default, or type the preferred option and press <ENTER>.

Command Prompt Cursor Menu Option (RMB)	**Overview**
Recent Commands	Lists recently used commands.
Input Settings 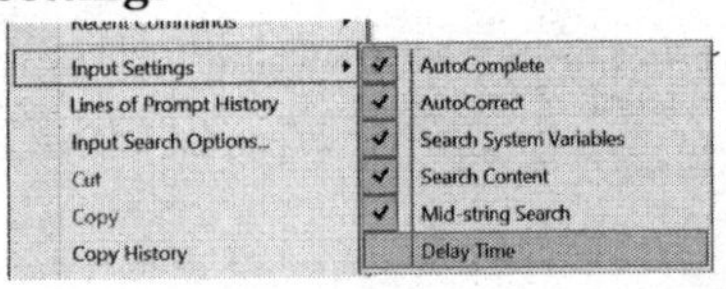	User can set how the command prompt responds to typed entries.
Lines of Prompt History	Sets the number of lines displayed in the command window.
Input Search Options	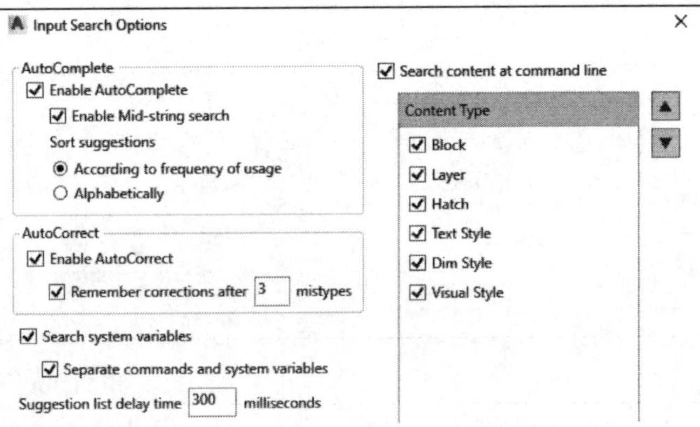
Transparency...	Sets the transparency of the command window.
Options...	Opens the Options dialog box to set user preferences.

- It is important to remember to read the Command Prompt, as this is your line of communication with AutoCAD.
- Use the keyboard <ENTER> button or the right button (RMB) on the mouse.
- When using the RMB, be sure that the cursor is in the drawing window.
- To disable the command options cursor menu, select Options, the User Preferences tab, "Right Click Customization" and "Repeat Last Command." Apply & Close.

Status Bar

Overview

The Application Status Bar is at the bottom of the AutoCAD window. Select (LMB) the buttons to turn the options ON or OFF, or use the corresponding function keys. Right-click (RMB) to access the Settings dialog box for the corresponding Status Bar options or other options that apply. The Status Bar shown has all options enabled. You can elect to turn off/disable options you don't use.

Status Bar Option	Overview	Function Key
COORDINATES	Displays the Cartesian coordinate for the cursor.	CTL+I
MODEL SPACE	Displays the active space—whether you are in model or layout mode.	
GRID	This switch turns the Grid ON and OFF. The Grid is a visual tool and does not restrict cursor selection. Grid spacing may or may not be equal to the Snap spacing. However, if the Grid spacing is set to 0, it will be equal to the Snap spacing.	F7
SNAP MODE	Snap ON will restrict the cursor to select points at designated X and Y increments. Snap spacing may or may not be equal to the Grid spacing. However, if the Grid spacing is set to 0, it will be equal to the Snap spacing.	F9
INFER CONSTRAINTS	Adds sketch constraints as you draw. For example, when you draw a horizontal line, a horizontal constraint will be added.	
DYNAMIC INPUT	Displays prompts in a tooltip near the cursor as you move through different commands.	
ORTHO MODE	Use Ortho (for orthogonal) ON when dragging the mouse to: Draw straight lines. Move, Copy, or Mirror objects along a linear plane. Rotate objects in 90-degree increments. ORTHO is either ON or OFF and does not have a Settings option.	F8
POLAR TRACKING	Turns Polar Snap ON/OFF. When Polar Snap is ON, the angular direction and the distance from the last point selected will be tracked and displayed according to the Polar Tracking settings.	F10

ISOMETRIC DRAFTING	Use to create an isometric view.	
OBJECT SNAP TRACKING	Object Snap Tracking (AUTOSNAP or OTRACK), when ON, will combine with OSNAP (which must also be ON) to allow the cursor to track along alignment paths based on other object snap points in the drawing. To use object snap tracking, you must turn on one or more object snaps.	**F11**
2D OBJECT SNAP	When Object Snap (OSNAP) is ON, the cursor will always gravitate to specified points on objects in the drawing. Unlike SNAP, which follows a grid pattern, OSNAP refers to objects in the drawing and will display object snap markers. When Object Snap (OSNAP) is ON, the cursor will always gravitate to specified points on objects in the drawing. Unlike SNAP, which follows a grid pattern, OSNAP refers to objects in the drawing and will display object snap markers.	**F3**
LINEWEIGHT	Line weights can be specified according to the LWT settings and applied to the lines being drawn when LWT is on. When LWT is off, objects will be drawn using the line weights as designated by the layer (ByLayer). Visibility of lineweight is controlled from the lineweight settings dialog box (choose it from the Format POP, or type *lineweight*). Select "Display Lineweight." Line weights can be specified according to the LWT settings and applied to the lines being drawn when LWT is on. When LWT is off, objects will be drawn using the line weights as designated by the layer (ByLayer). Visibility of lineweight is controlled from the lineweight settings dialog box (choose it from the Format POP, or type *lineweight*). Select "Display Lineweight."	
TRANSPARENCY	This sets the value for the system variable TRANSPARENCYDISPLAY to ON or OFF (1 for ON or) for OFF. Object transparency is controlled by layer. If TRANSPARENCYDISPLAY is set to OFF, the object transparency is overridden.	
SELECTION CYCLING	This tool allows you to tab through a selection set when there are elements overlapping or lying on top of each other.	
3D OBJECT SNAP	Snaps to grips on 3D solids.	**F4**
DYNAMIC UCS	This controls the appearance of the UCS icon when modeling in 3D.	**F6**
SELECTION FILTERING	Use to select edge, face, or vertex when editing 3D objects.	
GIZMO	Controls the visibility of gizmos used for editing 3D objects.	

ANNOTATION VISIBILITY	Display dimensions, notes, and other types of text used in the drawing.	
AUTO SCALE	Changes the size of text and dimensions depending on view scale.	
ANNOTATION SCALE	Displays the annotation scale of the current or active view. Model space should always show 1:1.	
WORKSPACE SWITCHING	Allows you to quickly switch between workspaces or create a new workspace environment.	
ANNOTATION MONITOR	Turns the annotation monitor on or off. When the annotation monitor is on, it flags all non-associative annotations by placing a badge on them. A non-associative annotation is not enabled as annotative and has no annotation scales.	
UNITS	Displays the current drawing units.	
QUICK PROPERTIES	Displays the Quick Properties dialog when an element is selected.	
LOCK UI	Locks the location and sizes of toolbars, panels, and dockable windows.	
ISOLATE OBJECTS	Allows you to create a selection set of elements and hide all other elements.	
GRAPHICS PERFORMANCE	Sets hardware acceleration on or off and provides access to display performance options. Improves the use of your hardware resources, but it is only available if you have an approved graphics card. Visit Autodesk's website and search for recommended hardware.	
CLEANSCREEN	Toggles just the drawing window visible.	**CTL+O**

- Select either the Status Bar button, or select the corresponding function key from the keyboard.
- A Status Bar option can be turned ON or OFF while using a draw or modify command. Therefore, beginning the Line command and deciding to turn ORTHO on or off while in the middle of the command is acceptable.
- To enable or disable the display of different status bar options, left click on the Customize icon and toggle the desired icon ON/OFF.

General Procedures

1. Select the Status Bar button to toggle it ON or OFF.
2. Right-click the Status Bar button to access the corresponding Settings dialog box.

Type **TRAYSETTINGS** at the command prompt to control the balloon notifications. Balloons will display when you plot, when updates are available, etc. To turn off the balloon notifications, you can simply disable the boxes and press 'OK'.

Left click on the menu icon on the Status Bar and a list of available buttons appears. A check mark next to the name indicates that the button is active and visible. To hide a button, simply left click on the name.

Note that the Status buttons have their own submenu.

Look at the status bar. At the far right, next to the Tray Settings menu is the System Variable Monitor.

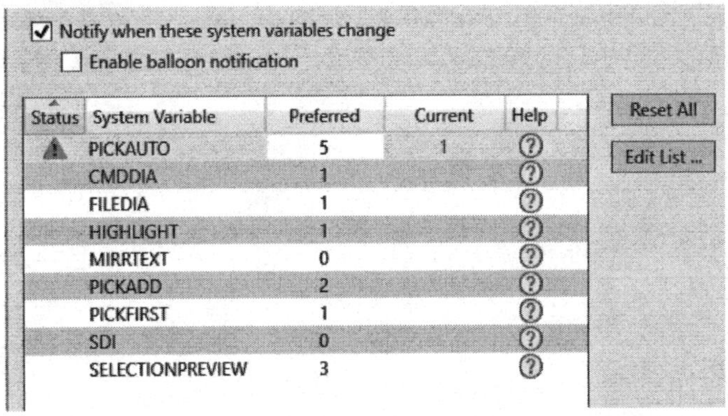

This control allows the user to keep track of various system variables. Most users really don't care or pay attention to system variables. The number indicates the option setting selected for that variable.
1 usually indicates ON or enabled.
0 usually indicates OFF or disabled.
If a different number is displayed, then another option is enabled.

Keyboard Options

Overview

Commands, command aliases, or *system variables* can be typed at the keyboard. It is important to remember to press <ENTER> to execute the command, and follow the Command Prompt prompts. When choosing a Command Prompt option, type the capitalized letter(s) of the desired option. Pressing <ENTER> or the spacebar will execute the command. When typing Text, however, the <ENTER> key is the same as a carriage return on a typewriter, and the spacebar will type a space. Function Keys are used to toggle some options ON or OFF.

Keyboard Option	Overview
ESC	Escape. Cancels all commands.
Enter	Executes a command.
Spacebar	Works like the <ENTER> key except when typing text.
Arrows	Moves the cursor position. In the case of the Command Prompt, the up and down arrows will bring the previously typed information to the last Command Prompt.
Ctrl	Use the Control key + single keys to begin selected commands as indicated in the Pull-Down menus (i.e., Ctrl+S will Save).

On the left side of the status bar, you see the Model and Layout tabs.
Model space is the default drawing space. All elements should be drawn 1:1. The Layout tabs are used to lay out sheets where views are placed.

- The Model Tab should be selected when creating a drawing.
- The cursor must be in the Drawing window in order to pick points for drawing objects, or select objects to modify.
- Right-click in the drawing window to execute a command, proceed with the next step of the command, or if the Command Prompt is blank, repeat the last command.
- Picking (LMB) in a blank area of the drawing window will initiate a selection window or box. You must pick the opposite corner whether you want to select an object or not, or press Escape to cancel the selection window.
- Close drawings that are not being used.

Command Alias	**Command Aliases are shortcut keys that can be typed to access a command when the Command Prompt is blank. Some of the command aliases include:**
A	Arc
B	Block Definition dialog box
C	Circle
CO	Copy
D	Dimension Style Manager dialog box
E	Erase
ED	Edit Text
F	Fillet
H	Boundary Hatch dialog box
I	Insert Block dialog box
L	Line
LA	Layers Properties Manager dialog box
M	Move
O	Offset
P	Real-Time Pan
PE	Edit Polyline
PL	Draw Polyline
PU	Purge
R	Redraw
Re	Regenerate Drawing

S	Stretch
T	Multiline Text
U	Undo (last command)
V	View dialog box
W	Write Block dialog box
X	Explode
Z	Zoom
Function Keys	Function Keys, located at the top or side of the keyboard, activate the following options:
F1	Activates the AutoCAD Help Menu
F2	Opens the AutoCAD Text Window
F3	Turns OSNAP (object snap) ON or OFF
F4	Toggles 3D Object Snap
F5	Toggles through the three Isoplanes: Top, Right, and Left.
F6	Toggles through the three coordinate options: ON, OFF or display Polar Coordinates.
F7	Turns the GRID ON or OFF
F8	Turns ORTHO ON or OFF
F9	Turns SNAP ON or OFF
F10	Turns POLAR Tracking ON or OFF
F11	Turns OTRACK (object snap tracking) ON or OFF
F12	Toggles Dynamic Input

General Procedures

1. Type the command, command alias, or system variable at the Command Prompt.
2. Press <ENTER> to execute the command, or follow the Command Prompt prompts.

Command Exercise

Exercise 1-3 – Start Page

Drawing Name: **(none, start from scratch)**
Estimated Time to Completion: 5 Minutes

Scope

Explore the Start tab.

1. Change the display of recent files.

Solution

1.

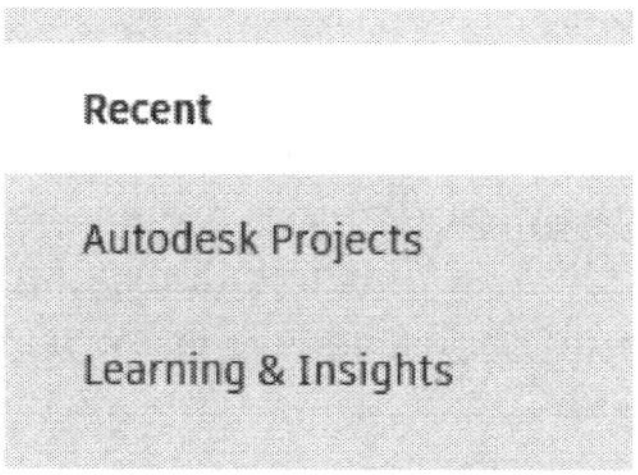

Click on the Start tab.
Notice that the Start tab is divided into two panels.
On the panel on the left, there are four links:

- Recent
- Autodesk Docs
- Learning & Insights

Highlight the **Recent** link.

2.

You can control how the recent drawings will be displayed using the two small icons located below the Recent heading.

3.

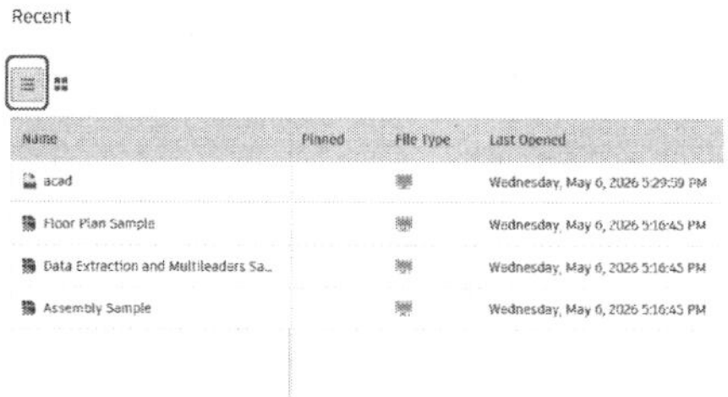

If the first icon is selected the recent drawing will be displayed with the file name and last opened date.

4.

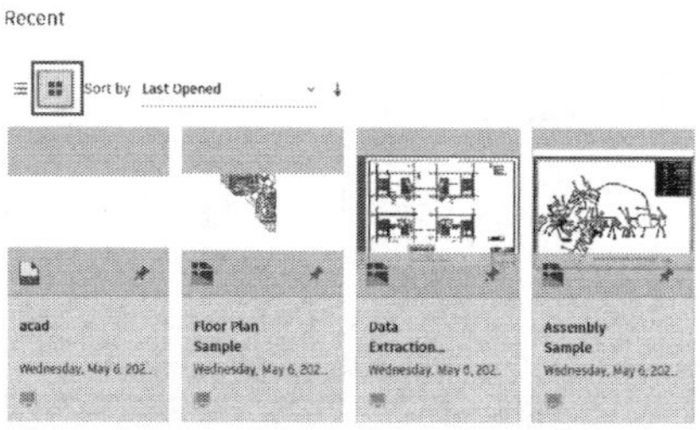

If the second icon is selected, the recent drawings will be displayed in preview mode with the file name along with the date last modified.

5. 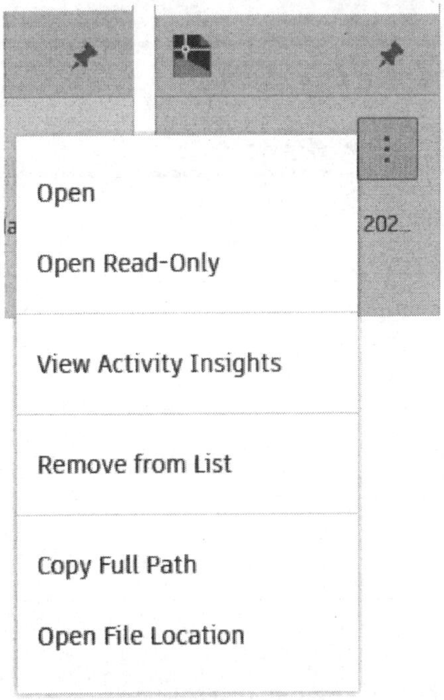

If you click on the three vertical dots next to the file name, you can elect to Open the drawing file or Open Read-Only.

6. 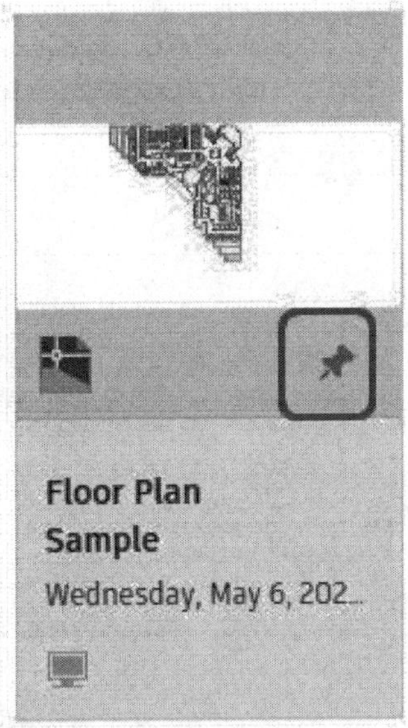

If you click the pin, you pin the drawing to the Recent page, so it is always available. This is useful if you need to refer to a drawing all the time for your work or if a drawing has blocks or other elements you might need.

Tips & Tricks

- You can turn off the Start Page by typing STARTMODE on the command line and then 0.
- If you press Ctl+Home, you will automatically switch from the active drawing back to the Start tab.
- If you have a drawing where you store blocks, linetypes, dimension styles, etc. you can pin it to the Start tab so it is always front and center.

Help Menu

Command Locator

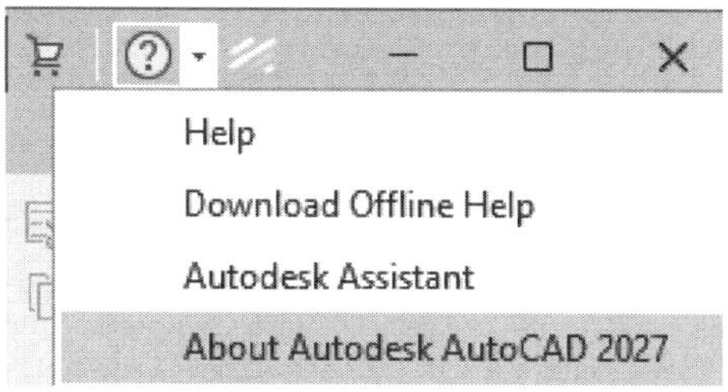

Command Overview

AutoCAD Help can be invoked at any time. If the Command Prompt is blank, the Help menu will open at one of the tabs, depending on which tab was selected the last time Help was used. If help is invoked while in the middle of a command, the Help menu will open to the page covering that command.

General Procedures

To access help when in the middle of a command:

1. Select the question mark in the toolbar.

To use the Help Contents tab:

1. Select Help Topics / Contents Tab.
2. Open a topic by double clicking on it, or single-click and select Open.

To use the Help menu Index tab:

1. Select Help Topics / Index Tab.
2. Begin to type the word.
3. Double-click the index entry, or single-click and select Display.

To use the Help menu Find tab:

1. Select Help Topics / Find Tab.
2. If the setup Wizard appears, select Next.
3. Begin to type the word.
4. Double-click the index entry, or single-click and select Display.

Command Locator

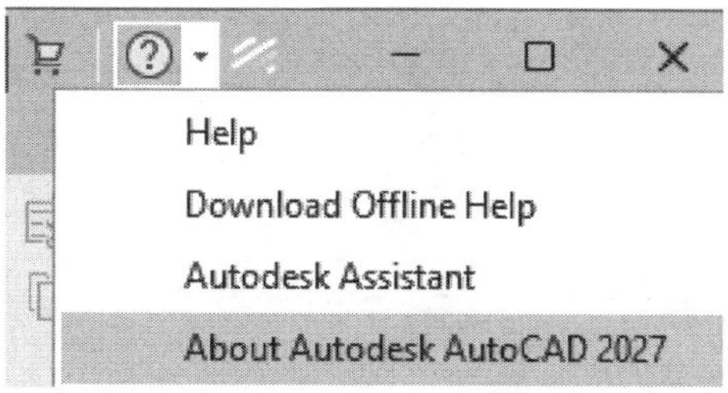

Autodesk Assistant

Command Overview

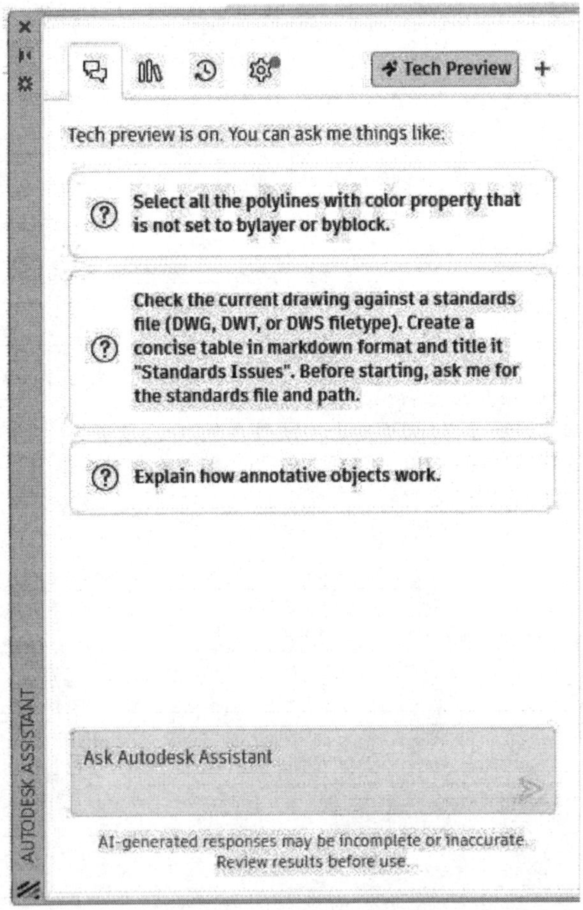

Autodesk Assistant is an AI chatbot that can provide guidance if you get stuck. You can save prompts if you find yourself asking the same questions more than once. You can save your chats to refer to at a later time.

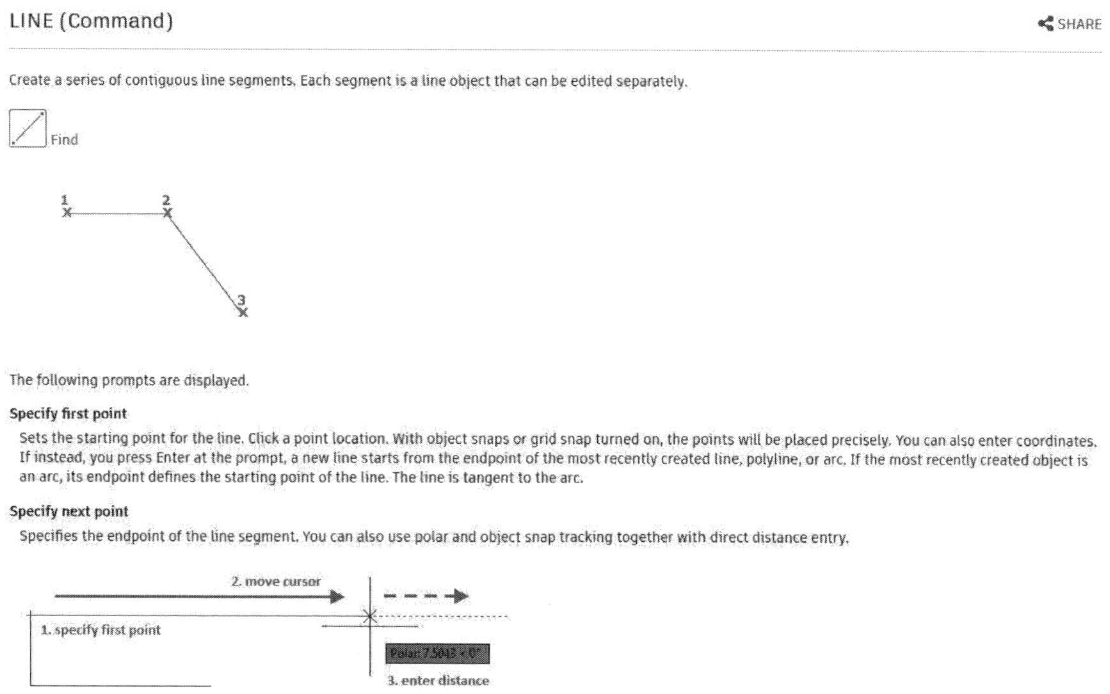
LINE (Command)

SHARE

Create a series of contiguous line segments. Each segment is a line object that can be edited separately.

Find

The following prompts are displayed.

Specify first point

Sets the starting point for the line. Click a point location. With object snaps or grid snap turned on, the points will be placed precisely. You can also enter coordinates. If instead, you press Enter at the prompt, a new line starts from the endpoint of the most recently created line, polyline, or arc. If the most recently created object is an arc, its endpoint defines the starting point of the line. The line is tangent to the arc.

Specify next point

Specifies the endpoint of the line segment. You can also use polar and object snap tracking together with direct distance entry.

If you start the LINE command and then press F1 before you select the first point, this dialog will appear.

Command Exercise

Exercise 1-4 – Dynamic Input

Drawing Name: **(none, start from scratch)**
Estimated Time to Completion: 5 Minutes

Scope

Control the appearance of Dynamic Input.

Solution

1. 

Click the + tab on the Launch page to create a new drawing.

2. 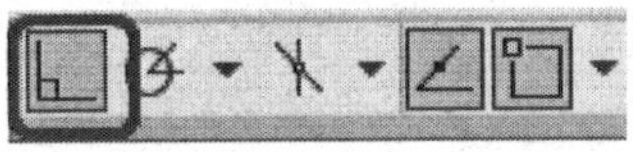
Verify that ORTHO is enabled.

   Toggle it on using the icon on the status bar or press F8.

3. 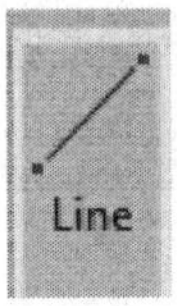

Start the LINE command.

4. 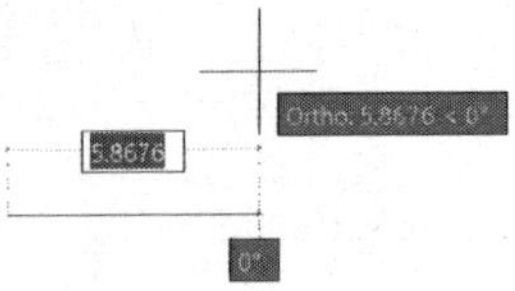

Left click in the window to place the line starting point.

   Move the cursor around the drawing window.

   Left click to place the second point of the line.

   Observe how the input prompts change.

5. RMB and select ENTER to exit the LINE command.

   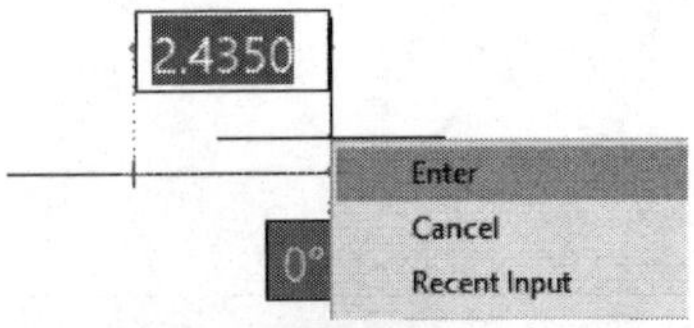

   Note how the coordinates in the input bar change depending on the cursor location.

6. 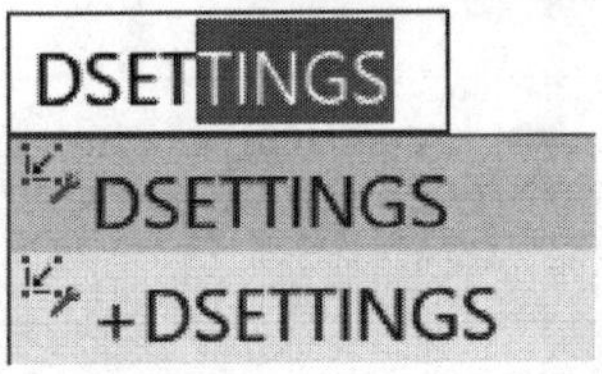

Type **DSETTINGS** on the command prompt.

   You can just start typing and AutoCAD will display the relevant commands. Use the up and down arrow keys to select the desired command or ENTER.

7. 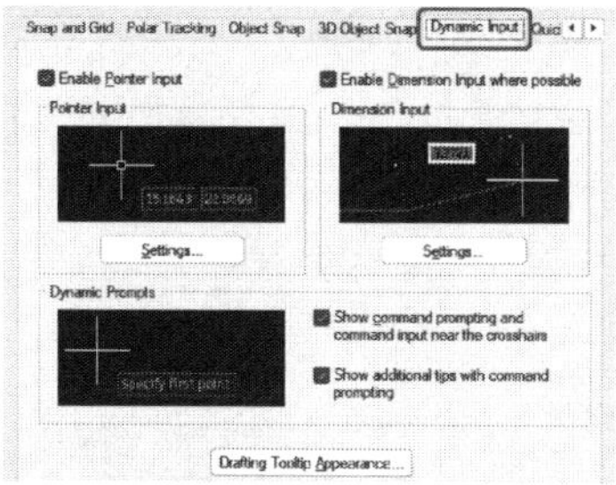

Activate the **Dynamic Input** tab.

8. 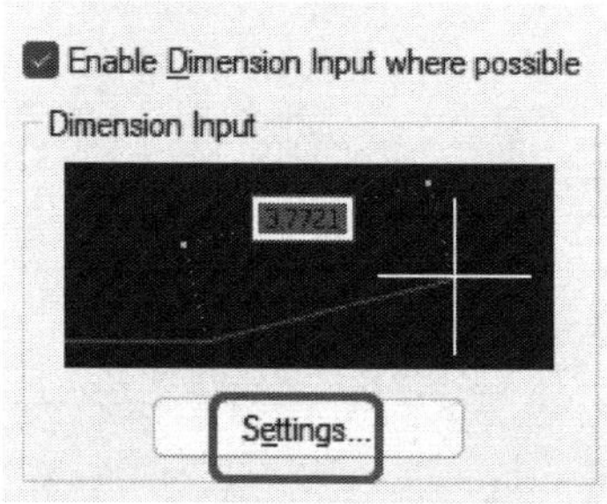

Select the **Settings** button under Dimension Input.

9. 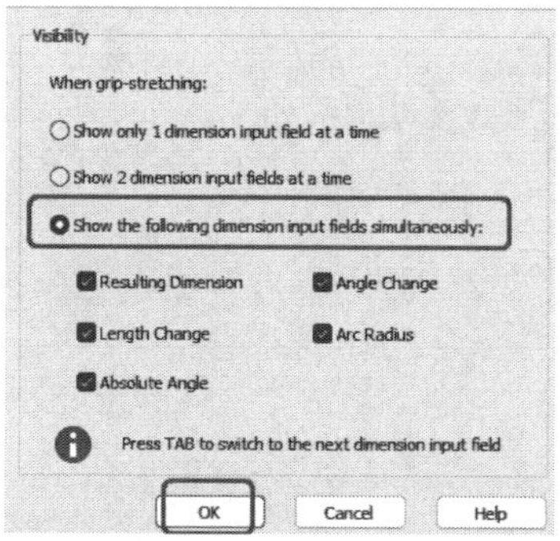

Enable **Show the following dimension input fields simultaneously**.
Enable all the options.
Click **OK**.

10. 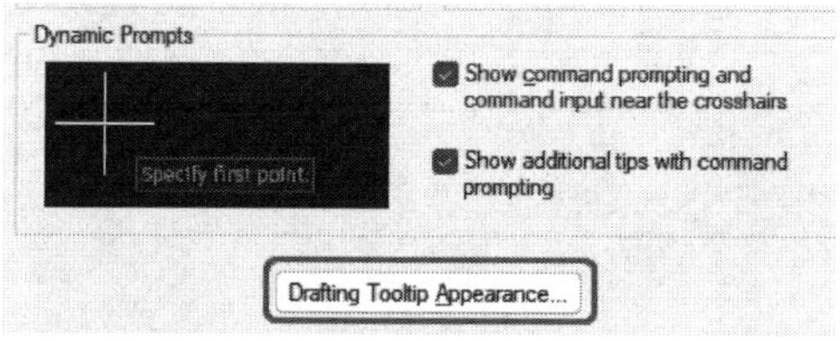

Select **Drafting Tooltip Appearance** under Dynamic Prompts.

11. 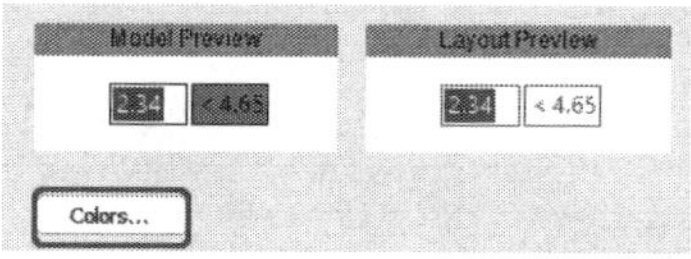

Select the **Colors** button.

12.

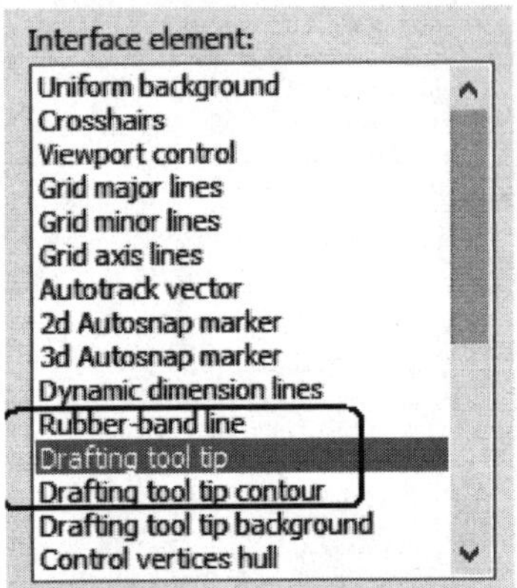

Highlight the **Drafting tool tip** in the Interface element box.

13.

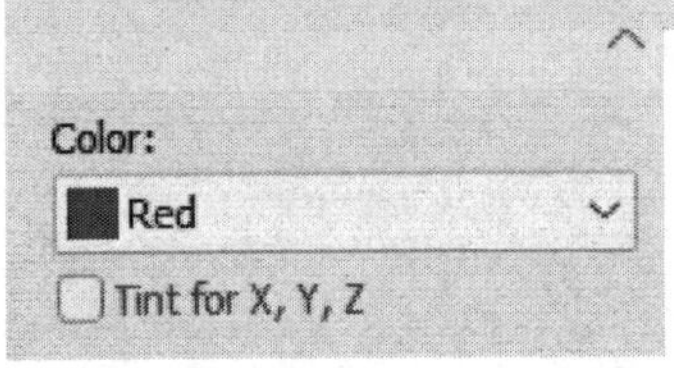

Set the color to **RED**.
Click **Apply & Close**.

14.

Note you can adjust the size of dimensions as they appear. This is especially helpful if you have vision problems.

Click **OK** twice to close the dialog.

Note how the display has changed.

15.

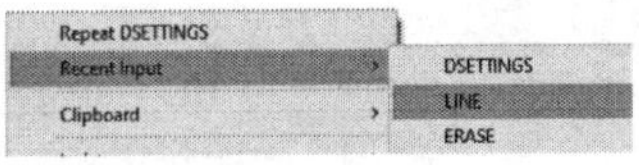

Start a LINE.

Right click in the display window.
Select **Recent Input→Line**.

16.

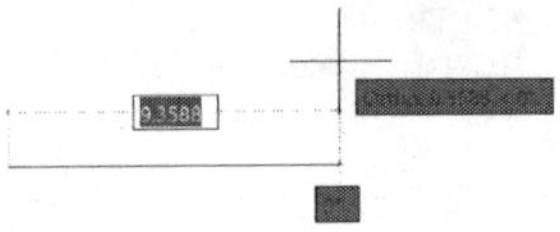

Pick a point to start the line.
Note the way the appearance of the interface has changed.

Press ESC on the keyboard to cancel out of the command.

Close without saving the file.

Profiles

Command Locator

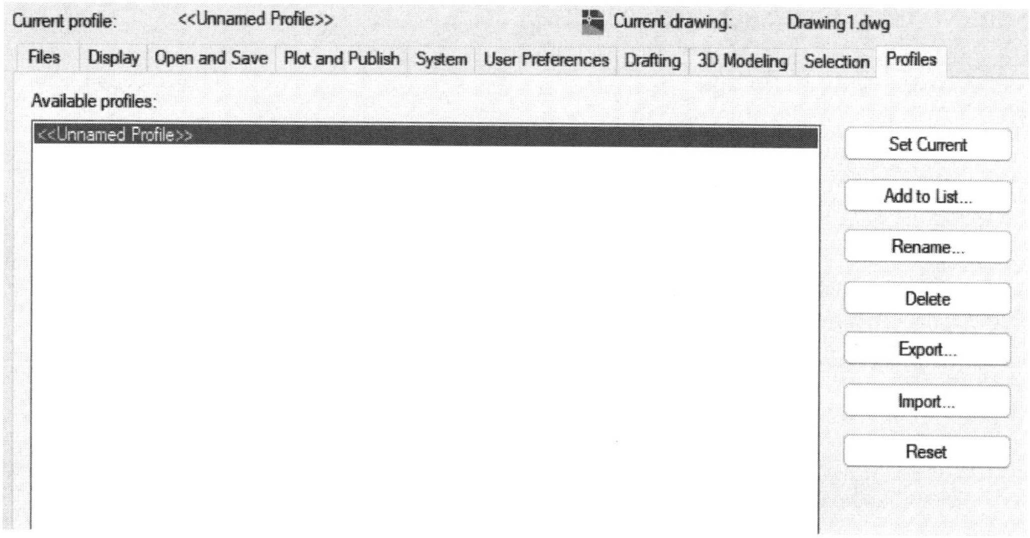

Command Overview

The Profiles Tab of the Options dialog box allows you to copy your Preferences settings to a personalized profile (.ARG file). This can be exported to the network or a floppy disk. When you use AutoCAD on another computer workstation, simply import your own .arg profile file.

Available Profiles – List all available profiles for the system.
Set Current – Makes the selected profile the current profile.
Add to List – Displays the Add Profile dialog box to save the selected profile under a different name.
Rename – Selecting this button will open the Change Profile dialog box allowing you to rename and change the description of the selected profile.
Delete – Deletes the selected profile (unless it is the current profile).
Export – Exports a selected profile as an .ARG file.
Import – Imports a selected profile that was created by using the Export option.
Reset – Resets the values in the selected profile to the system default settings.

- Most users set up their tool palettes and change the user environment to the way they like to work. If you are spending time on more than one work station—for example, working in a classroom or office and then also working at home—you can save your profile and import to any work station, so you don't have to set-up your work station each time.

Command Exercise

Exercise 1-5 – Create a Profile

Drawing Name: **pref4.dwg**
Estimated Time to Completion: 15 Minutes

Scope

Using the Profile tab in Options, copy the current profile as CAD–1 and CAD–2, then make CAD–1 the current profile. In the Display tab, deselect Scroll Bars, change the background color, and Apply. Open and rearrange some toolbars. Next use the Options / Profile command to make each profile current and view the changes made to the AutoCAD window.

1. 

Invoke the Options command by right-clicking in the display area of the screen and selecting **Options…**

2. 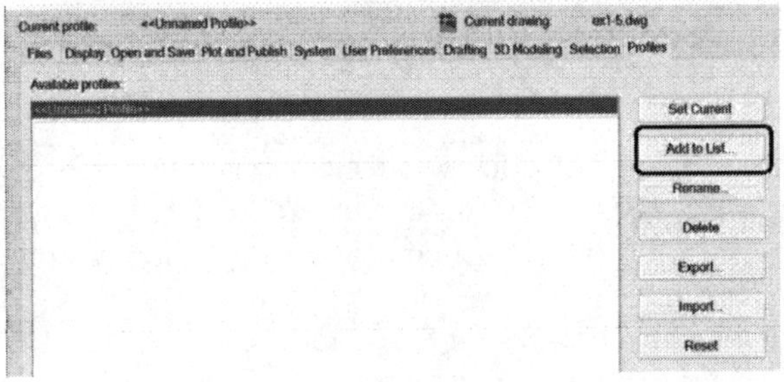

Select the *Profiles* tab and copy the current profile by using the **Add to List…** button.

3. 

Name the profile *CAD–1*.

Click **Apply & Close**.

4. 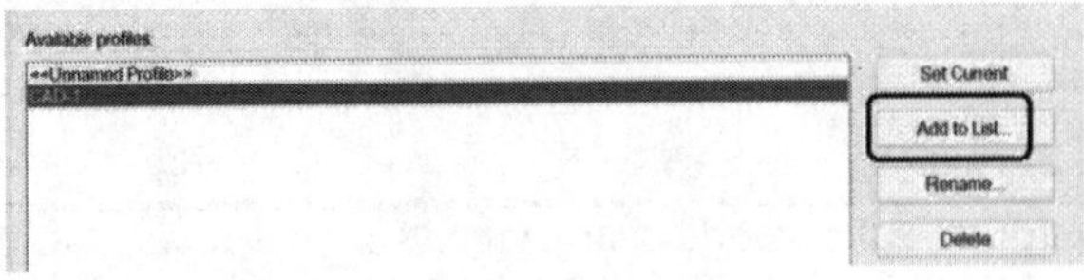

Highlight the *CAD-1* Profile and select **Add to List** to create another profile.

5. 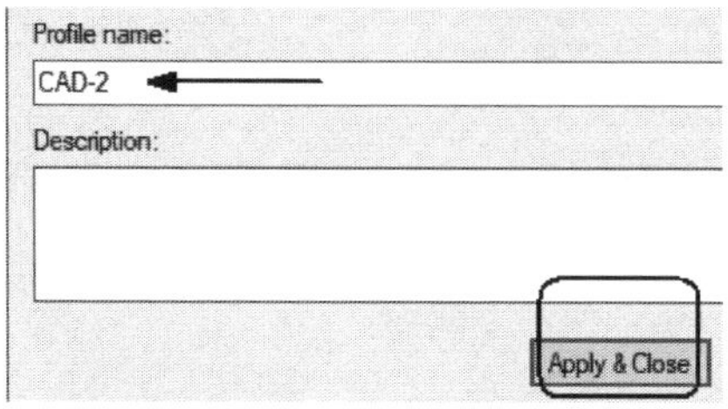

Name this profile *CAD-2.*

Click **Apply & Close**.

6. 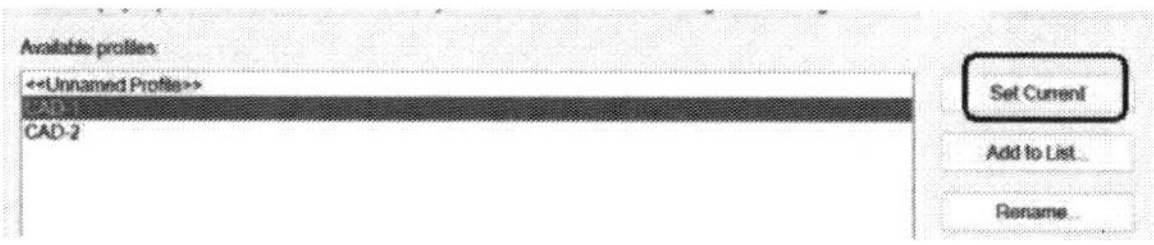

Highlight the *CAD-1* profile and select **Set Current**.

7. 

You will see the CAD-1 Profile listed as the current profile.

8. 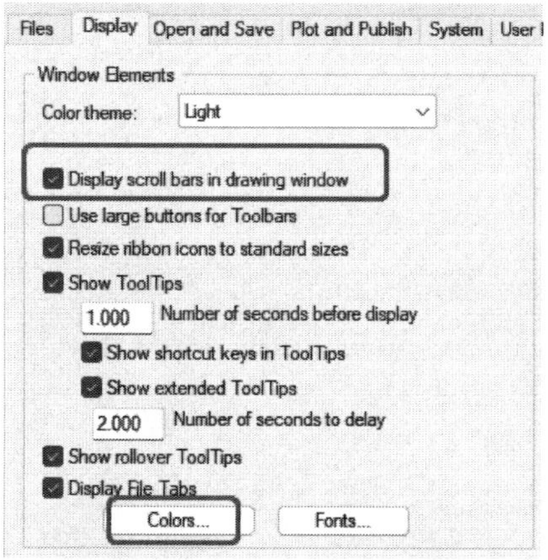

Switch to the **Display** tab.

Enable **Display Scroll Bars**.

Select the **Colors** button.

9. 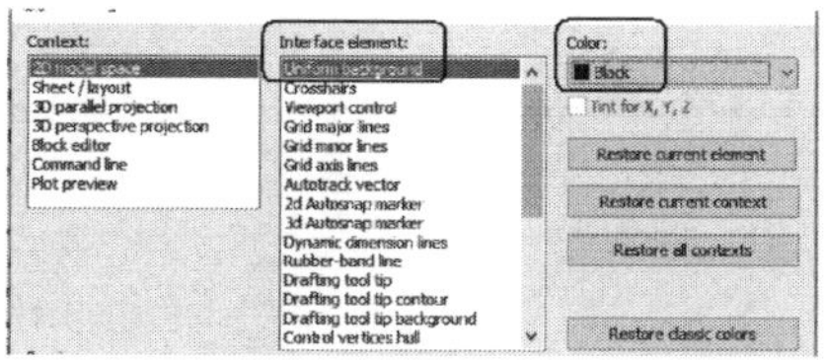

Change the Display Window background color to **Black.**

Click **Apply & Close** at the bottom of the dialog box.

The display background changes to Black.

10. 

Click **Apply**.

Notice that there are now scroll bars located on the right side and bottom of the screen.

11. Click **OK** to apply the changes and exit the Options dialog box.

12. 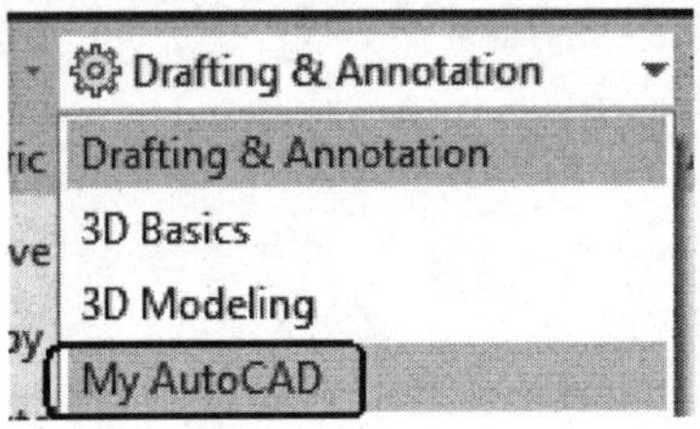

Change the workspace to **My AutoCAD**.

13. 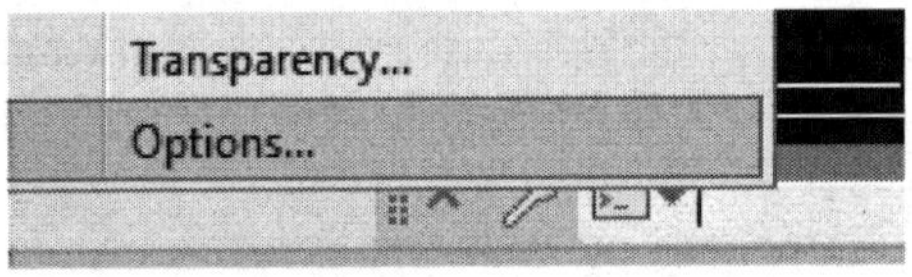

Place your cursor in the Command window.

Click the RMB and select **Options**.

14. 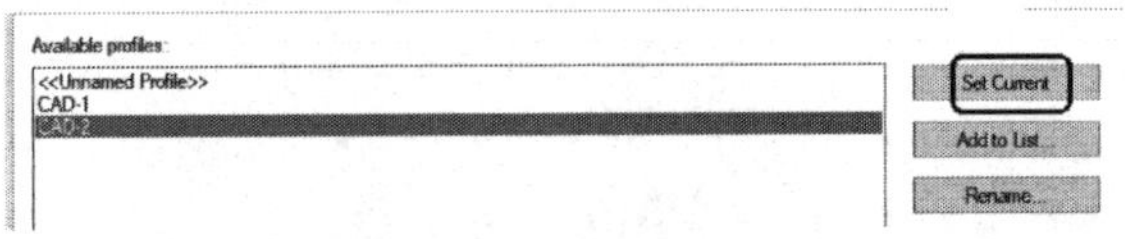

Select the **Profiles** tab.

Highlight the **CAD-2** profile and **Set Current**.

15. 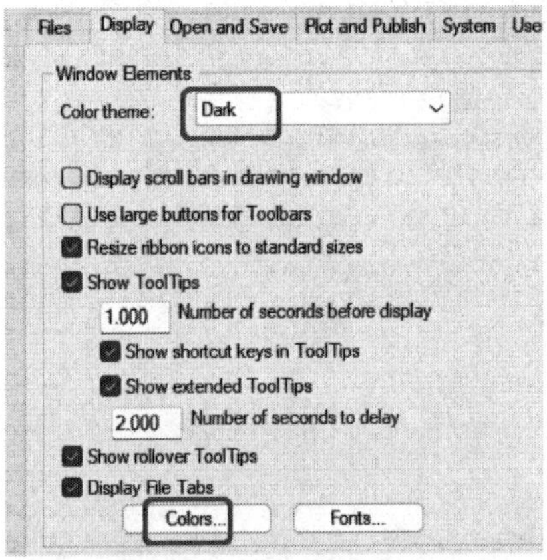

Switch to the **Display** tab.

Change the Color Theme to **Dark**.

Select the **Colors** button.

16. 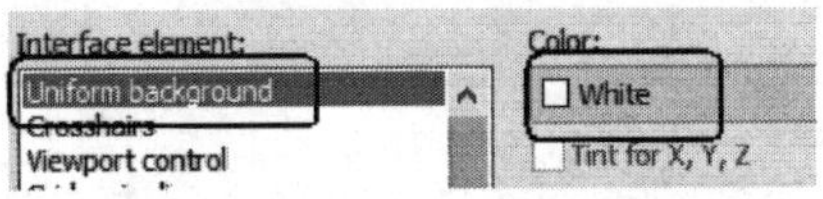

Change the Display Window background color to **White.**

17. 

Click **Apply & Close** at the bottom of the dialog box.

Click **OK** to apply the changes and exit the Options dialog box.

18. 

Observe how the user interface has changed.

Click the RMB and select **Options**.

19. 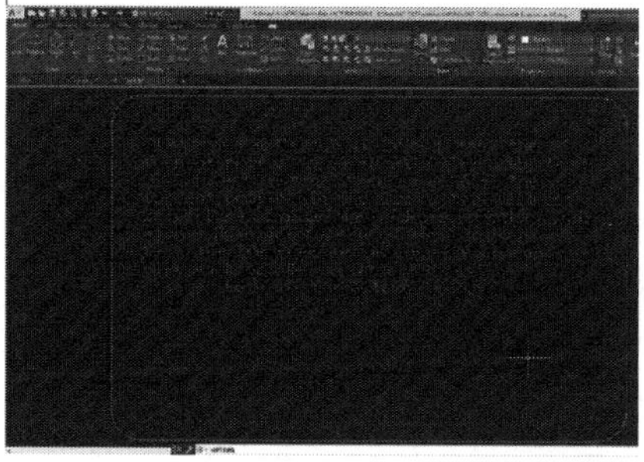

Set the **CAD-1** profile current.

Close the Options dialog box.

Note that the workspace has changed back to My AutoCAD.

The window background is black.

There are scroll bars displayed at the bottom and right side of the window.

20. 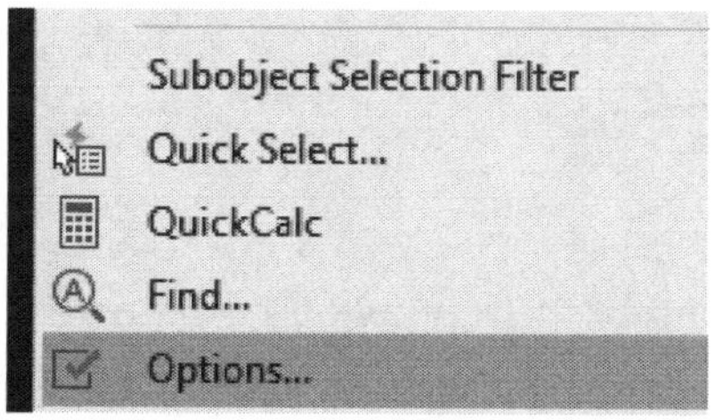

Place your cursor in the Command window.

Click RMB and select **Options**.

21. 

Set the **CAD-2** profile current.
Close the file without saving.

Once you get used to working with AutoCAD a certain way, you don't want to change. You have your options set up the way you like to work. If you change jobs or workstations, you want to keep all your settings. You can export your profile, so you don't need to go through all the different options again.

Command Exercise

Exercise 1-6 – Export a Profile

Drawing Name: **exportprofile.dwg**
Estimated Time to Completion: 5 Minutes

Scope

Export a profile for use at a different workstation.

Solution

1. 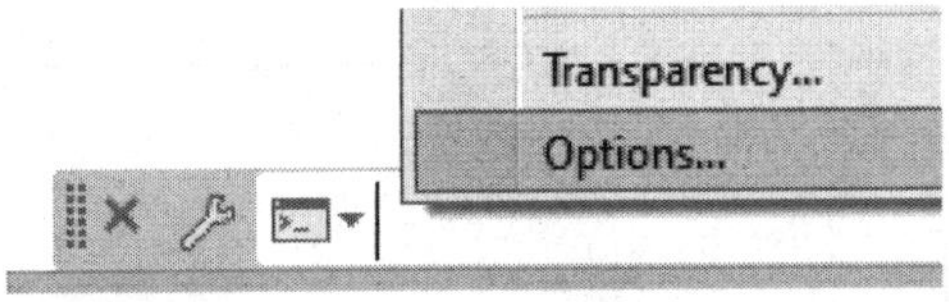

Place your cursor in the Command prompt window.

RMB and select **Options**.

2. 

Go to the **Profiles** tab.

Highlight the **CAD-1** profile.

Select **Export**.

3. 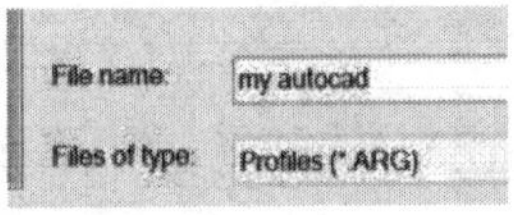

Browse to a folder to save the profile file.

Rename the file *my_autocad.arg*.

Click **Save**.

4. 

Click **OK** to exit the dialog.

Click the x on the drawing tab to close the drawing file.

Close the file without saving.

5. 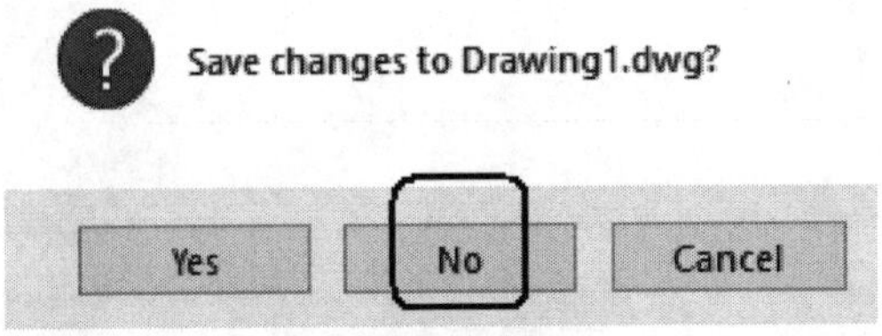

Click **No.**

6. 

Start a new drawing by clicking the + tab.

7. 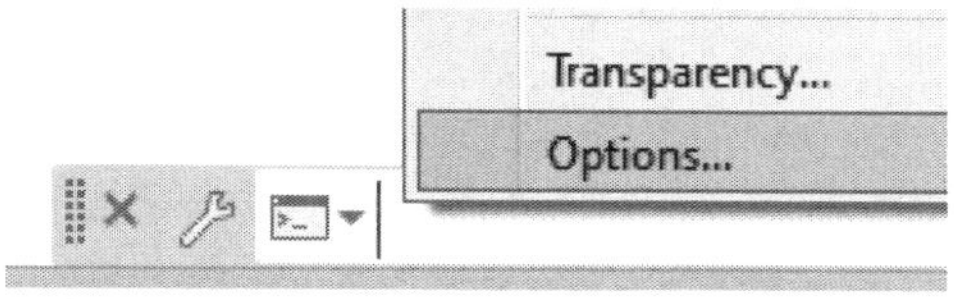

Place your cursor in the Command prompt window.

RMB and select **Options**.

8. 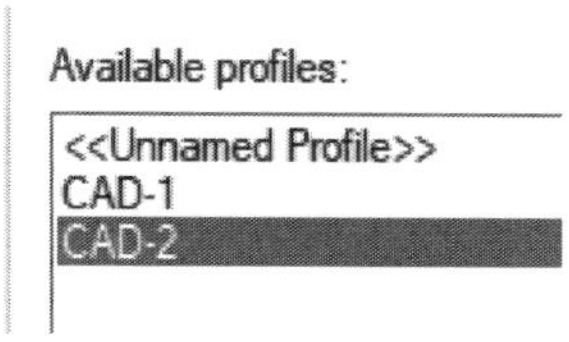

Select the Profiles tab.

Note that the profiles you created are stored on your workstation, so any drawing you open or create will now have the profiles available.

Click **OK** to close the dialog.

- Store your profile files on Google Drive or somewhere on the cloud so they will be available at any workstation.
- To import a profile, go to the Options/Profiles dialog and select Import. Then select the profile file you want to use.
- You can use the Autodesk Docs link to store your profile on the cloud.

Review Questions

1. Which is the Pick button and which is the <ENTER> button on the mouse?

2. Name the areas of the AutoCAD Screen:

3. How do you close the ribbon?

4. How do you open the ribbon?

5. What is the hotkey for Help?

6. How do you switch from one open drawing to another open drawing?

7. What happens if you press the enter button on the mouse when the cursor is:
   - ❑ In the drawing window?
   - ❑ Over the Command Prompt?

8. What does the Escape key do?

9. How can a dialog box be closed?

10. At a blank command prompt, what commands are initiated by typing the following letters?

E	**C**	**M**
A	**L**	**P**
R	**Z**	**U**

11. Where is the Quick Access toolbar?

12. What panel of the ribbon holds the LINE tool?

Review Answers

1. Which is the Pick button and which is the <ENTER> button on the mouse?
   Left Button (LMB): Pick
   Right Button (RMB): <ENTER>

2. Name the areas of the AutoCAD Screen:
   Title Bar, Quick Access Toolbars Drawing Window, Command Prompt, Status Bar, Ribbon

3. How do you close the ribbon?
   RIBBONCLOSE

4. How do you open the ribbon?
   RIBBON

5. What is the hotkey for Help?
   F1

6. How do you switch from one open drawing to another open drawing?
   Select the tabs at the top of the drawing window.

7. What happens if you press the enter button on the mouse when the cursor is:
   In the drawing window?
   A Shortcut Menu appears related to the last or current command.

   Over the Command Prompt?
   The Command Prompt Shortcut Menu appears.

8. What does the Escape key do?
   Cancels a command.

9. How can a dialog box be closed?
   Select OK, Close, the X in the upper right hand corner, or the Escape key

10. At a blank command prompt, what commands are initiated by typing the following letters?

E *Erase*	**C** *Circle*	**M** *Move*
A *Arc*	**L** *Line*	**P** *Pan*
R *Redraw*	**Z** *Zoom*	**U** *Undo*

11. Where is the Quick Access Toolbar?
    The docked toolbar at the top.

12. What panel of the ribbon holds the LINE tool?
    The DRAW panel.

Notes:

Lesson 2.0 – View Commands

Estimated Class Time: 1 Hour

Objectives

This Lesson will cover the different ways to view drawings. Learn to Pan and Zoom in *real time* and use the other Zoom options. Views can be Named and Saved, then Restored. The drawing window can be divided into Multiple Viewports.

- **Pan Realtime**
  Pan the drawing with the motion of the cursor in *real time*.
- **Zoom Realtime**
  Zoom the drawing with the up and down motion of the cursor in *real time*.
- **Zoom Window**
  Make a zoom window around an area to view close up.
- **Zoom Previous**
- **Zoom Options**
  Additional zoom options are located in the fly-out on the Standard Toolbar.
- **Regen**
  Regenerate the drawing to smooth out circles and arcs.
- **Named Views**
  Name and Save drawing Views and make them current when needed.
- **Multiple Viewports**
  Display different views of the drawing in multiple viewports.

Pan Realtime

Command Locator

Navigation Bar	**Pan**
Command	**Pan**
Alias	**P**
RMB Shortcut Menu	**Drawing Window**
Navigation Bar	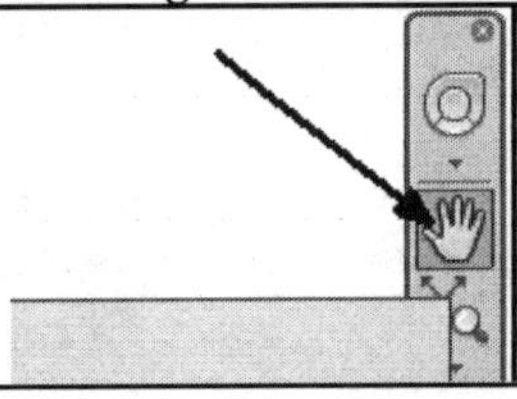

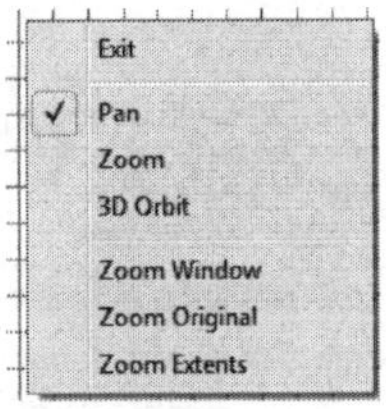

Pan Realtime Shortcut Menu

Real Time Pan / Zoom Shortcut Menu Options:	Overview
Exit	Exits the Realtime Pan or Zoom commands
Pan	Invokes the Realtime Pan command
Zoom	Invokes the Realtime Zoom command
3D Orbit	Rotates the drawing three-dimensionally
Zoom Window	Zooms to a window made by Clicking the pick button and dragging it around the area to view
Zoom Original	Displays the drawing in the original zoom setting
Zoom Extents	Zooms to the extents of the drawing objects

Command Overview

With the Pan Realtime command, pick a point in the drawing window. Click the LMB and drag the drawing view in real time. Right click (RMB) to access the shortcut menu and select Exit or one of the other options. The Escape key will also exit the Pan Realtime command.

General Procedures

1. Invoke the Pan Realtime command.
2. Pick a point in the drawing window (LMB), click and drag to pan the view.
3. Right-click (RMB) to access the shortcut menu and pick Exit.

Tips & Tricks

- The shortcut menus for Pan Realtime and Zoom Realtime are identical.
- When dragging the cursor in Pan Realtime, the mouse can be picked up and relocated in the drawing window if the cursor reaches the edge of the drawing window.

Zoom Realtime

Command Locator

Navigation Bar	**Navigation / Zoom**	
Command	**Zoom**	
Alias	**Z**	
RMB Shortcut Menu	**Drawing Window**	
	Navigation Bar	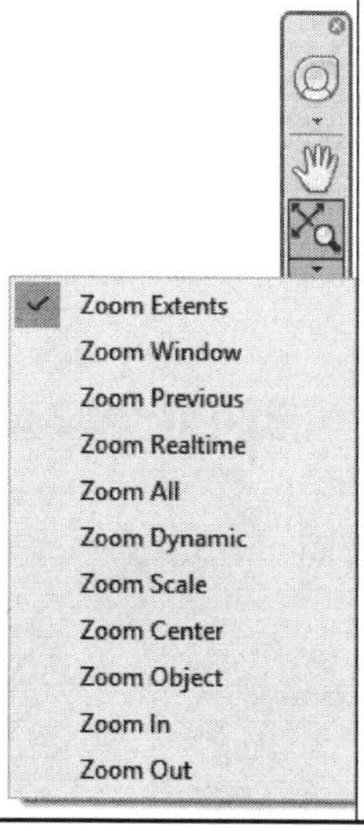

Command Overview

With the Zoom command, pick a point in the drawing window. Drag the mouse up or down to zoom in or out. Right click (RMB) to access the shortcut menu and select Exit or one of the other options. The Escape Key will also exit the Zoom command.

General Procedures

1. Invoke the Zoom command.
2. Pick a point in the drawing window (LMB), Click and drag up to zoom in and down to zoom out.
3. Right-click (RMB) to access the shortcut menu and select Exit or one of the other options.

Tips & Tricks

- Remember to drag up to zoom in and down to zoom out.
- When dragging the cursor in Zoom, the mouse can be picked up and relocated in the drawing window if the cursor reaches the top or bottom of the drawing window.

Zoom Window

Command Locator

Toolbar Menu	**Navigation / Zoom Flyout**
Command	**Zoom, Window**
Alias	**Z**

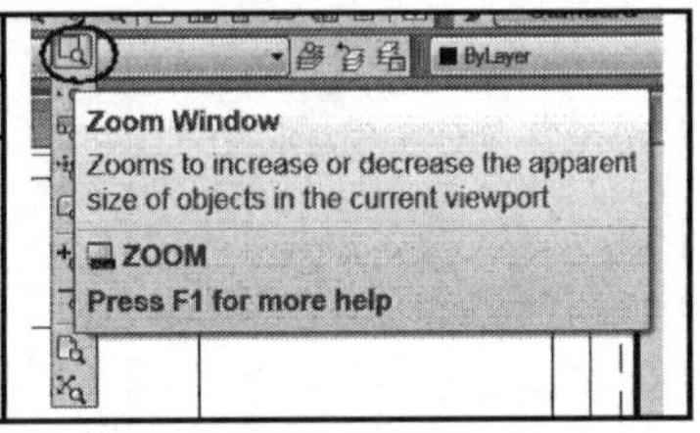

Command Overview

Use the Zoom window command to view a selected area of the drawing.

General Procedures

1. Invoke the Zoom Window command.
2. Pick the first corner of the view window, then drag the mouse and pick the opposite corner.

Tips & Tricks

- When the Zoom Window command is invoked, the opposite corner of the window must be made or Click Escape to cancel the Zoom command.
- When invoking the Zoom command, the Window option is a default. Just begin the first corner of the zoom window.
- Zoom commands can be used while in the middle of other commands.

Zoom Previous

Command Locator

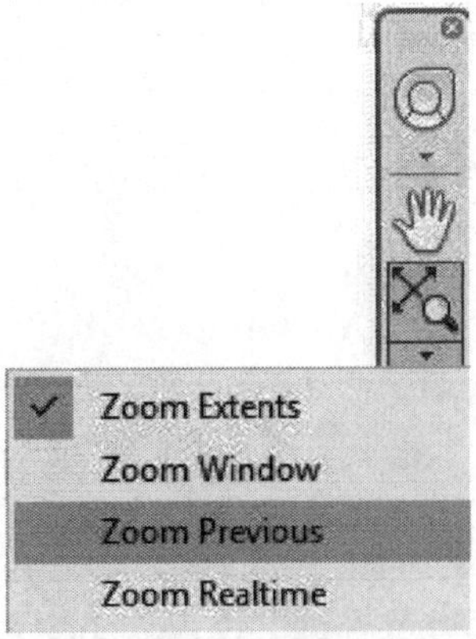

Toolbar Menu	**Navigation / Zoom Previous**
Command	**Zoom / P**
Alias	**Z / P**

Command Overview

The Zoom Previous command displays the previous view.

General Procedures

1. Invoke the Zoom Previous command using the button in the Standard toolbar. If typing the alias Z, Click <ENTER>, then type P (and <ENTER> for the Previous option).

> - Zoom previous can be accessed from the Zoom command by typing 'P' and Clicking <ENTER>.
> - Zoom Previous can go back until no previous views are found.

Zoom Options

Command Locator

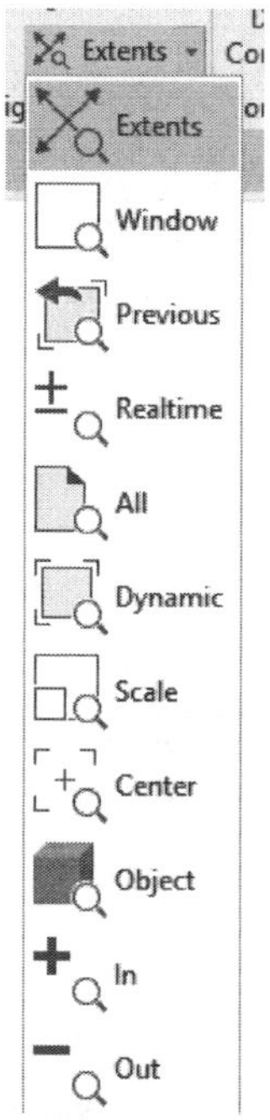

Toolbar Menu	**Navigation / Zoom Fly-out**
Command	**Zoom (type capitalized letter of the desired option)**
Alias	**Z (type capitalized letter of the desired option)**

Command Overview

Other zoom options are available within the Zoom command. These can be accessed from the fly-out button on the Standard Toolbar under the Zoom Window command. These options are also available by typing the capitalized letter of the desired option after invoking the Zoom command.

Zoom Option	Button	Overview
Zoom		Zoom Realtime – zoom in and out.
Zoom Previous		Zoom back through previous views.
Zoom Window		Zooms to a selected window.
Zoom Dynamic		Displays the zoom window. LMB to scale or pan the view window. RMB to display the Shortcut menu.
Zoom Scale		Zoom to a specific scale relevant to the last zoom or to actual scale in paper space (x/xp).
Zoom Center	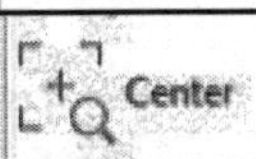	Makes a selected point in the drawing the Center of the drawing.
Zoom Object		Select an entity in your drawing and the view will adjust to center on the selected object.
Zoom In	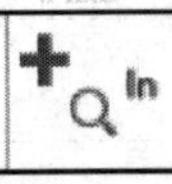	This will zoom at a scale of .5x.
Zoom Out		This will zoom at a scale of 2x.
Zoom All		This will zoom to view all of the geometry in the drawing as well as the area designated by the Drawing Limits.
Zoom Extents		This will zoom to view only the geometry in the drawing.

General Procedures

1. Invoke the Zoom command option from the fly-out in the Standard Toolbar.
2. If typing the alias Z, Click <ENTER>, then type the capitalized letter of the desired option and Click <ENTER>.

Tips & Tricks

- The most important Zoom options are Window, All and Extents.
- Zoom All or Extents occasionally to be sure bits of the drawing have not gotten thrown out into space.
- If the desired fly-out option is the visible button on the Standard Toolbar, simply select it. It is not necessary to display the fly-out list to select that option.

Command Exercise

Exercise 2-1 – Real Time Zoom

Drawing Name: **pan1.dwg**
Estimated Time to Completion: 10 Minutes

Scope

Zoom and Pan the drawing in real time. Use the RMB to switch between some basic zoom modes.

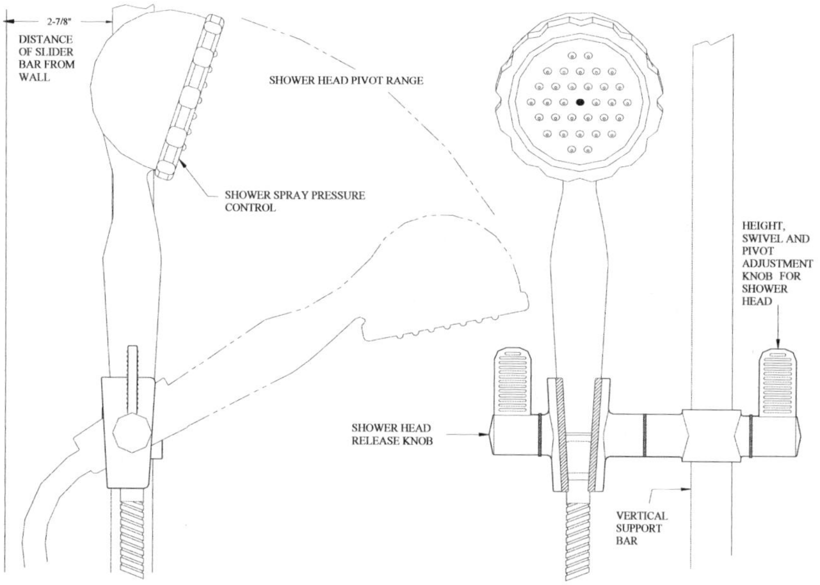

Solution

1.

On the Start tab:

Click **Open files…**

2.

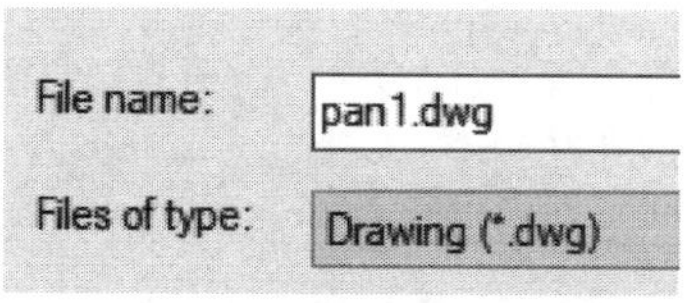

Browse to where you downloaded and saved the publisher's files.
Locate *pan1.dwg.*
Click **Open.**

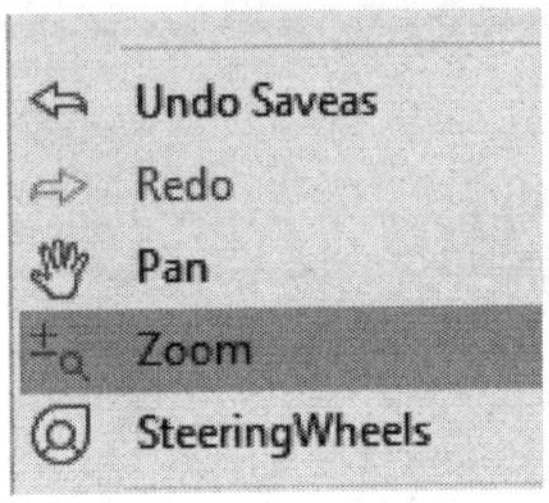

3. Invoke the Zoom command (z or zoom) or Right click in the screen and select Zoom.

4. *Click ESC or ENTER to exit, or right-click to display shortcut menu:*
Pick a point in the middle of the drawing window. Hold the LMB down and drag the mouse up and down. Notice how you zoom in as you move the mouse up and zoom out as you move the mouse down.

5. *Click ESC or ENTER to exit, or right-click to display shortcut menu:*
Hold the mouse down and drag the mouse to the top of the screen. Let go of the LMB and move the mouse to the center of the screen. Hold the LMB down and drag the mouse to the top of the screen. This allows you to continue to zoom in. Repeat the process but zoom out by dragging the mouse down instead of up.

6. *Click ESC or ENTER to exit, or right-click to display shortcut menu:*
Click the <ENTER> or <ESC> key to end the command.

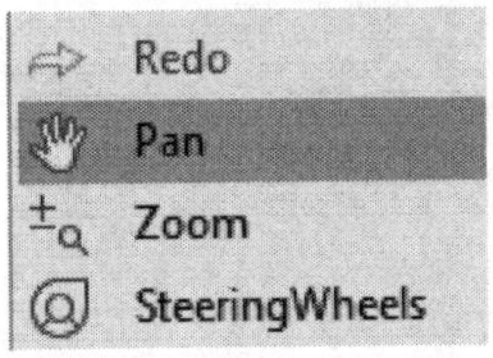

7. Invoke the Pan command (p or pan) or Right click in the screen and select Pan.

8. *Click ESC or ENTER to exit, or right-click to display shortcut menu:*
Select a location in the middle of the screen and hold your LMB down and drag your mouse up, down, right and left. Notice how the drawing pans as you move your mouse. Let go of the LMB, reposition the mouse and repeat the steps above to continue panning in one direction.

9. *Click ESC or ENTER to exit, or right-click to display shortcut menu:*
Click the RMB and select zoom from the view shortcut menu. Zoom in or out by holding the LMB down and dragging the mouse up and down.

10. *Click ESC or ENTER to exit, or right-click to display shortcut menu:*

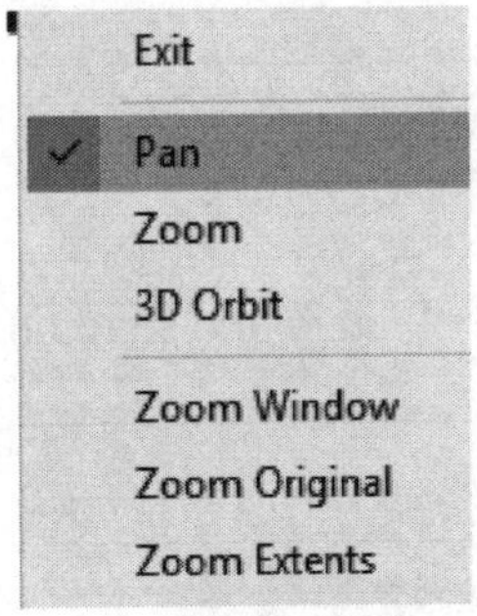

Click the RMB and switch back to Pan. Pan through the drawing.

11. *Click ESC or ENTER to exit, or right-click to display shortcut menu:*
    Click the RMB and switch to Zoom Window in the shortcut menu. You will create a window with your mouse that will represent the area to zoom in on. Position your mouse to create a rectangular window. Hold your LMB down and drag the mouse diagonally to create a window. Release the left mouse button to finish the command and zoom in on the drawing. Notice that this method is a *drag and release* and works slightly differently than the regular Zoom Window command.

12. *Click ESC or ENTER to exit, or right-click to display shortcut menu:*
    Click the RMB and select Zoom Extents. Notice how AutoCAD zooms to the extents of the drawing. Click the RMB and select the Zoom Original option in the shortcut menu. Notice how the drawing zooms to the original settings that existed when the ZOOM / PAN command was first invoked.
13. Close the file without saving.

The Microsoft IntelliMouse offers many user-friendly viewing options that are automatically invoked by using the Wheel on the IntelliMouse. Autodesk recommends using the Microsoft IntelliMouse with AutoCAD.

Command Exercise

Exercise 2-2 – Zoom

Drawing Name: **zoom1.dwg**
Estimated Time to Completion: 10 Minutes

Scope

Zoom this drawing out several times then use the Zoom Window option and pick just inside the corners of the red rectangle.

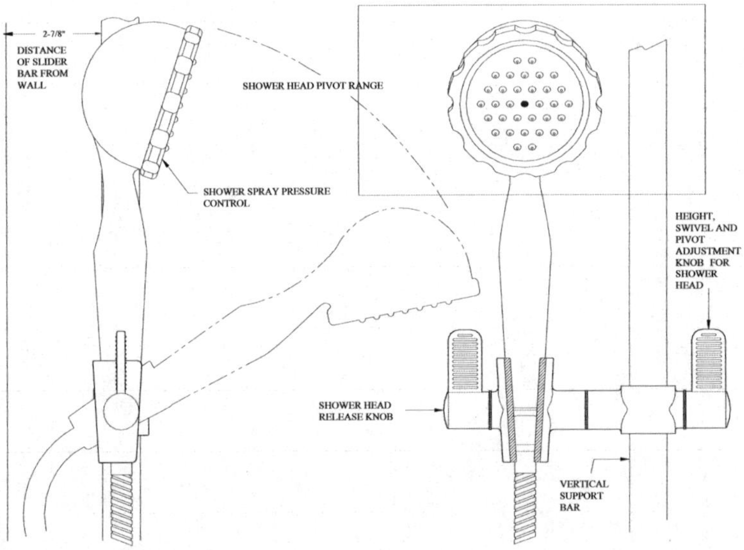

Solution

1. 

On the Quick Access Toolbar:

Click **Open.**

2. 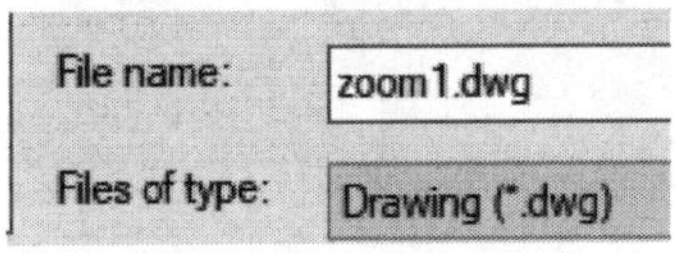

Browse to where you downloaded and saved the publisher's files.
Locate *zoom1.dwg.*
Click **Open.**

3. Invoke the Zoom command. Type **Z** and then use the scroll wheel on the mouse to zoom in and out.

4. *Click ESC or ENTER to exit, or right-click to display shortcut menu.*
Click the LMB in the middle of the drawing and drag down to zoom out of the drawing.

5. *Click ESC or ENTER to exit, or right-click to display shortcut menu.*
Click <ENTER> to end the command.

6. Invoke the Zoom Window command (z or zoom and <ENTER> once).
7. *[All/Center/Dynamic/Extents/Previous/Scale/Window/Object] <real time>:*
   Create a window with your mouse that will represent the area to zoom in on. Position your mouse inside a corner of the red box and click the LMB. Move the mouse diagonally to another corner of the box and click the LMB again. Notice how the Arcs and Circles are represented by small straight segments.

Extra: *From the <VIEW<ZOOM pull-down experiment with all the different zoom options available: Scale, Dynamic, Center, In, Out, Previous and All. Which method of viewing your drawing is the easiest?*

Tips & Tricks

- *You can invoke the Zoom Window function directly by typing Z <ENTER> and specifying the opposite corners of the Zoom Window (the Window option is the default).*

Command Exercise

Exercise 2-3 – Modifying the View Ribbon

Drawing Name: **zoom1.dwg**
Estimated Time to Completion: 5 Minutes

Scope

Activate the View Ribbon.
Modify which tabs and panels are available.

Solution

1. 

Verify that you are in the Drafting & Annotation workspace.

2. 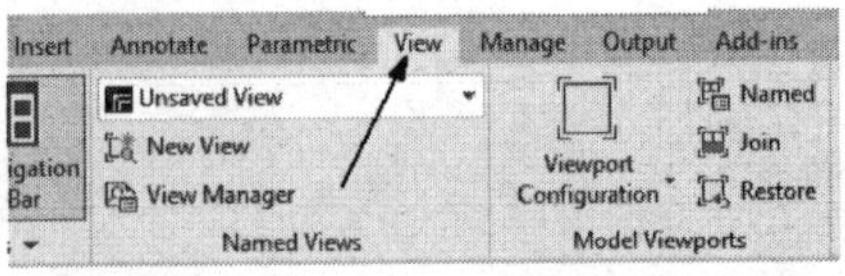

Select the **View** ribbon.

This displays the view tools.

3. 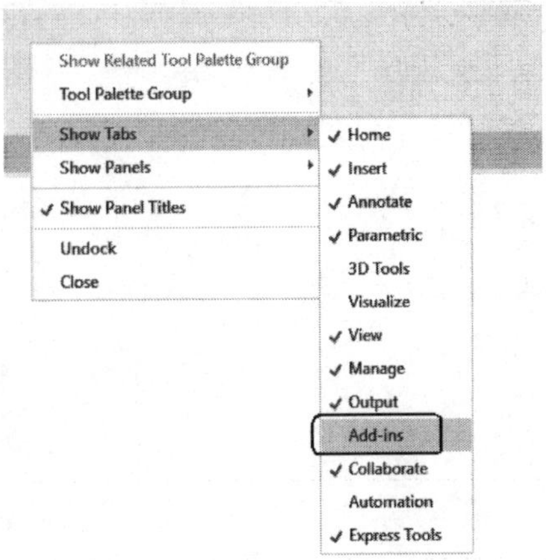

RMB anywhere on the ribbon.

If you expand the Show Tabs menu, you see the different tabs available for the ribbon.

Uncheck **Add-Ins.**

4. 

Notice the Add-Ins tab no longer appears on the ribbon.

5. 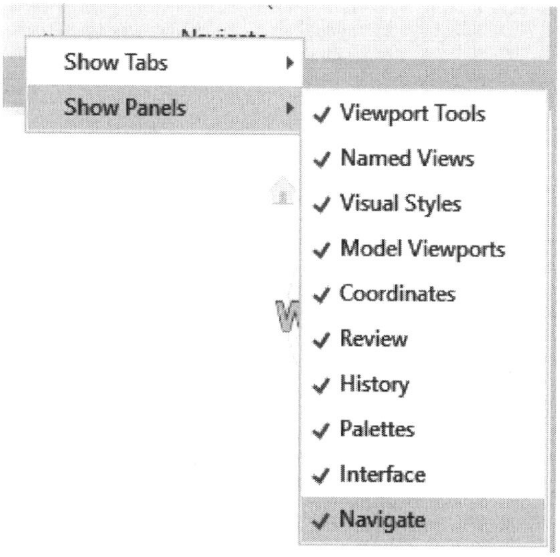

RMB on the ribbon again.

This time expand the Show Panels menu.

Place a check next to each name.

Observe how each panel is added to the ribbon.

> ➢ *Changes to the ribbon – like activating tabs and panels – are drawing-independent. Meaning when you change the ribbon, the changes remain regardless of which drawing file you are working on.*

Named Views

Command Locator

Command	**View**
Alias	**V**
Dialog Box	**View**
Ribbon	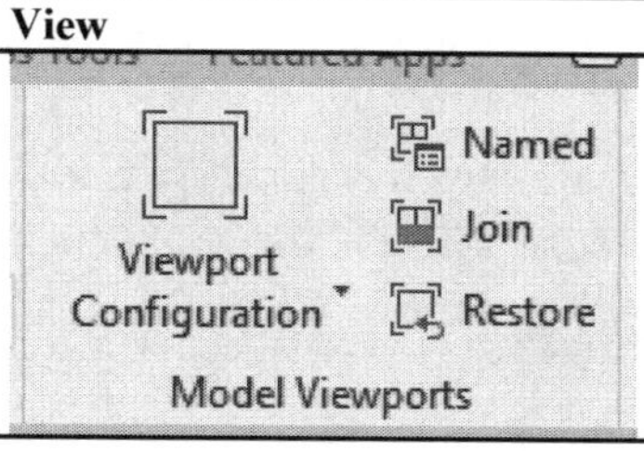

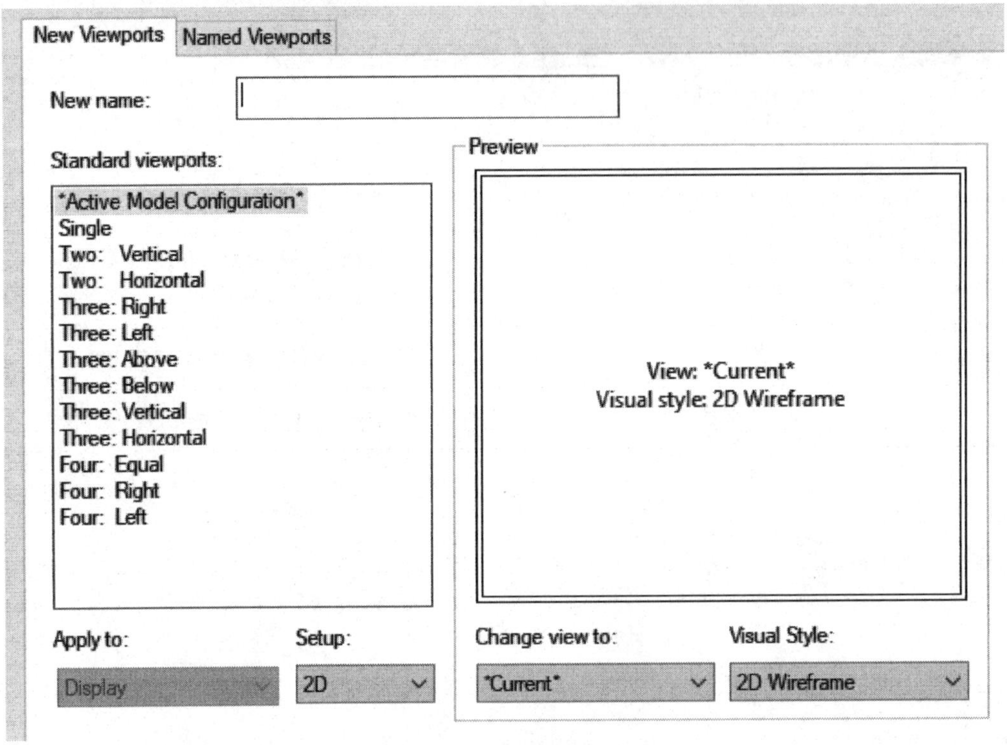

Viewports Dialog Box

Command Overview

Views can be saved and restored with the Named View command. This will save the time it takes to zoom out and into a frequently selected view. This tutorial will focus on the Named Views area of the View dialog box. New views can be Named as the Current display or defined by a new view (Define Window). Named Views from the list can be selected and set as the Current view.

General Procedures

1. Begin the Named Views command. Highlight 'Current' and select 'New'.
2. In the New View window, type the view name. Select 'Current display' or 'Define Window'. If Define Window is selected, select the cursor arrow and make a window around the desired view in the drawing. If this view is okay, select OK, otherwise try again.
3. Named Views can now be selected from the list and "Set Current."
4. To Delete or Rename a Named View, select it, then right click (RMB) and select the desired option.

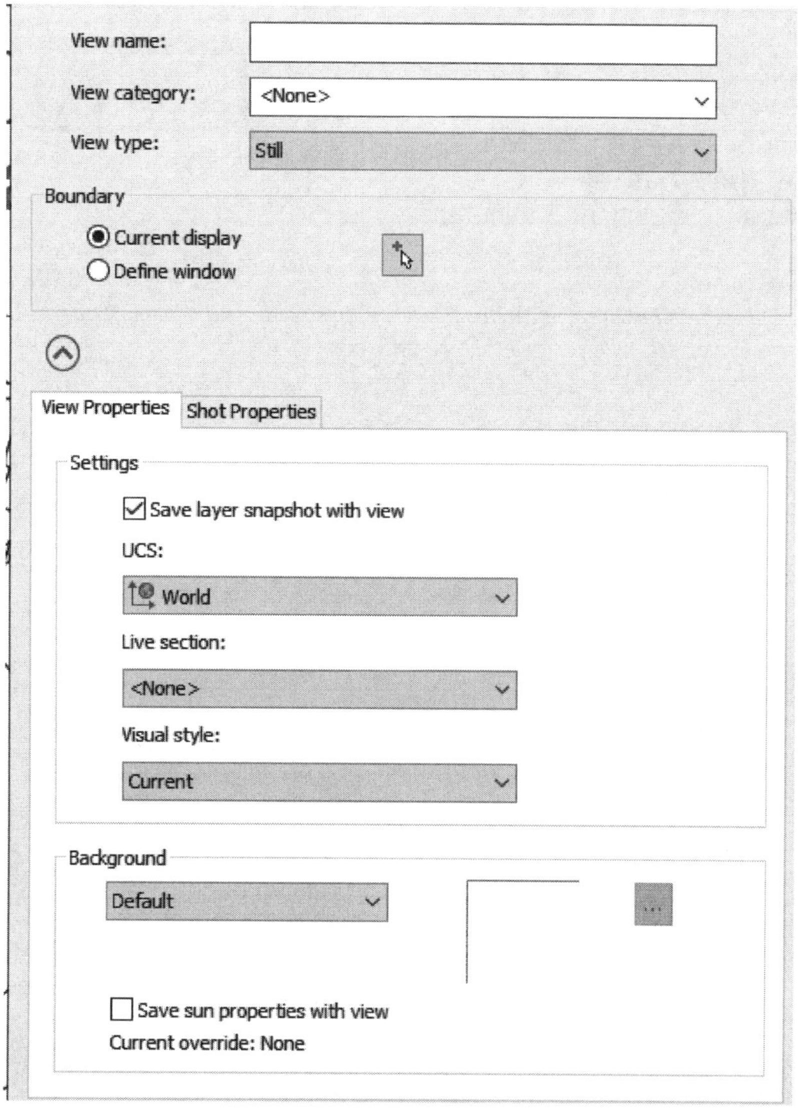

New Named View

View Name	Name of your saved view
View Category	The category is used in the Sheet Set Manager to organize your views. You can add a category or select one from the list. This entry is optional.
View Type	Options are Still, Cinematic and Recorded Walk.
Boundary	Sets the limits of the view.
Save layer snapshot View	Saves the current layer settings.
UCS Name	Allows you to set the view to a specific UCS.
Live section	Displays the live section applied when the view is restored. This option is only available when in the Model space.
Visual Style	Allows you to specify a visual style to be assigned to a view.
Background	Allows you to set a different background color than the current setting. This can only be done for model space views in shaded mode.

Command Exercise

Exercise 2-4 – Saving Named Views

Drawing Name: **nview1.dwg**
Estimated Time to Completion: 5 Minutes

Scope

Zoom into the specified area. With the Named Views command, name the view BALLAST and save it. Zoom All, then restore the named view.

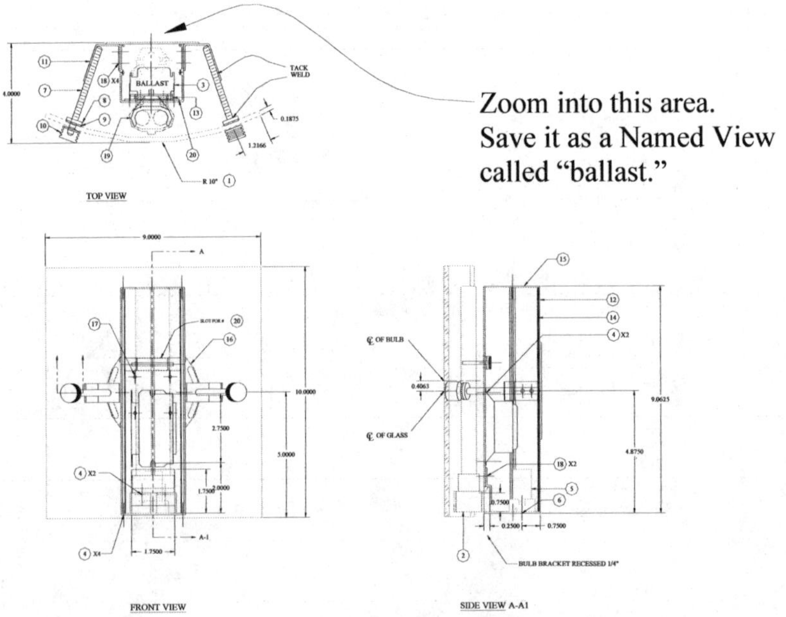

Solution

Enable the View ribbon in order to access the proper tools.

1.

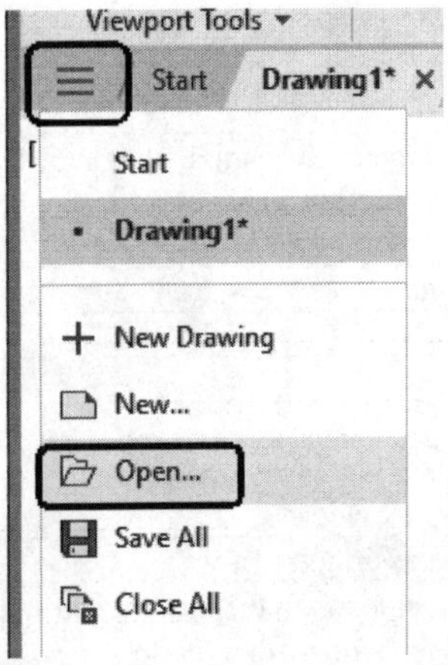

Left click on the three horizontal bars next to the Start tab.

Select **Open** from the list.

Open the *nview1.dwg*.

2. 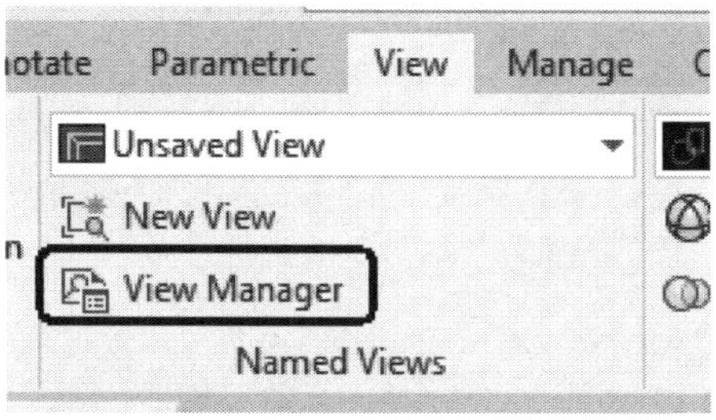

Go to the View ribbon.

Select **View Manager**.

3. 

Click the **New** button.

4. 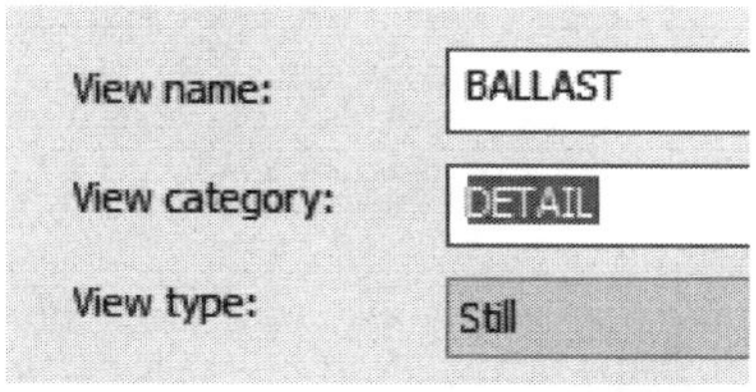

In the New View dialog box, fill out the information as shown. Click **OK**.

5. 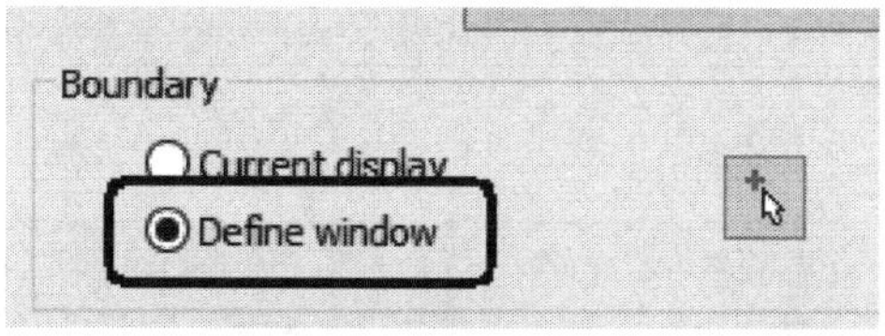

Enable **Define window**.

6. 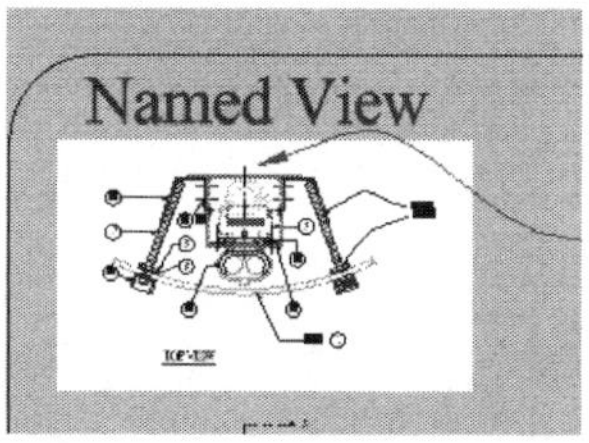

Window around the top view.
It should highlight.
Click ENTER.

7. 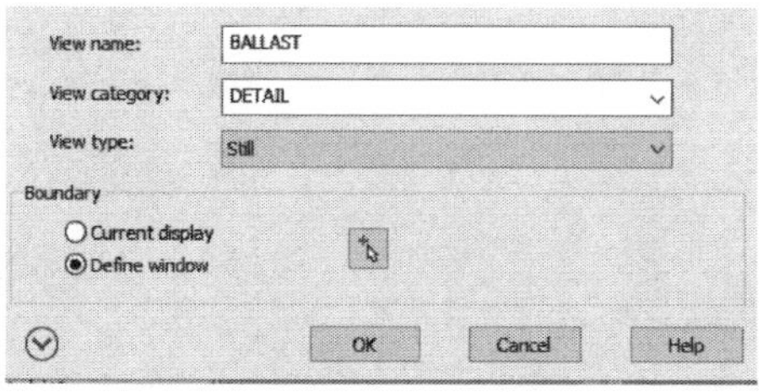

Click **OK**.

8. 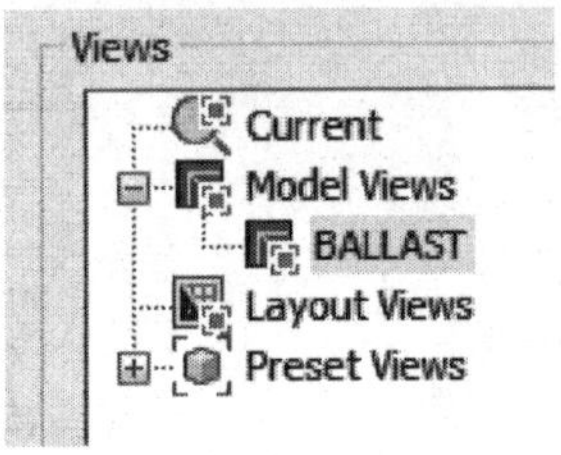

The view is listed in the left pane.

Click **OK** to close the View Manager dialog.

9. Double left click the scroll wheel on the mouse to zoom extents.

Notice that the entire drawing is now visible in the drawing window.

10. 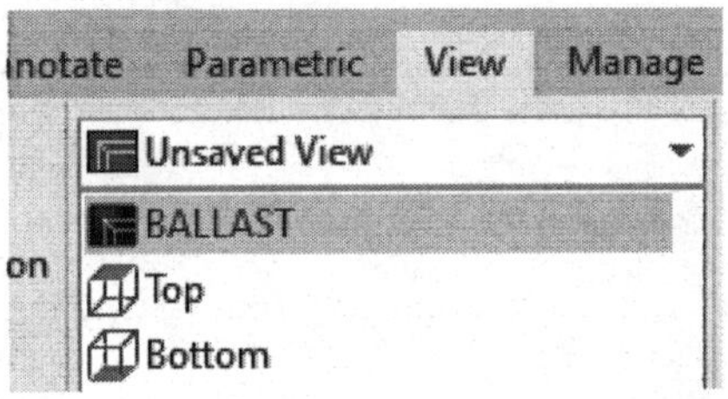

Select the BALLAST name in the Views list on the ribbon by left clicking on the name.

The drawing window now displays the BALLAST view you created at the beginning of the exercise.

Extra: *Practice saving other views in the drawing.*

Tips & Tricks

- Named Views are saved with the drawing file.
- Certain characters are not allowed for the View name.
- Remember to select Current display or Define window for the New Named View.
- You can save layer settings with Named Views to create different views for your layouts.
- The name can be up to 255 characters long and contain letters, digits, and the special characters dollar sign ($), hyphen (–), and underscore (_).
- Named Views can be placed on sheets.

Multiple Viewports

Command Locator

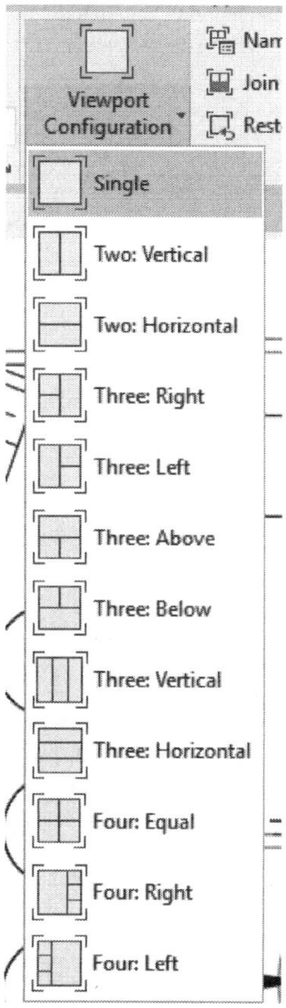

Command	**Viewports**
Alias	**Vports**
RMB Shortcut Menu	**List box**
Dialog Box	**Viewports**
Ribbon	**View/Model Viewports**

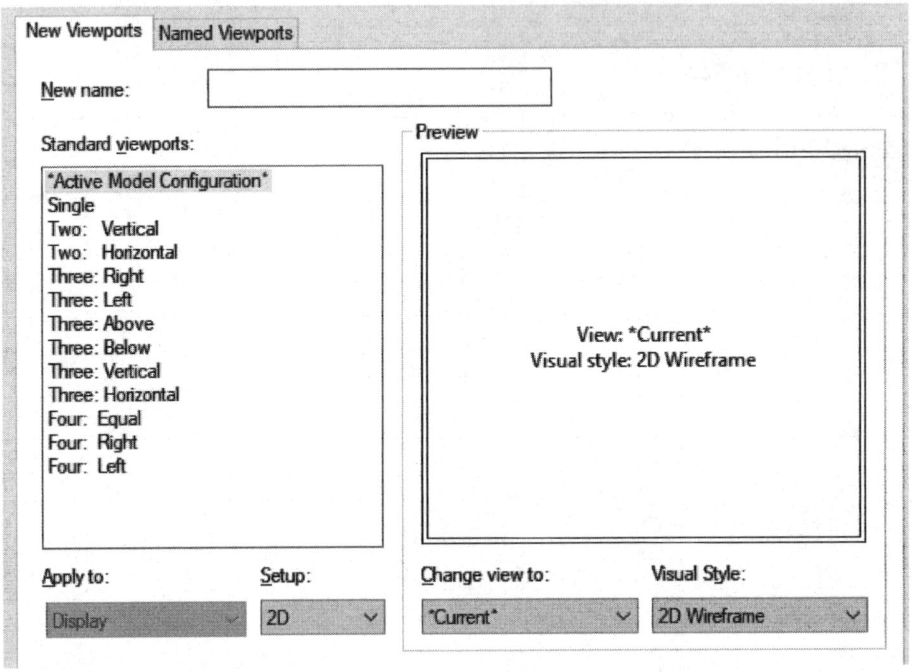

Command Overview

The Model view of the drawing can be divided into Multiple Viewports. Each viewport can display a different part of the drawing; however, only one viewport may be active. Tiled viewports configurations, including the views within each viewport, can be named and selected to be current later in the drawing.

General Procedures

To create one, two, three, etc. viewports:

1. Select the desired number of viewports from the Pull-Down (POP) menu, View / (select 1, 2, 3, or 4 viewports).
2. Follow the command line prompts. For three viewports, “Right” is the default location for the largest viewport.

To create viewports using the Viewports dialog box:

1. Type vports, or select the POP option View / Viewports / New Viewports…
2. Select the viewport configuration from the list.

To use Multiple Viewports:

1. Select a viewport to make it active.
2. Use any of the Zoom commands. To draw between viewports, click on one viewport and pick a point, then click on the other viewport to continue drawing the object.

To Save a Viewport Configuration:

1. From the Viewport dialog box, select the New Viewports tab.
2. Type in the New name for the current viewport configuration.
3. This name will appear in the list, and later can be selected and made current.

- An active viewport is the one with the bolder border around it. The cursor crosshairs will also be visible in the active viewport.
- Named Viewport configurations are saved with the drawing file.

Command Exercise

Exercise 2-5 – Multiple Viewports

Drawing Name: **vport1.dwg**
Estimated Time to Completion: 10 Minutes

Scope

Create four tiled viewports. Restore a named view in each viewport. Save the viewport configuration as V1. Join two adjacent views and save this as V2. Change to a single viewport. Restore the Saved viewport configurations.

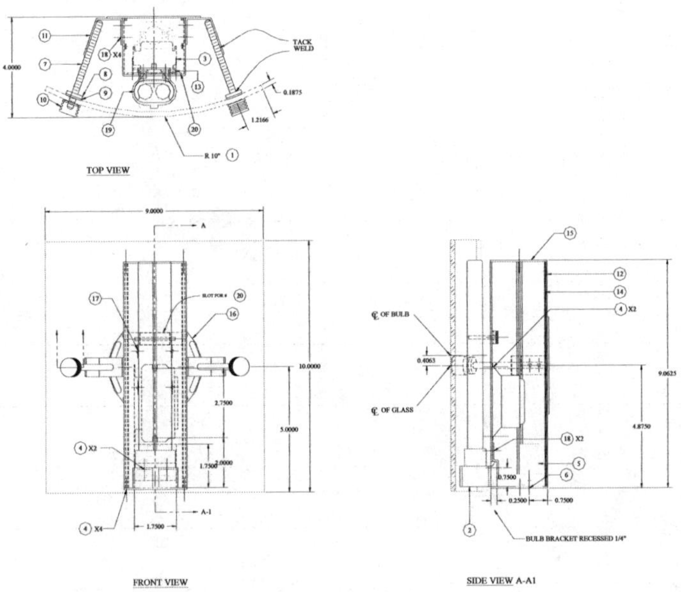

Solution

1. Start the exercise by creating four tiled viewports.

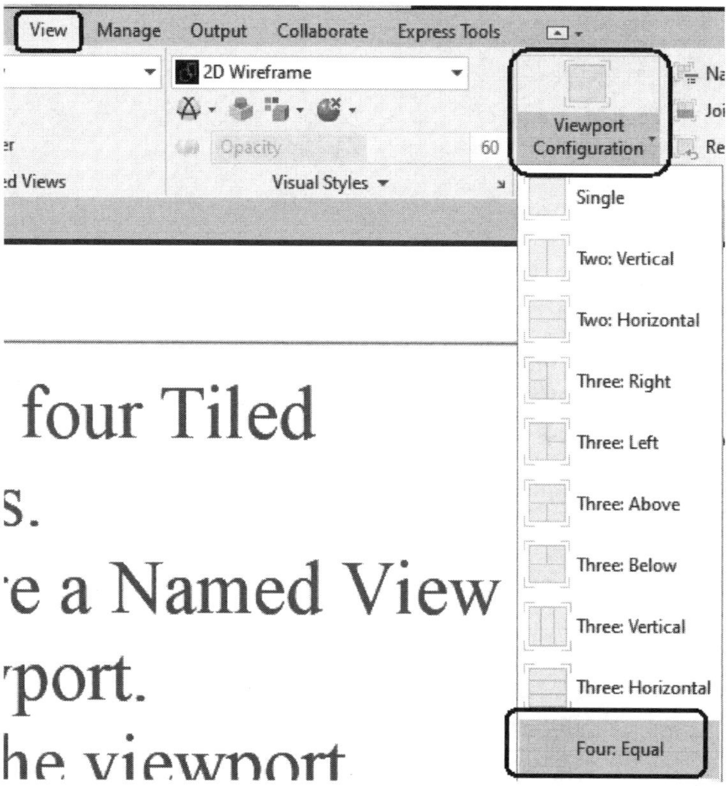

On the View ribbon:

Select **Viewport Configuration→Four:Equal**.

2. Notice how the drawing window is divided into 4 viewports. The same view is displayed in all four viewports. We will now restore different Named Views in each viewport.

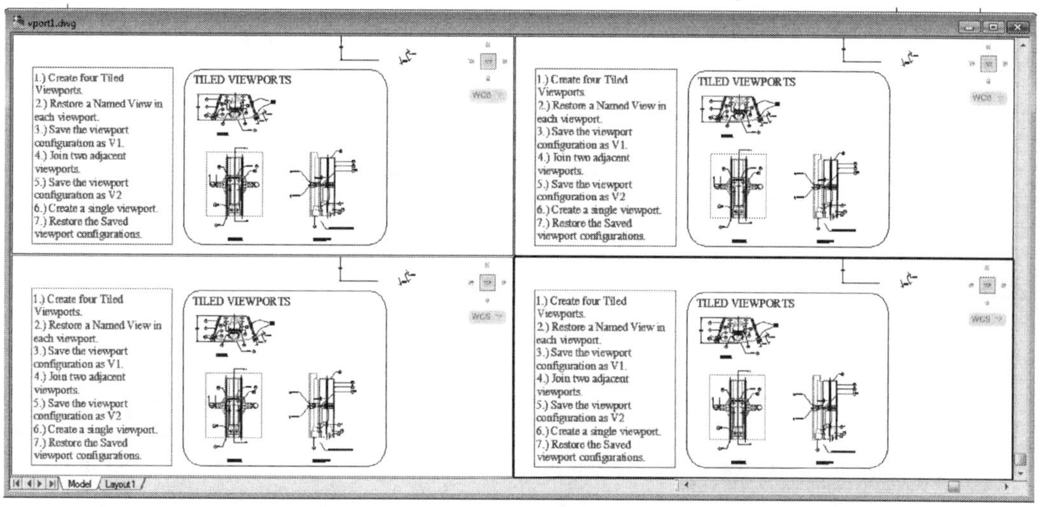

Four Viewports

3. Move your pointer to the upper left corner viewport and activate the viewport by clicking inside it with your LMB.

4. On the View ribbon, locate the View Manager with the view names listed.

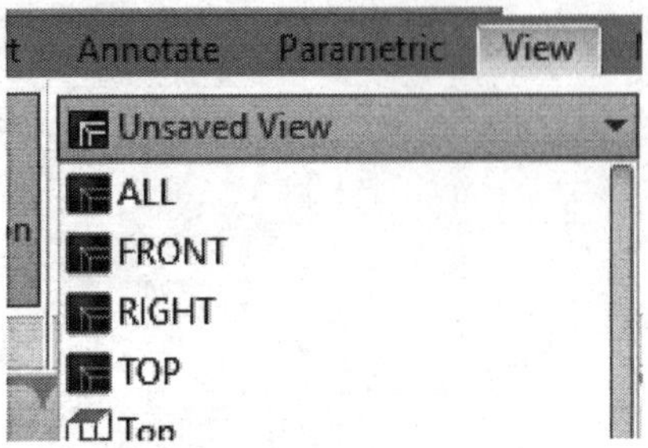

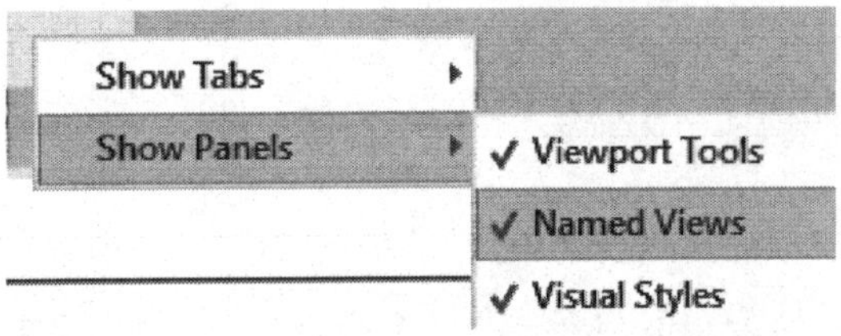

If you do not see the Views panel on the ribbon, you need to enable it.

Right click on the ribbon and select **Show Panels→Named Views**.

5. In the View list, select 'TOP' to set it current for the viewport.

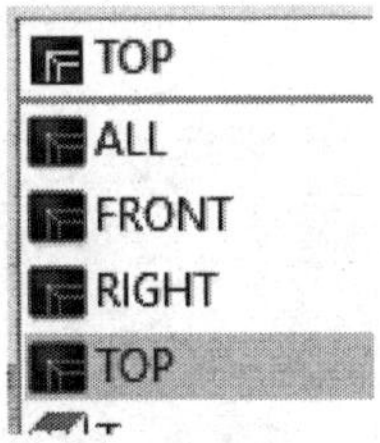

View Dialog Box

6. Move your cursor to the bottom left corner viewport and activate the viewport by clicking inside it with your LMB.

7. Select the FRONT view to assign it to the bottom left viewport.

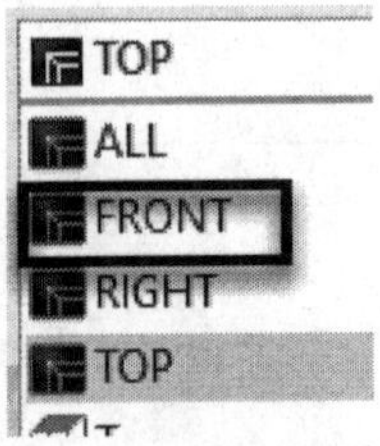

8. Move your cursor to the bottom right corner viewport and activate the viewport by clicking inside it with your LMB.

9. Select the RIGHT view to assign it to the bottom right viewport.

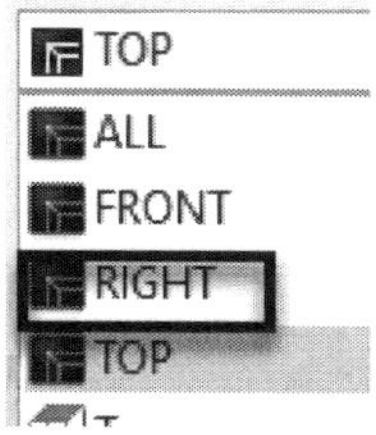

10. Your drawing may look similar to the next figure.

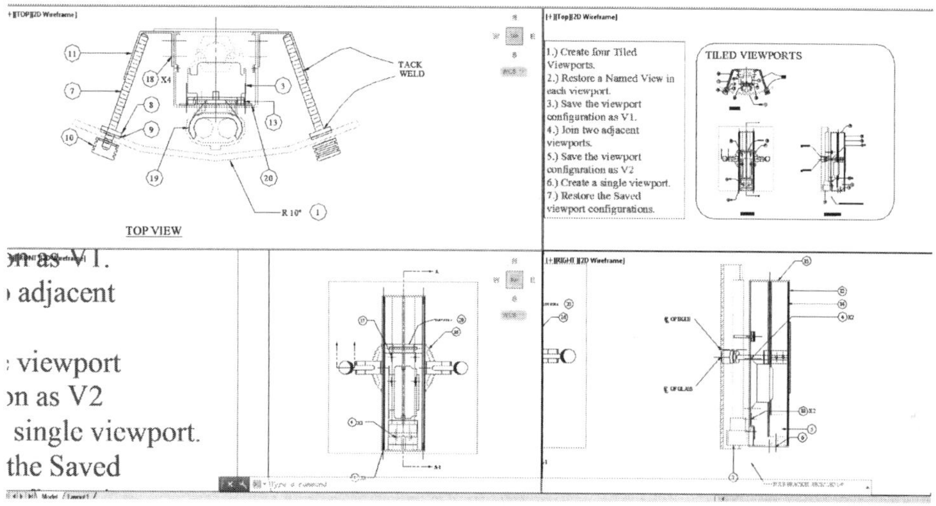

Four Viewports after Changing the Views

11. Once you have created the layout above, save the configuration. Select **Named** on the Model Viewports panel from the View ribbon.

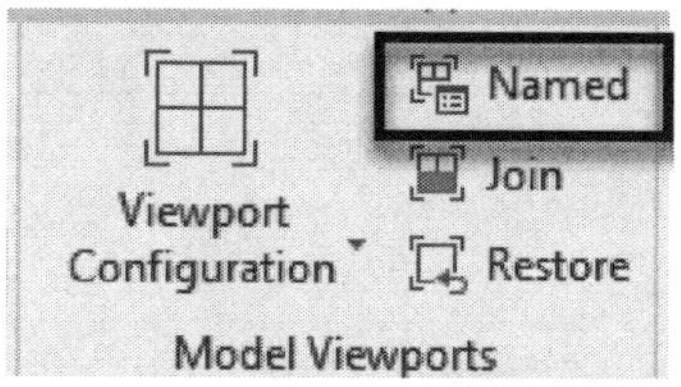

12. In the Viewports dialog box, select the New Viewports tab. Enter the information displayed in the following figure. Enter **V1** for the new name. Click **OK** to save. You have just saved a viewport configuration that can be restored at any time.

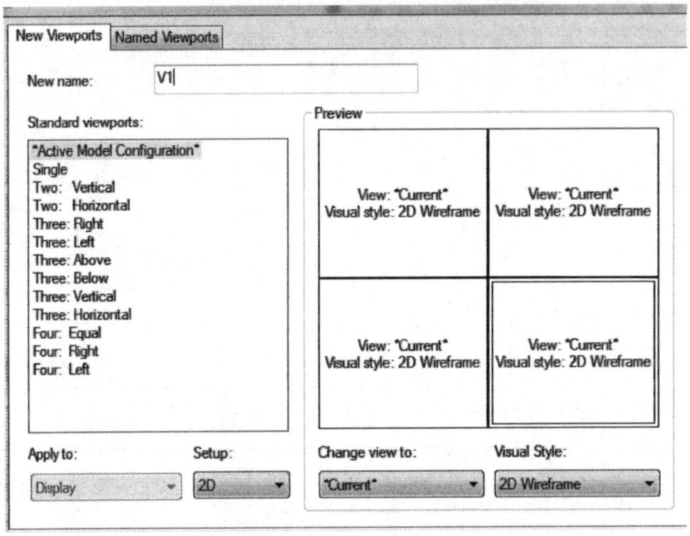

Viewports Dialog Box

13. Click on the **Restore** button on the ribbon.

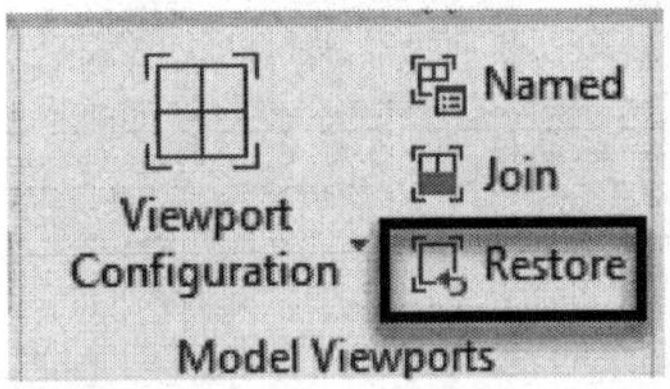

14. The display changes back to a single viewport.
    Double click the scroll wheel on the mouse to zoom extents.

15. Select **Named**.

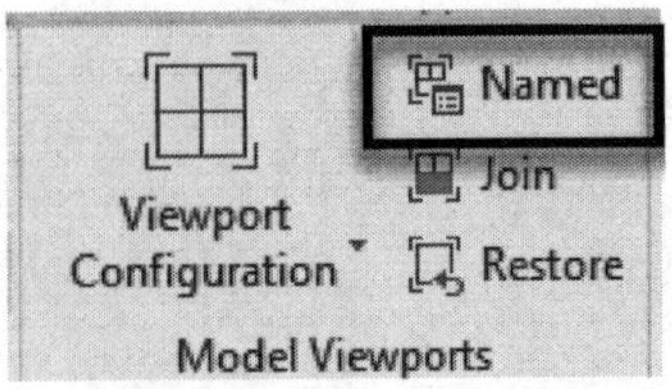

16. Left click on V1 – the named configuration you just created with four viewports. Click **OK**.

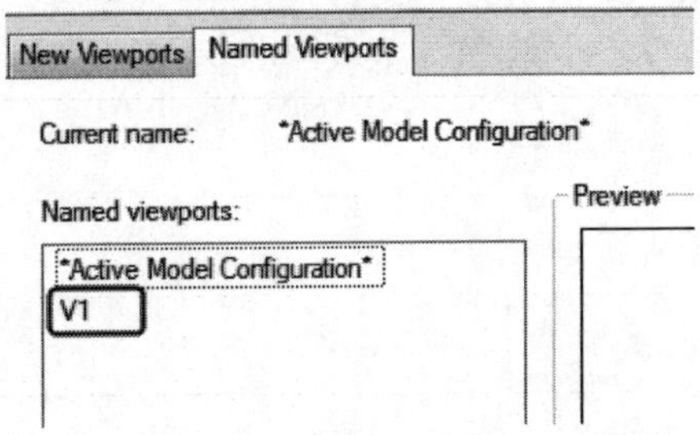

17. The V1 configuration is restored.

- *Use your RMB to activate a pop-up dialog box that will allow you to delete or rename your viewport configurations (Named Viewports) in the Viewports dialog box.*

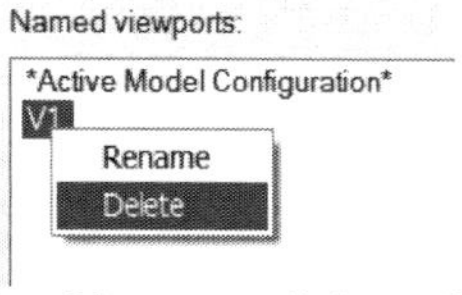

- You can click on the View Name in the upper left of the view to change the view.

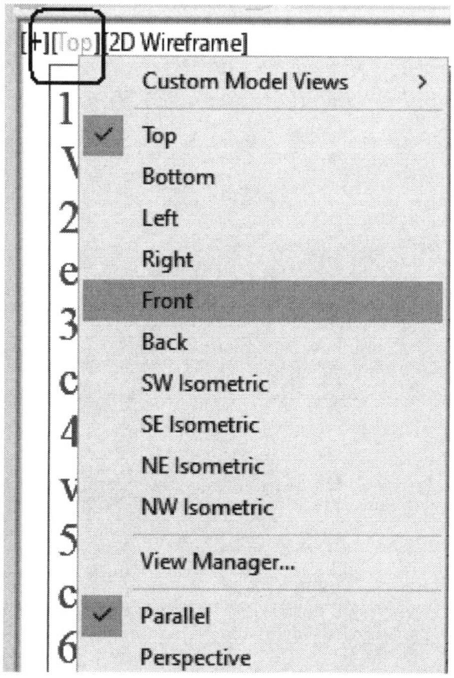

Lesson Exercise

Exercise 2-6

Viewing Drawings

Drawing Name: **Lesson 2 MCAD.dwg**
Estimated Time to Completion: 15 Minutes

Scope

Use the commands you have learned in Lesson Two to view the drawing. Determine which viewing commands are easier for you to use. Locate information on the drawing and fill out the table below. Follow the instructions on the drawing for creating a named view and tiled viewport layout. Save the file as Lesson 2 MCAD_complete.dwg.

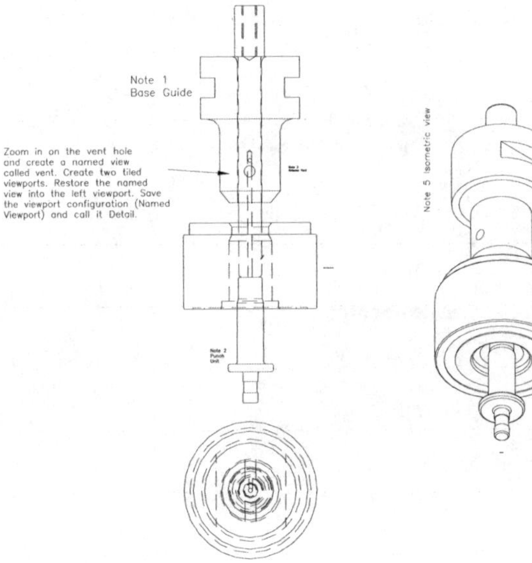

Hints

1. Choose a zoom command you feel comfortable with. The author likes the Zoom Window and Zoom Previous commands.
2. Note 6 is under the Isometric drawing. Note 7 is under the number 6 in Note 6.
3. Use the named views command and named viewports command to complete the second part of the exercise.

Lesson Exercise

Exercise 2-7

View Commands

Drawing Name: **Lesson 2 aec.dwg**
Estimated Time to Completion: **15 Minutes**

Scope

Using the commands learned in this Lesson, zoom and pan around the drawing. Examine the named views in the drawing and create named views of the kitchen, bath and small bedroom. View the drawing with multiple viewports.

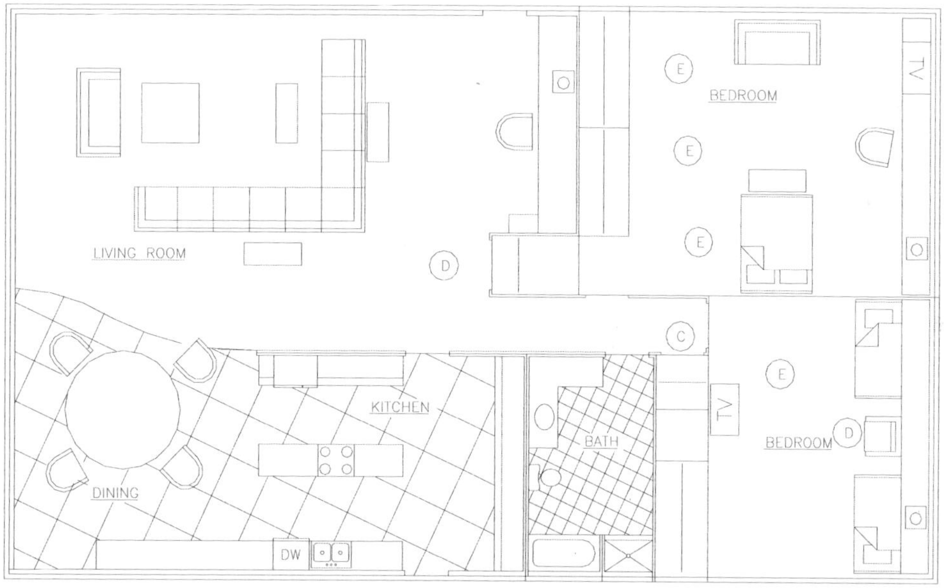

Hints

1. Use the different zoom options to become familiar with all of them.
2. Zoom in on the kitchen and create a named view of it. Do the same for the bathroom and small bedroom.
3. Use the Viewports command to bring up multiple viewports and show a different room in each viewport.

Review Questions

1. Identify the following icons by writing the command:

a		
b		
c	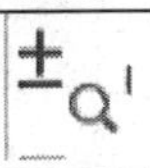	
d		
e		
f		
g		

2. What is the difference between Zoom Extents and Zoom All?

3. Which Zoom tools are available on the right click shortcut menu?

4. How do you make a viewport active? How can you tell that a viewport is active?

5. How many viewports can be active at the same time?
   - ❑ 1
   - ❑ 2
   - ❑ 3
   - ❑ As many as the user decides.

6. Can you create a new Viewport configuration (Named Viewport) if you activate the Viewport dialog box by selecting <VIEW<VIEWPORTS<NAMED VIEWPORTS… and Not <VIEW<VIEWPORTS<NEW VIEWPORTS…?

Review Answers

1. Identify the following icons by writing the command and the toolbars where they can be found:
    a. *Named View / Standard*
    b. *Pan Real-time / Standard*
    c. *Zoom / Standard*
    d. *Zoom Window / Standard & Zoom Toolbar*
    e. *Zoom Previous / Standard*
    f. *Zoom All / Standard & Zoom Toolbar*
    g. *Zoom Extents / Standard & Zoom Toolbar*

2. What is the difference between Zoom Extents and Zoom All?

    Zoom Extents will zoom only all of the geometry in the drawing. Zoom All will zoom everything - the drawing geometry and the drawing limits (grid area).

3. Which Zoom tools are available on the right click shortcut menu?

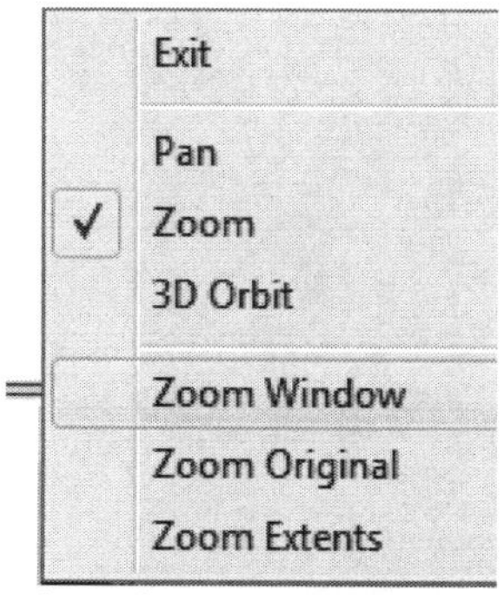

Zoom Window, Zoom Original, and Zoom Extents

4. How do you make a viewport active? How can you tell that a viewport is active?

    a. To make a viewport active, place the cursor in the viewport and select the left button on the mouse (LMB).

    b. An active viewport will have a slightly bolder border around it and will show the cursor crosshairs in it.

5. How many viewports can be active at the same time?

    ■ 1
    ❑ 2
    ❑ 3
    ❑ As many as the user decides.

    Only one viewport can be active in AutoCAD at one time.

6. Can you create a new Viewport configuration (Named Viewport) if you activate the Viewport dialog box by selecting <VIEW<VIEWPORTS<NAMED VIEWPORTS… and Not <VIEW<VIEWPORTS<NEW VIEWPORTS…?

    Yes, the viewport dialog box has two tabs: Named Viewports and New Viewports. Users can switch to either tab no matter how the dialog box was activated.

Notes:

Lesson 3.0 – Drawing Lines

Estimated Class Time: 2 Hours

Objectives

This section introduces AutoCAD commands for creating a simple drawing. Starting with a New drawing, the user will learn to draw lines using different methods.

- **Start From Scratch**
  - Use the New command to begin a new drawing from "scratch."
- **Line**
  - Draw line segments
  - Using Direct Distance Method
  - Using Polar Tracking
  - Using Cartesian Coordinates
  - Absolute Coordinates
  - Relative Coordinates
  - Polar Coordinates
  - Drag Method

- **Coordinate Entry**

- **Erase**
  - Deleting AutoCAD entities

- **Constraints**
  - Managing Geometric Constraints

Tips & Tricks

- Move the mouse after selecting each endpoint of the line. This will make it easier to see the last line segment created.
- Double click on ORTHO in the Status Bar (or press F8) to alternate between drawing straight or angled line segments.
- Typing U for Undo in the middle of the line command will undo the last line segment. Typing U after completing line segments (at the blank command prompt) will Undo the entire line command.

Start a New Drawing

Command Locator

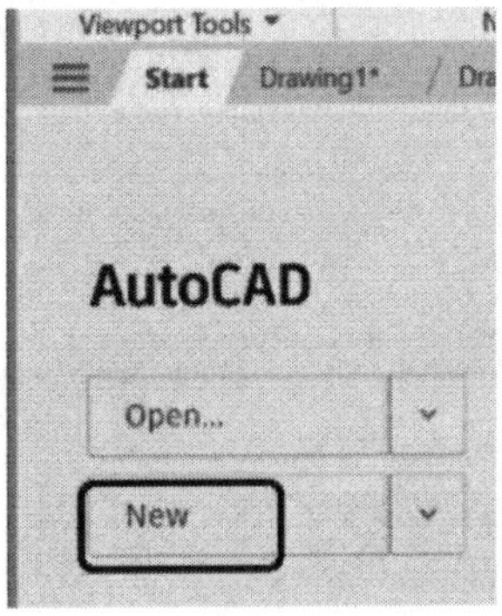

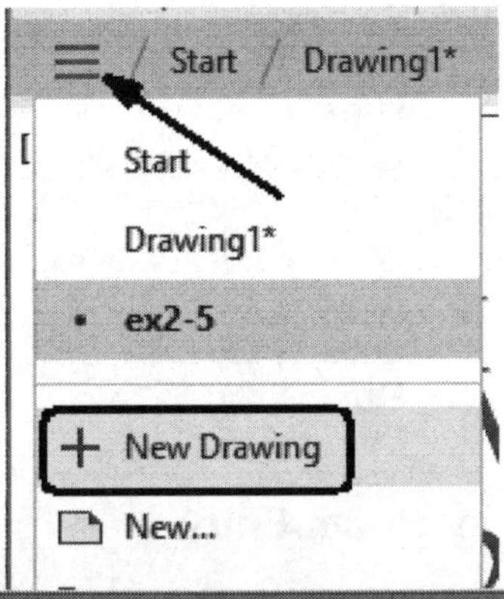

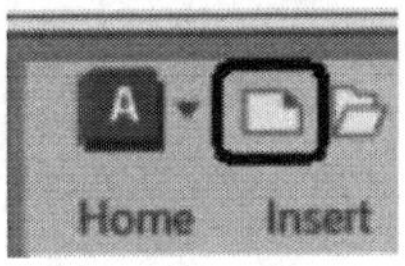

Command	**New**
Alias	**Ctrl+N**
Quick Access Toolbar	**New**
Application Menu	**New**
Start Tab	**New**
Folder tab	**Click the + tab**

For the exercises in this section, we will be using the *acad.dwt* template. This template setting was made when AutoCAD was installed. If you want to set a different default template to be used, go to the **Options** dialog and select the default template you wish to use.

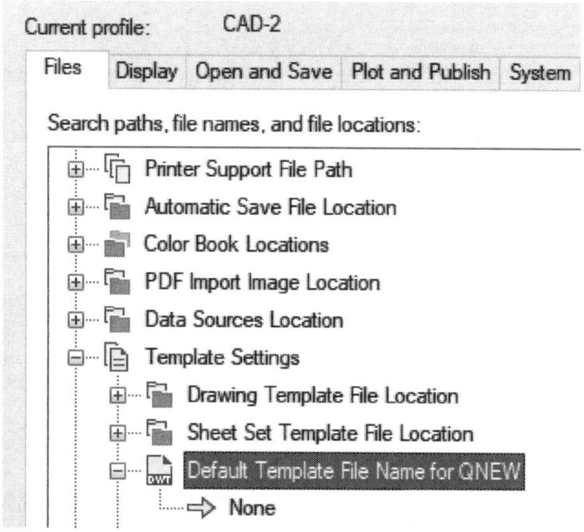

Command Overview

To Create a New drawing, choose New. Every time the New drawing command is invoked, a new drawing is created with the title Drawing1, Drawing2, Drawing3, etc.

General Procedures

1. Select the New button from the Standard Toolbar.

- Make it a habit to select the New file icon from the Quick Access Toolbar. This is a quicker way to access the command than from the Applications menu.
- Close drawings that are not being used.
- If you see an asterisk* next to the file name on the tab, it means there are unsaved changes.

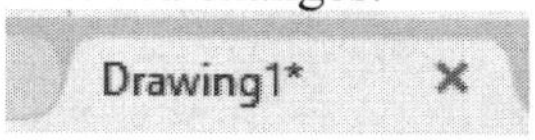

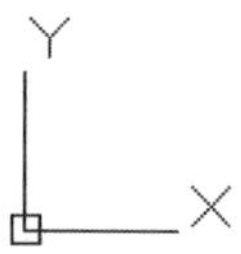

The graphics window uses a Cartesian coordinate system. The lower left corner of the screen shows a UCS (user coordinate system) icon. The icon shows x for horizontal and y for vertical. The z-axis is pointed toward the user. The UCS is located at the 0,0 or origin point.

You will see some numbers on the status bar. These numbers reflect the coordinate point (x, y) of your mouse. Move your mouse around and note how the coordinate values change.

- To toggle the display of coordinates on the status bar, left click on the Customize tool in the lower left of the screen and left click on Coordinates in the list.

Your graphics window in AutoCAD emulates a piece of paper. LIMITS controls the size of your piece of paper. When you start a new file, you can specify the size of paper you want to draw on using Wizards or Templates. AutoCAD really doesn't care where you draw in your graphics window. You can draw outside the limits with impunity.

AutoCAD allows you to draw geometry using four methods:

- **Absolute Coordinates**
- **Relative Coordinates**
- **Polar Coordinates**
- **Direct Entry**

Absolute Coordinates use absolute values relative to the origin.
Relative Coordinates use coordinates relative to the last point selected.
Polar Coordinates use a distance and angle relative to the last point selected.
Direct Entry allows the user to set ORTHO on (this is like using a ruler to draw a straight line), move the mouse in the desired direction, and then enter in the desired distance.

Line

Command Locator

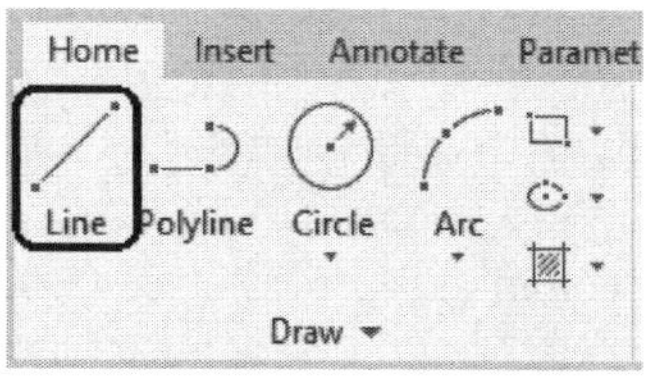

Command	**Line**
Alias	**L**
Home/Draw	**Line**

Command Overview

A line is defined by two endpoints. A line has 0 width and 0 thickness. When drawing a line, specify the first point, then specify the next point. Press the enter button on the mouse (with the cursor in the drawing window) to access the Line Shortcut menu. Type C to close two or more line segments. Use the LMB to pick the points.

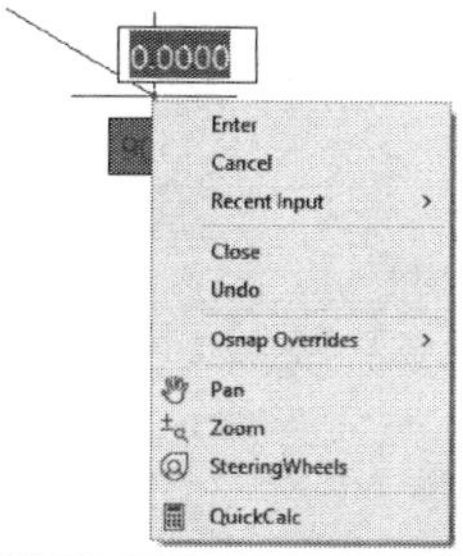

Line Shortcut Menu Option:	Overview
Enter	Select to exit the Line command.
Cancel	Cancels the command.
Recent Input	Lists the most recently entered point coordinates.
Close	Closes the line to form a closed polygon.
Undo	Undoes the last segment of the line.
OSnap Overrides	Allows the user to select an object snap.
Pan	Begins Real-Time Pan.
Zoom	Begins Real-Time Zoom.
Steering Wheels	Launches the Steering Wheel control.
QuickCalc	Launches a calculator.

General Procedures

1. Begin the line command by selecting the line icon in the Draw panel on the ribbon or typing L at the blank command prompt.
2. Select the first point, select the next point, and continue selecting the endpoints of each successive line segment.
3. Press the <ENTER> button on the mouse (with the cursor in the drawing window), then select <ENTER> to end the Line command.
4. Press <ENTER> to Repeat the Line command.

Tips & Tricks

- If you make an error selecting a point, right click and select Undo.
- If you escape out of a line and want to start at the point where you left off, start the LINE command and then press ENTER – the line will automatically start at the last end point selected.

Command Exercise

Exercise 3-1 – Line using Direct Distance Method

Drawing Name: **Begin a new drawing**
Estimated Time to Completion: 10 Minutes

Scope

Start a New drawing. Enable DYN. With ORTHO on, draw the object below. Drag the line in the desired direction and type the distance. Do not add the dimensions.

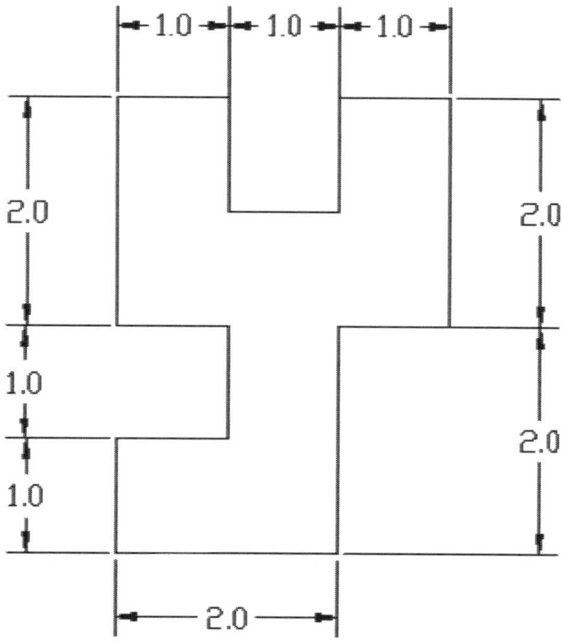

1. 

Start a New drawing by pressing the + tab.

2. 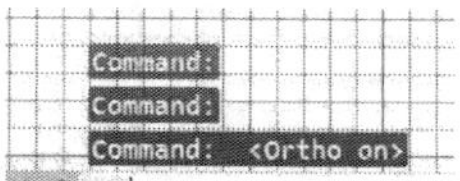

Turn **ORTHO** on by pressing <F8> until the command line says '<Ortho on>'.

3. 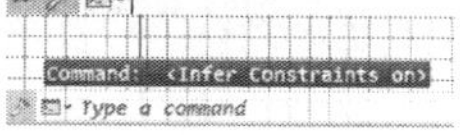

To see the geometric constraints as they are added, enable **Infer Constraints** or press **Ctrl+Shift+I**.

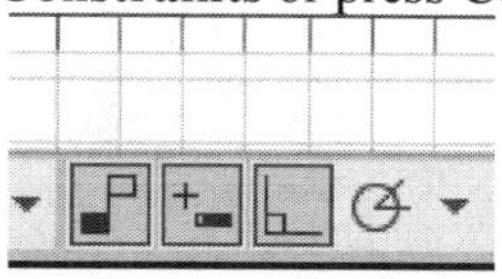

4. 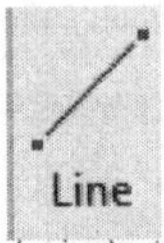

Invoke the **Line** command (l or line) on the Home ribbon.

5. 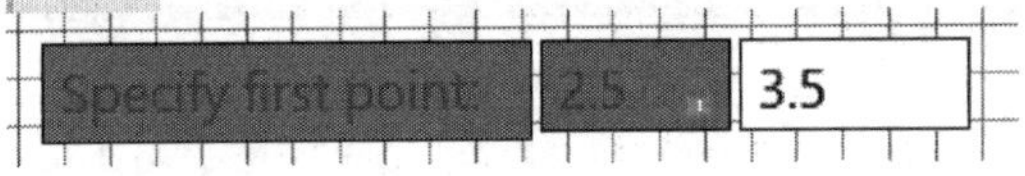

Specify next point or [Undo]:
Type **2.5** for the X-coordinate.
Use the TAB key to advance to the Y-coordinate square.
Type **3.5** for the Y-coordinate. Press **<ENTER>**.

6. 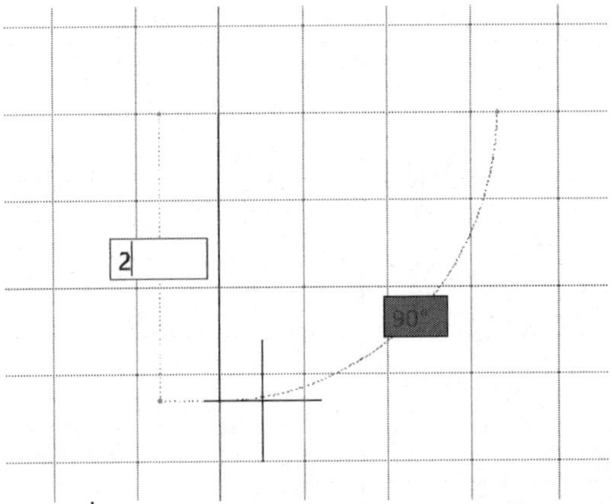

Specify next point or [Undo]:
Drag the cursor downward and type **2.00** and press <ENTER>.

7. 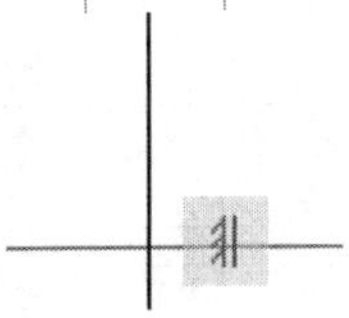

You will see a small icon next to the line. This is a geometric constraint.

A geometric constraint controls the geometry of an element. In this case, the symbol indicates that the line is vertical.

8. 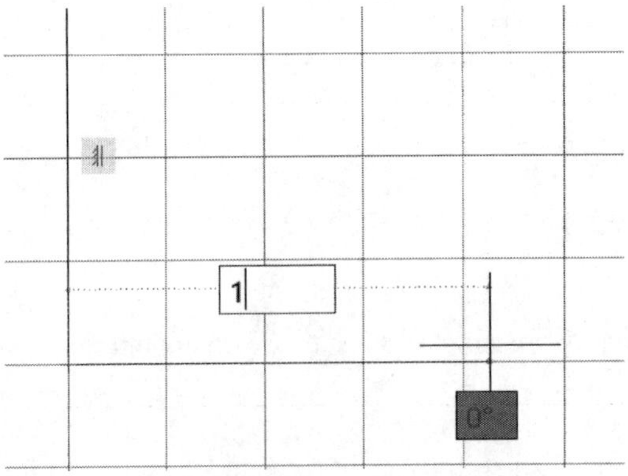

Specify next point or [Undo]:
Drag the cursor to the right and type **1.00** and press <ENTER>.

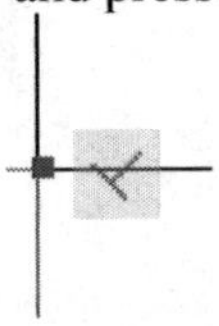

You should see another geometric constraint. This symbol indicates that the two lines are perpendicular to each other. Perpendicular means two lines form a 90°angle.

9.

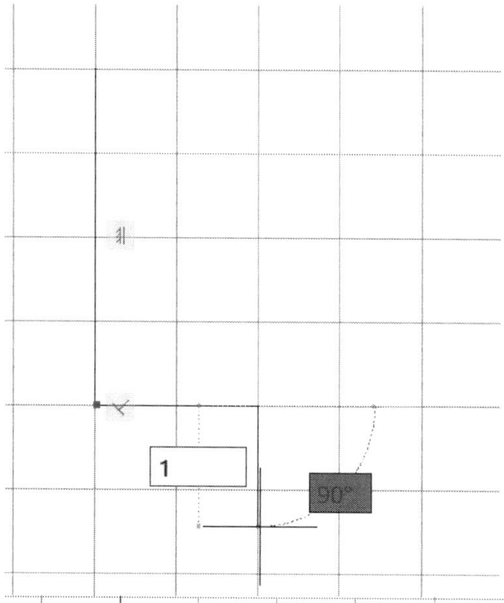

Specify next point or [Close/Undo]:
Drag the cursor downward and type **1.00** and press <ENTER>.

Another perpendicular symbol is added.

10.

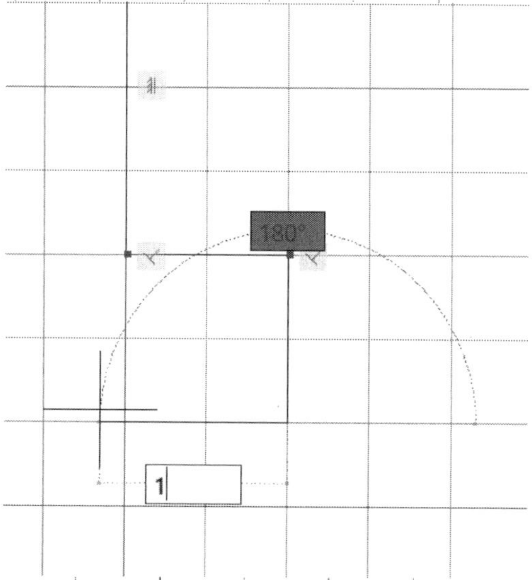

Specify next point or [Close/Undo]:
Drag the cursor to the left and type **1.00** and press <ENTER>.

11.

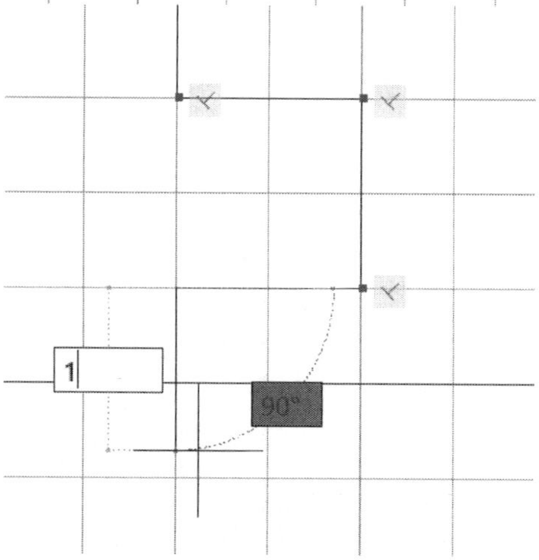

Specify next point or [Close/Undo]:
Drag the cursor downward and type **1.00** and press <ENTER>.

12.

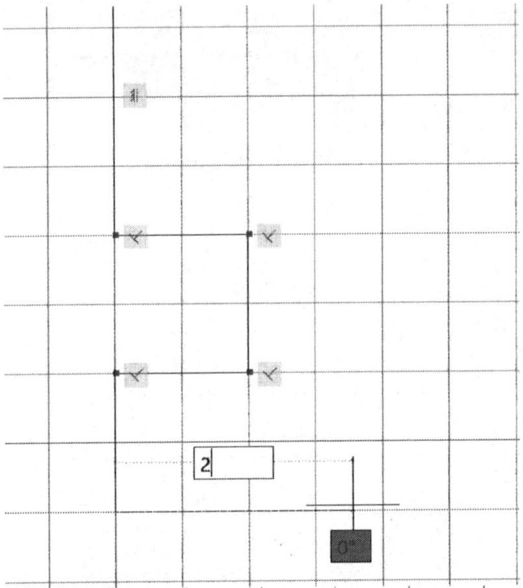

Specify next point or [Close/Undo]:
Drag the cursor to the right and type **2.00** and press <ENTER>.

13.

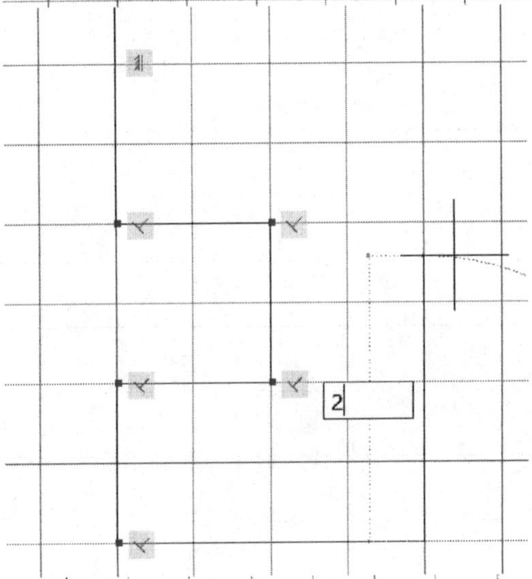

Specify next point or [Close/Undo]:
Drag the cursor up and type **2.00** and press <ENTER>.

14.

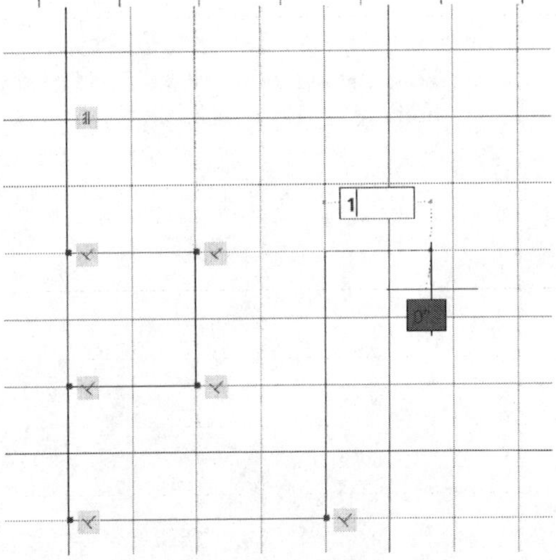

Specify next point or [Close/Undo]:
Drag the cursor to the right and type **1.00** and press <ENTER>.

15. 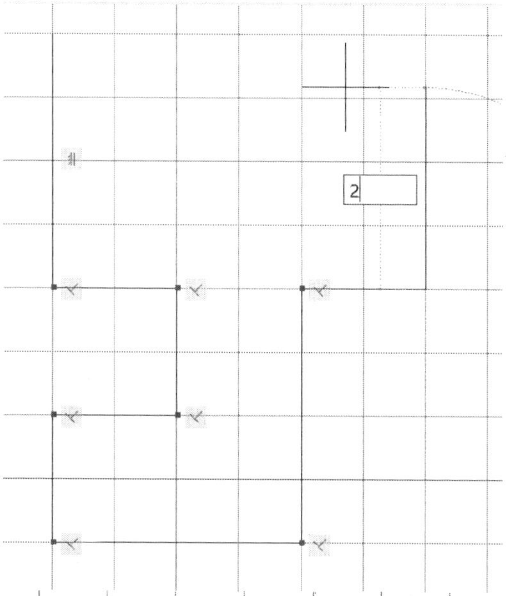

Specify next point or [Close/ Undo]:
Drag the cursor upward and type **2.00** and press <ENTER>.

16. 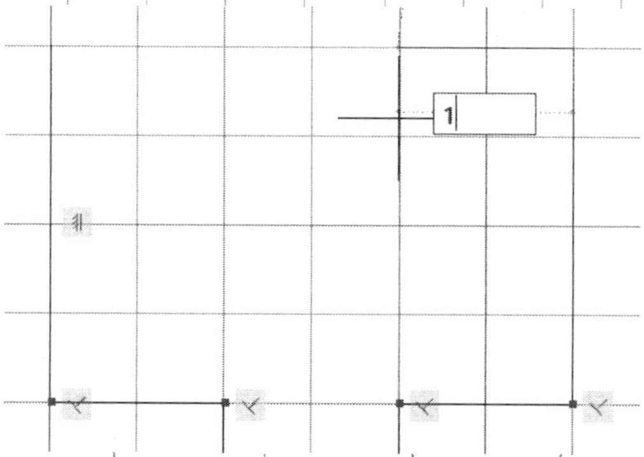

Specify next point or [Close/Undo]:
Drag the cursor to the left and type **1.00** and press <ENTER>.

17. 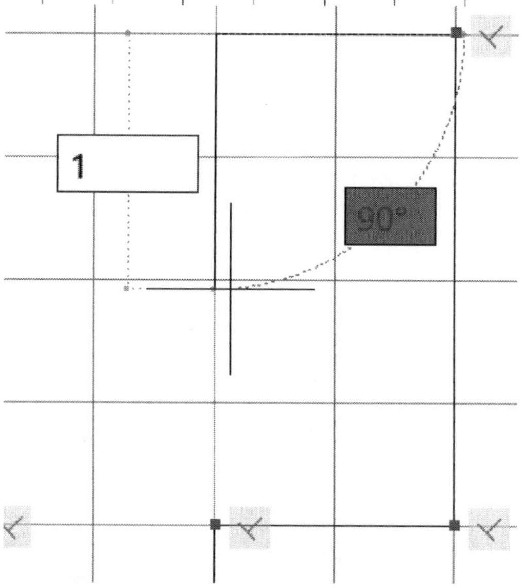

Specify next point or [Close/Undo]:
Drag the cursor downward and type **1.00** and press <ENTER>.

18. 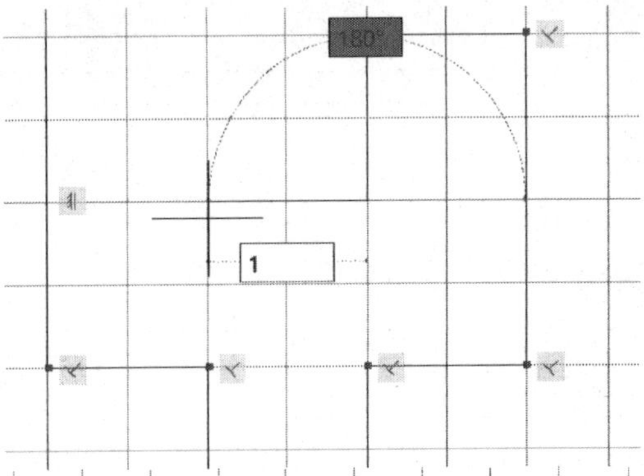

Specify next point or [Close/Undo]:
Drag the cursor to the left and type **1.00** and press <ENTER>.

19. 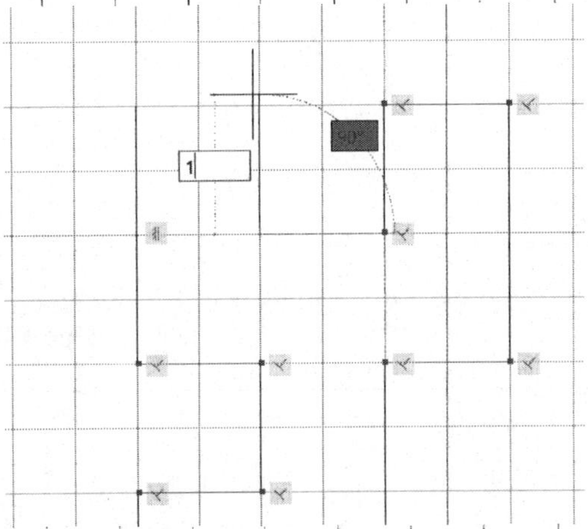

Specify next point or [Close/Undo]:
Drag the cursor upward and type **1.00** and press <ENTER>.

20. 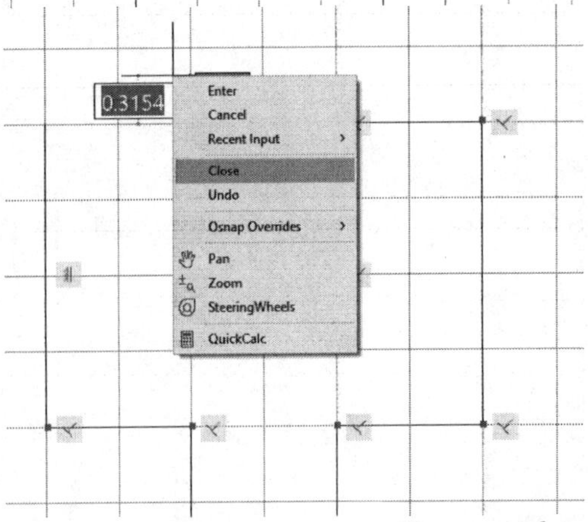

Specify next point or [Close/Undo]:
Right-click in the drawing area and select 'Close' or type 'C' and press <ENTER>.

The Close command will only work if you created a continuous line. If you exited the line command and started again, then you have to manually close the figure.

21. 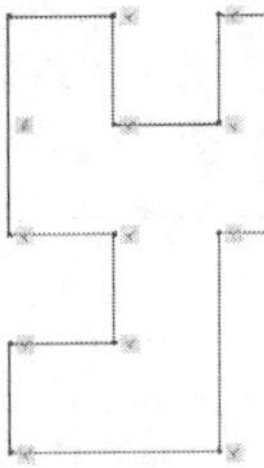

Your completed figure should look like this.

See if you can identify the different geometric constraints. You should see constraint symbols for vertical, horizontal and/or perpendicular.

To see the figure clearer, turn off the grid.

If the lines look crooked, then ORTHO is not on. You must begin again. Try to draw all of the line segments without starting and stopping the line command.

The Close option only works if you draw in one continuous line. Otherwise, you can simply draw a closing line from endpoint to endpoint.

Parametric Constraints

Command Locator

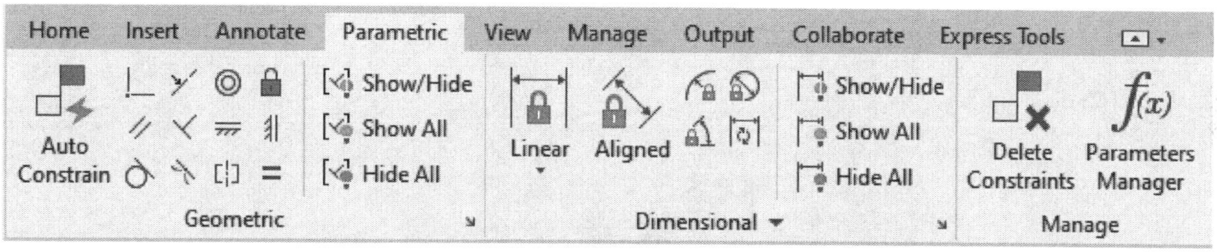

Parametric Ribbon	**Parametric**
Command	**Geomconstraint**

Command Overview

To see the parametric constraints ribbon, you should have the Drafting & Annotation Workspace enabled.

General Procedures

1. To apply a geometric constraint, select the type of geometric constraint desired, then select the element(s) to be constrained.

- Use inferred constraints - these are constraints which are automatically added as you draw.
- Hide geometric constraints when you are not actively constraining your sketch.
- Typing U for Undo in the middle of the line command will undo the last line segment. Typing U after completing line segments (at the blank command prompt) will Undo the entire line command.
- You can prevent constraints from automatically being applied by toggling OFF inferred constraints on the status bar or using the shortcut Ctl+Shift+I.

Command Exercise

Exercise 3-2 – Parametric Constraints

Drawing Name: **constraints1.dwg**
Estimated Time to Completion: 10 Minutes

Scope

Open 'constraints1.dwg.' Mouse over a constraint. Show all Constraints. Add a constraint. Delete a constraint. Hide all Constraints.

Solution

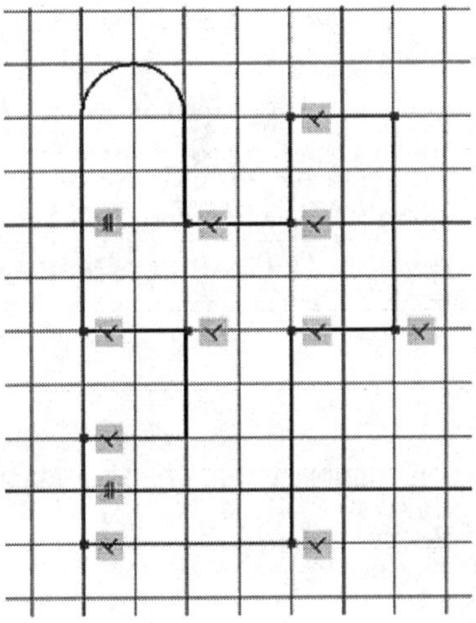

1.

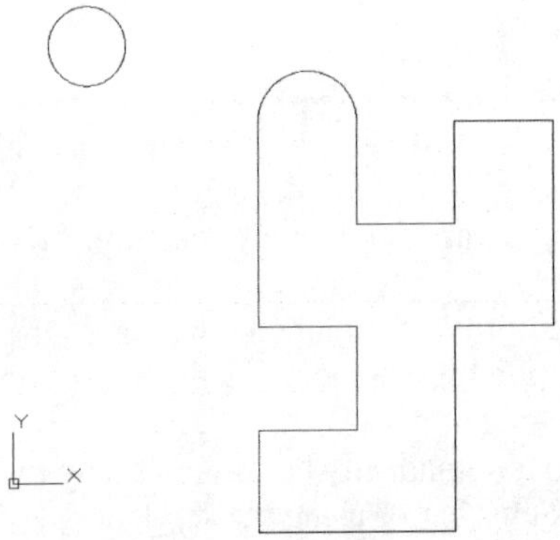

When the drawing is first opened, you should not see any geometric constraints. The geometric constraints have been hidden. Their display has been turned OFF.

Mouse your cursor over the drawing WITHOUT selecting anything. Don't left click. As you mouse over the lines, you should see a small symbol. The symbol indicates that a geometric constraint exists for that line. If no geometric constraint exists, you will not see the symbol. Mouse over the small circle and notice that no symbol appears.

2. 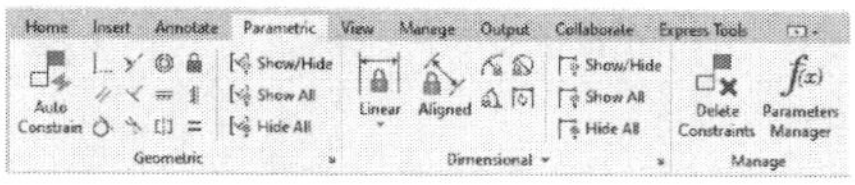

Activate the **Parametric** ribbon.

3. 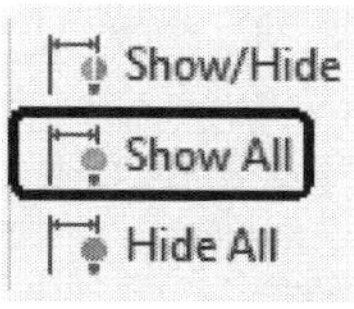

Select **Show All** to display all the geometric constraints currently applied.

Be sure to select from the Geometric panel, not the Dimensional!

4. 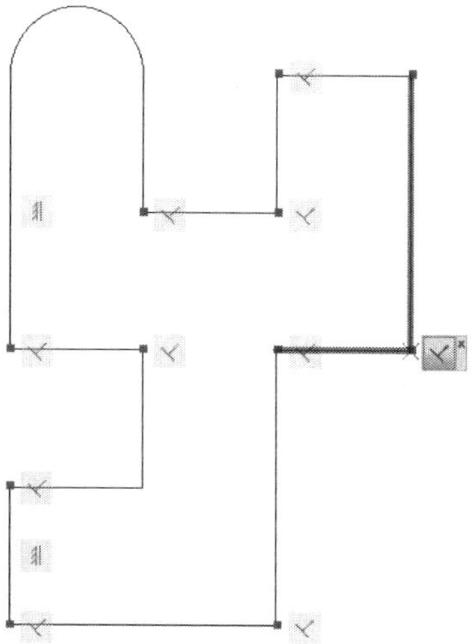

Use your left mouse button to rearrange the geometric symbols.
Hold down the left mouse button and drag the symbol to a new position.

5. 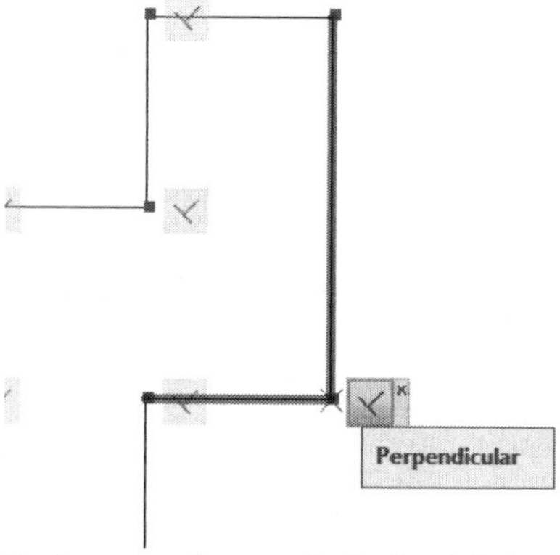

Place the left mouse button over one of the perpendicular symbols.

Notice that it will highlight the two lines that are perpendicular. You do not need to select the symbol. Just hover over it.

Let's move the small circle so it is concentric to the arc using a geometric constraint.

A concentric constraint means that two or more arcs/circles share the same center point. The elements can have different radii.

When you apply a geometric constraint, the FIRST element remains fixed and the SECOND element moves to be constrained.

6. 

Select the **Concentric** constraint.

7. 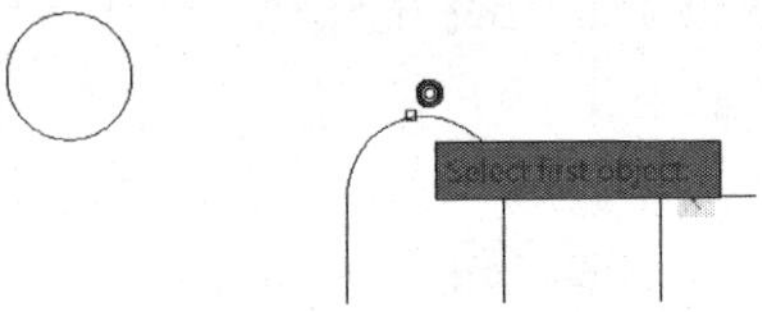

You will see a small Concentric symbol indicating that you are going to be applying that constraint type.
There is a prompt asking you to select the elements to be used for the constraint.

Select the arc first and then the circle.

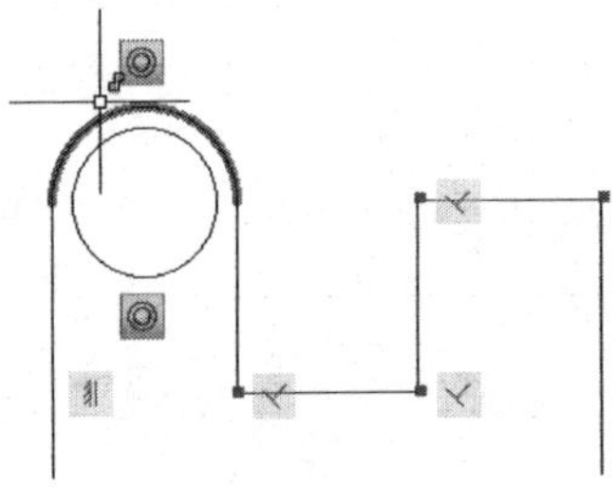

The circle popped into the correct position. You also see the concentric symbol on the arc and the circle.

8. 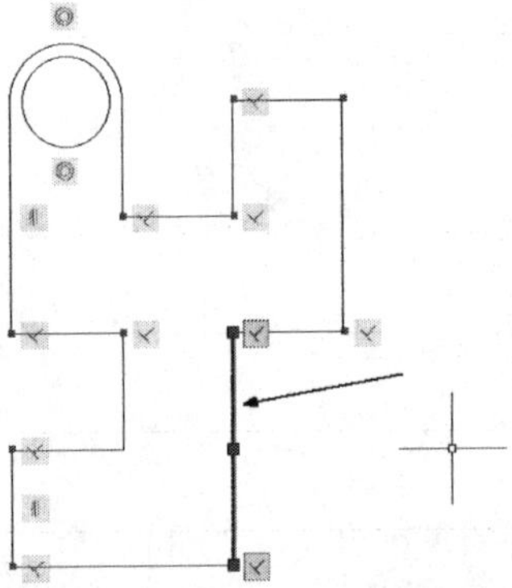

Select the line indicated.

9. 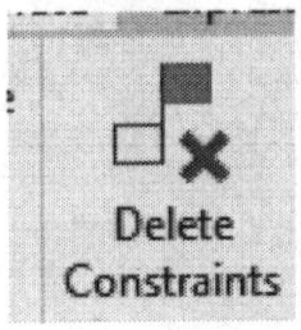

Select **Delete Constraints**.

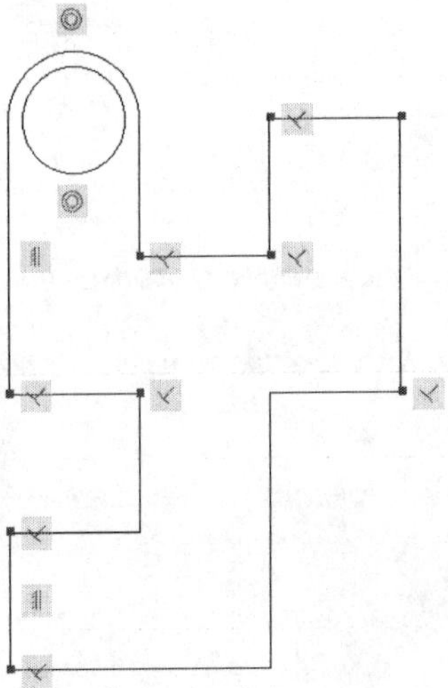

The perpendicular constraints on the selected line are deleted.

10. 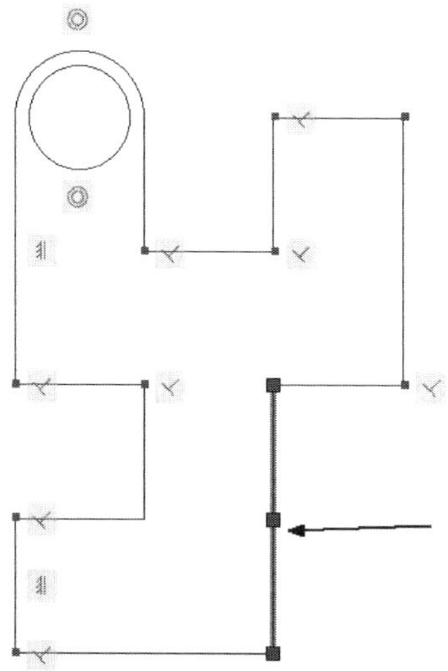

Select the same line.

11. 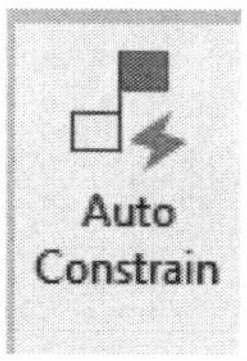

Select **Auto Constrain** from the ribbon.

This will add constraints to the selected line.
What constraints do you think will be added?

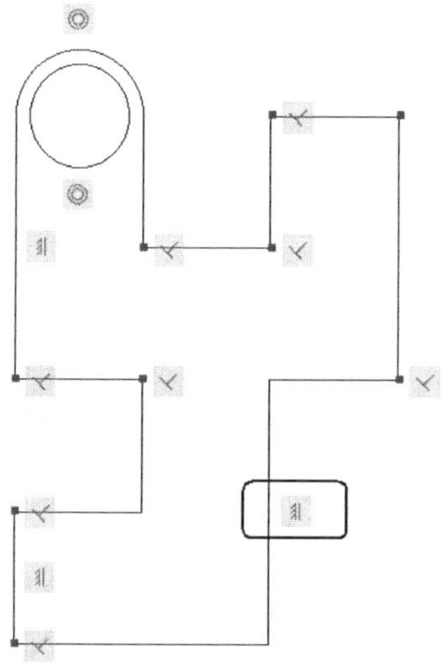

A vertical constraint is added.

In order to add a perpendicular constraint - you need to select TWO lines.

12. 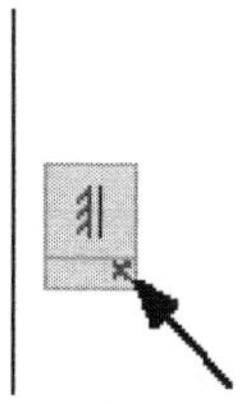

Select the vertical constraint.
Select the small x in the symbol box.

This hides the constraint.
It does not delete it.

13.

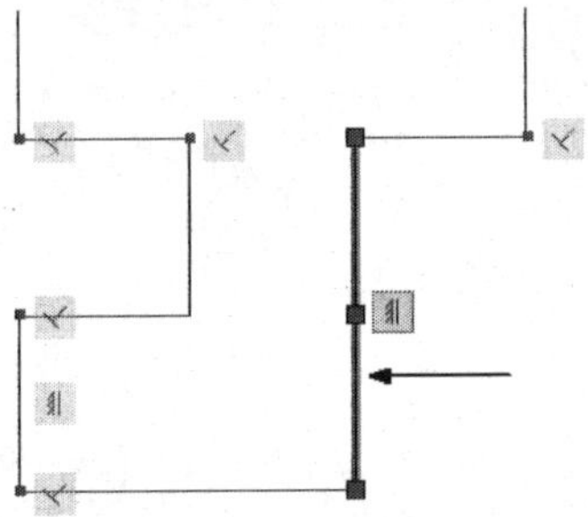

Select the vertical line.

The vertical symbol will appear while the line is selected.

14.

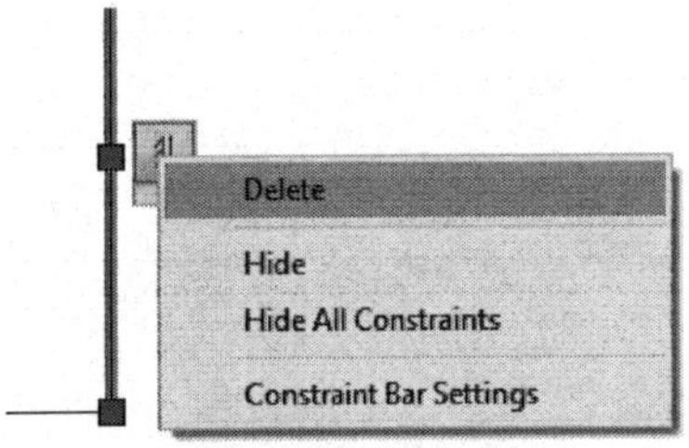

To delete the vertical constraint, select it, right click and select **Delete**.

Press ESC to release the selection.

15.

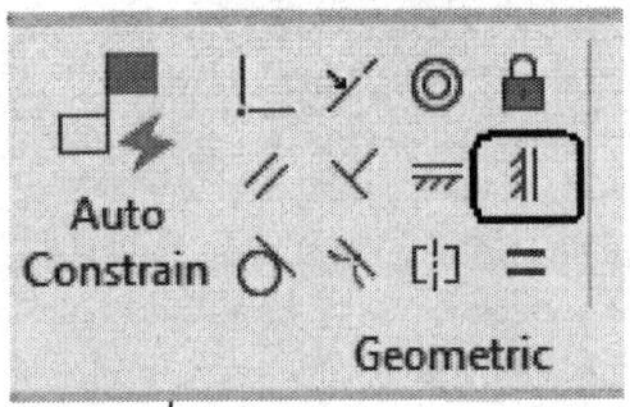

Select the vertical constraint tool on the ribbon.

16.

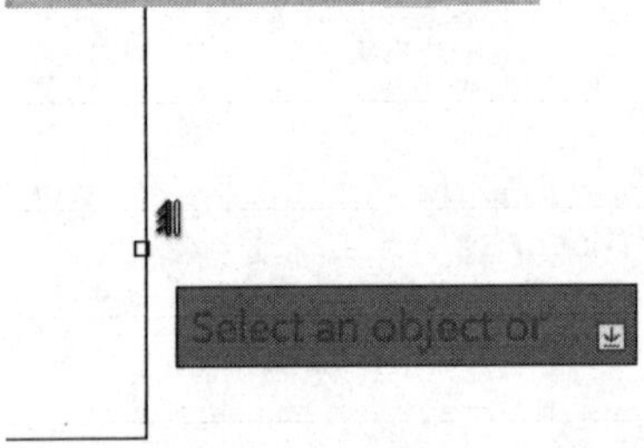

You will see the Vertical constraint icon and a prompt to select the element where the constraint is to be applied.

17.

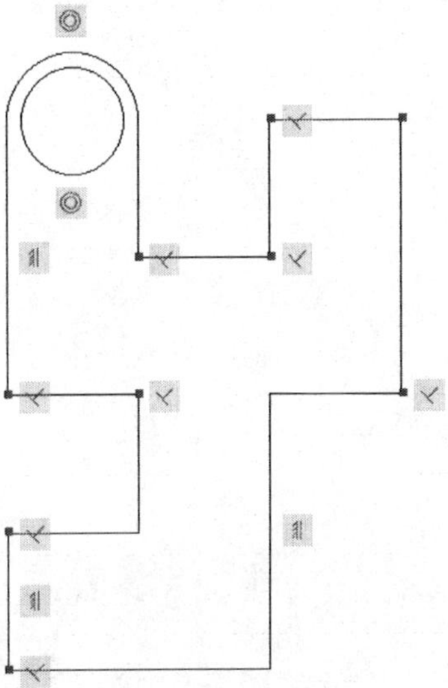

Select the vertical line.

You can only apply a vertical constraint if the constraint has been removed. Too many geometric constraints on the same element is not allowed.

18. 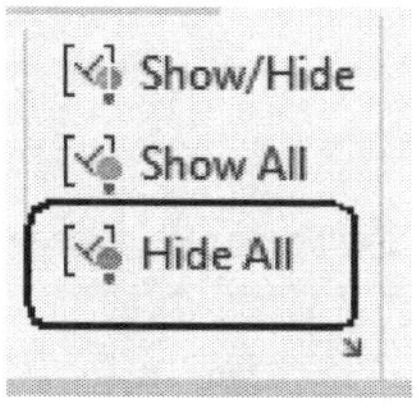

Select **Hide All**.
This hides all the geometric constraints.

19. Close without saving.

Polar Tracking

Polar tracking restricts cursor movement to specified angles. PolarSnap restricts cursor movement to specified increments along a polar angle.

When you create or modify objects, you can use polar tracking to display temporary alignment paths defined by the polar angles you specify. In 3D views, polar tracking additionally provides an alignment path in the up and down directions. In that case, the tooltip displays a +Z or -Z for the angle.

Polar angles are relative to the orientation of the current user coordinate system (UCS) and the setting for the base angle convention in a drawing, which is set in the Drawing Units dialog box.

Use PolarSnap™ to snap to specified distances along the polar alignment path. For example, in the following illustration you draw a two-unit line from point 1 to point 2, and then draw a two-unit line to point 3 at a 45-degree angle to the line. If you turn on the 45-degree polar angle increment, an alignment path and tooltip are displayed when your cursor crosses the 0 or 45-degree angle. The alignment path and tooltip disappear when you move the cursor away from the angle.

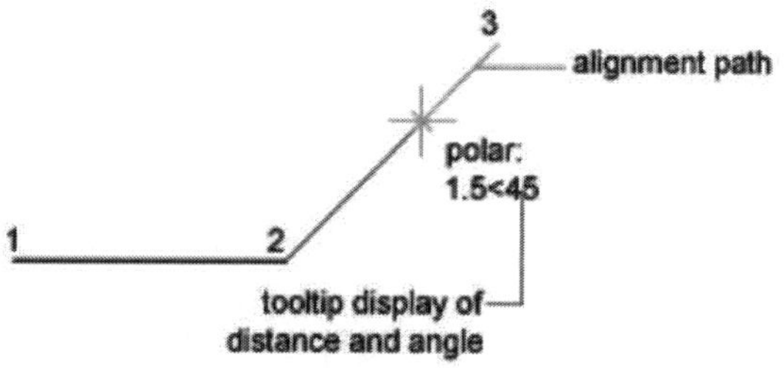

Use polar tracking to track along polar angle increments of 90, 60, 45, 30, 22.5, 18, 15, 10, and 5 degrees, or you can specify different angles. The following illustration shows the alignment paths displayed as you move your cursor 90 degrees with the polar angle increment set to 30 degrees.

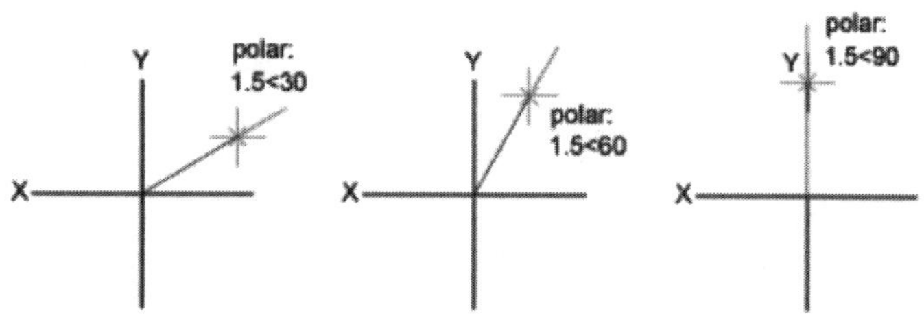

Command Exercise

Exercise 3-3 – Line Using Polar Tracking

Drawing Name: **Line2.dwg**
Estimated Time to Completion: 10 Minutes

Scope

Open 'line2.dwg' and draw the object shown in the example using the line command with POLAR enabled. Polar settings have already been made to create the necessary angles. When you have completed the third segment, type C to close the object. Press <ENTER> to repeat the line command, press <ENTER> again, and see that the line picks up from the last point selected.

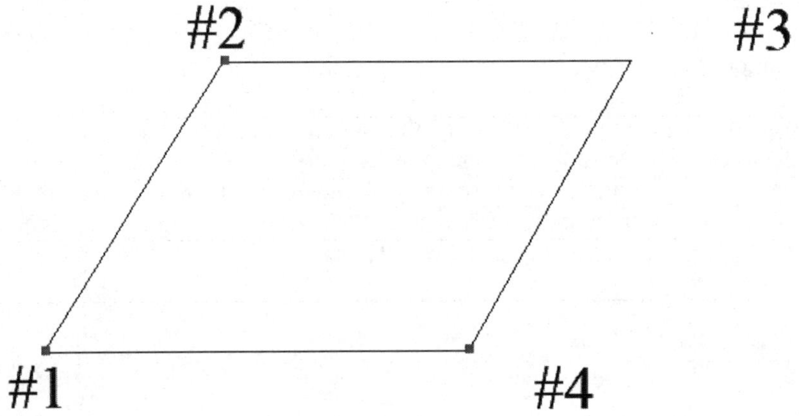

Solution

1. 

Turn **POLAR TRACKING** on.

2. 

Left click on the down arrow next to the Polar Tracking icon.

Select **Tracking Settings**.

3. 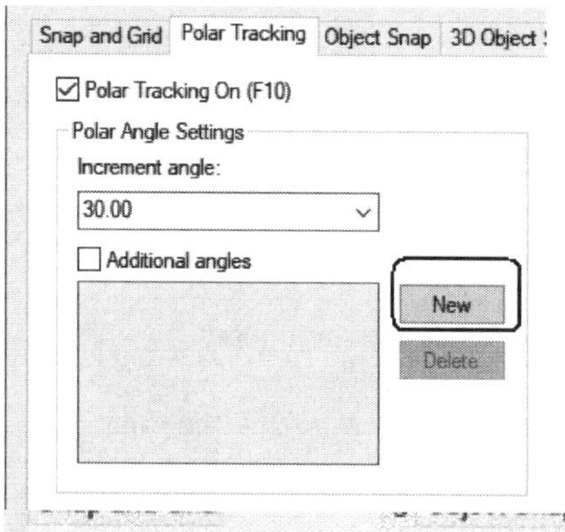

Select the **New** button to add an additional angle setting.

The increment angle shown may be different depending on your settings.

4. 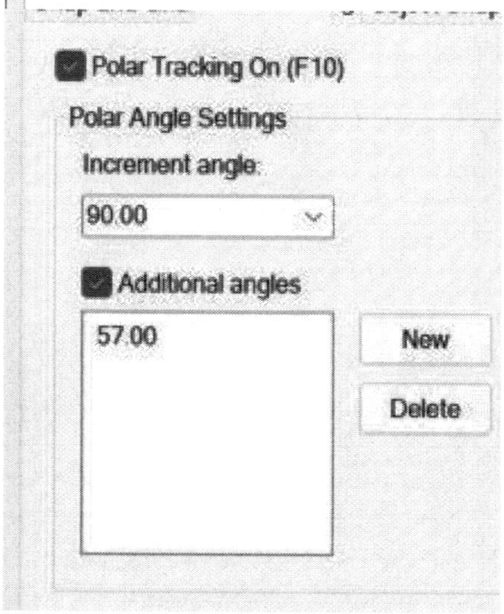

Type in **57.00** for the new angle value.

Click **OK.**

5. 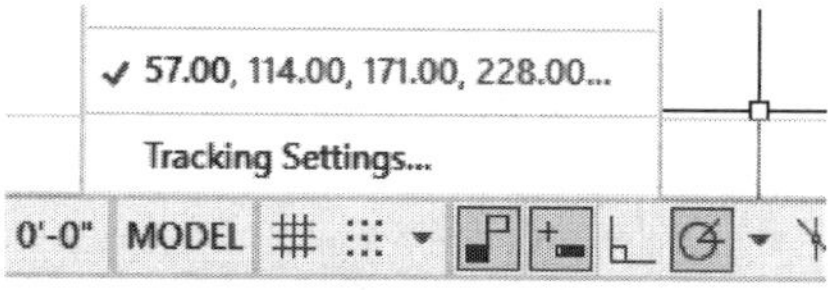

Left click on the down arrow next to the Polar Tracking icon.

Enable the **57.00** polar values.

6. 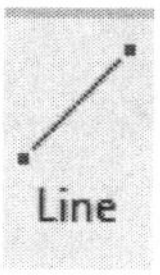

Invoke the **Line** command (l or line) from the Home tab on the ribbon.

7. 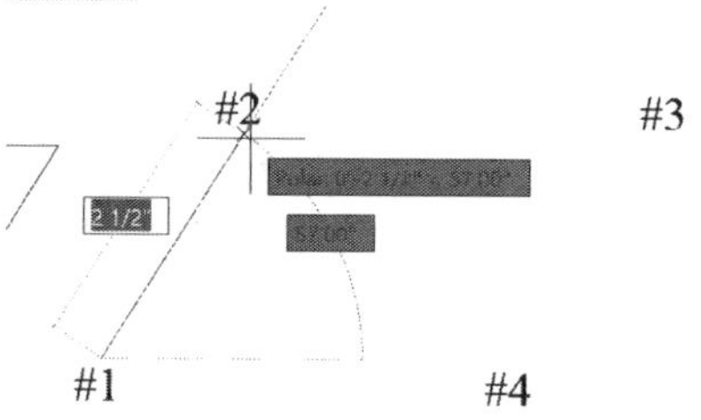

Specify first point:

Pick a start point of the line with your left mouse button near the #1 on the drawing.

Specify next point or [Undo]:

Pick a second point near the #2 on the drawing.

As you draw your line up to the #2, look for the Tooltip indicating the 57-degree angle.

8. 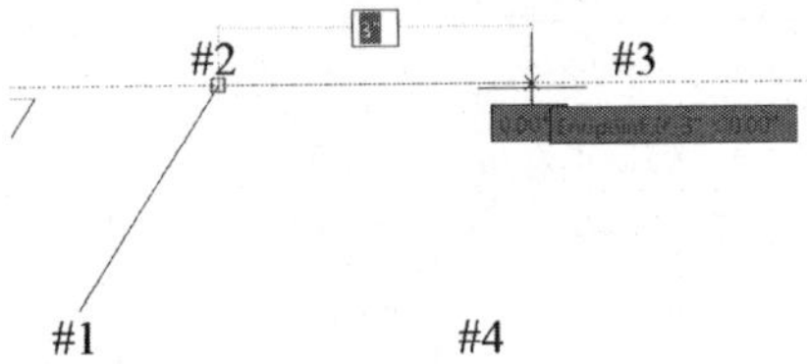

As you draw your line up to the #3, look for the Tooltip indicating the 0-degree angle.

Specify next point or [Undo]:
Move your mouse near #3 and click to complete the second line segment.

Press **ESC** to exit the LINE command.

9. 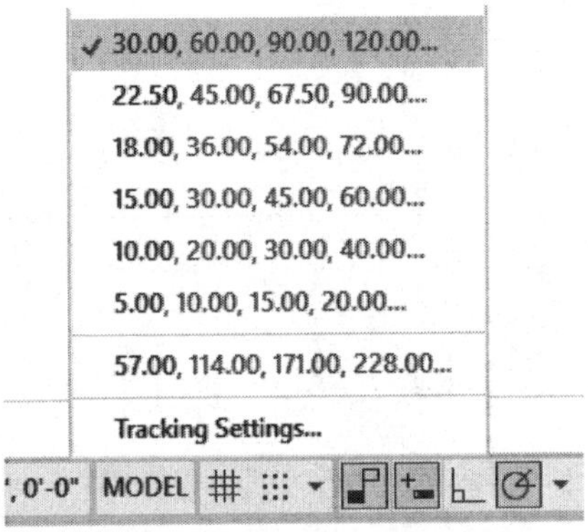

Left click on the down arrow next to the Polar Tracking icon.

Enable the **30.00** polar values.

10. 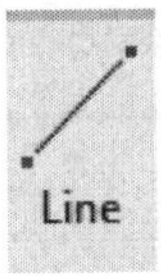

Select the **LINE** tool.

11. 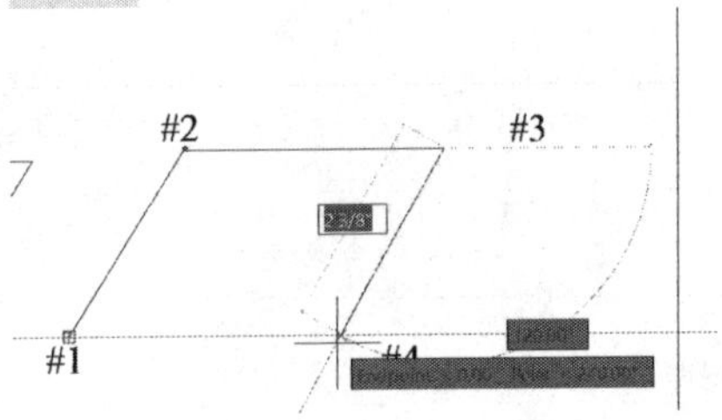

Press **ENTER** and the line will start where you left off at Point #3.

Specify next point or [Close/Undo]:
Use Object Tracking to line up your end point and set the Polar Angle to 120-degrees.

12. 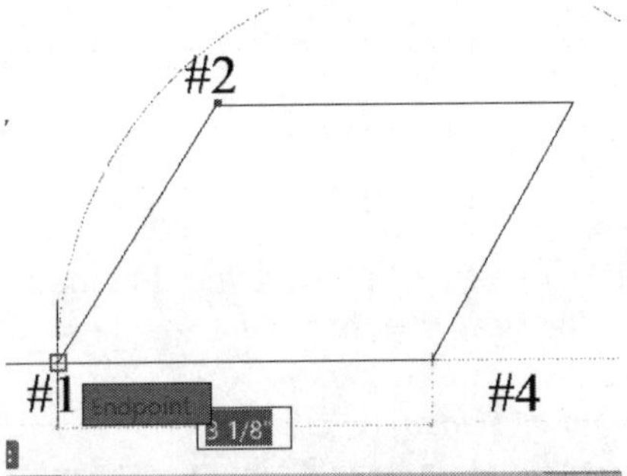

Specify next point or [Close/Undo]:
Place the final line segment by selecting the ENDpoint of the first line near Point #1.

13. 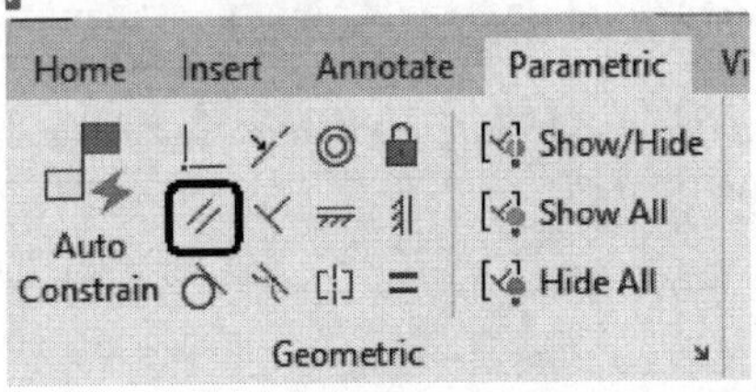

Open the Parametric ribbon.

Select the **PARALLEL** tool.

14.

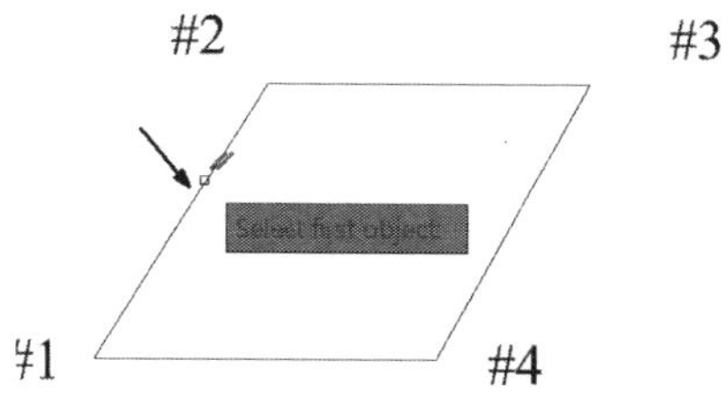

Select the line that goes from #1-#2.

15.

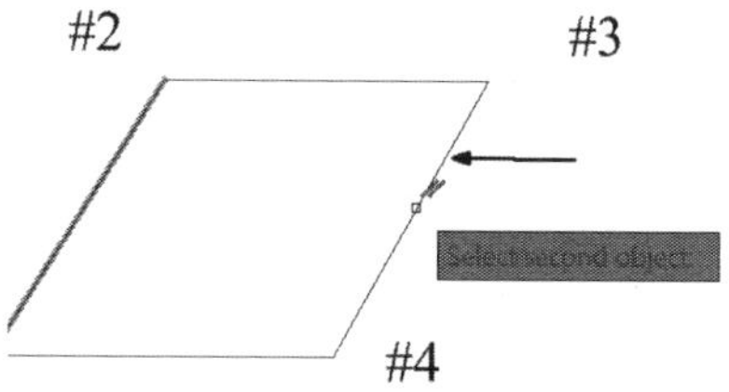

Select the line that goes from #3-#4.

16.

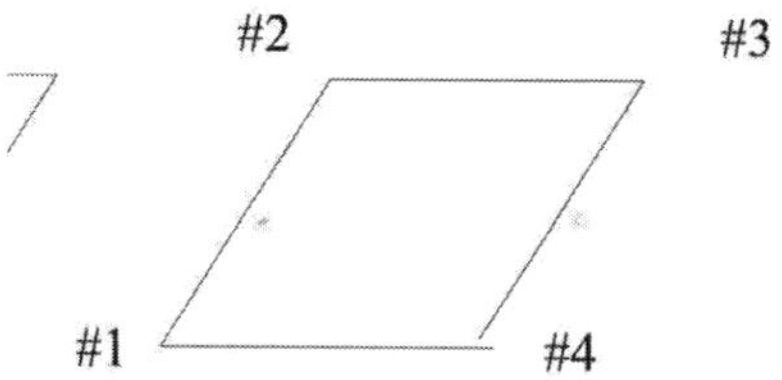

The lines are now parallel, but the figure is no longer closed.

17.

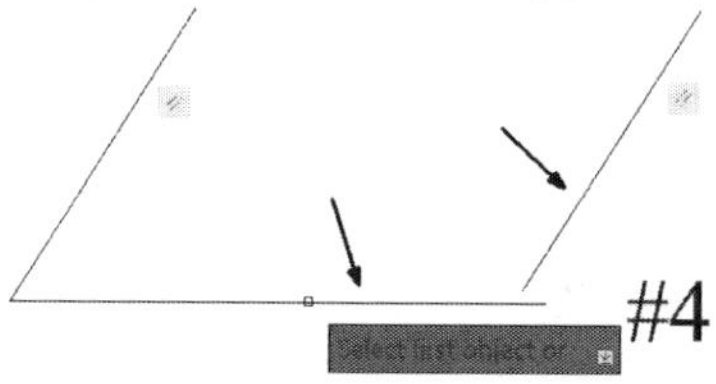

Type F for FILLET.
Select the two lines to create a closed polygon.

18.

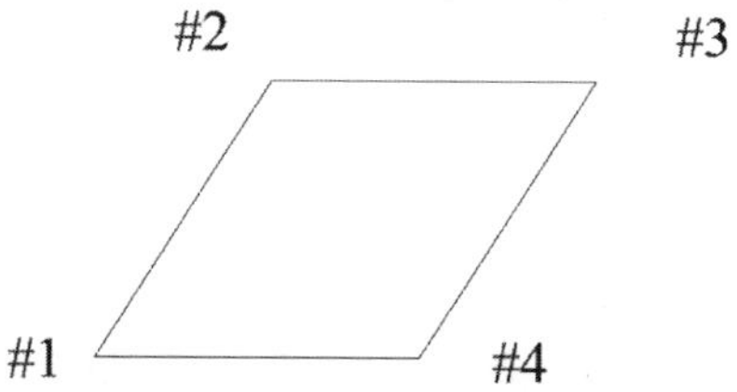

Close without saving.

- When you closed your object did it complete the parallelogram? If not, you may have stopped and restarted the line sequence, in which case the close option will refer to the new start point.
- Move your mouse as you work to see what line segments you have just completed.
- Click on ORTHO in the Status bar, or press the <F8> function key, whichever is more convenient at the time to create straight lines.
- Make a habit of using the <ENTER> key to complete your AutoCAD commands, and to repeat the last command used. Alternately, you may click the right mouse button and select the Repeat option.
- In order for Polar Tracking to click to specific angle values, you have to have them set. Use Settings in the Polar Tracking dialog to add angles you want to use in your drafting.

Cartesian Coordinates

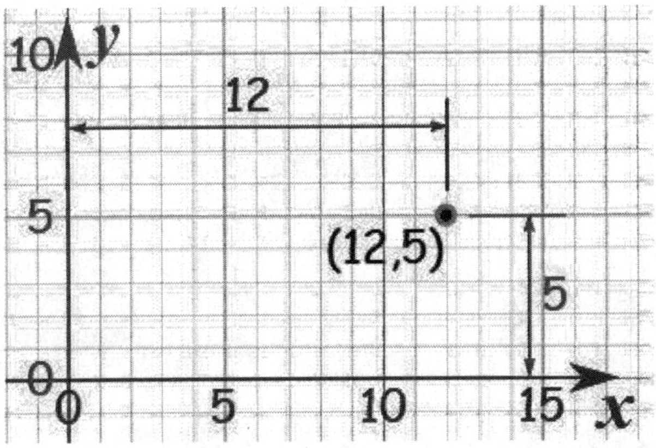

AutoCAD uses a Cartesian coordinate system – where x is the horizontal direction and y is the vertical direction. You can remember the difference between x and y by thinking x is a cross and x is across the page. The positive direction of x is towards the right. The negative direction of x is towards the left. The positive direction of y is up. The negative direction of y is down. Coordinates are always written X, Y with the X value first and the Y value second. So, a coordinate of 3,2 means three units to the right and two units up from the origin.

The status bar displays where the cursor is along the coordinate system. You can enter points using the coordinate system to place lines, circles and other elements. If you are drawing a survey map, the surveyor may provide you with a list of points to use to draw the outline of the building site. Those points are Cartesian coordinates.

Think of your drawing area as a blank piece of paper. The origin is located at 0,0. If you use absolute coordinates, you are selecting points based on their actual value on the grid. If you use relative coordinates, you are entering the distance in the X and Y direction from your current location. If you use polar coordinates, it is similar to a vector—where you enter a length and an angle. Polar coordinates usually use relative coordinates. The drag or direct entry method is the easiest method for most users—simply move your cursor in the direction you want to draw a line and enter in the distance/length of the line.

In order to ensure that you get the results you want, it is important to be cognizant of whether your drafting settings are set to relative or absolute coordinates.
To check your drafting settings, type DSETTINGS or DS.
Select the Dynamic Input tab.
Select the Settings button under Pointer Input.

If you want to use relative coordinates while in absolute coordinate mode, just type an @ before your coordinate entry; i.e. @3,1.

- *If your drawing did not turn out properly, make sure you had DYN OFF. To check your data entry, press F2 and the text window will open and you can review your entries.*

Coordinate Entry

Command Overview

Once the Units have been established, coordinates can be typed to specify points or distances. Always draw full scale. There are four ways to specify coordinates: absolute, relative, polar, and direct distance.

Coordinate Entry Method	*Overview*	*Examples*
Absolute Coordinates	The x and y coordinates are determined by an absolute Origin point of 0,0.	X,Y 1,5
Relative Coordinates	The x and y coordinates reference the last point selected in the drawing.	@x,y @3,5
Polar Coordinates	The distance and angle specified references the last point selected in the drawing.	@distance<angle @5<45
Direct Distance	Select the first point, then drag the cursor in the desired direction and type the distance.	Type the distance 4

General Procedures

Using Absolute Coordinates:

1. When prompted to specify a point, type the Absolute coordinates for x and y (x,y).
2. Type the Absolute Coordinate for each successive point (x,y).
   Typical Example: Inserting a Title Block or an Externally Referenced Drawing at a specific location.

Using Relative Coordinates:

1. When prompted to specify a point, select a point in the drawing.
2. Type the Relative Coordinate for each successive point (@x,y).
   Typical Example: Drawing a Rectangle.

Using Polar Coordinates:

1. When prompted to specify a point, select a point in the drawing.
2. Type the Polar Coordinate for each successive point (@distance < angle).
   Typical Example: Drawing lines or moving objects at a specified distance and angle other than orthogonal angles.

Using Direct Distance:

1. When prompted to specify a point, select a point in the drawing.
2. Turn ORTHO on and drag the cursor in the desired direction.
3. Type the distance and press <ENTER>.
   Typical Example: Drawing lines or using the Move, Copy or Stretch commands.

Tips & Tricks

- Always use object snap for selecting specific points in the drawing.
- Remember to separate the x and y coordinates by a comma. Example: 1,5 means the absolute coordinate where x=1 and y=5.
- It is not necessary to type the z coordinate when z = 0.
- Angles are typically measured counterclockwise. Angle 0 is typically East.
- Precede Relative and Polar coordinate information with an @ sign (over the number 2 on the keyboard) if drafting settings are set to Absolute Coordinates.
- ORTHO should be on when using the direct distance method.
- When drawing lines, or moving objects at specific angles (other than with ORTHO on), type the polar coordinate (example: @10<45) or use Polar Tracking Settings.
- Typing the minimum number of keystrokes is important for drawing efficiently. AutoCAD will fill in leading and trailing zeros and the appropriate Unit endings.
- AutoCAD will convert decimal equivalents to feet and inches.
- AutoCAD will assume inches, unless the foot mark ' is typed.
- The Coordinates Display can be turned on or off from the Status Bar by double clicking on it (LMB). If in the middle of a Draw or Modify command, a third option will display the distance and <angle.
- The DYN toggle can be used to display and enter coordinates.
- Use the Drafting Settings dialog to verify the mode of data entry you are using.

Command Exercise

Exercise 3-4 – Line Using Cartesian Coordinates

Drawing Name: **Begin a new drawing**
Estimated Time to Completion: 10 Minutes

Scope

Start a New Drawing using the acad.dwt template and draw the object shown in the example using the line command with Cartesian Coordinates. When you have completed the third segment, type C to close the object. Press <ENTER> to repeat the line command, press <ENTER> again, and see that the line picks up from the last point selected. Turn DYN off and ORTHO on for this exercise.

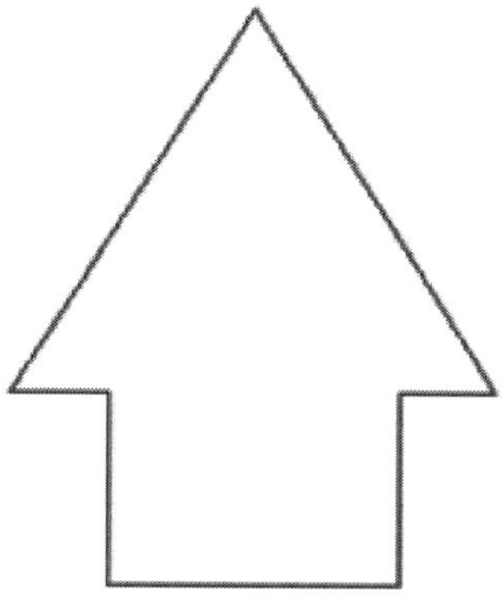

Solution

1. 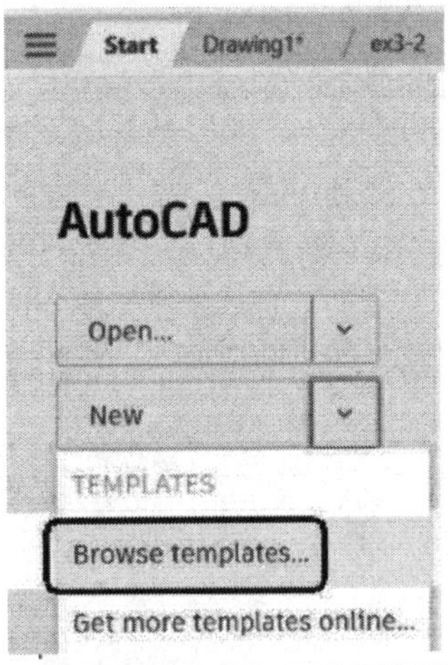

Click the Start tab.

Click **New→Browse templates.**

2. 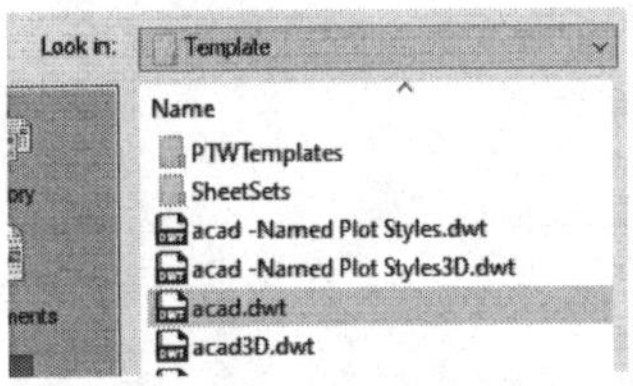

Select the *acad.dwt* template.

This starts a new drawing using the acad.dwt template.

3. 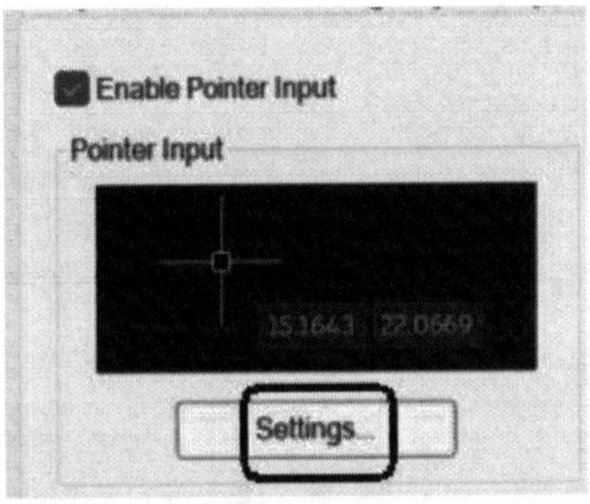

Type **DSETTINGS**.

Select the **Dynamic Input** tab.
Click **Settings** under Pointer Input.

4. 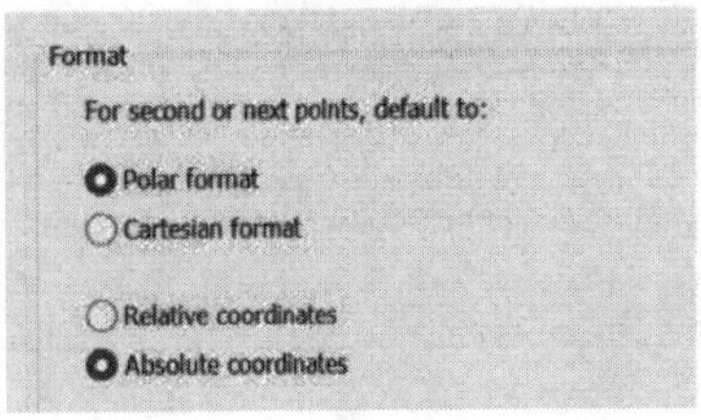

Enable **Absolute Coordinates.**
Click **OK** twice to close the dialog boxes.

5. 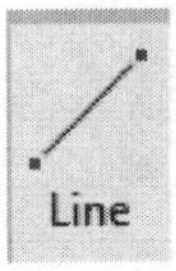

Invoke the **Line** command (l or line).

6.
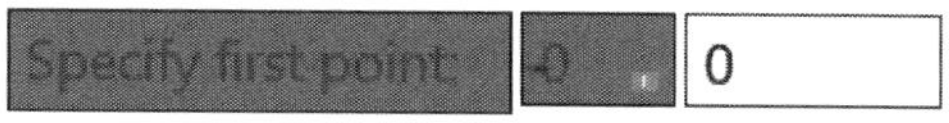

Specify first point: Type **0,0** at the command line.

7.

Specify next point or [Undo]: Type **3,0**.

8.

Specify next point or [Undo]: **3,2**

9.

Specify next point or [Close/Undo]: **4,2**

10.
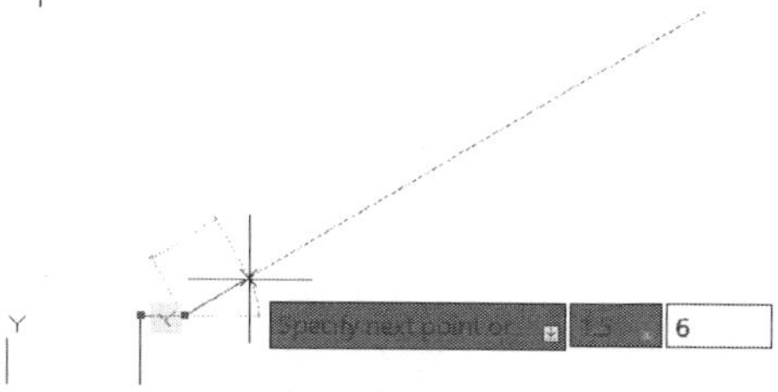

Specify next point or [Close/Undo]: **1.5,6**

11.

Specify next point or [Close/Undo]: **-1,2**

12.

Specify next point or [Close/Undo]: **0,2**

13.
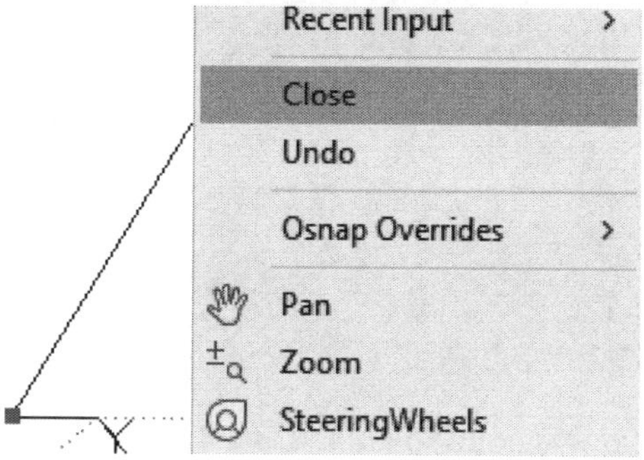

Specify next point or [Close/Undo]: Right-click in the drawing area and select 'Close' or type 'C' or 'CLOSE' and press <ENTER> at the command line to create the final line segment.

You can press U for UNDO if you make an error on any of the lines and restart. If you didn't make a continuous line, you can't use the CLOSE command. Type 0,0 instead.

Command Exercise

Exercise 3-5 – Absolute Coordinates

Drawing Name: **entry1.dwg**
Estimated Time to Completion: 10 Minutes

Scope

Start the line command. Draw the objects using the absolute coordinates in the order indicated. Connect the points using only the keyboard. Turn DYN off and ORTHO on.

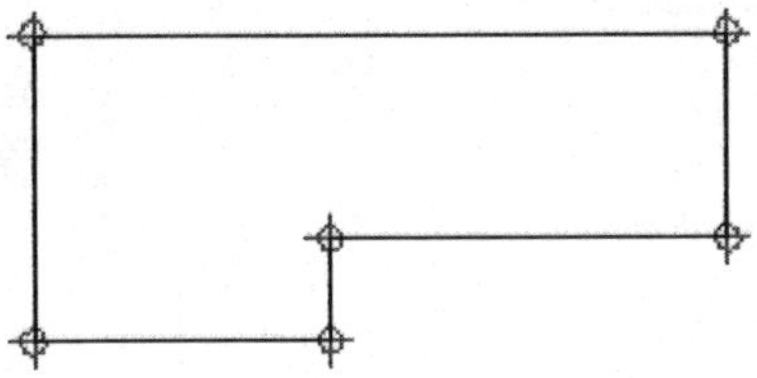

Solution

Before you start this exercise, you need to have your drafting settings set up to use absolute coordinates.

1. 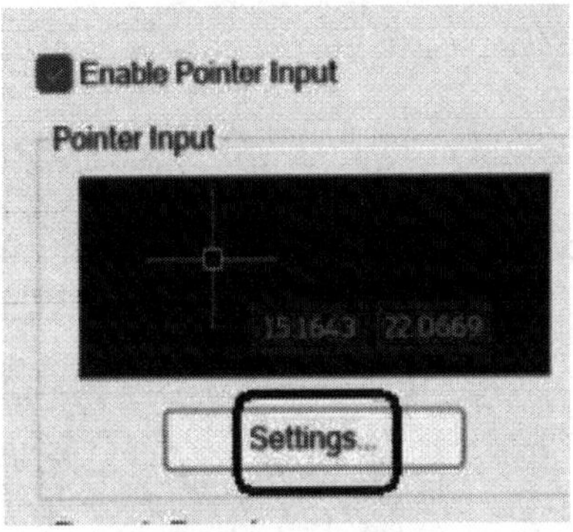

Type **DSETTINGS**.

Select the **Dynamic Input** tab.
Click **Settings** under Pointer Input.

2. 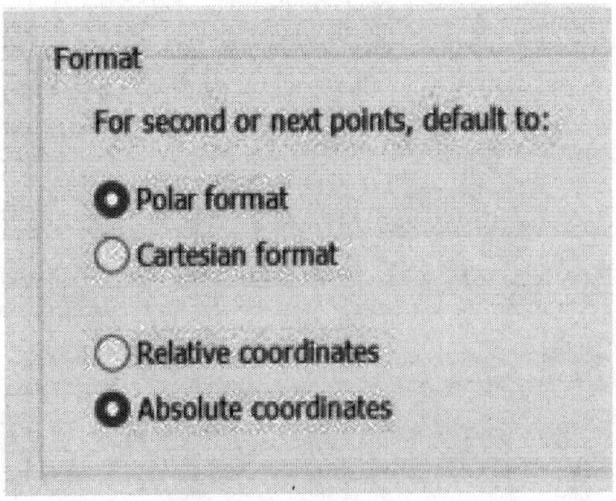

Enable **Absolute Coordinates**.
Click **OK** twice to close the dialog boxes.

3. 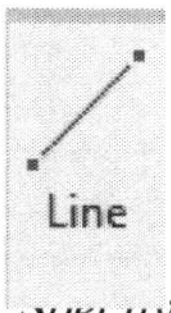

Invoke the **Line** command (l or line).

4. *Specify first point:*
Type **1,1** at the command line and press <ENTER>. Notice where the first point of the line is created.

5. *Specify next point or [Undo]:*
Type **4,1** at the command line and press <ENTER>.

6. *Specify next point or [Undo]:*
Type **4,2** at the command line and press <ENTER>.

7. *Specify next point or [Close/Undo]:*
Type **8,2** and press <ENTER>.

8. *Specify next point or [Close/Undo]:*
Type **8,4** and press <ENTER>.

9. *Specify next point or [Close/Undo]:*
Type **1,4** and press <ENTER>.

10. *Specify next point or [Close/Undo]:*
Type **1,1** and press <ENTER>.

11. *Specify next point or [Close/Undo]:*
Press the <ENTER> key to end the command.

Tips & Tricks

- *You can also use the close option to complete the exercise rather than typing in the final '1,1'.*

Command Exercise

Exercise 3-6 – Relative Coordinates

Drawing Name: **entry2.dwg**
Estimated Time to Completion: 10 Minutes

Scope

Start the line command. Draw the objects using the relative coordinates in the order indicated. Connect the points using only the keyboard. Turn DYN off and ORTHO on.

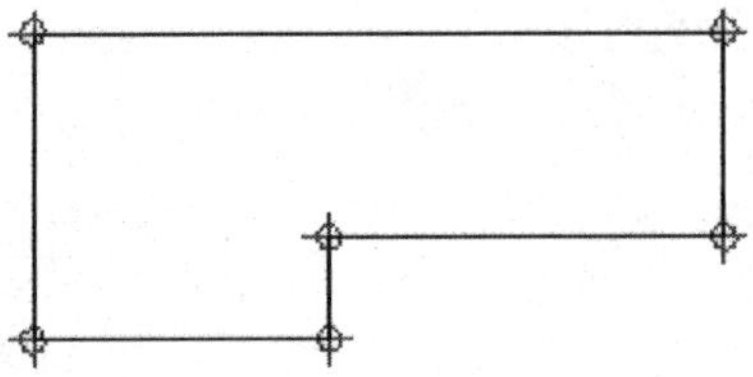

Solution

Before you start this exercise, you need to have your drafting settings set up to use relative coordinates.

1.

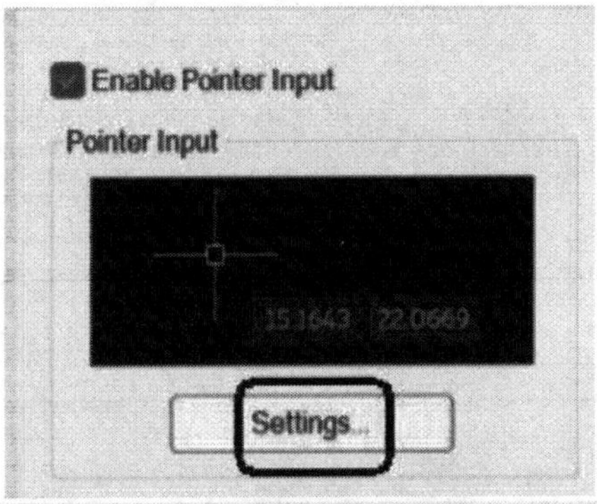

Type **DSETTINGS**.

Select the **Dynamic Input** tab.
Click **Settings** under Pointer Input.

2.

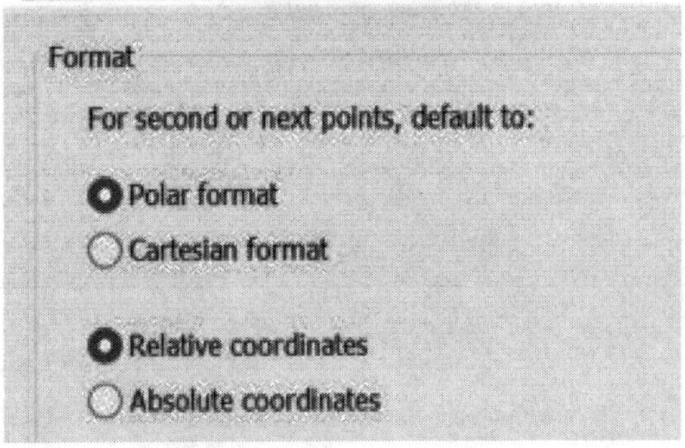

Enable **Relative Coordinates**.
Click **OK** twice to close the dialog boxes.

3. 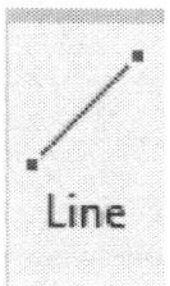

Invoke the **Line** command (l or line).

4. *Specify first point:*
Type **1,1** at the command line and press <ENTER>. Notice where the first point of the line is created.

5. *Specify next point or [Undo]:*
Type **3,0** at the command line and press <ENTER>.

6. *Specify next point or [Undo]:*
Type **0,1** at the command line and press <ENTER>.

7. *Specify next point or [Close/Undo]:*
Type **4,0** and press <ENTER>.

8. *Specify next point or [Close/Undo]:*
Type **0,2** and press <ENTER>.

9. *Specify next point or [Close/Undo]:*
Type **-7,0** and press <ENTER>.

10. *Specify next point or [Close/Undo]:*
Type **0,-3** and press <ENTER>.

11. *Specify next point or [Close/Undo]:*
Press the <ENTER> key to end the command.

Notice that absolute coordinates use the absolute values of X and Y. Relative coordinates tell AutoCAD how many units to move in the X or Y direction from the current location of the cursor.

***Extra:** What would you type in to create the shape in a clockwise fashion instead of counterclockwise direction? Try it.*

Command Exercise

Exercise 3-7 – Polar Coordinates

Drawing Name: **entry3.dwg**
Estimated Time to Completion: 5 Minutes

Scope

Start the line command. Draw the objects using polar coordinates in the order indicated. Connect the points using only the keyboard.

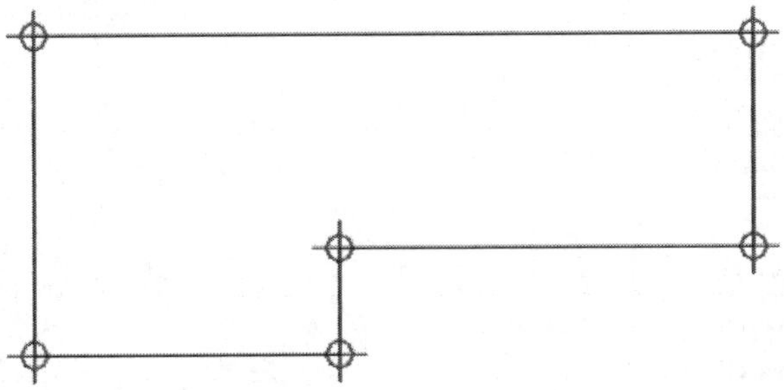

By using the @ symbol before the first number, you are specifying a relative coordinate. The < symbol indicates the angle to be used.

Solution

1.

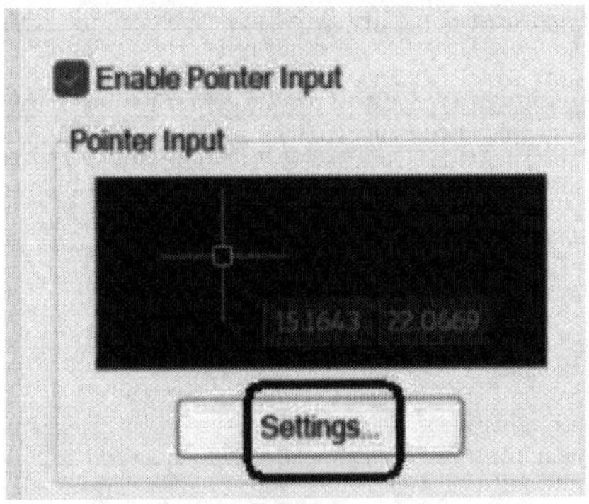

Type **DSETTINGS**.

Select the **Dynamic Input** tab.
Click **Settings** under Pointer Input.

2. 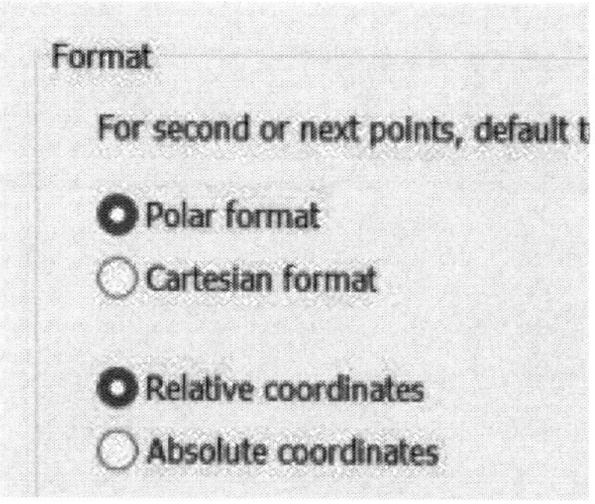

Enable **Relative Coordinates**.
Click **OK** twice to close the dialog boxes.

3. 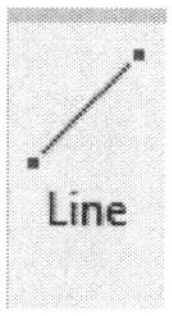

Invoke the **Line** command (l or line).

4. *Specify first point:*
Type **1,1** at the command line and press <ENTER>. Notice where the first point of the line is created.

5. *Specify next point or [Undo]:*
Type **@3<0** at the command line and press <ENTER>.

6. *Specify next point or [Undo]:*
Type **@1<90** at the command line and press <ENTER>.

7. *Specify next point or [Close/Undo]:*
Type **@4<0** and press <ENTER>.

8. *Specify next point or [Close/Undo]:*
Type **@2<90** and press <ENTER>.

9. *Specify next point or [Close/Undo]:*
Type **@7<180** and press <ENTER>

10. *Specify next point or [Close/Undo]:*
Type **@3<270** and press <ENTER>.

11. *Specify next point or [Close/Undo]:*
Press the <ENTER> key to end the command.

Extra: *What would happen if you typed @-3<180 in step 3 in the exercise? Try it.*

Command Exercise

Exercise 3-8 – Drag Method

Drawing Name: **entry4.dwg**
Estimated Time to Completion: 5 Minutes

Scope

Start the line command. Draw the objects using the direct entry method.

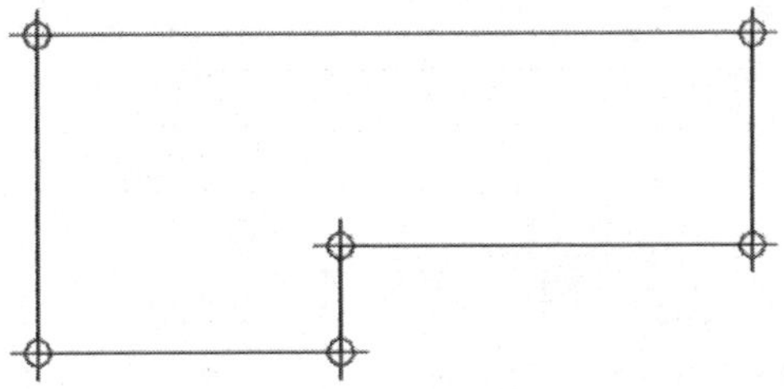

Solution

1. 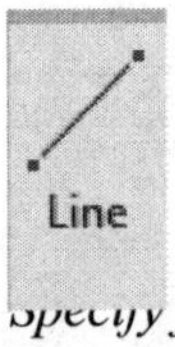

Invoke the **Line** command (l or line).

2. *Specify first point:*
Type **1,1** at the command line and press <ENTER>. Notice where the first point of the line is created.

3. 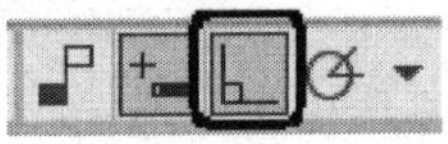 *Specify next point or [Undo]:*
Toggle ORTHO ON at the Status bar.

4. *Specify next point or [Undo]:*
Drag the mouse to the right, type **3** and press <ENTER>.

5. *Specify next point or [Close/Undo]:*
Drag the mouse upward, type **1** and press <ENTER>.

6. *Specify next point or [Close/Undo]:*
Drag the mouse to the right, type **4** and press <ENTER>.

7. *Specify next point or [Close/Undo]:*
Drag the mouse upward, type **2** and press <ENTER>.

8. *Specify next point or [Close/Undo]:*
Drag the mouse to the left, type **7** and press <ENTER>.

9. *Specify next point or [Close/Undo]:*
Drag the mouse downward, type **3** and press <ENTER>.

10. *Specify next point or [Close/Undo]:*
Press the <ENTER> key to end the command.

Command Exercise

Exercise 3-9 – Traverse

Drawing Name: **new**
Estimated Time to Completion: 30 Minutes

Scope

A *traverse* is a series of interconnected lines between a series of points. The connecting lines are called *courses*. The points are called *traverse stations*. The main purpose of a traverse survey is to find the distance between the traverse stations and angle of the courses. Imagine you are working as a junior civil engineer. A surveyor returns with a list of distances and angles and requests that you draw up the traverse using AutoCAD. The measurement uses relative coordinates and angles based on the azimuth.

An *azimuth* of a line is the horizontal angle between the given line and the datum line. An azimuth is measured clockwise from the North.

Solution

1. Start a new drawing.
   Turn off the SNAP.
   Turn off the GRID.

2. 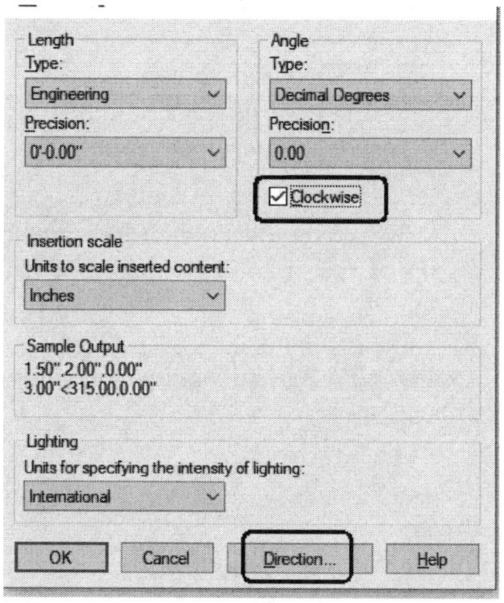

Type **UNITS.**

Set the Type to **Engineering**.

Set the Precision to **0'-0.00".**

Set the Angle Precision to **0.00**.
Enable **Clockwise**.

Click **Direction**.

3.

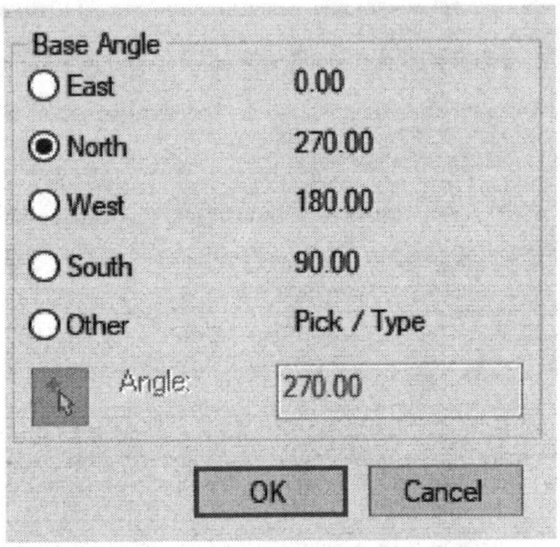

Enable **North**.

Click **OK**.

Close the UNITS dialog.

Engineering units should be displayed on the status bar.

4. 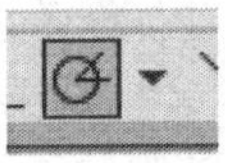 Enable **POLAR**.

5.

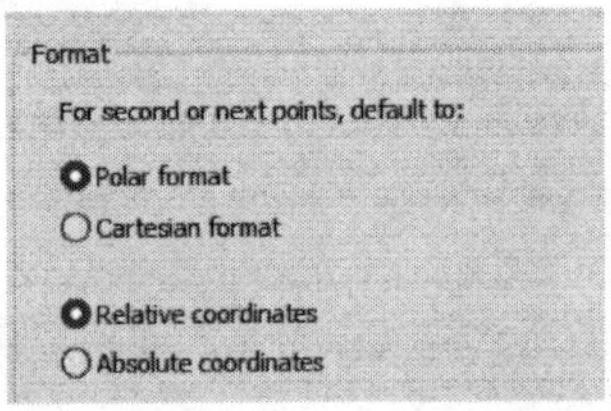

DSETTINGS should use Polar format and relative coordinates.

Keep in mind the surveyor measures the distance and angle from each survey point, not the origin.

6.

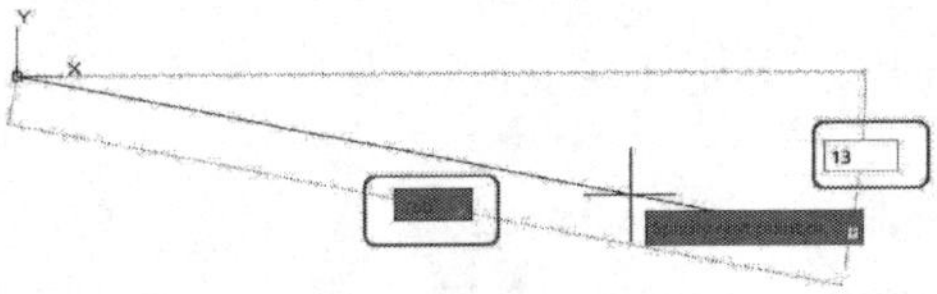

Start the LINE command.
The first coordinate should be 0,0.
The second coordinate should be:
260', 13°.

Drag the mouse down after selecting 0,0. Type in 260'. (Be sure to type in the ' or AutoCAD will assume you want 260 inches.)
Press TAB to advance to the angle value.
Type 13.

7.

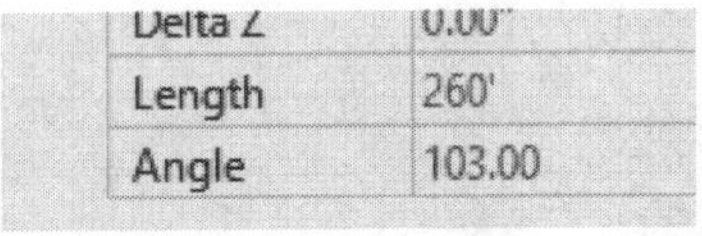

Select the line.
Right click and select **Properties**.

The dialog should show a length of 260' and an angle of 103.00.

Use the data provided by the surveyor to complete the traverse.
Be sure to use the apostrophe to indicate feet when entering the distance values.
Double check each line by selecting it and using Properties.
Press ENTER to start the line from the last point placed.

POINT	LENGTH (ft)	AZIMUTH
2	260	103
3	172	68
4	190	15
5	160	350
6	190	310
7	250	243
8	260	300
9	172	241
10	175	202
11	141	173
12	180	145
13	200	93
14		use the close command to close the traverse

When looking at the angle value, consider the angle of the line is being measured from the North Axis while AutoCAD's POLAR system might be displaying the angle from the East axis. If you use @ prior to typing the coordinates, you ensure your lines will be placed properly.

Your drawing should look similar to this:

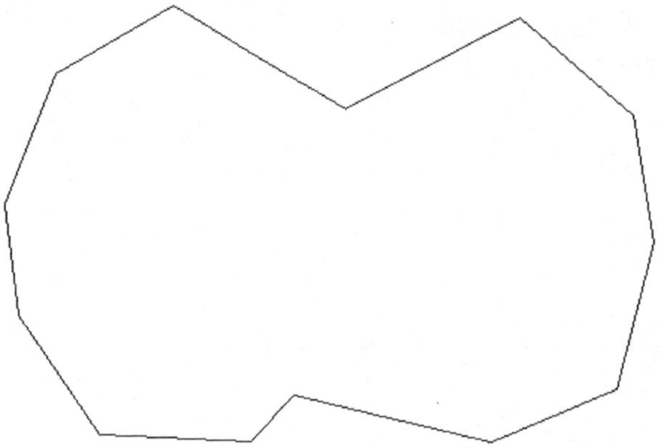

Erase

Command Locator

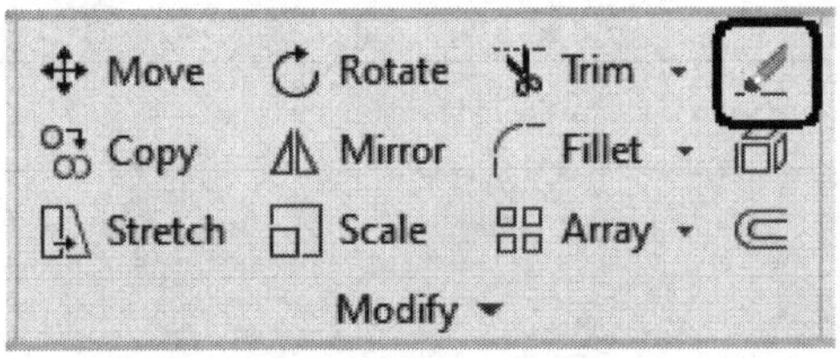

Home/Modify Panel	**Erase**
Command	**Erase**
Alias	**E**

Command Overview

Erase deletes selected objects. Press <ENTER> after selecting the objects to erase to execute the command. Type OOPS to bring back the last set of erased objects, even if other objects were drawn since the last erase.

General Procedures

1. Begin the erase command by selecting the Erase icon from the Modify Toolbar/Ribbon or typing E at the blank command prompt.
2. Place the cursor over the objects to erase and pick (LMB).

- If the cursor is not over an object, a selection window will appear. Make the other corner of the selection window.
- A Selection Window made from Left to Right will select only the objects completely in the window. *This is called a selection window.*
- A Selection Window made from Right to Left will select all objects the window crosses. *This is called a selection crossing.*
- Typing All (and pressing <ENTER>) will select all objects in the drawing to erase. Press <ENTER> to execute the command.

Command Exercise

Exercise 3-10 – Erase

Drawing Name: **erase1.dwg**
Estimated Time to Completion: 5 Minutes

Scope

Erase the objects in the drawing. Draw some more lines. Type OOPS to bring back the last set of erased objects. OOPS is different from UNDO. UNDO backs up the last set of issued commands. OOPS restores the last set of erased elements even if there was more than one command issued before you typed OOPS.

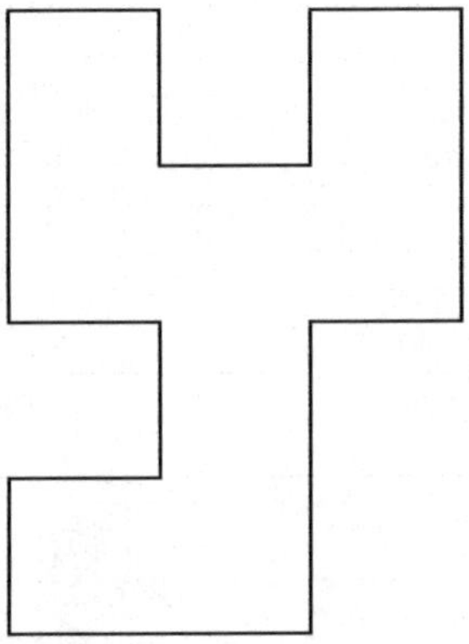

Solution

1. 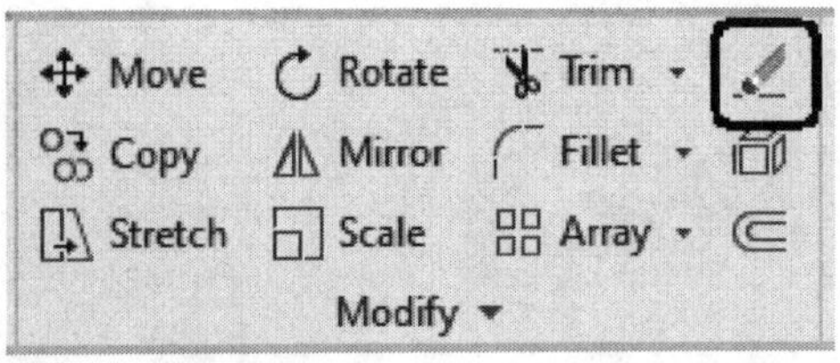

   Invoke the **Erase** command (e or erase) on the Home ribbon.

2. *Select objects:*
   Select the objects by typing **ALL** and pressing <ENTER>, picking each line individually, or using the Window method. When all the objects are highlighted, press <ENTER> to execute the Erase command.

3. Invoke the **Line** command (l or line).

4. *Specify first point:*
   Use your LMB to pick the start point of a line segment. Select any location on

the drawing.

5. *Specify next point or [Undo]:*
   Continue to use the LMB to create lines on the drawing.
6. *Specify next point or [Close/Undo]:*
   Press the <ENTER> key to end the line command.

7. Type **OOPS** at the command line and press the <ENTER> key.

> *Select all the objects to erase, then press <ENTER> to execute the command. To remove an object from the selection set, hold down the shift key and select the object again. See that it is removed from the selection set. Then press <ENTER>.*

Review Questions

1. How do you turn on the display of the coordinates in the status bar?

2. A user enters LINE 1,1 and then @0,2....what type of coordinates is she using?

3. To make sure you will always draw a straight line, what tray button should be enabled?

4. When using the POLAR method of coordinate entry, which tray button should be enabled?

5. When entering direct coordinates, which tray button should be disabled?

6. What is the difference between OOPS and UNDO?

Review Answers

1. How do you turn on the display of the coordinates in the status bar?
   Left click on the STATUS bar options icon and enable Coordinates

2. A user enters LINE 1,1 and then @0,2 ….what type of coordinates is she using?
   Relative

3. To make sure you will always draw a straight line, what tray button should be enabled?
   ORTHO

4. When using the POLAR method of coordinate entry, which tray button should be enabled?
   POLAR

5. When entering direct coordinates, which tray button should be disabled?
   DYN

6. What is the difference between OOPS and UNDO?
   UNDO reverses the last command entered. OOPS restores the last item(s) erased or deleted from the drawing.

Lesson 4.0 – Draw Commands

Estimated Class Time: 4 Hours

Objectives

This section introduces AutoCAD commands for creating a simple drawing. The user will learn to use the commands on the Draw panel of the Home ribbon.

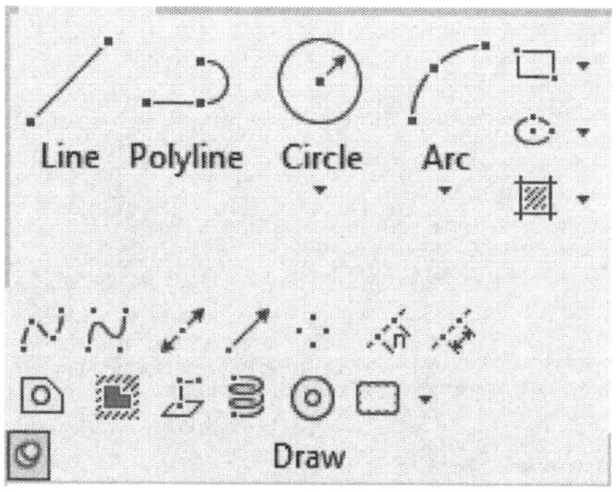

- **Polyline**
  Draw polylines.
- **Polygon**
  Draw multi-sided polylines.
- **Rectangle**
  Draw rectangular polylines.
- **Arc**
  Draw arcs several different ways.
- **Circle**
  Draw circles using six different methods.
- **Donut**
  Draw a donut – a circle with a thick outline.
- **Spline**
  Draw splines by using Points to control the spline shape.
- **Ellipse**
  Draw ellipses using two different methods.
- **Ellipse Arc**
  Draw an elliptical arc.
- **Add Selected**
  Adds selected elements using source properties.
- **Hatch**
  Adds a selected pattern to a closed boundary or region.

Polyline

Command Locator

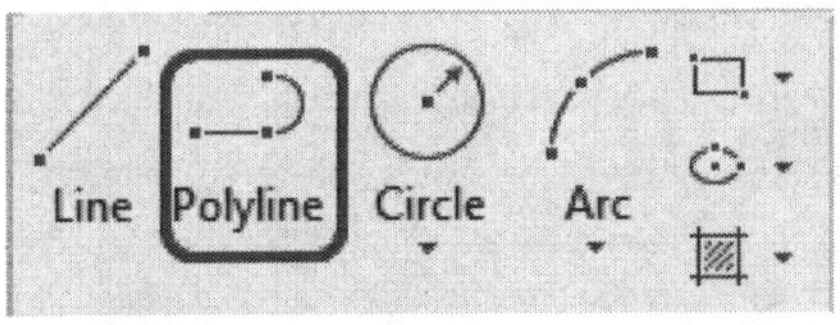

Home Ribbon	**Draw Panel/ Polyline**
Command	**Pline**
Alias	**PL**
RMB Shortcut Menu	**Drawing Window**

Command Overview

Polylines are essential to drawing in AutoCAD. Polylines are line and arc segments with common endpoints that are joined to make one object. A rectangle is an example of a polyline. Polylines can be more efficient because selecting one polyline segment will automatically select the entire polyline, and offsetting a Polyline will Offset all of the segments equally. Sometimes it is necessary to explode a Polyline, then use the Edit Polyline command to *join* all the line and arc segments. When drawing a Polyline, the user will be presented with many command line options; however, for all practical purposes, drawing a Polyline is much like drawing line segments.

Primarily, GIS drafters and architects use polylines. Mechanical drafters use polylines to create drawing borders, arrows and cutting plane lines. Cutting plane lines are used for section views.

A polyline is similar to a line, but it can have thickness. Additionally, you can “join” or connect more than one line to create a single object. Polylines can have varying thickness or widths.

You can draw your object using lines and arcs and convert it to polyline using the polyline edit command. You can convert polylines and polyarcs back to lines and arcs using the EXPLODE command.

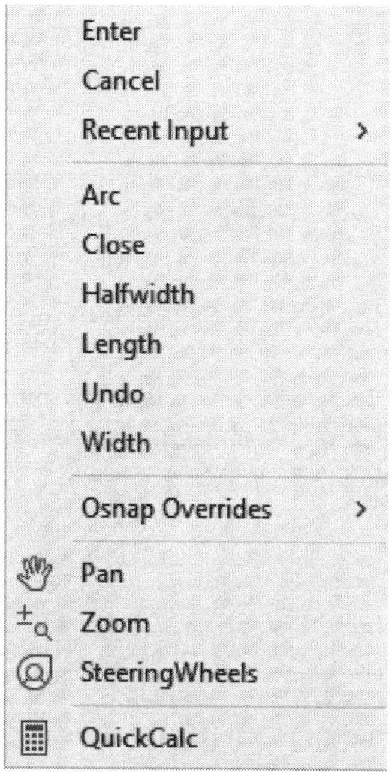

Polyline Option	Overview
Specify next point	This is the default option. Simply pick the next polyline point, much like drawing line segments.
Arc	This option, used within the Polyline command, will invoke the polyline Arc option, creating a Polyarc. There are a few ways to draw a polyline arc; one way is to simply drag the cursor in the desired direction (ORTHO on or off) and type the distance, then type L to return to the Polyline Line segment option.
Close	This option closes a polyline so that the first and last points are connected.
Halfwidth	This option will make the polyline width half the designated distance.
Length	The length option will extend the polyline being drawn a designated length.
Undo	The Undo option will undo the last polyline segment.
Width	Type W for width, then specify a start width and an ending width.

General Procedures

1. Invoke the Pline command.
2. Specify a start point.
3. Type W for width (and <ENTER>).
4. Specify a starting width (and <ENTER>) and an ending width (and <ENTER>). The default ending width is usually equal to the starting width, unless drawing an object such as an arrowhead.
5. Specify the next point using the methods learned in drawing line segments.
6. Optional: Type U (and <ENTER>) to Undo the last polyline segment without exiting the polyline command.
7. Optional: Type A (and <ENTER>) to go invoke the Arc option without exiting the polyline command. Type L (and <ENTER>) to return to the Line mode.
8. Optional: Type C (and <ENTER>) to Close the polyline.

Tips & Tricks

- It is more typical, and usually more practical, to draw regular line and arc segments and then use the Edit Polyline command to join them (see next section).
- When drawing a Polyline, the most common options used are Width and "Specify next point."
- The default polyline width is 0. When the width is changed, it will remain the latest width setting until changed again.
- Polyline starting and ending widths can be specified by picking points in the drawing window.
- Draw polylines in continuous segments. If the polylines are drawn as separate segments, the intersections will appear jagged. If the polyline is not closed, there will be a jagged edge at that opened intersection.
- Do not cross polyline segments.
  Example:

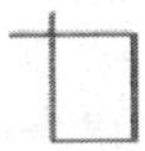

Sometimes it is easier for the beginner drafter to create the geometry using standard lines and arcs and then convert the geometry into polylines and polyarcs. To change a regular line to a polyline, use the PEDIT command. PEDIT can also be used to modify the width to an existing polyline and append geometry.

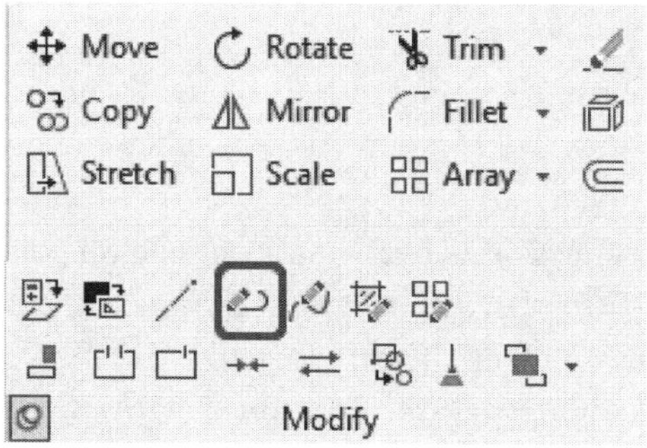

The Polyline Edit command can be initiated as follows:

Home Ribbon	**Modify Panel/ Edit Polyline**
Command	**Pedit**
Double Click	**Double left mouse click on polyline**
Alias	**PE**

The PEDIT command has several options:

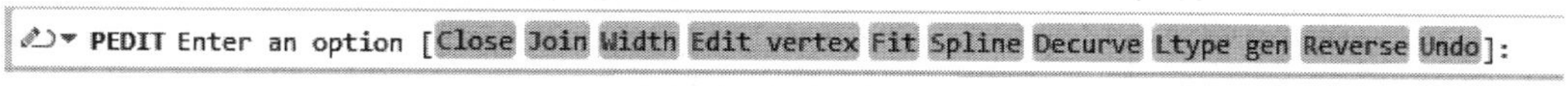

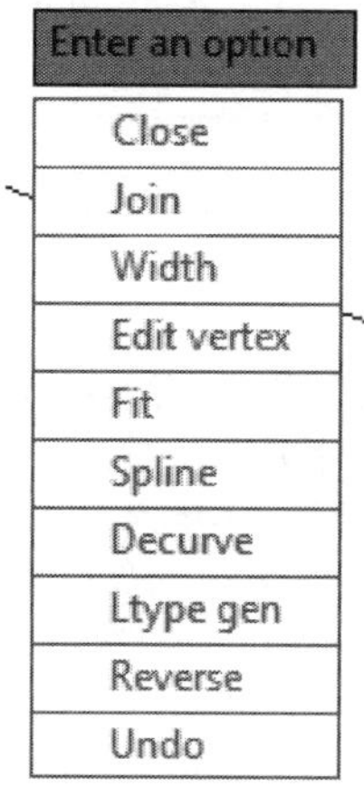

Close	Creates the closing segment of the polyline, connecting the last segment with the first. AutoCAD considers the polyline open unless you close it using the Close option.
Join	Adds lines, arcs, or polylines to the end of an open polyline and removes the curve fitting from a curve-fit polyline. For objects to join the polyline, their endpoints must touch unless you use the Multiple option at the first PEDIT prompt. In this case, you can join polylines that do not touch if the fuzz distance is set to a value large enough to include the endpoints.
Width	Specifies a new uniform width for the entire polyline.

Edit Vertex	Marks the first vertex of the polyline by drawing an X on the screen. If you have specified a tangent direction for this vertex, an arrow is also drawn in that direction.
Fit	Creates a smooth curve consisting of pairs of arcs joining each pair of vertices. The curve passes through all vertices of the polyline and uses any tangent direction you specify.
Spline	Uses the vertices of the selected polyline as the control points, or frame, of a curve. The curve passes through the first and last control points unless the original polyline was closed. The curve is pulled toward the other points but does not necessarily pass through them. The more control points you specify in a particular part of the frame, the more pull they exert on the curve. The technical term for this type of curve is *B-spline*. AutoCAD can generate quadratic and cubic spline-fit polylines.
Decurve	Removes extra vertices inserted by a fit or spline curve and straightens all segments of the polyline. Retains tangent information assigned to the polyline vertices for use in subsequent fit curve requests. If you edit a spline-fit polyline with commands such as BREAK or TRIM, you cannot use the Decurve option.
Ltype gen	Generates the linetype in a continuous pattern through the vertices of the polyline. When turned off, this option generates the linetype starting and ending with a dash at each vertex. Ltype Gen does not apply to polylines with tapered segments.
Reverse	Reverses the direction of the polyline.
Undo	Reverses operations as far back as the beginning of the PEDIT session.

- *The PLINEGEN system variable controls the linetype pattern display around and the smoothness of the vertices of a 2D polyline. Setting PLINEGEN to 1 generates new polylines in a continuous pattern around the vertices of the completed polyline. Setting PLINEGEN to 0 starts and ends the polyline with a dash at each vertex. PLINEGEN does not apply to polylines with tapered segments.*
- *PLINETYPE controls both the creation of new polylines with the PLINE command and the conversion of existing polylines in drawings from previous releases.*
- *0 Polylines in older drawings are not converted when opened; PLINE creates old-format polylines.*
- *1 Polylines in older drawings are not converted when opened; PLINE creates optimized polylines.*
- *2 Polylines in older drawings are converted when opened; PLINE creates optimized polylines.*
- *The CONVERT command can be used to optimize polylines created in AutoCAD R13 or earlier.*

Command Exercise

Exercise 4-1 – Polyline

Drawing Name: **pline1.dwg**
Estimated Time to Completion: 10 Minutes

Scope

Using the Polyline command with the Width, Arc and Line options, draw the object as indicated with a polyline width of '0.3'. Ortho should be on.

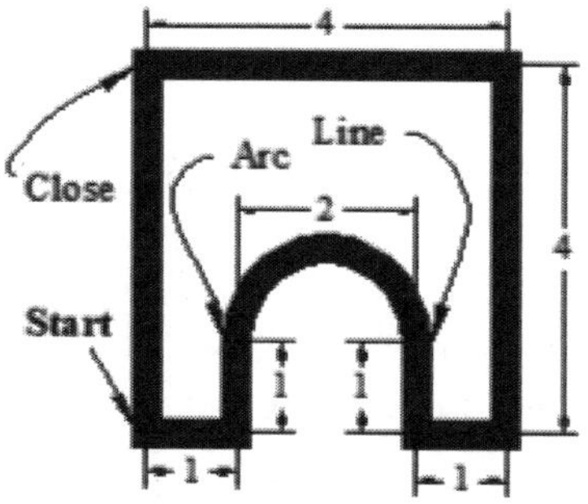

Solution

1. 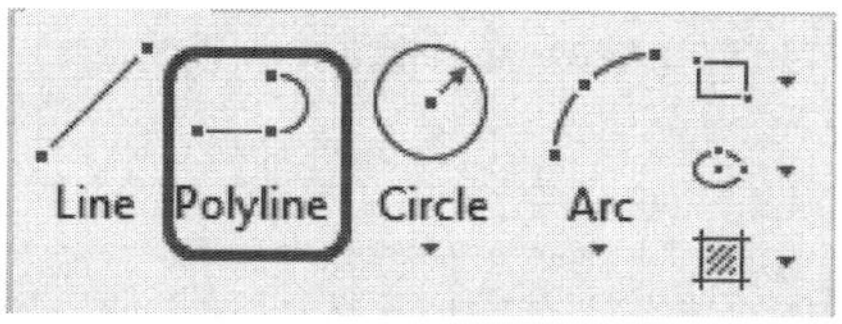

Invoke the Polyline command (pl or pline).

2. *Specify start point:*
Pick the start point with the LMB.
Type **6, 1** for the starting point.

3. 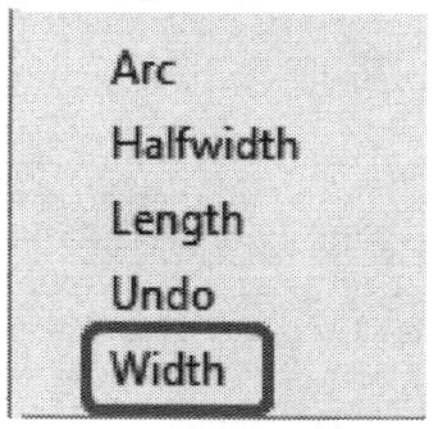

Specify next point or [Arc /Halfwidth/Length/Undo/Width]:
Right-click in the drawing window and select 'Width' or type 'W' for width and Click <ENTER>.

4. *Specify starting width <0.0000>:*
Type '0.3' and Click <ENTER>.

5. *Specify ending width <0.3000>:*
Click <ENTER>.

6. *Specify next point or [Arc/Close/Halfwidth/Length/Undo/Width]:*
Make sure ORTHO is ON. Drag the mouse to the right. Type '1' and Click

<ENTER>.

7. *Specify next point or [Arc/Close/Halfwidth/Length/Undo/Width]:*
   Drag the mouse upward. Type '1' and Click <ENTER>.

8. *Specify next point or [Arc/Close/Halfwidth/Length/Undo/Width]:*
   Right-click in the drawing window and select 'Arc' or type 'A' for arc and Click <ENTER>.

9. *Specify endpoint of arc or [Angle/CEnter/CLose/Direction/Halfwidth/Line/Radius/Second pt/ Undo/Width]:*
   Drag the mouse to the right. Type '2' and Click <ENTER>.

10. *Specify endpoint of arc or [Angle/CEnter/CLose/Direction/Halfwidth/Line/Radius/Second pt/ Undo/Width]:*
    Type 'L' for line and Click <ENTER>.

11. *Specify next point or [Arc/Close/Halfwidth/Length/Undo/Width]:*
    Drag the mouse downward. Type '1' and Click <ENTER>.

12. *Specify next point or [Arc/Close/Halfwidth/Length/Undo/Width]:*
    Drag the mouse to the right. Type '1' and Click <ENTER>.

13. *Specify next point or [Arc/Close/Halfwidth/Length/Undo/Width]:*
    Drag the mouse upward. Type '4' and Click <ENTER>.

14. *Specify next point or [Arc/Close/Halfwidth/Length/Undo/Width]:*
    Drag the mouse to the left. Type '4' and Click <ENTER>.

15. *Specify next point or [Arc/Close/Halfwidth/Length/Undo/Width]:*
    Right-click in the drawing window and select 'Close' or type 'C' for close to complete the exercise.

As the figure is created, you will see small symbols indicating geometric constraints which are automatically applied.

	Vertical
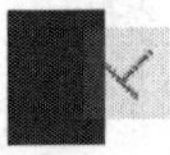	Perpendicular
	Tangent

Extra: *Explode the polyline. What happens? Undo the explode command. Move the objects by selecting the arc only. Notice that the entire polyline is selected.*

Command Exercise

Exercise 4-2 – Polyline

Drawing Name: **new drawing**
Estimated Time to Completion: 10 Minutes

Scope

Using the Polyline command with the Width and Line options, draw an arrow. ORTHO should be enabled.

Solution

1. 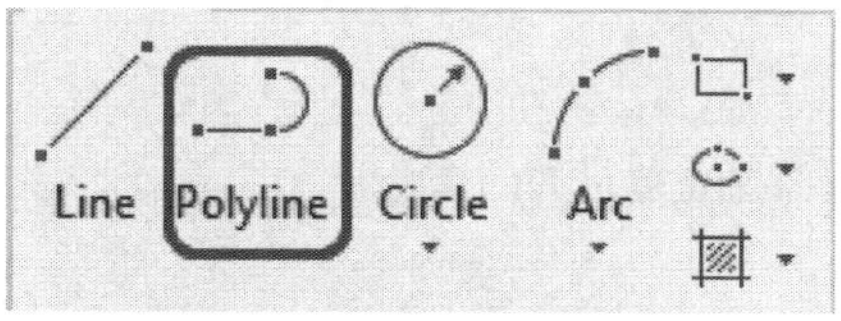

1. Invoke the Polyline command (pl or pline).

2. 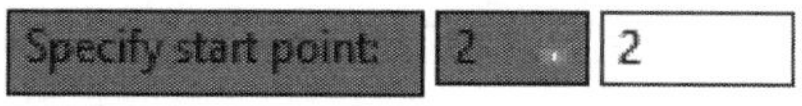

When prompted for the start point, enter **2,2**.

3. 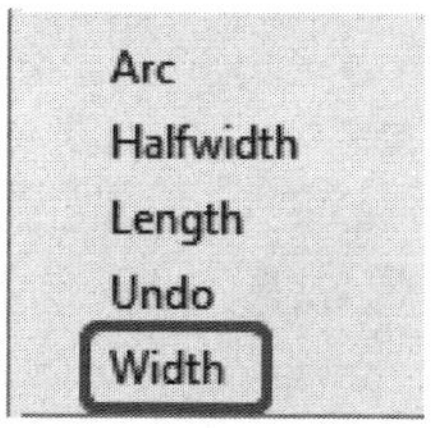

Right click and select **W** for width.

4. 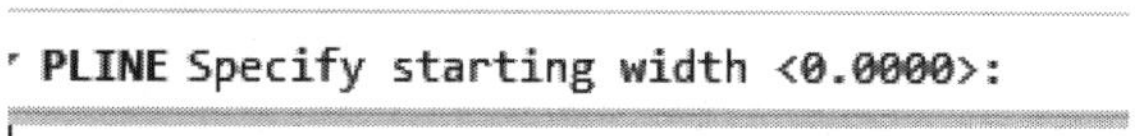

Set the starting width to **0**.

5. 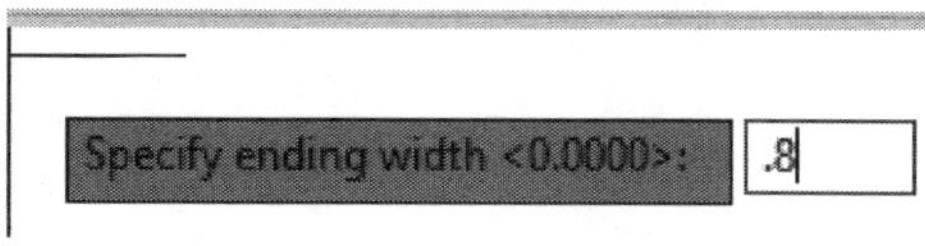

Set the ending width to **0.8**.

6. 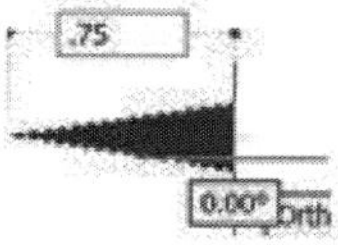

Specify the next point as **.75**. (Move the cursor towards the right.)

7. Right click and select **W** for width.

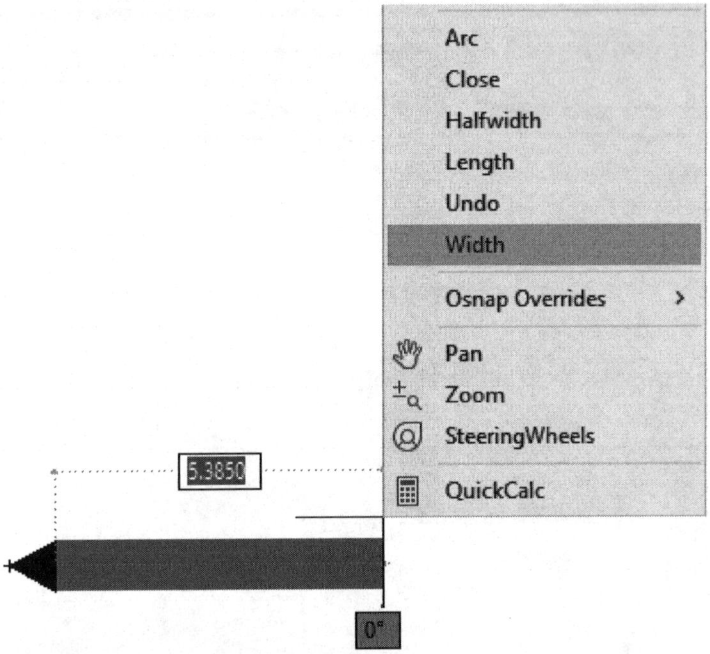

8. Set the starting width to **0.4**.

9. Set the ending width to **0.4**.

10. Set the distance to **5**. (Move the cursor towards the right.)

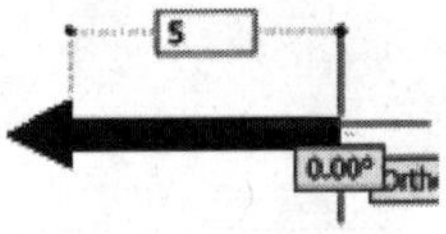

11. Click <**ENTER**> to exit the command.

- *Do not start and stop the polyline segments. Use the polyline UNDO option if an incorrect endpoint is selected.*

Polygon

Command Locator

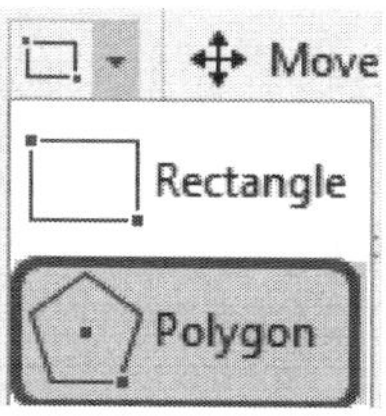

Home Ribbon	**Draw Panel/ Polygon**
Command	**Polygon**
Alias	**Pol**

Command Overview

Polygons are polylines with equal line segments. First determine the number of sides for the polygon then select a center point. A polygon may be either Inscribed (I) within or Circumscribed (C) around an imaginary circle. Typing the radius of this circle will determine the size of the polygon. A Polygon may also be constructed using the Edge option and specifying the length of the Polygon Edge.

General Procedures

1. Begin the Polygon command. Type the number of sides, and Click <ENTER>.
2. Specify the center of the Polygon.
3. Determine whether it is Inscribed (I) or Circumscribed (C) about the radius of the circle.
4. Specify the radius.

Tips & Tricks

- After specifying the number of sides to the polygon, type E (for Edge mode) to specify the length and direction of the polygon edge.
- There is no Polygon Center tool. Use the Geometric Center snap to locate the center of a polygon.

Command Exercise

Exercise 4-3 – Polygon

Drawing Name: **poly1.dwg**
Estimated Time to Completion: 20 Minutes

Scope

Practice the options for drawing a polygon:

1.) *Draw a 6-sided polygon making the overall radius 2, using the Inscribed option.*
2.) *Draw a 6 sided polygon making the overall radius 2, using the Circumscribed option.*
3.) *Draw a 6 sided polygon using the Edge option, with a length of 1. Notice that the angle of the polygon is determined by the cursor direction as it is dragged from the first pick point.*

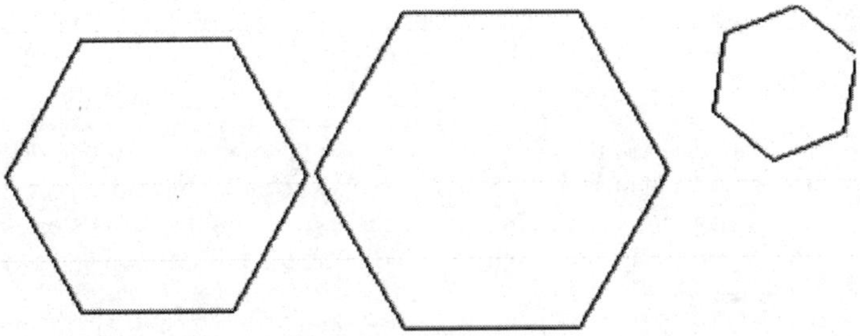

Solution

1. 
Turn ORTHO ON by Clicking F8.

2. 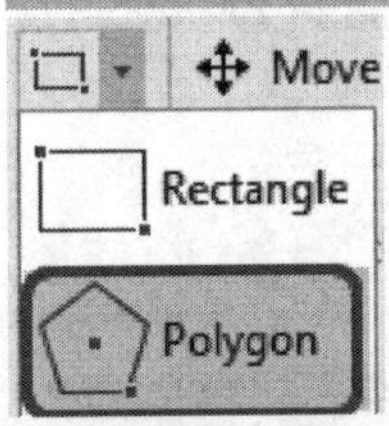

Invoke the Polygon command (polygon).
Enter number of sides <4>:
Remember the polygon tool is located below the RECTANGLE icon on the Draw panel.

3. 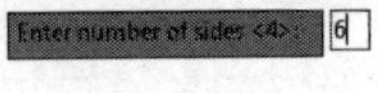
Type '6' at the command line for the number of sides and Click <ENTER>.

4. 
Specify center of polygon or [Edge]:
Type '2,4' for the center point.
Click ENTER.

5. 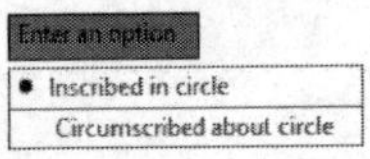

Enter an option [Inscribed in circle/Circumscribed about circle] <I>:
If the default value is <I> for inscribed, Click <ENTER> to accept

this value, right-click in the drawing window and select ‘Inscribed in circle’ or type ‘I’ and Click <ENTER>.

You can also click the desired option in the command prompt window.

6. 

Type ‘2’ and Click <ENTER> for the radius in which the polygon is inscribed.

7. 

Repeat the Polygon command with the RMB.

8. 

Enter number of sides <6>:
Click <ENTER> to accept the default.

9. 

Specify center of polygon or [Edge]:
Type ‘6.5,4’ and Click <ENTER>.

10. 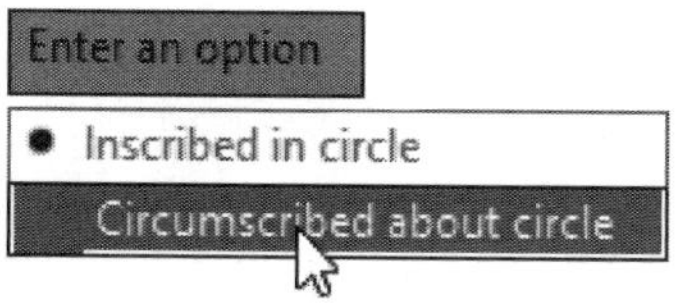

Enter an option [Inscribed in circle/Circumscribed about circle] <I>:
Right-click in the drawing window and select ‘Circumscribed about circle’ or type ‘C’ at the command line and Click <ENTER>

11. 

Specify radius of circle:
Type ‘2’ and Click <ENTER> for the radius of the circle about which the polygon is circumscribed.

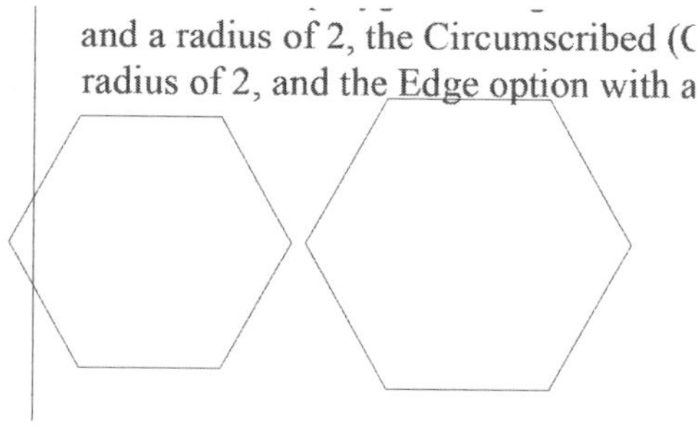

Both polygons have a radius of 2. Which polygon is larger? The circumscribed or inscribed?

12. Repeat the Polygon command with the RMB.

13. 

Enter number of sides <6>:
Click <ENTER> to accept the default.

14. 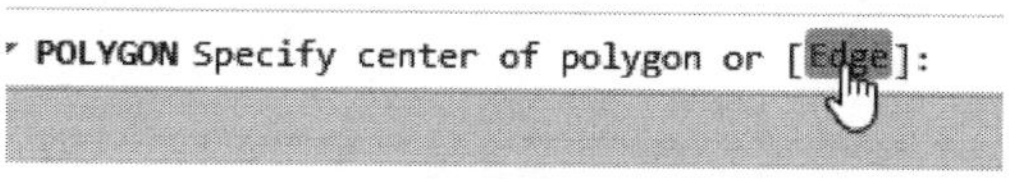

Specify center of polygon or [Edge]:
Right-click in the drawing window and select ‘Edge’ or type ‘E’ and Click <ENTER> for the edge

option or click on the Edge option in the command prompt window.

15. 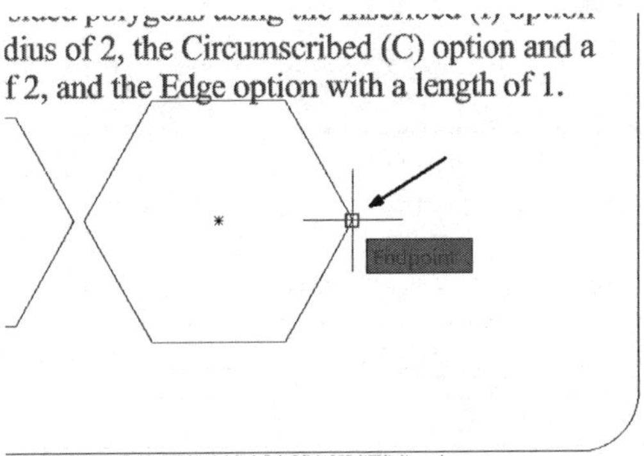

Specify first endpoint of edge:

Select the right vertex of the second polygon.

16. 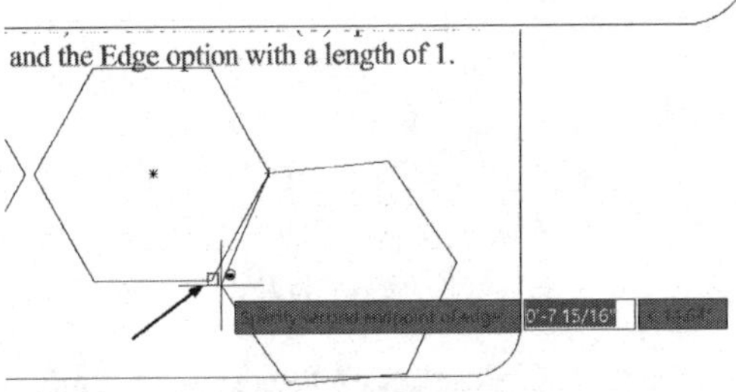

Specify second endpoint of edge:

Select the lower right vertex of the second polygon.

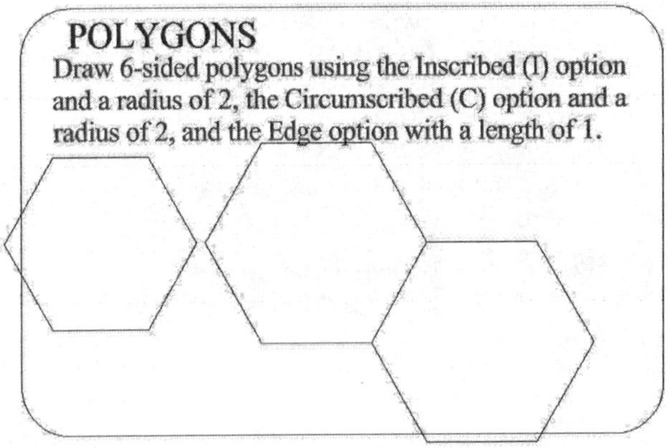

You should have three polygons in your drawing.

Tips & Tricks

➢ *Can the Center Object Snap be used to select the center of the polygon? Try it. How would you draw a line from the center point of one polygon to the next?*

Rectangle

Command Locator

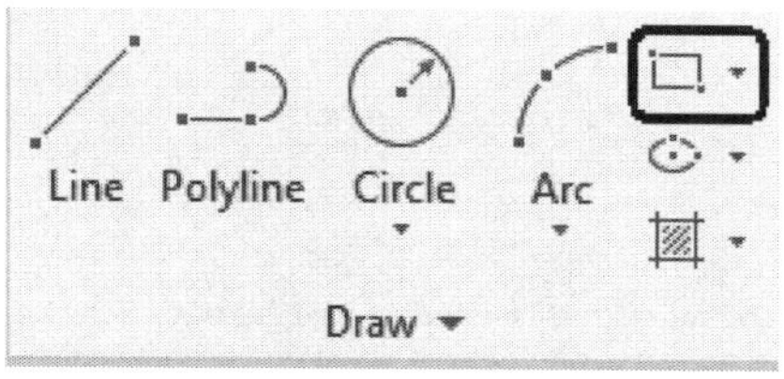

Home Ribbon	**Draw / Rectangle**
Command	**Rectangle**
Alias	**Rectang**
RMB Shortcut Menu	**Drawing Window (before select the first corner point)**

Command Overview

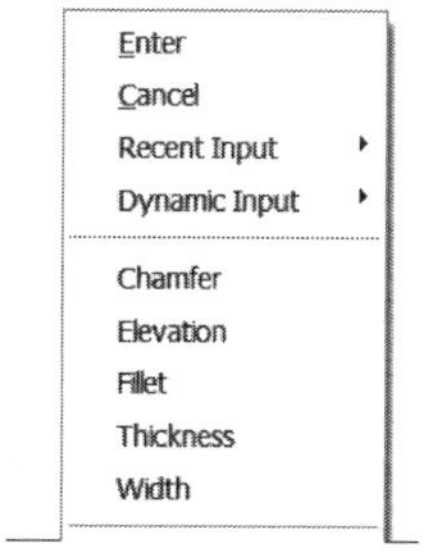

RMB Shortcut Menu for the Rectangle Command Before Selecting a Point

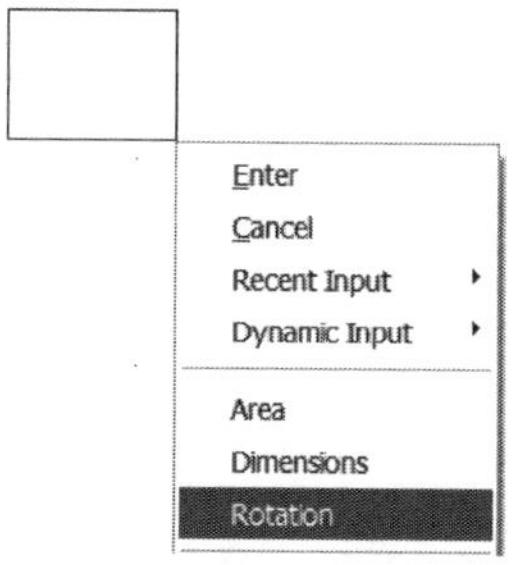

RMB Shortcut Menu for the Rectangle Command After Selecting a Point

Rectangles are polylines. All of the line segments are connected. Draw rectangles by designating the opposite corners.

General Procedures

To draw a rectangle by picking opposite corners:

1. Begin the rectangle command, and pick the first corner.
2. Drag the mouse and pick the opposite corner.

To draw a rectangle using coordinates:

1. Begin the rectangle command, and pick the first corner.
2. Type '@5,3' to create a 5 x 3 rectangle. The @ means "relative to the last point picked"; the first number is the distance in the x direction, and the second number is the distance in the y direction. The rectangle will be drawn 5 units to the right, and up 3 units. If a negative coordinate is typed, i.e., @-5,-3, the rectangle will be drawn to the left and down from the point picked.

Command Exercise

Exercise 4-4 – Rectangle

Drawing Name: **rect1.dwg**
Estimated Time to Completion: 5 Minutes

Scope

Draw rectangles as they are in the example. Turn Snap on to make the small rectangles. Turn Snap off to make the large rectangle.

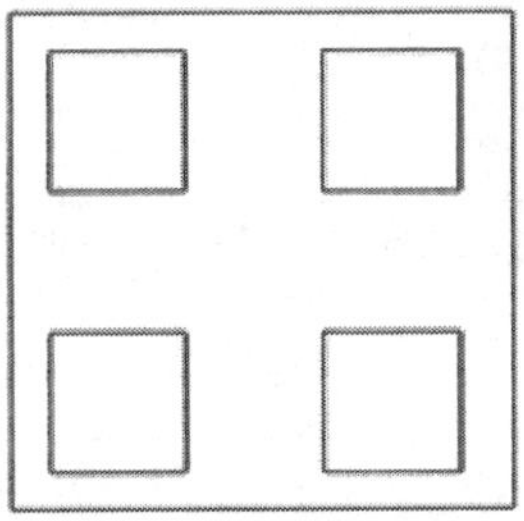

Solution

1.

Start by creating the small rectangles. Turn <Snap on> by Clicking the <F9> key, or use your LMB to toggle SNAP on at the Status Bar. Turn the GRID on to use as a guide, if you like.

2.

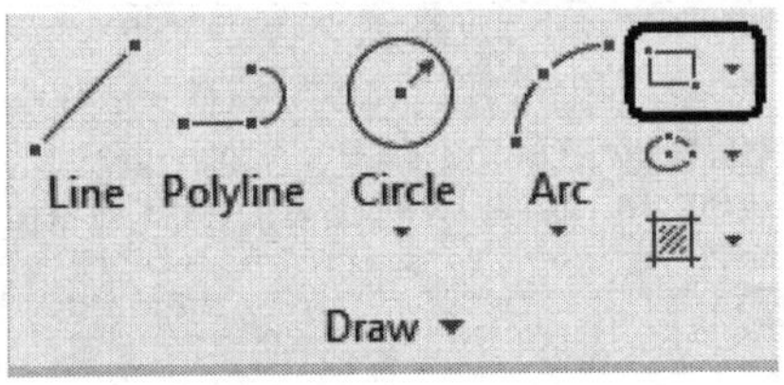

Invoke the **Rectangle** command (rectang).

3.

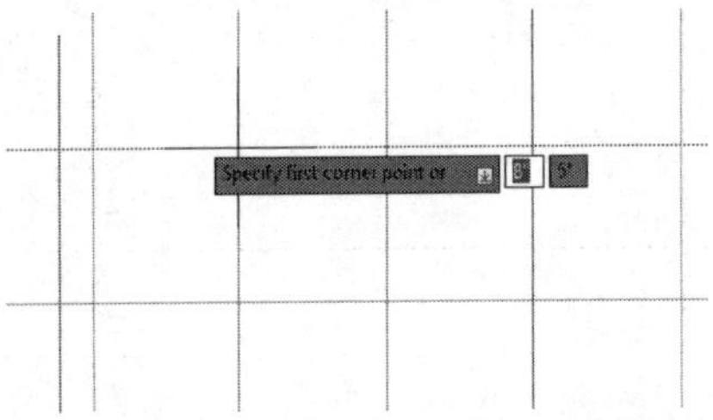

Specify first corner point or [Chamfer/Elevation/Fillet/Thickness/Width]
:

Position your pointer to the desired location and pick the first point with your LMB.

4. 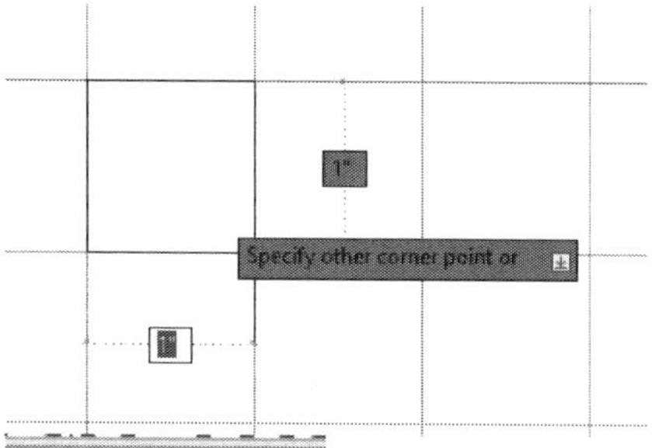

Specify other corner point:
Move your pointer diagonally to the second desired location and pick the point with your LMB.

5. 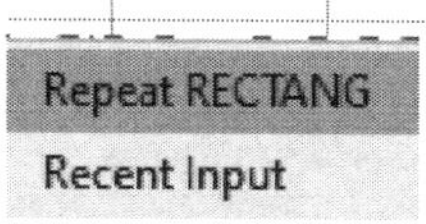

Repeat the Rectangle command by Clicking the RMB or the <ENTER> key.

Select the first corner for the rectangle and then the second corner. Repeat the command to finish the small rectangles.

6. 

Turn Snap off by Clicking the <F9> key or using the LMB to toggle snap off at the Status Bar.

7. 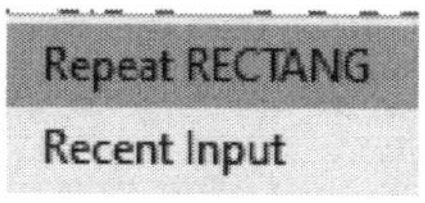

Repeat the Rectangle command by right-clicking in the drawing area and selecting 'Repeat'.

8. 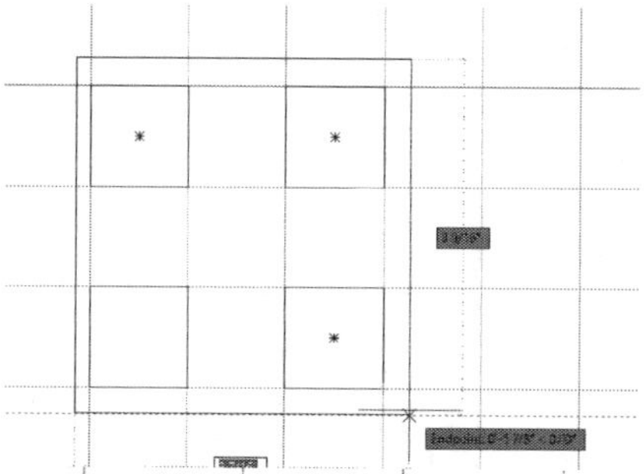

Specify first corner point or [Chamfer/Elevation/Fillet/Thickness/Width] :
Pick the first corner of the large rectangle with your LMB.

9. 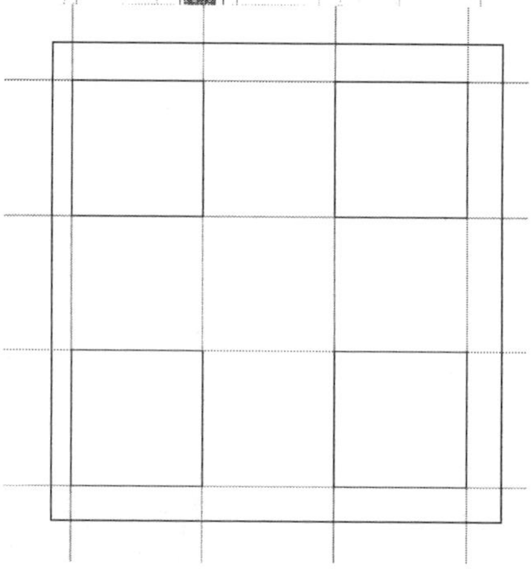

Specify other corner point:
Pick a second diagonal corner to complete the large rectangle.

- Use the Rectangle command rather than drawing four separate line segments. This is quicker to make, and a more efficient object, since it is a polyline.
- Beginners should ignore the other Rectangle options, which appear at the command line, until they have had more experience using AutoCAD. The Chamfer and Fillet options will automatically add those features to the corners of the rectangle. Width will change the width of the rectangle's lines. Thickness and Elevation are for 3D drawing. Area allows the user to set the area of the rectangle. The user is still prompted for the length of one side of the rectangle and AutoCAD performs the calculation to determine the length of the other side based on the area provided. Rotation allows you to create a rectangle at an angle.
- *You can toggle the SNAP on and off in the middle of the rectangle command. Try it.*
- You can use the Shift+RMB Center Object Snap to snap to the center of a rectangle.

Arc

Command Locator

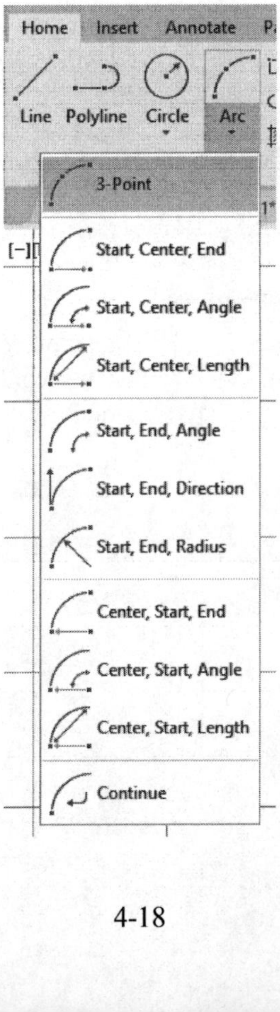

Home Ribbon	**Draw Panel/ Arc**
Command	**Arc**
Alias	**A**
RMB Shortcut Menu	**Drawing Window**

Command Overview

There are many arc options. We will look at the following Arc options: '3 points'; 'Start, Center, End'; and 'Start, End, Radius'. These Arc options will work in most instances.
Invoke the Arc command from the toolbar or by typing A at the command line. This will draw a '3-point' Arc through three consecutive points. Other Arc options can be selected from the Pull-Down menu. Arcs are constructed in a counterclockwise direction, except when drawing a 3-point Arc.

General Procedures

1. Begin the Arc command from the toolbar to draw a 3-point arc, or select one of the Arc options from the Pull-Down Menu.
2. Follow the Command Line prompts.
3. Click the RMB, with the cursor in the Drawing Window, to repeat the Arc command.

Tips & Tricks

- Arcs are constructed in a counterclockwise direction, except when drawing a 3-point Arc. You can flip the direction of the arc by Clicking the CTL key.
- Click the right button on the mouse to repeat the Arc command.
- When the cursor is in the Drawing Window, the Shortcut Menu (RMB) will provide an option to repeat the same Arc command.
- When the cursor is over the Command Line, the shortcut Menu (RMB) will provide an option to repeat the Arc command, but it will be the generic 3-point Arc.

Command Exercise

Exercise 4-5 – Arc

Drawing Name: **arc1.dwg**
Estimated Time to Completion: 10 Minutes

Scope

Draw the object on the left using the appropriate Arc and Object Snap options. Use running object snaps (Endpoint and Midpoint).

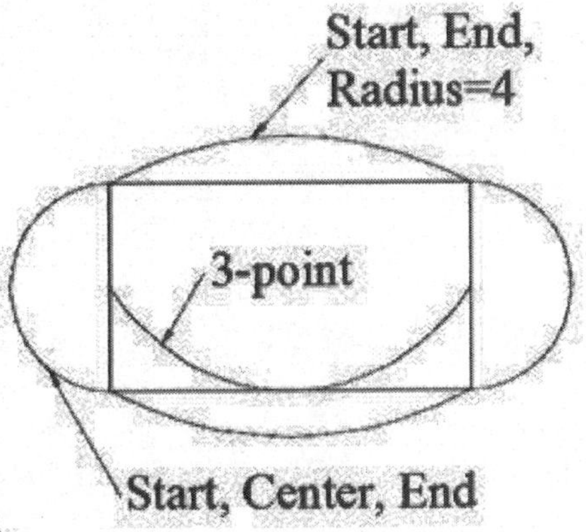

Solution

1. 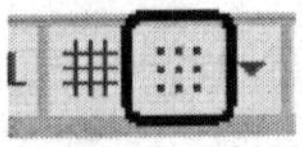

Toggle SNAP off.

2. 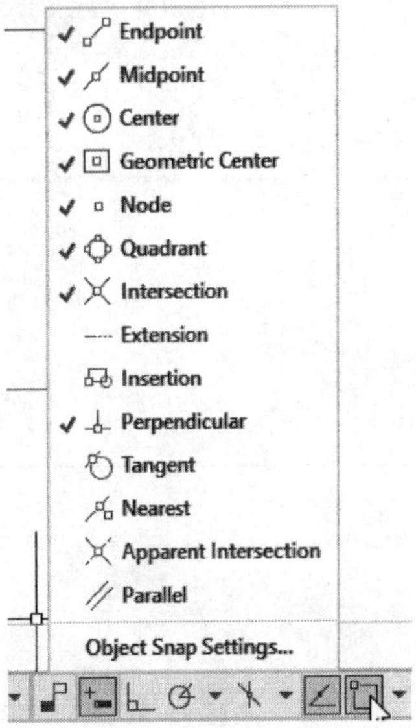

Click on the Object Snap Tracking button on the Status Bar.

3. 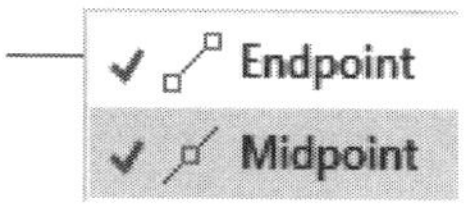

Enable **Midpoint** and **Endpoint** running object snaps as shown below.

4. 
Verify that both Object Snap On and Object Snap Tracking is enabled.

5. 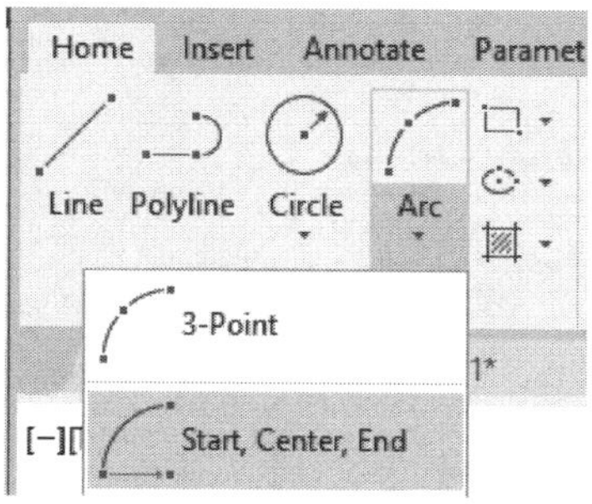

Invoke the Start, Center, End ARC command from the pull-down menu on the ribbon (<DRAW<ARC<START,CENTER,END…).

6. 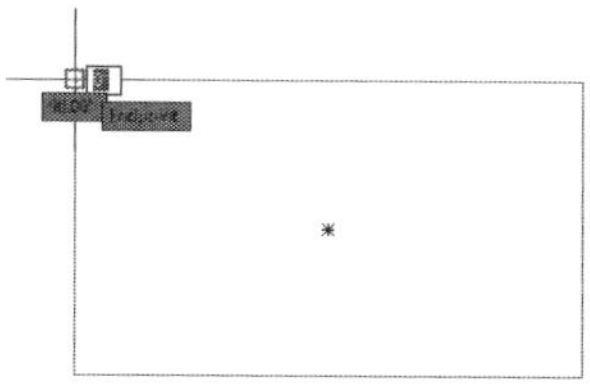
Specify start point of arc or [CEnter]:
Move near the upper left corner of the box until the desired Object Snap Marker appears. Select the point with the LMB.

7. 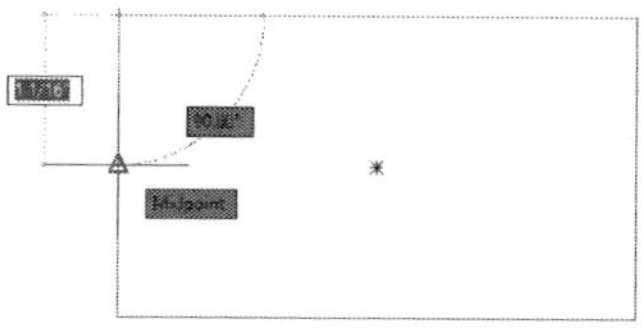
Specify second point of arc or [CEnter/ENd]: _c
Specify center point of arc:
Move the pointer near the middle of the left side of the box until the Midpoint Object Snap appears. Select the point with the LMB.

8. 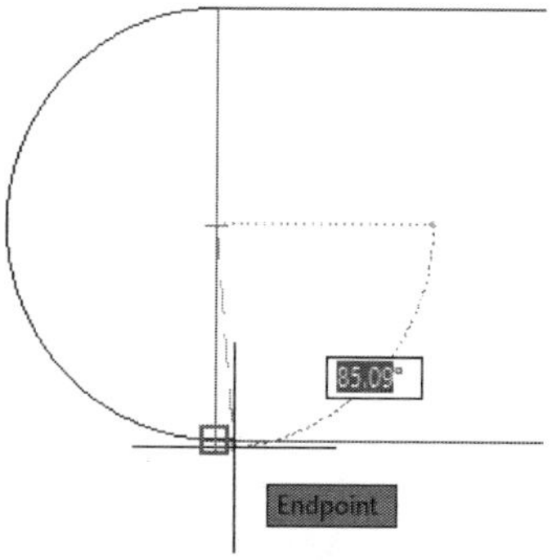

Specify end point of arc or [Angle/chord Length]:
Move near the bottom left corner of the box. Use your LMB when the Endpoint Object Snap appears.

9. 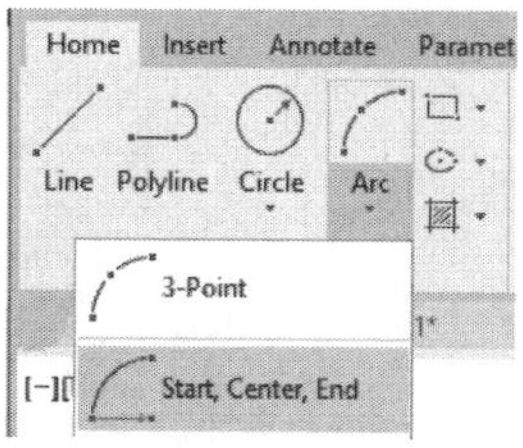

Invoke the Start, Center, End ARC command from the pull-down menu on the ribbon (<DRAW<ARC<START,CENTER,END…).

10.

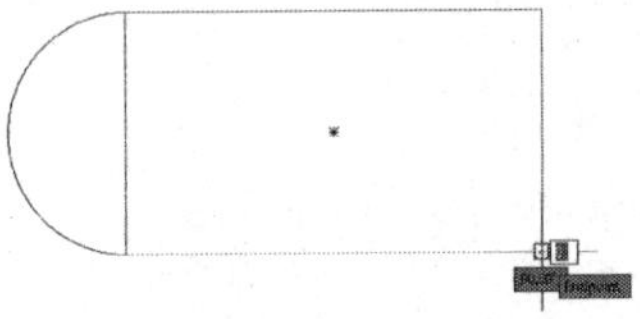

Specify start point of arc or [CEnter]:
Repeat the exact procedure for the right side of the box but start the arc at the lower right corner.

11.

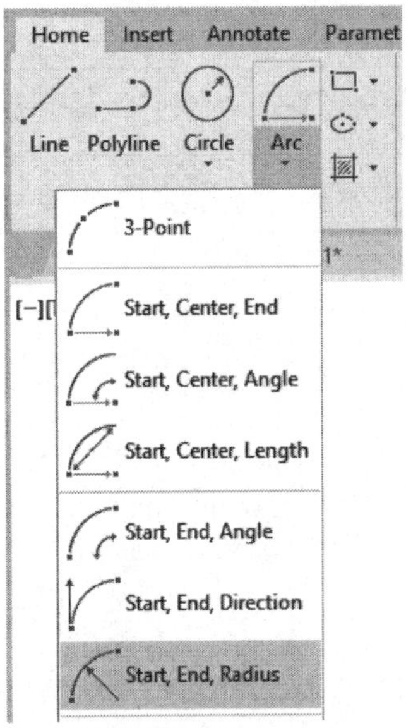

Invoke the Start, End, Radius Arc command from the pull-down menu on the ribbon
(<DRAW PANEL
<ARC<START,END,RADIUS).

12.

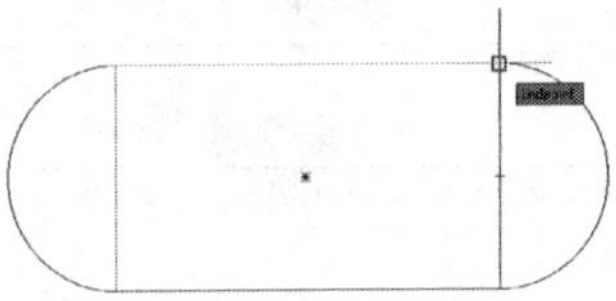

Specify start point of arc or [CEnter]:
Select a point near the upper right corner of the box. Remember to use the LMB when the desired Endpoint Object Snap Marker appears.

13.

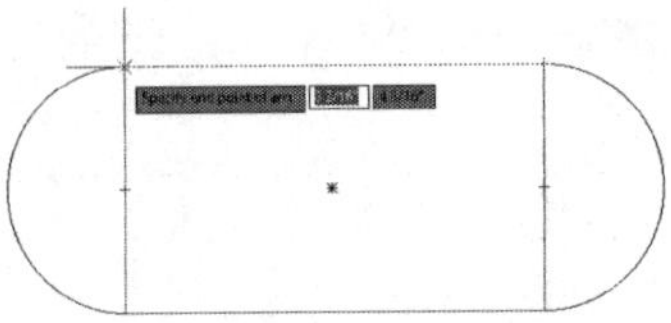

Specify second point of arc or [CEnter/ENd]:
Select the end point of the arc at the upper left corner of the box.

14.

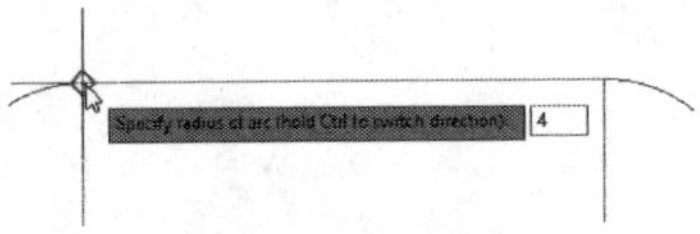

. Specify center point of arc or [Angle/Direction/Radius]: _r Specify radius of arc:
Type '4' for the radius of the Arc.

15. 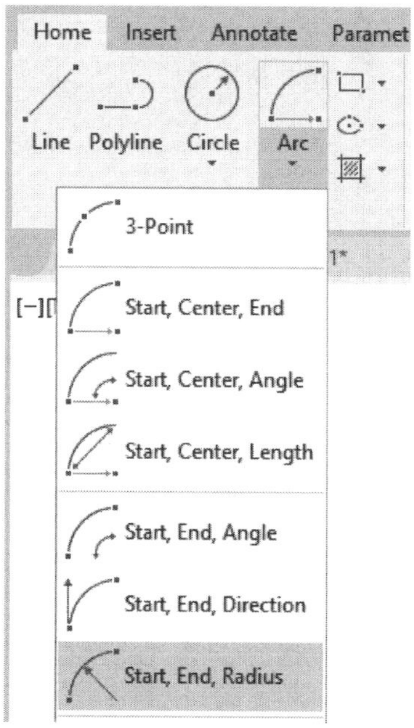

Invoke the Start, End, Radius Arc command from the pull-down menu on the ribbon
(<DRAW PANEL
<ARC<START,END,RADIUS).

16. 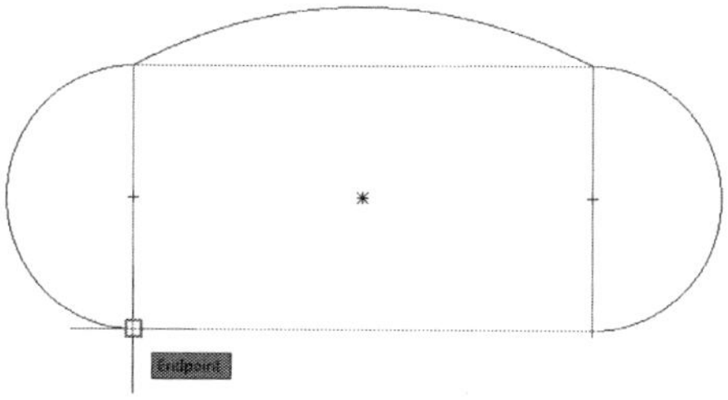

Select the lower left corner of the rectangle.

17. 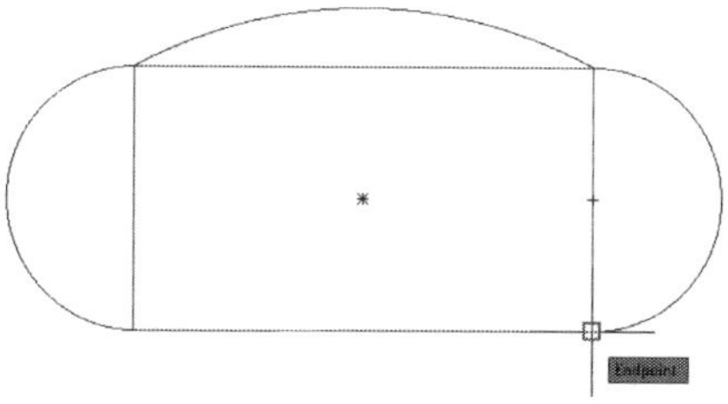

Select the lower right corner of the rectangle.

18. 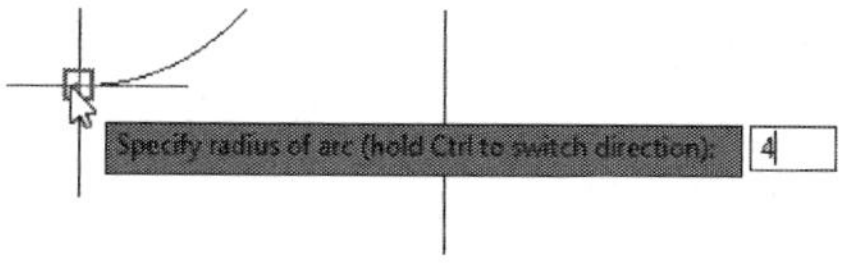

Specify center point of arc or [Angle/Direction/Radius]: _r Specify radius of arc:
Type '4' for the radius of the Arc.

19. 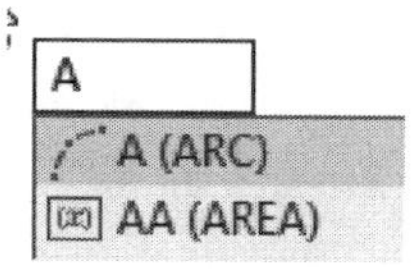

Invoke the Three Point Arc command by selecting it from the tool ribbon or by typing 'A' or 'ARC' at the command line and Clicking <ENTER>.

20. 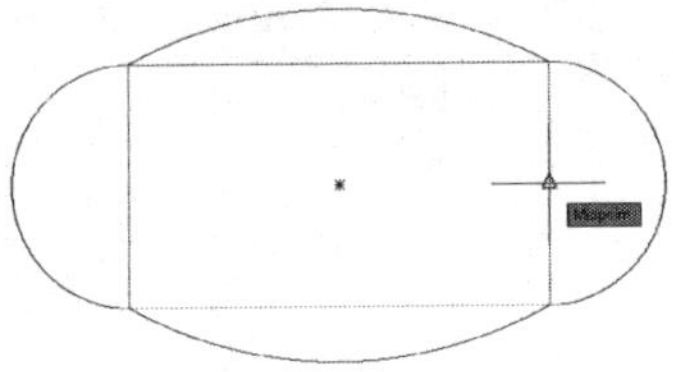

Specify start point of arc or [CEnter]:
Pick the midpoint of the right side of the box.

21. 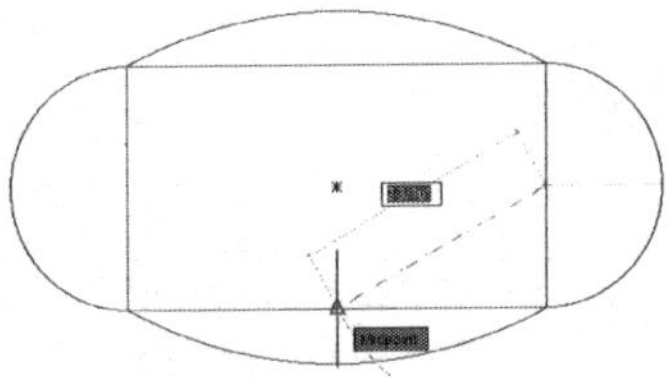

Specify second point of arc or [CEnter/ENd]:
Pick the midpoint of the bottom of the box.

22. 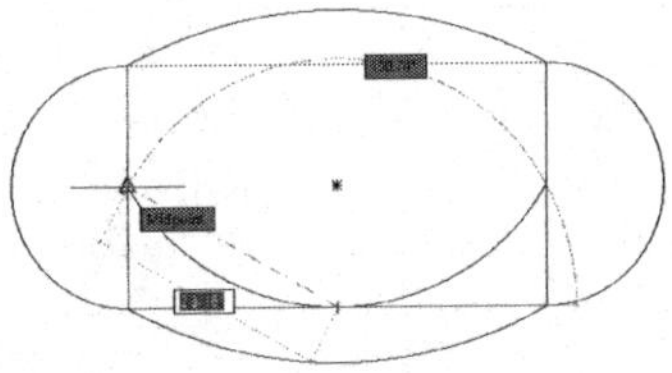

Specify end point of arc:
Pick the midpoint of the left side of the box. This will complete the arc.

- *Notice how the first two sets of arcs were created in a counterclockwise fashion. What happens if they were created in a clockwise fashion? Try it.*

Circle

Command Locator

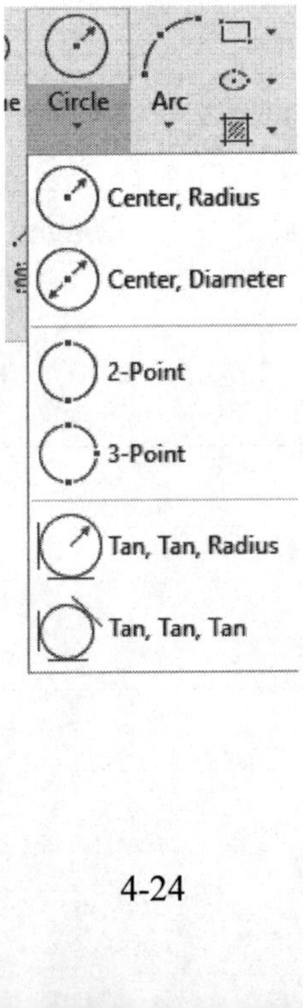

Ribbon Home	**Draw / Circle (select option)**
Command	**Circle**
Alias	**C**
RMB Shortcut Menu	**Drawing Window**

Command Overview

There are several ways to draw a Circle. The most common way is to pick the center point then designate a radius. Right click to view the shortcut menu for options. If a center point is selected first, the shortcut menu option for circle is Diameter. If no center point is selected, the shortcut menu will display other options.

Circle Options	**Overview**
Radius / Diameter	If a center point is selected, type or pick the Radius. Right-click to select the Diameter option or type D and <Enter>.
3P	Draws a circle by selecting 3 Points on the circumference.
2P	Draws a circle by selecting 2 Points on the diameter.
Tangent, Tangent, Radius	Draws a circle by selecting two Tangents and typing a radius.
Tangent, Tangent, Tangent	(Accessed from the Draw Pull-Down menu only.) Draws a circle by selecting three Tangents.

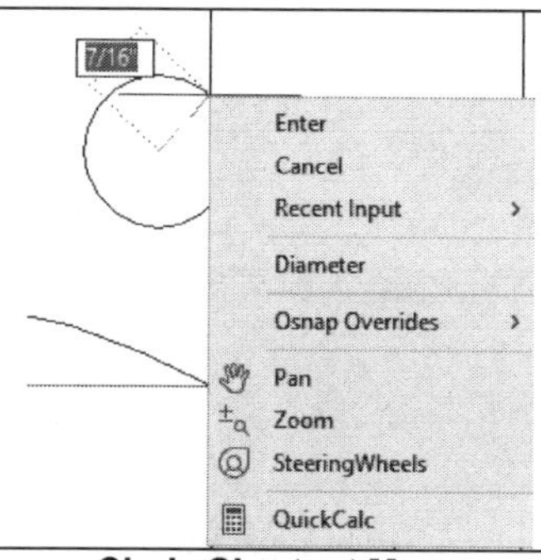

Circle Shortcut Menu (center point selected)

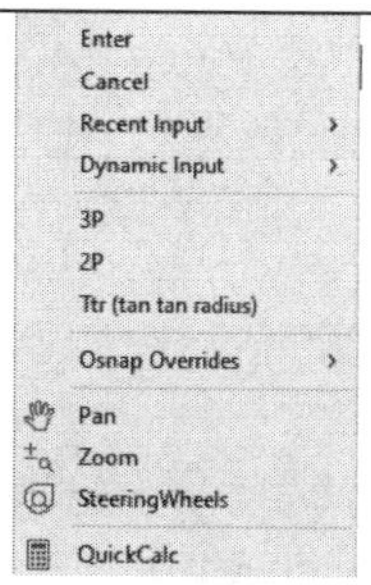

Circle Shortcut Menu (no center point selected)

General Procedures

1. Begin the Circle command, and pick the center point.
2. Type the radius, or Click <ENTER> and select the Diameter option. Then type the diameter.

Donut

Command Locator

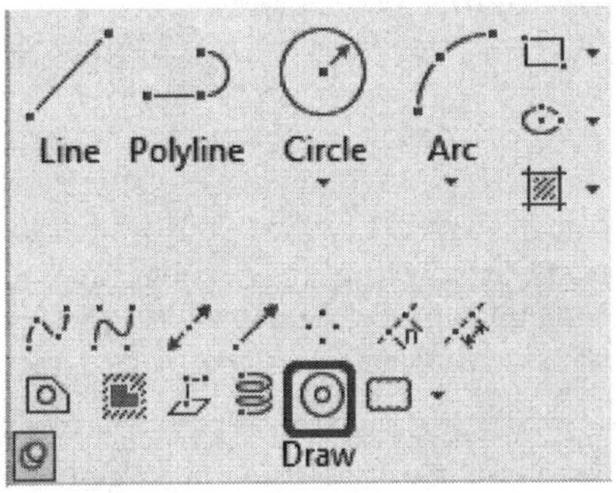

Home ribbon/Draw Panel	**Donut**
Pull Down Menu	**Draw / Donut**
Command	**Donut**
Alias	**DO**

Command Overview

A Donut has an inner diameter and an outer diameter. When prompted for inner and outer diameters, type it, or Click <ENTER> to accept the default.

General Procedures

1. Begin the Donut Command by typing DO (and <ENTER>) or selecting it from the Draw Pull-Down Menu.
2. Type the inside diameter or Click <ENTER> to accept the *default.*
3. Type the outside diameter or accept the *default.*
4. Specify the center of the donut by picking in the drawing window. <ENTER> to exit.

Tips & Tricks

- For a solid filled Donut, make the inner diameter zero (0).
- The diameters can also be determined by picking two points in the AutoCAD Window.

Command Exercise

Exercise 4-6 – Circle

Drawing Name: **circle1.dwg**
Estimated Time to Completion: 10 Minutes

Scope

Draw the large circle using the Tan, Tan, Tan option. With Snap On, draw the inner ring using the Center, Diameter (3) option. With Snap On, draw four circles the same size using the Center, Radius (0.25) option. Place a donut with an inside diameter of 0 and an outside diameter of 0.5 as designated.

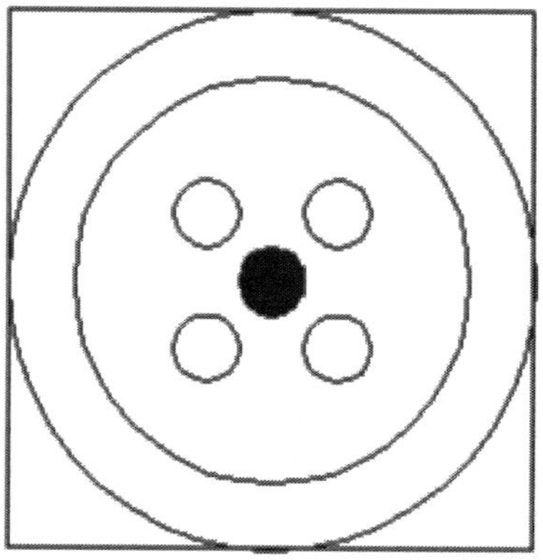

Solution

1. 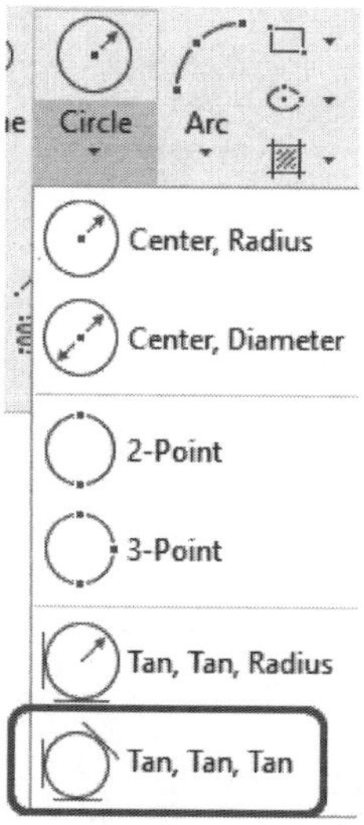

Invoke the circle command by using the **DRAW→CIRCLE→TAN, TAN, TAN** command from the Home ribbon.

2.

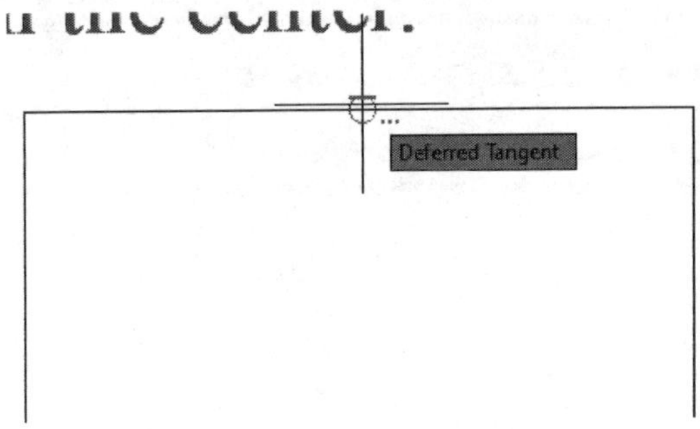

Specify first point on circle: _tan to
Select the top line segment of the box with the LMB. You will notice a symbol appearing when your pointer is on the line segment.

3.

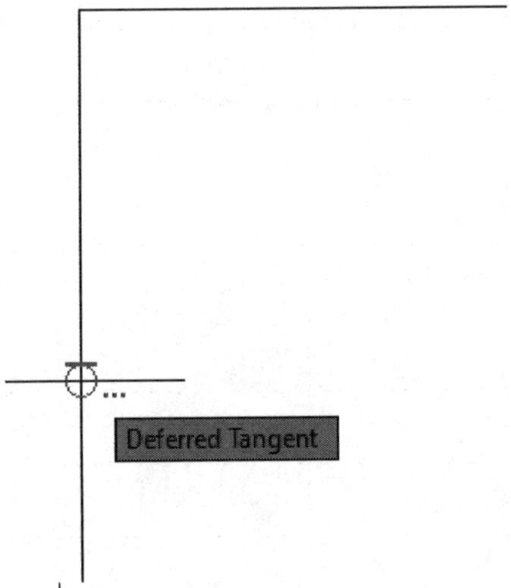

Specify second point on circle: _tan to
Select the left or right side of the box with the LMB. (Notice the symbol that appears.)

4.

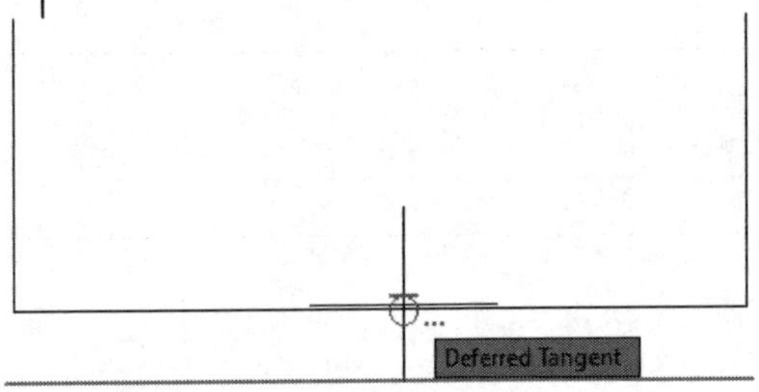

Specify third point on circle: _tan to
Select the bottom of the box with the LMB. (Notice the symbol that appears.) The Circle is automatically drawn.

5.

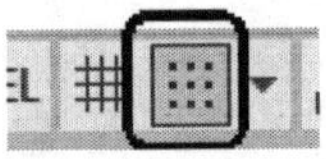

Turn Snap on with the <F9> key or use your mouse to toggle snap on at the Status Bar.

6. 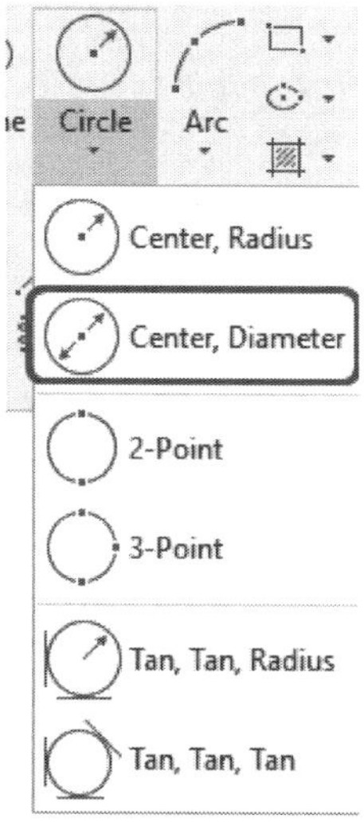

Invoke the circle command by using the **DRAW→CIRCLE→CENTER, DIAMETER** command from the pull-down menu.

7. 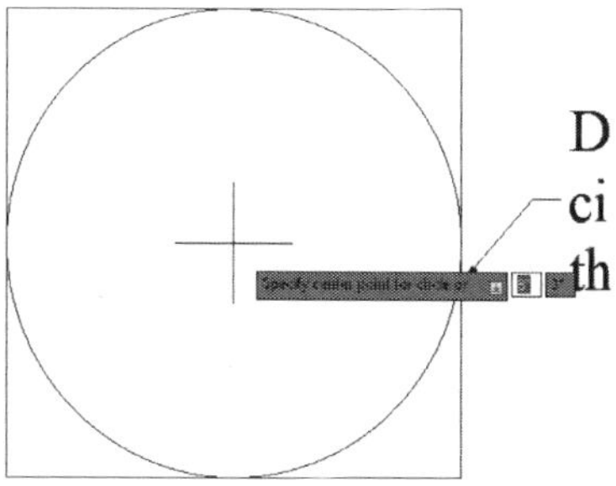

Specify center point for circle or [3P/2P/Ttr (tan tan radius)]:
Pick in the center of the box.

8. 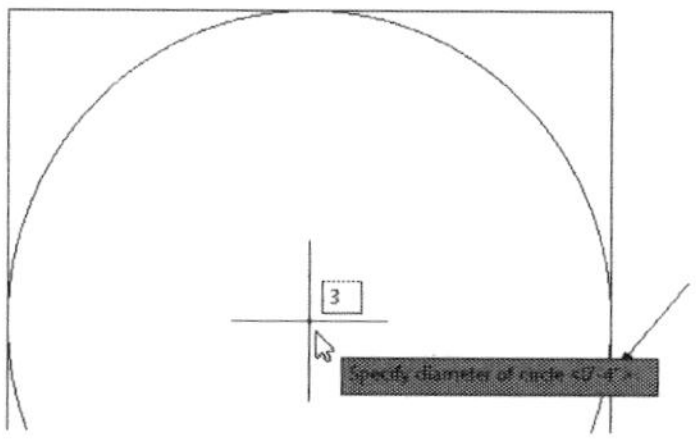

Specify diameter of circle:
Type '3' at the command line and Click <ENTER>.

9. 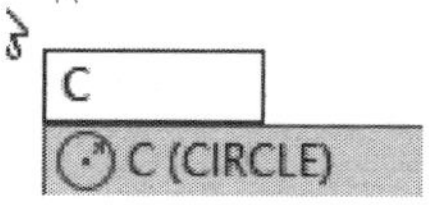

Invoke the circle command from the toolbar or by typing **C** or **CIRCLE** at the command line and Clicking <ENTER>.

10. 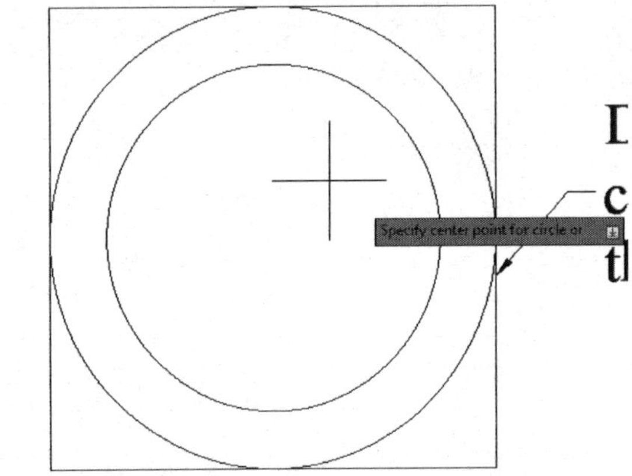

Specify center point for circle or [3P/2P/Ttr (tan tan radius)]:
Use your LMB to pick the desired center point of the first small circle.

Turning on the Grid may make it easier for you to place the four small circles.

11. 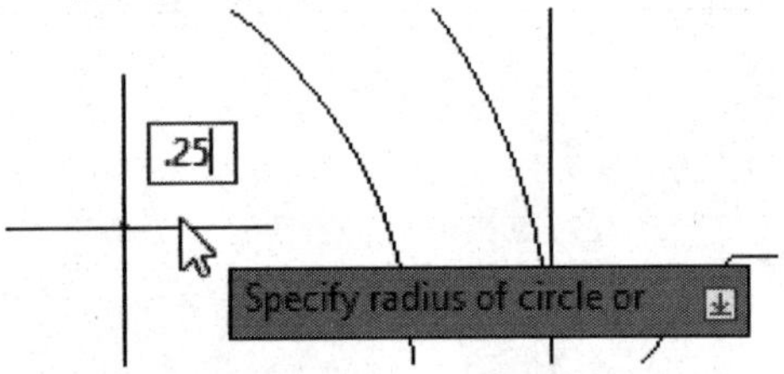

Specify radius of circle or [Diameter] <1.5000>:
Type **0.25** at the command line and Click <ENTER>.

12. 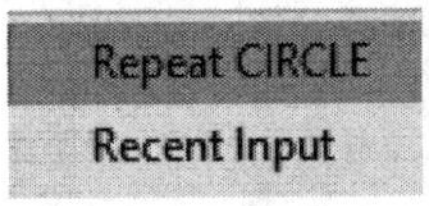

Repeat the Circle command by Clicking <ENTER> or the RMB.

13. 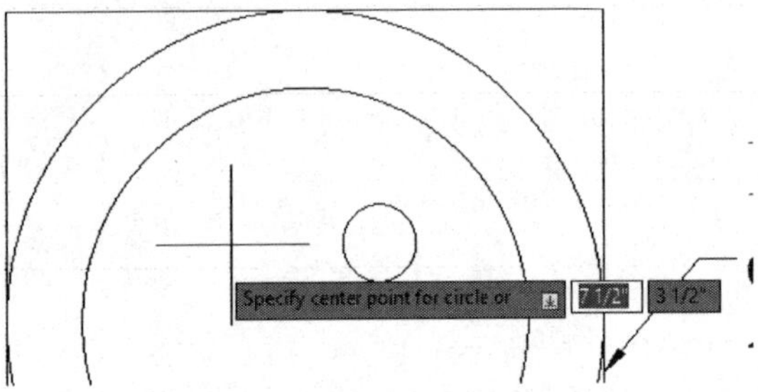

Specify center point for circle or [3P/2P/Ttr (tan tan radius)]:
Select the desired center point for the second small circle.

14. 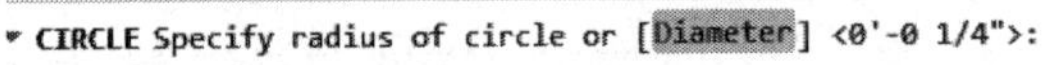

Specify radius of circle or [Diameter] <0.2500>:
Click <ENTER> to accept the radius setting of 0.25.

15.

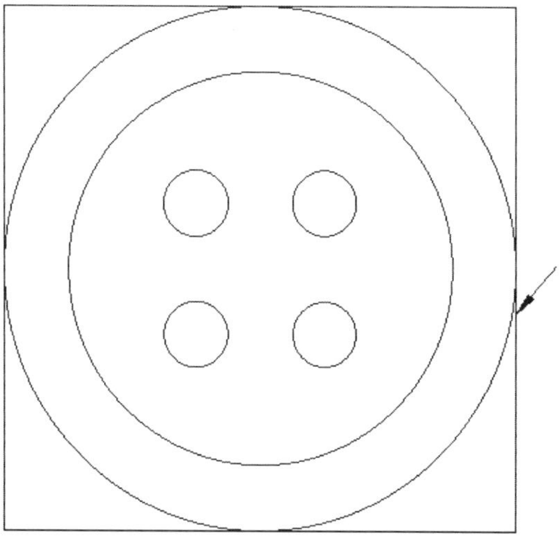

Repeat the command to complete the remaining circles.

16.

Invoke the Donut command by selecting Donut from the Draw panel on the Home ribbon or type **DO**.

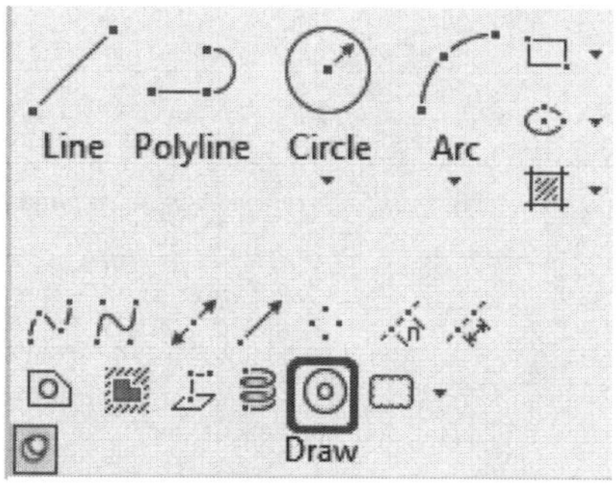

17.

Specify inside diameter of donut <0.5000>:
Type **0** and Click <ENTER>.

18.

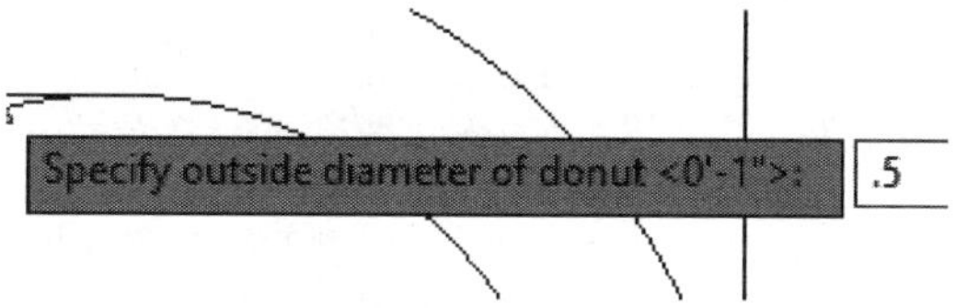

Specify outside diameter of donut <1.0000>:
Type **0.5** and Click <ENTER>.

19.

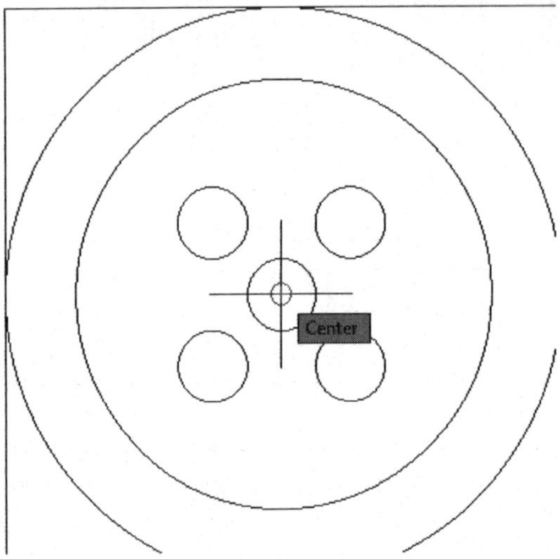

Specify center of donut or <exit>:
Use your LMB to pick the center point for the donut.

20.

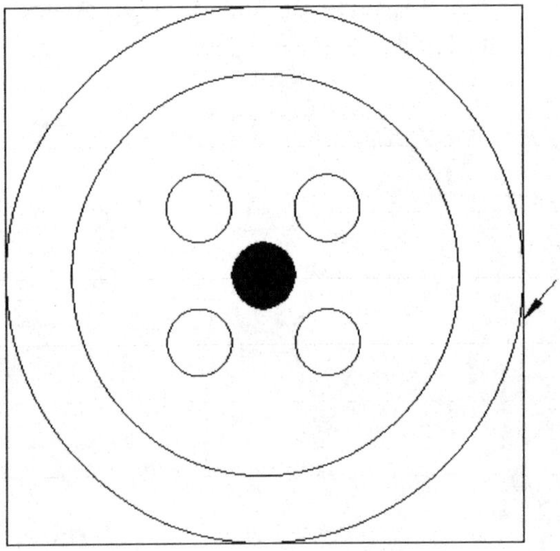

Specify center of donut or <exit>:
Click <ENTER> to end the command.

➤ *AutoCAD remembers the radius of the last circle that was created. If you start the Circle command by typing 'C' or 'Circle' you can enter a radius by default. If you would like to enter a diameter, type 'D' and Click <ENTER> after you have selected the center point of the circle and then enter the diameter of the circle.*

Spline

Command Locator

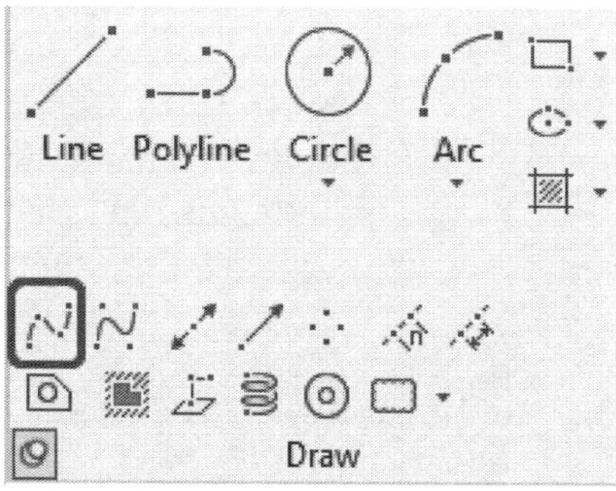

Home Ribbon	**Draw / Spline**
Command	**Spline**
Alias	**spl**

Command Overview

You can make a spline from a polyline using the Pedit command. An easy way to create a spline is to define the points where the arcs (both concave and convex) are to be placed and use those points to control your spline's shape.

General Procedures

1. Begin the Spline command.
2. Pick a point.
3. Pick a second point.
4. You can right click at this point to see the spline options.
5. Continue picking points until you are done. Click <ENTER> or 'Close' to exit the command.

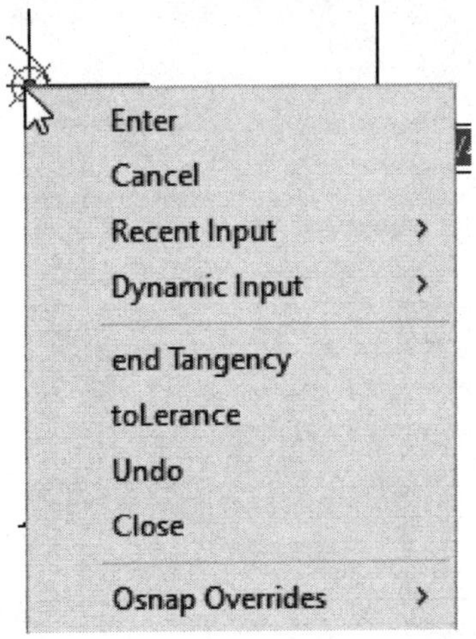

You can use the Fit tolerance option to define a spline using points. If you set the fit tolerance to 0, then the spline will pass through the selected points. If you set the fit tolerance to a number greater than 0, it will create a spline using the tolerance to get as close to the points as the tolerance allows. Dynamic Input only appears in the shortcut menu if the DYN button is enabled on the status bar.

Command Exercise

Exercise 4-7 – Spline

Drawing Name: **spline1.dwg**
Estimated Time to Completion: 5 Minutes

Scope

Use the points to assist you in creating your spline.

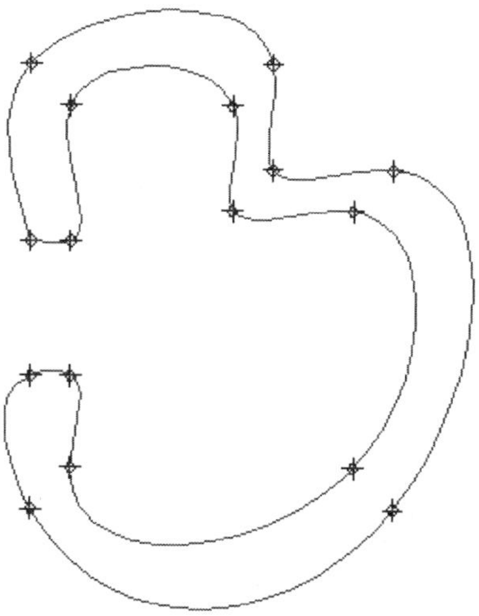

Solution

1. 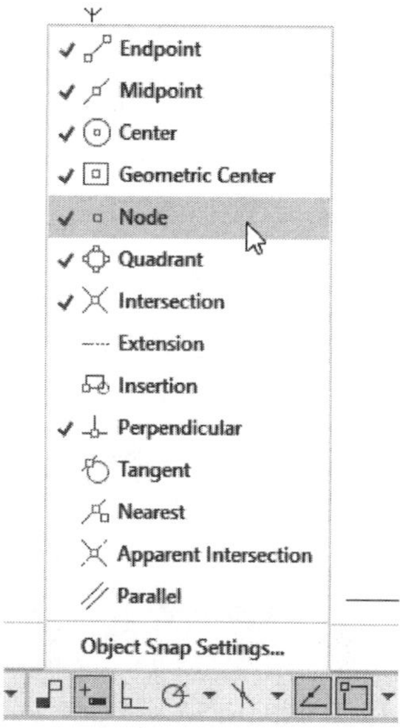

Enable the Node OSNAP.

2. 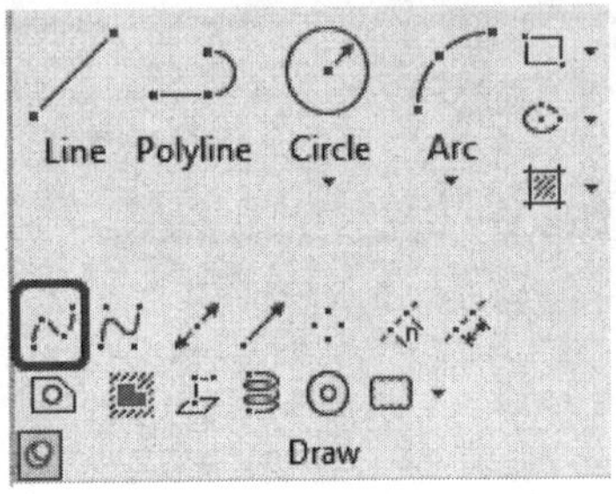

Invoke the **Spline** command.

3. 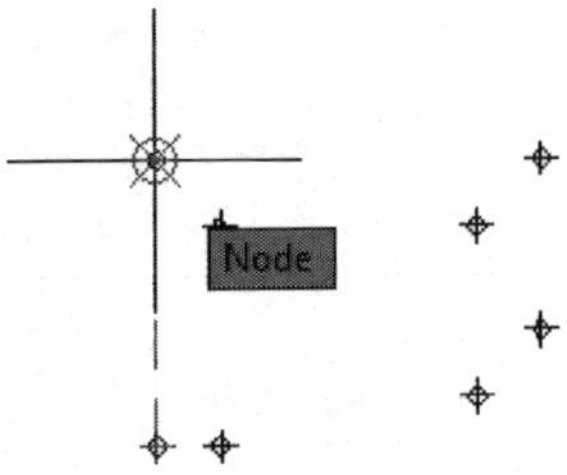

Select a point.

4. 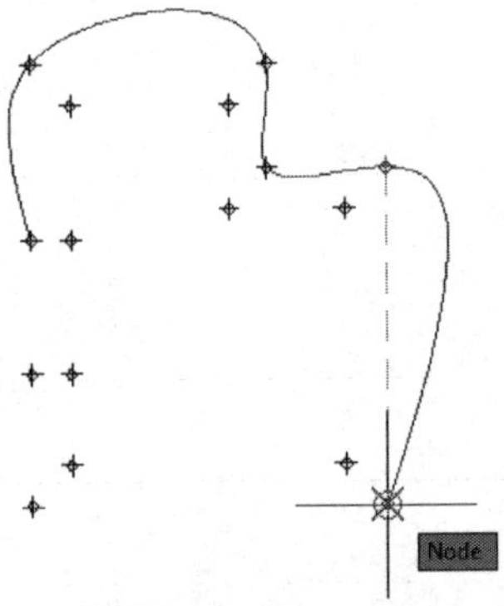

Follow the points along to create your spline object.

5. 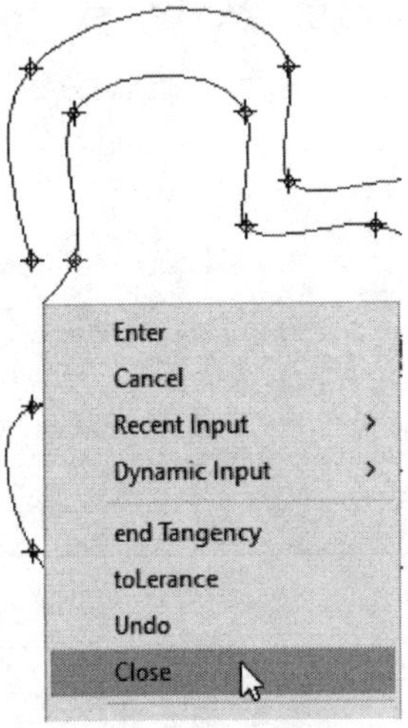

At the last point, right click and select **Close** and then <ENTER>.

Close will only work if you have created one continuous spline without stopping and restarting.

Ellipse

Command Locator

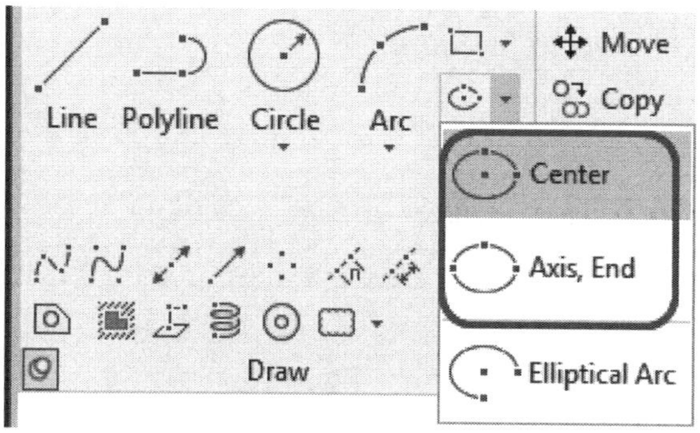

Home Ribbon	**Draw / Ellipse**
Command	**Ellipse**
Alias	**el**

Command Overview

The Ellipse command prompts for a center point, an axis end point, and then a radius distance to the perpendicular axis. Users can also determine the size of the ellipse based on rotation. Ellipse Arc allows the user to create a partial ellipse.

General Procedures

1. Begin the Ellipse command.
2. Pick a center point.
3. Pick a second point to indicate one axis end of the ellipse.
4. Move the mouse in a perpendicular direction from the second point to set the second axis. Enter a radius distance or select a point.

Command Exercise

Exercise 4-8 – Ellipse

Drawing Name: **ellipse1.dwg**
Estimated Time to Completion: 5 Minutes

Scope

Use the points to assist you in creating your ellipse.

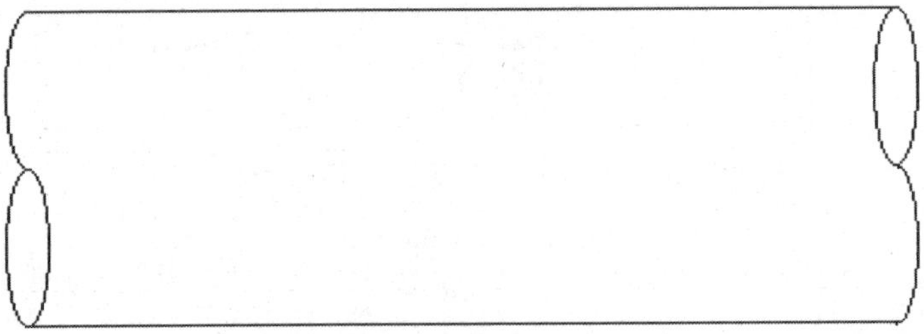

1.

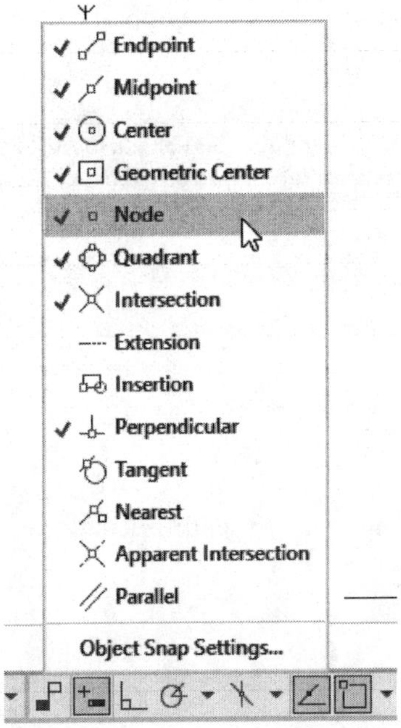

Enable the Node OSNAP.

2. 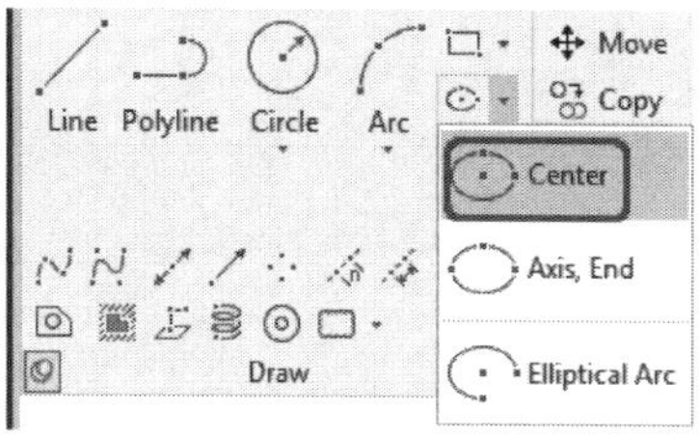

Invoke the **Ellipse** command using the **Center** option.

3. 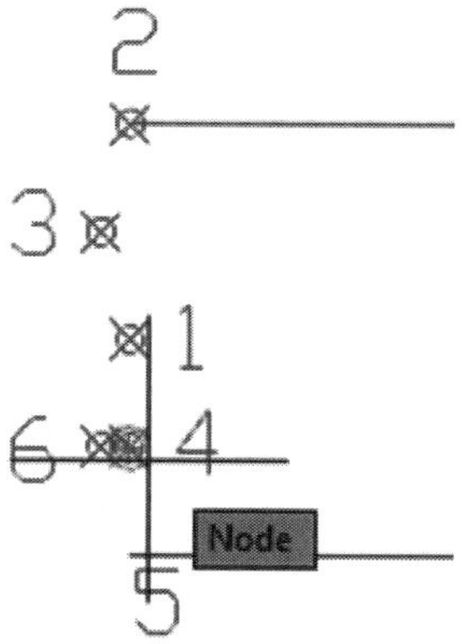

Select Point 4.

4. 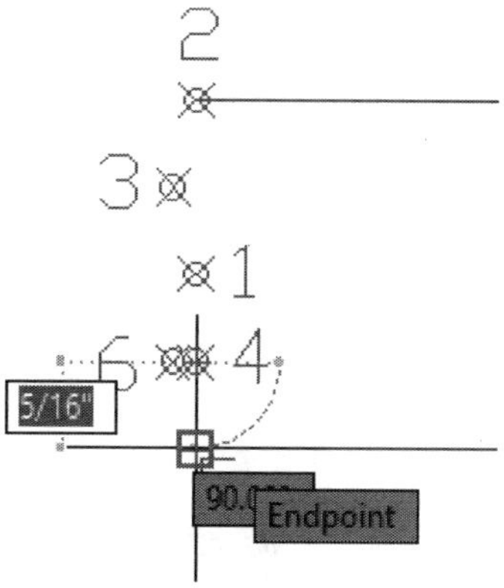

Select the endpoint located at Point 5.

5. 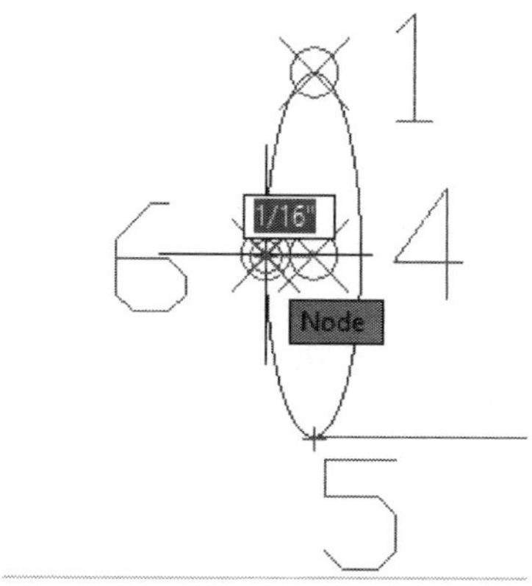

Select Point 6 when prompted for the distance to the other axis.

The ellipse is placed.

6. 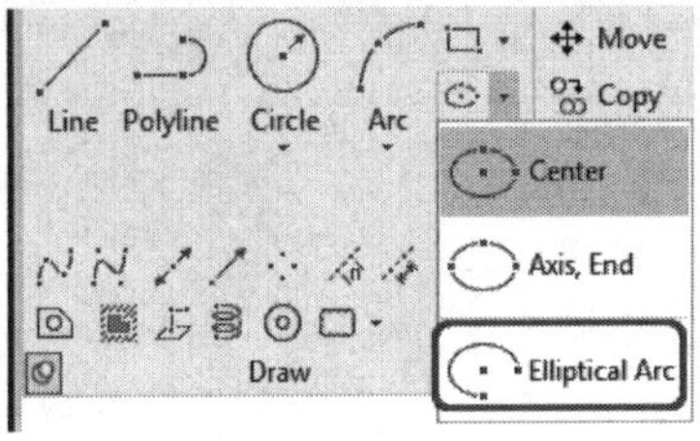

Select the **Elliptical Arc** tool.

7. 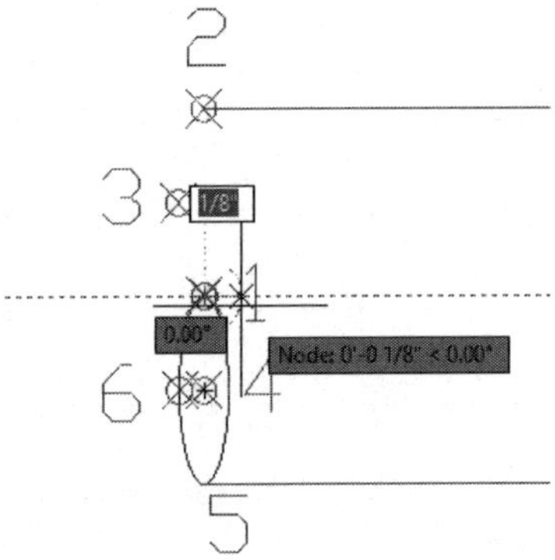

Select Point 1.

8. 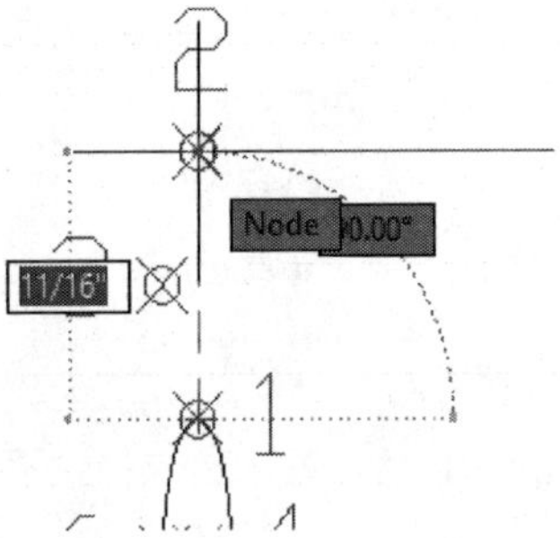

Select Point 2.

9. 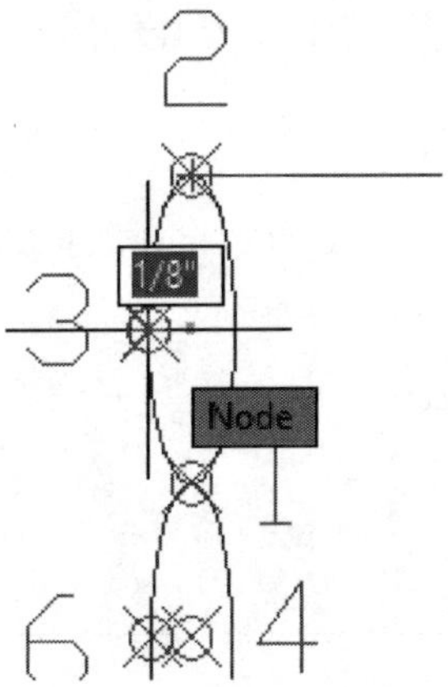

Select Point 3.

You will be prompted for the start and end points for the angle for the ellipse.

10. 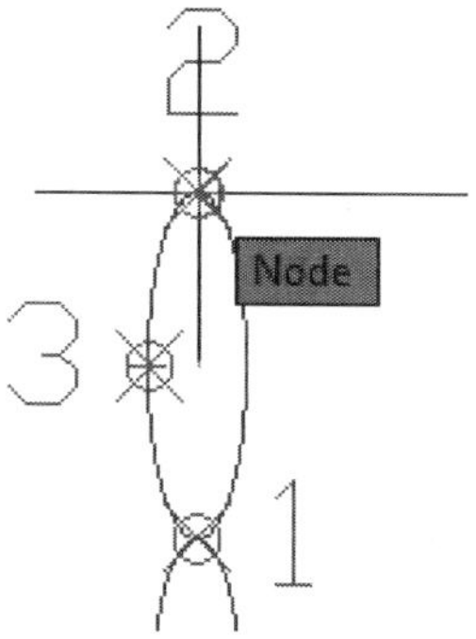

Select Point 2 as the start point for the ellipse.

11. 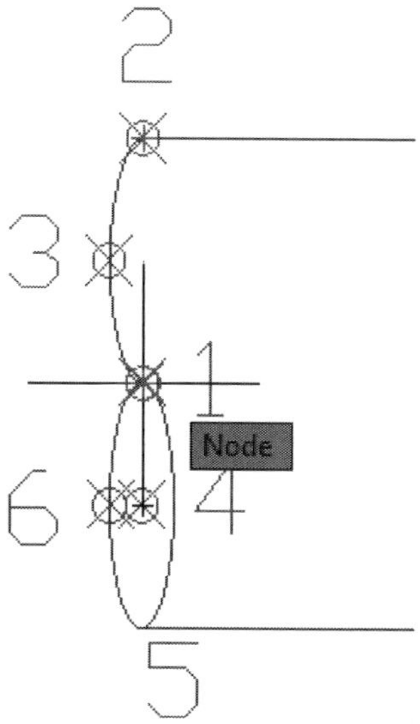

Select Point 1 as the end point for the angle.

One end of your wire is completed.

12. 

Repeat the steps for the other side.

Add Selected

Command Locator

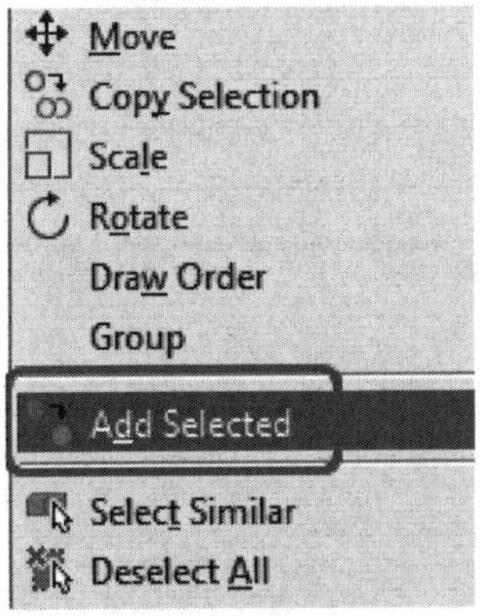

Shortcut Menu	**Select an object, right click and select Add Selected**
Command	**Add Selected**

Command Overview

With the ADD SELECTED command, you can create a new object using a source object. The new object will have the same layer, color, and line type as the source object; however, the user can define new location points and new sizes.

General Procedures

1. Select an object.
2. The command which is used to create the selected object is initiated.
3. Create a new object.
4. The new object has the same layer, color, linetype, etc. as the source object.

Command Exercise

Exercise 4-9 – Add Selected

Drawing Name: **addselected.dwg**
Estimated Time to Completion: **5 Minutes**

Scope

Use Add Selected to add lines and a circle.
Note that the new entities have the same properties as the source entities: layer, color, etc.

Solution

1. 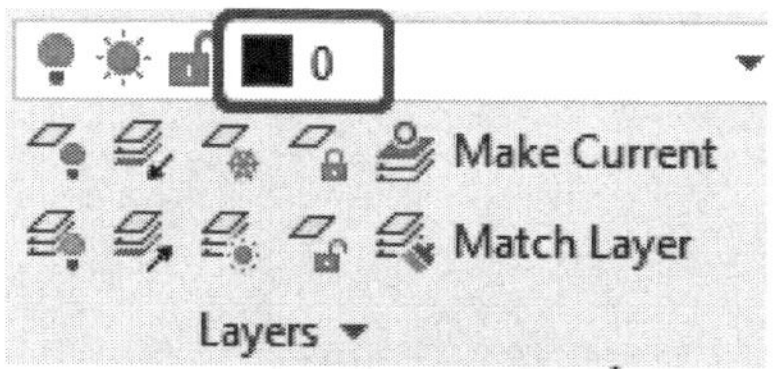

Note that the current layer is 0.

2. 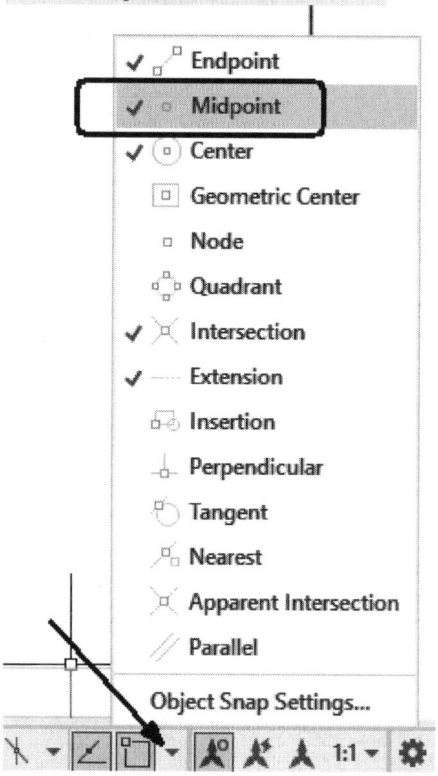

Right click on the OSNAP settings on the status bar.
Verify that the Midpoint OSNAP is enabled.

3.

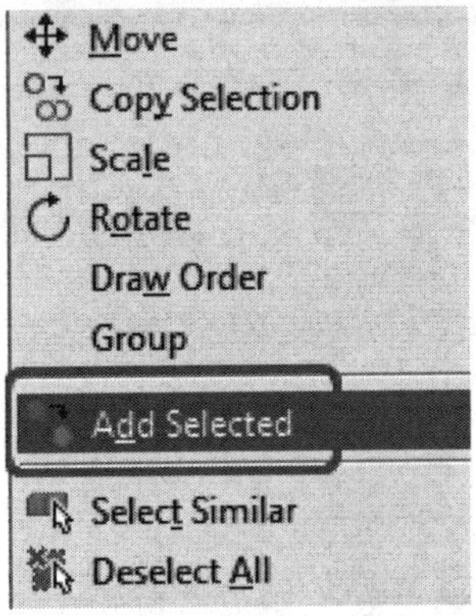

Select the vertical blue line.
Right click and select **Add Selected**.

4.

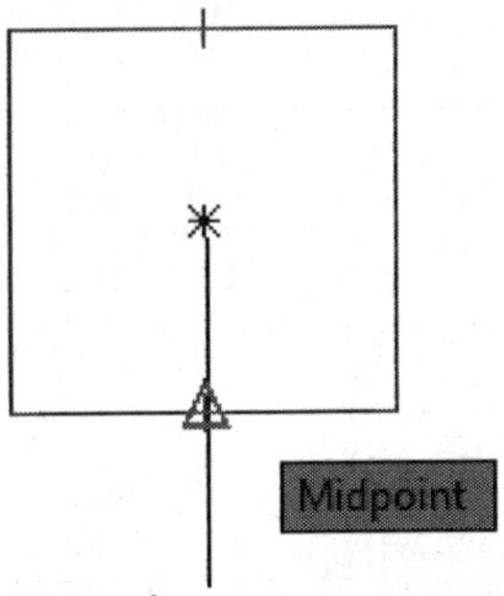

Select the top and bottom midpoints to place the new line.

Right click and select ENTER to exit ADD SELECTED mode.

5.

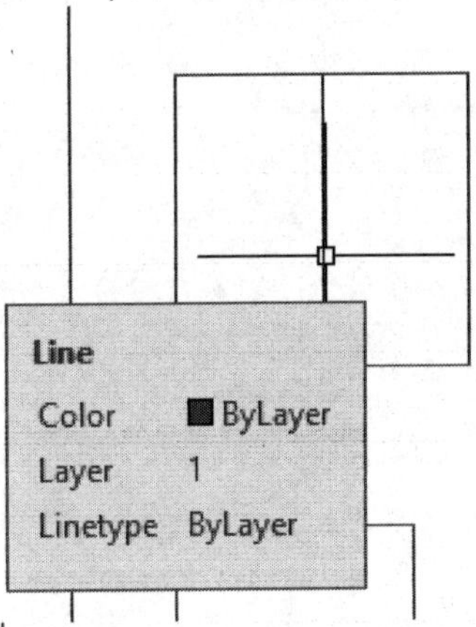

Note that the new line is placed on the same layer and is the same color as the line selected.

Verify that the current layer is still layer 0.

You can hover over any object in your drawing and you will see the name of the object, the layer, color, and linetype information.

6.

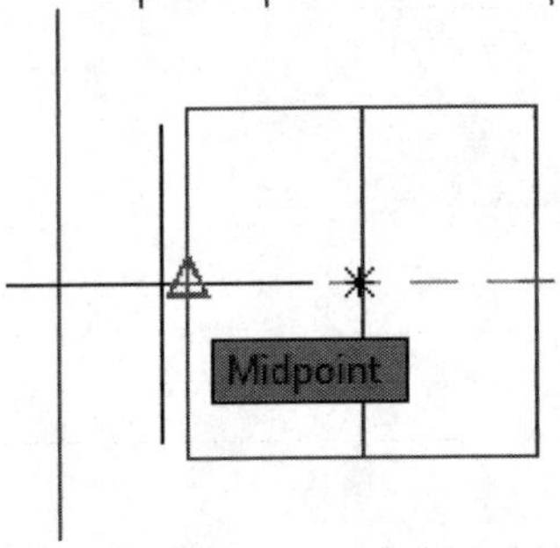

Repeat to place the horizontal blue line.

7. 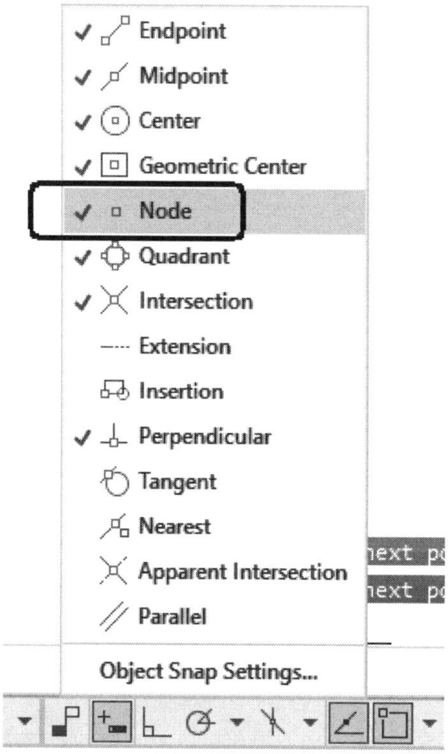

Enable the NODE object snap.

8. 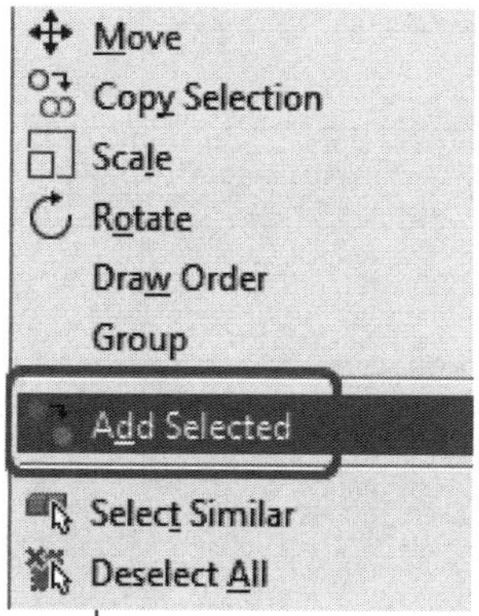

Select the orange circle.

Right click and select **Add Selected**.

9. 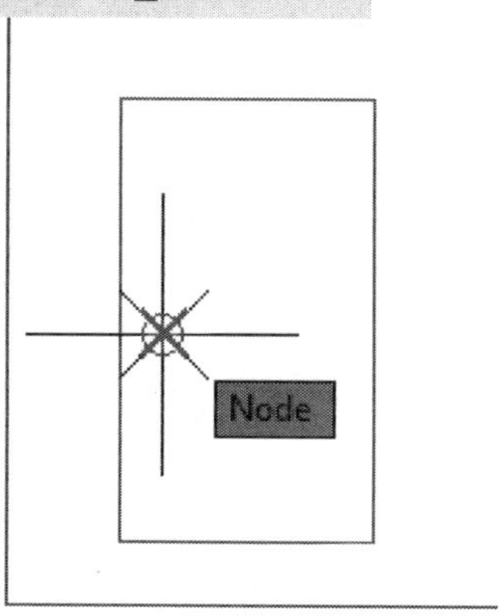

Select the point in the left-side door to place the circle.

10. 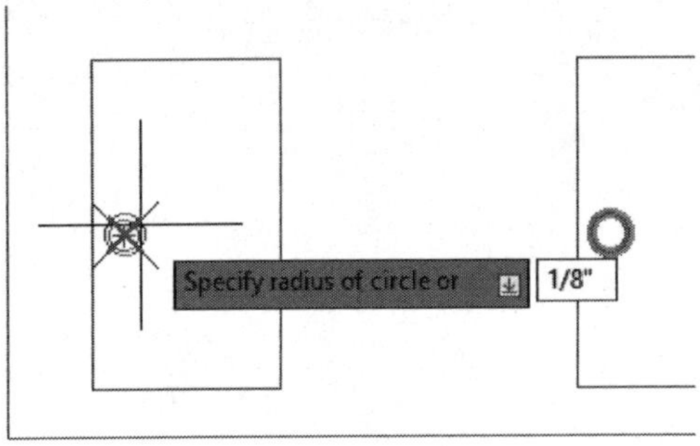

Specify a radius of 1/8″.

Note: You can change the radius of the circle.
AddSelected controls the type of object—circle, line, etc. and the color, linetype, and properties—but not the size.

11. 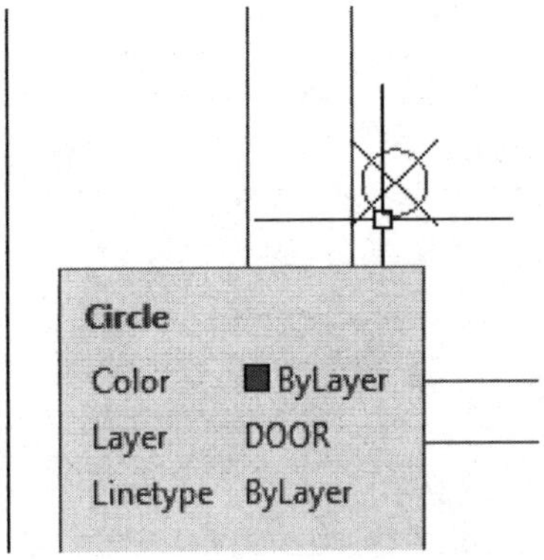

Note that the new circle has the same properties as the selected circle.

Verify that the current layer is still layer 0.

Section Exercise

Exercise 4-10 – Standard Bracket

Drawing Name: **create a new drawing**
Estimated Time to Completion: **15 Minutes**

Scope

Use the commands you have learned in the past section to create the three view orthographic drawing of the bracket in the figure below. Do not worry about a title block, drawing dimensions or hidden lines. Try to place the polygon and circle in the middle of the upper and lower plates. Remember to use the most efficient commands (i.e., Running Object Snap or Geometric Center).

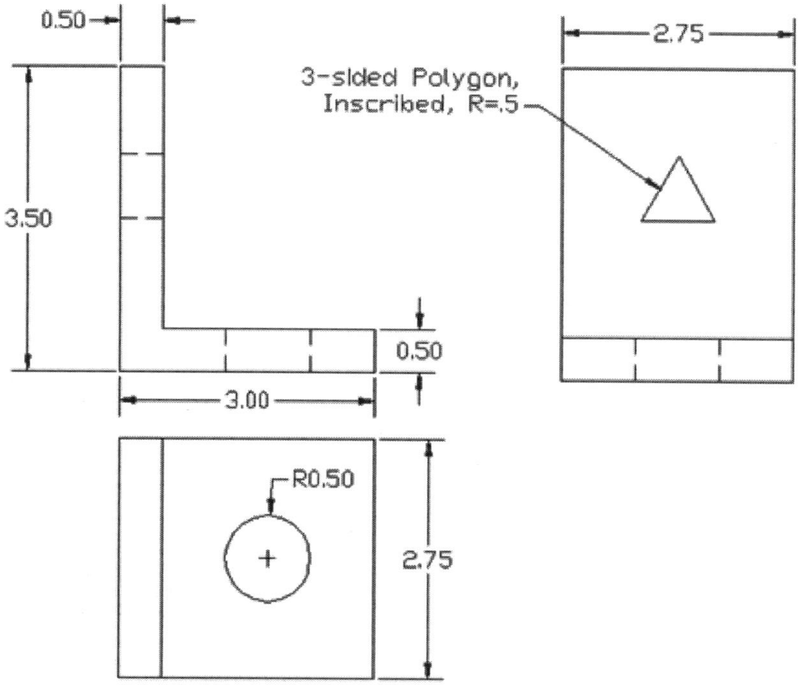

Hints

1. Start by setting the Endpoint, Midpoint, Intersection and Quadrant Running Object Snaps. Turn OTRACK on.
2. Try to use the Line and Rectangle commands to create the overall geometry. Try the Polygon command to create the Triangle, and the circle command to make the hole.
3. Use the ORTHO mode to create vertical and horizontal lines.

Section Exercise

Exercise 4-11 – Plate

Drawing Name: **create a new drawing**
Estimated Time to Completion: **15 Minutes**

Scope

Use the commands you have learned to create the orthographic drawing of the plate in the figure below. Do not worry about a title block, drawing dimensions or hidden lines. Try to locate the circle using the intersections. See how quickly you can draw the figure.

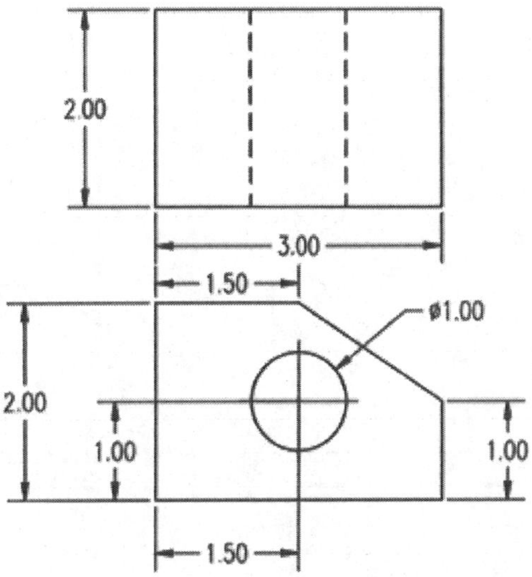

Hints

1. Start by setting the Endpoint, Perpendicular, and Quadrant Running Object Snaps. Turn OTRACK on.
2. Try to use the Line and Rectangle commands to create the overall geometry. Use the circle command to make the hole.
3. Use the ORTHO mode to create vertical lines.
4. Do not add the dimensions. They are just there to help you create the geometry.

Section Exercise

Exercise 4-12 – Simple House

Drawing Name: **create a new drawing**
Estimated Time to Completion: **15 Minutes**

Scope

Using the commands learned in this section, draw this simplified house.

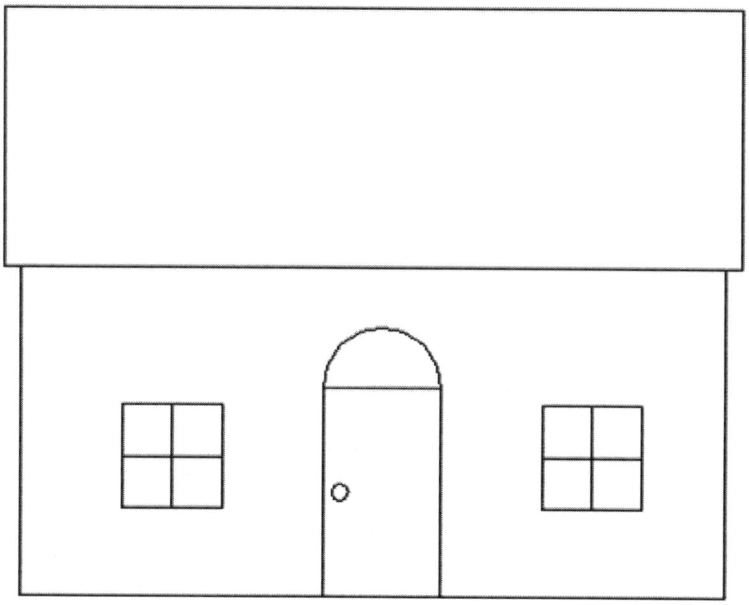

Hints

1. Use Rectangles for the basic shapes.
2. Use lines with midpoint object snaps for the window frames.
3. Create the arc using the Start, End, Direction option.

Hatch

Command Locator

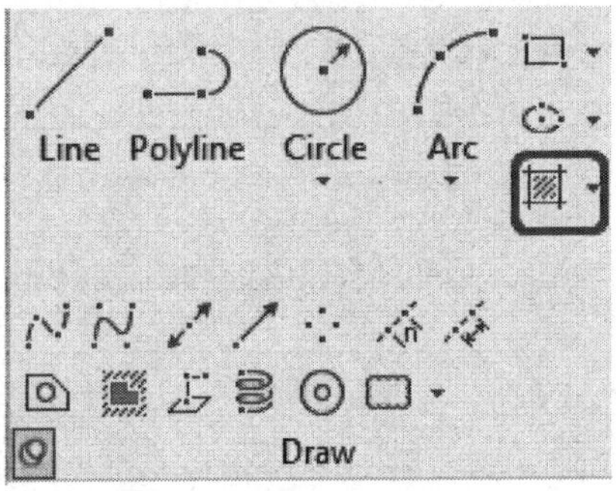

Home Ribbon	Draw/Hatch
Shortcut	**HA**
Command	**Hatch**

Command Overview

Hatch adds a pattern to a closed region or polygonal shape. Hatching is used to delineate materials or differentiate from one area to another.

General Procedures

1. Start the Hatch command.
2. Select the desired pattern from the ribbon.
3. Set the angle and scale as desired.
4. Select inside the area desired.
5. The area will preview.
6. If the result is OK, then Click ENTER or Close Hatch Creation on the ribbon.

Tips & Tricks

- *Use a Solid Hatch to completely fill an area.*

Command Exercise

Exercise 4-13 – Hatch

Drawing Name: **hatch1.dwg**
Estimated Time to Completion: **5 Minutes**

Scope

Use the Hatch Command to add a roof shake pattern to the roof on this house.

Solution

1. 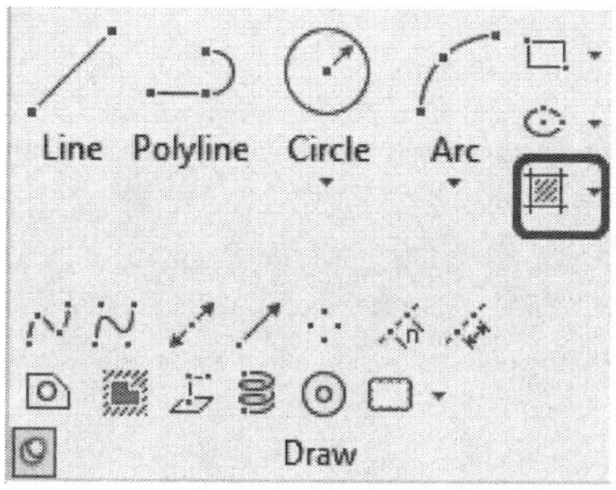

Select the **Hatch** command.

2. 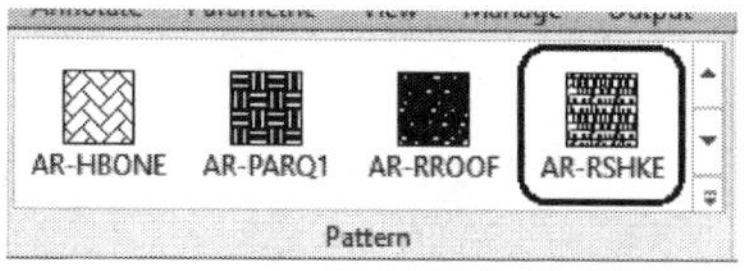

Locate the **AR-RSHKE** hatch pattern on the ribbon or right click and select Settings.

3. 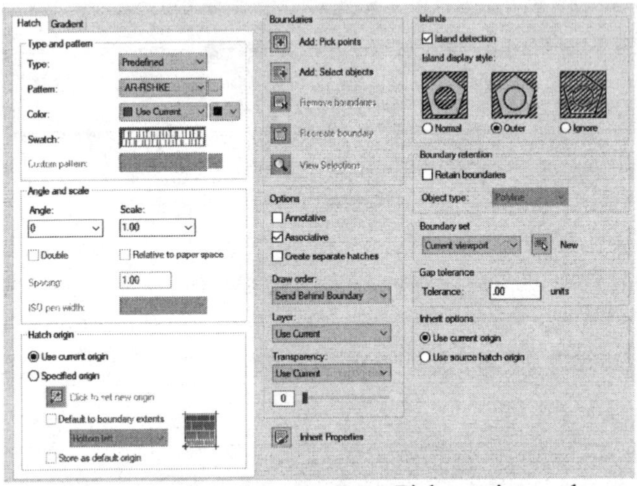

The settings dialog will allow you to select the pattern and color to be used for the Hatch pattern.

4. 

Pick a point on the roof.

5. 

You should see a preview of the roof hatch pattern.

6. 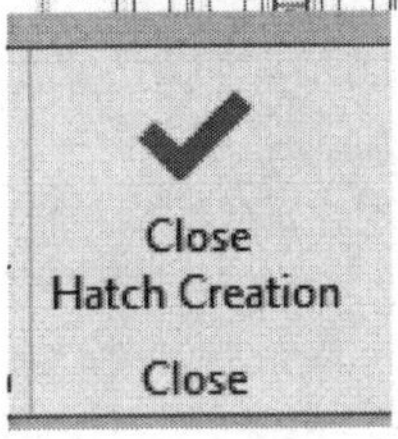

RMB and select ENTER or Click Close Hatch on the ribbon.

HPLAYER

Command Overview

HPLAYER allows you to set the layer used for hatches, so you don't have to constantly switch layers every time you place a hatch.

General Procedures

1. Type **HPLAYER**.
2. Type in the layer to be used for any hatches or click ENTER to use the current/active layer.

Command Exercise

Exercise 4-14 – HPLAYER

Drawing Name: **hplayer.dwg**
Estimated Time to Completion: **20 Minutes**

Scope

Use the HPLAYER system variable to set a layer as the default layer for new hatches and fills.

Solution

1. 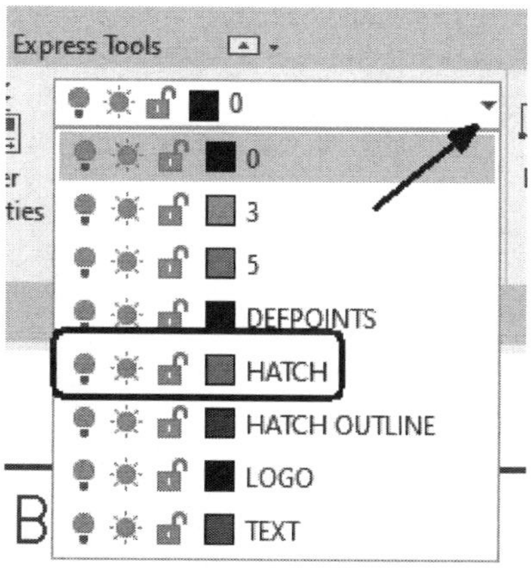

Go to the Layers list and check to see which layers are available.

Notice that one of the layers is called HATCH.

2. 

Verify that the current layer is 0.

3. 

Type **HPLAYER**.

4. 

Type **HATCH** when prompted for the layer to be assigned for hatches.

Click **ENTER**.

5. 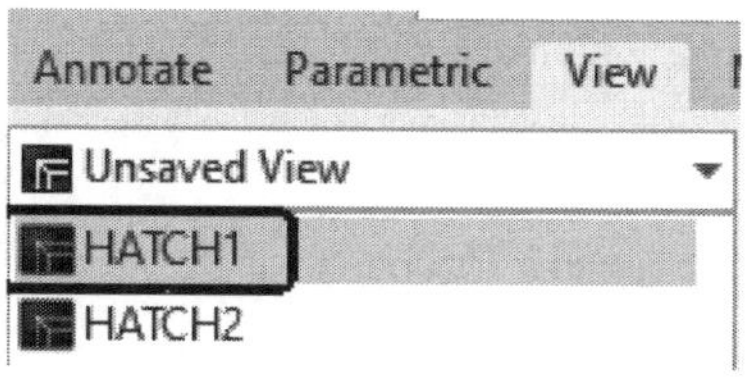

Activate the View ribbon.

Left click on the **HATCH1** named view to display.

6. 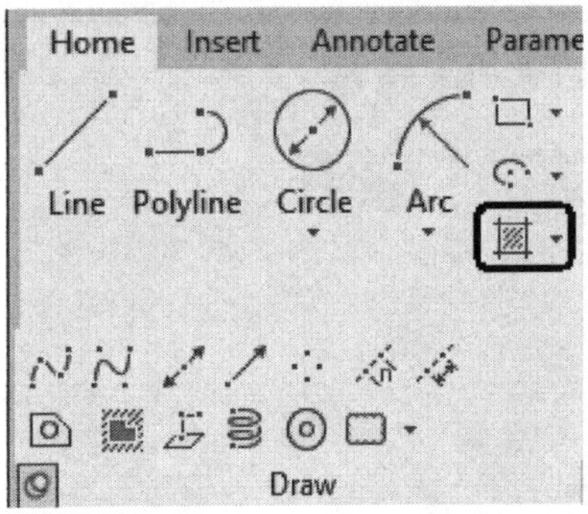

Activate the Home tab on the ribbon.

Select the **HATCH** tool.

7. 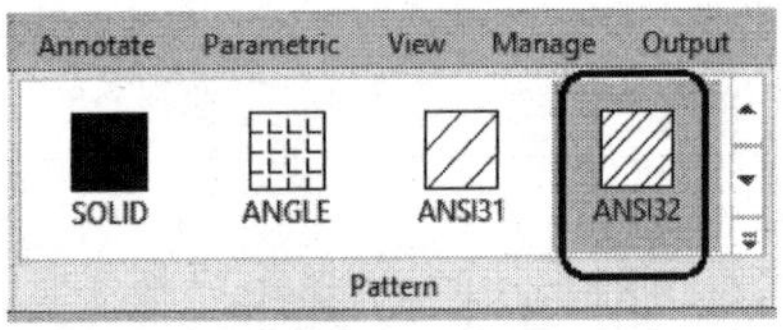

Select the **ANSI32** hatch pattern.

8. 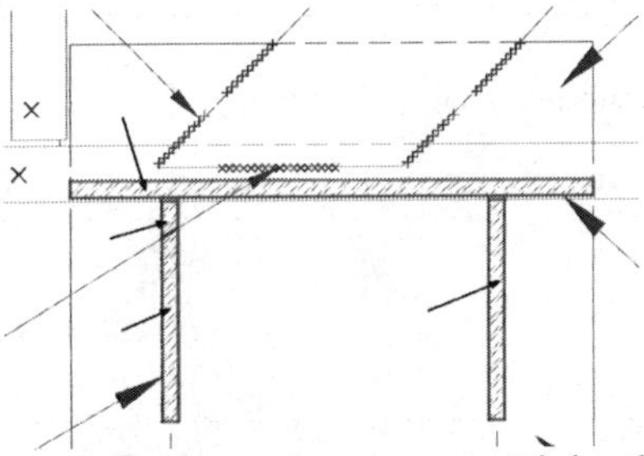

Left click inside the three areas indicated. These are steel plates.

Click **ENTER** to place the HATCH.

9. 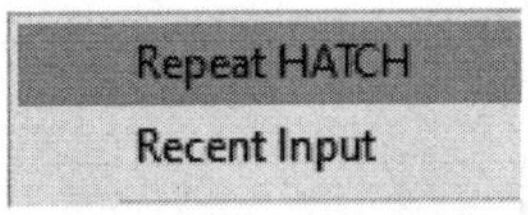

Right click and select **Repeat HATCH.**

10. 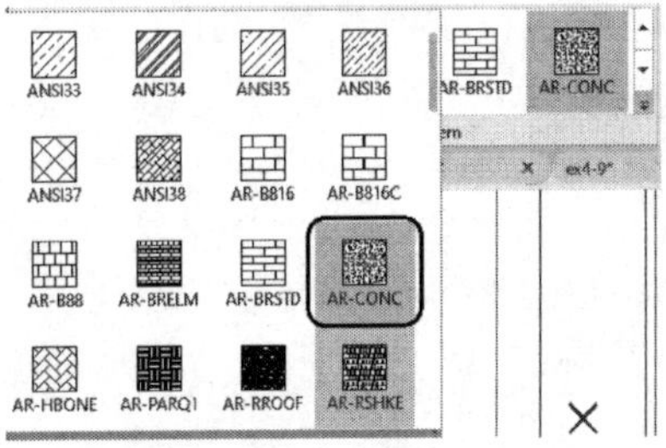

Use the scroll down arrow to scroll down the list of hatch patterns.

Select **AR-CONC.**

11. 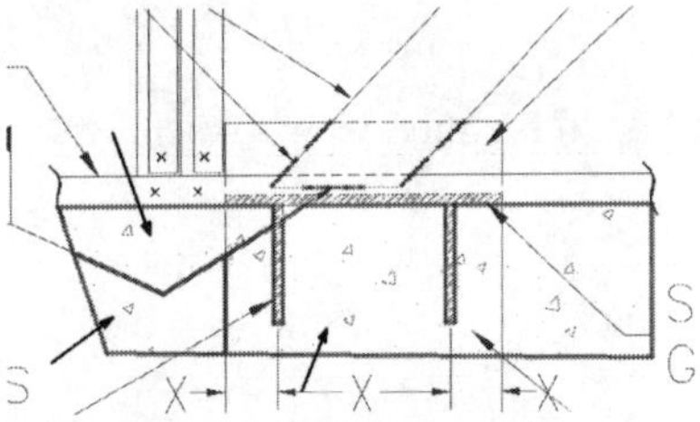

Left pick in the areas shown to place the hatch pattern.

Click **ENTER** to place the HATCH.

12.

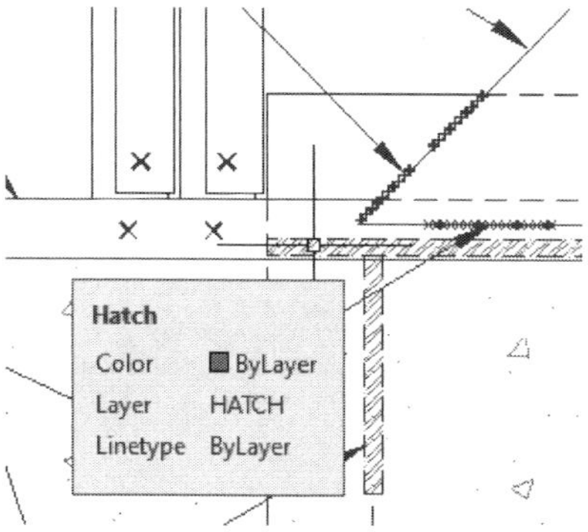

Select the hatch pattern placed on the plates.

Right click and select **Properties**.

You can also hover over the hatch to see the layer assigned.

13.

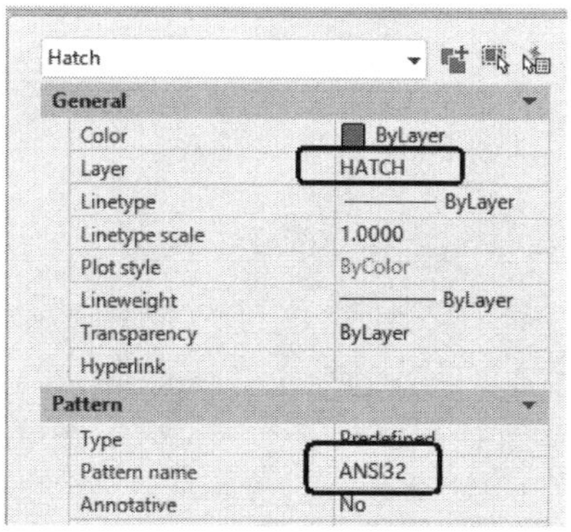

Verify that the hatch was placed on the HATCH layer—which was assigned using HPLAYER. Note that the hatch pattern name is listed correctly as ANSI32.

Command Exercise

Exercise 4-15 – Create a Hatch Layer

Drawing Name: **hplayer2.dwg**
Estimated Time to Completion: **15 Minutes**

Scope

Use the HPLAYER system variable to create a new layer and set it as a layer to be used as the default layer for new hatches and fills. The new layer uses the properties of the current layer; i.e., color and linetype.

Solution

1. 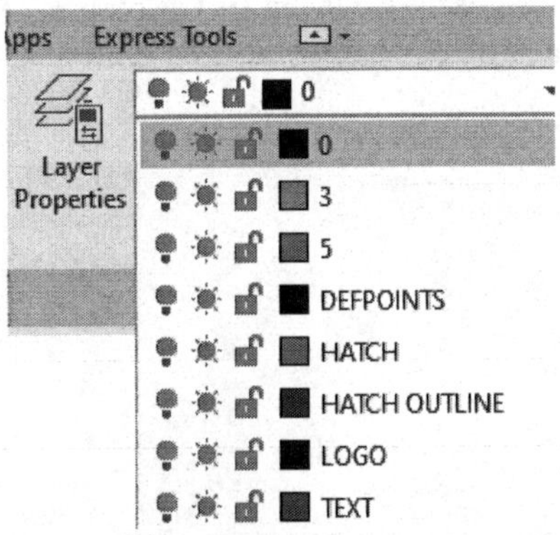

Go to the Layers list and check to see which layers are available.

Notice that there is no layer called HATCH2.

2. 

Verify that the current layer is **0**.

3. 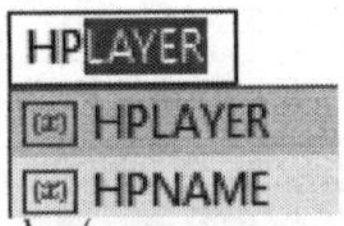

Type **HPLAYER**.

4. 

Type **HATCH2** when prompted for the layer to be assigned for hatches.

Press **ENTER.**

5. 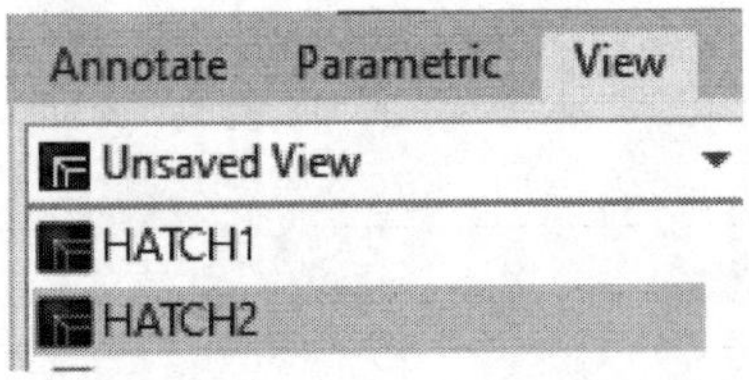

Activate the View ribbon.

Left click on the **HATCH2** named view to display.

6. 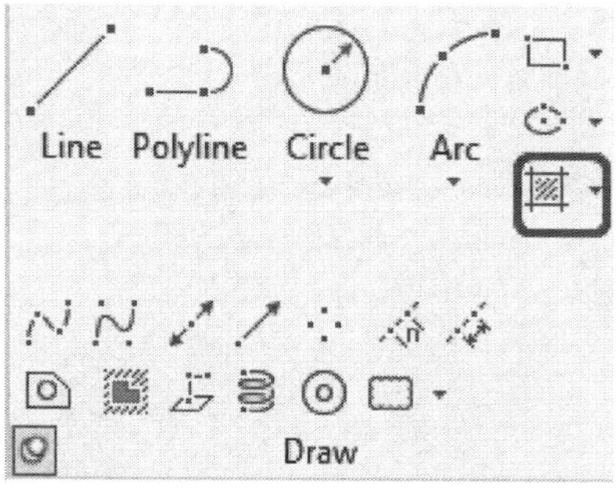

Activate the Home ribbon.

Select the **HATCH** tool.

7. 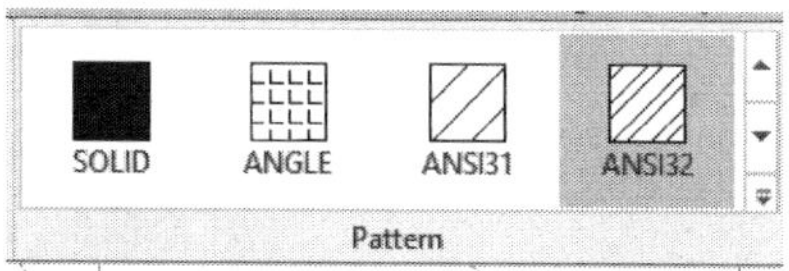

Select the **ANSI32** hatch pattern.

8. 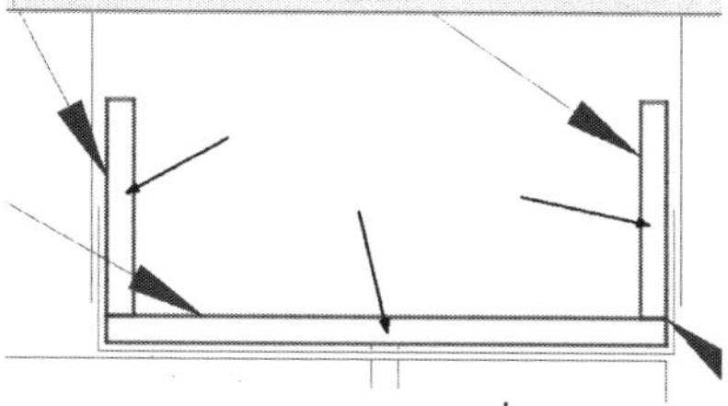

Left click inside the three areas indicated. These are steel plates.

Press **ENTER** to continue.

9. 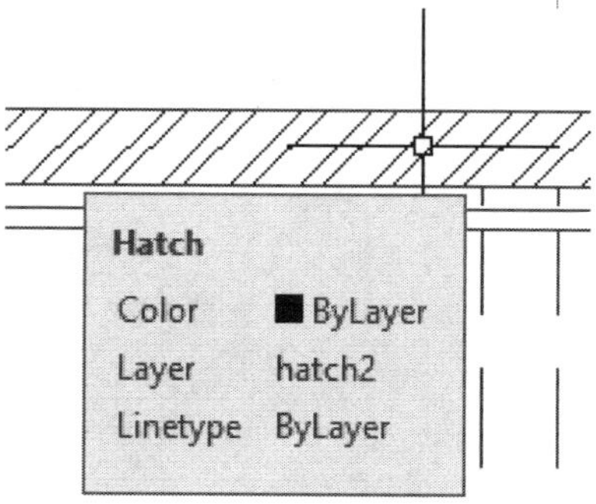

Select the hatch pattern placed on the plates.

Right click and select **Properties.**

10. 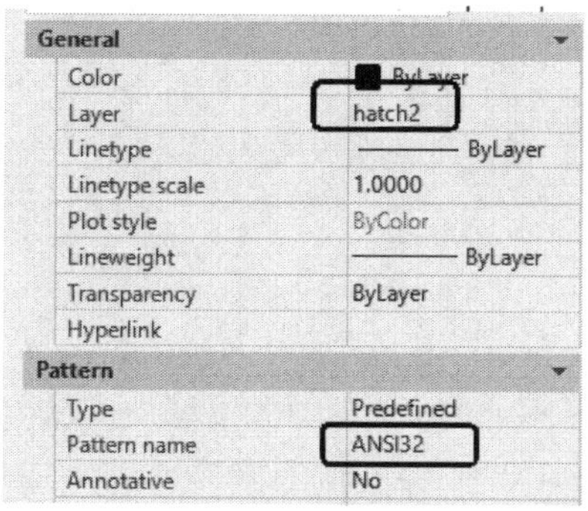

Verify that the hatch was placed on the HATCH2 layer—which was assigned using HPLAYER.

Note that the hatch pattern name is listed correctly as ANSI32.

11. 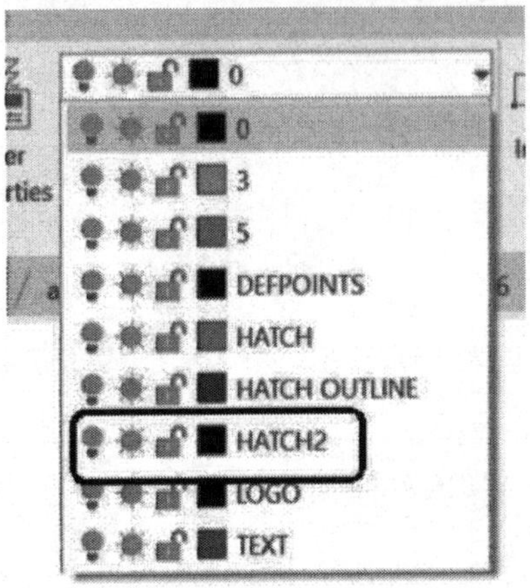

Check in the layers drop-down to see there is now a layer called HATCH2.

Notice that the layer created is case sensitive. So, it will appear in the layer list exactly as you typed it.

Review Questions

1. Identify the following icons by writing the name of the command and the toolbar where it can be found. *Extra: Write the command line shortcut, or alias.*

	Command

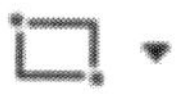	

2. Name the six options for creating a circle.

3. Name three options for creating an arc.

4. You construct a circle using the 2P option. What does this option prompt you for?

5. **T F** Using Add Selected automatically changes the active layer.

6. Identify the properties which are copied when using **Add Selected**.

   a) Color
   b) Layer
   c) Linetype
   d) Location

7. HPLayer is used to:

   a) Print a layer
   b) Create and/or assign a layer for hatches
   c) Add hatches
   d) Copy layers to hatches

Review Answers

1. Identify the following icons by writing the name of the command.

   Line / Draw / L

   Rectangle / Draw / REC

   Circle / Draw / C

   Arc / Draw / A

   Polygon / Draw / POL

2. Name the six methods for creating a circle.

   Center, Radius

   Center, Diameter

   2P

   3P

   Tan, Tan, Tan

   Tan, Tan, Radius

3. Name three methods for creating an arc.

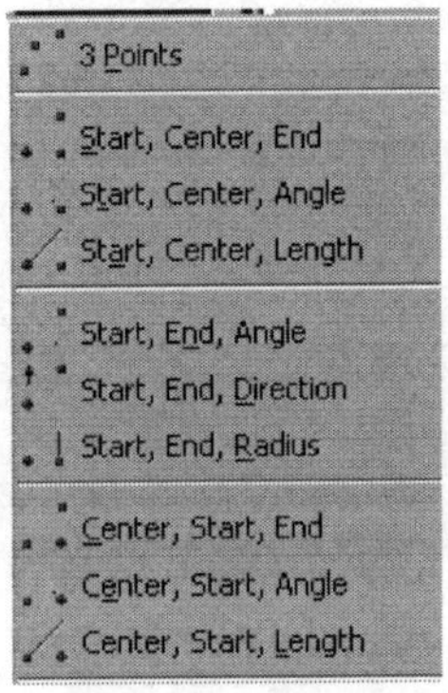

4. You construct a circle using the 2P option. What does this option prompt you for?

   The two end points of the diameter

5. *False*

6. *a, b, c*

7. *b*

Lesson 5.0 – Modify Commands

Estimated Class Time: 2 hours

Objectives

This section introduces AutoCAD commands for modifying objects in a simple drawing. This lesson reviews the following commands on the Modify tab:

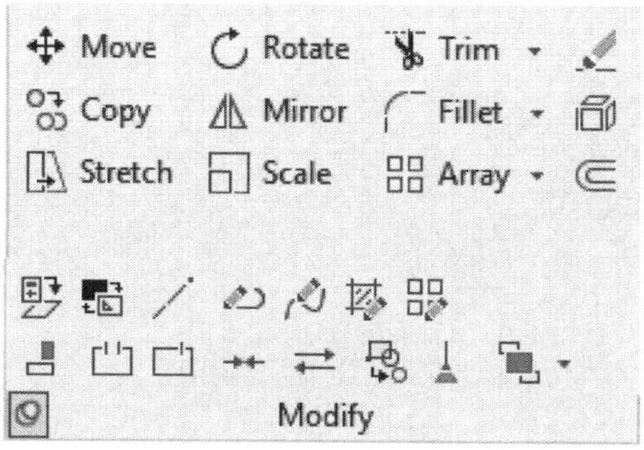

- **Copy**
  Copy selected objects to a new location.
- **Mirror**
  Mirror selected objects about a mirror line.
- **Offset**
  Offset selected objects a set distance.
- **Array**
  Rectangular and Polar Arrays.
- **Move**
  Move selected objects to a new location.
- **Rotate**
  Rotate selected objects to a new angle.
- **Scale**
  Scale objects to make them larger or smaller.
- **Stretch**
  Use stretch to lengthen and widen geometry.
- **Trim**
  Trim objects to a cutting edge.
- **Extend**
  Extend objects to a selected boundary.
- **Fillet**
  Add rounds or create corners.
- **Chamfer**
  Add beveled edges to objects.
- **Align**
  Adjust the position of elements so they are aligned on the same axis.
- **Undo and Redo**
  Undo previous commands and redo the "undo."

Copy

Command Locator

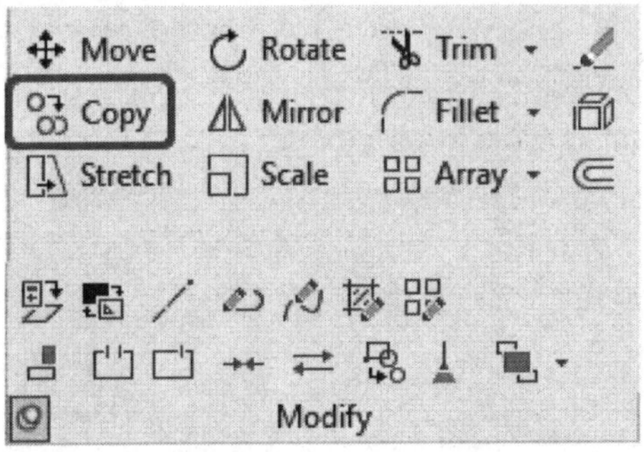

Home Ribbon	**Modify/Copy**
Command	**Copy**
Alias	**CO or CP**
RMB Shortcut Menu	**Drawing Window**

Command Overview

To copy an object, pick the base point, drag the mouse and pick the location for the copied object. Copy is automatically set to make multiple copies. You will continue to place copies until you Click <ESC> or <ENTER>.

General Procedures

To Create a single copy:

1. Invoke the Copy Command.
2. Select the objects to Copy, and Click <ENTER>.
3. Pick a point on or near the object as the base point.
4. Drag the mouse and pick the location for the copied object.
5. Click <ESC> to exit the command or right click and select <ENTER>.

Use Object Snaps for picking the base point and the new location.
If using direct distance to relocate the object, be sure ORTHO is ON.
Remember to use the LMB to pick the base point and the new location of the object.
Be sure SNAP (in the Status Bar) is off when selecting objects.
The Copy command is automatically in MUTLIPLE mode.

Command Exercise

Exercise 5-1 – Copy

Drawing Name: **copy1.dwg**
Estimated Time to Completion: 5 Minutes

Scope

Copy the objects in the rectangle on the left into the rectangle on the right.

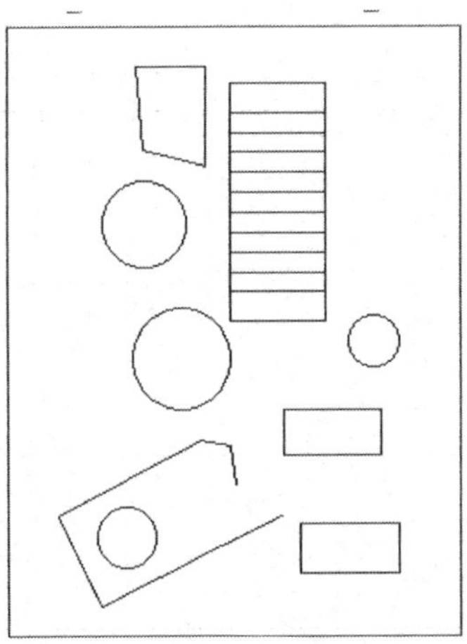

Solution

1. 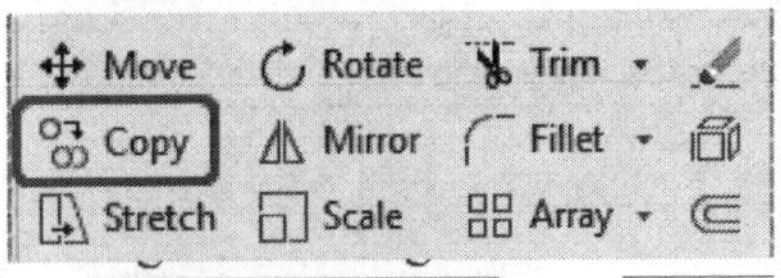

Invoke the Copy command (co or copy).

2. 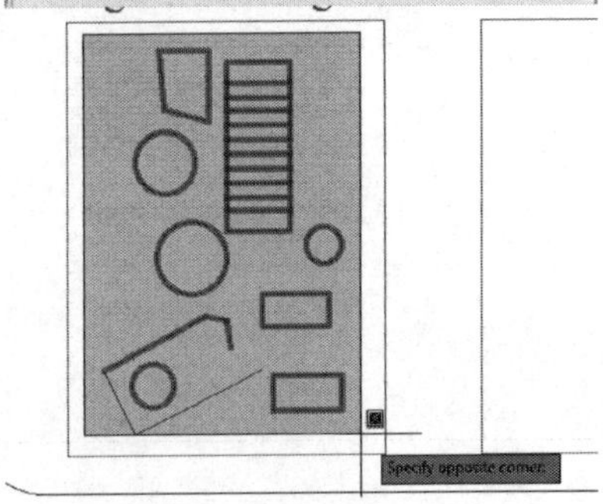

Select objects:
Select all of the objects using a window inside the red box. Click ENTER to complete the selection.

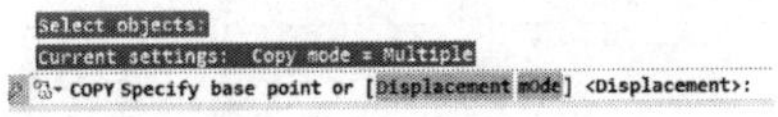

Notice on the command line that the Copy mode is displayed. The mode can be set to either Multiple or Single.

3.

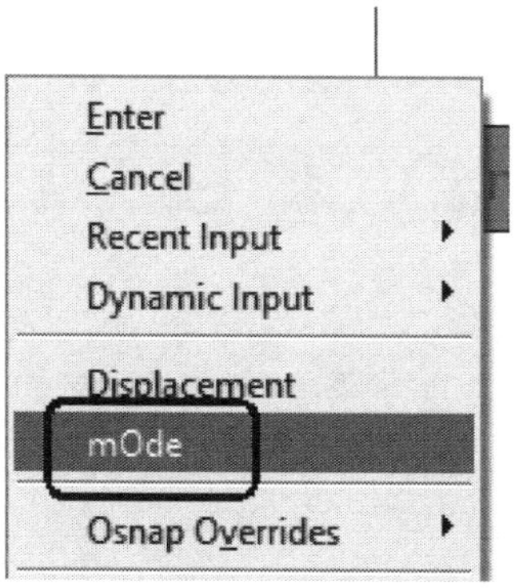

Right click and select **mOde.**

You can also type O as the shortcut key for mode.

4.

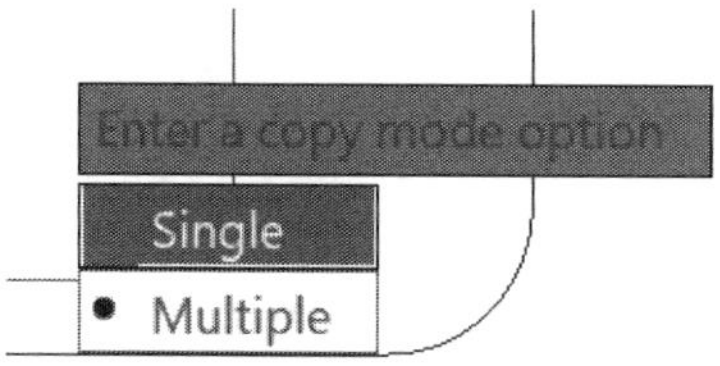

Select **Single**.

5.

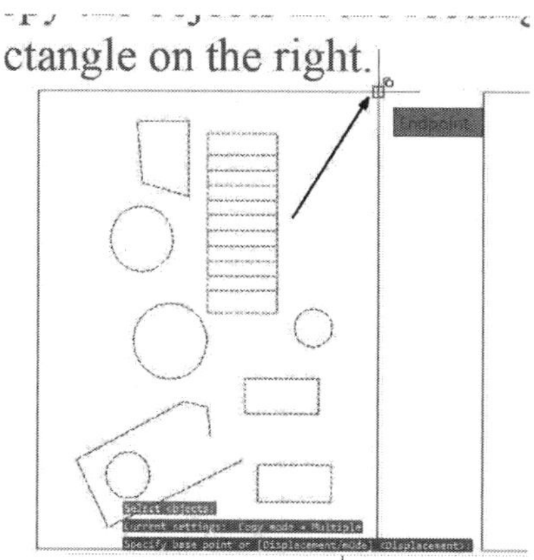

Specify base point or displacement:
Use your LMB to select the upper right corner of the red box with the objects. This is the point from which the objects will be copied.

6.

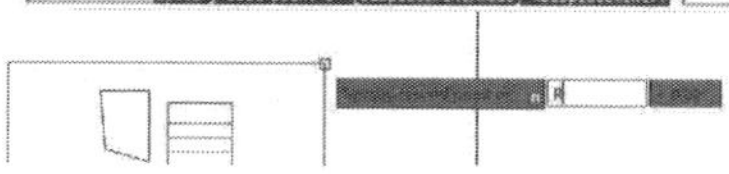

Specify second point of displacement or <use first point as displacement>:
Move your mouse to position the rectangles in the red box on the right and Click the LMB to specify the second point of displacement by selecting the upper right corner of the red box on the right.

> *If you get an oddly shaped window when trying to make a selection, it means you are holding down the left mouse button. Click once to start a selection window and then click a second time to define the window.*
> *You may also leave OSNAP on, and snap to a corner of the left red box for the base point and the same corner of the right red box for the second point of displacement.*

Command Exercise

Exercise 5-2 – Copy Multiple

Drawing Name: **copy2.dwg**
Estimated Time to Completion: 5 Minutes

Scope

Decorate the tree on the right by making multiple copies of the star as indicated in the drawing on the left.

Solution

1.

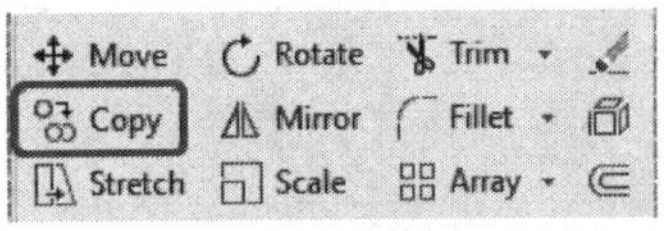

Invoke the Copy command (cp or copy).

2.

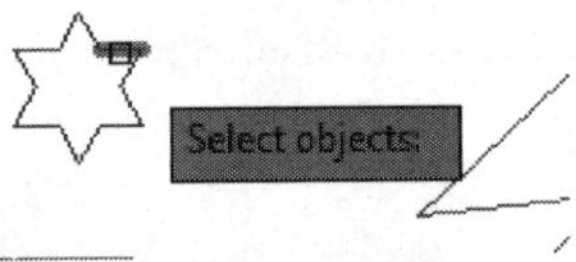

Select objects:
Select the star between the trees with the LMB. Close the selection set with the <ENTER> key or RMB.

3.

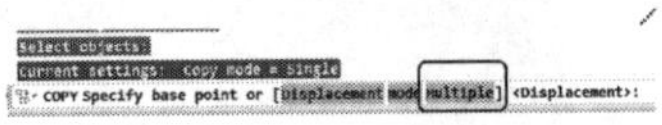

Check the command window. Notice that the COPY mode is currently set to SINGLE. However, the word MULTIPLE is displayed in the command window. Left click on the word **MULTIPLE** to switch to multiple mode.

4.

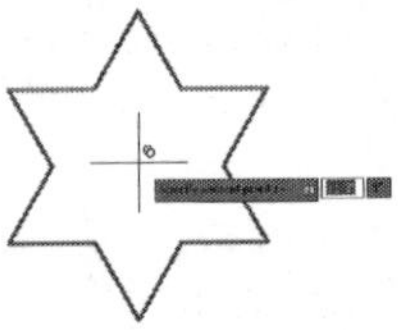

Specify base point:
You may want to turn OSNAP off. Use your LMB to select in the middle of the selected star. This is the point from which the stars will be copied multiple times.

5.

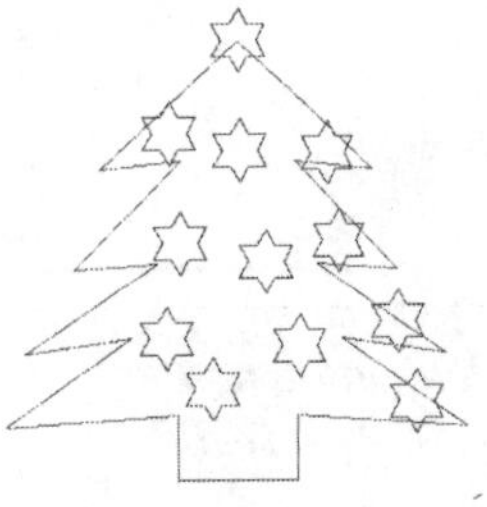

Specify second point of displacement or <use first point as displacement>:
Move your mouse to position the star on the tree on the right and Click the LMB to specify the second point of displacement. Move your mouse to another location and Click the LMB to copy another star. Repeat the process to decorate the tree. Right click and select <ENTER> to exit the command.

Command Exercise

Exercise 5-3 – Copy Array

Drawing Name: **copy3.dwg**
Estimated Time to Completion: 5 Minutes

Scope

Use the COPY command to array some AutoCAD elements.

Solution

1.

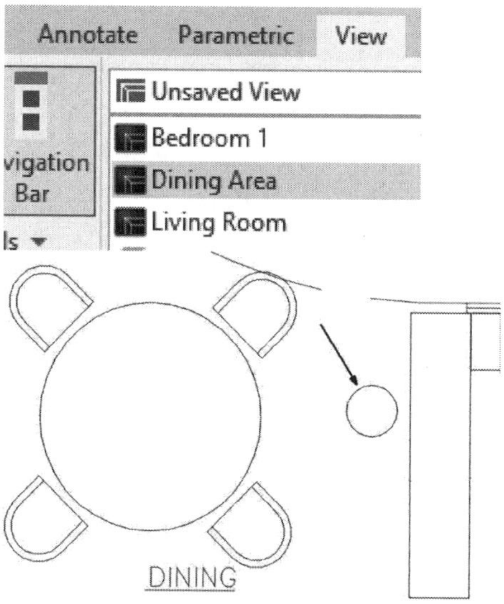

Switch to the View ribbon.

LMB on the **Dining Area** view to activate the named view.

The view zooms to the dining area.

We will be copying the stool (small circle).

2.

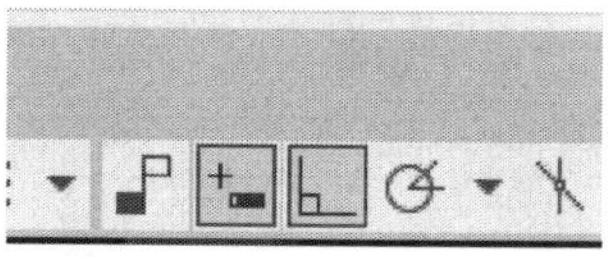

Enable **ORTHO** mode.

3.

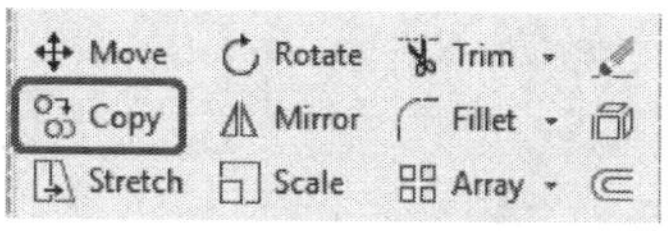

Switch to the Home ribbon.

Invoke the **Copy** command (cp or copy).

4.

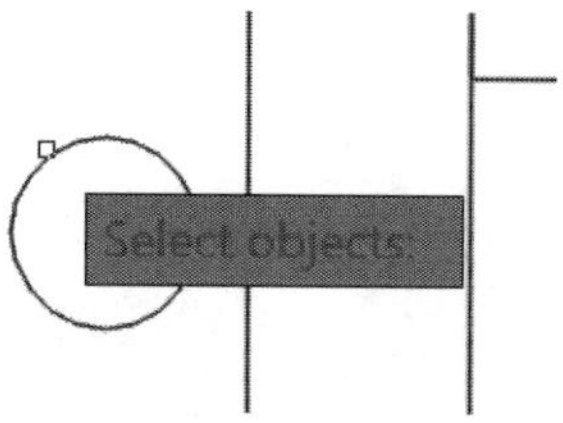

Select the small circle.

Click **ENTER**.

5. 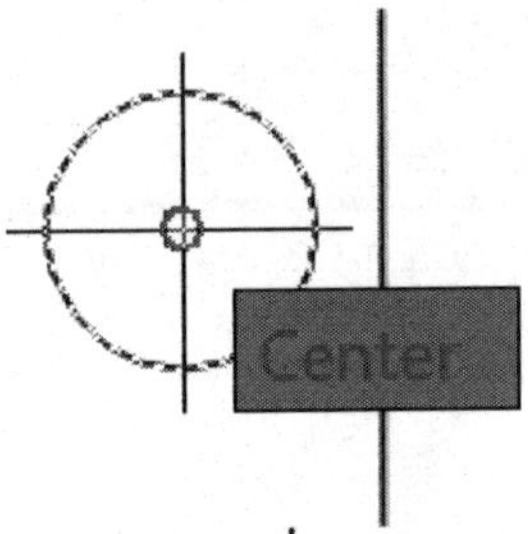

Select the Center of the stool (small circle) as the basepoint.

6. 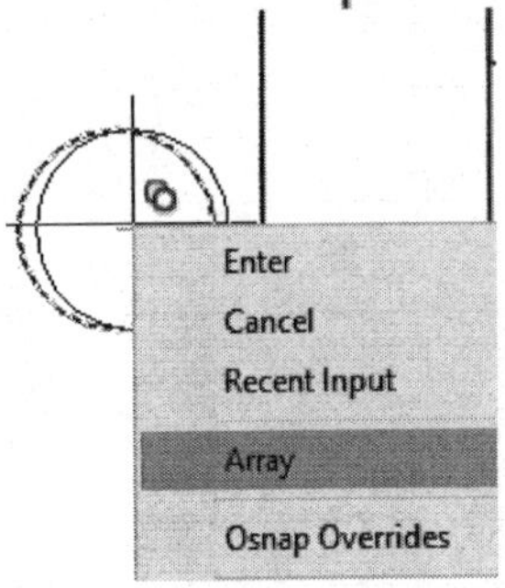

Right click and select **Array** or click on the word **Array** on the command prompt.

7. 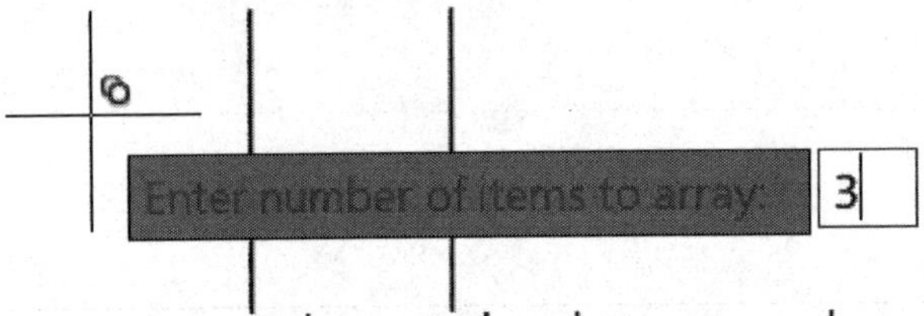

Type **3** as the number of items to array.

Click **ENTER**.

8. 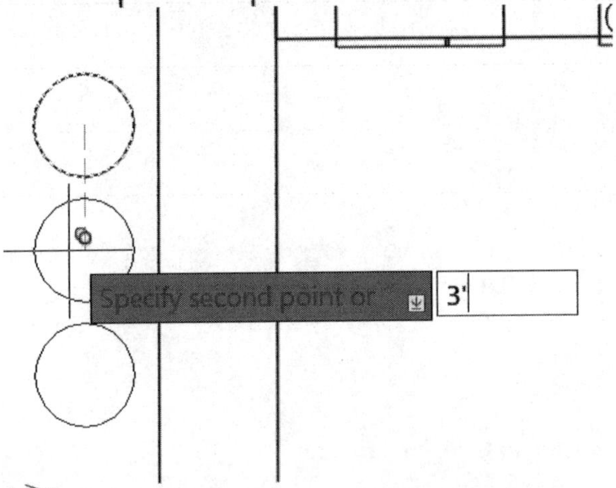

Move the mouse straight down.

Type **3'** to enter the distance between the elements.

Click **ENTER** to exit the command.

Hint: *Enable ORTHO to keep the stools aligned.*

9. 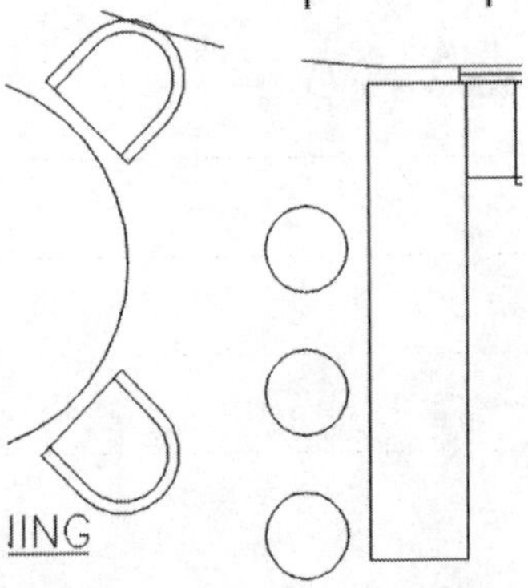

The stools are placed.

Mirror

Command Locator

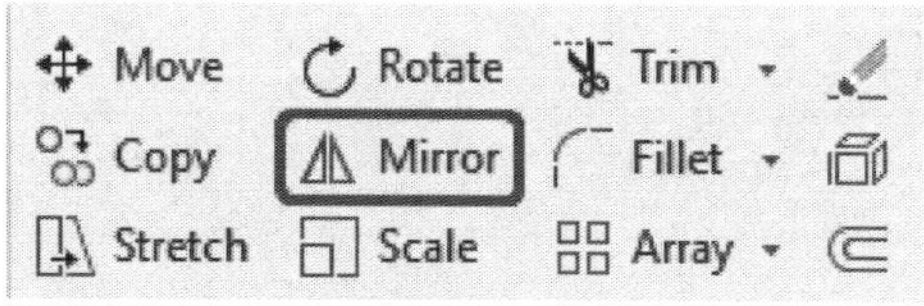

Home Ribbon	**Modify / Mirror**
Command	**Mirror**
Alias	**MI**
RMB Shortcut Menu	**Drawing Window**

Command Overview

Mirror selected objects around a mirror line with ORTHO on or off. Use the MIRRTEXT system variable to control whether text will mirror or not.

General Procedures

To use the Mirror command:

1. Invoke the Mirror Command.
2. Select the objects to mirror, and Click <ENTER>.
3. Pick the first point of the mirror line. Drag the mouse and pick the second line.
4. At the prompt Delete source objects? [Yes/No] <N>, Click <ENTER> to accept the default or type Y to delete the source objects.

To use the Mirror command without mirroring text:

1. Type MIRRTEXT, and Click <ENTER>.
2. Type 0 to turn MIRRTEXT off.
3. Proceed with the Mirror command.

Command Exercise

Exercise 5-4 – Mirror

Drawing Name: **mirror1.dwg**
Estimated Time to Completion: 5 Minutes

Scope

Mirror the lines below using the endpoints of the upper and lower lines for the Mirror Line.

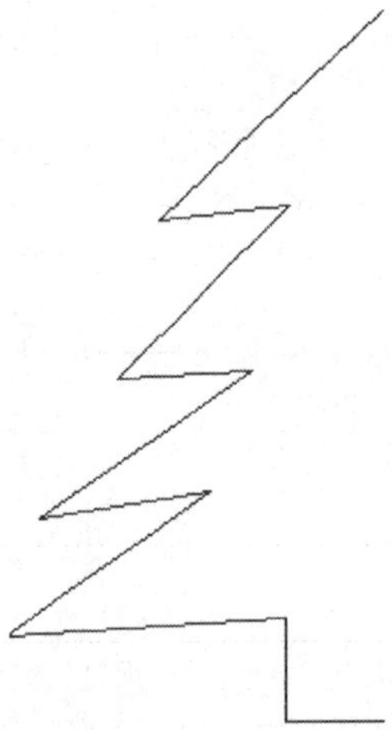

Solution

1. 

Enable **ORTHO** mode.

2. 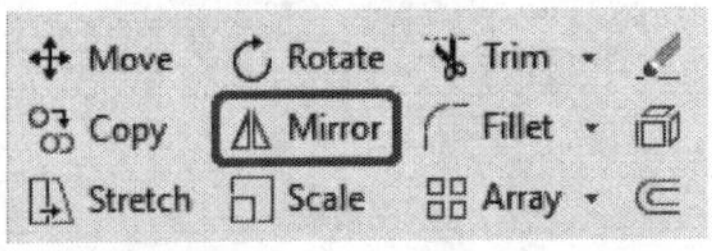

Invoke the Mirror command (mirror).

3. 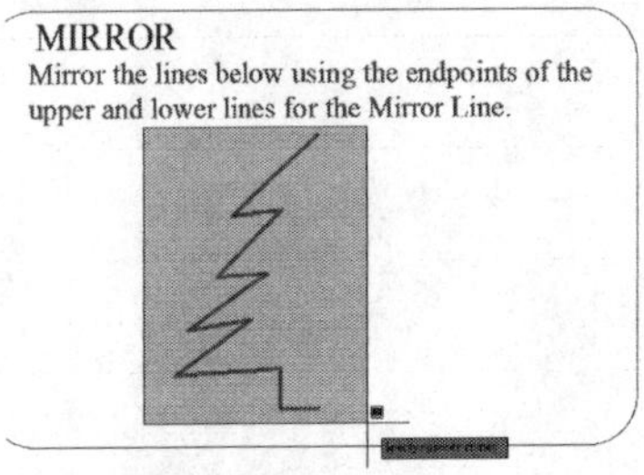

Select objects:
Select the left side of the tree and Click <ENTER> to end the selection.

4. 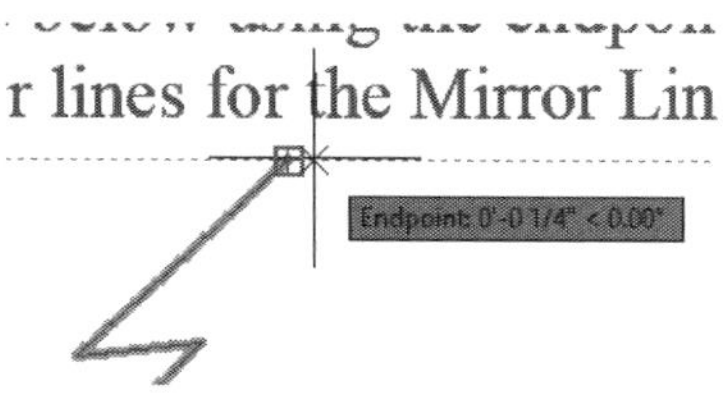

Specify first point of mirror line:
Make sure OSNAP is on. Pick the endpoint of the line that will represent the top of the tree with the LMB.

5. 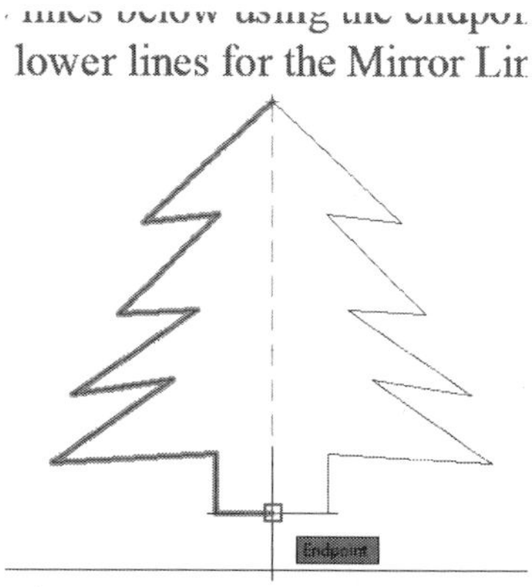

Specify second point of mirror line:
Use the LMB and object snap to select the end point that represents the bottom of the tree.

6. 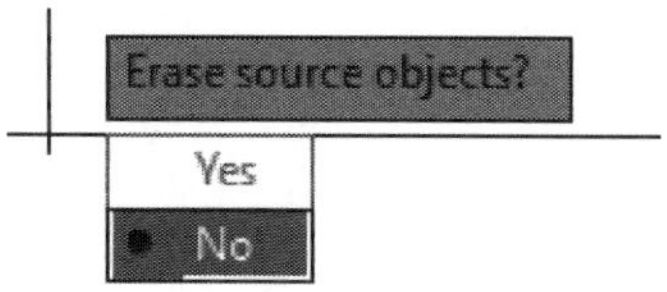

Erase source objects? [Yes/No] <N>:
Right-click in the drawing area and select 'No' or just Click <ENTER> to accept the default (N).

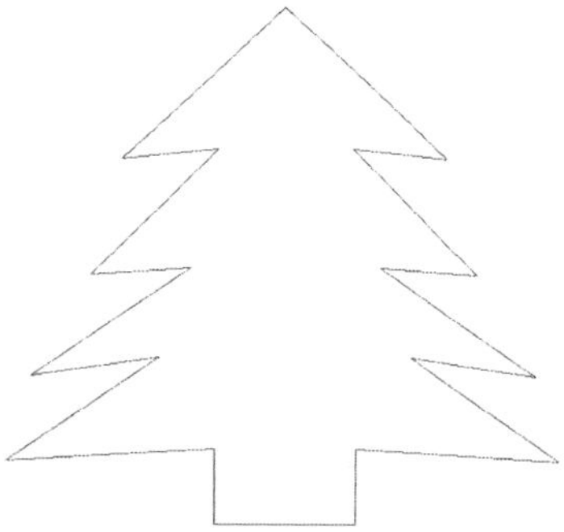

Extra: *Mirror the word MIRROR. Type 'MIRRTEXT' at the command line and Click <ENTER>. Type 0 <ENTER>. Mirror the word MIRROR again. What is the difference? Try it.*

Command Exercise

Exercise 5-5 – Mirror Text

Drawing Name: **mirror2.dwg**
Estimated Time to Completion: 5 Minutes

Scope

Turn the mirror text system variable MIRRTEXT off, and mirror the objects using the endpoints of the upper and lower lines for the mirror line.

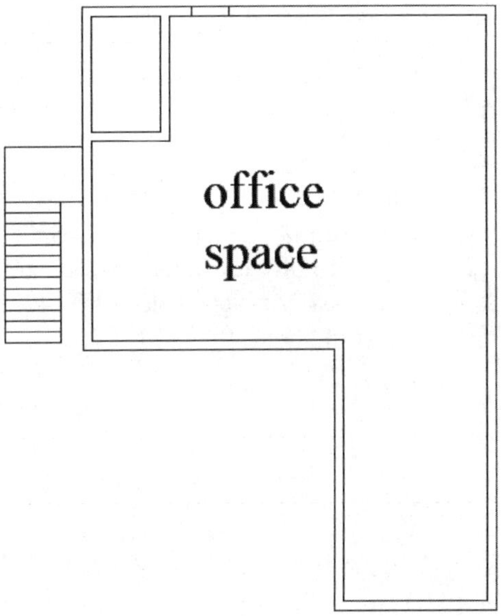

Solution

1. 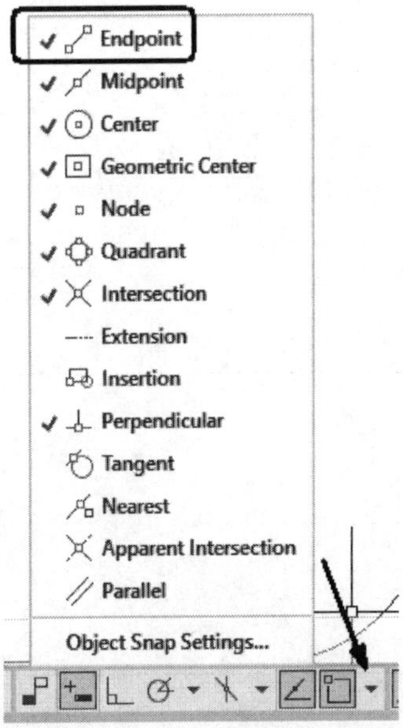

Start the exercise by making sure the Endpoint running object snap is activated.

2. 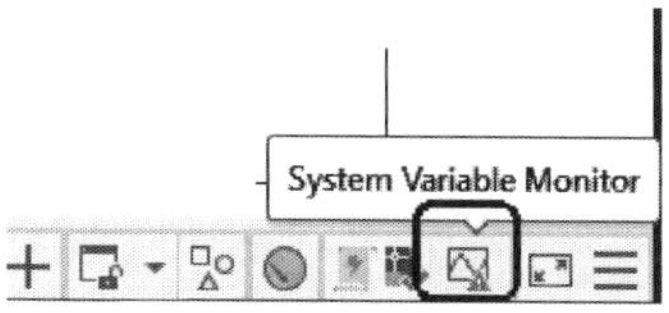

On the Status Bar, click on the **System Variable Monitor**.

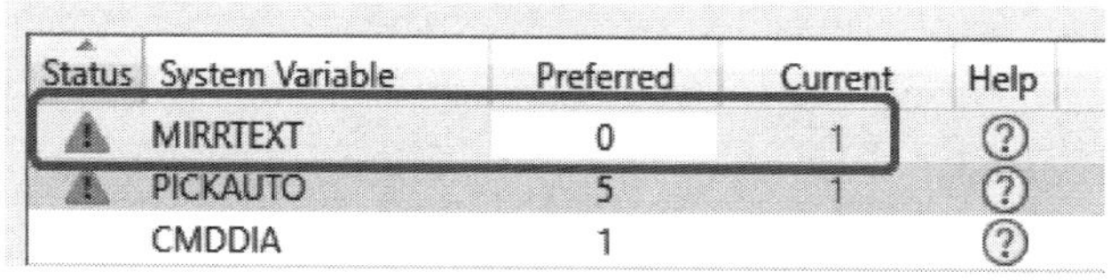

The MIRRTEXT system variable controls if text is mirrored.

It is currently set to 1 – meaning ON.

We want to change it to 0.

Click **OK**.

This dialog only tells us the current values of system variables. It does not allow us to modify them.

3. 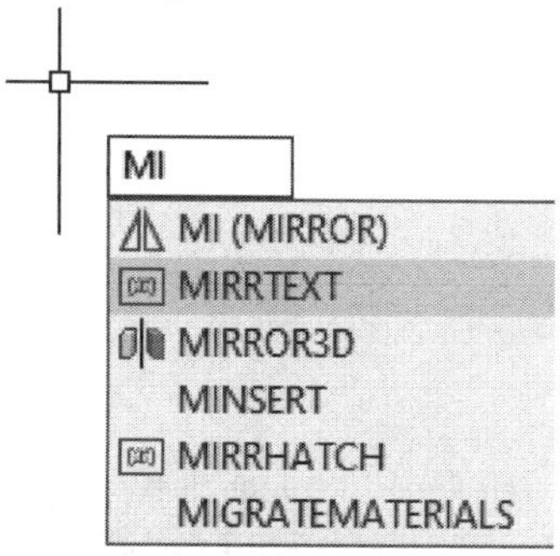

Place the cursor anywhere in the drawing area. Type 'MI' and notice how AUTOCOMPLETE provides a list of commands that start with MI. Select MIRRTEXT from the list and Click <ENTER>.

4. 

Enter new value for MIRRTEXT <1>:
Type '**0**' and Click <**ENTER**>.

5. 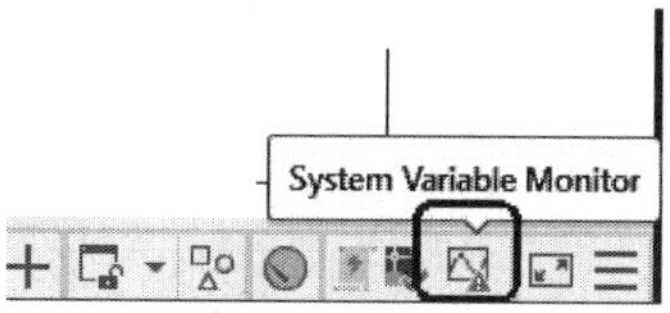

On the Status Bar, click on the **System Variable Monitor**.

6. 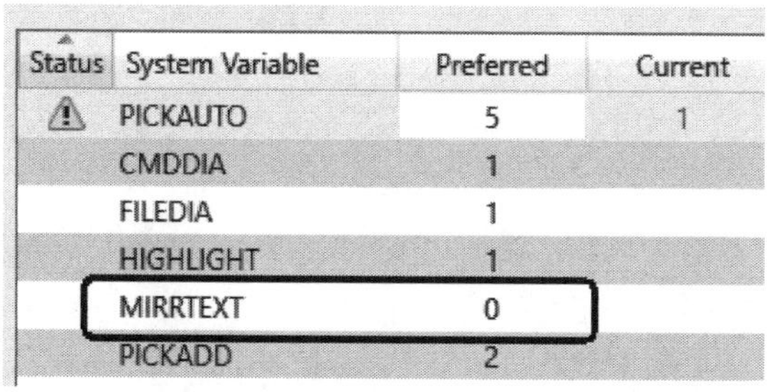

The MIRRTEXT variable shows it is set to 0.

Click **OK**.

7. 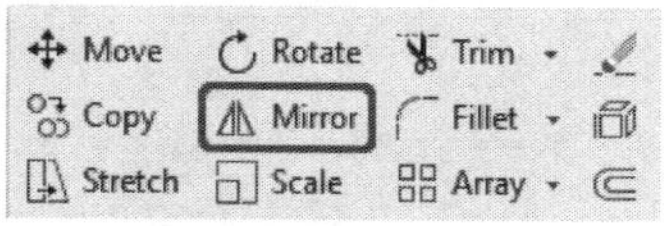

Invoke the Mirror command (mirror).

8. 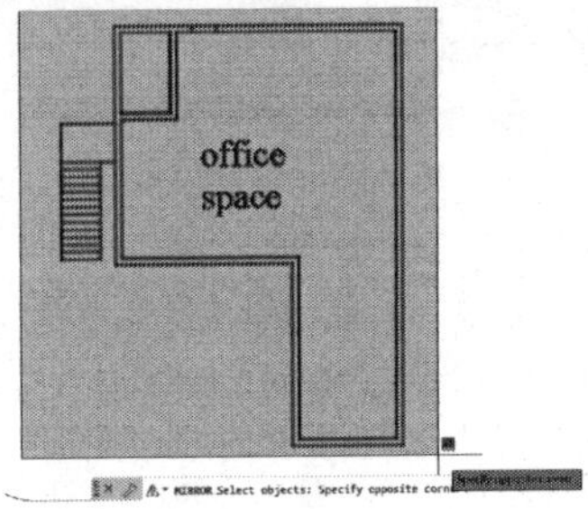

Select objects:
Select the objects that make up the office space. Include the text.

9. *Select objects:*
Close the selection set by Clicking <ENTER>.

10. 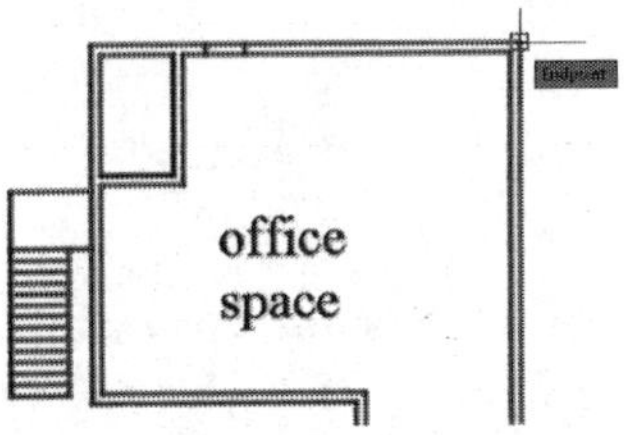

Specify first point of mirror line:
Select the upper right hand corner of the office space. Remember to use the object snap.

11. 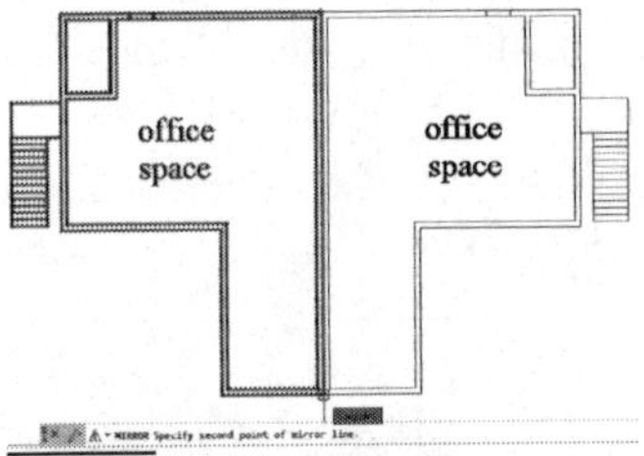

Specify second point of mirror line:
Toggle ORTHO on. Move the mouse near the bottom right corner of the office space and click the LMB.

12. 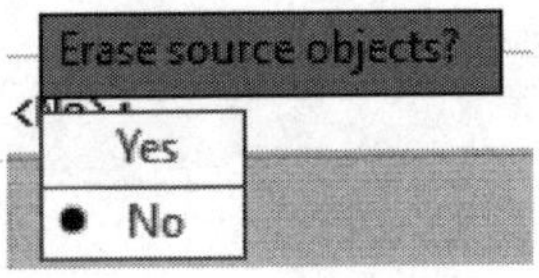

Erase source objects? [Yes/No] <N>:
Right-click in the drawing area and select 'No' or just Click <ENTER> to accept the default option of 'No'.

13. 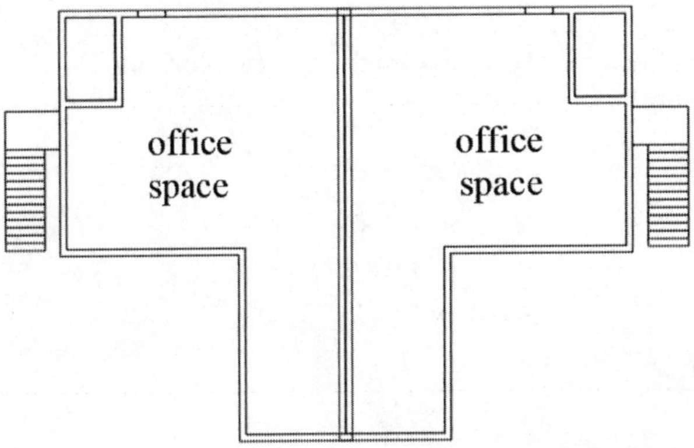

Notice that the text is not mirrored.

Offset

Command Locator

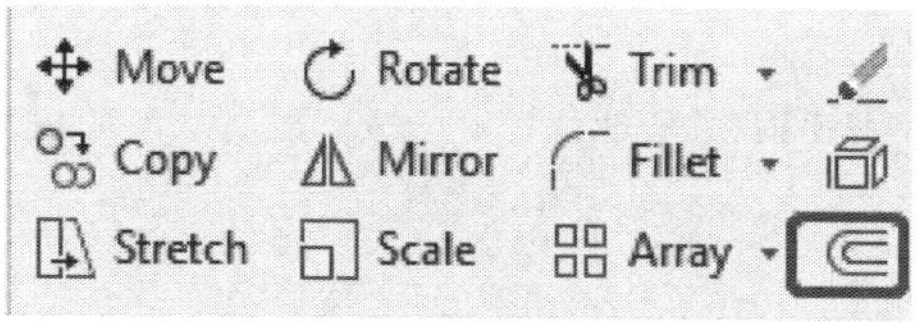

Home Ribbon	**Modify / Offset**
Command	**Offset**
Alias	**O**
RMB Shortcut Menu	**Drawing Window**

Command Overview

To Offset a single object, first set the offset distance by picking two points in the Drawing Window, or typing the offset distance. Select the object to offset and the side to offset.

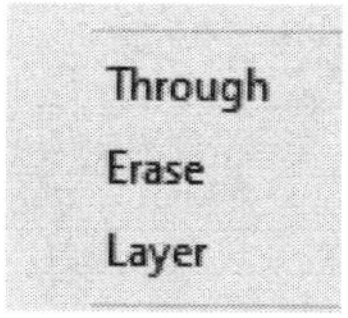

Offset Option	**Overview**
Through	Use this option to use a second object or point to set the distance for the offset.
Erase	Use this option to delete the source object after it is offset.
Layer	Use this option to set what layer the offset/new object will be assigned. You can set the new object to the current layer or the layer used by the source object.

General Procedures

1. Invoke the Offset Command.
2. Type the Offset distance.
3. Select the object to Offset, then pick the side to offset the object.

Command Exercise

Exercise 5-6 – Offset

Drawing Name: **offset1.dwg**
Estimated Time to Completion: 5 Minutes

Scope

Offset the objects with an offset distance of 0.25.

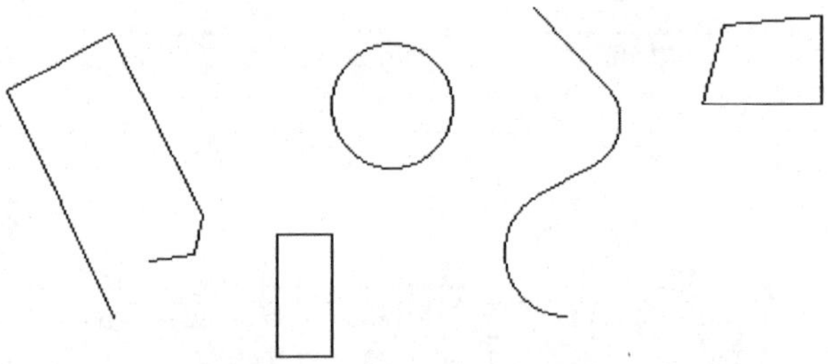

Solution

1. 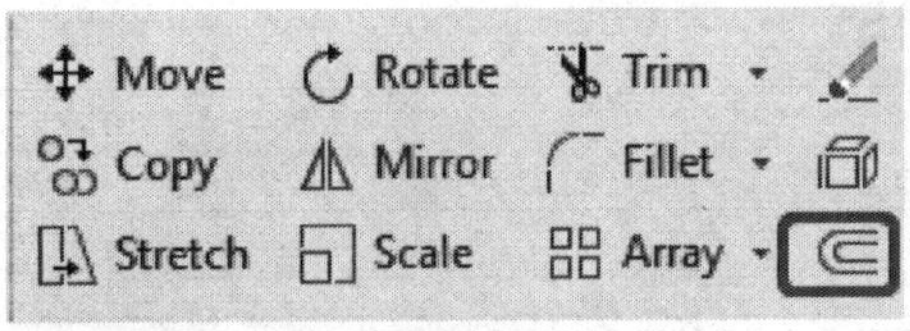

Start the Offset command (o or offset).

2. 

Specify offset distance or [Through] <Through>:
Type '0.25' at the command line and Click <ENTER>.

3. 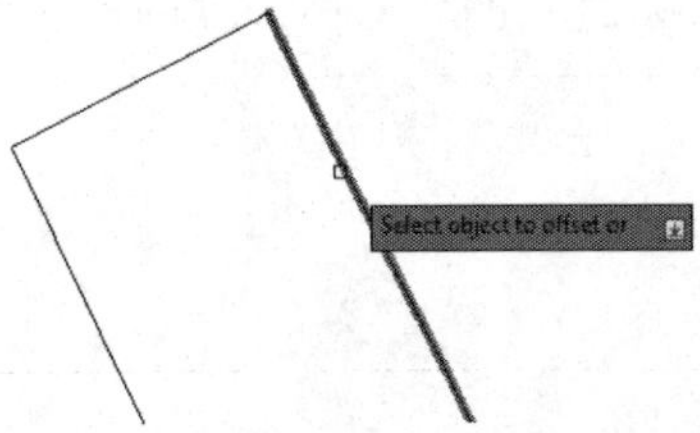

Select object to offset or <exit>:
Select the desired object with the LMB.

4. 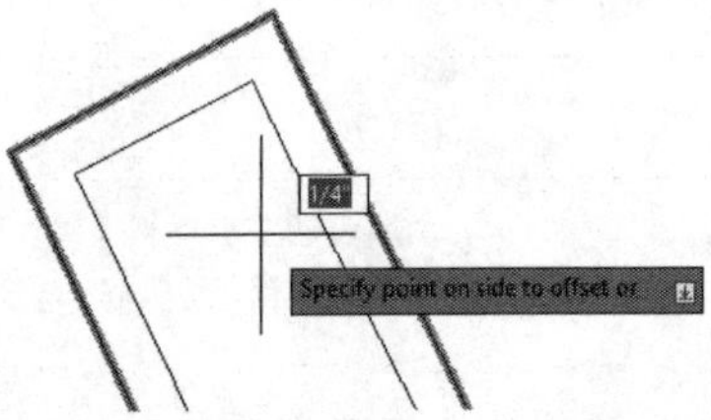

Specify point on side to offset:
Select the side of the object to create the offset on.

5.

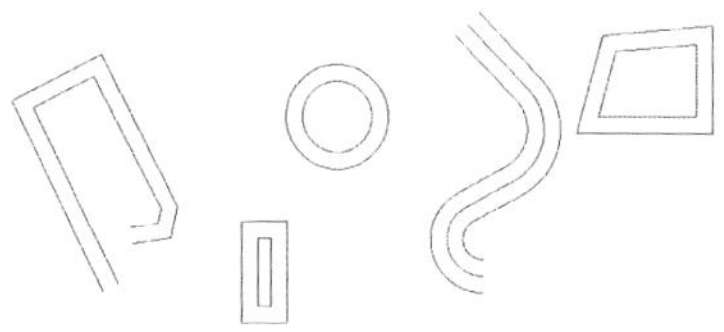

Select object to offset or <exit>:
Repeat the process offsetting all the objects on the screen.

- Offset lines, circles, arcs and polylines.

Array

Command Locator

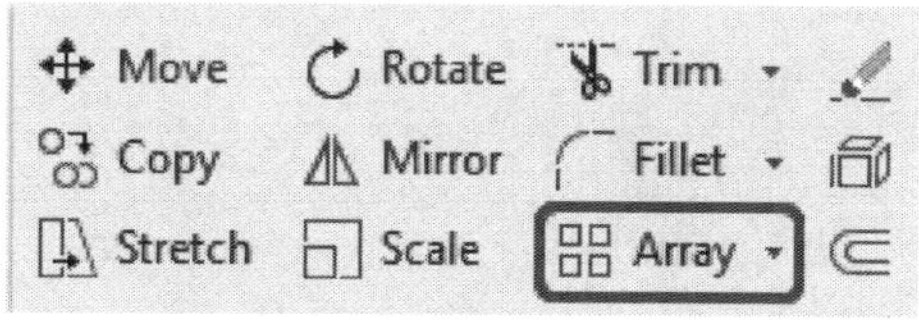

Home Ribbon	**Modify / Array**
Command	**Array**
Alias	**AR**
RMB Shortcut Menu	**Drawing Window**

Command Overview

A rectangular array copies the objects into rows and columns with designated distances between the objects. Columns are copied in the positive X direction, and Rows are copied in the positive Y direction. A negative distance will copy the objects in the negative X and Y directions, respectively.

A path array distributes an object along a line, arc, spline, or polyline at equal distances.

A polar array copies objects around a center point. Specify the total number of objects, the angle to fill (360 degrees or less) and whether the objects should be rotated.

General Procedures

To create a Rectangular Array:

1. Invoke the Array command.
2. Select the objects to Array and Click <ENTER>.
3. Right click to set the number of rows.
4. Enter the number of rows, then enter the number of columns.
5. Right click and select Spacing.
6. Type the distance between the rows and the columns.
7. Click ENTER to accept the array that is previewed.

To create a Path Array:

1. Invoke the Array command.
2. Select the objects to Array and Click <ENTER>.
3. Select the path.
4. Enter the number of elements to place.
5. Specify the distance between the elements or whether to divide the path distance by the number of elements (equal spacing).

6. Click ENTER to accept the array that is previewed.

To create a Polar Array:

1. Invoke the Array command.
2. Select the objects to Array and Click <ENTER>.
3. Specify the center point of the array.
4. Enter the total number of items for the array or specify the angle to fill.
5. Click <ENTER> for 360, or type the angle.
6. Click <ENTER> to accept the default to rotate the arrayed objects.

Tips & Tricks

- For Rectangular Array, a negative distance between columns will array the objects in the negative x (-x) direction (right to left). A negative distance between rows will array objects in the negative y (-y) direction (below one another).
- For Path Array, you can change the orientation so elements are tangent or centered on a path.
- For Polar Array, a negative angle arrays objects in a counterclockwise direction.
- For Rectangular Array, one row or one column will array objects in one direction only.
- The MINSERT command (typed) will insert blocks in rows and columns. Individual blocks cannot be deleted or Exploded.
- For Rectangular Array, you can set an angle to array from.

Command Exercise

Exercise 5-7 – Rectangular Array

Drawing Name: **arrayr1.dwg**
Estimated Time to Completion: 5 Minutes

Scope

Create a 3 x 2 rectangular array of the object with a spacing of 1.5.

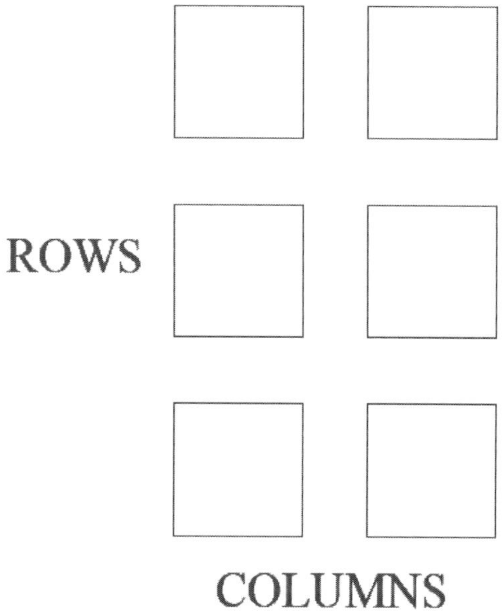

Solution

1.

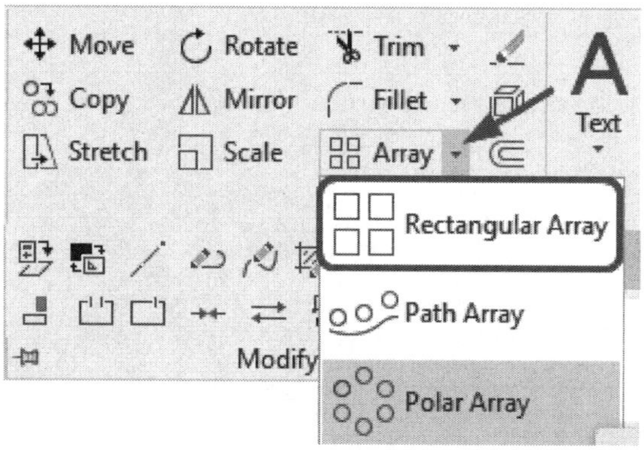

Invoke the **Rectangular Array** command (array).

2. 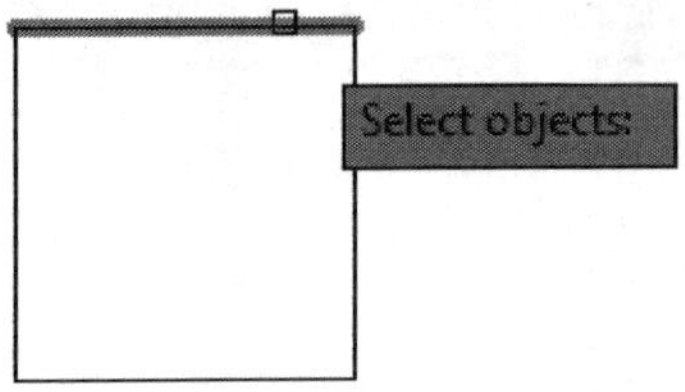

Select the rectangle on the right.

3. Click <ENTER> when it has been selected.

4. 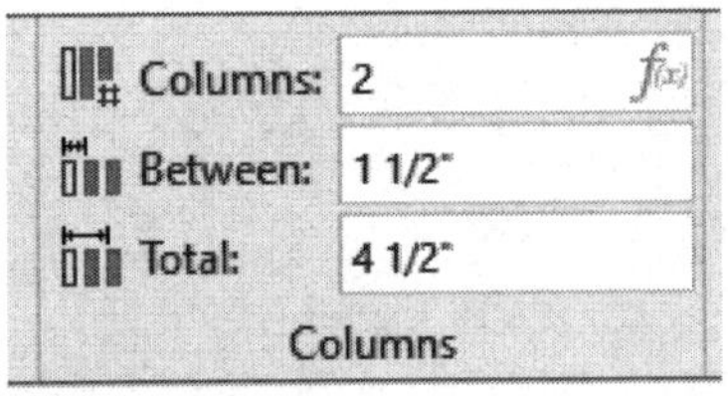

On the ribbon, set the Columns to 2.

5. 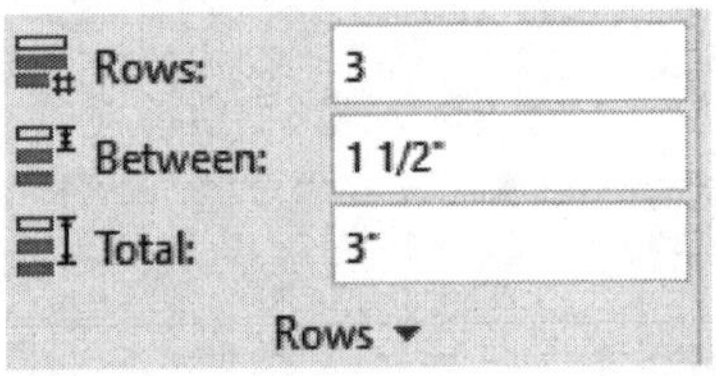

Verify that the Rows are set to 3.

6. 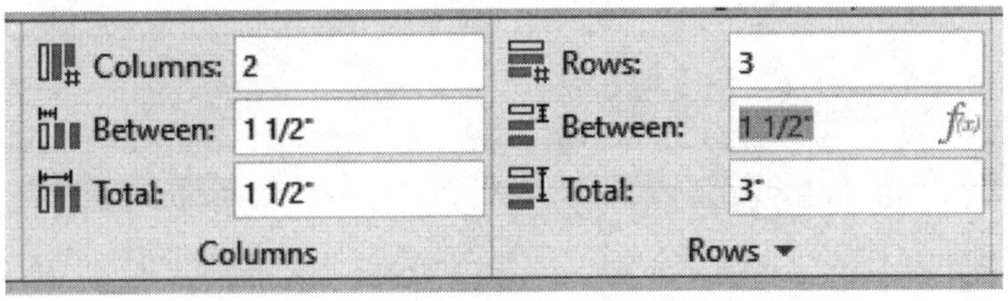

Verify that the distance between the rows and columns is set to 1 1/2″.

7. 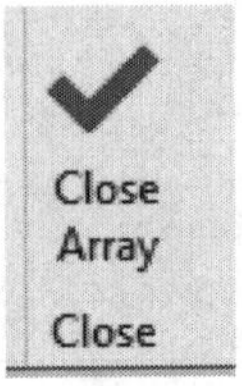

Select **Close Array** on the ribbon.

Command Exercise

Exercise 5-8 – Rectangular Array at an Angle

Drawing Name: **arrayr2.dwg**
Estimated Time to Completion: 5 Minutes

Scope

Create a 3 x 2 rectangular array of the object with a spacing of 1.5 at a minus 30-degree angle.
The ability to create a rectangular array at an angle is available using the "Classic" Array dialog box.

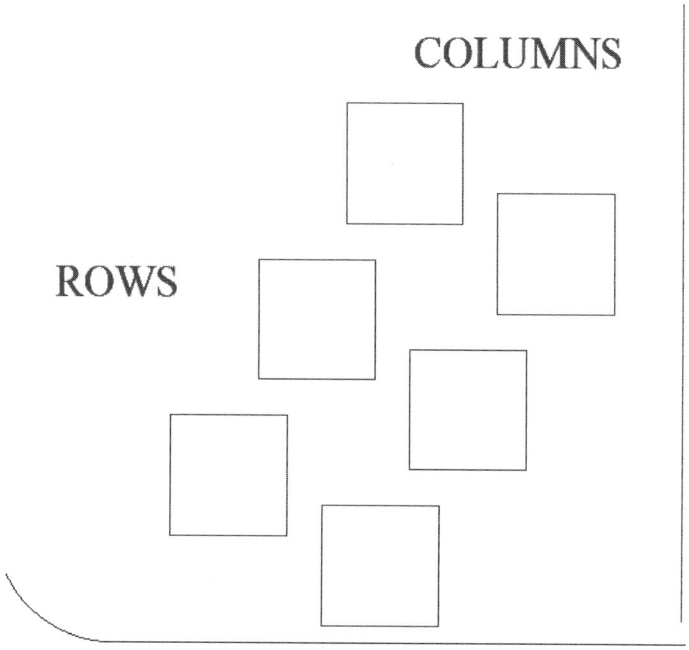

Solution

1.

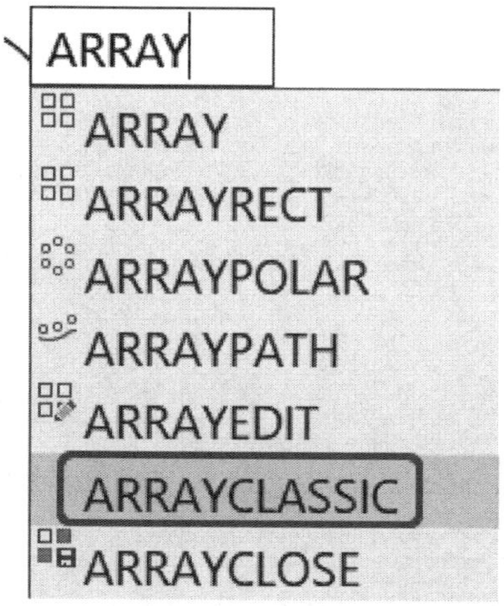

Start typing anywhere in the window. Type ARRAY… and use the Auto-Fill to select **ARRAYCLASSIC**.

2. 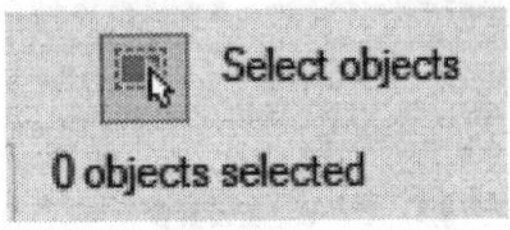

In the dialog box, select the **Select objects** tool.
Select the rectangle on the right.
Click <ENTER> when it has been selected.

3. 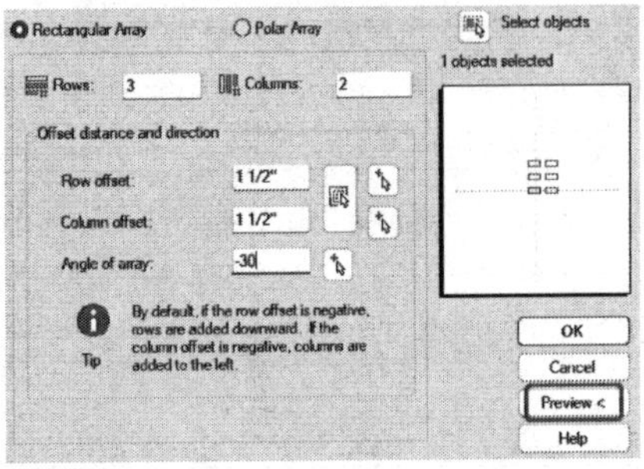

In the dialog box:
- Set the Rows to **3**.
- Set the Columns to **2**.
- Set the Row Offset to **1 1/2″**.
- Set the Column Offset to **1 1/2″**.
- Set the Angle of array to **-30.00**.
- Click the **Preview** button.

Note the angle is a negative value.

4. 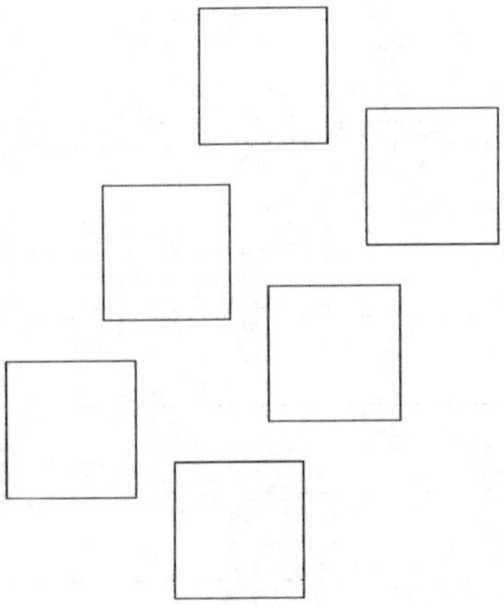

If the preview looks like the figure on the right, Click the right mouse button to accept. If it doesn't, Click ESC and double-check the settings in the dialog box.

The most common error students make is they forget to type a minus sign for the angle.

Command Exercise

Exercise 5-9 – Polar Array

Drawing Name: **arrayp1.dwg**
Estimated Time to Completion: 5 Minutes

Scope

Array the hex object using the polar array option as indicated in the drawing. The number of items is 8 (total).

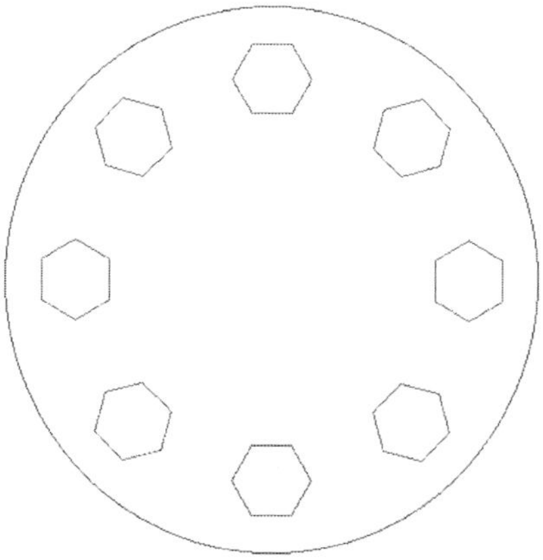

Solution

1. Enable the **CENTER** Osnap.

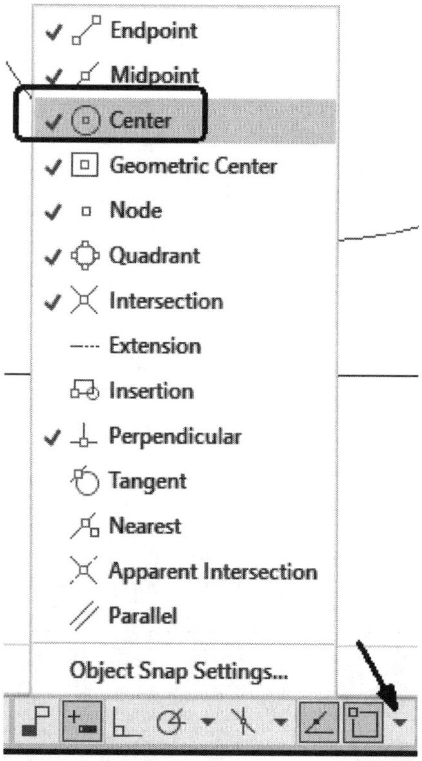

2. 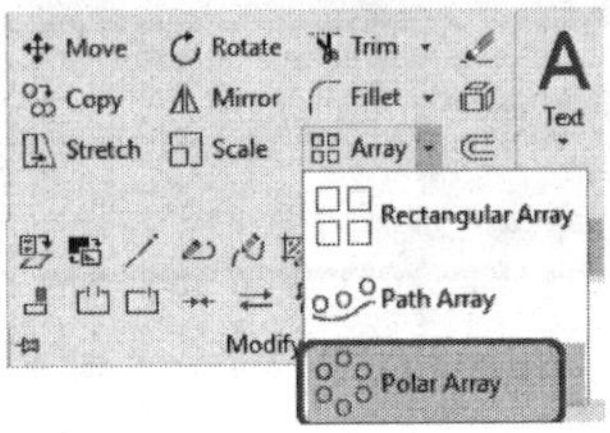

Invoke the Polar Array command (arraypolar).

3. 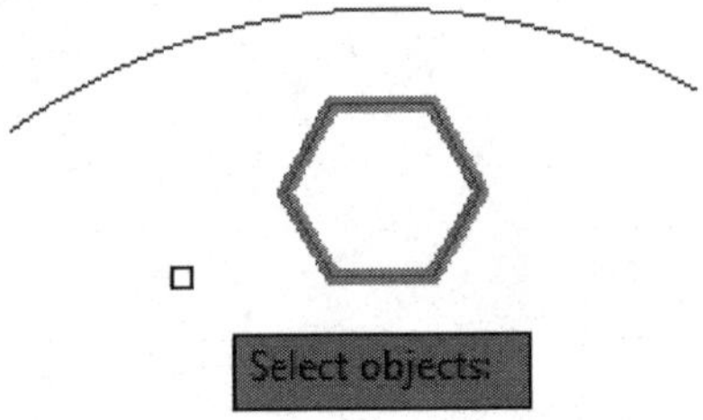

Select the polygon on the right.
Click <ENTER> to complete the selection.

4. 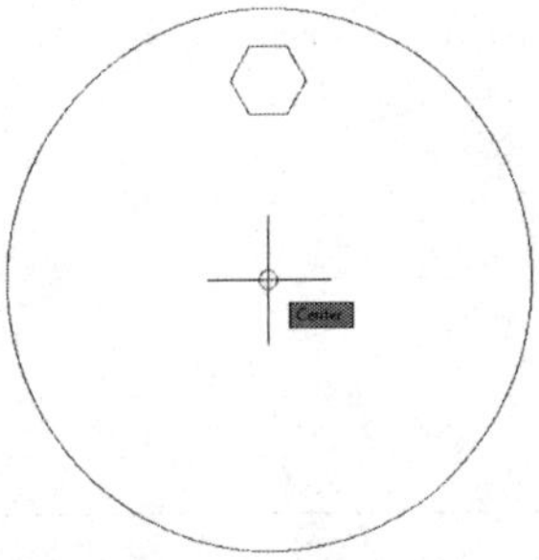

You are prompted to select the center point for the array.
Pick the center of the circle as the base point.

5. 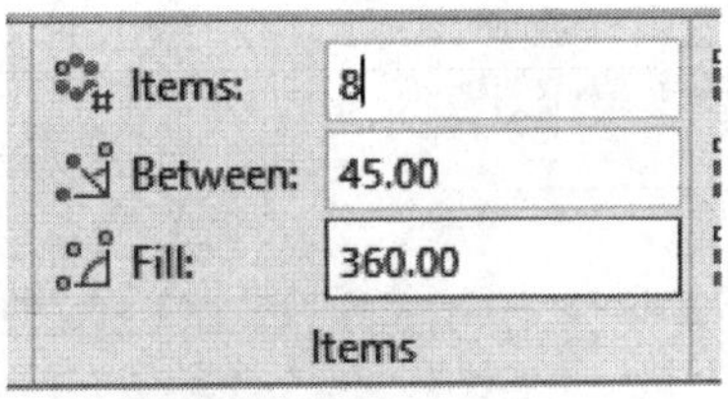

On the ribbon:
Set the number of items to **8**.
AutoCAD will automatically calculate the space between the objects.

6. 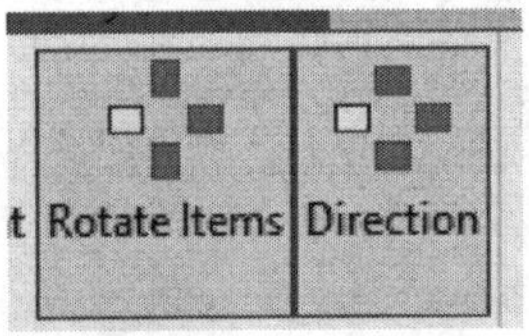

Verify that the **Rotate items** button is shaded (enabled) on the ribbon.

7. 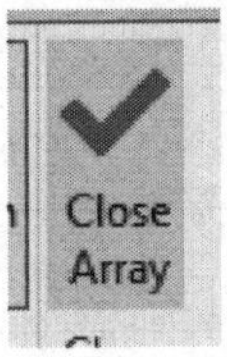

Select **Close Array** or Click ENTER to exit the command.

Extra: *Undo the polar array and repeat the exercise. Do not rotate the objects as they are copied.*

Command Exercise

Exercise 5-10 – Path Array

Drawing Name: **arraypath.dwg**
Estimated Time to Completion: 5 Minutes

Scope

Array the circle object using the path option as indicated in the drawing. The number of items is 6 (total).

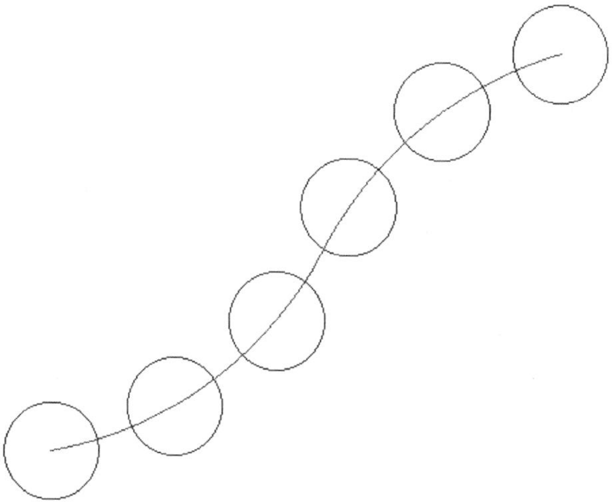

Solution

1. 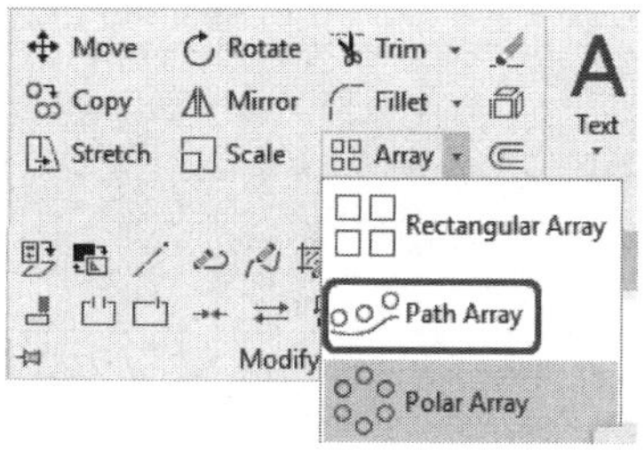

Invoke the **Array** command (arraypath) using the Path option.

2. 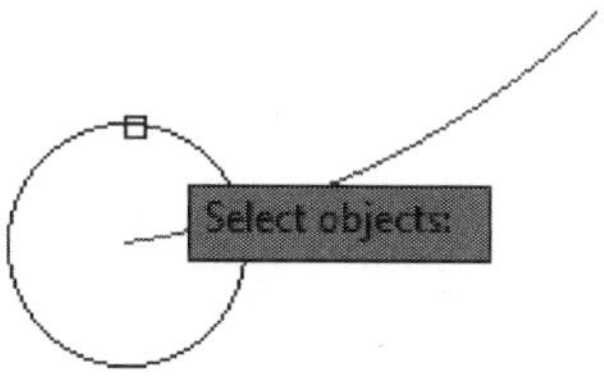

Select the circle on the right side of the view.
Click <ENTER> to complete the selection.

3. 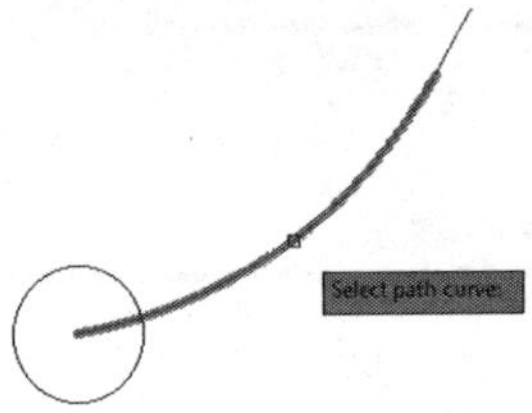

Select the path curve.

4. 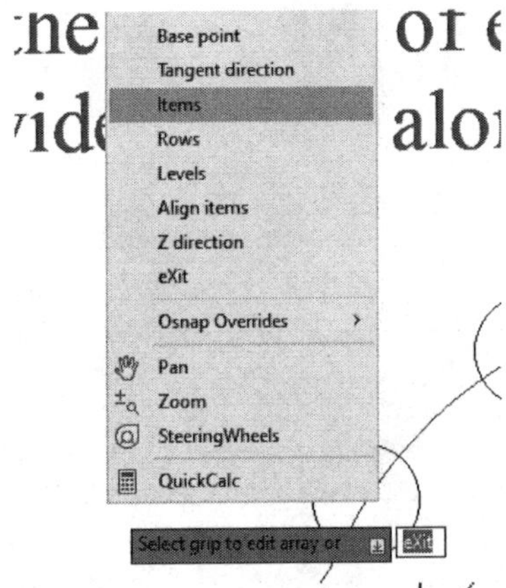

Right click anywhere in the drawing window and select **Items** from the shortcut menu.

You'll be asked to specify the distance between items along the path.

5. 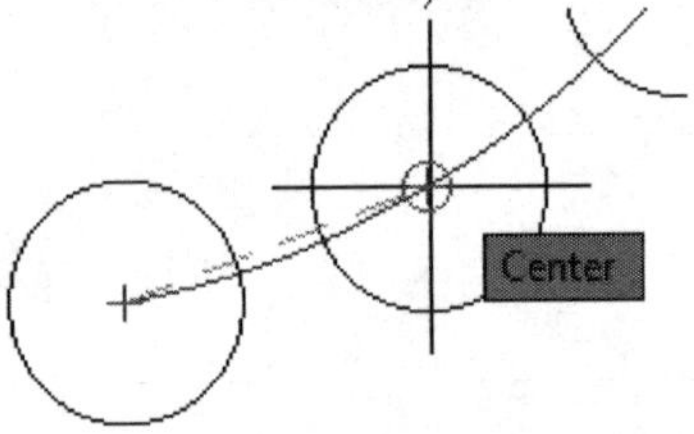

Use the completed drawing on the left side to help set the spacing distance.

Select two center points on two of the circles on the path on the left to set the distance between the circles.

6. 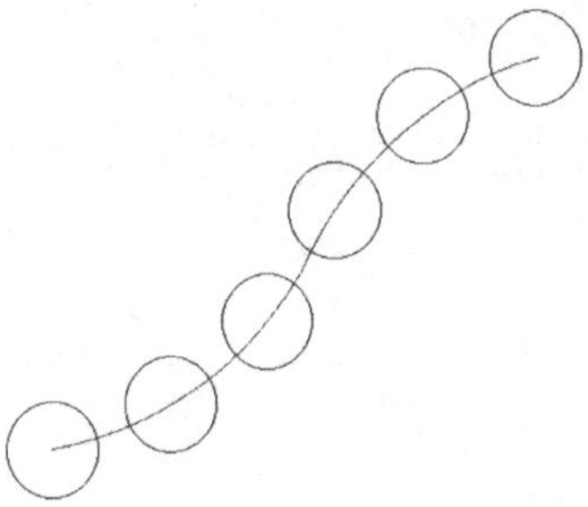

You will then be offered the maximum number of items that will fill the path as 6.

Click <ENTER> to accept the default of spacing the items evenly along the path.

7. Click <ENTER> to accept the preview of the array and exit the command.

Command Exercise

Exercise 5-11 – Associative Array

Drawing Name: **assocarray.dwg**
Estimated Time to Completion: 10 Minutes

Scope

Array the square object using the rectangular array. Use the Associative option on the left side. Turn off Associative for the right array. Explore the difference.

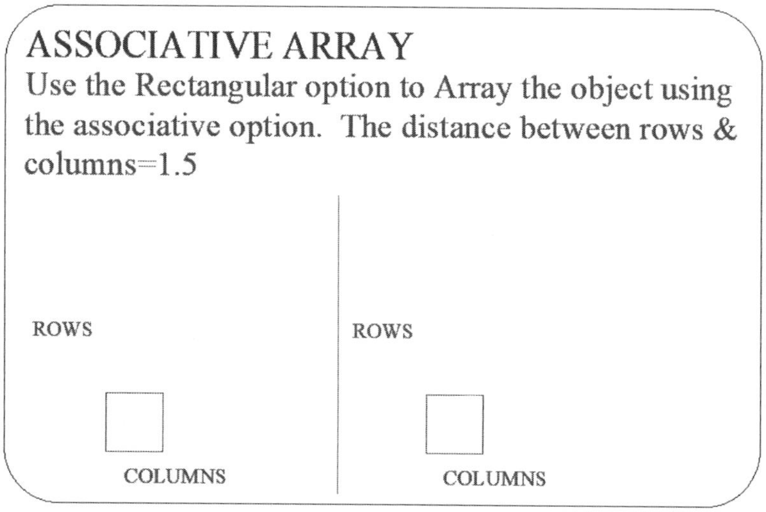

Solution

1.

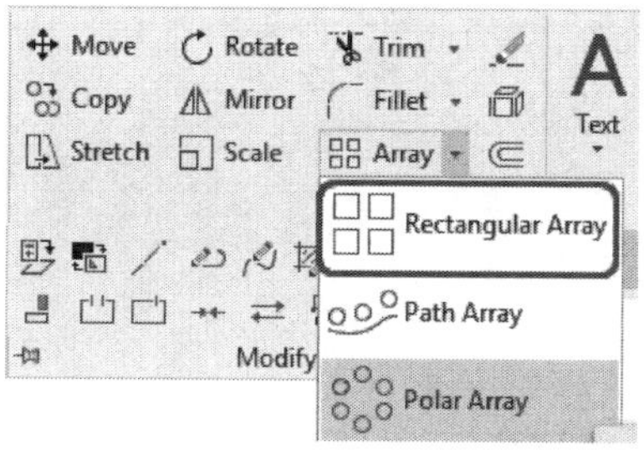

Invoke the Array command (array) using the Rectangular option.

2.

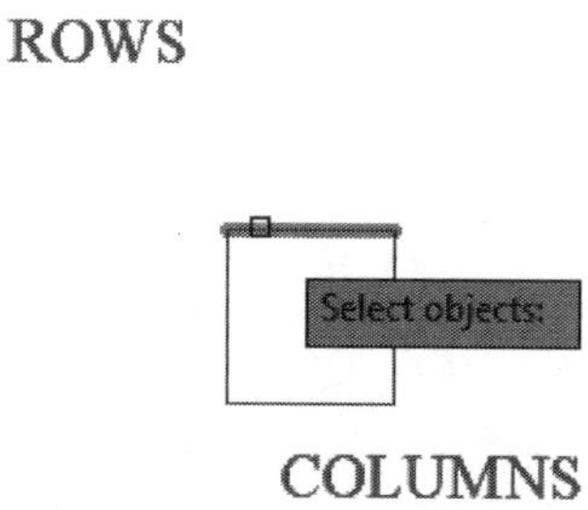

Select the square on the left side of the view. Click <ENTER> to complete the selection.

3. 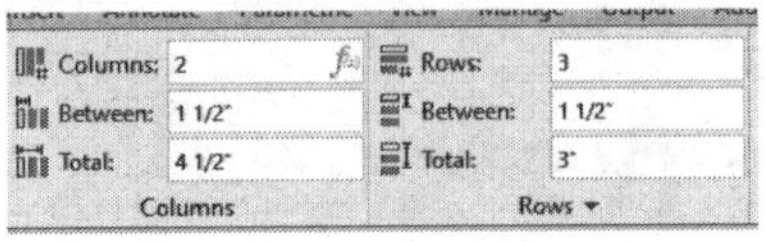

On the ribbon:
Set the Columns to 2.
Set the Rows to 3.
Set the distance between rows to 1 1/2″.
Set the distance between columns to 1 1/2″.

4. 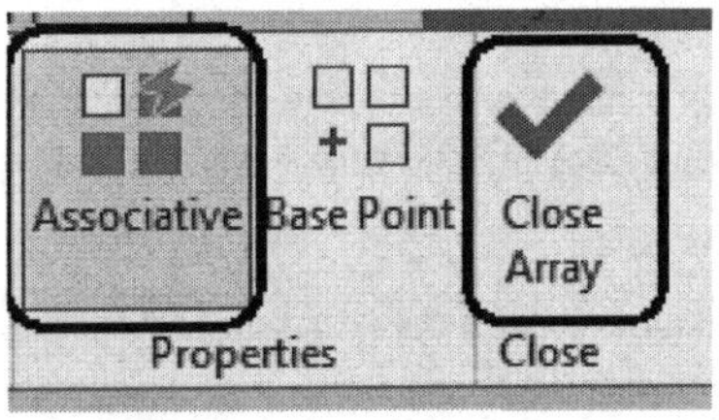

Enable **Associative**.
Click **Close Array**.

5. 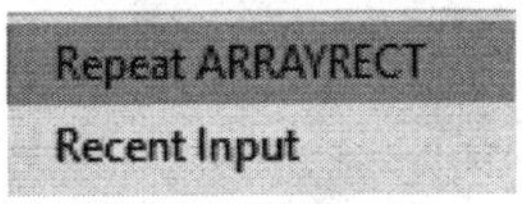

Invoke the Array command (arrayrect) using the Rectangular option.

You can right click and select Repeat ARRAYRECT.

6. 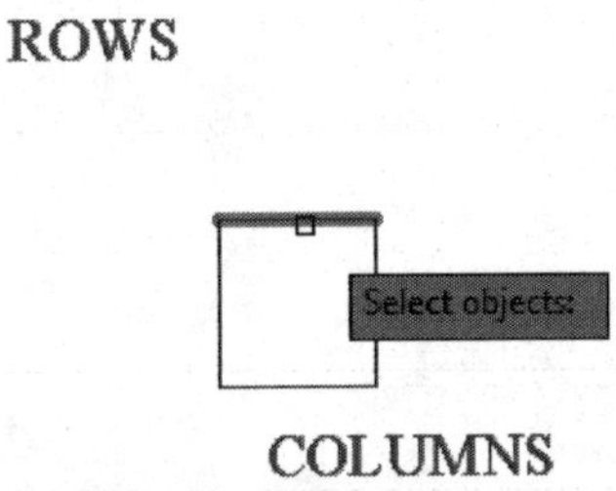

Select the square on the right side of the view.
Click <ENTER> to complete the selection.

7. 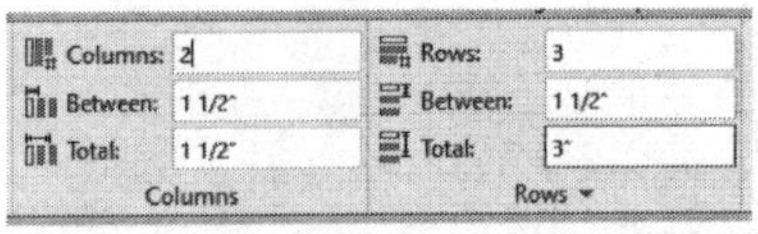

On the ribbon:
Set the Columns to **2**.
Set the Rows to **3**.
Set the distance between rows to **1 1/2″**.
Disable **Associative**.
Click **Close Array**.

8. 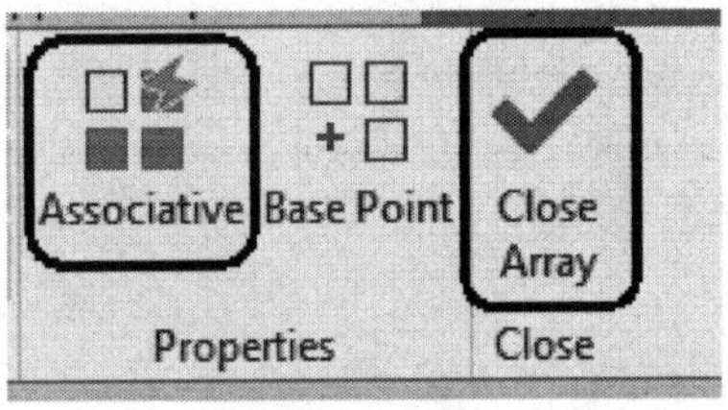

9. 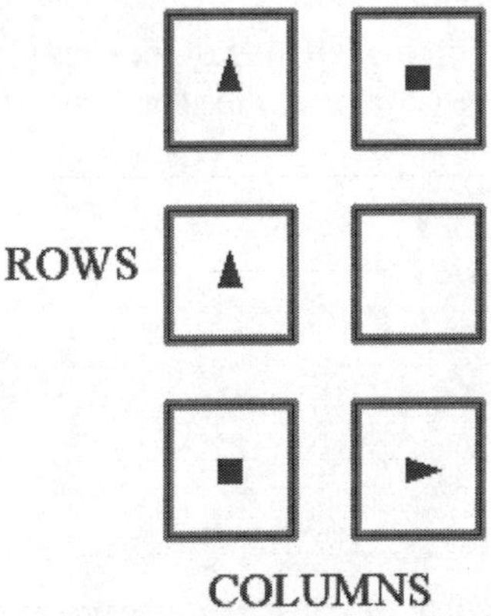

Select the array on the left (the array created as an associative array).
The ribbon will allow you to modify the array.

10.

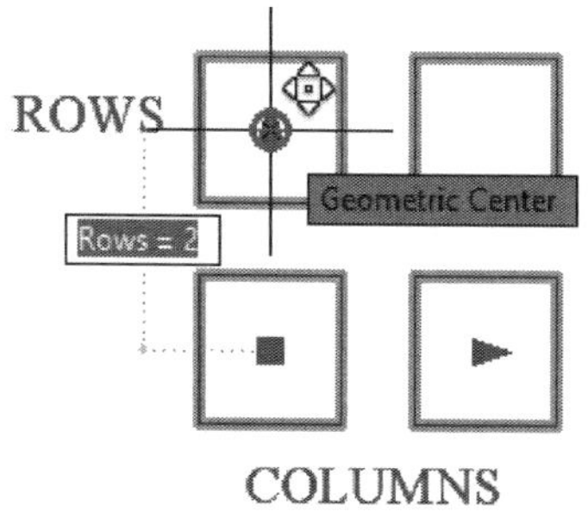

Change the number of rows to **2**.
Change the number of columns to **3**.

You can use the grips or the ribbon to modify the array.

11.

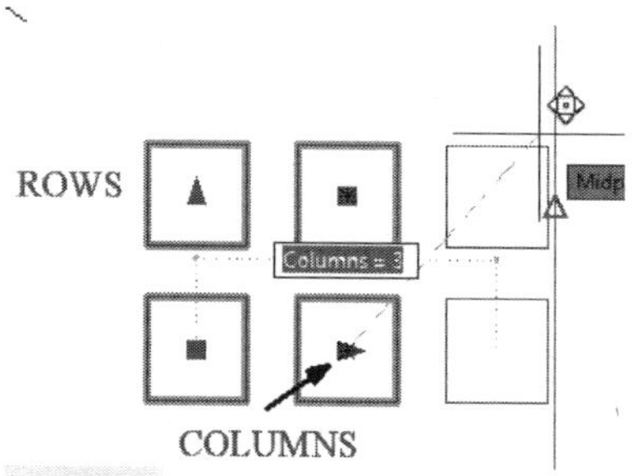

Select the arrow grip and move the cursor to change the count or modify the count in the edit box.

12.

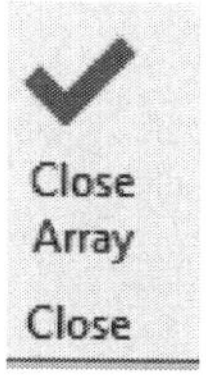

Close the Array to exit editing.

13.

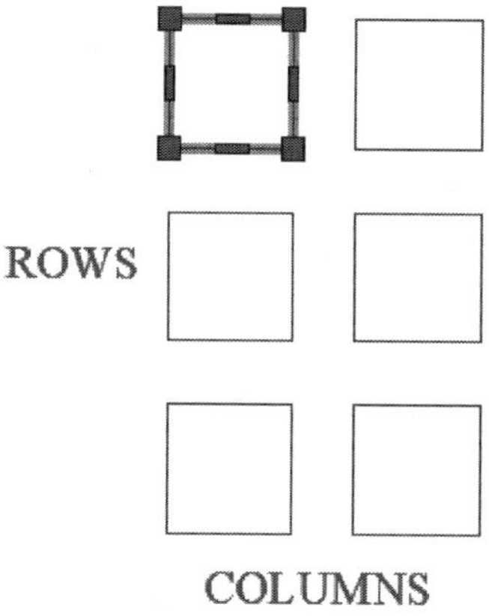

Select one of the squares on the right array (the array created as the non-associative array).

Note that it acts as an independent element. The array was created as a non-associative array.

Move

Command Locator

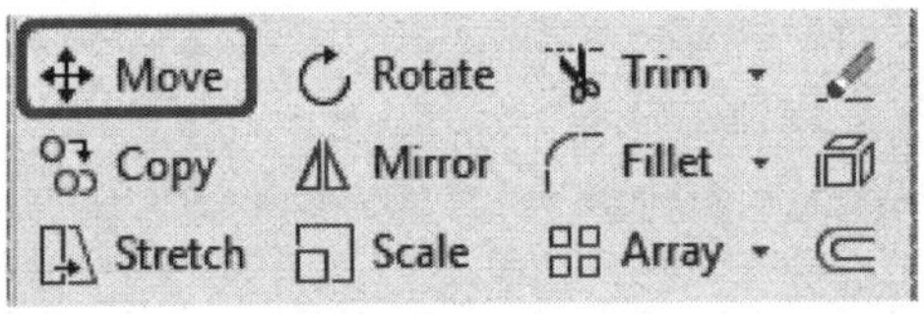

Home Ribbon	Modify / Move
Command	Move
Alias	M

Command Overview

To move an object, pick the base point, drag the object and pick or use any of the methods previously discussed to input coordinates.

General Procedures

1. Invoke the Move Command.
2. Select the objects to move and Click <ENTER>.
3. Pick a point on or near the object for the base point.
4. Drag the mouse and pick the new location or use absolute, relative coordinates, polar coordinates, or the direct distance method to relocate the object.

Tips & Tricks

Use Object Snaps for picking the base point and the new location.
If using the direct distance to relocate the object, be sure ORTHO is ON.
Remember to use the pick button (LMB) to select the base point and the new location of the object.
Be sure SNAP (in the Status Bar) is off when selecting objects.
Use ORTHO TRACKING to help align objects being moved.

Command Exercise

Exercise 5-12 – Move

Drawing Name: **move1.dwg**
Estimated Time to Completion: 5 Minutes

Scope

Turn Snap off and Move the blue objects into the red rectangle.

Solution

1. 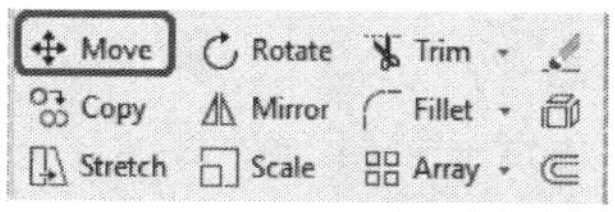

Invoke the Move command (m or move).

2. 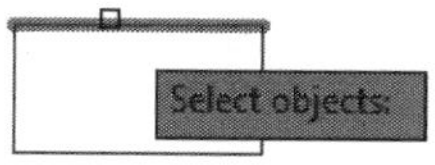

Select objects:
Start by selecting one of the blue rectangles with the LMB. Close the selection set with the <ENTER> key or RMB.

3. 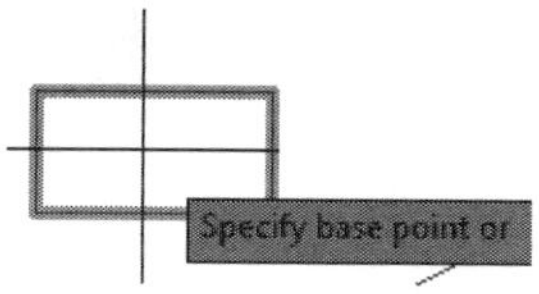

Specify base point or displacement:
You may want to turn OSNAP off. Use your LMB to select in the middle of the rectangle. This is the point from which the rectangle will be moved.

4. 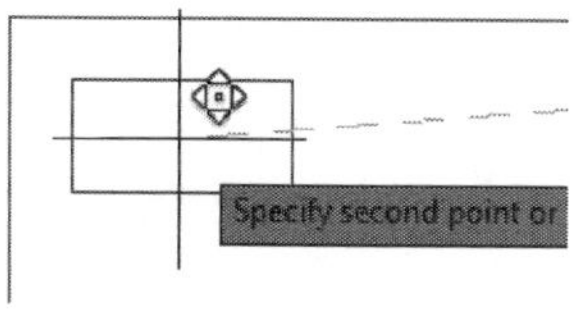

Specify second point of displacement or <use first point as displacement>:
Move your mouse to position the rectangle in the red box and Click the LMB to specify the second point of displacement.

5. 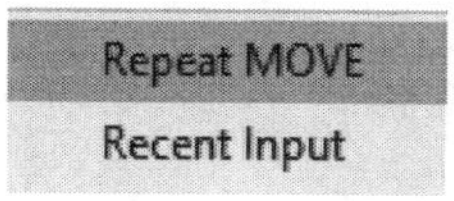

Repeat the Move command with the RMB (m, move or <ENTER>).

6. 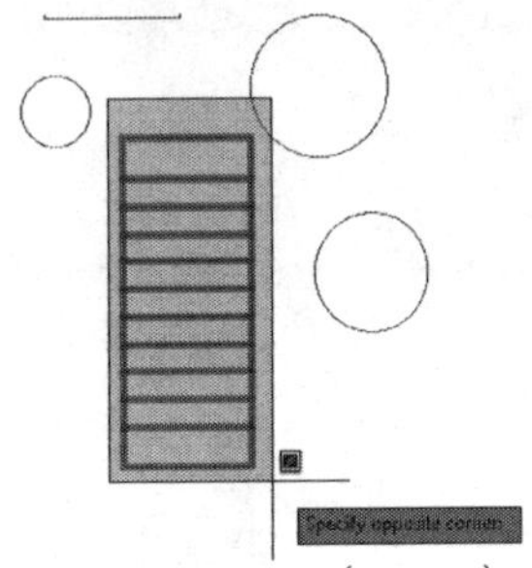

Select objects:
Select another object.

7. 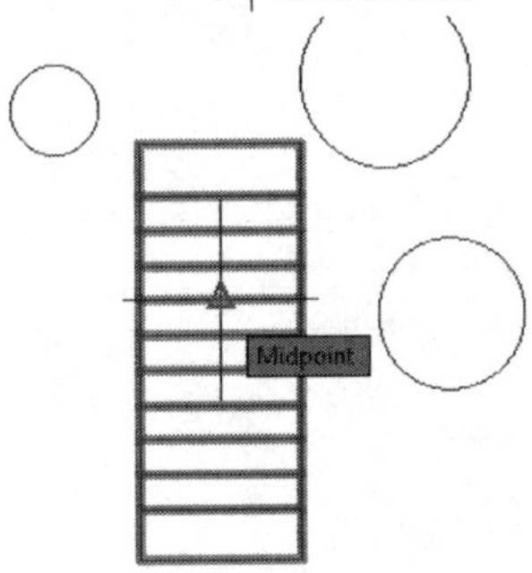

Specify base point or displacement:
Pick near the middle of the object. This will be the point from which it is moved.

8. 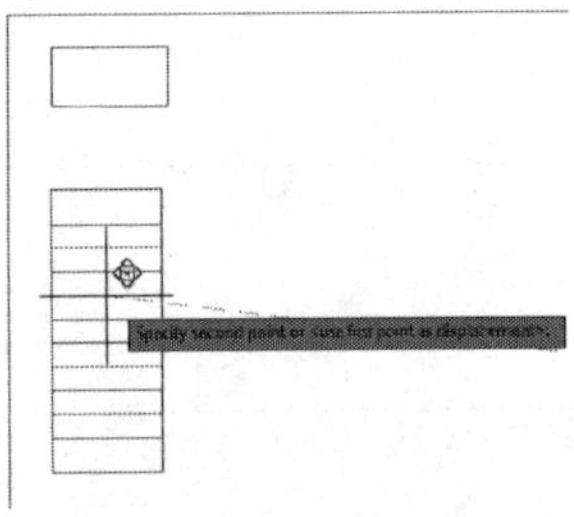

Specify second point of displacement or <use first point as displacement>:
Select a point inside the red box for the second point.

9. 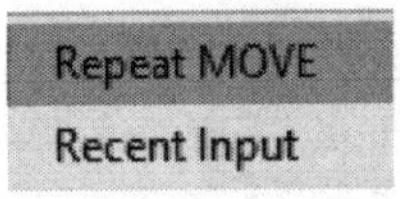

Repeat the Move command with the RMB (m, move or <ENTER>) and move the rest of the objects into the red box, one at a time or in groups.

10. 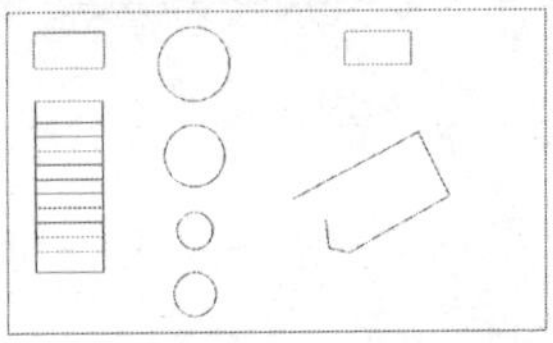

See if you can use the MOVE command to rearrange the objects.

Extra: *Undo the command and repeat the exercise using different methods of selecting objects. Try selecting using a window, then try selecting using a crossing; then try selecting using the Fence option.*

Rotate

Command Locator

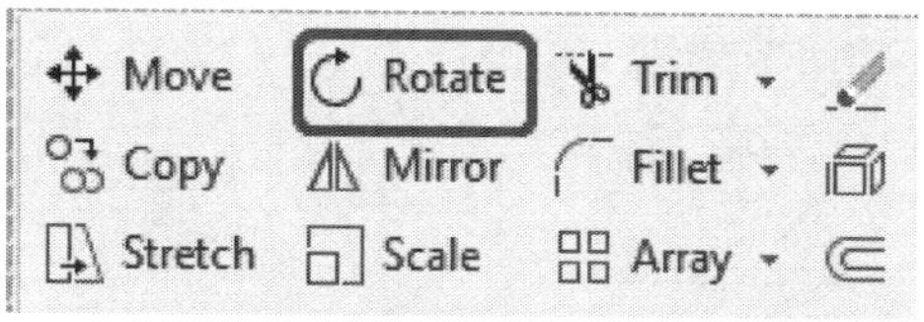

Home Ribbon	**Modify / Rotate**
Command	**Rotate**
Alias	**RO**
RMB Shortcut Menu	**Drawing Window**

Command Overview

Rotate selected objects in a counterclockwise direction with a positive rotation angle. Rotate in a clockwise direction with a negative angle. The Reference option permits the user to reference the angle of an existing line in the drawing and type a new angle.

General Procedures

To use the Rotate command:

1. Invoke the Rotate Command.
2. Select the objects to rotate, and Click <ENTER>.
3. Pick a base point on or near the object.
4. Type the rotation angle or drag the mouse and pick the rotation angle.

To use the Rotate command with the Reference option:

1. Invoke the Rotate Command.
2. Select the objects to rotate, and Click <ENTER>.
3. Pick a base point on or near the object. Type R for reference, or Click the RMB and select Reference from the shortcut menu.
4. Using Object Snap, select the endpoints of the line to reference. This will determine the precise reference angle.

Command Exercise

Exercise 5-13 – Rotate

Drawing Name: **rotate1.dwg**
Estimated Time to Completion: 5 Minutes

Scope

Rotate the objects as indicated in the drawing.

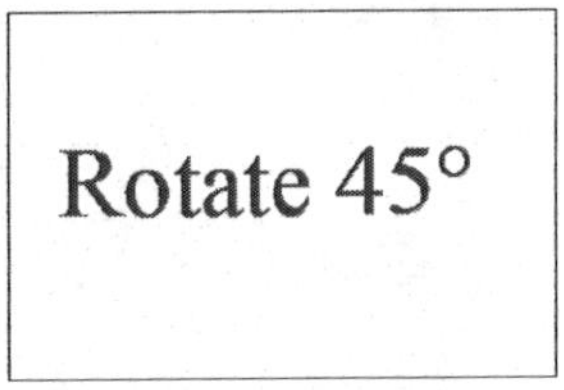

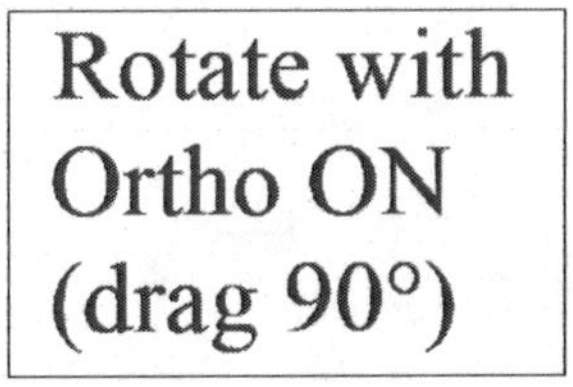

Solution

1. 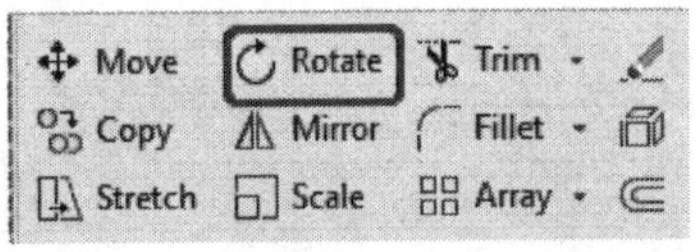

Invoke the Rotate command (rotate).

2. 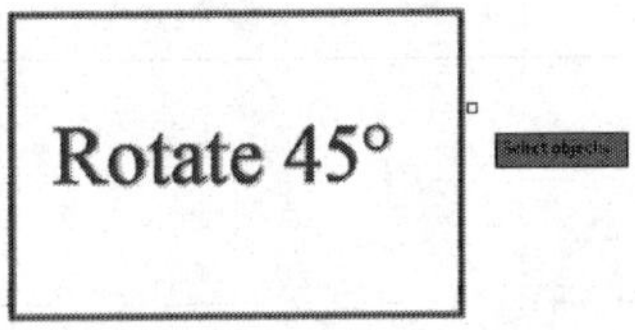

Select objects:
Select the box and text on the left.

3. *Select objects:*
Click <ENTER> to close the selection set.

4. 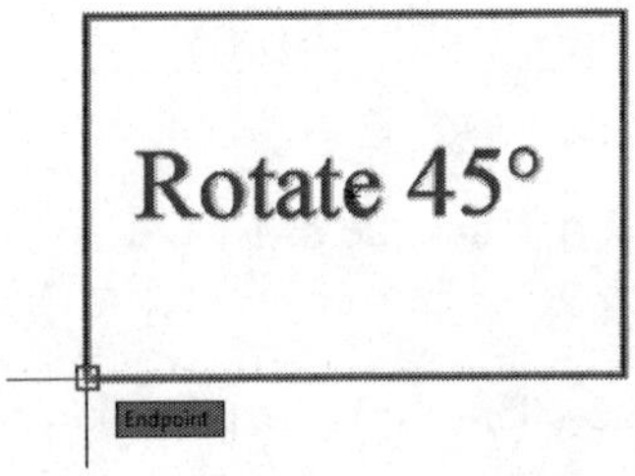

Specify base point:
Pick the left lower corner of the rectangle. This is the point about which the objects will be rotated.

5. 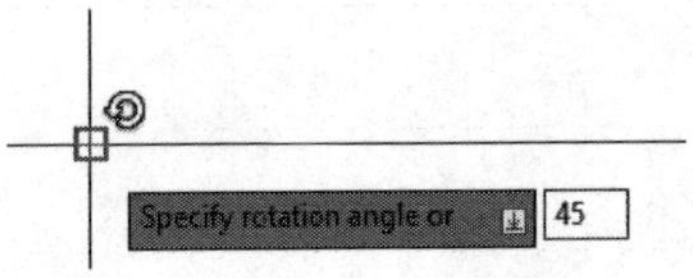

Specify rotation angle or [Reference]:
Type '45' and Click <ENTER>.

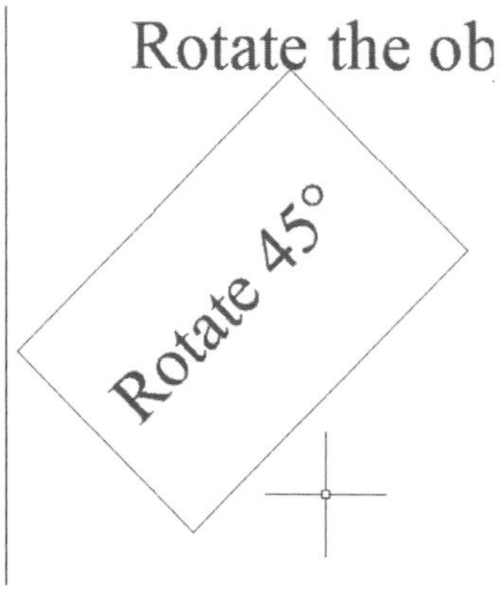

The rectangle and text are rotated.

6. 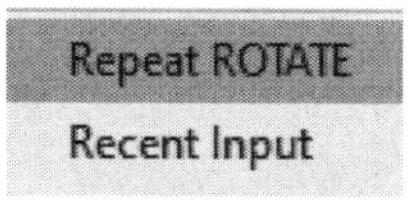

Repeat the Rotate command with the RMB (rotate or <ENTER>).

7. 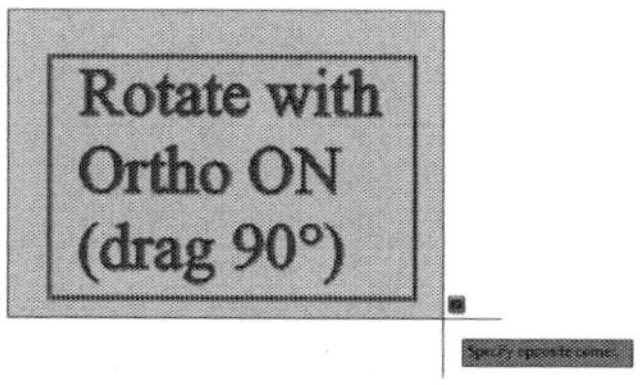

Select objects:
Select the box and text on the right.

8. *Select objects:*
Click <ENTER> to close the selection set.

9. 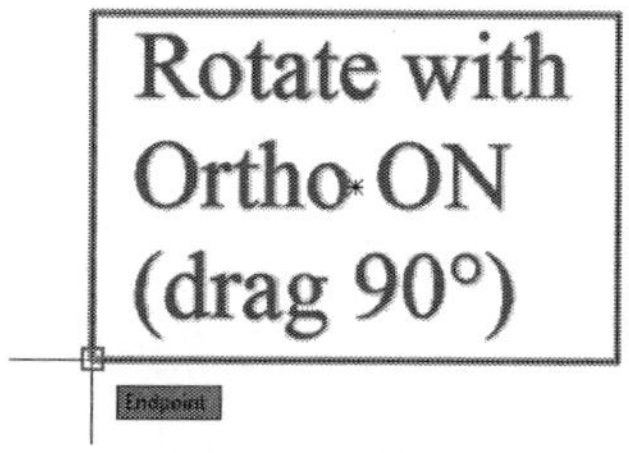

Specify base point:
Select the end point on the lower left as the base point.

10. 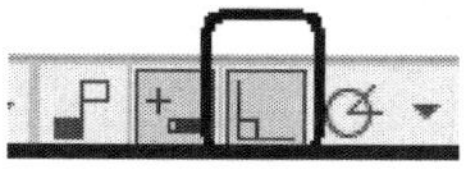

Toggle ORTHO on.

Pick a point inside the box on the right with the LMB.

11. 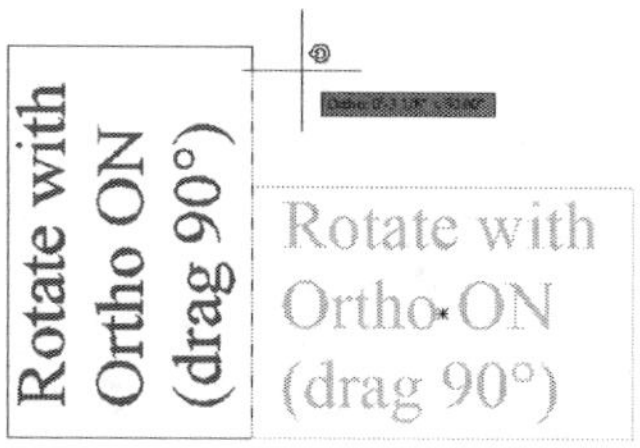

Specify rotation angle or [Reference]:
Drag the mouse upward and click to rotate the objects 90 degrees counterclockwise.

Command Exercise

Exercise 5-14 – Rotate and Copy

Drawing Name: **rotate2.dwg**
Estimated Time to Completion: 5 Minutes

Scope

Use Rotate to Copy and Rotate an object.

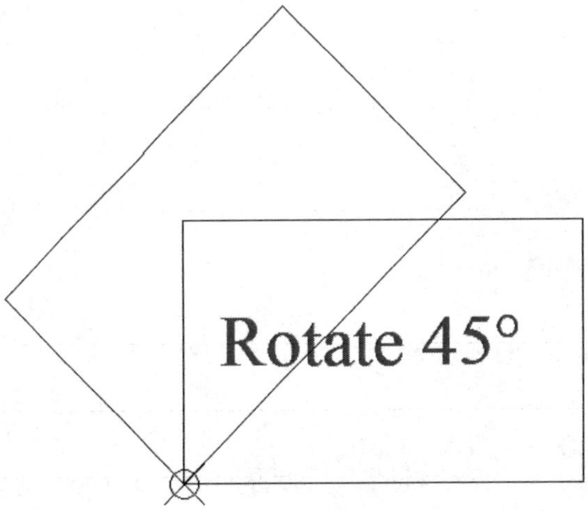

Solution

1. 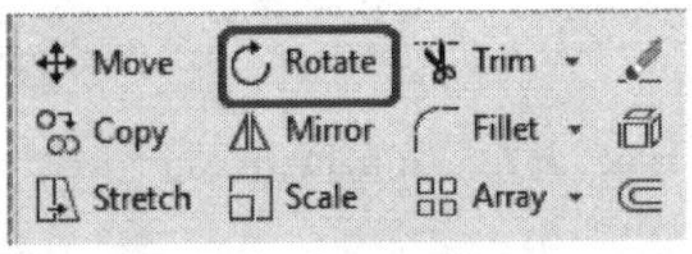

Invoke the Rotate command (rotate).

2. *Select objects:*
Select the rectangle with the LMB.

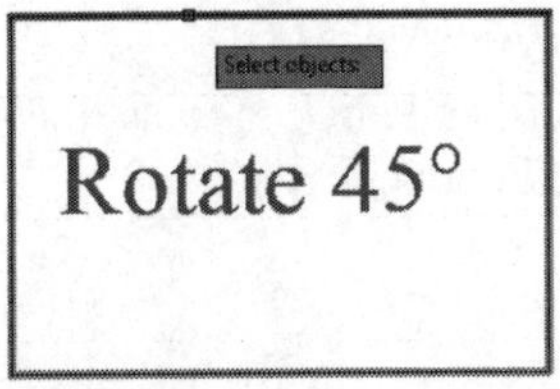

3. *Select objects:*
Close the selection set by Clicking <ENTER>.

4.

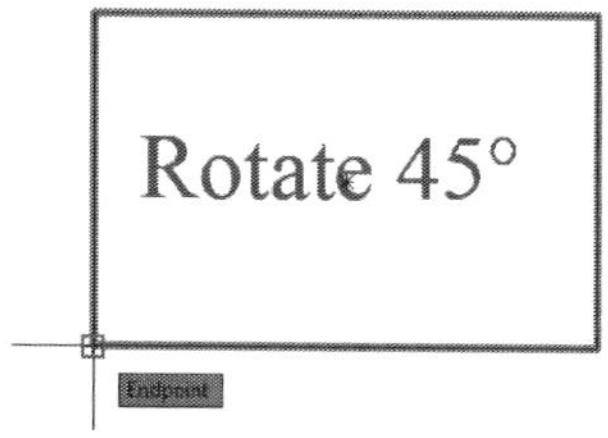

Specify base point:
Pick the lower left corner of the rectangle.
Remember to use Object Snaps.

5.

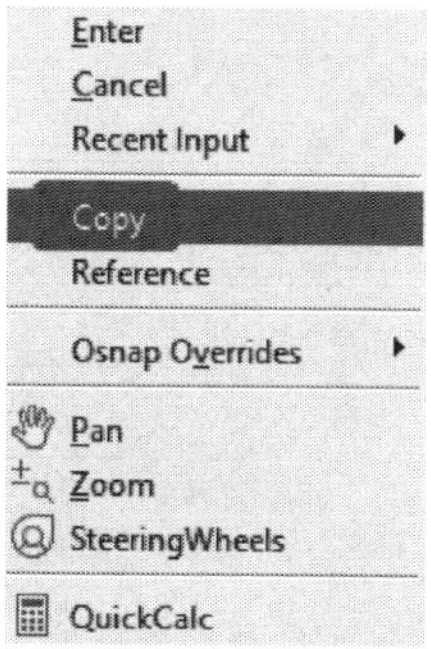

Click the RMB and select **Copy** from the shortcut menu.

6.

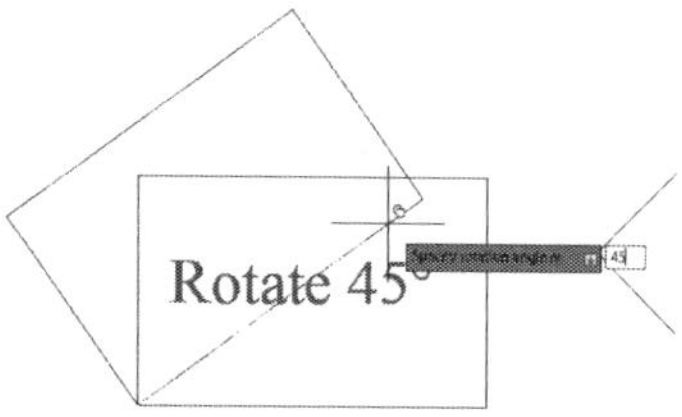

Type **45** as the rotation angle.

Click ENTER.

Turn ORTHO on to rotate in 90 degree increments, relative to the current rotation angle.

When rotating the object with ORTHO on, keep the cursor close to the base point to make it easier to rotate the object.

Toggle through the Coordinates display by selecting F6 or double clicking the coordinates in the Status Bar to view the distance and angle option.

When using the Reference option to straighten objects, it is more accurate to reference the angle of a line in the drawing using the object snap than to try to find the angle of the line and rotate it in the negative direction.

Objects will be rotated around the rotation base point.

The Rotate Command has a COPY option, so that you can create a copy in addition to rotating selected objects.

Command Exercise

Exercise 5-15 – Rotate Using Reference

Drawing Name: **rotate3.dwg**
Estimated Time to Completion: 5 Minutes

Scope

Straighten the object using the reference option with rotate.

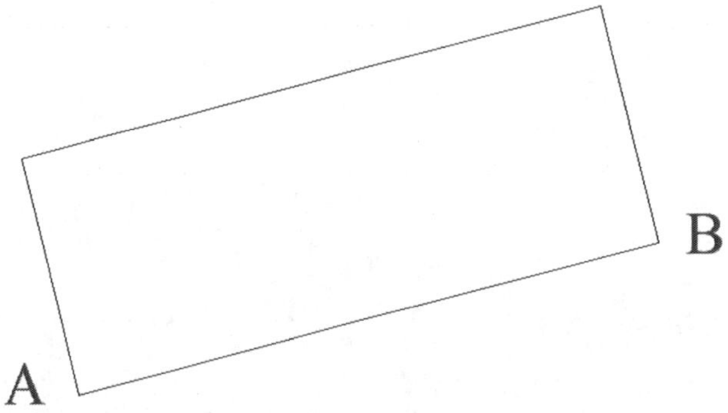

Solution

1. 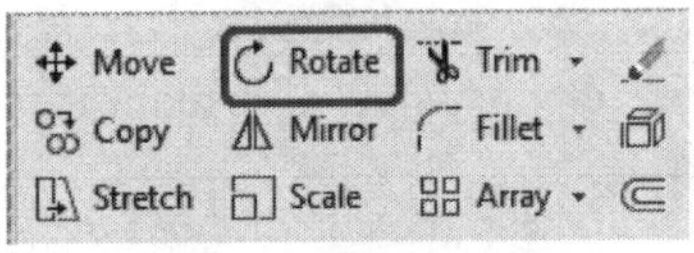

Invoke the Rotate command (rotate).

2. 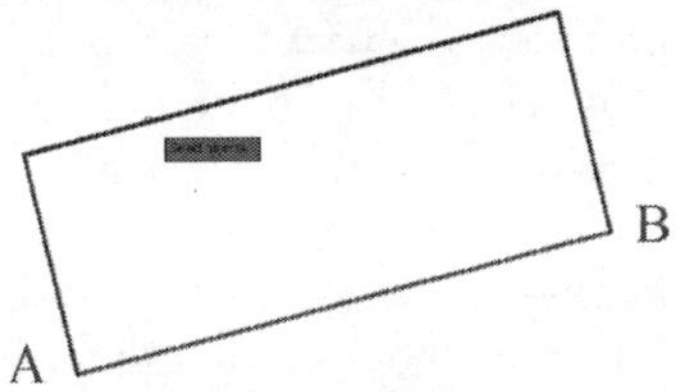

Select objects:
Select the rectangle with the LMB.

3. *Select objects:*
Close the selection set by Clicking <ENTER>.

4. 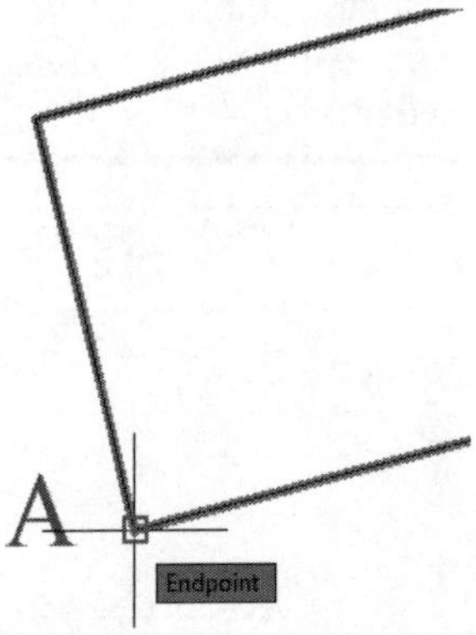

Specify base point:
Pick the lower left corner of the rectangle (A).
Remember to use Object Snaps.

5. 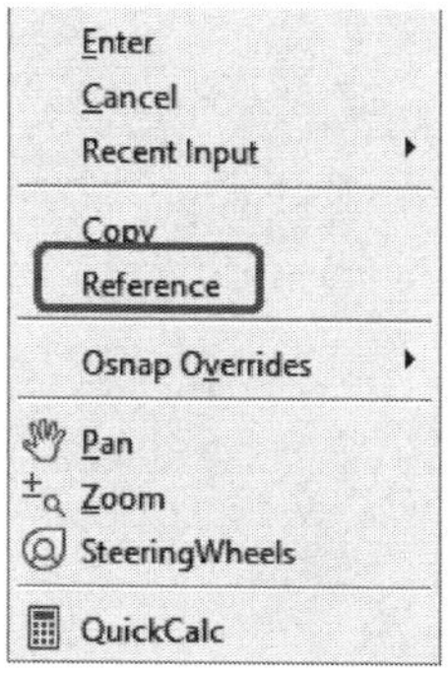

Specify rotation angle or [Reference]:
Right-click in the drawing area and select 'Reference' or type 'R' for Reference and Click <ENTER>.

6. 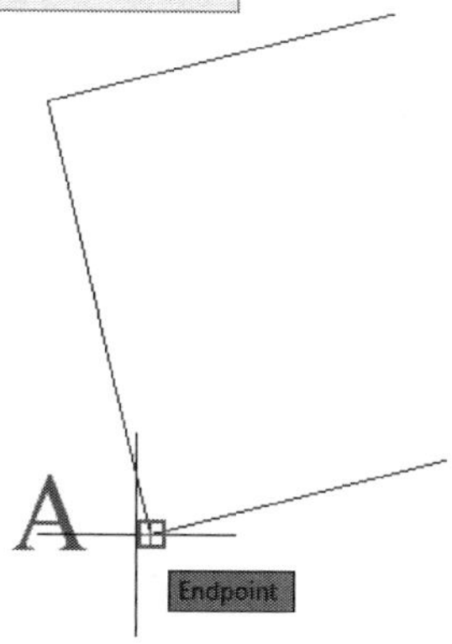

Specify the reference angle <0>:
Pick the same point on the rectangle (A).

7. 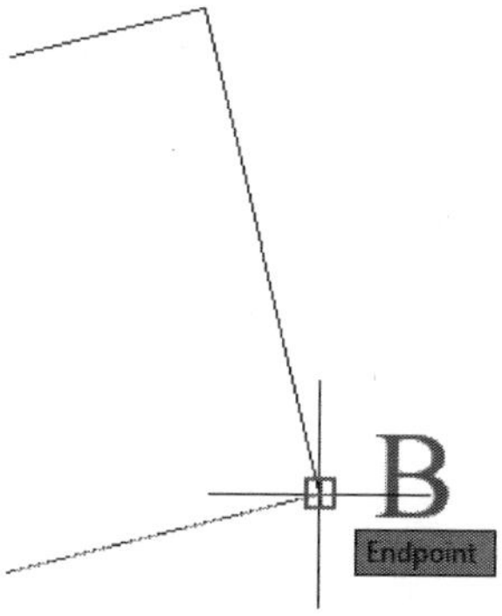

Specify second point:
Pick the lower right corner of the rectangle (B).

8. 

Specify the new angle or [Points] <0>:
Type '0' at the command line and Click <ENTER>.
(The Points option allows you to select two points to specify the new angle.)

9. 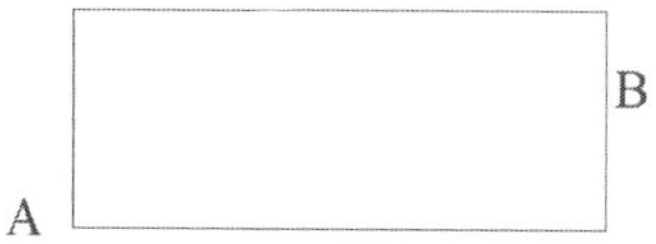

The rectangle is now horizontal.

Scale

Command Locator

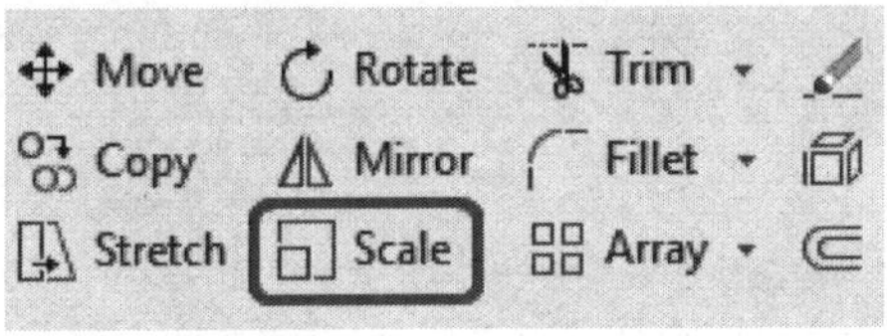

Home Ribbon	**Modify / Scale**
Command	**Scale**
Alias	**SC**
RMB Shortcut Menu	**Drawing Window**

Command Overview

Scale objects *up* or *down* from a selected base point. Use the Reference option to reference a known length, then type the new length to scale the object proportionately.

General Procedures

To use the Scale command:

1. Invoke the Scale Command.
2. Select the objects to Scale, and Click <ENTER>.
3. Pick a base point on or near the object.
4. Type the Scale Factor and Click <ENTER>.

To use the Scale command with the Reference option:

1. Invoke the Scale Command.
2. Select the objects to Scale, and Click <ENTER>.
3. Pick a base point on or near the object. Type R for reference (and Click <ENTER>), or Click the RMB and select Reference from the shortcut menu.
4. Use Object Snaps to specify the reference length, or type the reference length, if known.
5. Type the new length.

Command Exercise

Exercise 5-16 – Scale

Drawing Name: **scale1.dwg**
Estimated Time to Completion: 5 Minutes

Scope

Scale the images as indicated in the drawing.

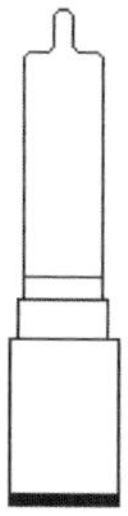

Scale Factor = **.5**

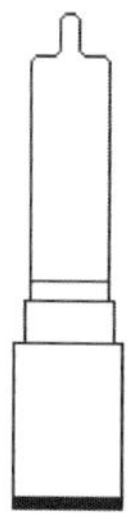

Scale Factor = **2**

Solution

1. 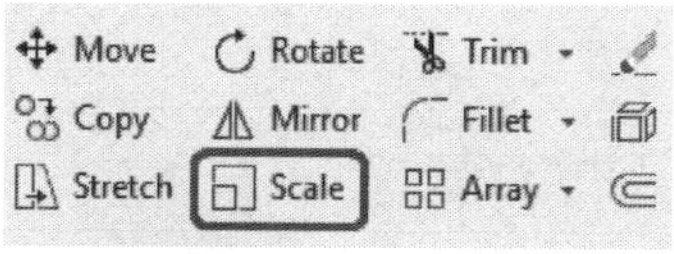

Invoke the Scale command (scale).

2. 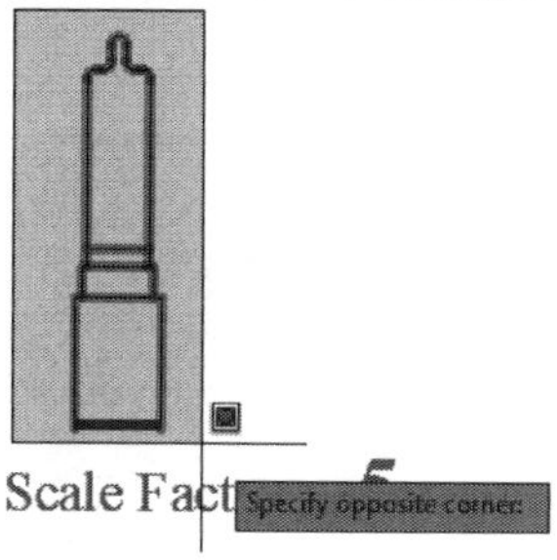

Select objects:
Use a window to select the objects that make up the part on the left.

Select objects:
Click <ENTER> to close the selection set.

3. 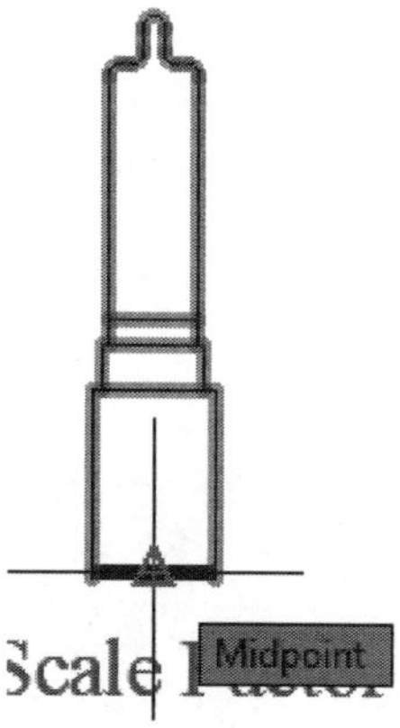

Specify base point:
Select a point near the base of the part.

Hint: Use the midpoint.

4. 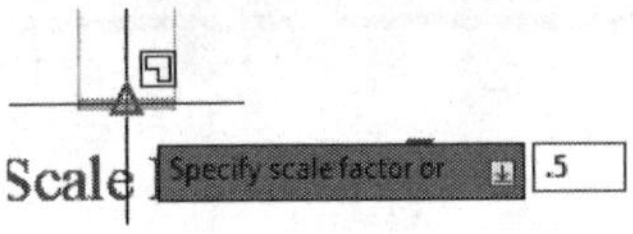

Specify scale factor or [Reference]:
Type **0.5** and Click <ENTER>.

5. 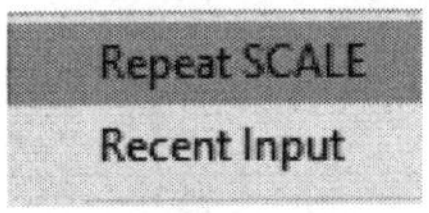

Repeat the Scale command with the RMB (scale or <ENTER>).

6. 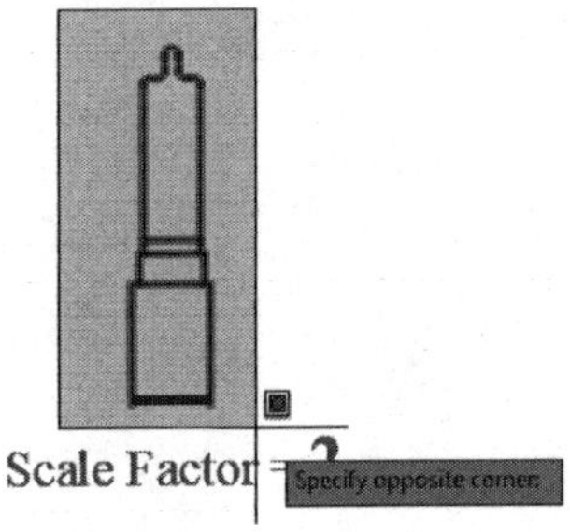

Select objects:
Use a window to select the objects that make up the part on the right.

Select objects:
Click <ENTER> to close the selection set.

7. 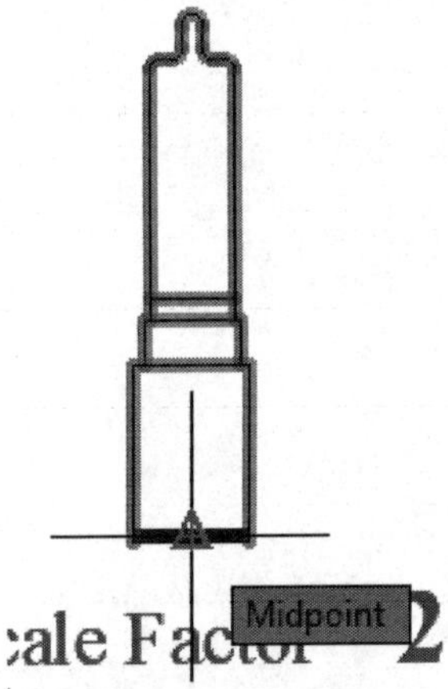

Specify base point:
Select a point near the base of the part.

8. 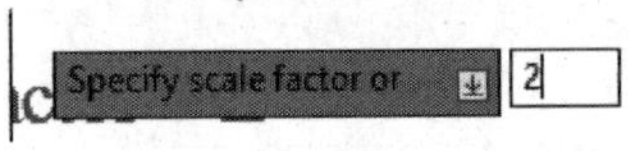

Specify scale factor or [Reference]:
Type **2** and <ENTER>.

- If you want to keep the original object even after changing the scale, then click on the "Copy" option from the command line when prompted for the scale factor.

Command Exercise

Exercise 5-17 – Scale Using Reference

Drawing Name: **scale2.dwg**
Estimated Time to Completion: 5 Minutes

Scope

Using the Reference option, scale the object so that the overall height is 4.

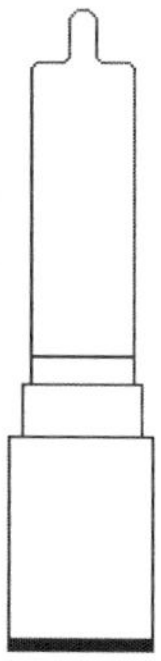

Scale Factor = **4**

Solution

1. 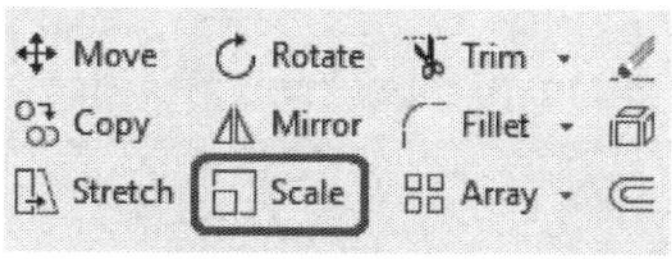

Invoke the Scale command (scale).

2. 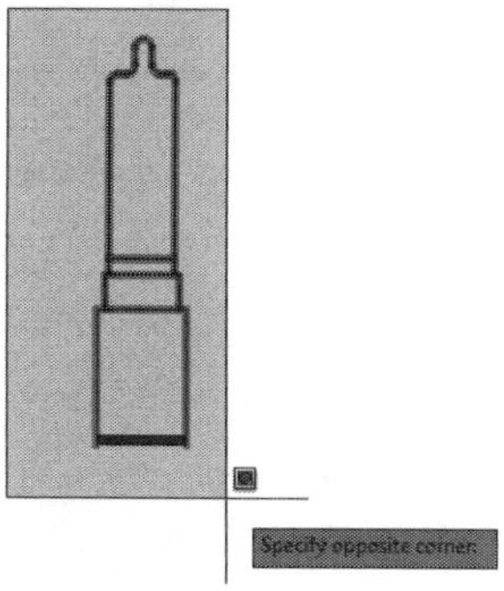

Select objects:
Use a window to select the objects that make up the part on the right.
Select objects:
Click <ENTER> to close the selection set.

3.

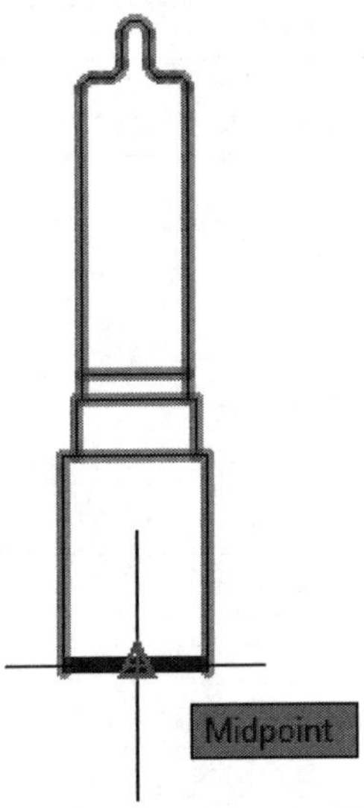

Specify base point:

Select the Midpoint of the base with the LMB. Remember to use the Object Snap.

4.

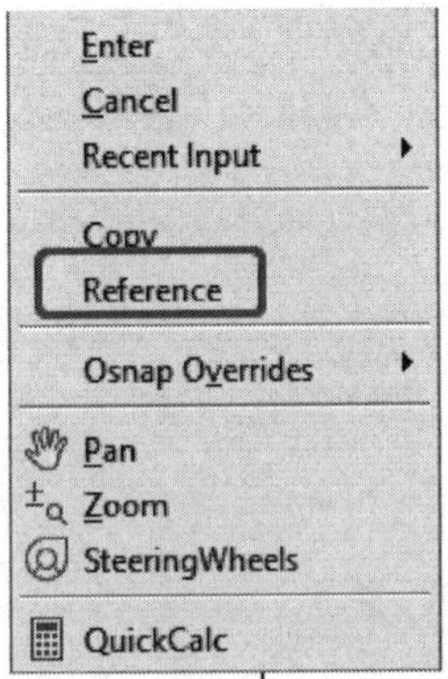

Specify scale factor or [Reference]:

Right-click in the drawing window and select **Reference** or type **R** for Reference and Click <ENTER>.

5.

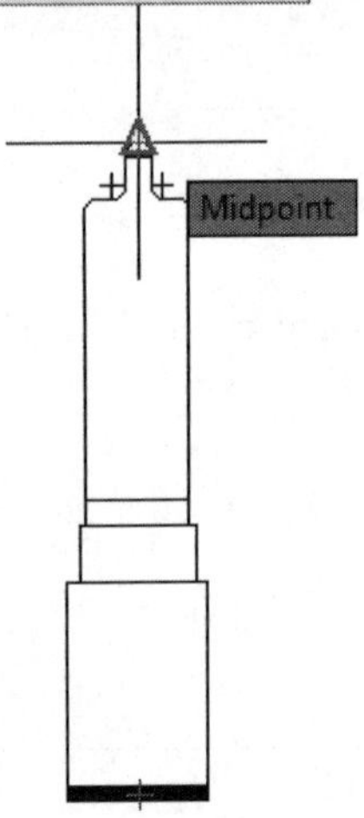

Specify reference length <1>:

Pick the Midpoint or Quadrant of the top with the LMB.

6.

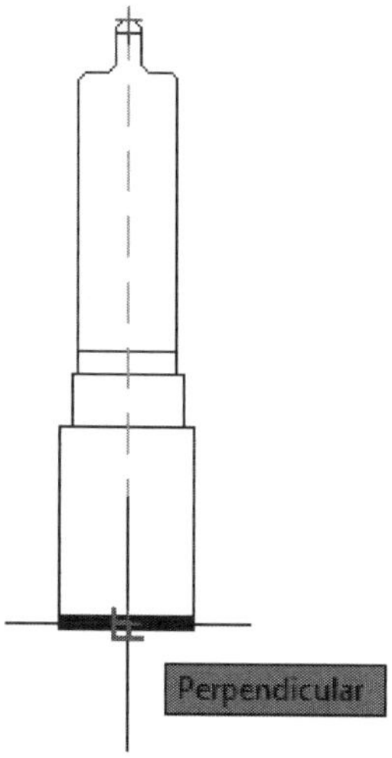

Specify second point:

Pick the Midpoint or Perpendicular to the bottom with the LMB. Remember to use the running object snap.

7.

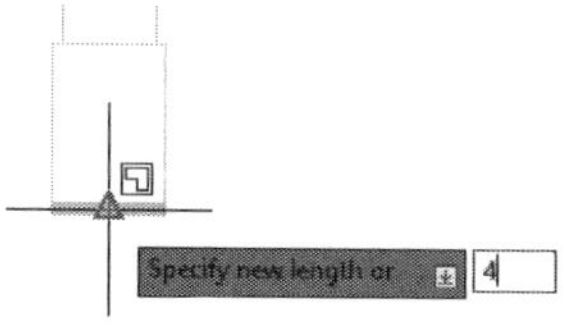

Specify new length:

Type **4** and Click <ENTER>.

Stretch

Command Locator

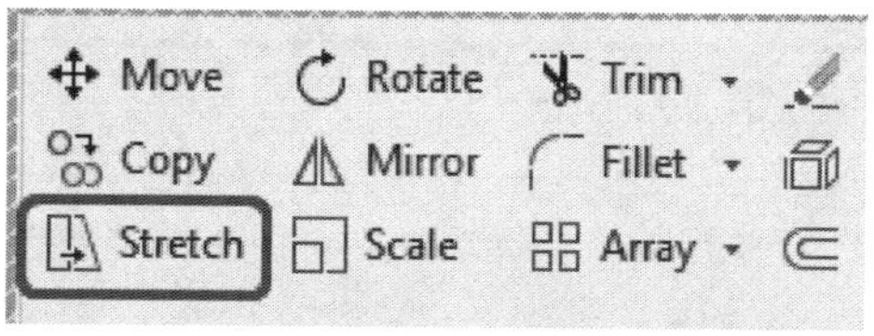

Home Ribbon	**Modify→Stretch**
Command	**Stretch**
Alias	**s**

Command Overview

Learning how to use the Stretch command is tricky at first. Always use a Crossing Window or Crossing Polygon to select the objects to stretch. The endpoints or vertices of the objects selected will be stretched, or *moved*, to a new location, while the objects outside of the selection window will remain anchored. Once the objects are selected, Click <ENTER> and pick a base point, then with ORTHO on, drag the object in the desired direction and type a distance.

General Procedures

1. Begin the Stretch command.
2. Select objects using the automatic Crossing Window option (right to left). Frame the object so that the endpoints to be moved are completely within the selection box.
3. Pick a base point on or near the object.
4. Select the second point of displacement, drag the object in the desired direction (with ORTHO on) and type the distance.

Tips & Tricks

Circles cannot be stretched with this command but can be stretched using grips (grips will be covered at the end of this chapter).

Objects that are completely within the selection window will be moved.

If a crossing window is not used, only the objects completely within the window will be moved, and not stretched.

Blocks cannot be stretched.

When selecting the Second point of displacement, use the direct distance method with ORTHO on. Drag the cursor in the desired direction and type the distance.

When selecting points (base point or second point of displacement), picking points with or without Object Snap, Relative Coordinates, or Polar Coordinates are all acceptable methods. However, the direct distance with ORTHO on works best.

Command Exercise

Exercise 5-18 – Stretch

Drawing Name: **stretch1.dwg**
Estimated Time to Completion: 5 Minutes

Scope

Use the crossing window option to select objects to stretch.

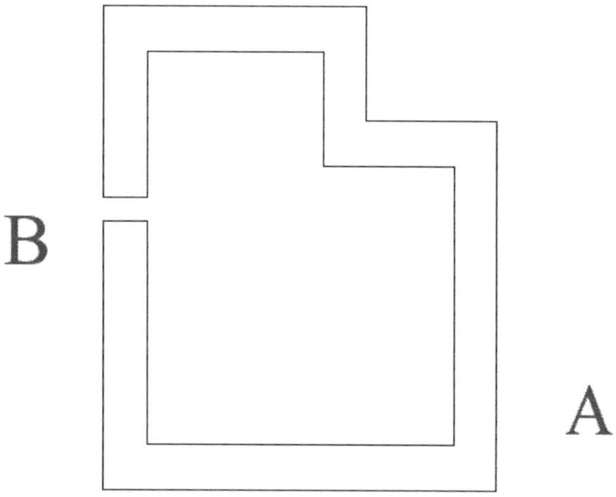

Solution

1. 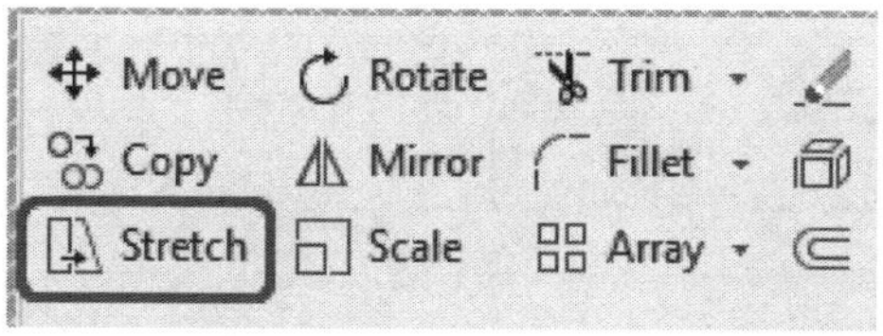

Invoke the Stretch command (stretch).

2. 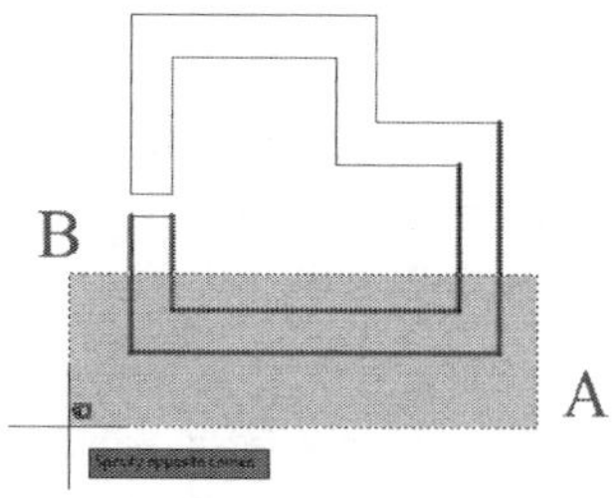

Select objects:
Use a crossing window to select the lower half of the object.

LMB at Point A then LMB at Point B.

Select objects:
Click <ENTER> to continue.

3. 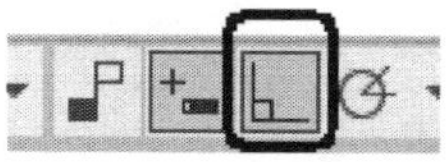

Turn ORTHO on.

4.

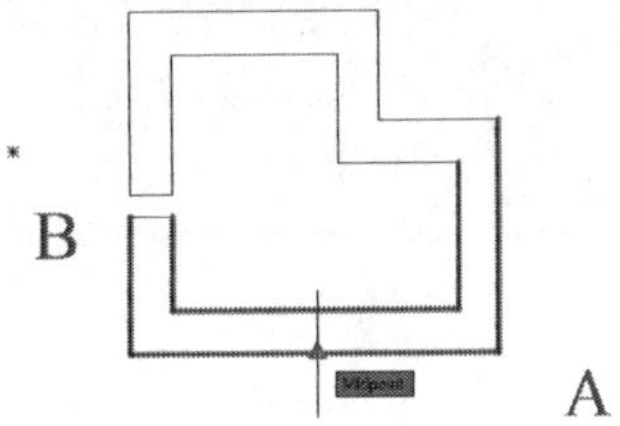

Specify base point or displacement:

Pick a point from which the part will be stretched with the LMB. ***(Hint:*** *Using the midpoint of the bottom horizontal line works well.)*

5.

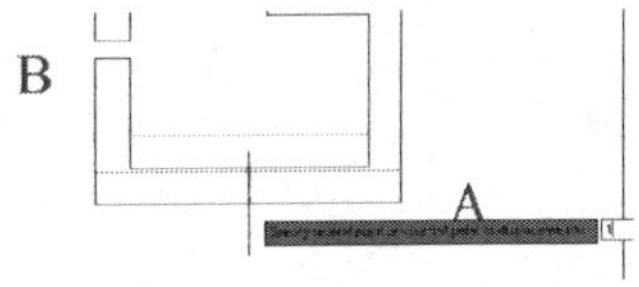

Specify second point of displacement:

Drag the mouse downward. Type '1' at the command line and Click <ENTER>.

Notice that the line segments that are fully contained in the crossing selection window are moved while the lines that are crossed are stretched.

Trim

Command Locator

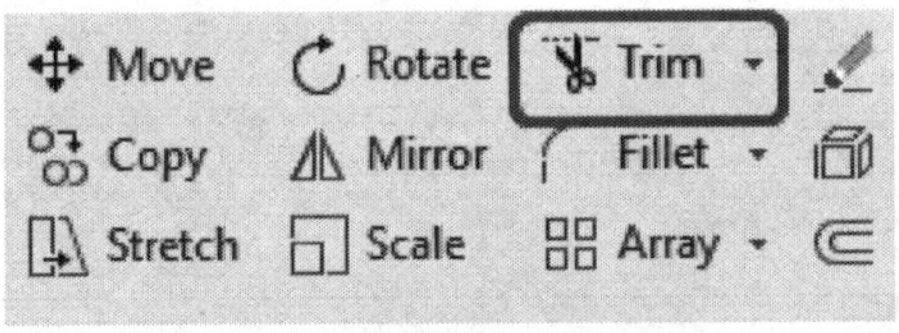

Home Ribbon	**Modify / Trim**
Command	**Trim**
Alias	**TR**
RMB Shortcut Menu	**Drawing Window**

Command Overview

Trim objects to a cutting edge. The cutting edge may or may not cross the object to trim. If the objects do not cross or intersect, the Edge mode must be set to "Extend." The Project option is for 3D. Undo is an option that can be used within the Trim command, without completely exiting the command.

Users are no longer required to select a cutting edge.

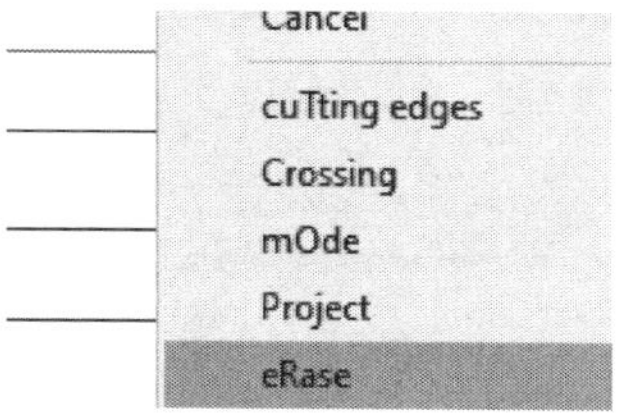

Trim Option	Overview
Cutting edges	*Allows users to specify which elements to use as cutting edges. If no cutting edge is selected, all elements in the drawing may be used as a cutting edge.*
Crossing	*The crossing option is used to designate the objects which are to be retained following the Trim operation.*
Mode	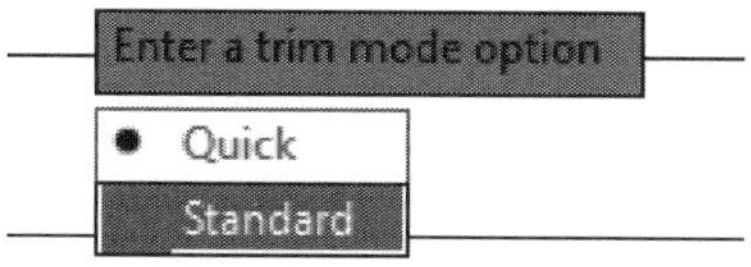 *If you select the Standard option, you can specify the cutting edges to be used for trimming. Otherwise, all elements in the drawing will be used as a cutting edge.*
Project	*The Project option is used when you are working in 3D space and you wish to trim using objects which may be at a different elevation or work plane.*
Erase	*Deletes selected objects – temporarily suspends the trim command to allow the user to erase unwanted objects and then returns to the Trim command.*

General Procedures

Regular Trim (No Extend):

1. Invoke the Trim command.
2. Select the objects to trim.

Trim using the Extend option:

1. Invoke the Trim command.
2. Type E (for Edge) and Click <ENTER>.
3. Type E (for Extend) and Click <ENTER>.
4. Select the objects to trim.

Tips & Tricks

An object must be crossed by the cutting edge to be trimmed (unless the Edge mode Extend option is selected and the object would cross the cutting edge if extended).

A circle must be crossed twice by the cutting edge in order to be trimmed.

- The object will be trimmed on the side of the cutting edge where it is selected.
- Selecting Multiple lines to trim is acceptable, such as lines that trim to each other.

Command Exercise

Exercise 5-19 – Trim

Drawing Name: **trim1.dwg**
Estimated Time to Completion: 5 Minutes

Scope

Trim the lines outside the red box and select the line individually. Repeat the exercise but select the lines to trim using the Fence (F) option.

Solution

1. 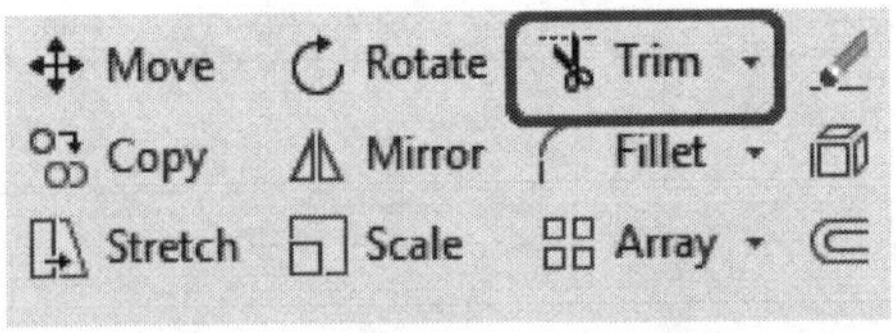

Invoke the Trim command (trim).

2. 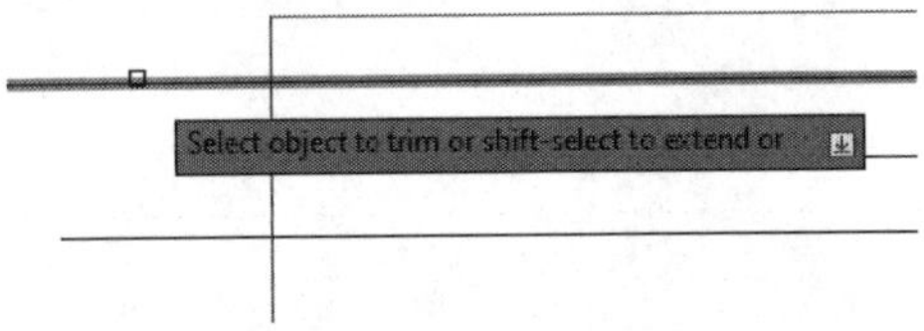

Select object to trim or [Project/Edge/Undo]:
Use the left mouse button to select the portion of the top black line that extends outside the left side of the red box.

3. 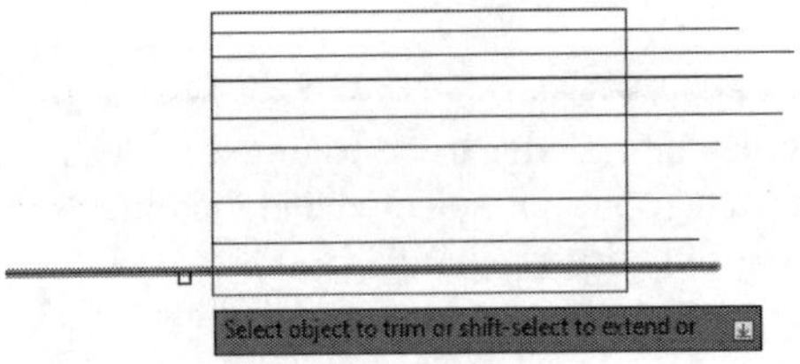

Select object to trim or [Project/Edge/Undo]:
Repeat the process for all the lines along the left side of the red box.

4. 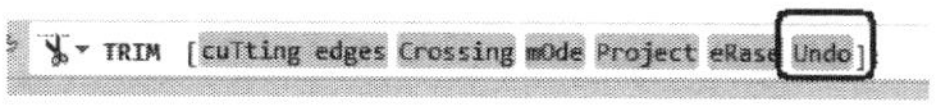

Click **Undo** on the command line.

Notice that the Undo only restores the last line trimmed, not all the lines that were trimmed.

5. 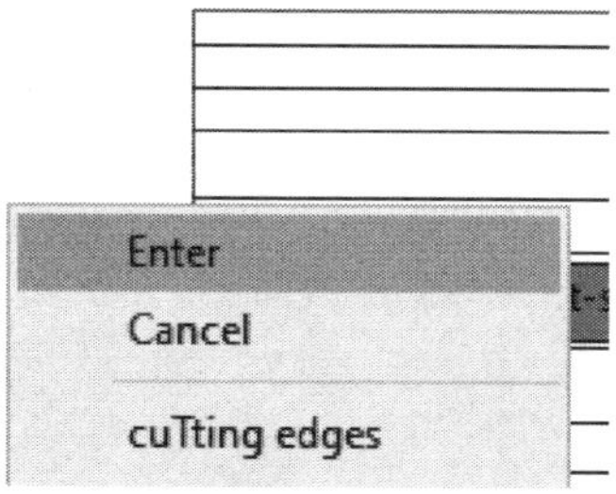

Click <ENTER> .

This exits the TRIM command.

6. 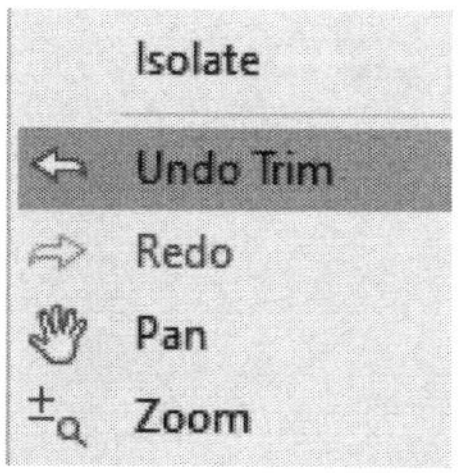

Right click and select **Undo Trim**.

Notice that this Undo restored all the trimmed lines.

7. 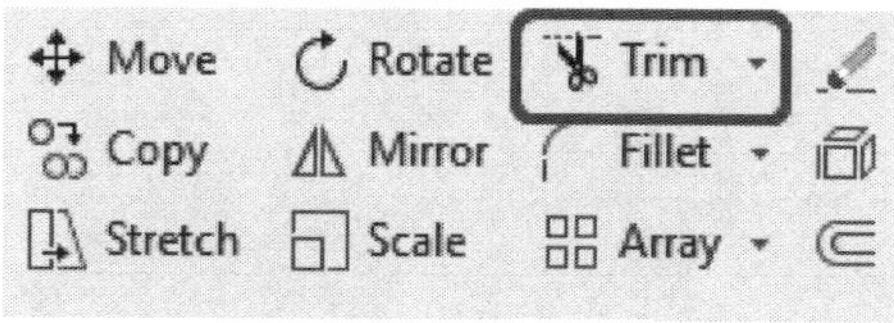

Invoke the Trim command (trim).

8. 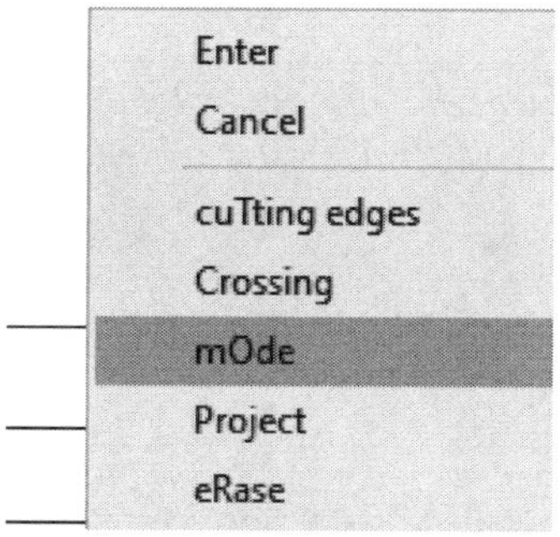

Right click and select **mOde**.

9. 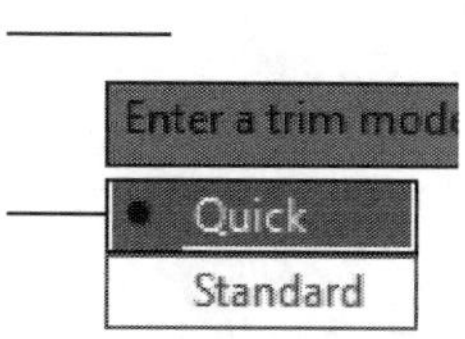

Select **Quick**.

10\. 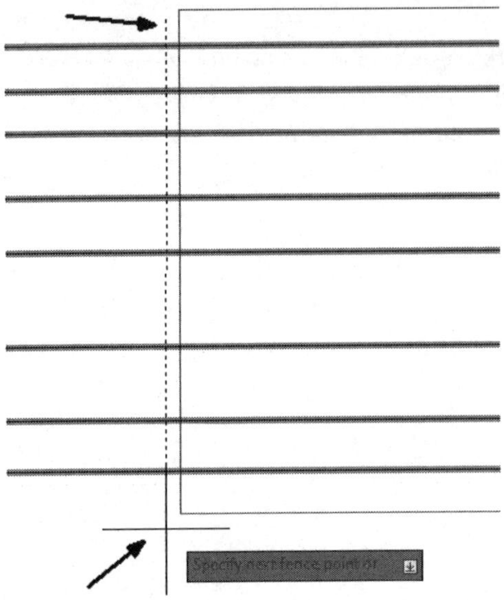

Click to select a point above the top line to be trimmed.

Trace a line straight down.

Click below the last line to complete the trim.

11\. 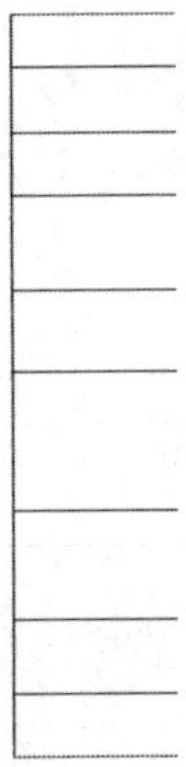

All the lines on the left side should be trimmed.

Note that you were automatically entered into 'fence' mode.

12\. 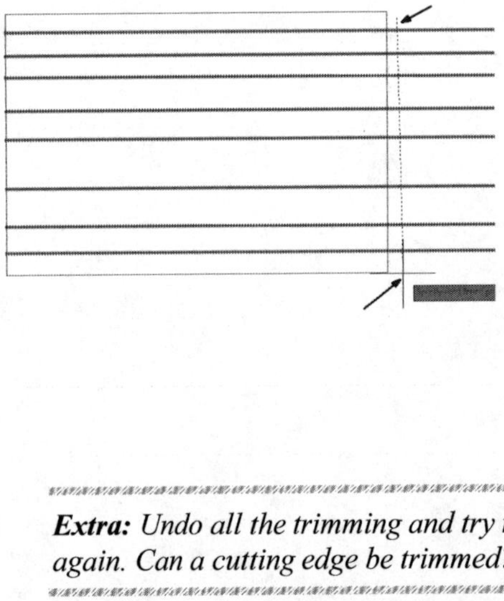

You should still be in the TRIM command. If not, you can simply REPEAT TRIM or select the TRIM tool.

Select a point on the right side above the line to be trimmed.

Trace a line down and select a point below the last line to be trimmed.
Click ENTER to exit the TRIM command.

Extra: *Undo all the trimming and try removing the lines inside the red box. Undo again. Can a cutting edge be trimmed? Try it. Trim the red rectangle and the lines.*

Extend

Command Locator

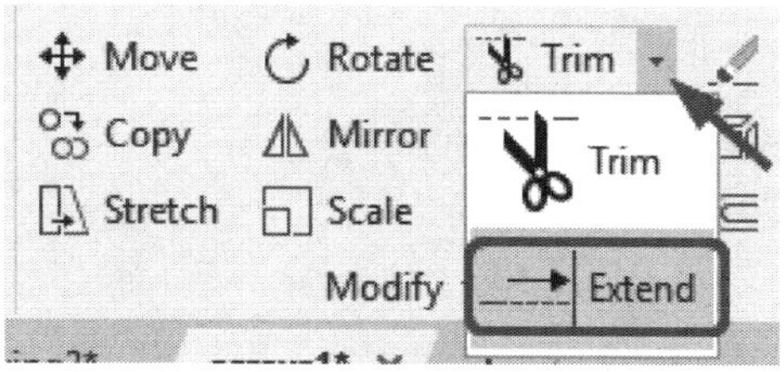

Home Ribbon	**Modify / Extend**
Command	**Extend**
Alias	**EX**
RMB Shortcut Menu	**Drawing Window**

Command Overview

Extend objects to a boundary by selecting the object towards the end to be extended. The boundary may or may not reach the object being extended. If the objects do not reach the boundary, the Edge mode must be set to "Extend." Typically, this option is set to "No Extend." The Project option is for 3D. Undo can be used as an option within the Extend command without completely exiting the command.

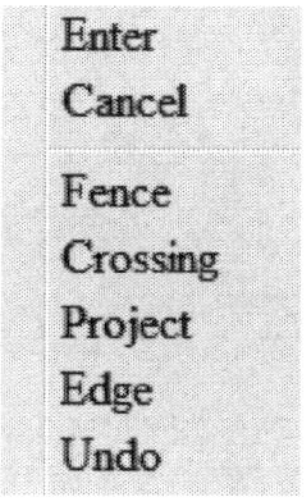

Extend Option	**Overview**
Fence	When this option is selected, the user draws an imaginary fence line that is used as the cutting edge.
Crossing	The crossing option is used to designate the objects which are to be retained following the Trim operation.
Project	The Project option is used when you are working in 3D space and you wish to trim using objects which may be at a different elevation or work plane.
Edge	The Edge object is also used when working in 3D space to designate either a projected edge or an edge which is actually intersecting the object to be trimmed.

General Procedures

Regular Extend (No Extend):

1. Invoke the Extend command.
2. Select the boundary edges, and Click <ENTER>.
3. Select the objects to extend towards the boundary edge.

Trim using the Extend option:

1. Invoke the Extend command.
2. Select the boundary edges, and Click <ENTER>.
3. Type E (for Edge) and Click <ENTER>.
4. Type E (for the Extend option) and Click <ENTER>.
5. Select the objects to extend towards the boundary edge.

- The Undo option will undo one step at a time without exiting the Extend command.
- An object must be able to meet the boundary edge to be trimmed (unless the Edge mode Extend option is selected and the object would meet the boundary edge if extended).
- Select the object to Extend anywhere on the half that is closest to the boundary.
- You can extend arcs to a boundary.

Command Exercise

Exercise 5-20 – Extend

Drawing Name: **extend1.dwg**
Estimated Time to Completion: 5 Minutes

Scope

Extend the black elements to the sides of the red rectangle.

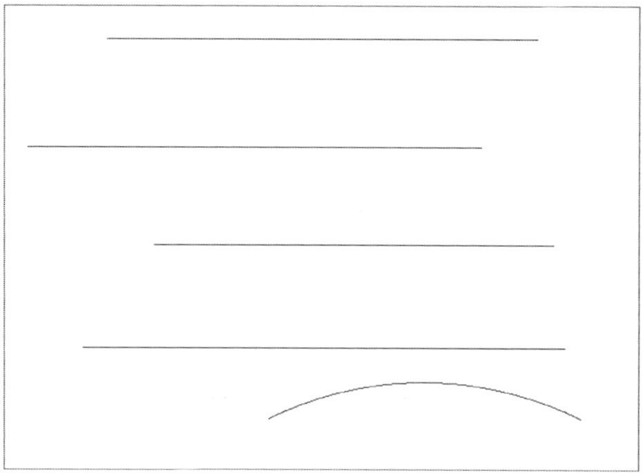

Solution

1. 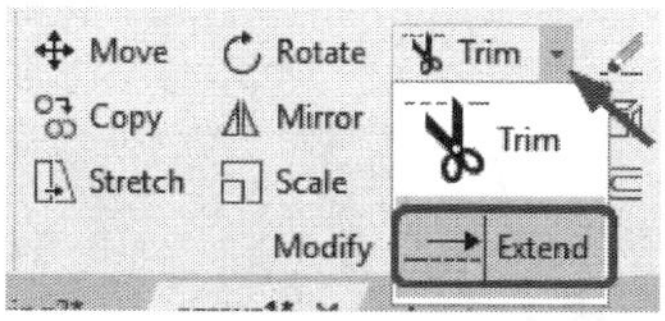

Invoke the Extend command (extend).

2. 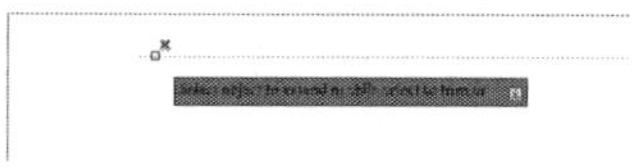
Select object to extend or [Project/Edge/Undo]:
Pick on the left side of the top black line.
Notice that the line extends from the side of the line you have selected.

3. 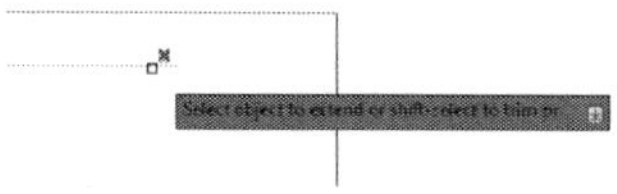
Select object to extend or [Project/Edge/Undo]:
Pick the other side of the same line.

4. 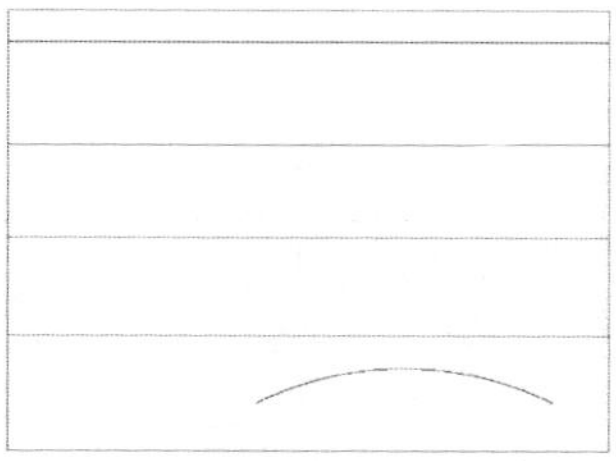
Select object to extend or [Project/Edge/Undo]:
Repeat the process with the rest of the lines.

Try clicking a point above and below the objects to be extended.

5. 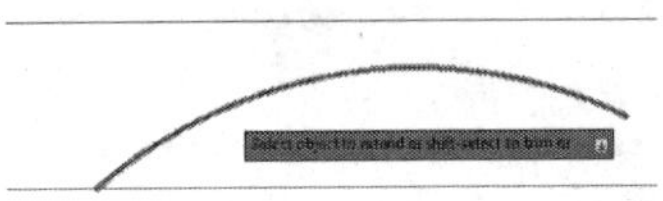

Select the left end of the arc to extend to the bottom horizontal line of the red outline.

6. 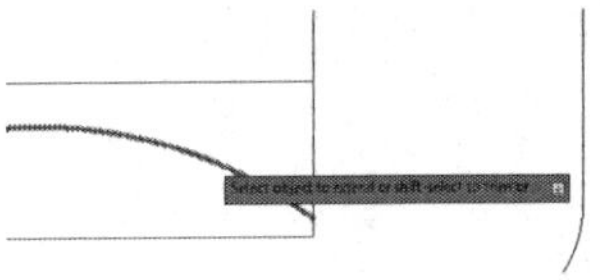

Select the right end of the arc to extend to the right vertical line of the red outline.

Exit the command by clicking ESC.

Extra: *Create a line segment that is outside the red box. Start the Extend command and use the red box as the boundary edge. Extend the line to the outside of the rectangle and then extend the line through the rectangle to the opposite side.*

Fillet

Command Locator

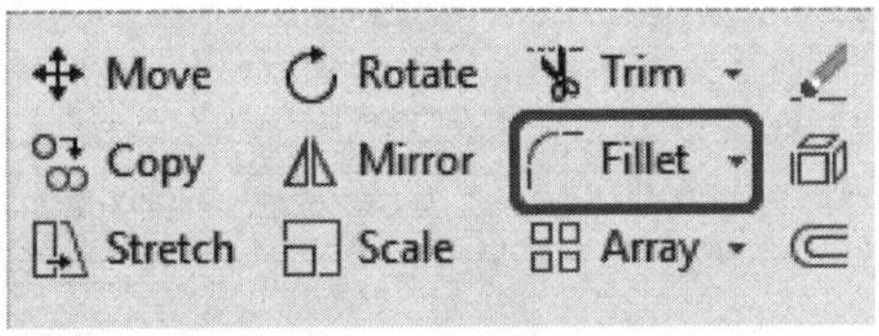

Home Ribbon	**Modify / Fillet**
Command	**Fillet**
Alias	**F**
RMB Shortcut Menu	**Drawing Window**

Command Overview

Radius corners with the FILLET command. Clean up corners with the Fillet radius set to 0.

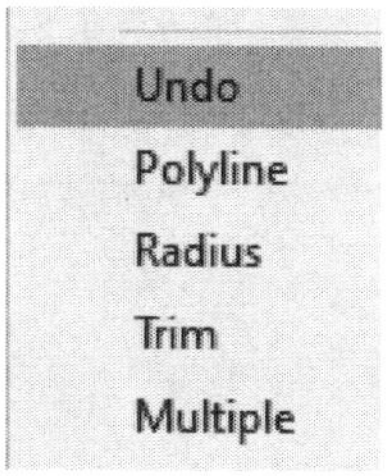

Fillet Option	Overview
Undo	Reverses the fillet that was just placed.
Polyline	Type P to fillet all of the corners of a polyline at once.
Radius	Type R to change the Radius of the fillet. This setting remains until it is changed again. The default radius setting when starting a new drawing is .50.
Trim	Type T to invoke the Trim or No Trim options. No trim (N) will leave the original lines when making a fillet.
Multiple	Type M to create more than one fillet. Works similar to the Multiple option of the Copy command.

General Procedures

1. Begin the Fillet command.
2. To change the current radius, type R (and <ENTER>). Type the desired radius (and <ENTER>). Click <ENTER> to repeat to the Fillet command.
3. Select the first object, then select the second object.

It is not necessary to set the radius to fillet parallel lines.
Fillet can be used on any lines or arcs that are separate polylines, or at the arc intersections of polylines.
Set a Radius value of 0 to create a 90-degree angle and trim corners.
You cannot select all of the segments in one step. You must repeat the fillet command for each corner, unless the object is a polyline and the Fillet command is used with the Polyline option.

Command Exercise

Exercise 5-21 – Fillet

Drawing Name: **fillet1.dwg**
Estimated Time to Completion: 5 Minutes

Scope

Use the fillet command with a fillet radius of 0 to clean up the corners of the lines as indicated. Remember to change the fillet radius first.

Solution

1. 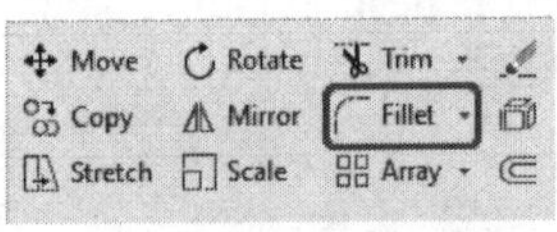

Invoke the Fillet command (f or fillet).

2. 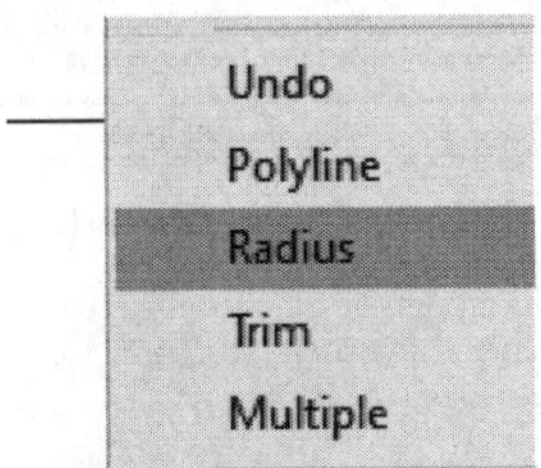

Select first object or [Polyline/Radius/Trim]:
Right-click in the drawing window and select 'Radius' or type 'R' for Radius and Click <ENTER>.

3. 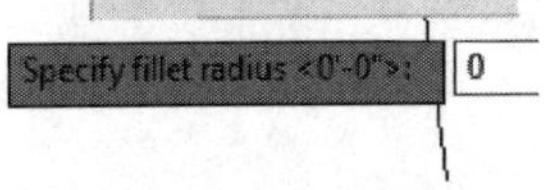

Specify fillet radius <0.5000>:
Type '0' and Click <ENTER>.

4. 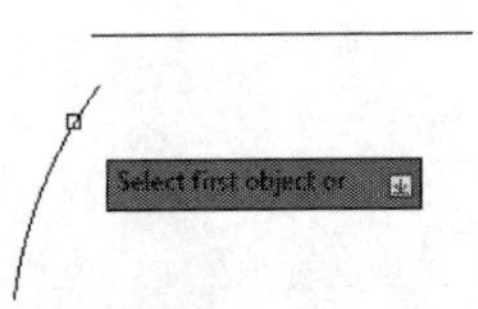

Select first object or [Polyline/Radius/Trim]:
Use the LMB to select the arc.

5. 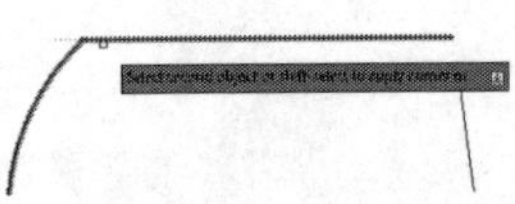

Select second object:
Use the LMB to select the top line segment.

6. 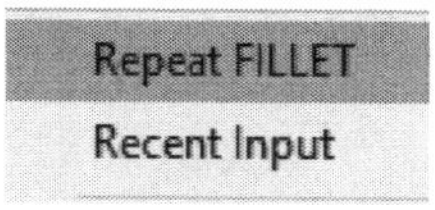

Repeat the Fillet command with the RMB (f, fillet or <ENTER>).

7. 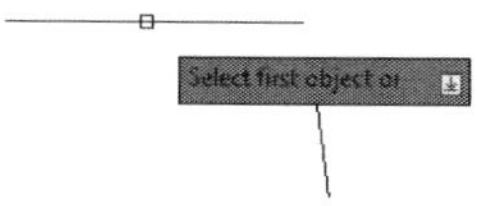

Select first object or [Polyline/Radius/Trim]:
Select the top line with the LMB.

8. 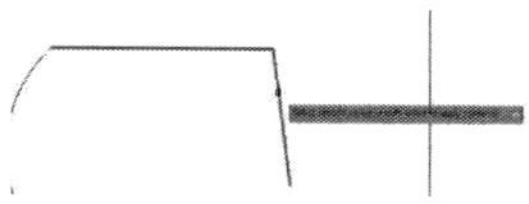

Select second object:
Pick the line on the right side with the LMB.

9. 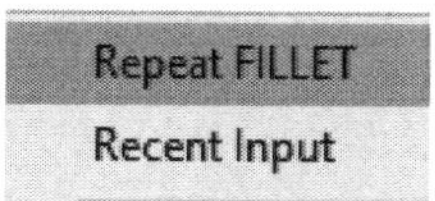

Repeat the Fillet command with the RMB (f, fillet or <ENTER>).

10. 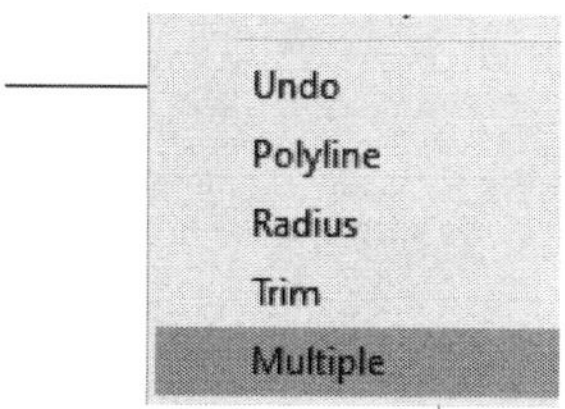

Right click and select **Multiple**.

11. 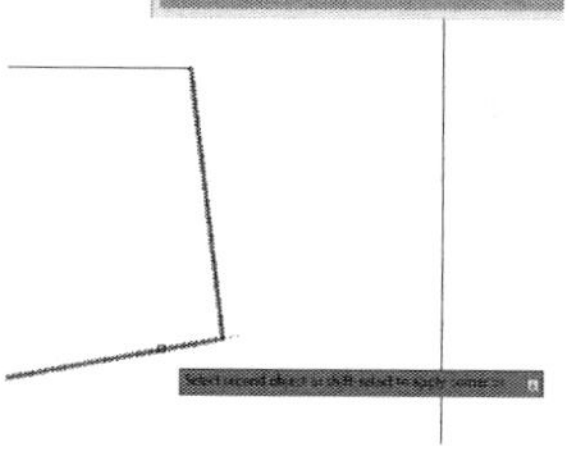

Add a fillet to the right lower corner.

12. 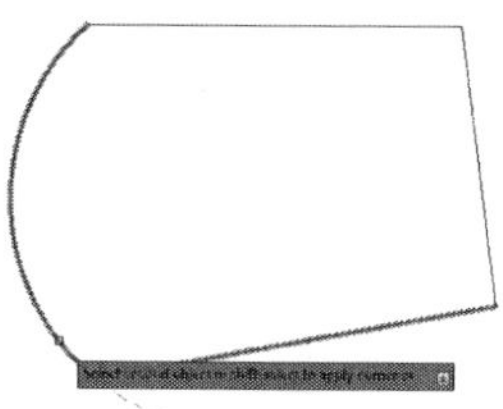

Add a fillet to the left lower corner.

Notice that the fillet command re-started without you having to invoke it.

Command Exercise

Exercise 5-22 – Fillet a Polyline

Drawing Name: **fillet2.dwg**
Estimated Time to Completion: 5 Minutes

Scope

Use the fillet command with a fillet radius of .25 to add a radius to a polyline.

Solution

1. 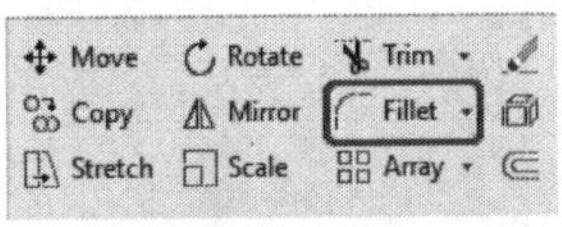

Invoke the Fillet command (f or fillet).

2. 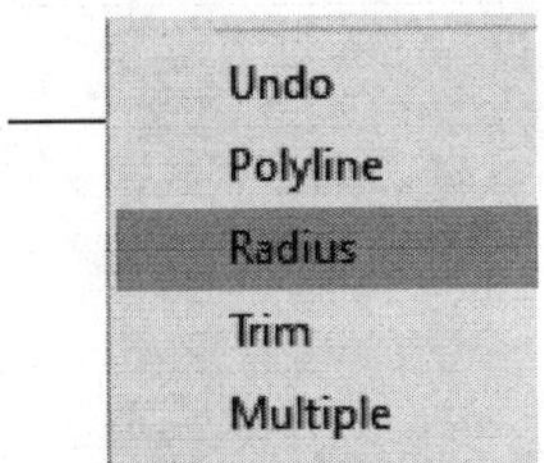

Select first object or [Polyline/Radius/Trim]:
Right-click in the drawing window and select 'Radius' or type 'R' for Radius and Click <ENTER>.

3. 

Type **.25** for the radius value.

4. 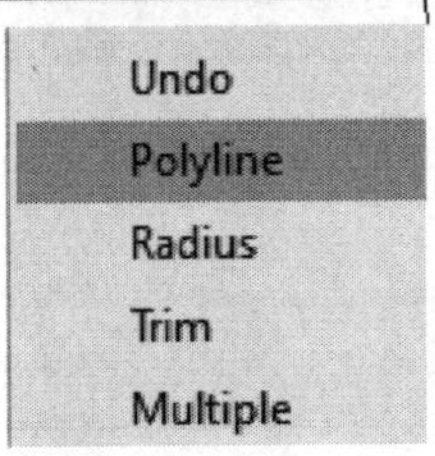

Right click and select **Polyline**.

5. 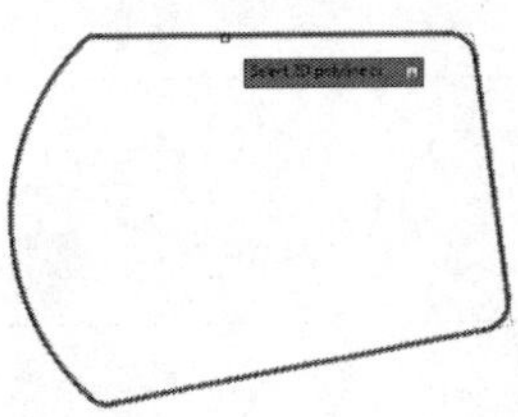

Select the right polyline.

It will preview what it will look like with the fillets.

Chamfer

Command Locator

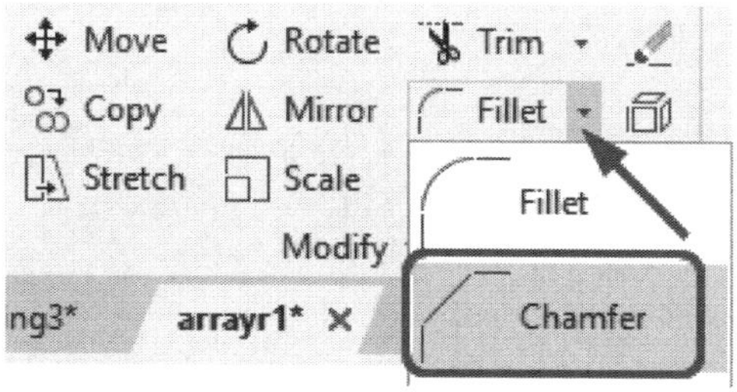

Home Ribbon	**Modify / Chamfer**
Command	**Chamfer**
Alias	**CHA**
RMB Shortcut Menu	**Drawing Window**

Command Overview

Chamfer is used to add a beveled edge to a corner.

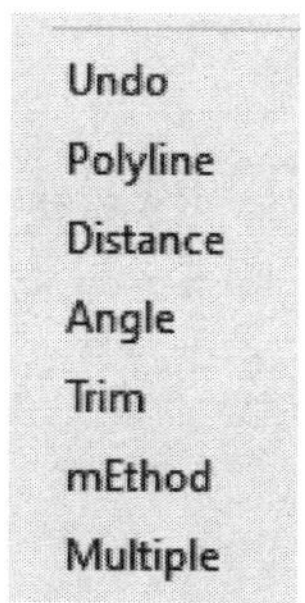

Chamfer Option	Overview
Undo	Reverses the chamfer that was just placed.
Polyline	Type P to chamfer all of the corners of a polyline at once.
Distance	Type D to change the distance of the chamfer. This setting remains until it is changed again. The distance is measured from the edge. You can set different distances for the two sides of the chamfer.
Angle	Type A to set the angle of the chamfer. This setting remains until it is changed again.
Trim	Type T to invoke the Trim or No Trim options. No trim (N) will leave the original lines when making a chamfer.
Method	Allows you to switch between using a distance or angle to place the chamfer.

Multiple	Type M to create more than one chamfer. Works similar to the Multiple option of the Copy command.

General Procedures

1. Begin the Chamfer command.
2. To change the current distance, type D (and <ENTER>). Type the desired distance (and <ENTER>). Click <ENTER> to repeat to the Chamfer command.
3. Select the first object, then select the second object.

Chamfers can be added to lines or polylines, not arcs or splines. You cannot select all of the segments in one step. You must repeat the chamfer command for each corner, unless the object is a polyline and the chamfer command is used with the Polyline option.

Command Exercise

Exercise 5-23 – Chamfer

Drawing Name: **chamfer1.dwg**
Estimated Time to Completion: 5 Minutes

Scope

Use the chamfer command to add a bevel to a rectangle. Use the No Trim option to retain the corners.

Solution

1.

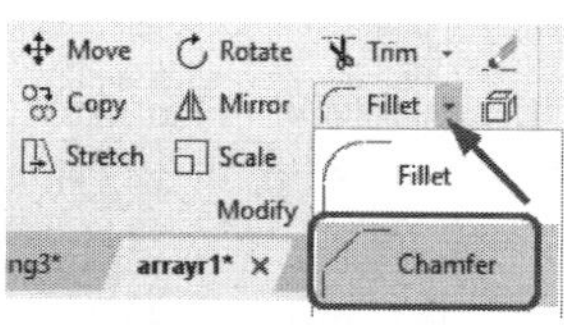

Invoke the Chamfer command (CHA or chamfer).

2.

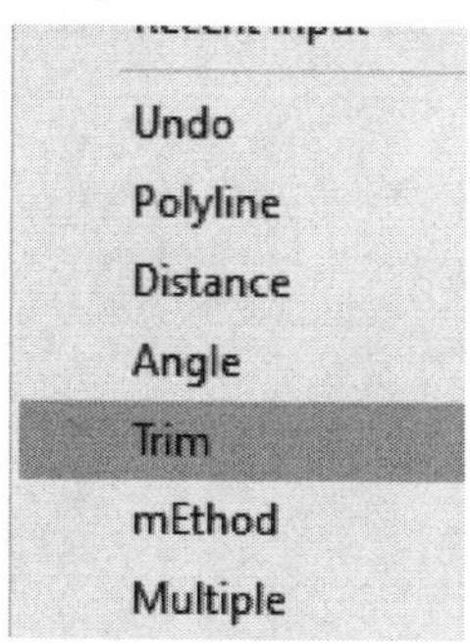

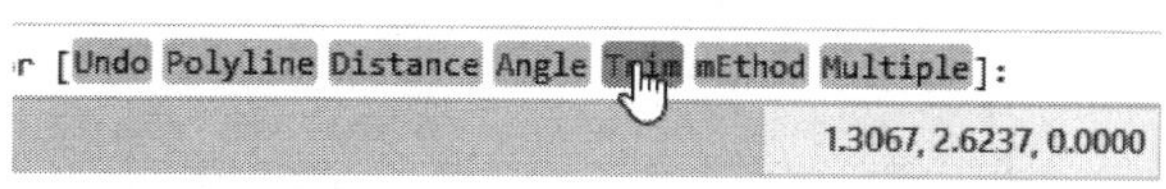

Select first line or [Undo/Polyline/Distance/Angle/Trim/Method/ Multiple]:

Right-click in the drawing window and select 'Trim' or type 'T' for Trim or click on the Trim option on the command line.

3.

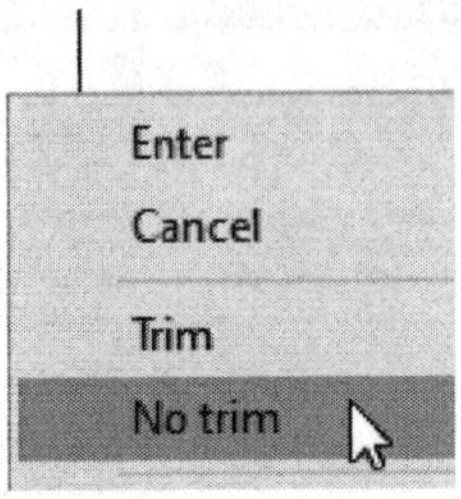

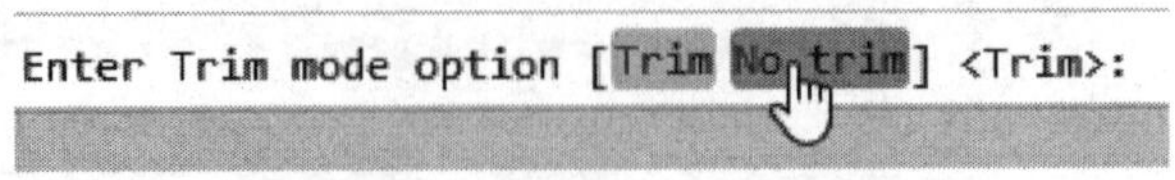

Right-click in the drawing window and select 'No Trim' or click on the No Trim option on the command line.

4.

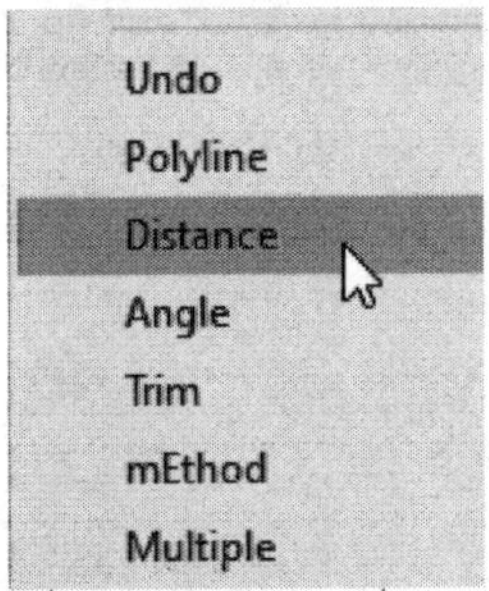

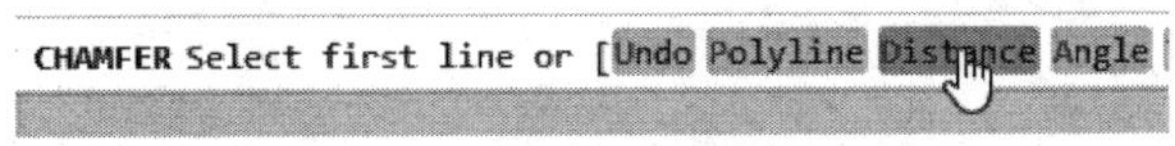

Right-click in the drawing window and select 'Distance' or type 'D' or click on the Distance option on the command line.

5.

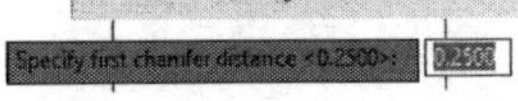

Specify first chamfer distance <0.25>

Type .25 for the first chamfer distance.

6.

Specify second chamfer distance <0.25>

Type .125 for the second chamfer distance.

Click <ENTER>.

7.

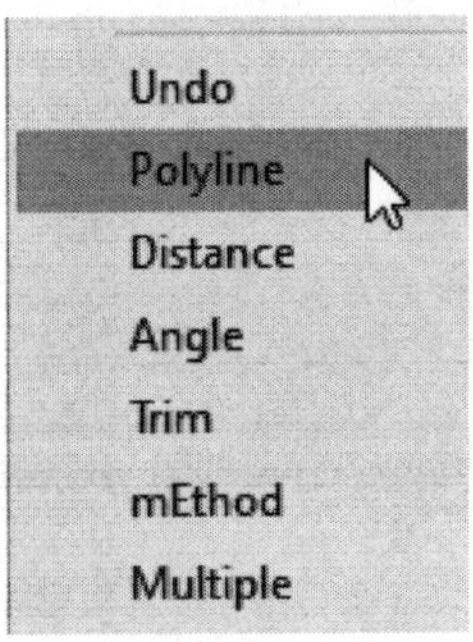

Select first line or [Undo/Polyline/Distance/Angle/Trim/Method/ Multiple]:

Right-click in the drawing window and select 'Polyline' or type 'P' or click on the Polyline option on the command line.

8.

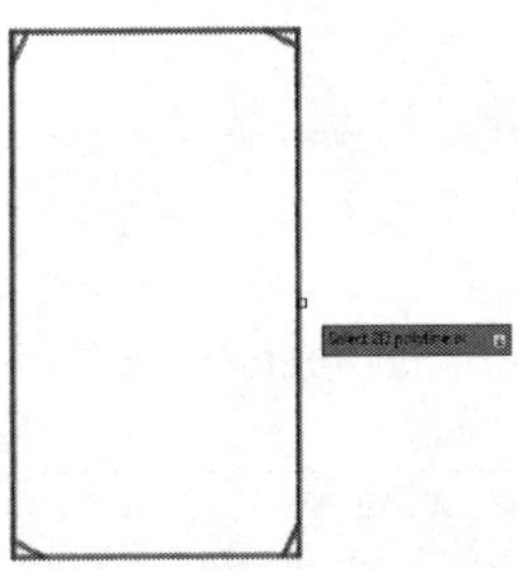

Select the rectangle to add the chamfer.

Notice how the chamfer is rotated as you go around the polyline.

Blend Curves

Command Locator

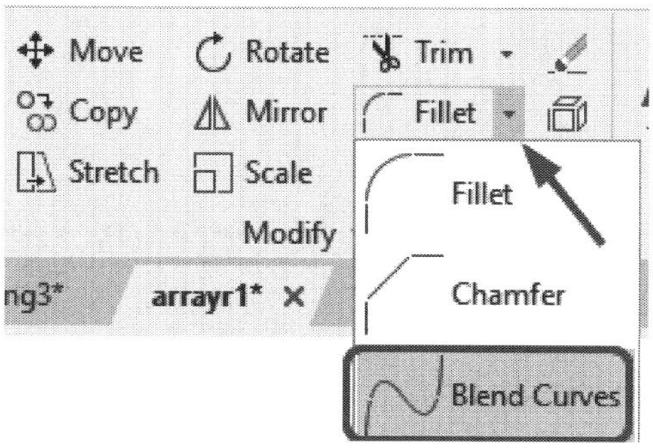

Home Ribbon	**Modify / Blend Curves**
Command	**Blend**
RMB Shortcut Menu	**Drawing Window**

Command Overview

Blend is used to add a spline between arcs, lines, or splines to blend them together. The length of the pre-existing lines/arcs/splines is not changed. The shape of the placed spline depends on the mode of continuity – whether it is set to tangent or smooth.

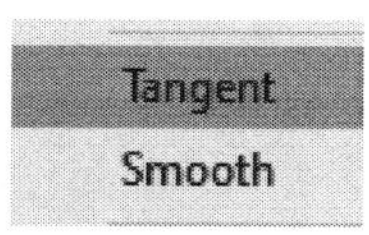

Blend Option	Overview
Tangent	Adds a spline that is tangent to both selected objects.
Smooth	Adds a spline that is smooth between both selected objects.

General Procedures

1. Begin the Blend command.
2. To determine the continuity of the added spline, right click and select Continuity.
3. Select Tangent or smooth to determine whether the spline will be tangent to both objects or smooth.
4. Select the first object, then select the second object.

Command Exercise

Exercise 5-24 – Blend

Drawing Name: **blend1.dwg**
Estimated Time to Completion: 10 Minutes

Scope

Use the Blend command to add splines to other elements, like arcs and lines, to create an enclosed area.

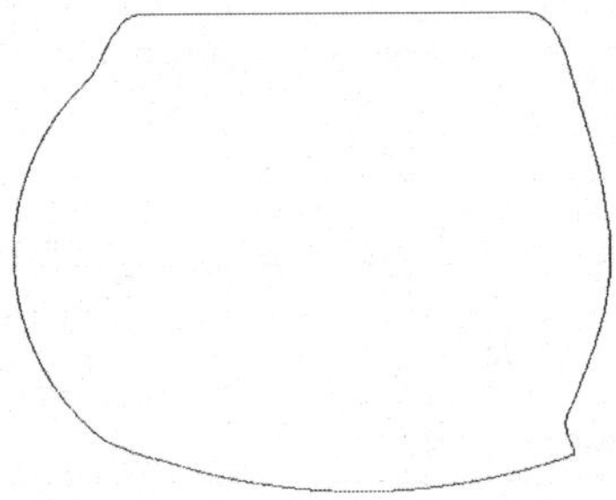

Solution

1.

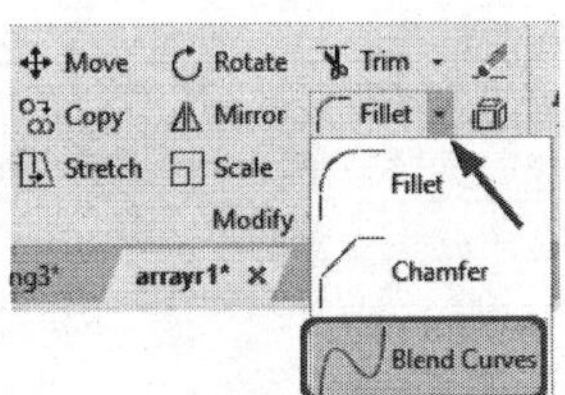

Invoke the **Blend Curves** command.

2.

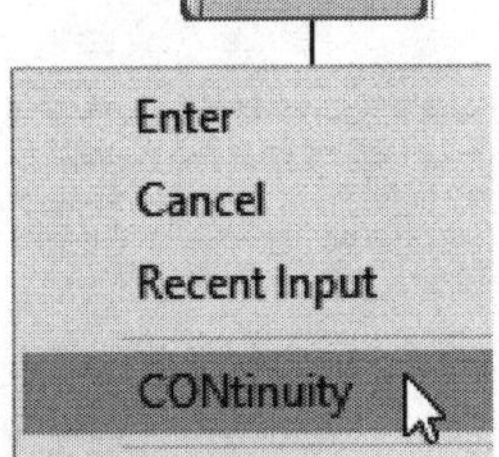

Right click and select **CONtinuity**.

3.

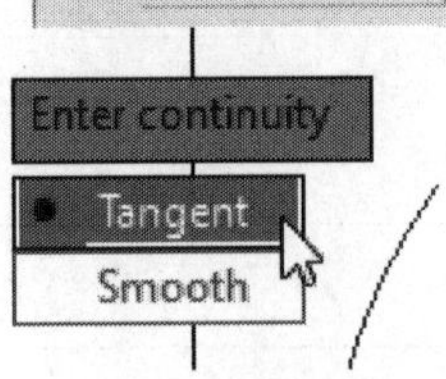

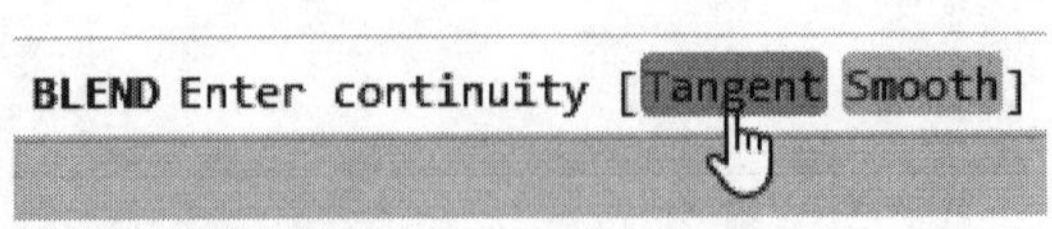

Enable **Tangent**.

4.

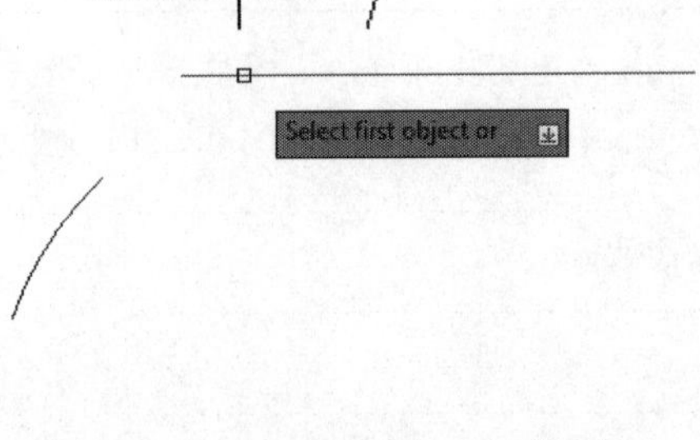

Select first object or:
Select near the left end of the horizontal line.

5.

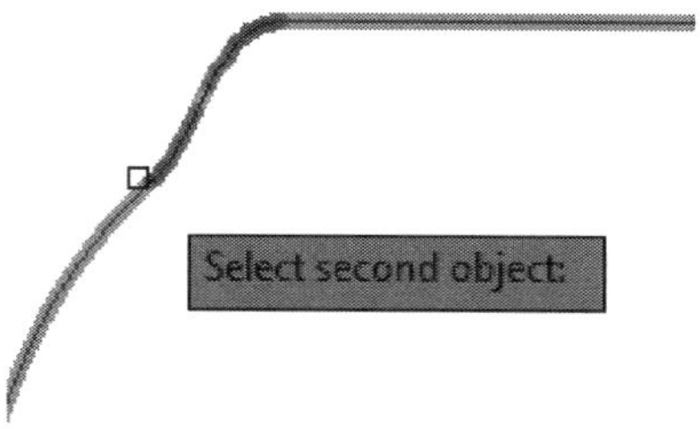

Select second object:
Select near the top end of the left arc.

6.

Right click to **Repeat Blend**.

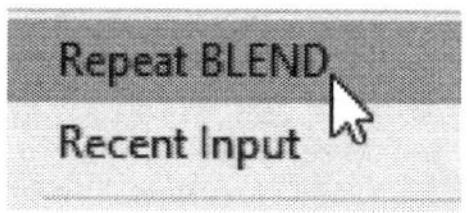

7.

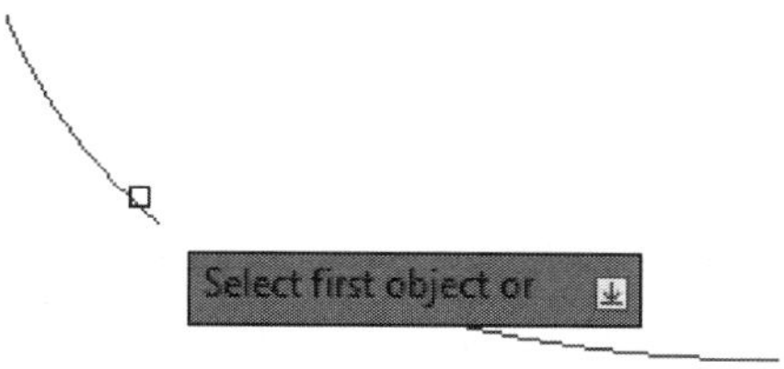

Select first object or:
Select near the bottom end of the left arc.

8.

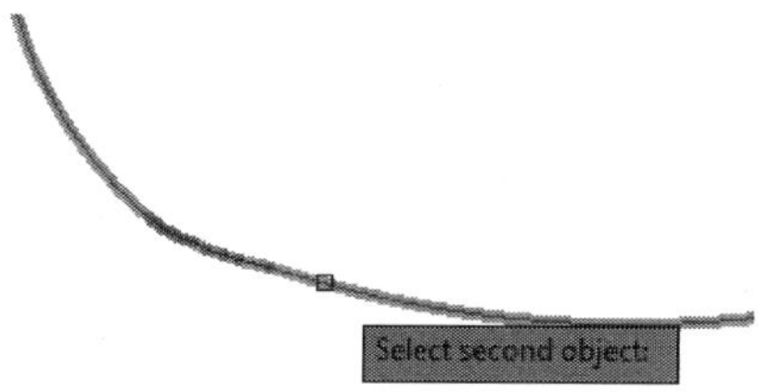

Select second object:
Select near the left side of the bottom arc.

9.

Right click to **Repeat Blend**.

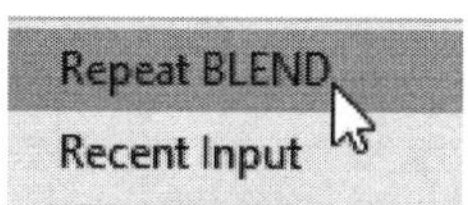

10.

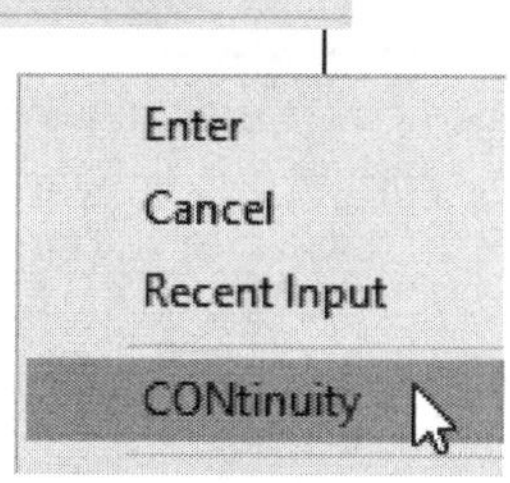

Right click and select **CONtinuity**.

11.

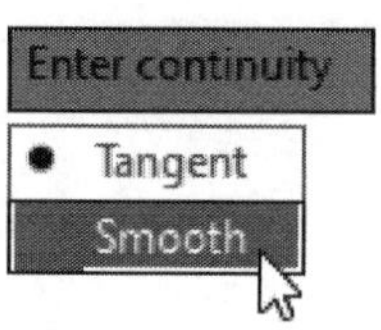

Enable **Smooth**.

12.

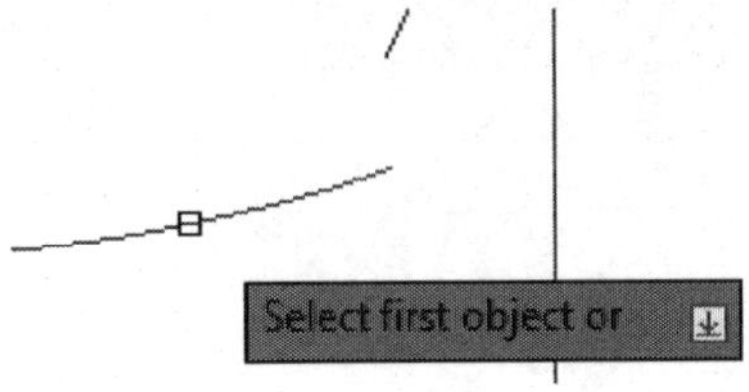

Select first object or:
Select near the right end of the bottom arc.

13.

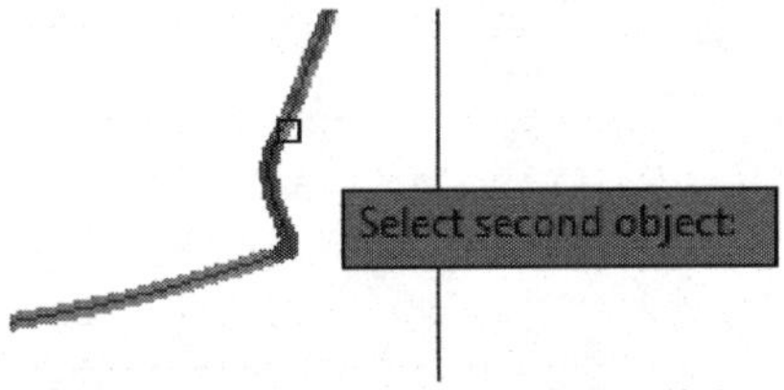

Select second object:
Select near the bottom end of the right spline.

14.

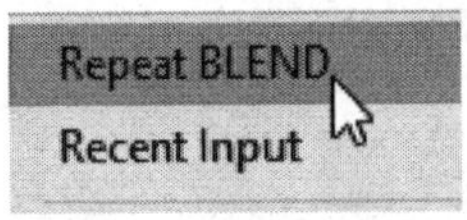

Right click to **Repeat Blend**.

15.

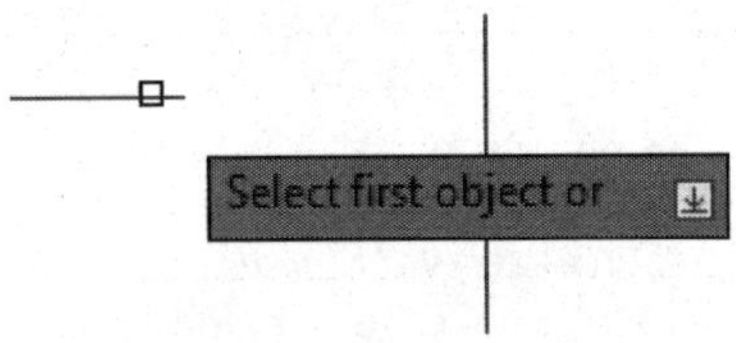

Select first object or:
Select near the right end of the horizontal line.

16.

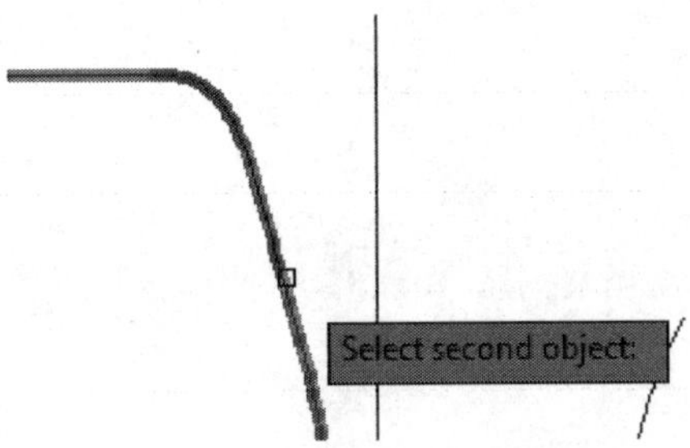

Select second object:
Select near the top end of the spline.

Tips & Tricks

- Blended curves are useful when creating toposurfaces or landscaping elements.
- In order to add a blended curve to a circle, trim out the circle to change it to an arc.

Undo and Redo

Command Locator

Home Ribbon	**Edit / Undo and Edit / Redo**
Command	**Undo or Redo**
Alias	**U (no alias for redo)**
RMB Shortcut Menu	**Drawing Window (for Undo options)**
Shortcut Keys	**Ctrl+Z for Undo, Ctrl+Y for Redo**

Command Overview

Type U for undo or select the button in the Standard Toolbar. This will reverse previous commands. Undo can be taken all the way back to the beginning of the drawing. Redo must immediately follow the Undo command and will reverse the last Undo commands in order.

General Procedures

1. Select the Undo button or type U at the command line, and Click <ENTER>.
2. Click the <ENTER> key to repeat the undo command until satisfied.

Be careful not to Click the <ENTER> key too many times.
Use U rather than typing the entire UNDO command.
The Undo shortcut menu appears only when the entire word 'UNDO' is typed.
Use the **Mark** option for Undo to mark a point before you start an edit sequence. You can then undo back to the point you have bookmarked.
➢ Both the Undo and Redo commands have a drop-down list so you can see how far back or forward you want to go.

Command Exercise

Exercise 5-25 – Undo and Redo

Drawing Name: **undo1.dwg**
Estimated Time to Completion: 5 Minutes

Scope

Draw several lines, circles and rectangles. Undo your drawing several steps back. Next try to Redo several steps. Notice that both Undo and Redo keep track of the commands issued.

Solution

1. 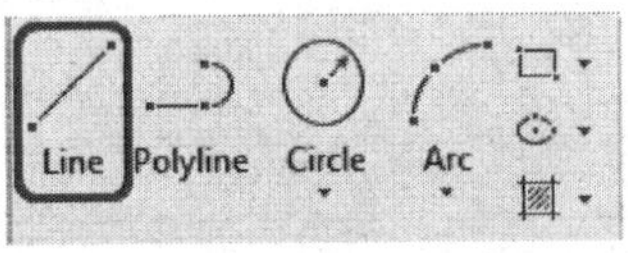

Invoke the **Line** command (l or line) and create several lines on the drawing.

2. 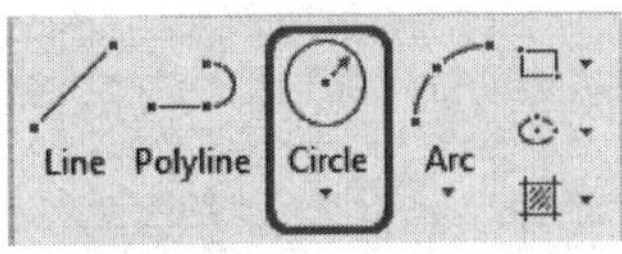

Invoke the **Circle** command (c or circle) and create several circles on the drawing.

3. 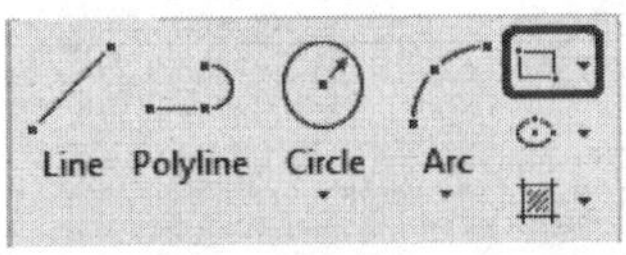

Invoke the **Rectangle** command (rectang) and create several rectangles on the drawing.

4. 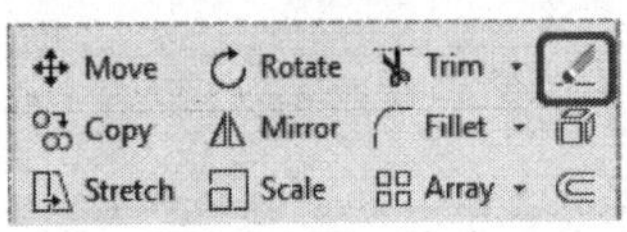

Invoke the **Erase** command (e or erase) and erase one or two of the objects you have just created.

5. 
Invoke the **Undo** command by using the standard Windows icon at the top of the screen or typing 'U' at the command line.

6. 
Invoke the **REDO** command by using the standard Windows icon at the top of the screen.

Command Exercise

Exercise 5-26 – Modify Commands Review

Drawing Name: **Lesson 5 AEC.dwg**
Estimated Time to Completion: 15 Minutes

Scope

Using the modify commands, furnish the apartment as shown.

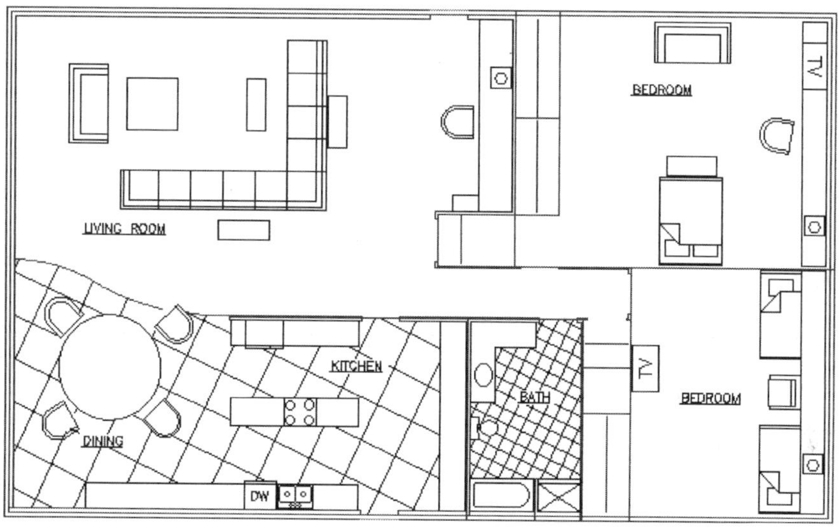

Hints

1. Copy the chairs and sofa sections.
2. Use the mirror command to create the second single bed.
3. Move most of the pieces into place.
4. Use the Array command to array the chairs around the dining table.

Command Exercise

Exercise 5-27 – Modify Commands Review 2

Drawing Name: **Lesson 5 Electrical.dwg**
Estimated Time to Completion: 30 Minutes

Scope

Using the modify commands to create the circuit diagram.

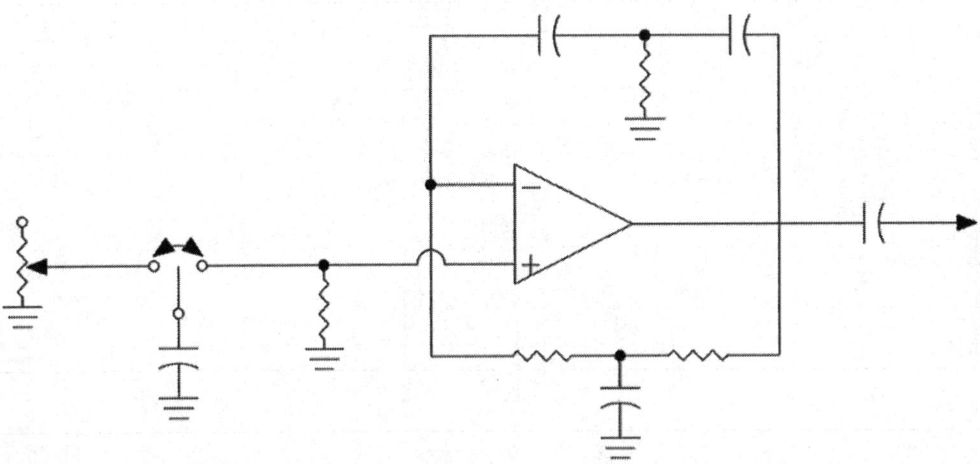

Hints

1. The symbols are provided in the drawing.
2. Use Copy and Rotate to place the symbols.
3. Draw lines to connect the symbols.

Review Questions

1. You construct a circle. You now want to copy the circle. What option can you use at the Select objects prompt to select the last object you created?
2. You wish to mirror some text. What value should MIRRTEXT be set to to ensure that the text mirrors properly?
3. You need to duplicate an object in a rectangular pattern. What command allows you to do this?
4. You enter the TRIM command. When prompted to select the cutting edges, you Click the <ENTER> key. What is the result?
5. You wish to offset an object and delete the source object. What is the best way to do this?

6. Identify the following icons that are all located in the Modify Toolbar:

a. ____________________ 

b. ____________________ 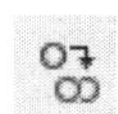

c. ____________________ 

d. ____________________ 

e. ____________________ 

f. ____________________ 

g. ____________________ 

h. ____________________ 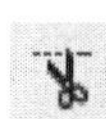

i. ____________________ 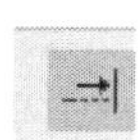

7. Typing the letter R at the command line invokes which command?
   - ❑ Scale
   - ❑ Rotate
   - ❑ Redraw
   - ❑ Regen

8. What does the R option stand for in the Scale command?

9. What does the U option stand for in the trim and extend commands?
10. Explain the similarities between the Copy and Move commands.
11. Can you trim a line that is acting as a cutting edge? Try it.

Review Answers

1. *Type L at the command line to select the last object created.*

2. *Set **MIRRTEXT** to 1.*

3. *ARRAY*

4. *All objects in the drawing may now be used as a cutting edge.*

5. *Use the **ERASE** option for OFFSET.*

6.

   a. erase
   b. copy
   c. mirror
   d. offset
   e. move
   f. scale
   g. rotate
   h. trim
   i. Extend

7. *Redraw*
8. *Reference*
9. *Undo*
10. *The steps to move an object are similar to copying an object. The major difference is that the copy command leaves the original object in place.*
11. *Yes. Cutting edges can be trimmed as long as they cross another object.*

Lesson 6.0 – Selecting Objects

Estimated Class Time: 1 Hour

Objectives

This section introduces different methods of selecting objects and what to do with the objects once they are selected.

- **Selecting Objects**
- **Quick Select**
- **Quick Properties**

Selecting Objects

Command Overview

Knowing how to select objects is an important aspect to being able to manipulate objects inside of AutoCAD. Typically, one begins with a specific Modify command, then selects the objects to modify. When an object is selected, it will be highlighted. Continue to select (or de-select) objects at the "Select objects" prompt, then Click <ENTER> to continue. Objects can be selected individually, with the selection window, or by invoking one of the options at the *Select object* prompt.

Select Object Option	Key	Overview
Pick		Place the cursor over the object and pick it using the LMB.
Window (Left to Right)		Making a selection window from left to right will create a window in which only the objects that are completely within the window will be selected. Place the cursor in the blank area of the drawing to the left of the objects to select and pick (LMB). Drag the mouse to the right to display the selection window, and pick the opposite corner.
Window (Right to Left)		Making a selection window from right to left will create a crossing window. All objects that are crossed by this window will be selected. Place the cursor in the blank area of the drawing to the right of the objects to select and pick (LMB). Drag the mouse to the left to display the selection window, and pick the opposite corner.
Deselecting objects		To deselect a previously selected object, Click the shift key and select it again using any of the selection methods.
Last	L	At the Select objects prompt, type L to select the last object drawn.
All	ALL	At the Select objects prompt, type ALL to select all objects in the drawing.
Fence	F	At the Select objects prompt, type F to initiate the Fence option. All objects crossed by the fence line will be selected.

Window Polygon	WP	At the Select objects prompt, type WP to initiate a Window Polygon. Create the polygon by picking points around the objects to select. This will be easier if ORTHO is off. Only objects completely within the Window Polygon will be selected.
Crossing Polygon	CP	At the Select objects prompt, type CP to initiate a Crossing Polygon. Create the polygon by picking points that cross the objects to select. This will be easier if ORTHO is off. All objects crossed by the Polygon will be selected.
Previous	P	At the Select objects prompt, type P to select the Previous objects selected.

General Procedures

1. Select a Modify Command.
2. At the Select object prompt, initiate a Selection option (remember to Click <ENTER>).
3. When all of the desired objects have been selected, Click <ENTER> to continue with the Modify Command.

Tips & Tricks

- After objects have been selected, Click <ENTER> to continue, even if all objects have been selected.
- If the selection window is accidentally initiated, try to utilize the crossing window to select the object. If there is no way to properly cross the object with a window to select it (right to left), make a window that selects nothing and try to select the object again without exiting the modify command.
- It is very difficult to select objects if SNAP is ON.
- Objects may also be selected first, then a Modify command can be selected. When objects are selected first, they will be highlighted and will display small boxes at various points of the object. These boxes are called Grips and will be covered in greater detail in the section on Advanced Commands.
- At the Select objects prompt, type S to view the list of command line options. Type the capitalized letter(s) of the Select Object option, and Click <ENTER>. It is not necessary to view this list in order to invoke the select object option.
- If you want to select all the similar objects (for example, all circles), select one circle, right click and use 'Select Similar'.
- Dashed lines displayed on the screen when using selection methods indicate that objects that are touched or crossed are selected. Solid lines indicate that only objects fully contained will be selected.

AutoCAD uses cursor badges to provide contextual feedback.
A selection badge indicates when you are creating a crossing or window selection.

The green window with the symbol on the left indicates a crossing selection and the blue window with the symbol on the right indicates a window selection.

If you prefer not to see the cursor badges, you can turn off the display by typing CURSORBADGE.
Enter 1 to turn OFF the display. Enter 2 to turn ON the display.

If you hold down the left mouse button while moving the mouse, you get an irregularly shaped object which can be used to select objects. This is called LASSO selection.

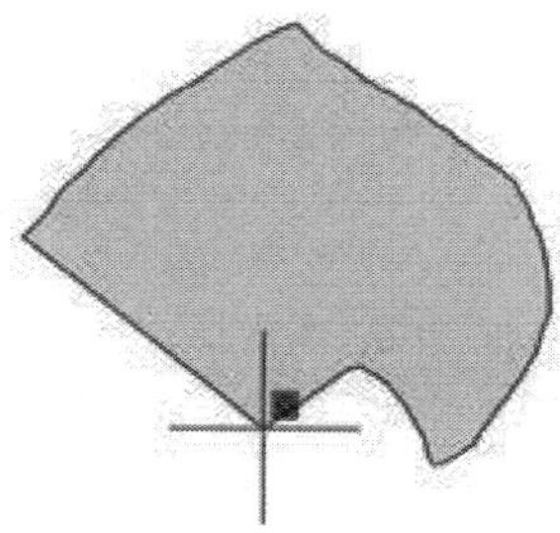

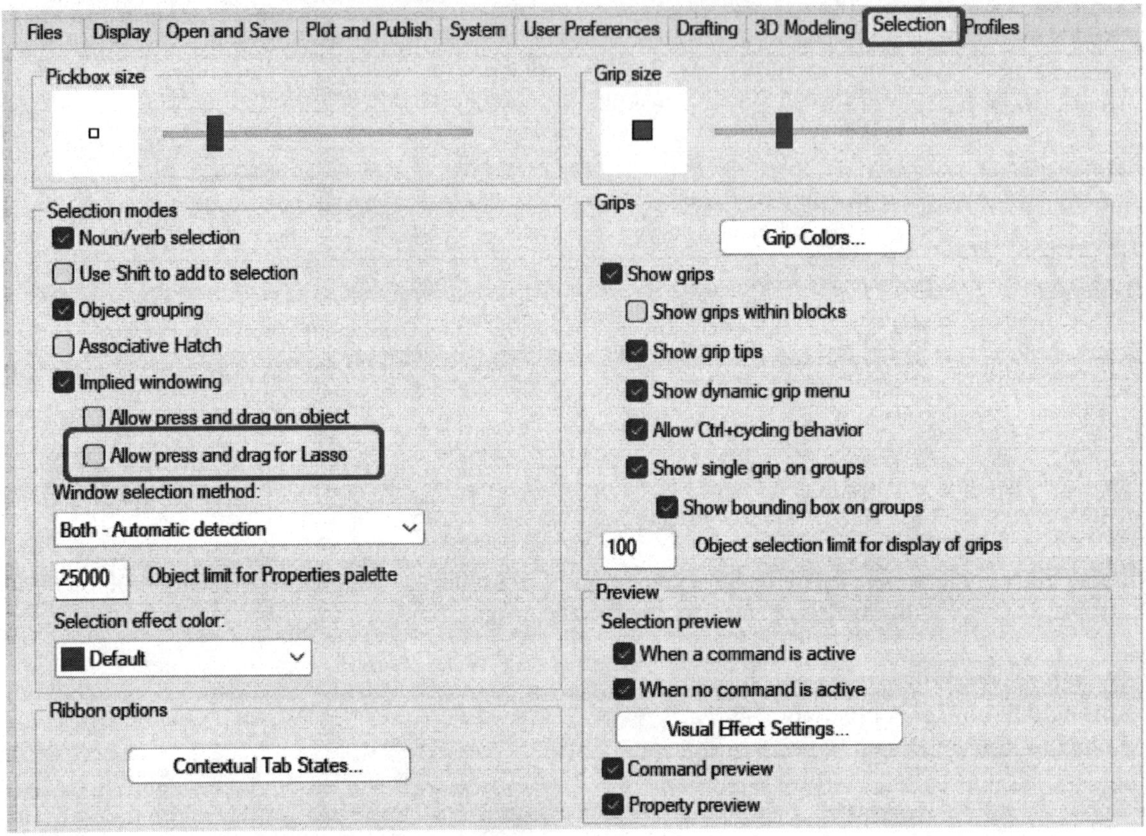

Many users dislike the LASSO selection method. To disable, go to OPTIONS. Select the Selection tab. Disable **Allow press and drag for Lasso**.

Command Exercise

Exercise 6-1 – Selecting Objects

Drawing Name: **select1.dwg**
Estimated Time to Completion: 5 Minutes

Scope

Using the erase command, practice selecting the blue and red objects in the drawing. Optional: use the select objects as indicated. Use the fence (F) option to select the red lines on the left. Use the Window Polygon (WP) to select the blue objects on the right.

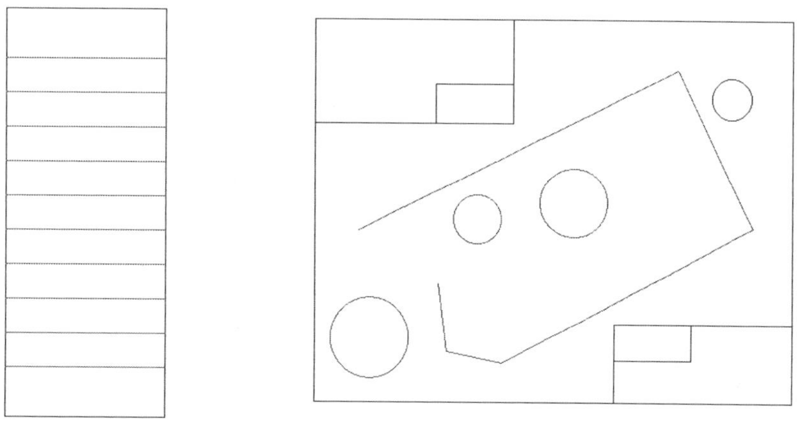

Solution

1. 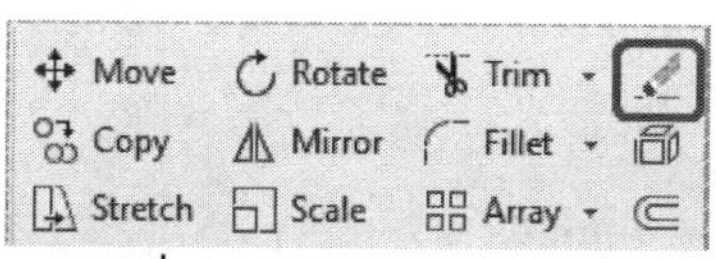

Invoke the Erase command (e or erase).

2. 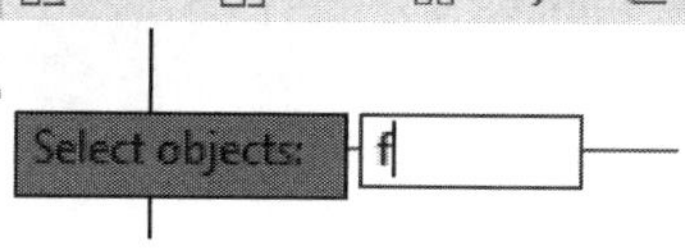

Select objects:
Activate the Fence option by typing 'F' and Clicking <ENTER>.

3. 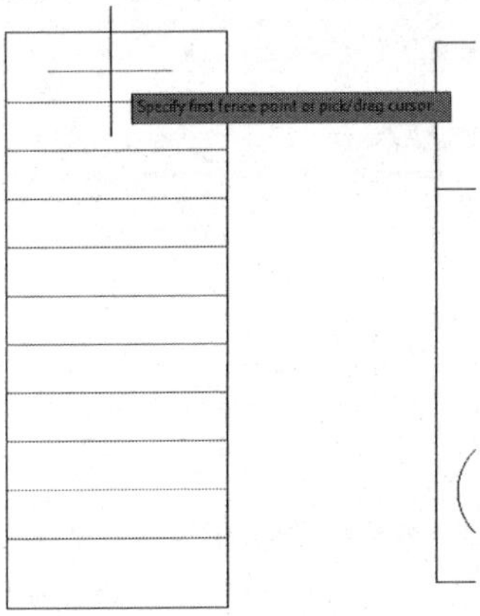

First fence point:

Pick just above the top red line with the LMB. You may want to toggle OSNAP off.

4. 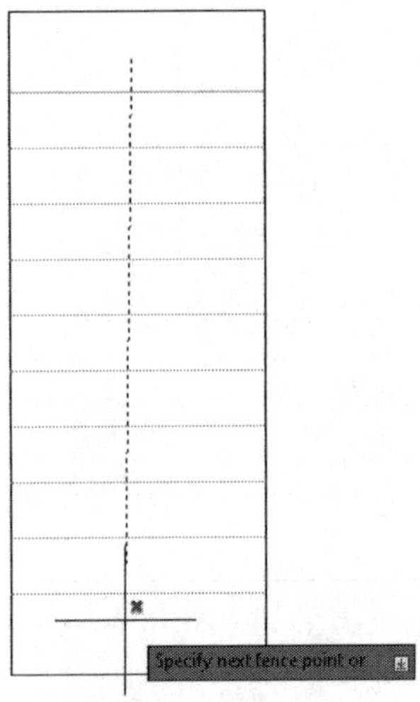

Specify endpoint of line or [Undo]:

Pick just below the bottom red line with the LMB. Click <ENTER> to close the selection set.

Select objects:

Click <ENTER> again to erase the selected lines.

5. 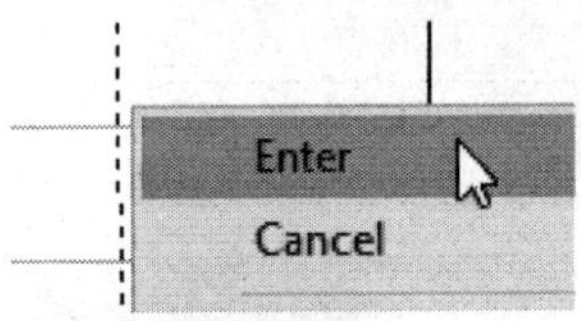

Specify endpoint of line or [Undo]:

Click the <ENTER> key to close the selection set.

6. 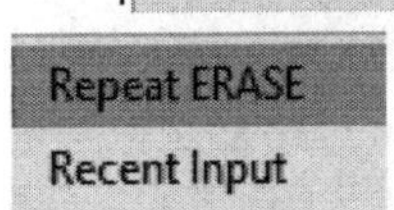

Repeat the Erase command with the RMB (e, erase or <ENTER>).

7. 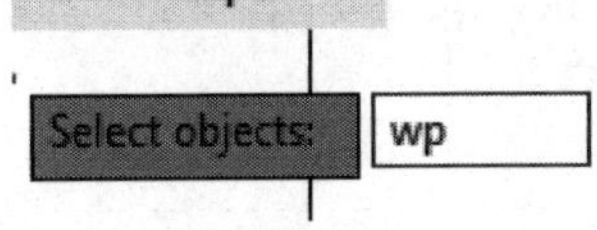

Select objects:
Activate the Window Polygon option by typing 'WP' and Clicking <ENTER> (make sure ORTHO is off).

8. 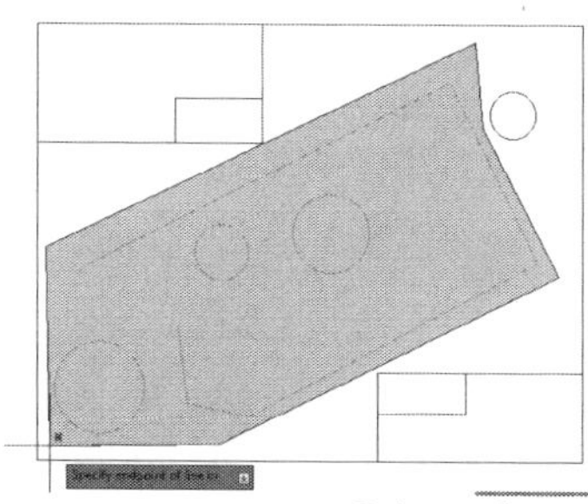

First polygon point:
Create a polygon around the blue objects similar to that shown in the figure to the right.

Select the objects with a window polygon.

9. 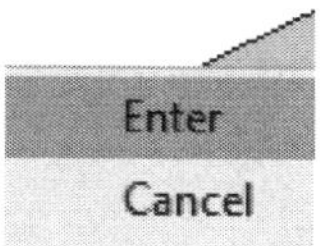

Select objects:
Right click and select <ENTER> to finish the window polygon.

10. 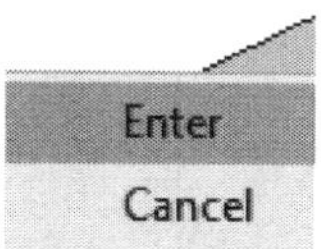

Select objects:
Click the <ENTER> key again to complete the exercise by erasing the selection set.

Extra: *Use the Undo Command to bring the erased objects back. Experiment with different methods of selecting objects. Can you use the Fence selection method followed by the Crossing Polygon method to create a single selection set? Try it. Use the <Shift> key to remove an object from your selection set.*

Tips & Tricks

- If you have a partially opened drawing, only objects that are currently loaded can be selected with the Quick Select command. Any objects in the drawing that are not currently loaded cannot be found by the command.
- You can also access the Quick Select filter using the Properties dialog.
- If you select more than one object accidentally, you can use the drop-down list in the Properties dialog to select the desired object.

Command Exercise

Exercise 6-2 – Selecting Objects Using Properties

Drawing Name: **select2.dwg**
Estimated Time to Completion: 5 Minutes

Scope

Use the Properties dialog to filter out selected objects.

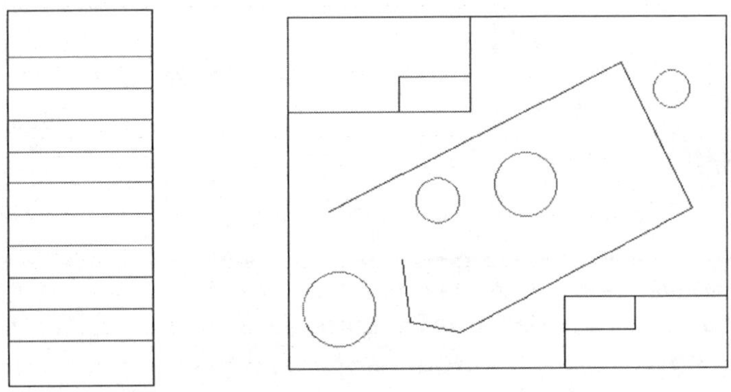

Solution

1. 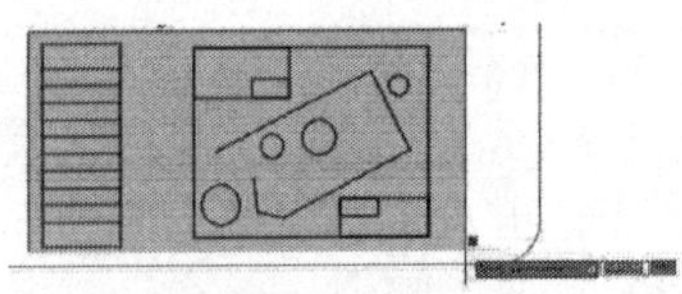

   Window around all the objects so that they are highlighted.

2. 

   Right click and select 'Quick Properties'.

3. 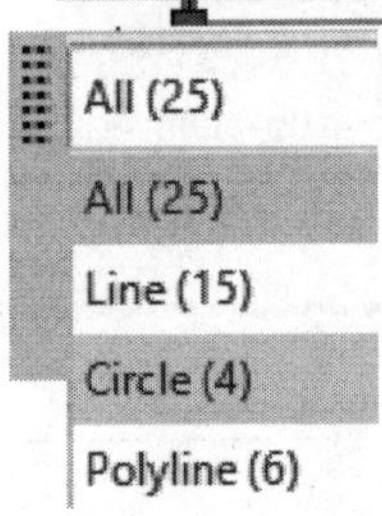

   A small dialog will appear.

   From the drop-down list, select **Circle**.

4. 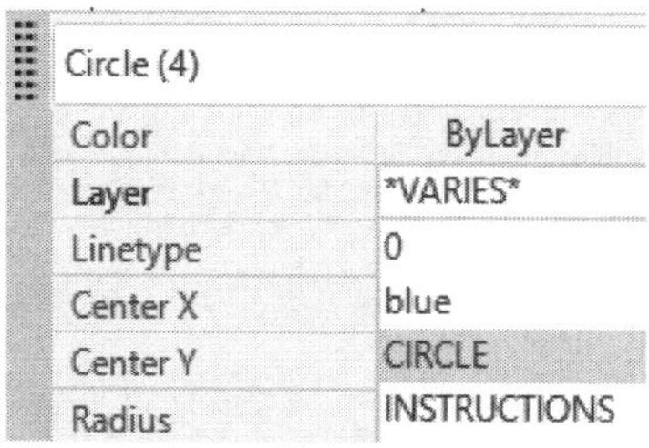

Select the **Circle** layer from the drop-down list for layers.

5. The circles will be moved to the circle layer.

Click ESC to release the selection.

- *You can only change the settings for SELECTSIMILAR when nothing is selected.*

Command Exercise

Exercise 6-3 – Selecting Objects Using Properties

Drawing Name: **select3.dwg**
Estimated Time to Completion: 5 Minutes

Scope

Use Select Similar to target similar objects.

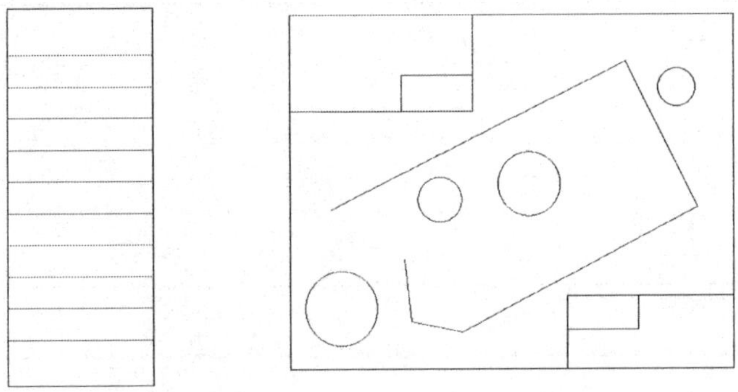

Solution

1. Select the black circle located on the far right.

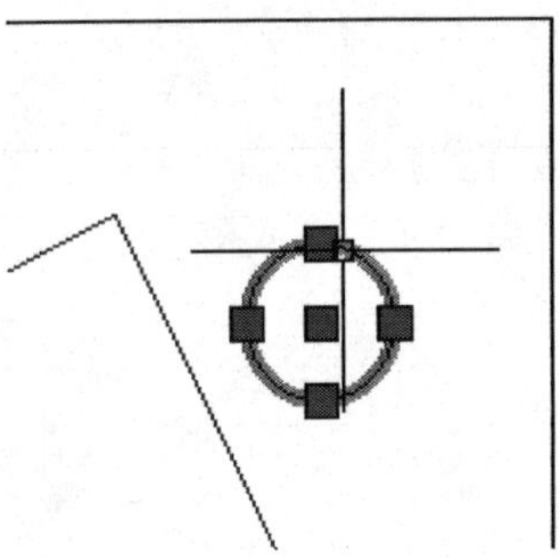

2.

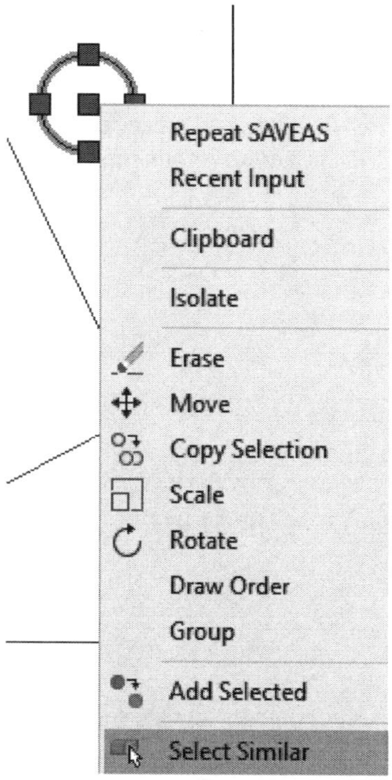

Right click and left pick on 'Select Similar'.

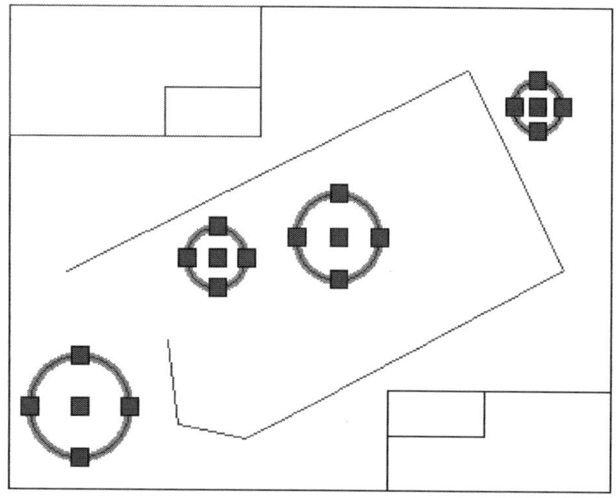

The other circles are selected.

Click ESC to deselect.

3.

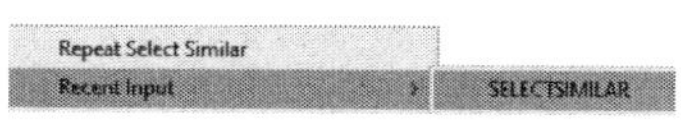

Make sure nothing is selected/highlighted. Click ESC to release selections, if necessary.

Right click and select 'Recent Input →SELECTSIMILAR'.

4. Right click and select 'Settings'.

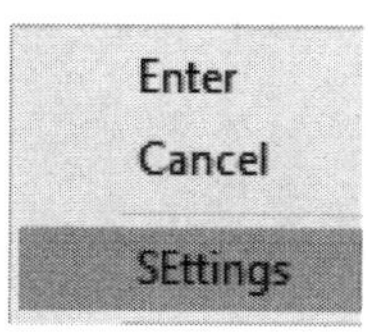

5. 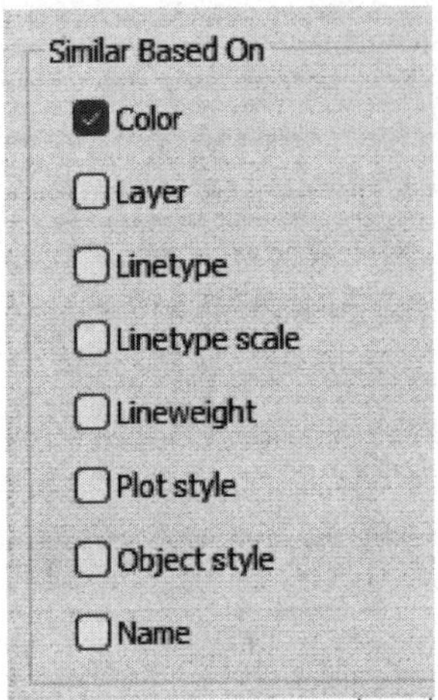

Uncheck all the choices except for Color. Click 'OK'.

This means that objects with the same color are selected. If Name was enabled, all objects with the same name would be selected, like objects named 'circle'.

6. 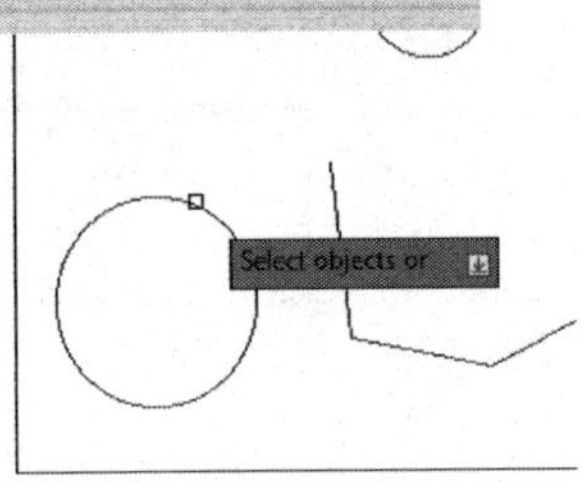

Select the lower blue circle. Click 'ENTER'.

7. 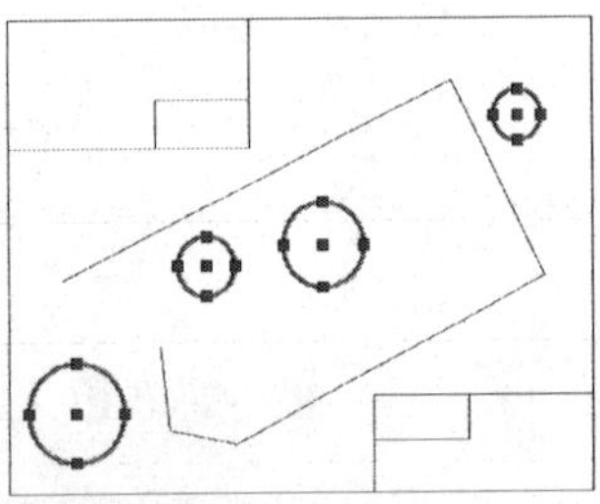

Now all the circles are selected.

8. 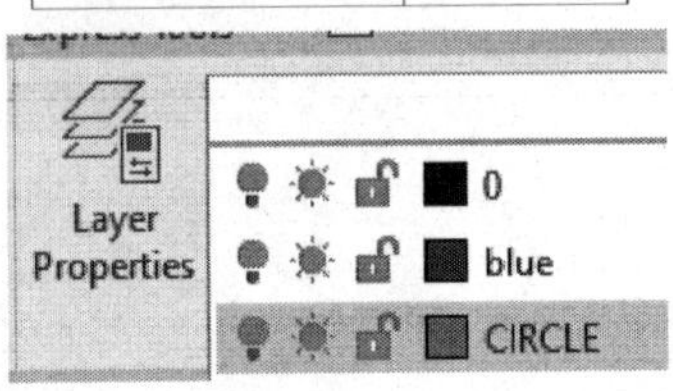

Select the CIRCLE layer from the drop-down layer list on the ribbon.
Note that the circles all change color to match the layer.

Click ESC to release the selection.

Quick Select

Command Locator

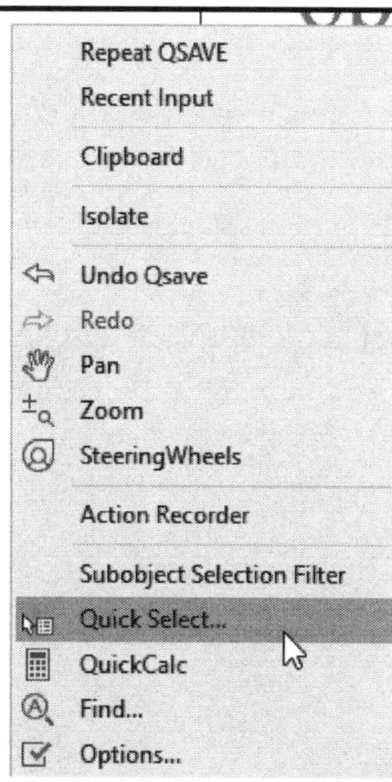

Command	**qselect**
RMB Shortcut Menu	**Quick Select…**
Dialog Box	**Quick Select**

Command Overview

The Quick Select command allows you to specify filtering criteria and then decide how you want AutoCAD to create the selection set from that criterion. You are given the option to restrict the filter selection to currently selected entities or allow it to apply to the entire drawing. The Quick Select dialog box then presents you with the option to choose the object type. These options are "Multiple," or choose the drop-down list which will display every type of entity currently in the drawing. After selecting the object type, you can further filter the selection set by choosing one of the entity's properties and then selecting an operator and value for that property. You are then given the option of how to apply this filter to the current selection set. You can choose to Include or Exclude the filter entities from the current selection set. Lastly you can decide whether or not to append to the current selection set.

General Procedures

Using Quick Select to create a filtered selection set:

1. Invoke the Quick Select command.
2. In the Quick Select dialog box, select the entity type in the Object Type drop down list.
3. In the Properties list, if applicable select a specific property for the objects being selected and set the operator and value fields accordingly.
4. Select whether to "Include objects in new selection set" or "Exclude objects from new selection set."
5. Select whether or not to "Append to current selection set."
6. Click 'OK'.

Command Exercise

Exercise 6-4 – Quick Select

Drawing Name: **qselect1.dwg**
Estimated Time to Completion: 10 Minutes

Scope

Using Quick Select, select all lines in the drawings and place on the lines layer. Next select all polylines in the drawing and place on the polyline layer. Repeat the process for all Mtext, Text, and blocks.

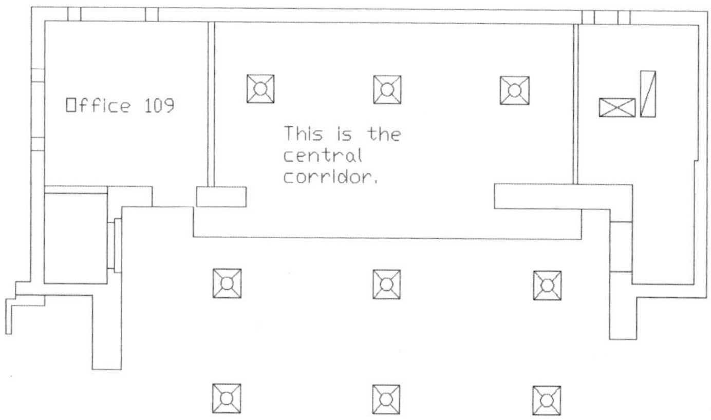

Solution

1.

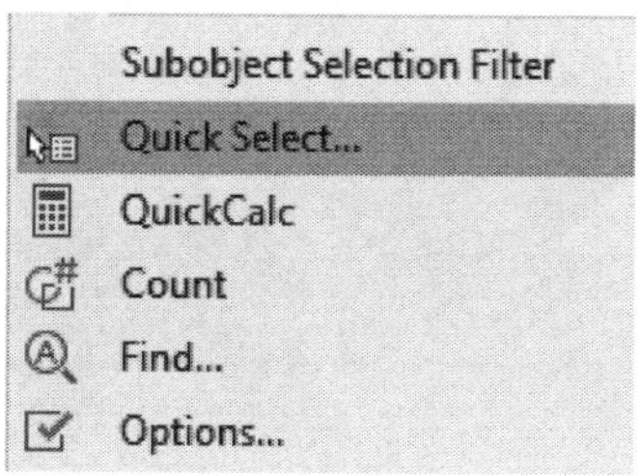

Right click in the window and select **Quick Select**.

2. 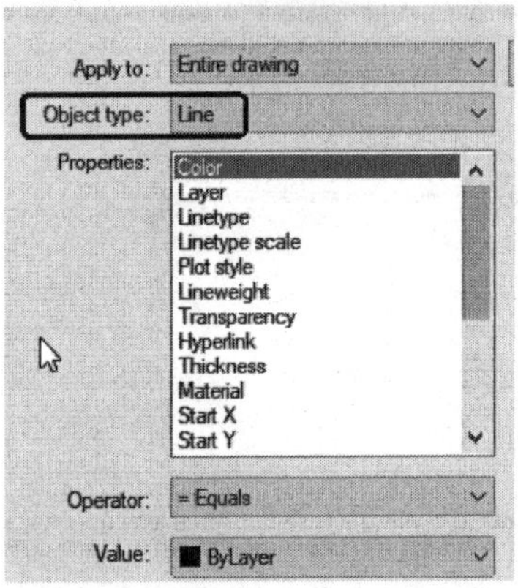

Select 'Line' in the Object Type drop down list.

In the properties section, select 'Color', 'Equal =' as Operator, and 'Bylayer' as value.

3. 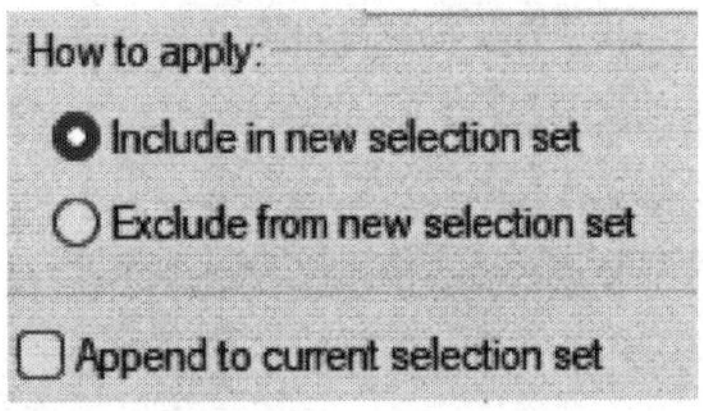

In the 'How to apply' section, choose 'Include in new selection set.'

Uncheck the 'Append to selection set' if it is currently checked and select 'OK'.

4. 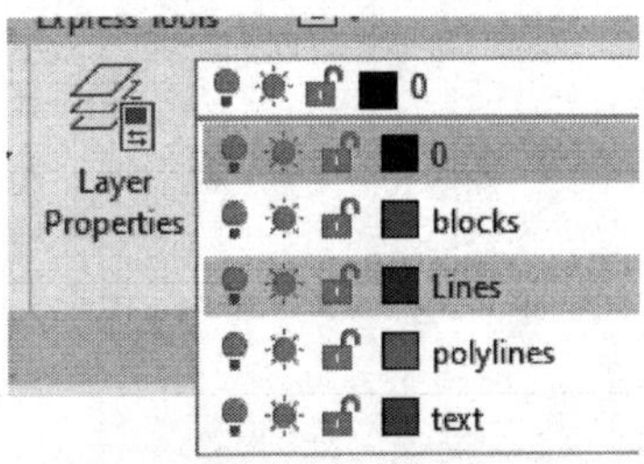

With all the lines selected in the drawing, use the Layer drop down list on the object properties tool bar and select the Lines layer. This will place the selected entities on the Lines layer.

Press <ESC> to clear the selection set.

5. 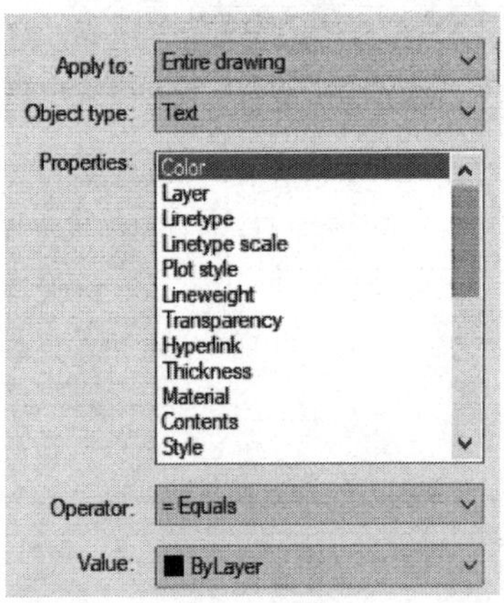

Repeat the above process for Polylines, Text, Mtext, and Blocks.

Extra: *You select several objects, including lines, circles, and rectangles. How can you filter the selection so that you change the layer of only the rectangles?*

Quick Properties

Command Locator

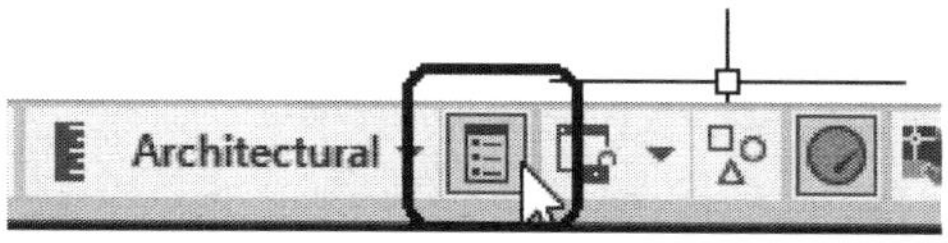

Status Toolbar	**Quick Properties toggle**
Command	**Quickproperties**
RMB Shortcut Menu	**Quick Properties…**
Shortcut Key	**Ctl+Shift+P**
Dialog Box	**Quick Properties**

To enable Quick Properties, use the Quick Properties toggle located on the Status Bar. In order to enable the Quick Properties toggle, it needs to be enabled on the status bar first.

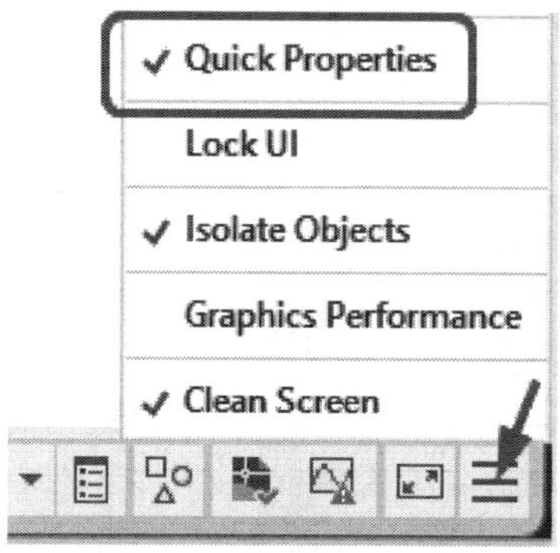

To add Quick Properties to the status bar, left click on the customization button on the far right of the status bar and enable Quick Properties. You can also type QPMODE on the command line and type 1 to enable.

If no selection is made, the Quick Properties dialog is not available. You can customize what Properties are displayed/included in the dialog. The Options buttons allow you to control where the dialog will appear when any object is selected.

Command Exercise

Exercise 6-5 – Customize Quick Properties

Drawing Name: **qprops1.dwg**
Estimated Time to Completion: 10 Minutes

Scope

Learn how to set which fields will appear in the Quick Properties dialog.

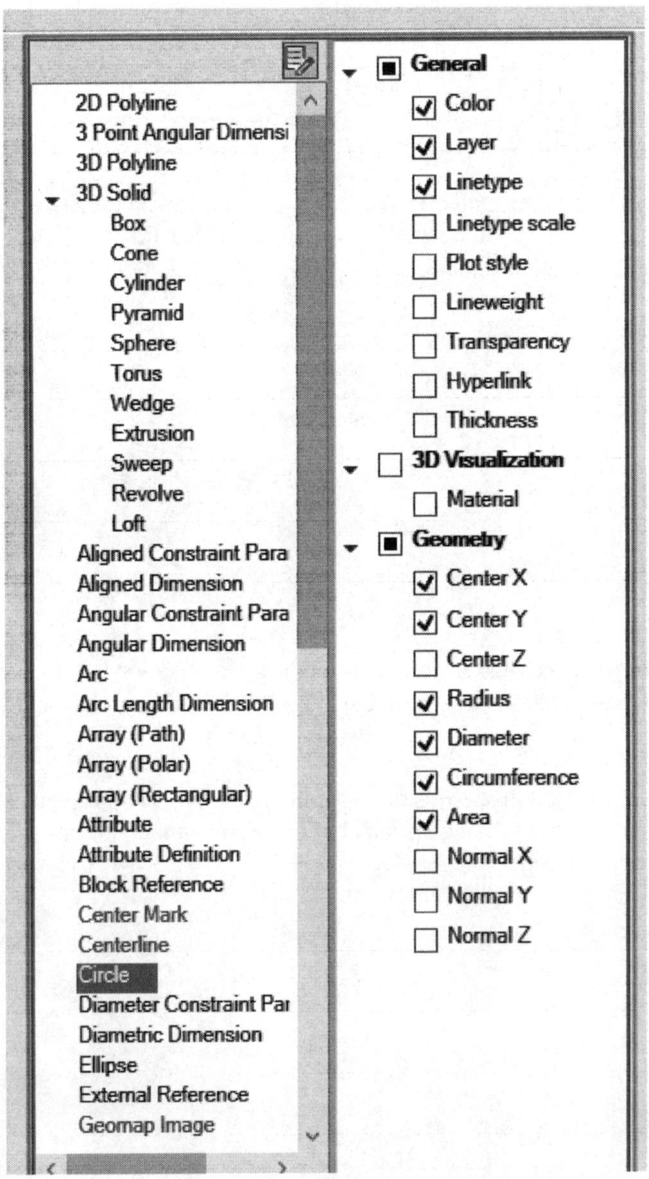

Solution

1. 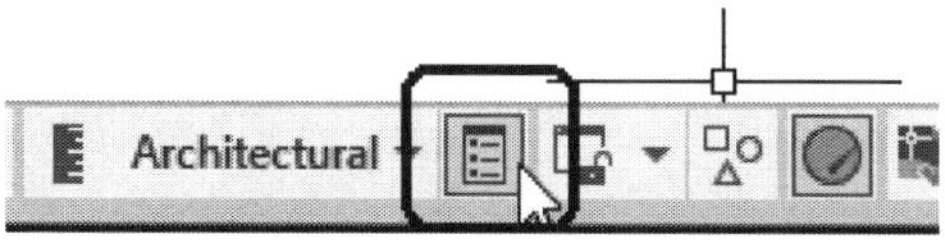

Toggle **Quick Properties** ON using the Status Bar button.

2. 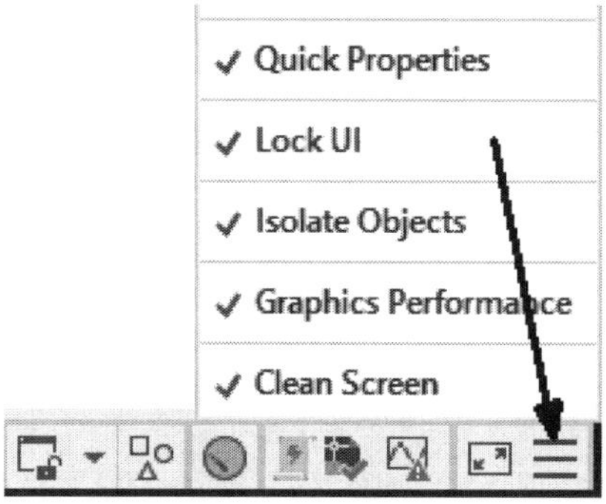

If you don't see Quick Properties on the Status Bar, use the menu to enable Quick Properties.

3. Select a line in the drawing.

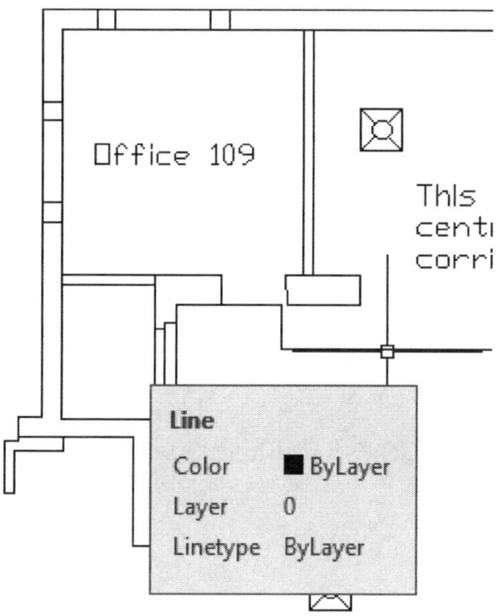

You can hover over an element to display the element information.

The Quick Properties dialog will display information about the line. Note which properties are listed: Color, Layer, Linetype, etc.

4. 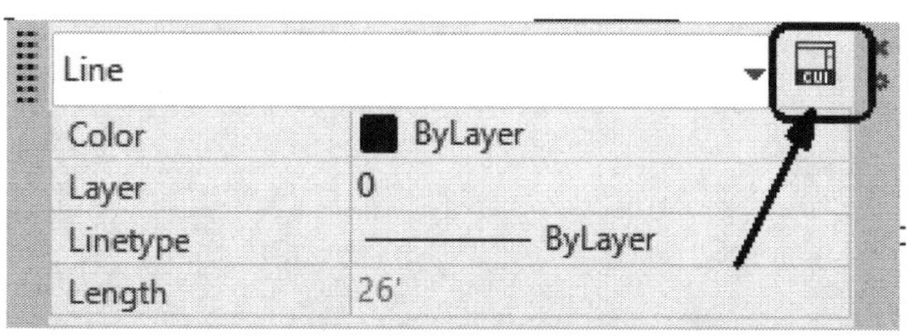

Select the **Customize** button.

5\.

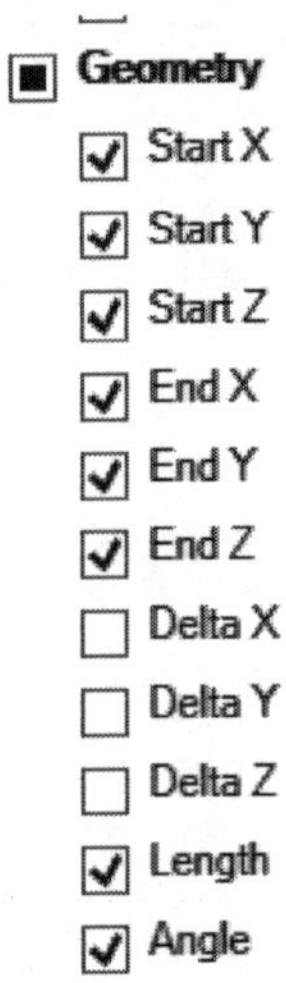

In the right hand pane, you see a list of properties that can be displayed in the Quick Properties dialog.

A checkmark indicates it will be displayed.

Place a check mark in front of the Start X, Start Y, Start Z, and End X, End Y, End Z and Length.

These display the start and end coordinates of the selected line.

6\. Press **Apply** and **OK** to close the dialog.

7\.

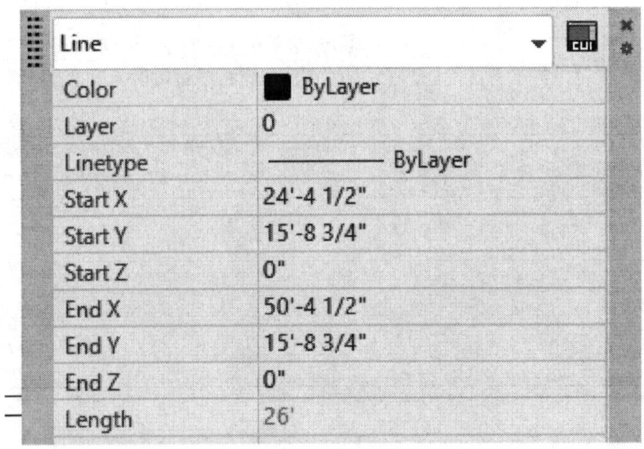

Select a line again.

Notice how the Quick Properties have changed.

Click **ESC** to release the selection.

8\.

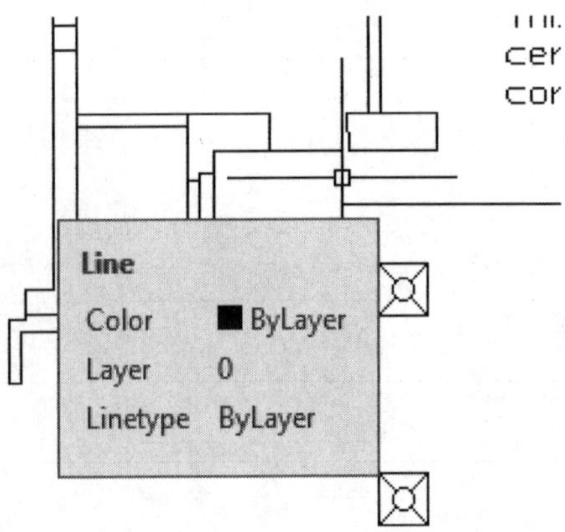

Select a different line.

9. 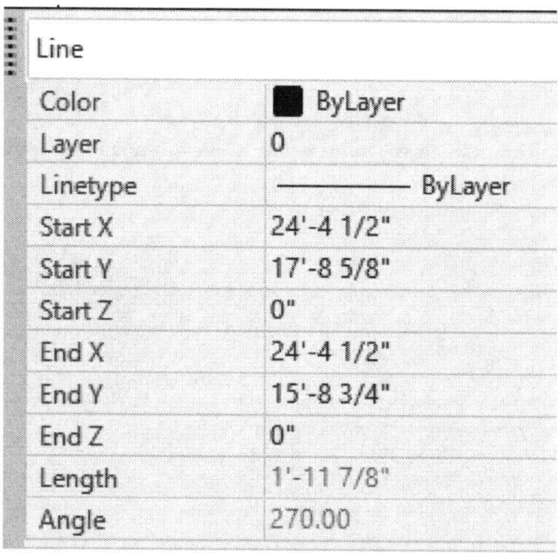

Quick Properties displays the selected properties.

Note: Your Quick Properties may show different values depending on which line you selected.

Command Exercise

Exercise 6-6 – Quick Properties

Drawing Name: **qprops2.dwg**
Estimated Time to Completion: 5 Minutes

Scope

Learn how to use Quick Properties to modify objects easily.

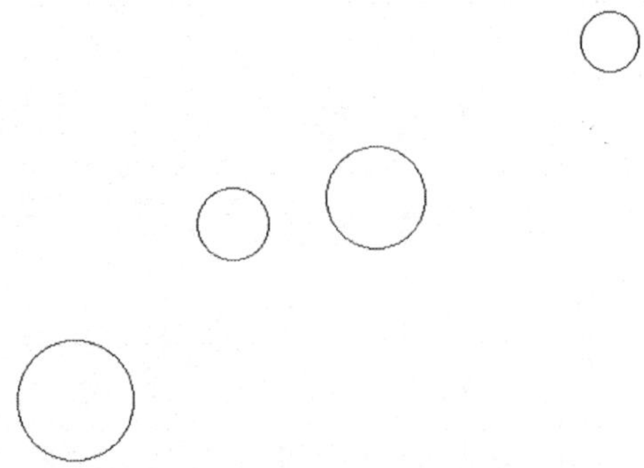

Solution

1. 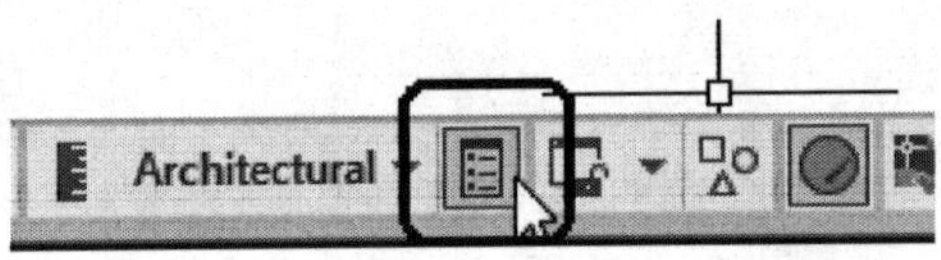

Toggle **Quick Properties** ON using the Status Bar button.

2. 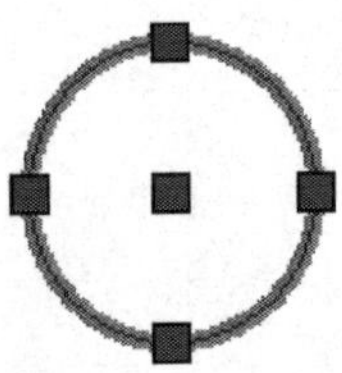

Select a circle.

The Quick Properties dialog should pop up immediately.

3. 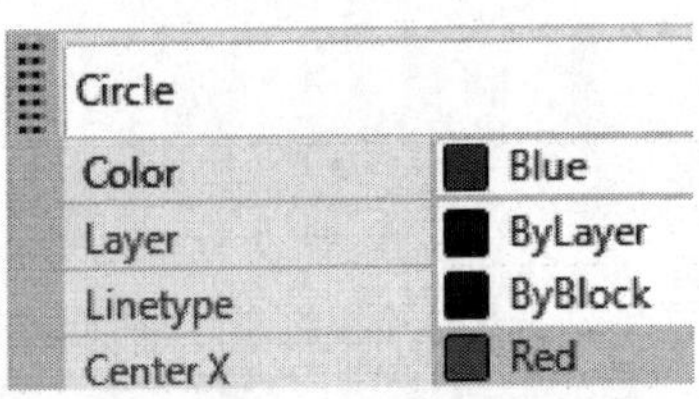

Change the Color to **Red**.

4.

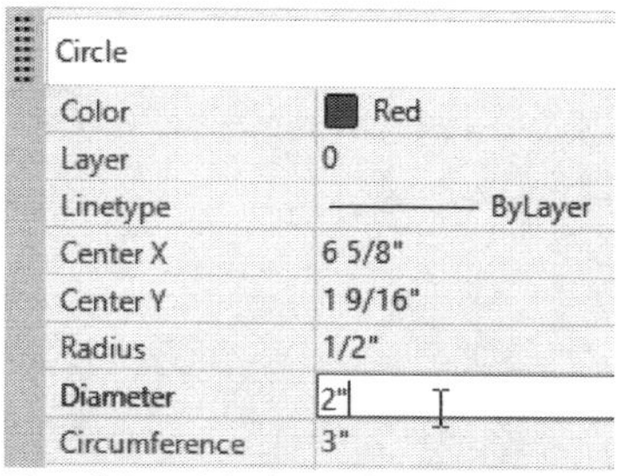

Change the Diameter to **2″**.

Click **ESC** to deselect the circle.

5. Try this with the other circles.

Selection Cycling

Command Locator

Selection cycling is used when creating or modifying a 3D model. Some edges or faces are often hidden. Rather than rotate the model, the user can use selection cycling to pick the desired entity.

It also is useful when you have a drawing with overlapping elements.

To use selection cycling, toggle the Selection Cycling button on the Status Bar. You can also type SUBOBJSELECTIONMODE on the command prompt and enter 1 to enable.

As you position your cursor, a dialog will appear to aid you in your selection by displaying the object's information.

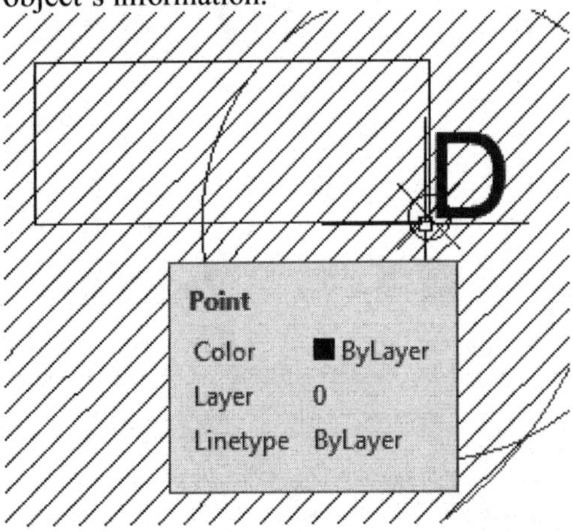

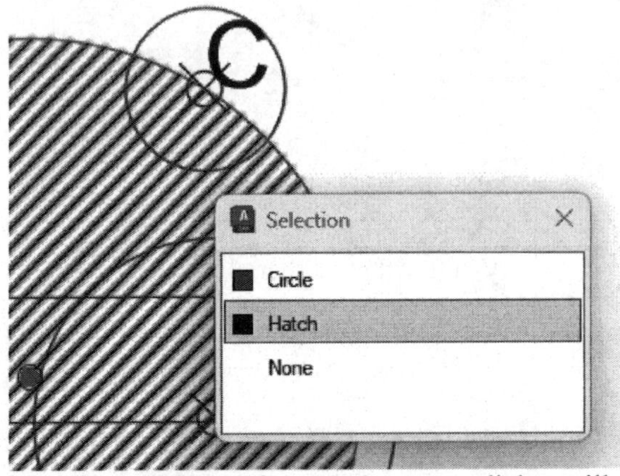

Once you click to select an element, a dialog will appear listing all the overlapping elements to confirm your selection. If you mouse over an item in the list, it will highlight in the drawing.

You can use the shortcut keys in the list to the right to help filter your selections.

	Vertex filtering is on	Shift + F2
	Edge filtering is on	Shift + F3
	Face filtering is on	Shift + F4
	History subobject filtering is on	Shift + F5
	Subobject filtering is off	Shift + F1

To set the Selection Cycling settings, you can access the Drafting Settings dialog and select the Selection Cycling tab. To launch the Drafting Settings dialog, type DS on the command prompt. You can also right click on the status bar icon and select Selection Cycling Settings...

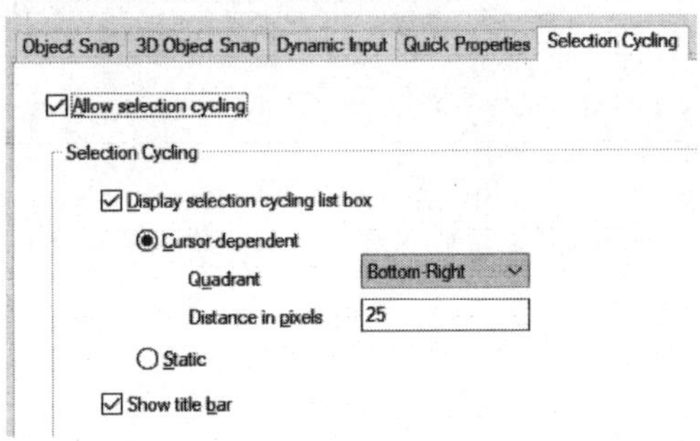

Command Exercise

Exercise 6-7 – Selection Cycling

Drawing Name: **selcycling1.dwg**
Estimated Time to Completion: 5 Minutes

Scope

Use Selection Cycling to select each letter and modify it to a number.

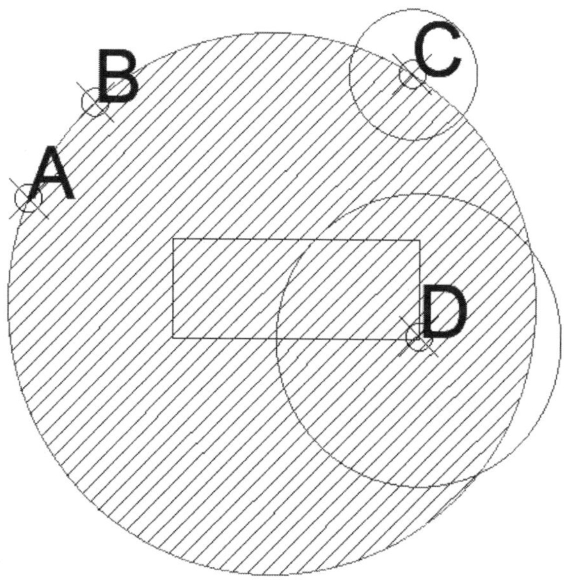

Solution

1. Verify that the Selection Cycling toggle is set to ON in the status toolbar.

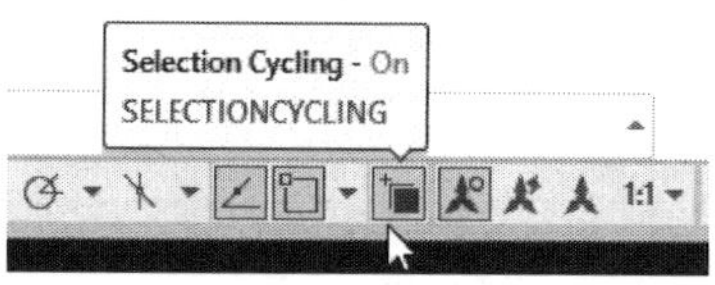

2.

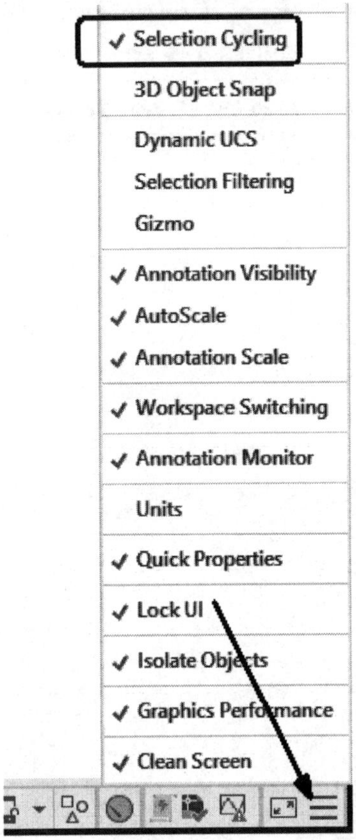

If you don't see Selection Cycling on your Status Bar, click on the Status Bar menu and enable.

3.

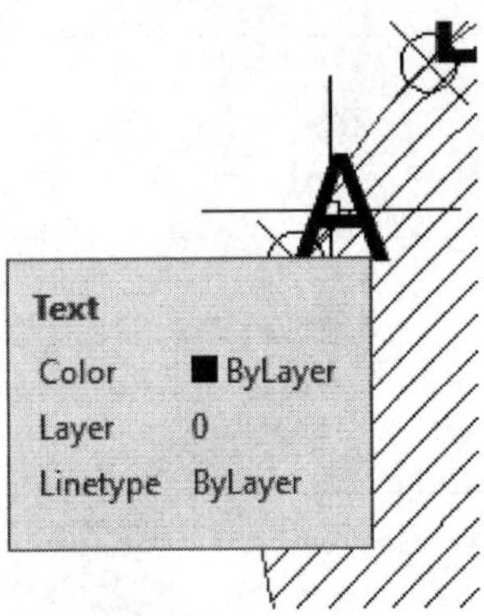

Hover your cursor over the letter A.

You should see a dialog showing Text. You also should see a double rectangle indicating that the Text is lying on top of other objects.

Left click on the **A.**

4.

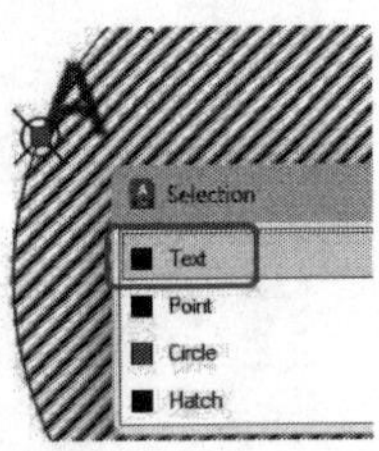

A list will appear with the objects that can be selected in the area where you clicked.

Left click on **Text** to modify the text.

5. 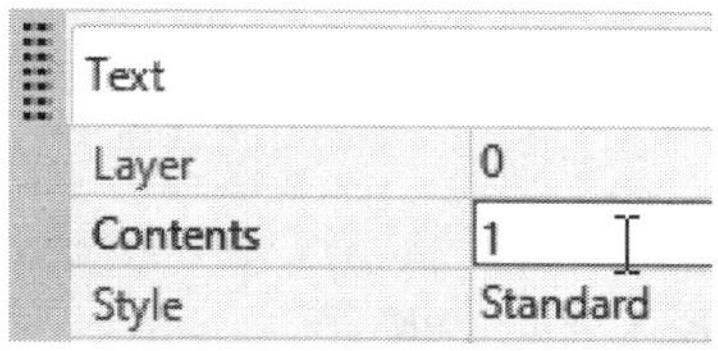

In the Quick Properties dialog, change the Contents of the Text to **1.**

Press **ENTER** and the value will update.

Click ESC to release the selection.

6. Repeat to change B to 2, C to 3, and D to 4.

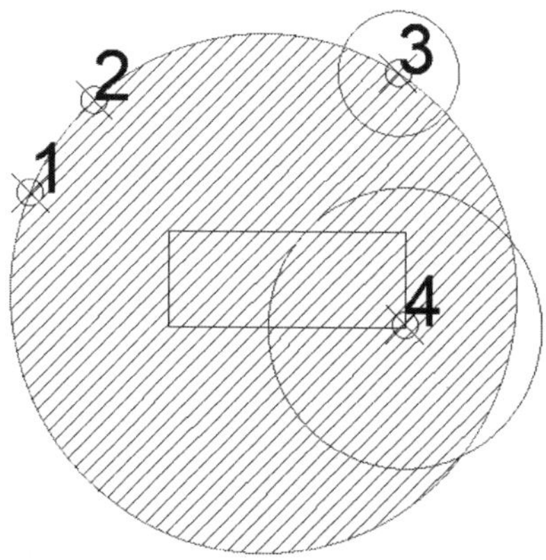

Review Questions

1. Name three methods of selecting an object.

2. Quick Select is used to filter through a drawing or selection to quickly select objects. Which object in the list below can be selected using the Quick Select dialog?

   a. Lines
   b. Circles
   c. Dimensions
   d. Polygons
   e. All of the above

3. To customize the properties in the Quick Properties dialog:

   a. Go to Options and select the Properties
   b. Go to Settings and select the Quick Properties tab
   c. Right click on the Quick Properties dialog and select Customize
   d. All of the above

4. True or False:
   You can determine where the Quick Properties will appear when an object is selected.

5. In order to change the settings for Select Similar:

   a. You cannot have anything selected
   b. Right click on the Select Similar toggle and choose 'Settings'
   c. Right click in the Graphics window and choose 'Options'
   d. B or C

6. To deselect an object:

   a. Press Esc

   b. Press the Shift and pick the object again

   c. Press Enter

   d. A and B

Review Answers

1. Name three methods of selecting an object.

   Pick, Window, Crossing, Fence

2. Quick Select is used to filter through a drawing or selection to quickly select objects. Which object in the list below can be selected using the Quick Select dialog?

   e. All of the above.

3. To customize the properties in the Quick Properties dialog:

   c. Right click on the Quick Properties dialog and select Customize.

4. True or False:
   You can determine where the Quick Properties will appear when an object is selected.

   True

5. In order to change the settings for Select Similar:

   a. You cannot have anything selected.

6. To deselect an object:

   d. Press Esc and/or Press the Shift and pick the object again.

Notes:

Lesson 7.0 – Object Properties

Estimated Class Time: 3 Hours

Objectives

This section will focus on the Object Properties Toolbar. Object properties include Color, Layer, Linetype, Linetype Scale, Lineweight, and Thickness. The Match Properties and Properties commands can be used to change specific features as well as the properties of a selected object. Layers will help keep the drawing information organized. Use the drop-down Layer Control list to make a layer current or change a layer state. Use the Layer Properties Manager dialog box to create new Layers. These settings can be saved to a drawing that can be used as a prototype or template for other drawings.

- **Layer Manager**

  Control the Layer states from this drop-down list.

- **Make an Object's Layer Current**

  Select an object in the drawing and make the layer it is on the current layer.

- **Color Control**

  Control the Color of the objects being drawn.

- **Linetype Control**

  Control the Linetype of the objects being drawn.

- **Lineweight Control**

  Control the Lineweight of the objects being drawn.

- **Layer Properties Manager**

  Use the Layer Properties Manager dialog box to create a system of layers for the current drawing.

- **Match Properties Command**

  Match the properties of a selected object to other objects.

- **Properties Command**

  Change the object properties as well as specific features of a selected object.

- **Layer States**

  Layer states are used when you have a lot of layers and you want to save a setting with some layers frozen, locked, and on.

When you start AutoCAD, the only line type available is CONTINUOUS. This is the linetype used primarily for object lines. In order to keep file sizes small, the user must load any other desired linetype before he can draw using that line style.

Once you load a linetype it remains in the drawing's database even if you don't have any geometry with that linetype. To keep your file size small, you should routinely run the PURGE command to eliminate unused linetypes and layers.

The architectural industry has set up layer standards defining colors and linetypes to be used when creating drawings. The mechanical engineering industry has not developed a standard to be used for layers. Each company usually creates their own standards to be used for all technical documents. This ensures that the drawings have a uniform appearance.

One method to ensure that all drafters comply with a company's standards is to use a template set up with layers and linetypes. Use of templates is discussed later in this text.

AutoCAD 2004 and above come with a CAD Standards tool to help you ensure that drawings meet company standards.

Layers are used to organize your drawing. Industry standard is to place object lines, hidden, dimensions, etc. each on a separate layer. Many drafters organize their drawings by placing object types on separate layers. For example, fasteners, doors, walls, gears might each be placed on a separate layer. Layer names should be short but easy to understand.

You can use the Layer Control and Linetype control to set up your layers to use the different linetypes and colors.

Layer Manager

Command Locator

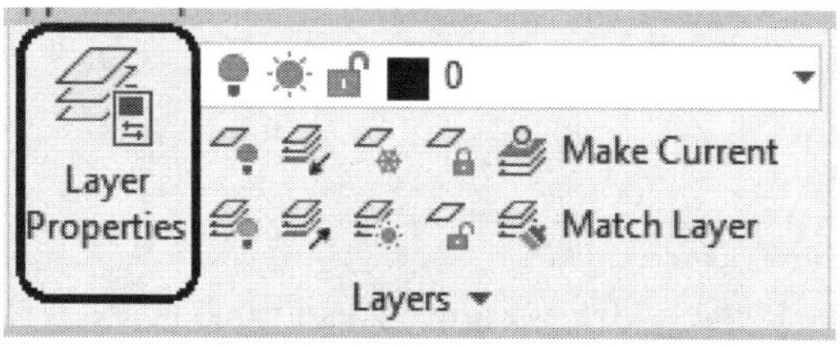

Command	**Layer**
Alias	**la**
Dialog Box	**Layer Manager**

Command Overview

Layers may be conveniently selected from the Layer Control drop-down list. Layers may be made current, or the *layer state* may be changed. The options include On or Off, Freeze or Thaw, Lock or Unlock, and making a layer plottable or not. A layer may be made current by selecting it from the list. When the command line is blank, the properties of a selected object will be identified in the Object Properties Toolbar and can be placed on a different Layer by selecting a different Layer from the drop-down list. This feature applies to the Color, Linetype, and Lineweight Controls as well.

Layer State	Overview
Make a Layer Current	Select the name of the layer in the drop-down list to make it current. Objects drawn on the current layer will have the properties assigned to that layer.
Turn a Layer On or Off	Select the light bulb to turn that layer on (yellow). Select it again to turn it off (gray). A layer is not visible when it is turned off; however, it may be current. A layer that is off and current at the same time would be odd, because the new objects drawn would be invisible until the layer is turned on again.
Freeze or Thaw in All Viewports	Select the sun to freeze that layer (snowflake). Select the snowflake to thaw that layer (sun). A layer is not visible when it is frozen. It is also completely ignored in a regeneration, which will make the regeneration time faster. A layer that is made current cannot be frozen.
Lock or Unlock a layer	Objects on a Locked layer cannot be changed. When a layer is locked current, objects may be drawn on that layer, but cannot be changed.
Make a layer plottable or non-plottable	Whether a layer is plotted or not can be controlled by selecting this feature. This way the layer may be visible, but will not plot.

General Procedures

To make a Layer current:

1. Select the down arrow in the Layer list.
2. Select the layer (name) to make it current.

To change a Layer state:

1. Select the down arrow in the Layer list.
2. Select the desired option: On/Off, Freeze/Thaw, Lock/Unlock, Plot/no plot.

To move objects from one Layer to another:

1. With the Command Line blank (Click Escape), select the objects to change.
2. Select the down arrow in the Layer list, and select the desired layer.
3. Click Escape two times to deselect the object and cancel the *grips*.

Tips & Tricks

One method to ensure that all drafters comply with a company's standards is to use a template set up with layers and linetypes. Use of templates is discussed later in this text.

AutoCAD 2004 and above come with a CAD Standards tool to help you ensure that drawings meet company standards.

Command Exercise

Exercise 7-1 – Layer Control

Drawing Name: **layerc1.dwg**
Estimated Time to Completion: 15 Minutes

Scope

Using Layer Control drop down list, draw the objects on the appropriate layer. Make the layer current before you draw. Practice the Freeze and Thaw options.

Solution

1.

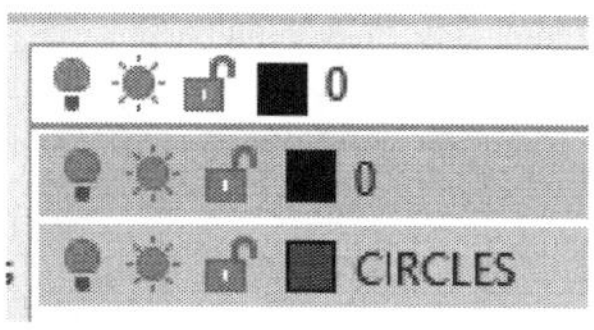

Select the **CIRCLES** layer in the Layer Control drop-down list.

This makes the CIRCLES layer active or current.

2.

Invoke the **Circle** command (c or circle).

3.

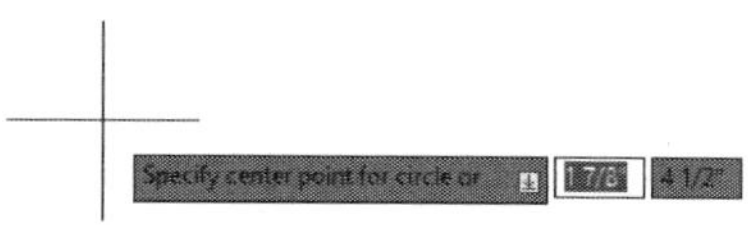

Specify center point for circle or [3P/2P/Ttr (tan tan radius)]:
Pick a point on the screen with the LMB.

4. 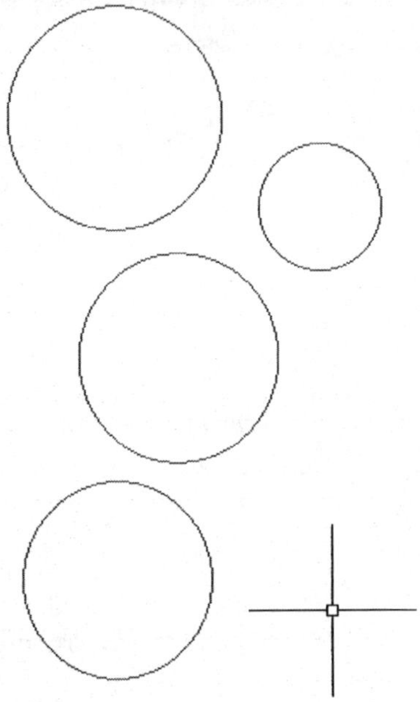

Repeat the circle command and create more circles on the Circles layer.

If you hover over a circle, AutoCAD will display information about the circle – including what layer it is on.

5. 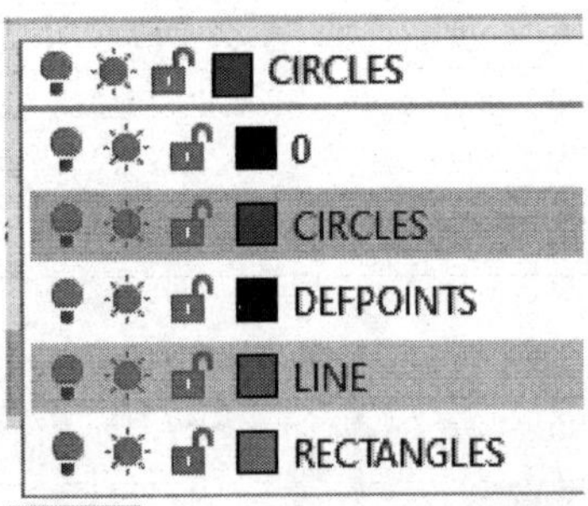

Use the Layer Control drop down list to select the LINE layer as the current layer.

6. 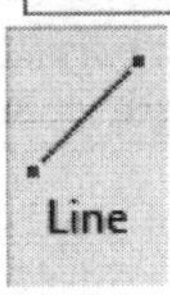

Invoke the **Line** command (l or line).
Specify first point:
Use the LMB to pick the first point.

7. 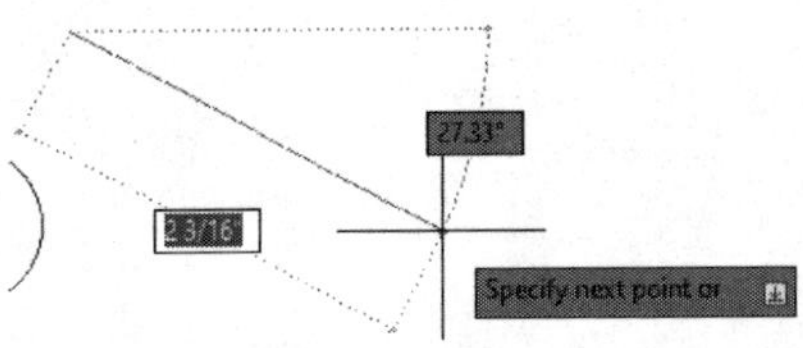

Specify next point or [Undo]:
Use the LMB to pick the second point. Notice that the line is green.

8. 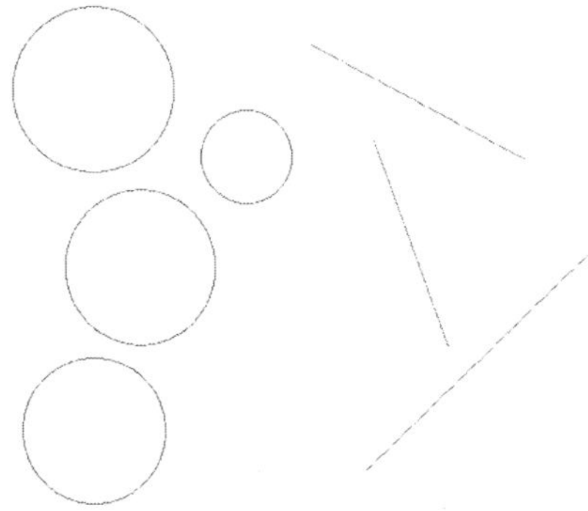

Create more line segments on the LINE layer and Click <ENTER> to end the command.

9. 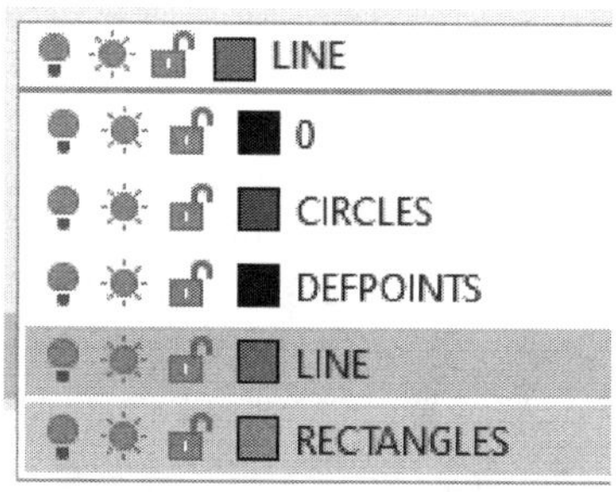

Use the Layer control drop-down list to select the **RECTANGLES** layer.

10. 

Start the RECTANGLE command.
Specify first corner point or [Chamfer/Elevation/Fillet/Thickness/Width]:
Use the LMB to select the first corner of the rectangle.

11. 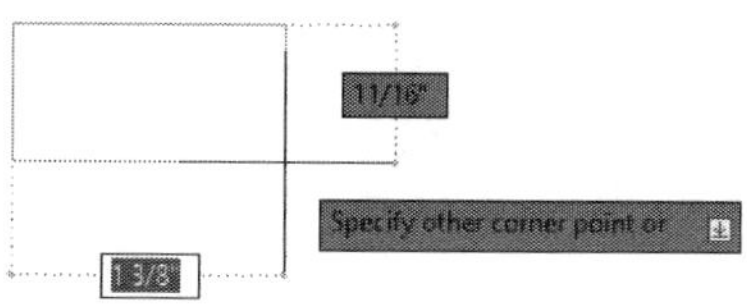

Specify other corner point:
Use the LMB to specify the second point of the rectangle.

12. 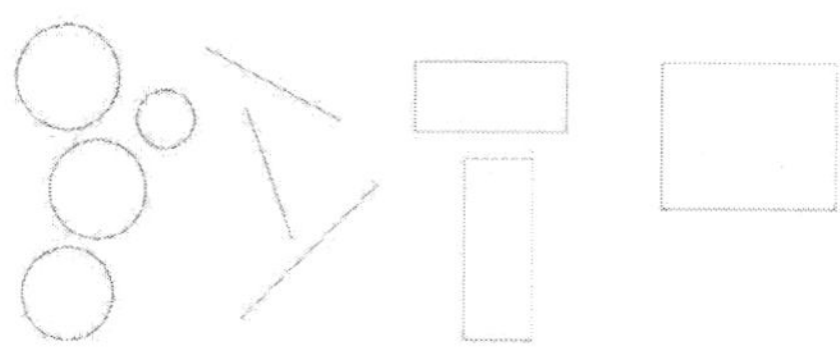

Repeat the rectangle command to create multiple rectangles on the RECTANGLES layer.

13. 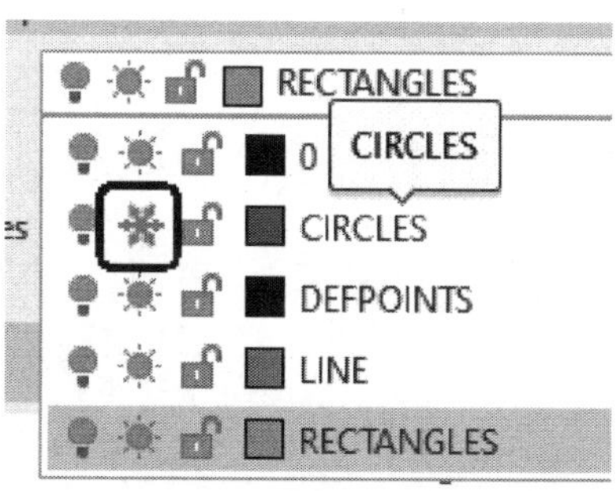

Freeze the CIRCLES layer by selecting the Layer Control drop-down list and selecting the Freeze / Thaw icon for a layer that is not current.

14. 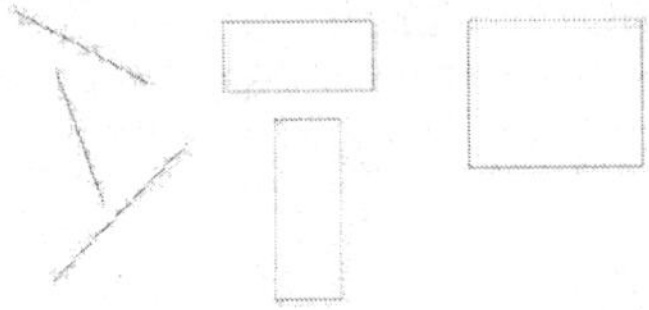

Note that the icon changes to a snowflake. Because the CIRCLES layer is frozen, the circles are no longer visible.

15. 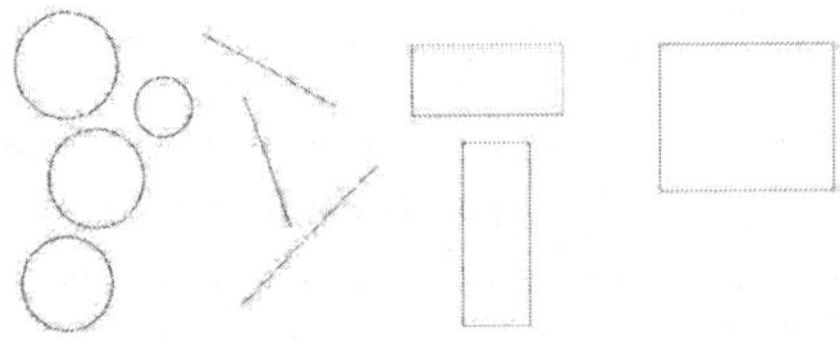

Left click on the Freeze/Thaw icon next to the Circles layer. This will thaw the layer and the icon will show as a sun.

Note that the circles are visible when the layer is thawed.

Extra: *Try freezing the current layer. What happens? Try turning a layer ON and OFF. Try drawing on a layer that is OFF. To toggle a layer ON/OFF, left click on the light bulb icon.*

You can draw on a layer that is turned OFF. But you cannot draw on a layer that is frozen. AutoCAD will not REGEN objects on a frozen layer. Locking a layer is a good way to filter the selection of objects. Entities on a locked layer cannot be edited.

Make an Object's Layer Current

Command Locator

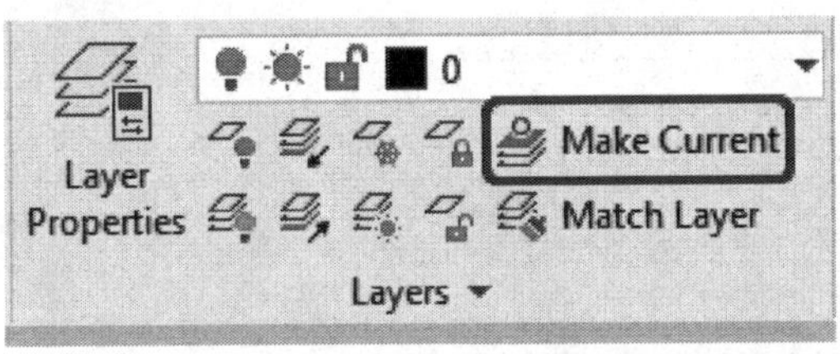

Command	**LAYMCUR**

Command Overview

Make a layer current by selecting an object in the drawing on that layer.

General Procedures

1. Select the Make Object's Layer Current button from the Properties toolbar.
2. Select the desired object.

Color Control

Command Locator

Command	**Color**
Alias	**COL**
Dialog Box	**Select Color**

Command Overview

This option controls the color of the objects currently being drawn. Typically, the colors of objects in the drawing should be determined *by the layer*, and it is not advisable to mix colors in the same layer. This is because the user will usually want to know at a glance that all objects that are Blue, for instance, are on a particular layer. Be sure that "ByLayer" appears in the Color Control box. When an object is selected with the Command Line blank, selecting a color from the drop-down list will automatically apply the color to the selected object.

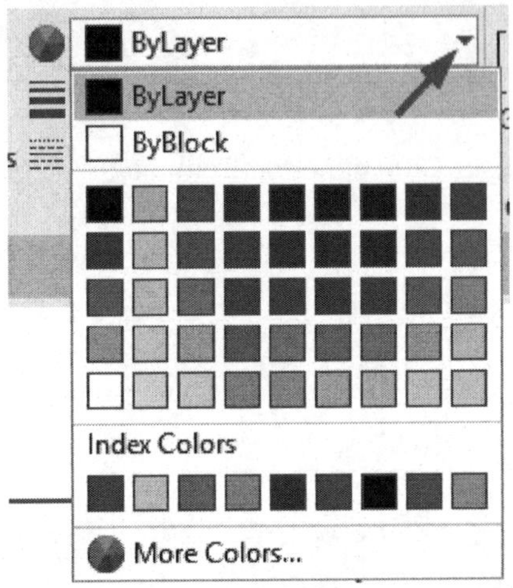

General Procedures

1. Select the down arrow in the Color Control list.
2. Select "ByLayer."

Tips & Tricks

- When drawing, make sure that the word "BYLAYER" appears in the Color Control window. This is a suggestion, but not the rule. This ensures that objects use the color assigned to the layer.
- The Color Control list will appear gray when in the middle of a command. Click Escape to cancel the command and the Color Control list will be accessible.
- Selecting "Other…" from the Color Control drop down list will display the Select Color dialog box and full Color Spectrum.

Linetype Control

Command Locator

Command	**Linetype**
Alias	**LTYPE**
Dialog Box	**Linetype Manager**

Command Overview

This option controls the Linetype of the objects currently being drawn. It is typical that a variety of linetypes may be present on the same layer, such as Continuous, Center and Hidden. However, it is best to leave the Linetype Control setting to ByLayer. Selecting "Other…" from the drop-down list will display the Linetype Manager dialog box. The user can load additional linetypes into the drawing using either this dialog box or the Layer Properties Manager dialog box.

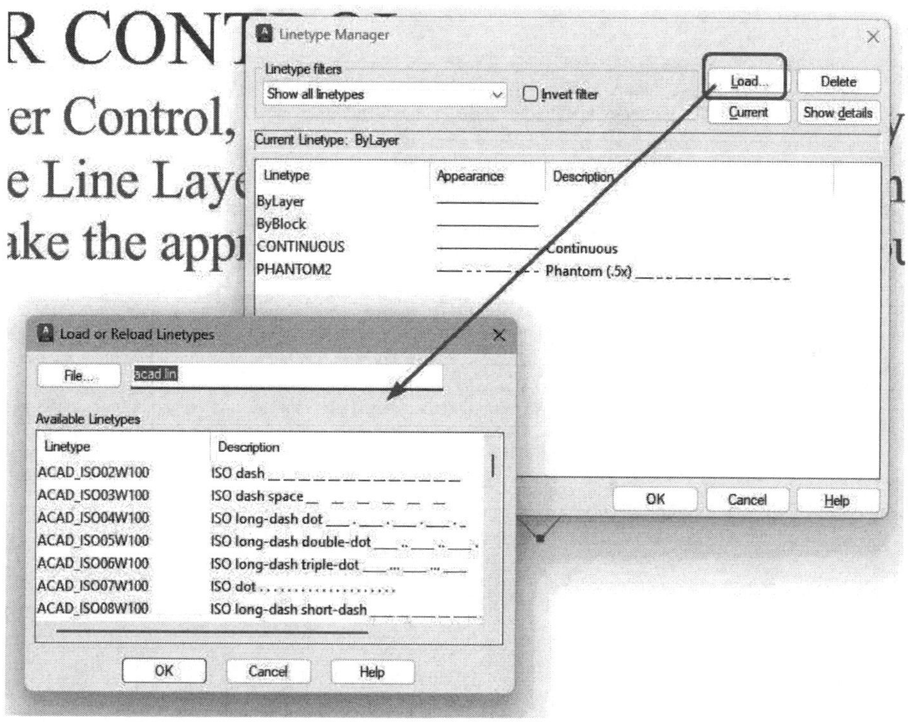

General Procedures

To load a linetype into the drawing:

1. Select the down arrow in the Linetype Control list.
2. Select "Other…"
3. From the Linetype Manager dialog box, select Load, then scroll through the list to find and select the linetypes to load into the drawing. Hold down the Control key to select alternate linetypes; hold down the Shift key to select several linetypes. Then select OK (two times) to exit.

- Verify that the word "ByLayer" appears in the Linetype Control window. If making another linetype current for a specific reason, remember to change it back to ByLayer. This means that objects drawn on the active layer will use the assigned linetype.
- Linetypes can be assigned to a Layer. This will be covered further on in this chapter.
- The system variable, LTSCALE, will globally control the scale of the linetypes in the drawing.
- Linetypes beginning with ACAD_ISO are for Metric drawings.

Lineweight Control

Command Locator

Command	**Lineweight**
Alias	**LWEIGHT**
Dialog Box	**Lineweight Settings**

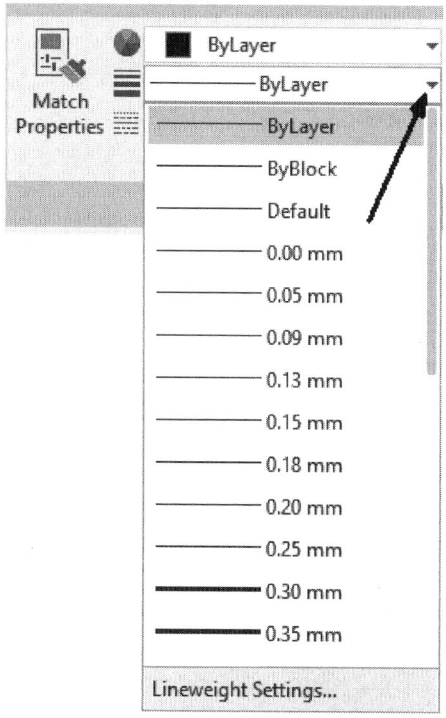

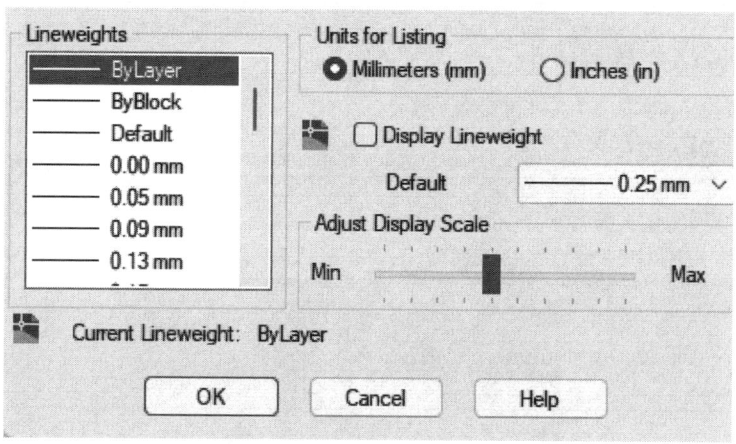

To access lineweight settings, scroll down to the bottom of the lineweight drop-down list.

Command Overview

The lineweight of the objects in the drawing can be controlled individually or by the Layer when set to ByLayer. You will learn how to determine linetypes by the Layer in the section that covers the Layer Properties Manager dialog box.

General Procedures

To make a lineweight the current setting:

1. Select the down arrow in the Linetype Control list.
2. Select the desired linewidth.

To change the lineweight of an existing object:

1. With the Command Line blank, select the objects in the drawing to change.
2. Select the down arrow in the Linetype Control list.
3. Select the desired linewidth. Once the lineweights of the objects have changed, Click Escape two times to cancel the selection.

- Verify that the word "ByLayer" appears in the Lineweight Control window. If selecting another lineweight current for a specific reason, remember to change it back to ByLayer. This means that objects drawn on the active layer will use the assigned lineweight.
- Lineweights can be assigned to a Layer.
- Lineweights will not be visible unless "Display Lineweight" is selected in the Lineweight Settings dialog box.

Layer Properties Manager

Command Locator

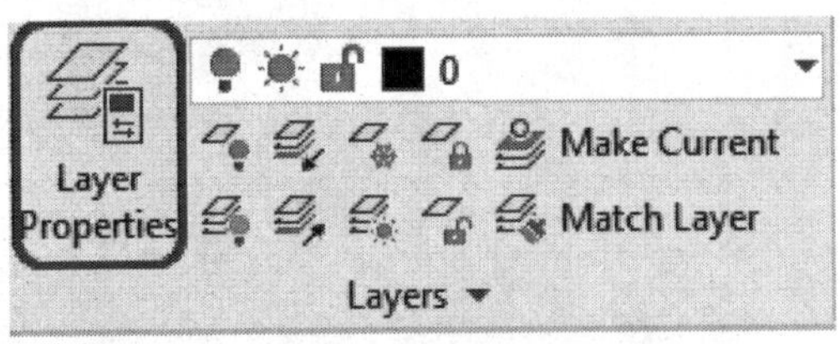

Command	**Layer**
Alias	**LA**
RMB Shortcut Menu	**Inside the Layer Dialog box**
Dialog Box	**Layer Properties Manager**

Command Overview

Use the Layer Properties Manager dialog box to create drawing Layers with specified Names, Colors, Linetypes, Lineweights, and Plot Styles (plot colors) and Plot variables (plottable or not). The layer lists may be sorted in ascending or descending order by double-clicking the heading, such as Name. Layer 0 is a default standard layer and cannot be renamed or deleted. This makes it a good "working layer." Other layers may only be deleted if there is no geometry on those layers and they are not "current." Layers may be made current, frozen, thawed, locked, unlocked, turned on or off from this dialog box. Once objects are created, they may be moved to other layers using the Match Properties, or the Properties commands, or by selecting the object with the Command line blank and selecting the layer to move it to from the drop-down list (shown in the previous section). Create a system of layers to save as a prototype or template drawing.

Feature	Overview
Named Layer Filters	This section controls what layer names are visible. For all practical purposes, the words "Show all layers" should be visible in the text window and the Invert Filter and Apply to Object Properties toolbar options should not be checked.
New	Select this button to create a New layer. The default name will be Layer1, Layer2, Layer3, etc. Type in a different layer name, or select the layer name twice to rename it.
Delete	This option allows selected layers to be deleted, only if the layer contains no geometry, or is not current.
Current	Select this option to make a highlighted layer current. A layer that is current cannot be frozen. You can also use the "Make Object's Layer Current" icon found in the Object Properties Toolbar to make a layer current. Select the object whose layer will become current.

Layer List Heading	Icon	Overview
Name		Lists the layer name. Select two times to rename a layer. Spaces and certain characters are not allowed. To select a layer in the dialog box, pick it (LMB); to deselect it, pick it again, select another layer or pick in the blank area of the dialog box. To select all layers, right-click (RMB) in the blank area and choose "Select All."
On / Off		Turns selected layers on or off. A layer that is turned OFF may still be current but will not be visible. This is an odd state because objects drawn on that layer will not be seen until the layer is turned back on.
Freeze / Thaw in all VP		Freezes or thaws selected layers in all view ports. A frozen layer is not visible and cannot be made current.
Lock / Unlock		Locks or unlocks selected layers. It is possible to lock a current layer and draw on a locked layer but not modify the objects on that layer until it is unlocked.
Color		Pick the color for the corresponding layer(s) to access the Select Color dialog box. Pick a color from the Standard Colors or the Full Color Palette to apply to a selected layer.

Linetype		Pick the linetype for the corresponding layer(s) to access the Select Linetype dialog box. Pick a linetype from "Loaded linetypes" list to apply to a selected layer. Select the Load button to access and select from the "Available linetypes" list.
Lineweight		Pick the lineweight for the corresponding layer(s) to access the Lineweight dialog box. Pick a lineweight from the list to apply to a selected layer.
Transparency		Sets the level of transparency for the layer; if level is set to 0, then layer is not transparent. Transparency can be set from 0 – 90, where 90 is fully transparent.
Plot Style		Controls how layers are plotted.
Plot		Makes a layer plottable or not.

General Procedures

1. Invoke the Layer command.
2. In the Layer Properties Manager dialog box, select New. Name the layer.
3. Select the corresponding color to access the Select Color dialog box, pick a color, then select OK.
4. Select the corresponding linetype to access the Select Linetype dialog box, and pick a linetype from the list. If the desired linetype is not in the list, select "Load…" and pick a linetype from the list. Select OK or Cancel to exit the Linetype dialog boxes.
5. Select OK to close the Layer Properties Manager dialog box.

Command Exercise

Exercise 7-2 – Drawing on Layers

Drawing Name: **layers1.dwg**
Estimated Time to Completion: 15 Minutes

Scope

In the layers dialog box, create the designated layers and draw the object using the appropriate layers. Do not simply copy the objects from the left side to the right side! Learn to create layers. Use the Grid and Snap tools to help you align the lines and rectangles.

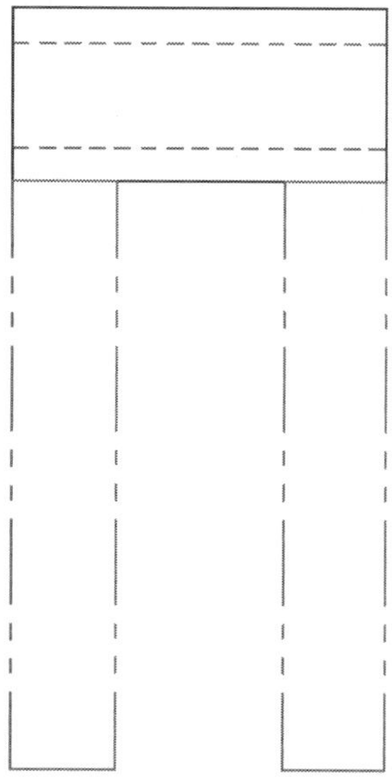

Solution

1. 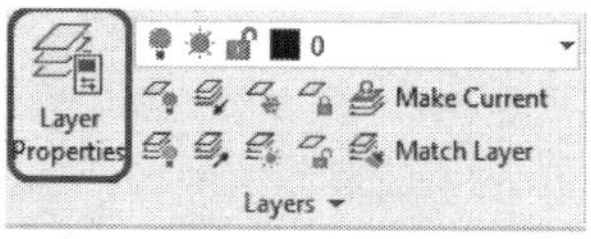

Invoke the **Layers** command (layer) to open the Layer Properties Manager.

2. 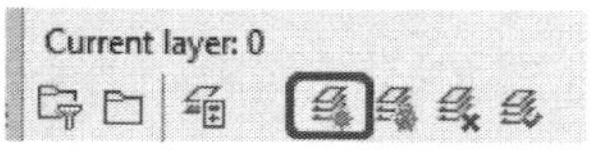

In the Layer Properties Manager dialog box Click the **New** button with the LMB.

This will create a new layer called 'Layer1' in rename mode.

3. 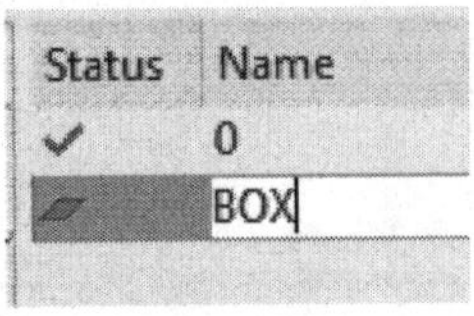

In the dialog box, rename LAYER1 to **BOX**.

4. 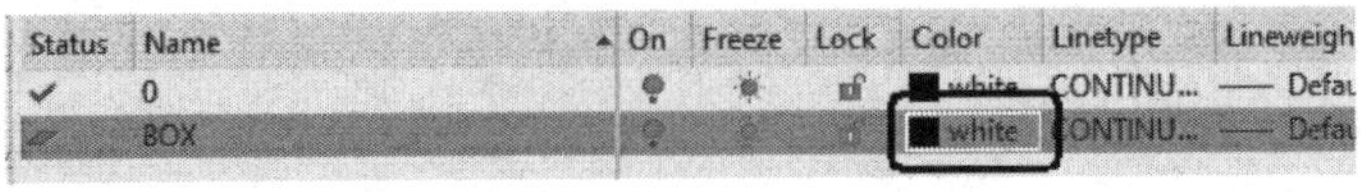

Use the LMB to select the color box to change the color associated with the BOX layer.

5. 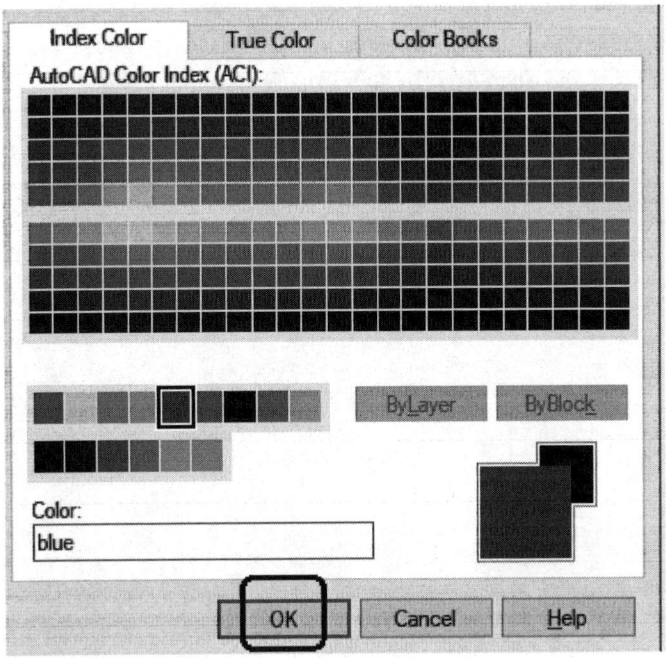

Use the LMB to select BLUE from the Standard Colors section in the Select Color dialog box.

Click **'OK'** to complete the change.

6. 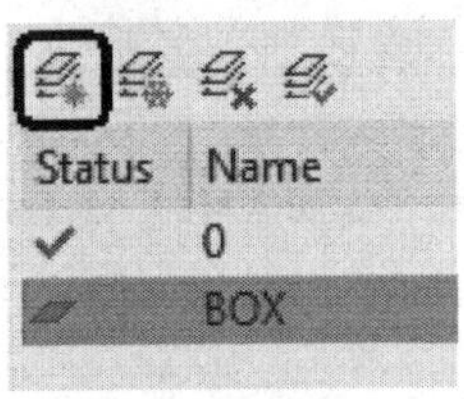

Create a third layer by Clicking the **New** button in the Layer Properties Manager dialog box.

7. 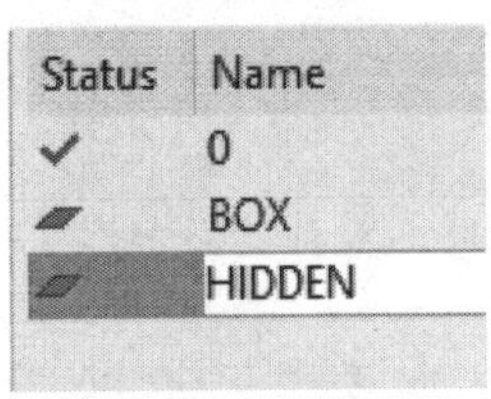

Rename the new layer to **HIDDEN**.

8. 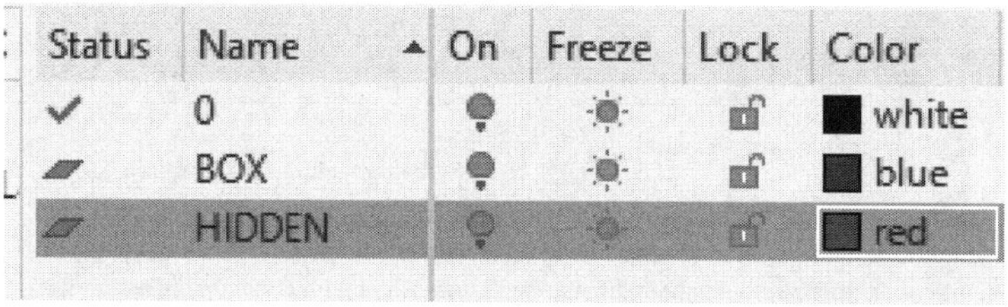

Set the color to **RED**.

9. 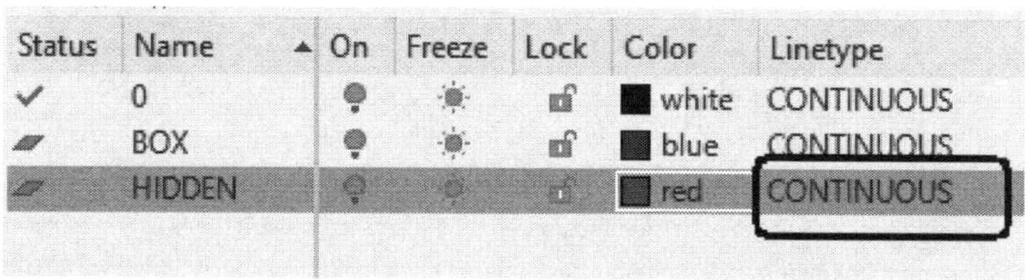

Use the LMB and Click on the Word CONTINUOUS under Linetype for the HIDDEN layer.

This will activate the Select Linetype dialog box.

10. 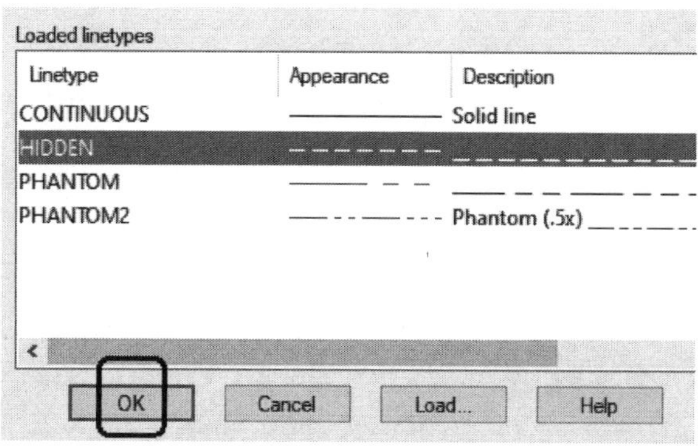

Use the LMB to select the **HIDDEN** Linetype.

Click '**OK**'.

11. 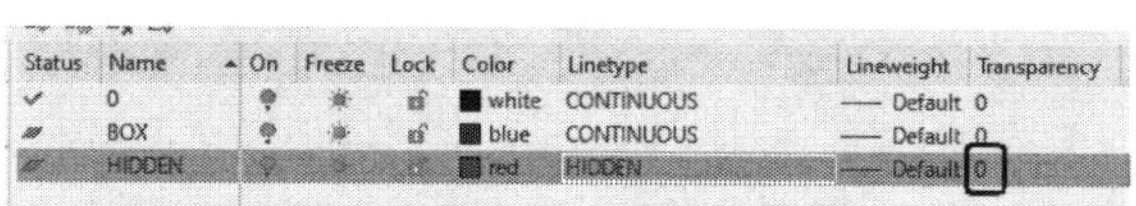

LMB on the **0** under the Transparency column.

12. 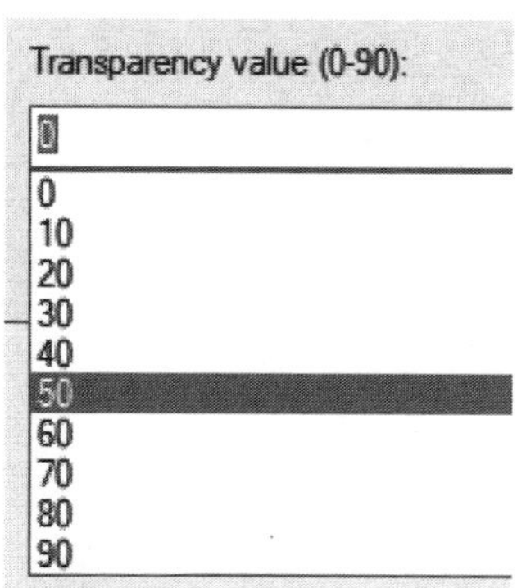

Enter the value **50** in the dialog or select from the drop-down list.

Click **OK** to continue.

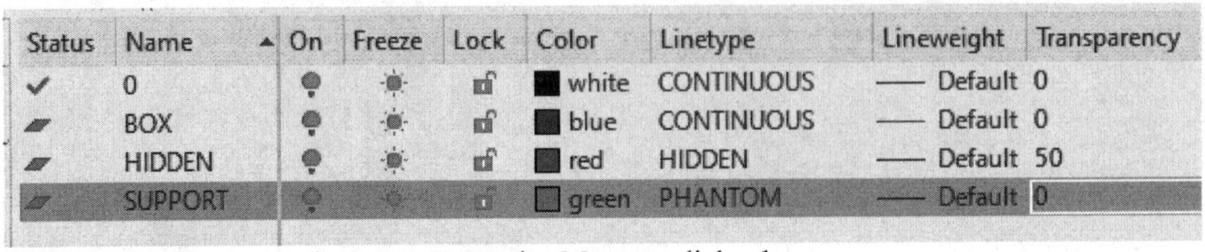

13. Click the **New** button in the Layer Properties Manager dialog box.
Rename the new layer to **SUPPORT**.
Change the color to **green**.
Set the linetype to **PHANTOM**.
Transparency should be set to **0**.

14. 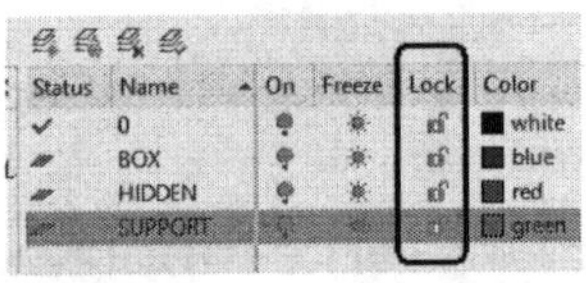

Make sure that your layers are UNLOCKED or you will not be able to edit any objects you place on that layer.

15. 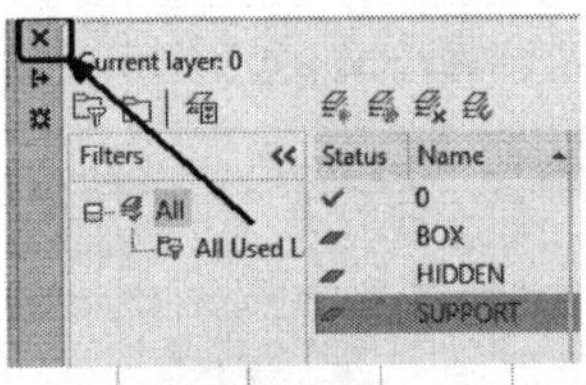

When you have finished creating the three layers, close the dialog box by clicking the 'x' button in the upper corner.

16. 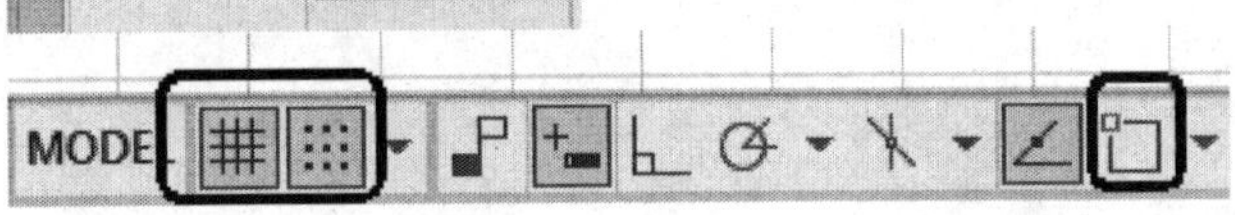

Turn ON GRID and SNAP.

Turn OFF object snaps.

Use the grid to help you place the lines and rectangles.

17. 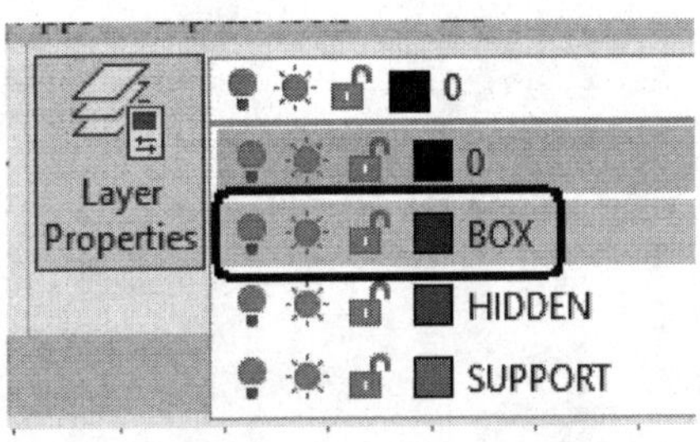

Start by setting the BOX layer current before you create the blue box.

Select the **BOX** layer from the Layer Dropdown list in the Object Properties toolbar.

18. 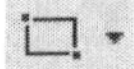

Invoke the **Rectangle** command (rectang).
Use your mouse and LMB to create the blue rectangle.

19. 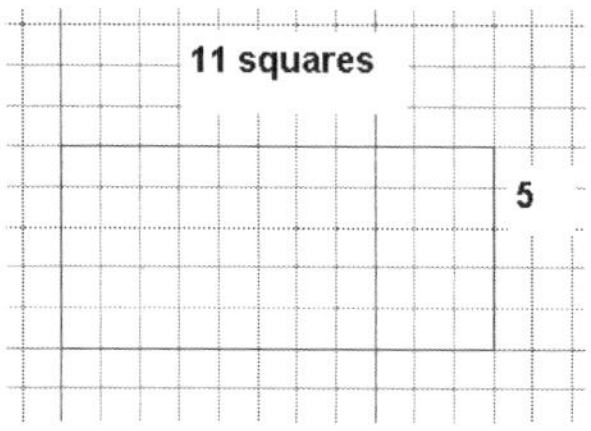

The rectangle is 11 grid squares in the horizontal direction and five grid squares in the vertical direction.

20. 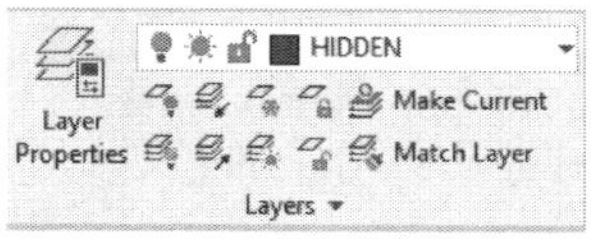

Set the **HIDDEN** layer current.

21. 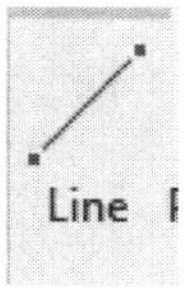

Select the **LINE** tool from the Draw panel on the ribbon.

22. 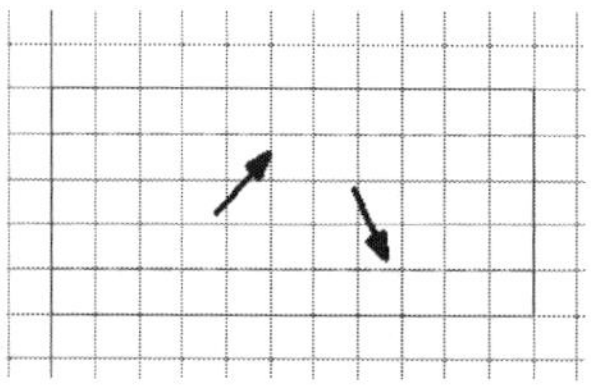

Draw the two horizontal lines inside the blue rectangle.

The lines are located one grid below the top of the rectangle and one grid above the bottom of the rectangle.

23. 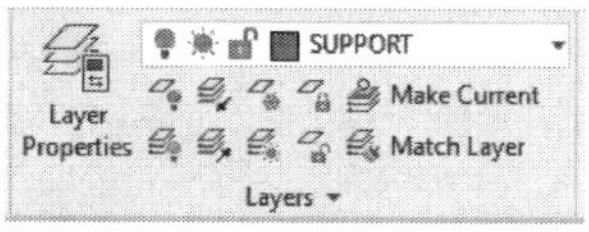

Set the SUPPORT layer current.

24. 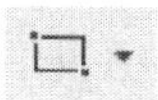 Select the RECTANGLE tool from the Draw panel on the ribbon.

25. 

Place two green rectangles.

Each rectangle is three grid squares in the horizontal direction and seventeen grid squares in the vertical direction.

EXTRA: *Type LTSCALE at the command line and change the linetype scale to 0.75. View the changes to your drawing. Repeat LTSCALE, and change it to 0.25. View the drawing, then set it back to 0.5. From the Layer Properties dialog box change the colors associated with the layers you created. Change the linetype of the layers. View your drawing.*

Tips & Tricks

- Use the Freeze option instead of Off. Layers that are frozen are completely ignored in a regeneration, and hence will speed regeneration time.
- Deleting a selected Layer or linetype is similar to the PURGE command.
- A layer can be renamed any time. This will help to organize the information in the drawing.
- Layer 0 cannot be renamed or deleted.
- The Color, Linetype and Lineweight Control options in the Properties Toolbar should be set to Bylayer. In this way these options will be determined by the layer.
- The system variable LTSCALE controls the global scale of the linetypes in the drawing. The effects of LTSCALE apply to linetypes that contain spaces and dashes (i.e., the hidden or the center linetypes).
- Refer to Scale Factor Chart to help determine an appropriate LTSCALE.
- You can create more than one layer at a time by typing a comma at the end of your layer name.
- Transparency controls how bright objects appear.
- To rename a layer: double click on the name with the LMB to activate a cursor that will allow you to type a new name.
- Double clicking on a layer will also set it to be the current layer.
- Use the shortcut ALT+C to set a selected object's layer current.

Command Exercise

Exercise 7-3 – Creating Layers

Drawing Name: **new drawing** (use the acad.dwt template)
Estimated Time to Completion: 10 Minutes

Scope

Practice creating layers, loading linetypes and assigning linetypes and colors to the layers.

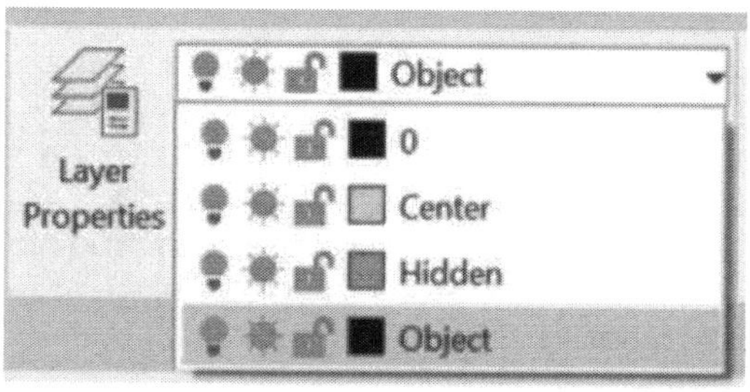

Solution

1. 

Select the + tab to start a new drawing.

2. 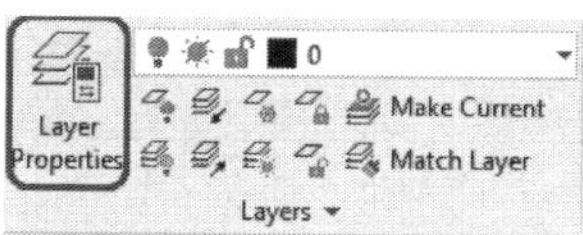

Invoke the **Layers** command (layer) to open the Layer Properties Manager.

3. 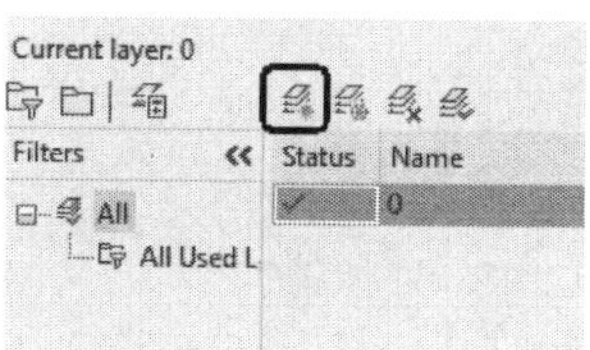

In the Layer Properties Manager dialog box Click the **New** button with the LMB.

This will create a new layer called 'Layer1' in rename mode.

4. 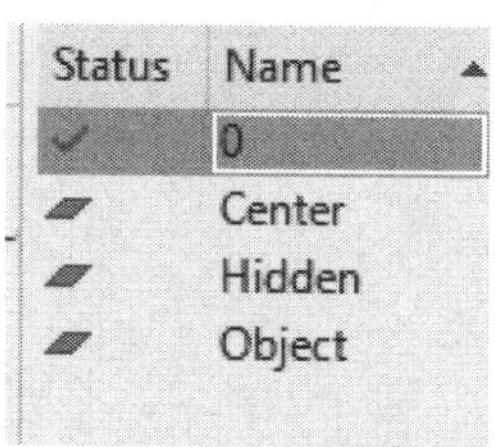

Create three layers:
   - Object
   - Hidden
   - Center

If you type a comma after you enter the layer name, AutoCAD will automatically drop a line so you can add the next layer.

Your layers are automatically organized in alphabetical order.

5. 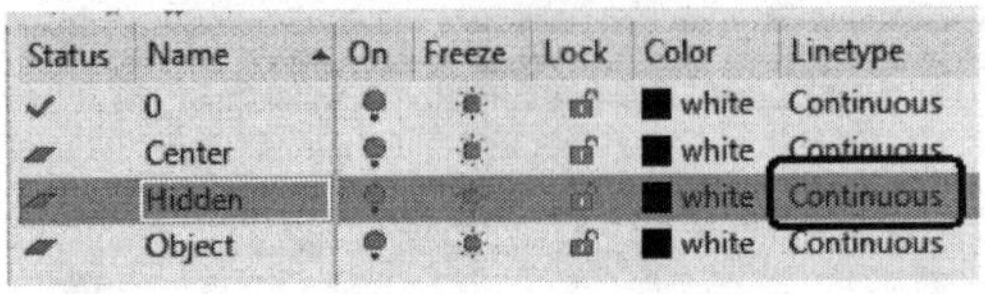

Highlight the **Hidden** layer.

Pick the word **Continuous** to assign a different linetype.

6. 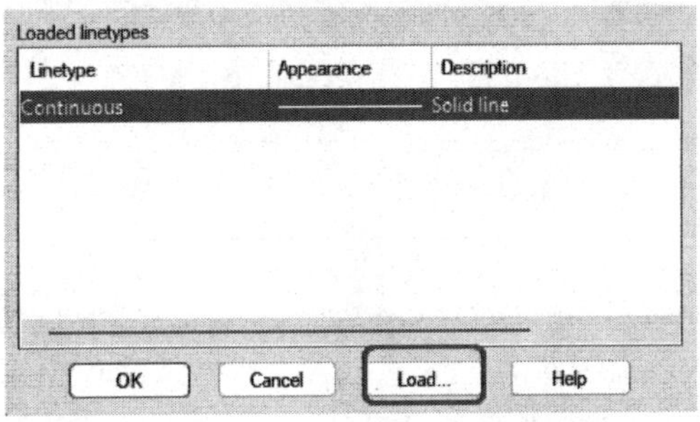

Click the **LOAD** button.

7. 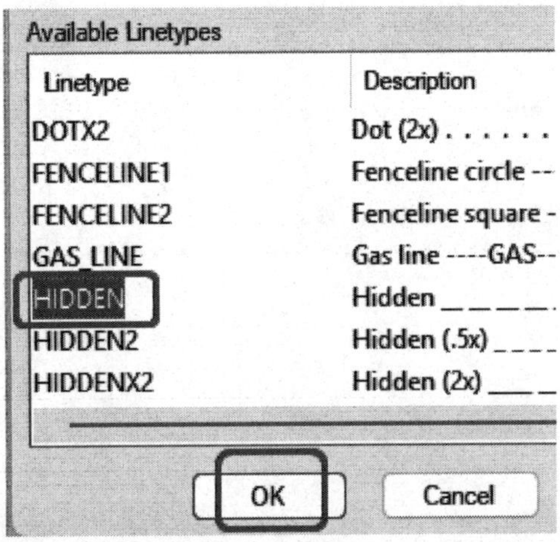

Use the scroll bar on the right side of the dialog to locate the Hidden linetype.

Select the **Hidden** linetype.

Click **OK**.

This loads the selected linetype into the active drawing.
You can select more than one linetype to load by holding down the ***Control*** *key.*

8. 

HIDDEN is now listed as a loaded linetype.

Highlight **HIDDEN**.

Click **OK**.

This assigns the HIDDEN linetype to the selected layer.

9. 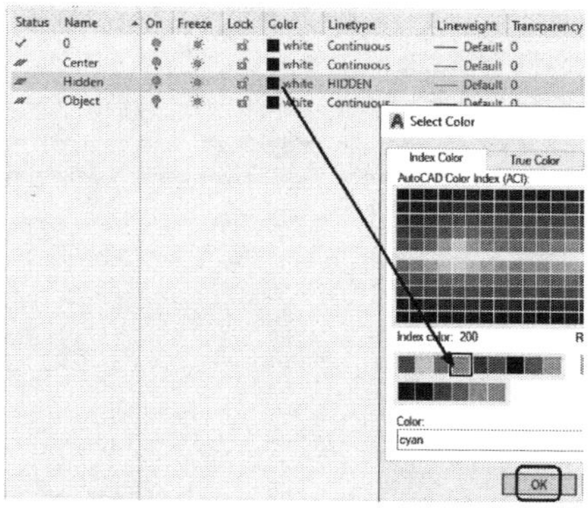

Highlight the HIDDEN layer.

Pick the Color button.

Select the **Cyan** color.

Click **OK**.

The Cyan color has now been assigned to the Hidden layer.

10. 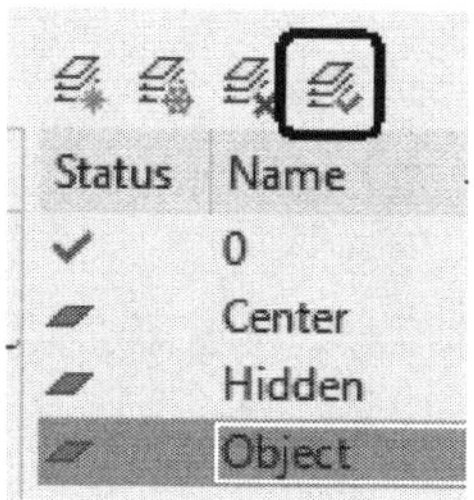

Highlight **Object** and select the Set Current icon.

You can also use Alt-C as a shortcut.
This sets the Object Layer current.

We want the Object layer to be the Current layer – the layer where any entities we create are placed.

Close the Layer Manager dialog.

11. 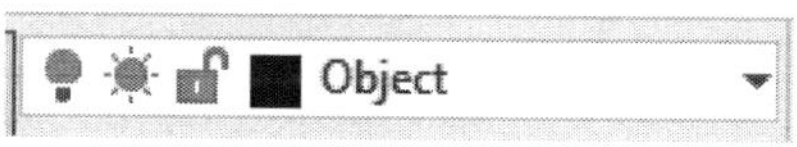

The Current Layer is noted at the top bar of the Layer dialog.
You also see a green check next to the current layer.

12. 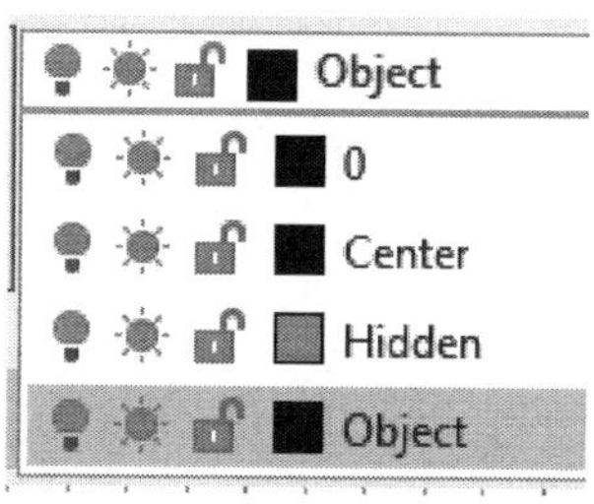

Left click on the drop-down arrow in the layer list.

Notice that the layers are listed in alphabetic order.
You can set a layer current by selecting it from the drop-down list.
You can quickly assign an object to a layer by selecting it and then selecting the layer from the drop-down list.

EXTRA: *Assign the Center layer the color yellow. Load the CENTER linetype and assign it to the Center layer.*

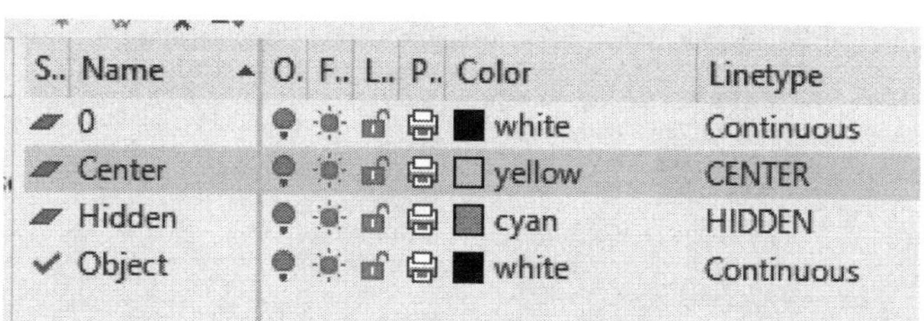

Command Exercise

Exercise 7-4 – Rename Layers

Drawing Name: **layers2.dwg**
Estimated Time to Completion: 5 Minutes

Scope

In the Layer Properties dialog box, Rename layer #1 to WINDOW. Make the House Layer current. Select all, then Freeze all.

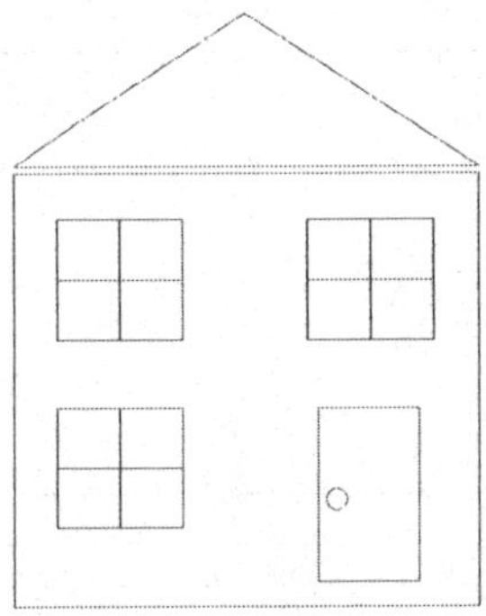

Solution

1. 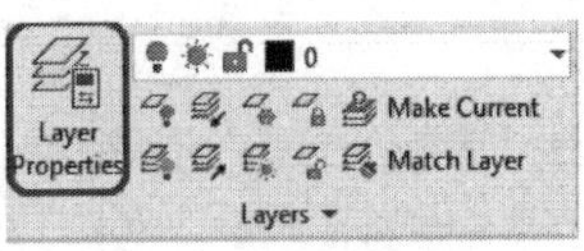

Invoke the **Layers** command (layer) to open the Layer Properties Manager.

2. 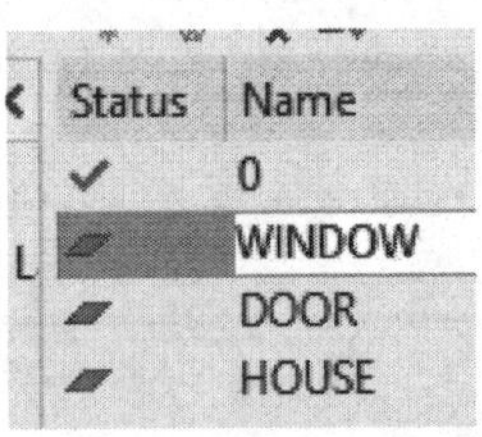

In the Layer Properties Manager, double click on the name of Layer '1' to rename it to **WINDOW**.

You also can right click and select Rename Layer or Click F2.

3. 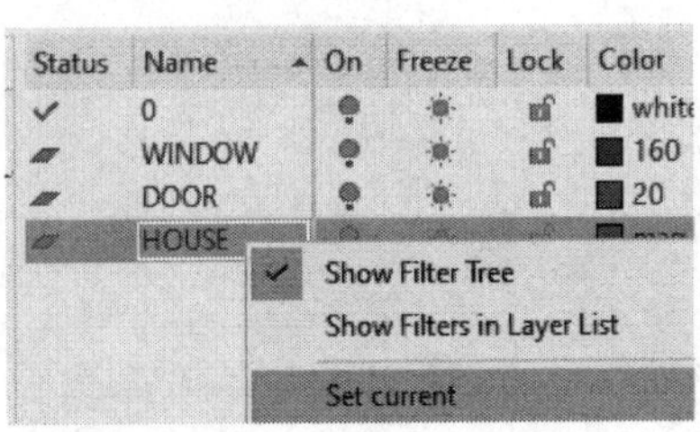

Select the **HOUSE** layer and set it current by Clicking the 'Current' button.

You can also right click and select 'Set current'.

4. 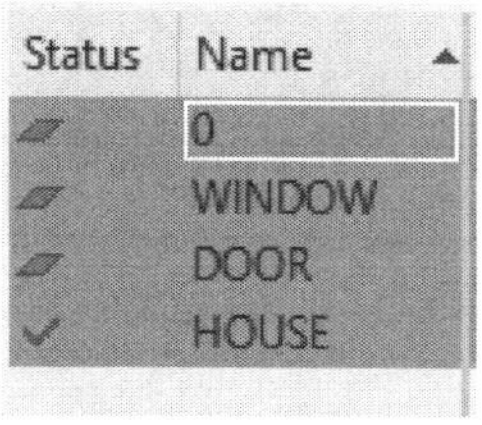

Hold down the <SHIFT> key to select all the layers so they are highlighted.

5. 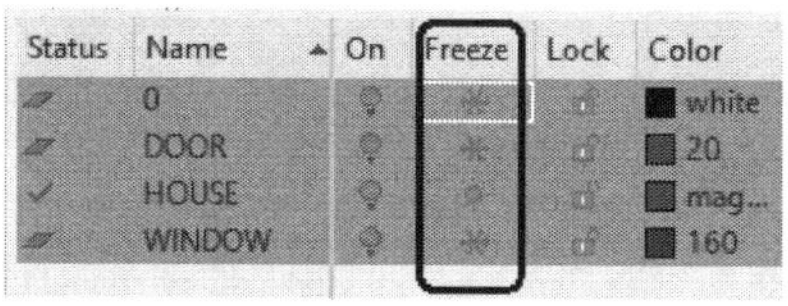

LMB click the sun in the Freeze column on the first row.

6. 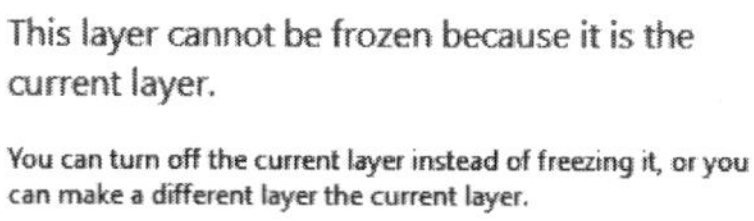

A warning message will appear.

Click **Close.**

All the layers will be frozen except for the current layer – House.

7. 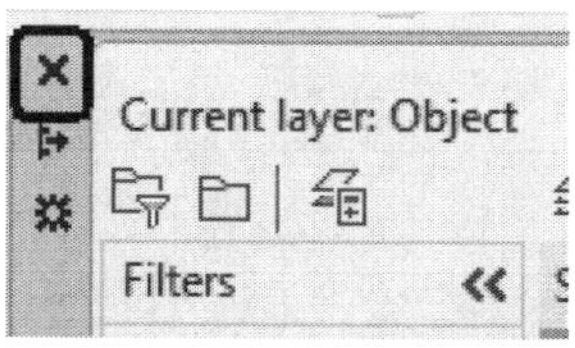

Close the layer properties dialog by Clicking the X in the corner.

Extra: *Try Freezing and Thawing different layers. Try turning different layers ON or OFF.*

- *Remember visually turning layers OFF is similar to Freezing, but time can be saved during regeneration if a layer is Frozen.*

When you first start out as a drafter, chances are you won't be creating drawings from scratch. Instead, you will be given legacy drawings to work on. (A legacy drawing is an older drawing that needs to be updated to comply with engineering changes or standards.) Your first step upon opening up a legacy drawing should be to identify how the drawing is organized; i.e. which objects are on which layers. Once you have determined how the drawing is organized, you may opt to move objects onto different layers to make it easier to work on the drawing or in order to comply with your company's CAD standards.

There is more than one tool inside of AutoCAD to help you identify which elements are assigned to each layer. Every user has their own individual preference on which tool to use. There is no wrong answer. Use the tool that is the most comfortable for you.

Layer Translator

Command Locator

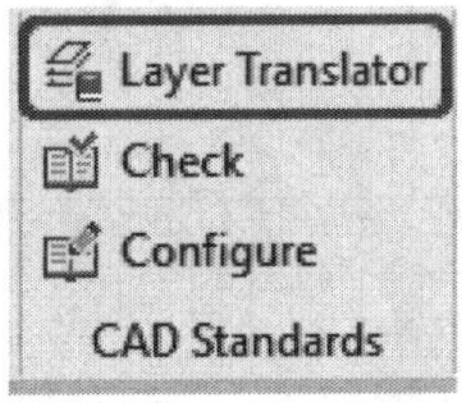

Manage Ribbon/CAD Standards	**Layer Translator**
Command	**LAYTRANS**
Dialog Box	**Layer Translator**

Command Overview

Reassigns the layers in a current drawing to specified layer standards. Normally this is done when you receive a drawing from an outside source or if someone within your company failed to follow the company's standards. You can map layers in the current drawing to rename layers, change layer properties, etc. All elements on the designated layers are moved to the selected layers.

You can also use the Layer Translator to view elements on different layers and control which layers are visible.

You can purge/delete any layers which have no elements assigned. Eliminating empty layers reduces the drawing size and makes the drawing more manageable.

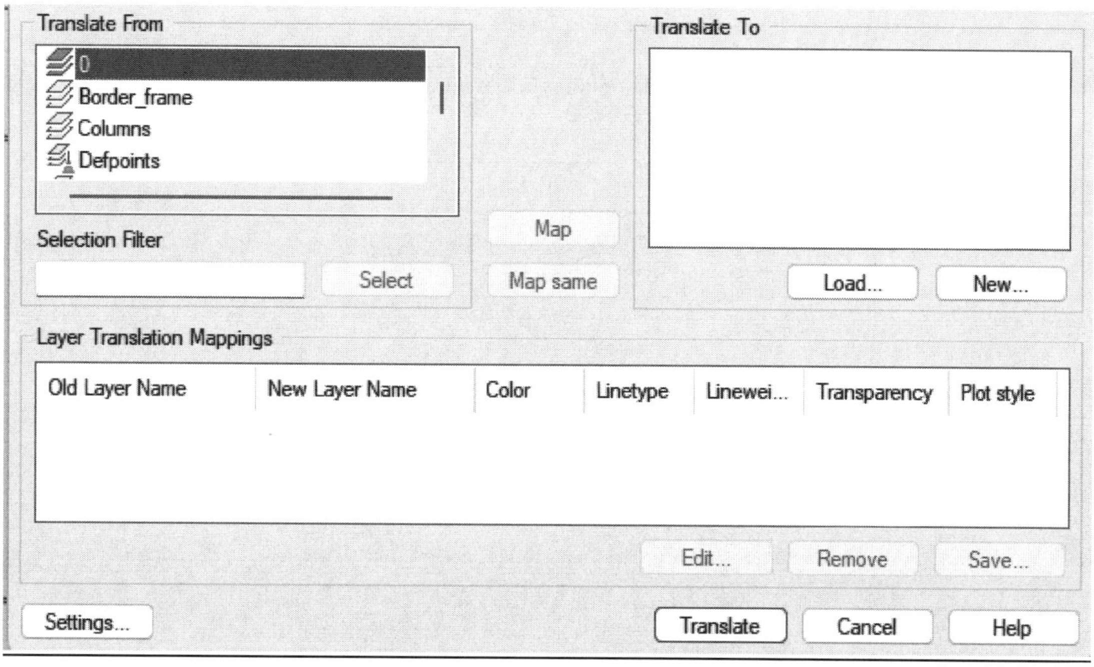

The color of the icon preceding the layer name indicates whether or not the layer is referenced in the drawing. A dark icon indicates that the layer contains elements; a white icon indicates the layer is empty. Unreferenced layers can be deleted from the drawing by right-clicking in the Translate From list and choosing Purge Layers.

Selection Filter	Specifies layers to be selected in the Translate From list, using a naming pattern that can include wild cards. The layers identified by the selection filter are selected in addition to any layers previously selected. AutoCAD allows the use of several different wildcard symbols. The most common is the * which allows you to type in a character string and searches the layer names to match that string.
Map	Moves elements on the Translate From layer to the layer selected in Translate To.
Map Same	Moves elements to all layers that have the same name in both lists.
Translate To	Lists the layers you can use for the current drawing. If the current drawing does not have this layer defined, the layer is created with the desired properties.
Load	Loads layers in the Translate To list using an existing drawing, usually a standards drawing. You can load layers from more than one file. If you load a file that contains layers with the same name as layers already loaded, the duplicate layer names are ignored.
New	Defines a new layer to be added to the Translate To list. Basically, you can create a new layer to be used in the active drawing 'on the fly'. You cannot

	create a new layer with the same name as an existing layer.
Settings	Launches the Settings dialog box where you can customize the layer translation.
Translate	Starts the layer translation process. If you have not saved the current layer mapping, you will be prompted to see if you want to save the mappings.

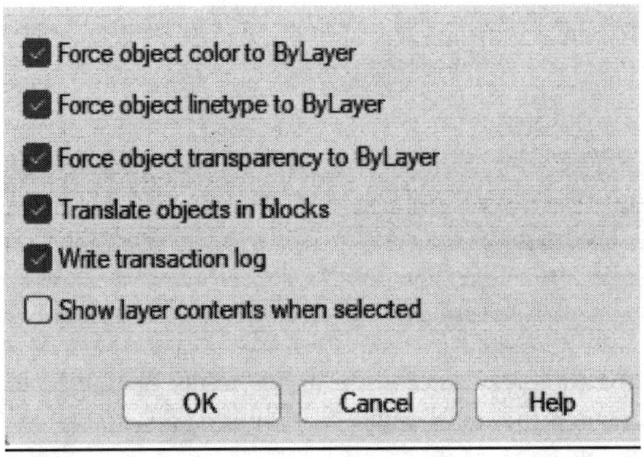

Use the Settings to control how layer properties are managed when elements are moved from one layer to another.

General Procedures

1. Invoke the Laytrans command.
2. Use Settings to manage the layer properties.
3. Click on Load to select a drawing with the layers you want to use for the current drawing.
4. In the Translate From panel, select the layer you want to re-assign. In the Translate To, select the layer you want to use instead of the layer selected in the Translate From panel.
5. Click Translate to replace the existing layers with the selected layers. You will be prompted if you want to save your mapping settings to use in other drawings.

Command Exercise

Exercise 7-5 – Identifying Layers

Drawing Name: **Floor Plan.dwg**
Estimated Time to Completion: 10 Minutes

Scope

Use the Layer Translator to identify the layers in a drawing.

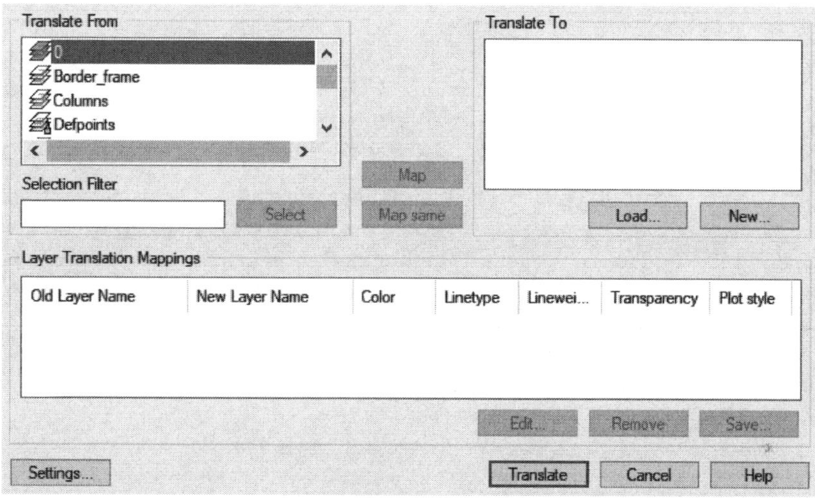

Solution

1.

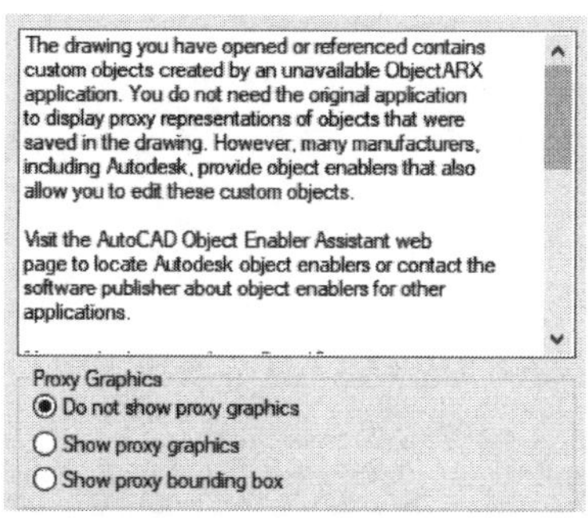

If this dialog appears when you open the drawing,

Select **Do not show proxy graphics.**

Click **OK.**

2.

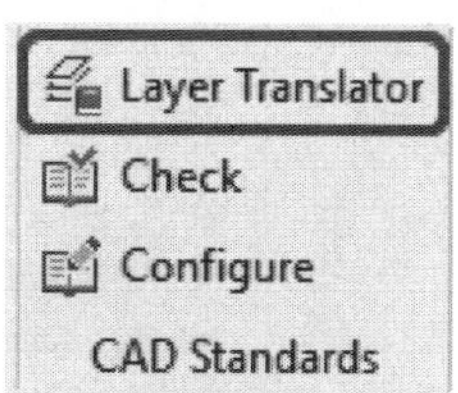

Activate the **Manage** tab on the ribbon.
Select the **Layer Translator** on the CAD Standards panel.

3. 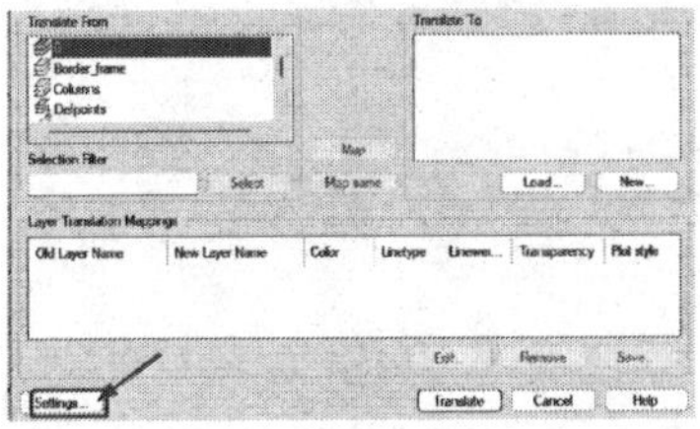

Select **Settings**.

4. 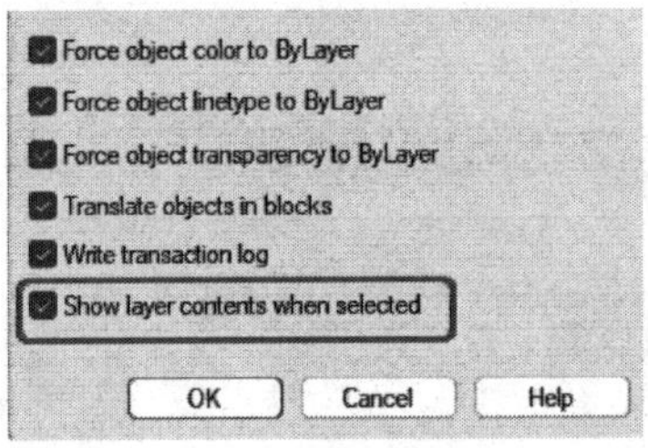

Enable **Show layer contents when selected.**

Click **OK**.

5. 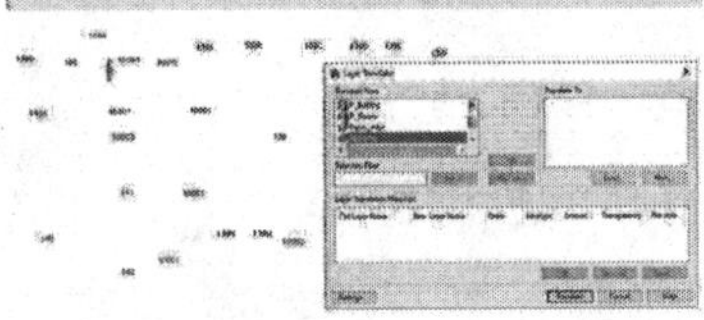

Move the Layer Translator dialog to the side so you can see the drawing.

Select each layer in the Translate From list. Note which objects are visible when which layers are highlighted. You can use the up and down arrows on the keyboard to scroll through the layers.

Note that several layers don't have anything on them.

6. Close the Layer Translator.

Close the file without saving.

➢ If you don't want to see the proxy graphics dialog when you open drawings, go to OPTIONS, select the Open and Save tab, disable the Show Proxy Information dialog box.

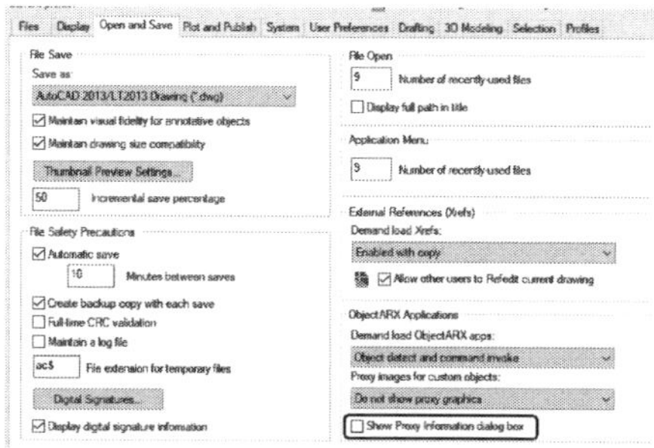

Command Exercise

Exercise 7-6 – Using the Layer Translator

Drawing Name: **elevation.dwg**
Estimated Time to Completion: 15 Minutes

Scope

Often you will work on a file with objects residing on the wrong layer. The Layer Translator makes it easy for you to organize drawings according to your company standards.

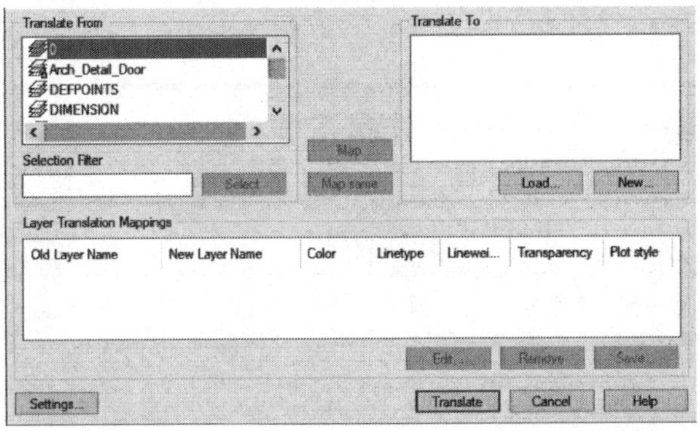

Solution

1. 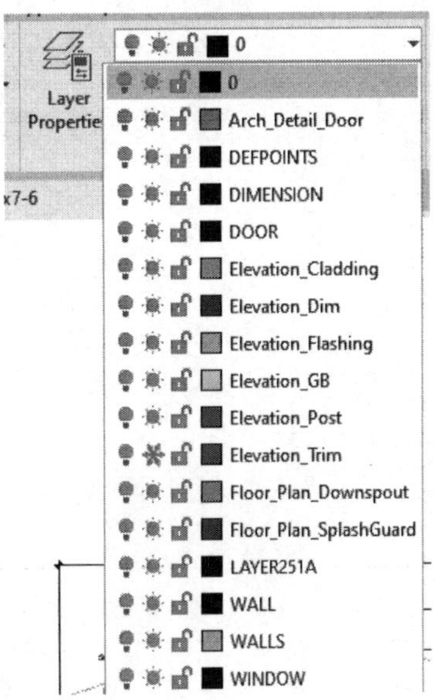

Check the layer drop-down list to see what layers currently exist in the drawing.

2. 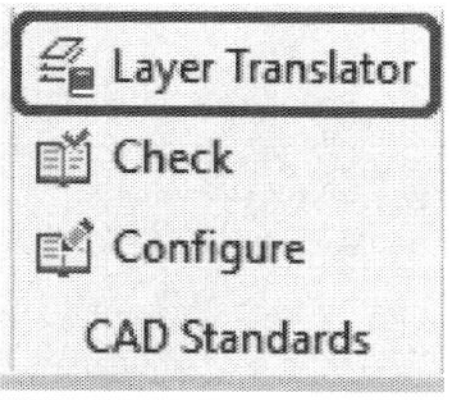

Activate the **Manage** tab on the ribbon.

Select the **Layer Translator** on the CAD Standards panel.

3. 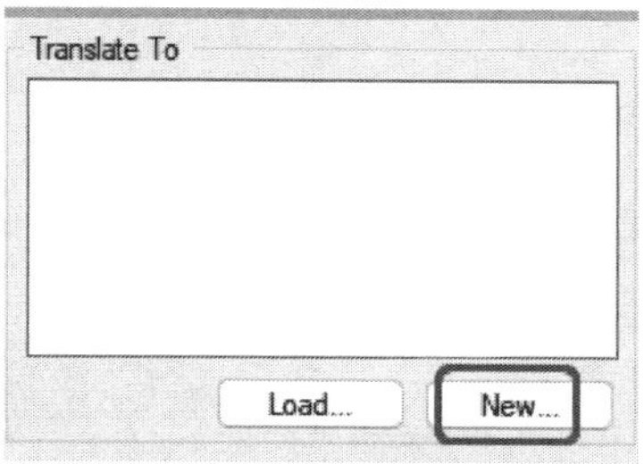

Select the **New** button.

4. 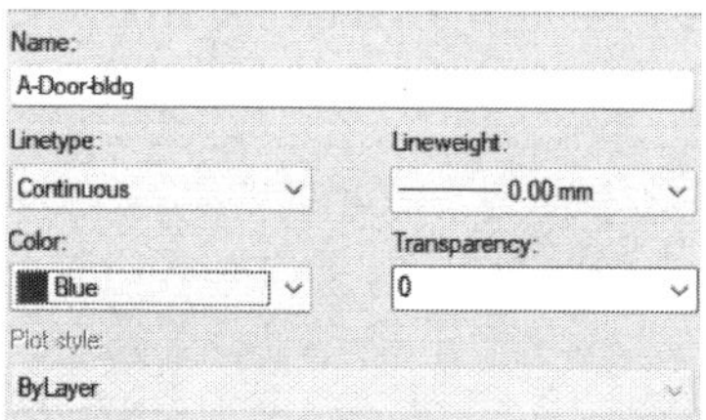

In the New Layer dialog:
In the Name field, enter **A-Door-bldg**.
Set the Color to **Blue**.

Click **OK**.

Note that the A-Door-bldg. layer is listed in the Translate To list.

5. 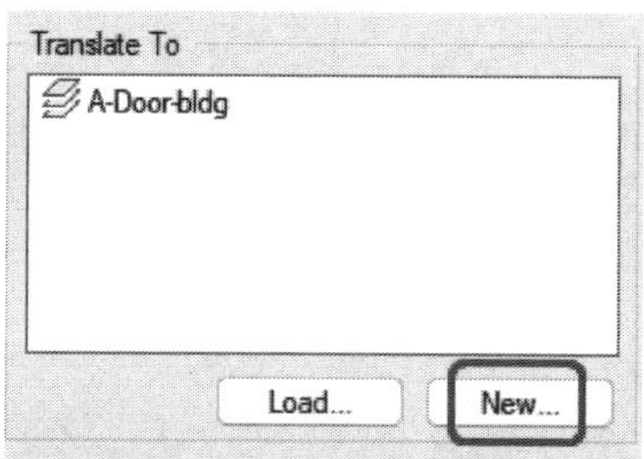

Select the **New** button.

6. 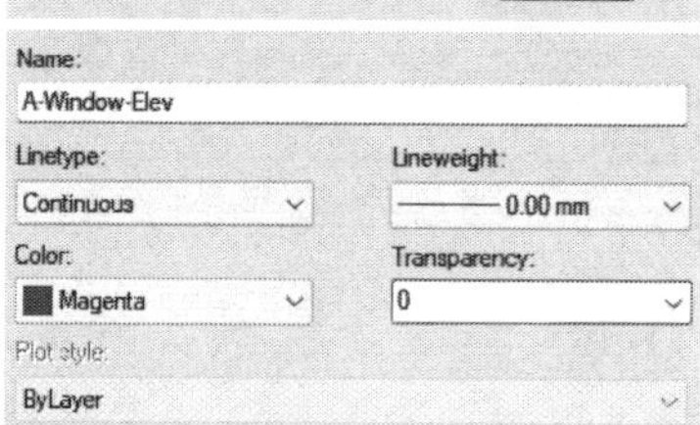

In the New Layer dialog:

In the Name field, enter **A-Window-Elev**.

Set the Color to **Magenta**.

Click **OK**.

7. 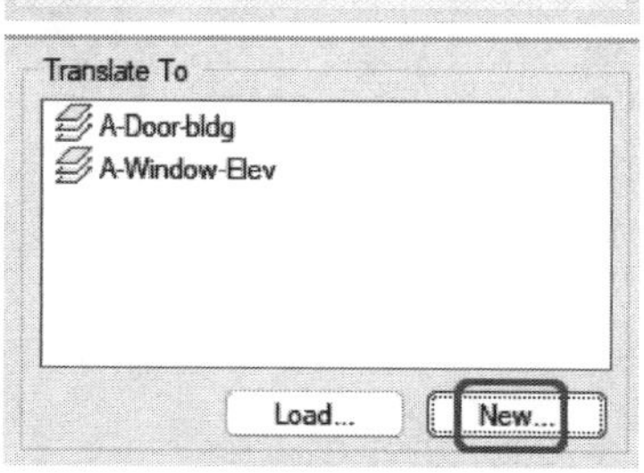

Select the **New** button.

8. 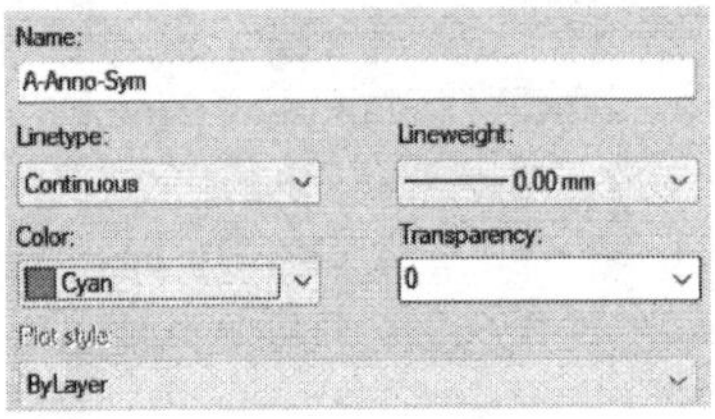

In the New Layer dialog:

In the Name field, enter **A-Anno-Sym**.

Set the Color to **Cyan**.

Click **OK**.

9. 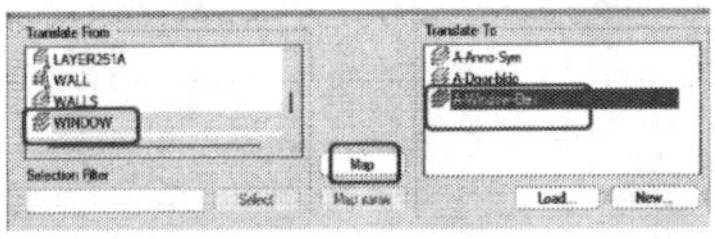

Highlight **WINDOW** in the Translate From window.
Highlight **A-Window-Elev** in the Translate To window.
Select **Map**.

10. 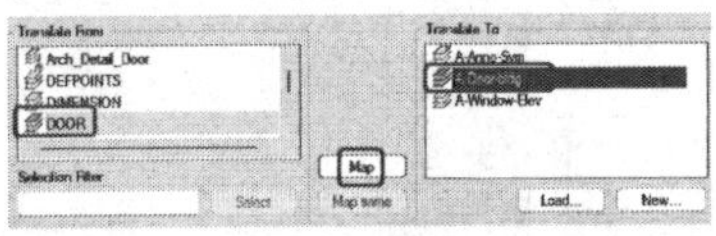

Highlight **DOOR** in the Translate From window.
Highlight **A-Door-bldg** in the Translate To window.
Select **Map**.

11. 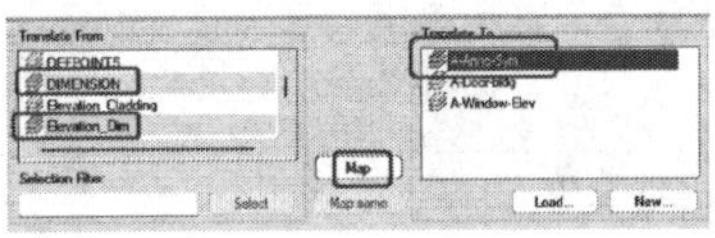

Hold down the Control key.

Highlight **DIMENSION** and **Elevation_Dim** in the Translate From window.

Highlight **A-ANNO-SYM** in the Translate To window.
Select **Map**.

You can map more than one layer at a time.

The list of layers to translate are listed in the lower panel.

12. 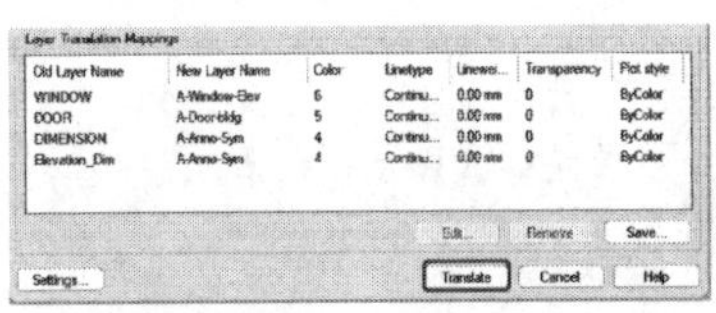

Select **Translate**.

13. 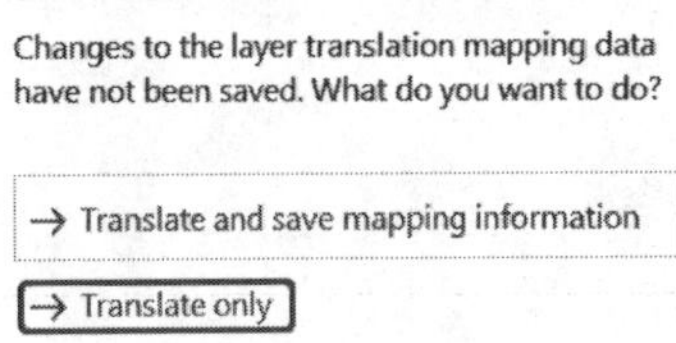

Select **Translate Only**.

You may wish to Save your mapping settings if you plan to translate more than one drawing from the same source.

14. 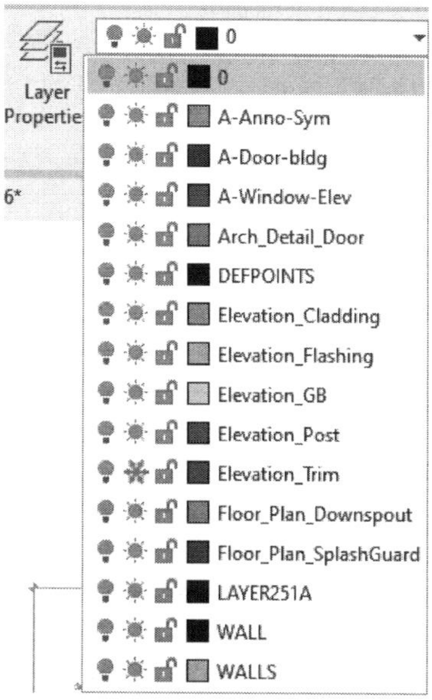

Check your layer drop-down list.

Note that the new layers have been created and that the Doors, Windows, Dimension and Elevation_Dim layers have been purged. The objects on those layers have been moved to the assigned layers.

15. Close the drawing without saving.

Extra: Create a new layer called A-Wall-bldg with the color Black and move objects on the WALL layer to the new layer using the Layer Translator.

Command Exercise

Exercise 7-7 – Using the Layer Translator with a CAD Standards drawing

Drawing Name: **cad_standards.dwg, aia.dwg**
Estimated Time to Completion: 10 Minutes

Scope

Many companies will set up a standards drawing which contains the company's standard layers, title block, notes, and blocks. You can use the standards drawing to fix the layer names and properties of legacy drawings, third-party drawings, or drawings which were set up incorrectly.

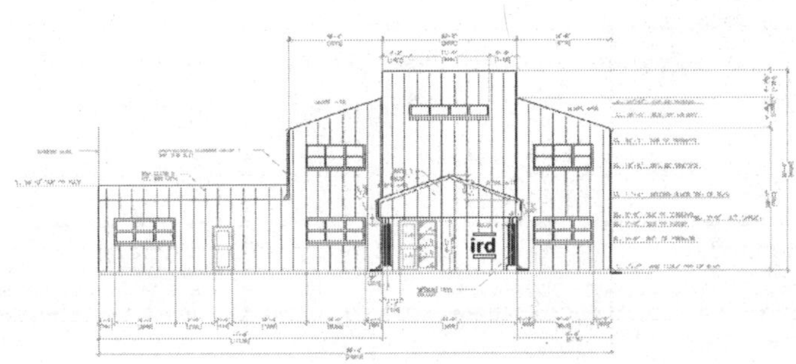

Solution

1. 

Open the ***cad_standards.dwg.***

2. 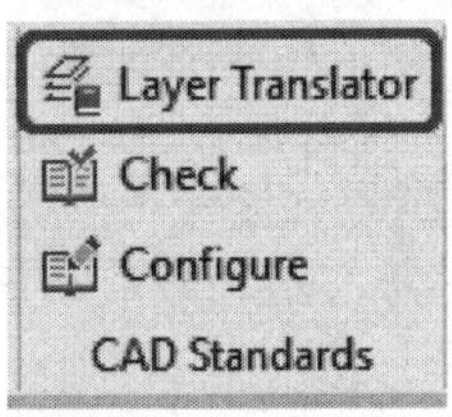

Activate the **Manage** tab on the ribbon.

Select the **Layer Translator** on the CAD Standards panel.

3. 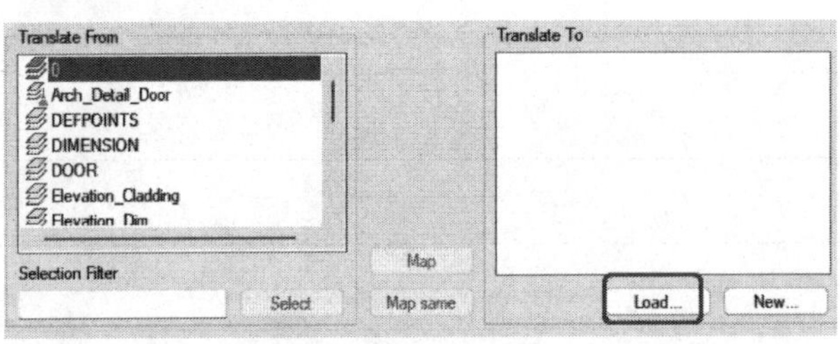

Click **Load**.

4. 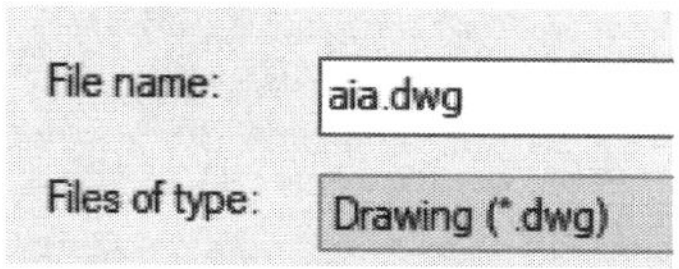

Locate the *aia.dwg*.

We will use this drawing as our CAD Standards drawing.

Click **Open**.

5. 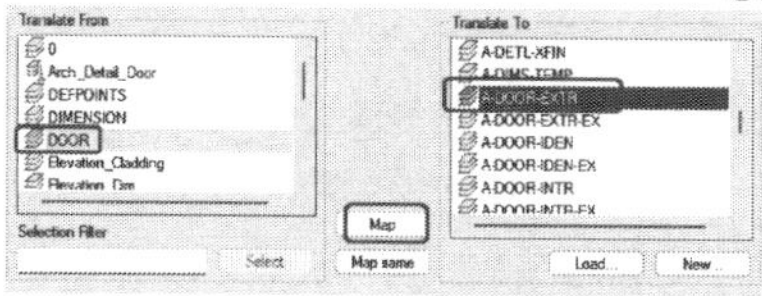

In the Translate From panel:
Select **DOOR**.
In the Translate To panel:
Select **A-DOOR-EXTR**.

Click **Map**.

6. 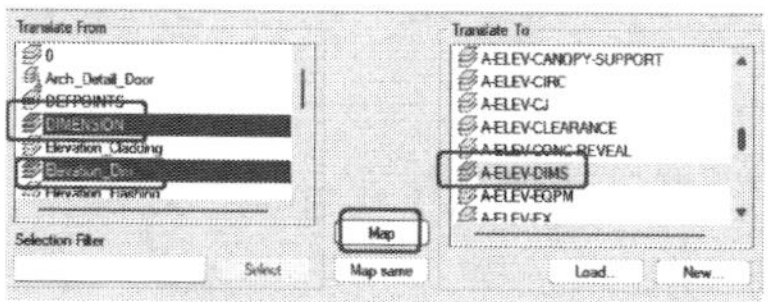

In the Translate From panel:
Select **DIMENSION**.
Hold down the CTL key.
Select **Elevation_Dim**.

In the Translate To panel:
Select **A-ELEV-DIMS**.

Click **Map**.

7. 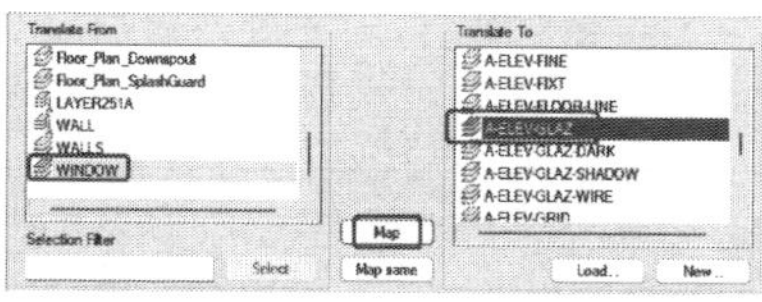

In the Translate From panel:
Select **WINDOW**.
In the Translate To panel:
Select **A-ELEV-GLAZ**.

Click **Map**.

8. 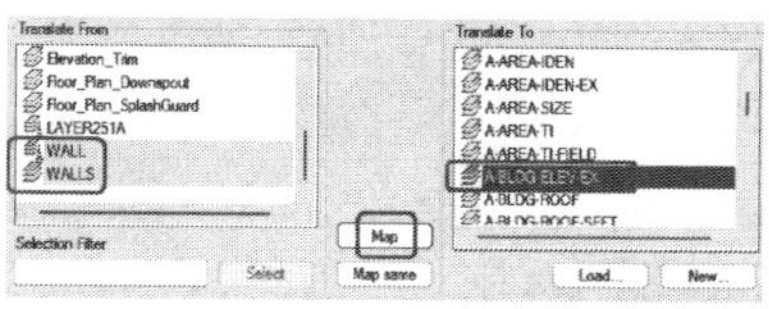

In the Translate From panel:
Select **WALL**.
Hold down the CTL key.
Select **WALLS**.

In the Translate To panel:
Select **A-BLDG-ELEV-EX**.

Click **Map**.

9. 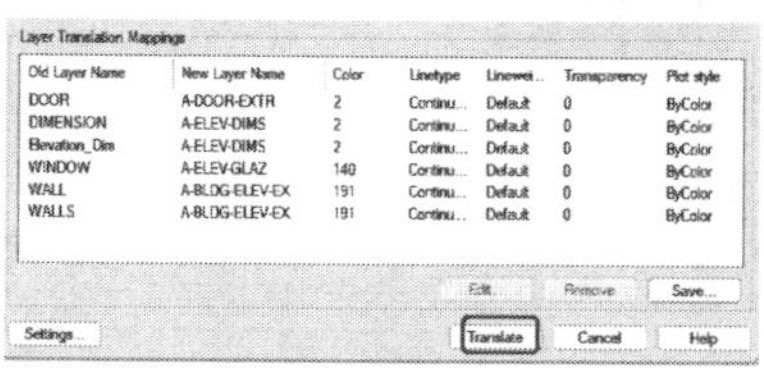

Select **Translate**.

10. 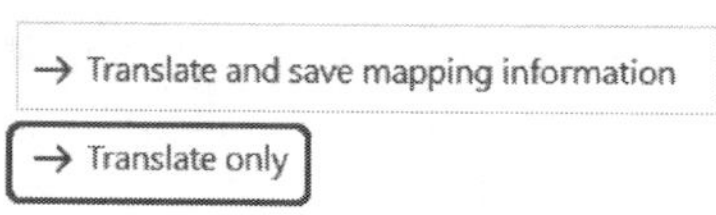

Select **Translate Only**.

11. Close the drawing without saving.

Layer Walk

Command Locator

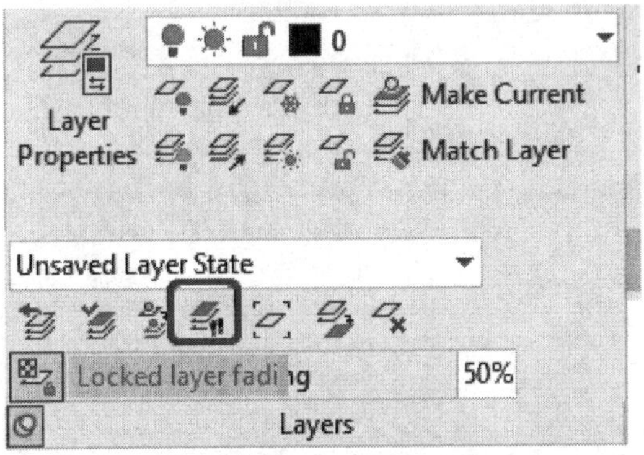

Manage Ribbon/CAD Standards	**Layer Translator**
Command	**LAYWALK**
Dialog Box	**Layer Walk**

Command Overview

Dynamically displays objects on layers that you select in the layer list.

You can use the Layer Walk dialog box to select layers to turn on, thaw, or freeze.

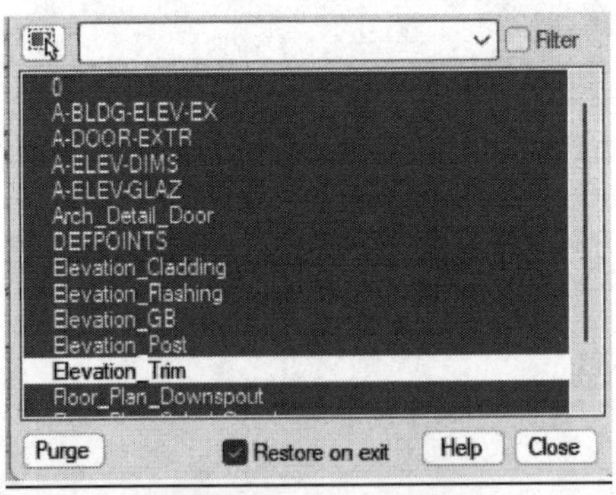

Select Object	Selects objects and their layers.
Filter List	A Filter can be used to display a list of layers that comply with that filter.
Purge	When selected layers are not referenced, purges them from the drawing. For a list of layers that can be purged, right-click anywhere in the Layer list and click Select Unreferenced. In the Layer list, the unreferenced layers are highlighted. You can purge those layers.
Restore on exit	Returns layers to their previous state when you exit the dialog box. If the check box is cleared, any changes you made are saved.

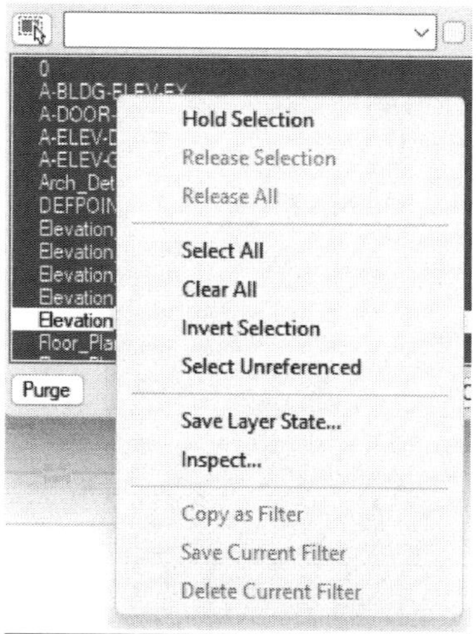

Hold Selection	Turns on the Always Show option for selected layers. An asterisk (*) is displayed to the left of each layer held.
Release Selection	Turns off the Always Show option for selected layers.
Release All	Turns off the Always Show option for all layers.
Select All	Selects and displays all layers.
Clear All	Clears all layers.
Invert Selection	Clears current layers and selects and displays all other layers.
Select Unreferenced	Selects all unreferenced layers. Use with the Purge button to remove unused layers.
Save Layer State	Saves the current selection of layers as a layer state that can be used by the Layer States Manager.
Inspect	Displays the number of layers in the drawing, the number of layers selected, and the number of objects on the selected layers. 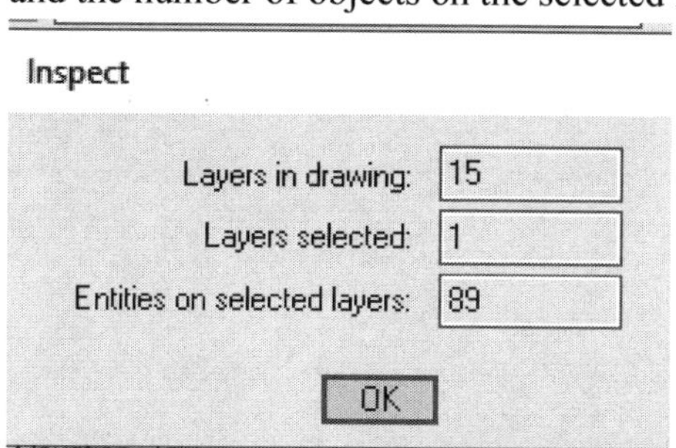
Copy as Filter	Displays the name of the selected layer in the Filter text box. Can be used to create wildcards.
Save Current Filter	Saves the current filter so that it is available in the Filter list for reuse.
Delete Current Filter	Removes the current filter from the filter list.

General Procedures

1. Invoke the LAYWALK command.
2. Click on the layers to see what elements reside on each layer. You can select more than one layer by using the CTL key. To see how many elements are residing on a layer, right click and select Inspect.

Command Exercise

Exercise 7-8 – Using LAYWALK

Drawing Name: **Floor Plan.dwg**
Estimated Time to Completion: 5 Minutes

Scope

Use the Layer Translator to identify the layers in a drawing.

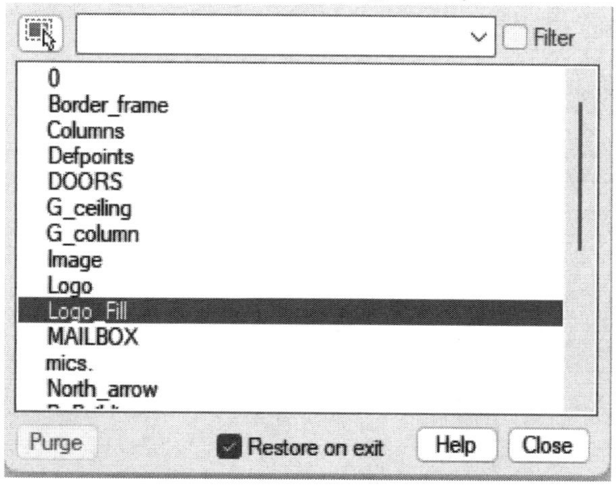

Solution

1.

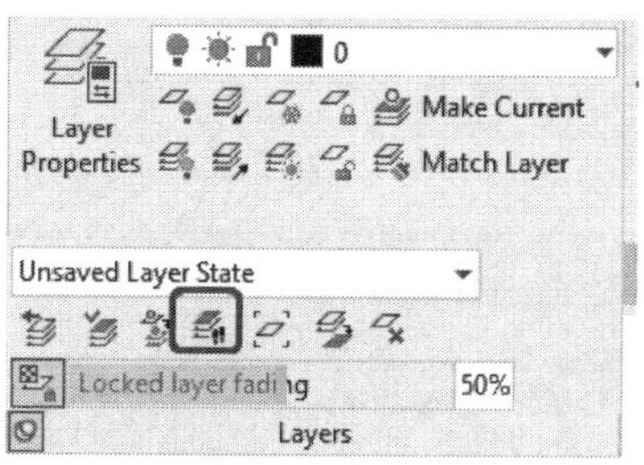

Invoke the **LAYWALK** command.

2.

Can you identify how many layers are in the drawing?

Answer: **24**

3. 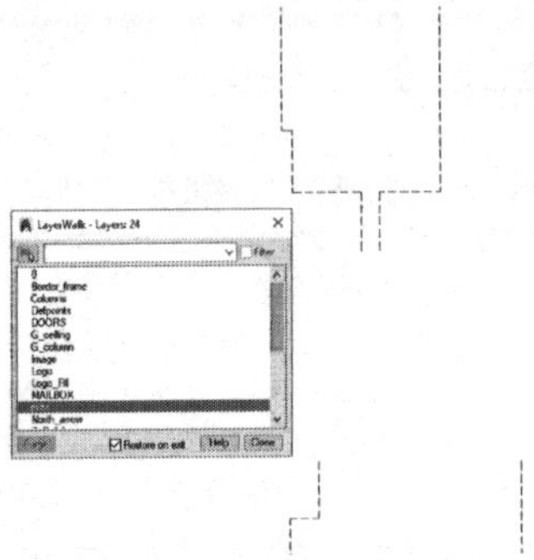

Move the LayerWalk dialog to the side so you can see the drawing.

Select each layer in the Translate From list. Note which objects are visible when which layers are highlighted.

Note that several layers don't have anything on them.

4. Close the LayerWalk dialog box.

Close the file without saving.

Extra: *Both LAYWALK and LAYTRANS allow the user to identify what elements reside on layers and understand how a drawing is organized. How are these tools different?*

Match Properties

Command Locator

Pull Down Menu	**Modify / Match Properties**
Command	**Matchprop**
Alias	**MA**
RMB Shortcut Menu	**Drawing Window**
Dialog Box	**Property Settings**

Command Overview

Object Properties of a selected object can be matched to other objects in the drawing. Select the Source object first, then select the destination object(s). The Matching Properties command will apply the Color, Layer, Linetype, Linetype Scale, Lineweight, Thickness (for 3D), and Dimension, Text, and Hatch styles. Type S to invoke the Settings option or Click the RMB to access the shortcut menu and select Settings. Remove the checkmark from any items not to match.

General Procedures

1. Select the Match Properties command from the Properties panel on the Home tab.
2. Select the Source object.
3. Select the destination objects.
4. Click <ENTER> to Exit the command.

Tips & Tricks

- This option is similar to the Microsoft Word *Property Painter*.
- If you have a lot of drawings open, type SAVEALL to save all the work in every drawing and then CLOSEALL to close all the files.
- To help remember what object to pick first, think of dipping your paintbrush in a can of paint and then painting the object you want to modify.

Command Exercise

Exercise 7-9 – Match Properties

Drawing Name: **match1.dwg**
Estimated Time to Completion: 5 Minutes

Scope

Using the Match Properties command, match the properties of the colored objects to the similar objects on layer 0 (Black or White). Zoom Window for a close-up view of the drawing.

drawing.

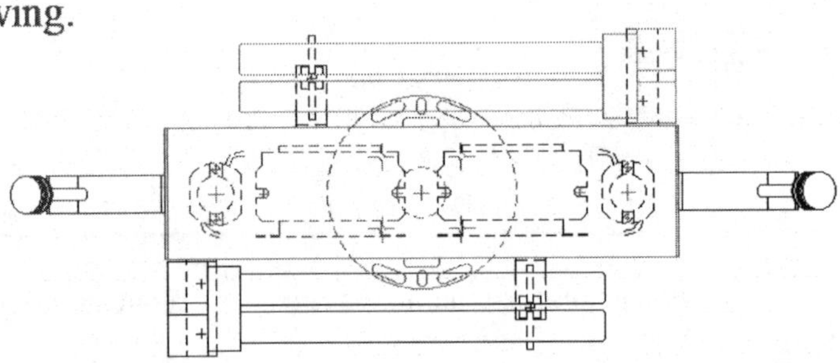

Solution

1.

Invoke the **Match Properties** (matchprop) tool.

2.

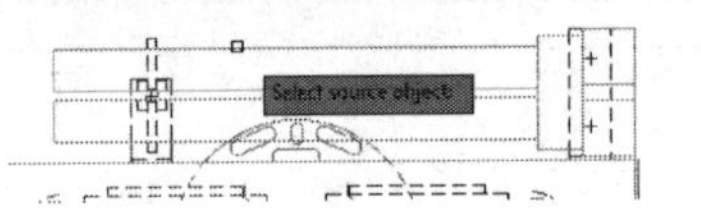

Select source object:
Use the LMB to select the Cyan colored object at the top of the assembly.

3.

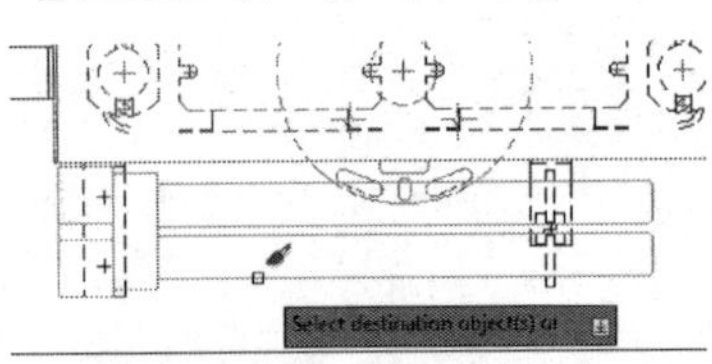

Select destination object(s) or [Settings]:
Pick the corresponding part at the bottom of the assembly.

Notice that if you hover over the destination object it will preview the property changes.

4.

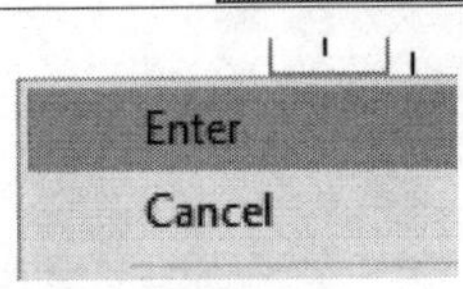

Select destination object(s) or [Settings]:
Click the <ENTER> key to end the command.

5. 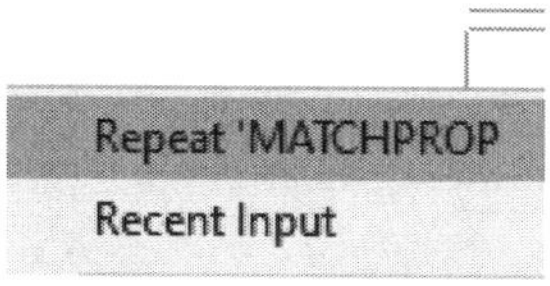

Repeat the process by repeating the Match Properties command. Select the source object first and then apply the properties of the source object to the desired part in the assembly.

Hint: *The properties of the dark blue object can be applied to multiple objects.*

drawing.

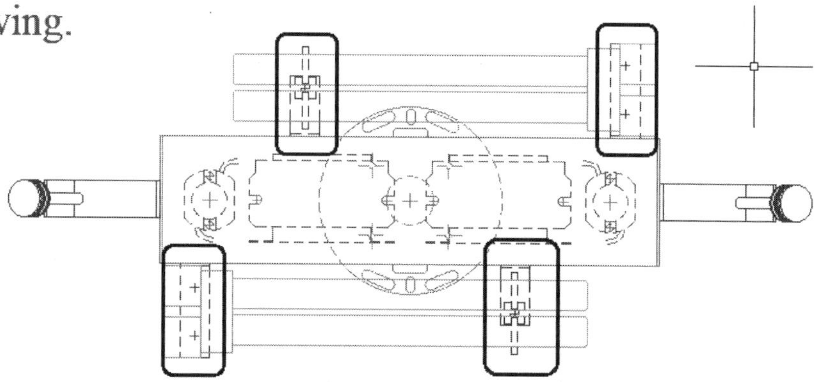

Layer Filters

Command Locator

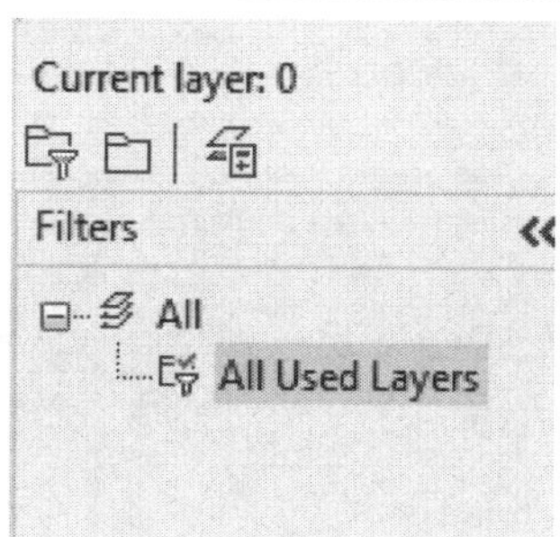

	Alt-P	New Property Filter
	Alt-G	New Group Filter

Command Overview

Whenever you have a lot of layers in your drawings, it will probably take you longer to locate the one you need. If they belong to some groups, e.g. different floor plans in your drawing, it will make sense to group (filter) them in Layer Properties Manager as well. You will be able to manage your layers more quickly. Group Filters can be created manually, by grouping the layers you want, or automatically, by grouping layers according to their properties (Layer Property Filter).

You can create two types of layer filters:

- *Properties filter: Defines the filter based on layer property; i.e., color, linetype, or letter pattern (For example, all layers with Door in the name).*
- *Group filter: Define the filter by selecting a group of layers. Select any layers you like to place in the group.*

General Procedures

1. Open the Layer Properties dialog. (LA)
2. Right click in the filter tree panel. If you don't see the filter tree panel, select the >> box and **Expand the Layer filter** tree or right click in the Layers dialog and select **Show Filter Tree**.
3. Click the New Property Filter button. The Layer Filter Properties dialog will launch.

Layer Filter Properties

Filter Name	Lists the name of the layer properties filter.
Filter Definition	Displays the layer properties that determine which layers are included in the layer filter. You can specify one or more properties to be used.
Status	Click the desired status to include the layer in the filter. — The layer status does not matter. — The layer is in use. — The layer is not in use. — The layer is in use, and a property override is turned on in a layout viewport. — The layer is not in use, and a property override is turned on in a layout viewport.
Name	Enter a layer name, either full or partial. You can use * as a wildcard character.
On	Select a cell in the On column, and then select whether it should be On/Off/Blank. Blank indicates that the setting does not matter.
Filter Preview	Allows the user to verify the filter settings when the selected filter is active.

Command Exercise

Exercise 7-10 – Create a Group Layer Filter

Drawing Name: **layerfilters.dwg**
Estimated Time to Completion: 15 Minutes

Scope

Use LAYWALK to identify what elements are on each layer.
Create a layer filter.
Note how the layer list updates depending on which layer filter is active.

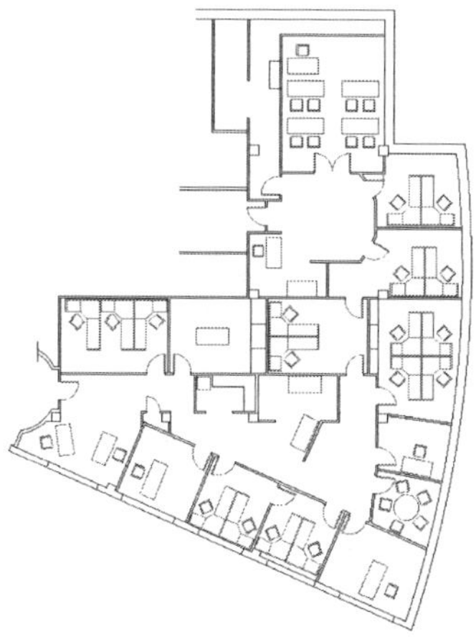

Solution

1.

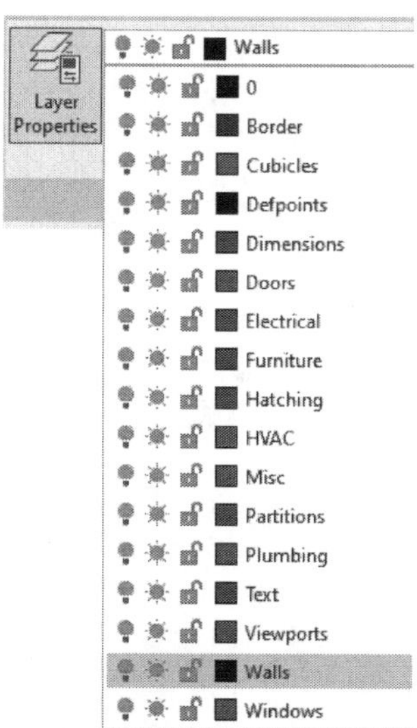

On the Home tab, check out the list of layers available in the drop-down list.

2. 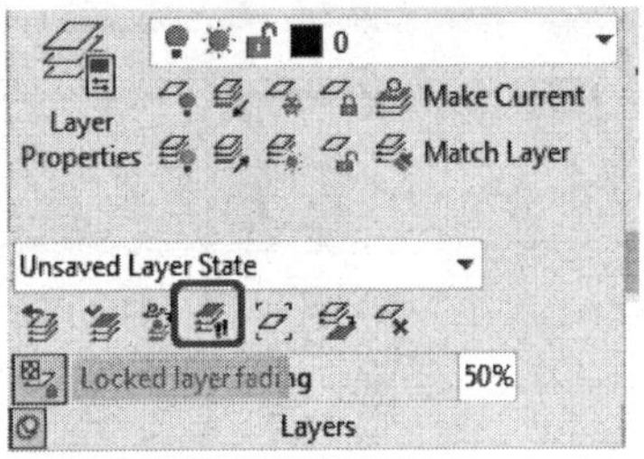

Select the **LAYWALK** tool.

3. 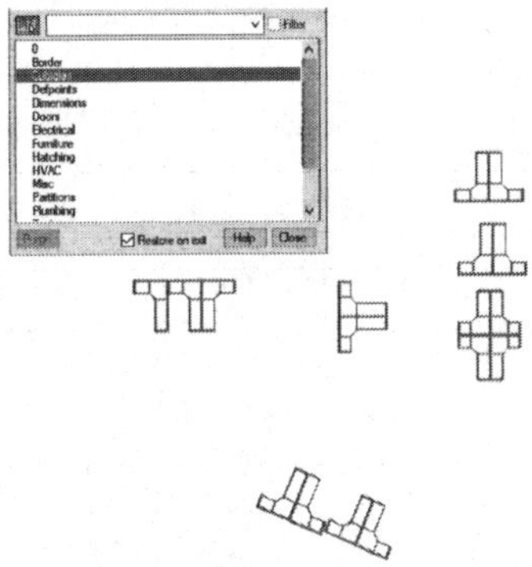

Move the dialog box to the side so you can observe how the display updates.

Highlight the **Cubicles** layer.

Note how all the elements on the Cubicles layer are isolated.

Close the Layerwalk dialog box.

4. 

Select **Layer Properties** from the ribbon.

5. 

Select **New Group Filter**.

6. 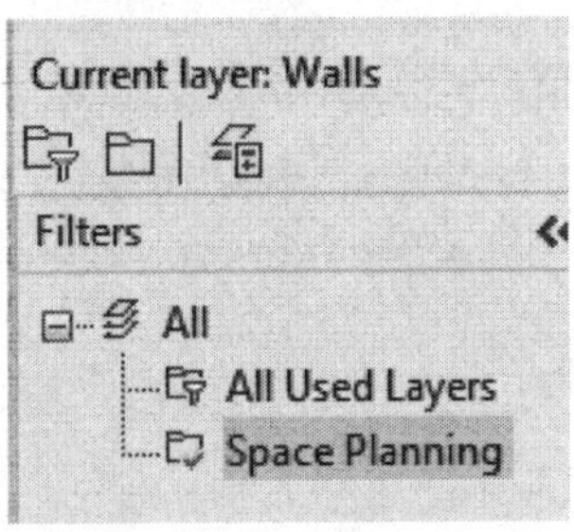

Rename the filter **Space Planning**.

Notice that no layers are listed because no layers have been assigned to this filter.

7. 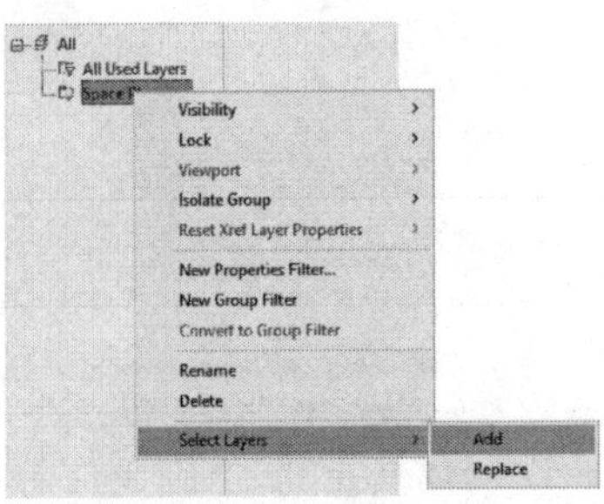

Right click on the Space Planning filter name. Highlight **Select Layers→Add**.

8.

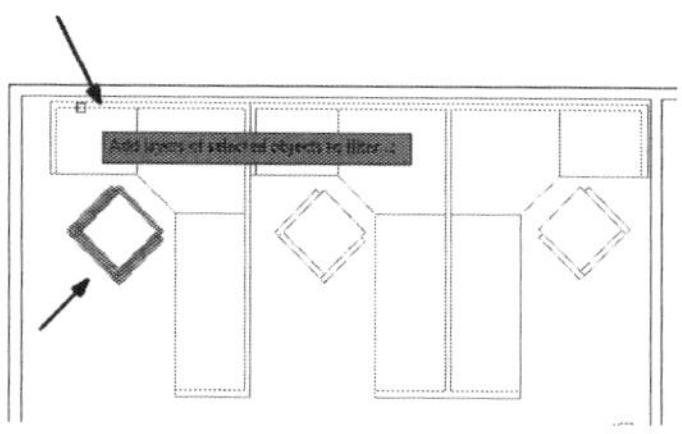

In the Display Window, select a chair and a desk cubicle.

Click **ENTER**.

9.

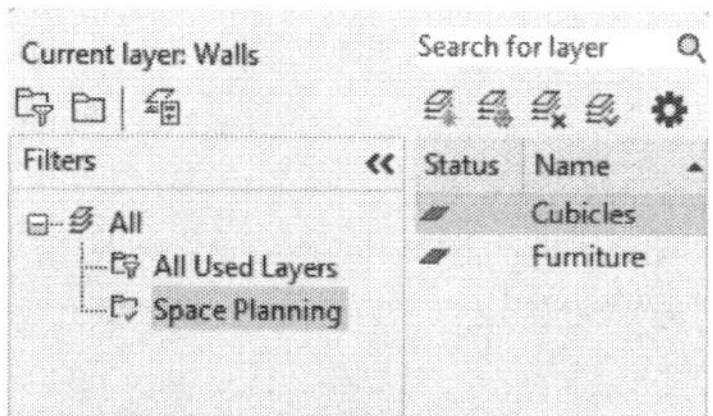

The layers associated with the chair and desk cubicle are listed in the filter.

Close the Layers Properties Manager dialog.

10.

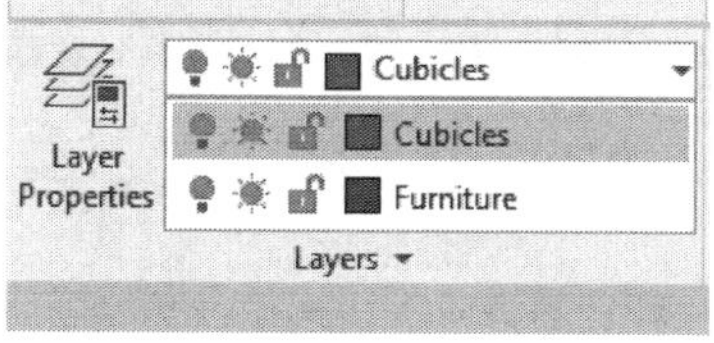

Set the **Cubicles** layer as the current layer.

Notice that only the layers in the active filter are available in the drop-down list.

11.

Open the Layer Properties dialog box.

12.

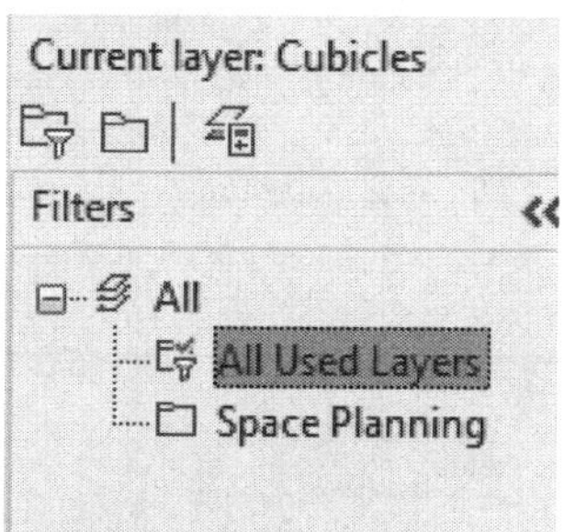

Left click on **All Used Layers** to make that filter active.

13.

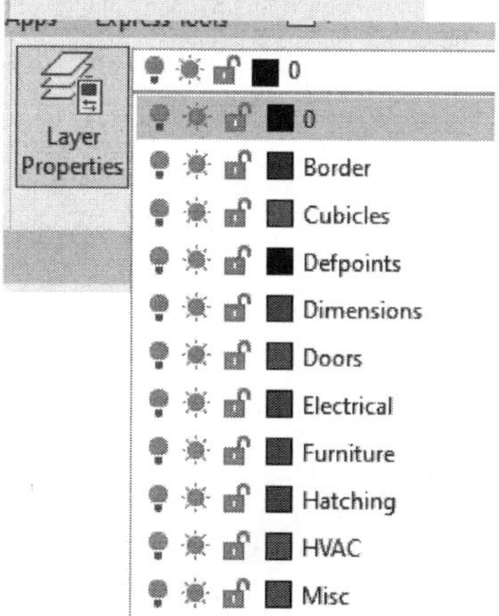

Set **Layer 0** as the current layer.

Notice that the drop-down layer list now shows all the used layers.

14. 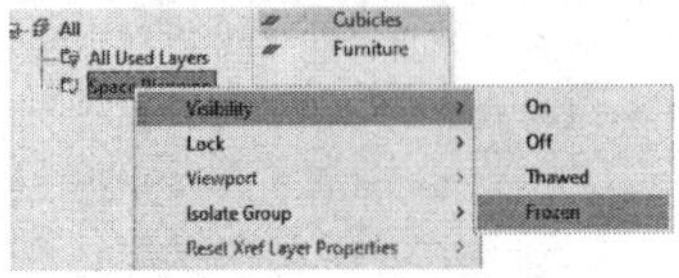

Highlight the Space Planning filter.
Right click and select **Visibility→Frozen**.

All elements on the layers belonging to the Space Planning filter will be hidden.

15. 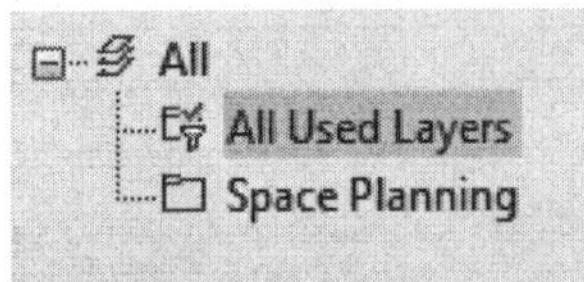

Verify that the All Used Layers filter is active.
Close the layer dialog.

16. 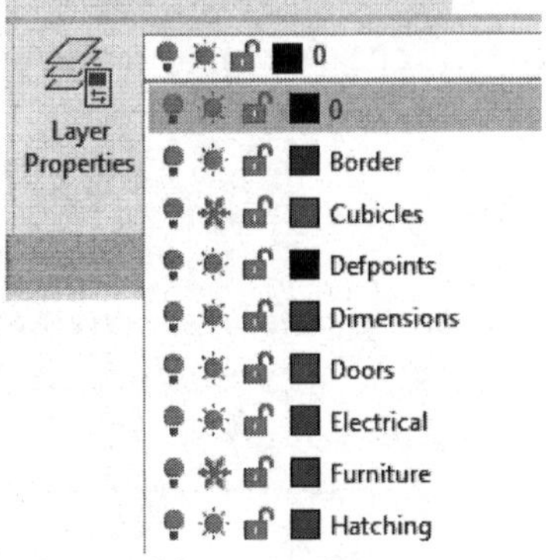

Check the layer drop-down list and see that it now displays all the used layers.

Note that the display has changed since two of the layers have been frozen.

17. Close without saving.

- *You can use layer filters to hide the layers used in external references. Create a property layer filter called NOXREF. In the Name column, type ~*|*. To create the | symbol, Click and hold the ALT key and then Click 1,2,4 from the numeric keypad. The tilde ~ removes items from the layer list.*

Command Exercise

Exercise 7-11 – Create a Properties Layer Filter

Drawing Name: **layerfilters2.dwg**
Estimated Time to Completion: 10 Minutes

Scope

Use LAYWALK to identify what elements are on each layer.
Create a layer filter.
Note how the layer list updates depending on which layer filter is active.

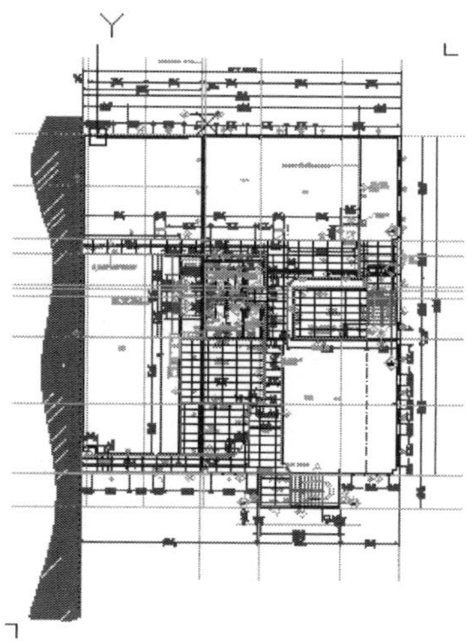

Solution

1.

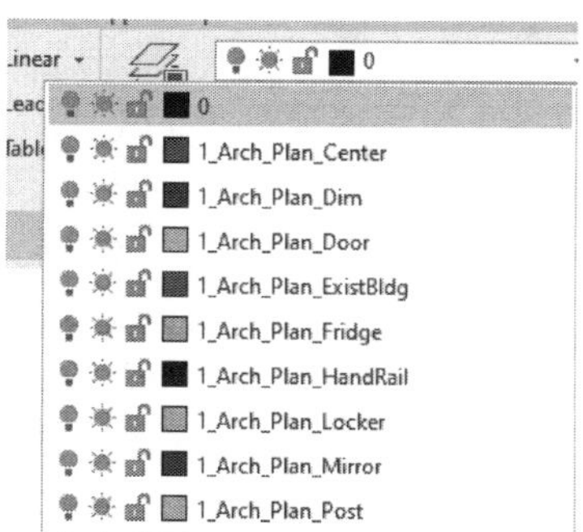

On the Home tab on the ribbon, check out the list of layers available in the drop-down list.

2. 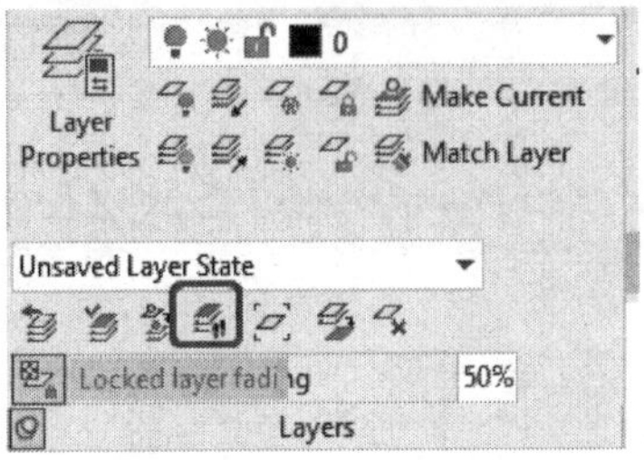

Select the **LAYWALK** tool.

3. 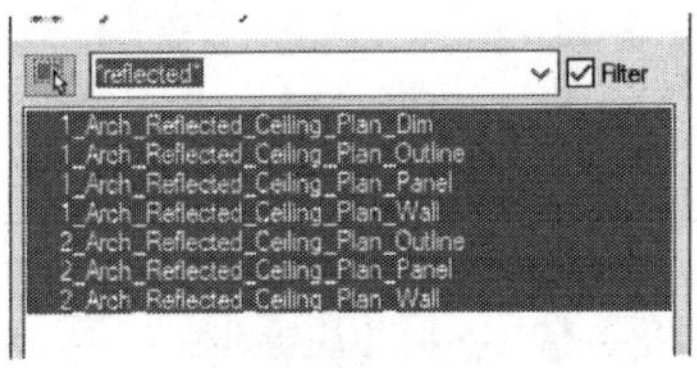

Type ***reflected*** in the filter box.
Click **ENTER**.

Filter will automatically be enabled.

4. 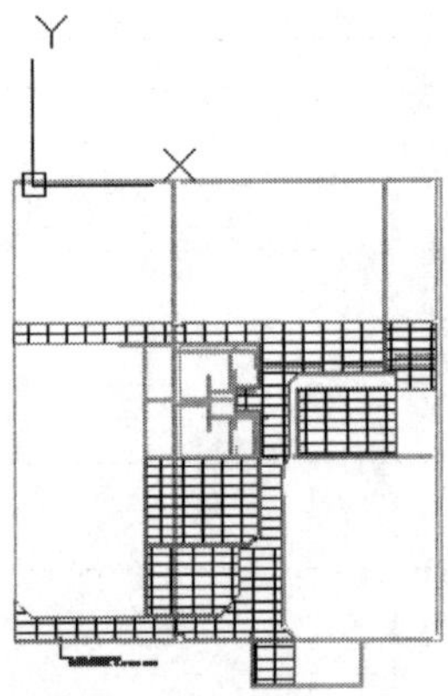

All the layers that contain the word reflected are selected. You see the reflected ceiling plan.

Close the Layer Walk dialog box.

Note that the display is restored when the dialog box is closed.

5. 

Select **Layer Properties** from the ribbon.

6. 

Select **New Properties Filter**.

7. 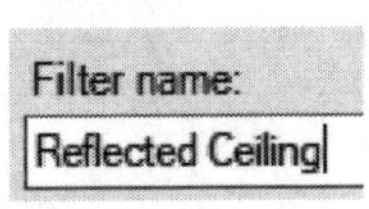

Type **Reflected Ceiling** for the Name.

8. 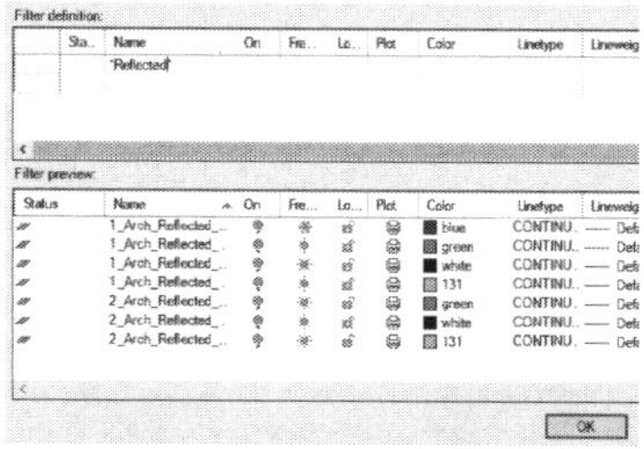

Type ***Reflected*** in the Name field.

All the layers with the word "reflected" are listed as part of the layer filter.

Click **OK**.

9. 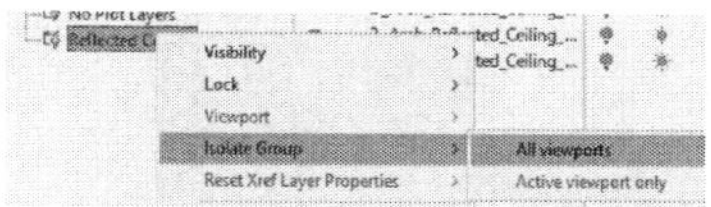

Highlight the **Reflected Ceiling** property filter. Right click and select **Isolate Group→All viewports.**

10. 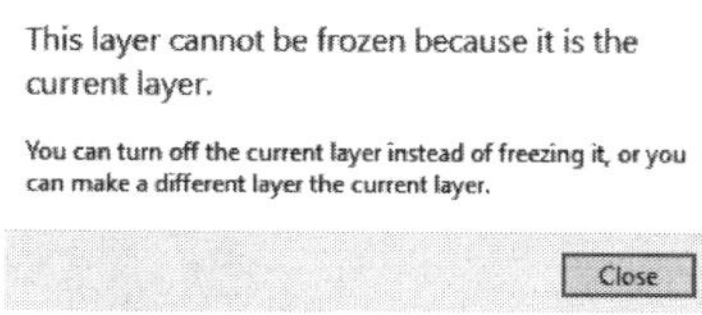

If you get an error dialog that you cannot freeze current layer, that is layer 0 which is current. You can just click Close to dismiss the dialog.

11. 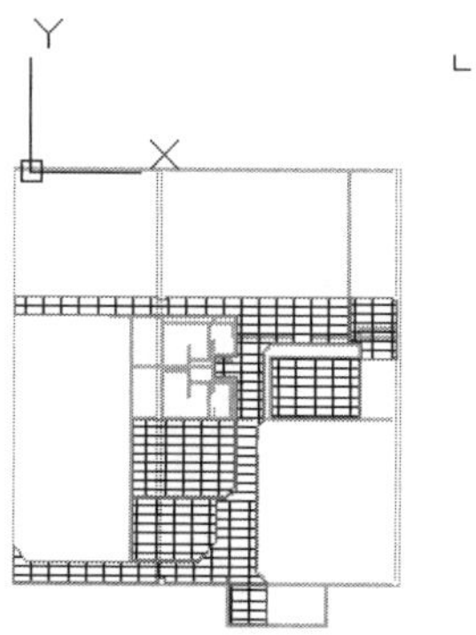

Only those layers which are part of the filter group are visible.

12. 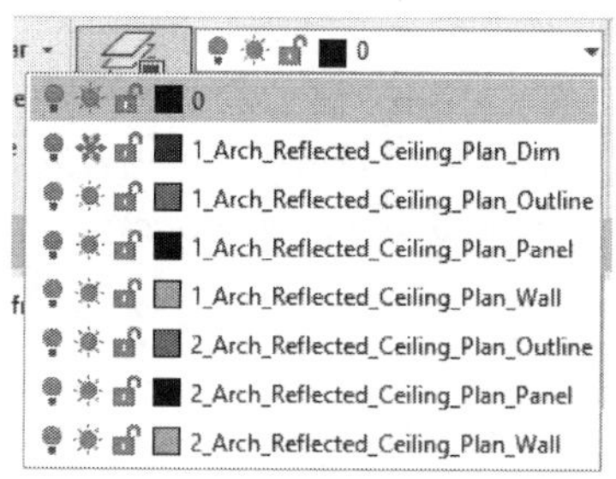

Check the Layer drop-down list.
Only layers which are part of the filter group are listed.

13. Close the file without saving.

Layer States

Command Locator

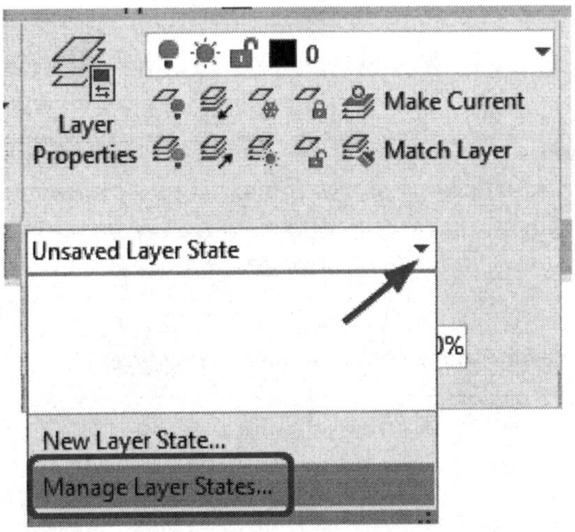

Command	**LAYERSTATE**
Dialog Box	**Layer States Manager**

Command Overview

Layer states are used to save configurations of layer properties and states. For example, you might want a layer to be red sometimes and blue other times. You may need certain layers to be locked, off or frozen when you are editing one part of the drawing, but unlocked, on, or thawed when you are editing another part.

You could spend time setting up how you want the layers to be and then lose those changes, or you can save the layer settings as layer states to be re-used when you need them.

General Procedures

1. Create a default layer set.
2. Set the layers and layer properties how you want them.
3. Open the Layer Properties dialog. (LA)
4. Click Alt+S to launch the Layer States dialog.
5. Click New and type a name and description for the layer state. Click OK.
6. Uncheck any states or properties that you don't want to save. For example, if you don't save the Color property, the color won't be affected when you restore the layer state. Therefore, if you change a layer's color and restore the layer state, the layer will remain the new color.
7. If you want your drawing to exactly match the way it looks now, check the Turn Off Layers Not Found in Layer State check box in the main section of the dialog box. When you check this box, any new layers that you create afterwards are turned off when you restore the layer state.
8. Click Close to save the layer state.

You can continue to display desired states and save them until you have all the layer states that you need.

To restore a layer state, open the Layer States Manager, choose the layer state and click Restore.

Layer States	Lists the layer states that have been saved in the drawing.
Don't List Layer States in Xrefs	Excludes the layer states that were saved in externally referenced drawings. ***Note:*** *Layer states that were saved in xrefs cannot be edited.*
New	Displays the New Layer State to Save dialog box, where you can create a layer state by providing a name and entering an optional description.
Save	Saves the *current* layer settings in the drawing to the selected layer state, replacing the previously saved settings. The Layer Properties to Restore settings are also saved as part of the layer state. When you select this layer state in the Layer States list, the check boxes update to match the saved settings. ***Note:*** *The Save button is used only when you want to save the current layer settings to the current layer state. When you create or edit a layer state, the layer state is automatically saved, and you only need to close the dialog box.*
Edit	Displays the Edit Layer State dialog box, where you can modify a selected layer state, which is then automatically saved.
Rename	Renames the selected layer state.
Delete	Eliminates the saved layer state.
Import	Displays a standard file selection dialog box, where you can select a DWG, DWS, DWT file, or a previously exported layer state (LAS) file. Once you select the file for import, the Select Layer States dialog box is displayed, where you can select the layer states to import.

Export	Displays a standard file selection dialog box, where you can save the selected layer state to a layer state (LAS) file.
Restore	Restores the layer settings saved in the specified layer state, depending on which settings are checked in the Layer Properties to Restore column.
Close	Closes the Layer States Manager.
Restore Options	**Turn Off Layers Not Found in Layer State** Layers created after the layer state was saved are turned off. The intent of this setting is to preserve the visual appearance of the drawing at the time that the layer state was saved. **Apply Properties as Viewport Overrides** Applies the selected layer state as layer property overrides to the *current* layout viewport. This option is available when the Layer States Manager is opened when a *layout* viewport is current.
Layer Properties to Restore	Applies only the specified layer property settings when the specified layer state is restored. • The Visibility in Current VP option is available only for layout viewports • The On/Off and Frozen/Thawed options are available only for model space viewports The following rules apply if you restore a layer state when the current viewport is a *layout* viewport and the Visibility in Current VP is turned on: • Layers that should be turned off or frozen in the layout viewport are set to VP Freeze Layers that should be visible in the layout viewport are also turned on and thawed in model space

- *In Layer States Manager dialog box you can choose which layer properties to restore. For example, if color is turned on, then all changes you have made after saving layer state will be ignored when restoring layer state. Edit button allows you to add/remove layers to saved layer state and change their properties.*
- *Layer states are saved in the drawing. To share them among drawings, you need to export them. Each layer state has its own LAS file. To export a layer state, select it in the Layer States Manager, and choose Export. In the Export Layer State dialog box, enter a name, choose a location, and click Save.*
- *To import a saved layer state, open the Layer States Manager, and click the Import button. In the Import Layer State dialog box, choose Layer States (*.las) from the Files of Type drop-down list. Choose the LAS file that you want, and click Open.*
- *You can save layer states in your templates for maximum ease and to maintain CAD standards. Layer states can be an important method for controlling how your drawings look and speeding up the drawing and editing process.*

You can use layer states to create different layouts of the same drawing.

1. Create the layer states you wish to apply to each layout.
2. Select the layout.
3. Activate model space in the layout.
4. Select the desired layer state.
5. Enable the 'Turn off layers not found in layer state' option.
6. Enable 'Apply properties as viewport overrides.'
7. Click on Restore.
8. Rename the layout with the layer state name, if desired.

Command Exercise

Exercise 7-12 – Save a Layer State

Drawing Name: **layerstates.dwg**
Estimated Time to Completion: 20 Minutes

Scope

Create two layer states and save them.
Switch from one layer state to another and observe how the display changes.

Solution

1. 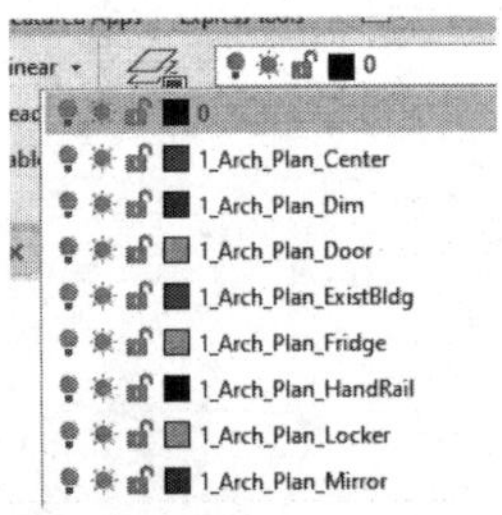

Select the layers drop-down list.

Note all the layers that exist in the drawing.

2. 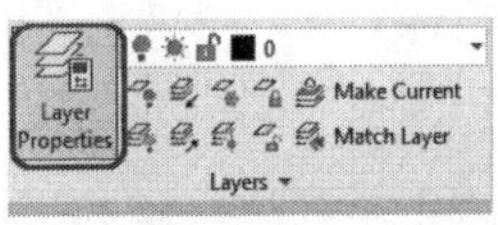

Launch the Layer Properties dialog box.

3. 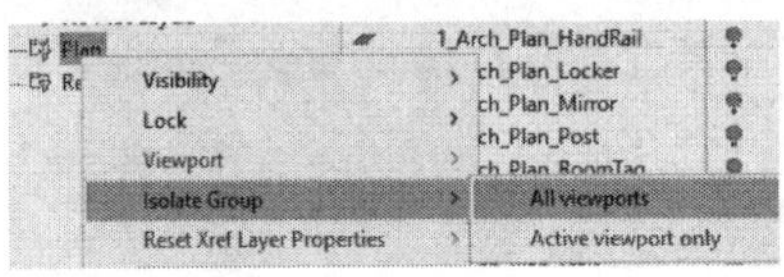

Highlight the **Plan** layer filter.

Right click and select **Isolate Group→All viewports**.

4. 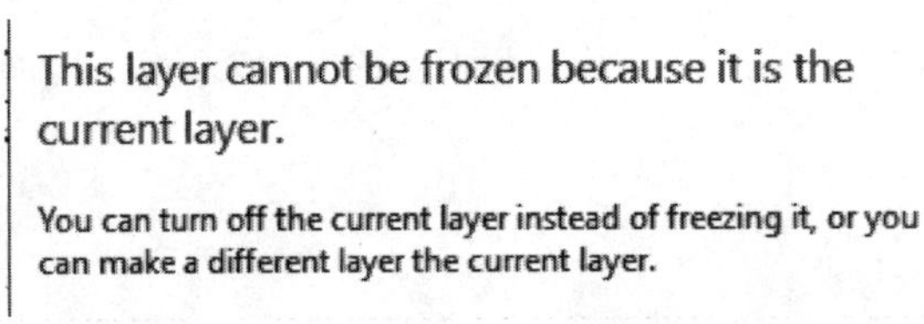

Close this dialog.

It pops up because Layer 0 is the current layer.

5. 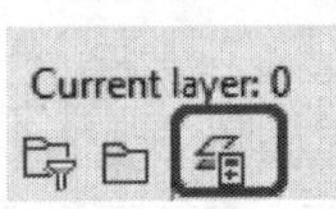

Launch the **Layer States Manager**.

6. 

Select **New**.

7.

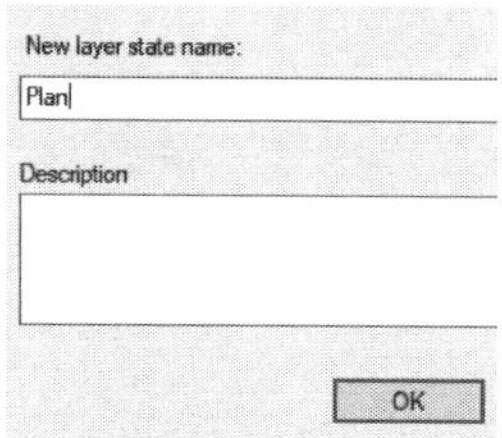

Type **Plan** for the new layer state name.
Click **OK**.

The current layer settings are saved to the layer state.

8. Select **Close**.
Close all the dialog boxes.

9.

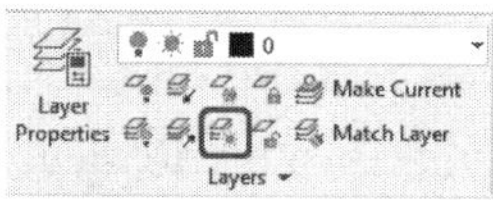

Select the **Thaw All** tool to thaw all the layers.

10.

Launch the Layer Properties dialog box.

11.

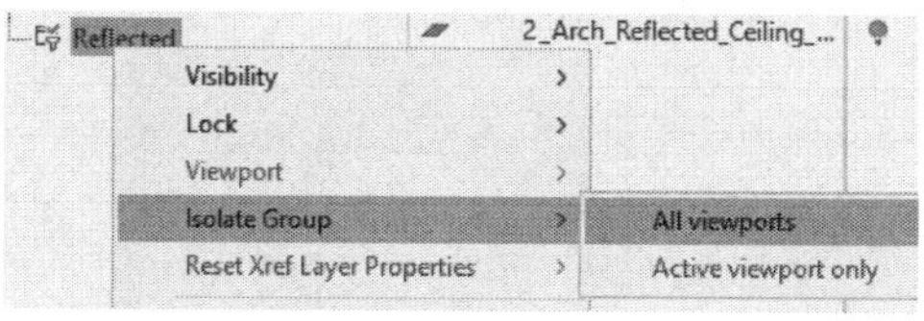

Highlight the **Reflected** layer filter.
Right click and select **Isolate Group→All viewports**.

The view display updates.

Close the dialog warning that Layer 0 was not frozen because it is the current layer.

12.

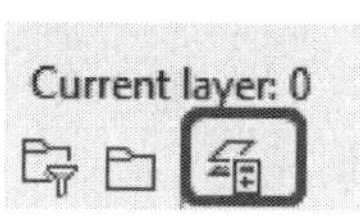

Launch the **Layer States Manager**.

13.

Select **New**.

14.

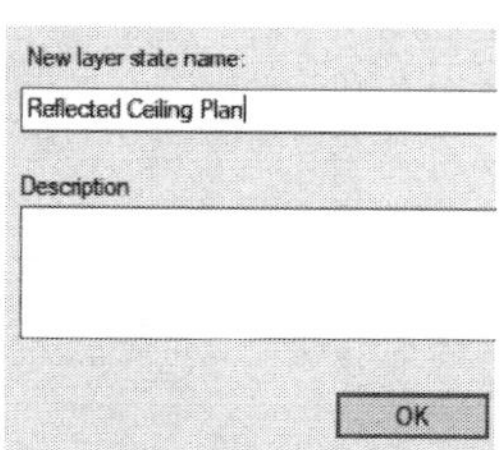

Type **Reflected Ceiling Plan** for the new layer state name.
Click **OK**.

The current layer settings are saved to the layer state.

15. *Note that there are two layer states listed.*

Close all the dialog boxes.

16.

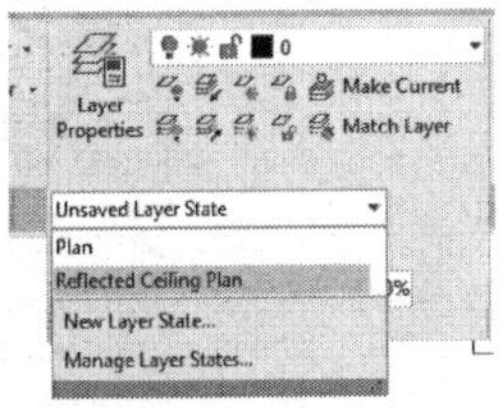

Expand the Layers pane. *Note there are two saved layer states listed.*

Select the **Plan** layer state by left clicking on it. *Notice how the display changes.*

17.

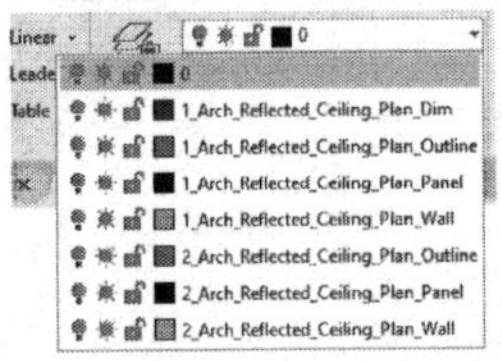

The layer drop-down list is still set to the Reflected layer filter.

18.

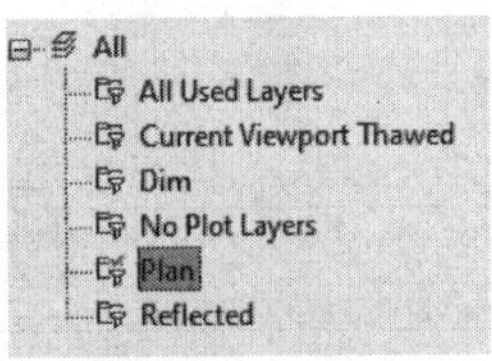

Open the Layer Properties dialog.
Change the layer filter to **Plan**.

19.

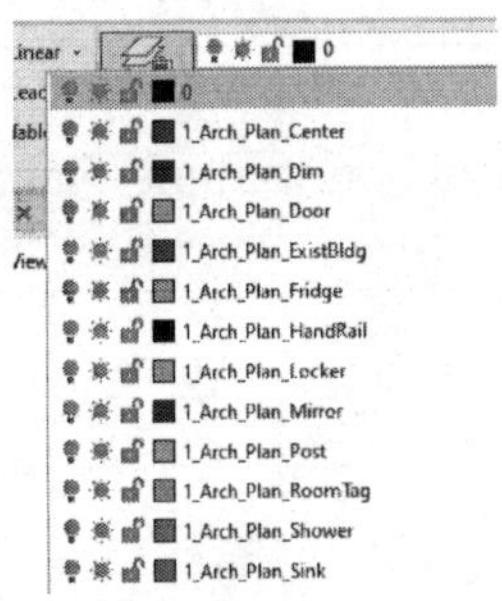

The layer drop-down list updates to the Plan layer list. Activate the **Reflected Ceiling Plan** layer state.

Notice that the display changes, but the layer drop-down does not update. Layer states and layer filters operate independently.

20.

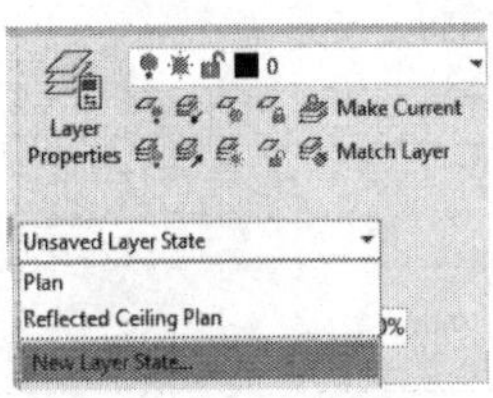

Expand the **Layers** panel on the ribbon.

Use the drop-down list to switch between the two layer states you created.

21. Close the file without saving.

Command Exercise

Exercise 7-13 – Apply a Layer State to a Layout

Drawing Name: **layerstate-layouts.dwg**
Estimated Time to Completion: 15 Minutes

Scope

Create two layouts and apply a different layer state to each layout.

Solution

1. 

There are two layouts in the drawing: One called **Plan** and one called **Reflected Ceiling Plan**.

Verify that the Plan layout is active. The name should be bold. To activate a layout, just click on the tab.

2. 

Launch **Layer Properties**.

3. 

Highlight the **All Used Layers Filter**.

4. 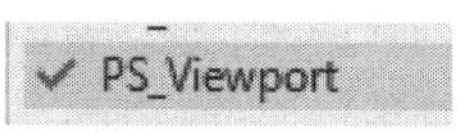

Set the **PS_Viewport** layer current.

5. 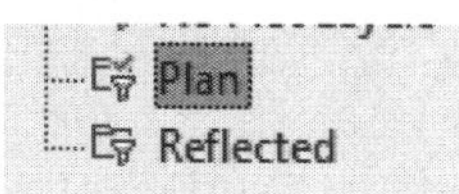

Set the **Plan** layer filter as active to control what layers are listed in the layer drop-down list.

6. Close the Layer Properties dialog.

7.

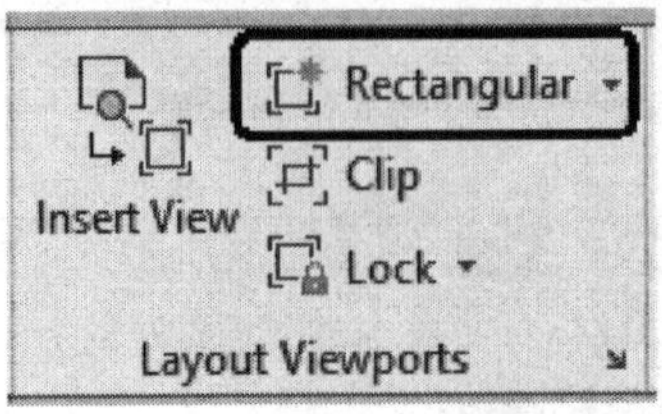

On the Layout ribbon, select **Rectangular**.

You will only see the Layout tab if you are on a sheet layout.

8.

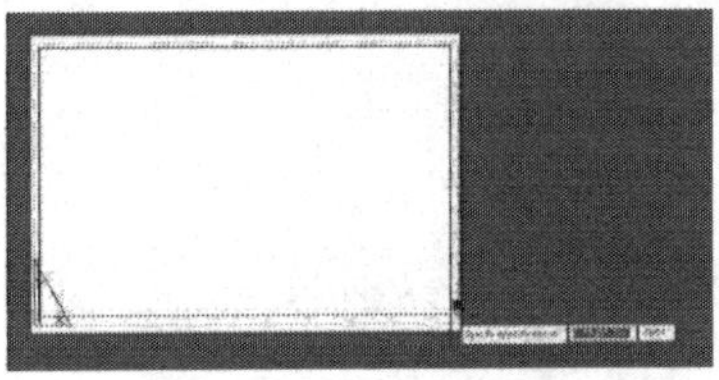

Select the upper left corner of the layout and the lower right corner of the layout.

This places a rectangular viewport, displaying the model space.

9.

Notice that the status bar shows that you are in Paper space.

10.

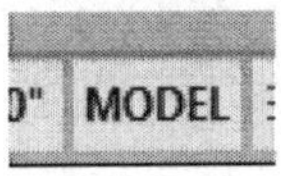

Double left click on the layout sheet inside the rectangle.
This activates Model space.
The status bar updates to display MODEL.
The viewport is displayed in bold.

11.

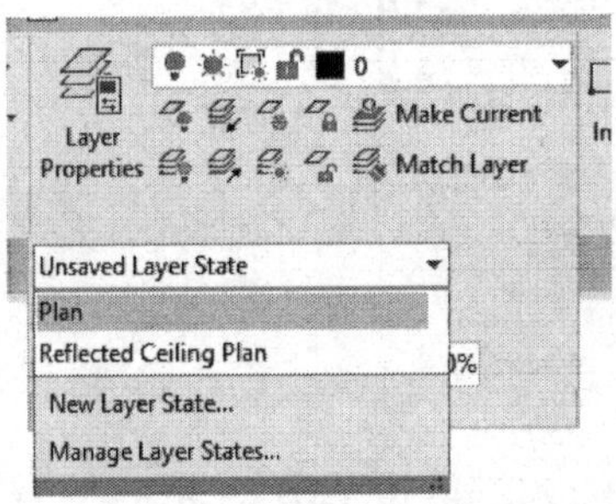

Switch to the Home ribbon.
Select the **Plan** layer state.

Notice how the layout updates to the Plan layer state.

12.

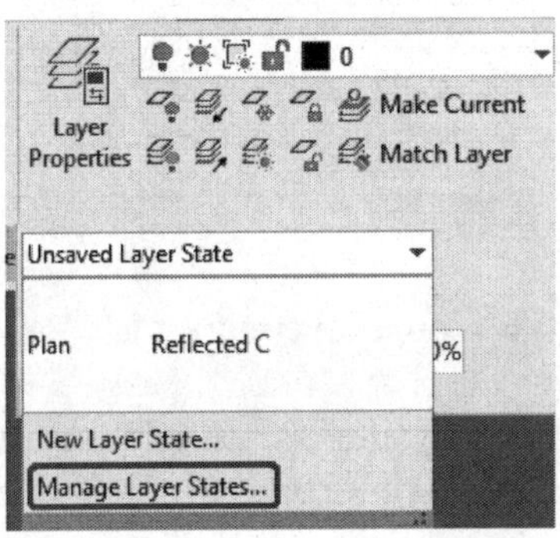

Select **Manage Layer States**.

13. 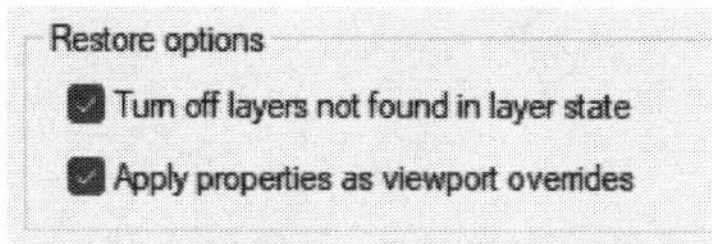

Verify that the Restore options are both enabled.

Close the dialog.

14. 

Activate the **Reflected Ceiling Plan** layout.

15. 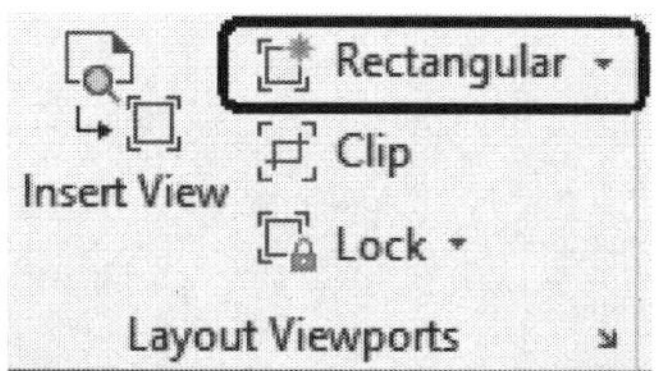

On the Layout ribbon, select **Rectangular**.

16. 

Select the upper left corner of the layout and the lower right corner of the layout.

This places a rectangular viewport, displaying the model space.

17. 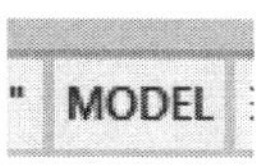

Double left click on the layout sheet.
This activates Model space.

The status bar updates to display MODEL. The viewport is displayed in bold.

18. 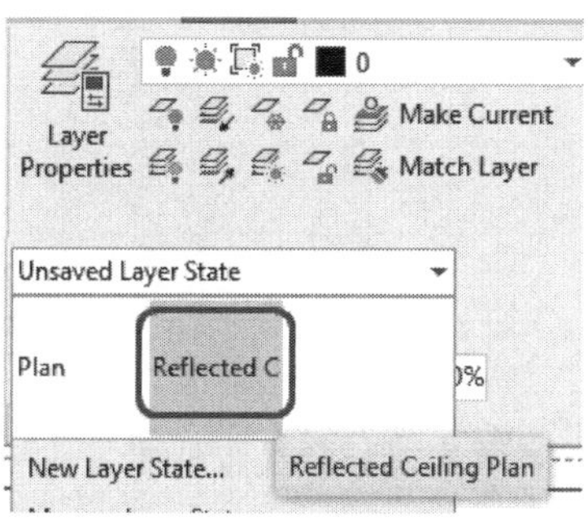

Switch to the Home ribbon.

Select the **Reflected Ceiling Plan** layer state.

19. 

Click on the word **MODEL** on the status bar to switch back to PAPER space.

20. 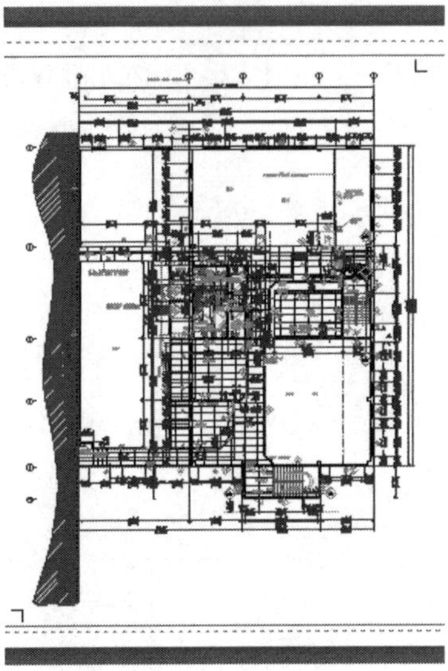

Toggle between the two layouts to compare the sheets.

21. Close without saving.

Command Exercise

Exercise 7-14 – Publish Layouts with Layer States

Drawing Name: **layerstate-publish.dwg**
Estimated Time to Completion: 10 Minutes

Scope

Publish the two layouts to a PDF using the Sheet Set Manager.

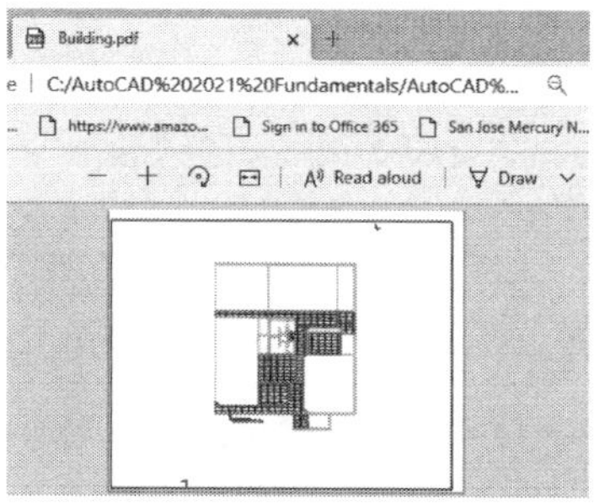

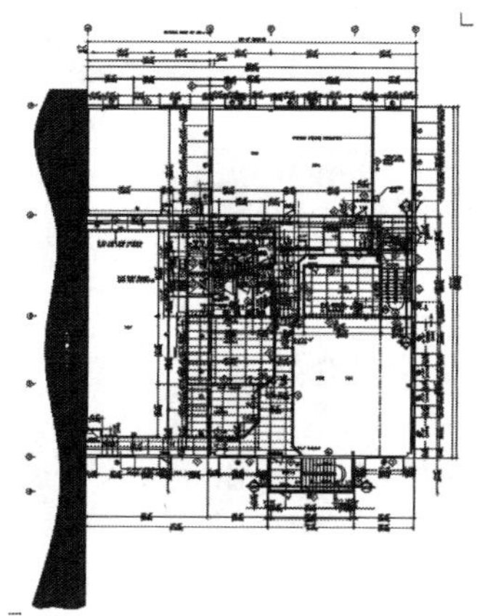

Solution

1. 

Type **SSM** to launch the Sheet Set Manager.

2. 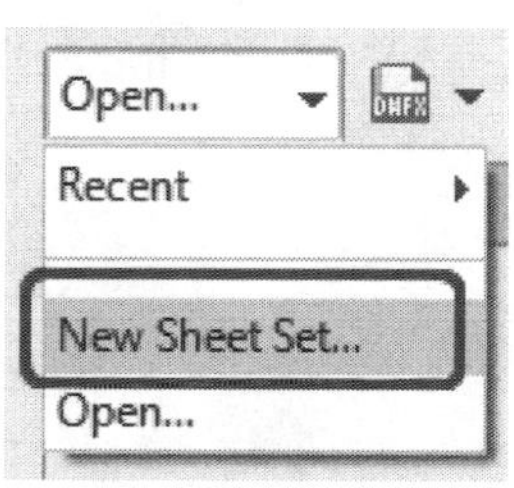

Select the drop-down arrow and select **New Sheet Set.**

3. 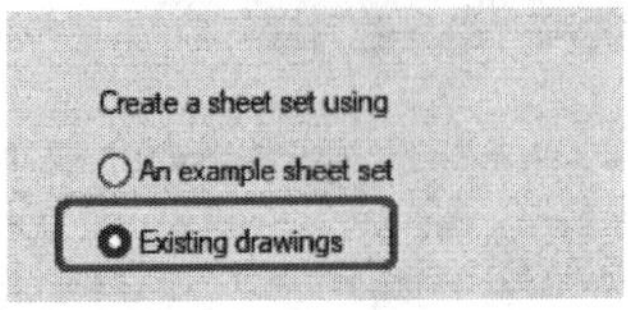

Enable **Existing drawings.**

Click **Next**.

4. 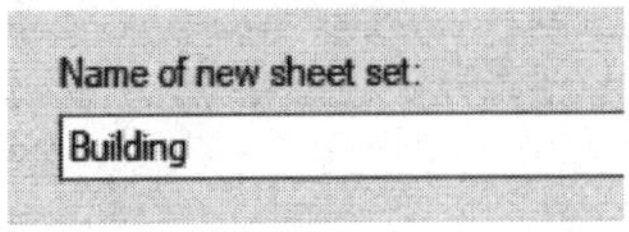

Type **Building** as the name of the new sheet set.

Click **Next.**

5. 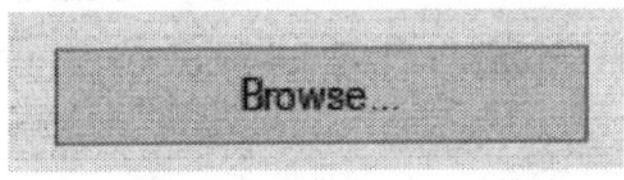

Click **Browse.**

6. 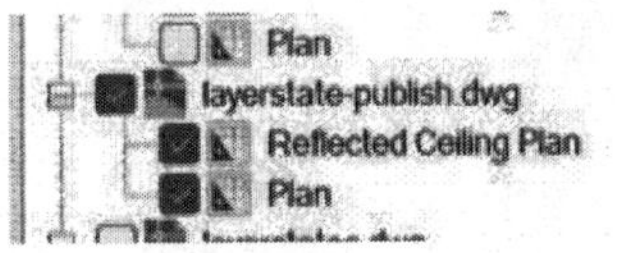

Browse to where the file is located and select the two layouts.

Clear any other selections.

7. 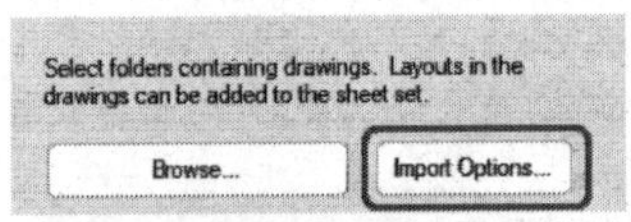

Select **Import Options**.

8. 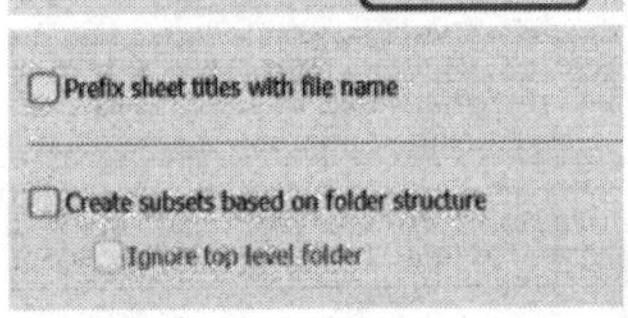

Uncheck **Prefix sheet titles with file name**.

Uncheck **Create subsets based on folder structure**.

Click **OK**.

Click **Next**.

9. 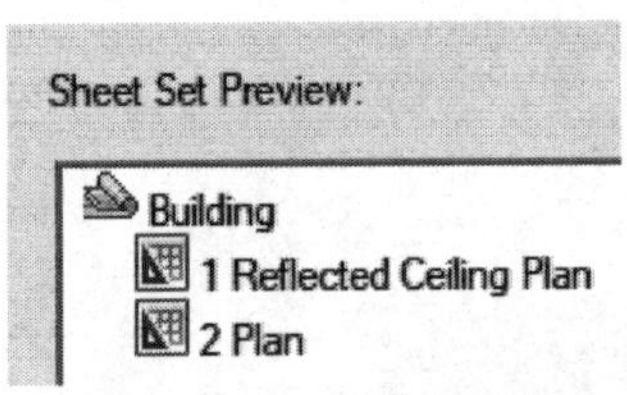

Verify that only the two desired sheets are listed.

Click **Finish**.

10. 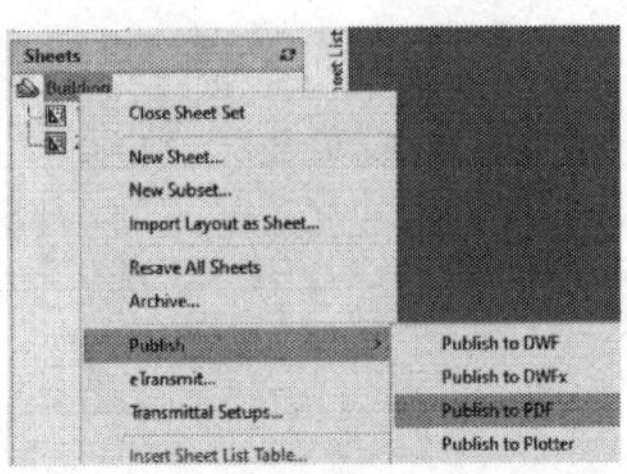

Highlight the Building sheet set.
Right click and select **Publish→Publish to PDF**.

Browse to where you want to save the PDF and select **Select**.

11. 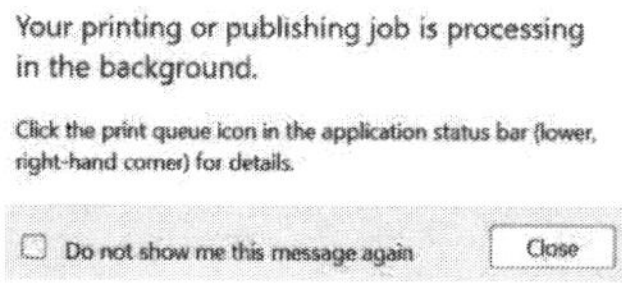

Click **Close** to close the dialog.

12. 
You will see a small printer icon in the lower right of the status bar indicating that a print job is active.

13. 

When the plot is finished, you will see a small bubble indicating that the file is ready.

14. Locate the PDF where it was saved. Open it and review.

Properties

Command Locator

Command	**PROPERTIES**
Dialog Box	**Properties**
Ribbon/View	**Properties**

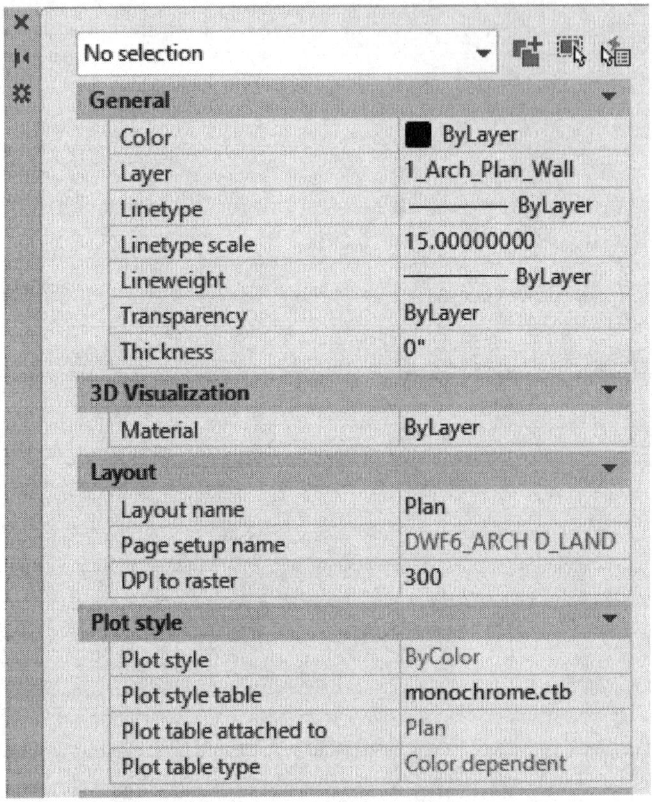

Command Overview

The Properties of selected objects can be changed using the Properties command. The list in the Properties dialog box will correspond to the objects that are selected. Objects may be selected before or after the Properties command is invoked. The most common features to change are Layer and Linetype. When one item is selected, the Properties dialog box will display options relevant to the features of that object, such as the radius or diameter of a circle, or the contents of selected Text. The Properties dialog box can be moved to select items in the drawing that may appear behind it. Click Escape to deselect objects and pick new objects to modify.

General Procedures

1. Invoke the Properties command, then select the object(s) to change.
2. Select the option to change from the list and select or type the new option.
3. Click Escape to deselect the objects.
4. Select the X in the upper right-hand corner to close the dialog box.

Command Exercise

Exercise 7-15 – Change Properties

Drawing Name: **change1.dwg**
Estimated Time to Completion: 10 Minutes

Scope

Using the Properties command, place the shaft on the SHAFT layer, the bellows on the BELLOWS Layer, and the CV joints on the CV Layer.

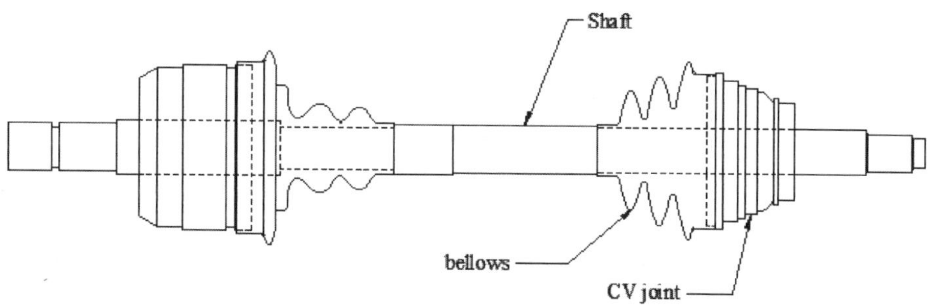

Solution

1. 

Toggle OFF Quick Properties on the status bar.

2. 

Activate the View tab on the ribbon.

Launch the **Properties** palette (properties).

3. 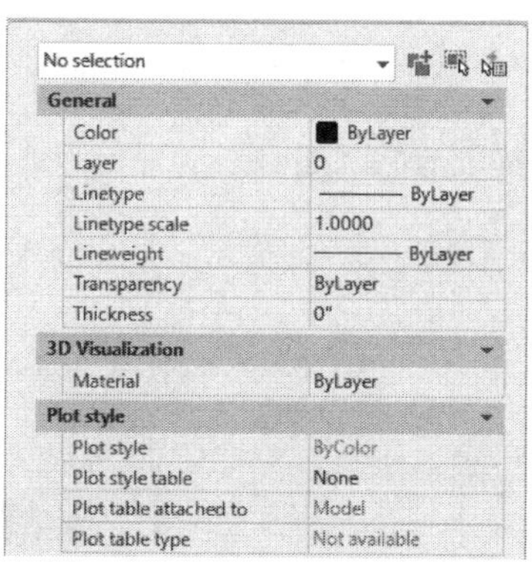

Your Properties palette will look similar to the following figure.

4. 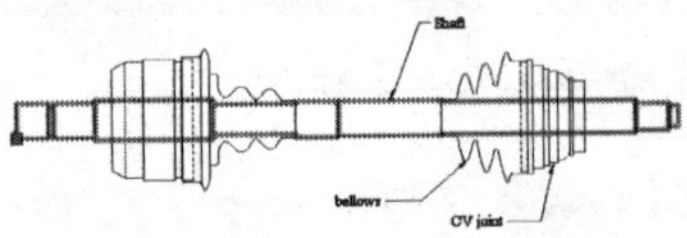

Use the LMB to select the Shaft.

5. 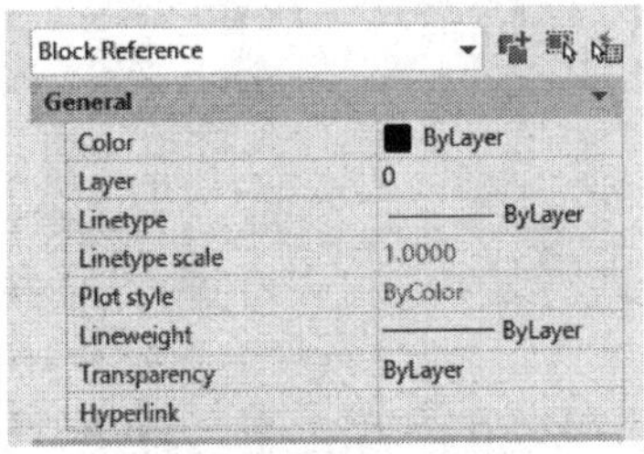

Notice that it is highlighted when selected and the information in the Properties Dialog box changes.

6. 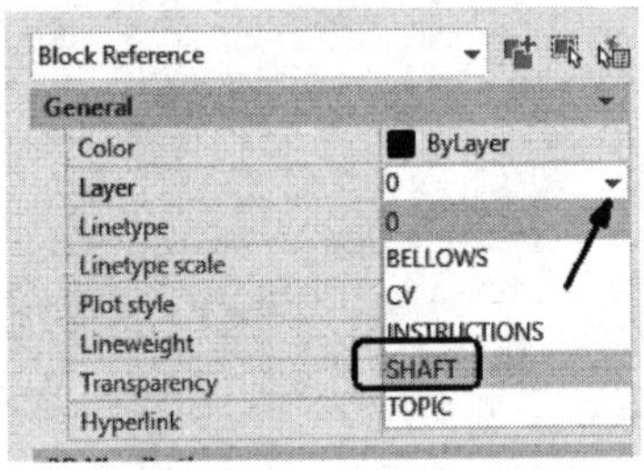

Change the layer the shaft is on to the SHAFT layer.

Pick 0 next to the word Layer in the Properties dialog box.

In the drop-down list that appears select the SHAFT Layer.

Notice that the Shaft changes color. Click the <ESC> key to clear the selection.

Click <ESC> to release the selection.

7. 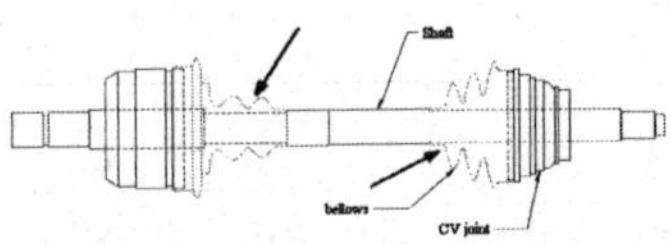

Select the two Bellows with the LMB.

Notice how the information in the Properties Dialog box changes.

8. 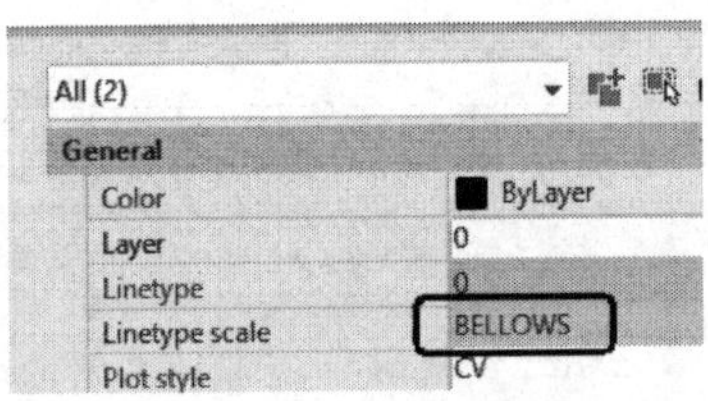

Activate the drop-down list next to the word Layer and select BELLOWS.

Note that the Properties dialog displays that two items have been selected.

Click <ESC> to release the selection.

9. 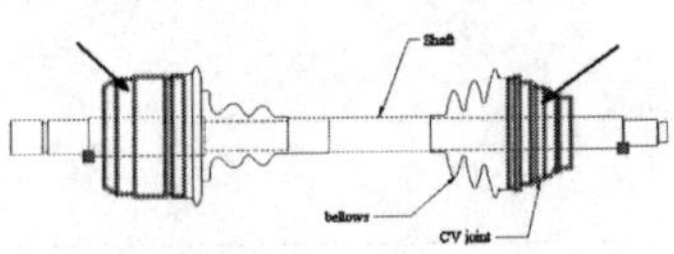

Select the two CV joints.

10. 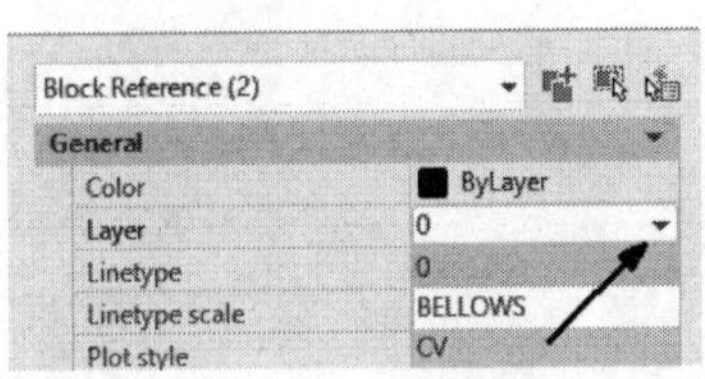

Change the layer in the Properties dialog box to CV.

Click <ESC> to release the selection.

Extra: *Try undocking the Properties dialog box from the side of the screen and float it in the drawing area. If it is already floating, try to dock it.*

- The linetype scale will be multiplied by the global LTSCALE for the objects selected. This change will only affect linetypes other than Continuous.
- The beginner's rule is that the colors of objects should be set to BYLAYER.
- Only layers that are already created will be available in the Select Layer list.
- Only linetypes that have already been loaded will be available in the Select Linetype list.

Command Exercise

Exercise 7-16 – Change Properties (Reprised)

Drawing Name: **change2.dwg**
Estimated Time to Completion: 10 Minutes

Scope

Using the Properties command, change the radius of the circle to 2, the layer to "Circle" and the center point to the midpoint of the line. Perform all these changes in the Properties dialog box. Using the Properties dialog, switch between the circle and the line selection. Change the layer for the line.

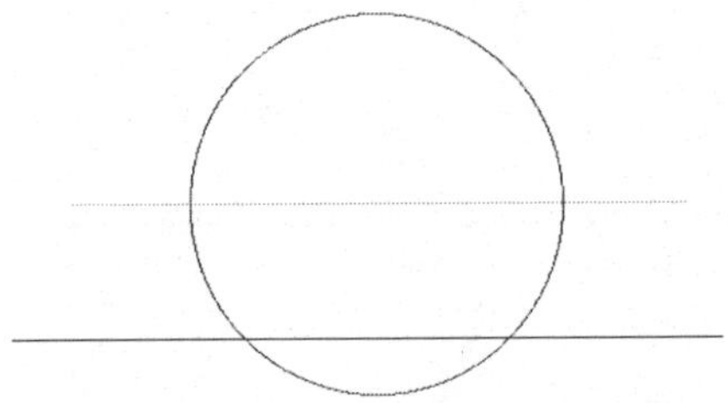

Solution

1.

Toggle OFF Quick Properties on the status bar.

2.

Activate the View ribbon.

Launch the **Properties** palette (properties).

3.

Select the circle and the line using window or crossing.

4.

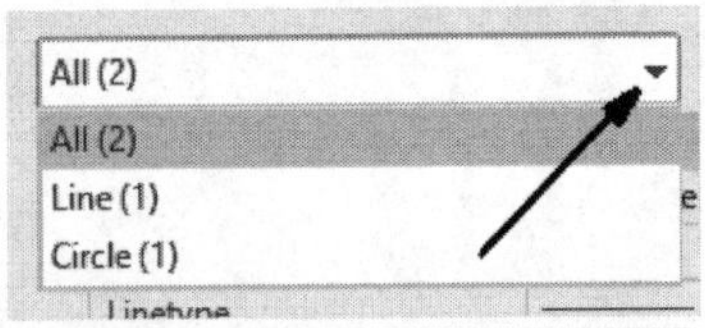

Two items are listed in the Properties dialog.
Select the drop-down arrow.

5.

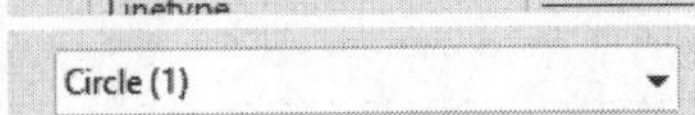

Select the Circle in the list.

6. 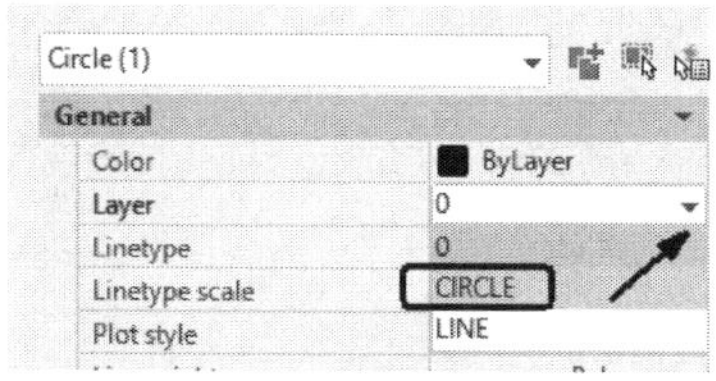

Change the layer to the CIRCLE layer in the properties dialog box.

7. 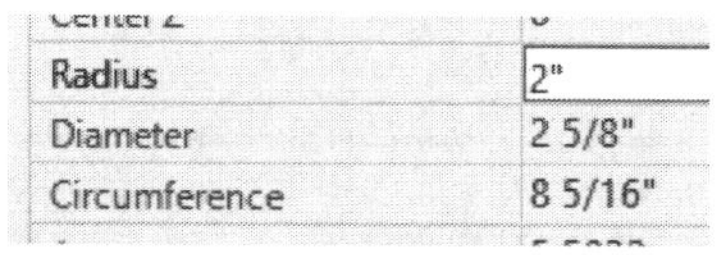

Select the Radius property and change it to 2”.

8. 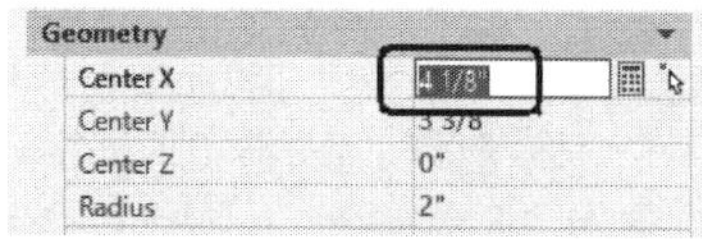

Under the Geometry properties of the circle LMB inside the Center X property.

9. 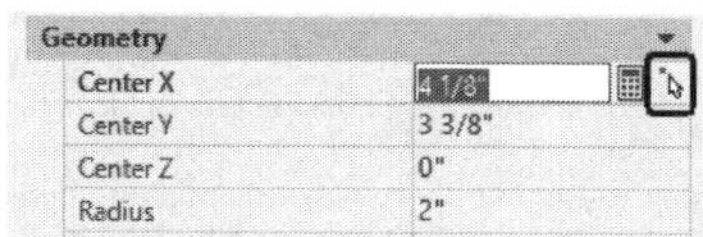

Pick the pointer icon that appears next to the Center X property in the dialog box.

10. 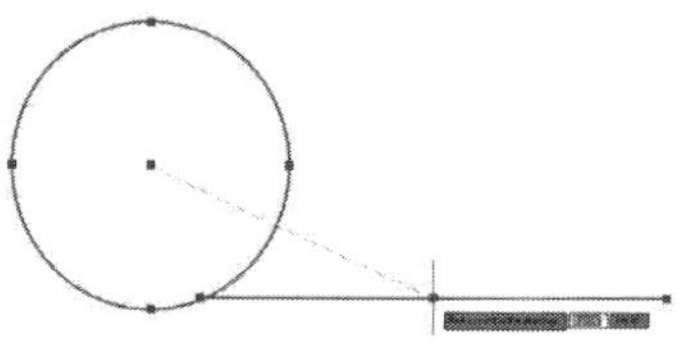

Pick a point in the drawing.
Use your OSNAP to select the midpoint of the line.

Notice how the circle has been changed.

11. 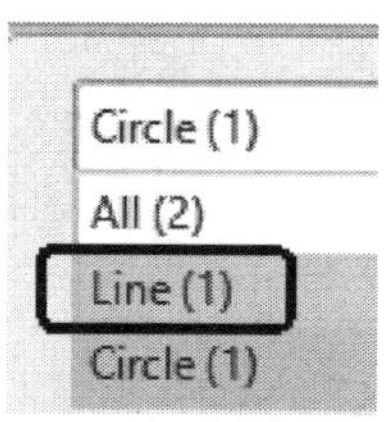

Select the Line from the drop-down list on the Properties dialog.

12. 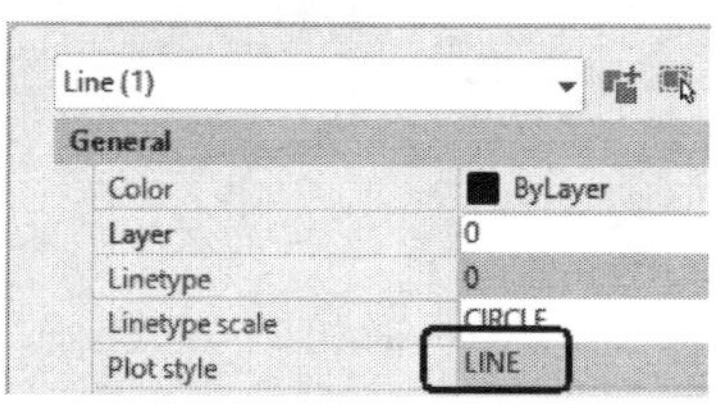

Assign the Line to the **LINE** layer.

13. 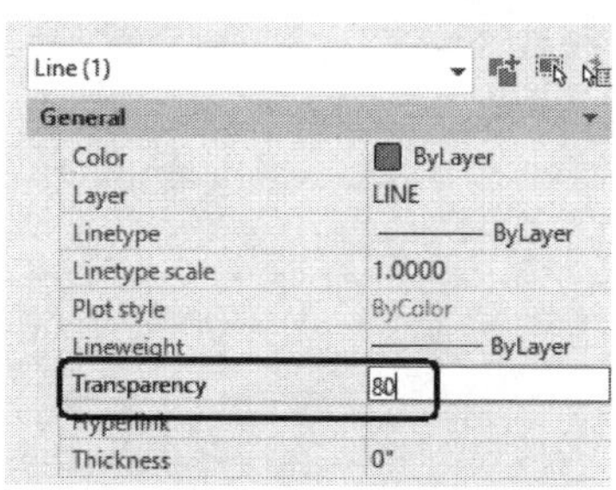

Set the Transparency of the line to 80.

14. 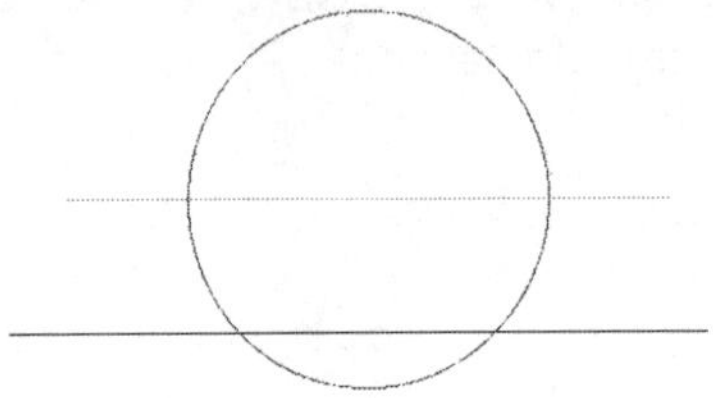

Click <ESC> to release the selection set.

Note how the objects have changed.

Extra: *Try changing the Area and Circumference of the circle using the Properties palette.*

Command Exercise

Exercise 7-17 – Organize a Drawing

Drawing Name: **Lesson 7 MCAD.dwg**
Estimated Time to Completion: 15 Minutes

Scope

Use the commands you have learned to organize the drawing into different layers. Create a Layer for each part in the assembly. Use the Properties tools to place the corresponding part on the correct layer.

Layer Name:	*Color:*
NUT	*GREEN*
UPPERBODY	*RED*
LOWERBODY	*YELLOW*
POST	*91*
PLATE	*65*
SHOULDERSCREW	*CYAN*
BILL_OF_MATERIAL	*YELLOW*
TEXT	*250*

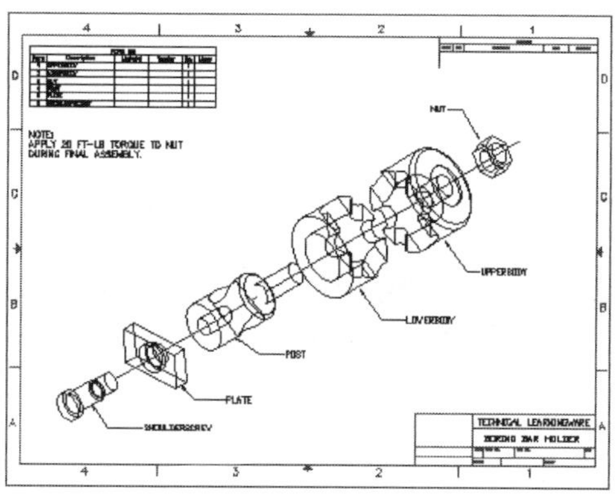

Solution

Hints

1. Start by creating the 8 new layers using the Layers Command. Notice that a layer for the title block already exists.
2. Use the Properties Command and different selection methods to make sure each part is on the correct layer.

Command Exercise

Exercise 7-18 – Organize a Drawing (Reprised)

Drawing Name: **Lesson 7 AEC.dwg**
Estimated Time to Completion: 15 Minutes

Scope

Use the commands you have learned to organize the drawing into different layers. Use the Layer Translator tool to use the aia.dwg as the CAD standard. Use the Properties tools to place elements on the correct layer.

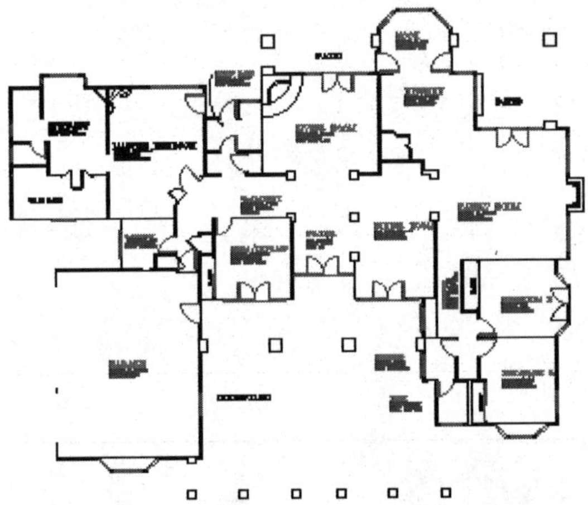

Solution

Hints

Place walls on the layer for walls, place doors on the layer for doors, etc. Walk through the drawing to see how it is currently organized before moving elements to new layers.

Review Questions

1. Identify the following icons and briefly describe each function:

A.		
B.		
C.		

2. What are the two options (what the image represents and its opposite) for the individual icons in the layers control dialog box?

	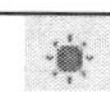

3. What is the difference between FREEZE and OFF when controlling layers?

4. You can turn the current layer OFF. Can you FREEZE the current layer? Can you draw on a layer that is OFF? Try it.

5. What command will remove used layers thus decreasing the file size of your drawing?
   - ❑ CLEAN
   - ❑ DRAIN
   - ❑ PURGE
   - ❑ FLUSH

6. What does it mean to choose the color BYLAYER?

   ❑ Objects choose their own color randomly.
   ❑ Objects default to the 0 layer and are black or white depending on the drawing window background color.
   ❑ Objects take on the color of the current layer they are assigned to.
   ❑ Objects take on an assigned color no matter what layer they are on.

7. What does the LTSCALE command do?

8. How can you control the Match Properties command so only specific features are matched like Line Type? Try it.

9. True or False
   When using the MATCHPROP command, you can select more than one source object.

10. True or False
    When using the MATCHPROP (Match properties) command, you can match properties from objects in one drawing to another drawing that is opened.

11. True or False
    If you create objects on layer 0, they cannot be moved to a different layer.

Review Answers

1. Identify the following icons and briefly describe each function:

    A. *Layer Properties Command, opens the Layers dialog box*

    B. *Match Properties, matches the properties of one or more objects to the first selected*

    C. *Make Object's Layer Current, makes the layer of the selected object current*

2. What are the two options (what the image represents and its opposite) for the individual icons in the layers control dialog box?

    A. *Freeze & Thaw*

    B. *On & Off*

    C. *Lock & Unlock*

3. What is the difference between FREEZE and OFF when controlling layers?

    The layers are not visible. Frozen layer is ignored in a regeneration (saving time when you regen), and a layer that is simply turned Off will still be processed in a regeneration (saving no time in a regen). Therefore, use FREEZE instead of OFF.

4. You can turn the current layer OFF. Can you FREEZE the current layer? Can you draw on a layer that is OFF? Try it.

    You cannot FREEZE the current layer. You can turn OFF the current layer. You can draw on a layer that is turned OFF. It is not recommended to draw on layers that are turned off, though, because you cannot see what you are drawing.

5. What command will remove used layers thus decreasing the file size of your drawing?

    PURGE

    The Purge command will delete unused layers and other objects such as linetypes, blocks, etc. You may also delete unused layers and linetypes in the Layers dialog box.

6. What does it mean to choose colors BYLAYER?

    Objects take on the color of the current layer they are assigned to.

    Objects will take on the color of the current layer when the color control is set to ByLayer. In the Object Properties dialog box, selecting BYLAYER will assign color to the selected object according to the layer it is on.

7. What does the LTSCALE command do?

    LTSCALE is a system variable that controls the linetype scale.

8. How can you control the Match Properties command so only specific features are matched like Line Type? Try it.

    Right click and select Settings to enable/disable Match Property Options.

9. True or False
    When using the MATCHPROP command, you can select more than one source object.

    False

10. True or False
    When using the MATCHPROP (Match properties) command, you can match properties from objects in one drawing to another drawing that is opened.

    False

11. True or False
    If you create objects on layer 0, they cannot be moved to a different layer.

    False

Lesson 8.0 – Drafting Settings and Object Snaps

Estimated Class Time: 2 Hours

Objectives

Students will practice setting different drafting and object snap settings and using the active settings to control how geometry is drawn.

- **Drafting Settings**
- **Object Snaps**
- **Creating Orthographic Views**

Drafting Settings: Snap and Grid

Command Locator

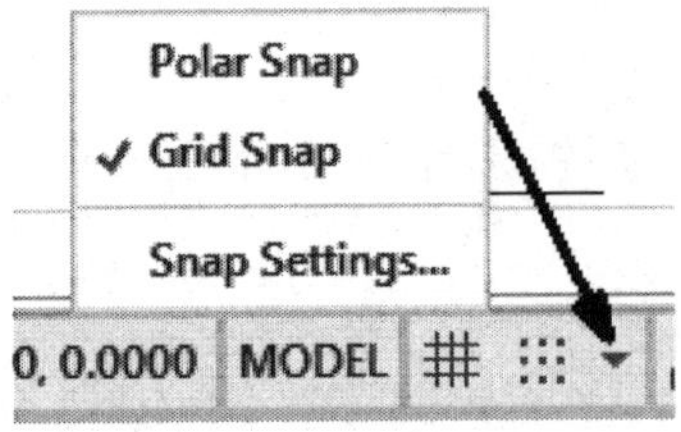

Command	**dsettings**
Alias	**ds**
RMB Shortcut Menu	**SNAP, GRID, POLAR, OSNAP or OTRACK in the Status Bar**
Dialog Box	**Drafting Settings**

Command Overview

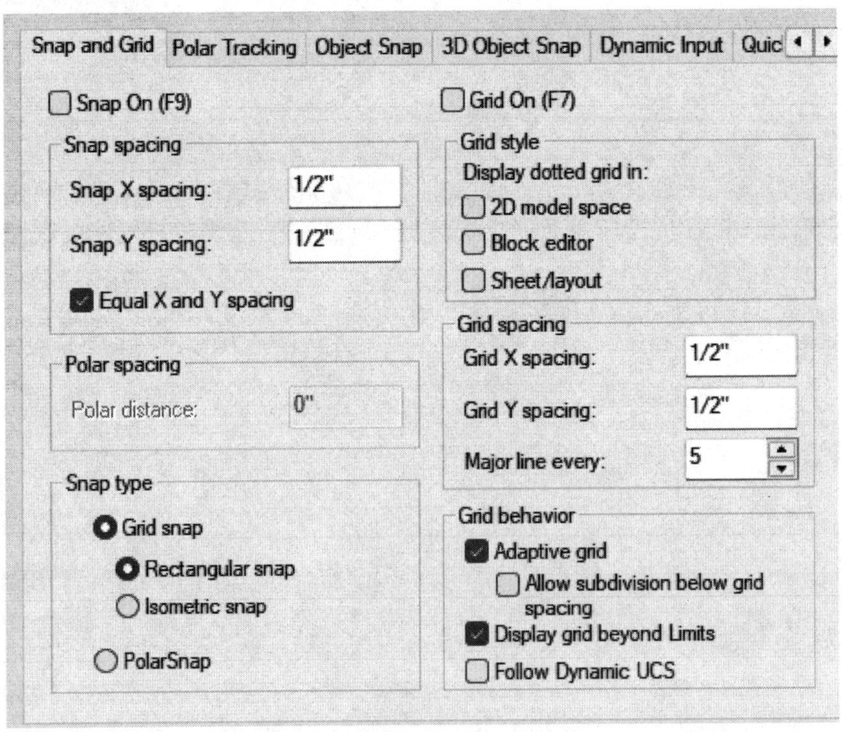

The Drafting Settings dialog box contains seven tabs:

- *Snap and Grid*
- *Polar Tracking*
- *Object Snap*
- *3D Object Snap*
- *Dynamic Input*
- *Quick Properties*
- *Selection Cycling*

Select the Status Bar option using the LMB to turn these functions ON or OFF. Use the RMB to access the Drafting Settings dialog box. You can quickly enable and disable object snaps by mousing over the OSNAP button and selecting/deselecting the preferred OSNAPs.

General Procedures

1. Type DS to launch the Drafting Settings dialog box.
2. Select the tab for the options you want to change or set.
3. Make the desired changes.
4. Click OK to close the dialog box.

- *Use the Isometric Snap option in the dialog box above to create an isometric drawing. Turn Ortho ON and use the F5 function key or Ctrl+E to toggle through the isoplanes.*
- *You can use temporary overrides to turn different drafting settings on or off. All these overrides use the SHIFT key plus a letter or symbol. Notice that the on/off overrides use keys on the left/right side of the keyboard. To turn a setting ON, use the left SHIFT key plus letter/symbol. To turn OFF a setting, use the right SHIFT key plus letter/symbol.*

DSETTING OVERRIDE	ON	OFF
OSNAP	SHIFT + A	SHIFT + ‘
ORTHO	SHIFT	SHIFT
OBJECT SNAP TRACKING	SHIFT+Q	SHIFT +]
OSNAP TRACKING	SHIFT+D	SHIFT+L
ENDPOINT OSNAP	SHIFT+E	SHIFT+P
MIDPOINT OSNAP	SHIFT+V	SHIFT +M
CENTER OSNAP	SHIFT+C	SHIFT+,

Command Exercise

Exercise 8-1 – Drafting Settings

Drawing Name: **drsettings1.dwg**
Estimated Time to Completion: 5 Minutes

Scope

In the Drafting Settings dialog box, Set the Grid spacing to 1,1. Set the Snap Spacing to .5,.5. Turn the Snap and Grid ON. Select OK. Notice how the snap and grid spacing changes.

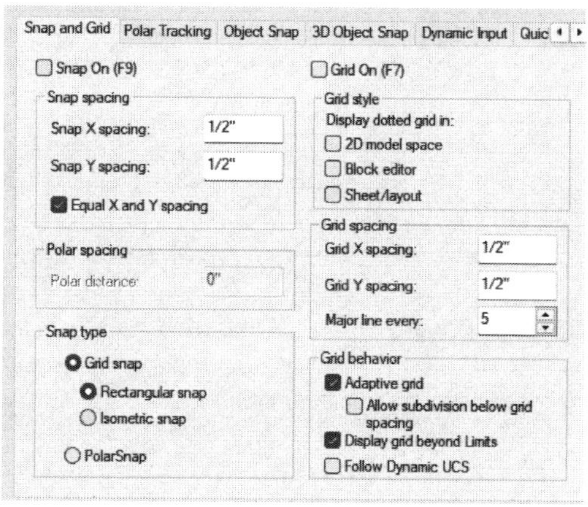

Solution

1.

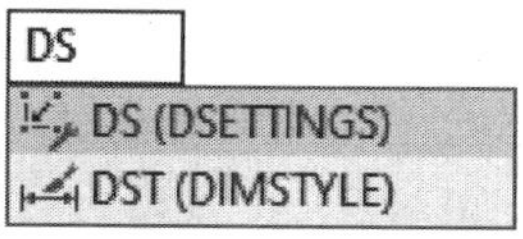

Activate the Drafting Settings dialog box by typing 'DSETTINGS' at the command line and Clicking <ENTER> or select the down arrow next to the Object Snap icon on the task bar and select **Object Snap Settings.**

2.

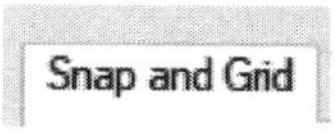

Select the **Snap and Grid** tab.

3. 

Enable **Snap On**.
Enable **Grid On**.

4. 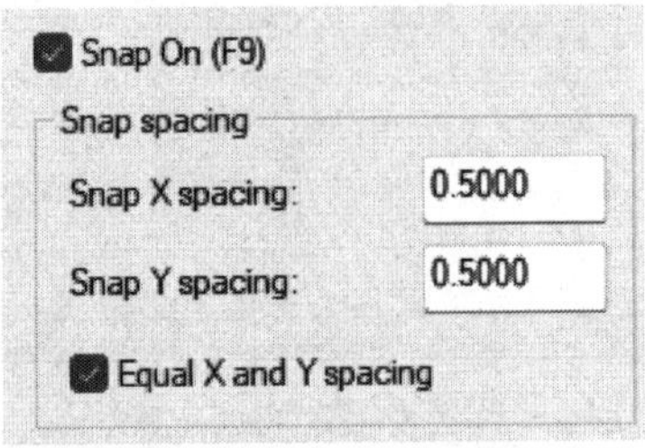

Set the Snap X spacing to **.50**.

Enable **Equal X and Y spacing**.

5. 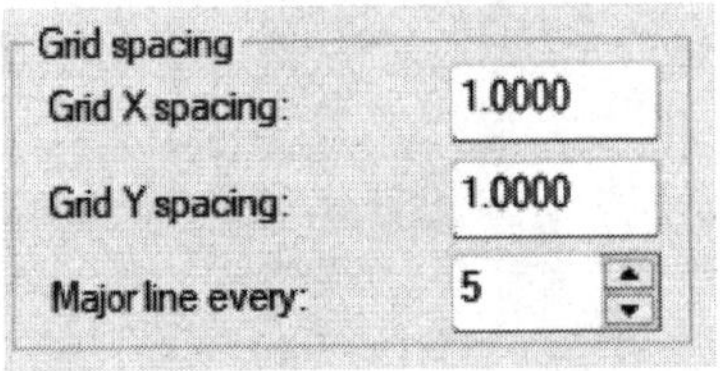

Set the Grid spacing to **1.0**.

Click **OK**.

6. 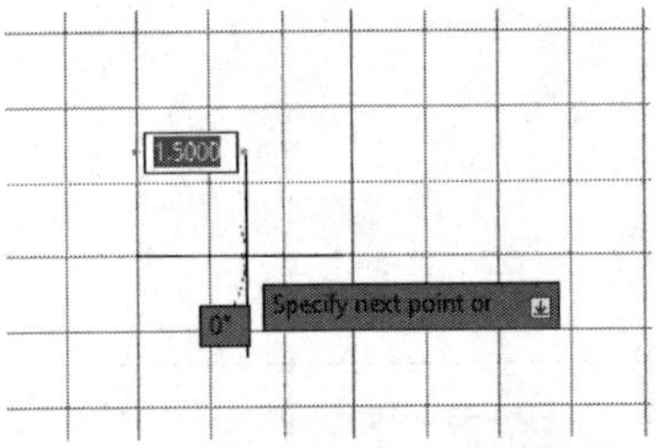

Notice how the Grid spacing defaults to the Snap spacing.

Start the LINE command.

Move the mouse around the screen and notice how the cursor snaps to the grid at .50 intervals.

Extra: *What happens if you set the snap spacing to 1,1 and Grid spacing to .3,.3? Try it.*

Drafting Settings: Polar Tracking Tab

Command Locator

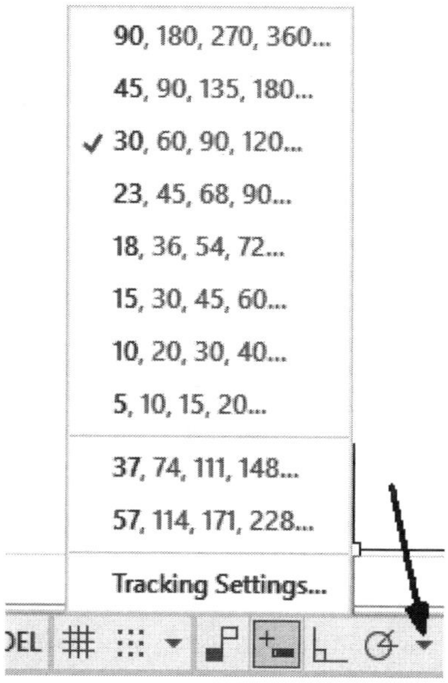

Command	**dsettings**
Alias	**ds**
RMB Shortcut Menu	**SNAP, GRID, POLAR, OSNAP or OTRACK in the Status Bar**
Dialog Box	**Drafting Settings**

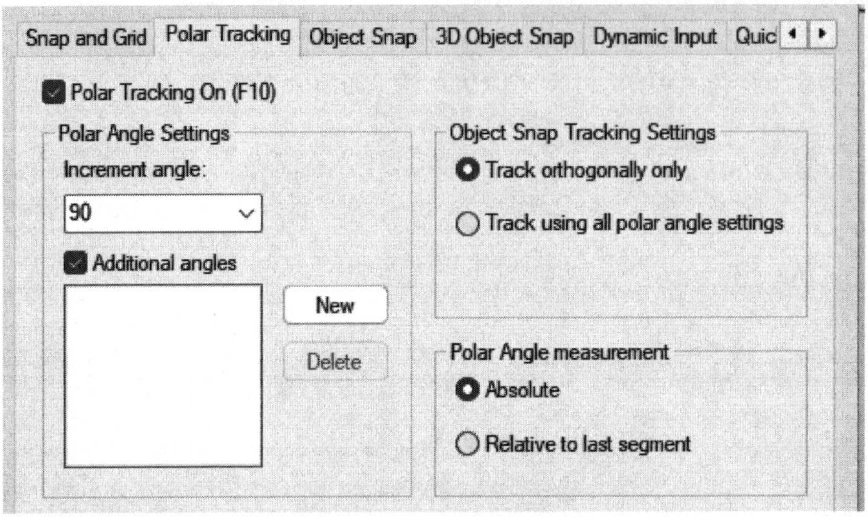

Command Overview

Polar Snap works independently from SNAP. With Polar Snap turned ON incremental angles will be displayed as the line being dragged approaches that angle. Set the "Incremental angle" from the drop down list, or add "New" angles.

General Procedures

1. Right-click on POLAR in the Status Bar to open the Drafting Settings dialog box and select the Polar Tracking tab.
2. Select the desired "Incremental angle" from the drop-down list. Check "Track orthogonally only" and "Absolute" Polar Angle measurement.
3. "Track orthogonally only" and "Absolute" Polar Angle measurement should also be selected.
4. Using the Line command, pick the first point, then drag the line to see the Polar Angle display.

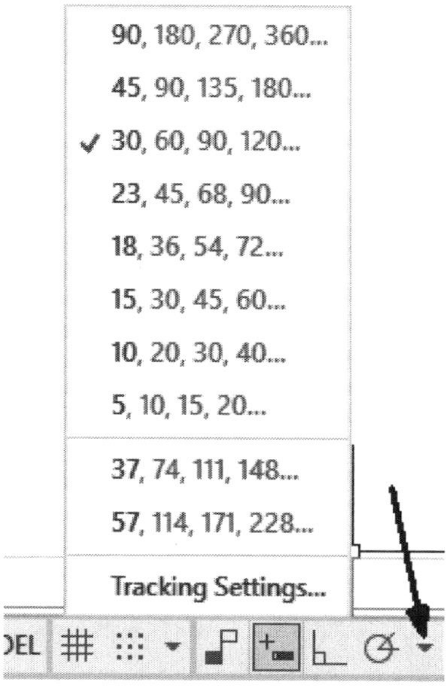

Selecting the Down Arrow next to the Polar icon on the Status Bar allows the user to select different combinations of angles to be used when tracking as well as creating new tracking settings.

- *With the desired polar angle displayed, type the length of the line and Click the <ENTER> key.*
- *Select "Relative to last segment" to see the Polar Angle in relation to the angle of the last object drawn.*

Command Exercise

Exercise 8-2 – Polar Snap

Drawing Name: **polar_osnap.dwg**
Estimated Time to Completion: 10 Minutes

Scope

Draw the shape indicated using the LINE command and POLAR OSNAP of 45 degrees. You do not need to add dimensions. The dimensions are for reference only.

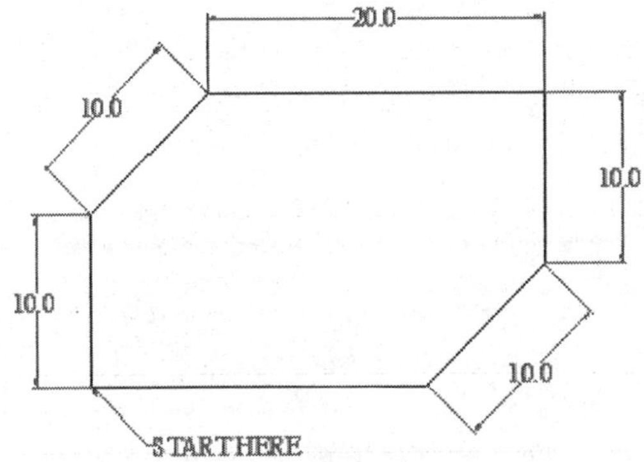

Solution

1. 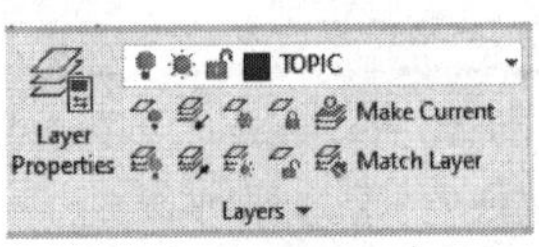

Make the **TOPIC** layer current.

2. 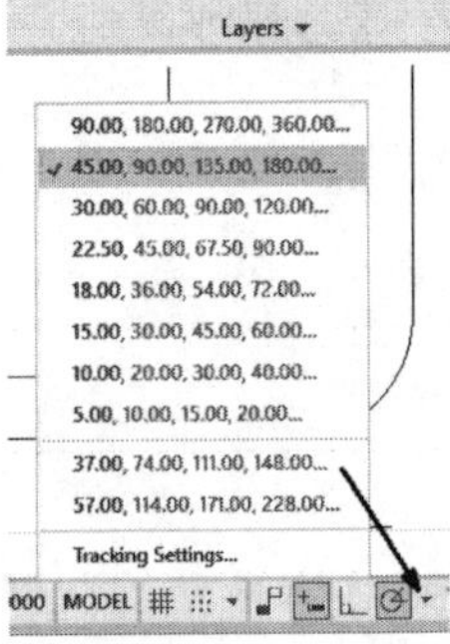

Set the POLAR OSNAP to use the **45 degree** increments.

3. 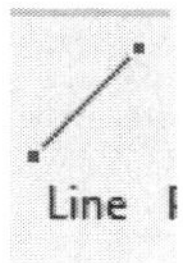

Start the **LINE** command.

4. 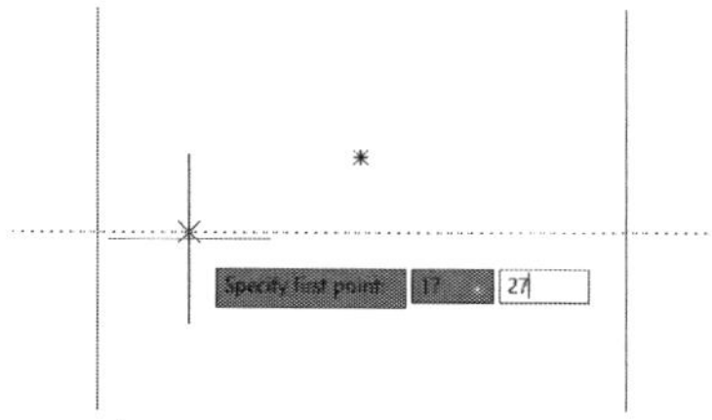

Type **17, 27** as the starting point.

5. 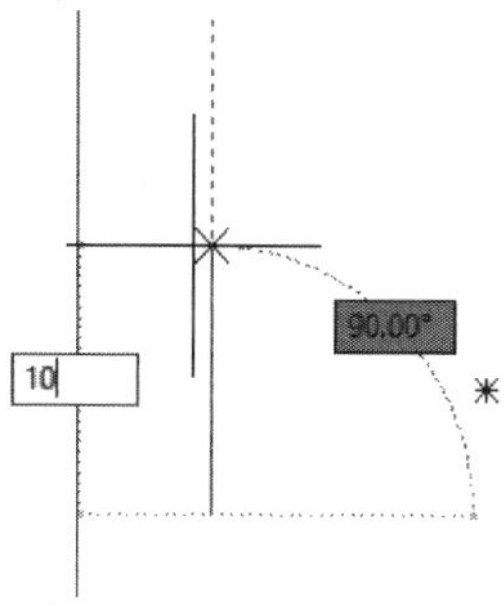

Drag the mouse up and type **10** for the distance.

6. 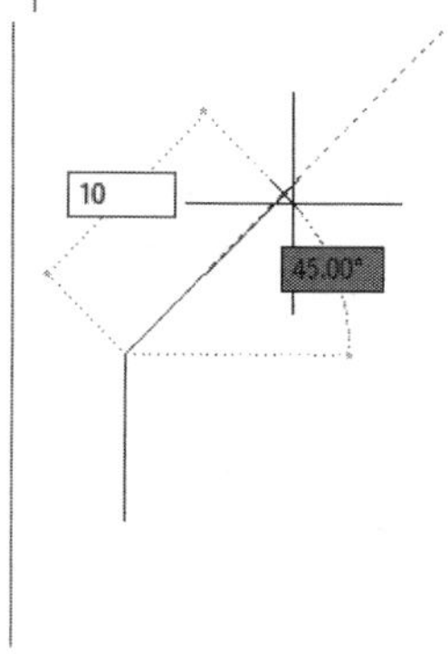

Move the cursor so that you see the **45 degree** OSNAP.
Type **10** for the distance.

7. 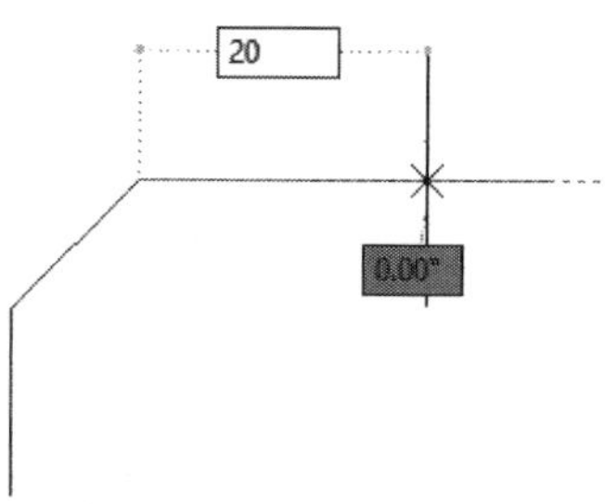

Move the mouse to the right.
Type **20** for the distance.

8. 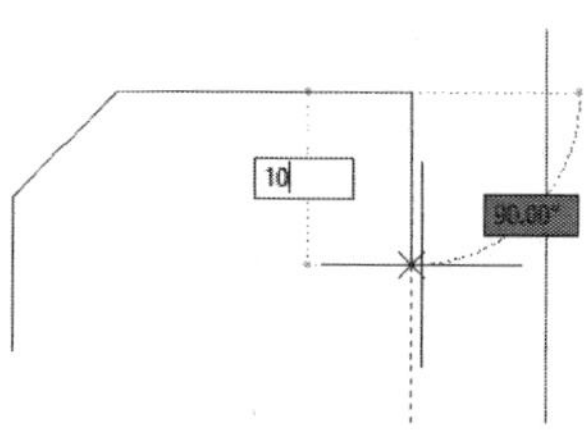

Move the mouse down.
Type **10** for the distance.

9.

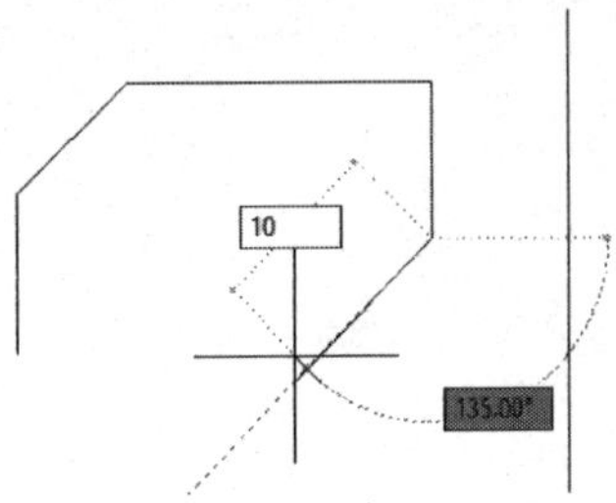

Move the cursor until the **135 degree** OSNAP is displayed.
Set the distance to **10**.

10.

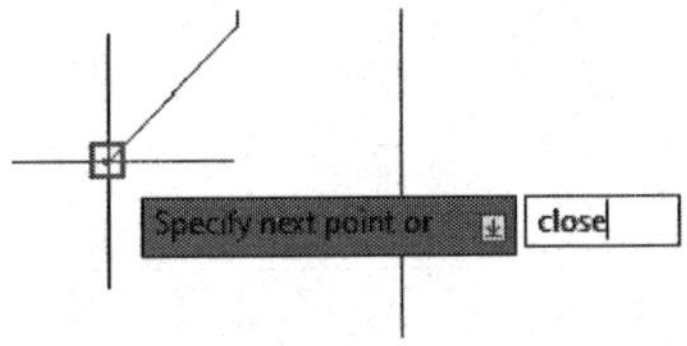

Type **CLOSE** to close the object.

11.

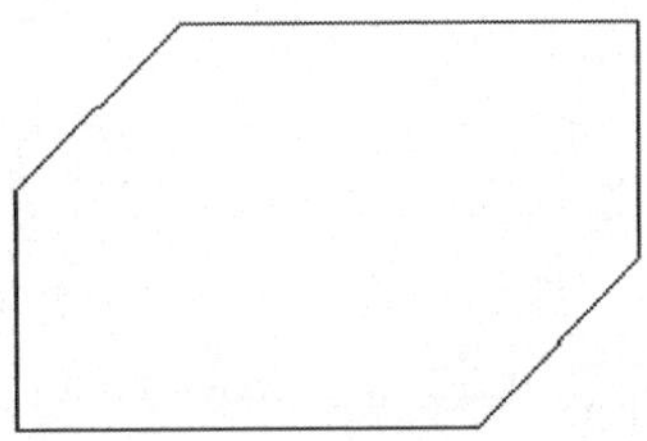

The object should look like this.

***Extra:** What are some other ways you can use POLAR OSNAP to create the object? Go back and review the different ways we used the LINE command.*

Drafting Settings: Object Snap

Command Locator

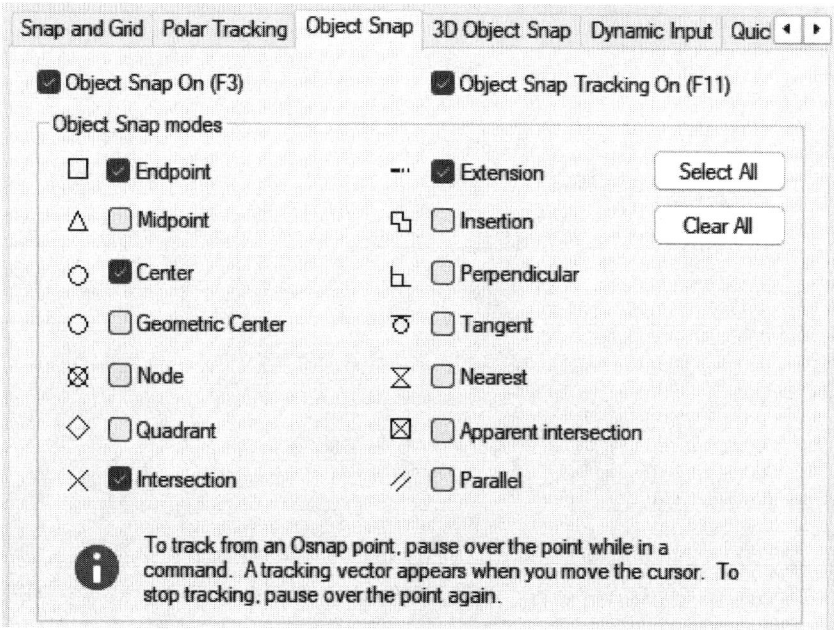

Command	**dsettings**
Alias	**ds**
RMB Shortcut Menu	**SNAP, GRID, POLAR, OSNAP or OTRACK in the Status Bar**
Dialog Box	**Drafting Settings**

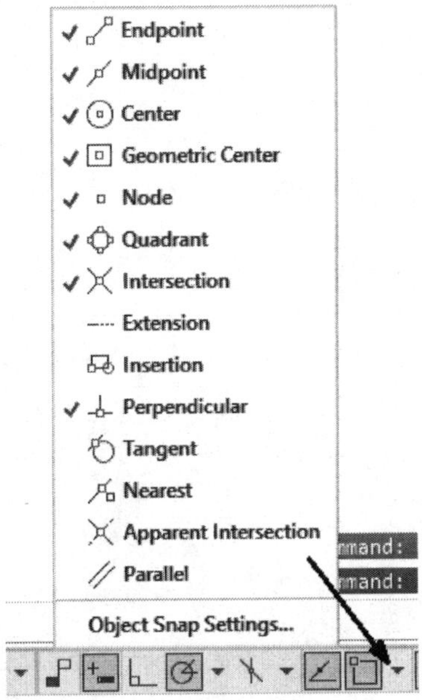

Command Overview

Object Snaps are used in combination with other commands. Use an object snap option when prompted to select a point and a specific object snap is desired. Unlike the OSNAP settings, which keep the OSNAP option "running," these object snaps are used for single selections.

General Procedures

1. Begin a Draw (or Modify) command.
2. When prompted for a selection point, choose an Object Snap option.
3. Place the cursor over the object, and when the marker appears at the desired location, use the LMB to select.

Tips & Tricks

- *The Object Snap symbols help to indicate where the selection point will be placed. The Object Snap toolbar can also be used to select the desired Object Snap. Move your pointer near the circumference of a circle when using the Center Object Snap.*

Object Snap Option	Button	Overview
Endpoint	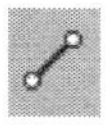	selects the endpoint of a line or arc.
Midpoint		selects the midpoint of a line or arc.
Intersection	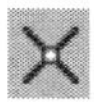	selects the intersection or projected intersection of two lines.
Apparent Intersect	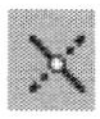	selects the virtual intersection of an existing line and the extension of another line.
Extension	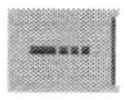	selects a point extending from a line's endpoint.
Center		selects the center of a circle or arc.
Geometric Center		selects the center of a polygon.
Quadrant		selects one of the four quadrants of a circle or arc.
Tangent		makes the object drawn, tangent to the object selected.
Perpendicular		makes the object drawn perpendicular to the object selected.
Parallel		draws an object parallel to the selected object.
Node	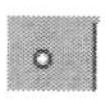	selects a point – you must have placed a point using the POINT command.
Insert		selects the point on the object where it was inserted–works for blocks, xrefs, and text.
Nearest		selects a point on the object selected at the location where it was picked.
None		turns off all active object snap settings during the active command.
OSNAP Settings		opens the Drafting Settings dialog box.

Command Exercise

Exercise 8-3 – Object Snap

Drawing Name: **osnap1.dwg**
Estimated Time to Completion: 15 Minutes

Scope

Practice using single object snaps. Draw the objects shown using the object snaps as indicated.

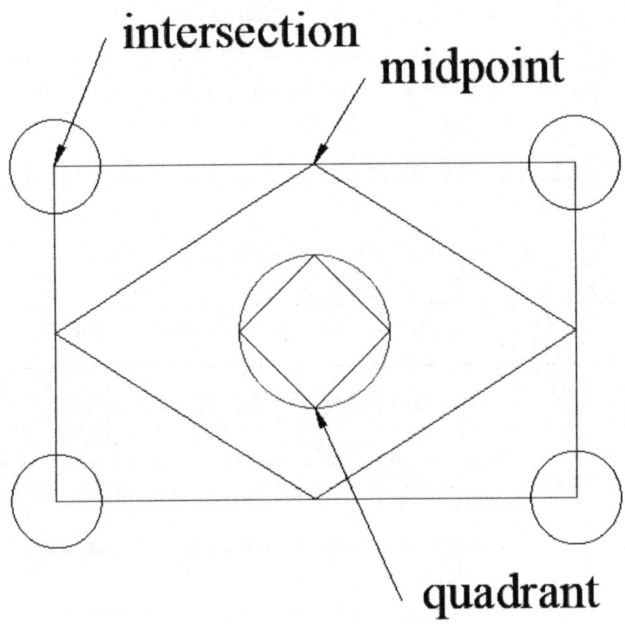

Solution

1. 

Make sure Running Object Snap is turned off. Use your LMB to toggle OSNAP off at the status bar. When OSNAP is off there is no blue indicator on the icon.

2. 

Create the four circles first.

Invoke the Circle command (c or circle).

3.

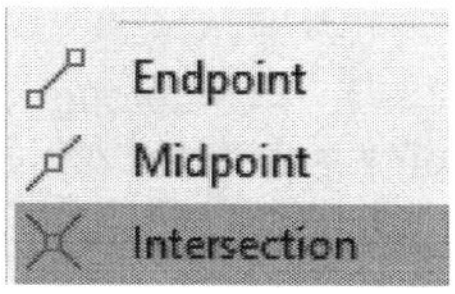

Specify center point for circle or [3P/2P/Ttr (tan tan radius)]:
Before you pick the first center point of the circle hold your <Shift> key down and Click the RMB to bring up the Object Snap shortcut menu.

Select **Intersection**.

4.

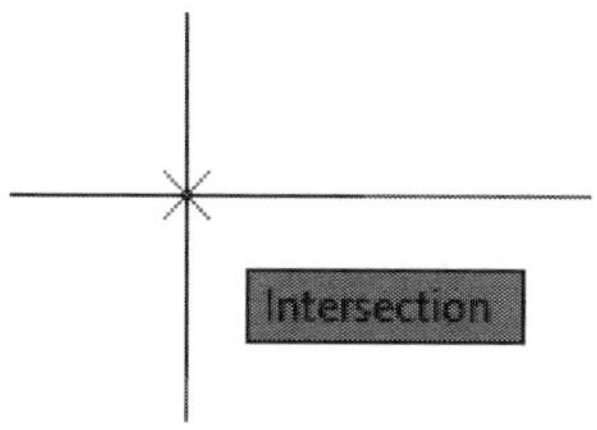

Specify center point for circle or [3P/2P/Ttr (tan tan radius)]: _int of
Move your pointer near the desired intersection until the Intersection Object Snap Marker appears. Pick the point with your LMB. Notice how the center of the circle is exactly at the intersection of the 2 lines.

You should see a cursor badge indicating that you are selecting an intersection prior to the left picking.

5.

Specify radius of circle or [Diameter]:
Type **0.5".**

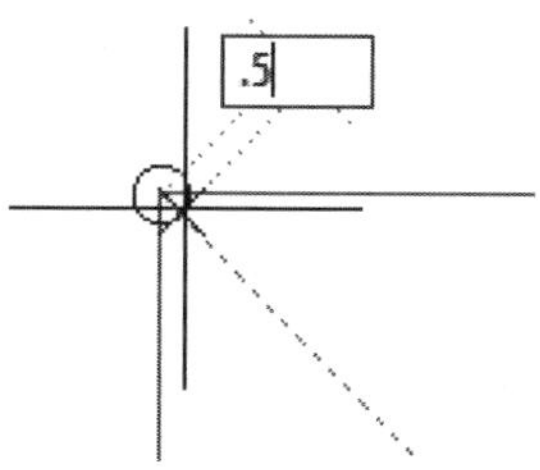

6.

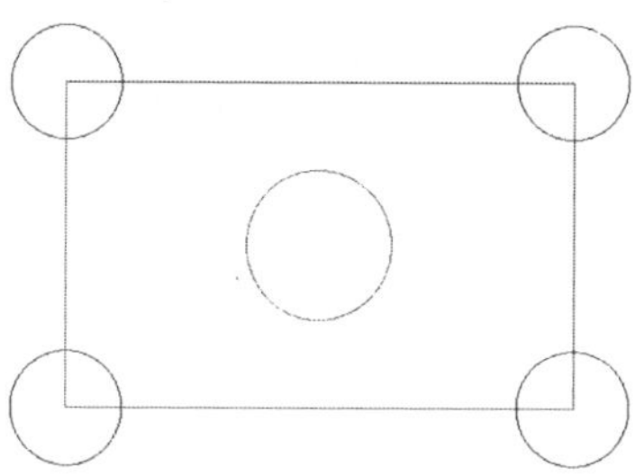

Repeat the process to complete the remaining circles.
You can Click ENTER to accept the default value for the radius.

7.

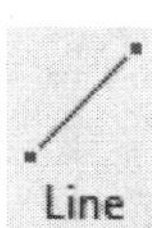

Invoke the Line command (l or line).

8. 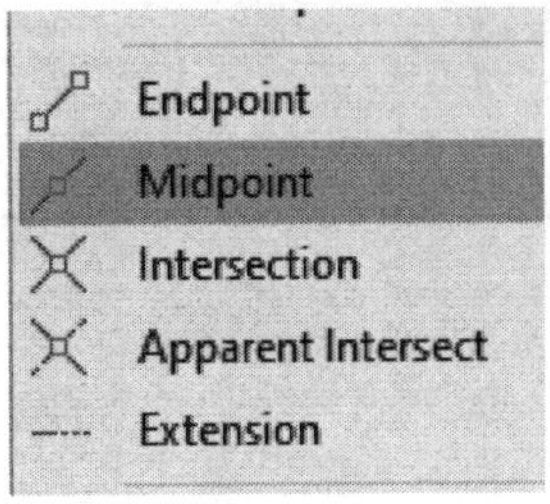

Specify first point:
Before you pick the start point of the line hold your <Shift> key down and Click the RMB. This will bring up the Object Snap shortcut menu.

Select **Midpoint**.

9. 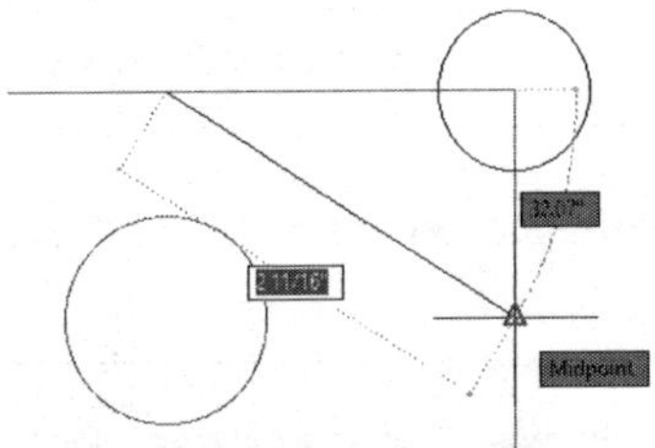

Specify first point: _mid of
Move your pointer near one of the sides of the box until the Midpoint Object Snap Marker appears.

Select the point with the LMB.

10. 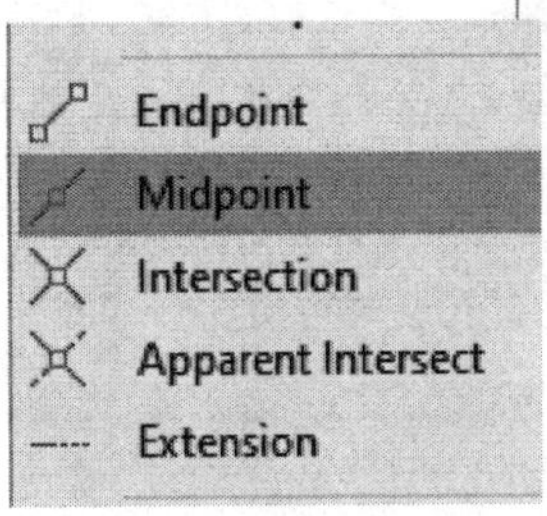

Specify next point or [Undo]:
Hold your <Shift> key down and Click the RMB to activate the Object Snap shortcut menu.

Select **Midpoint**.

11. 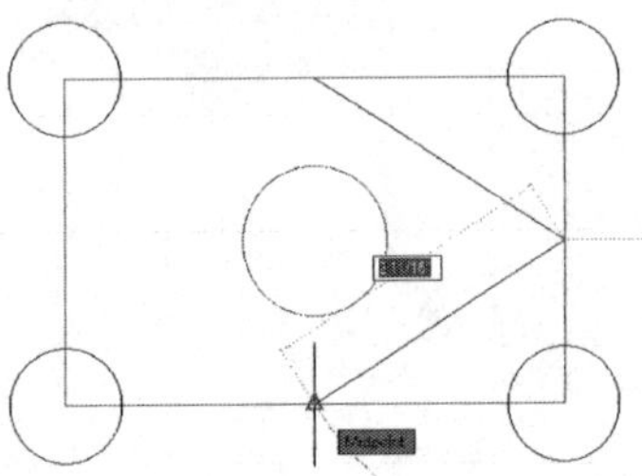

Specify next point or [Undo]: _mid of
Move your pointer to the desired side of the box to complete the first line segment.

12. 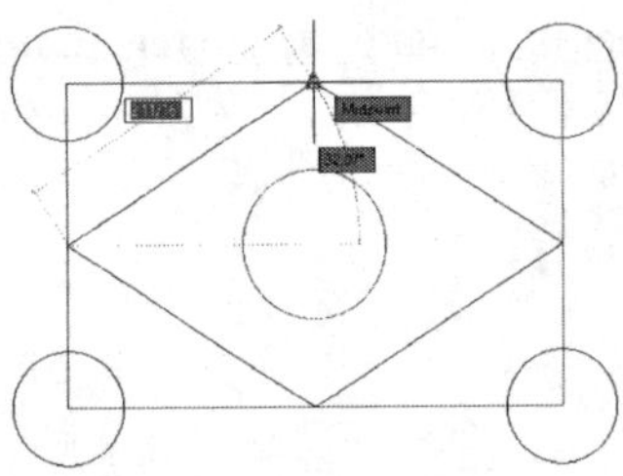

Specify next point or [Close/Undo]:
Repeat the process using the midpoint object snap to place the four line segments in the Box.

Click ENTER to exit the LINE command.

13. 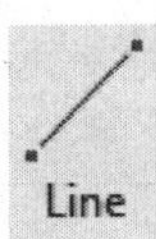

Finish the exercise by creating the 4 line segments in the center circle.

Invoke the Line command (l or line).

14. 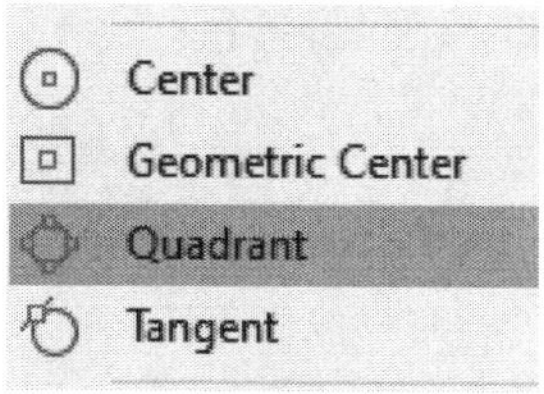

Specify first point:
Hold the <Shift> key down and Click the RMB to activate the Object Snap shortcut menu.

Select the **Quadrant** object snap.

15. 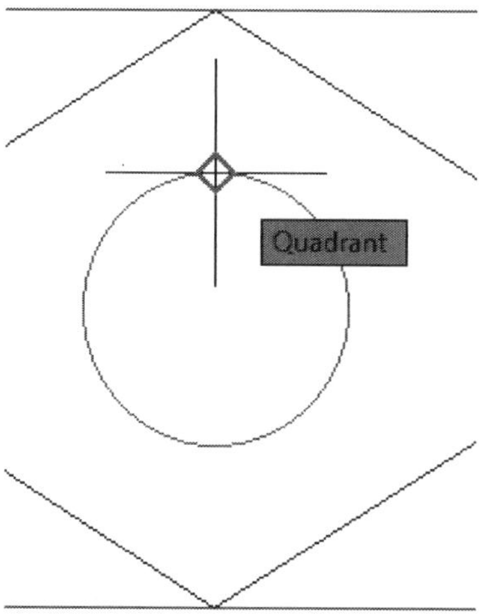

Specify first point: _qua of
Move the pointer near the top of the center circle and Click the LMB once; the Quadrant Object Snap Marker appears.

16. 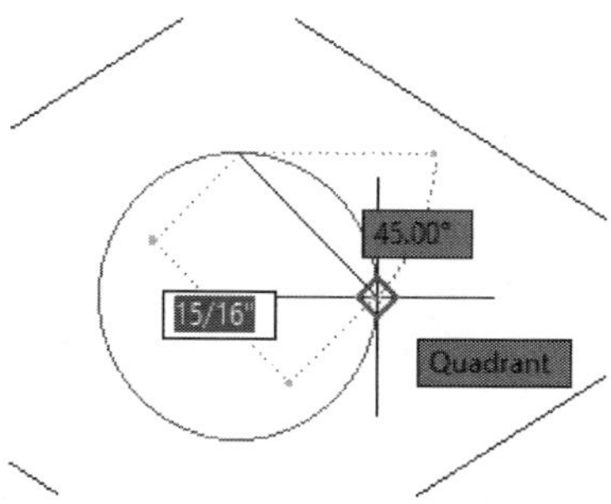

Specify next point or [Undo]:
Repeat the process of using the <Shift> RMB to activate the shortcut menu.

Remember to select the Quadrant Object Snap before selecting a point with the LMB.

You should see a cursor badge displaying the quadrant point prior to left picking.

17. 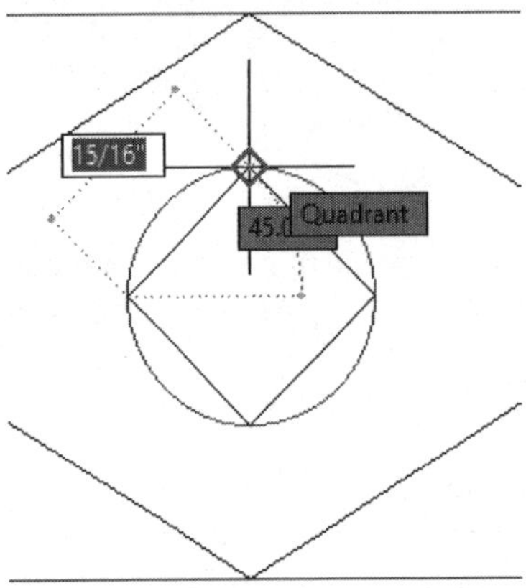

Complete the diamond shape using the QUAdrant OSNAP.

18. 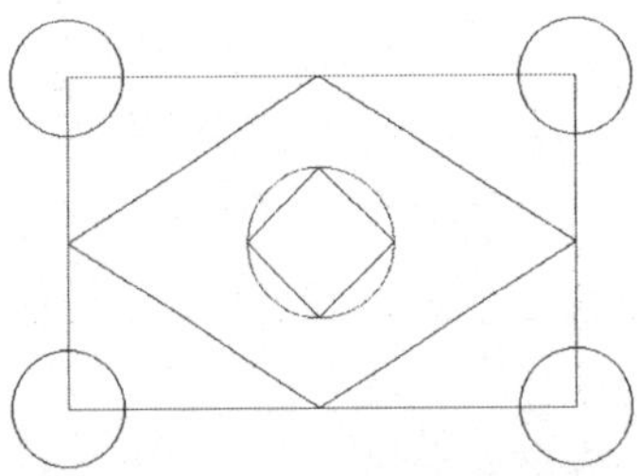

Your drawing should look like this at completion.

Close without saving.

Tips & Tricks

- *AutoCAD will not display lines when using a Perpendicular or Tangent Object Snap until an end point is selected. This occurs because the first point is dependent on the second point selected when using Tangent and Perpendicular Object Snaps.*
- *Be aware of the cursor badges—they are there to help guide you and reinforce your selections to prevent you from making the wrong left pick.*

Command Exercise

Exercise 8-4 – Object Snap (Reprised)

Drawing Name: **osnap2.dwg**
Estimated Time to Completion: 15 Minutes

Scope

Using the single object snap option, draw the object on the left using the object snaps as indicated each time you select a point.

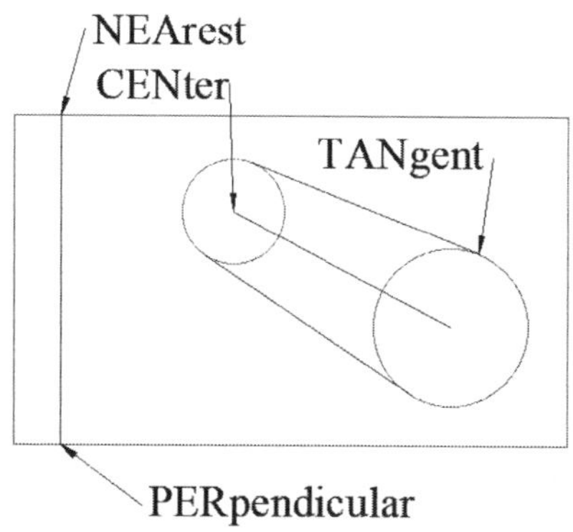

Solution

1.  Make sure Running Object Snap is turned off. Use your LMB to toggle OSNAP off at the status bar. When OSNAP is off there is no blue indicator on the icon.

2. 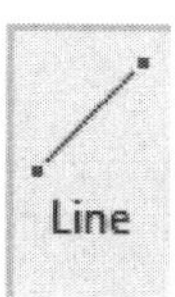

Start by creating the vertical line using the Perpendicular and Nearest Object Snaps.

Invoke the **Line** command (l or line).

3.

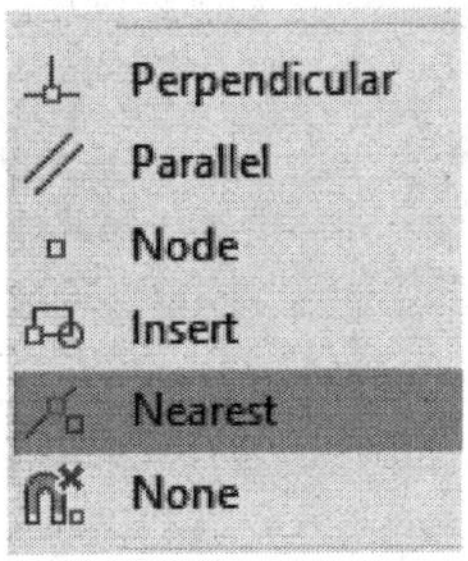

Specify first point:

Hold the <Shift> key down and Click the RMB to activate the Object Snap shortcut menu.

Select the **Nearest** Object Snap.

4.

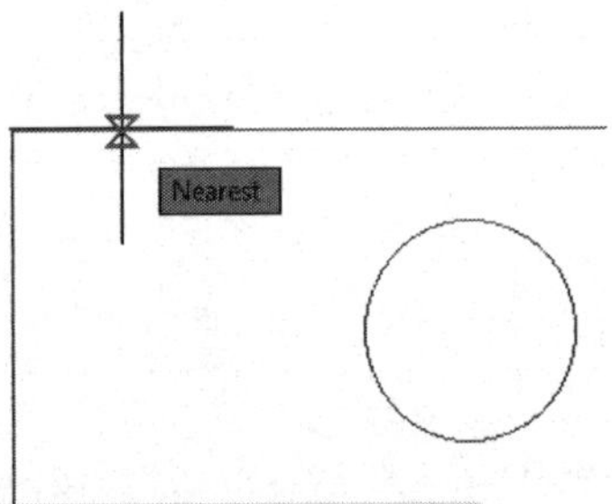

Specify first point: _per to

Move the pointer to the top of the box and Click the LMB when the Nearest Object Snap Marker appears.

5.

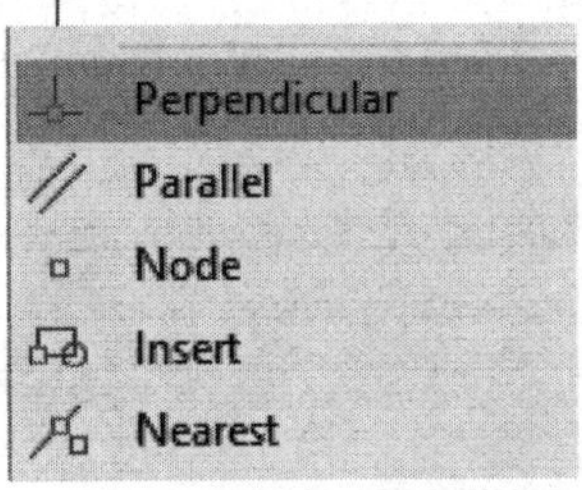

Specify next point or [Undo]:

Hold the <Shift> key down and Click the RMB to activate the Object Snap shortcut menu.

Select the **Perpendicular** Object Snap.

6.

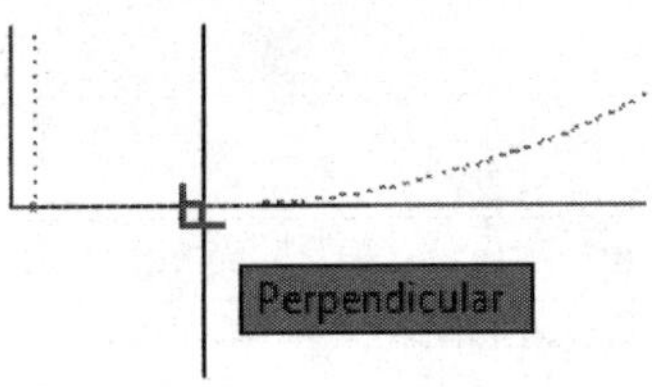

Specify next point or [Undo]: _nea

Move the pointer to the bottom of the box and select the desired point that will create the vertical line segment.

Notice that the line is perpendicular to the bottom line segment and positioned at the second point you have selected.

7.

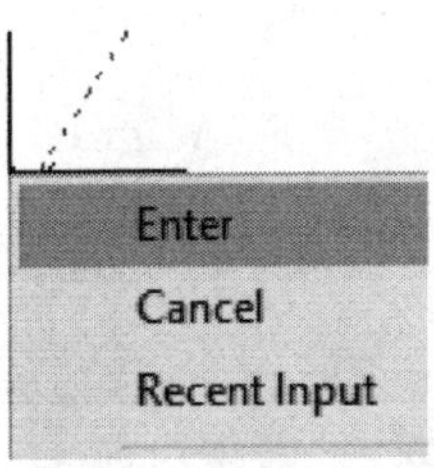

Right click and select **ENTER** to exit the LINE command.

8.

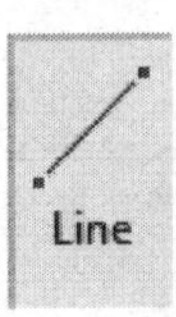

Create the two lines that are tangent to the circles.

Start by invoking the **Line** command (l or line).

9.

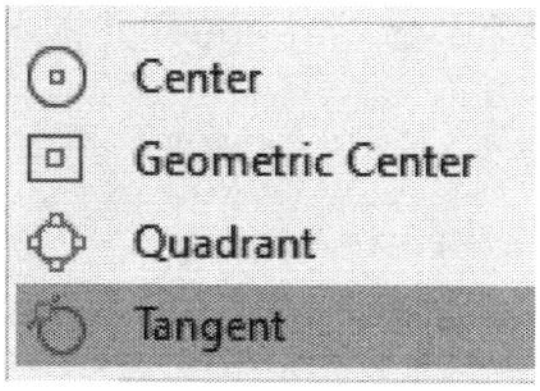

Specify first point:
Hold your <Shift> key down and Click the RMB to activate the Object Snap shortcut menu.

Select **Tangent**.

10.

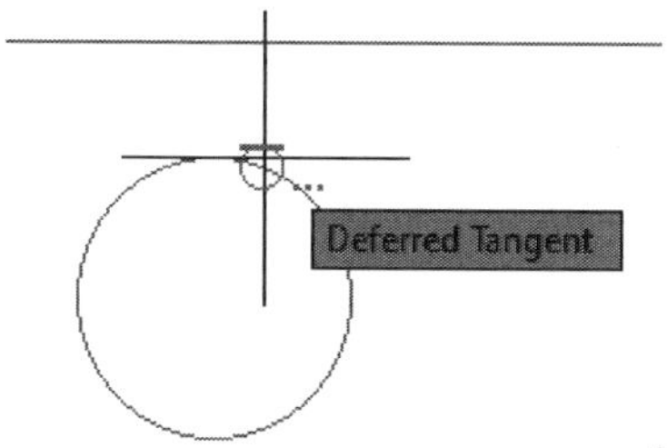

Specify first point: _tan to
Move the pointer to the general area for the start point of the line and Click LMB when the Tangent Object Snap Marker appears.

11.

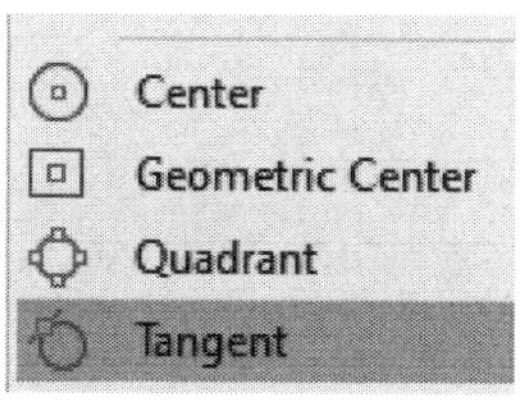

Specify next point or [Undo]:
Hold your <Shift> key down and Click the RMB to activate the Object Snap shortcut menu.

Select **Tangent**.

12.

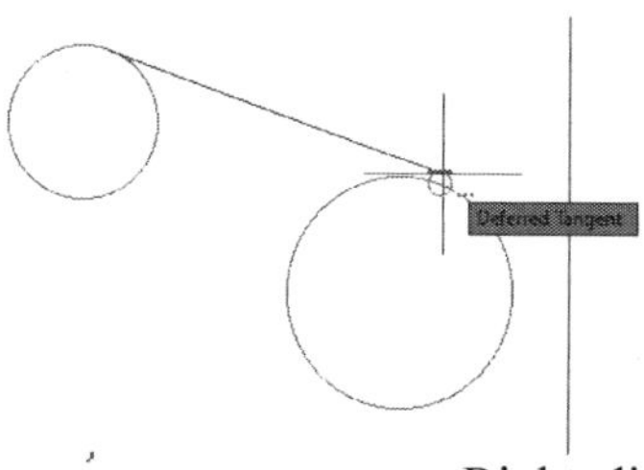

Specify first point: _tan to
Move the pointer to the general area for the end point of the line and Click LMB when the Tangent Object Snap Marker appears.

13.

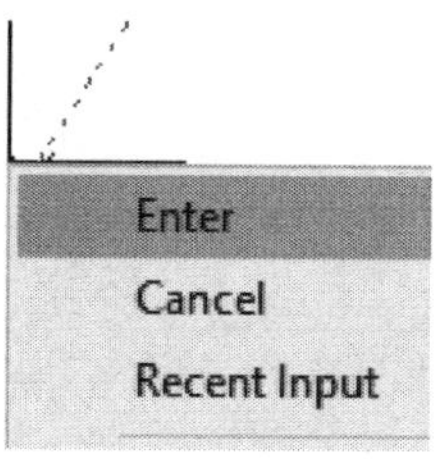

Right click and select **ENTER** to exit the LINE command.

14. 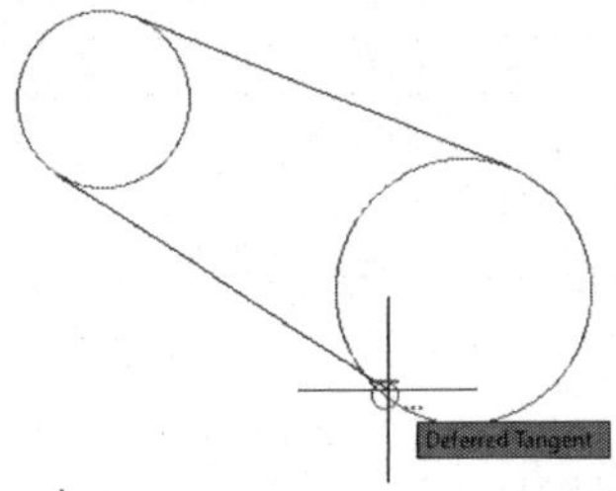

Repeat the process for the second line that is tangent to the 2 circles.

15. 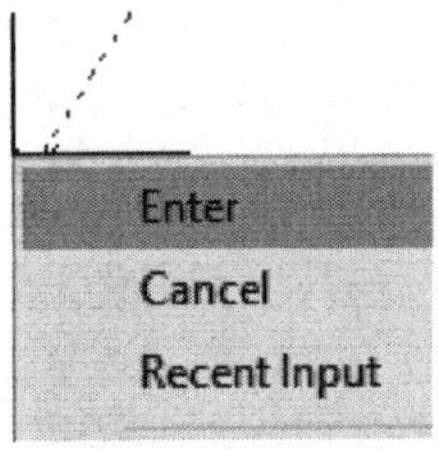

Right click and select **ENTER** to exit the LINE command.

16. 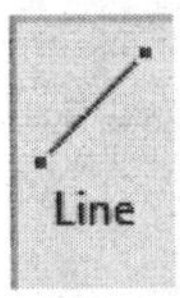

Finish the exercise by creating a line from the center point of the first circle to the center point of the second circle.

Invoke the **Line** command (l or line).

17. 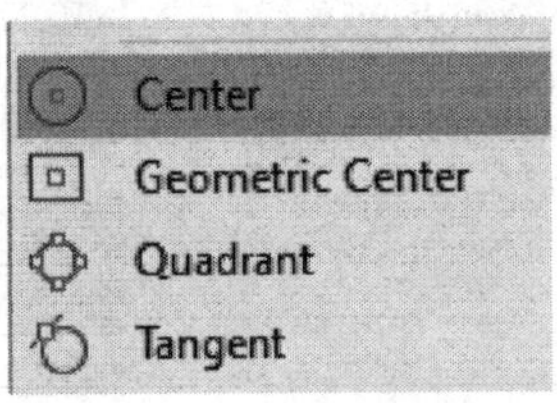

Specify first point:
Hold your <Shift> key down and Click the RMB to activate the Object Snap shortcut menu.

Select **Center**.

18. 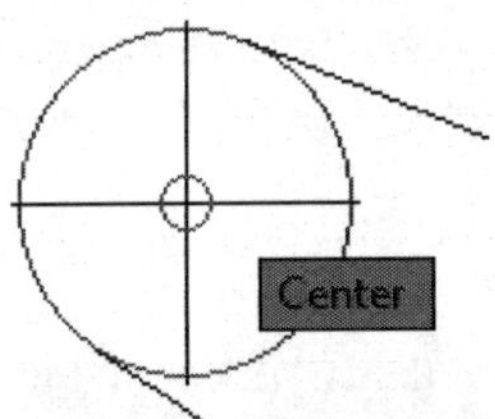

Specify first point: _cen to
Move the pointer to the center of the circle for the start point of the line and Click LMB when the Center Object Snap Marker appears.

19. 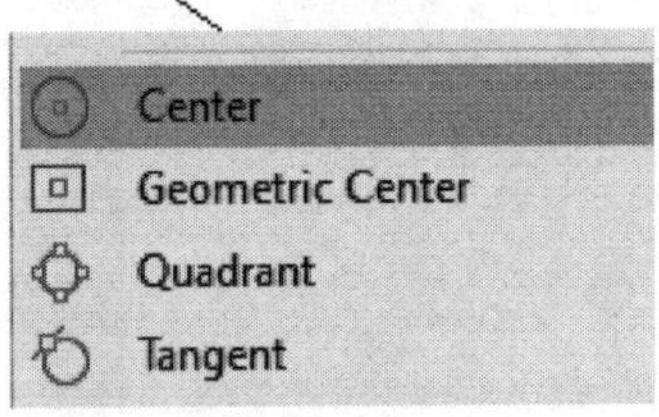

Specify next point or [Undo]:
Hold your <Shift> key down and Click the RMB to activate the Object Snap shortcut menu.

Select **Center.**

20. 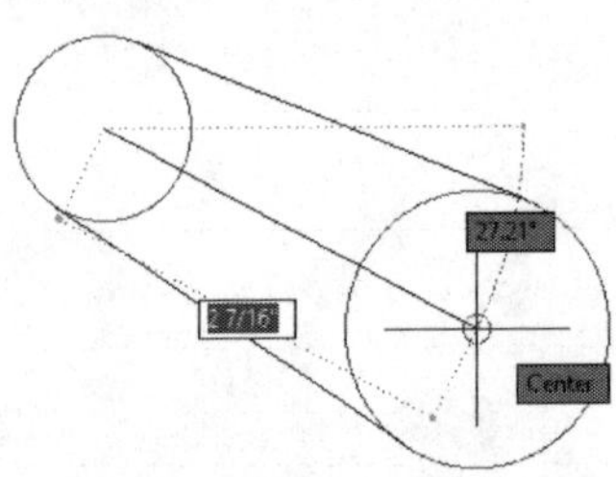

Specify next point or [Undo]: _cen of
Move the pointer to the center of the second circle for the end of the line. Click the LMB when the Center Object Snap Marker appears.

21. 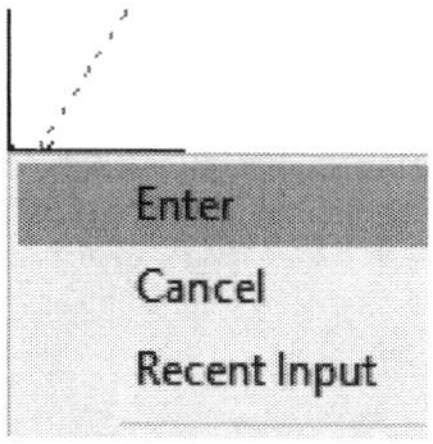

Right click and select **ENTER** to exit the LINE command.

22. 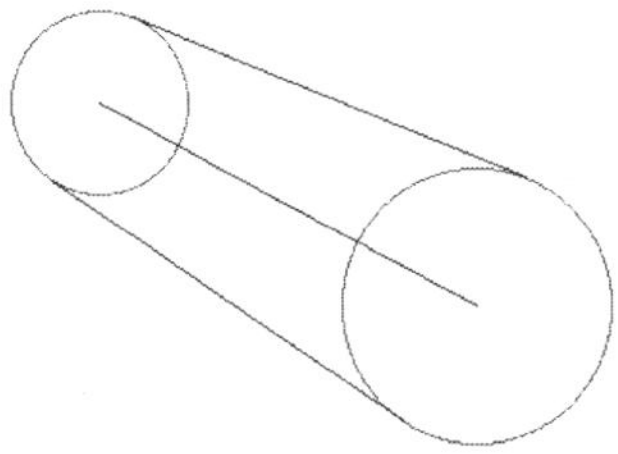

Close without saving.

Command Exercise

Exercise 8-5 – Running Object Snap

Drawing Name: **osnap3.dwg**
Estimated Time to Completion: 15 Minutes

Scope

Draw the object on the left using Running Object Snaps. Double click on OSNAP, or select <TOOLS<DRAFTING SETTINGS. Activate the Endpoint, Midpoint and Quadrant running object snaps. Note that this exercise is similar to the previous single object snap exercise, except that Object Snap options will remain ON.

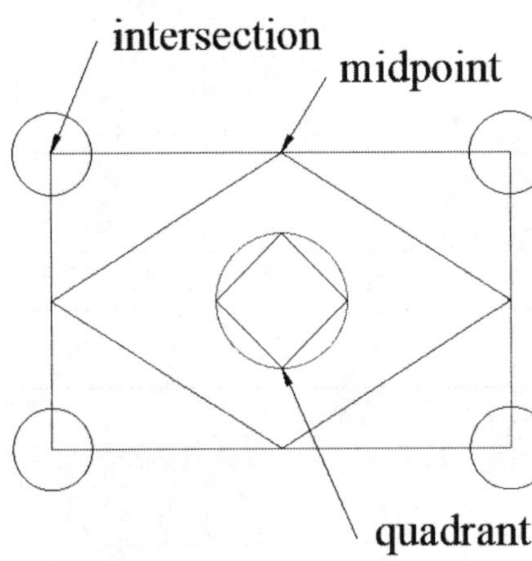

Solution

1. 

Start by making sure the Running Object Snaps are set.

Use your LMB to toggle OSNAP on at the status bar.

When the OSNAP toggle is ON, it will show as blue.

2.

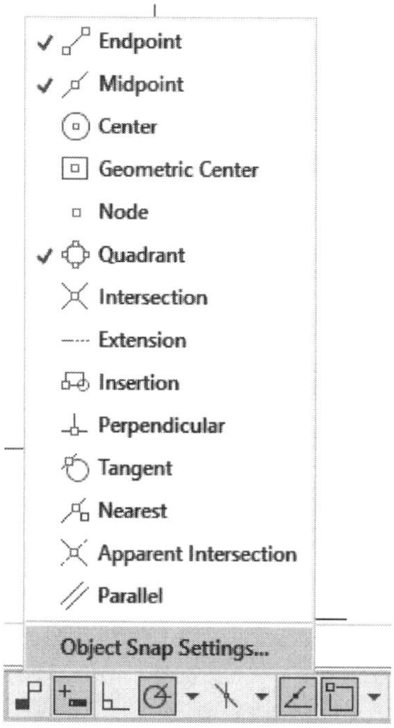

Set the correct running object snaps by left clicking on the down arrow next to the OSNAP icon.

Enable:

- Endpoint
- Midpoint
- Quadrant

A check mark indicates the option is ENABLED.

3.

Invoke the **circle** command (c or circle).

4.

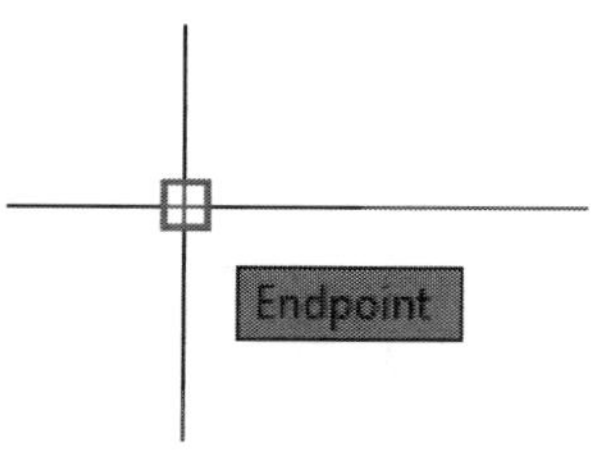

Specify center point for circle or [3P/2P/Ttr (tan tan radius)]:
Move your pointer to near one of the desired corners until the End Object Snap Marker appears.

Pick the point with the LMB.

5.

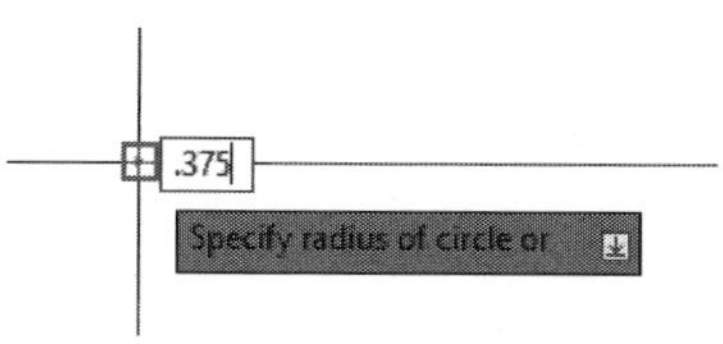

Specify radius of circle or [Diameter]:

Type **.375** for the radius value.

Click **ENTER.**

6.

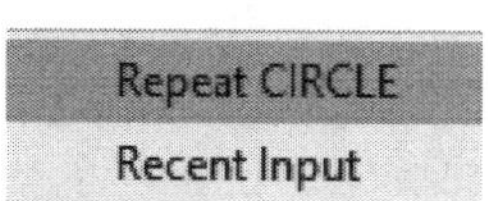

Repeat the circle command by Clicking <ENTER> or right-clicking in the drawing window and selecting **'Repeat CIRCLE'**.

7.

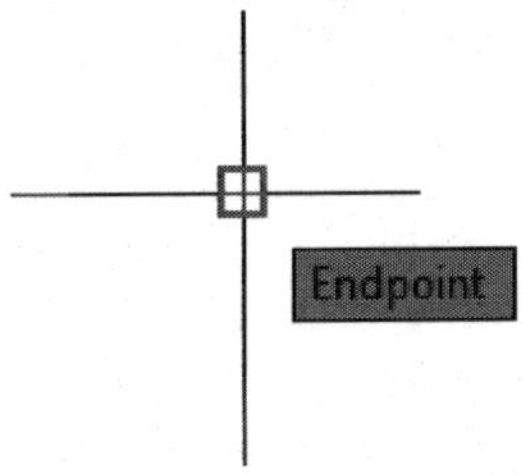

Specify center point for circle or [3P/2P/Ttr (tan tan radius)]:

Move your pointer to the next corner until the desired End Object Snap Marker appears.

Pick with your LMB.

8.

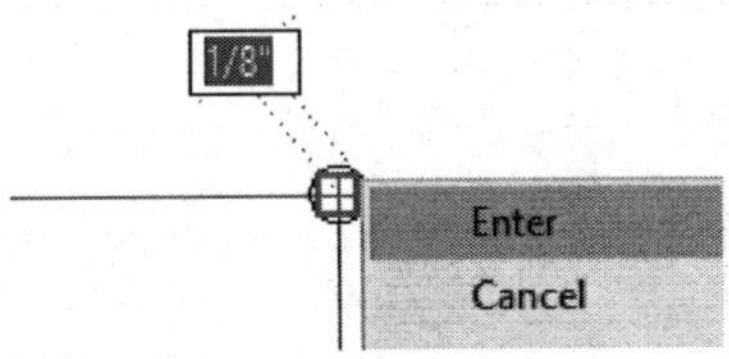

Specify radius of circle or [Diameter] <x.xx>:

Click <ENTER> to finish the second circle with the same radius.

9.

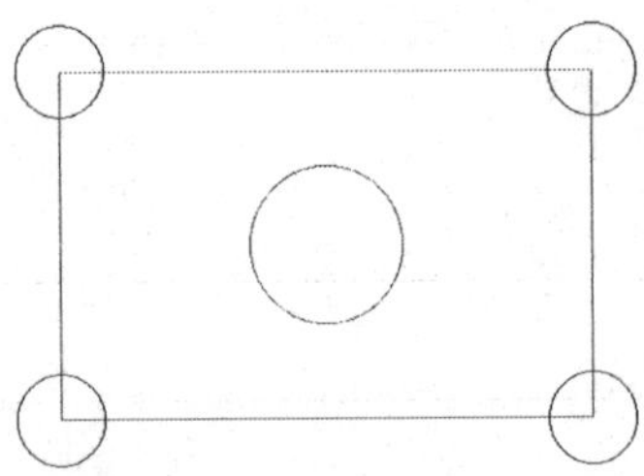

Repeat the process to complete the remaining circles.

10.

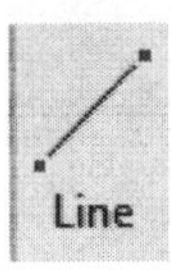

Invoke the line command (l or line).

11.

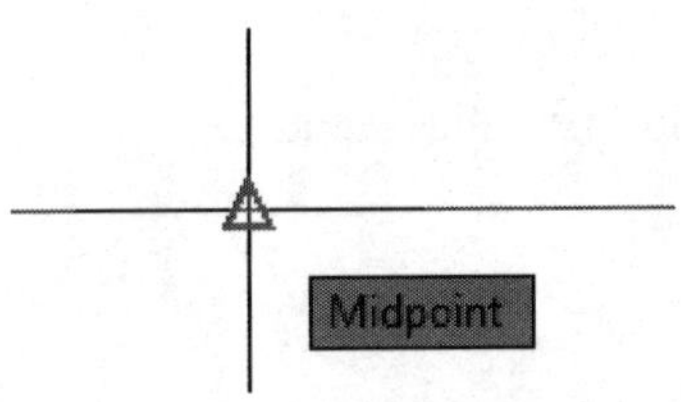

Specify first point:

Move your pointer to one of the sides of the box. You will see the Midpoint Object Snap Marker appear.

Pick with your left mouse button.

This creates the start point of the line.

12.

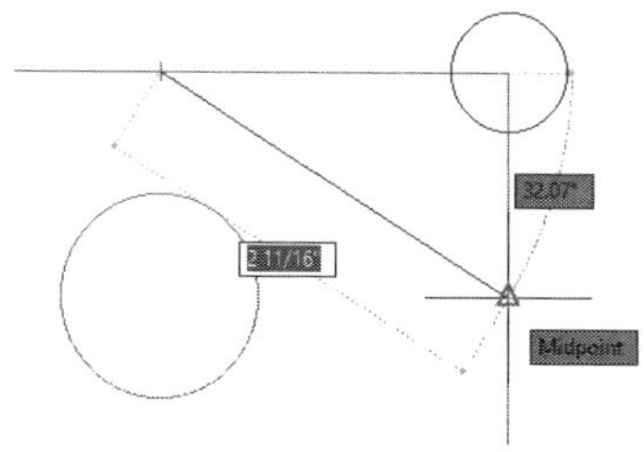

Specify next point or [Undo]:

Move your pointer to another side to complete the first line segment.

Remember to use your LMB when the desired object snap marker appears.

Let the cursor *snap* into the Object Snap marker.

13.

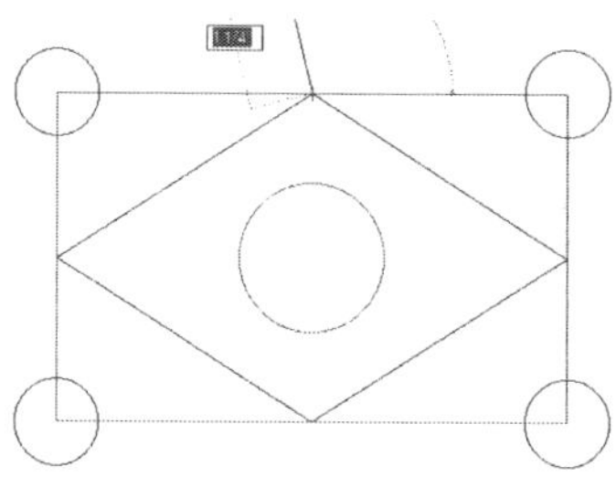

Repeat the command to complete the four line segments.

14.

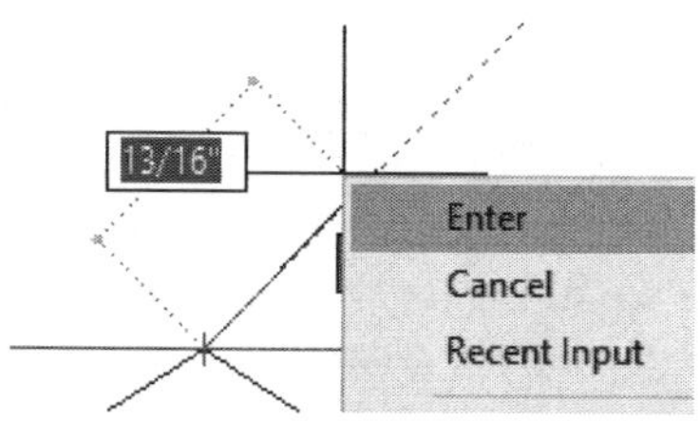

Right click and select **ENTER** to exit the LINE command.

15.

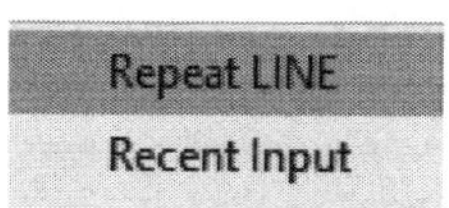

Invoke the line command (l or line).

16.

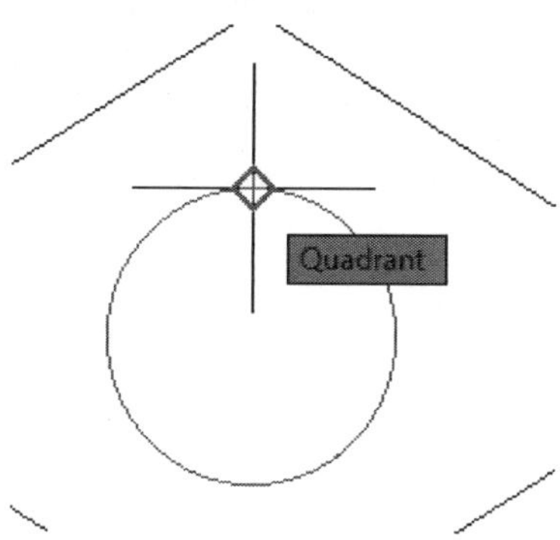

Specify first point:

Move your pointer near the top quadrant of the center circle.

Click the LMB to select the start point of the line segment.

17.

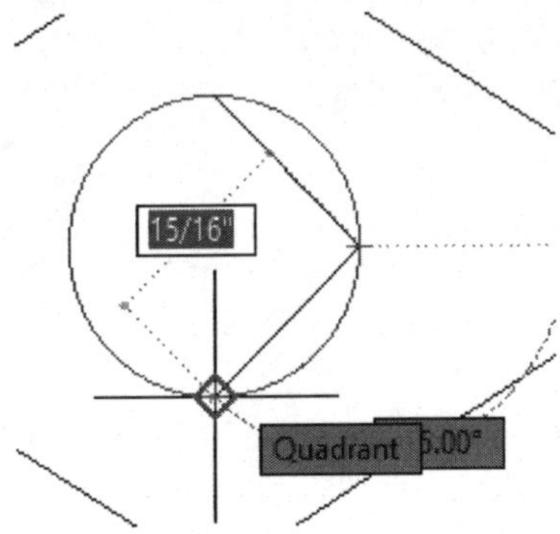

Specify next point or [Undo]:
Repeat the process by moving the pointer near the desired quadrant and Clicking the LMB when the Quadrant Object Snap appears.

18.

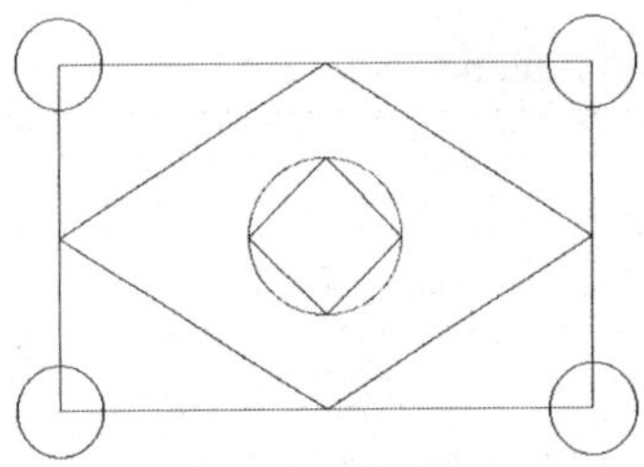

Close without saving.

Tips & Tricks

- *Before you start drafting, set running object snaps. Most commonly used object snaps are Endpoint, Midpoint, Intersection and Center.*
- *Use your <Tab> key to cycle through the different object snaps that overlap each other (i.e., Quadrant and Center or multiple object snap options that are close together).*
- *Remember to use the regular Intersection object snap to find the Intersection or Extended Intersection of two objects. Apparent Intersection is for 3D. Choosing an object snap option from the toolbar, shortcut menu, or by typing the alias will override Running Object Snap.*

Object Tracking AKA AUTOSNAP

Command Locator

Command	**AUTOSNAP**
Status Bar	**AUTOSNAP**
Shortcut	**F11**

Command Overview

Tracks the cursor along vertical and horizontal alignment paths from object snap points. Object snap tracking works in conjunction with object snaps. Use object snap tracking to track along alignment paths that are based on object snap points. Acquired points display a small plus sign (+). After you acquire a point, horizontal, vertical, or polar alignment paths relative to the point are displayed as you move the cursor over their drawing paths. For example, you can select a point along a path based on an object endpoint or midpoint or an intersection between objects.

Note: You can track Perpendicular or Tangent object snap from the last picked point in a command even if the object snap tracking is off.

If you use the command AUTOSNAP, you are prompted to enter a number. The number coincides with which object snaps should be enabled and used for object tracking.

This command used to be OTRACK but has been renamed.

Value	Description
0	Turns off the AutoSnap marker, tooltips, and magnet. Also turns off polar tracking, object snap tracking, and tooltips for polar tracking, object snap tracking, and Ortho mode
1	Turns on the AutoSnap marker
2	Turns on the AutoSnap tooltips
4	Turns on the AutoSnap magnet
8	Turns on polar tracking
16	Turns on object snap tracking
32	Turns on tooltips for polar tracking, object snap tracking, and Ortho mode
63	*0+1+2+4+8+16+32 = 63* This is the initial registry value until changed by the user.

- *Use Perpendicular, End, and Mid object snaps with object snap tracking to draw to points that are perpendicular to the end and midpoints of objects.*
- *Use the Tangent and End object snaps with object snap tracking to draw to points that are tangent to the endpoints of arcs.*
- *Use object snap tracking with temporary tracking points. At a point prompt, enter **tt**, then specify a temporary tracking point. A small + appears at the point. As you move your cursor, AutoTrack alignment paths are displayed relative to the temporary point. To remove the point, move the cursor back over the +.*
- *After you acquire an object snap point, use direct distance to specify points at precise distances along alignment paths from the acquired object snap point. To specify a point prompt, select an object snap, move the cursor to display an alignment path, then enter a distance at the prompt.*
- *Use the Automatic and Shift to Acquire options set on the Drafting tab of the Options dialog box to manage point acquisition. Point acquisition is set to Automatic by default. When working in close quarters, Click Shift to temporarily avoid acquiring a point.*
- *To facilitate creating section lines, an AutoTrack* extension *capability is available in paper space. For example, acquisition points between the centers of two circles along a diagonal can be used to extend a section line along the angle between those points. The acquisition points can be extracted from objects created either in model space or in paper space.*

Command Exercise

Exercise 8-6 – Auto Tracking

Drawing Name: **new drawing**
Estimated Time to Completion: 20 Minutes

Scope

Enable Object Snaps and Object Tracking in order to draw the figure. Enable ORTHO ON.

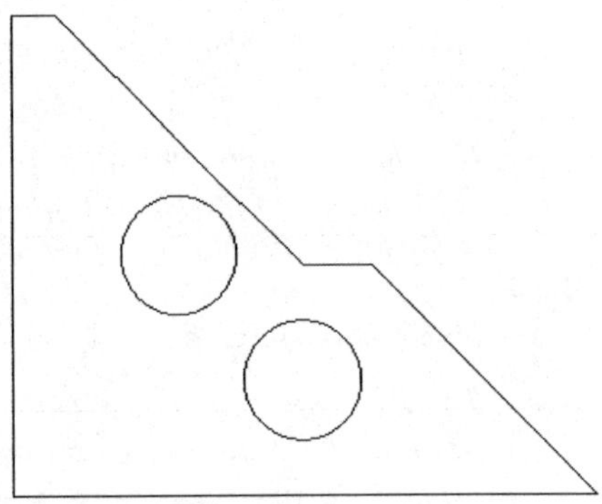

Solution

1.  Start a new drawing by clicking on the + tab.

2.  Left click on the down arrow next to the OSNAP tool on the status bar.

3. 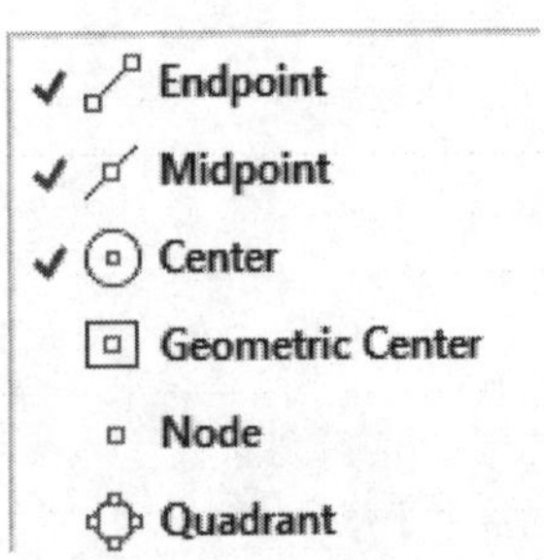

LMB on Endpoint, Midpoint, and Center to enable those OSNAPs.

4. 

Turn ORTHO **ON.**

You can Click F8 to enable ORTHO.

The icon will display as blue when it is enabled.

5. 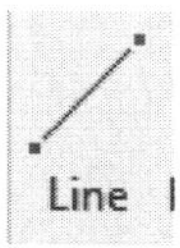

Start the **Line** command.

6. 

Specify the first point as **0,8.**

7. Move the cursor down and enter **8.**

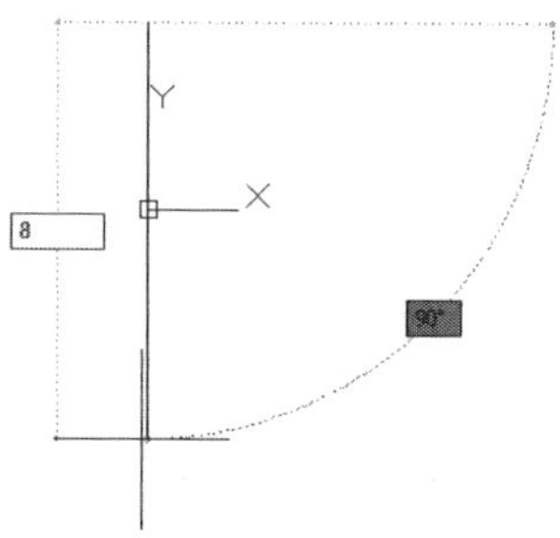

8. 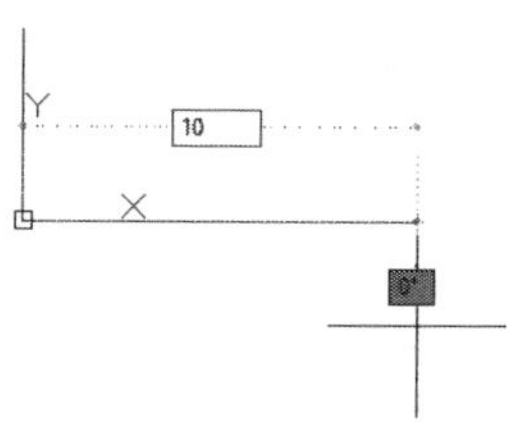

Specify next point or [Undo]:
Move the cursor towards the right until a temporary polar tracking path of 0 degrees displays as shown in the next figure.

Type **10** and Click <ENTER> while this path is showing.

Exit the **LINE** command.

9. 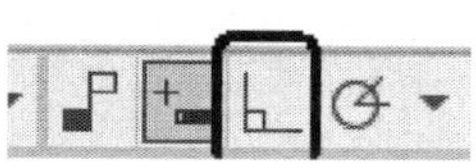

Disable the **ORTHO** toggle.

To disable, Click F8 or left click on the ORTHO icon.

10. Enable the **45 degree** setting on the Polar Tracking list.

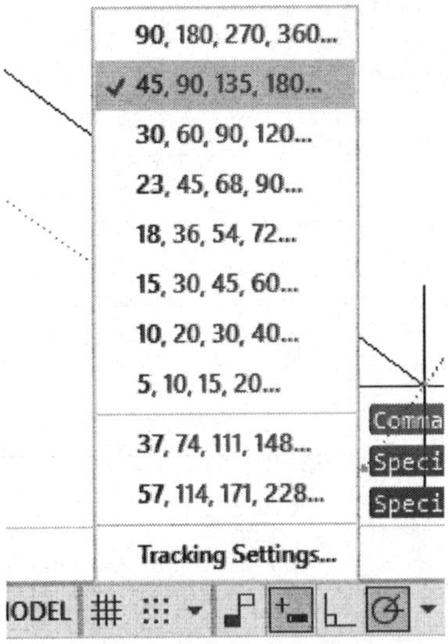

11. Verify that Polar Tracking, Object Snap Tracking, and Object Snap are all enabled.

They should be displayed in blue.

12. Start the **Line** command.

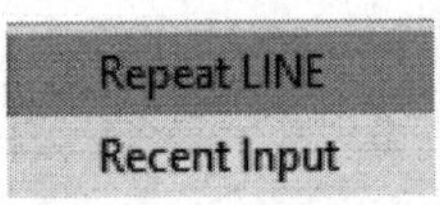

13. Start the line at the endpoint of the horizontal line.

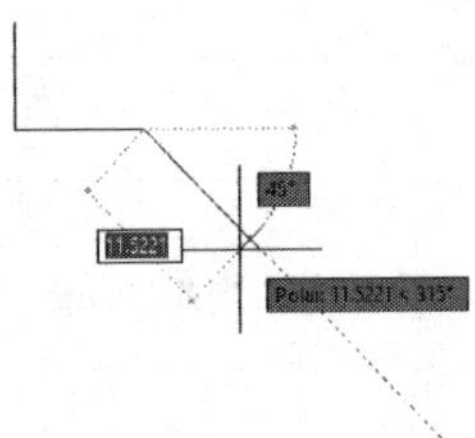

If you Click ENTER, the line should pick up where you left off.

14. *Specify next point or [Close/Undo]:*
Move the cursor near the midpoint of the vertical line until it is acquired (a + sign shows up at the midpoint and a tooltip also appears). Then move the cursor to the right to display the tracking path through the midpoint until you also have a polar tracking path of 135 degrees. Then click to select that point.

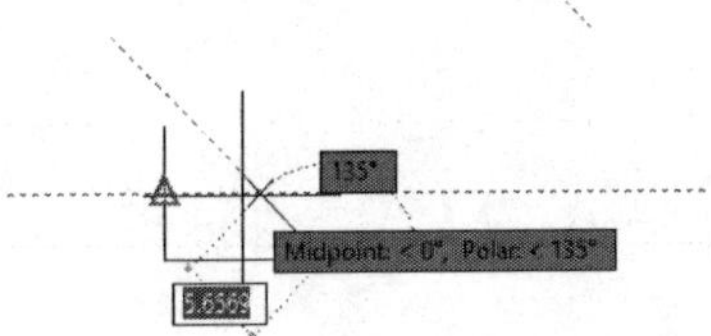

15. 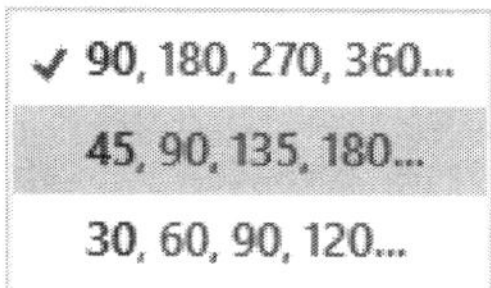

Switch the POLAR TRACKING settings to use the ***90,180,270,360*** *option.*

To do this, just left click on the down arrow next to the Polar Tracking icon and then left click on the **90,180,270,360** option.

16. 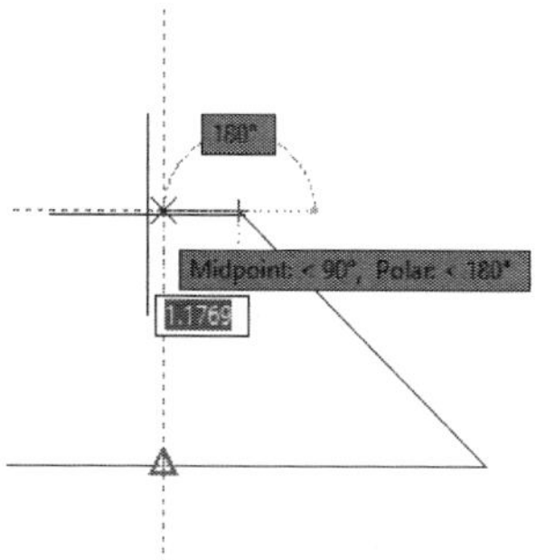

Specify next point or [Close/Undo]:
Move the cursor near the midpoint of the horizontal line until it is acquired (a + sign shows up at the midpoint and a tooltip also appears). Then move the cursor upward to display the tracking path through the midpoint until you also have a polar tracking path of 180 degrees as shown.

Then click to select that point.

17. 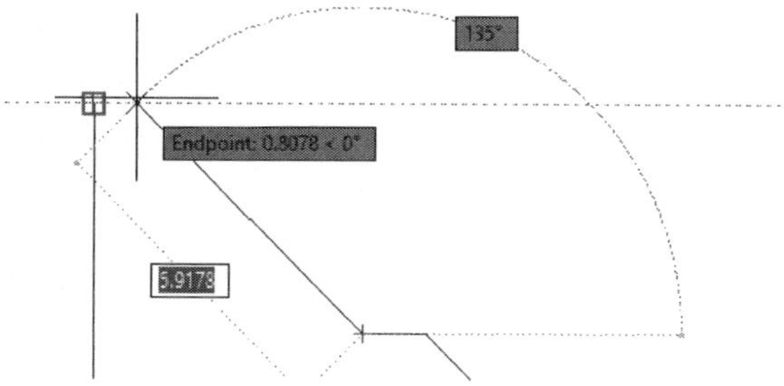

Specify next point or [Close/Undo]:
Move the cursor near the upper endpoint of the vertical line until it is acquired (a + sign shows up at the endpoint and a tooltip also appears). Then move the cursor to the right to display the tracking path through the endpoint until you also have a polar tracking path of 135 degrees. Then click to select that point.

18. 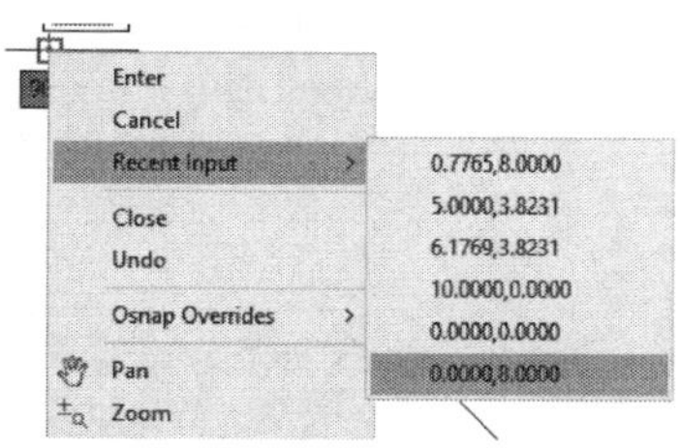

Right click and select **Recent Input.**

Select **0,8** as the closing point.

19. 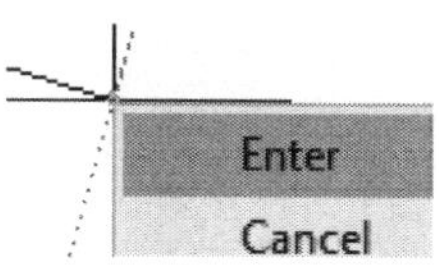

Click <ENTER> to exit the LINE command.

20. 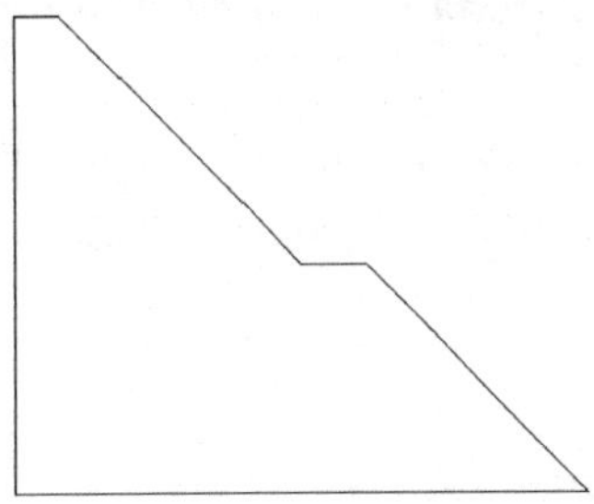

Your figure should look like this.

I have the UCSICON turned OFF.

To turn off the UCSICON, type **UCSICON, OFF**.

21. 

Invoke the **Circle** command (c or circle).

22. 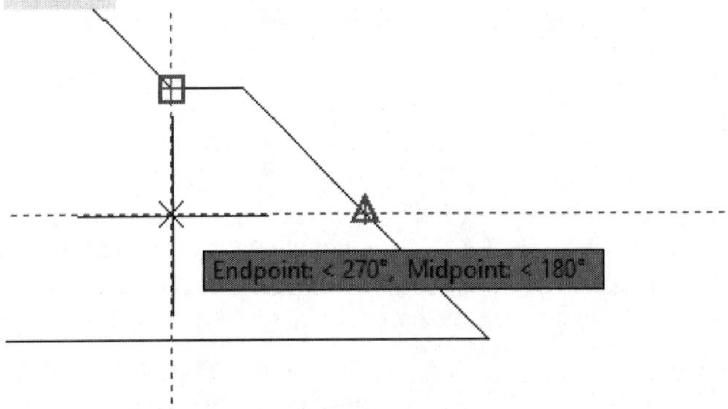

Specify center point for circle or [3P/2P/Ttr (tan tan radius)]: Move the cursor near endpoint of the upper horizontal line until it is acquired (a + sign shows up at the midpoint and a tooltip also appears).

Then move the cursor near midpoint of the lower angled line until it is acquired. Finally, move to the left until tracking paths display through both of the midpoints as shown in the next figure. Then click to select that point as the center point for the circle.

23. 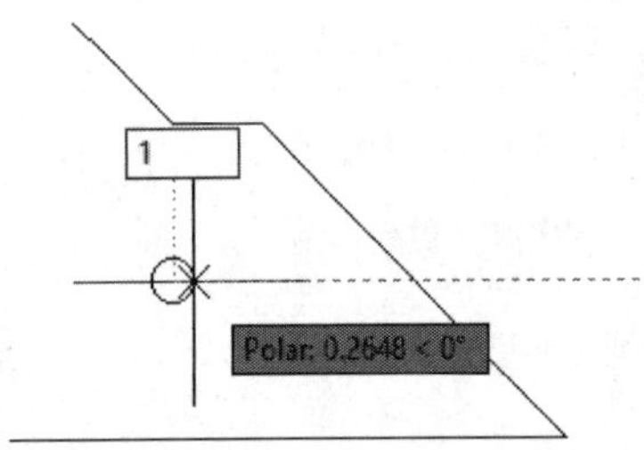

Specify radius of circle or [Diameter] <x.xx>:
Type **1.0** and Click <ENTER>.

24. 

Invoke the **Circle** command (c or circle).

25.

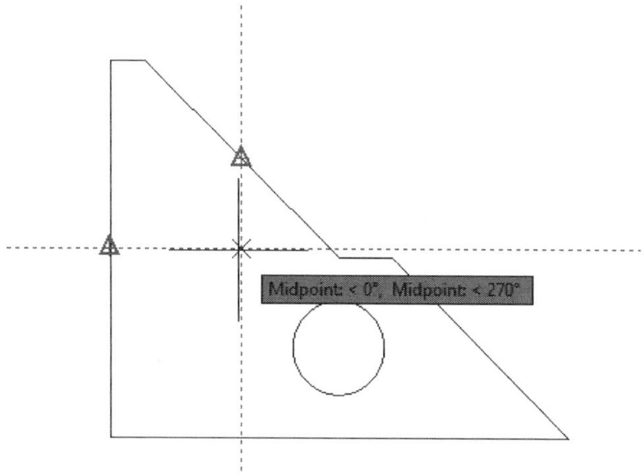

Specify center point for circle or [3P/2P/Ttr (tan tan radius)]:
Move the cursor near midpoint of the vertical line until it is acquired (a + sign shows up at the midpoint and a tooltip also appears). Then move the cursor near midpoint of the upper inclined line until it is acquired. Finally, move downward until tracking paths display through both of the midpoints as shown in the next figure. Then click to select that point.

26.

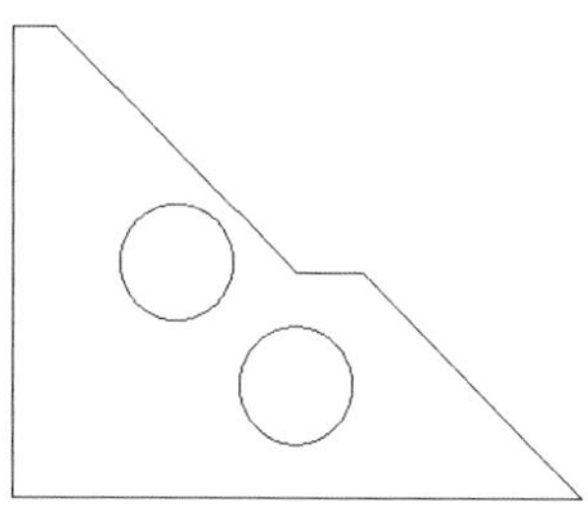

Specify radius of circle or [Diameter] <x.xx>:
Type **1.0** and Click <ENTER>.

Save as *ex8-6.dwg.*

Extra: *Draw a line with a random angle, then draw another line that is parallel to it. Use the Parallel Object Snap option.*

Command Exercise

Exercise 8-7 – Geometric Center OSNAP

Drawing Name: **osnap5.dwg**
Estimated Time to Completion: 15 Minutes

Scope

Use the Geometric Center Osnap to place a triangle in the center of an octahedron.

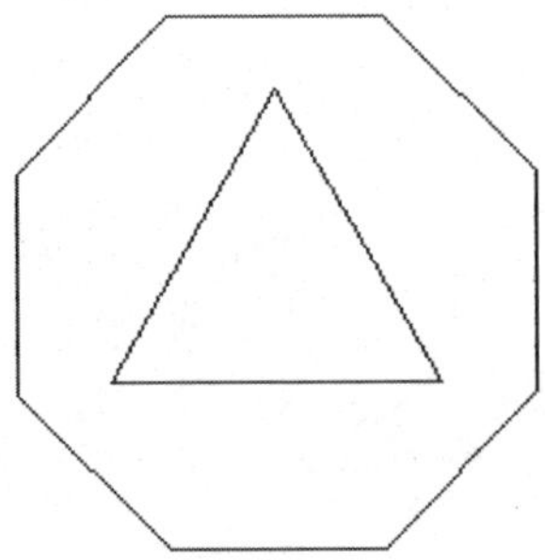

Solution

1.  Left click on the down arrow next to the OSNAP tool on the status bar.

2. 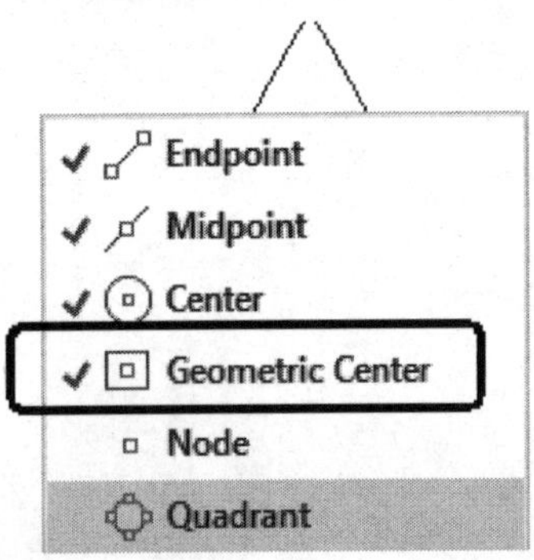

LMB on Geometric Center to enable.

3. 

Select the **Move** tool.

4.

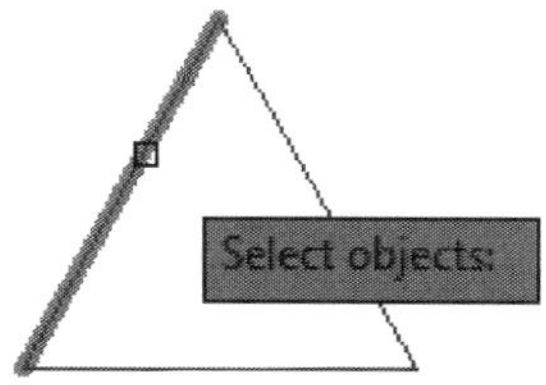

Select the triangle on the right.

Click **ENTER**.

5.

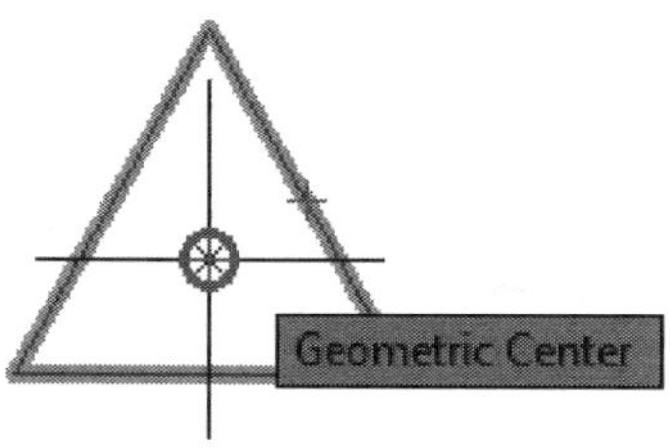

Hover the cursor over the triangle until the Geometric Center is shown.

Left click to select.

6.

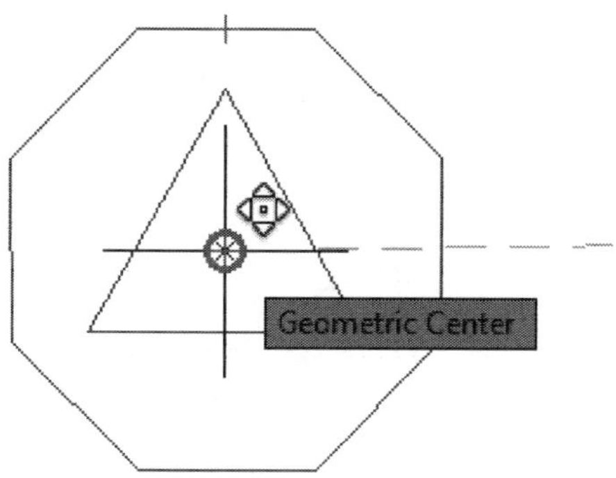

Move the cursor over the polygon.

Left click when the Geometric Center is displayed.

2D Drawings

With the implementation of 3D CAD, the mechanical industry is moving away from 2D drawings. 2D drawings are still being used heavily in civil, architectural, and electrical fields. Mechanical 2D drawings are used for quoting, fabrication, and inspection. Civil 2D drawings are used to lay out site plans, foundation work, parking lots, and roads. Architectural 2D drawings are used for floor plans, ceiling plans, and elevations. Electrical 2D drawings are used for schematics and circuit board layouts. AutoCAD is used to create 2D drawings in all of these industries. It is helpful to be familiar with how to create the various required views for each industry.

Creating Orthographic Views

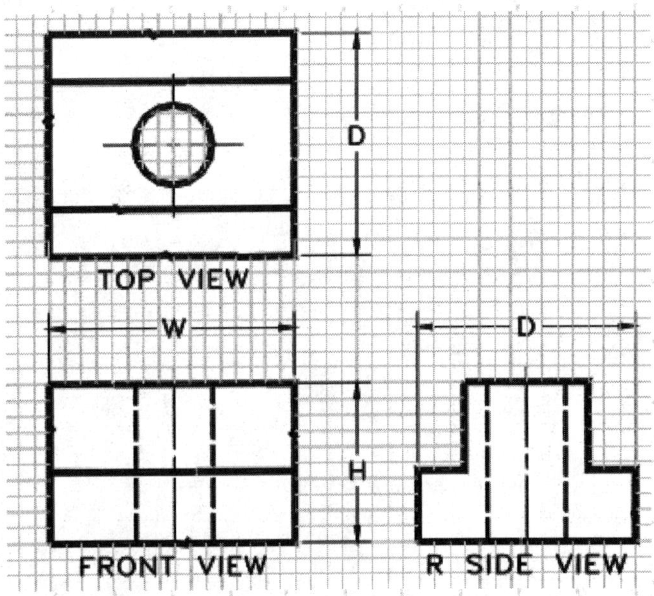

In the US and Canada, the orthographic views for mechanical drawings use third angle projection.

The rest of the world uses first angle projection.

All countries start with a front view and then project the remaining views.

Third angle projection places a top and right side view in addition to the front view.

First angle projection places the front view, the bottom view, and the right view.

Because many companies use sources outside of the US, it is important to be able to read a drawing regardless of whether first angle or third angle projection is used.

One way to help visualize the different views is to imagine a glass box around the object you want to draw and think how it would appear if each side were *projected* onto the side of the box.

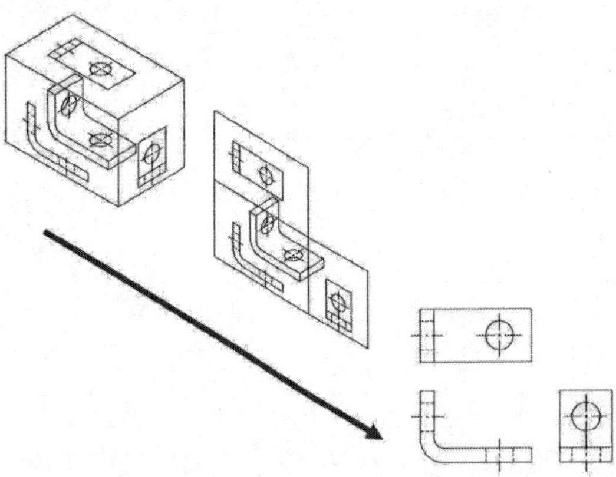

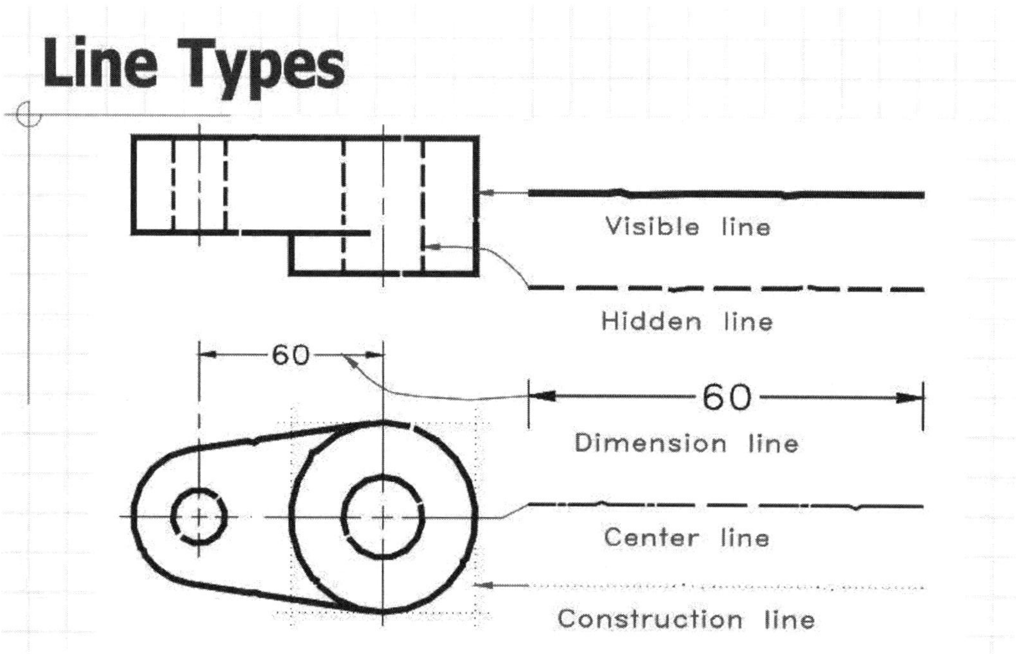

Different linetypes are used to designate the object outline, center lines, and hidden lines. This is why it is important to create layers and assign the desired colors and linetypes.

Tips & Tricks

- Remember to select the Object Snap each time before picking a point.
- When specifying the center of a circle, be sure to pick the circumference.
- The "Apparent Intersection" Object Snap is for 3D modeling.
- Selecting two object snaps in a row, such as Endpoint and Midpoint, will cancel both Object Snap selections (it doesn't understand the "endpoint of the midpoint").
- If the wrong Object Snap option is mistakenly selected, pick in a blank area of the Drawing Window, then select the proper Object Snap option again.
- Single object snaps can be used in combination with the running OSNAP settings.

View Selection

- If the object has an obvious top, then it must be the top view
- Minimize the number of hidden lines
- Use the most descriptive view as the front view
- Conserve space by choosing the depth to be the smallest dimension

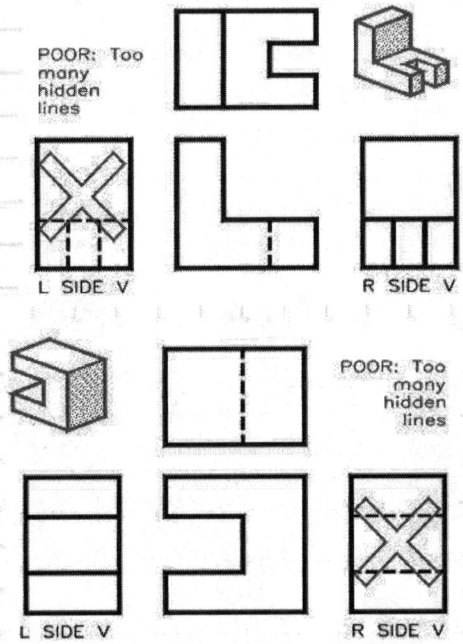

Section Exercise

Exercise 8-8 – Drawing Layout

Drawing Name: **new drawing**
Estimated Time to Completion: 20 Minutes

Scope

The goal of this exercise is to create an orthographic layout without using any construction lines. Use OTRACK, OSNAP, and OFFSET. If you have to draw and erase any lines, you have not done the exercise properly. Dimensions are for reference. You do not have to place dimensions or create a dimension layer.

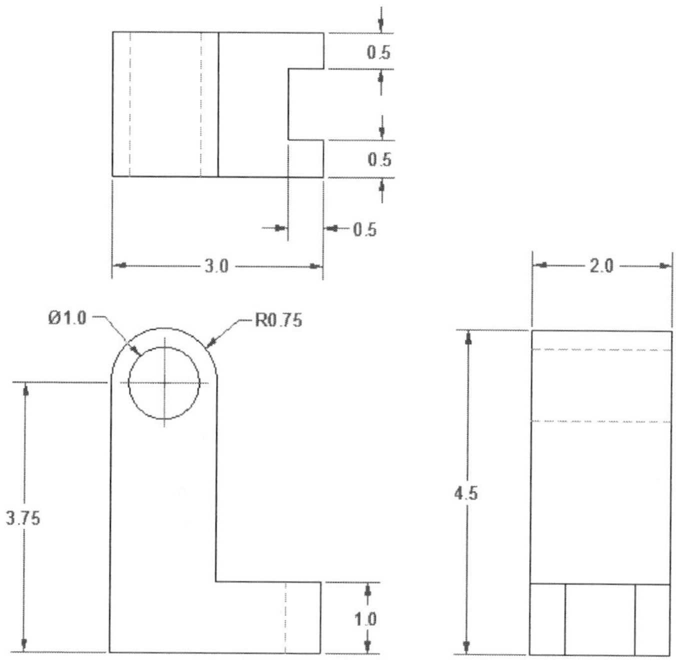

Solution

1. 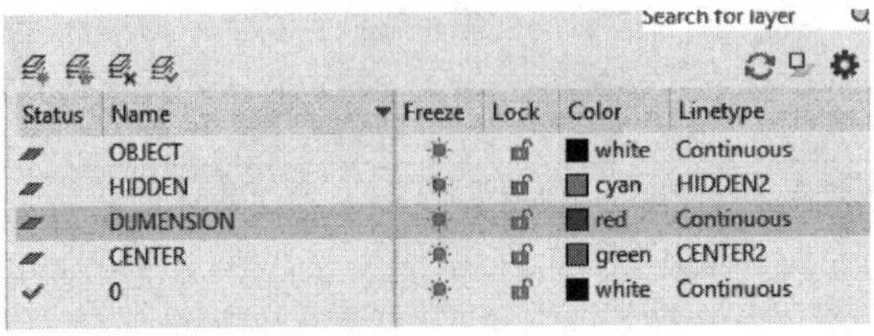

Search for layer

Status	Name	Freeze	Lock	Color	Linetype
	OBJECT			white	Continuous
	HIDDEN			cyan	HIDDEN2
	DIMENSION			red	Continuous
	CENTER			green	CENTER2
✓	0			white	Continuous

Set up layers for object, hidden, and center lines.

2. 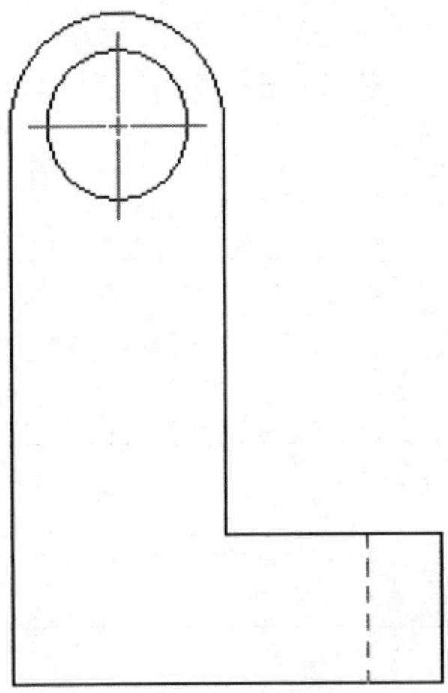

Draw the front view of this object.

3. 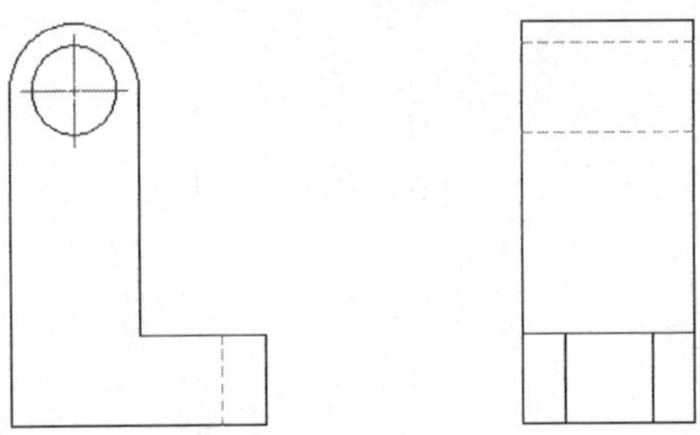

Draw the right side view using object tracking and osnaps.

HINT: *Use Extension, Quadrant, and Perpendicular OSNAPS for the hidden lines.*

4.

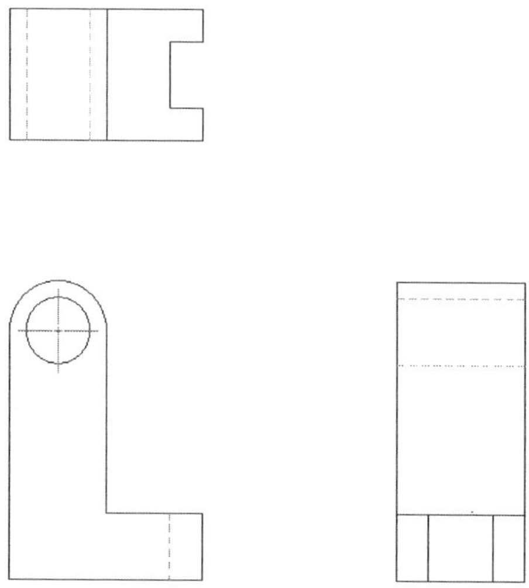

Draw the top side view using object tracking and osnaps.

Section Exercise

Exercise 8-9 – Drawing Layout

Drawing Name: **new drawing**
Estimated Time to Completion: 30 Minutes

Scope

The goal of this exercise is to create an orthographic layout without using any construction lines. Use OTRACK, OSNAP, and OFFSET. If you have to draw and erase any lines, you have not done the exercise properly. Dimensions are for reference. You do not have to place dimensions or create a dimension layer.

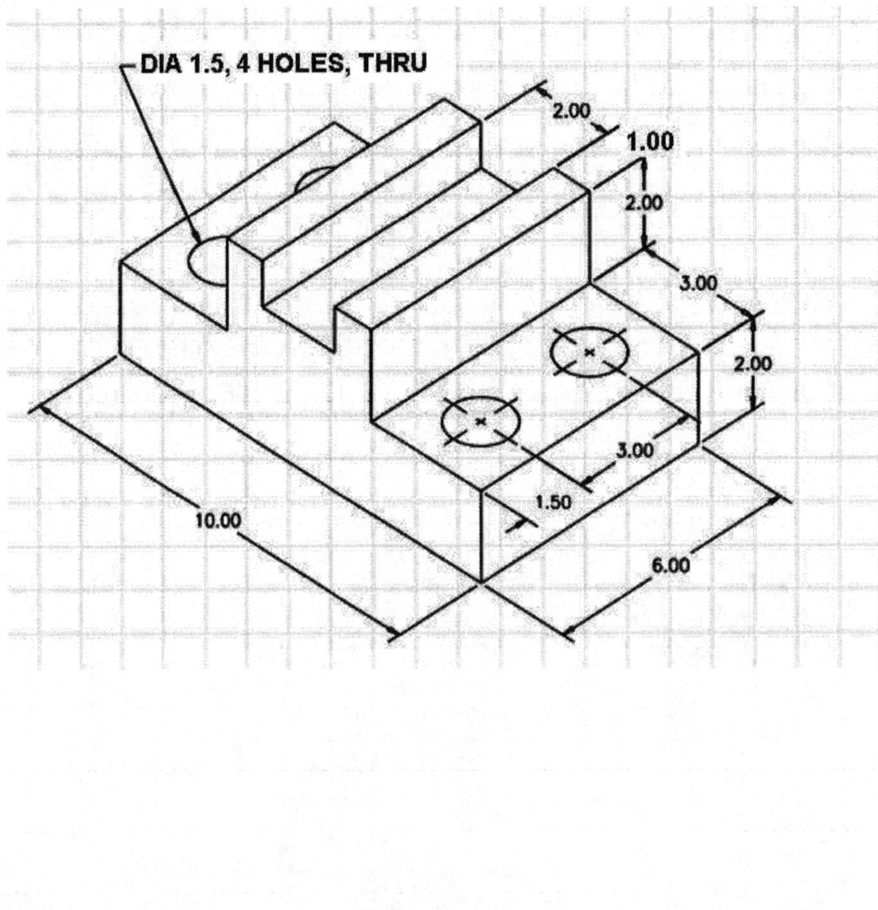

Solution

1. 

Set up layers for object, hidden, and center lines.

2. 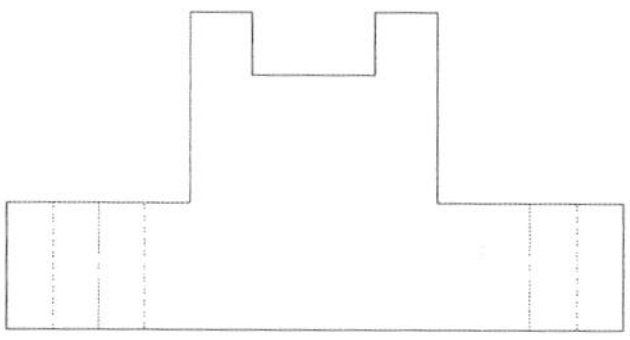

Draw the front view of the object.

3. 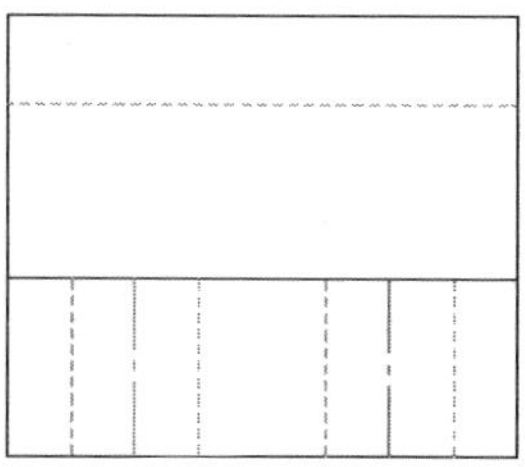

Draw the right side view using object tracking and osnaps.

HINT: *Use OFFSET. Set the OFFSET layer to use the current layer so you don't have to change the properties.*

4. 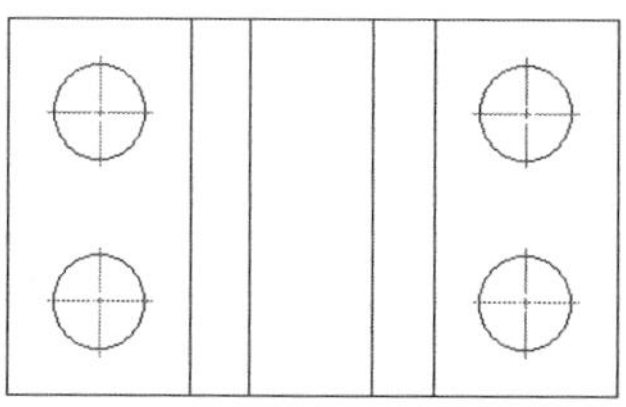

Draw the top side view using object tracking and osnaps.

HINT: *Place one circle and then use MIRROR to create the additional circles.*

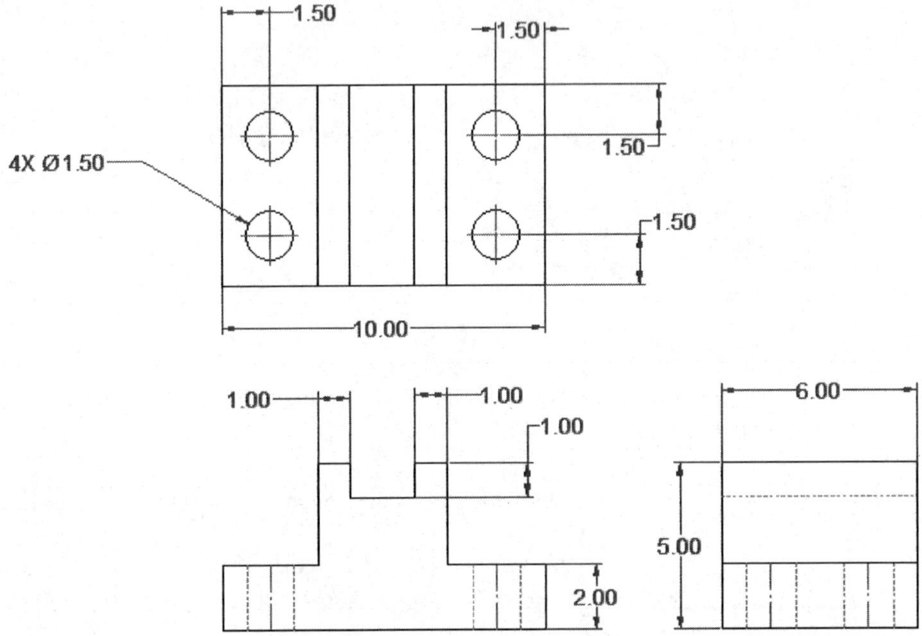
1.50
1.50
1.50
4X Ø1.50
1.50
10.00
1.00
1.00
1.00
6.00
5.00
2.00

Section Exercise

Exercise 8-10 – Plate

Drawing Name: **new drawing**
Estimated Time to Completion: 20 Minutes

Scope

The goal of this exercise is to create an orthographic layout without using any construction lines. Use OTRACK, OSNAP, and OFFSET. If you have to draw and erase any lines, you have not done the exercise properly. Dimensions are for reference. You do not have to place dimensions or create a dimension layer.

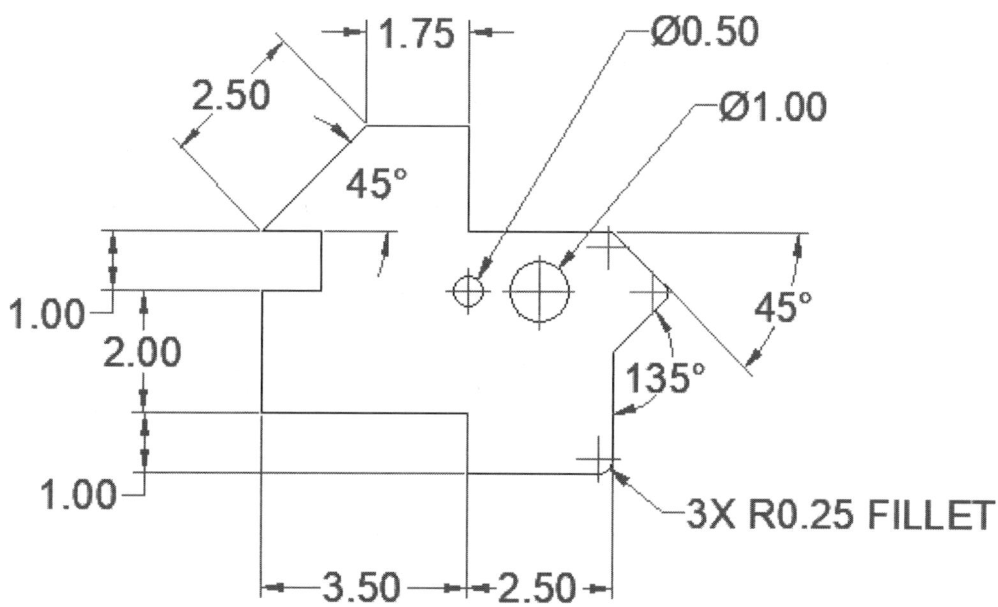

Section Exercise

Exercise 8-11 – Clamp

Drawing Name: **new drawing**
Estimated Time to Completion: 20 Minutes

Scope

The goal of this exercise is to create an orthographic layout without using any construction lines. Use OTRACK, OSNAP, and OFFSET. If you have to draw and erase any lines, you have not done the exercise properly. Dimensions are for reference. You do not have to place dimensions or create a dimension layer.

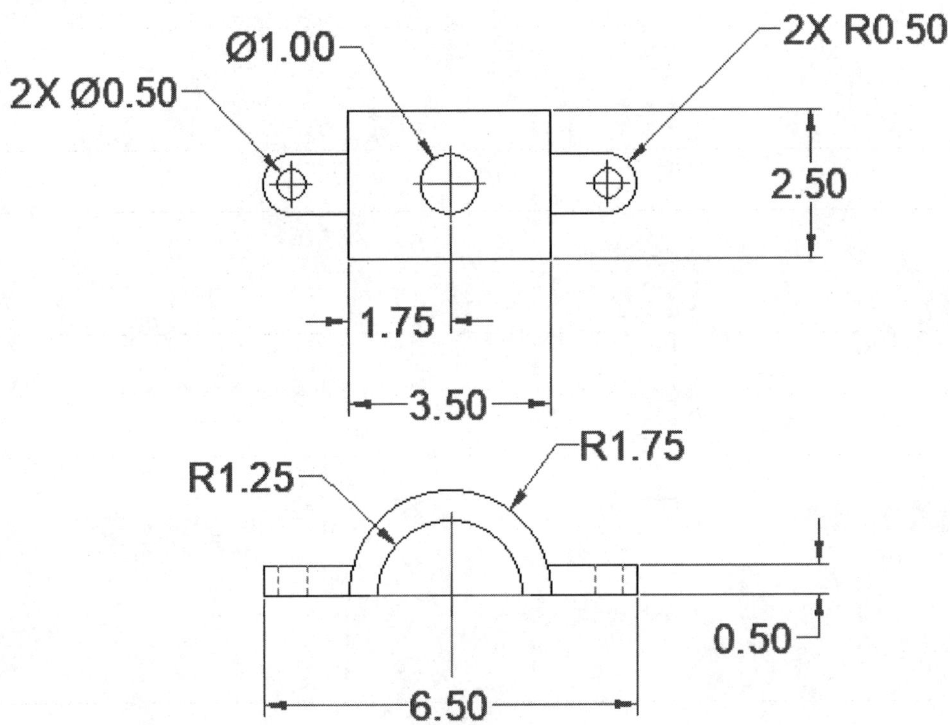

Set the units to Decimal.

Use object tracking with PERpendicular, CENter, QUADrant, and ENDpoint for best results.

You do not need to add the dimensions.

The 1 unit diameter circle is located in the geometric center of the rectangle.

Review Questions

1. Identify the following object snap options:

a. 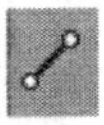 ________________

b.  ________________

c. 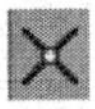 ________________

d.  ________________

e.  ________________

f.  ________________

g.  ________________

h.  ________________

i.  ________________

2. How can you access an object snap option for a single selection (not OSNAP)?

3. What control in the Status Bar turns the Object Snap Settings ON or OFF?

4. What does the DSETTINGS command do?

   ❑ Invokes the Object Snap Pop-up Menu
   ❑ Allows you to adjust the running object snap settings
   ❑ Toggles the OSNAP command on and off
   ❑ Nothing

5. How would you select the exact center of a circle? How would you select the exact center of a 6 or 4 or 3 sided polygon? Try it.

6. The features MIDPOINT, INTERSECTION, PERPENDICULAR, and ENDPOINT are located and set in which menu?

   A. Options

   B. Object Snap Settings

   C. Drafting Settings

7. To "SNAP" to the middle of a line, use the:

   A. Center" snap.
   B. "Middle" snap.
   C. "Midpoint" snap.

8. True or False

   Several running objects snaps are on, more than one object snap may be eligible at a given location. You can Click the CTRL key to cycle through the possibilities before you specify the object snap.

Review Answers

1. Identify the following object snap options:

   a. Endpoint

   b. Perpendicular

   c. Intersection

   d. Center

   e. Nearest

   f. Midpoint

   g. Tangent

   h. Quadrant

   i. Object Snap Settings

2. How can you access an object snap option for a single selection (not OSNAP)?

   Click the <Shift> key and RMB to access the Object Snap Pop up dialog box.

3. What control in the Status Bar turns the Object Snap Settings ON or OFF?

   OSNAP

4. What does the DSETTINGS command do?

   Invokes the Object Snap Pop-up Menu
   Allows you to adjust the running object snap settings *(You can toggle OSNAP on and off)*
   Toggles the OSNAP command on and off
   Nothing

5. How would you select the exact center of a circle? How would you select the exact center of a 6, 4 or 3 sided polygon? Try it.

   Use the Geometric Center Osnap to select the center of a polygon. Use the Center Osnap to select the center of a circle.

6. The features MIDPOINT, INTERSECTION, PERPENDICULAR, and ENDPOINT are located and set in which menu?

   B. Object Snap Settings

7. To "SNAP" to the middle of a line, use the:

   C. "Midpoint" snap.

8. True or False

   Several running objects snaps are on, more than one object snap may be eligible at a given location. you can Click the CTRL key to cycle through the possibilities before you specify the object snap.

   False

Notes:

Lesson 9.0 – Dimensions

Estimated Class Time: 2 Hours

Objectives

Dimensioning a drawing is easy. If placed correctly, the dimensions will be as accurate as the drawing. Students will learn how to create Dimension Styles to suit the drawing specifications. Dimensions can be created in English/Standard or Metric units, or both. Edit selected dimensions or make changes to the Dimension Style for a global update.

- **Dimensions**

  Place dimensions using different dimension tools.

- **Ordinate Dimensions**
- **Dimension Space**
- **Dimension Break**
- **Dimension Style**

  Control the appearance of dimensions, including text color and size, arrowheads, and spacing.

- **Edit Dimension Location**

  Use grips to edit the placement of dimensions.

- **Edit Dimension Text**
- **Edit Dimension Properties**

  Edit dimensions globally by modifying the dimension styles or individually with the Properties command.

- **Dimensional Constraints**
- **Center Mark and Center lines**

Dimensions

If you are a mechanical drafter, you will be expected to use ANSI standards when applying dimensions. If you are an architectural drafter, you will be expected to apply AIA standards.

Architects will often create many different styles to manage the requirements of different counties and cities. Most mechanical drafters will create one style for standard (inch) dimensioning and one style for metric. Dimensioning styles for mechanical drawings are dictated by the American Society of Mechanical Engineers (ASME). A copy of the standards can be purchased through the ASME website at www.asme.org. The current dimensioning standards are ASME Y14.5M-2009. Most mechanical design jobs require drafters to be familiar with ANSI dimensioning standards.

Some simple rules to keep in mind when applying ANSI standards:

- Center the dimension. You can use GRIPS or DIMTEDIT to shift the dimension text position to get it centered.
- Always place your dimensions between views.
- Always place overall dimensions (length, height, and width).
- Place the shortest dimensions closest to the object.
- Never place dimensions on top or inside of the object.
- Leaders are placed at a 30, 45, or 60 degree angle.
- When dimensioning holes, use a diameter dimension NOT a radius.
- Never dimension to hidden or center lines.
- Do not double dimension (that is, apply a dimension that is already shown in a different view or the same view).
- When using inches, Click leading zeros.

Command Locator

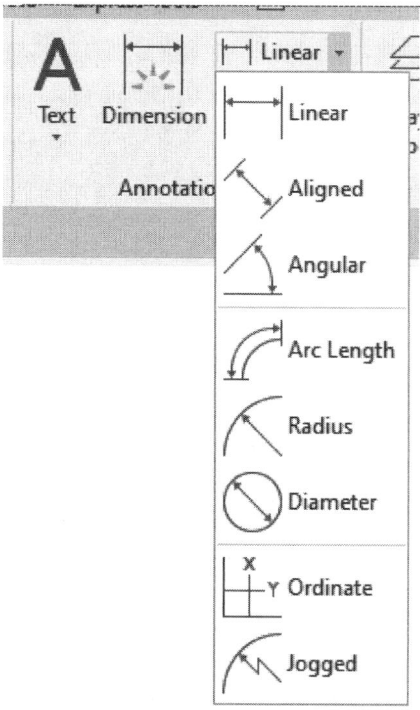

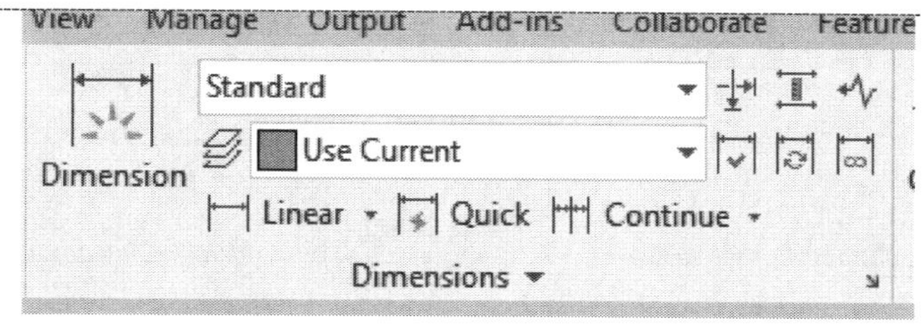

Ribbon	**Home or Annotate**
Command	DIMLINEAR,DIMALIGNED,DIMANG…

Command Overview

Learn how to dimension a drawing using the dimension variables. Dimensions will be as accurate as the drawing, provided the objects were chosen correctly. To open the Dimension Toolbar, place the cursor over any icon and Click the right button on the mouse, then place a checkmark before "Dimension." This section will cover individual dimension commands, how to select the object to dimension and pick the dimension location. The easiest way to adjust the dimension locations after they have been placed is to use the Grips. Dimension Style and Edit Dimension commands and options will be covered in the next section.

Dimension Command	**Button**	***Overview***
Linear Dimension		This option is for horizontal or vertical dimensions. Use object snap to select the first and second extension line origin or Click return to select the object. Drag the cursor and pick to place the dimension.
Aligned Dimension		This option will align a dimension with an angled line. Use object snap to select the first and second extension line origin or Click return to select the object. Drag the cursor and pick to place the dimension.
Arc Length		Dimension the length of an arc.
Ordinate Dimension		Places ordinate dimensions. Right click to select the Origin option to set the origin for the Ordinate Dimension.
Radius		Select a circle or arc for the Radius Dimension. Drag the cursor and pick to place the dimension.
Jogged		Places a jogged leader on a circle or arc.
Diameter Dimension		Select a circle or arc for the diameter dimension. Drag the cursor and pick to place the dimension.
Angular Dimension		This option will place an angular dimension between selected lines. Select two angular lines and pick the dimension location.
Quick Dimension		Quick Dimension (QDIM) allows the user to select an object that contains multiple lines and place multiple dimensions with the Continuous, Staggered, Baseline, Ordinate, Radius, Diameter, datum, Point, and Edit options.
Baseline Dimension		This option builds a baseline dimension from the first extension line of a linear, aligned or angular dimension. Begin with the linear, aligned or angular dimension first, using object snaps to select the origin points. Next invoke Baseline Dimension and select the next extension line origin. Continue then Click <ENTER> to exit the command.
Continued Dimension		This option creates continuous dimensions from the second extension line of a linear, aligned or angular dimension. Begin with the linear, aligned or angular dimension first, using object snaps to select the origin points. Next invoke the Continued Dimension and select the next extension line origin. Continue then Click <ENTER> to exit the command.
Dimension Space		Dimension Space allows you to quickly adjust the spacing between linear dimensions so that they do not overlap.
Dimension Break		This creates a gap in the extension line of a dimension. Select the dimension, then select the object (a line or point) where you wish to place the gap.
Tolerance		Places a GD&T symbol.

Dimension Command	Button	*Overview*
Center Mark	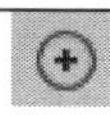	Select a circle or arc to place a center mark in the drawing. Center mark styles can be modified in the Dimension Style dialog box.
Inspection		Select existing dimensions to be used for inspection purposes.
Jogged Linear	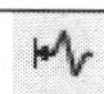	Add a jog to an existing dimension so that it can be foreshortened as needed.
Dimension Edit	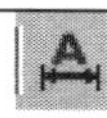	Shifts dimension text.
Dimension Text Edit	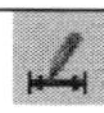	Edit the value of dimension text.
Dimension Update	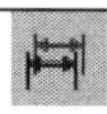	Update the dimension style applied to a dimension.
Dimension Style drop-down		Use this drop-down box to select a dimension style on the fly.
Dimension Style		Launches the Dimension Style Manager dialog.

General Procedures

For Linear or Aligned dimensions:

1. Select the desired dimension command.
2. Use the appropriate Object Snaps to select the dimension line origin points. Drag the cursor and pick the dimension location.

Note: To dimension a single line segment, Click <ENTER>, then select the line.

For Radius, Diameter, or Center Mark dimensions:

1. Select the desired dimension command.
2. Pick the Circle, Arc, or Line to dimension. Drag the cursor and pick the dimension location.

Note: Center Mark will simply be placed at the center.

For Baseline or Continued Dimensions:

1. Begin by placing a Linear, Aligned or Angular Dimension, using Object Snaps to select the origin points.
2. Invoke the Baseline or Continued Dimension. Using Object Snaps, pick the next dimension line origins. When finished, Click <ENTER> to Exit the command.

For Quick Dimensions (QDIM):

1. Invoke the Quick Dimension command.
2. Window the objects to be dimensioned, or pick them individually, and Click <ENTER>.
3. Specify the dimension line position by dragging in the desired direction. The default dimension option will appear in parentheses.
4. Pick to place the dimension, or type the capitalized letter of the desired option and <ENTER>. Then pick (LMB) to place the dimension.

- Use Object Snaps or set the OSNAP settings when selecting dimension line origin points.
- Do not explode dimensions. Associativity to the object will be lost and the dimension will be broken into as many as 10 separate objects.
- Adjust dimension locations after they are placed using grips.
- Begin the Baseline and Continued dimensions by placing a Linear, Aligned or Angular dimension first.
- Leader text will have "no wrap" unless a width is specified.

Command Exercise

Exercise 9-1 – Linear and Aligned Dimensions

Drawing Name: **dim1.dwg**

Estimated Time to Completion: 15 Minutes

Scope

Dimension the object as indicated using Linear and Aligned Dimensions

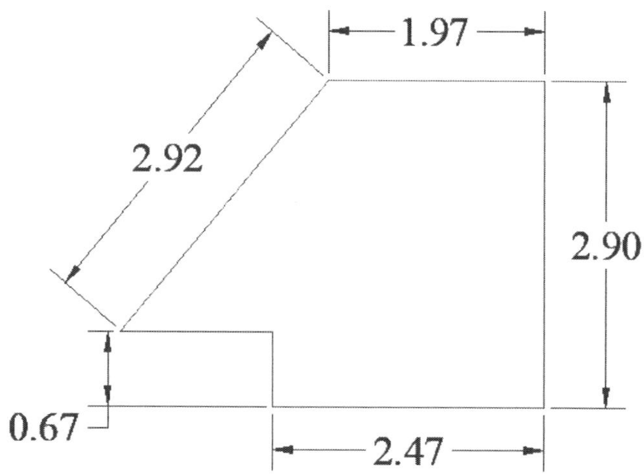

Solution

1. 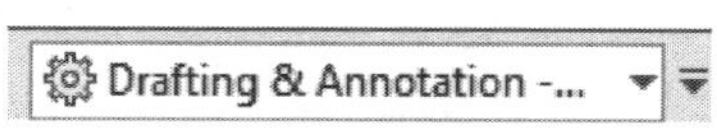

*Set **Drafting and Annotation** workspace current.*

2. 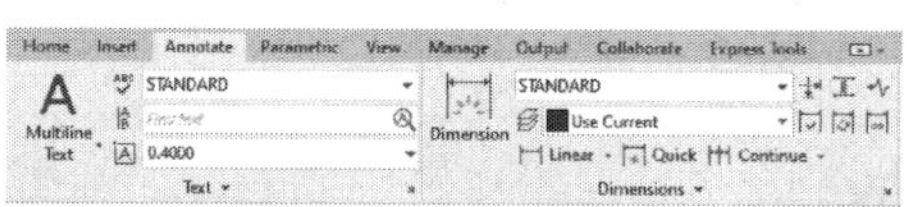
Switch to the Annotate ribbon.

3. 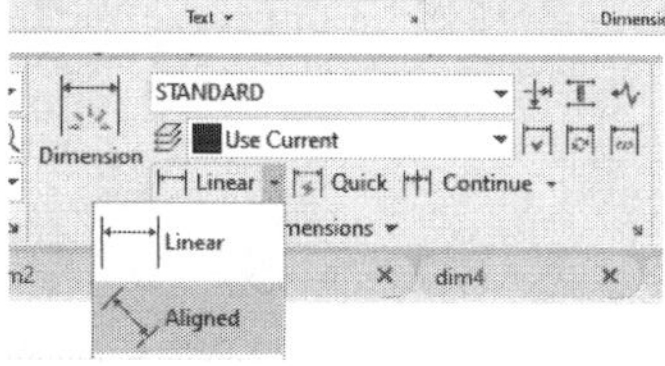

Invoke the Aligned Dimension command (dimaligned).
Locate the **Aligned** tool in the Dimensions panel.

4. 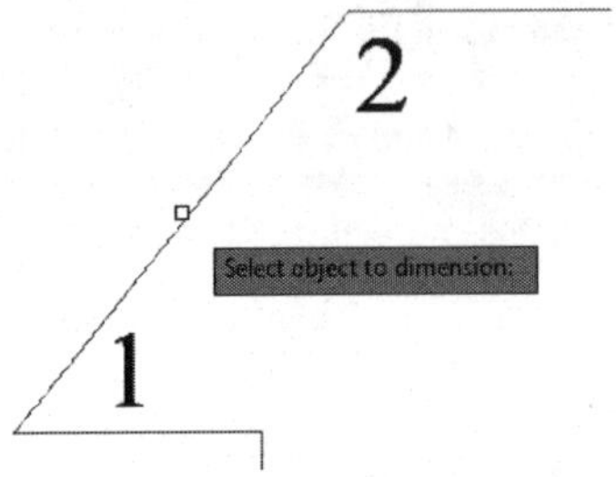

Specify first extension line origin or <select object>:
Click <ENTER> to select the object.

Select object to dimension:
Select the angled line between 1 and 2.

5. 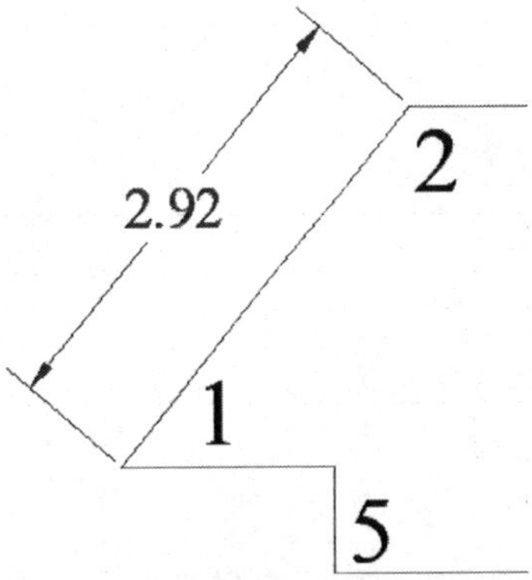

Specify dimension line location or [Mtext/Text/Angle]:
Select a location for the dimension with the LMB.

6. 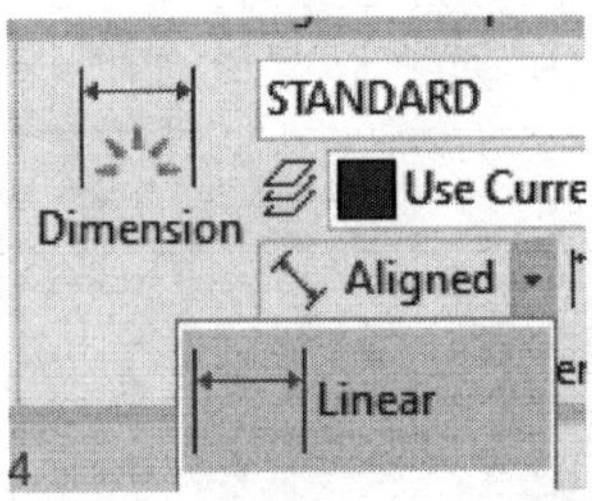

Invoke the Linear Dimension command (dimlinear).
Select the Linear Dimension command.

7. 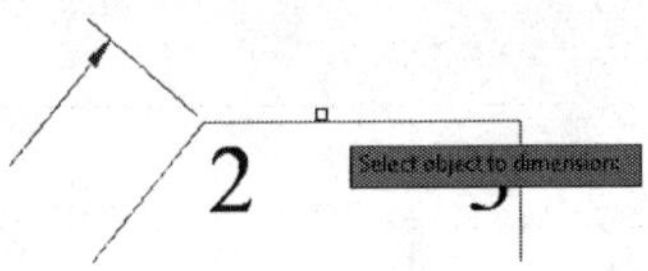

Specify first extension line origin or <select object>:
Click <ENTER> to select the object.

Select object to dimension:
Select the line between 2 and 3.

8. 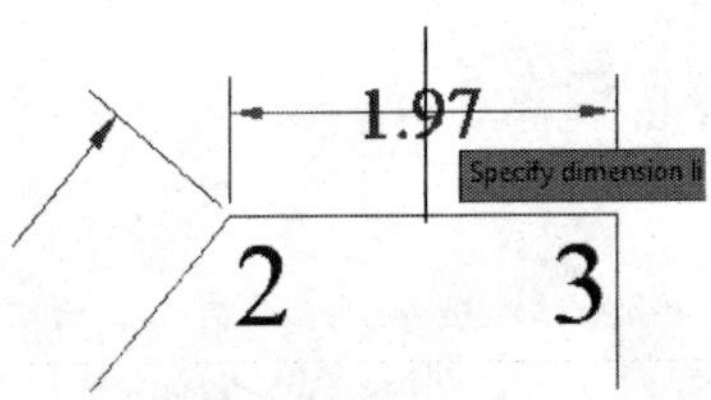

Specify dimension line location or [Mtext/Text/Angle/Horizontal/Vertical/Rotated]:
Select a location for the horizontal dimension with the LMB.

9. 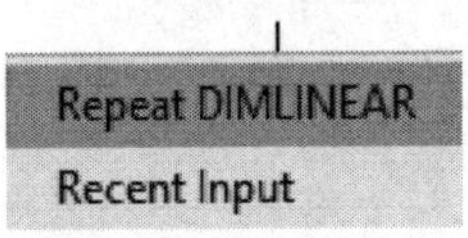

Repeat the Linear Dimension command with the RMB (dimlinear or <ENTER>).

10. 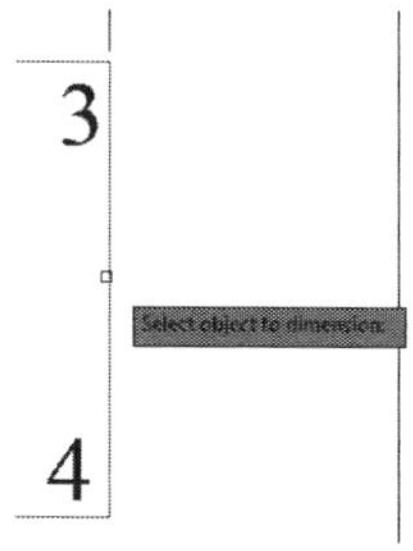

Specify first extension line origin or <select object>:
Click <ENTER> to select the object.

Select object to dimension:
Select the line between 3 and 4.

11. 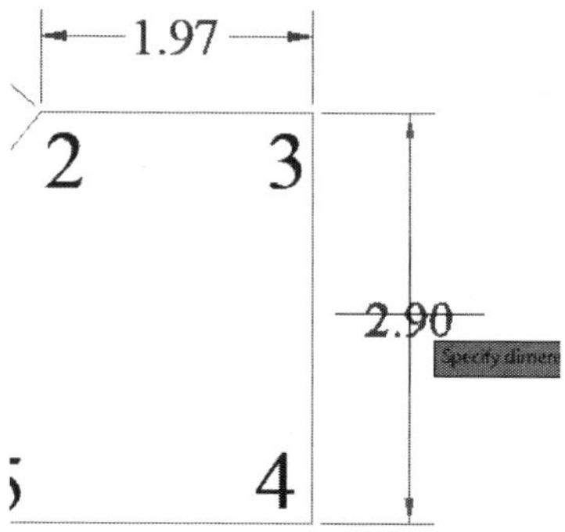

Specify dimension line location or [Mtext/Text/Angle/Horizontal/Vertical/Rotated]:
Select a location for the vertical dimension with the LMB.

12. 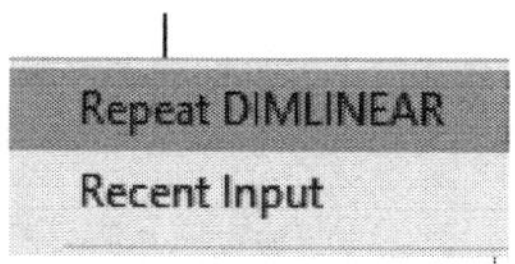

Repeat the Linear Dimension command with the RMB (dimlinear or <ENTER>).

13. 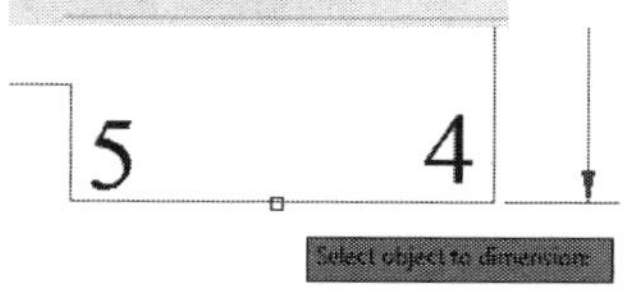

Specify first extension line origin or <select object>:
Click <ENTER> to select the object.

Select object to dimension:
Select the line between 4 and 5.

14. 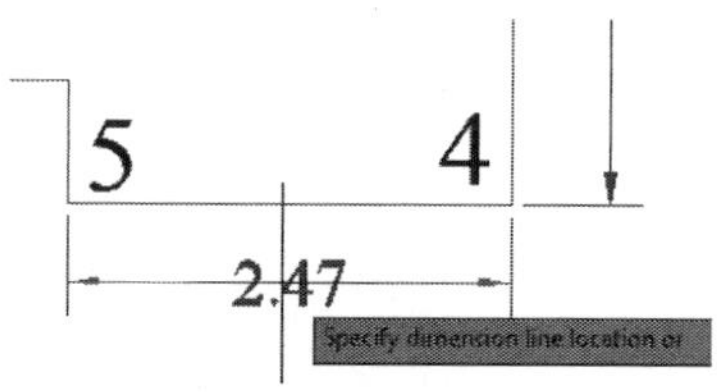

Specify dimension line location or [Mtext/Text/Angle/Horizontal/Vertical/Rotated]:
Select a location for the horizontal dimension with the LMB.

15. 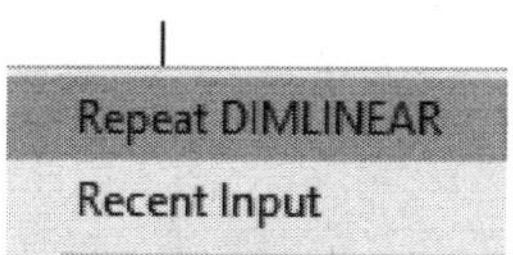

Repeat the Linear Dimension command with the RMB (dimlinear or <ENTER>).

16. 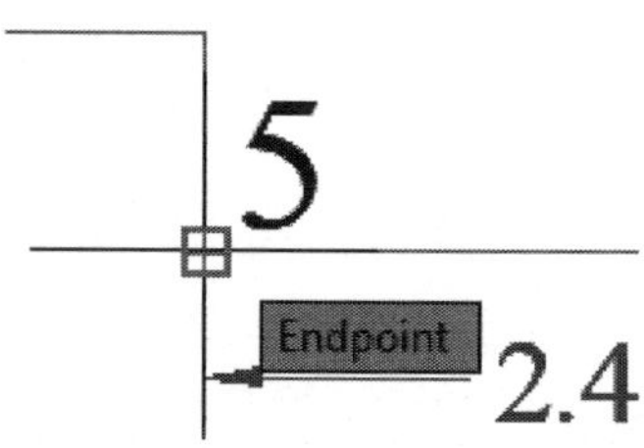

Specify first extension line origin or <select object>:
Select the endpoint of corner #5.

17. 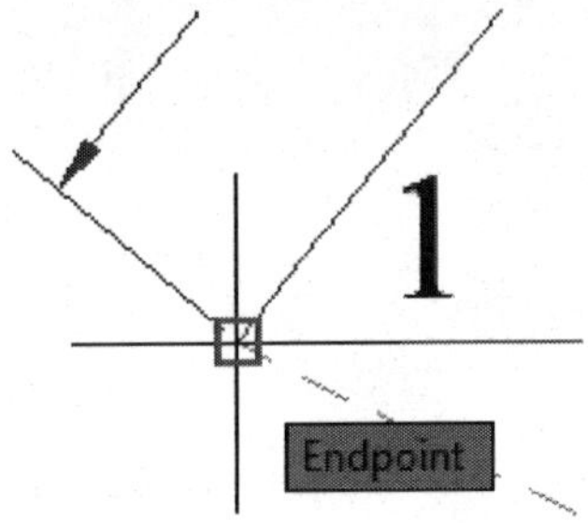

Specify second extension line origin:
Select the endpoint of corner #1.

18. 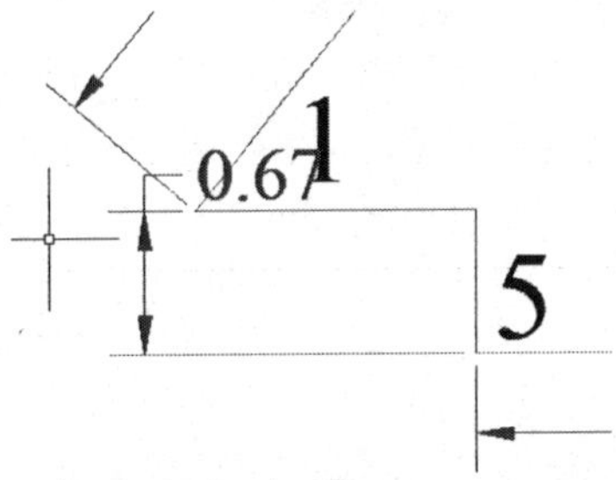

Specify dimension line location or [Mtext/Text/Angle/Horizontal/Vertical/Rotated]:
Select a location for the vertical dimension with the LMB.

19. 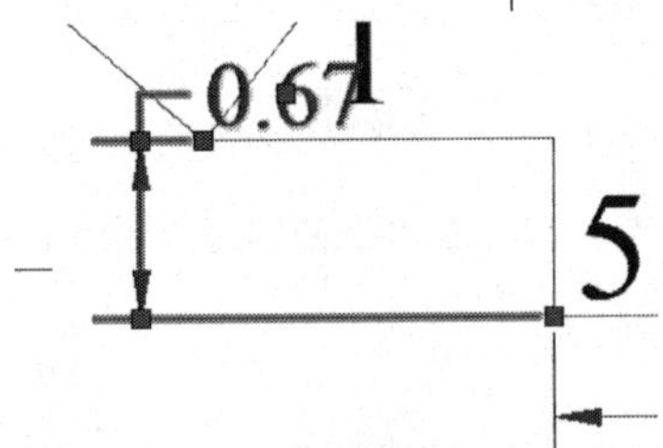

Select the vertical dimension that was just placed.

20. 

Select the grip on top of the text.

21. 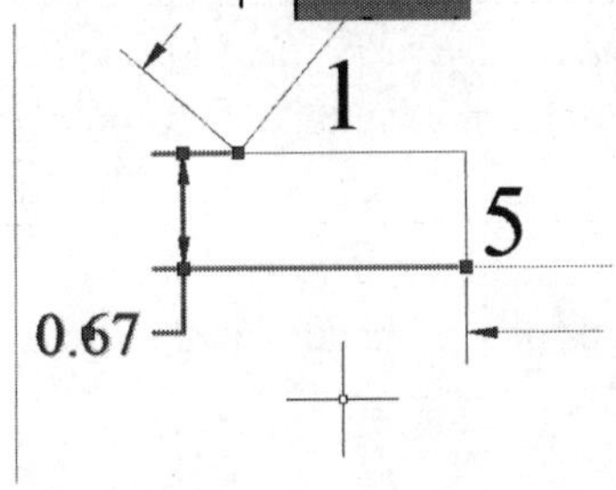

Move the text down.

Note: *If you select the entire line segment instead of the corners of the object for the first and second origin points, the dimension line will run over the object and no gap will be visible between the object and the dimension line.*

Command Exercise

Exercise 9-2 –Continuous and Baseline Dimensions

Drawing Name: **dim2.dwg**
Estimated Time to Completion: 15 Minutes

Scope

OSNAP should be enabled with ENDPOINT. Workspace should be set to Drafting & Annotation.

Dimension the object as indicated using Continuous and Baseline Dimensions.

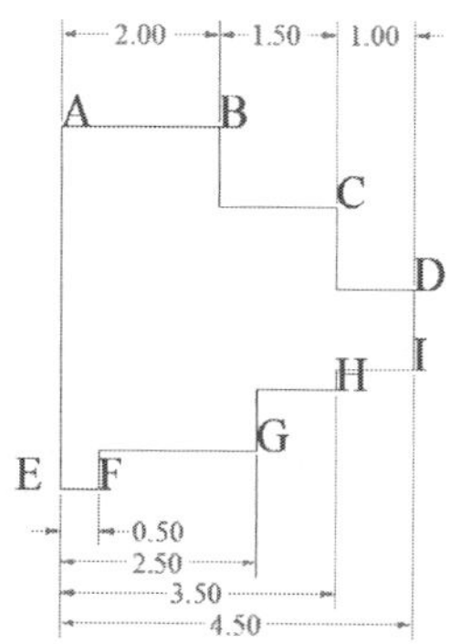

Solution

1. 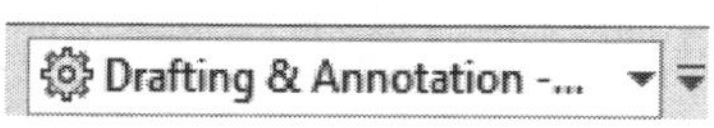

*Set **Drafting and Annotation** workspace current.*

2. 

Activate the Annotate tab on the ribbon.

3. 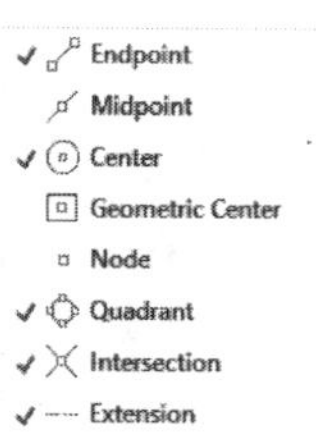

Make sure the **Intersection** Running Object Snap is active.

4. 

Select the **Linear Dimension** command from the Dimensions panel on the ribbon.

5. 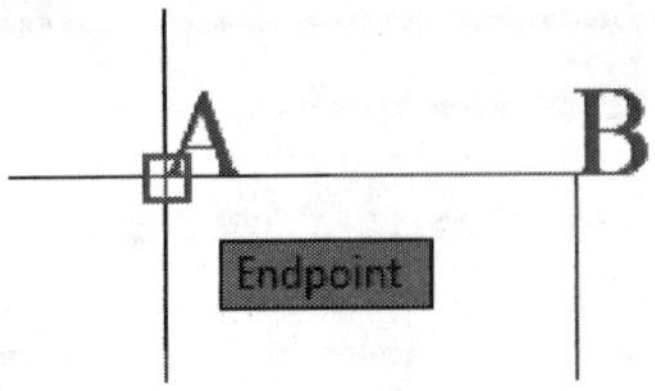

Specify first extension line origin or <select object>:
Pick the upper left corner of the object A with the LMB.

6. 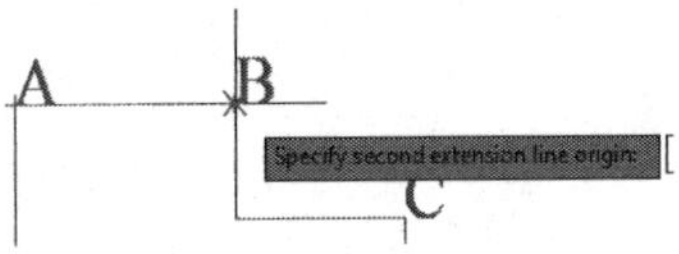

Specify second extension line origin:
Pick corner B with the LMB.

7. 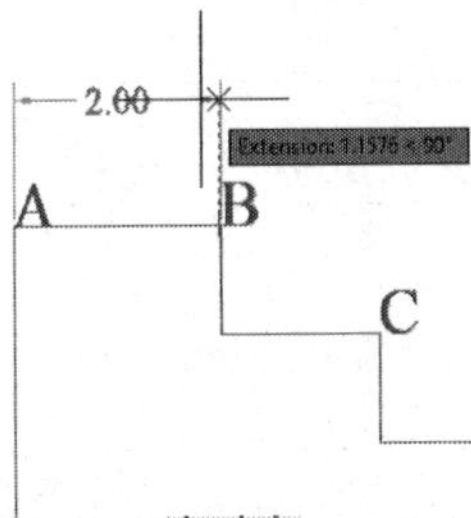

Specify dimension line location or [Mtext/Text/Angle/Horizontal/Vertical/Rotated]:
Select a location for the dimension with the LMB.

8. 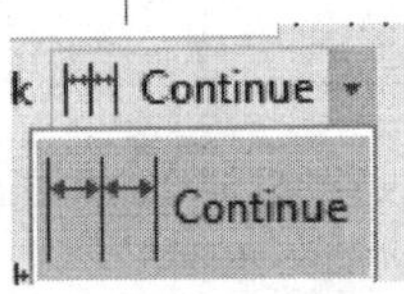

Invoke the **Continue Dimension** command (dimcontinue).

9. 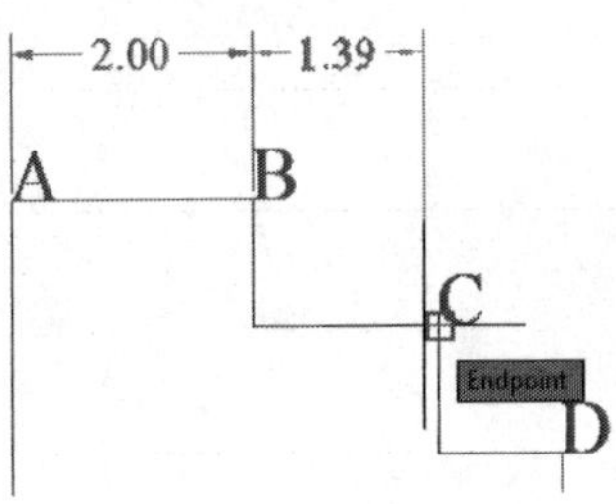

Specify a second extension line origin or [Undo/Select] <Select>:
Select corner C.

10. 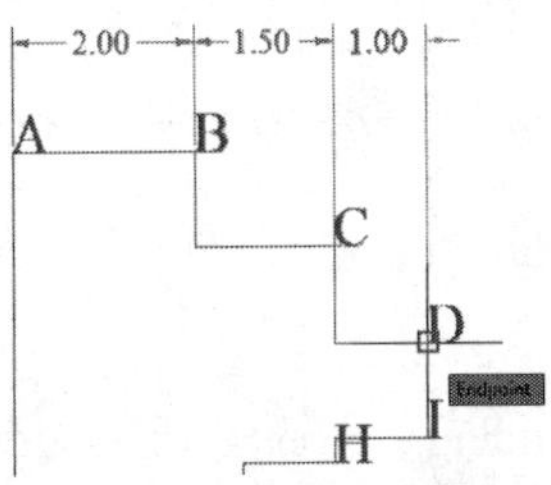

Specify a second extension line origin or [Undo/Select] <Select>:
Select corner D.

11. 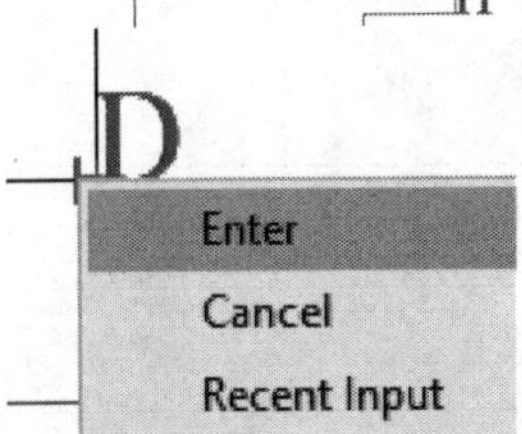

Specify a second extension line origin or [Undo/Select] <Select>:
Right click and select <ENTER> to end the command.

12. 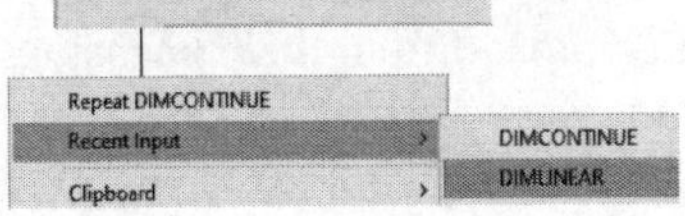

Invoke the Linear Dimension command (dimlinear).

13. 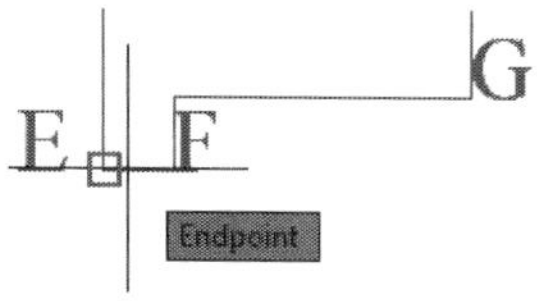

Specify first extension line origin or <select object>:
Select the lower left corner E of the object with the LMB.

14. 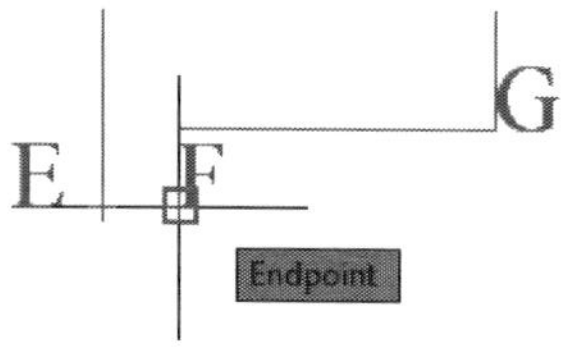

Specify second extension line origin:
Select corner F.

15. 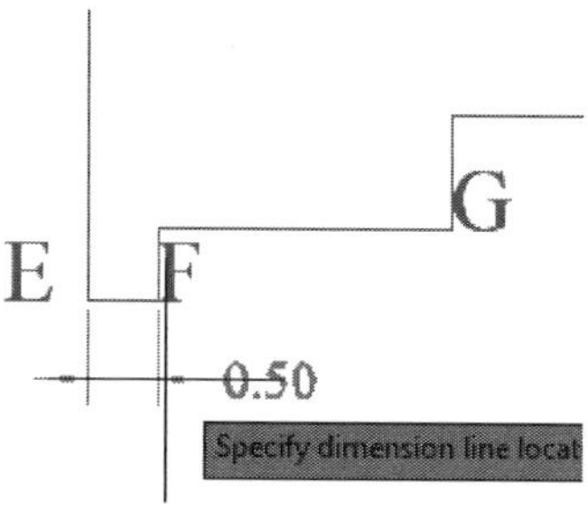

Specify dimension line location or [Mtext/Text/Angle/Horizontal/Vertical/Rotated]:
Select a location for the dimension with the LMB.

16. 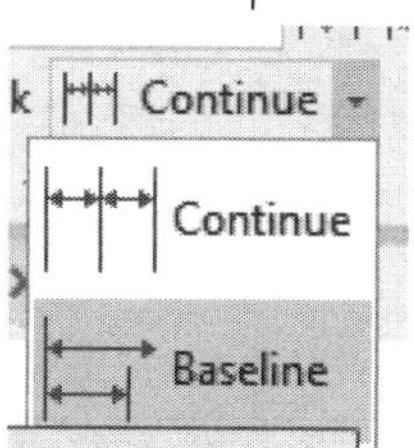

Invoke the **Baseline Dimension** command (dimbaseline).

17. 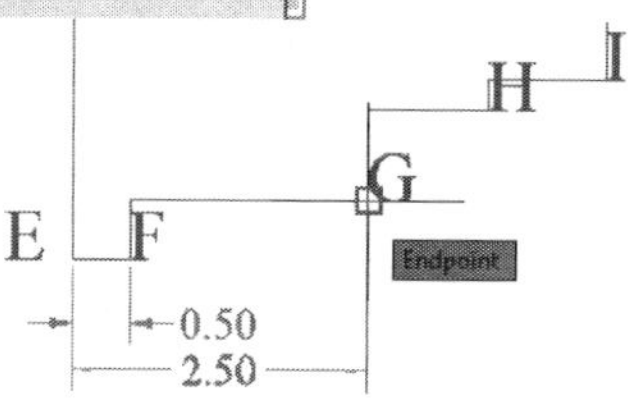

Specify a second extension line origin or [Undo/Select] <Select>:
Select corner G.

18. 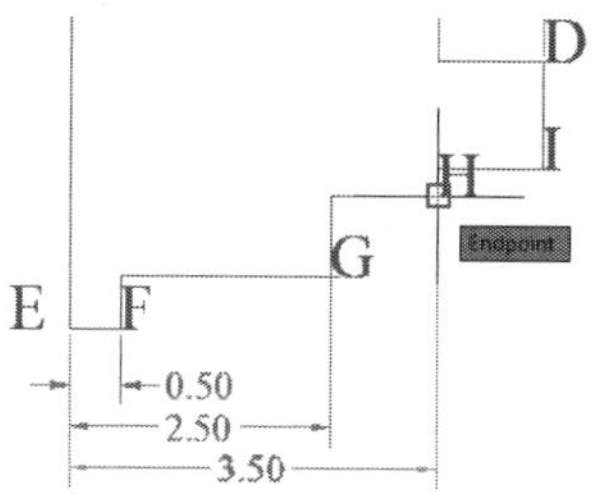

Specify a second extension line origin or [Undo/Select] <Select>:
Select corner H.

19. 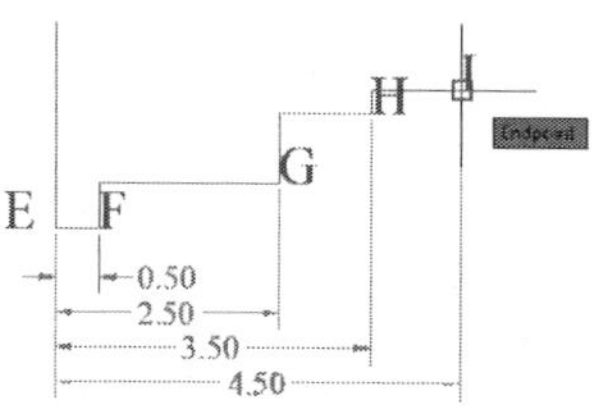

Specify a second extension line origin or [Undo/Select] <Select>:
Select corner I.

20. 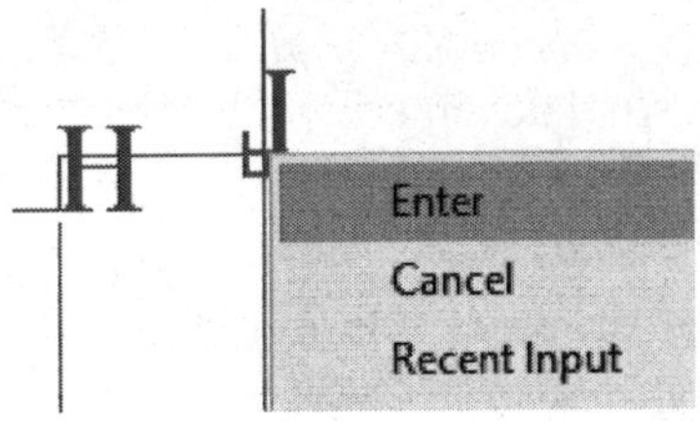

Select base dimension:
Right click and select <ENTER> to end the command.

***Note:** You will get the best results if you start with a linear, angular, or aligned dimension and immediately follow with the Baseline or Continued Dimension command.*

Command Exercise

Exercise 9-3 – Angular, Radius and Diameter Dimensions

Drawing Name: **dim3.dwg**
Estimated Time to Completion: 15 Minutes

Scope

Dimension the object as indicated using Angular, Radius, Diameter Dimensions, and Center Mark.

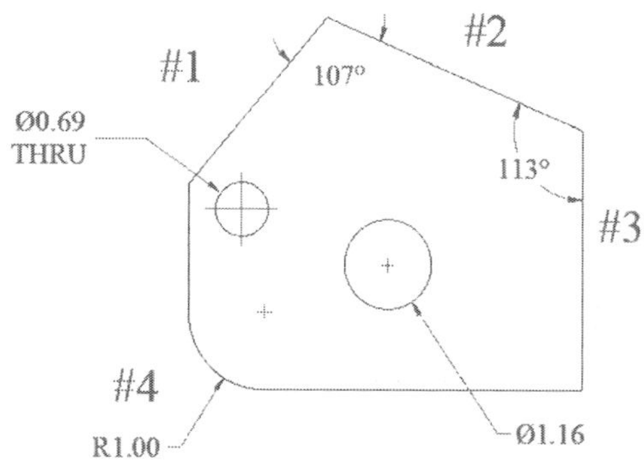

Solution

1.

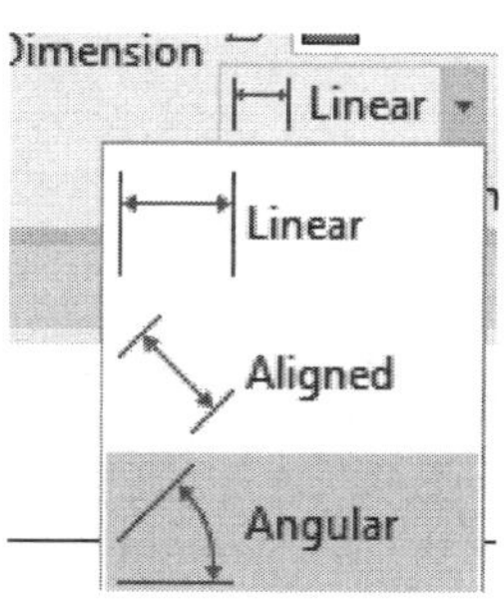

Invoke the Angular Dimension command (dimangular).

2.

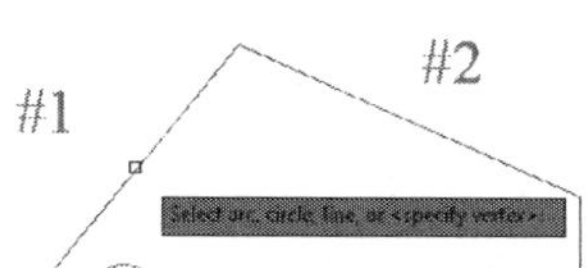

Select arc, circle, line, or <specify vertex>:
Pick the line segment marked #1.

3.

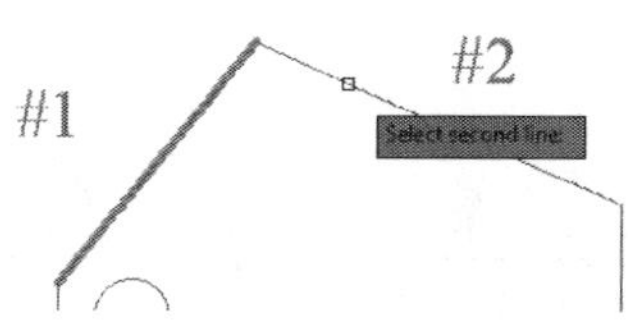

Select second line:

Pick the line segment marked #2.

4. 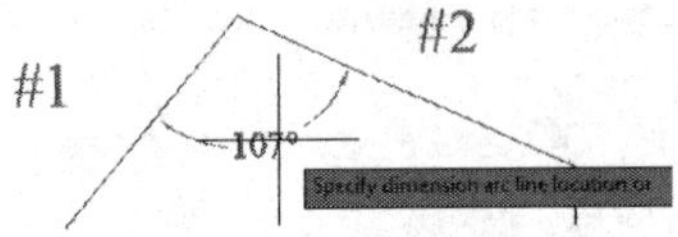

Specify dimension arc line location or [Mtext/Text/Angle]:
Select a location for the dimension.

5. 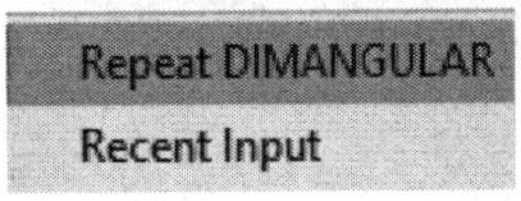

Repeat the Angular Dimension command with the RMB (dimangular or <ENTER>).

6. 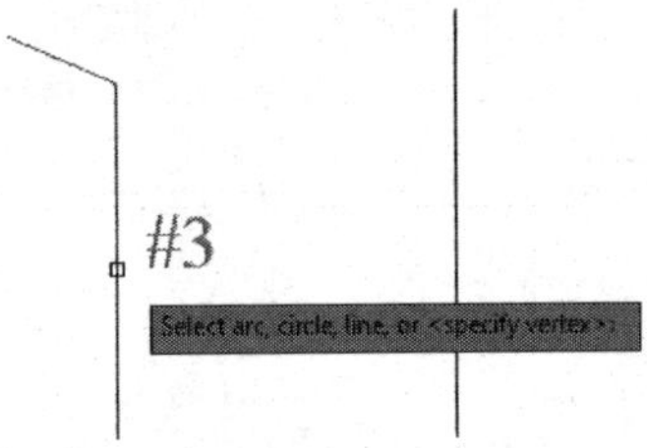

Select arc, circle, line, or <specify vertex>:
Pick the line segment marked #3.

7. 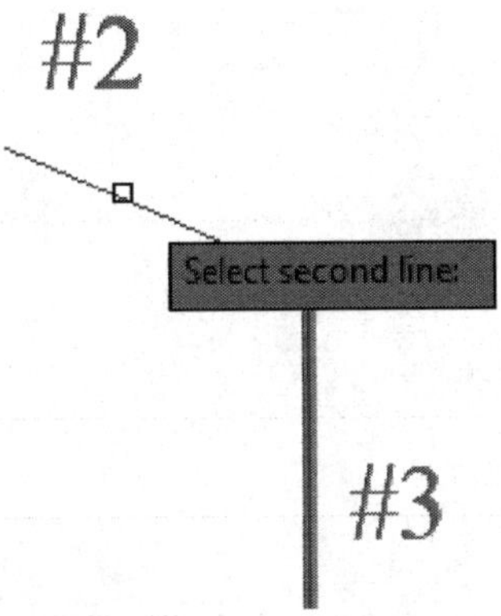

Select second line:
Pick the line segment marked #2.

8. 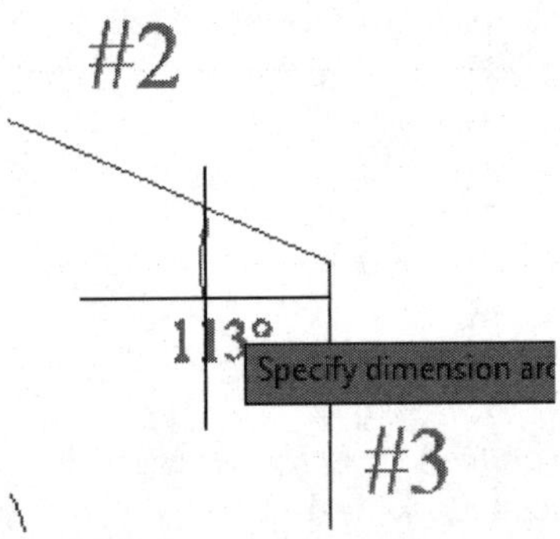

Specify dimension arc line location or [Mtext/Text/Angle]:
Select a location for the dimension.

9. 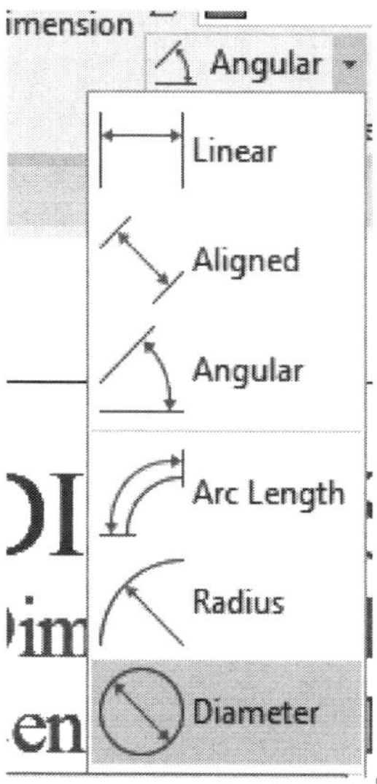

Invoke the Diameter Dimension command (dimdiameter).

10. 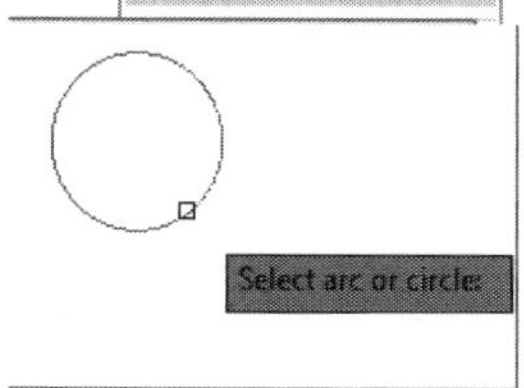

#3 *Select arc or circle:*

Select the large circle.

11. 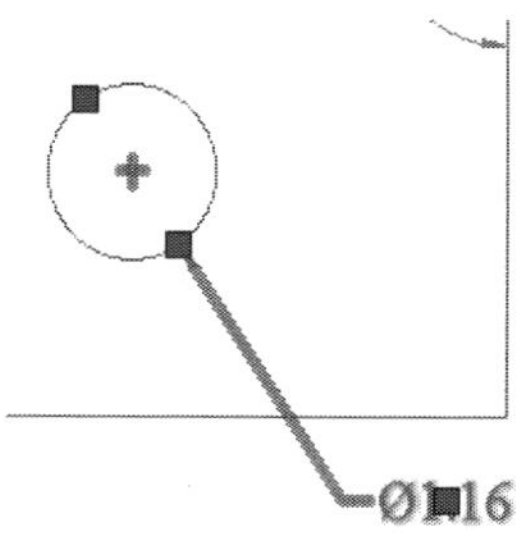

#3 *Specify dimension line location or [Mtext/Text/Angle]:*
Select a location for the dimension.

12. 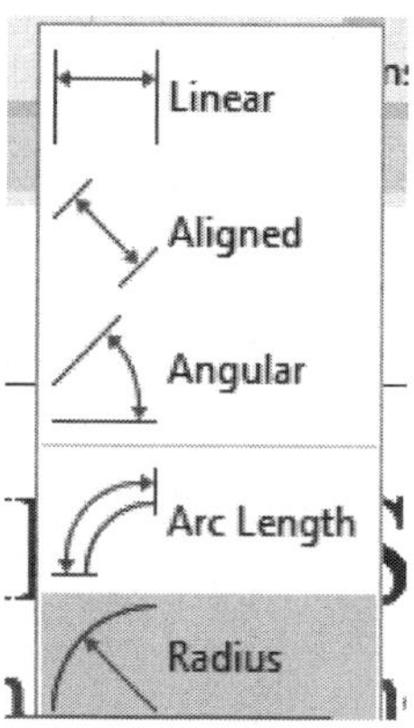

Invoke the **Radius Dimension** command (dimradius).

13. 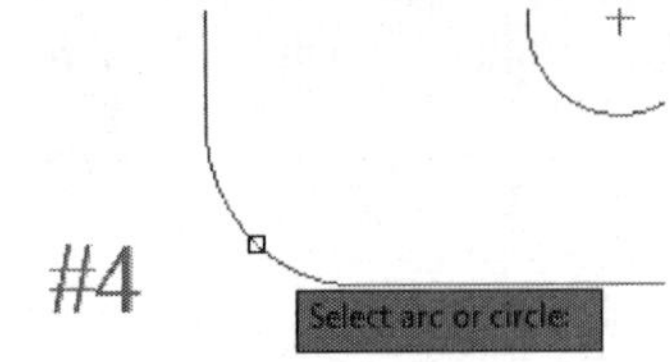

Select arc or circle:
Select the arc marked #4.

14. 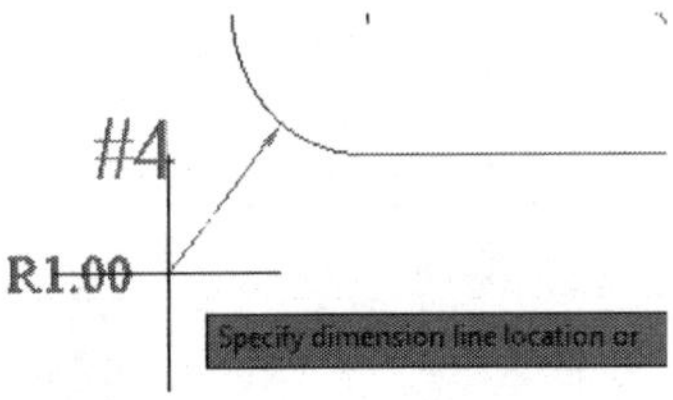

Specify dimension line location or [Mtext/Text/Angle]:
Select a location for the dimension.

15. 

Invoke the **Center Mark** command (dimcenter).

16. 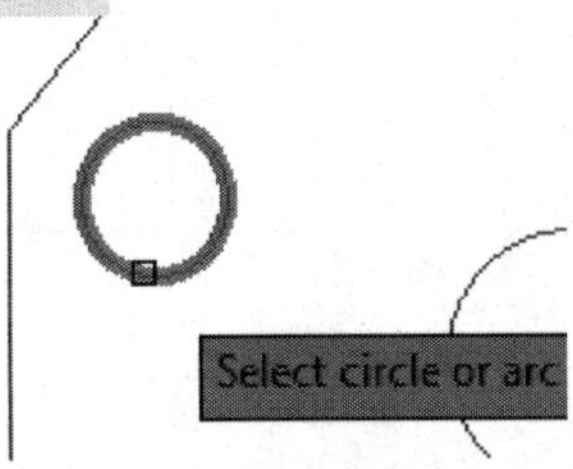

Select arc or circle:
Select the small circle.

Click **ENTER** to exit the command.

In the Drafting & Annotation workspace, you need to expand the Dimensions panel to see the Center Mark tool. To expand use the down arrow next to the word 'Dimensions'.

17. 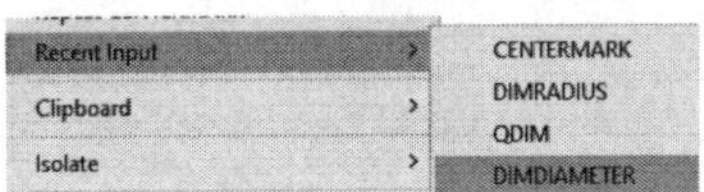

Invoke the Diameter Dimension command (dimdiameter).

18. 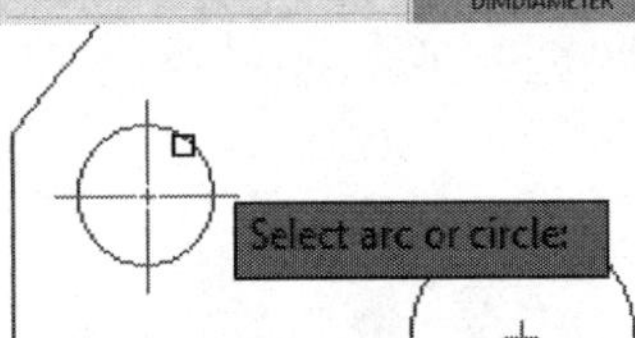

Select arc or circle:
Select the small circle.

19. 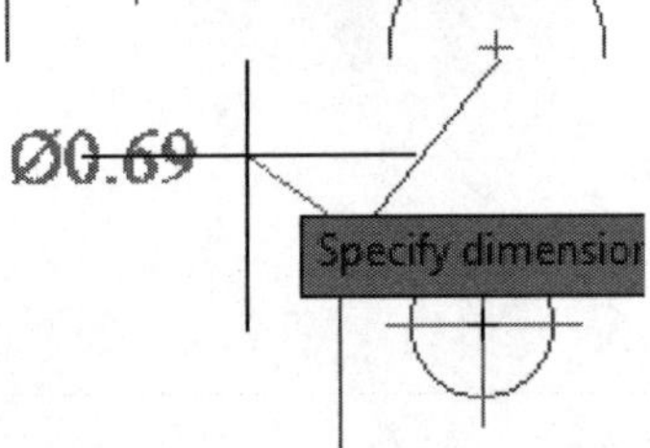

Specify dimension line location or [Mtext/Text/Angle]:
Select a location for the dimension.

20. 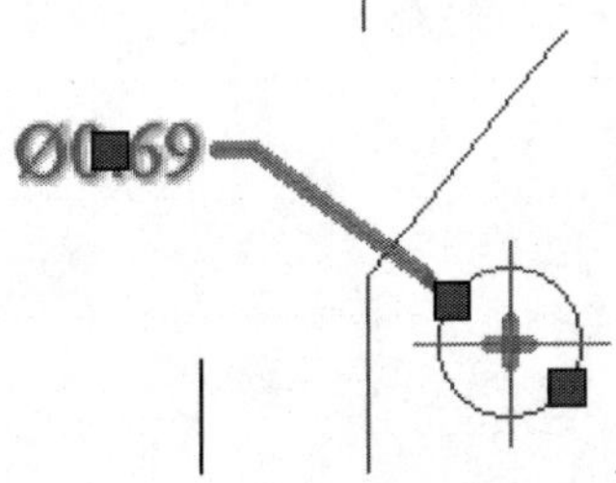

Select the diameter dimension that was just placed.

21. 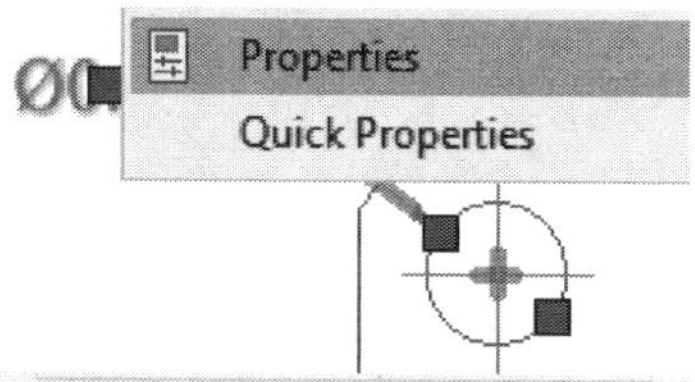

Right click and select **Properties**.

22. 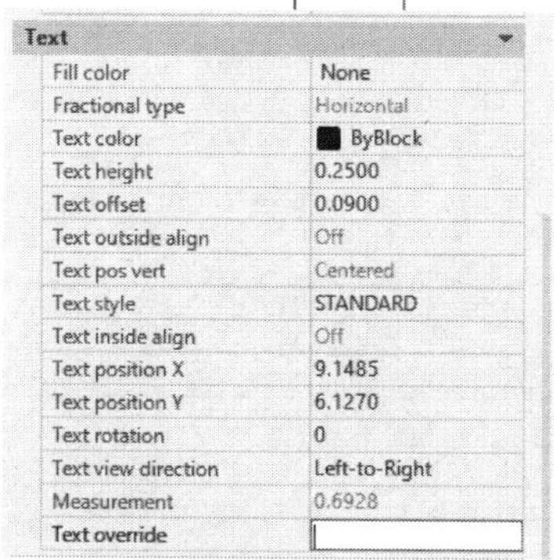

Text	
Fill color	None
Fractional type	Horizontal
Text color	ByBlock
Text height	0.2500
Text offset	0.0900
Text outside align	Off
Text pos vert	Centered
Text style	STANDARD
Text inside align	Off
Text position X	9.1485
Text position Y	6.1270
Text rotation	0
Text view direction	Left-to-Right
Measurement	0.6928
Text override	

Use the scroll bar to scroll down to locate the Text override field.

23. 

Type '<> **THRU**' in the field. Click <ENTER>.

24. 

Click **<ESC>** to release the selection.

The dimension updates.

Click on the dimension.

Position your cursor after the 0.69 value and click ENTER.

This drops the THRU onto a second line.

Click anywhere outside the text box to exit.

25. Right click and select **ENTER**.

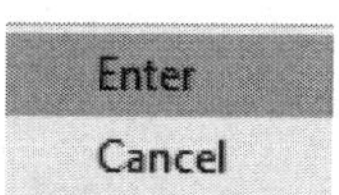

<> is used to indicate the default text or dimension assigned to the object.

Centerline

Command Locator

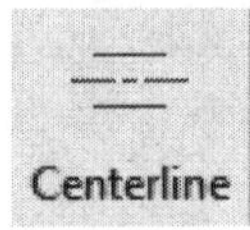

Ribbon/Annotate /Centerlines	**Centerline**
Command	**Centerline**

Command Overview

This tool will add a center line in between two parallel or non-parallel lines. To add a center line select the Centerline tool from Centerlines panel of the Annotate tab and click on the two lines.

The center line will be automatically added in between the selected lines. If the lines are intersecting then the center line will pass through the angle bisector of the lines.

Several system variables control the appearance of centerlines.

SYSTEM VARIABLE	DESCRIPTION
CENTERLAYER	Controls the layer the centerline is assigned
CENTERLTSCALE	Controls the linetype scale of the centerline
CENTERLTYPE	Controls the linetype used by the centerline
CENTERMARKEXE	Controls the size of the centerline – whether it extends beyond the selected lines

Tips & Tricks

You can select each object to expose their grips, allowing you to alter their length or positioning.

Command Exercise

Exercise 9-4 – Centerline Annotations

Drawing Name: **centerline.dwg**
Estimated Time to Completion: 25 Minutes

Scope

Add a centerline to the holes in the top and front view.
Set the layer to be used for the centerline using the CENTERLAYER command.

Solution

1. 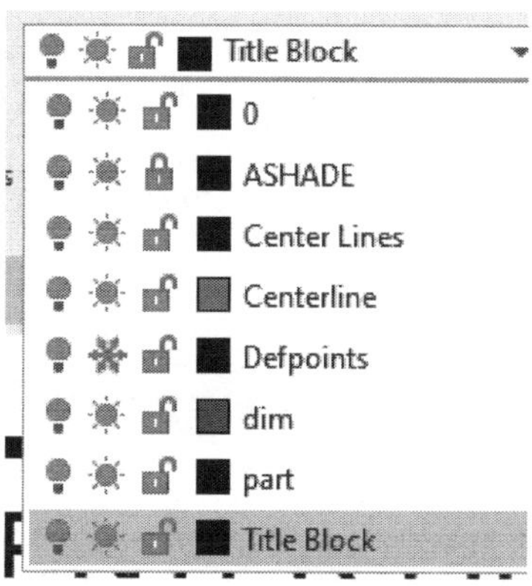

Use the drop-down layer list on the Home tab on the ribbon to see what layers are currently in the drawing.

2. 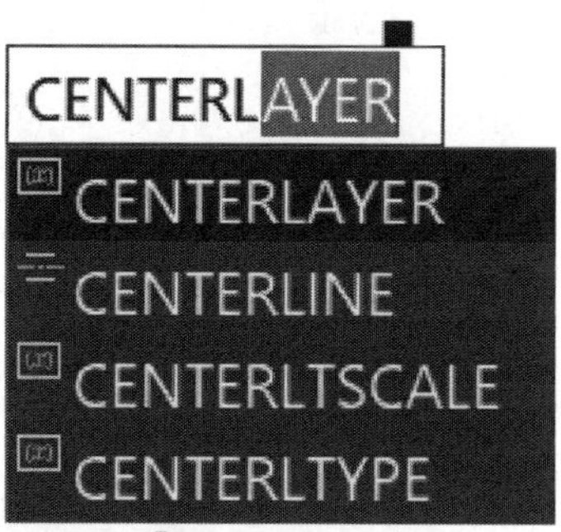

Type **CENTERLAYER** at the command prompt.
Autofill will display the command as you start typing.

3. 
Type **Centerline** for the value of the layer.
This will place any center lines on the centerline layer regardless of the current layer.

4. 

Set the current layer to **0**.

5. 

Type CENTERLINE at the command prompt.

Autofill will display the command as you start typing.

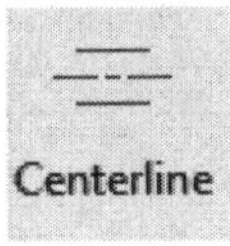

Activate the **Annotate** ribbon.

Select the **Centerline** tool from the Centerlines panel.

6. 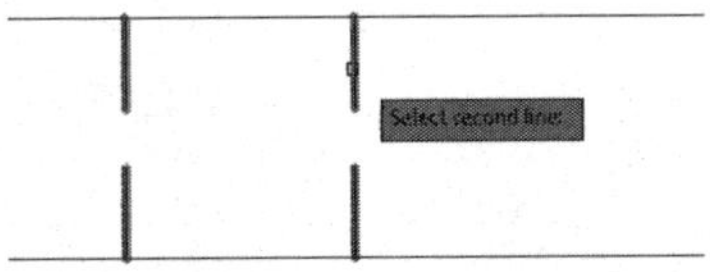

Select the two hidden lines designating the left hole in the front view.

7. 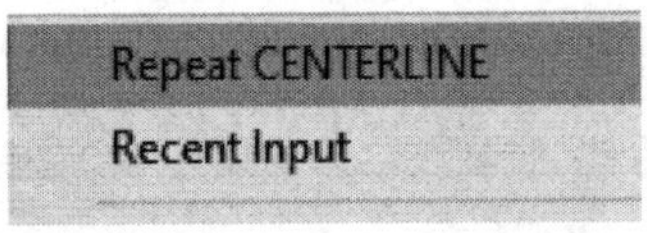

Right click and select **Repeat CENTERLINE**.

8. 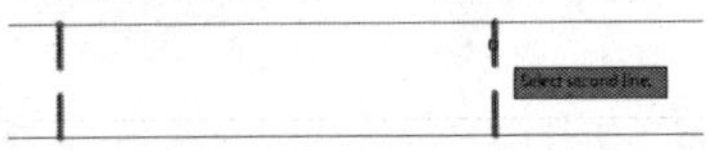

Select the two hidden lines designating the middle hole.

9. 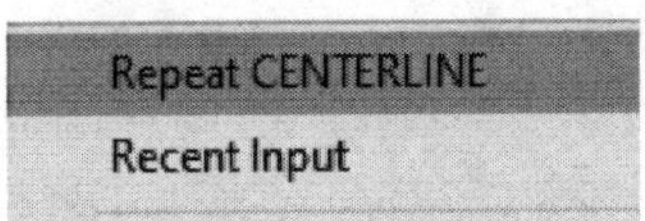

Right click and select **Repeat CENTERLINE**.

10. 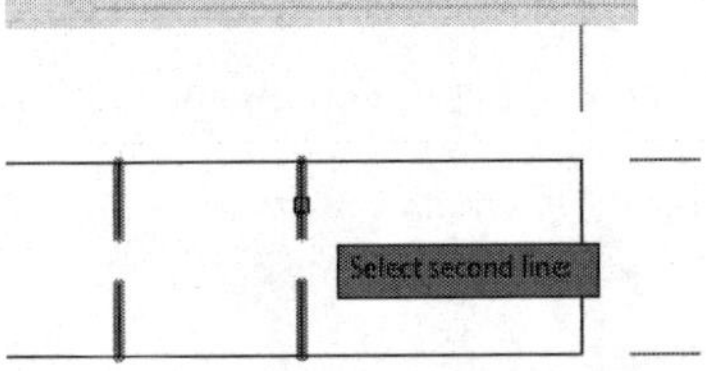

Select the two hidden lines designating the right hole.

11. 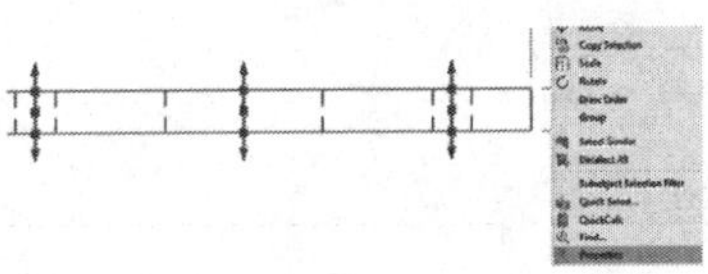

Select the three centerlines which were placed.

Right click and select '**Properties**'.

12. 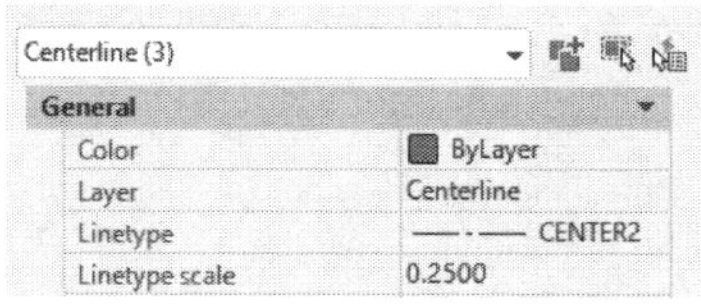

Change the Linetype scale to 0.2500.

Notice that the center lines were automatically placed on a layer called Centerline per the earlier setting.

Click ESC to release the selection.

13. 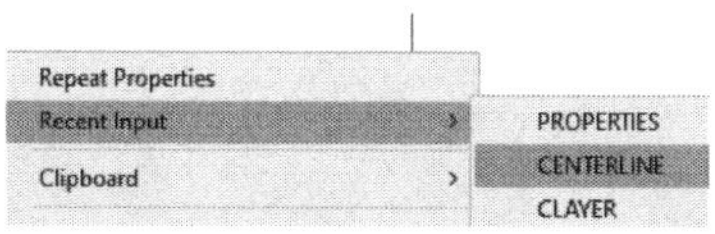

Right click in the display window.

Select **Recent Input → CENTERLINE**.

14. 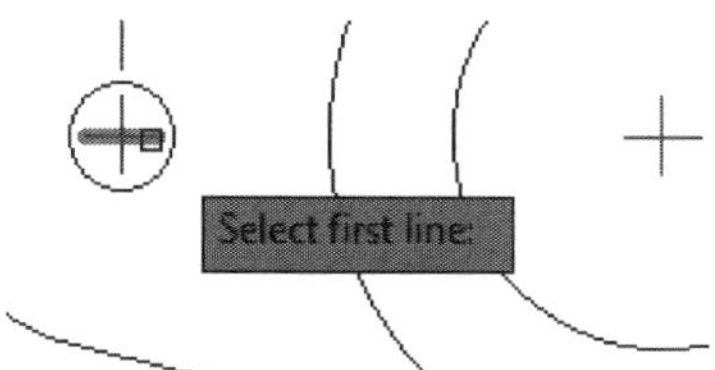

Select the horizontal line of the center mark for the circle on the left.

15. 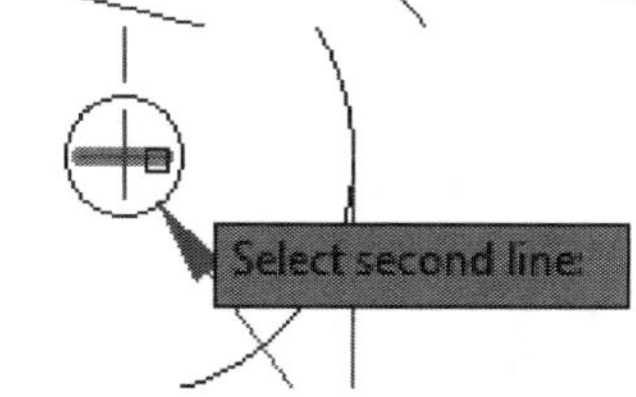

Pan over to the right side of the top view.

Select the horizontal line of the center mark for the circle on the right.

16. 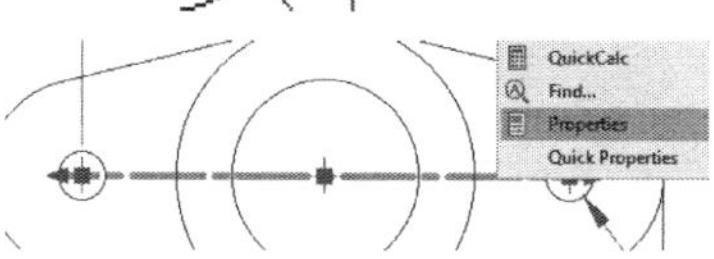

Select the centerline.

Right click and select '**Properties**'.

17. 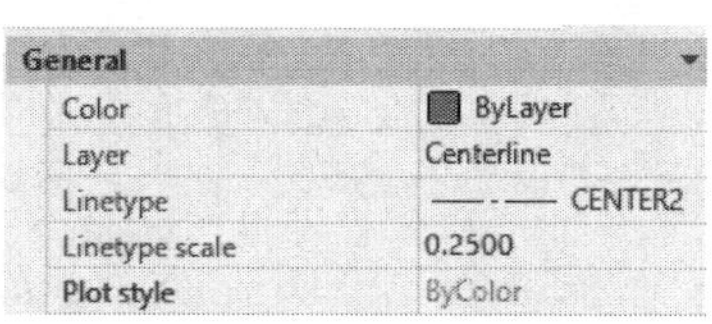

Verify that the centerline was placed on the correct layer and has the correct properties.

Click **ESC** to release the selection.

Extra: *What system variable could be used to set the LTSCALE for the CENTERLINE so you wouldn't have to use PROPERTIES to change the centerline after it was placed? Try using the system variable and then re-do the exercise.*

Quick Dimension

Command Locator

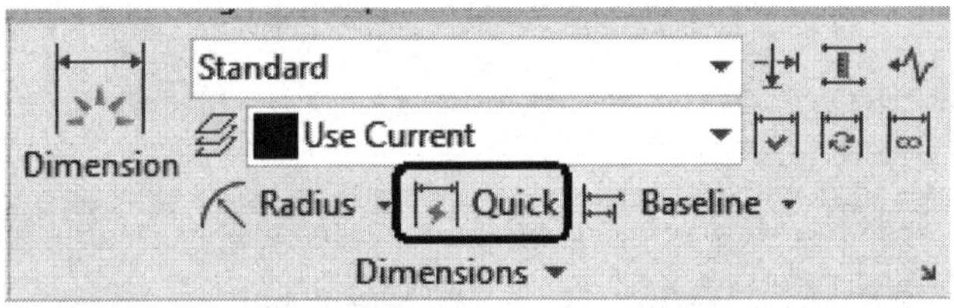

Ribbon/Annotate/Dimensions	**QDIM**
Command	**QDIM**
RMB Shortcut Menu	Continuous, Staggered, Baseline,Ordinate, Radius, Diameter, datumPoint, Edit, Settings

Command Overview

Creates a series of dimensions quickly from selected objects. With QDIM, you can create a string of dimensions using two picks to select the objects to be dimensioned (select the objects using a window), one click to confirm the selection and one pick to place the dimensions.

General Procedures:

1. Start the **QDIM** command.
2. Right click and select the type of desired dimensions.
3. Window around the geometry to be dimensioned.
4. Left click to place the dimensions.

Command Exercise

Exercise 9-5 – Quick Dimensions - Continuous

Drawing Name: **qdim1.dwg**
Estimated Time to Completion: 5 Minutes

Scope

Use the Quick Dimension command to place continuous dimensions.

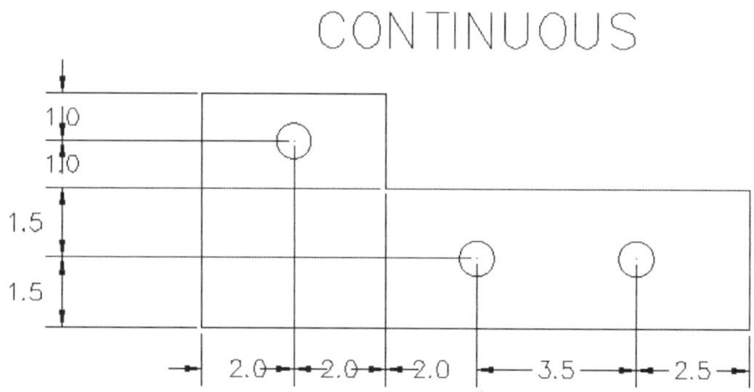

Solution

1. 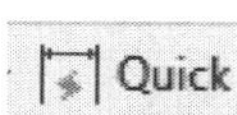

Activate the **Annotate** tab on the ribbon.

Invoke the **Quick Dimension** command (qdim).

2. 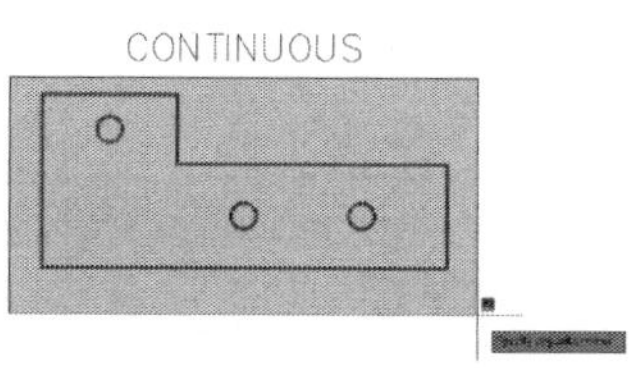

Select geometry to dimension:
Select all of the geometry underneath the word 'CONTINUOUS' using a WINDOW selection.

3. *Select geometry to dimension:*
Click <ENTER> when all of the geometry is selected.

4. 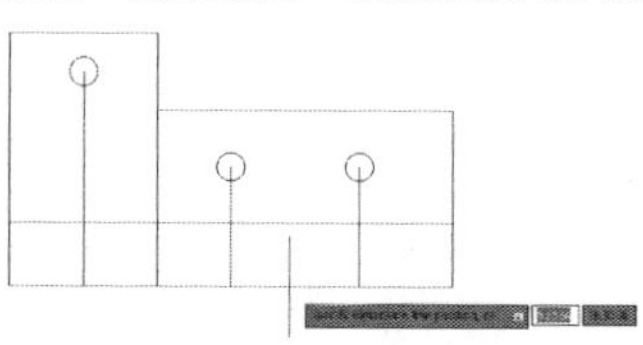

[Continuous/Staggered/Baseline/Ordinate/Radius/ Diameter/datumPoint/Edit] <Continuous>:
Select a placement point below the geometry to create the horizontal dimensions.

5. 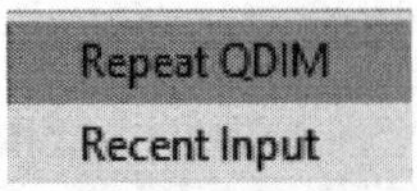

Repeat the **Quick Dimension** command with the RMB (Click <ENTER> or qdim).

6. 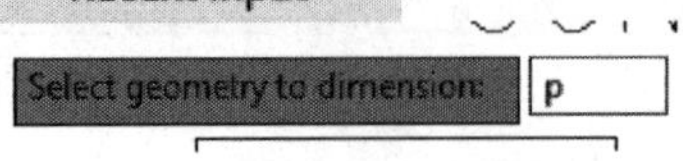

Select geometry to dimension:
Select the same set of geometry (type 'P' and Click <ENTER>).

7. *Select geometry to dimension:*
Click <ENTER> when all of the geometry is selected.

8. 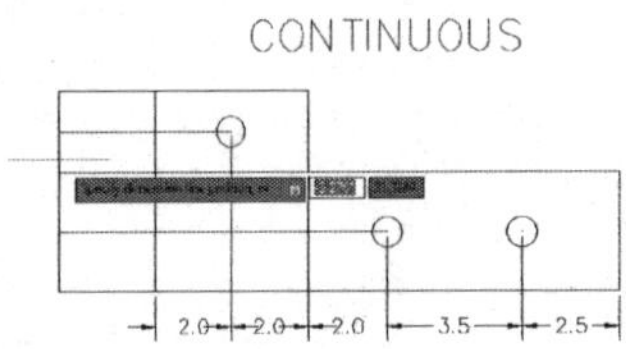

[Continuous/Staggered/Baseline/Ordinate/Radius/Diameter/datumPoint/Edit] <Continuous>:
Select a placement point to the left of the geometry to create the vertical dimensions.

Command Exercise

Exercise 9-6 – Quick Dimensions - Staggered

Drawing Name: **qdim2.dwg**
Estimated Time to Completion: 5 Minutes

Scope

Use the Quick Dimension command to place staggered dimensions.

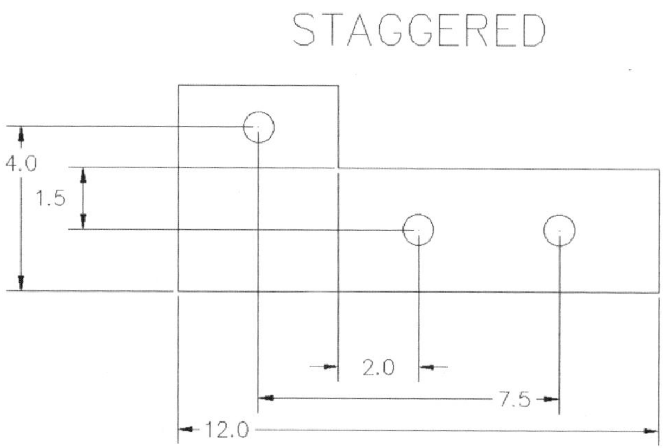

Solution

1. 

Type **QDIM** on the command line.

2. 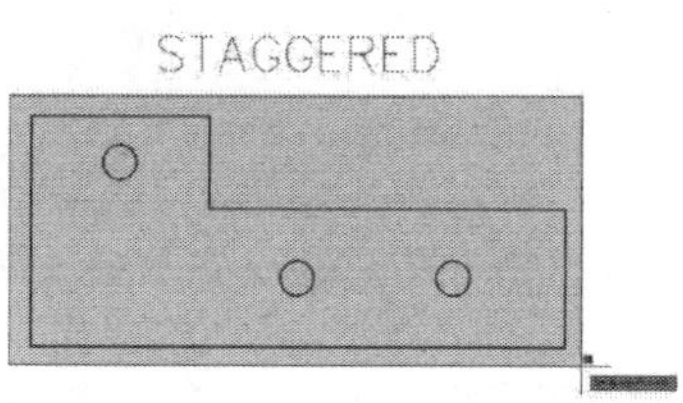

Select geometry to dimension:
Select all of the geometry underneath the word 'STAGGERED' using a window selection.

3. *Select geometry to dimension:*
Click <ENTER> when all of the geometry is selected.

4.

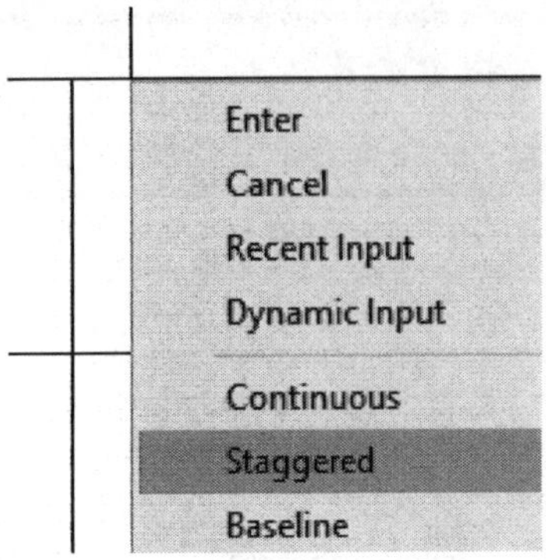

[Continuous/Staggered/Baseline/Ordinate/Radius/Diameter/datumPoint/Edit] <Continuous>:
Right-click in the drawing area and select '**Staggered**' or type 'S' and Click <ENTER> to select staggered dimensions.

5.

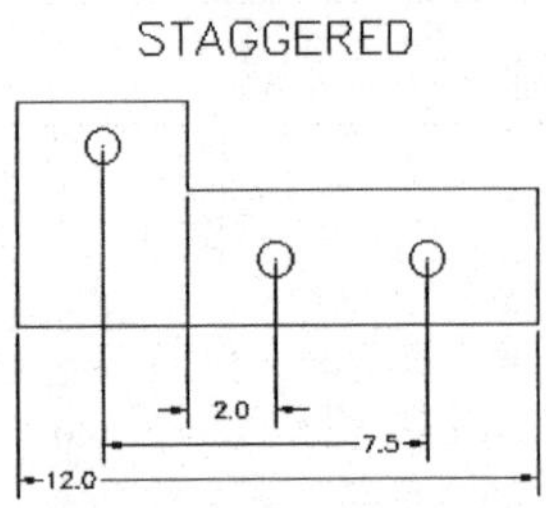

[Continuous/Staggered/Baseline/Ordinate/Radius/Diameter/datumPoint/Edit] <Staggered>:
Select a placement point below the geometry to create the horizontal dimensions.

6.

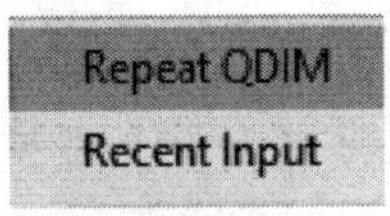

Repeat the **Quick Dimension** command with the RMB (Click <ENTER> or qdim).

7.

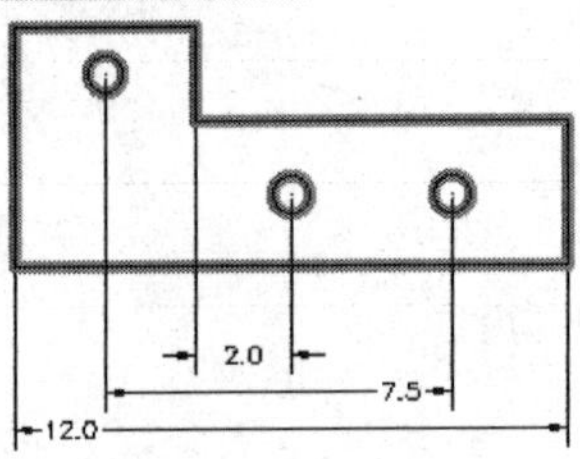

Select geometry to dimension:
Select the same set of geometry (type 'P' and Click <ENTER>).

8. *Select geometry to dimension:*
Click <ENTER> when all of the geometry is selected.

9.

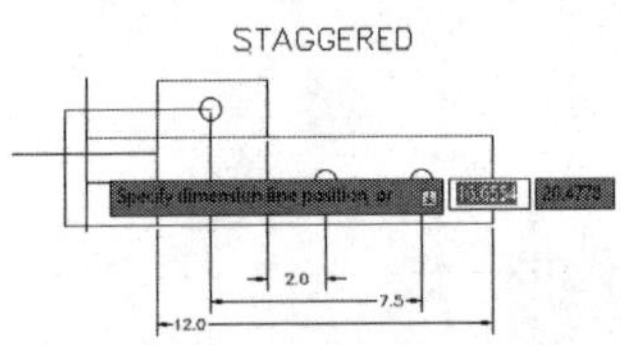

[Continuous/Staggered/Baseline/Ordinate/Radius/Diameter/datumPoint/Edit] <Staggered>:
Select a placement point to the left of the geometry to create the vertical dimensions.

10. 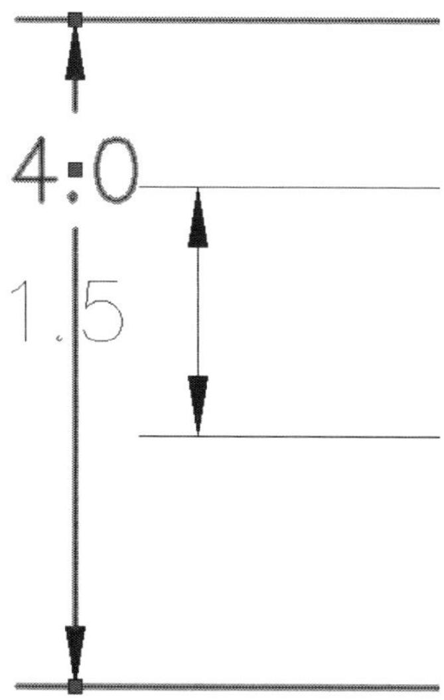

To adjust the position of the dimension:

Select the dimension so it highlights.

11. 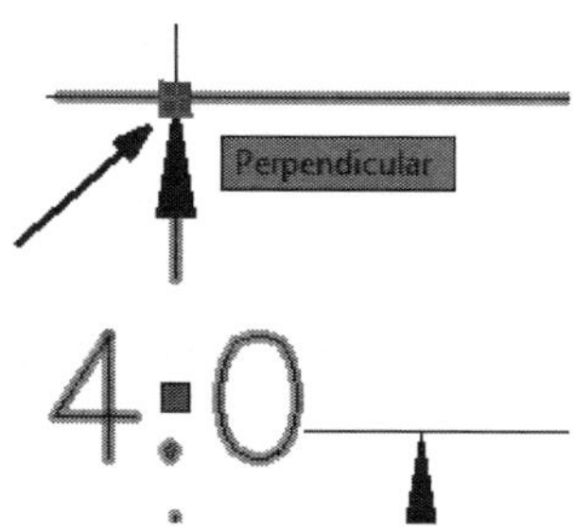

Select one of the end grips (blue square).

12. 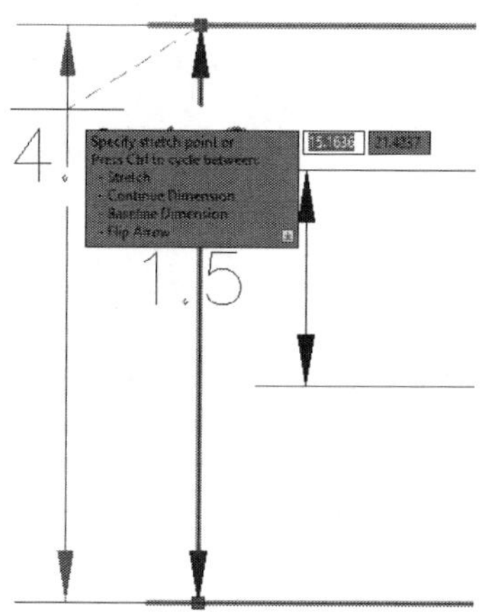

Drag to a new position. LMB to place.

Click **ESC** to release the selection.

Command Exercise

Exercise 9-7 – Quick Dimensions - Baseline

Drawing Name: **qdim3.dwg**
Estimated Time to Completion: 5 Minutes

Scope

Use the Quick Dimension command to place baseline dimensions.

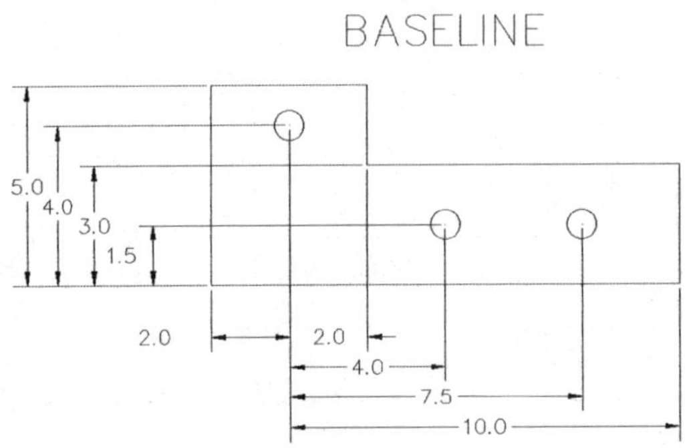

Solution

1. 

Select the **Quick Dimension** tool on the Annotate tab on the ribbon.

2. 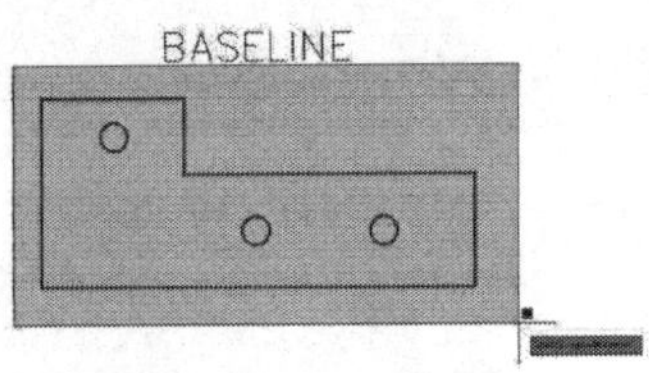

Select geometry to dimension:
Select all of the geometry underneath the word 'BASELINE'.

Select geometry to dimension:
Click <**ENTER**> when all of the geometry is selected.

3. 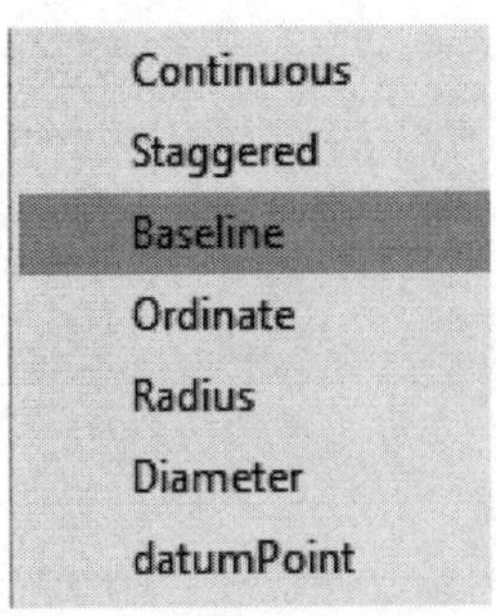

[Continuous/Staggered/Baseline/Ordinate/Radius/Diameter/datumPoint/Edit] <Staggered>:
Right-click in the drawing area and select '**Baseline**' or type 'B' and Click <ENTER> to select baseline dimensions.

4. 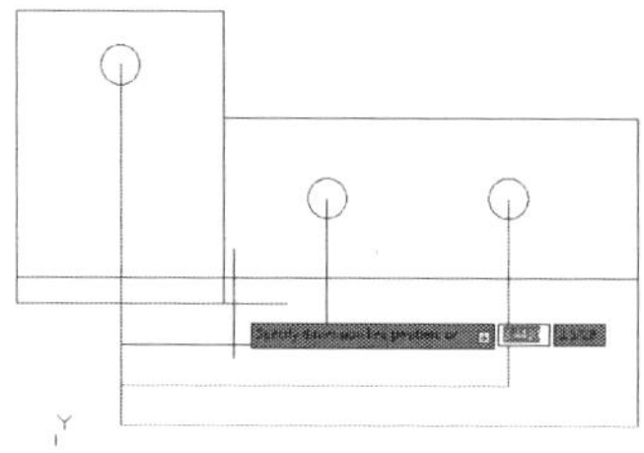

[Continuous/Staggered/Baseline/Ordinate/Radius/

Diameter/datumPoint/Edit] <Baseline>:
Select a placement point below the geometry to create the horizontal dimensions.

5. 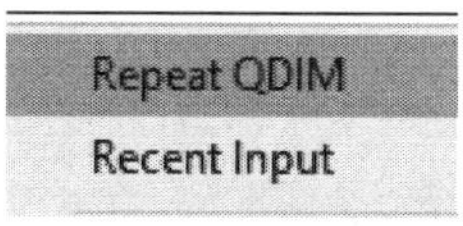

Repeat the **Quick Dimension** command with the RMB (Click <ENTER> or qdim).

6. 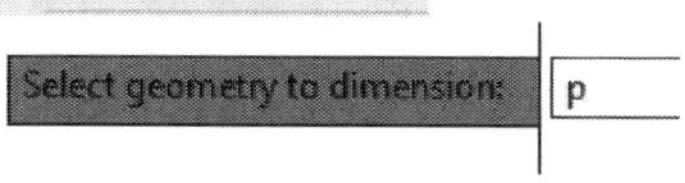

Select geometry to dimension:
Select the same set of geometry (type 'P' and Click <ENTER>).

Select geometry to dimension:
Click <ENTER> when all of the geometry is selected.

7. 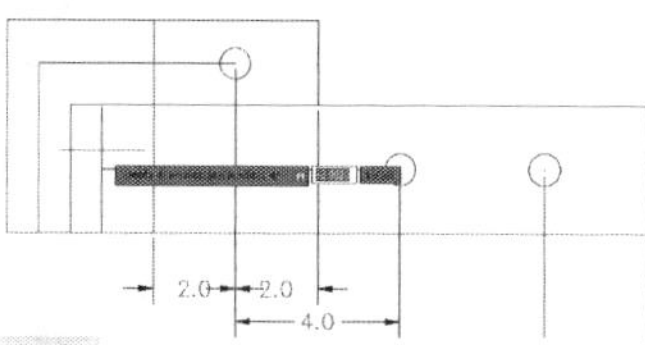

[Continuous/Staggered/Baseline/Ordinate/Radius/
Diameter/datumPoint/Edit] <Baseline>:
Select a placement point to the left of the geometry to create the vertical dimensions.

8. 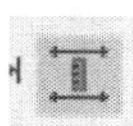

Use GRIPs to adjust the position of dimensions as needed.

You can also use the DIMSPACE tool to adjust the spacing of the dimensions.

Command Exercise

Exercise 9-8 – Quick Dimensions - Ordinate

Drawing Name: **qdim4.dwg**
Estimated Time to Completion: 5 Minutes

Scope

Use the Quick Dimension command to place ordinate dimensions.

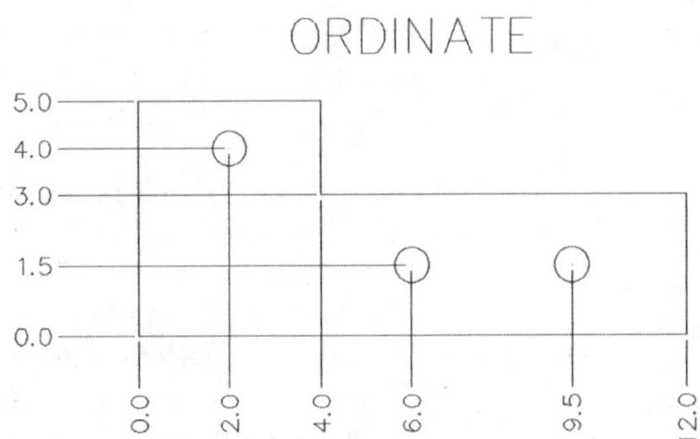

Solution

1. 

Type **QDIM** at the command prompt.

2. 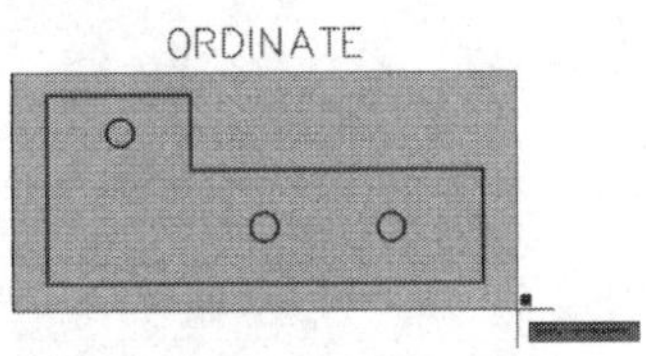

Select geometry to dimension:
Select all of the geometry underneath the word **'ORDINATE'**.

Select geometry to dimension:
Click <**ENTER**> when all of the geometry is selected.

3. 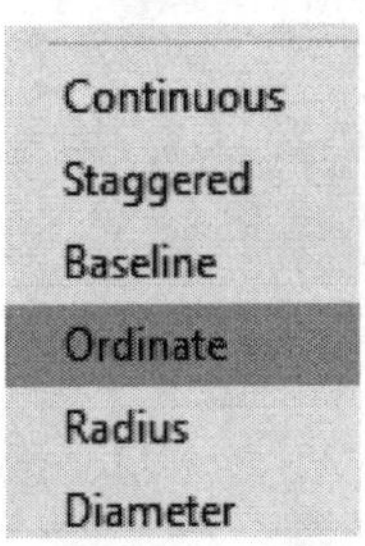

[Continuous/Staggered/Baseline/Ordinate/Radius/Diameter/datumPoint/Edit] <Baseline>:
Right-click in the drawing area and select **'Ordinate'** or type 'O' and Click <ENTER> to select ordinate dimensions.

4. 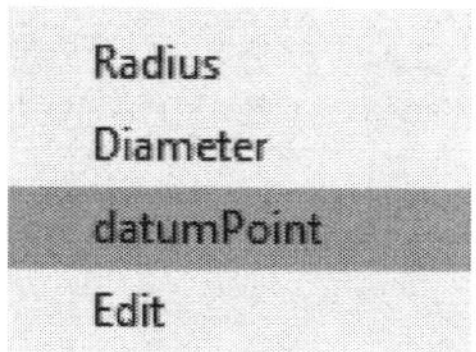

[Continuous/Staggered/Baseline/Ordinate/Radius/Diameter/datumPoint/Edit] <Ordinate>:
Right-click in the drawing area and select **'datumPoint'** or type 'P' and Click <ENTER> to select a new datum point.

The datumPoint is the 0,0 or origin.

5. 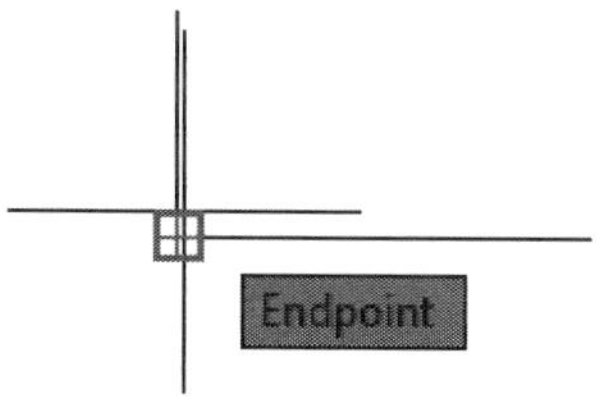

Select new datum point:
Using an object snap, select the lower left corner of the geometry.

6. 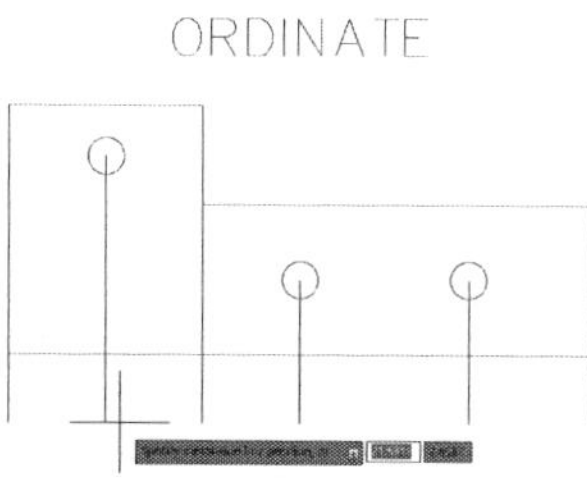

[Continuous/Staggered/Baseline/Ordinate/Radius/Diameter/datumPoint/Edit] <Ordinate>:
Select a placement point below the geometry to create the horizontal dimensions.

7. 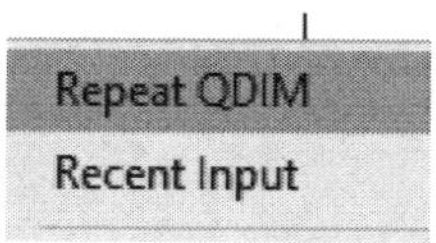

Repeat the **Quick Dimension** command with the RMB (Click <ENTER> or qdim).

8. 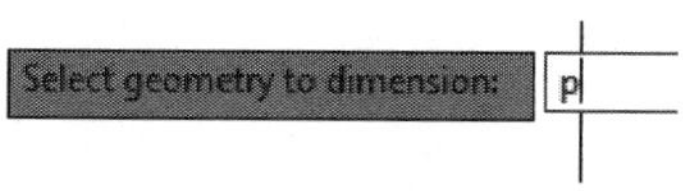

Select geometry to dimension:
Select the same set of geometry (type 'P' and Click <ENTER>)
Select geometry to dimension:
Click <**ENTER**> when all of the geometry is selected.

9. 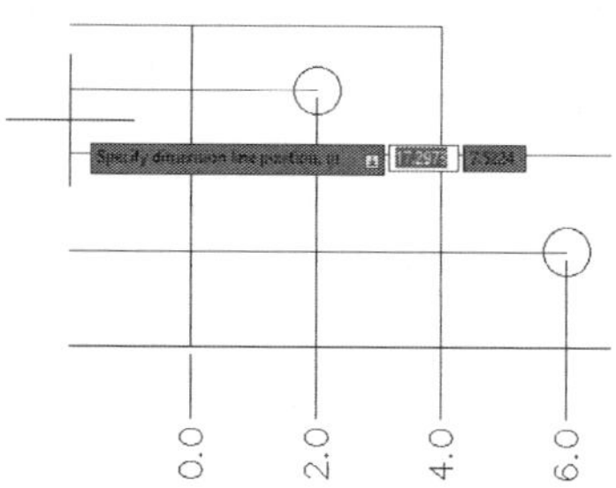

[Continuous/Staggered/Baseline/Ordinate/Radius/Diameter/datumPoint/Edit] <Ordinate>:
Select a placement point to the left of the geometry to create the vertical dimensions.

Command Exercise

Exercise 9-9 – Quick Dimensions - Edit

Drawing Name: **qdim5.dwg**
Estimated Time to Completion: 5 Minutes

Scope

Use the Quick Dimension command to edit ordinate dimensions.

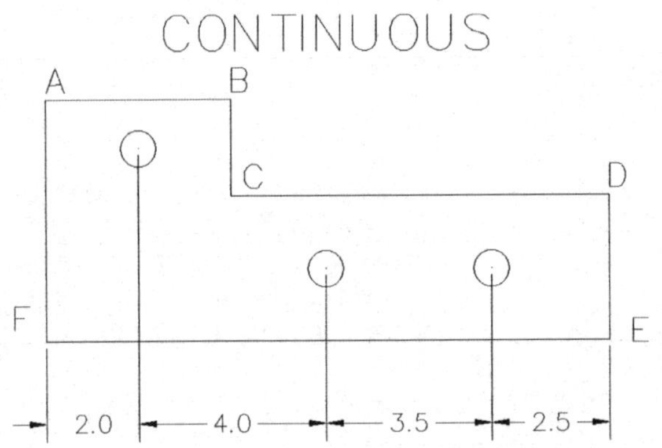

Solution

1. 

Invoke the **Quick Dimension** command (qdim).

If you are using the Drafting & Annotation workspace, you need to switch to the Annotate ribbon.

2. 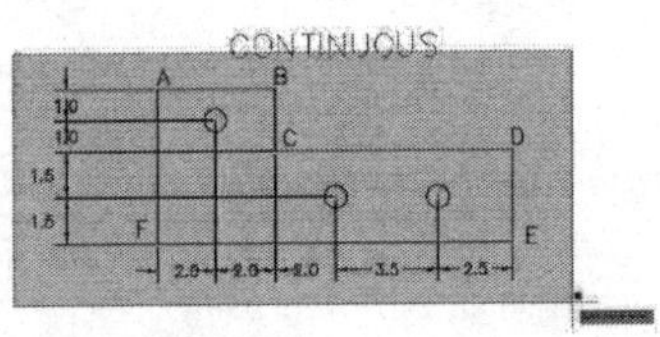

Select geometry to dimension:
Select all of the geometry underneath the word 'CONTINUOUS'.

Select geometry to dimension:
Click <**ENTER**> when all of the geometry is selected.

3. 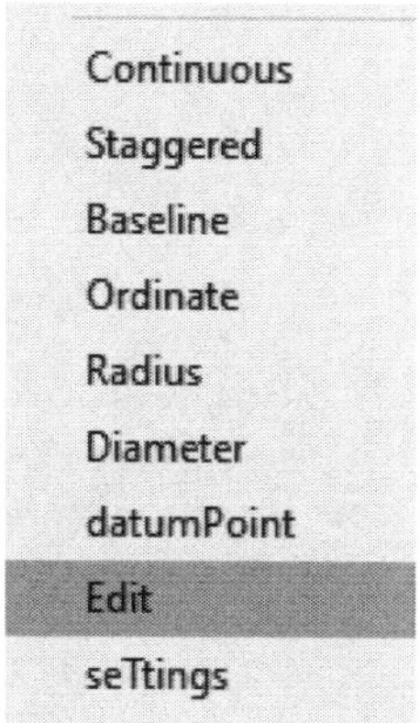

[Continuous/Staggered/Baseline/Ordinate/Radius/Diameter/datumPoint/Edit] <Ordinate>:
Right-click in the drawing area and select '**Edit**' or type 'E' and Click <ENTER> to edit the dimension points.

4. 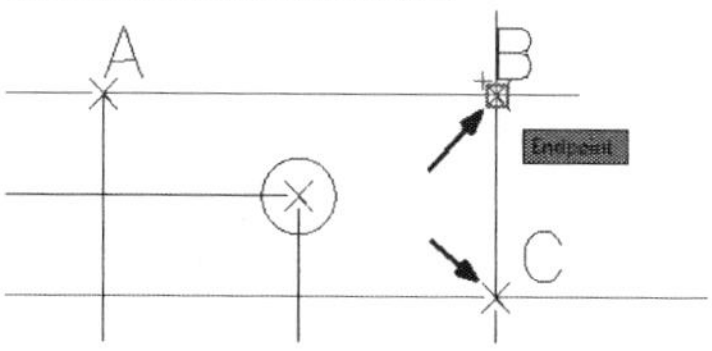

Indicate dimension point to remove, or [Add/eXit] <eXit>:
Select the points B and C as indicated.

Remove the Indicated Points.

Indicate dimension point to remove, or [Add/eXit] <eXit>:
Click <**ENTER**> to exit edit mode.

5. 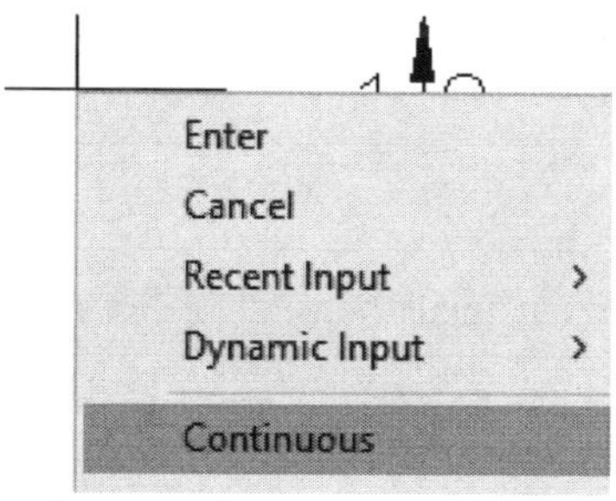

[Continuous/Staggered/Baseline/Ordinate/Radius/Diameter/datumPoint/Edit] <Ordinate>:
Right-click in the drawing area and select '**Continuous**' or type 'C' and Click <ENTER> to change back to continuous dimensions.

6. 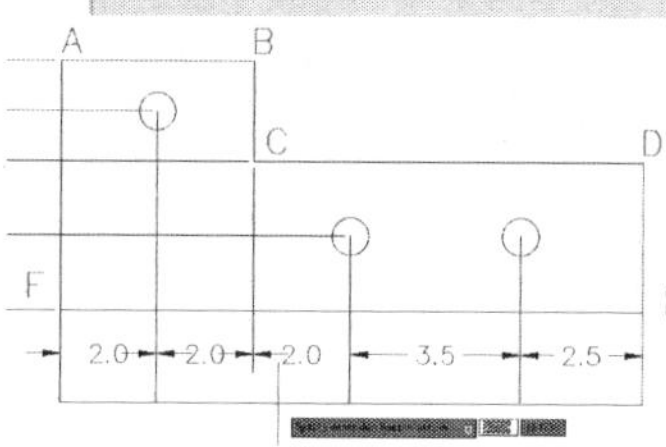

[Continuous/Staggered/Baseline/Ordinate/Radius/Diameter/datumPoint/Edit] <Continuous>:
Select a placement point below the geometry to create the horizontal dimensions.
Note: You have to switch to the type of dimension style you want to use or whichever style was last selected is the default. Notice that the vertical dimensions are erased.

Automatic Dimensions

Command Locator

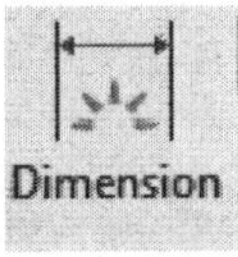

Ribbon/Annotate/Dimensions	**Dimension**
Command	DIM
RMB Shortcut Menu	Angular/Baseline/Continue/Ordinate/Align/Distribute/Layer/Undo

Command Overview

Creates a series of dimensions quickly from selected objects.

General Procedures:

1. Start the **DIM** command.
2. Select the geometry to be dimensioned.
3. Move the cursor to position and define the type of dimension to place. The dimension will preview.
4. Left click to place the dimension.

Tips & Tricks

- *If object snaps are interfering with object selection or dimension placement, either zoom in or Click F3 to turn off running object snaps.*
- *When specifying points for a linear dimension, the direction that you move the cursor determines whether you create a horizontal, vertical, or aligned dimension.*
- *To prevent creating an aligned dimension, turn on Ortho mode by Clicking F8.*

Command Exercise

Exercise 9-10 – Automatic Dimensions

Drawing Name: **dim4.dwg**
Estimated Time to Completion: 10 Minutes

Scope

Dimension the object using the automatic dimension tool. Practice changing the cursor position to place different dimension types.

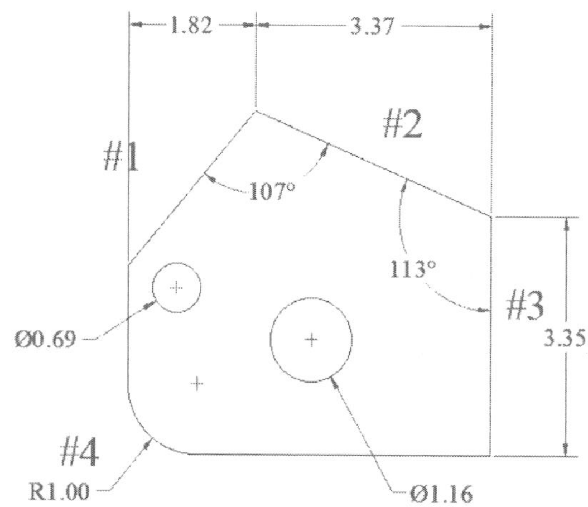

Solution

1.  Turn OSNAPS **OFF**.

2. 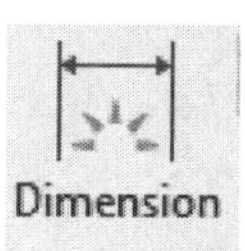

Invoke the **Dimension** command (**dim**) on the Annotate tab on the ribbon.

3. 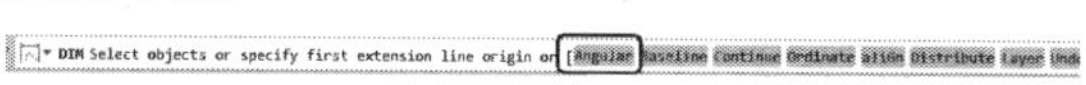 Click on **Angular**.

4. 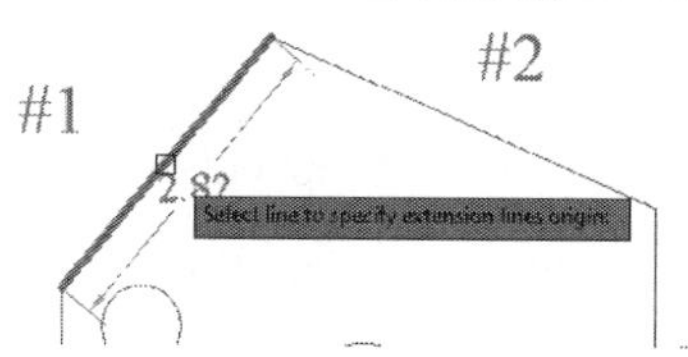

Select arc, circle, line, or <specify vertex>:
Pick the line segment marked #1.

5.

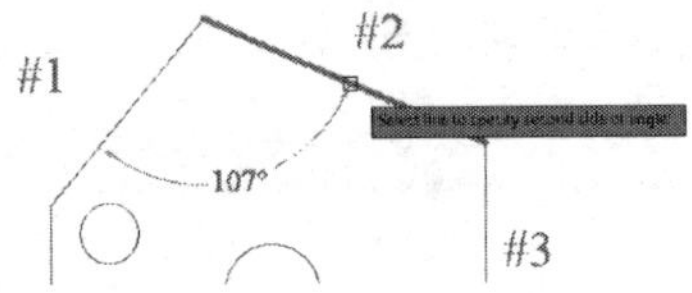

Select second line:
Pick the line segment marked #2.

Note that the preview changes to an angular dimension.

6.

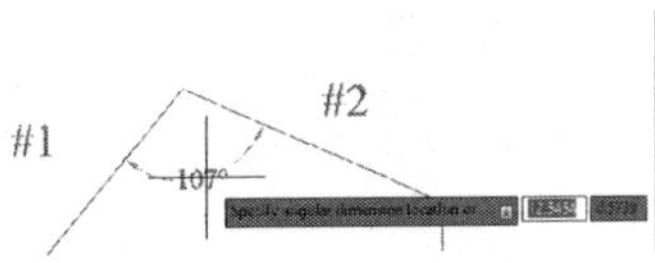

Specify dimension arc line location or [Mtext/Text/Angle]:
Select a location for the dimension.

Note that you are still in the dimension command.

7.

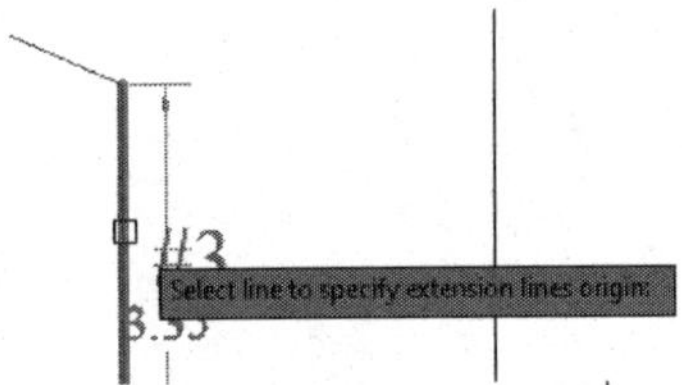

Select arc, circle, line, or <specify vertex>:
Pick the line segment marked #3.

Ignore the vertical dimension that is previewed.

8.

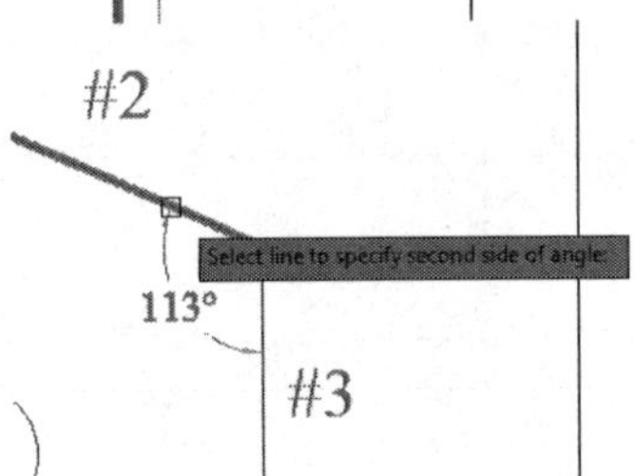

Select second line:
Pick the line segment marked #2.

9.

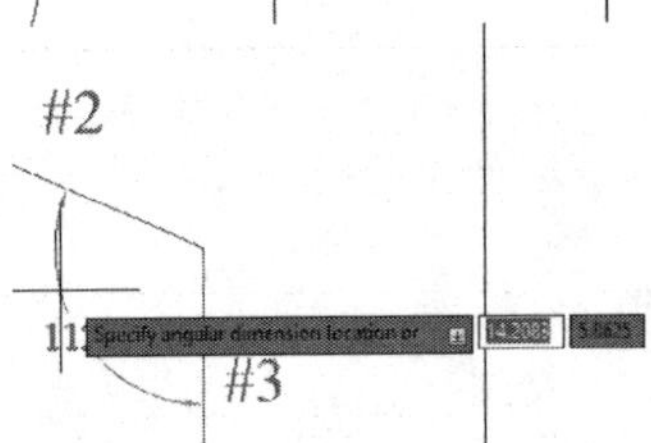

Specify dimension arc line location or [Mtext/Text/Angle]:
Select a location for the dimension.

10.

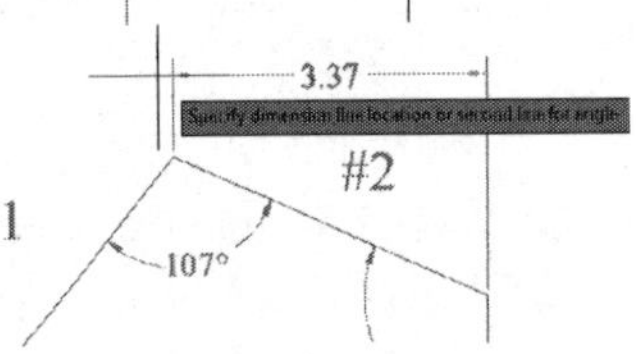

Select Line #2.

Pull the dimension straight up and place.

Note that the direction you move the cursor will determine what type of dimension is placed—aligned, horizontal, or vertical.

11.

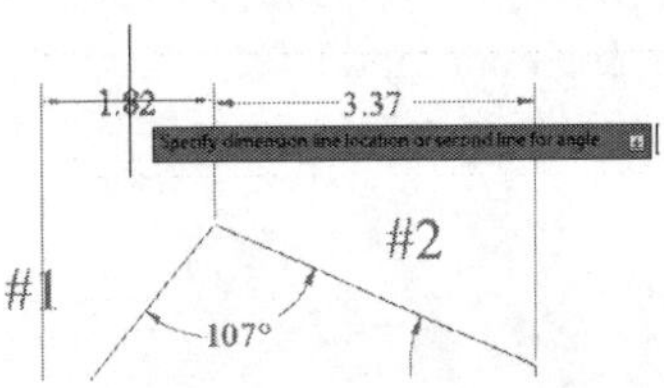

Select Line #1.

Pull the dimension straight up and place.

Note that if you select the endpoint of the previous dimension you can align the two dimensions.

12. 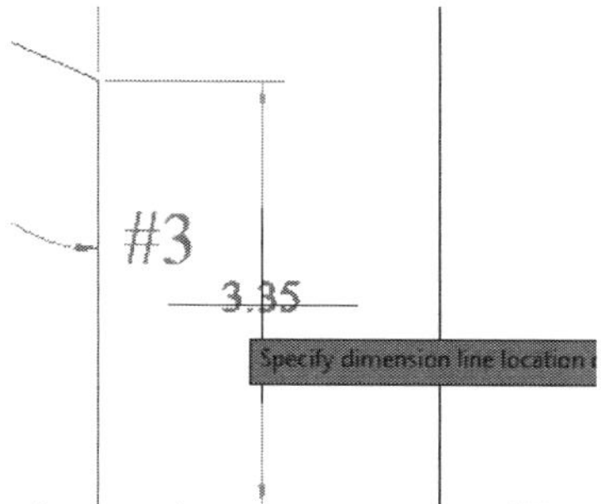

Select Line #3 and place a vertical dimension to the right of the line.

13. 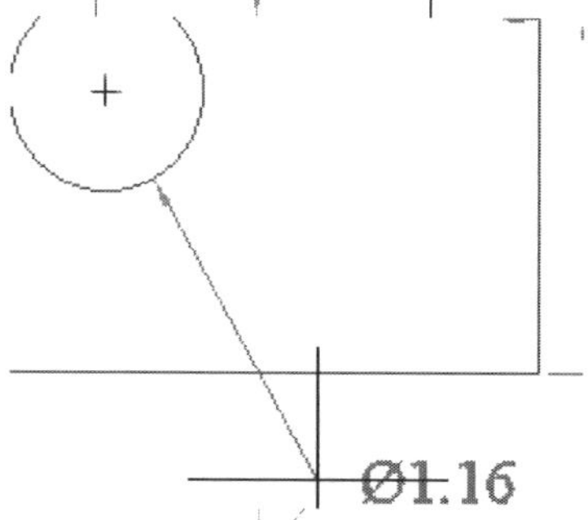

Select the large circle.

Select the outside circumference of the circle, not the center or inside the circle. Do not select any of the QUAD snaps.

Place the dimension outside the figure.

14. 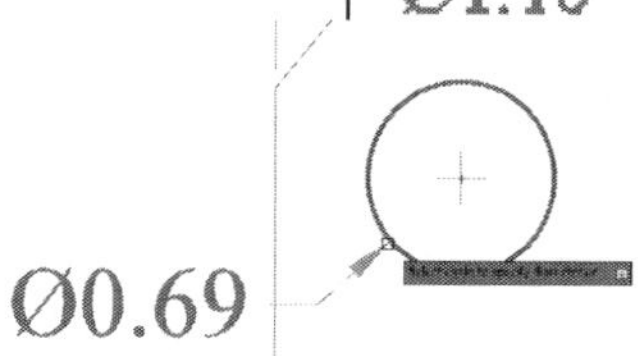

Repeat for the small circle.

15. 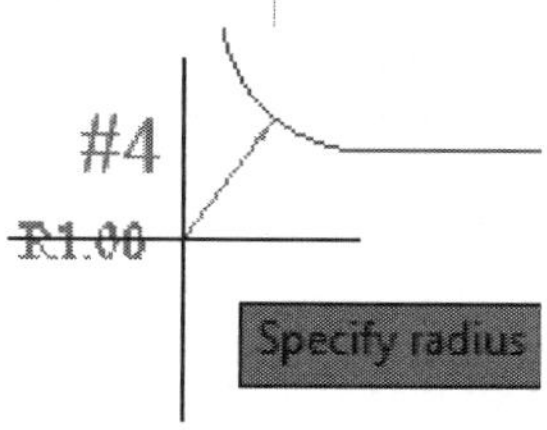

Select the radius of the fillet to place the last dimension. Left pick to place the dimension outside the figure.

Ordinate Dimension

Command Locator

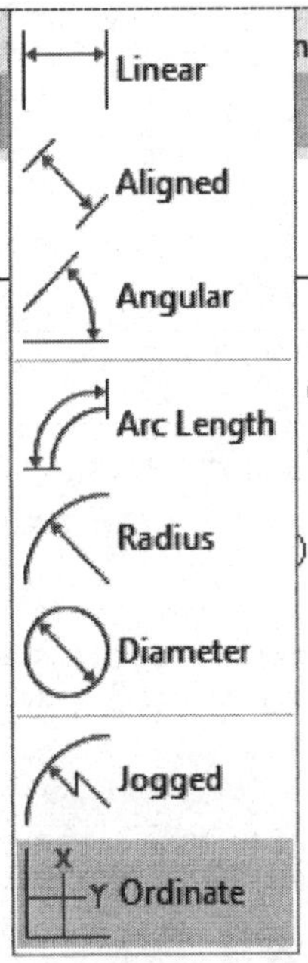

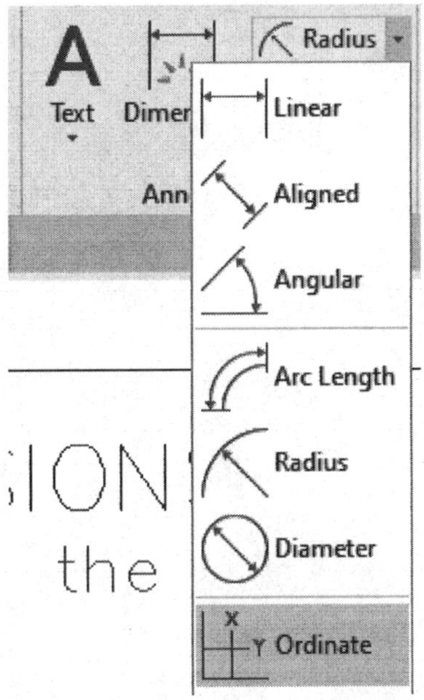

Ribbon/Annotate/Dimensions	**DIMORDinate**
Ribbon/Annotation	**DIMORDinate**
Shortcut	**DIMORD**

Command Overview

This dimension tool places ordinate dimensions in both the horizontal and vertical directions. You can add and delete points as well as set the origin.

In order for the dimensions to appear properly, you need to set the origin, or 0,0 coordinate, that all the dimensions are measured from. To do that, use the UCS command to identify the 0,0 point by selecting an endpoint or vertex of the geometry.

General Procedures:

1. Set the Origin for the ordinate dimensions using the UCS command. Type UCS, Origin, select the point to be used for the 0,0 location for the ordinate dimensions.
2. Start the **DIMORD** command.
3. Select the endpoint for the ordinate dimension extension line.
4. Select the location for the dimension text.

Tips & Tricks

- *If you do not want jogs in the **ordinate** leaders, turn on Ortho mode [F8].*
- *Set the UCS origin BEFORE placing ordinate dimensions.*

Command Exercise

Exercise 9-11 – Ordinate Dimensions

Drawing Name: **dimord.dwg**
Estimated Time to Completion: 10 Minutes

Scope

Use the Ordinate Dimension tool to place vertical and horizontal dimensions. Set the Origin for the Ordinate Dimension by setting the UCS.

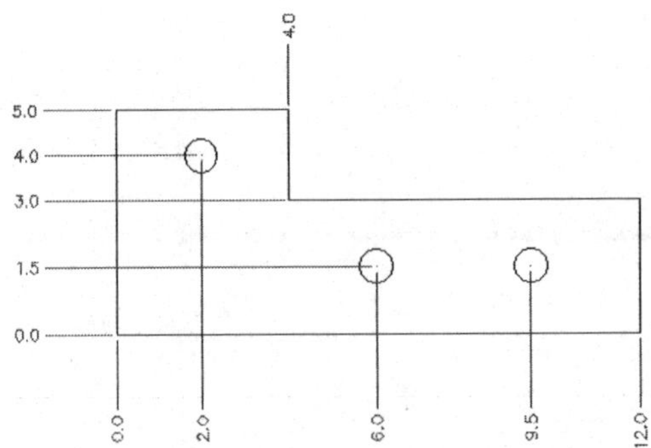

Solution

1.  Turn OSNAPS **ON**.

2. 

Type **UCS** on the command line.

3. 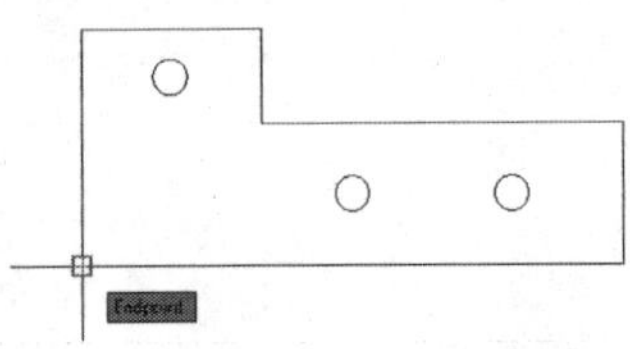 Select the lower left corner of the object to set the origin for the ordinate dimensions.

   Click <**ENTER**> when prompted to specify the X-axis.

4. 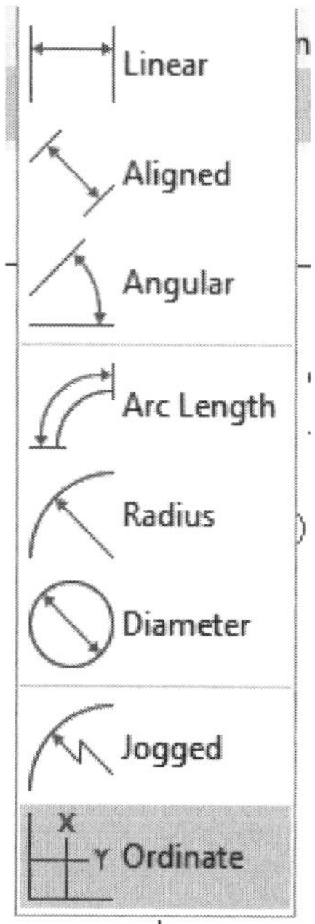

Select the **Ordinate** Dimension tool.

The prompt will ask you to select a feature.

5. 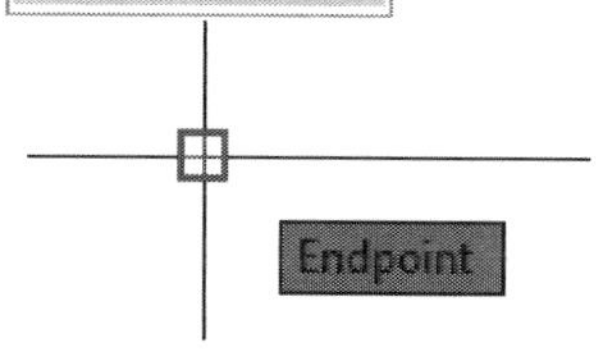

Select the same point as the origin.

6. 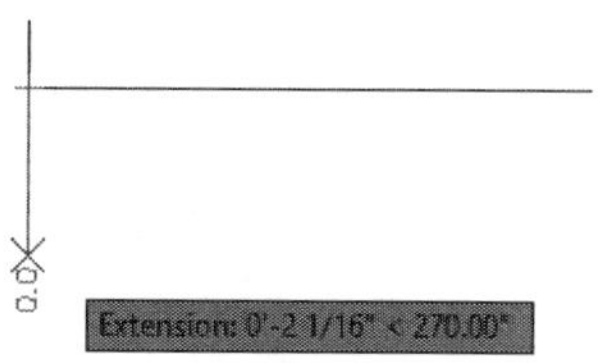

Bring the mouse down vertically to place the dimension.

LMB to place.

7. 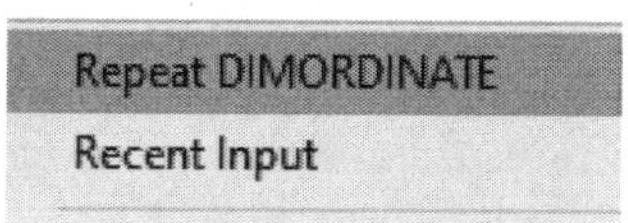

Right click and select **Repeat DIMORDINATE.**

8. 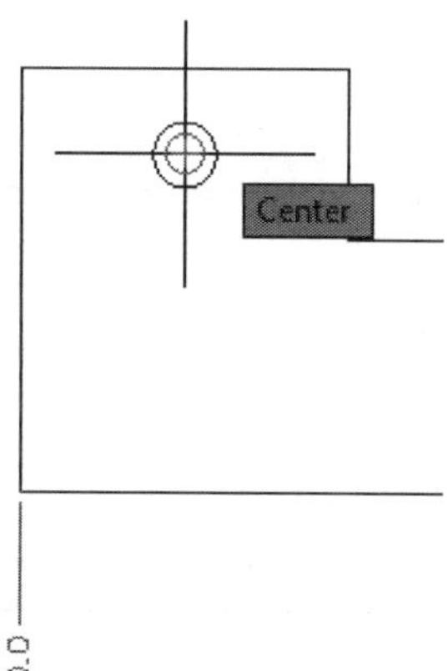

Select the center of the circle.

9. 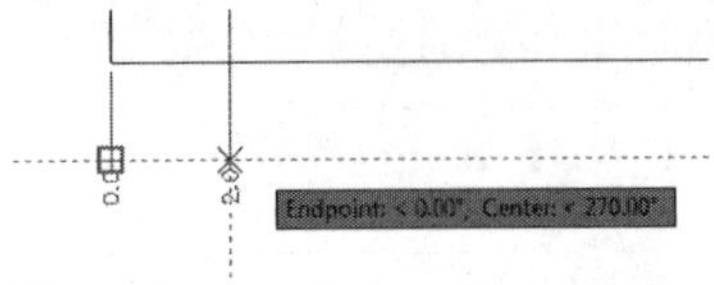

Use Object Tracking to line up the next ordinate dimension.

10. Place the remaining dimensions using the DIMORDINATE tool.

Dimension Space

Command Locator

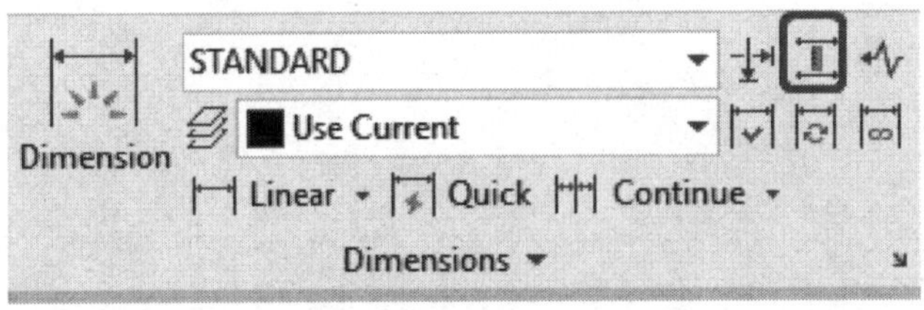

Ribbon/Annotate/Dimensions	**Dimension Space**
Command	**DIMSPACE**

Command Overview

This dimension tool aligns and/or spaces linear and angular dimensions. It uses the spacing value set in the DIMDLI system variable. You can also set the spacing value within the command.

General Procedures:

1. Start the **DIMSPACE** command.
2. Select the dimension to be used as the anchor for the spacing.
3. Set the spacing value or click ENTER to accept the system value setting.
4. Select the dimensions to be repositioned.

Tips & Tricks

Use (getdist) to set the distance between dimensions "on the fly"

Command Exercise

Exercise 9-12 – Dimension Space

Drawing Name: **dimspace.dwg**
Estimated Time to Completion: 5 Minutes

Scope

Use the DIMSPACE tool to adjust the spacing of the overlapping linear dimensions. It can also be used to align dimensions.

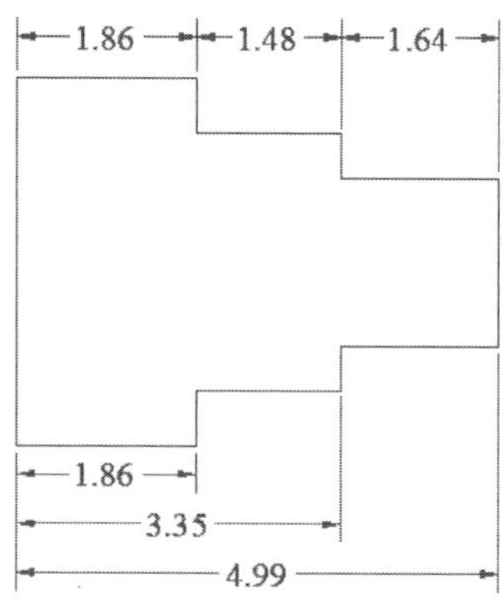

Solution

1. 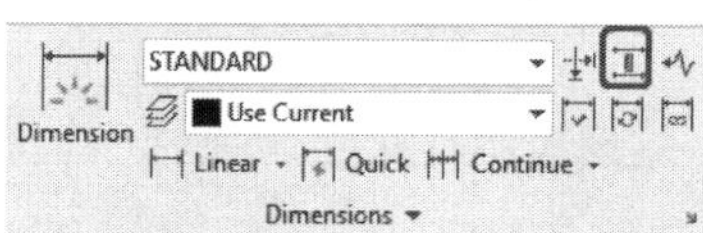

Select the **DIMSPACE** tool.

2. 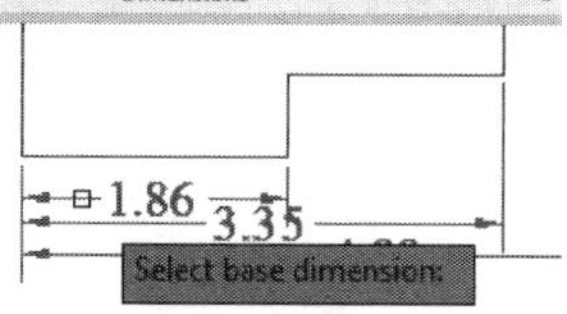

Select the lower 1.86 dimension.

It will highlight when you mouse over it to indicate it will be selected.

3. 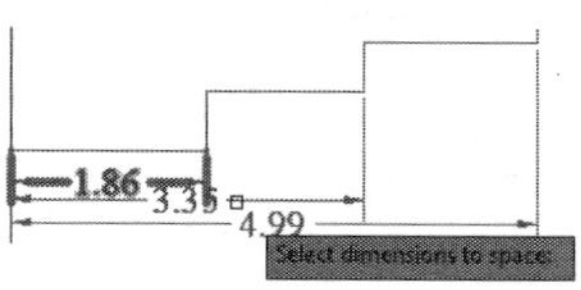

Select the **3.35** dimension.

4. 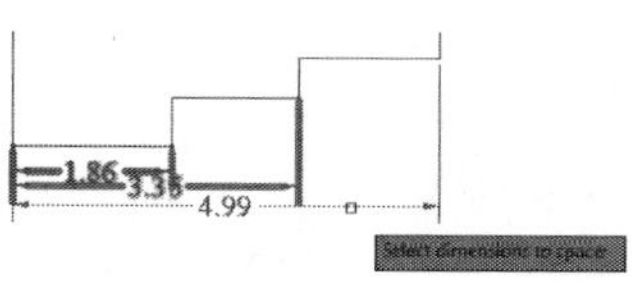

Select the **4.99** dimension.

Click **ENTER** to complete the selections.

5. 

You will be prompted to enter a spacing value or select Auto.

Auto is the default and uses the value stored in the DIMDLI system variable.

6. 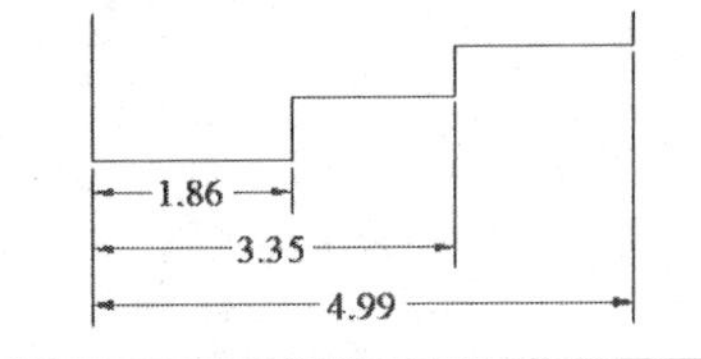

The dimensions will adjust to the correct spacing.

7. 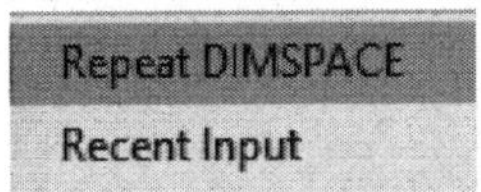

Right click and select **Repeat DIMSPACE**.

8. 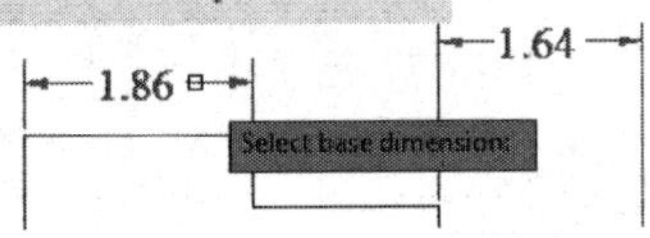

Select the upper 1.86 dimension.

It will highlight when you mouse over it to indicate it will be selected.

9. 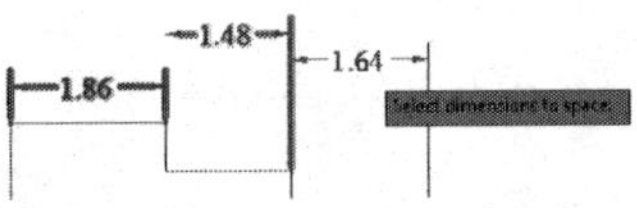

Select the 1.48 and 1.64 dimensions.

Click **ENTER** to complete the selection.

10. 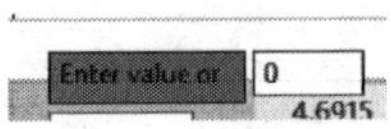

Type **0** for the value.

11. 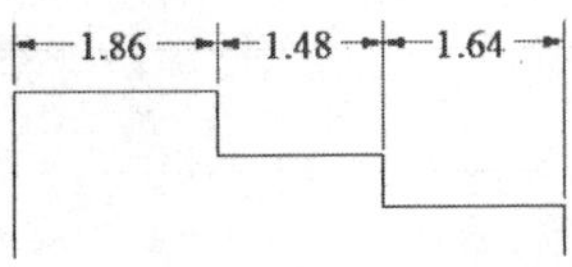

The dimensions are now aligned.

Dimension Break

Command Locator

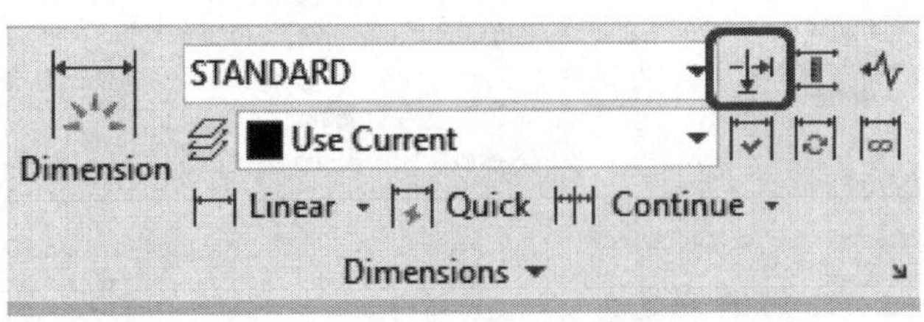

Ribbon/Annotate/Dimensions	**Dimension Break**
Command	**DIMBREAK**
RMB Shortcut Menu	**Auto/Restore/Manual**

Command Overview

This dimension tool places or removes gaps in the extension lines of dimensions. This is used to create a cleaner drawing. The AUTO option requires the user to select an object such as a line to be used as the midpoint for the gap. The RESTORE option removes any breaks placed in the dimensions. The MANUAL option requires the user to select two points to define the gap. If the AUTO option is used, the gap will adjust if the selected object or the dimension is modified.

General Procedures:

1. Start the **DIMBREAK** command.
2. Select the dimension to place the gap (to be broken).
3. Select the geometry to use to break the dimension (this can be another dimension or another element).

To remove a gap that was placed using DIMBREAK:

1. DIMBREAK <enter>
2. Select the object that you would like to remove the break from.
3. R <enter> To use the "Remove" function of the tool. This will remove the breaks from the selected object.

If you have applied Dimbreaks to either a dimension or a multileader and need to remove them, please don't erase the objects and recreate them. You can use the DIMBREAK command that created the dimbreak to remove the gaps.

Command Exercise

Exercise 9-13 – Dimension Break

Drawing Name: **dimbreak.dwg**
Estimated Time to Completion: 15 Minutes

Scope

Use the DIMBREAK tool to place gaps in the extension lines using the AUTO and MANUAL methods. Use the RESTORE option to eliminate the breaks.

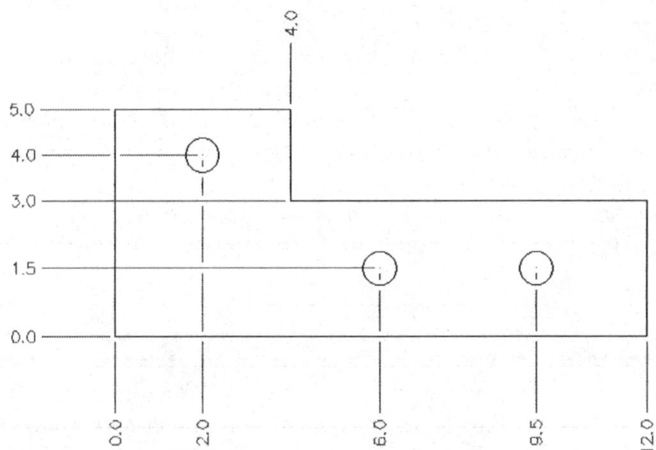

Solution

1. 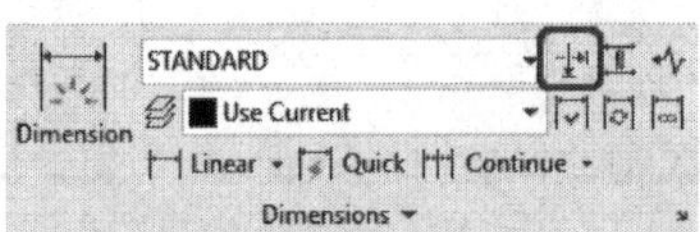

Select the **DIMBREAK** tool from the Annotate tab on the ribbon.

2. 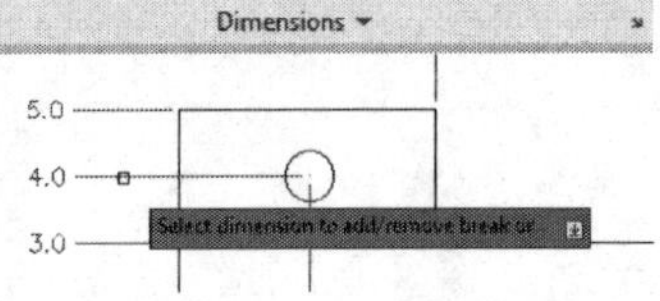

Select the 4.0 vertical dimension.

3. 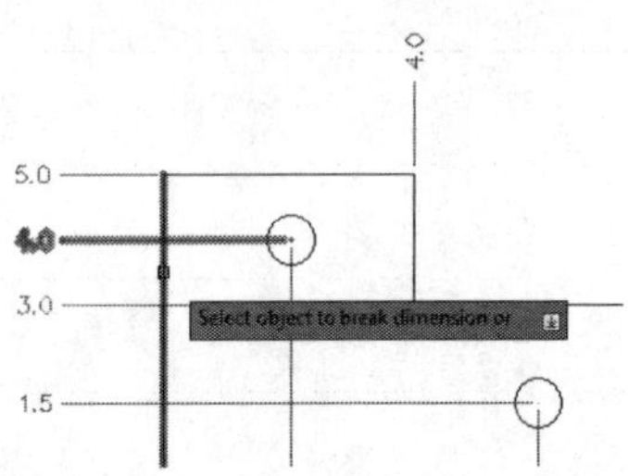

Select the polygon object.

4.

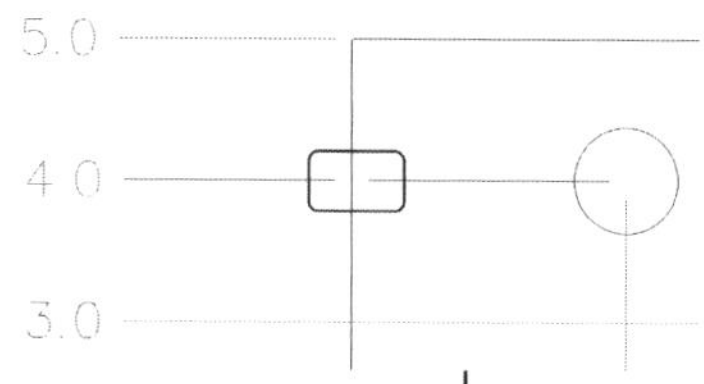

A gap is placed in the dimension.

Click **ENTER** to exit the command.

5.

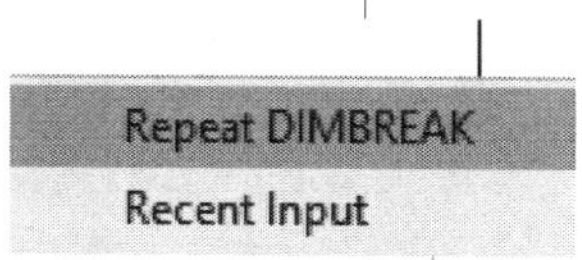

Right click and select **Repeat DIMBREAK**.

6.

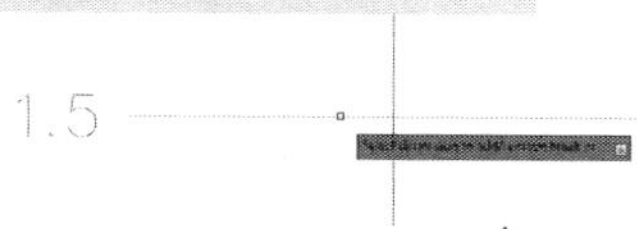

Select the 1.5 vertical dimension.

7.

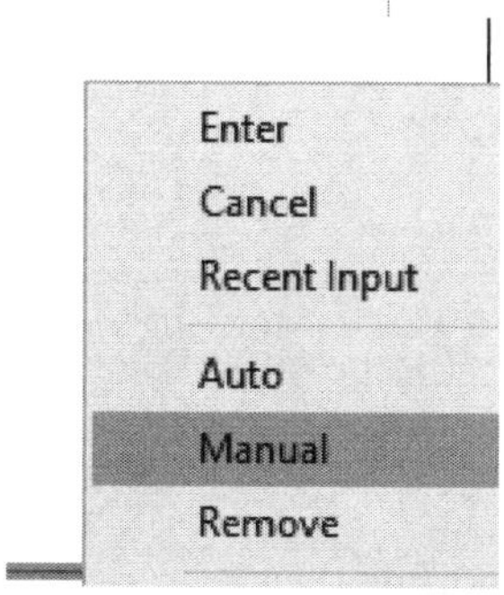

RMB and select **Manual**.

8.

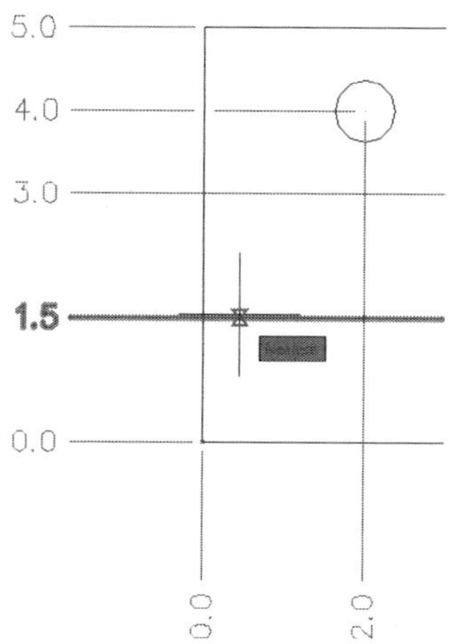

Select a location to the right of the horizontal 0.0 dimension line between the circle and the 1.5 dimension as your first point.

Refer to image.

9.

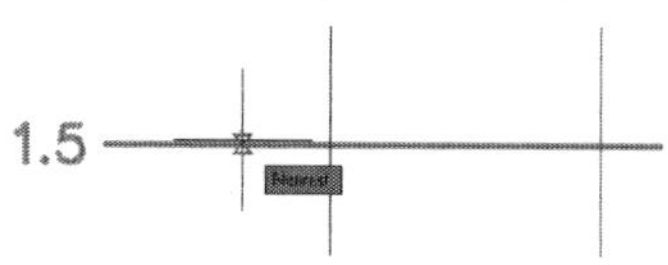

Select a point between the object and the extension line as the second point.

Shift + Right click to use an NEA osnap.

10. 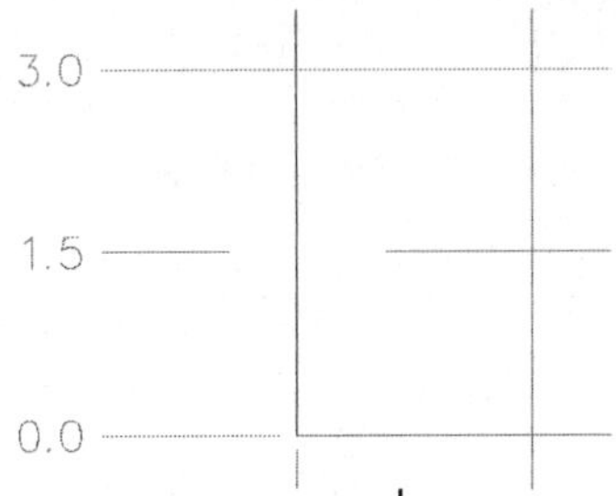

Note the gap created.

Compare the manual gap placed with the AUTO gap placed.

11. 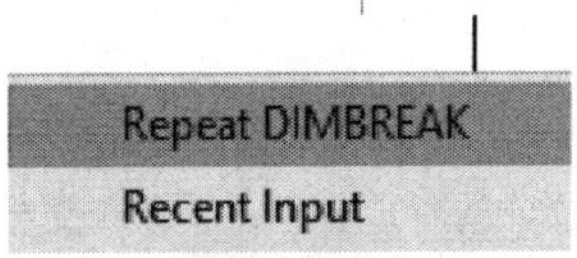

Right click and select **Repeat DIMBREAK**.

12. 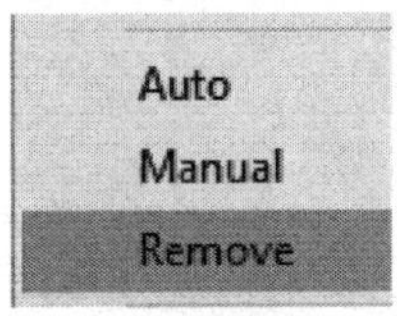

Select the 1.5 vertical dimension you just modified.

RMB and select **Remove**.

The gap is removed.

13. 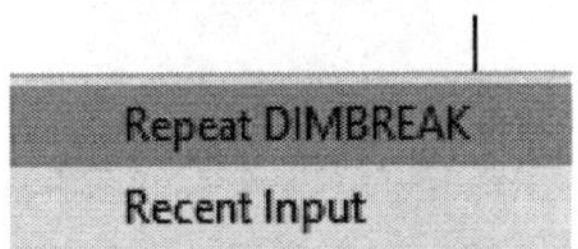

Right click and select **Repeat DIMBREAK**.

14. 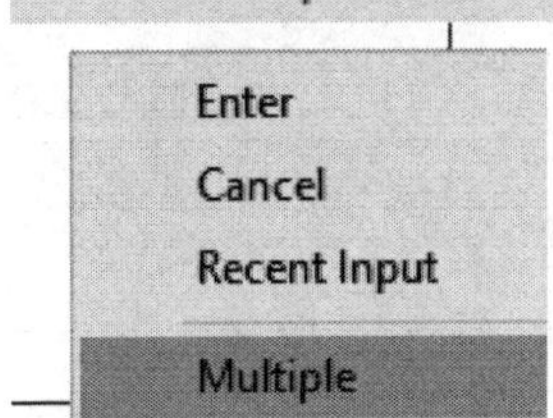

RMB and select **Multiple**.

15. 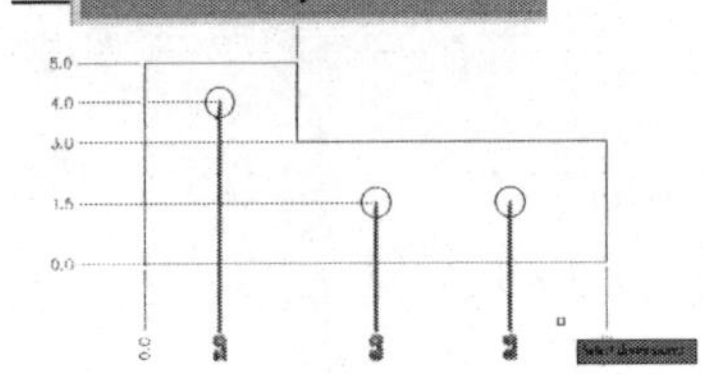

Select the three middle horizontal dimensions.

Click **ENTER** to indicate you are done selecting.

16. 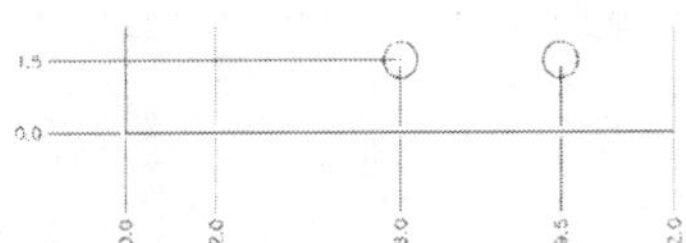

RMB and select **ENTER**.

A gap is automatically placed for all three dimensions without having to select the object.

Dimension Style

Command Locator

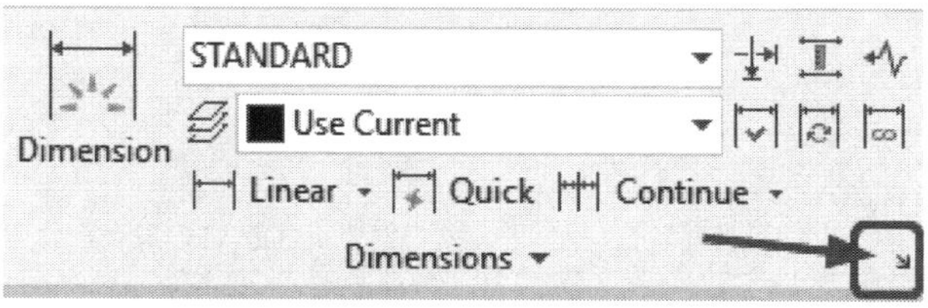

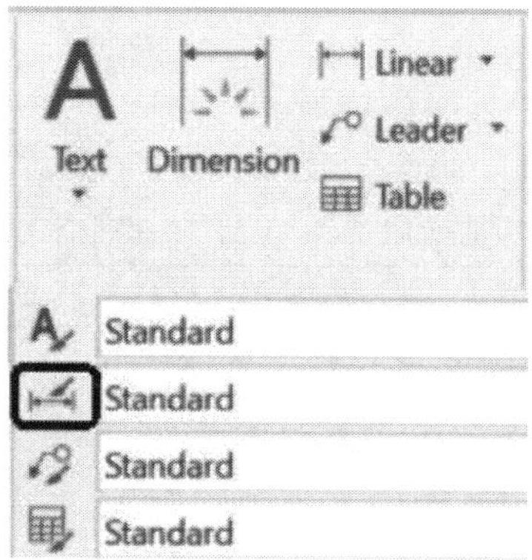

Ribbon/Home/Dimension Pull-down	**DIMSTYLE**
Ribbon/Annotate/Dimensions	**DIMSTYLE**
Command	**Dimstyle**
Alias	**D**
Dialog Box	**Dimension Style Manager**

Command Overview

The Standard Dimension Style is sufficient for most beginners. However, it may be necessary to make minor changes to the Standard Dimension Style or create additional Dimension Styles. The Dimension Style Manager dialog box lists and previews selected dimension styles. Select Modify to access the Modify Dimension Style options. Changes made to the Dimension Styles will globally affect the dimensions in the drawing that reference the style being modified, unless the change was made to an individual dimension.

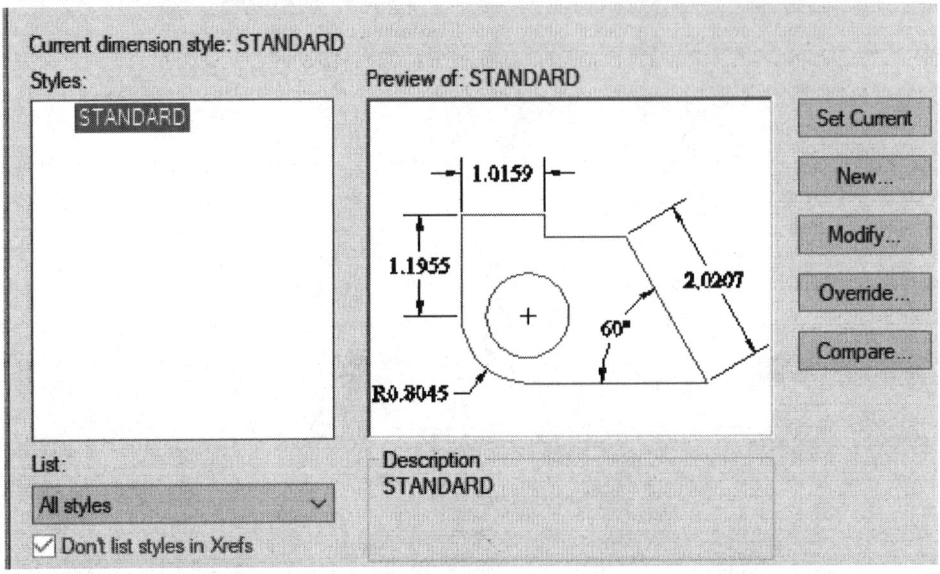

*Use the **Dimension Style Manager** dialog box to make global changes to dimensions in the drawing. This will automatically apply modifications made to the dimension style. When creating a subset from a dimension style with changes to specific dimensions, select New, then choose the type of dimension from the list alongside "Use for." Then select Continue to make the desired changes.*

Dimension Style Manager	Overview
Current Dimstyle	Displays the name of the current dimension style.
Styles:	Lists the dimension styles in the drawing.
List	Controls the display of either all dimension style names in the drawing or only the dimension styles in use.
Preview of : Standard	Shows a Preview image of the current [Standard] dimension style.
Set Current	Makes a selected dimension style current.
New…	Invokes the New Dimension Style dialog box where a new style name can be typed, starting with or based on a selected dimension style, for all or selected dimensions (linear, angular, radial…etc.).
Modify…	Invokes the Modify Dimension Style dialog box. Changes made to the current dimension style will be applied to dimensions placed in the drawing using that style (see next section).
Override…	Works similar to the Modify option; however, changes will be applied to dimensions placed after the Override modifications have been made.
Compare…	Compares selected dimension styles and displays the differences.

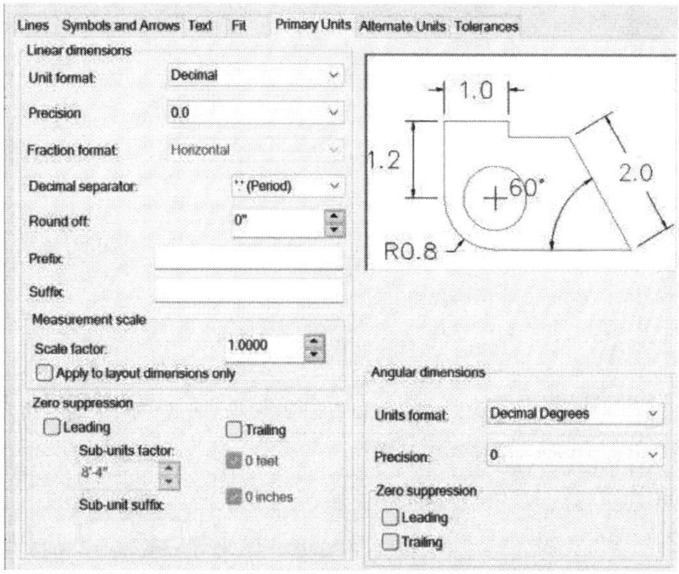

Modify Dimension Style dialog box tab	Overview	Typical Options to Change
Lines and Arrows	Controls the features of the Extension Lines and Arrowheads.	Offset from origin, colors, and linetype
Symbols and Arrows	Controls the size and the style of arrowheads.	Arrowhead style Center Marks for Circles
Text	Controls the text style, and where the text is located in relation to the dimension lines.	Text Alignment: Horizontal or Aligned with dimension line
Fit	Controls the placement of dimension text.	Sets text above, below, or beside dimension line Set the dimension as annotative
Primary Units	Controls the type and precision of dimension linear and angular units. Controls measurement scale factor when objects in the drawing have been scaled.	Linear Dimensions: Unit Format Precision Angular Dimensions: Units Format Precision Measurement Scale: Scale Factor
Alternate Units	Controls the display of Alternate Units, the Unit format, and the Multiplier for alternate units.	Display Alternate Units Precision
Tolerances	Controls Tolerance Format.	Tolerance Format Method Precision Values

General Procedures

To Create a New Dimension Style:

1. Invoke the Dimension Style command.
2. Select a dimension style to start with from the drop-down list. Select the New button, then type the New Style Name, or accept the default name.
3. Select Continue to access the Modify Dimension Style dialog box.

To Modify a Dimension Style:

1. Invoke the Dimension Style command.
2. Select the dimension style, then select the Modify button.
3. Select the appropriate tab in the Modify Dimension Style dialog box. Select OK and Close to Continue.

To Delete a Dimension Style:

1. Invoke the Dimension Style command.
2. Select the dimension style from the list, then right-click (RMB) to access the shortcut menu.
3. Select delete. The dimension style will not be deleted if it is current, or if there are any dimensions in the drawing using that dimension style.

To make a change to a specific feature of an existing Dimension Style Properties:

1. Invoke the Dimension Style command.
2. In the Dimension Style Manager box, select the dimension style to change, then select the New button.
3. From the New Dimension Style dialog box select the dimension type (Angular, Radius, etc.) from the "Use for" list. Select Continue.
4. Select the options to change from the corresponding tab in the Modify Dimension Style dialog box. Then select OK to exit.

- The Purge command can also be used to delete unreferenced Dimension Styles. Select File / Drawing Utilities / Purge (select option or All).
- The Standard Dimension Style will be adequate for most beginners.
- When creating a new dimension style, base the new style on Standard, and apply changes to it, leaving Standard alone, unless only minor changes are needed.
- Make global modifications to dimensions in the drawing by changing the Dimension Style. Existing dimensions should automatically update. If for some reason they do not update, select the dimension Update command from the Dimension toolbar or from the Dimension pull-down menu.

DIMLAYER

Command Locator

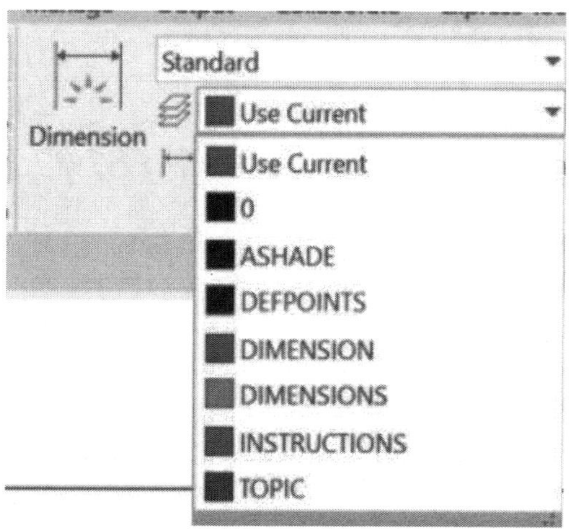

Ribbon/Annotate/Dimensions	DIMLAYER drop-down
Command	**DIMLAYER**

Command Overview

Assigns new dimensions to the specified layer. By default, this is set to use the Current or Active layer. To ensure that dimensions are placed on the correct layer, set the DIMLAYER to use the desired layer.

General Procedures:

1. Switch to the Annotate tab on the ribbon.
2. Select the desired layer from the layer drop-down list in the Dimensions panel.

Command Exercise

Exercise 9-14 – Dimension Styles

Drawing Name: **dimsty1.dwg**
Estimated Time to Completion: 20 Minutes

Scope

Dimension the object on the left using the standard dimension style. Create a new Dimension Style called TEST based on the Standard dimension style with overall scale (Geometry) of 2 (remember to set current). Dimension the object on the right.

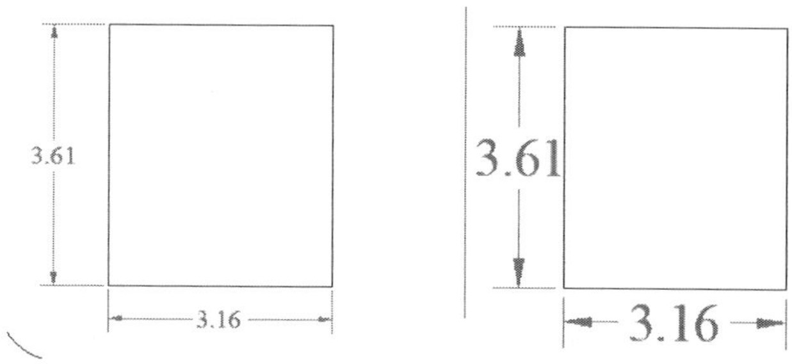

Solution

1.

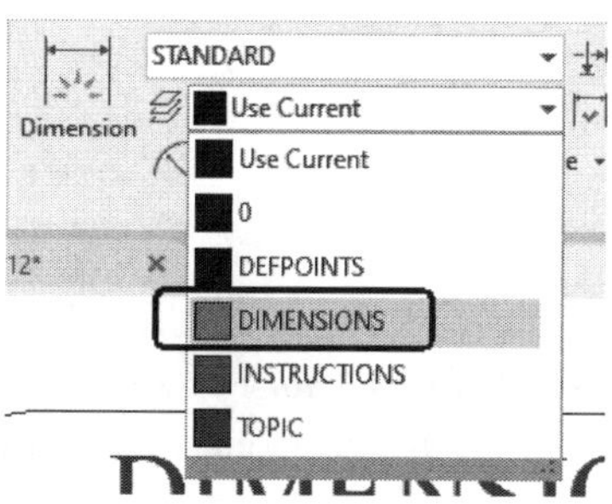

Switch to the **Annotate** tab on the ribbon.

Set the DIMLAYER to **DIMENSIONS**.

This will place any new dimensions on the DIMENSIONS layer automatically.

2.

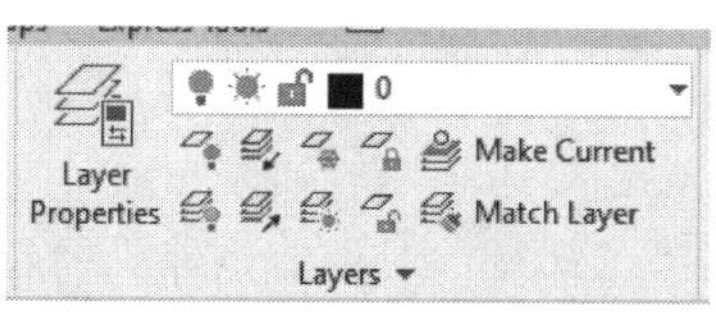

Switch to the **Home** ribbon.

Note that the current layer is **0**.

3.

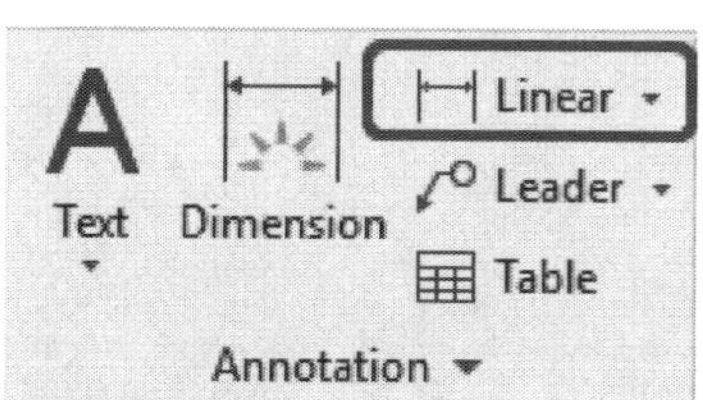

Invoke the **Linear Dimension** command (dimlinear).

Specify first extension line origin or <select object>:
Click <ENTER> to select an object.

4. 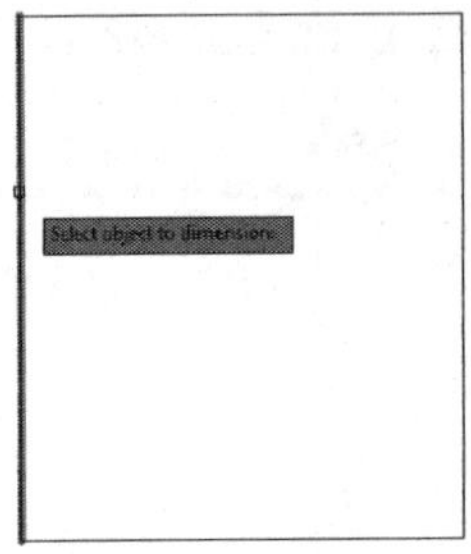

Select object to dimension:
Select the left side of the left box.

5. 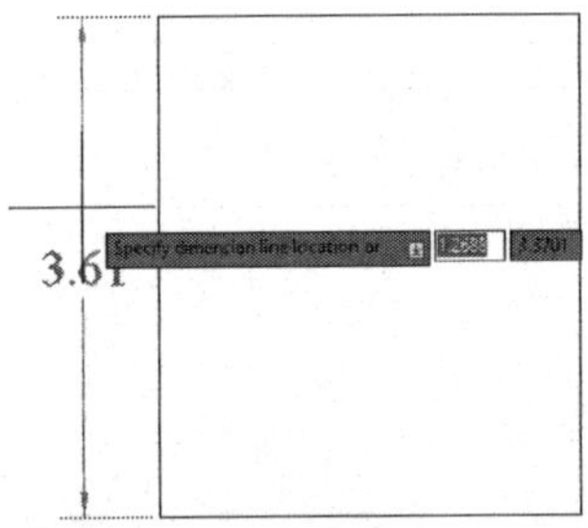

Specify dimension line location or
[Mtext/Text/Angle/Horizontal/Vertical/Rotated:
Select a location for the vertical dimension.

6. 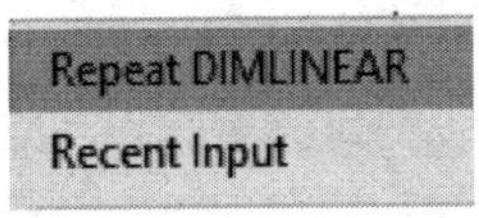

Repeat the Linear Dimension command with the RMB (dimlinear or <ENTER>).

7. 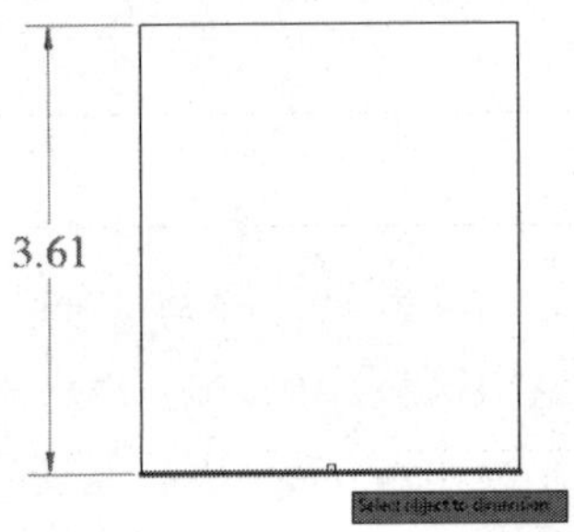

Specify first extension line origin or <select object>:
Click <ENTER> to select an object.

Select object to dimension:
Select the bottom of the left box.

8. 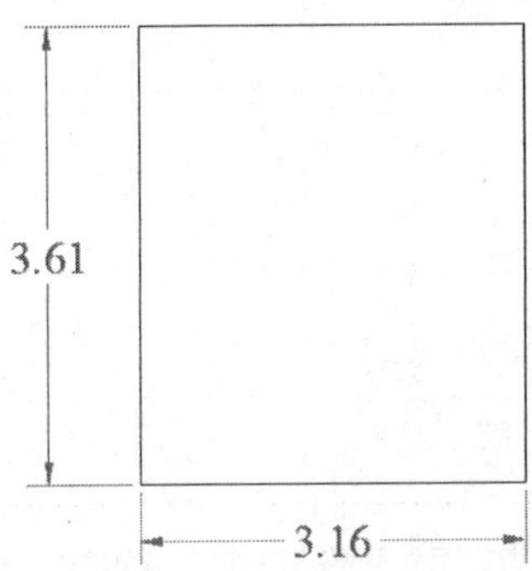

Specify dimension line location or
[Mtext/Text/Angle/Horizontal/Vertical/Rotated:
Select a location for the horizontal dimension.

Notice that the dimensions are placed on the DIMENSION layer.

9. 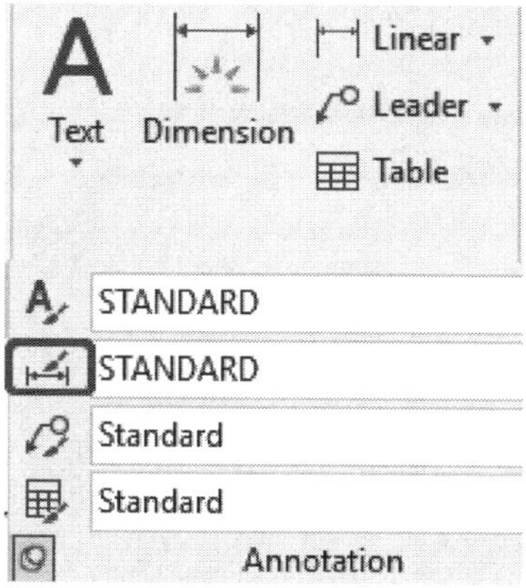

Invoke the Dimension Style command (**dimstyle**).

Expand the Annotation panel on the Home tab.

Click on the **DIMSTYLE** icon.

10. 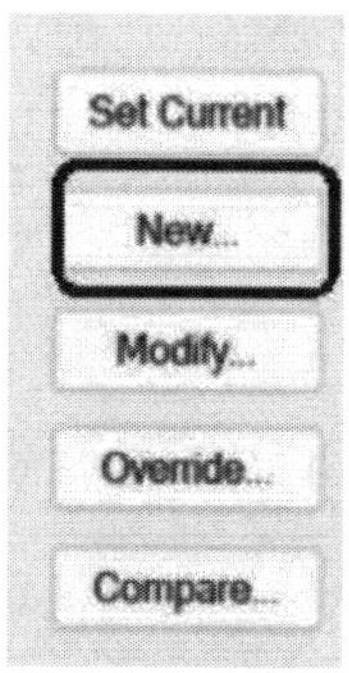

In the Dimension Style Manager dialog box, Click **New…** to create a new dimension style.

11. 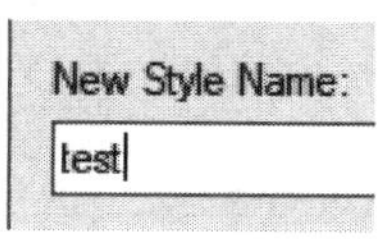

In the Create New Dimension Style dialog box, enter the new name **test** for the new dimension style based on the standard dimension style and Click **Continue**.

12. 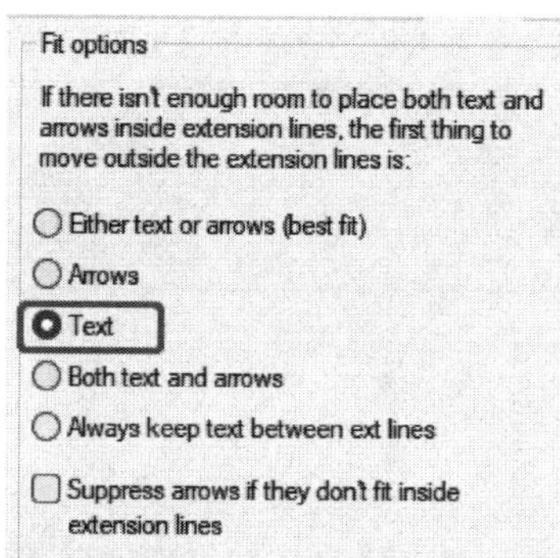

Select the **Fit** tab:

Under Fit options:
Enable **Text**.

Notice how the radial dimension changes in preview window.

13. 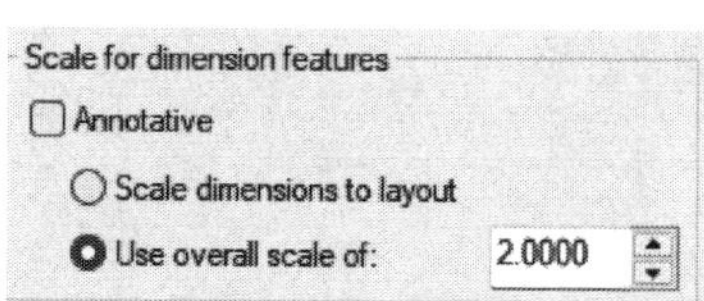

Under Scale for dimension features:

Change the overall scale to **2**.

14. 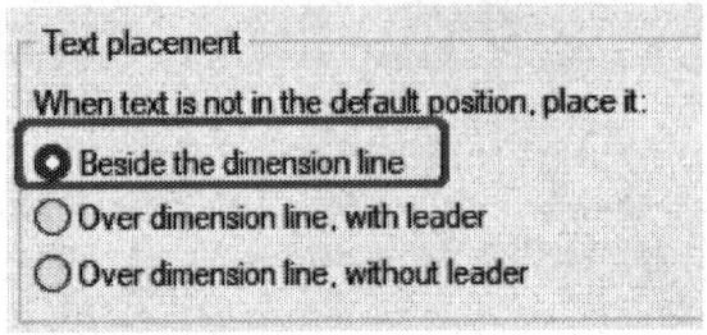

Under Text placement:

Enable **Beside the dimension line**.

15. 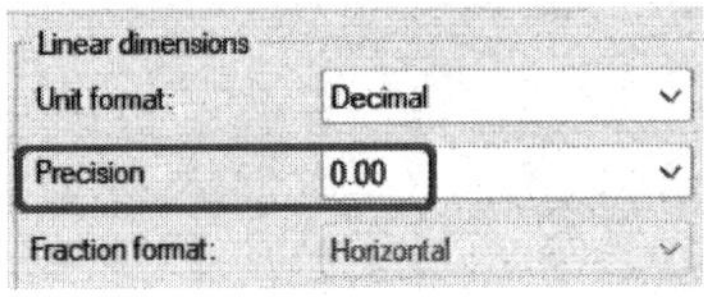

Select the **Primary Units** tab.

Under Linear Dimensions:

Set the Precision to **0.00**.

In mechanical design, you want to keep the precision for your dimensions to three decimal places or less. A good rule of thumb is that every decimal place adds 10% to the cost of fabrication.

Note how the Preview window display updates to reflect the changes.

16. 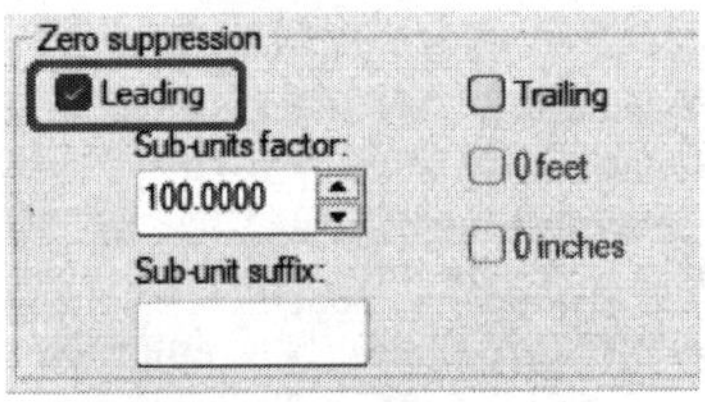

Enable **Leading** under Zero suppression.

17. 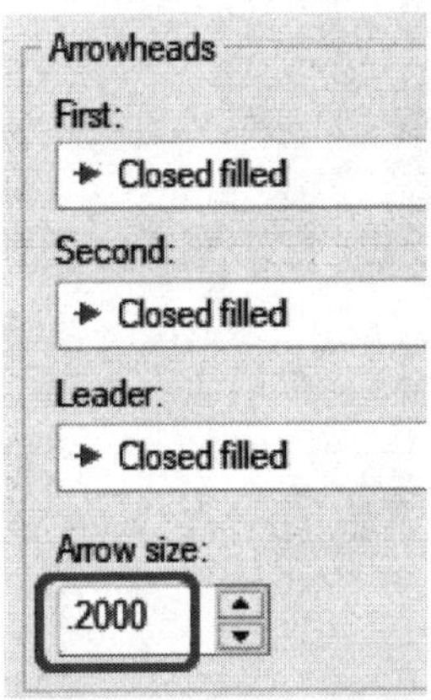

Select the **Symbols and Arrows** tab.

Under Arrowheads:

Set the Arrow size to **0.200**.

Click **OK**.

18. 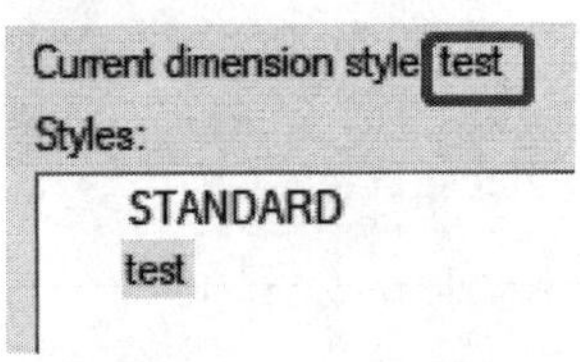

Note that the current dimension style is set to the new style.

Click **Close** to continue.

19. 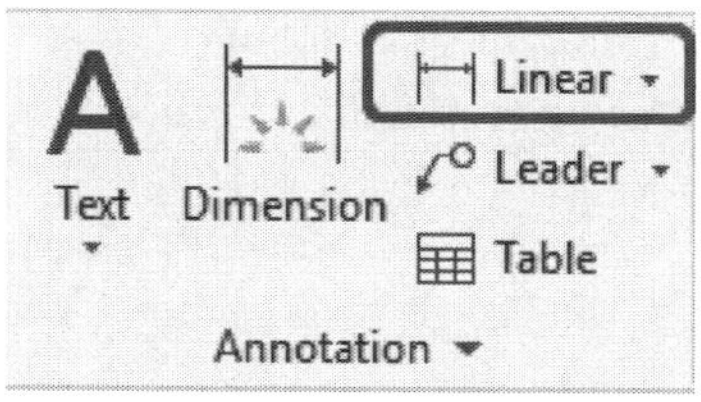

Invoke the Linear Dimension command (dimlinear).

20. 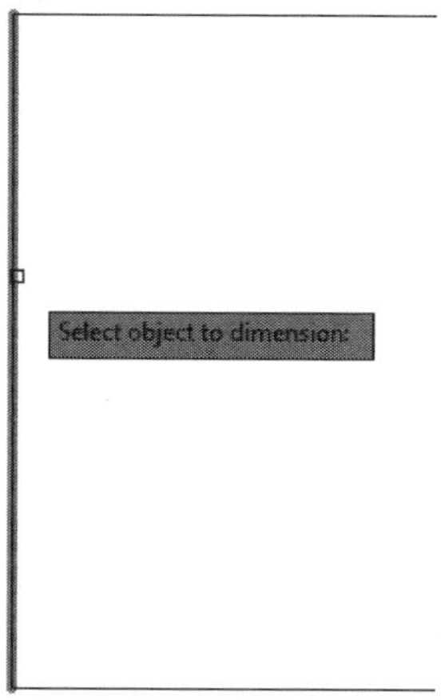

Specify first extension line origin or <select object>:
Click <ENTER> to select an object.

Select object to dimension:
Select the left side of the box on the right.

21. 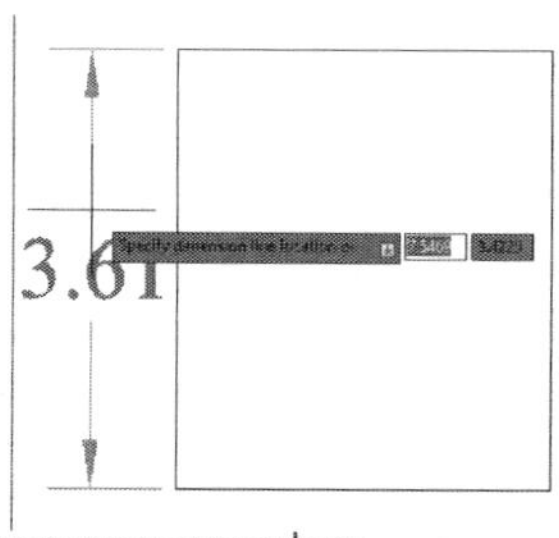

Specify dimension line location or [Mtext/Text/Angle/ Horizontal/Vertical/Rotated:
Select a location for the vertical dimension.

22. 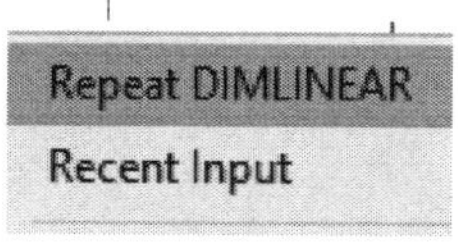

Repeat the Linear Dimension command with the RMB (dimlinear or <ENTER>).

23. 

Specify first extension line origin or <select object>:
Click <ENTER> to select an object.

Select object to dimension:
Select the bottom of the box on the right.

24. 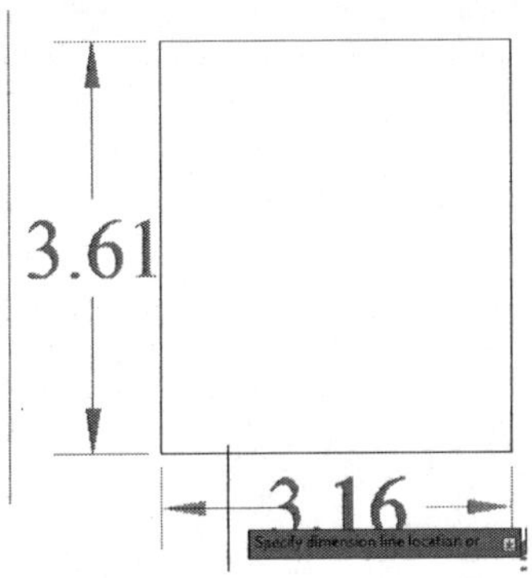

Specify dimension line location or [Mtext/Text/Angle/Horizontal/ Vertical/Rotated: Select a location for the horizontal dimension.

25. 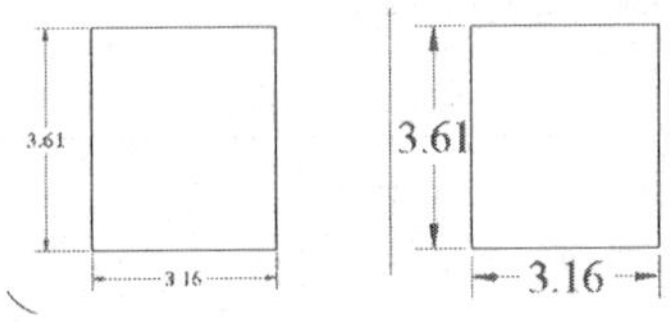

Compare the two dimension styles.

Architectural Dimensions

Architectural drawings, such as floor plans and site plans, require that you use an architectural style of dimensioning. AutoCAD comes with a pre-set architectural dimension style if you select the Tutorial-iArch.dwt, the architectural template provided with AutoCAD, or you can create your own.

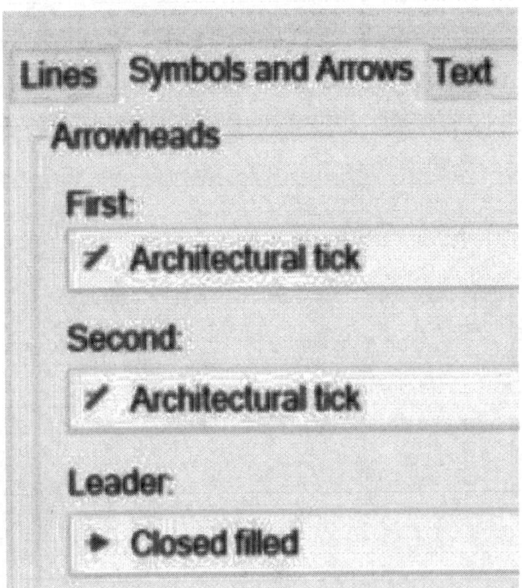

Most architectural dimension styles use tick marks instead of arrowheads on the dimension lines.
This setting is controlled in the Symbols and Arrows tab of the Dimension Style dialog.

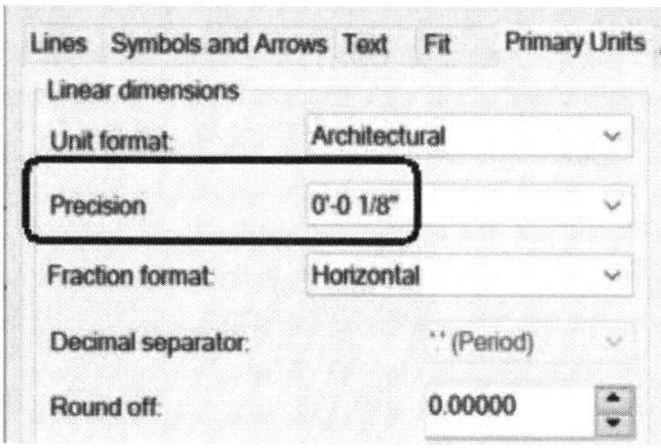

Another setting that needs to be checked for architectural dimensions is Primary Units. For those users wanting to use Feet-Inches, set the Unit Format to Architectural. I normally set my precision for 1/8" or 1/4". By default, AutoCAD sets the Precision to 1/16" which would be difficult, if not impossible, for most contractors to meet.

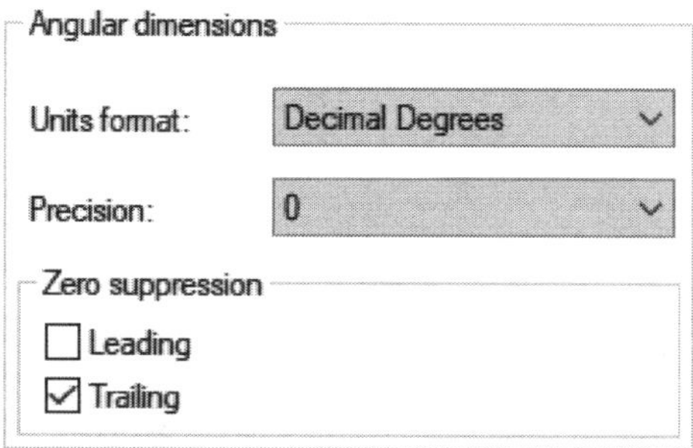

I also set the precision on my angular dimensions to 0.

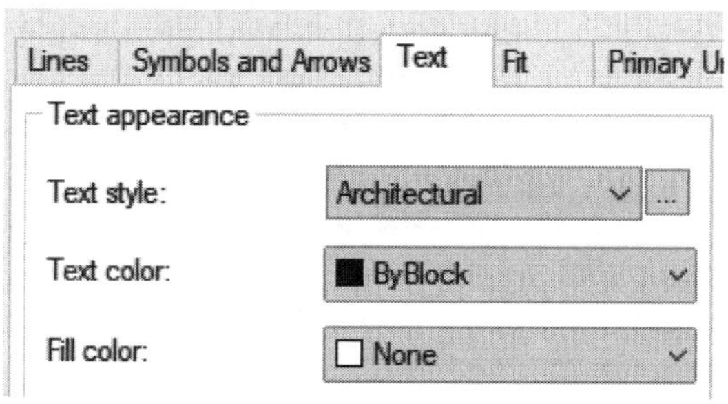

You also want to specify the Text style you want to use for your dimension style. Many architectural firms use a custom font. Before you can specify that font to be used in a dimension style, it needs to be set up as a text style.

Command Exercise

Exercise 9-15 – Architectural Dimension Style

Drawing Name: **archdims.dwg**
Estimated Time to Completion: 5 Minutes

Scope

Create an architectural dimension style.

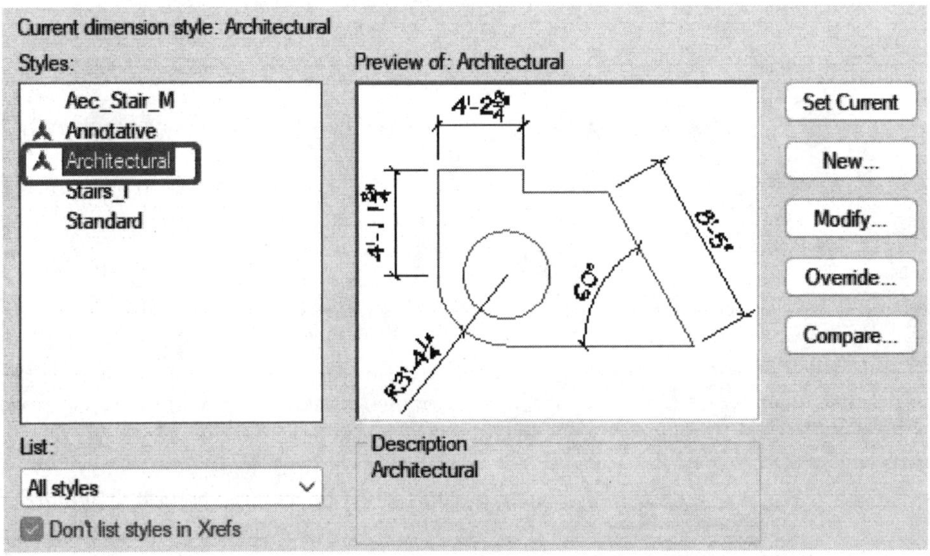

Solution

1.

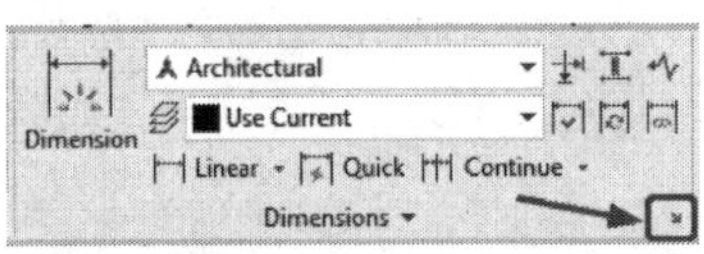

Activate the **Annotate** ribbon.

Select the arrow in the corner of the Dimension panel to launch the Dimension Style dialog box.

Or

Type **DIMSTYLE** at the command prompt.

2.

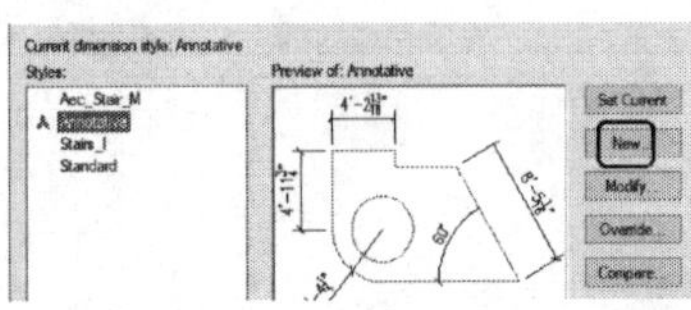

Highlight the **Annotative** dimension style which is active.

Click the **New** button to create a new architectural dimension style.

3.

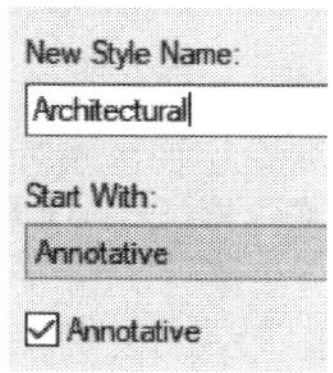

Type **Architectural** in the Style Name field.

Enable **Annotative**.

Click **Continue**.

4.

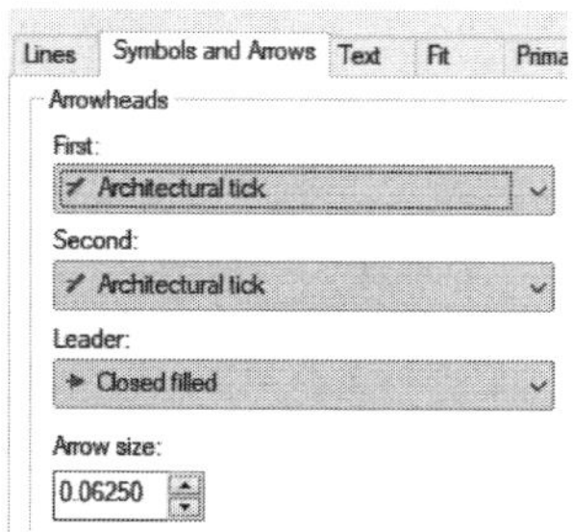

Select the **Symbols and Arrows** tab.

Note that the architectural tick is selected for the arrowheads.

5.

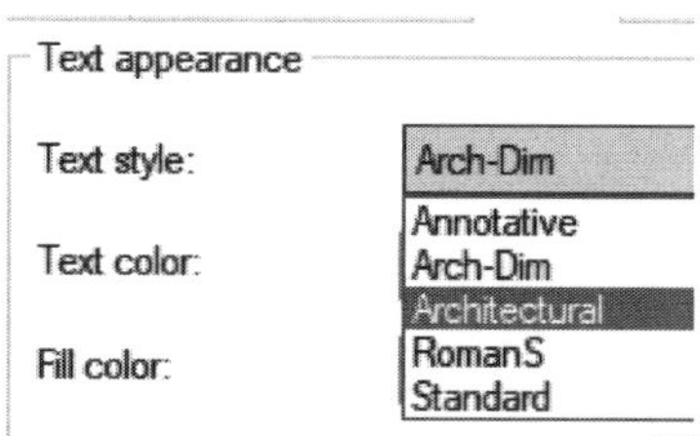

Select the **Text** tab.

Select the **Architectural** text style from the drop-down list.

6.

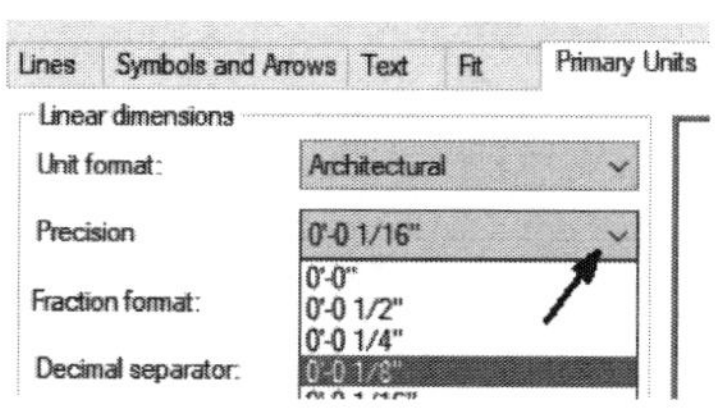

Select the **Primary Units** tab.

Set the Precision to **1/8"** for Linear Dimensions.

7.

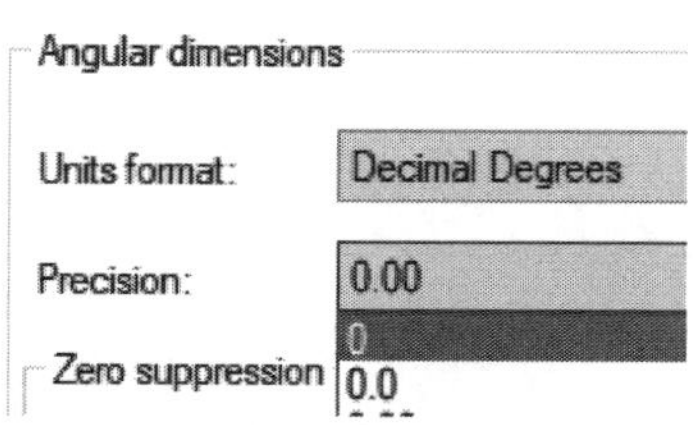

Set the Precision for Angular Dimensions to **0**.

Click **OK**.

8.

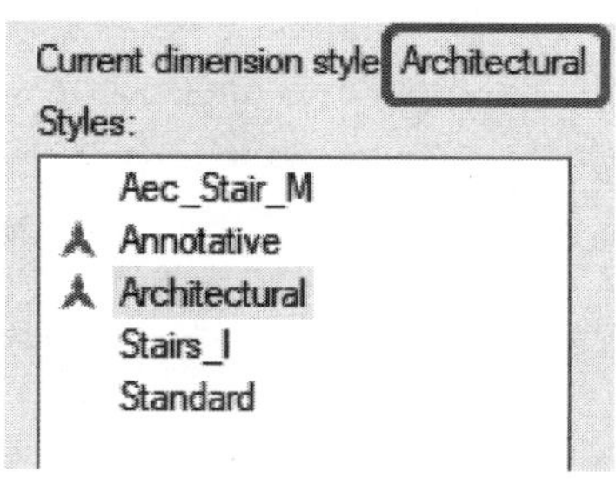

Note that the Current dimension style is set to **Architectural**.

The preview window should update.

Close the dialog.

9.

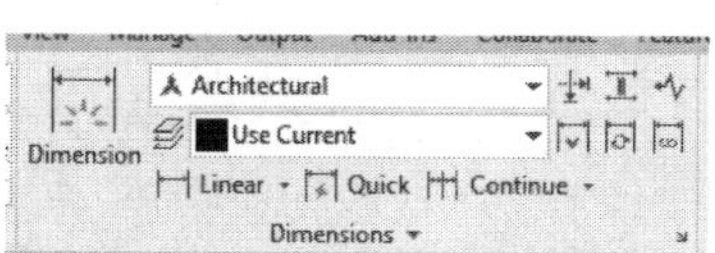

Note that the Dimension style is set to **Architectural** on the Annotate ribbon.

Save the drawings as *ex9-15.dwg*.

Command Exercise

Exercise 9-16 – Architectural Dimensions

Drawing Name: **archdims2.dwg**
Estimated Time to Completion: 15 Minutes

Scope

Add dimensions to a floor plan.

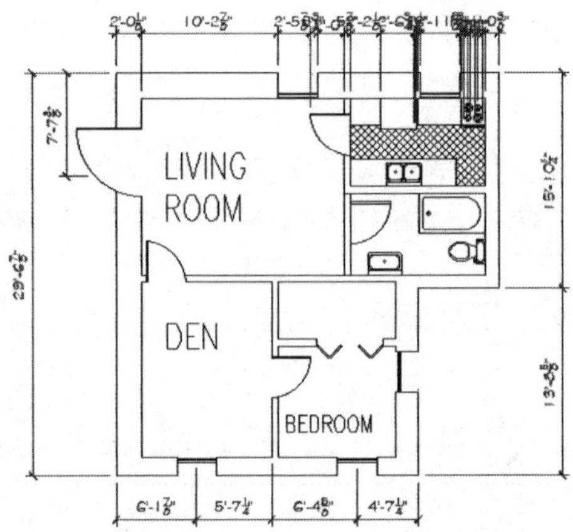

Solution

1. 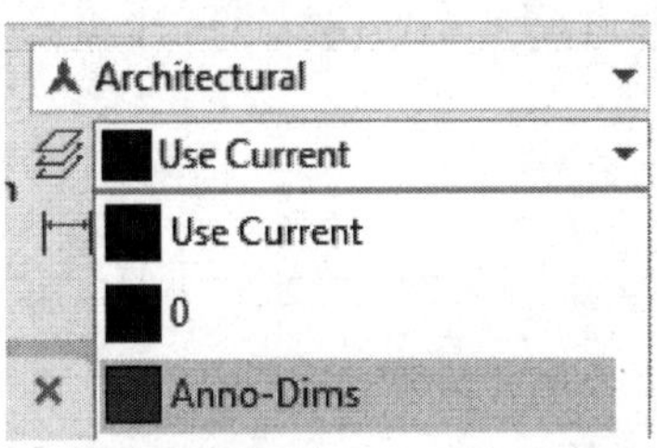

Activate the **Annotate** tab on the ribbon.

Set the DIMLAYER to **Anno-Dims**.

2. 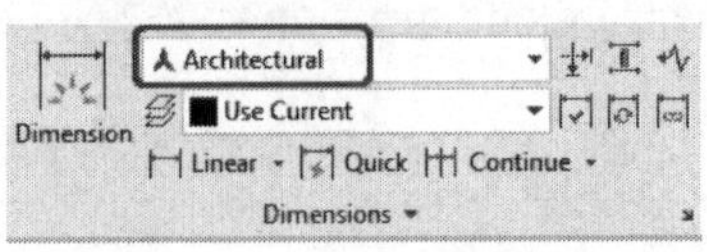

Verify that the **Architectural** dimension style is selected on the Dimensions panel.

3. 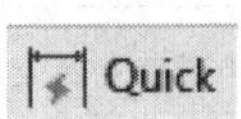

Select the **Quick Dimension** tool from the Dimensions panel on the Annotate tab.

4. 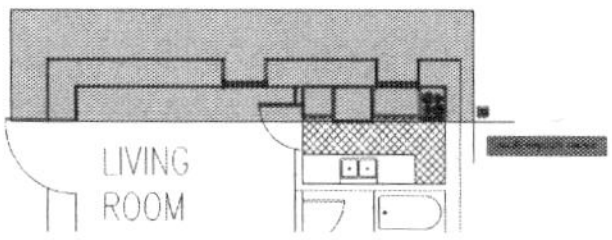

Window around the top of the floor plan.

Click **ENTER** to complete the selection.

5. 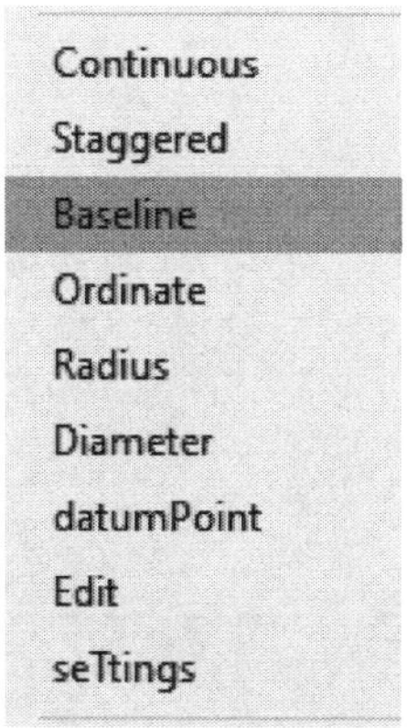

Right click and select **Baseline**.

6. 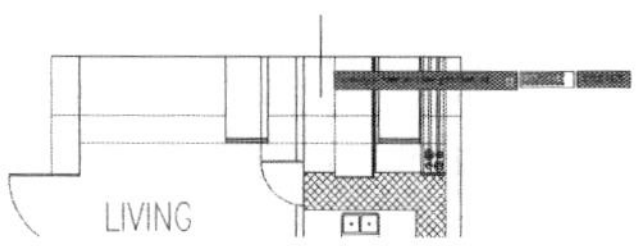

Left click above the view to place the dimensions.

7. 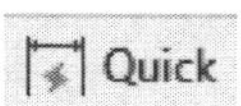

Select the **Quick Dimension** tool from the Dimensions panel on the Annotate tab.

8. 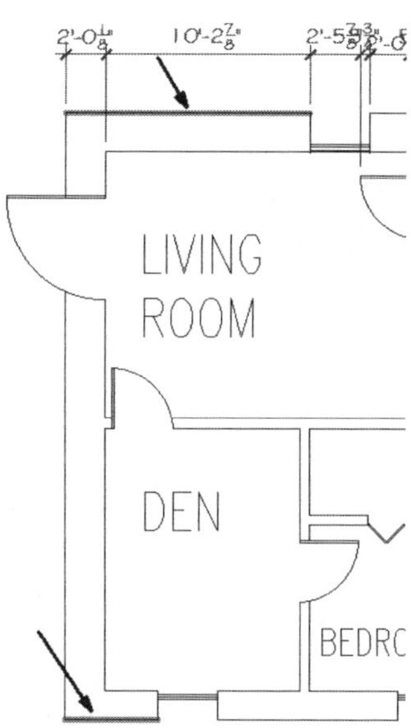

Select the top horizontal line of the view and the bottom horizontal line of the view.

Click **ENTER** to indicate you are done with selecting elements.

9. 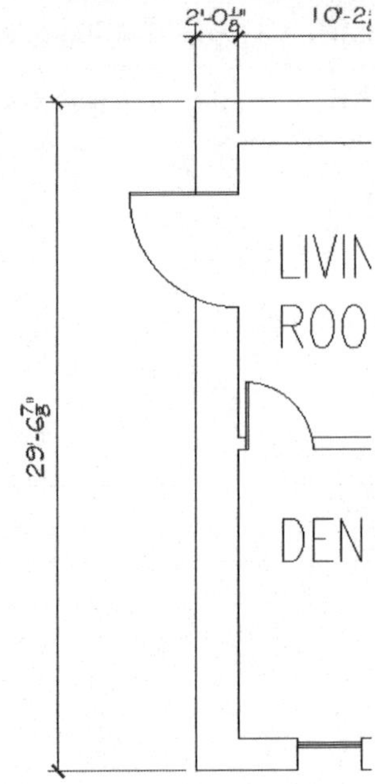

Left click to place the dimension to the left of the view.

10. 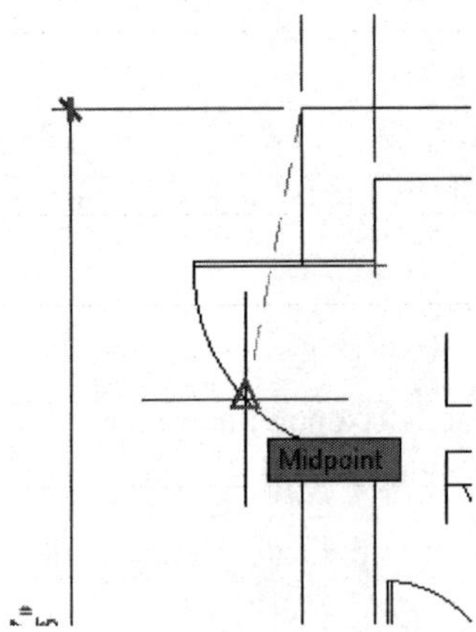

Add a linear dimension using the top horizontal line and the midpoint of the door swing.

11. 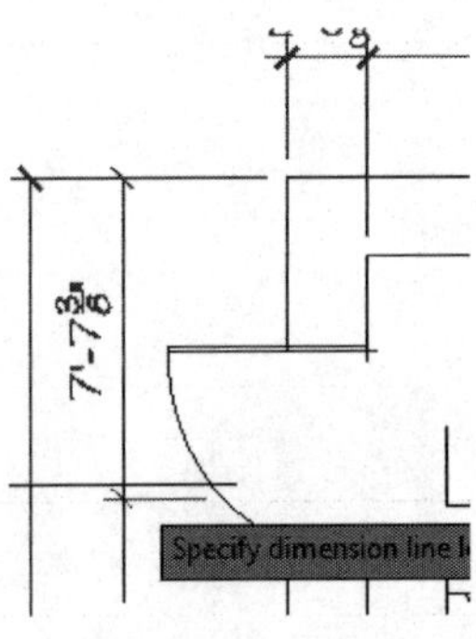

Left click to place the dimension.

12.

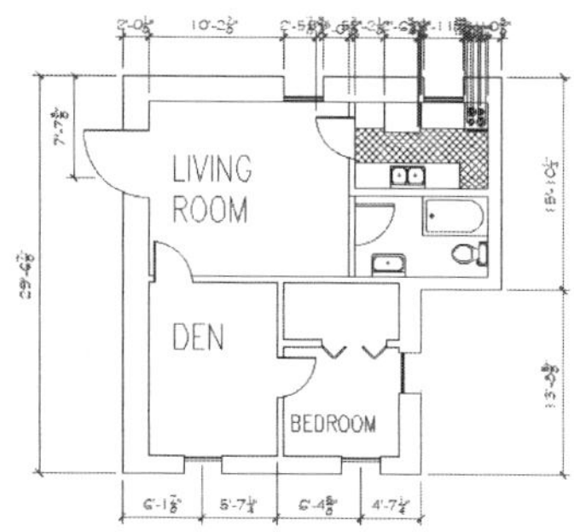

Use the dimension tools to place the remaining dimensions.

Edit Dimension Location

Command Overview

The placement of the dimension lines and text can be adjusted using Grips. With the command line blank, select the dimension. Select the grip at either arrow point, or on the dimension text, drag the cursor then pick the new location. The location of the dimension text can be moved closer to one extension line or the other using the same method. This is also a good way to move the extension line origin points, should they be incorrectly selected.

General Procedures:

To move the dimension line:

1. With the Command line blank, select the dimension.
2. Select either the text, or arrowhead grip. The default grip mode will be Stretch.
3. Stretch the dimension line and pick the new location. Click Escape two times to cancel the grip selection.

To move the dimension text:

1. With the Command line blank, select the dimension.
2. Select the dimension text. The default grip mode will be Stretch.
3. Drag the dimension text toward one extension line or the other, or to a new location. Click Escape two times to cancel the grip selection.

To move a dimension origin point:

1. Zoom into the area where the dimension origin point should meet the object (intersection, endpoint…etc.). With the Command line blank, select the dimension.
2. Select the dimension origin point. The default grip mode will be Stretch.
3. Use Object Snap to drag the origin point to the correct location on the object. Click Escape two times to cancel the grip selection.

Note: *Sometimes both the object and the dimension may be selected and the origin point dragged to the grip of the object being dimensioned.*

- *Remember to Click the Escape key two times to cancel the grip selection. Clicking <ENTER> will repeat the last command (which may have been the Erase command!).*

Edit Dimension Text

Command Overview

AutoCAD dimensions are associated with the object being dimensioned; therefore, if the dimension text appears to be incorrect, it is either because the dimension line origin points were incorrectly selected, or the drawing is incorrect. Check first to see that the origin points are at the correct location (see previous section). If this seems to be correct, then go back and correct the drawing. The Edit Text command (DDEDIT) should be used to add annotation to the dimension text and <u>not</u> to delete or overwrite existing dimension text. In the Multiline Text Editor, the dimension text will be represented as the greater than and less than symbols < >. Place the cursor before or after these symbols to type additional text. Do <u>not</u> overwrite or delete the < > symbols representing the dimension text. Deleting or typing over these symbols will break associativity between the dimension and the objects being dimensioned. It is better to make corrections to the geometry in the drawing. The Text Editor ribbon is a contextual ribbon that appears only when text is being edited.

General Procedures:

1. Invoke the Edit Text command.
2. Select the dimension to edit.
3. Place the cursor before or after the < > symbols and type additional annotation. Select OK to exit.

- Never delete these < > symbols, or type in between these symbols.
- By maintaining *associativity* between the dimension and the object being dimensioned, changes made to the object will automatically update the dimension text.
- If you ever accidentally delete or modify a dimension, you can select the dimension and type <> and the true dimension will automatically be recovered.

Edit Dimension Properties

Command Overview

When changing dimensions properties, decide first whether this change should apply globally to the dimension style, or to a single dimension.

For instance, if the precision of the primary units of a dimension style are set to four decimal places, and the user wants the precision of radial dimensions to always be two decimal places, then a subset style for Radius dimensions needs to be created from the original dimension style. Use the Dimension Style Manager dialog box to make the desired changes, and all of the radial dimensions in the drawing will be automatically updated to reflect the change.

If you want to change only a selected dimension in the drawing, use the Properties command. Changes made to individual dimensions will usually not update globally if a change is later made to that Dimension Style.

The Styles panel is a drop down under Annotation on the Home ribbon. It allows you to select the current dimension style, the current text style and the current table style. Simply select the style you want to make active from the drop-down list.

Use the ***Properties*** *dialog box to change individual dimensions in the drawing. Select the dimension in the drawing to display the dimension properties in the dialog box. Select the plus sign + before the property to access the options to change.*

General Procedures:

To make a change to an individual dimension:

1. Invoke Properties command.
2. Select the dimension to change (move the Properties dialog box if necessary).
3. Select the option to change. If there is a plus + sign before the option to change, select the plus sign first, then select the option to change. Type or select the new option.
4. Select OK to exit.

Tips & Tricks

- *When editing dimensions, determine whether you want to apply the change globally by making the change to the Dimension Style, or individually by using the Properties command.*
- *Changes made to individual dimensions will usually not update if a change is later made to that Dimension Style.*

Command Exercise

Exercise 9-17 - Edit Dimensions

Drawing Name: **dimedit1.dwg**
Estimated Time to Completion: 15 Minutes

Scope

Use the Properties command to modify the dimensions as indicated.

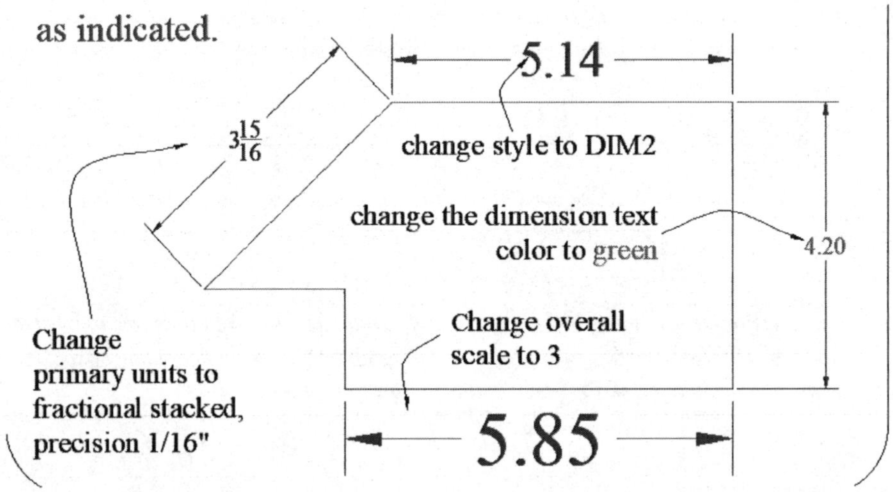

Solution

1. 

Switch to the **View** ribbon.

Launch the **Properties** palette.

2. 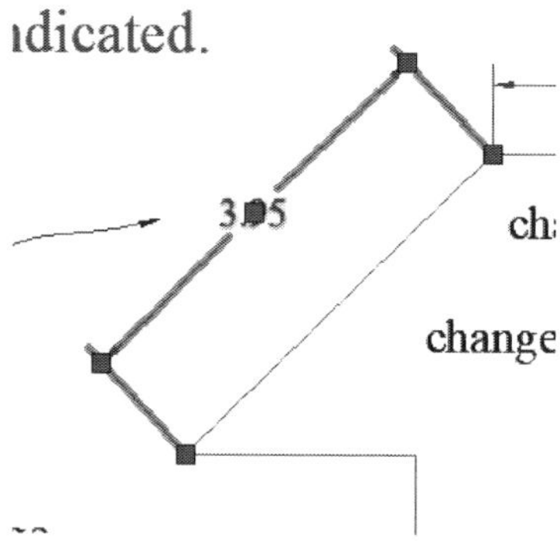

Select the aligned dimension that will be changed to fractional stacked.

3. 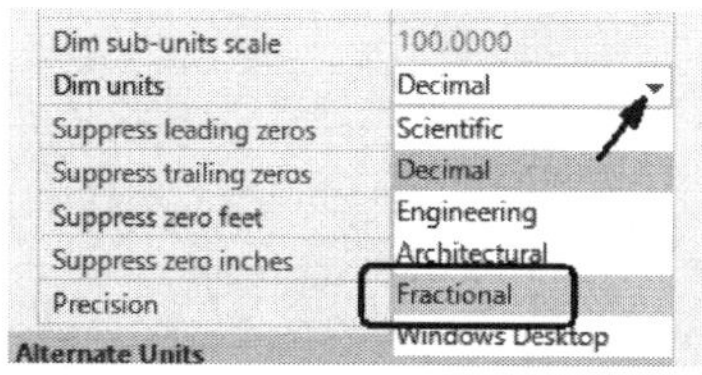

In the Properties dialog box, scroll down and change the 'Dim units' to **Fractional**.

4. 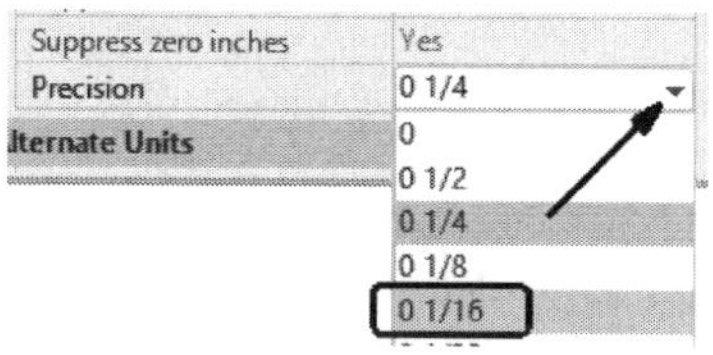

Change the 'Precision' to '**0 1/16**'.

5. 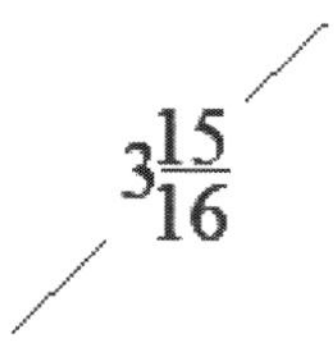

Notice how the Dimension changes.

Click the <**Esc**> key once to clear the selection.

6. 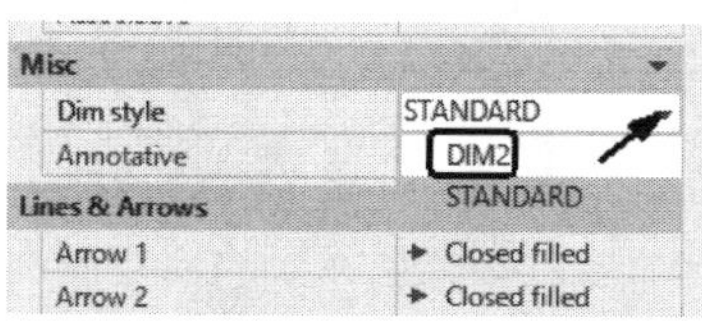

Pick the top horizontal dimension that will have its style changed to **DIM2**.

Notice how the Dimension changes.

Click the <**Esc**> key once to clear the selection.

7. 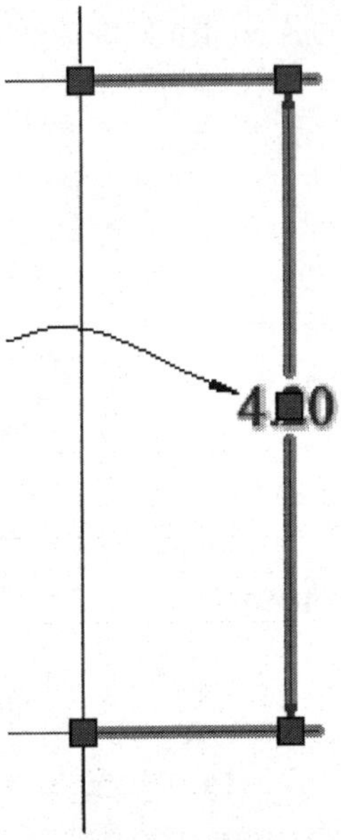

Pick the vertical dimension that will have its text color changed to green.

8. 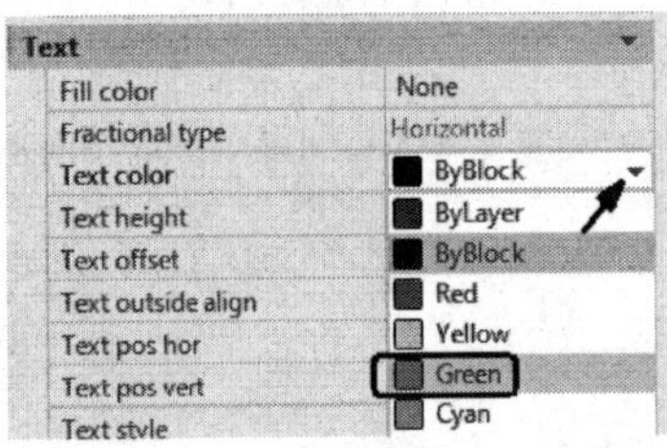

Scroll down the Properties palette to change the 'Text color' to **Green.**

Notice how the Dimension changes.

Click the <**Esc**> key once to clear the selection.

9. 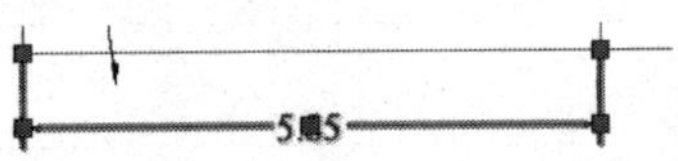

Pick the lower horizontal dimension that will have its overall scale changed to 3.

10. 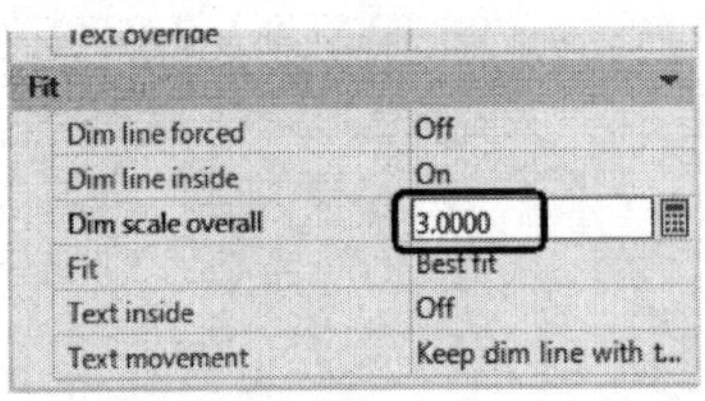

Scroll down to the Fit heading and change the 'Dim scale overall' setting to **3**.

Notice how the Dimension changes.

Click the <Esc> key once to clear the selection.

Close the **Properties** palette.

Command Exercise

Exercise 9-18 – Edit Dimension Text

Drawing Name: **dimedit2.dwg**
Estimated Time to Completion: 15 Minutes

Scope

Use the Properties command to edit the top dimension. Use the Edit Text command to make changes to the bottom dimension.

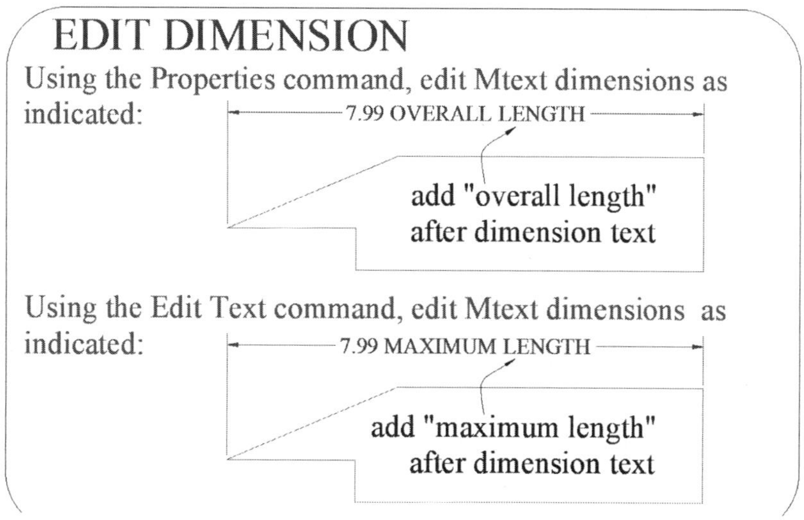

Solution

1.

Switch to the **View** tab on the ribbon.

Launch the **Properties** palette.

2.

Pick the top dimension with the LMB.

3.

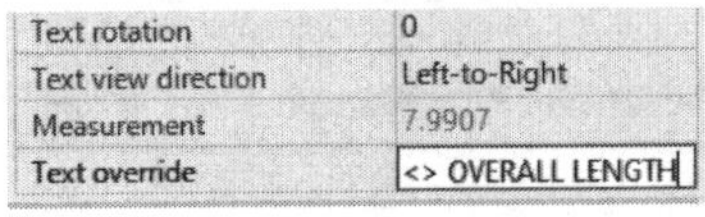

In the Properties dialog box, change the Text override to **<> OVERALL LENGTH**.

Close the dialog box and Click <**ESC**> once to clear the selection.

4.

*Type **TEXTEDIT.***

Select an annotation object or [Undo]:

You also can just double click on the dimension text to edit.

<Select the lower dimension text>

5.

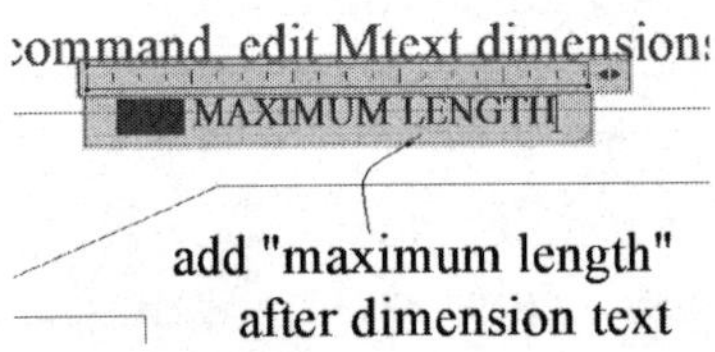

Type in the desired text in the edit field. Use the arrows on the text box to expand the text box.

6.

Select **Close Text Editor** on the ribbon.

You also could click ESC to release the selection.

Command Exercise

Exercise 9-19 - Edit Dimensions Using Grips

Drawing Name: **dimedit3.dwg**
Estimated Time to Completion: 15 Minutes

Scope

Use the Align Text Option in the Dimensions Menu.
Use Grips to adjust the dimensions as indicated.

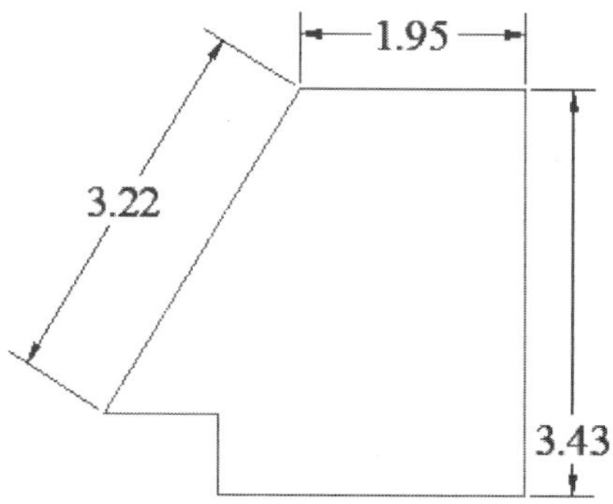

Solution

1.

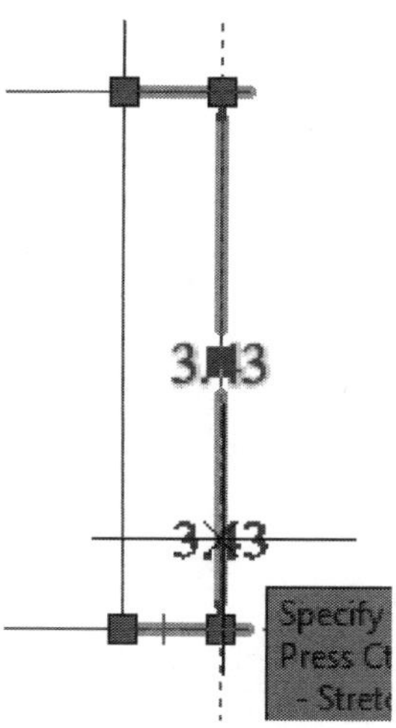

Pick the **3.43** vertical dimension on the right side figure.

Use the grip on the text to position the text.

Click <ESC> to release the selection.

2. 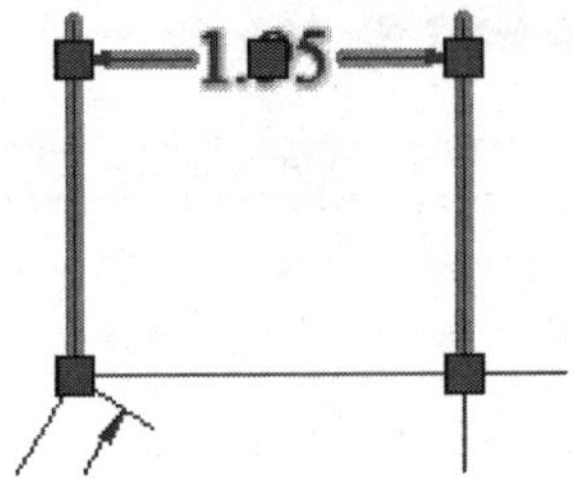

Pick the horizontal dimension at the top of the object on the right.

3. 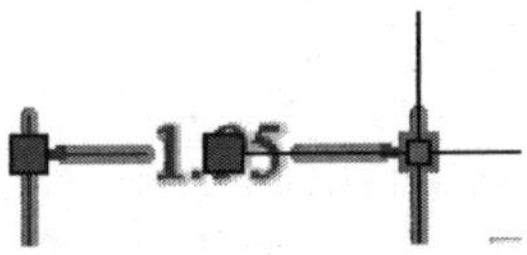

Select one of the end grips along the dimension line.

4. 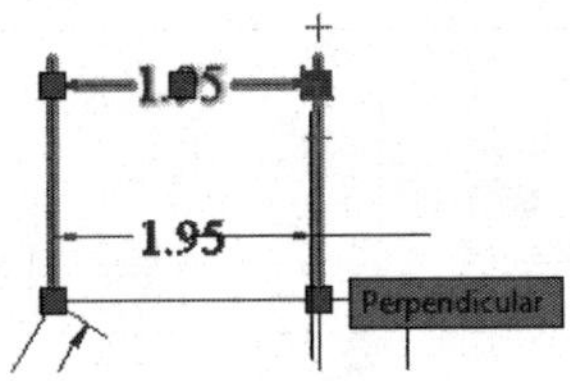

Specify stretch point or [Base point/Copy/Undo/eXit]: Move the dimension down closer to the top line segment and click again.

Click <**ESC**> once to clear the selection.

5. 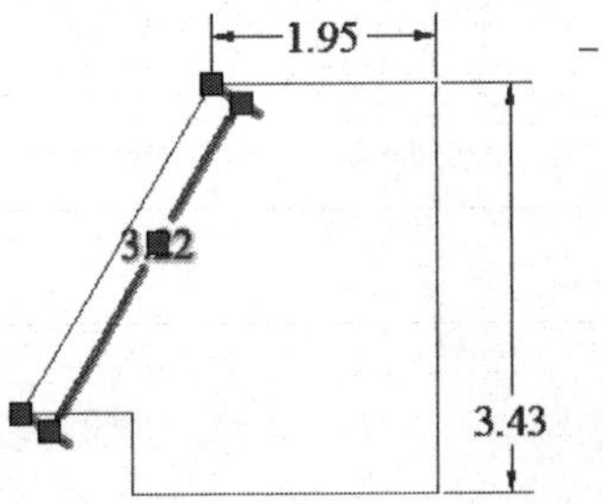

Pick the Aligned dimension.

6. 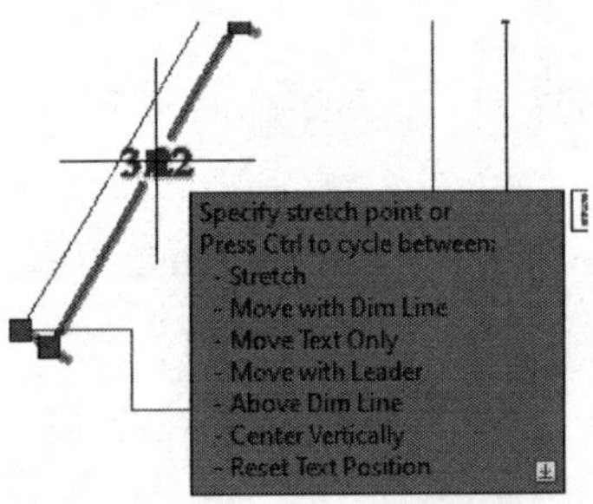

Select the grip over the text.

7.

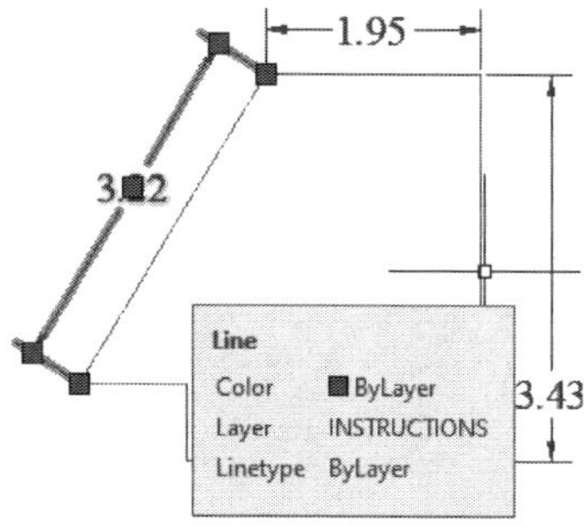

Specify stretch point or [Base point/Copy/Undo/eXit]: Move the dimension away from the line segment and click again to place.

Click <**ESC**> to deselect.

When using the Stretch tool to modify objects, turn ORTHO ON.

Command Exercise

Exercise 9-20 – Edit Dimension Using Stretch

Drawing Name: **dimedit4.dwg**
Estimated Time to Completion: 15 Minutes

Scope

Use the Stretch command to modify the part. Notice that the dimensions will change automatically.

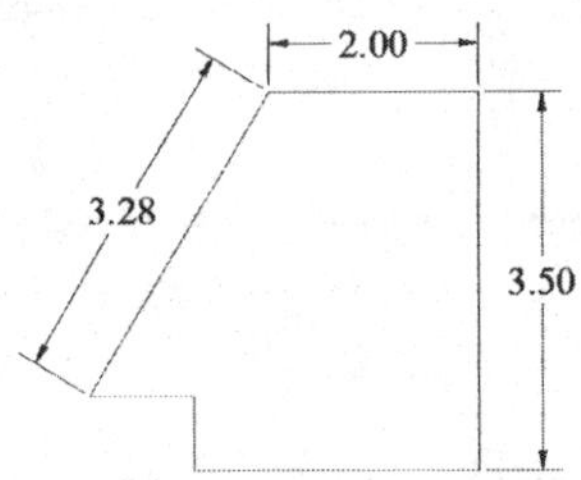

Solution

1.

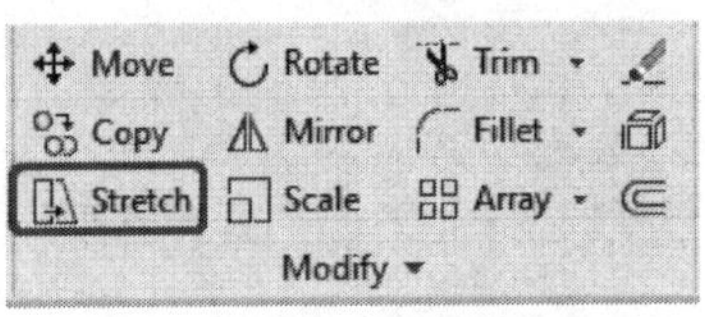

Turn **ORTHO ON**.

Invoke the Stretch command (stretch) on the Home tab on the ribbon.

2.

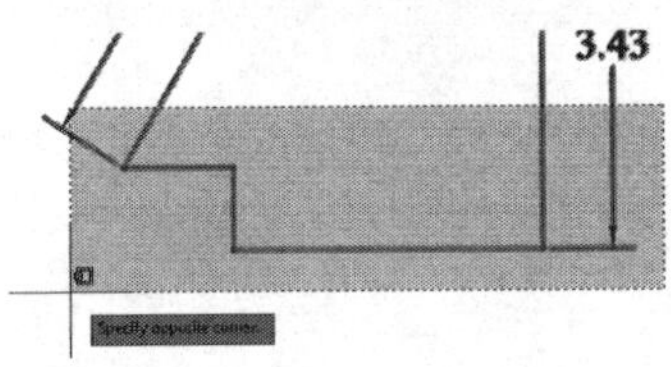

Select objects:
Using a crossing window, select the bottom portion of the part, and include crossing over the dimensions.

Select objects:
Click <ENTER>

3. 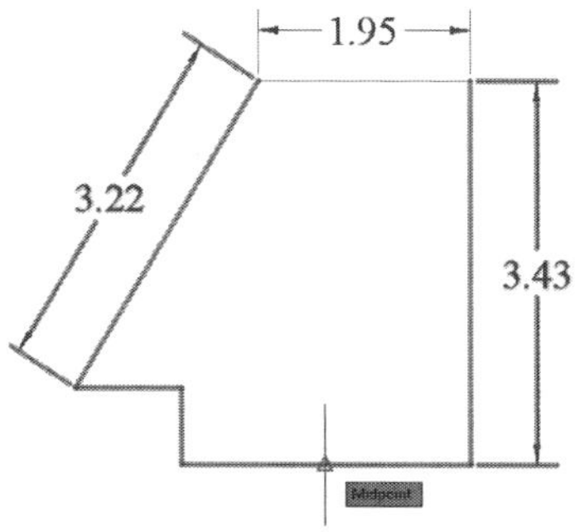

Specify base point or displacement:
Pick a base point near the center of the object.

4. 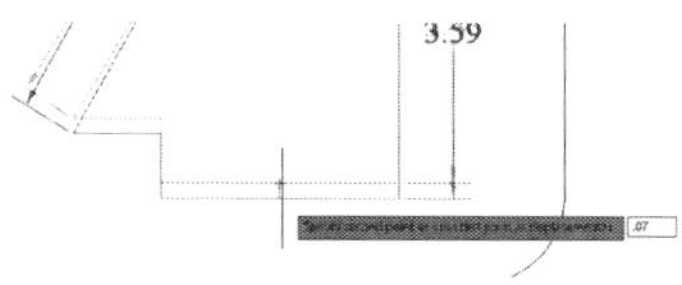

Specify second point of displacement:
Drag the object down; type '0.07' and Click <ENTER>.

Notice how the part changes as well as the dimensions.

5. 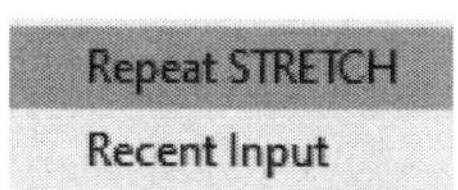

Repeat the Stretch command with the RMB (stretch or <ENTER>).

6. 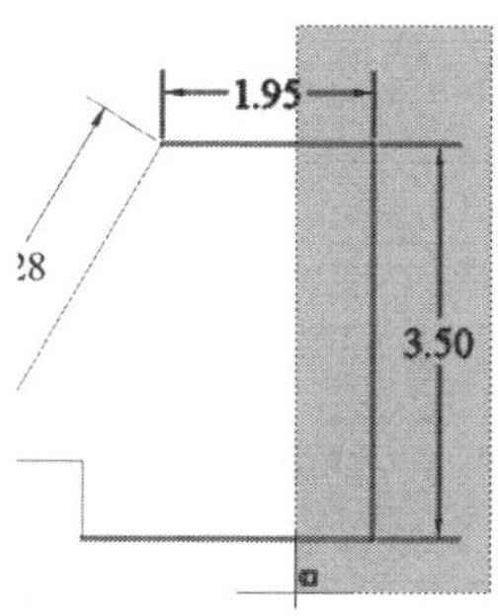

Select objects:
Using a crossing window, select the right side, and include crossing over the horizontal dimension.

Select objects:
Click <ENTER>

7. 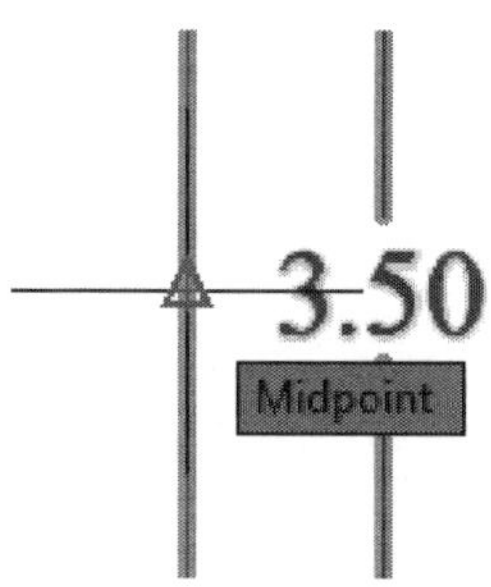

Specify base point or displacement:
Pick a base point near the center of the object.

8. 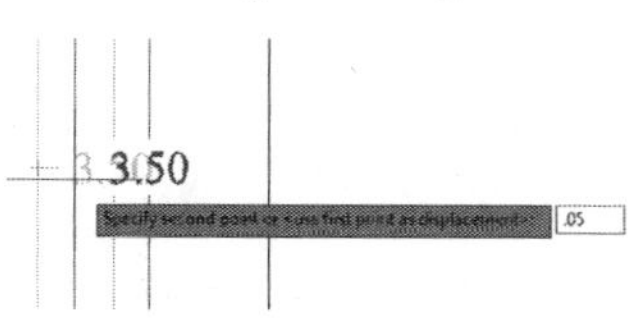

Specify second point of displacement:
Drag the object to the right and type '0.05' and Click <ENTER>

Section Exercise

Exercise 9-21 – Dimension a Drawing

Drawing Name: **new dwg**
Estimated Time to Completion: 30 Minutes

Scope

Create a drawing from scratch using standard orthographic views and dimensions.

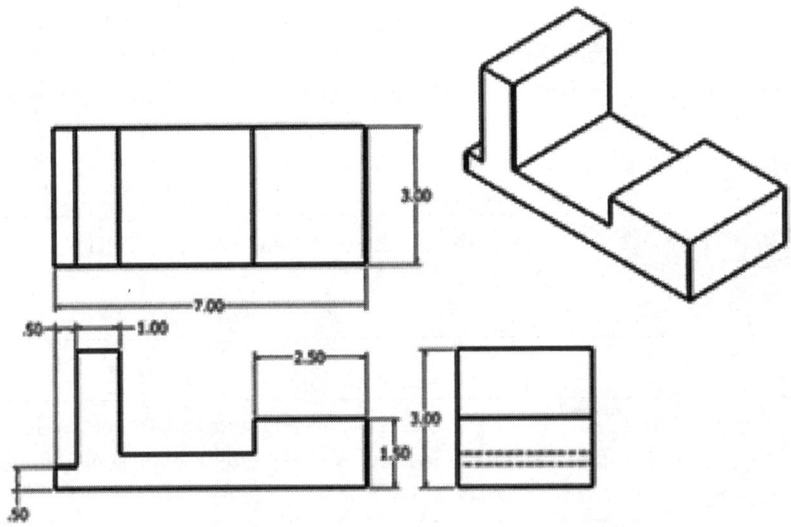

Solution

Set Drawing Unit Precision to 2.

Create three layers:

Object	Green	Continuous
Hidden	Cyan	Hidden
Dimension	Red	Continuous

Draw a front, top, and right side view as shown.

Section Exercise

Exercise 9-22 – Dimension a Drawing

Drawing Name: **new dwg**
Estimated Time to Completion: 30 Minutes

Scope

Create a drawing from scratch using standard orthographic views and dimensions.

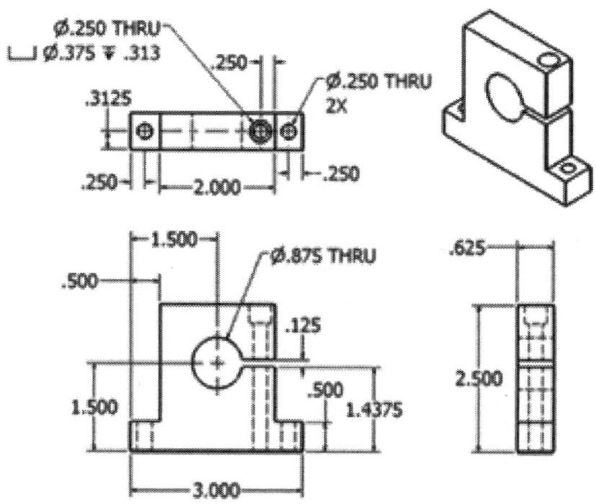

Solution

Set Drawing Unit Precision to 3.

Create three layers:

Object	Green	Continuous
Hidden	Cyan	Hidden
Dimension	Red	Continuous

Draw a front, top, and right side view as shown.

Section Exercise

Exercise 9-23 – Create a Floor Plan

Drawing Name: **new dwg**
Estimated Time to Completion: 30 Minutes

Scope

Create a floor plan from scratch. Create an architectural dimension style using millimeter units. Create layers for the dimensions, walls, and hatch. You do not have to place the room labels or plumbing fixtures.

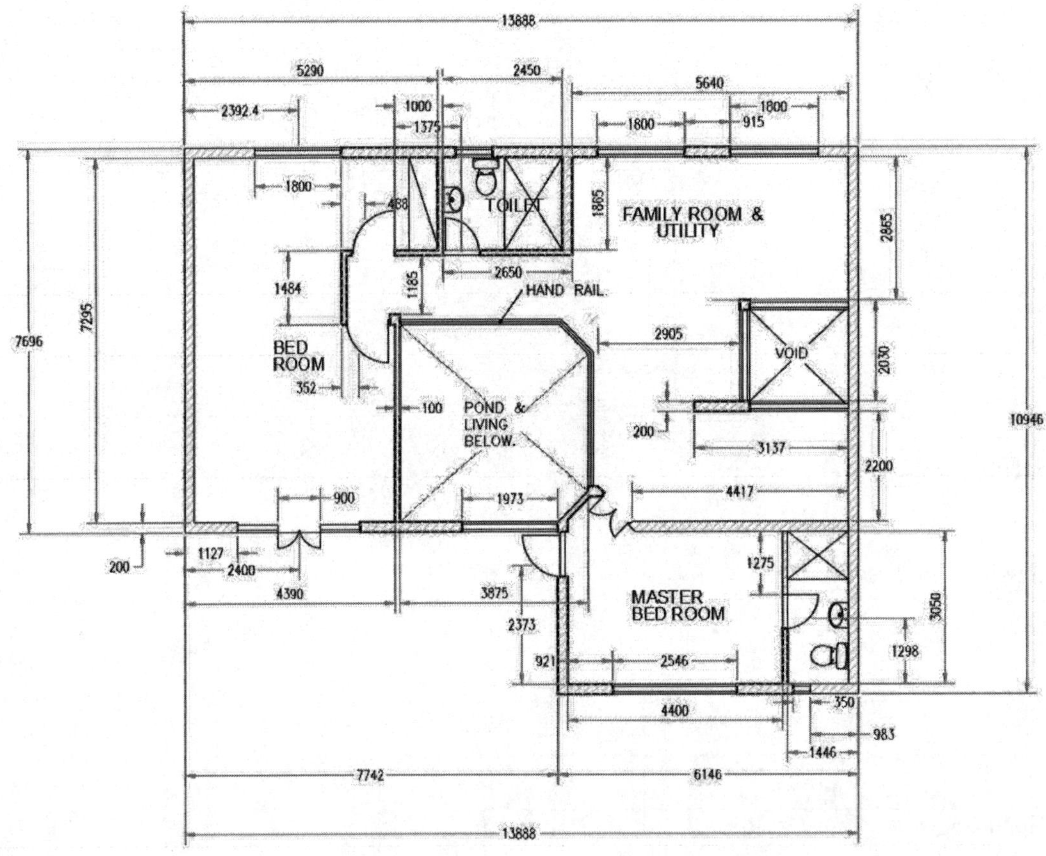

Annotative Objects

Annotative is a property that can be applied to:

- Text
- Blocks
- Attributes
- Hatches
- Dimensions
- Geometric Tolerances
- Multileaders

When AutoCAD was first developed, there was only model space. Paper space was added in Release 11, in the early 1990s.

While most mechanical drafters and designers, could manage their designs using model space only – simply by plotting to a larger piece of paper. Architects complained that buildings would exceed any paper size when drawn 1:1. Architects wanted to create layouts at different scales to show the building floor plans, elevations, sections, and construction details.

Initially, architects would create a dimension style or text style for different view scales and that worked fairly well. But, they asked if AutoCAD could automate that process.

AutoCAD added annotative scaling in 2006, more than a decade after they introduced paper space.

There are three different approaches to display text and dimensions at different scales:

- Create multiple representations of the same annotation objects on different layers using different styles.
- Create annotation in paper space only – not in model space.
- Use annotative properties

AutoCAD has three icons on the status bar that can be used to control annotative objects in a drawing.

 Displays annotative objects using the annotation scale. When turned off, annotative objects are displayed at the current scale.

 Automatically adds annotation scales to all annotative objects, when the annotation scale changes.

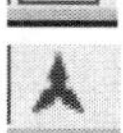 Sets the current annotation scale for annotative objects in model space.
Best practice is to use the same annotative scale for objects as the view.

Command Exercise

Exercise 9-24 – Annotative Objects Part 1

Drawing Name: **annotative_objects.dwg**
Estimated Time to Completion: 30 Minutes

Scope

Switch between model space and paper space. Set the annotative and view scales for a viewport. Verify the annotative scales applied to annotative objects.

1.

In the lower right of the screen, left click on the tab named SECTIONS AND DETAILS.

Zoom out to see the entire sheet.

2.

This layout tab represents a piece of paper.
If you look on the status bar, you will see the word PAPER.
This indicates you are in PAPER SPACE.

There can only be ONE model space, but you can have as many as 256 layouts for PAPER SPACE or sheets of paper.

Think of a viewport like a window into model space.

We can reach through the window and manipulate inside the model space by double clicking inside the viewport.

3.

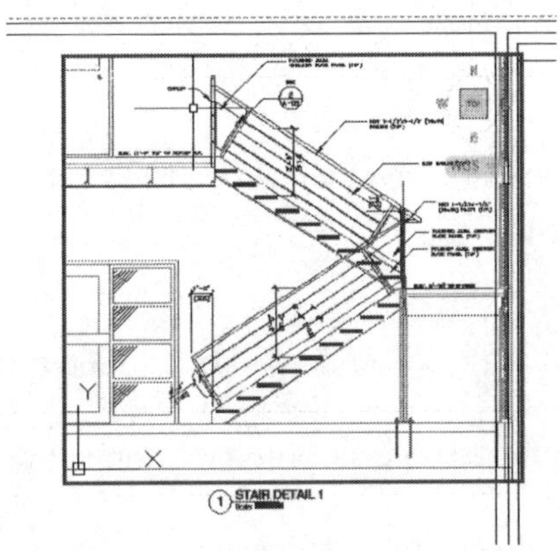

Locate the view called **Stair Detail 1.**

Double click inside the viewport.

We can tell model space is active because the viewport is now bold.

If you look at the task bar, you will see MODEL.

If you change the view scale inside of MODEL space, all the views in model space will be that view scale. MODEL space should always be 1:1.

4. 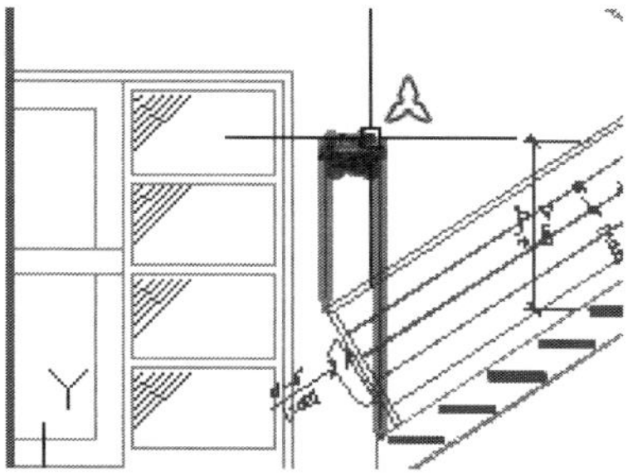

Hover the mouse over a dimension.

A symbol appears next to the dimension to indicate the dimension is annotative. This means the dimension will change size depending on the scale of the viewport.

5. 

Click on the lock on the status bar.

This unlocks the viewport display. This allows you to change the viewscale and reposition the view inside the viewport.

6. 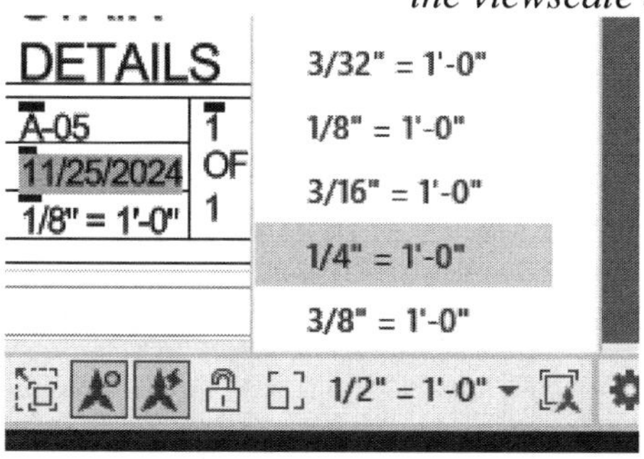

On the status bar, set the view scale to ¼" = 1'-0".

This will affect model space since you are in model space.

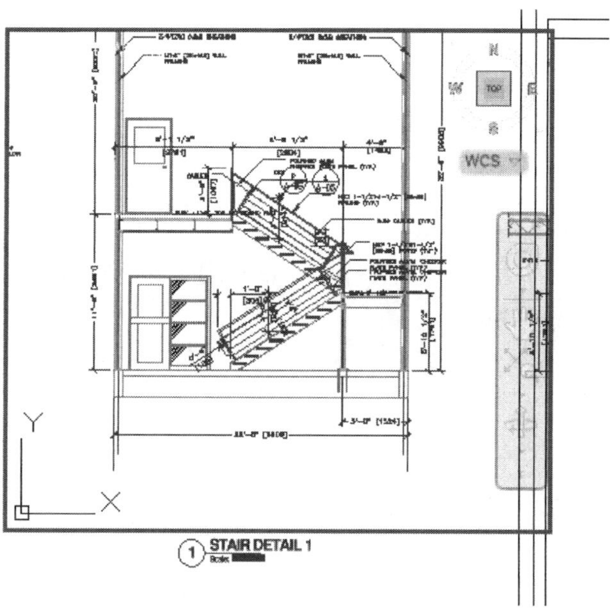

The view will re-scale. Note the annotations scale with the view.

Click outside the viewport anywhere on the sheet to return to PAPER space.

Verify you are in PAPER space by checking the status bar.

7.

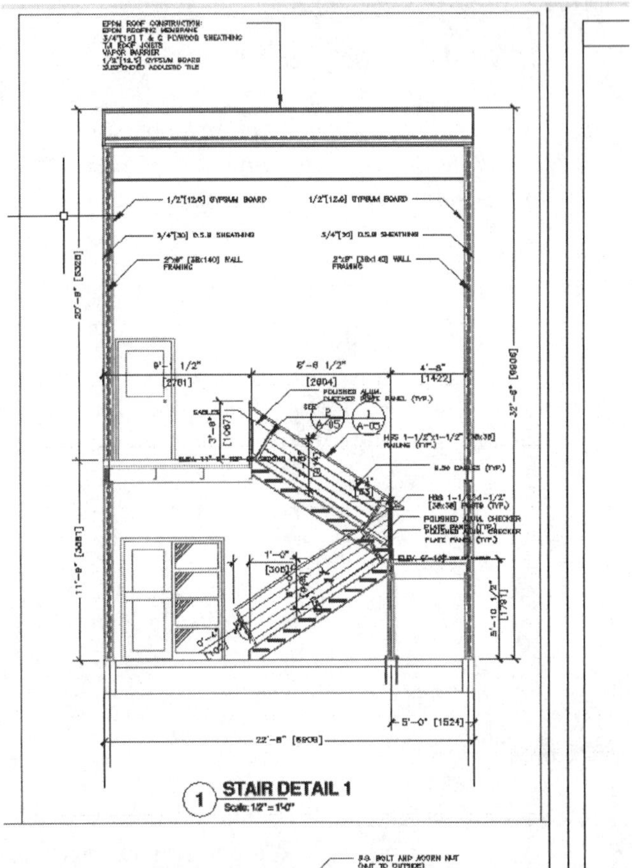

Adjust the position and size of the viewport so it displays the entire view.

Note that the view tag is placed in PAPER space.

Move the view tag so it is below the view.

8.

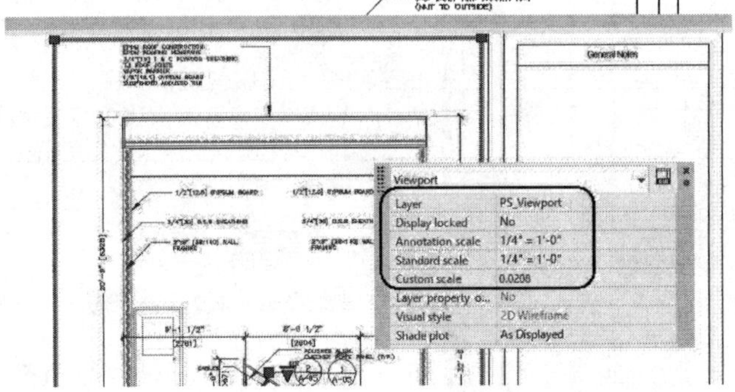

Select the viewport.
Right click and select **Quick Properties.**

Note that the Annotation scale is ¼"= 1'-0".
The Standard Scale is ¼" = 1'0".

The annotation scale and standard scale should always be the same for viewports.

9. Set the Display locked to **Yes**.

10.

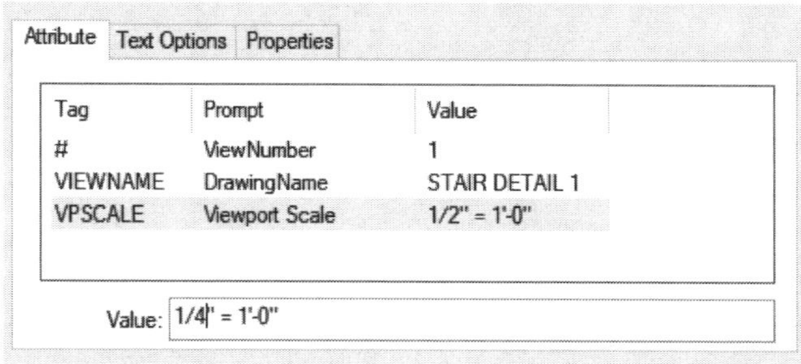

Click **ESC** to release the viewport selection.

Double left click on the view tag.
This brings up the Attribute Editor.

Change the VPSCALE to **¼" = 1'-0".**
This reflects the view scale applied to that view.

Click **OK**.

11.

Left click on the MODEL tab.
This is the MODEL SPACE view.

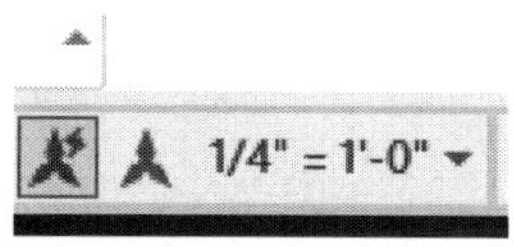

Note the view scale is set to ¼"=1'-0".

12.

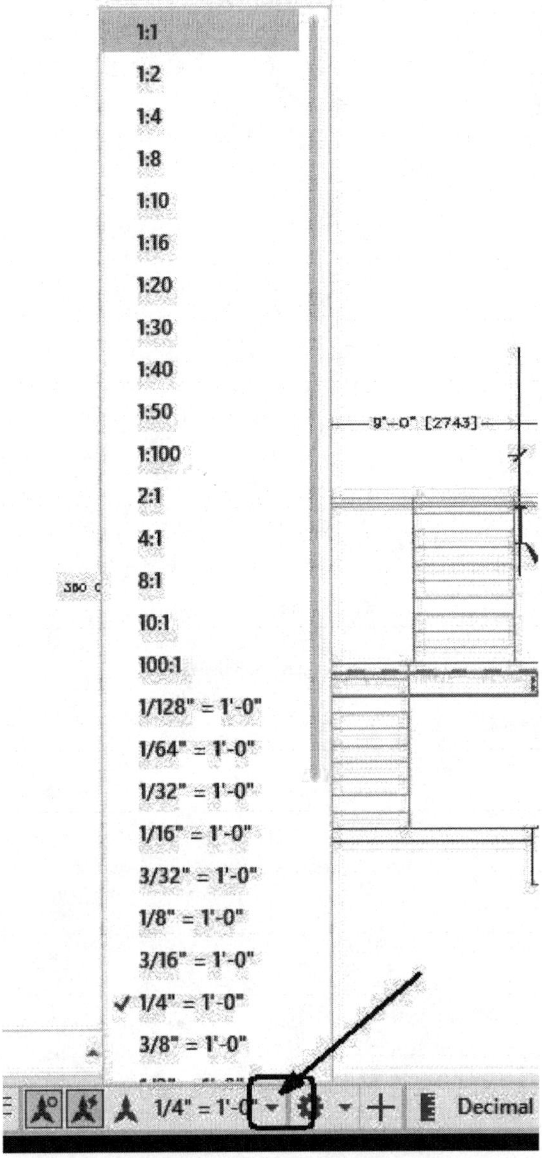

The MODEL view should always be set to 1:1.

Change the view scale to **1:1**.

You will see the dimensions and callouts change size.

13.

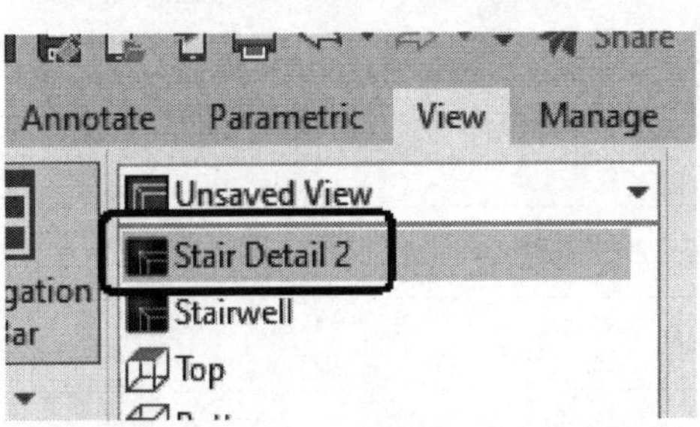

Open the View ribbon.
Activate the **Stair Detail 2** view.

14.

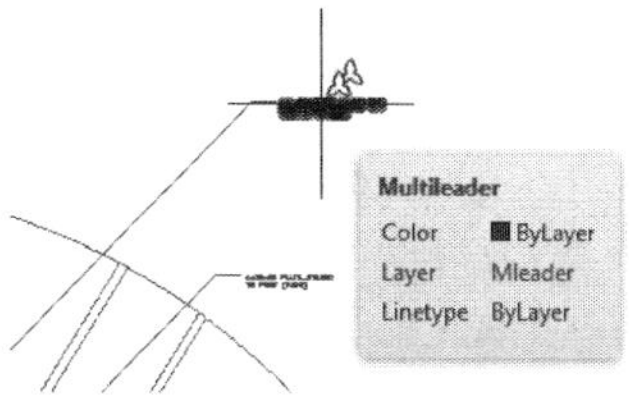

If you hover the mouse over a multileader, you will see two annotation symbols. This indicates the multileader has more than one view scale applied.

Select the multileader.

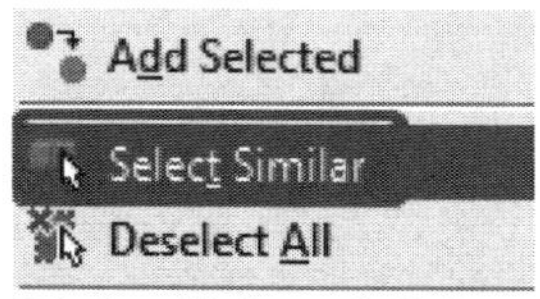

Right click and **Select Similar**.
This will select all the multileaders in the drawing.

15.

Right click and select **Properties**.

16.

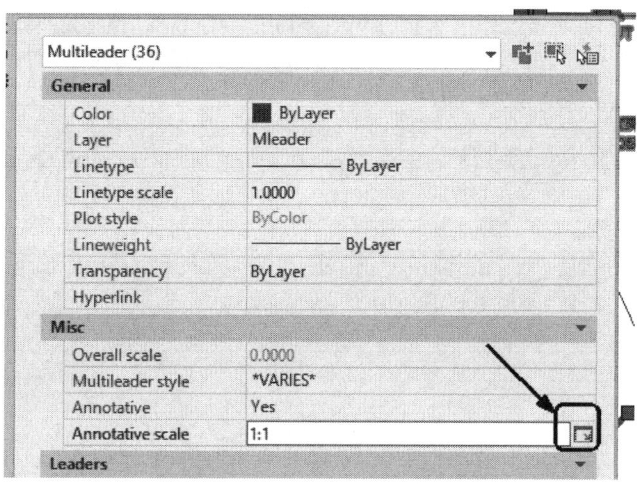

Note that 36 multileaders are selected.
They are using more than one multileader style.
Click in the Annotative scale property.
A small dialog box will appear on the far right.
Click on the dialog box.

17.

A list of object scales is displayed.

These are all the view scales that are applied to the multileaders.

Click OK.

18. 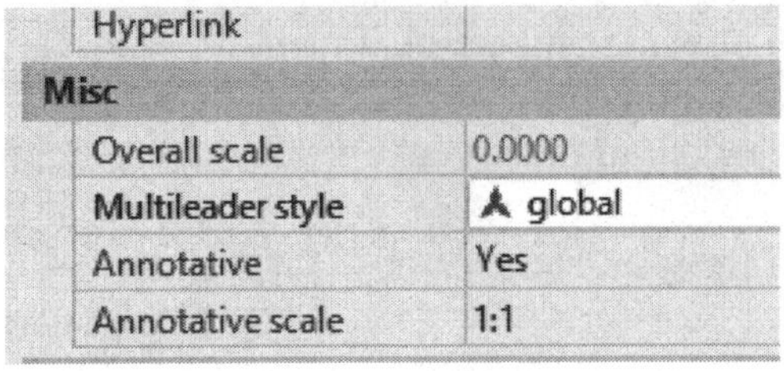

Set the Multileader style to global.

Note that the style has an annotative symbol next to the name to indicate that it is annotative.

19. Close the file.

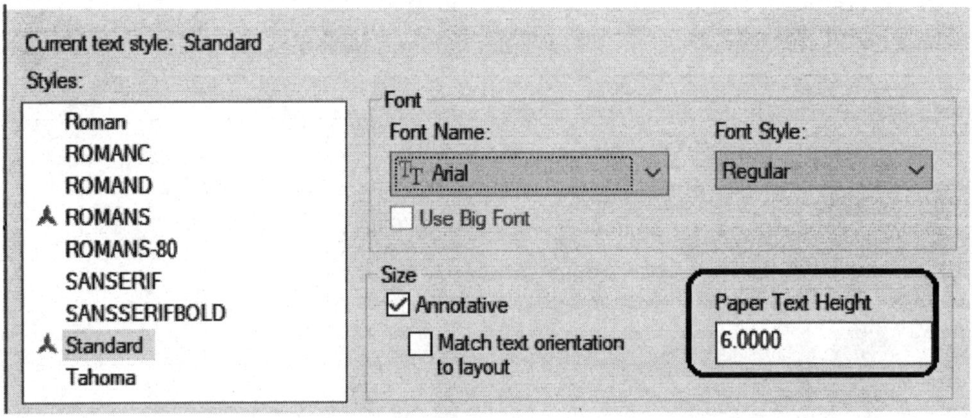

Determining the paper text height can be challenging for annotative objects. Consider what view scale will be applied to the view to figure out what paper text height should be used. The best formula is paper text height x scale factor = text height.

For example, if you want a paper text height of ¼" in a viewport scaled at ½" = 1'0" (factor of 24), you would calculate .25 * 24 = 6".

With annotative text, AutoCAD automatically calculates and displays the annotative object based on the paper text height defined in the style and the assigned view scale.

Command Exercise

Exercise 9-25 – Annotative Objects – Part 2

Drawing Name: **annotative_objects_2.dwg**
Estimated Time to Completion: 20 Minutes

Scope

Add an annotative object to a view. Verify the object scales for the annotative object. Add a viewport to a layout. Modify the attributes for a block.

1.

Switch to the **Model** tab in the lower right of the screen.

2.

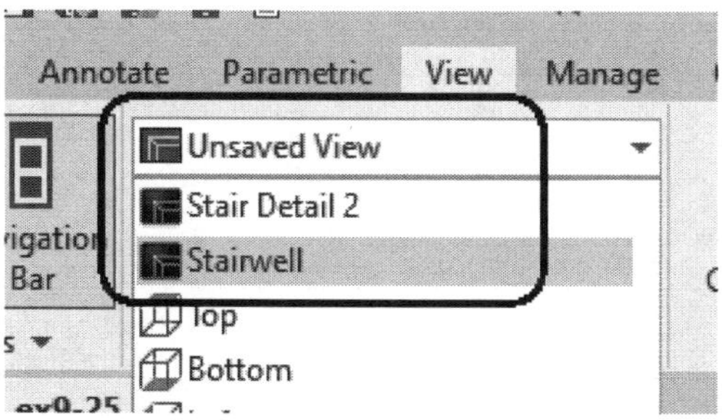

Open the View ribbon.

Select the **Stairwell** named view.

3.

Open the Home ribbon.

Set the **TEXT** layer as current.

4.

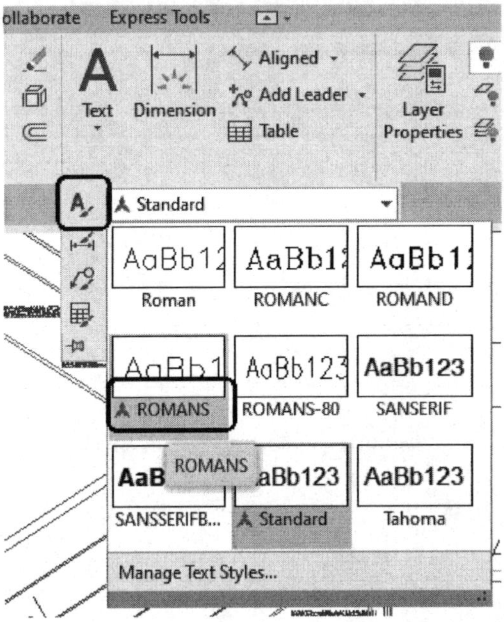

Expand the Annotation panel on the Home ribbon.

Locate the **ROMANS** text style and set it as the current text style.

5.

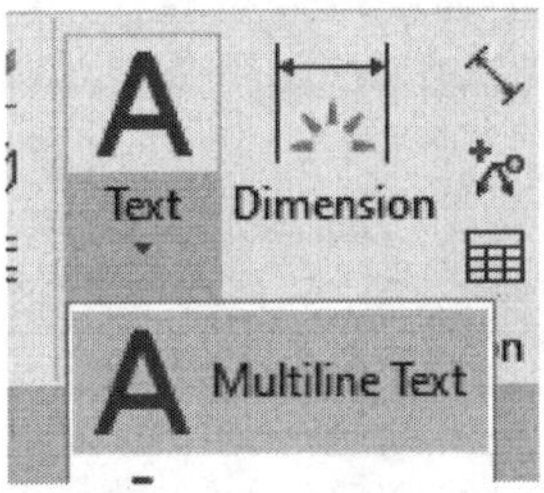

Select the MTEXT tool from the Home ribbon.

You can also type MT for MTEXT.

6.

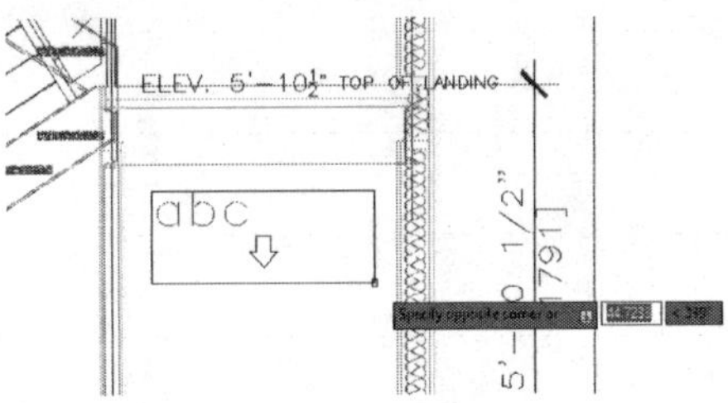

Select the two points in the view to define the MTEXT window.

7.

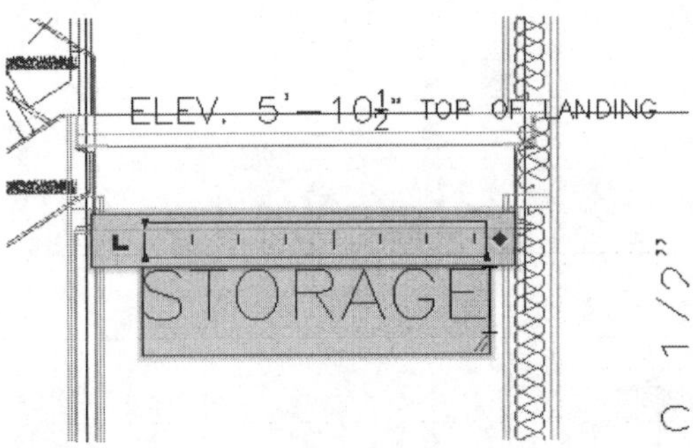

Type **STORAGE** in the window.

8. 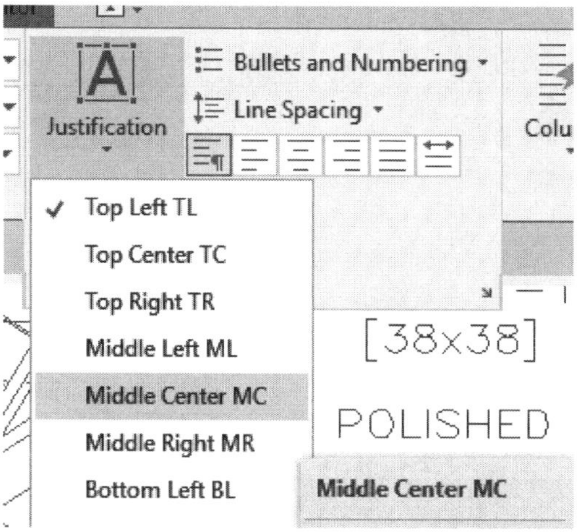

Set the Justification to **MIDDLE CENTER.**

9. 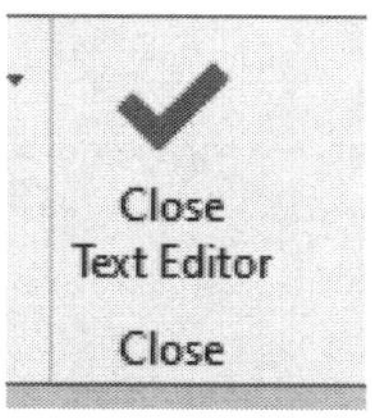

Close the Text Editor.

10. 

Switch to the **SECTIONS AND DETAILS** layout.

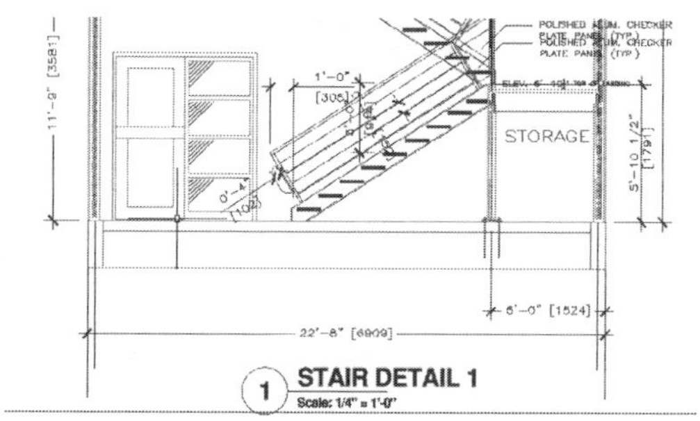

Look at the STAIR DETAIL 1 view.

You should see the mtext that was just added.

11. 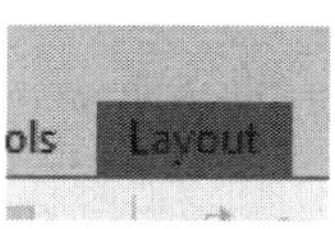

Open the Layout ribbon.

12. 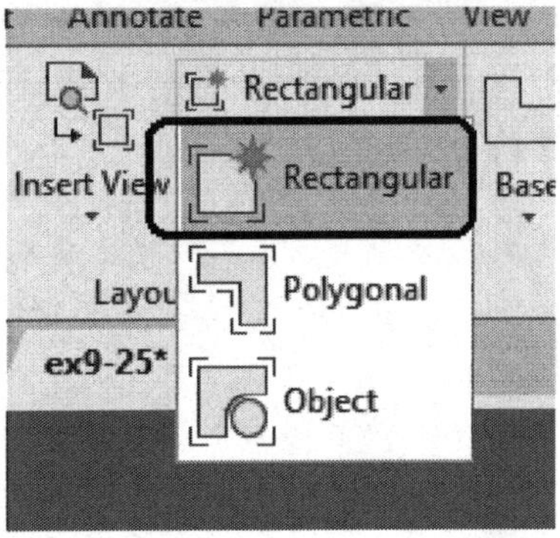

Select **Rectangular** to place a rectangular viewport.

13. 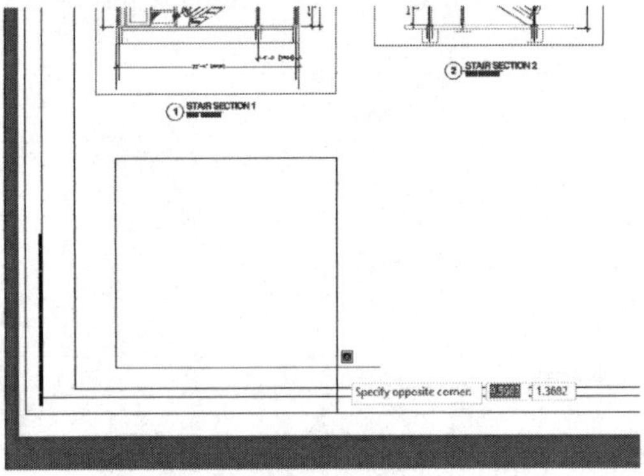

Draw a rectangle in the lower left corner of the sheet to place the viewport.

14. 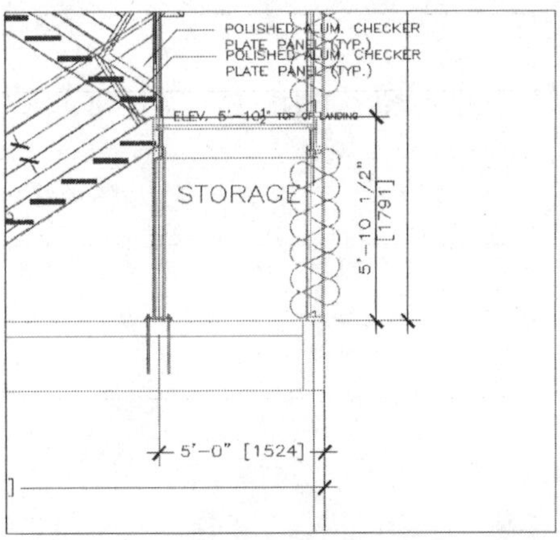

Double click inside the viewport to activate MODEL space.

Zoom into the storage area under the stairs.

15. 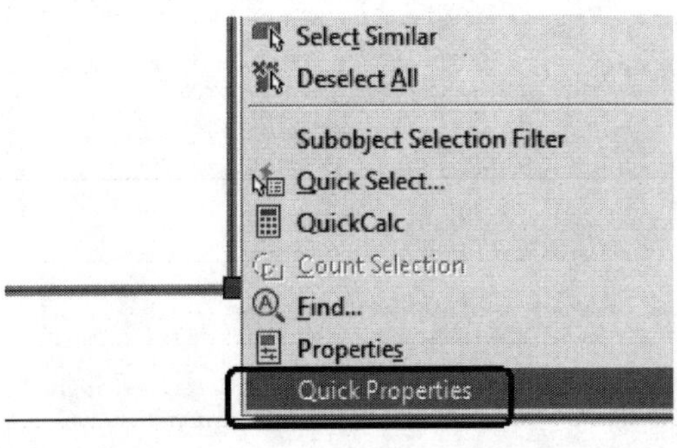

Select the viewport.
Right click and select **Quick Properties**.

16. 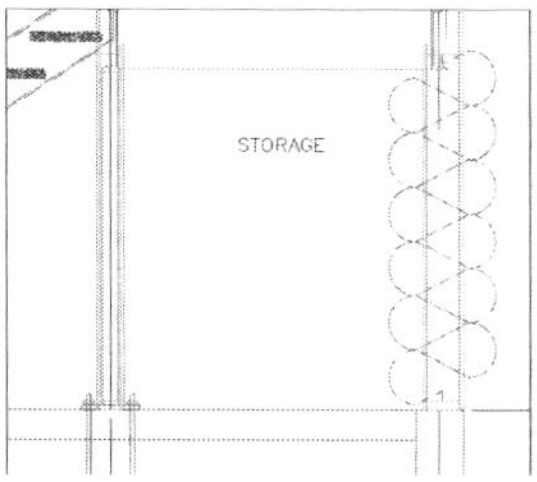

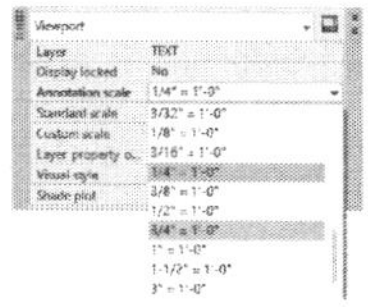

Set the Standard Scale to ¾" = **1'-0"**.

17. 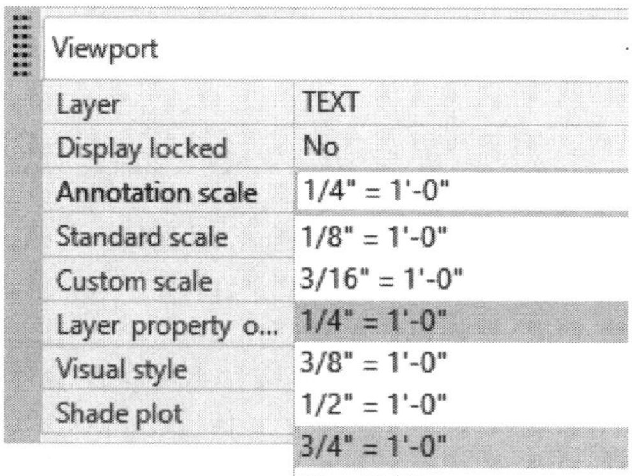

Set the Annotation scale to ¾" = **1'-0"**.

Note that the MTEXT is visible, but all the dimensions have disappeared.

You don't see the dimensions because the object scale needs to be added.

18. 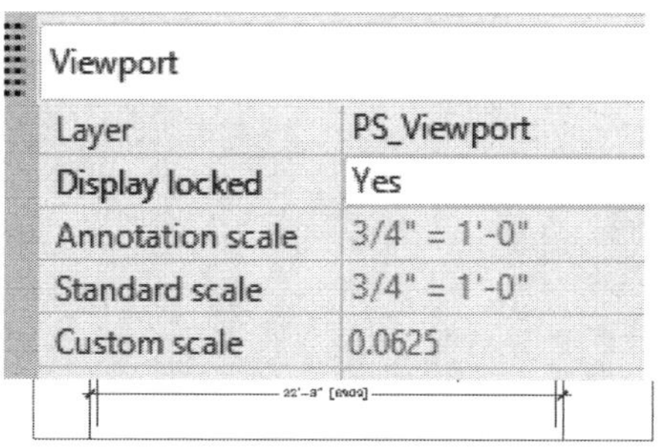

Set the Layer to **PS_Viewport.**
Set Display locked to **Yes.**

Click **ESC** to release the selected viewport.

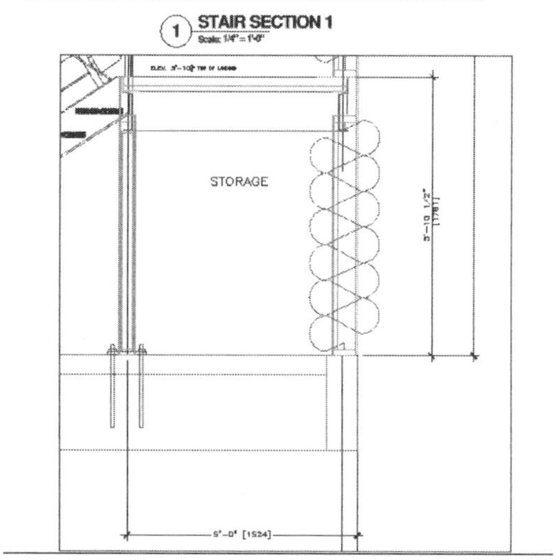

The viewport should look like this.

19.

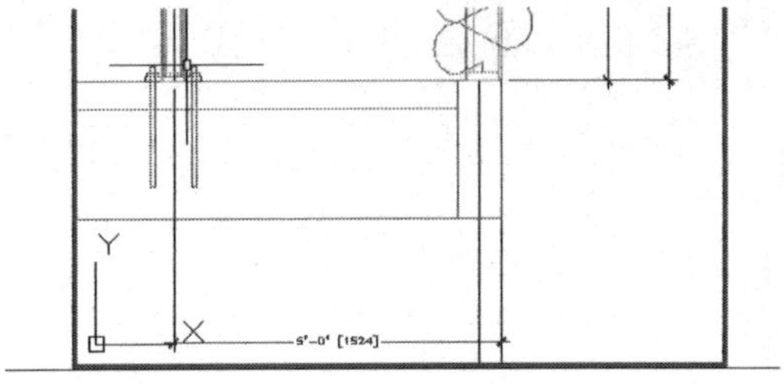

Double click inside the viewport to activate MODEL space.

20.

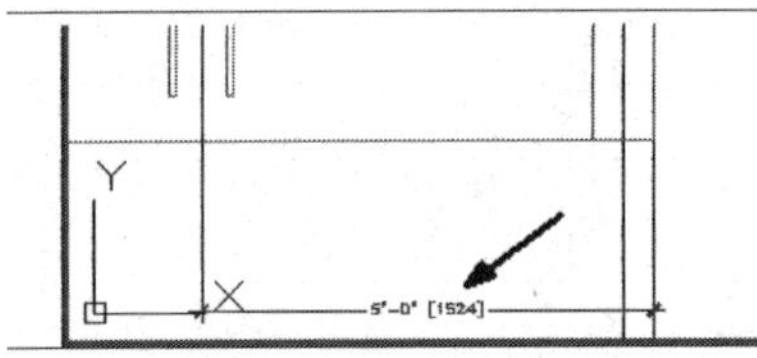

Select the 5'-0" horizontal dimension below the STORAGE area.

21.

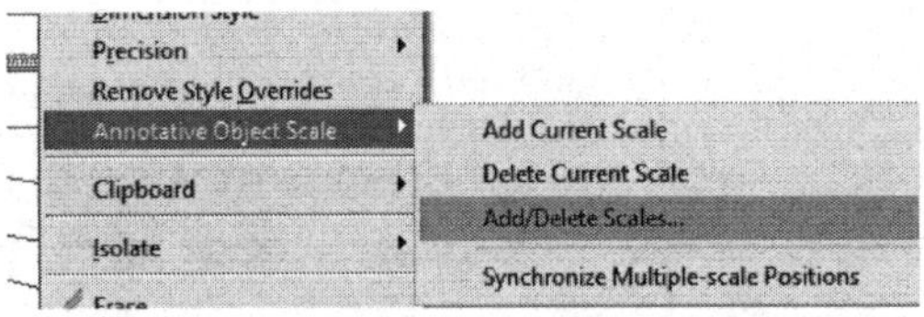

Right click and select **Annotative Object Scale→Add/Delete Scales.**

This option is available on the right click menu if only one annotative object is selected.

22.

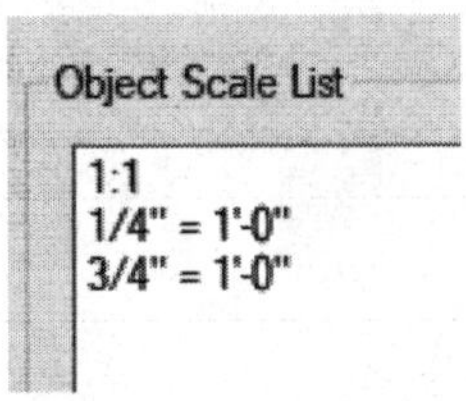

Notice that the ¾" scale was automatically added.

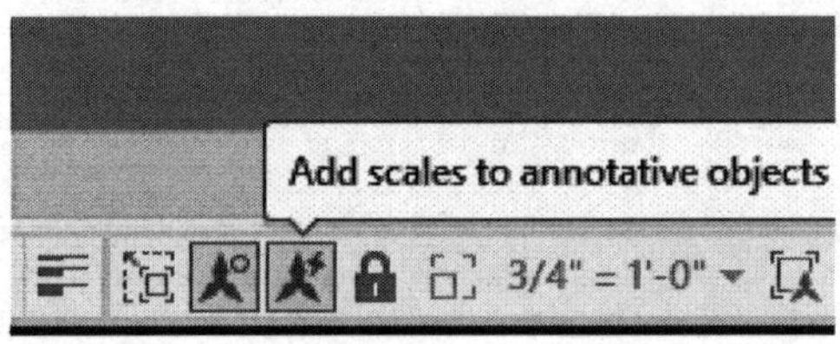

This is because this icon is enabled.
If you did not enable the icon, then add the ¾" scale.

Click **OK**.

23.

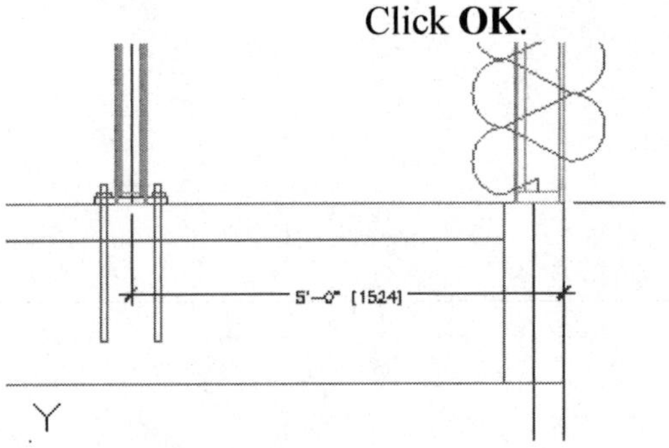

Move the dimension up so it is closer to the storage area.

24. 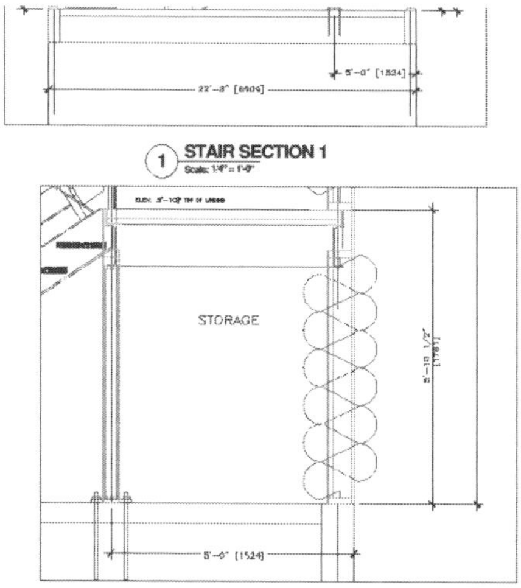

Exit MODEL space.

Adjust the viewport size using the viewport grips.

25. 

Copy the vewport tag and place below the Storage area viewport.

26. 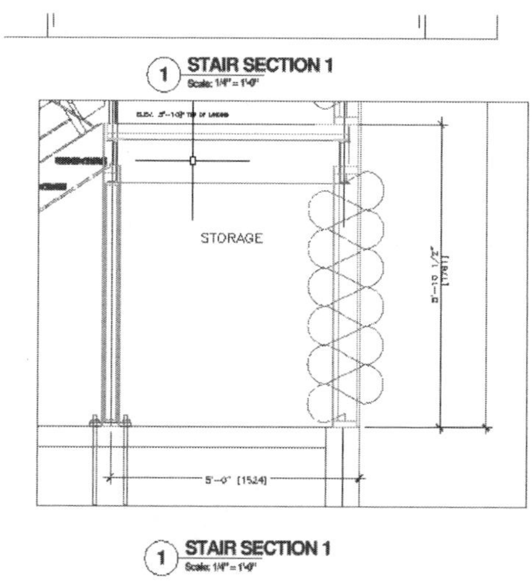

Double click on the copied view tag to modify the attributes.

27. 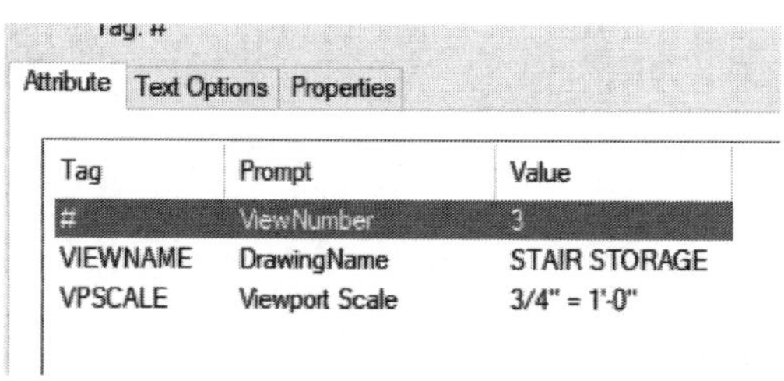

Change the ViewNumber to **3**.
Change the Viewname to **STAIR STORAGE.**
Change the Viewport Scale to **¾" = 1'-0".**

Click **OK**.

28. Save as *ex9-25.dwg*.

Review Questions

1. Which dimensioning units are most often used for Mechanical technical drawings?
   A. Decimal
   B. Engineering
   C. Architectural
   D. Scientific

2. The _______ dialog box is used to control dimension styles and variables.
   A. DIMENSION
   B. DIMSTYLE
   C. Dimension Style Manager
   D. STYLE

3. **T F** The DIMASO system variable governs the creation of associative dimensioning.

4. **T F** The size of dimension arrows cannot be modified.

5. The default dimension style is called:
   A. DEFAULT
   B. STANDARD
   C. OVERRIDE
   D. STYLE1

6. **T F** The DIMSTYLE command allows you to change the text style of the dimension.

7. **T F** Adding text to an existing dimension text is not possible.

8. **T F** Horizontal, vertical, aligned, and rotated dimensions cannot be associative dimensions.

9. **T F** You can trim and extend associative dimension extension lines.

10. **T F** Dimension Styles cannot be named.

11. **T F** To remove the jog symbol from a jogged linear dimension, use the erase command and then the join command to clean up the gap.

12. **T F** If you modify a dimension style, all dimensions using that style in the drawing update automatically.

Review Answers

1. Which dimensioning units are most often used for Mechanical technical drawings?

   A. Decimal

2. The _______ dialog box is used to control dimension styles and variables.

   C. Dimension Style Manager

3. **T F** The DIMASO system variable governs the creation of associative dimensioning.

   True

4. **T F** The size of dimension arrows cannot be modified.

   False

5. The default dimension style is called:

   B. STANDARD

6. **T F** The DIMSTYLE command allows you to change the text style of the dimension.

   True

7. **T F** Adding text to existing dimension text is not possible.

   False

8. **T F** Horizontal, vertical, aligned, and rotated dimensions cannot be associative dimensions.

   False

9. **T F** You can trim and extend associative dimension extension lines.

   False

10. **T F** Dimension Styles cannot be named.

    False

11. **T F** To remove the jog symbol from a jogged linear dimension, use the erase command and then the join command to clean up the gap.

    False

12. **T F** If you modify a dimension style, all dimensions using that style in the drawing update automatically.

    True

Notes:

Lesson 10.0 – Text Tools

Estimated Class Time: 2 Hours

Objectives

This section will cover how to use text. Learn to type text in either single or multiple lines, edit text and use multi-leaders (notes with arrows). Create text styles choosing from a variety of fonts.

- **Single Line Text**

  Type a single line of text for simple notes.
- **Multiline Text**

  Use the Multiline Text editor to create paragraphs of text or sentences that can be stretched into wider or narrower paragraphs using Grips.
- **Text Style**

  Create several Text Styles for specific text requirements.
- **Edit Text**

  Use the Edit Text command to change the content of Single Line or Multiline text. Use the Properties command to change other features of the text in the drawing.
- **Fields**

  Fields are tied to drawing properties and can be used as a more dynamic and powerful version of attributes.
- **Tables**

  Tables may be used for tabulated drawings, parts lists, and material lists. Fields, attributes and texts can all be inserted into a table.
- **Mleaders**

  A multileader object typically consists of an arrowhead, a horizontal landing, a leader line or curve, and either a multiline text object or a block.

Single Line Text

Command Locator

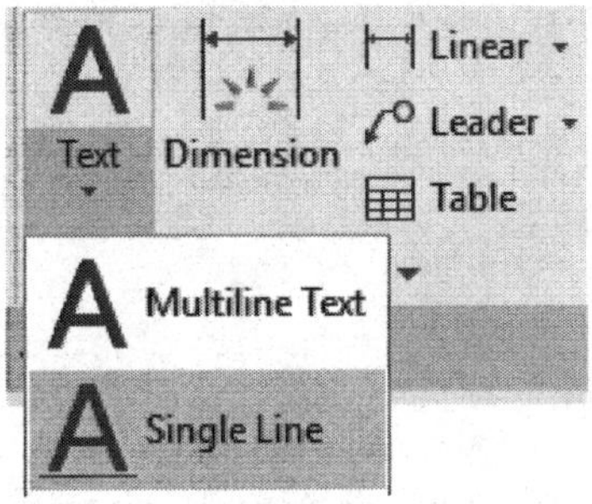

Command	**TEXT**
Ribbon/Home/Annotation	**TEXT**
Ribbon/Annotate/Text	**TEXT**
Alias	**DT**
RMB Shortcut Menu	**Justify/Style**

Command Overview

Text can be typed as a single line at a time with the TEXT command. Text can be moved, copied, rotated, scaled or changed after it has been placed in the drawing. When typing text, the spacebar will create a space, and the <ENTER> key will act as a carriage return and bring the cursor to the next line. The <ENTER> button on the mouse (RMB) will not work with text. Use the <ENTER> key on the keyboard. The easiest way to use the Single Line Text command is to pick a start point and follow the prompts for the Text height and Text rotation angle, then begin typing. It is important to Click <ENTER> twice to end the TEXT command. This is because the first time <ENTER> is Clicked, the cursor will move to the next line, but the text will not be placed until <ENTER> is Clicked again. Single Line Text is best when used for simple notes that contain only a few words or a short sentence.

TEXT Option	Overview
Start point	Pick a start point for the text in the Drawing Window.
Specify height	Type in a height, or Click <ENTER> to accept the default text height.
Specify rotation angle	Type in a rotation angle or Click <ENTER> to accept the default rotation angle.

Two less common options within the TEXT command are Justify and Style. Type J (and <ENTER>) to access the Justification options. The more common Justification options are Align, Fit, Center, Middle, and Right. Justifications will not display until the TEXT command is completely executed. The default start point is Left Justification and need not be typed.

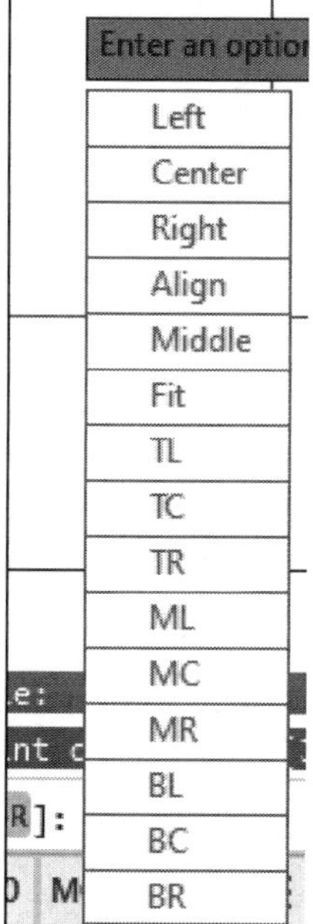

Justification	Overview
Align	Aligns the text between two points, scaling the text height proportionately.
Fit	Fits the text between two points, maintaining the text height.
Center	Centers the text at the (bottom center).
Middle	Centers the text right in the middle of the text.
Right	Justifies the text to the right.

General Procedures:

1. Begin the Single Line Text command by typing **DT** (and <ENTER>).
2. Pick a start point in the Drawing Window.
3. Type the text height, or Click <ENTER> to accept the default Text height.
4. Click <ENTER> to accept the default rotation angle (0) or type a new angle.
5. Type the first line of text. Click <ENTER>. Type the second line of text. Click <ENTER> twice to complete the dtext command.

Command Exercise

Exercise 10-1 – Single Line Text

Drawing Name: **text1.dwg**
Estimated Time to Completion: 5 Minutes

Scope

Create the two lines of text as indicated in the drawing using the Single Line text command.

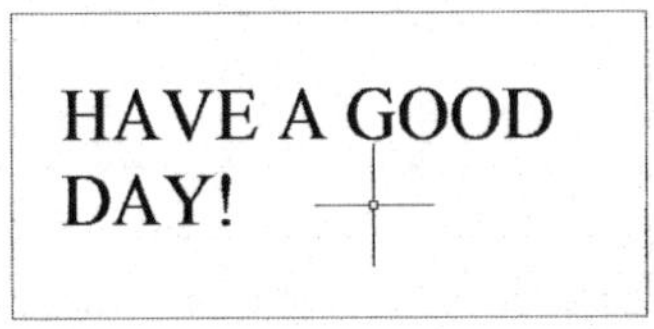

Solution

1. 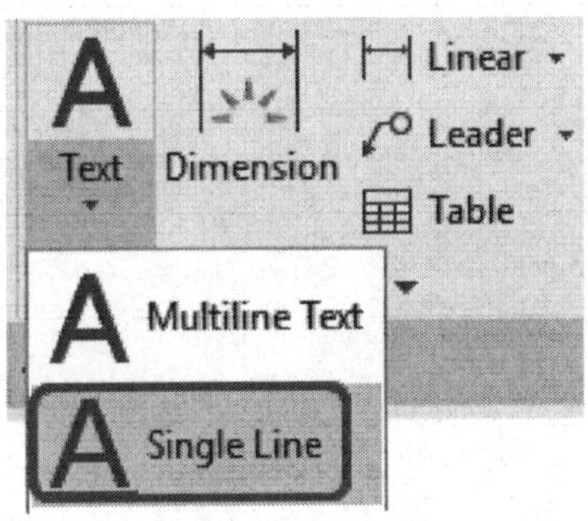

Invoke the Single Line Text command.
From the Annotation panel on the Home tab, select **Text→ Single Line Text** (or type *dt, dtext* or *text*).

2. 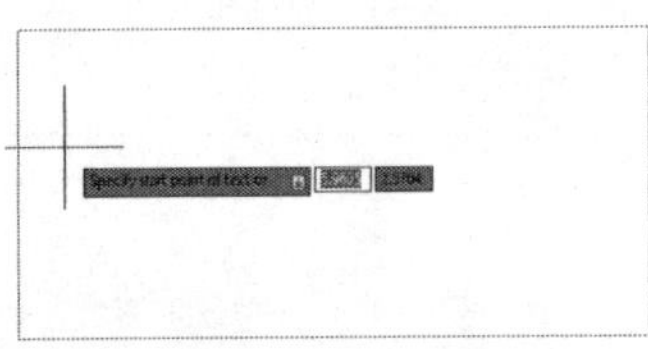

Specify start point of text or [Justify/Style]:
Use the LMB to pick the start point of the text.
Remember that the text will be created from this pick point.

3. 

Specify height <0.2000>:
Type **0.4** and Click <ENTER>.

4. 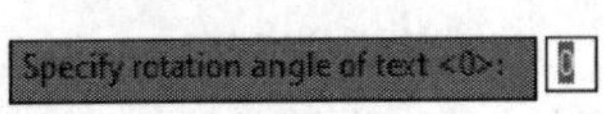

Specify rotation angle of text <0>:
Type **0** and Click <ENTER> or simply Click <ENTER> to accept the default value.

5.

Type the first line of text **HAVE A GOOD** and Click <ENTER> once.

6.

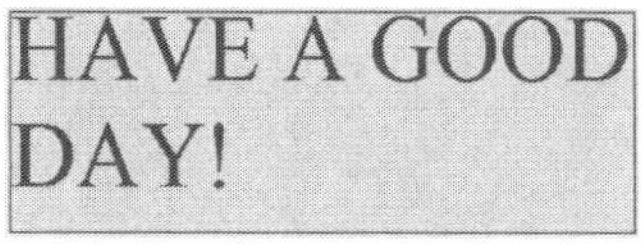

Type the second line of text **DAY!**.

7.

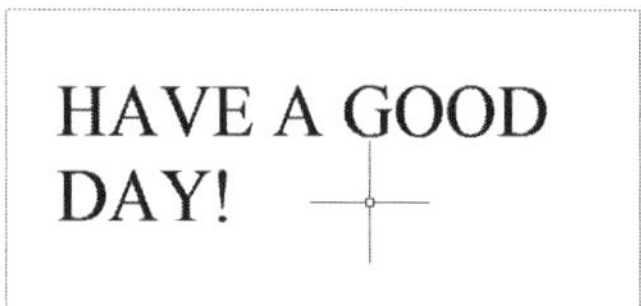

LMB outside of the textbox and Click <ESC> to exit the command.

- Single Line Text (DTEXT) is referred to as dynamic or *displayed* text because it is displayed on the screen as it is being typed.
- When the Dtext (Single Line Text) command is repeated, the last line of text will be highlighted to show the height and rotation. Clicking enter will automatically place the text cursor under the last line of text. The cursor can be moved at any time to locate new start points.
- Remember to Click <ENTER> at the Keyboard.
- You will not be prompted for a text height if one is specified in the current text style.

Command Exercise

Exercise 10-2 – Single Line Text Options

Drawing Name: **text2.dwg**
Estimated Time to Completion: 30 Minutes

Scope

Recreate the single line text. Use the different methods of justifying the text. Note that the text justifications will not be displayed until the Enter key is Clicked twice to complete the DTEXT command.

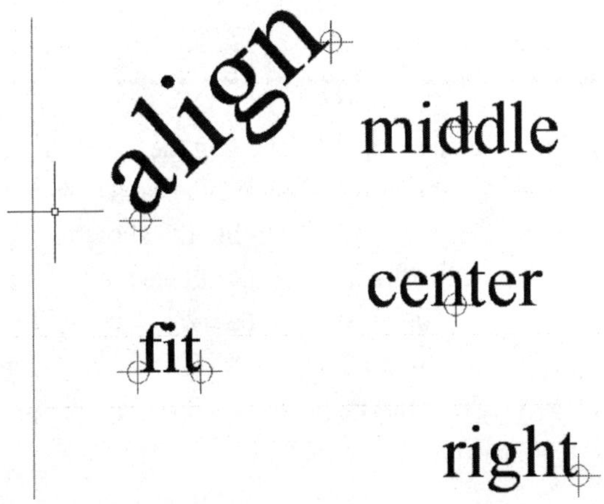

Solution

1. 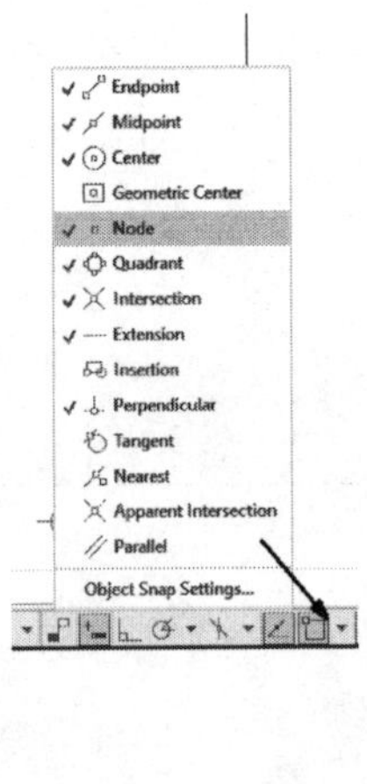

Enable the **Node** OSNAP.

2. 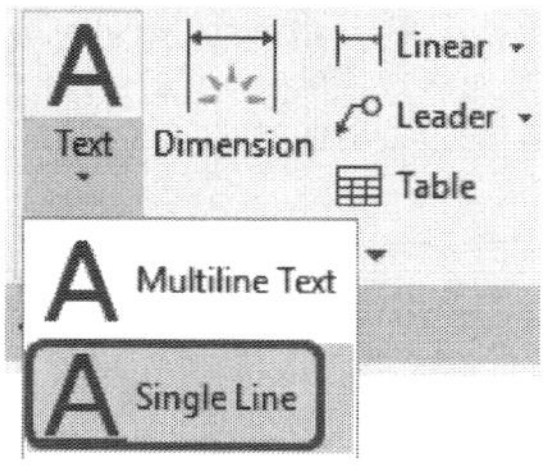

Invoke the '**Single Line Text**' command.

3. 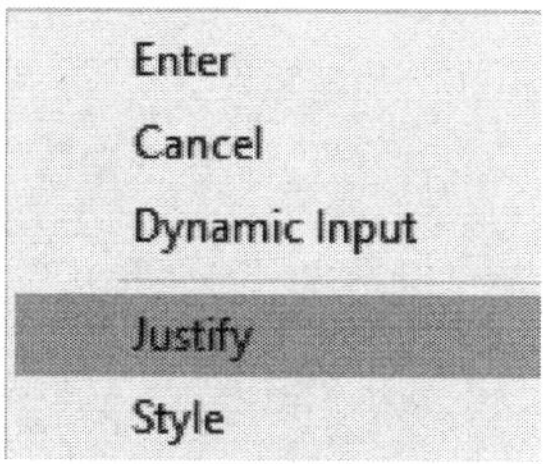

When prompted for a starting point, type **J** for justify or RMB and select '**Justify**'.

A shortcut menu will appear.

4. 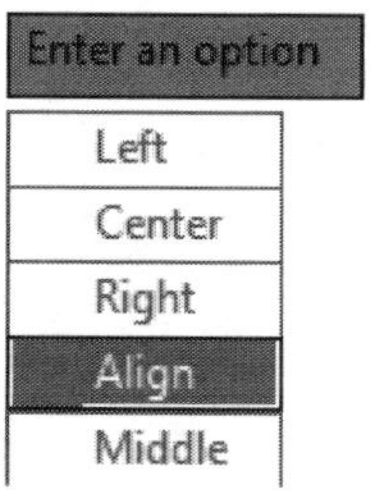

Select **Align**.

5. 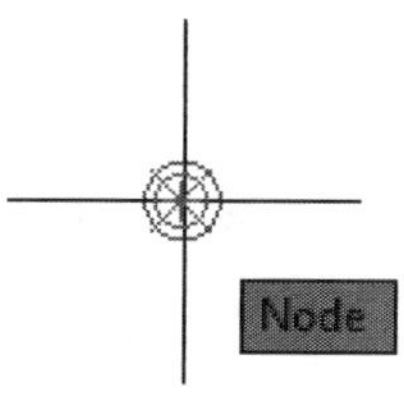

Specify first endpoint of text baseline:
Pick the first point with the LMB.

6. 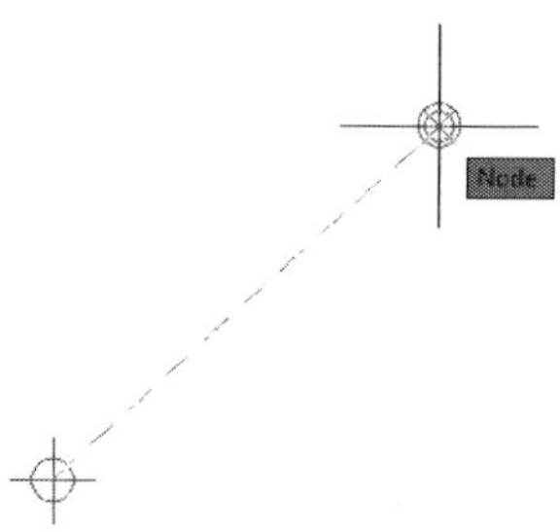

Specify second endpoint of text baseline:
Select the second align point with the LMB.

7. 

Type **align** and LMB outside the text box.

Click <ESC> to exit the command.

8. Invoke the 'Single Line Text' command

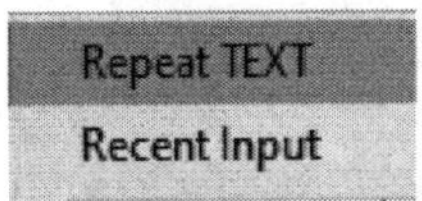

9. 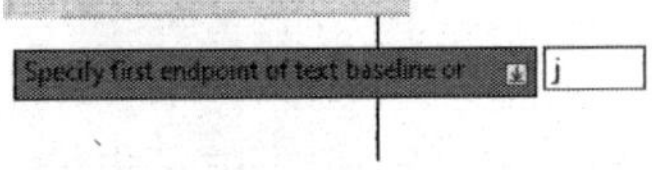

Type **J** for Justify.
Click <ENTER>.

10. 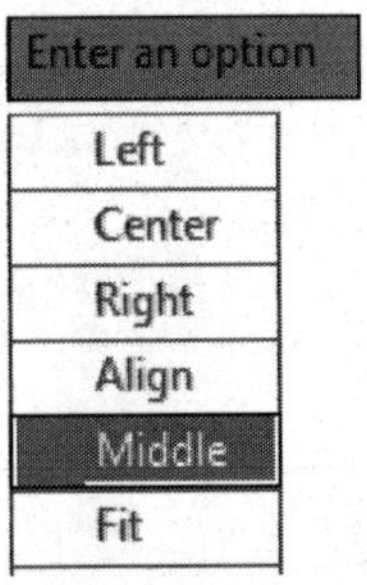

LMB on **Middle**.

11. 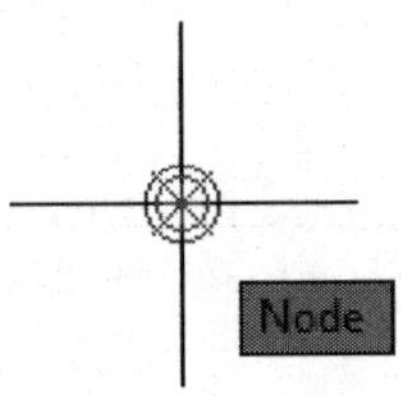

With the Node OSNAP enabled, pick the node to be used for the middle text.

12. 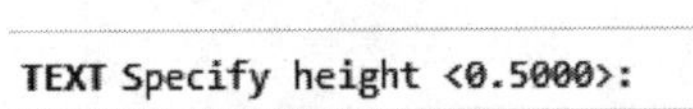

Specify height <0.5000>:
Click <ENTER>.

13. 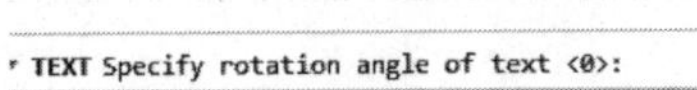

Specify rotation angle of text <0>:
Click <ENTER>.

14. 

Enter text:
Type **middle** and Click <ENTER>.

Click <ESC> to exit the command.

15. 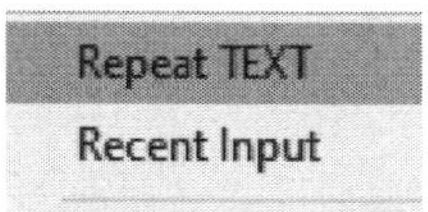

Repeat the **Single Line Text** command with the RMB (dt, dtext, text or <ENTER>).

16. 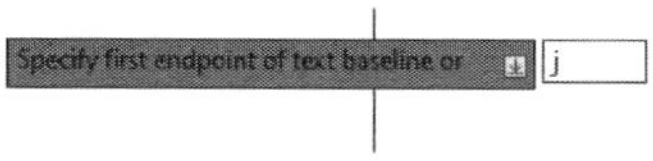

Type **J** for Justify.
Click <ENTER>.

17. 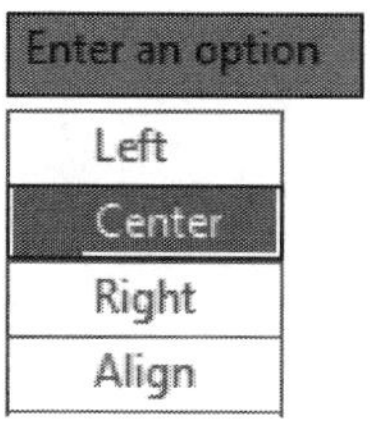

Select **Center** or type '**C**' for Center.
Click <ENTER>.

18. 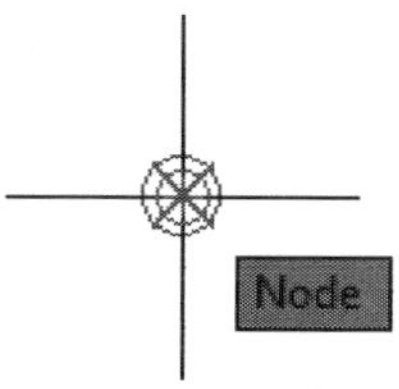

Specify center point of text:
Pick the center point with the LMB.

Specify height <0.5000>:
Click <ENTER>.

Specify rotation angle of text <0>:
Click <ENTER>.

19. 

Enter text:
Type **center.**
Click <ENTER>.

Click <ESC> to exit the command.

20. 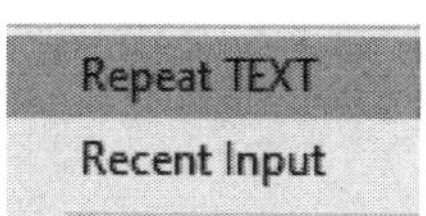

Repeat the Single Line Text command with the RMB (dt, dtext, text or <ENTER>).

21. 

Type **J** for Justify and Click <ENTER>.

22. 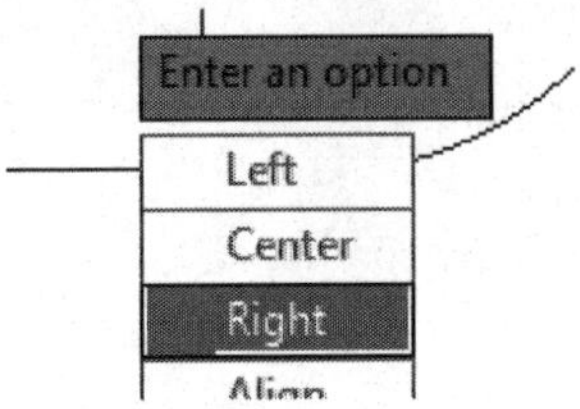

Select **Right.**
Click <ENTER>.

23. 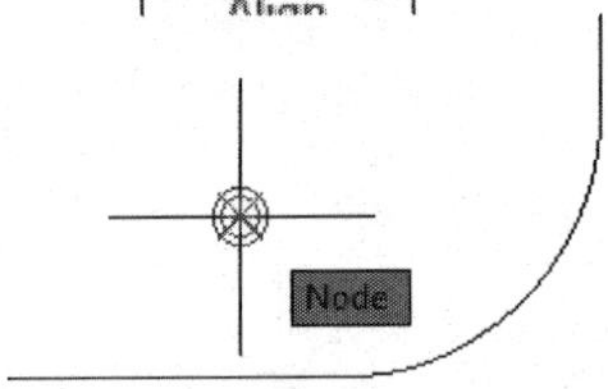

Specify right end point of text:
Pick the right end point with the LMB.

Specify height <0.5000>:
Click <ENTER>.

Specify rotation angle of text <0>:
Click <ENTER>.

24. 

Enter text:
Type **right** and Click <ENTER>.

Click <ESC> to exit the command.

25. 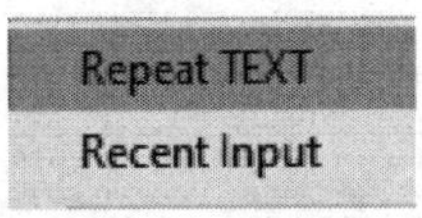

Repeat the Single Line Text command with the RMB (dt, dtext, text or <ENTER>).

26. 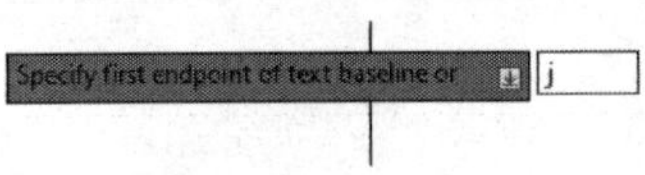

Type **J** for Justify and Click <ENTER>.

27. 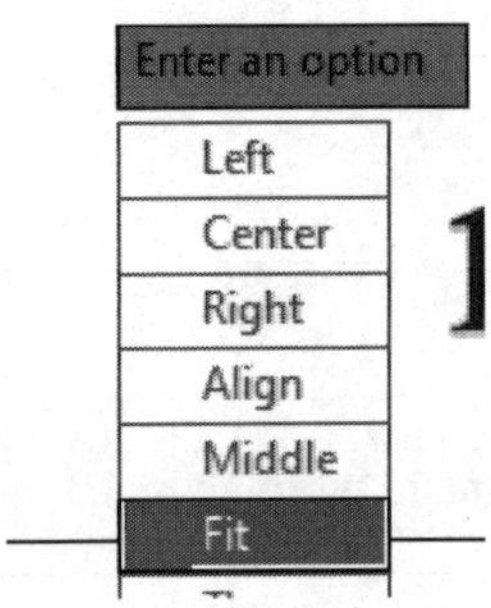

Select **Fit** or type **F** for Fit and Click <ENTER>.

28. 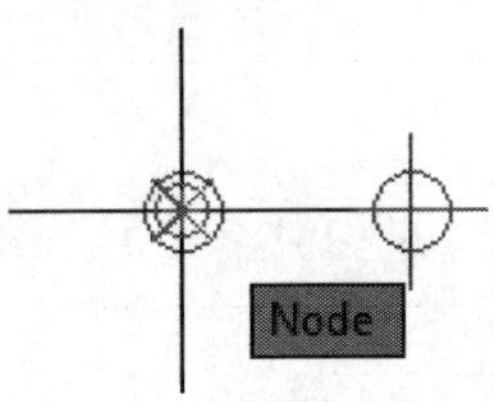

Specify first endpoint of text baseline:
Pick the first point with the LMB.

29.

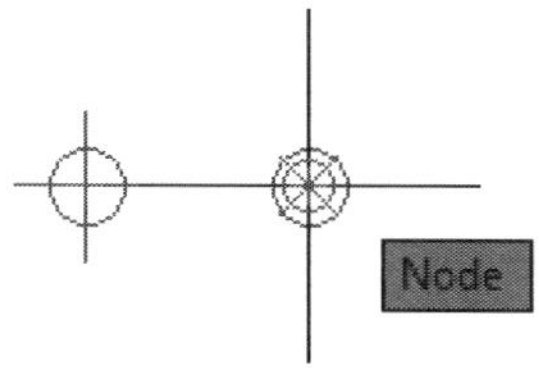

Specify second endpoint of text baseline:
Pick the second point with the LMB.

Specify height <0.5000>:
Click <ENTER>.

30.

Enter text:
Type **fit** and Click <ENTER>.

Click <ESC> to exit the command.

Multiline Text

Command Locator

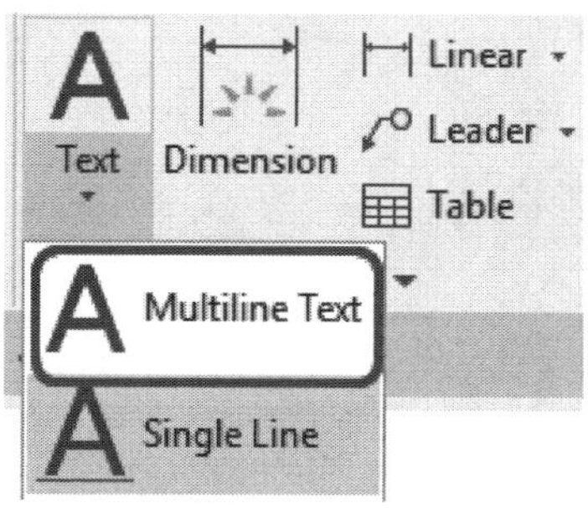

Command	**MTEXT**
Ribbon/Home/Annotation	**Multiline TEXT**
Ribbon/Annotate/Text	**MultilineTEXT**
Alias	**MT**

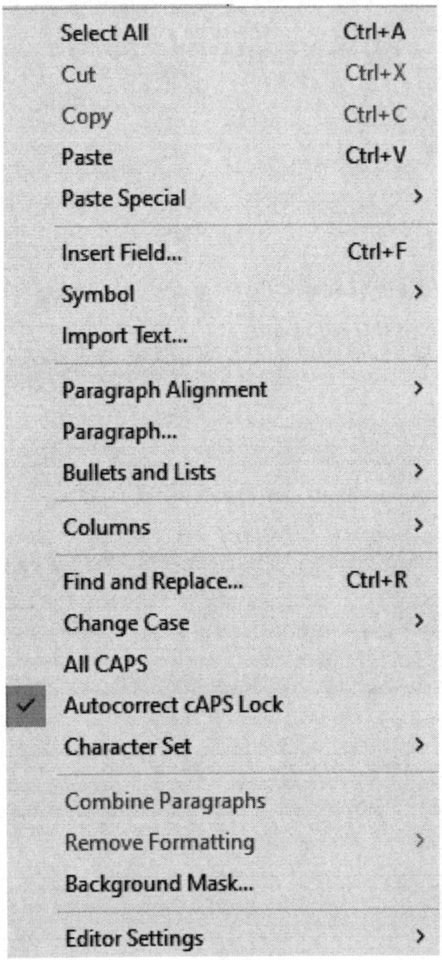

If you RMB click in the MTEXT window, you have several more options available to you, including placing Indents and Tabs, inserting symbols, inserting fields, and modifying the text.

Command Overview

Create paragraphs of text with the Multiline Text command. Define the area where the Multiline text should appear in the drawing by picking the opposite corners of the text box in the drawing window. Type the text in the Multiline Text Editor dialog box. Multiline Text can be moved, rotated, scaled, copied or changed after it has been placed in the drawing. Use the grips to adjust the paragraph width. When typing in the text editor, the spacebar will create a space, and the <ENTER> key will act as a carriage return and bring the cursor to the next line. The cursor may be placed between letters by picking once (LMB). A double click will select an entire word and a triple click will select the entire sentence. The <ENTER> button on the mouse (RMB) when placed within the Multiline Text Editor dialog box will invoke a shortcut menu with options to Cut, Copy, and Paste selected text. To resize the Multiline Text Editor, select a corner of the window with the LMB and drag. The Editor contains four tabs: Character, Properties, Line Spacing, and Find/Replace. Begin the Multiline text command, specify the first corner, then the opposite corner of the window. Type text in the Multiline Text Editor, use the available options, then select OK to place the text in the drawing. The Edit Text command will open the same Text Editor dialog box with the selected text for editing.

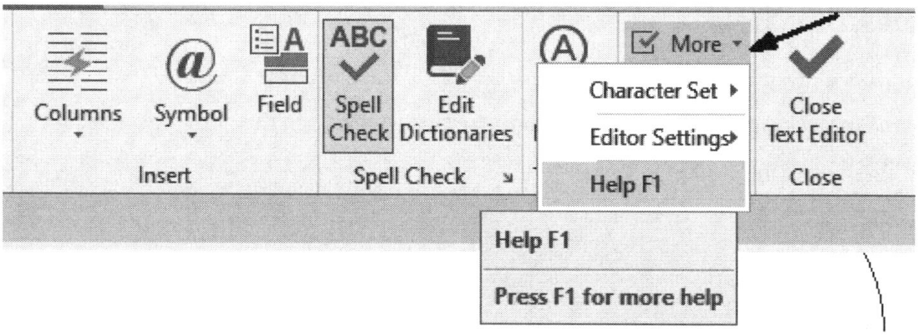

*If you select the **More** button at the far right of the MTEXT dialog, you can control the appearance of the MTEXT dialog box.*

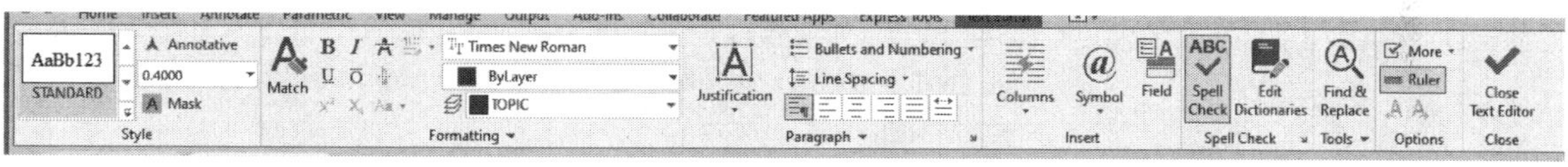

Multiline Text Editor Option	Overview
Font	Change the font of selected words with this option. This option should be used when changing only a few selected words. If a global font change is preferred, use the Text Style command.
Font height	Change the height of selected words.
Bold	Make selected text Bold, when applicable to the font.
Italics	Make selected text *Italic,* when applicable to the font.
Underline	Underlines selected text.
Undo	This option will undo the last step in the dialog box.
Redo	This option will undo the last undo.
Stack	This option will stack selected words or text when separated by a forward slash.
Color	This option will make selected text a different color. Select a color from the list. Color changes to selected text will override color changes applied to the layer or the object.

General Procedures:

1. Invoke the Multiline Text command by typing T or selecting the icon from the draw toolbar.
2. Specify Text area by picking the first corner, then the opposite corner in the drawing Window.
3. Type the Multiline Text Editor dialog box.
4. Select OK to exit.

- In the Multiline Text editor, single click (LMB) to insert words or letters. Double click to highlight the entire word. Triple click to select the entire sentence.
- Clicking the <ENTER> button on the mouse (RMB), with the cursor in the text box, will bring up the cursor menu with the Windows Edit options.
- Type text using the space bar (and not <ENTER>) to allow sentences to wrap.
- After exiting the multiline text dialog box, use grips to adjust the width of the Multiline Text.
- Documents to be imported into the text editor should be saved in Text (.txt) or Rich Text Format (.rtf).
- Exploding Multiline text will make single lines of text.

Command Exercise

Exercise 10-3 – Multiline Text

Drawing Name: **mtext1.dwg**
Estimated Time to Completion: 5 Minutes

Scope

Use the Multiline text command to create the text as indicated.

Solution

1. 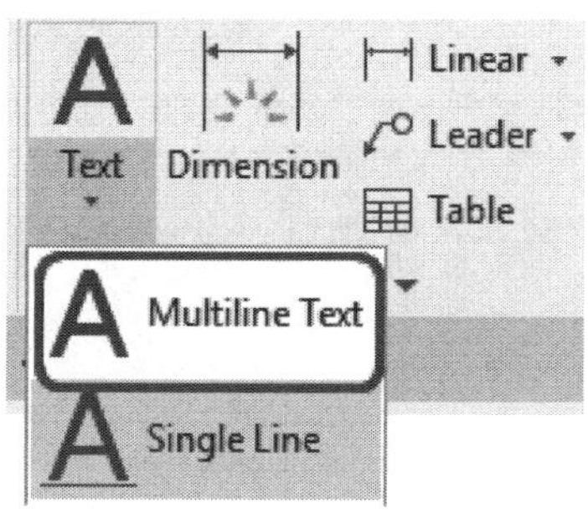

Invoke the Multiline Text command (mt or mtext).

2. 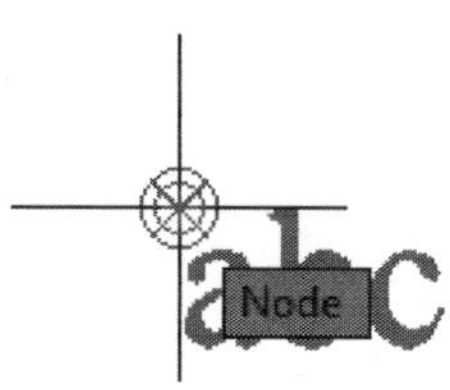

Specify first corner:

Use the Node Object Snap to select the upper left point.

3. 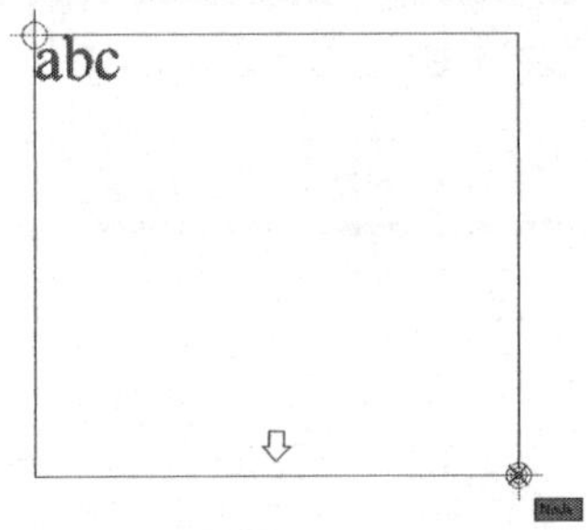

Specify opposite corner or [Height/Justify/Line spacing/ Rotation/Style/Width]:

Use the Node Object Snap to select the lower right point.

4. 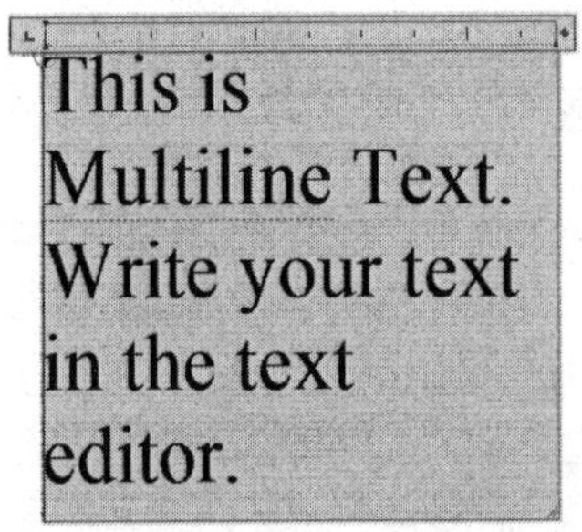

Type the text as shown on the left side of the screen.

5. 

Use your mouse to highlight the words **'text editor**.'.

6. 

Enable the **Underline** option on the ribbon.

7. 

Click **Close Text Editor** on the Ribbon to close the dialog or left click outside the mtext box.

Command Exercise

Exercise 10-4 – Formatting Multiline Text

Drawing Name: **mtext2.dwg**
Estimated Time to Completion: 10 Minutes

Scope

Use the Multiline text command to create the text as indicated.

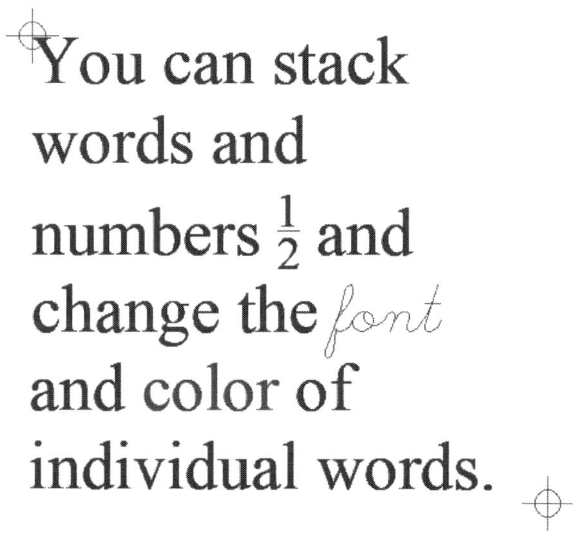

Solution

1.

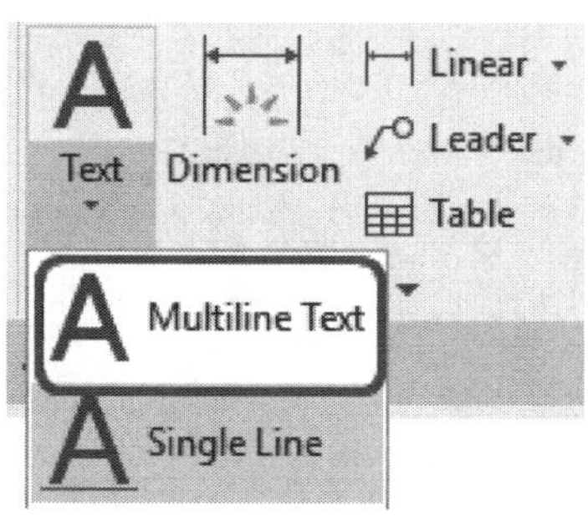

Invoke the Multiline Text command (mt or mtext).

2. 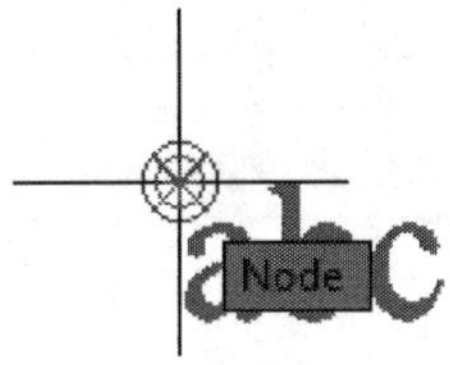

Specify first corner:

Use the Node Object Snap to select the upper left point.

3. 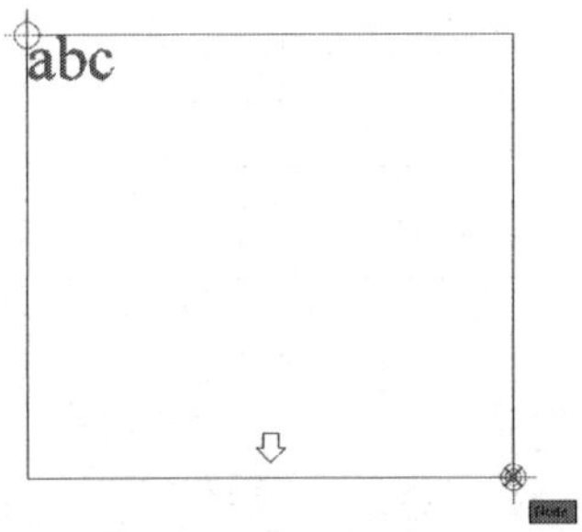

Specify opposite corner or [Height/Justify/Line spacing/ Rotation/Style/Width]:

Use the Node Object Snap to select the lower right point.

4. 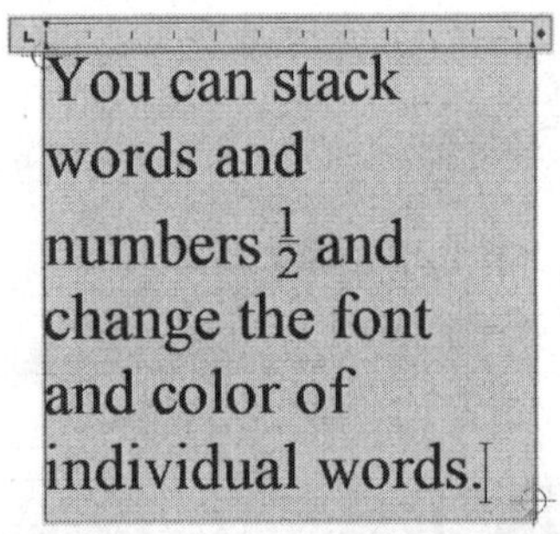

Type the text as shown on the left side of the screen.

Notice how the fraction automatically stacked the numbers.

5. 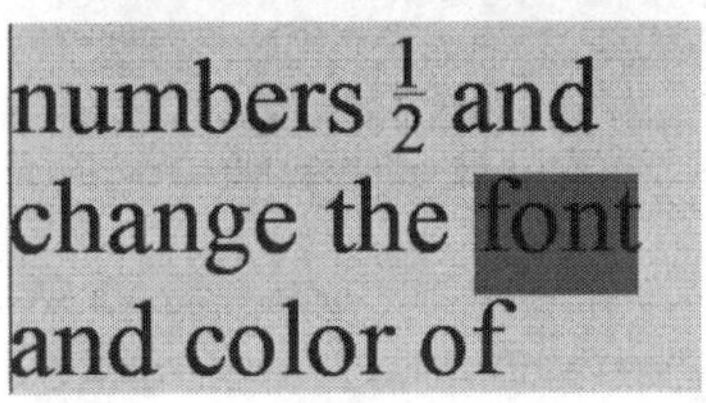

Use your mouse to highlight the word '**font**'.

6. 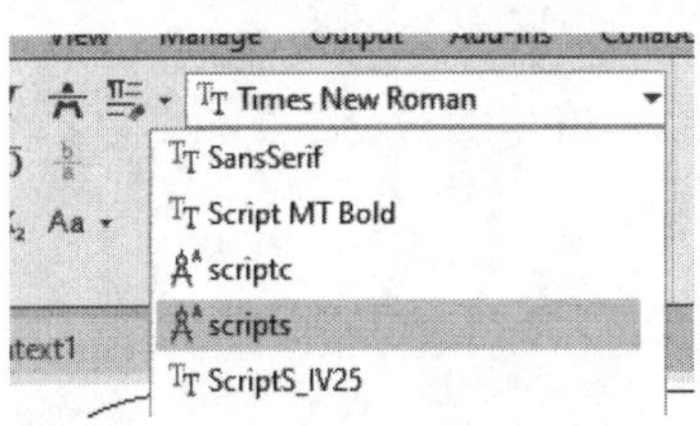

Select **scripts** from the drop-down list on the ribbon.

Hint: *You can start typing the font name and the list will automatically take you to that font.*

Note that the text will preview as you mouse over different font styles.

7. 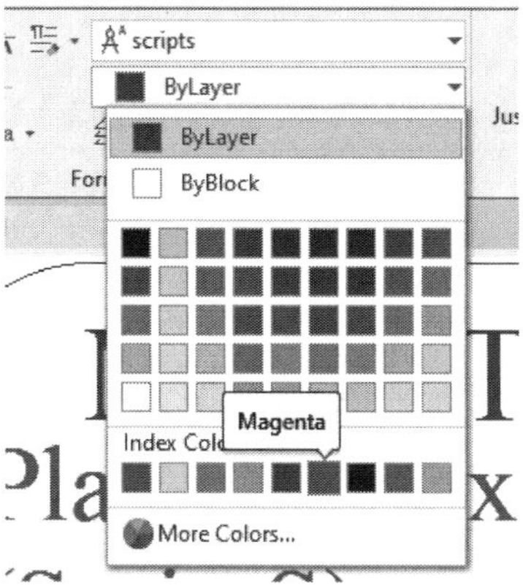

Change the color of the word to **magenta** using the ribbon.

8. 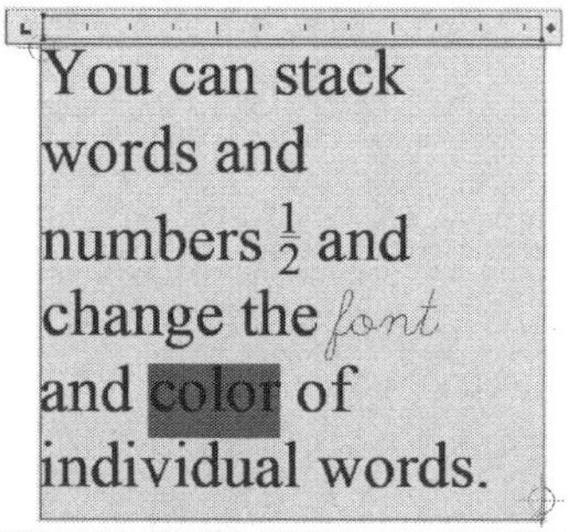

Highlight the word **color**.

9. 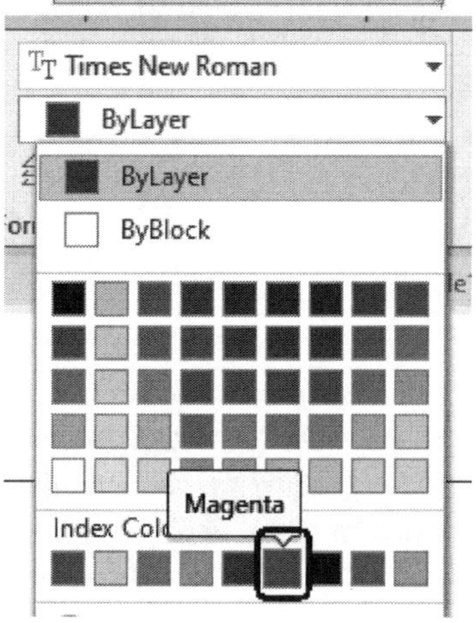

Change the color of the word to **magenta** using the ribbon.

10. 

Click **Close Text Editor** on the Ribbon to close the dialog or left click outside the mtext box.

Text Style

Command Locator

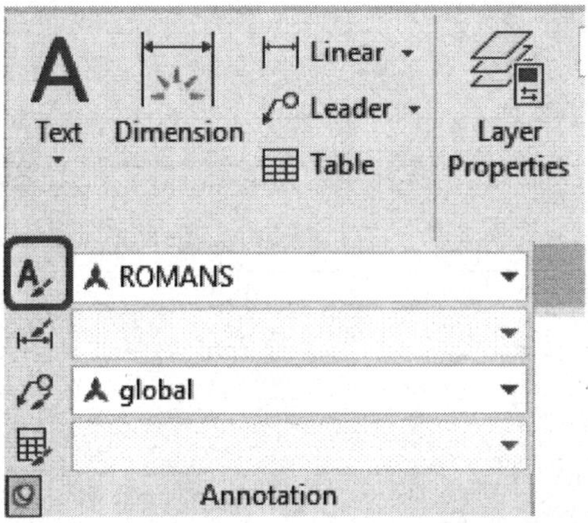

Ribbon/Home/Annotation	**Annotation pull-down**
Command	**Style**
Alias	**ST**
Dialog Box	**Text Style**

Command Overview

In addition to the Standard Text Style, additional styles can be created. Text will be typed in the current text style and may be changed from one style to another. Applying a different font to a Text Style will globally change the font of any text in the drawing that has been typed in that style. AutoCAD supports most Windows fonts including TrueType fonts. Text Styles may be deleted or Purged only if there is no text in the drawing referencing that style, or it is not the current style.

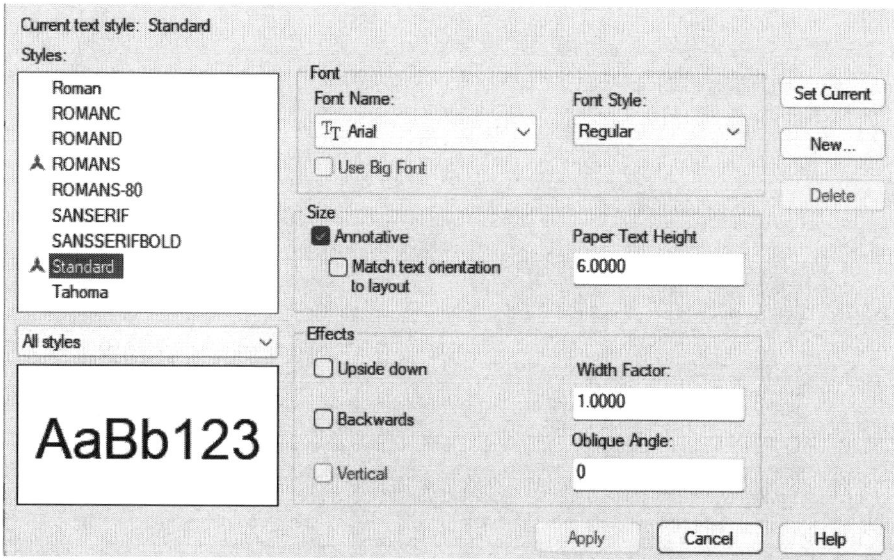

Text Style Option	Overview
Style Name	The current style will be at the top of the list of Text Style in the drawing. The default style is Standard with the txt.shx font.
New	Select this button to make a new Text Style. The default name will be style1, but it may be renamed.
Rename…	Select this button to rename a selected Text Style.
Delete	Select this option to delete a selected Text Style. There cannot be text in the drawing using that Style.
Font	Select a Font from the Font Name list. The default font for the Standard style is txt.shx. AutoCAD supports most Windows fonts including TrueType fonts.
Font Style	Font style options will be displayed according to the Font selected. Some fonts do not have Font style options.
Font Size	When the Text Style height is 0.0, the user will always be prompted for a text height when using the DTEXT command. Text style height can be pre-set; however, it is always possible to change the height of text in the drawing. When Annotative is enabled, the text will automatically be scaled depending on the annotative scale. Instead of creating text styles for different text heights, you can use annotative scale to control the size of the text.
Effects	These are hardly used options that include Upside down, Backwards, and Vertical. A Width factor of 1.0 is a normal width. Greater than 1 is a wider letter, and less than 1 is a narrower letter. Oblique Angle creates a slant letter.
Set Current	Select this button to apply changes to the Text Style before exiting the dialog box.

AutoCAD Text Scale Charts

ARCHITECTURAL

The chart lists drawing scale factors and AutoCAD text heights for common architectural drafting scales.

All text shown in inches:
(1/8 = 1/8"); (3 = 3"); (1 1/2 = 1 1/2"); (48 = 48"), etc...
To get feet, divide by 12

Drawing Scale	Drawing Scale Factor	1/64" Plotted Text Height	1/32" Plotted Text Height	1/16" Plotted Text Height	3/32" Plotted Text Height	1/8" Plotted Text Height	3/16" Plotted Text Height	1/4" Plotted Text Height	3/8" Plotted Text Height	1/2" Plotted Text Height	3/4" Plotted Text Height	1" Plotted Text Height
1/16" = 1' - 0"	192	3	6	12	18	24	36	48	72	96	144	192
1/8" = 1' - 0"	96	1 1/2	3	6	9	12	18	24	36	48	72	96
3/16" = 1' - 0"	64	1	2	4	6	8	12	16	24	32	48	64
1/4" = 1' - 0"	48	3/4	1 1/2	3	4 1/2	6	9	12	18	24	36	48
1/2" = 1' - 0"	24	3/8	3/4	1 1/2	2 1/4	3	4 1/2	6	9	12	18	24
3/4" = 1' - 0"	16	1/4	1/2	1	1 1/2	2	3	4	6	8	12	16
1" = 1' - 0"	12	3/16	3/8	3/4	1 1/8	1 1/2	2 1/4	3	4 1/2	6	9	12
1-1/2" = 1' - 0"	8	1/8	1/4	1/2	3/4	1	1 1/2	2	3	4	6	8
3" = 1' - 0"	4	1/16	1/8	1/4	3/8	1/2	3/4	1	1 1/2	2	3	4

Use this text height chart as a reference when defining your text styles.

General Procedures:

Making changes to the Standard Text Style:

1. Invoke the Text Style command.
2. Select a different Font from the drop down list.
3. Select Apply, then Close the dialog box.

Creating a New Text Style:

1. Invoke the Text Style command.
2. Select "New" and type a name for that style (or accept the default name).
3. Select a Font from the drop down list. Optional: Type the Height for the new text style.
4. Select Apply, then Close the dialog box.

- Use the dialog box to make a Text Style current.
- Changes applied to a Text Style will globally affect any text in the drawing referencing that style.
- Avoid having an excessive number of Text Styles. Some common text styles might be made for notes, dimensions, and the Title Block.
- You can use PURGE to eliminate any unused text styles from your drawing.
- You can import text styles from one drawing to another using the Design Center.
- You can store text styles in your template for easier access.

Command Exercise

Exercise 10-5 – Defining Text Styles

Drawing Name: **style1.dwg**
Estimated Time to Completion: 10 Minutes

Scope

Create a text style called TEXT1 and apply a text height of 0.4 and the font called Arial to that style. Type the text as indicated in the new style.

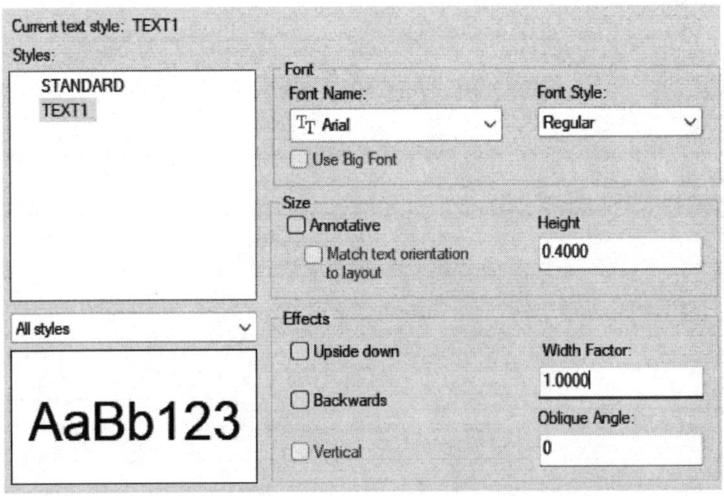

Solution

1.

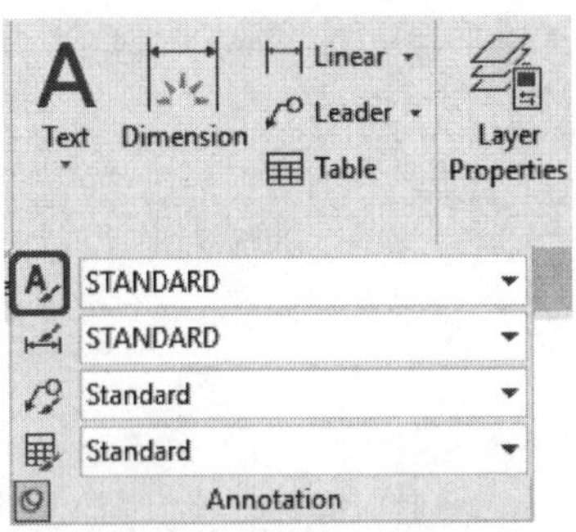

From the Home ribbon, select the **Text Style** tool on the Annotation pull-down.

2.

Click the **New** button in the Text Styles dialog box.

3. 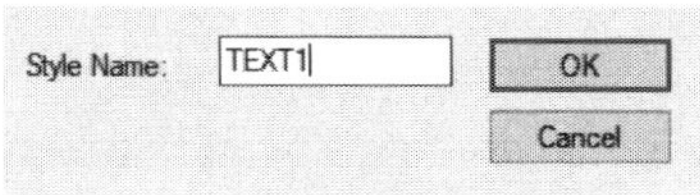

In the New Text Style dialog box, enter **TEXT1** for the name of the new text style and Click **OK**.

4. 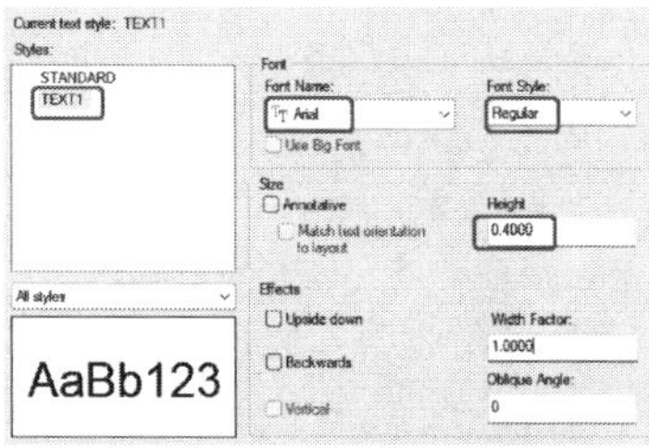

Fill in the remaining information in the Text Style dialog box.

Set the Font Name to **Arial**.
Set the Font Style to **Regular**.
Set the Height to **0.4**.

5. 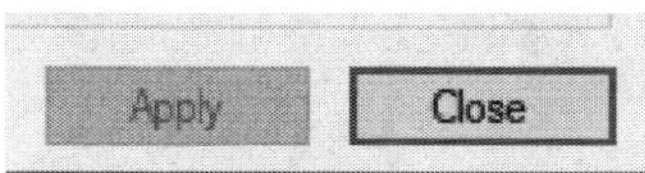

Click the **Apply** button first and then the **Close** button to apply the changes to TEXT1 and then close the dialog box.

6. 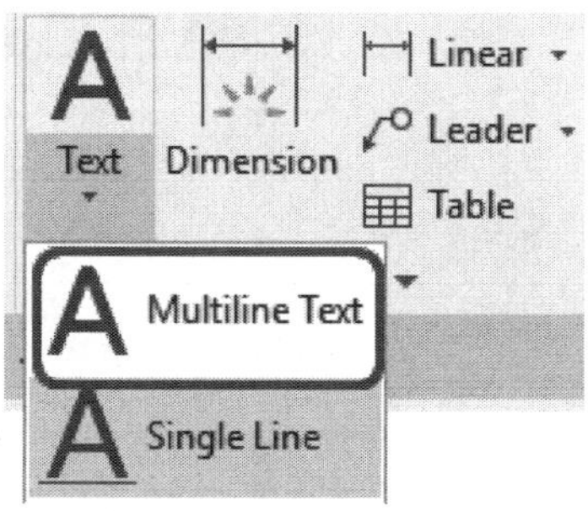

Invoke the **Multiline Text** command (mt or mtext).

7. 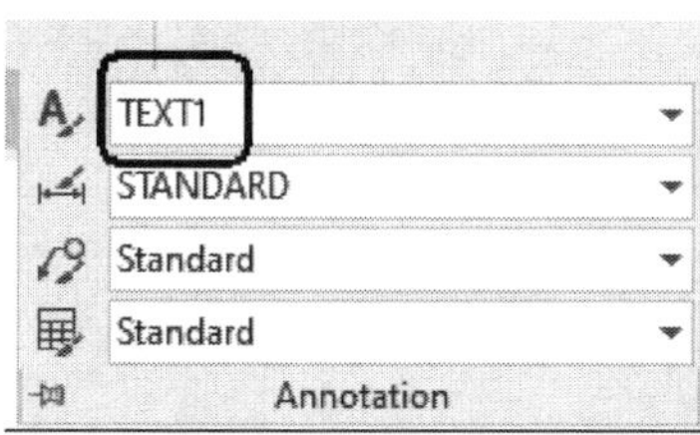

Specify first corner:
Notice that the current style is TEXT1.

8. 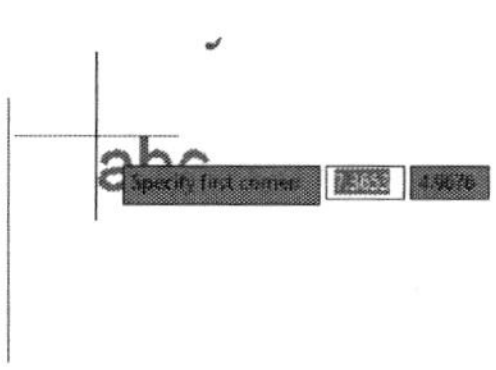

Pick the upper left corner of the multiline text window with the LMB.

9. 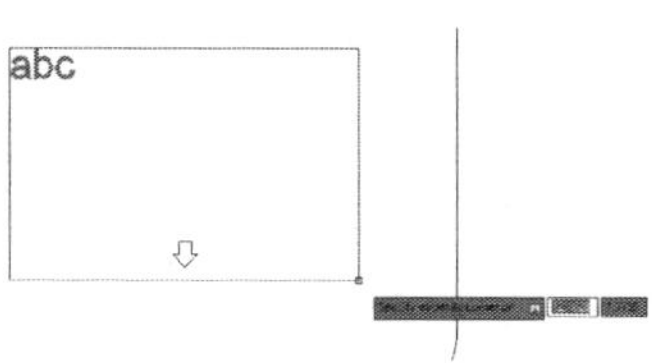

Specify opposite corner or [Height/Justify/Line spacing/ Rotation/Style/Width]:
Pick the lower right corner of the multiline text window.

10. 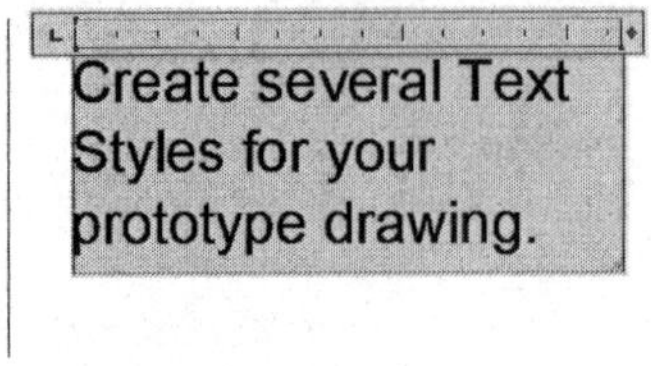

Type the desired text into the Multiline Text Editor.

11. 

Click **'Close Text Editor'** to exit.

Command Exercise

Exercise 10-6 – Define an Architectural Text Style

Drawing Name: **archtext.dwg**
Estimated Time to Completion: 10 Minutes

Scope

Create a text style called Architectural. Set the font to Tahoma and make the text style annotative. Select all the MTEXT in the drawing and apply the new style.

Solution

1.

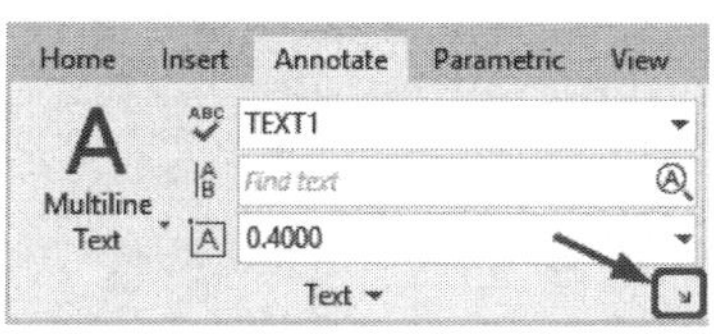

Activate the Annotate ribbon.

Select the arrow in the corner of the Text panel to launch the Text Style dialog box.

Or

Type **STYLE** at the command prompt.

2.

Click the **New** button in the Text Styles dialog box.

3. 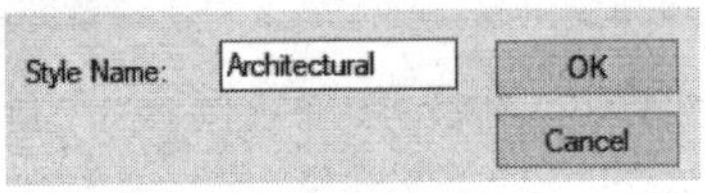

Type **Architectural** in the Style Name field.

Click **OK**.

4. 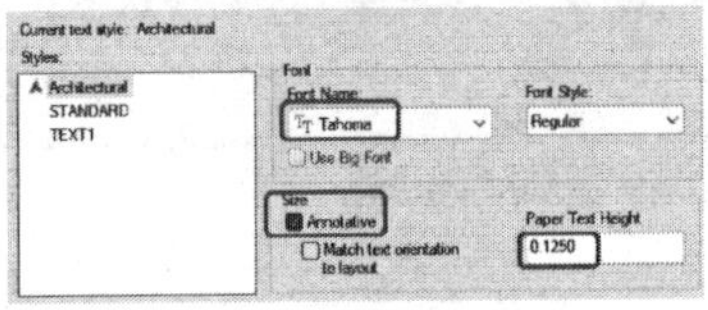

Change the Font Name to **Tahoma**.

Enable **Annotative** under Size.

Set the Paper Text Height to **0.125**.

Click **Apply**.

5. 

*Note that the Current text style is set to **Architectural.***

Close the dialog.

6. 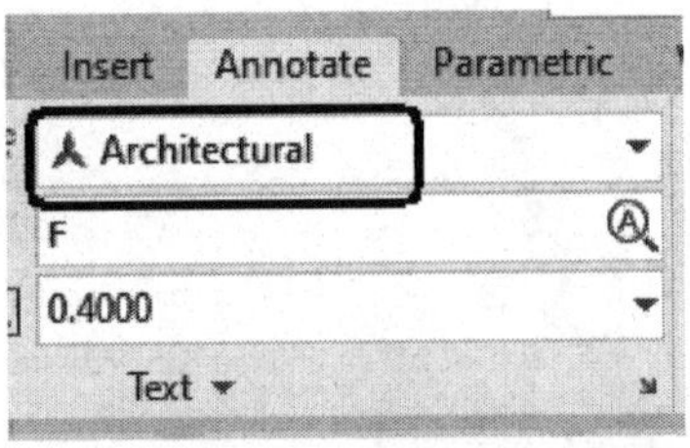

In the Text panel on the Annotate ribbon, note that the Architectural text style is set as the current text style.

7. 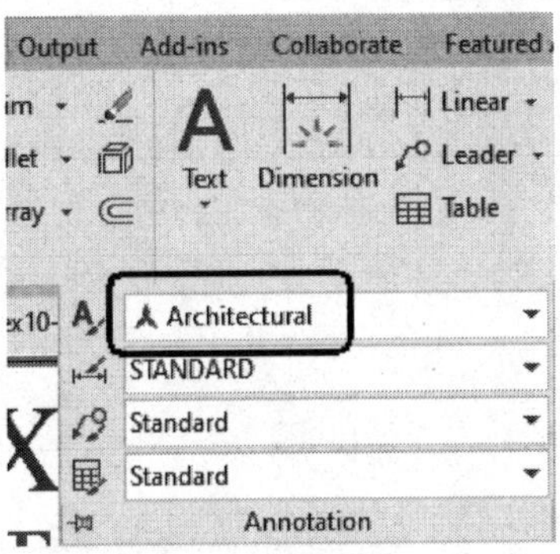

Activate the Home ribbon.

Expand the Annotation panel.

Note that the Architectural text style is listed as the current text style.

8. 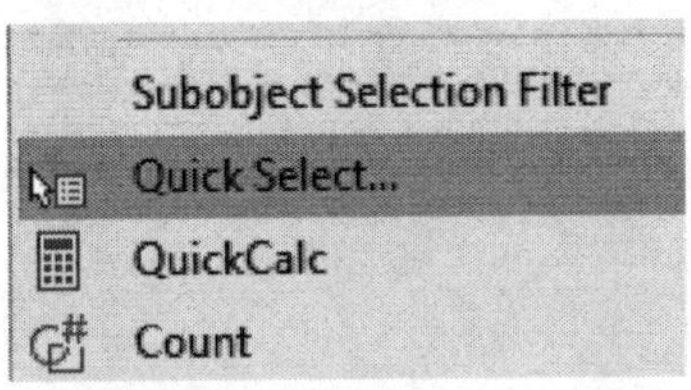

Select all the MTEXT in the drawing.

Right click in the drawing window.

Select **Quick Select**.

9. 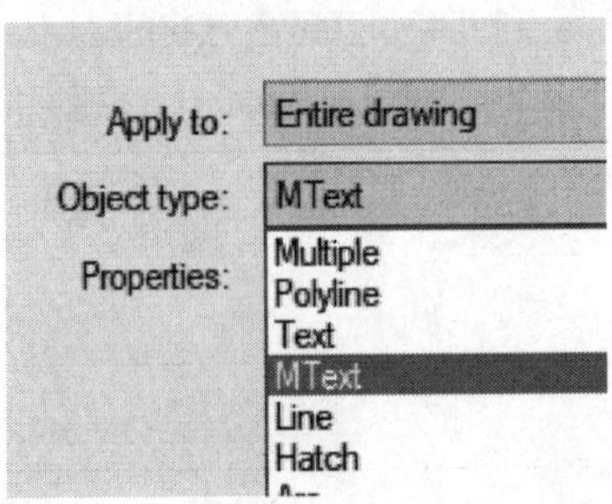

Set the Object Type to **Mtext**.

Click **OK**.

The MTEXT elements in the drawing are selected.

10. 

Right click and select **Properties**.

11. 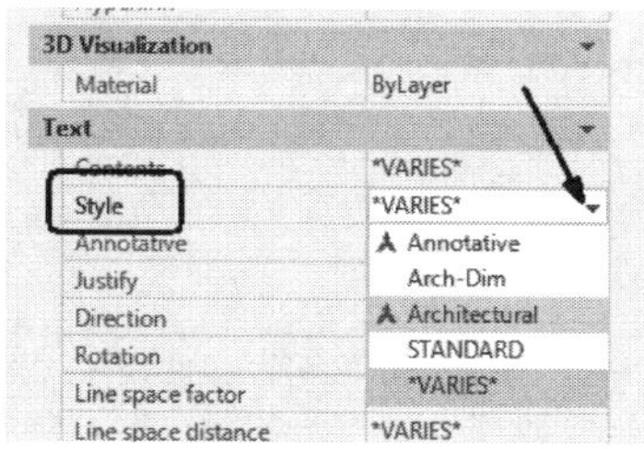

Under Style, select the **Architectural** style.

Close the Properties palette.

Click **ESC** to release the selection.

12. Save as *ex10-6.dwg*.

Edit Text

Command Locator

Command	**Ddedit**
Alias	**ED**
RMB Shortcut Menu	**Text Window**
Dialog Box	**Edit Text (when Single Line text is selected)** **Multiline Text Editor (when Multiline text is selected)**
	Double left click on the text object to edit

Command Overview

Use the Edit Text command to change the contents of Text in the drawing. For Single Line text, this will display the single line Text Editor. Text may also be edited using the Properties command. This contains additional options to change the text properties.

General Procedures:

1. Invoke the Edit Text command (ED). Select the text to edit.
2. Make corrections to the text by typing over the highlighted text, or place the cursor between letters or words and type.
3. Select OK to exit.

- Place the cursor in the text area and Click the RMB to Copy, Cut, Paste, or Delete selected text.
- The Edit Text command works with dimension text, Multiline Text, and Single Line Text.
- To exit the Edit Text mode, simply left click outside the text edit box.

Command Exercise

Exercise 10-7 – Edit Text

Drawing Name: **etext1.dwg**
Estimated Time to Completion: 5 Minutes

Scope

Edit the Single Line and Multiline Text using the Edit Text (DDEDIT) command. Edit the text on the right to be like the text on the left.

HAVE A GOOD DAY!

The Text command
issues the Multiline
Text option.

Solution

1. 

Select an annotation object or [Undo]:
Double left click to edit the "This is Single Line Text."

2. 

In the Edit Text dialog box, type over the existing text.
Type **HAVE A GOOD DAY!** and Click <ENTER>.

3. 

LMB click on the multiline text to activate the edit box.

4. 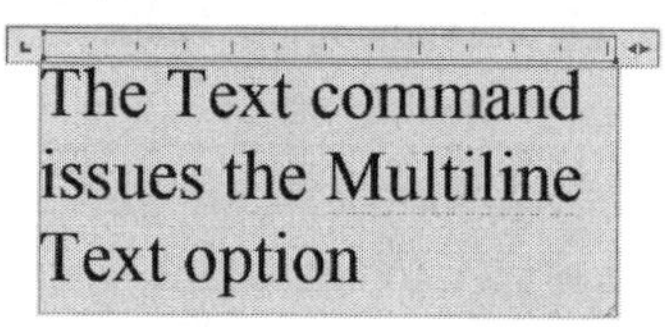

Modify the text and Click LMB outside the text edit box to exit.
Click <ESC> or right click and select <ENTER> to exit the command.

Extra: *Try copying and pasting from the multiline text on the left to the multiline text on the right using Ctl+C to copy and Ctl+V to paste.*

Command Exercise

Exercise 10-8 – Modify Text Properties

Drawing Name: **etext2.dwg**
Estimated Time to Completion: 5 Minutes

Scope

Edit the Single Line and Multiline text using the Quick Properties tool.

HAVE A GOOD DAY!

Multiline text can be
adjusted with grips.
Let the text wrap
naturally, using the
space bar instead of
the Enter key.

Solution

1. 

Enable **Quick Properties**.

The tool is enabled if it is highlighted in blue.
If you don't see the tool, enable it using the Customize tool on the task bar.

2. 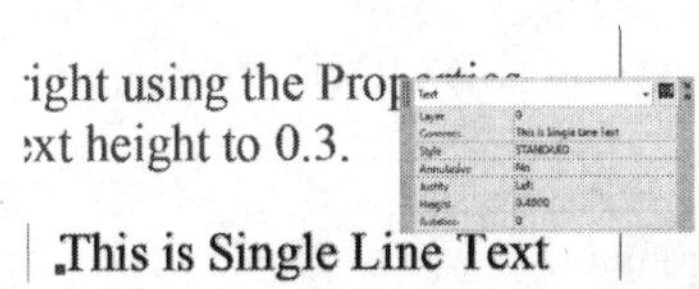

Use the LMB to select the single line of text located on the right side of the drawing.

3. 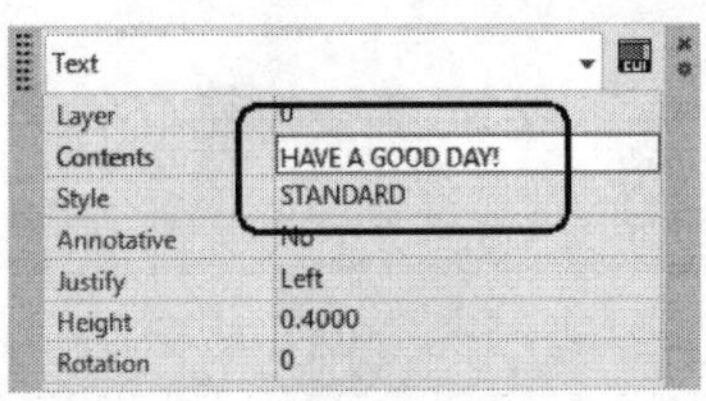

In the Quick Properties dialog box, highlight the existing text and change it to **HAVE A GOOD DAY!**

4.

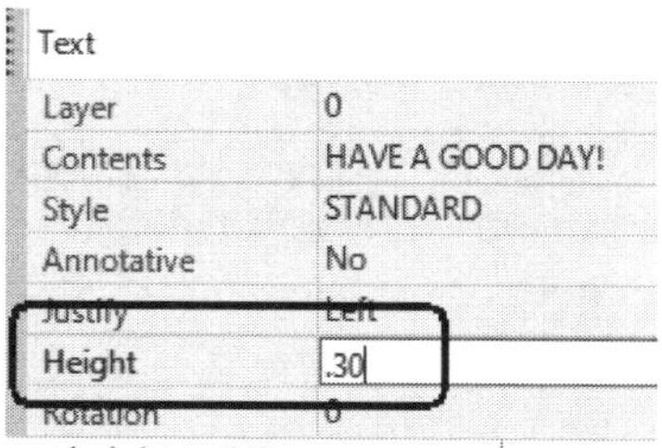

Adjust the Height to **0.3** in the Quick Properties dialog.

Click the <ESC> button to release the selection.

Notice how the text changes.

5.

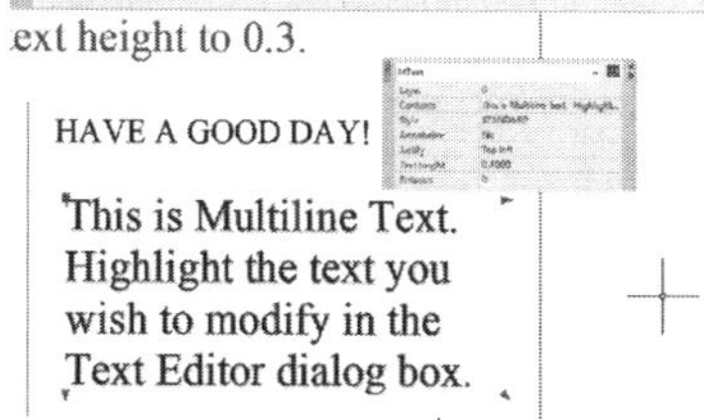

Use the LMB to pick the Multiline Text.
Notice the Quick Properties dialog box updates.

6.

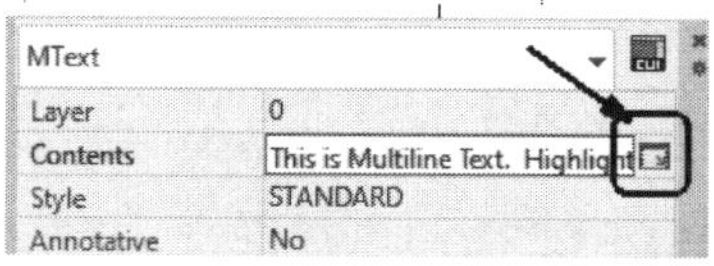

Pick the Button next to the Contents of the text.

This will activate the Multiline Text Editor.

You will only see the button if you left click in the Contents field.

This is the same as double left clicking on the text.

7.

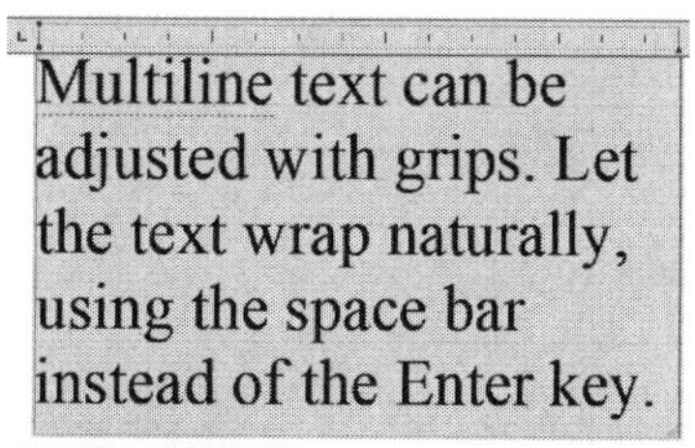

Highlight the existing text and delete it.

Type in the new text.

8.

Click **Close Text Editor**.

9.

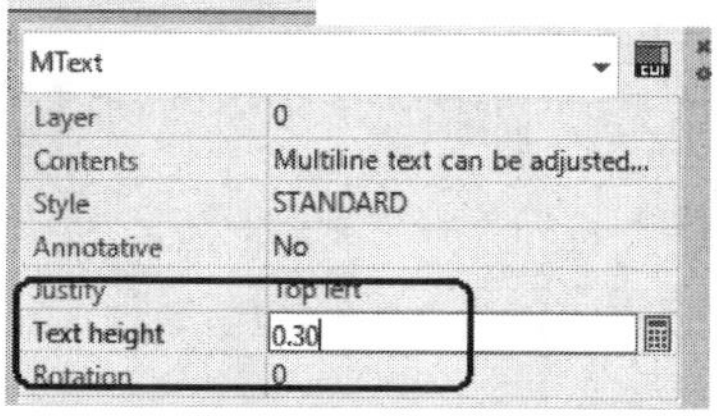

Re-select the edited MTEXT.
Back in the Quick Properties dialog box, change the height to **0.3000**.

Click the <ESC> button to release the selection.

Notice how the text changes.

Command Exercise

Exercise 10-9 – Modify Text Using Grips

Drawing Name: **etext3.dwg**
Estimated Time to Completion: 5 Minutes

Scope

Using grips, move and stretch the multiline text paragraph into the box.

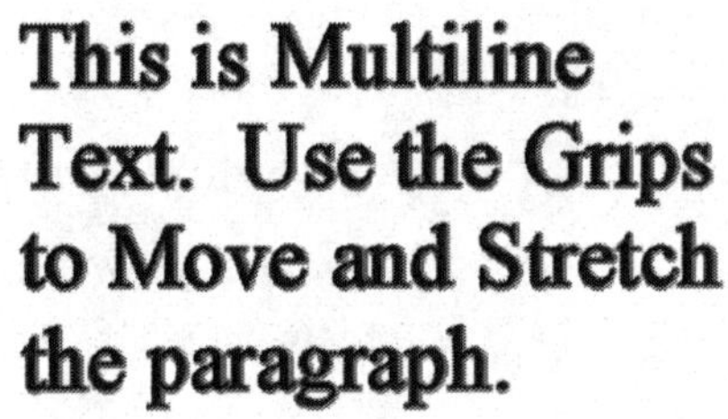

Solution

1. 

   Make sure the command line is clear.

   Enable OSNAPs.

2. 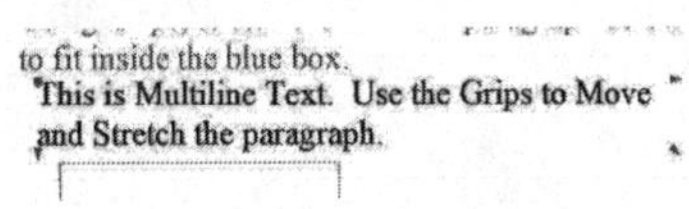

   Select the black multiline text.

   Notice how the grip points appear.

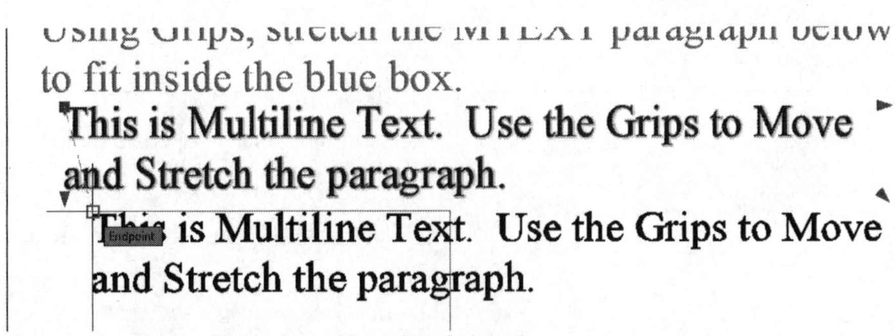

3. *Specify stretch point or [Base point/Copy/Undo/eXit]:*

   Click the upper left grip point on the text; it will turn red. Move to the upper left endpoint of the box and click again. The text will move down to the box.

4. 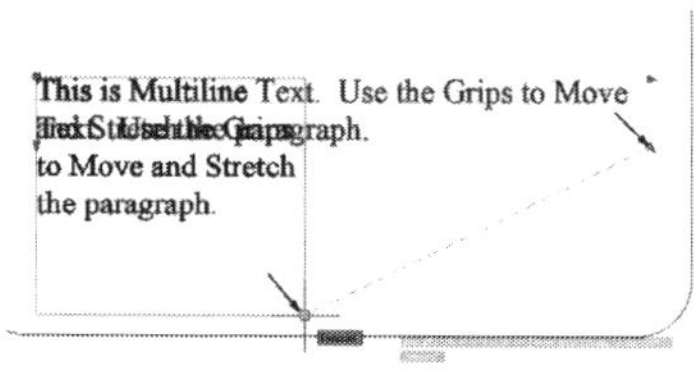

Specify stretch point or [Base point/ Copy/Undo/eXit]:

Click the lower right grip point on the text. Move to the lower right corner of the box and click again.

The text will stretch itself to fit inside the box.

Click <ESC> to release the selected text.

5. 

Unlock and Freeze the Topic layer.

6. 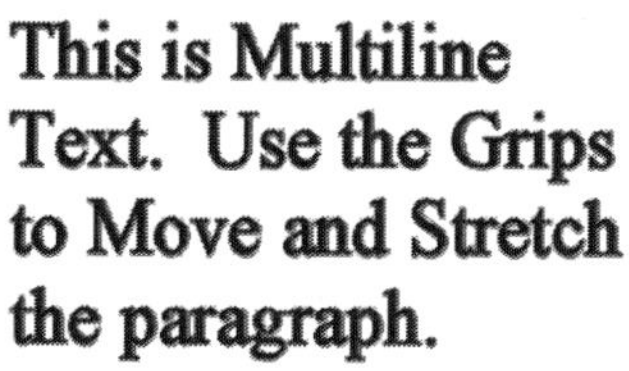

Notice how you can use a rectangle to locate and format multiline text.

Fields

Command Locator

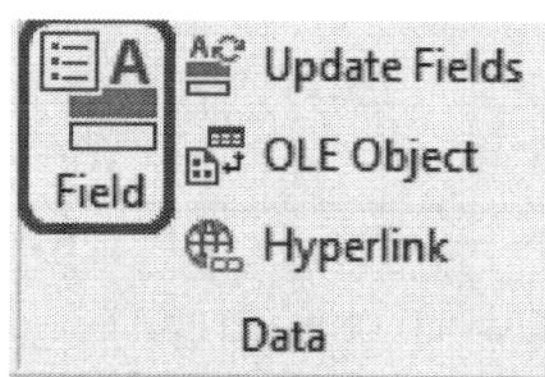

Ribbon/Insert/Data	**Field**
Command	**Field**
Alias	**Ctl+F**

Command Overview

Fields can be used in MTEXT or attribute definitions. You can use fields to display the area of a polygon or for title block information. Fields are also used in sheet sets. You can access the command by right clicking in the MTEXT window and selecting *Insert Field.*

There are several system variables that control how fields work. FIELDDISPLAY allows you to turn off the gray box under any defined fields. The gray box is not printed even when it is visible. FIELDEVAL sets how fields are updated upon saving the drawing, plotting the drawing, or on Regen. FIELDUPDATE is used to update fields manually.

When you insert the field, there are two options available: Text Height and Justification.

General Procedures:

Inserting a Field:

1. Go to Insert, Field.
2. Select the field data to use under the Field Category list.
3. Select the format (Upper Case/Lower Case/Sentence Case/Title Case) to be used for the field.
4. Click OK to close the dialog.
5. Select the insertion point for the field.

- The insertion point of the field is the upper left corner of the text.
- The Date field can only be updated using the UPDATEFIELD command.
- Spell check does not work on the values stored in fields.
- Fields are linked but not attached to objects. This means you can move the object and the field will not move with it. To have the field move with an assigned object, use **Group**.

Command Exercise

Exercise 10-10 – Adding Fields to Objects

Drawing Name: **fields1.dwg**
Estimated Time to Completion: 10 Minutes

Scope

Adding Fields to an object.

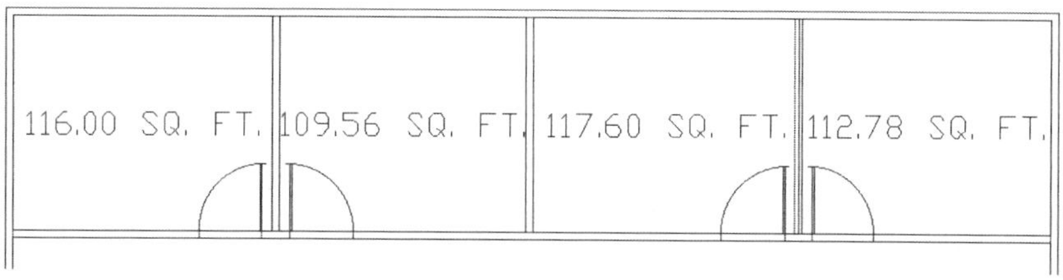

Solution

1. 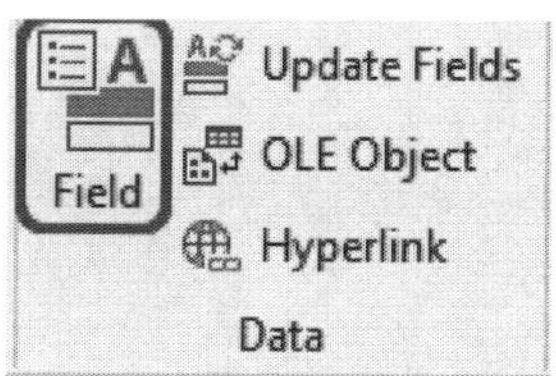

Activate the **Insert** ribbon.
Select the **Field** tool.

2. 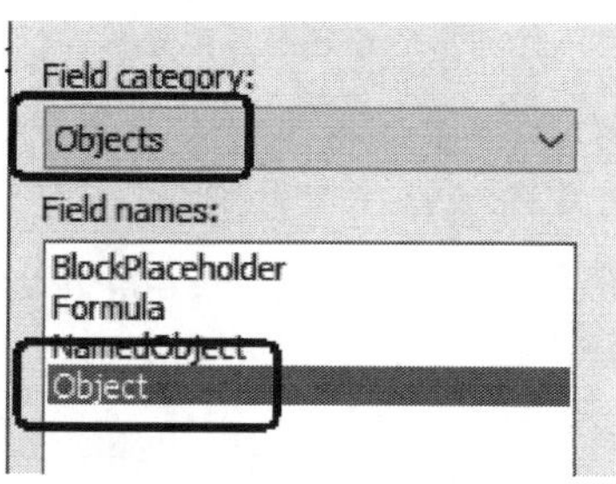

Under the Field Category, select **Objects**.

Highlight **Object** under Field names.

3. 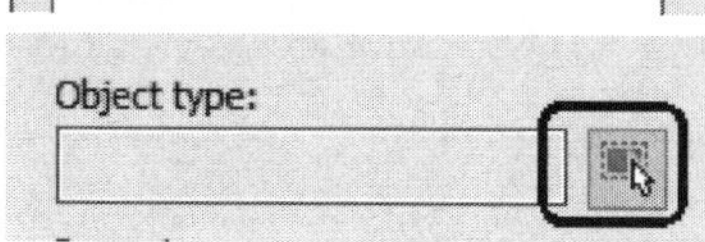

Select the **Select Object** tool.

4.

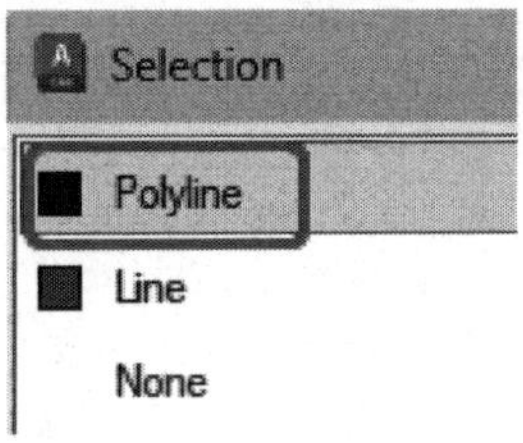

Select the first rectangle in the upper left corner.

***Hint**: Use the Selection Filter tool to help you select the rectangle.*

A selection box should appear to allow you to choose the Polyline.

A rectangle is considered a polyline.
Make sure you select the rectangle and not a line or the object properties will not display properly.

5.

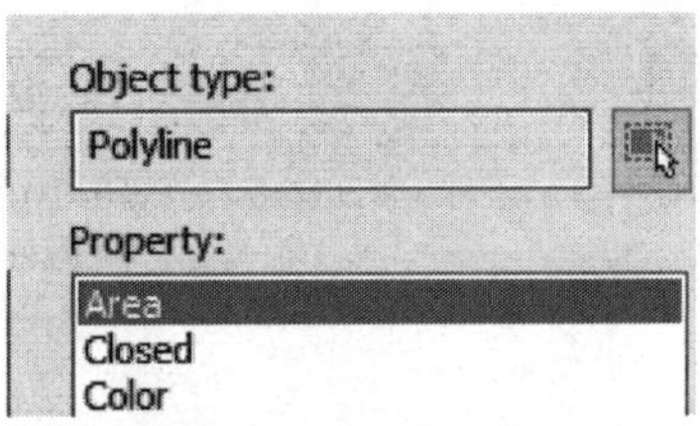

Highlight **Area** under Property.

6.

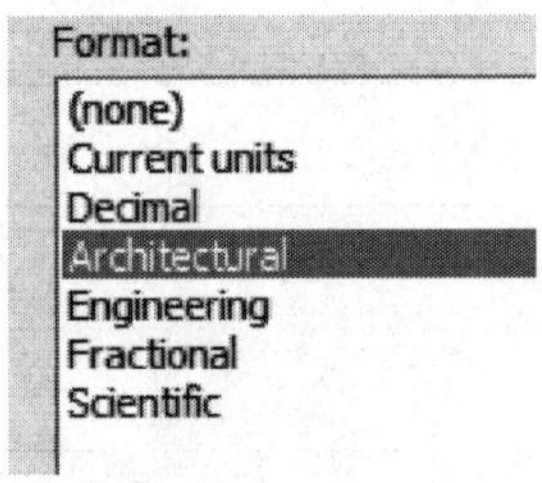

Select **Architectural** under Format.

7.

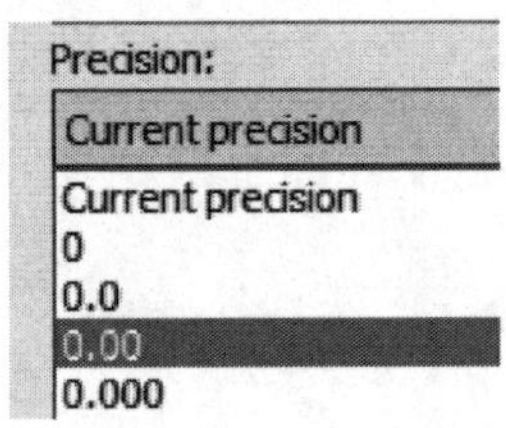

Set the Precision to two decimal places.

Note you will see a preview of what the text will look like in the Preview box.

Click **OK**.

8.

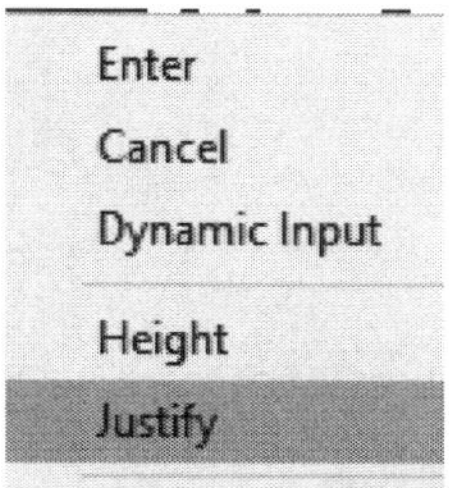

RMB and select **Justify**.

9.

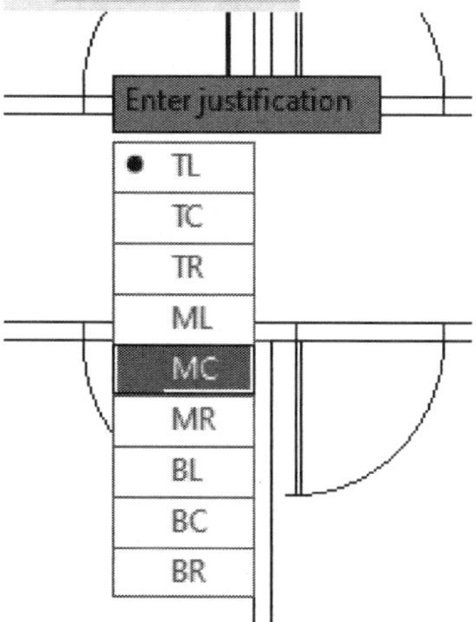

Select **MC** for Middle Center.

10.

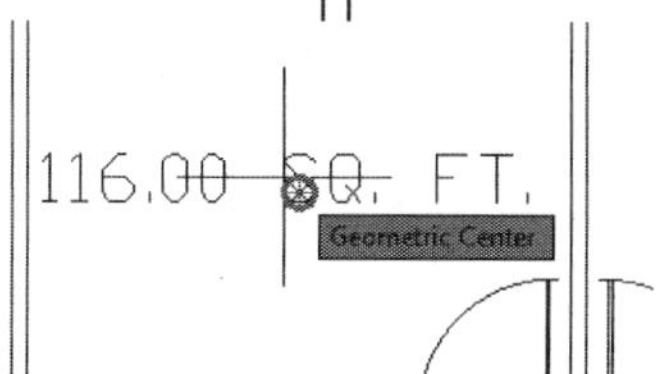

With Justification set to MC for Middle Center, use the Geometric Center of the rectangle to place the field.

11.

If you don't want to see the shading that indicates the text is a field, type FIELDDISPLAY, 0.

Extra: *Repeat for the other rooms in the layout.*

Tables

Command Locator

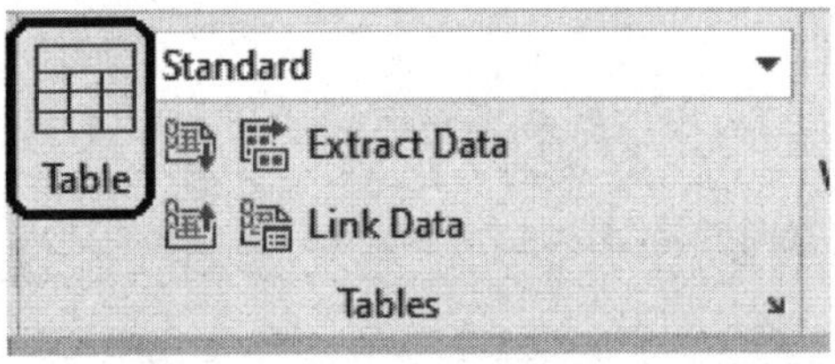

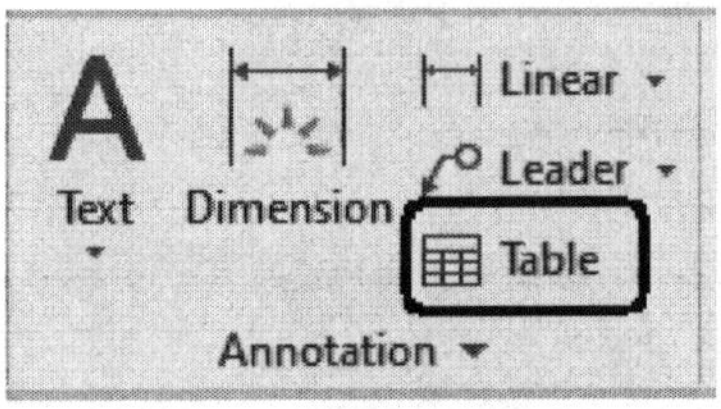

Ribbon/Home	**Annotation/Table**
Ribbon/Annotate	**Tables**
Command	**table**
Alias	**tb**

Command Overview

Tables are used in drawings to help organize information. Tables can be defined with a specific number of columns and rows. You can save table styles to be re-used in other drawings.

General Procedures:

Inserting a Table:

1. Go to Draw, Table.
2. Select the number of columns, the column size, and the number of rows.
3. Click OK to close the dialog.
4. Select the insertion point for the table.

- Tables can be exported to Excel or a text file.
- It is helpful to create text styles for the font styles to be applied to cells. Simply select the cell(s) and assign the desired text style.
- Columns can be combined to create headers.
- Borders can be turned off and on to create more elaborate tables.
- Cells can be colored to provide shading.
- *To change the colors used to indicate the cells and rows when a table is activated, select the table. Right click and select Table Indicator color. Select the desired color and Click OK.*

Command Exercise

Exercise 10-11 – Creating a Table

Drawing Name: **table1.dwg**
Estimated Time to Completion: 15 Minutes

Scope

Insert a table into a drawing to provide additional information.

WIRING MAP		
P1	P2	WIRE COLOR
1	1	BLUE
2	2	ORANGE
3	3	BLACK
4	4	RED
5	5	GREEN
6	6	YELLOW
7	7	BROWN
8	8	WHITE

Solution

1.

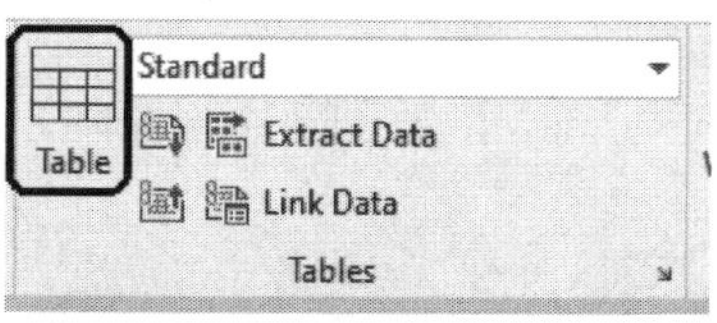

Activate the **Annotate** ribbon.

Select the **Table** tool.

2.

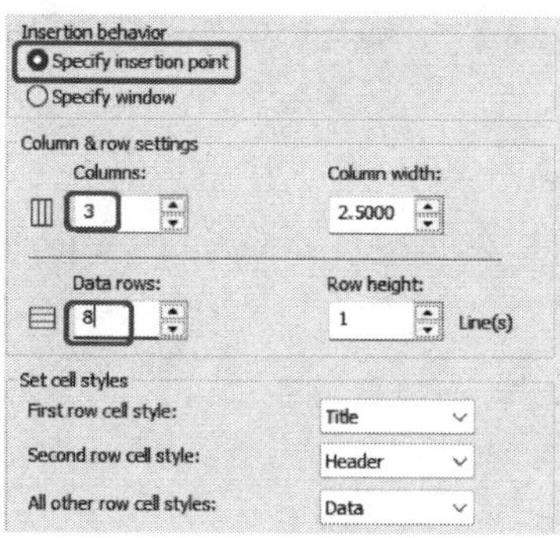

Enable **Specify insertion point**.
Set the Columns to **3**.
Set the Data rows to **8**.

Click **OK**.

3. 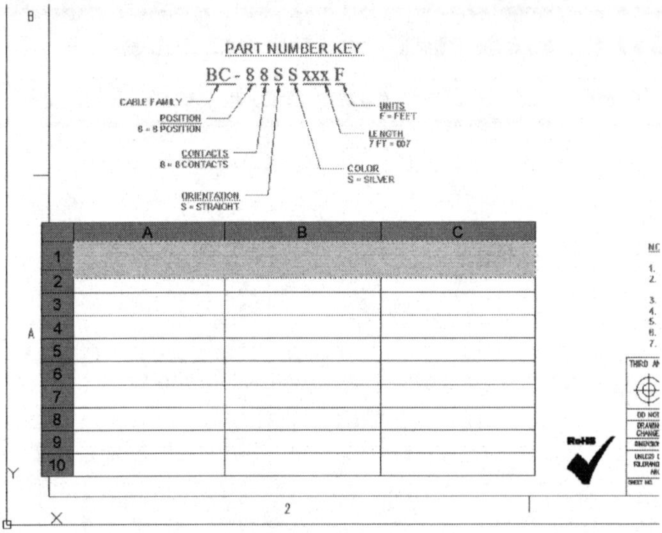

Click to place the table in the lower left of the drawing.

4. Fill in the table as shown.

Use the TAB key to advance to the next cell.

WIRING MAP		
P1	P2	WIRE COLOR
1	1	BLUE
2	2	ORANGE
3	3	BLACK
4	4	RED
5	5	GREEN
6	6	YELLOW
7	7	BROWN
8	8	WHITE

5. 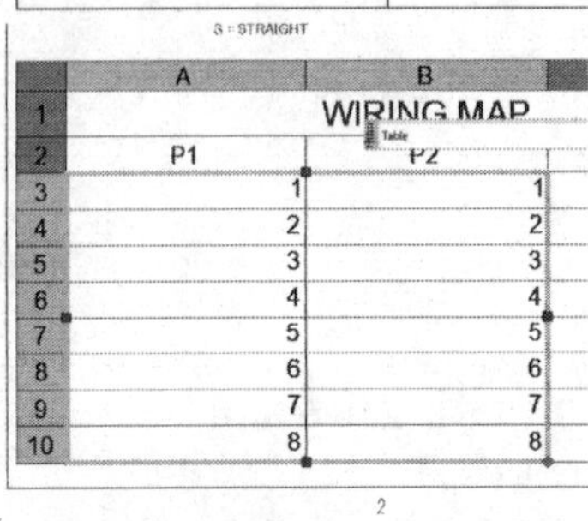

Highlight the pin number cells.

Click Cell A3 and Cell B10 to select all the cells.

6. 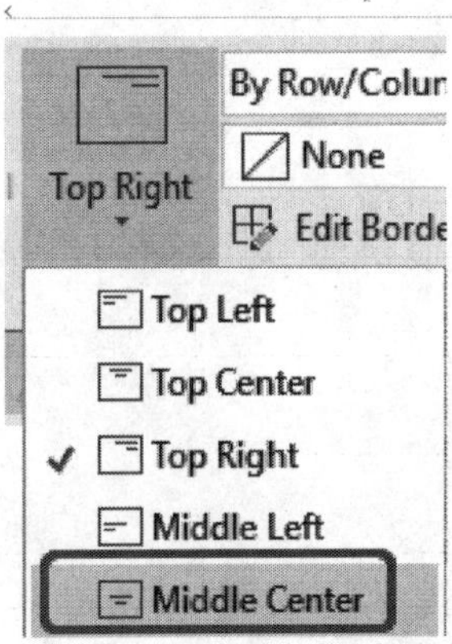

Select **Middle Center** to change the justification of the cells.

Click **ESC** to release the selection.

Command Exercise

Exercise 10-12 – Extracting a Table

Drawing Name: **table2.dwg**
Estimated Time to Completion: 20 Minutes

Scope

Creating a table by extracting data from a drawing.

Door Schedule			
Part Number	Name	Width	Count
D-001	SingleDoor	600	1
D-002	SingleDoor	800	2
D-003	SingleDoor	650	6

Solution

1.

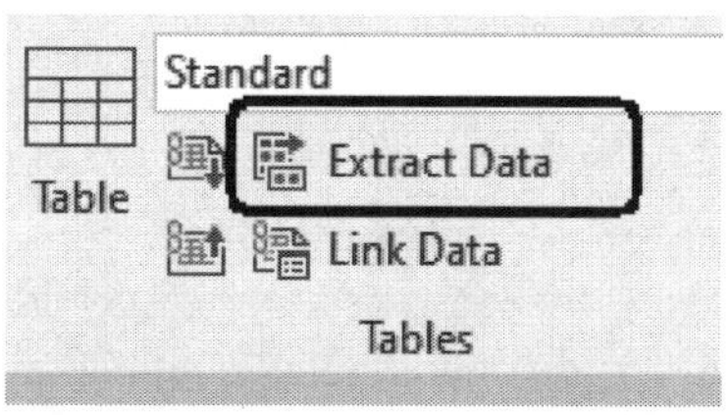

Activate the **Annotate** ribbon.

Select the **Extract Data** tool.

2.

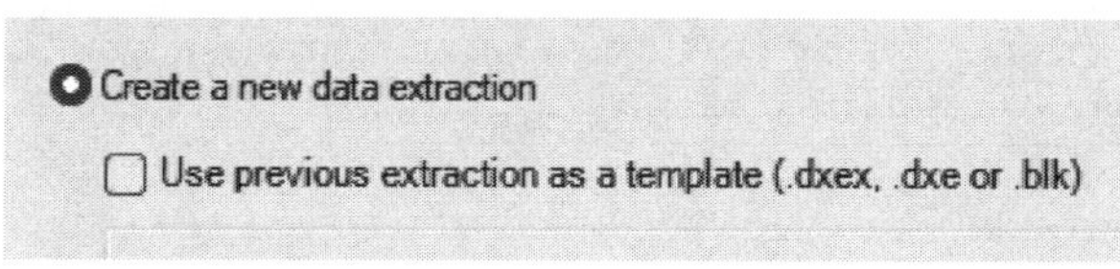

Enable **Create a new data extraction.**

Click **Next**.

3.

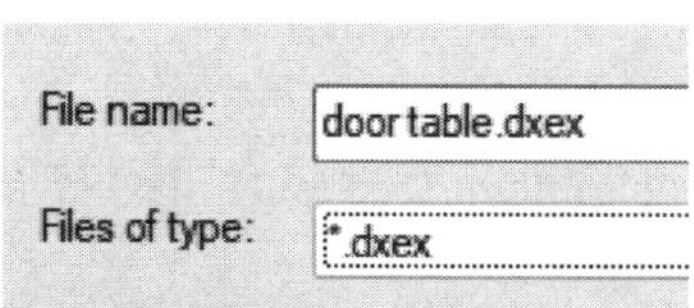

Browse to the folder where you are saving your work.

Name the file **door table**.

Click **Save**.

4.

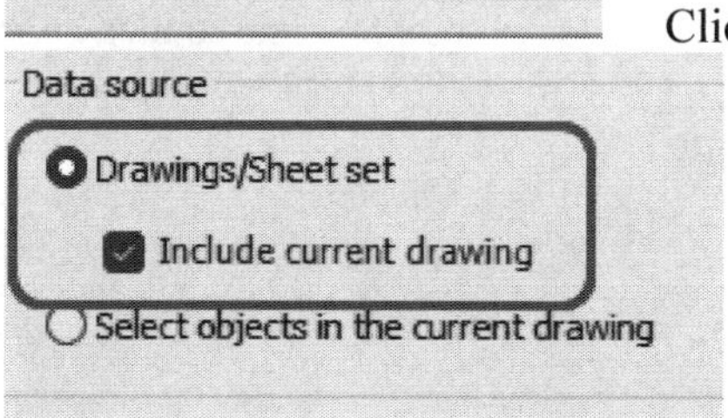

Enable **Drawings/Sheet set**.
Enable **Include current drawing**.

Click **Next**.

5.

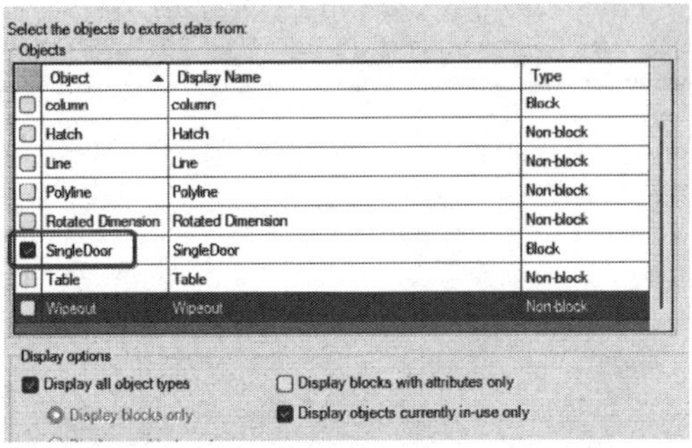

De-select all the objects.

Select **SingleDoor**, which is a block.

Click **Next**.

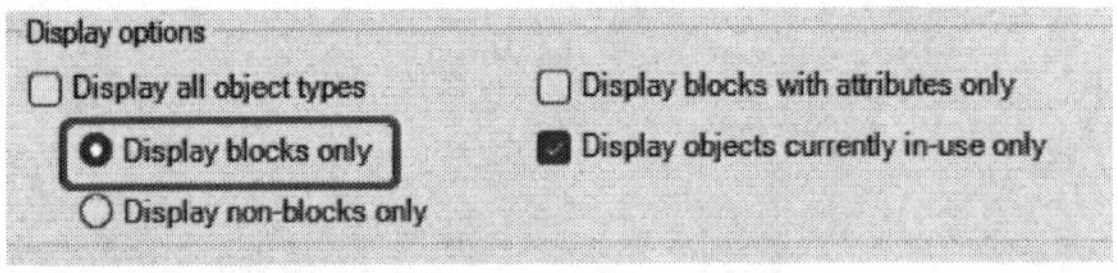

Hint: *Disable Display all object types. You can enable Display blocks only to shorten the list.*

6.

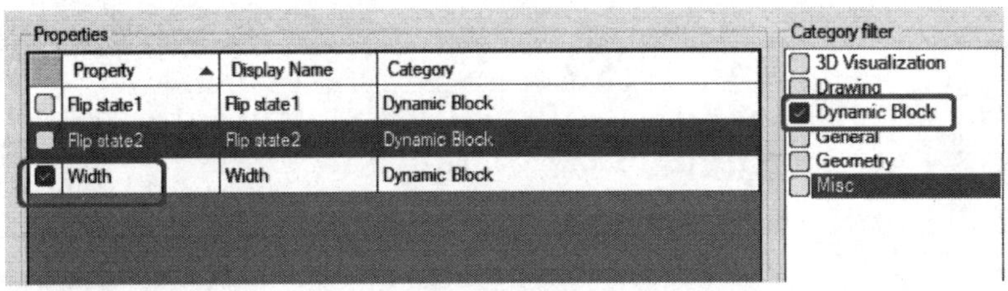

Enable **Dynamic Block**.

Enable **Width**.

Click **Next**.

7.

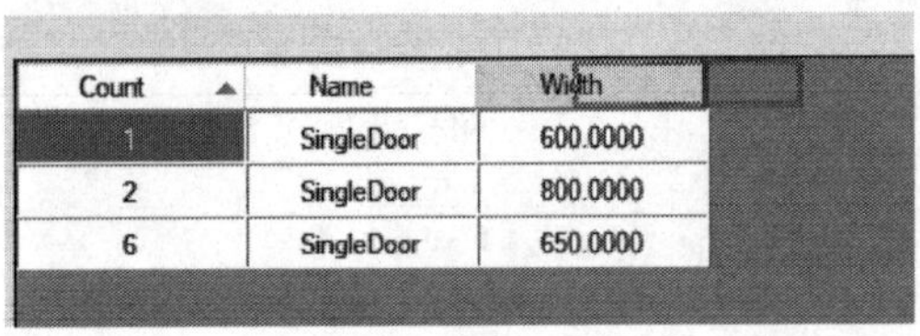

Hold the LMB over the Count header and drag to the right.

8.

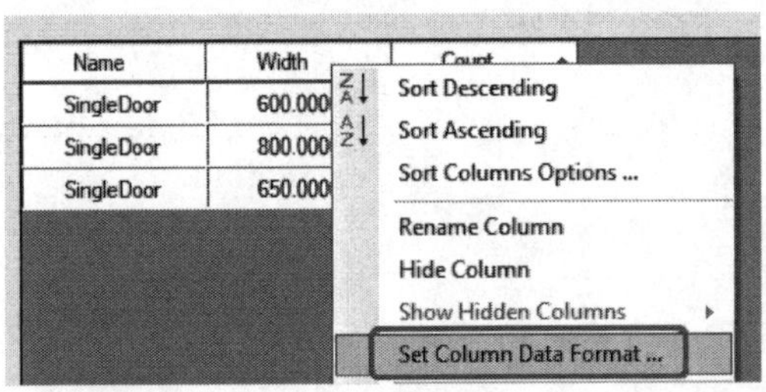

Right click on the Width column.

Select **Set Column Data Format…**

9.

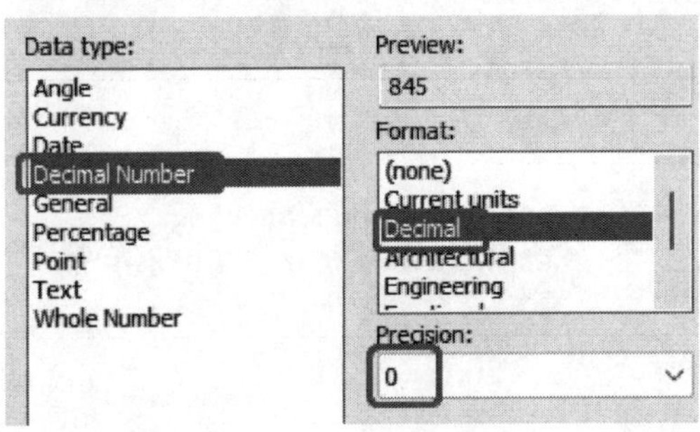

Highlight **Decimal Number** under Data Type.
Highlight **Decimal** under Format.
Select **0** under Precision.

Click **OK**.

10.

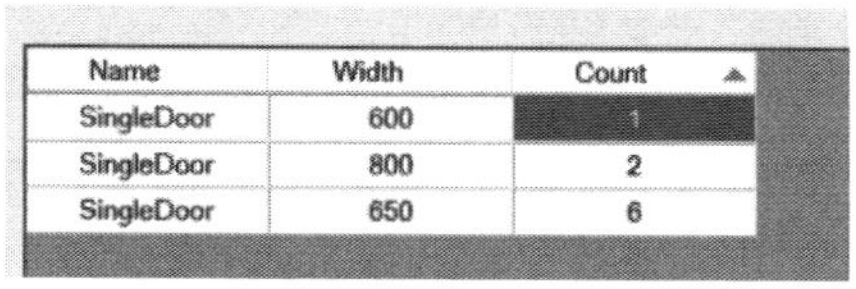

The table updates.

Click **Next**.

11.

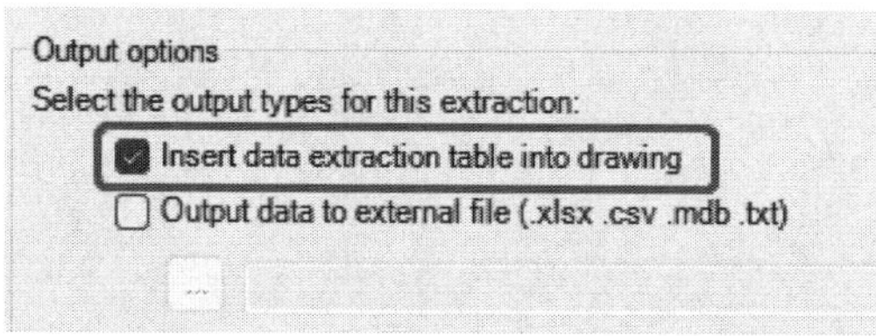

Enable **Insert data extraction table into drawing.**

Click **Next**.

12.

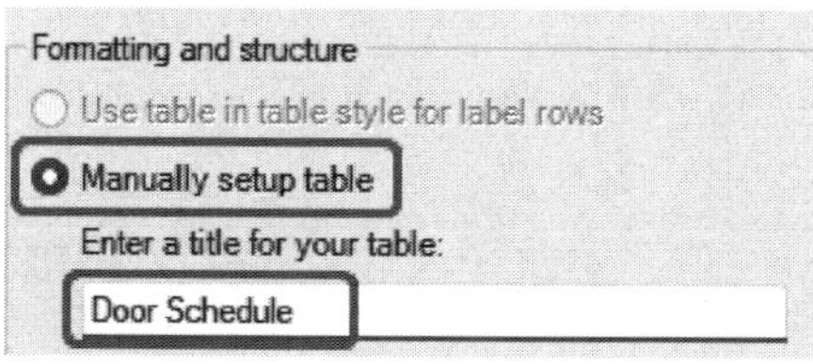

Type **Door Schedule** in the title field.

Click **Next**.

13.

Click **Finish**.

14.

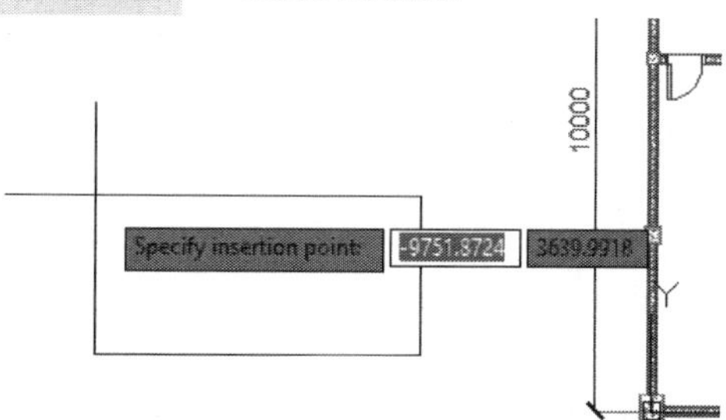

Click to the left of the floor plan to place the door schedule.

15.

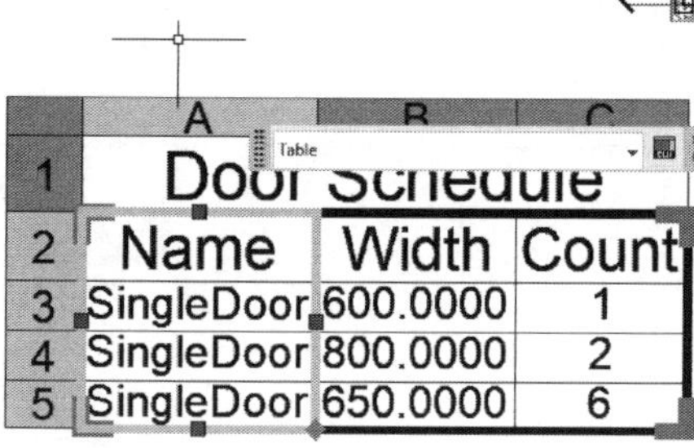

Highlight the first column.

Hint: *Click on Cell A2.*
Hold down the SHIFT key and click on Cell A5 to select the column.

16.

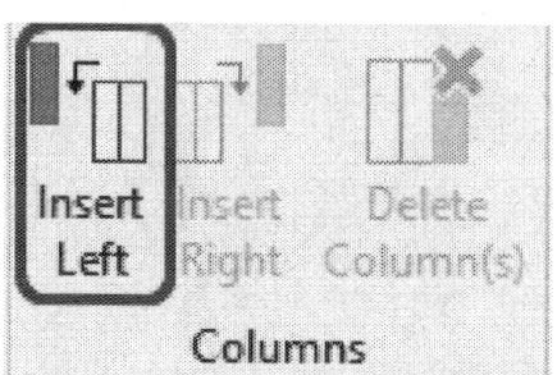

On the ribbon in the Columns panel:

Select **Insert Left.**

17.

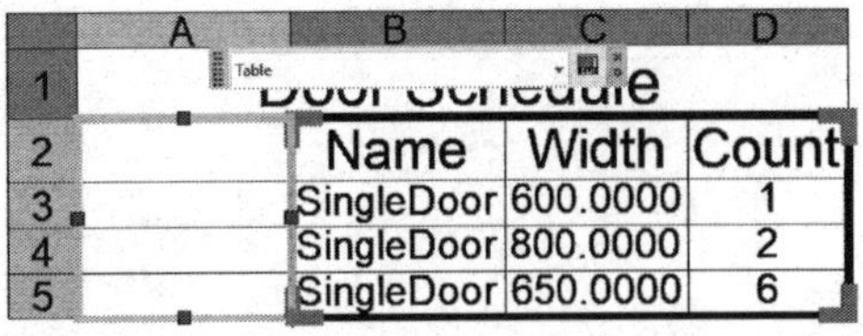

Select the new column.

Hint: *Click on Cell A2.*
Hold down the SHIFT key and click on Cell A5 to select the column.

18.

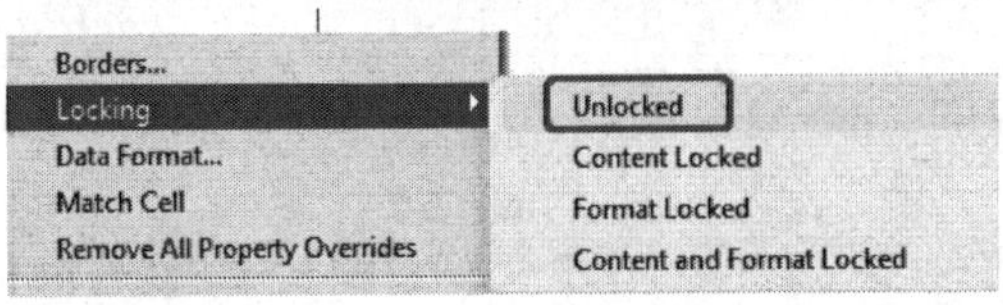

Right click and select **Locking→Unlocked**.

19.

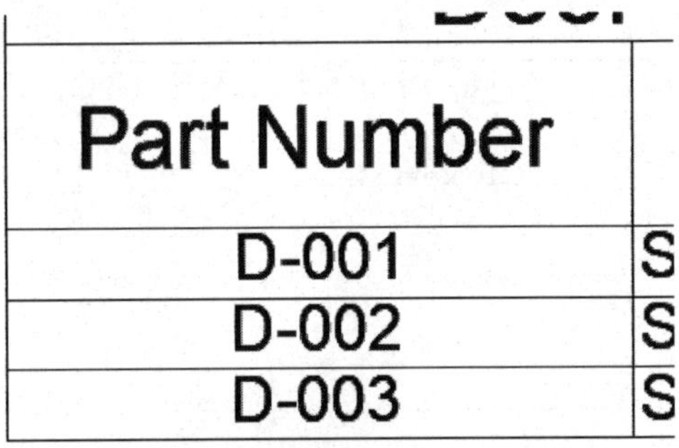

Type **Part Number** in the Header cell.

Add part numbers to each row.

20.

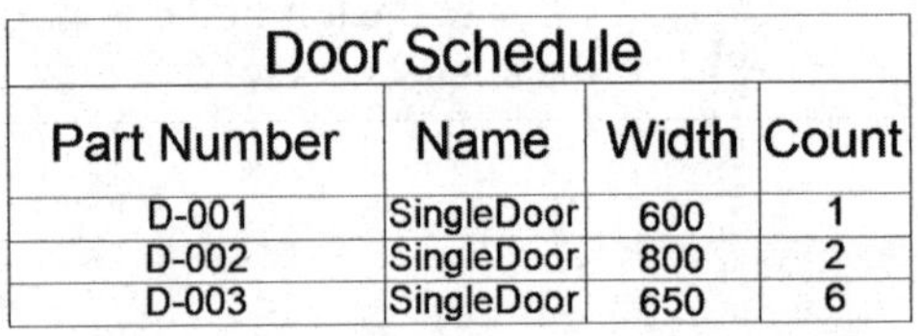

Door Schedule			
Part Number	Name	Width	Count
D-001	SingleDoor	600	1
D-002	SingleDoor	800	2
D-003	SingleDoor	650	6

Click **ESC** to release the selection.

Extra*: Change the Column Header* ***Count*** *to* ***Qty****. To change the header, you need to unlock the cell first.*

Command Exercise

Exercise 10-13 – Exporting a Table

Drawing Name: **table3.dwg**
Estimated Time to Completion: 5 Minutes

Scope

Exporting a table.

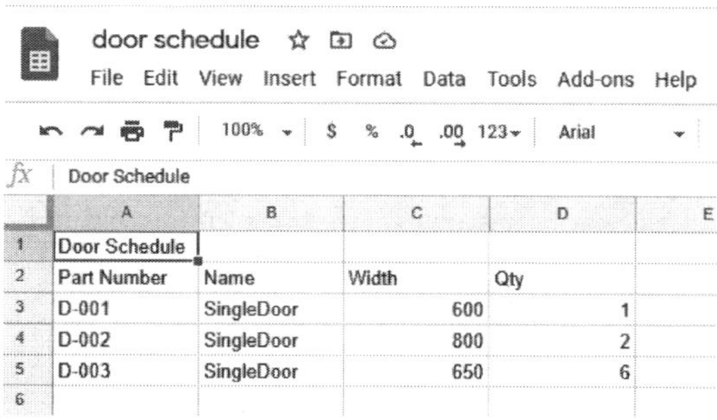

Solution

1. Select the table in the drawing.

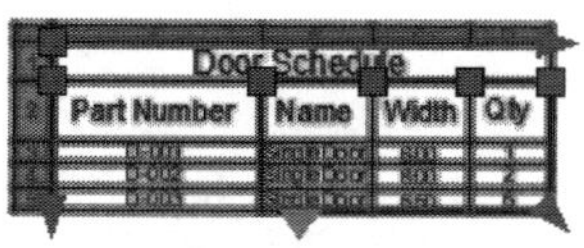

2. Right click and select **Export**.

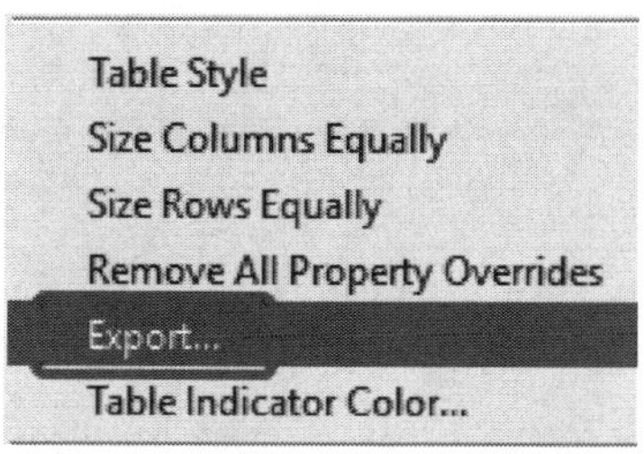

3. Browse to the folder where you want to save the file.

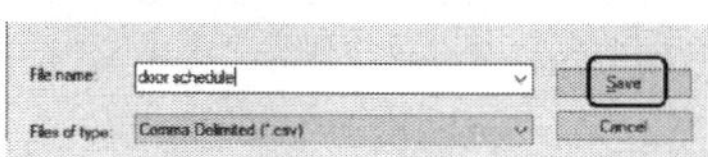

Type **door schedule** for the file name.

Click **Save**.

Note that the file is saved as a csv file.

4. Launch EXCEL or open Google sheets.

5. Select **Open** in Excel.

   Set the Files of type to Text Files.

   OR

   Upload the csv file in Google sheets.

6. 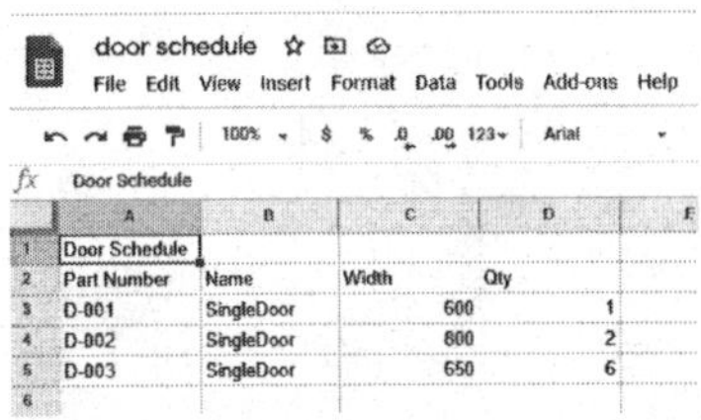

   You will have to format the columns to get the table to look proper in Excel, but Google Sheets does an excellent job of importing the data.

Tips & Tricks

- *You can only import text from a txt or rtf file. To import a Word file, save as txt or rtf.*
- *To open a csv file in Excel, you need to set the Files of Type to 'Text files' or you won't be able to see the file listed.*

Command Exercise

Exercise 10-14 – Adding Blocks to a Table

Drawing Name: **table4.dwg**
Estimated Time to Completion: 10 Minutes

Scope

Adding blocks and symbols to a table.

LEGEND	
SYMBOL	DESCRIPTION
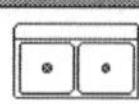	SINK - DOUBLE 36 IN
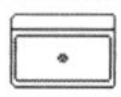	SINK - SINGLE 30 IN

Solution

1. 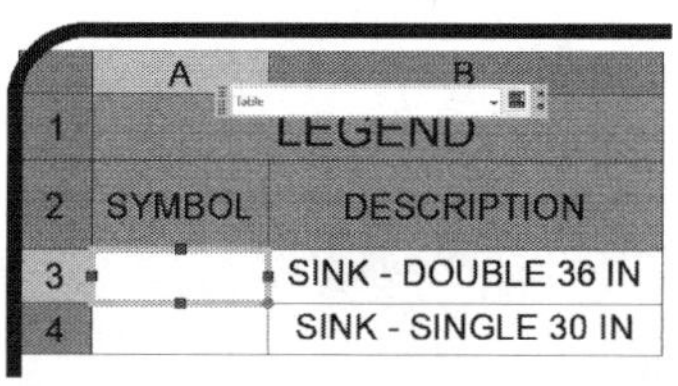

Select the 3A cell.

2. 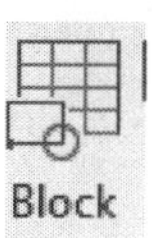

Select the **Insert Block** tool from the Insert panel on the ribbon.

3. 

Select the **Sink-double-36 in top** from the drop-down.

These blocks are pre-loaded in the drawing.
If you need to locate a block, use the Browse button.

4. 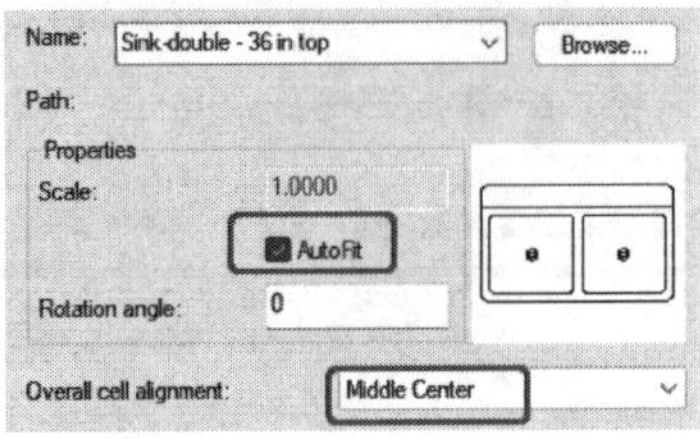

Enable **Autofit** to scale the block to the cell size.

Set the **Overall cell alignment** to **Middle Center**.

Click **OK**.

5. 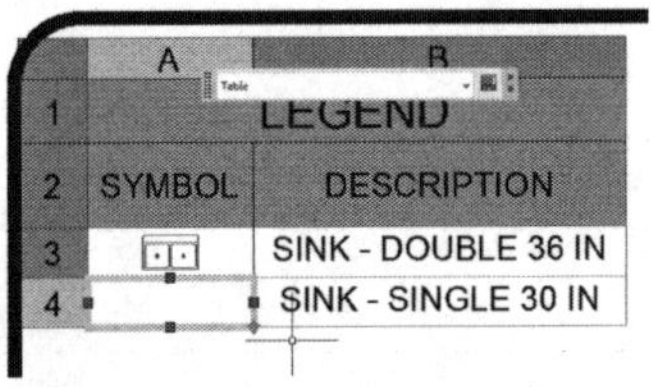

Select the 4A cell.

6. 

Select the **Insert Block** tool from the Table ribbon.

7. 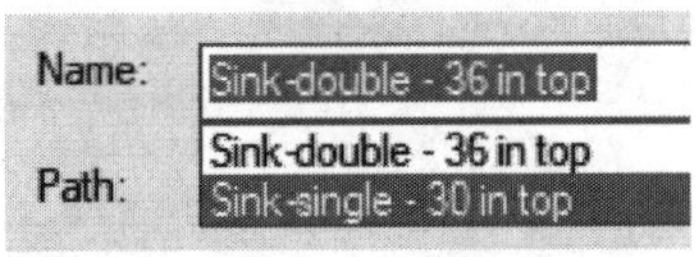

Select the **Sink-single-30 in top** from the drop-down.

8. 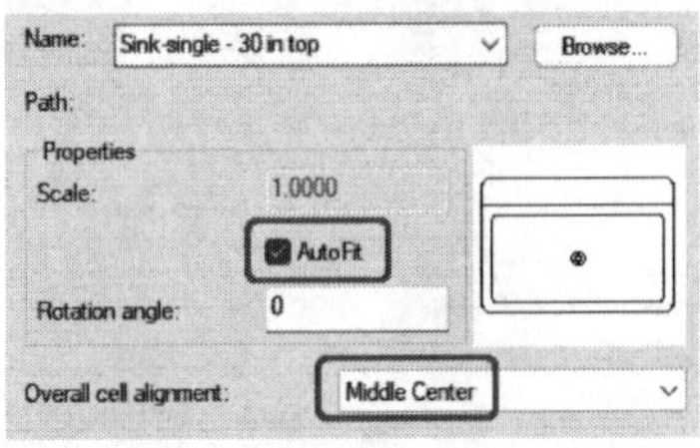

Enable **Autofit** to scale the block to the cell size.

Set the **Overall cell alignment** to **Middle Center**.

Click **OK**.

9. 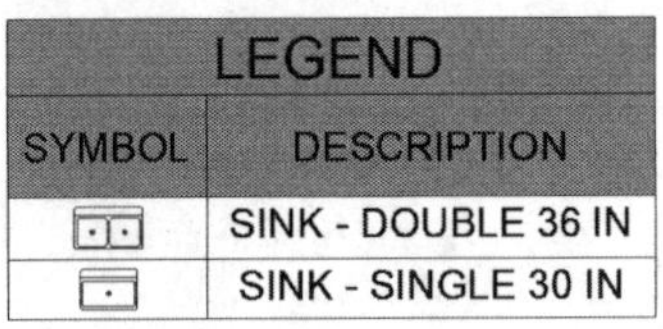

The legend is completed.

Click **ESC** to release the selection.

Multi-Leader (MLEADER)

Command Locator

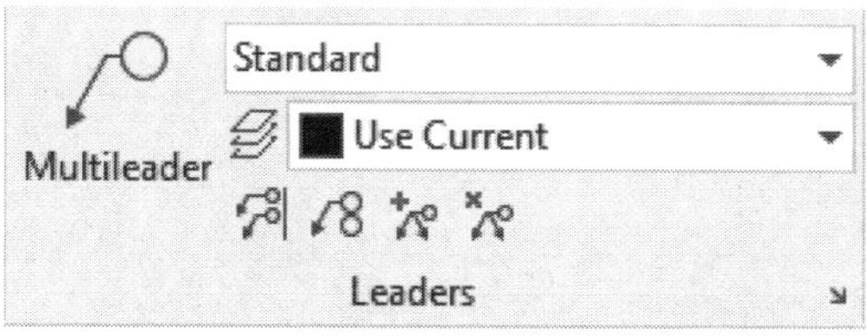

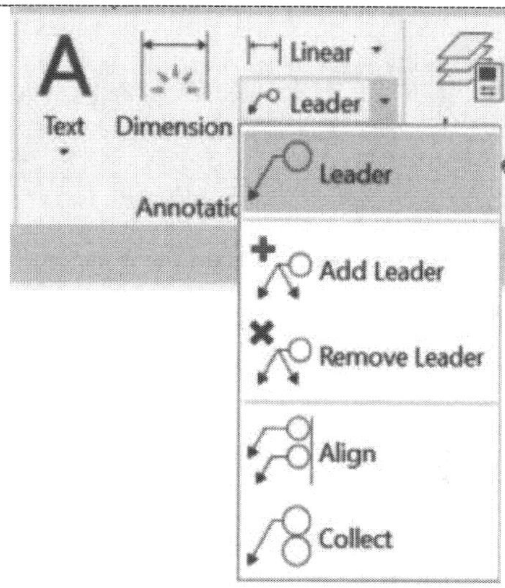

Command	MLEADER
Ribbon/Home/Annotation	**LEADER**
Ribbon/Annotate/Leaders	**MULTILEADER**
Alias	**MLD**

Command Overview

Multileaders can be created arrowhead first, leader landing first, or content first. If a multileader style has been used, the multileader can be created from that specified style. You can add a leader to existing MTEXT using the MLEADER command.

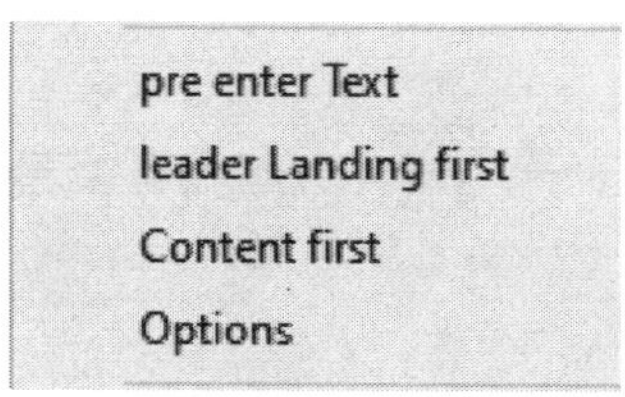

RMB Option	Overview
Select Mtext	User is prompted to select an existing multiline text object to use for the multileader object.
Leader arrowhead location first	User picks a location to place the arrowhead for the multileader.

Leader Landing first	User picks a location to place the landing (the horizontal line) for the multileader.
Content First	User is prompted to select the position for the text or block associated with the multileader.
Point selection	User picks two points to define the mtext box used for the mtext label associated with the multileader. When you have completed entering the text, click ESC or click outside.

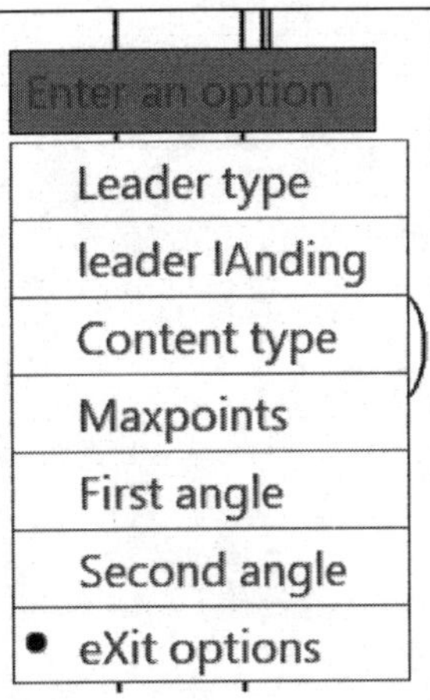

Options	**Overview**
Leader Type	Specifies how the leader line is handled. • **Straight.** Creates a straight multileader line. • **Spline**. Creates a spline multileader line. • **None.** Creates a multileader with no leader line.
Leader lAnding	Specifies whether to add a horizontal landing line. If you enter Yes, you are prompted to set the landing line length.
Content type	Specifies the type of content that will be used for the multileader. • **Block.** Specifies a block within your drawing to associate with the new multileader. • **Mtext.** Specifies that multiline text is included with the multileader. • **None.** Specifies that no content is displayed at the end of the leader line.
Maxpoints	Specifies a maximum number of points, or segments, for the new leader line.
First angle	Constrains the angle of the first point in the new leader line.
Second angle	Constrains the second angle in the new leader line.

General Procedures:

1. Begin the Multileader command by typing **MLD** (and <ENTER>).
2. Pick a start point in the Drawing Window.
3. Type the text height, or Click <ENTER> to accept the default Text height.
4. Click <ENTER> to accept the default rotation angle (0) or type a new angle.
5. Type the first line of text. Click <ENTER>. Type the second line of text. Click <ENTER> twice to complete the dtext command.

Command Exercise

Exercise 10-15 – Adding a Multi-Leader

Drawing Name: **mleader1.dwg**
Estimated Time to Completion: 5 Minutes

Scope

Adding a multi-leader to a drawing.

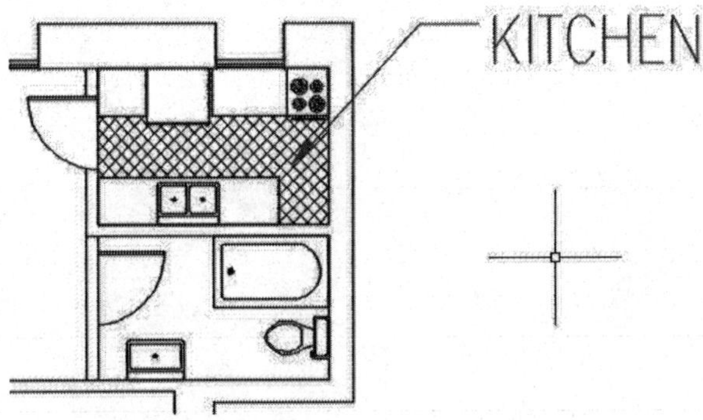

Solution

1.

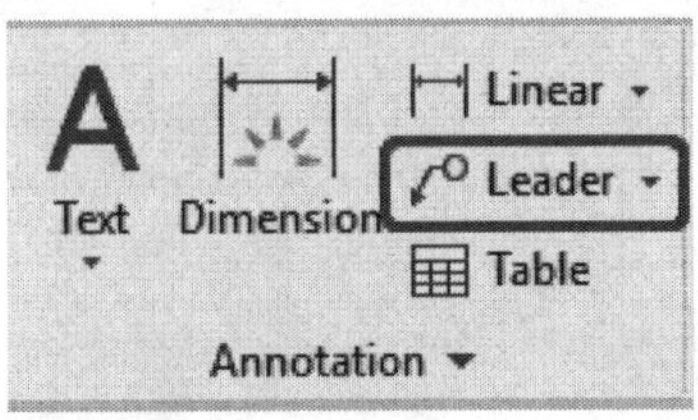

Activate the Home ribbon.

Select the Leader tool from the Annotation panel.

2.

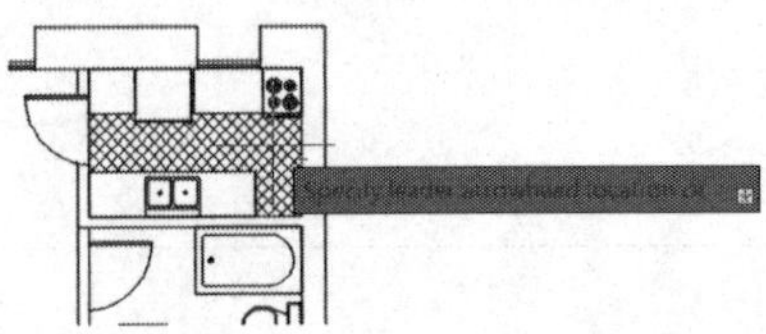

Click inside the kitchen area to specify the arrowhead position.

3. 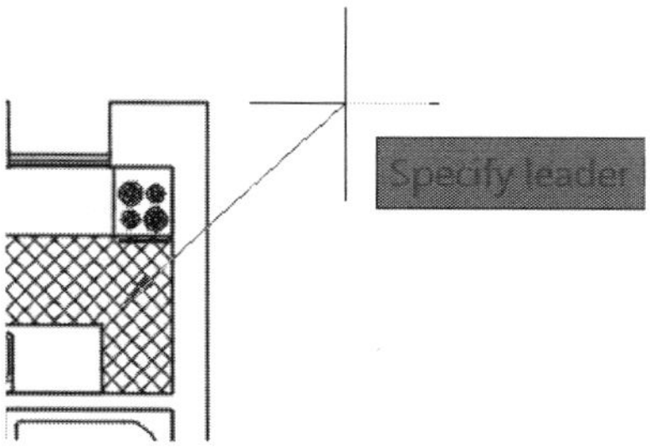

Drag the mouse up and to the right to select the start point of the landing.

4. 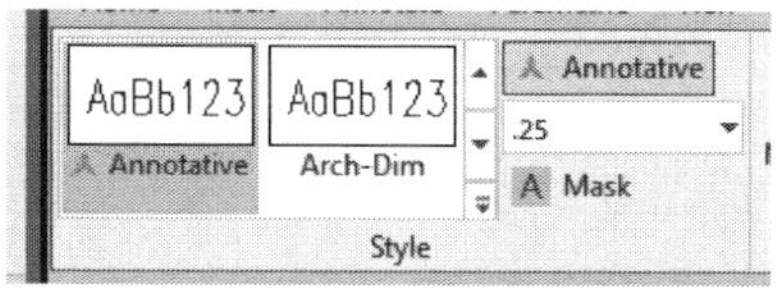

On the ribbon, set the text style to **Annotative** and the text height to **0.25**.

5. 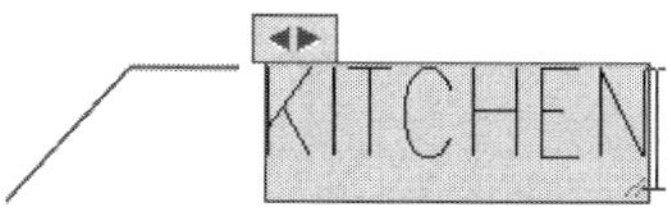

Type **KITCHEN**.

Click outside the text box to exit the command.

6. Close the drawing.

Command Exercise

Exercise 10-16 – Converting Mtext to a Multi-Leader

Drawing Name: **mleader2.dwg**
Estimated Time to Completion: 10 Minutes

Scope

Adding a multi-leader to existing mtext.

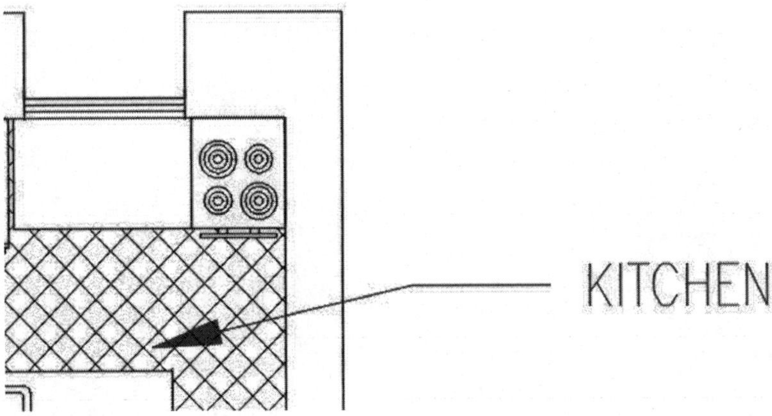

Solution

1. 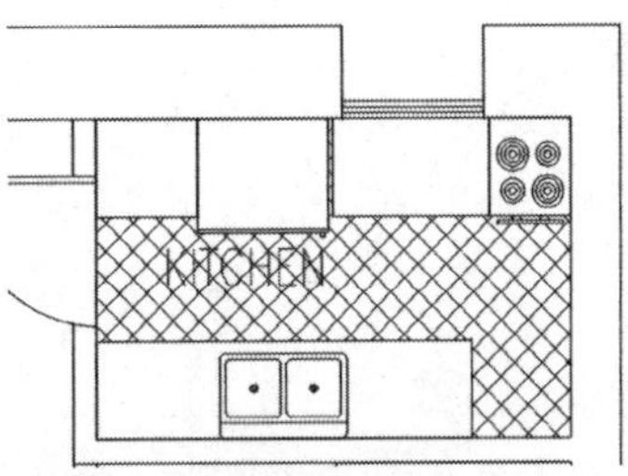

Zoom into the kitchen area.

2. 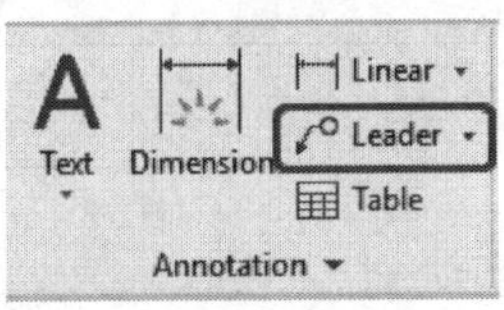

Type **MLD** or select the LEADER tool to start the MLEADER command.

3.

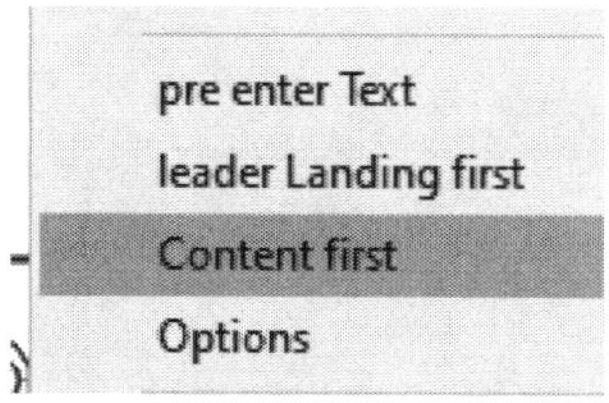

RMB and click **Content first** or type **C** for Content first.

4.

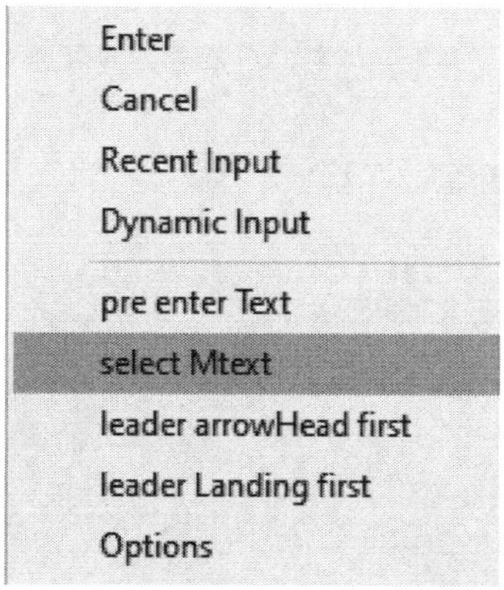

Right click and click **Select Mtext**.

5.

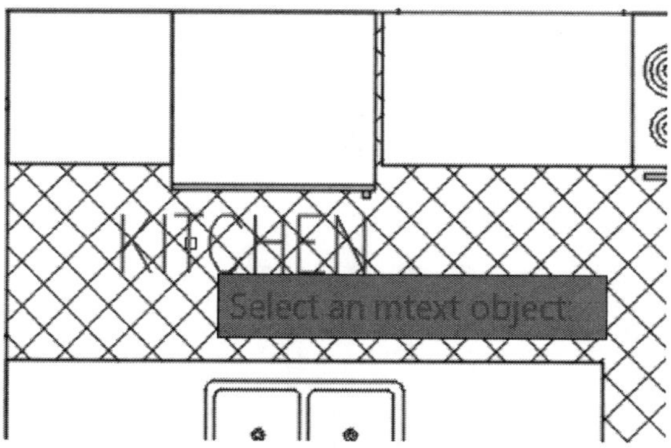

Click on the word KITCHEN to select.

6.

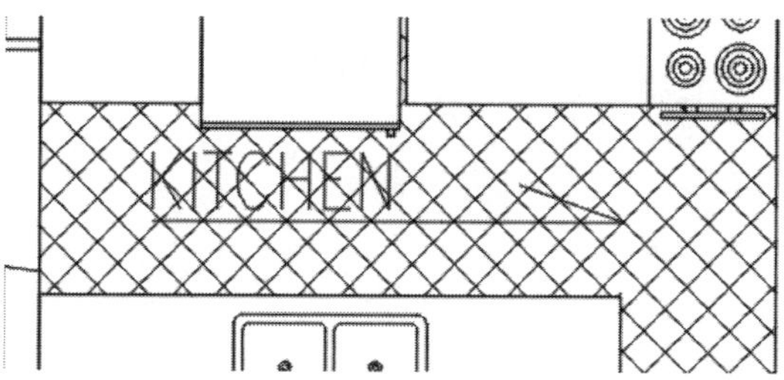

Click inside the kitchen area to place the arrowhead.

7.

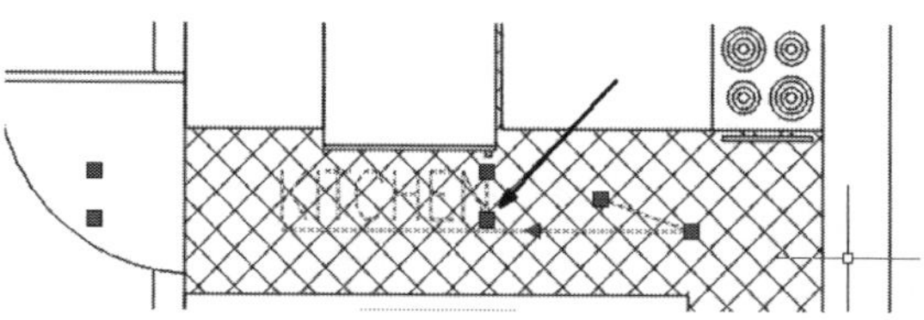

Select the MLEADER object you just placed.

Click on the indicated grip to move the mtext outside the kitchen area.

8.

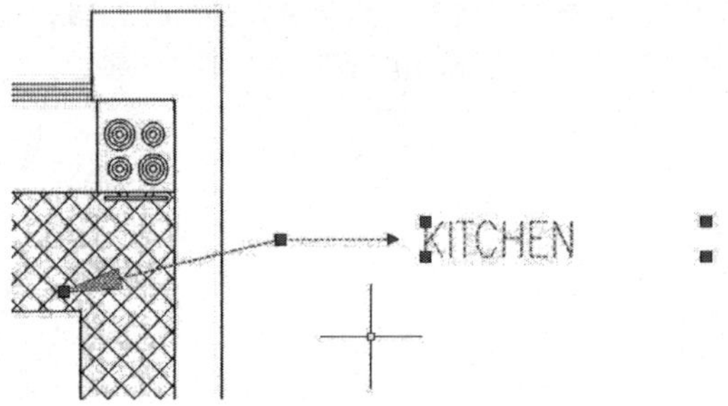

Use the grips to adjust the arrow position, add an angle to the mleader, and adjust the size of the landing.

Click ESC to release the selection.

9.

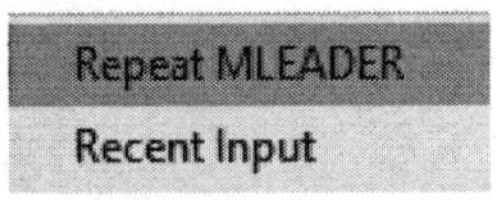

RMB and select **Repeat MLEADER**.

10.

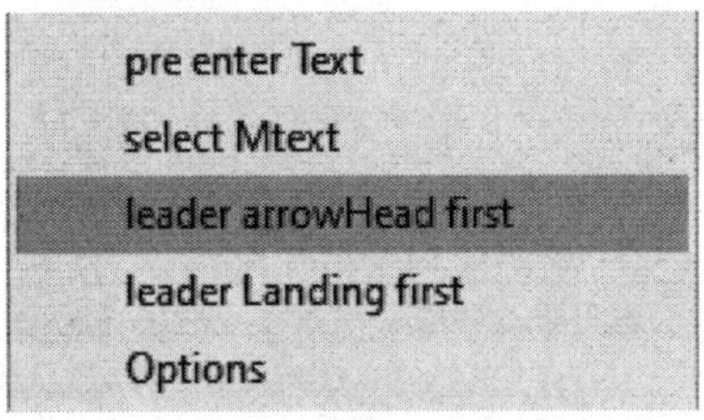

Right click and select **leader arrowHead first**.

11.

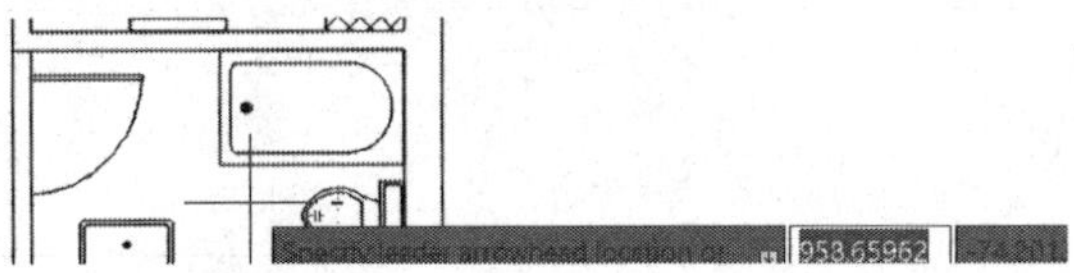

Click inside the bathroom to place the arrowhead.

12.

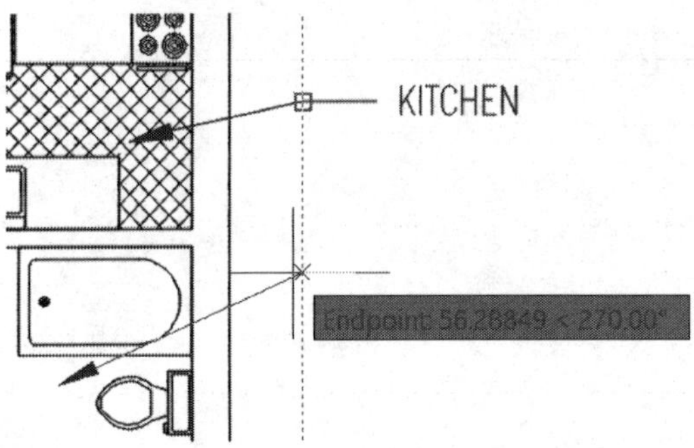

Move the mouse outside of the floor plan.

See if you can line up the start of the landing with the other multi-leader.

Click to place.

13.

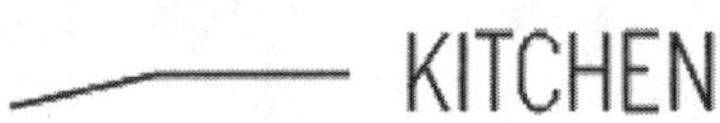

Type **BATHROOM**.

Click outside the text box to exit and complete the command.

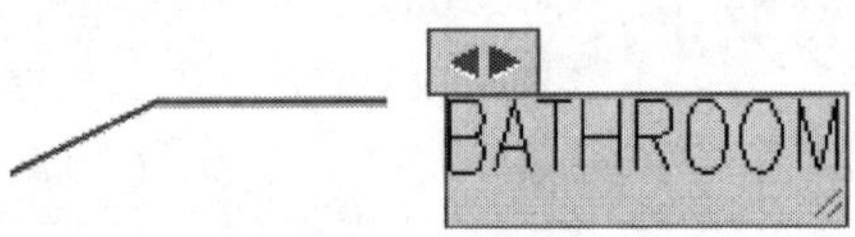

Section Exercise

Exercise 10-17 – Adding Callouts to a Drawing

Drawing Name: **Lesson 10 - Mechanical.dwg**
Estimated Time to Completion: 15 Minutes

Scope

Create a layer called Callouts. Assign the layer the color blue. Make this the current layer.
Add multi-leaders to drawing to call out different features of the jeep.
Convert the MTEXT to a multileader and position the arrowhead properly.
Place all multi-leaders on the Callouts layer.

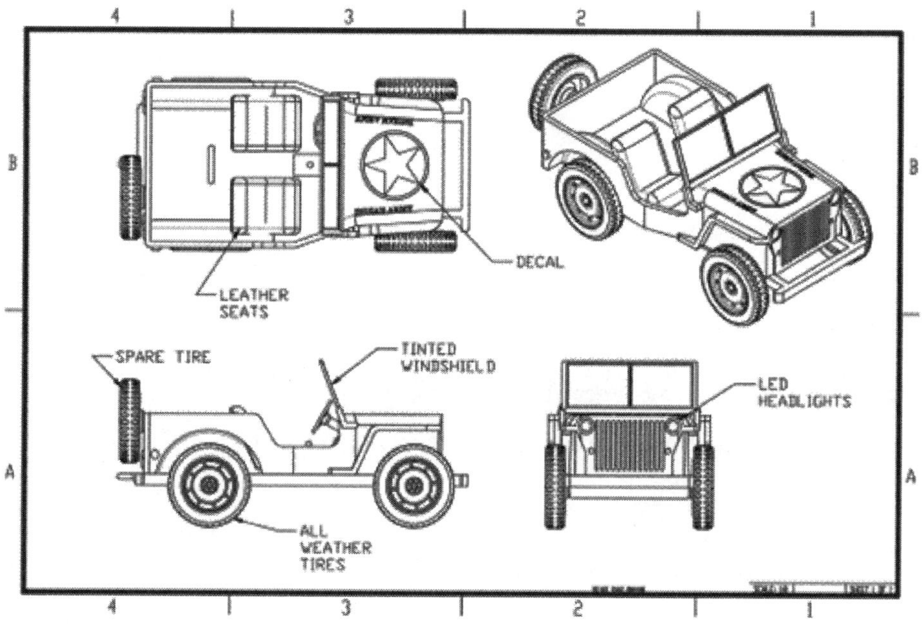

Hints:

Create the Callouts layer.
Assign the layer the color blue.
Use the RMB to REPEAT MLEADER.

Combine Text (TXT2MTXT)

Command Locator

Command	TXT2MTXT
Ribbon/Insert/Import	**COMBINE TEXT**

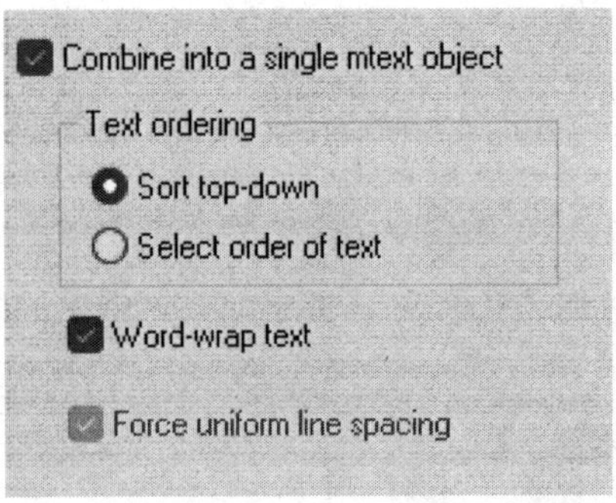

Settings allows you to determine the method used when combining text objects.

Combine into a single mtext object	Combines selected text objects into a single mtext object.
Text ordering - Sort top-down	Specifies the order of the selected text by descending vertical position.
Text ordering - Select order of text	Specifies the order of the selected text by manual selection.
Word-wrap text	Combines all the lines of text into a single line, and then wraps any text that exceeds the width of the mtext object to the next line.
Force uniform line spacing	Applies consistent interline spacing and paragraph spacing when word wrap is turned on. Paragraph spacing is 50% larger than interline spacing.

Command Overview

The selected text objects are replaced by one or more multiline text objects. If possible, the text size, font, and color differences between text objects are maintained.

General Procedures:

1. Begin the Combine Text command by typing **TXT2MTXT** (and <ENTER>).
2. Select the text objects to be combined.
3. Click ENTER to accept the selections.

Command Exercise

Exercise 10-18 – Combine Text

Drawing Name: **ctext.dwg**
Estimated Time to Completion: 10 Minutes

Scope

Convert single line text to MTEXT

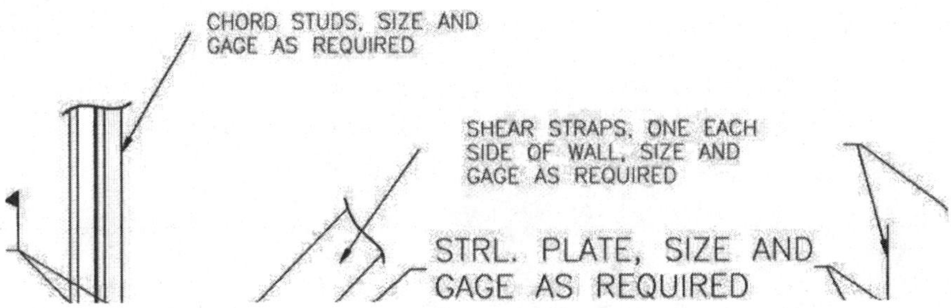

Solution

1. 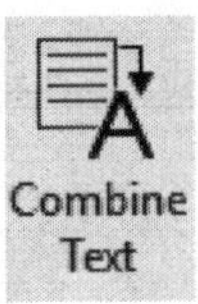

   Switch to the Insert ribbon.

   Select **Combine Text** from the Import panel.

2. 

   Select the single line text that is CHORDS, STUDS, SIZE, AND

   Then select the single line text that is GAGE AS REQUIRED.

   Click ENTER.

3.

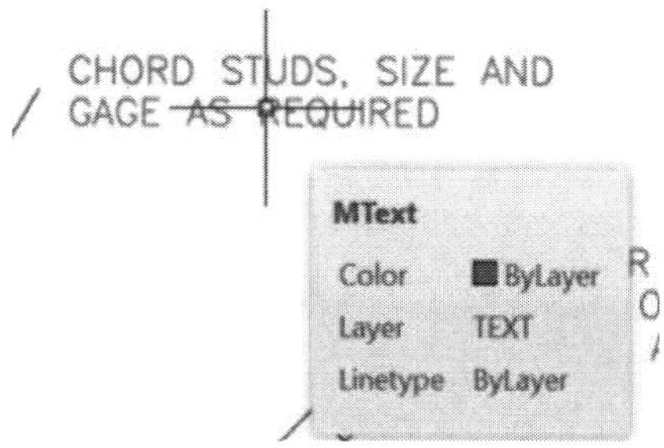

Hover the mouse over the text you just selected.

You will see that it has been converted to MTEXT.

4.

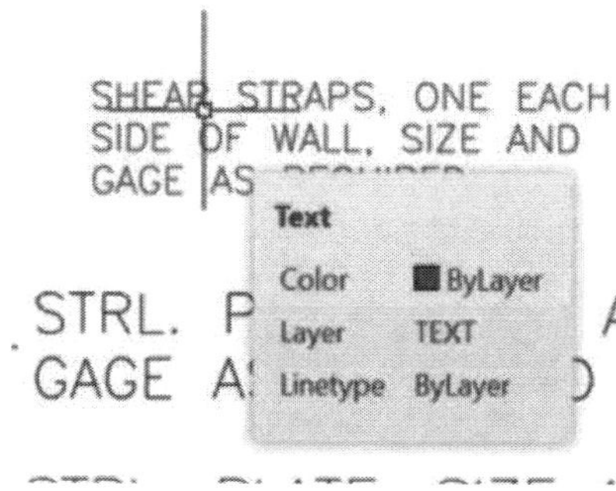

Hover the mouse over the other single line text.

You will see that it is single line text.

5.

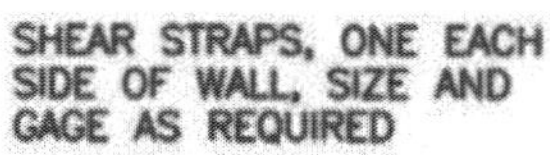

Use the COMBINE TEXT command to combine the single line text into mtext.

Review Questions

1. To change the justification of text in the MTEXT dialog, select here.

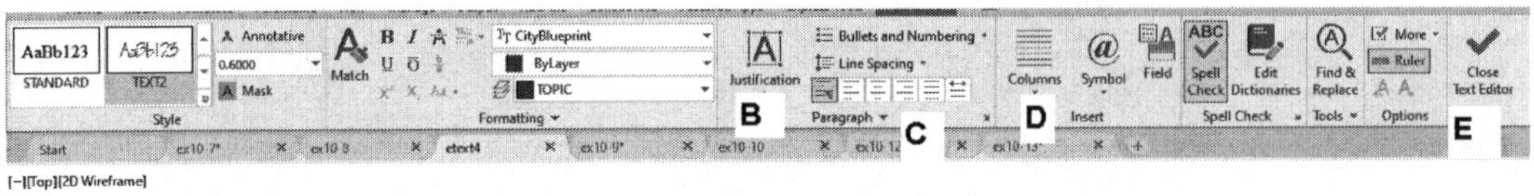

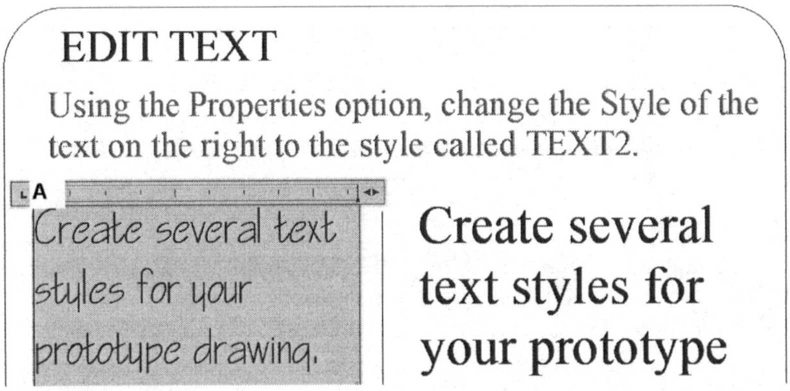

2. **T F** If a text height is specified in the text style, the user will not be prompted for the text height.

3. **T F** Fields can be applied to objects.

4. In order to import a text file into MTEXT, the file should be this format:
   - ❑ Txt or rtf
   - ❑ Doc or csv
   - ❑ Xls or csv
   - ❑ Txt or doc

5. Data exported from a table will be in this format:
   - ❑ Xls
   - ❑ Csv
   - ❑ Txt
   - ❑ Dwg

6. **T F** You can control the text style inside of tables.

7. **T F** You cannot add or delete columns or rows from a table once it has been placed.

8. **T F** You can control the appearance of the MTEXT dialog.

9. **T F** If you explode Multiline text it becomes single line text.

10. **T F** You can edit multiline text, but it becomes single line text.

11. **T F** You can create numbered and bulleted lists with Mtext.

12. **T F** Changes made to a text style affect all text objects that use the style.

Review Answers

1. To change the justification of text in the MTEXT dialog, select here.

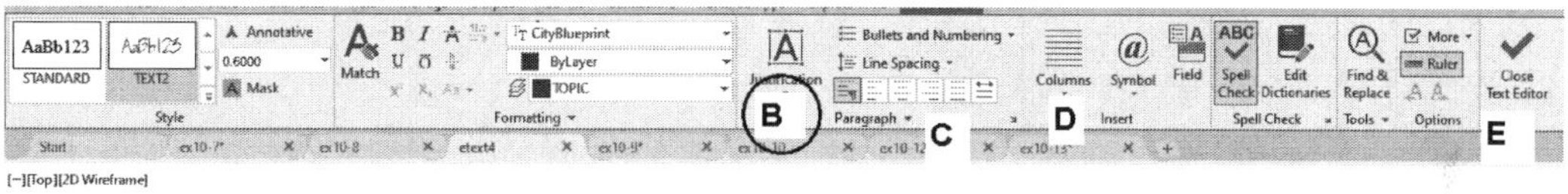

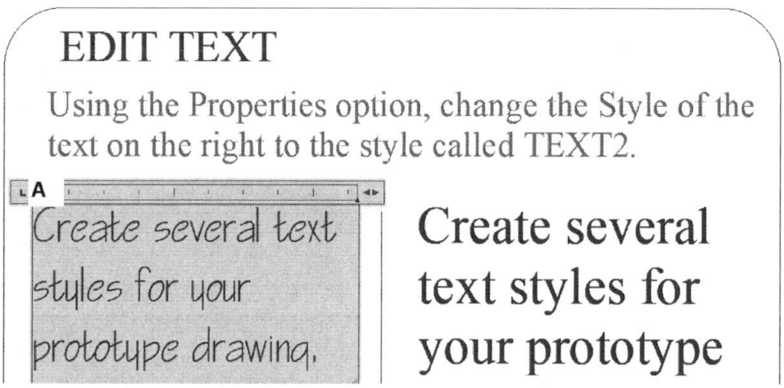

2. **T F** If a text height is specified in the text style, the user will not be prompted for the text height.

   True

3. **T F** Fields can be applied to objects.

   True

4. In order to import a text file into MTEXT, the file should be this format:

   Txt or rtf

5. Data exported from a table will be in this format:

   Csv

6. **T F** You can control the text style inside of tables.

   True

7. **T F** You cannot add or delete columns or rows from a table once it has been placed.

   False

8. **T F** You can control the appearance of the MTEXT dialog.

   True

9. **T F** If you explode Multiline text it becomes single line text.

   True

10. **T F** You can edit multiline text, but it becomes single line text.

    False

11. **T F** You can create numbered and bulleted lists with Mtext.

    True

12. **T F** Changes made to a text style affect all text objects that use the style.

    True

Lesson 11.0 – Blocks and Templates

Estimated Class Time: 4 Hours

Objectives

Students will learn how to create blocks, Title blocks and templates using drawing tools, fields, and attributes.

- **Templates**
  Templates are used as the starting point for a drawing and can store layers, linetypes, text styles and dimension styles.
- **Title Blocks**
  Titleblocks are used to track a drawing's name, part number, revision level, and other important information.
- **Fields**
  Fields can be linked to drawing properties.
- **Attributes**
  Attributes store data and are easily edited.
- **The Define Attribute Command**

One of the options when you create a drawing is to use a template. Many companies set up and use templates to ensure their drafters comply with their internal standards. Templates are great because you only need to set up your layers, title blocks, and dimension styles once.

Technical drawings require a title block and a border.

You will notice that there are four arrows on the border, one on each side. The arrows are a leftover from the days when technical drawings were done on vellum.

Drafters would create drawings using multiple sheets. Each sheet would act as a layer. The arrows were used to line up the views so that the overlays would match.

Most companies have a title block template that contains their company name and logo, as well as company address and contact information. As drafters, you need to know how to create and modify title blocks in case the company information changes and how to insert title blocks for use in your drawings.

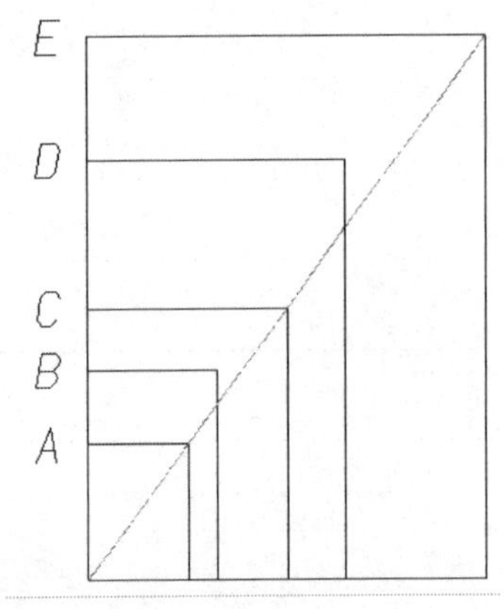

Each title block size is double the previous size:

A size: 8 ½ x 11

B size: 11 x 17

C size: 17 x 22

D size: 22 x 34

E size: 34 x 44

In AutoCAD, all models and views are drawn 1:1. That way we can compare elements to make sure they fit together. For architectural plans, you want to be able to overlay the site plan and the floor plan to make sure everything lines up. If everything is drawn at the same scale (Hint: 1:1), the different layouts can be placed on top of each other and appear proper. In order to plot, we place the title block on a layout tab, scale the title block, place viewports on the layout tab, and then scale the plot.

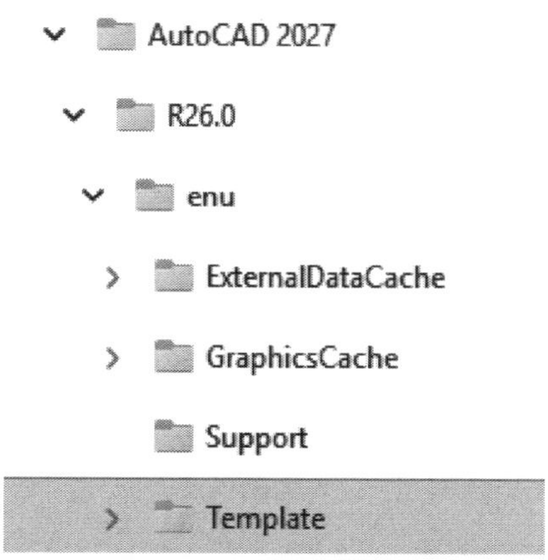

AutoCAD comes with standard title block templates. They are located in the Templates subdirectory under *Users\<User Name>\AppData\ Local\Autodesk\ AutoCAD 2027\R26\enu \Template.*

Many companies will place their templates on the network so all users can access the same templates. In order to make this work properly, set the Options so that the templates folder is pointed to the correct path.

By adding attributes and fields to a title block, we can easily modify the text values and we can later learn how to export the attribute values to create a database for our parts drawings.

Define Attribute

Command Locator

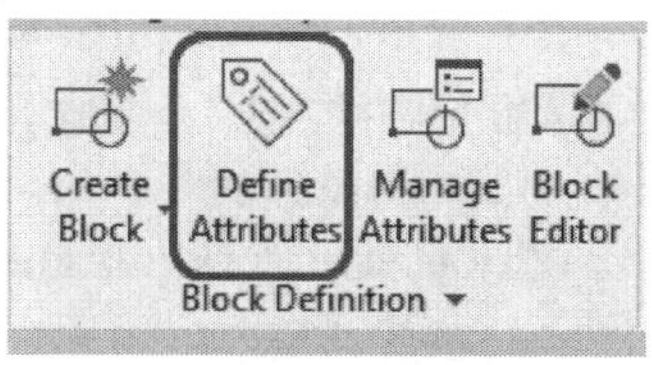

Ribbon/Insert	**Define Attribute**
Command	**ATTDEF**
Alias	**ATT**
Dialog Box	**Define Attribute**

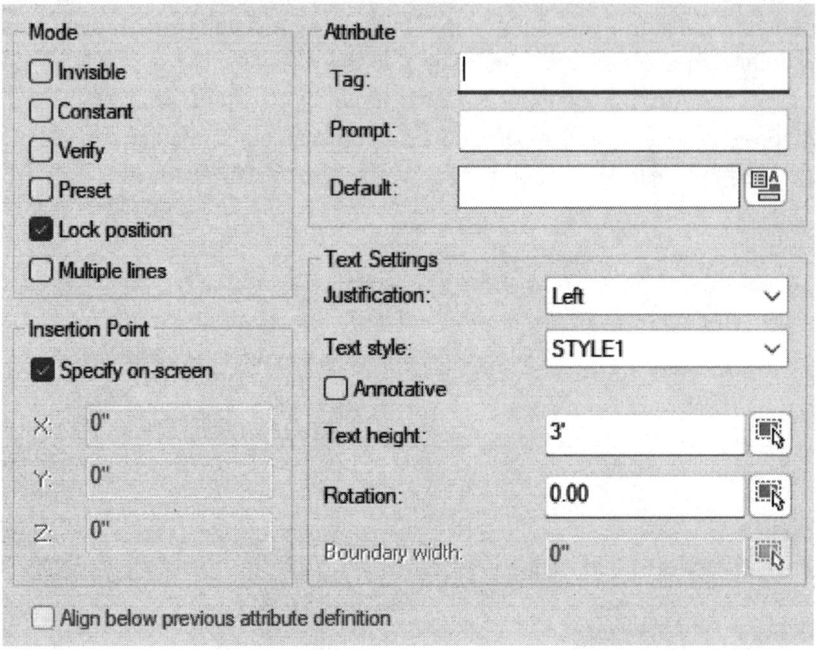

Command Overview

The Define Attribute dialog allows fields to be used as attributes. Field data is set up in the File Properties dialog. Once you enter the data in this dialog, the fields will automatically update in any corresponding locations.

There are four modes of Attribute definitions:

· *Invisible*
· *Constant*
· *Verify*
· *Preset*

Invisible attributes are used to store information in a drawing that is not seen in normal mode. Some companies will create a set of invisible attributes that list the layer standards. Drafters then turn the attribute display on so they can see the layer standards and turn them off when they are ready to plot their drawings. Other companies use invisible attributes to store cost information for parts. They don't want the customer to see how much the material costs, but they need the information to estimate project costs.

Constant attributes are used when the value does not change, such as company name, but the information is needed for extraction to a database.

Verify mode prompts the user with a Yes/No after they enter the attribute value to give them a chance to recheck their entry.

Preset sets the attribute to its default value when you insert a block containing a preset attribute.

Lock Position fixes the position of the attribute so it cannot be moved.

Multiple lines allows you to create an attribute using the MTEXT editor. You can use the editor to determine the width of your paragraph.

General Procedures:

1. Start the **ATTDEF** command.
2. Fill in the dialog box with the desired properties.
3. Click to place the attribute or use specified coordinates.
4. Click OK to close the dialog.

Tips & Tricks

To control the display of attributes use the command ATTDISP. Normal is normal/default viewing mode. ON allows you to see invisible and visible attributes. OFF makes all attributes invisible.

Command Exercise

Exercise 11-1 – Define Attribute

Drawing Name: **ANSI B title block.dwg**
Estimated Time to Completion: 60 Minutes

Scope

Add attributes and fields to a title block.

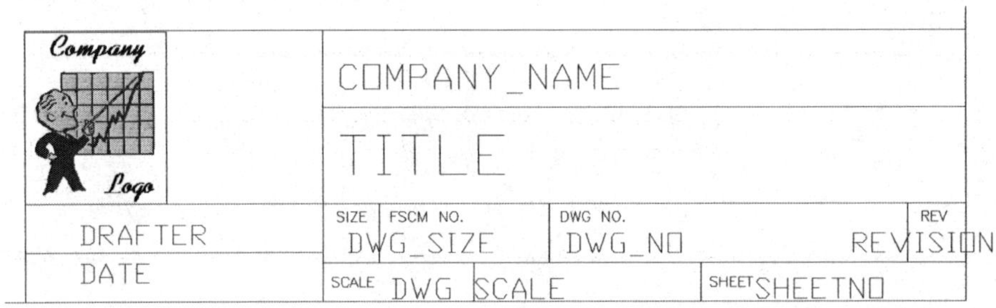

Solution

1. 

Verify that the active workspace is **Drafting & Annotation**.

2. 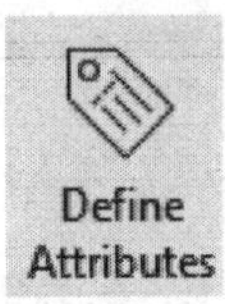

Activate the **Insert** ribbon.

Select the **Define Attributes** tool.

3. 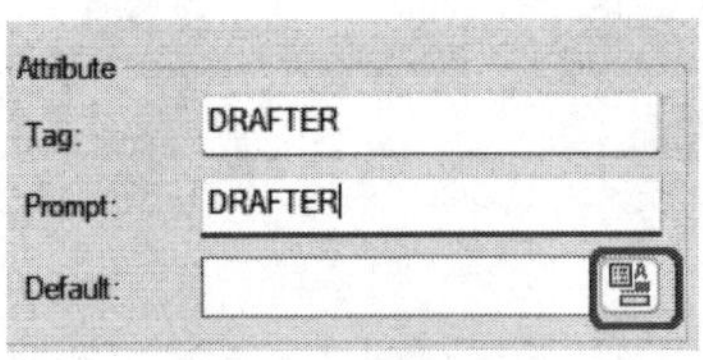

Enter **DRAFTER** in the Tag field.

Enter **DRAFTER** in the Prompt field.

Then select the **Insert Field** button.

4. 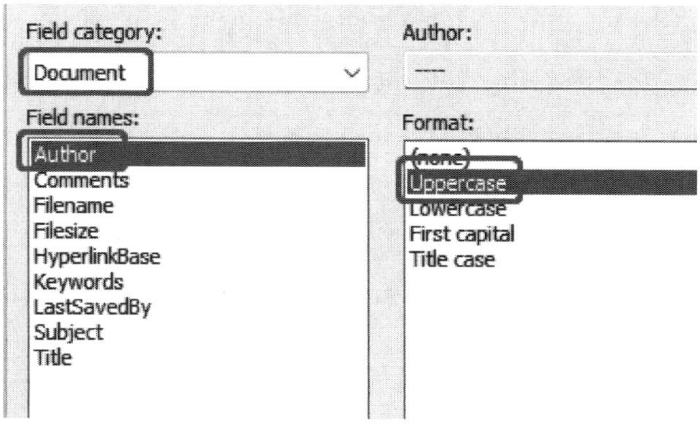

In the Field category, select **Document**.

Highlight **Author** in the Field Names window.
Highlight **Uppercase** in the Format window.

Click **OK**.

5. 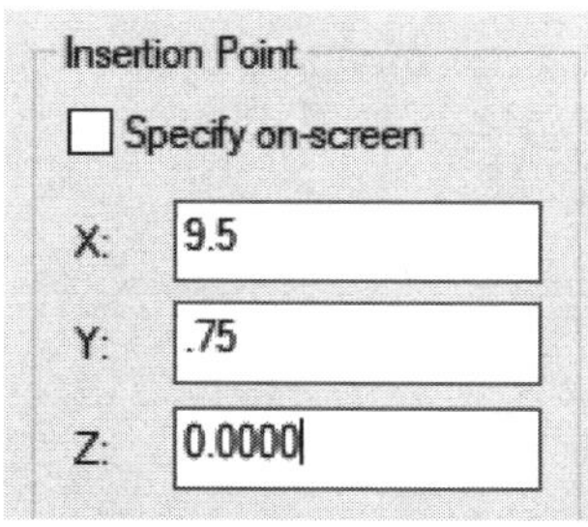

Under Insertion Point:

Set X to **9.5**.

Set Y to **0. 75**.

Set Z to **0**.

6. 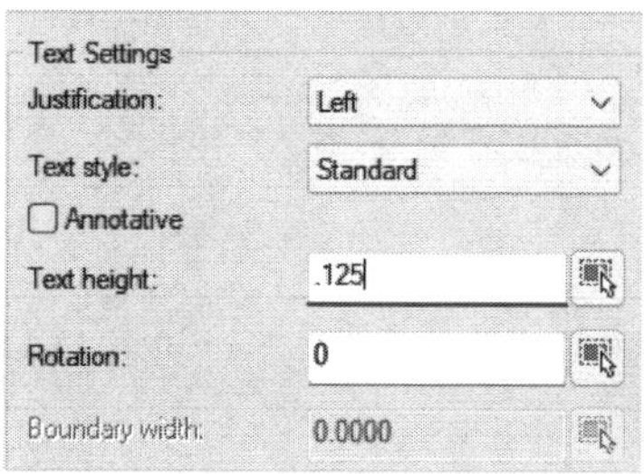

Under Text Options:
Set the Height to **.125**.

Click **OK**.

7. 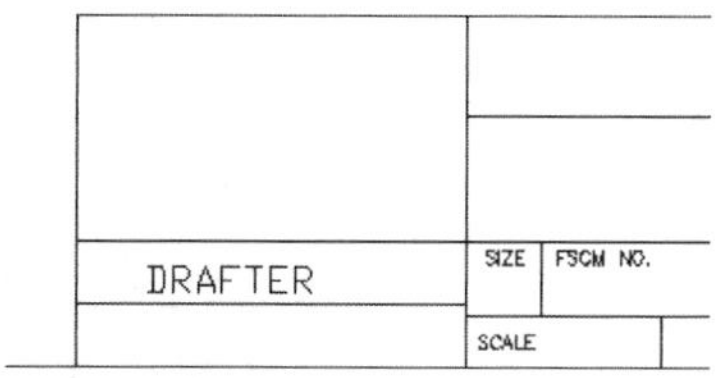

The field appears in the title block.

8. 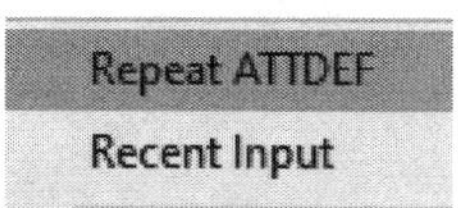

Right click and select **Repeat ATTDEF** from the shortcut menu.

9. 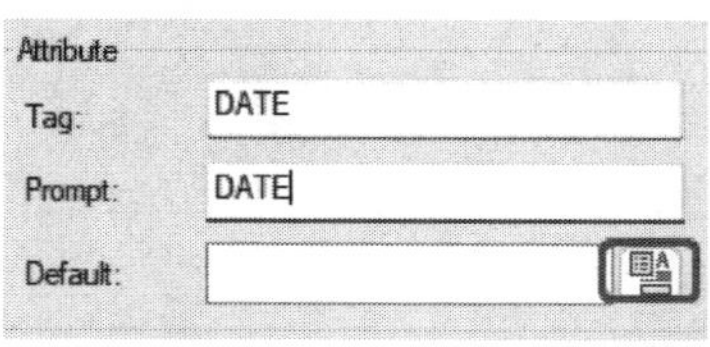

Enter **DATE** in the Tag field.

Enter **DATE** in the Prompt field.

Then select the **Insert Field** button.

10. In the Field category, select **Date & Time**.

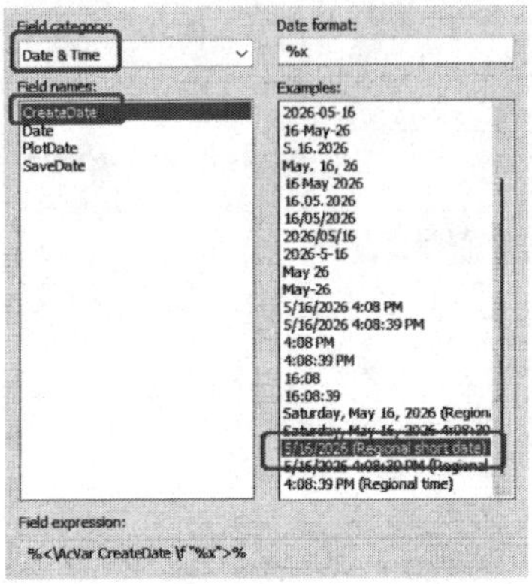

Highlight **CreateDate** in the Field Names window.

Highlight the **Regional short date** in the list.

Click **OK**.

You will see a preview of what the date will look like in the Default field.

11.

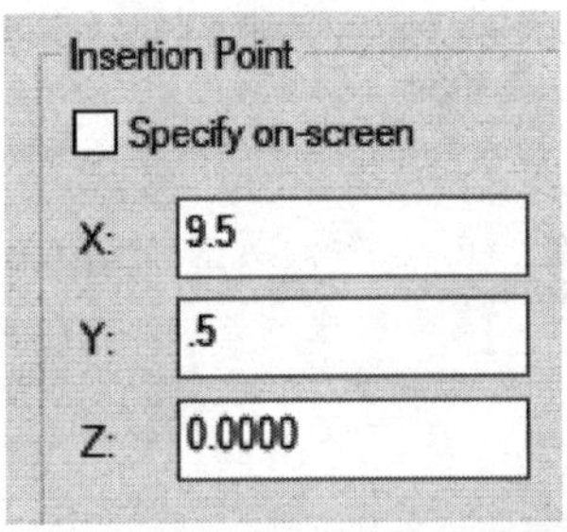

Under Insertion Point:

Set X to **9.5**.

Set Y to **0.5**.

Set Z to **0**.

12.

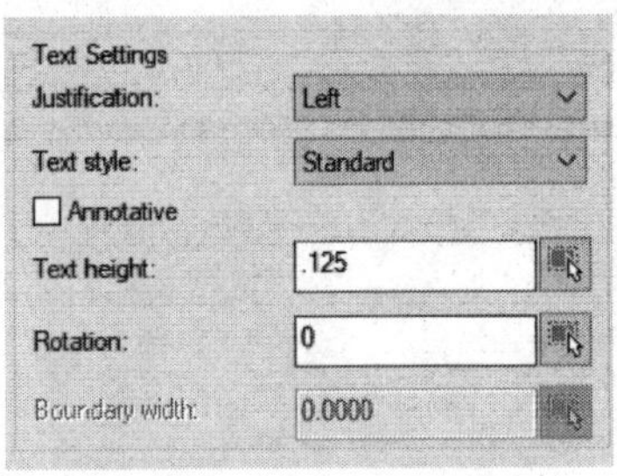

Under Text Options:

Set the Height to **.125**.

Click **OK**.

13.

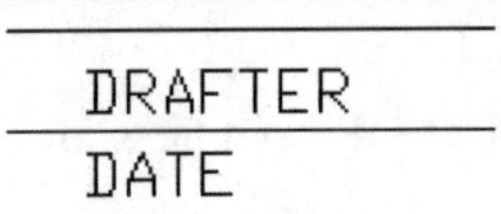

The field appears in the title block.

14.

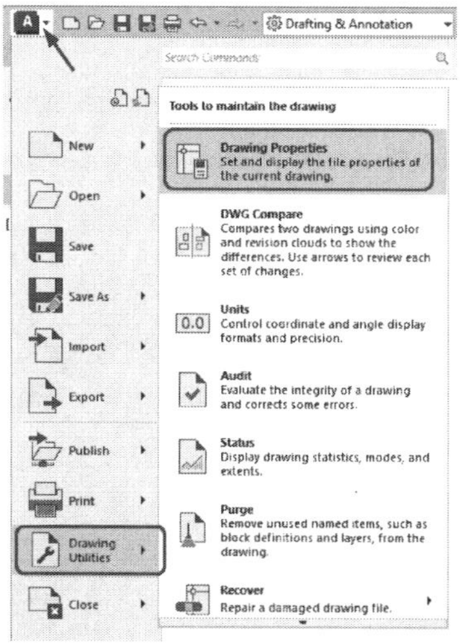

Go to the **Application Menu** (the capital A in the upper left corner)→**Drawing Utilities→ Drawing Properties**.

15.

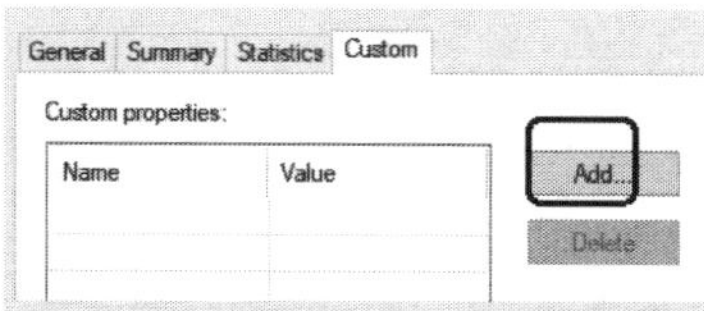

Select the **Custom** tab.

Click the **Add** button.

16.

Type **Company Name** in the Custom property name field.

Type your school or company name in the Value field.

Click **OK** twice.

17.

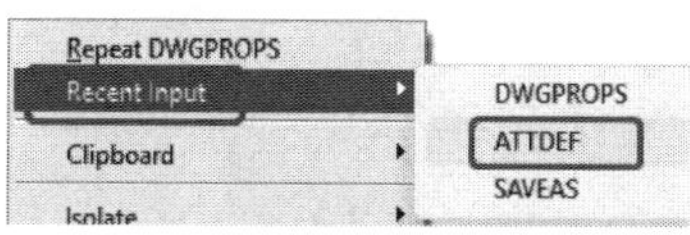

Right click and select **Recent Input→ATTDEF** from the shortcut menu.

18.

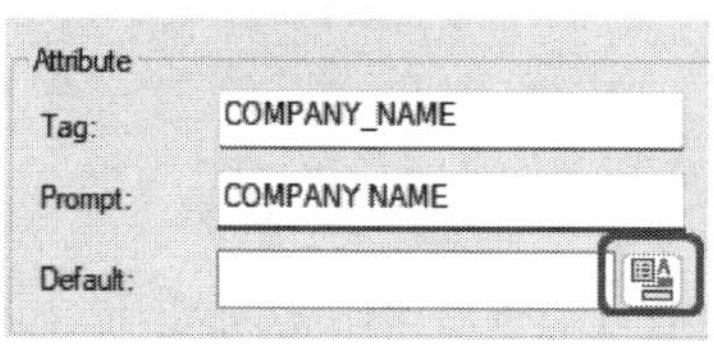

Enter **COMPANY_NAME** in the Tag field.

Enter **COMPANY NAME** in the Prompt field.

Note that the Tag field does not allow spaces.

Select the **Insert Field** button.

19.

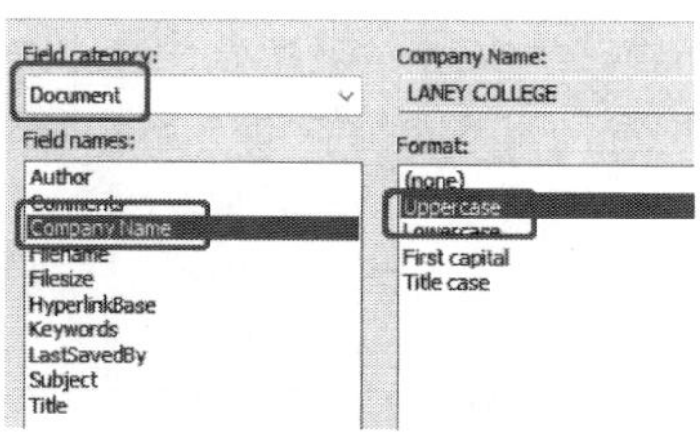

In the Field category, select **Document**.

Highlight **Company Name** in the Field Names window.

Highlight **Uppercase** in the format field.

Click **OK**.

20. 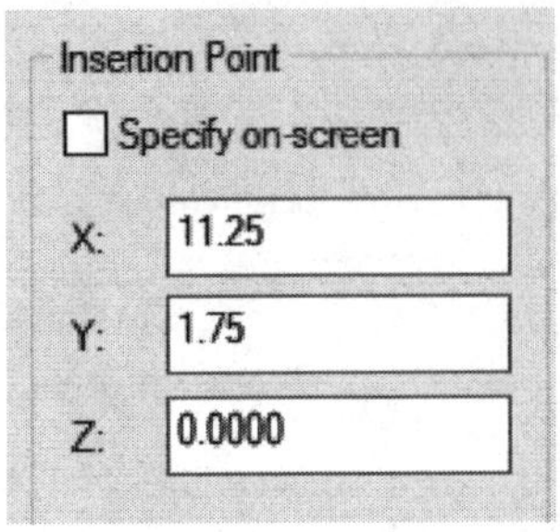

Under Insertion Point:

Set X to **11.25**.

Set Y to **1.75**.

Set Z to **0**.

21. 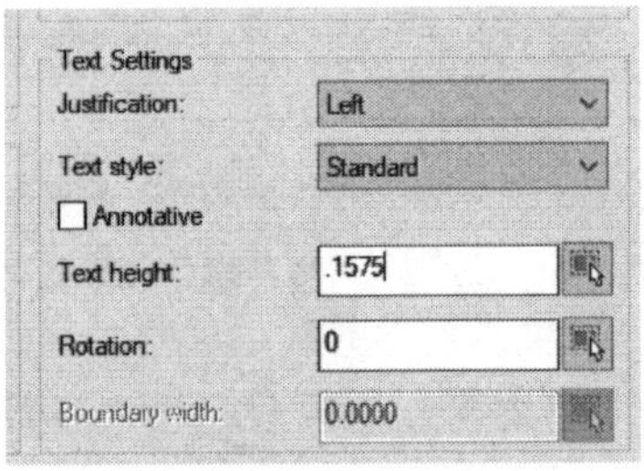

Under Text Options:

Set the Height to **.1575**.

Click **OK**.

22. 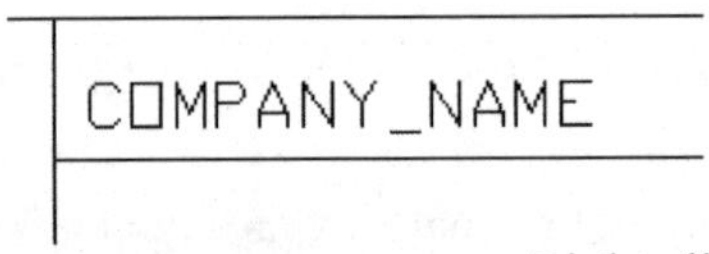

The field appears in the title block.

23. 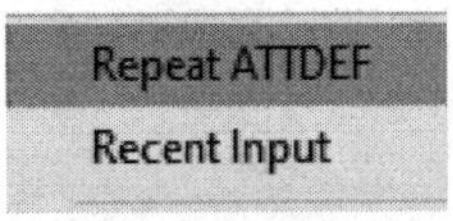

Right click and select **Repeat ATTDEF** from the shortcut menu.

24. 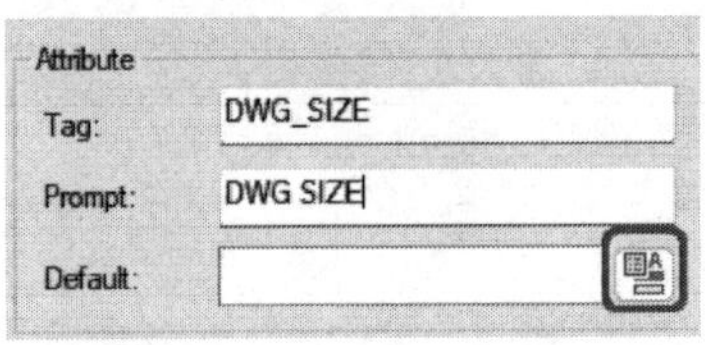

Enter **DWG_SIZE** in the Tag field.

Enter **DWG SIZE** in the Prompt field.

Then select the **Insert Field** button.

25. 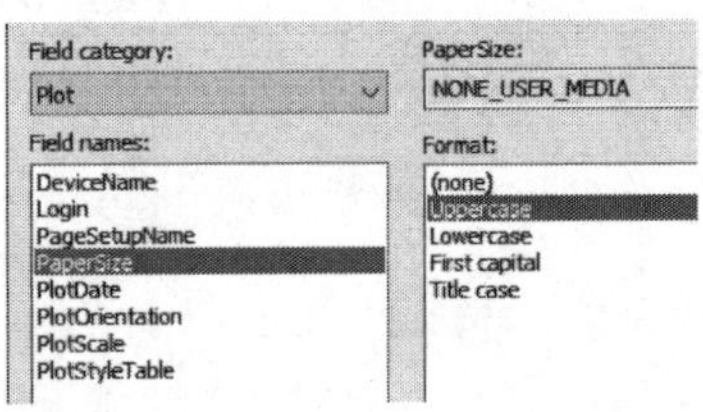

In the Field category, select **Plot**.

Highlight **PaperSize** in the Field Names window.

Highlight **Uppercase** in the format field.

Click **OK**.

By using a field for the paper size, the paper size will adjust based on the layout size used...you can change the paper size and the field will automatically update.

26. 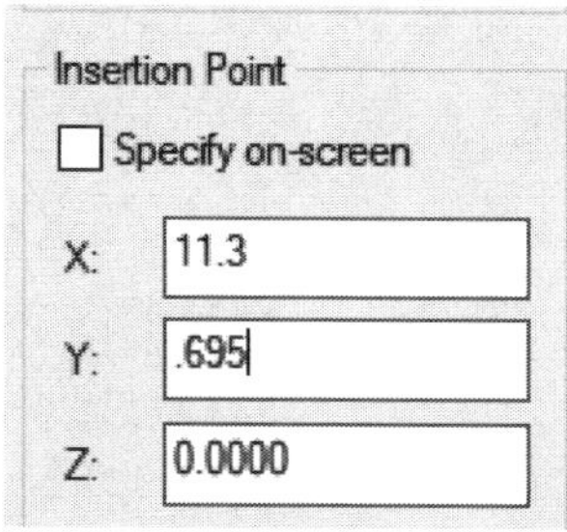

Under Insertion Point:
Set X to **11.3**.
Set Y to **0.695**.
Set Z to **0**.

27. 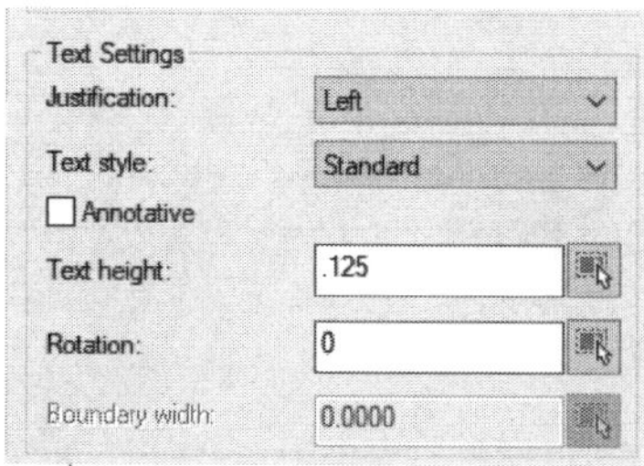

Under Text Options:
Set the Justification to **Center**.
Set the Height to **.125**.

Click **OK**.

28. 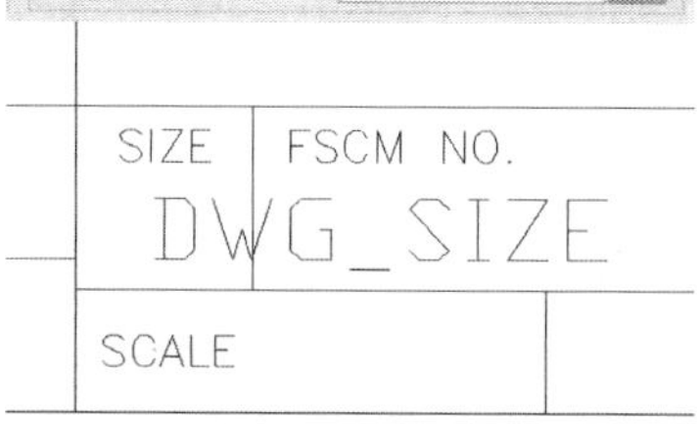

The field appears in the title block.

Don't worry about the field going outside the box as it will only be one character.

29. 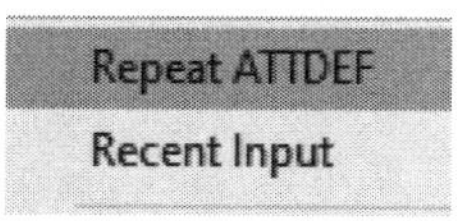

Right click and select **Repeat ATTDEF** from the shortcut menu.

30. 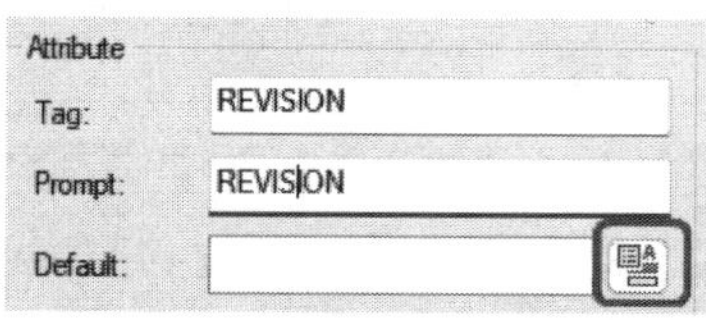

Enter **REVISION** in the Tag field.

Enter **REVISION** in the Prompt field.

Then select the **Insert Field** button.

31. 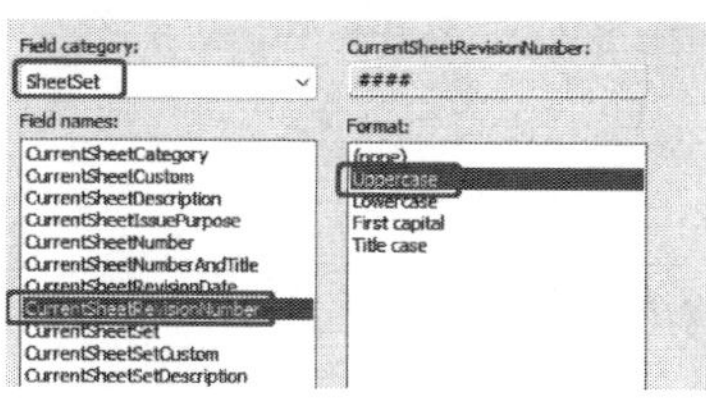

In the Field category, select **SheetSet**.

Highlight **CurrentSheetRevisionNumber** in the Field Names window.

Highlight **Uppercase** in the format field.

Click **OK**.

By using a field for the sheetset, you can have multiple layouts in a drawing and use the revision on that specific layout for the revision number.

32. 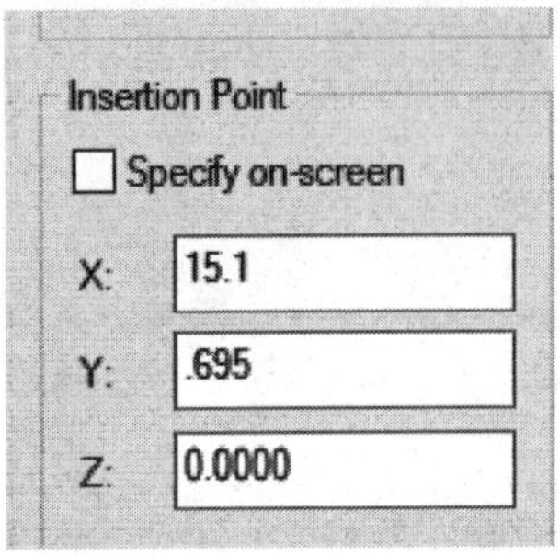

Under Insertion Point:

Set X to **15.1**.

Set Y to **0.695**.

Set Z to **0**.

33. 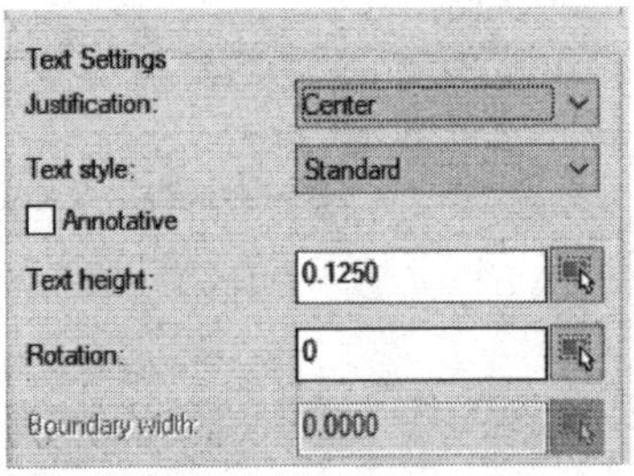

Under Text Options:

Set the Justification to **Center**.

Set the Height to **.125**.

Click **OK**.

34. 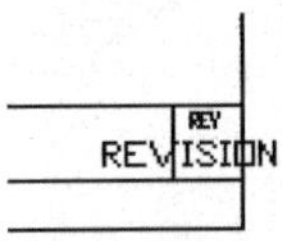

The field appears in the title block.

Don't worry about the field going outside the box as it will only be one to three characters.

35. 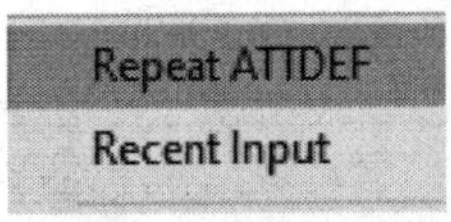

Right click and select **Repeat ATTDEF** from the shortcut menu.

36. 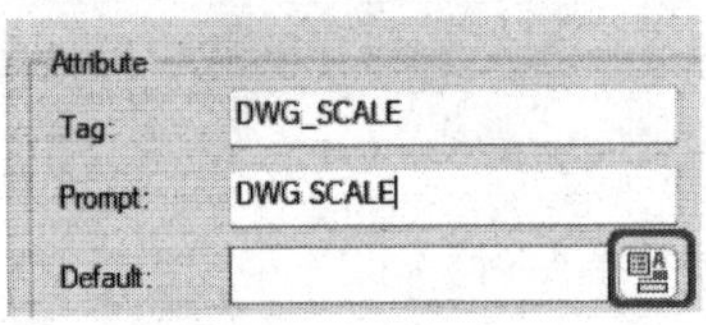

Enter **DWG_SCALE** in the Tag field.

Enter **DWG SCALE** in the Prompt field.

Then select the **Insert Field** button.

37. 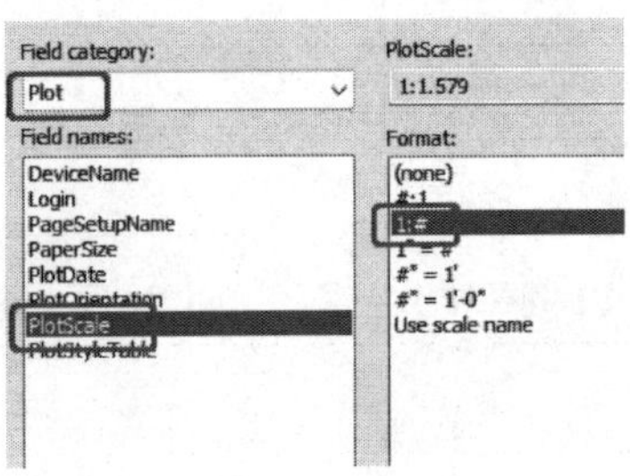

In the Field category, select **Plot**.

Highlight **PlotScale** in the Field Names window.

Highlight **1:#** in the format field.

Click **OK**.

By using a field for the plot scale, you can have multiple layouts in a drawing and use the plot scale on that specific layout.

38. 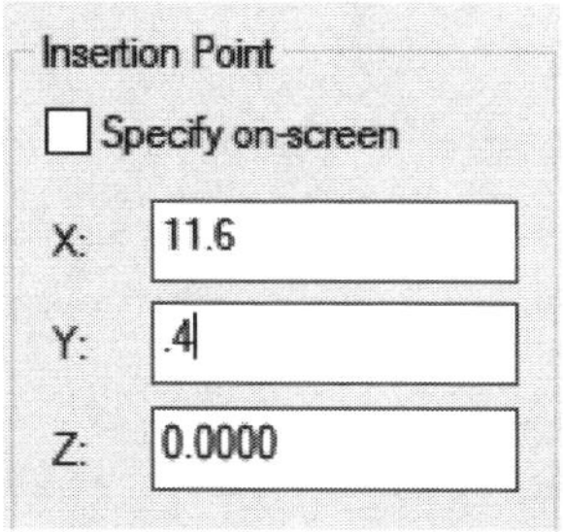

Under Insertion Point:

Set X to **11.6**.

Set Y to **0.40**.

Set Z to **0**.

39. 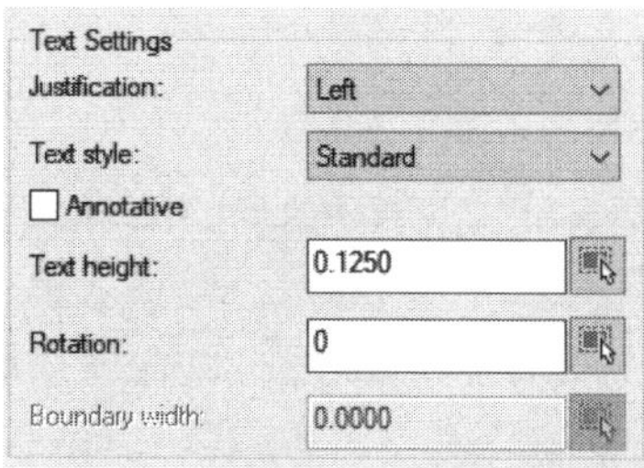

Under Text Options:

Set the Justification to **Left**.

Set the Height to **.125**.

Click **OK**.

40. 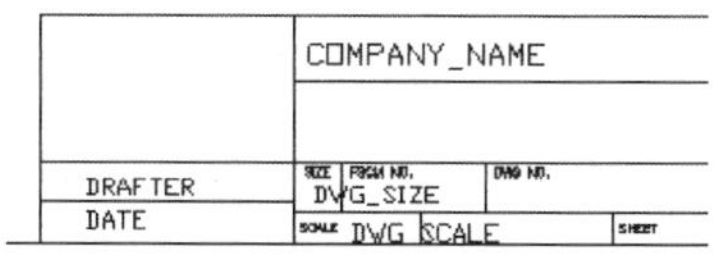

The field appears in the title block.

Don't worry about the field going outside the box as it will only be a few characters.

41. 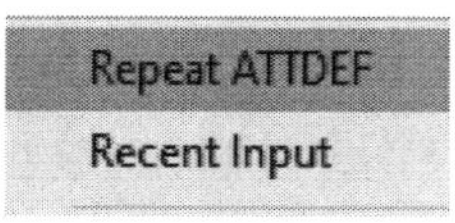

Right click and select **Repeat ATTDEF** from the shortcut menu.

42. 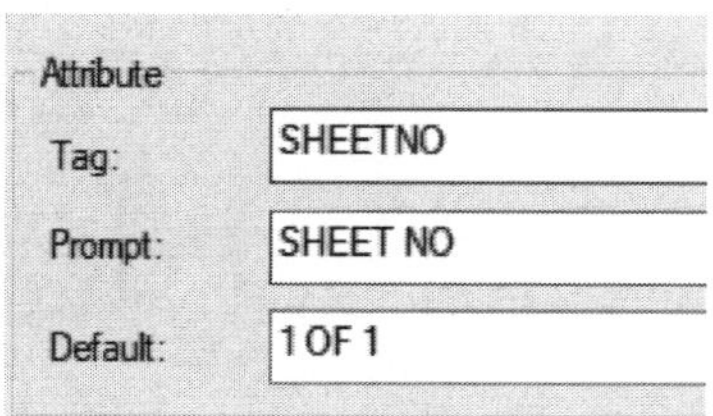

Enter **SHEETNO** in the Tag field.

Enter **SHEET NO** in the Prompt field.

Enter **1 OF 1** in the Default field.

43. 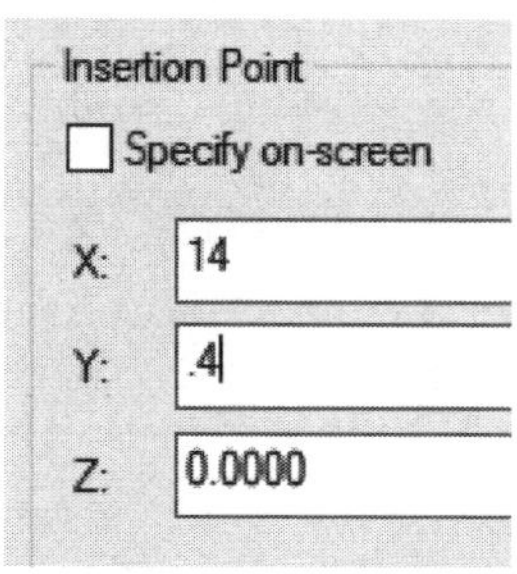

Under Insertion Point:

Set X to **14**.

Set Y to **0.40**.

Set Z to **0**.

44. 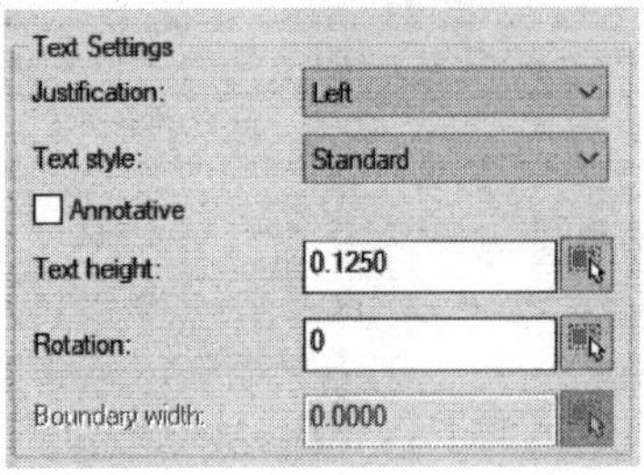

Under Text Options:

Set the Justification to **Left**.

Set the Height to **.125**.

Click **OK**.

45. 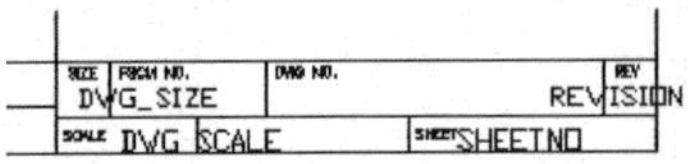

The field appears in the title block.

46. 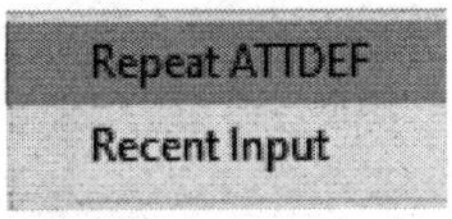

Right click and select **Repeat ATTDEF** from the shortcut menu.

47. 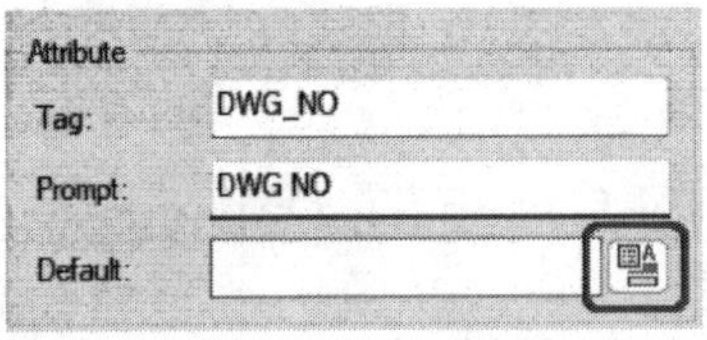

Enter **DWG_NO** in the Tag field.

Enter **DWG NO** in the Prompt field.

Select the **Insert Field** button.

48. 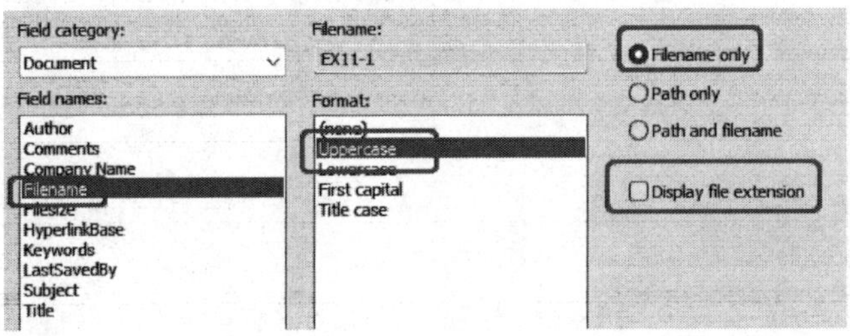

In the Field category, select **Document**.

Highlight **Filename** in the Field Names window.

Highlight **Uppercase** in the format field.

49. Enable **Filename only**.

Disable **Display file extension**.

This removes the .dwg from the file name.

Click **OK**.

50. 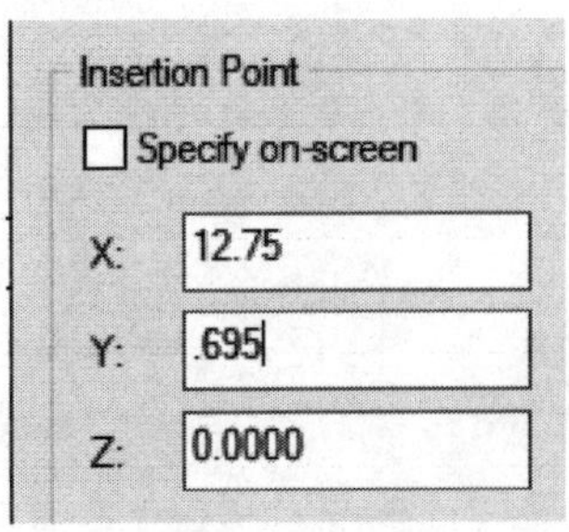

Under Insertion Point:

Set X to **12.75**.

Set Y to **0.695**.

Set Z to **0**.

51.

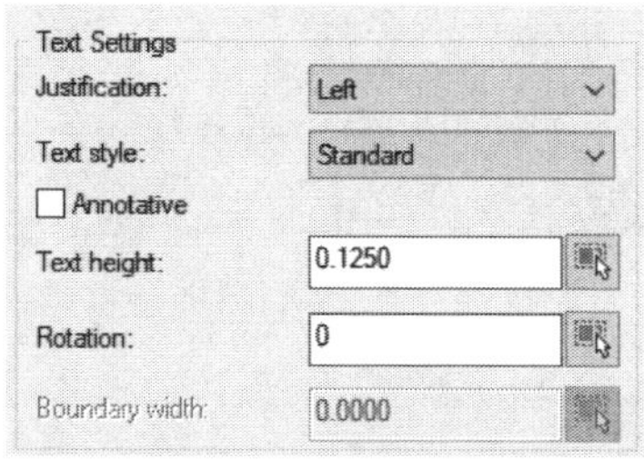

Under Text Options:

Set the Justification to **Left**.

Set the Height to **.125**.

Click **OK**.

52.

The field appears in the title block.

53.

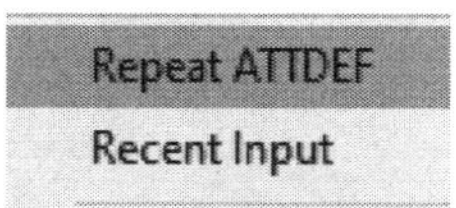

Right click and select **Repeat ATTDEF** from the shortcut menu.

54.

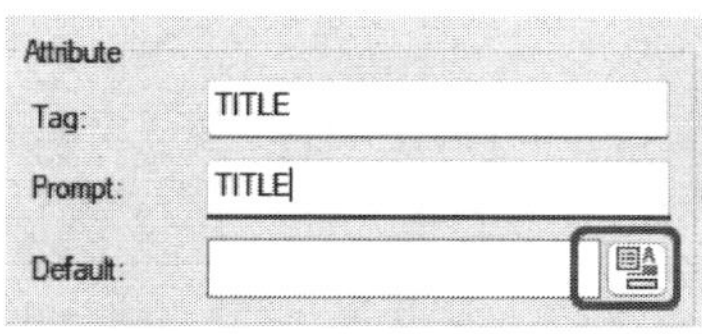

Enter **TITLE** in the Tag field.

Enter **TITLE** in the Prompt field.

Select the **Insert Field** button.

55.

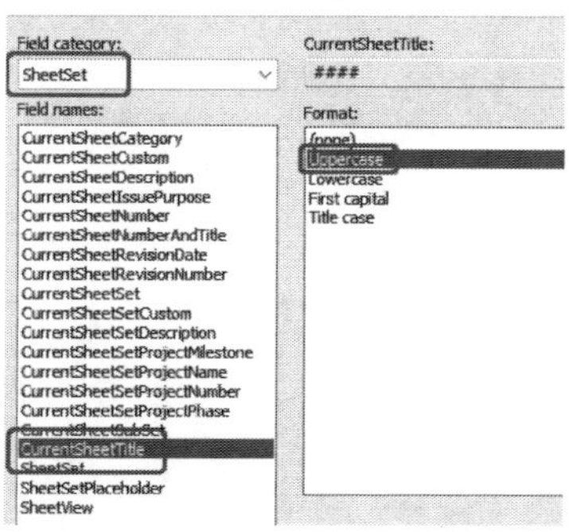

In the Field category, select **SheetSet**.

Highlight **CurrentSheetTitle** in the Field Names window.

Highlight **Uppercase** in the format field.

Click **OK**.

56.

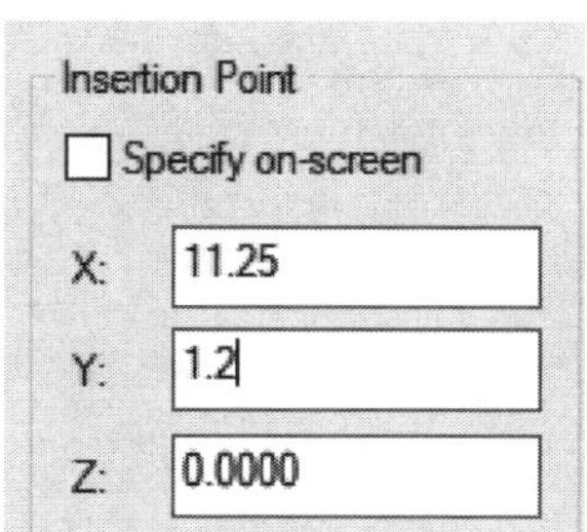

Under Insertion Point:

Set X to **11.25**.

Set Y to **1.2**.

Set Z to **0**.

57. 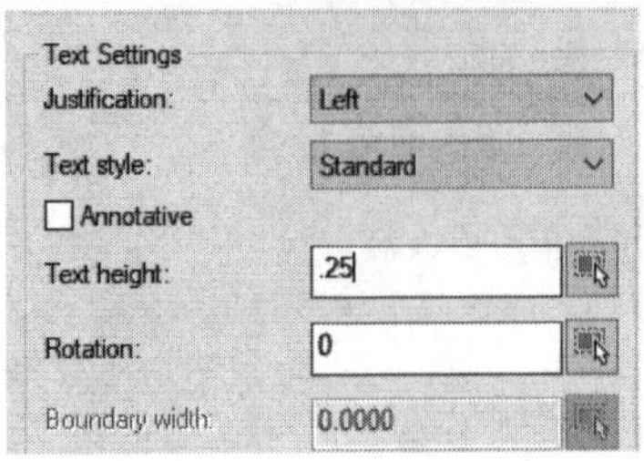

Under Text Options:

Set the Justification to **Left**.
Set the Height to **.25**.

58. *The title block should appear as shown.*

You'll notice that some of the attributes don't fit properly in the title block. This is OK. The values will fit just fine.

You can adjust the position of any of the attributes using the MOVE tool.

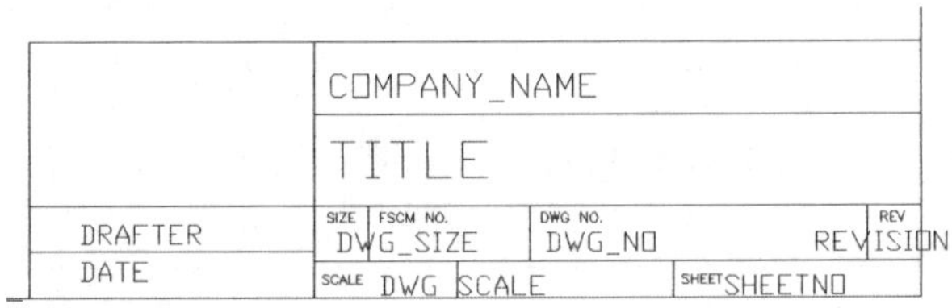

59. 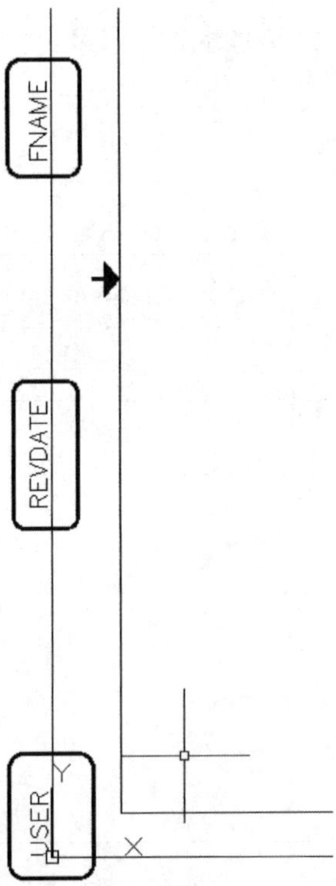

Erase the pre-defined attributes in the title block located on the left vertical side.

60. 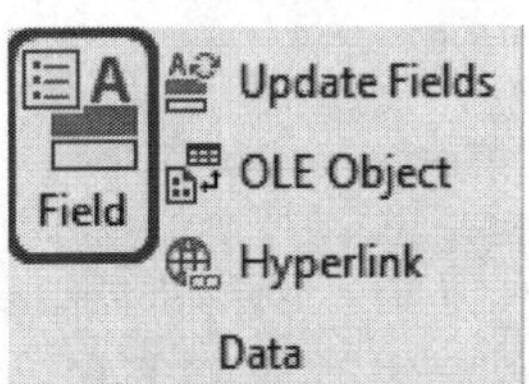

Select the **Field** tool from the Insert ribbon.

61. 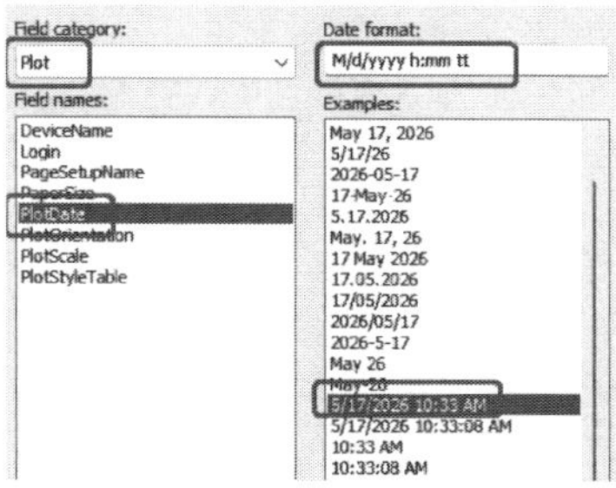

In the Field category, select **Plot**.

Highlight **PlotDate** in the Field Names window.

Highlight **M/d/yyyy h:mm tt** in the format field.

Click **OK**.

62. 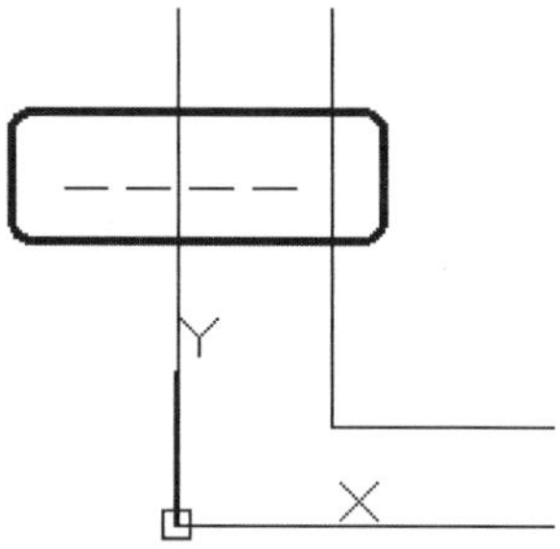

Place the field above the lower left corner of the title block.

63. 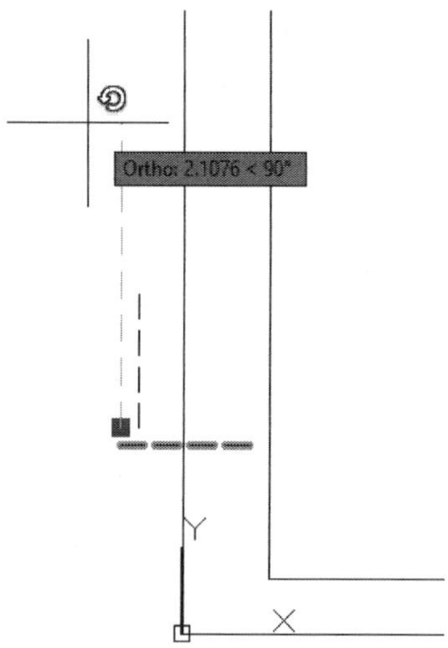

Rotate the field so that it is vertical.

This will act as a plot stamp for the sheet when it is plotted.

Click **ESC** to release the selection.

Many companies like to see their logo in the title block. AutoCAD allows you to insert graphics into drawings. Any image file (gif, jpg, bmp, etc.) can be inserted.

64. 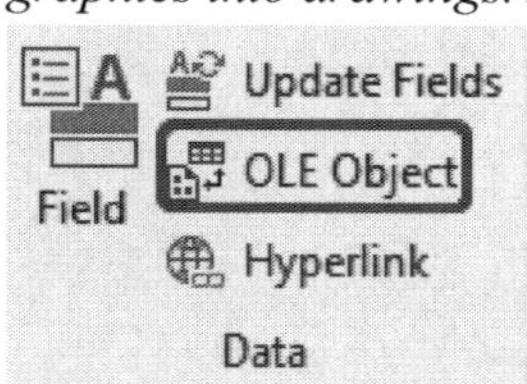

On the Insert ribbon, select **OLE Object** on the Data panel.

65. 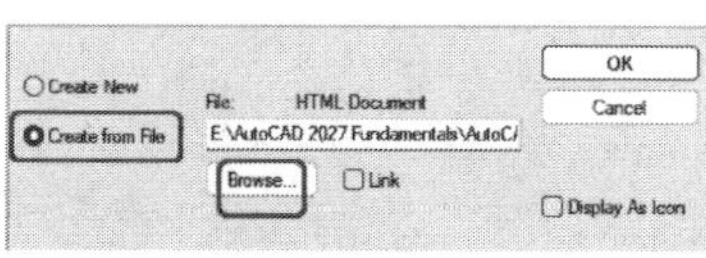

Enable **Create from File**.

Use the **Browse** button to locate the image file.

Use the image file provided in the textbook downloads or use an image of your choice.

Click **OK**.

66. 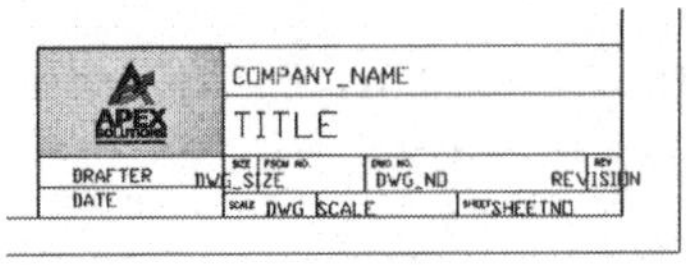

Position the graphic as shown.

You can use the grips on the image to move and stretch the image file.

67. Save the file as '*Custom-B.dwg*'.

- *Address, phone, and other data may also be defined as custom properties.*
- *Right click and use Recent Input to access your most recent commands. Simply select the command you want to use from the list.*
- *Custom Properties must be defined before they are available as fields.*
- *It is a good idea to save any custom blocks, toolbars, etc. in a separate directory away from AutoCAD. That way you can easily back up your custom work to use on another workstation and if you need to reinstall AutoCAD for any reason, you will not lose your work.*
- *Use a BMP image file to embed it into an AutoCAD file. Otherwise, it is just a link or reference.*
- *Think of an attribute as a box and the value as the item stored in the box. The attribute name is the name of the box and acts as a pointer to what's inside. Many students confuse the attribute name with the value.*

Page Setup Manager

Command Locator

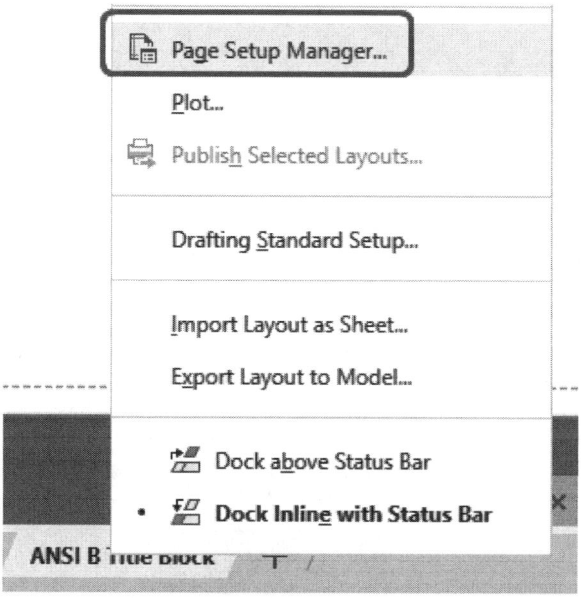

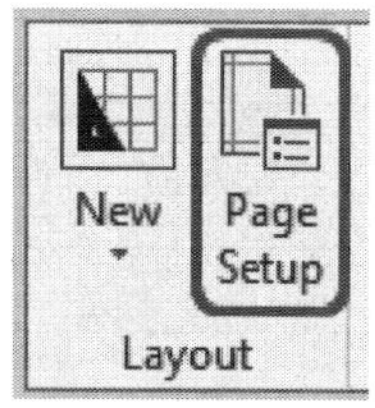

Ribbon/Layout/	**PAGESETUP**
Command	**PAGESETUP**
Dialog Box	**Page Setup Manager**

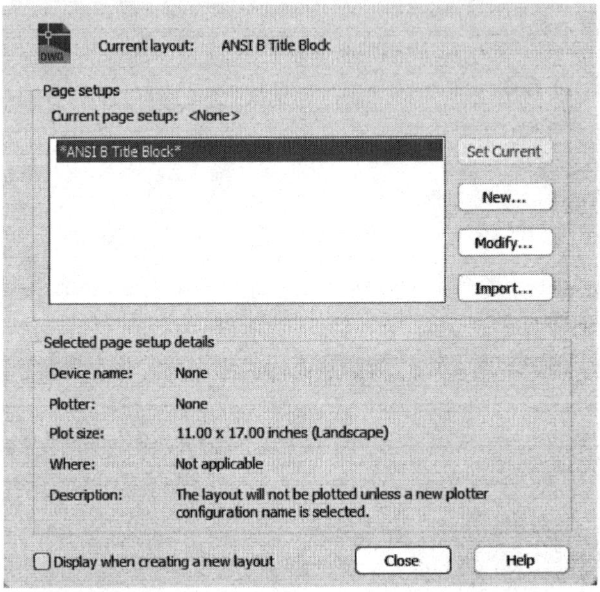

The Page Setup Manager is used to set up how drawings should be plotted and assigned to different layout tabs. A page setup is a collection of plot device and other settings that determine the appearance and format of your final output. These settings are stored in the drawing file and can be modified and applied to other layouts.

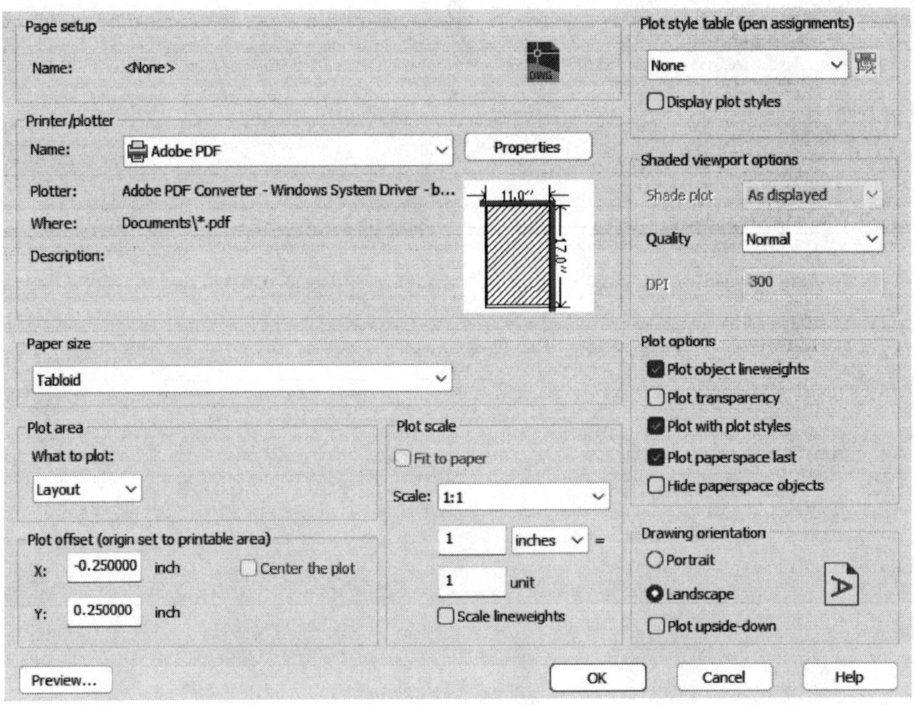

Page Setup

Name

Displays the name of the current page setup.

Icon

Displays a DWG icon when the Page Setup dialog box is opened from a layout, and displays a sheet set icon when the Page Setup dialog box is opened from the Sheet Set Manager.

Printer/Plotter

Specifies a configured plotting device to use when plotting or publishing layouts or sheets.

Name

Lists the available PC3 files or system printers from which you can select to plot or publish the current layout or sheet. An icon in front of the device name identifies it as a PC3 file or a system printer.

Properties

Displays the Plotter Configuration Editor (PC3 editor), in which you can view or modify the current plotter configuration, ports, device, and media settings.

If you make changes to the PC3 file using the Plotter Configuration Editor, the Changes to a Printer Configuration File dialog box is displayed.

Plotter

Displays the plot device specified in the currently selected page setup.

Where

Displays the physical location of the output device specified in the currently selected page setup.

Description

Displays descriptive text about the output device specified in the currently selected page setup. You can edit this text in the Plotter Configuration Editor.

Partial Preview

Shows an accurate representation of the effective plot area relative to the paper size and printable area. The tooltip displays the paper size and printable area.

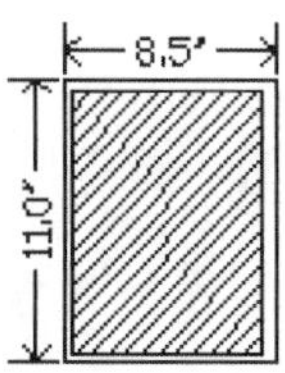

Paper Size

Displays standard paper sizes that are available for the selected plotting device.

If the selected plotter does not support the layout's selected paper size, a warning is displayed, and you can select the plotter's default paper size or a custom paper size.

A default paper size is set for the plotting device when you create a PC3 file with the Add-a-Plotter wizard. For information about this wizard, see "Set Up Plotters and Printers" in the *Driver and Peripheral Guide*. The paper size that you select in the Page Setup dialog box is saved with the layout and overrides the PC3 file settings.

The actual printable area of the page, which is determined by the selected plotting device and paper size, is indicated in the layout by a dashed line.

If you are plotting a raster image, such as a BMP or TIFF file, the size of the plot is specified in pixels, not in inches or millimeters.

Plot Area

Specifies the area of the drawing to be plotted.

Layout/Limits

When plotting a layout, plots everything within the printable area of the specified paper size, with the origin calculated from 0,0 in the layout.

When plotting from the Model layout, plots the entire drawing area that is defined by the grid limits. If the current viewport does not display a plan view, this option has the same effect as the Extents option.

Extents

Plots the portion of the current space of the drawing that contains objects. All geometry in the current layout is plotted. The drawing may be regenerated to recalculate the extents before plotting.

Display

Plots the view in the current viewport in the current layout.

View

Plots a view that was previously saved with the VIEW command.

Window

Plots any portion of the drawing that you specify. When you specify the two corners of the area to plot, the Window button becomes available.

Click the Window button to use the pointing device to specify the two corners of the area to be plotted, or enter coordinate values.

Plot Offset

Specifies an offset of the plot area relative to the lower-left corner of the printable area or to the edge of the paper, depending on the setting made in the Specify Plot Offset Relative To option (Options dialog box, Plot and Publish tab). The Plot Offset area of the Page Setup dialog box displays the specified plot offset option in parentheses.

The printable area of a drawing sheet is defined by the selected output device and is represented by a dashed line in a layout. When you change to another output device, the printable area may change.

You can offset the geometry on the paper by entering a positive or negative value in the X and Y offset boxes. The plotter unit values are in inches or millimeters on the paper.

Center the Plot

Automatically calculates the *X* and *Y* offset values to center the plot on the paper.

X

Specifies the plot origin in the *X* direction relative to the setting of the Plot Offset Definition option.

Y

Specifies the plot origin in the *Y* direction relative to the setting of the Plot Offset Definition option.

Plot Scale

Controls the relative size of drawing units to plotted units.

***Note**: If the Layout option is specified in Plot Area, the layout is plotted at 1:1 regardless of the setting specified in Scale.*

Fit to Paper

Scales the plot to fit within the selected paper size and displays the custom scale factor in the Scale, Inch =, and Units boxes.

Scale

Defines the exact scale for the output. Also controls the coordinate and distance values on a layout in paper space.

Custom defines a user-defined scale. You can create a custom scale by entering the number of inches (or millimeters) equal to the number of drawing units.

Note: You can modify the list of scales with SCALELISTEDIT.

Inch(es) =/mm =/Pixel(s) =

Specifies the number of inches, millimeters, or pixels equal to the specified number of units.

Inch/mm/pixel

Specifies inches or mm for display of units. The default is based on the paper size and changes each time a new paper size is selected.

Pixel is available only when a raster output is selected.

Unit

Specifies the number of units equal to the specified number of inches, millimeters, or pixels.

Scale Lineweights

Scales lineweights in proportion to the plot scale. Lineweights normally specify the linewidth of output objects and are output with the linewidth size regardless of the scale.

Plot Style Table (Pen Assignments)

Sets the plot style table, edits the plot style table, or creates a new plot style table.

Name (Unlabeled)

Displays the plot style table that is assigned to the current Model tab or layout tab and provides a list of the currently available plot style tables.

If you select New, the Add Plot Style Table wizard is displayed, which you can use to create a new plot style table. The wizard that is displayed is determined by whether the current drawing is in color-dependent or named mode.

Edit

Displays the Plot Style Table Editor, in which you can view or modify plot styles for the currently assigned plot style table.

Display Plot Styles

Controls whether the properties of plot styles assigned to objects are displayed on the screen.

Shaded Viewport Options

Specifies how shaded or rendered viewports are plotted and determines their resolution levels and dots per inch (dpi).

Note: *Shaded viewport plotting of rendered views is not supported in AutoCAD LT.*

Shade Plot

Specifies how views are plotted. To specify this setting for a viewport on a layout tab, select the viewport and then, on the Tools menu, click Properties.

From the Model tab, you can select from the following options:

- **As Displayed:** Plots objects the way they are displayed on the screen.
- **Wireframe:** Plots objects in wireframe regardless of the way they are displayed on the screen.

- **Hidden:** Plots objects with hidden lines removed regardless of the way they are displayed on the screen.

The options for plotting visual styles include (not available in AutoCAD LT):

- **3D Hidden:** Plots objects with the 3D Hidden visual style applied regardless of the way the objects are displayed on the screen.
- **3D Wireframe:** Plots objects with the 3D Wireframe visual style applied regardless of the way the objects are displayed on the screen.
- **Conceptual:** Plots objects with the Conceptual visual style applied regardless of the way the objects are displayed on the screen.
- **Realistic:** Plots objects with the Realistic visual style applied regardless of the way the objects are displayed on the screen.
- **Rendered:** Plots objects as rendered regardless of the way they are displayed on the screen.

Quality

Specifies the resolution at which shaded or rendered viewports are plotted.

You can select from the following options:

- **Draft**: Sets rendered and shaded model space views to be plotted as wireframe.
- **Preview**: Sets rendered and shaded model space views to be plotted at one quarter of the current device resolution, to a maximum of 150 dpi.
- **Normal**: Sets rendered and shaded model space views to be plotted at one half of the current device resolution, to a maximum of 300 dpi.
- **Presentation**: Sets rendered and shaded model space views to be plotted at the current device resolution, to a maximum of 600 dpi.
- **Maximum**: Sets rendered and shaded model space views to be plotted at the current device resolution with no maximum.
- **Custom**: Sets rendered and shaded model space views to be plotted at the resolution setting that you specify in the DPI box, up to the current device resolution.

DPI

Specifies the dots per inch for shaded or rendered views, up to the maximum resolution of the current plotting device.

Plot Options

Specifies options for lineweights, transparency, plot styles, shaded plots, and the order in which objects are plotted.

Plot Object Lineweights

Specifies whether lineweights assigned to objects and layers are plotted.

Plot Transparency

Specifies whether object transparency is plotted. This option should only be used when plotting drawings with transparent objects.

Attention: For performance reasons, plotting transparency is disabled by default. To plot transparent objects, check the Plot Transparency option. This setting can be overridden by the PLOTTRANSPARENCYOVERRIDE system variable. By default, the system variable honors the setting in the Page Setup and the Plot dialog boxes.

Plot with Plot Styles

Specifies whether plot styles applied to objects and layers are plotted.

Plot Paper Space Last

Plots model space geometry first. Paper space geometry is usually plotted before model space geometry.

Hide Paper Space Objects

Specifies whether the HIDE operation applies to objects in a paper space viewport. This option is available only from a layout tab. This setting is reflected in the plot preview, but not in the layout.

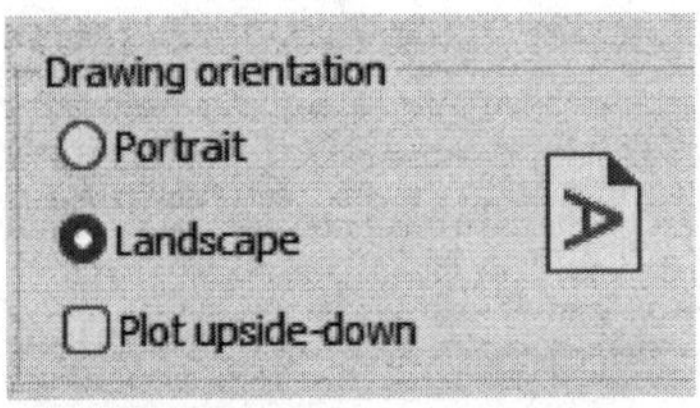

Drawing Orientation

Specifies the orientation of the drawing on the paper for plotters that support landscape or portrait orientation.

Portrait

Orients and plots the drawing so that the short edge of the paper represents the top of the page.

Landscape

Orients and plots the drawing so that the long edge of the paper represents the top of the page.

Plot Upside-Down

Orients and plots the drawing upside-down.

Icon

Indicates the media orientation of the selected paper and represents the orientation of the drawing on the page as a letter on the paper.

Note: *The orientation of plots is also affected by the PLOTROTMODE system variable.*

Preview

Displays the drawing as it will appear when plotted on paper by executing the PREVIEW command.

Command Overview

Creates and saves the appearance and format for printing your drawing.

General Procedures:

1. Start the **PAGESETUP** command.
2. Create a new set of options or modify an existing page setup.
3. Specify the plotter to be used, the papersize, the plotscale, etc.
4. Assign the named page setup to the layout tab.

Tips & Tricks

Save all your different page setups to a template file. Then use the import option to import the desired page setup to your active file from the template. You can also use the command PSETUPIN to import a desired page setup to your active file.

Command Exercise

Exercise 11-2 – Inserting a Title Block

Drawing Name: **new drawing**
Estimated Time to Completion: 15 Minutes

Scope

Insert the Custom-B title block into a drawing layout. Use the Page Setup Manager to modify a drawing layout.

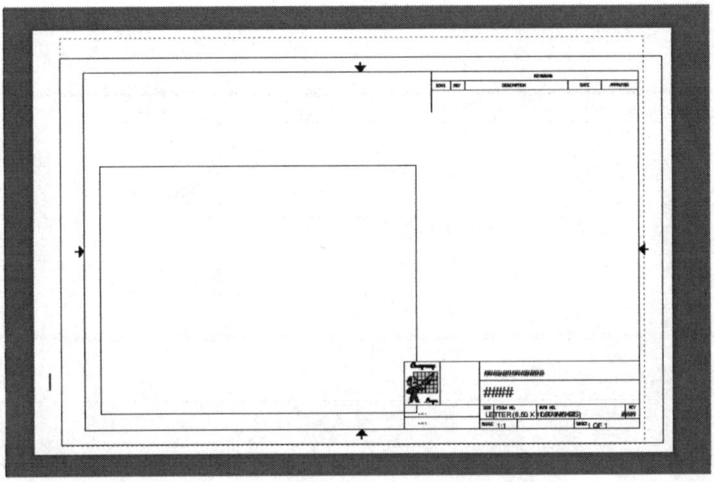

Solution

1. 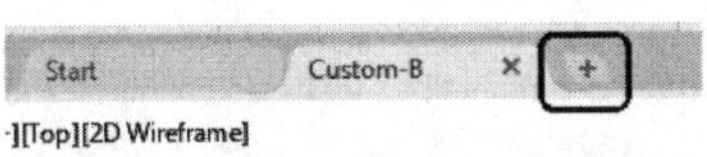

Start a new drawing using the plus tab.

2. 

Select the **Layout1** tab.

3. 

Activate the **Insert** ribbon.

4.

Select **Insert** from the Block panel.

Select the **Blocks from Libraries** option in the drop-down.

5.

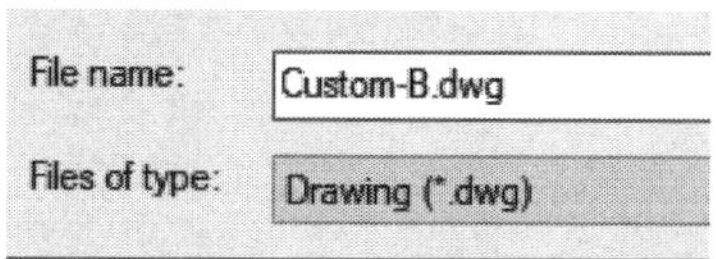

Browse for the Custom B title block created in Exercise 11-1.

Click **Open**.

6.

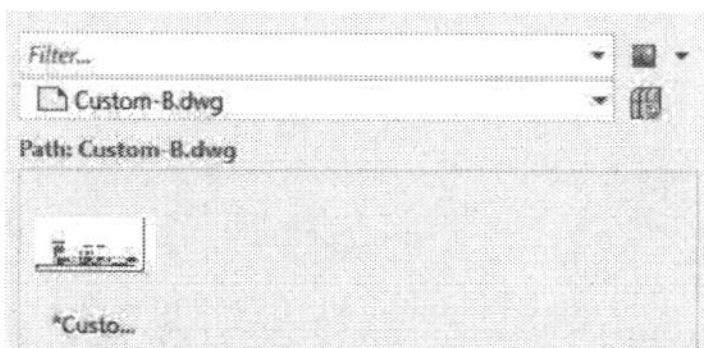

There will be a brief pause while AutoCAD loads the file.

7.

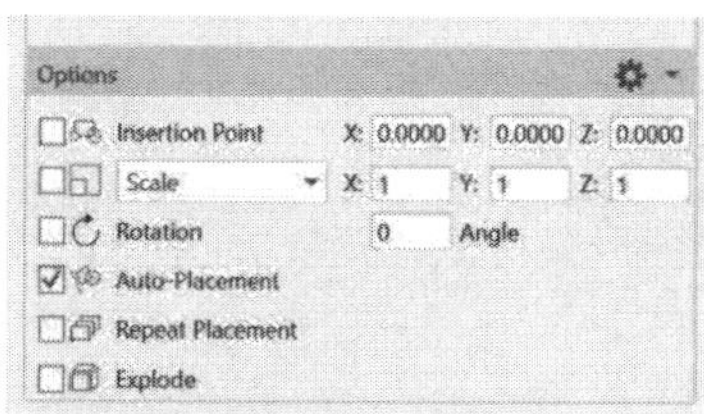

Disable the Insertion point, the scale, and rotation options.

8.

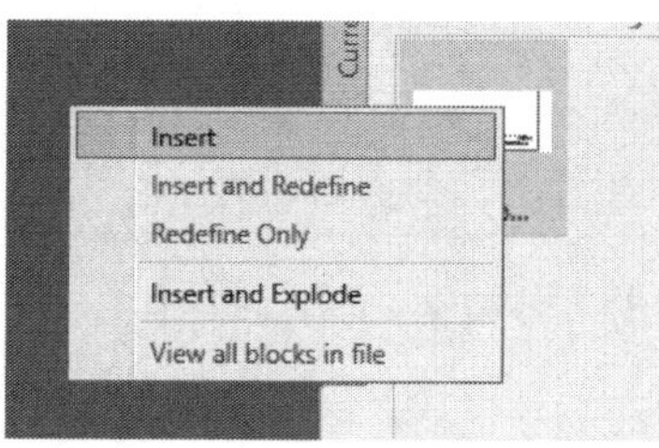

Right click on the loaded file and select **Insert**.

9.

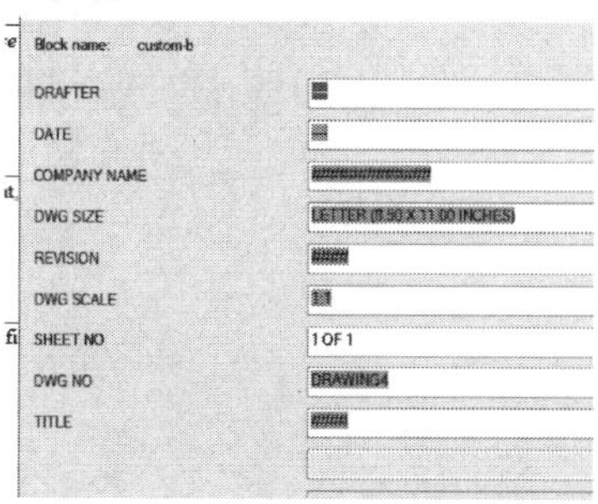

The Edit Attributes dialog will appear.

Any attributes which are controlled by field properties are shaded. Non-shaded fields can be modified.

Click **OK**.

10. 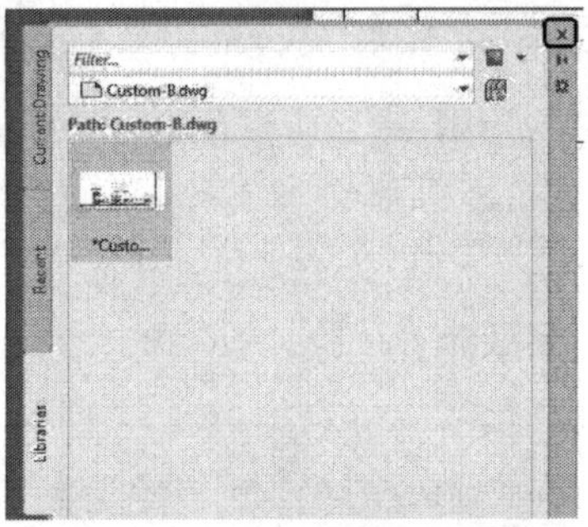

Close the Blocks palette.

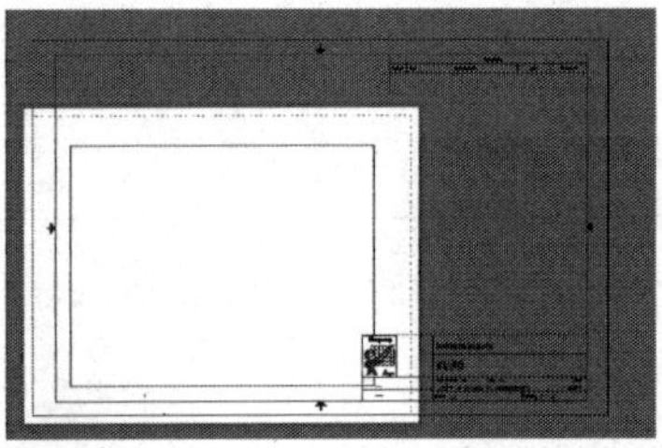

The title block is too large for the sheet.

11. 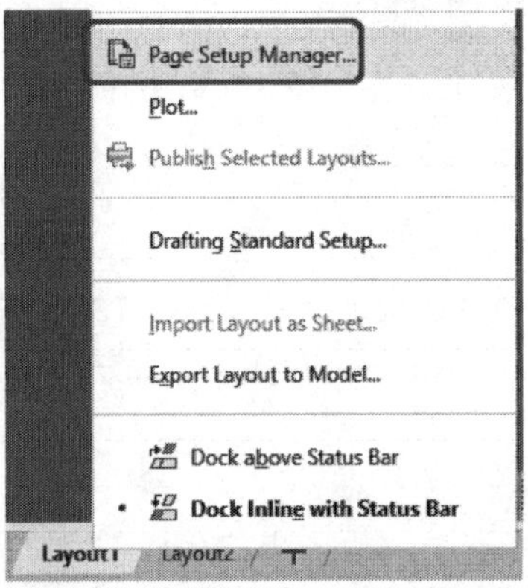

Right click on the layout tab.

Select **Page Setup Manager.**

12. 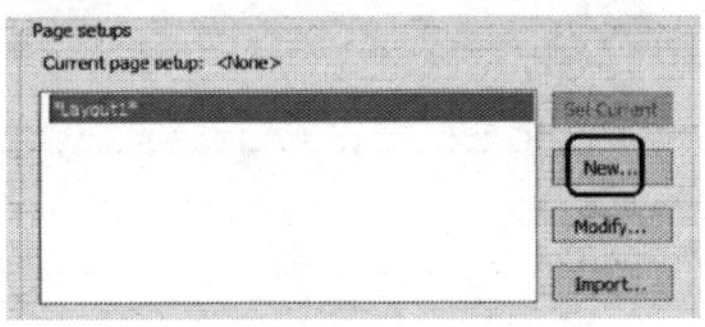

Select **New**.

13. 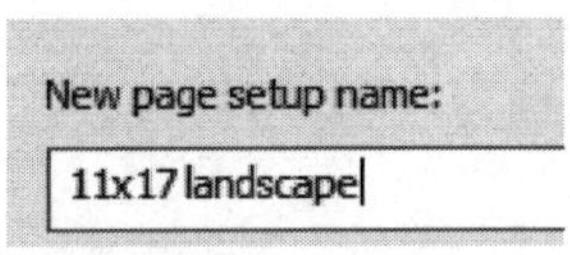

Type **11x17 landscape** for the new page setup name.

Click **OK**.

14. 

Set the Paper size to **ANSI B (11.00 X 17.00 Inches)**.

15. 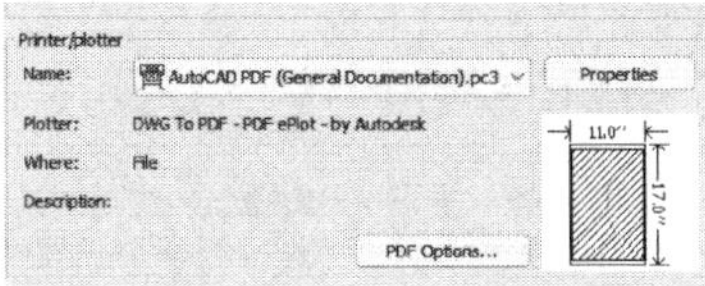

Set the Printer/plotter name to **AutoCAD PDF (General Documentation).pc3**.

16. 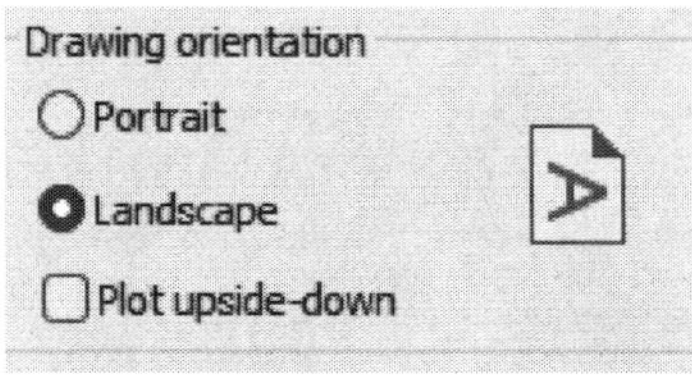

Set the Drawing orientation to **Landscape**.

Click **OK**.

17. 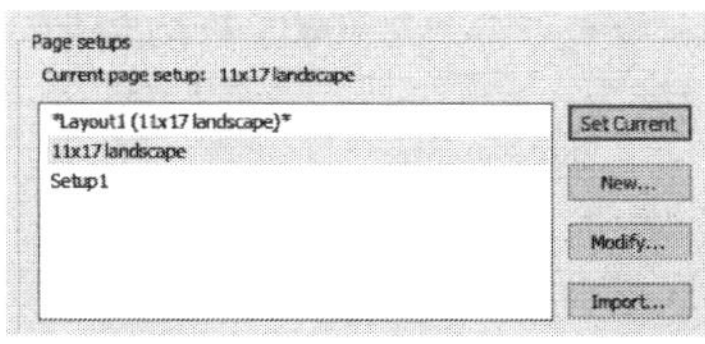

Highlight the **11x17 landscape** page setup.

Click **Set Current**.

Click **Close**.

18. 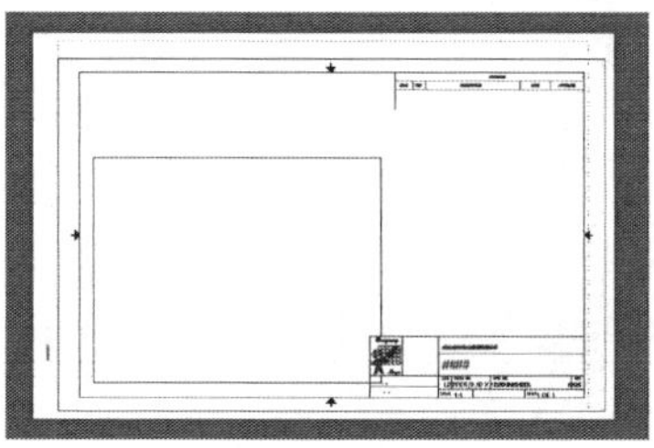

The title block now fits on the sheet.

Save as *ex11-2.dwg*.

Command Exercise

Exercise 11-3 – Create a Template

Drawing Name: **new dwg**
Estimated Time to Completion: 20 Minutes

Scope

Define the standard layers to be used in your template. Define a dimension style to be used. Insert a title block onto a layout sheet. Set up the layout sheet. Use the Sheet Set Manager to control the field data on the title block.

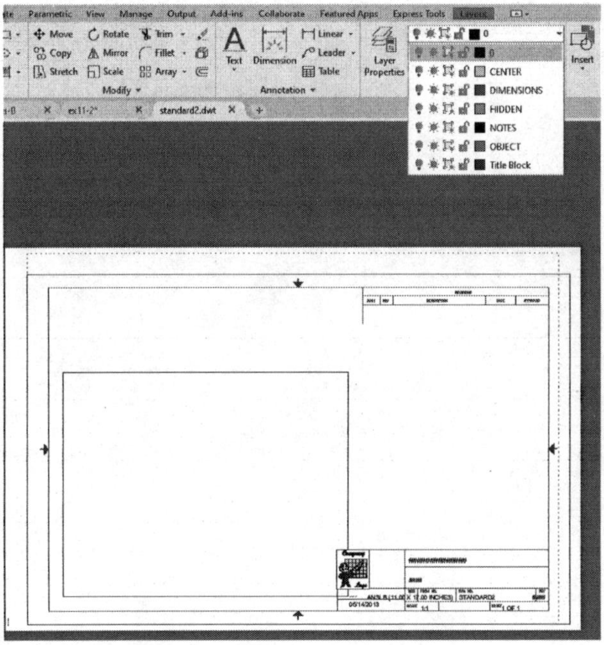

Solution

1. 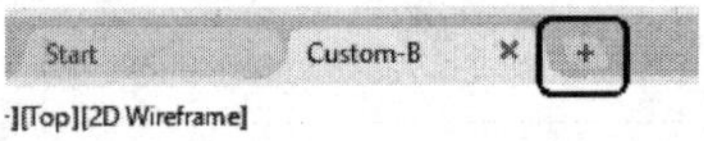 Start a new drawing.

2. 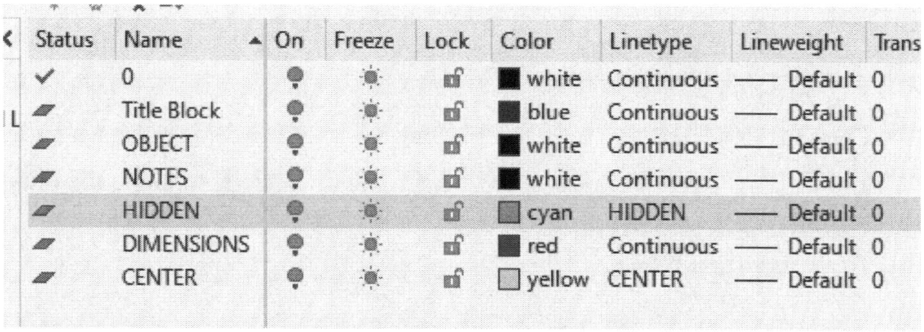

3. Set up your layers:

4. 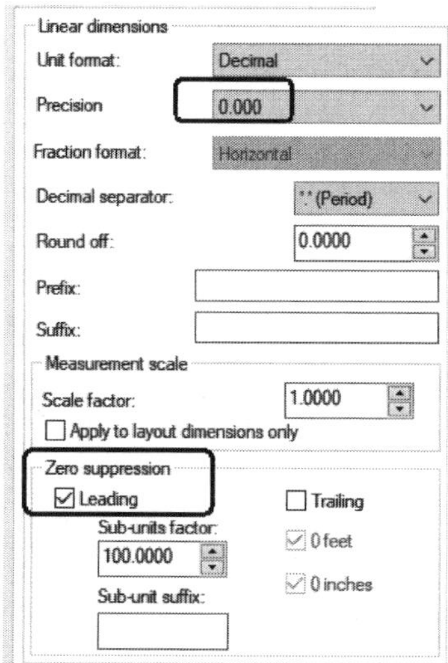

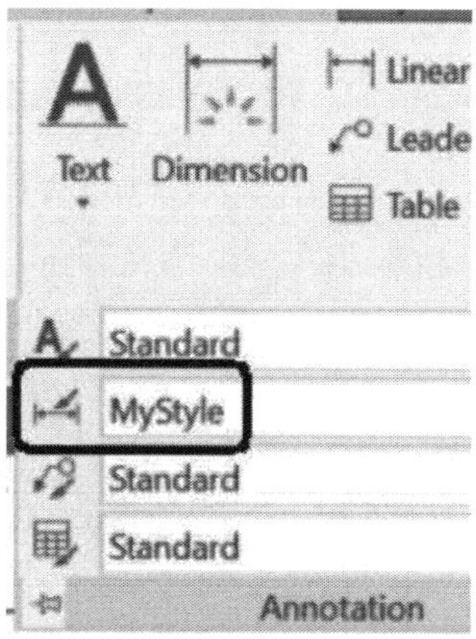

Set up your dimension style:
Open the **DIMSTYLE** dialog.
Click **New**.
Type **MyStyle** for the new dimstyle name.

Select the **Primary Units** tab.
Set the Precision to **0.000**.
Suppress **Leading Zeros.**

5.

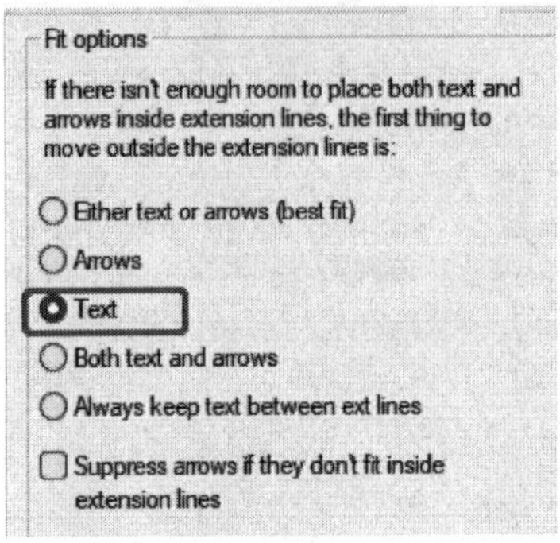

Select the **Fit** tab.

Set the Fit to **Text**.

Click **OK** and **CLOSE** to close the dialog.

6.

Return to the MODEL tab.

Set the limits.
Type **LIMITS** on the command line.

Set the lower left corner to **0,0**.

7.

Set the upper right corner to **34, 22**.

8.

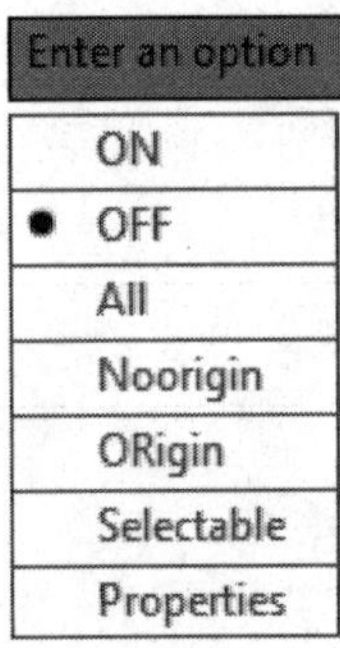

Turn the UCSICON off.
Type **UCSICON** on the command line.

Type **OFF**.

9.

Activate **Layout 1**.

10.

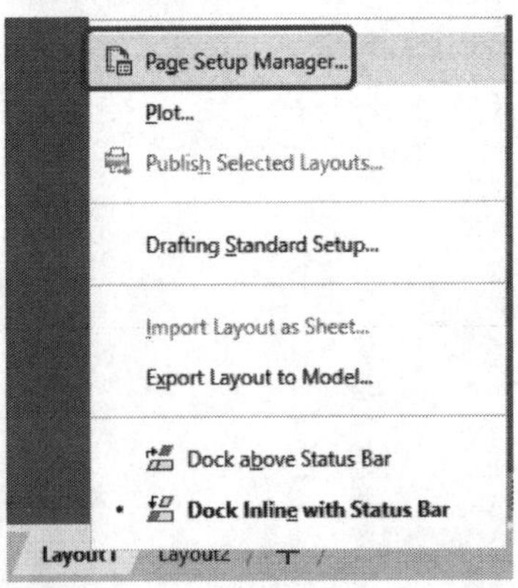

Right click on the Layout tab and select **Page Setup Manager** from the shortcut menu.

11. 

Select **New**.

12. 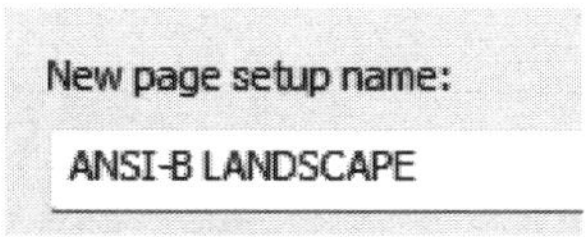

Type **ANSI-B LANDSCAPE** for the new setup name.

Click **OK**.

13. 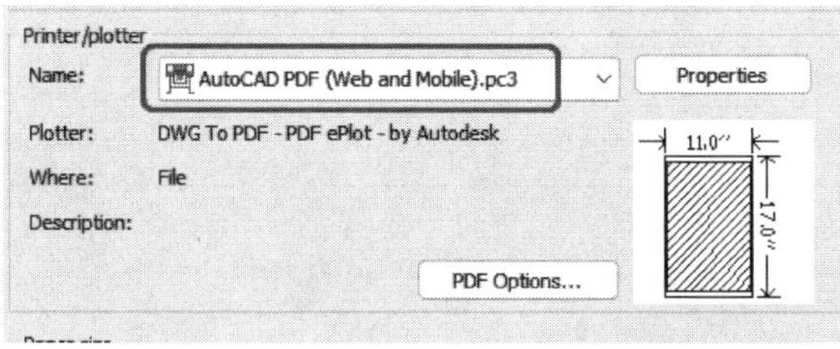

Set the Printer/plotter to**AutoCAD PDF (Web and Mobile).pc3**.

AutoCAD includes a built-in PDF converter.

14. 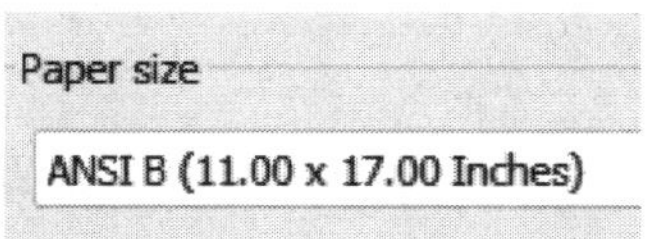

Set the Paper Size to **ANSI B (11 x 17.00 Inches)**.

15. 

Set the Plot style table to **Grayscale.ctb**.

Click **OK**.

16. 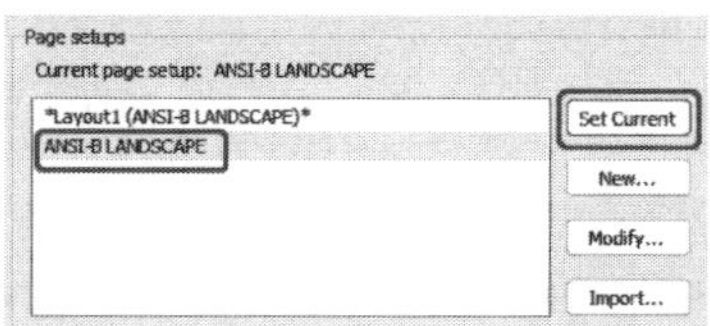

Highlight the **ANSI-B LANDSCAPE** page setup.

Click **Set Current**.

Note that it shows the current page setup.

Verify that the page setup details are correct.

Click **Close**.

17.

Select **Insert** from the Block panel.

Select the **Blocks from Libraries** option in the drop-down.

18.

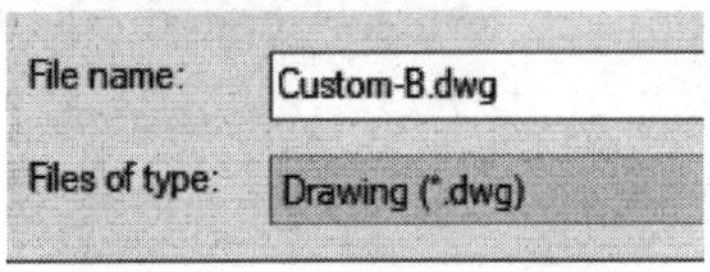

Browse for the Custom B title block created in Exercise 11-1.

Click **Open**.

19.

There will be a brief pause while AutoCAD loads the file.

20.

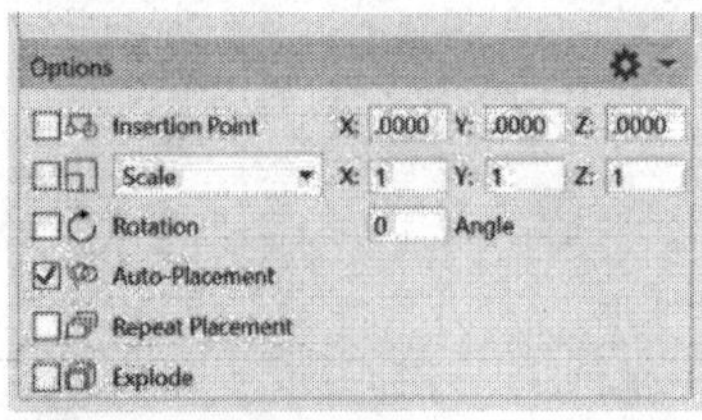

Disable the Insertion point, the scale, and rotation options.

21.

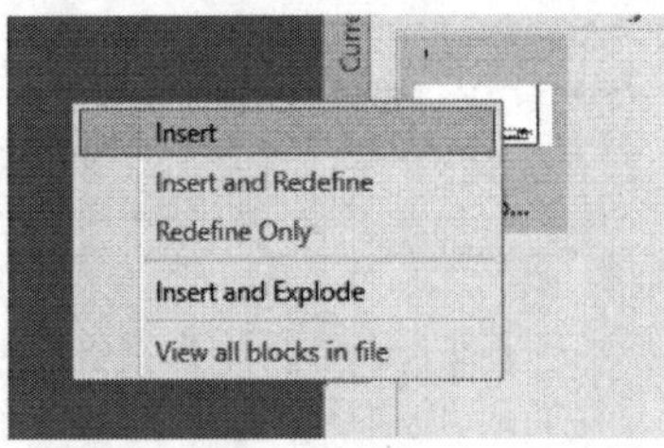

Right click on the loaded file and select **Insert**.

22.

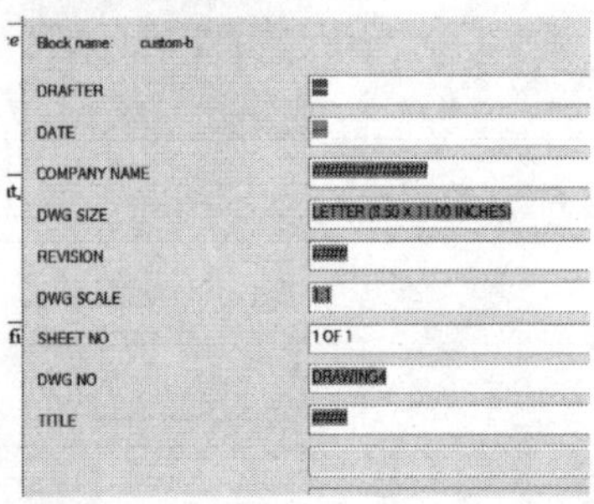

The Edit Attributes dialog will appear.

Any attributes which are controlled by field properties are shaded. Non-shaded fields can be modified.

Click **OK**.

23. 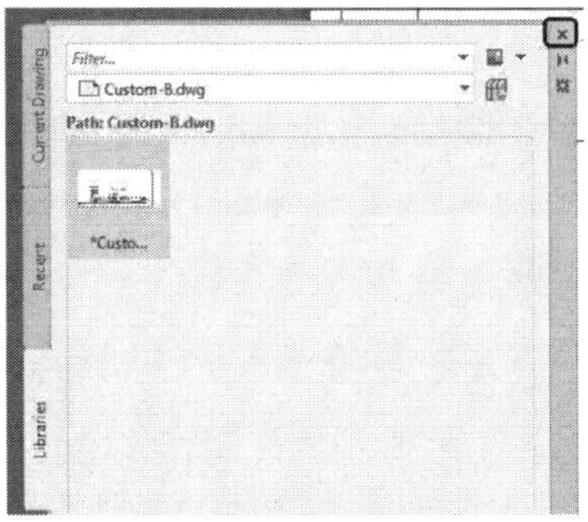

Close the Blocks palette.

24. 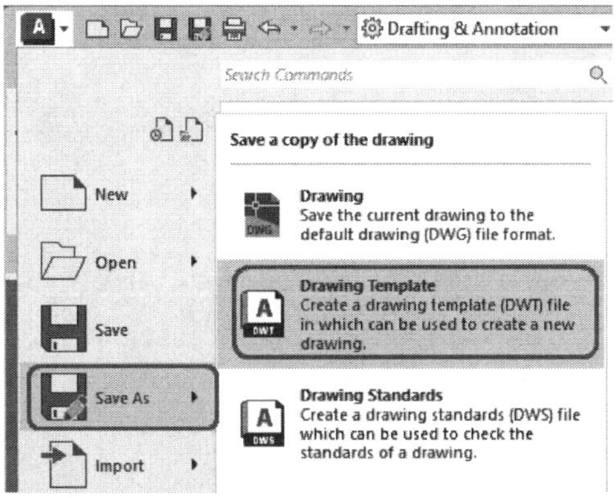

Go to **Application Menu→Save As→Drawing Template**.

25. 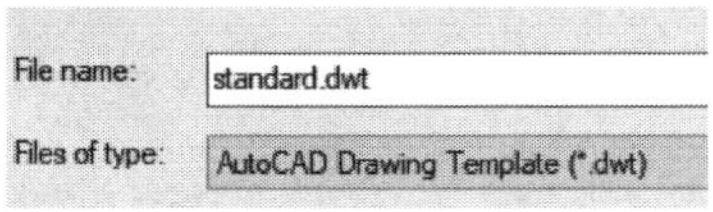

Browse to your work folder.

Call your template *standard.*

Click **Save**.

Store your template in a directory away from AutoCAD – NOT in the Templates subdirectory. That way you can back up and copy your template to a different workstation as needed.

26. 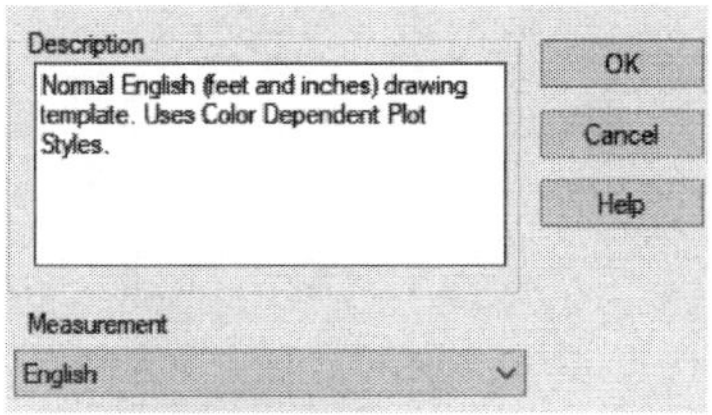

Enter a description for your template.

Click **OK**.

27. 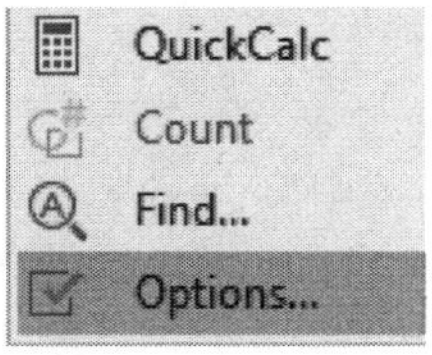

Right click in the AutoCAD drawing window and select **Options**.

28. 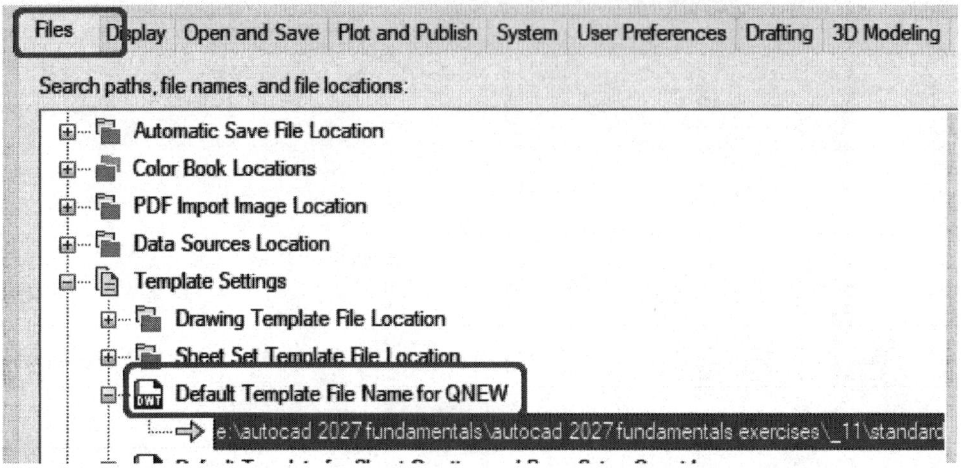

Select the Files tab.

Under Template Settings, set the Default Template File Name for QNEW to use the standard.dwt file you just created.

Click **OK**.

29. Save and close the template file.

Command Exercise

Exercise 11-4 – Use a Template

Drawing Name: **new drawing**
Estimated Time to Completion: 5 Minutes

Scope

Test the new template file.

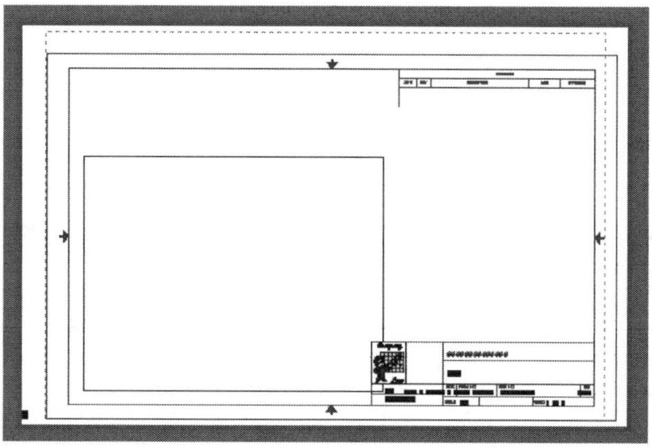

Solution

1. 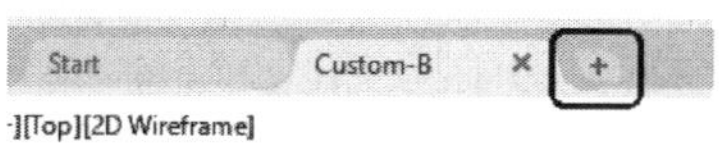

Start **QNEW** to start a new drawing.

Use the standard.dwt template created in Exercise 11-3.

2. 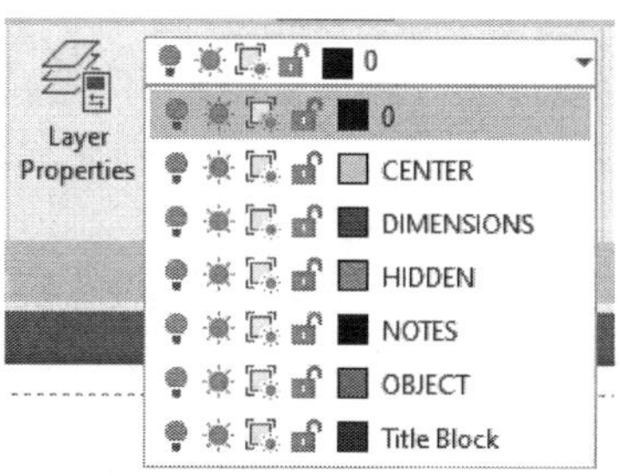

Note your layers are already set up.

3. 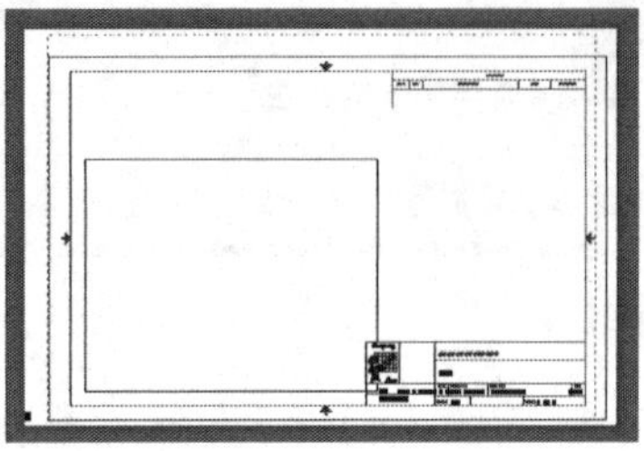

Activate **Layout 1**.

Note the layout has the title block ready to go.

A Word about Blocks

Blocks are useful and boost productivity. Blocks allow you to re-use objects. There are two types of blocks—local and global. Local blocks are created 'on the fly' and used inside a single drawing. A global block is a separate drawing—like the title block template—which can be inserted into another drawing. Local blocks are created using the Create Block tool. Global blocks are created using the Write Block tool.

Blocks can be edited and modified. However, if you edit a block, it is only modified in the existing drawing—it does not update the external drawing file.

You can explode a block—which basically 'unblocks' the object and restores it back to the basic elements. Blocks can include text, fields, and attributes.

There are a great number of blocks available for use and download on the internet, in the Design Center, and in the Autodesk resource area. Before you create common objects from scratch, like doors, windows, furniture, plants, etc., do a search for blocks. You may be surprised what you find.

Many companies consider their block libraries proprietary. They have spent time and money creating the blocks they use in their drawings, and they don't want competitors using their blocks. To avoid this, many companies will type EXPLODE ALL before they send out a drawing to ensure any blocks cannot be used or they will only send drawings out in pdf format to protect their intellectual property.

As you work in industry and start using blocks, you may start collecting your own favorite blocks to use in your career.

If you think you will use an object or drawing more than once, chances are you have a potential block.

Block

Command Locator

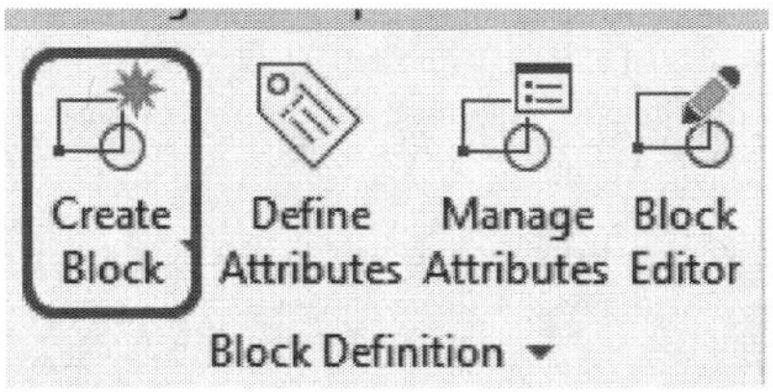

Ribbon/Insert	**BLOCK**
Command	**BLOCK**

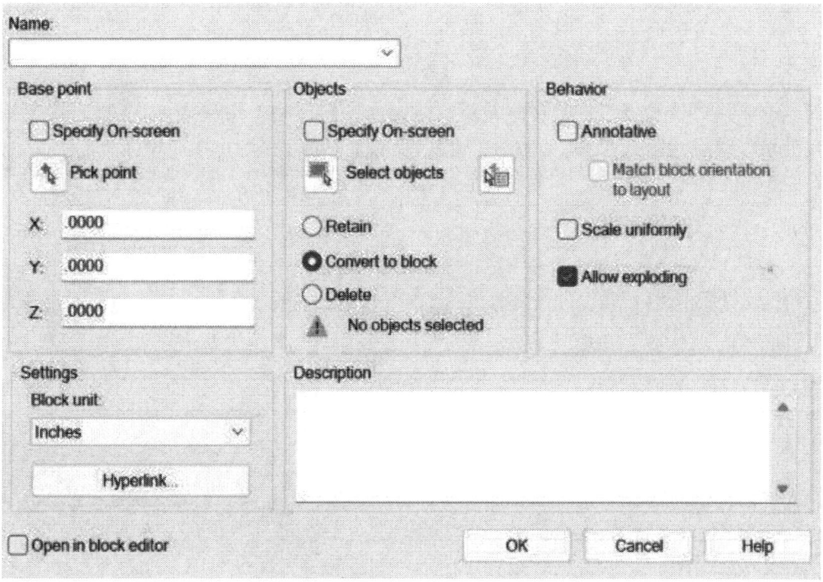

Name Assigns a name to the block.

Base point Assigns an insertion point for the block. If no point is selected, then the block is automatically defined in relation to the 0,0,0 position.

Block unit Specifies unit of measurement:

Hyperlink Adds a hyperlink to a part. This may be used to link a block to a vendor website, so users can purchase the item.

Objects Allows the user to select which elements are used to define the block.

Retain/Convert to Block/Delete Retain keeps the selected elements as they are. Convert to block converts the selected elements to the block definition. Delete erases the selected elements, but the block definition is saved.

Open in Block Editor Opens the block editor once the OK button is pushed. The Block Editor allows the user to add constraints, controls to flip, rotate or stretch the block, as well as other advanced settings.

Annotative Sets the block to be annotative—which means the block will automatically scale in viewports.

Quick Select

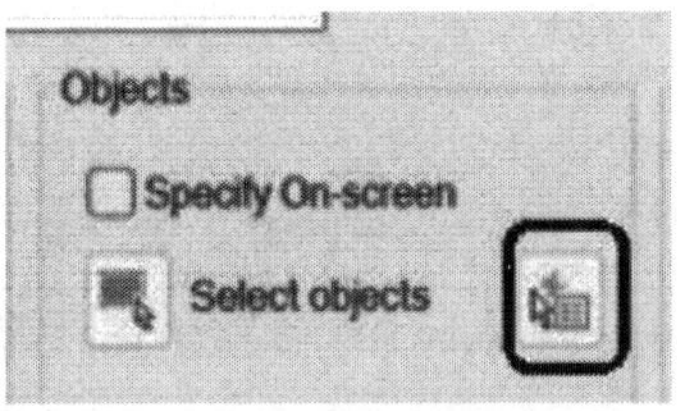

The Quick Select tool allows you to select elements for a block based on their properties.

Match Block Orientation to Layout Ensures the block will orient correctly if the paperspace layout is set to landscape or portrait. This option is only available if the block is annotative.

Scale uniformly If the block is scaled and this is enabled, then the resolution of the block is maintained.

Allow Exploding If this is disabled, the block cannot be exploded back to the original elements.

Command Overview

Groups elements into a single element.

General Procedures:

1. Select the objects desired for a block.
2. Select the point to be used for the insertion/base point for the block.
3. Determine how the existing elements are to be managed after the block is created (retain as individual elements, delete or convert to the block definition).
4. Determine how the block should react in paper space—Annotative or non-annotative.
5. Set the block units. By default the block will use the existing or current unit settings.
6. Click OK.

WBLOCK

Command Locator

Ribbon/Insert	Write Block
Command	WBLOCK
Alias	W

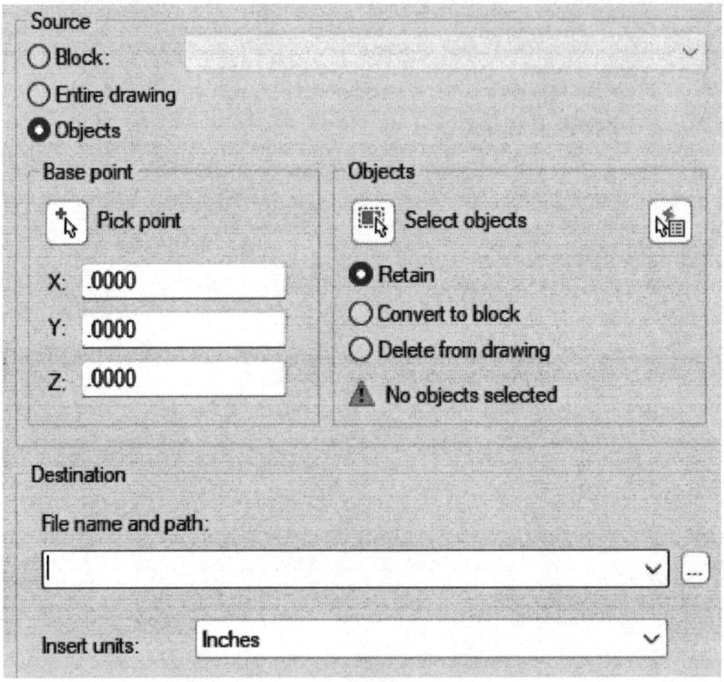

File Name and path Browse to the folder where you want to store your block and enter in the desired name.

Base point Assigns an insertion point for the block. If no point is selected, then the block is automatically defined in relation to the 0,0,0 position.

Insert units Specifies unit to be used when block is inserted.

Objects Allows the user to select which elements are used to define the block.

Quick Select

The Quick Select tool allows you to select elements for a block based on their properties.

Retain/Convert to Block/Delete Retain keeps the selected elements as they are.
Convert to block converts the selected elements to the block definition.
Delete erases the selected elements, but the block definition is saved.

Command Overview

Creates an external file using selected elements.

General Procedures:

1. *Select the objects desired for a block.*
2. *Select the point to be used for the insertion/base point for the block.*
3. *Determine how the existing elements are to be managed after the block is created (retain as individual elements, delete or convert to the block definition).*
4. *Set the block units. By default the block will use the existing or current unit settings.*
5. *Browse to the location where the block file should be saved and name the block.*
6. *Click OK.*

- *Blocks created on layer 0 will adopt the properties of the layer where they are placed.*
- *Blocks created on layers other than 0 will retain the properties of their birth layer.*
- *Blocks can be stored internally in a drawing file or externally as a separate file.*

Command Exercise

Exercise 11-5 – Create a Block

Drawing Name: **mblock.dwg**
Estimated Time to Completion: 45 Minutes

Scope

Create some blocks and use them to furnish an empty room.

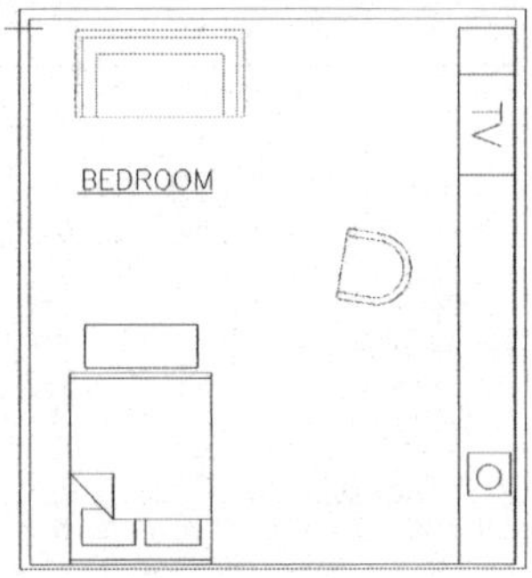

Solution

1. 

Verify that the current layer is set to **0.**

2. 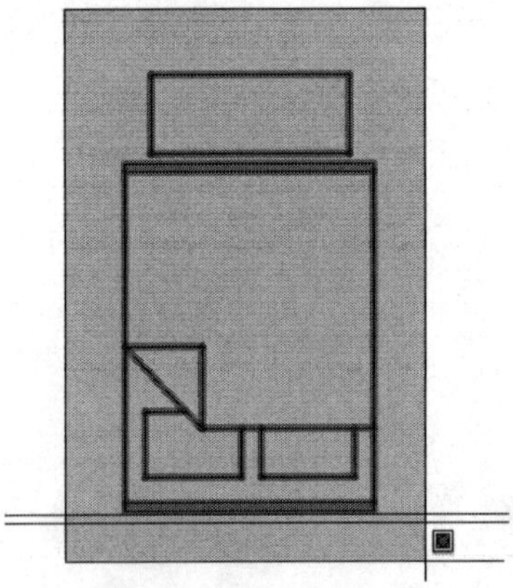

Window about the bed to select all the lines that define the bed object.

3. 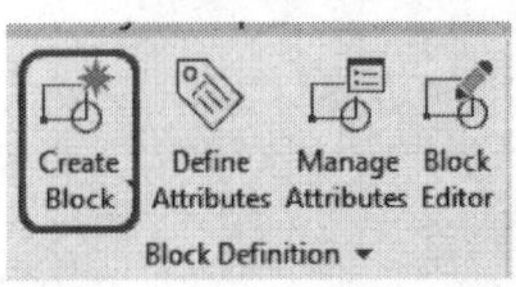

On the Insert ribbon on the Block Definition panel, select **Create Block.**

4. 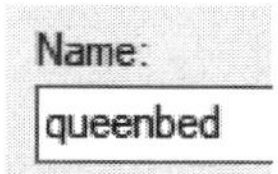

Type **queenbed** in the Name field.

5. 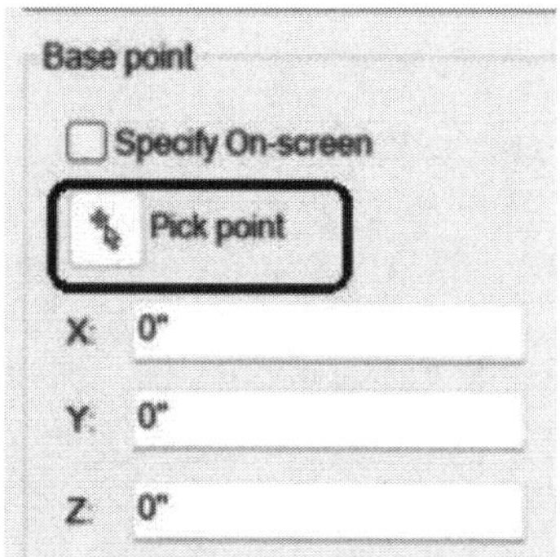

Select the pick point icon to set the Base point.

6. 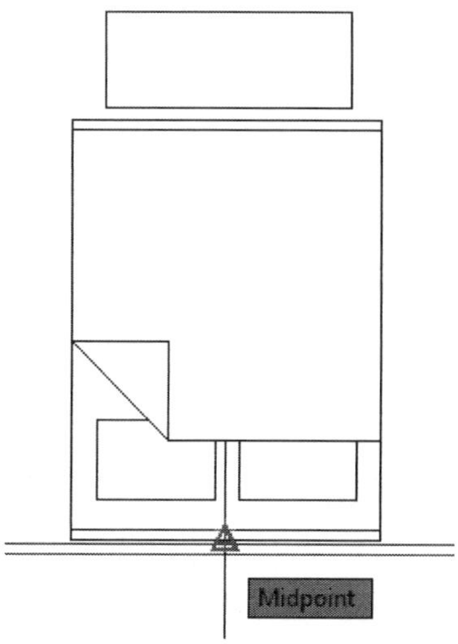

Select bottom midpoint of the bed (by the pillows or head of the bed) as the Base point.

7. 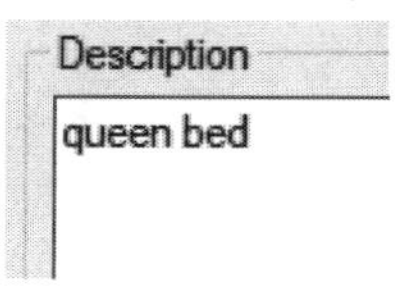

Type **queen bed** in the description.

8. 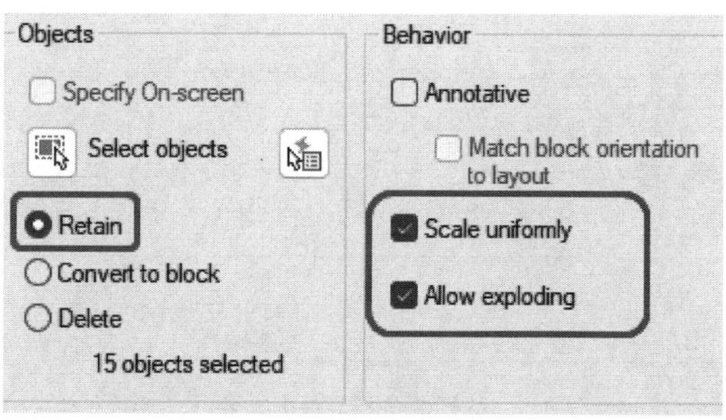

Disable **Annotative.**
Enable **Allow Exploding**.
Enable **Retain**.
Enable **Scale uniformly.**

9.

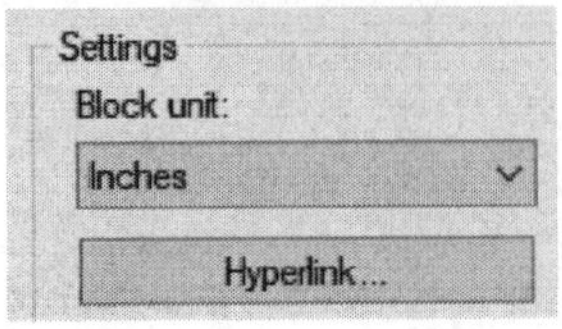

Set the Block unit to **Inches.**

By default the dialog may be set to the wrong units, so be sure to check this.

10.

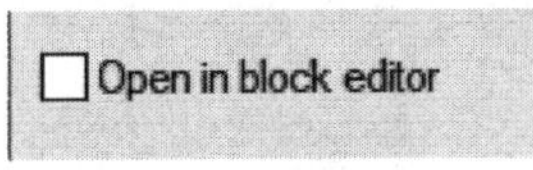

Uncheck **Open in block editor.**
Click **OK.**

11.

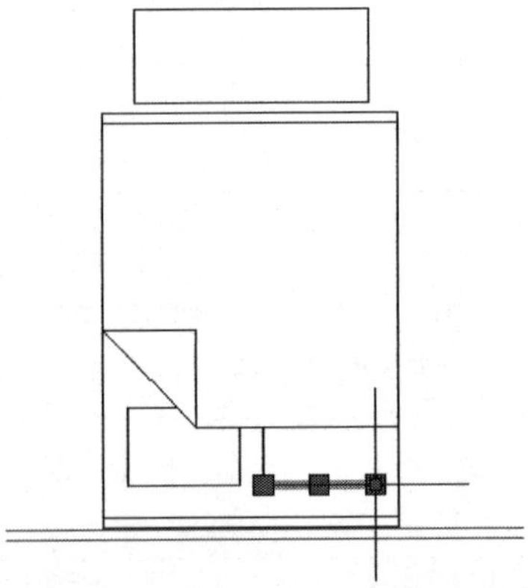

Select one of the lines that is part of the pillow.
Note that the elements are still individual elements since you used the Retain option when creating the block. Notice that the element is on Layer 0.

Click **ESC** to release the selection.

12.

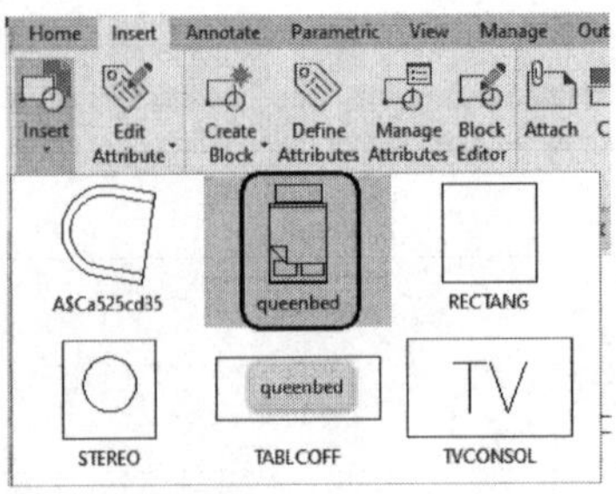

On the Insert ribbon:
Select the scroll bar under the Insert tool.
Note that all the local blocks in the drawing are listed. You can also use the Insert tool on the Block panel on the Home ribbon.

Select the **queenbed** block you created.

13.

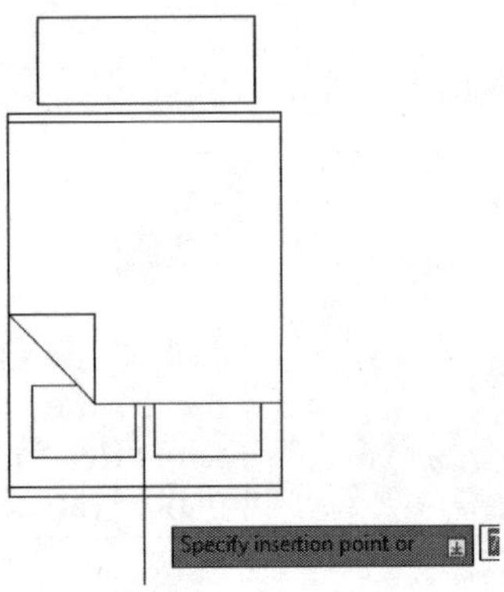

Notice that the cursor is located at the selected base point (the midpoint of the block) as you drag the block into the drawing.
If you did not select a base point, the insertion point is automatically set to 0,0,0.

14. 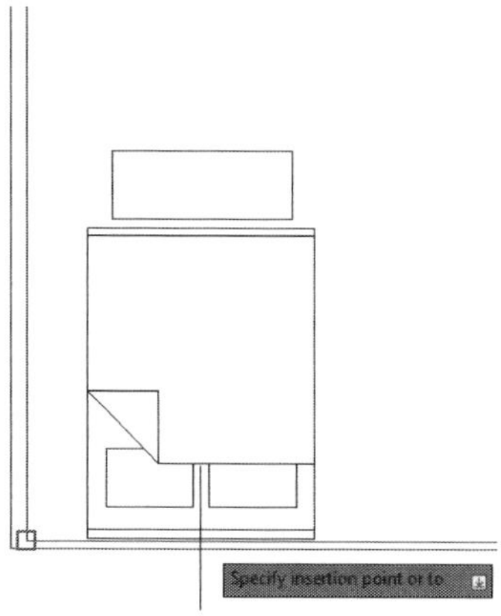

Place the bed in the empty bedroom on the right using the NEA Osnap to place it along the bottom wall.

15. 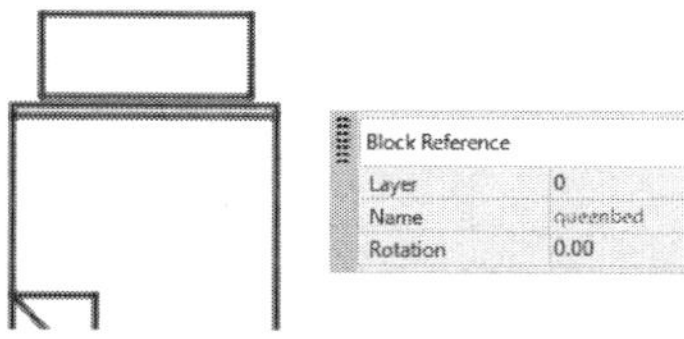

Select the block that was placed.
On the Quick Properties palette, you should see the Name and the Layer set to 0.
Blocks that are created on Layer 0 will adopt the properties of the current layer when placed.

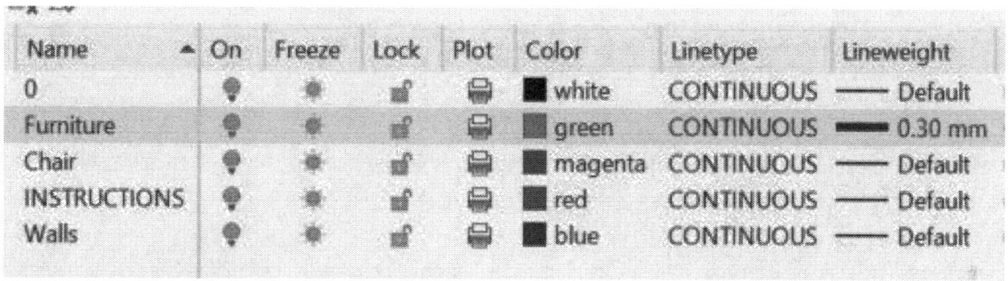

16. Create a new layer called **Furniture.**
Set the Color to **Green.**
Set the Lineweight to **0.30 mm.**

17. 

Set the Current Layer to **Furniture.**

18. 

Select **Write Block** from the Insert ribbon.

19. 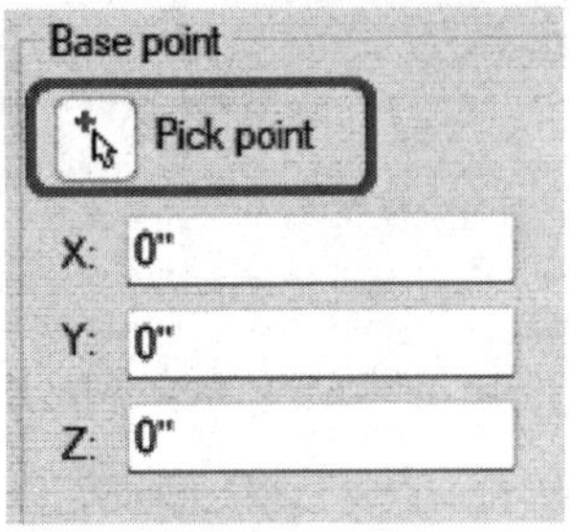

Select the **Pick point** icon under Base point.

20. 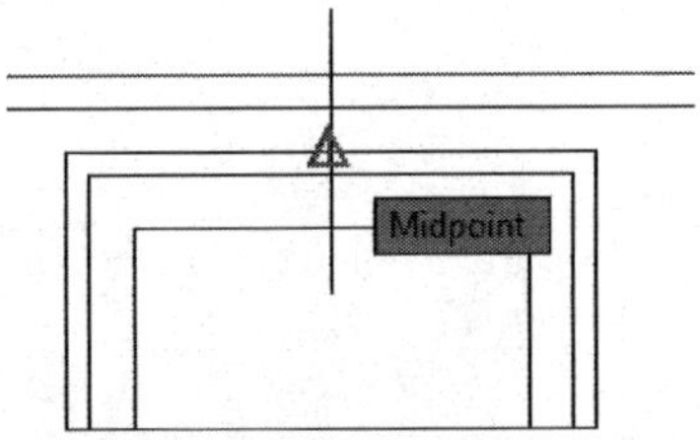

Select the top midpoint (rear of the sofa) for the sofa's Base point.

21. 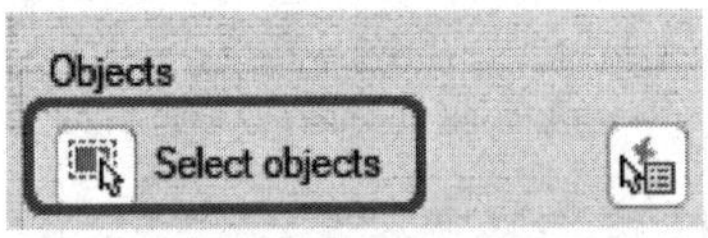

Select the **Select objects** icon under Objects.

22. 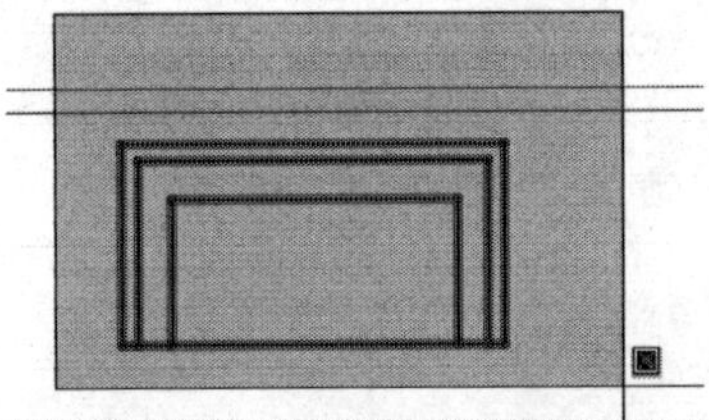

Window around the entire sofa to select it.
Click **ENTER**.

23. 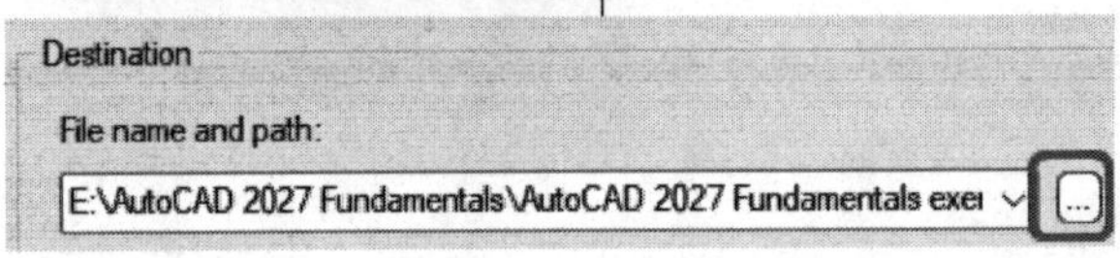

Click the Browse … button next to File name and path.

24. 

Browse to your work folder and save the block as **mysofa.dwg**.
Click **Save**.

25. 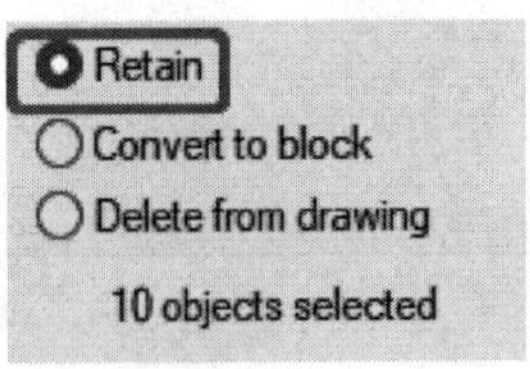

Enable **Retain**.

Set the Insert units to **Inches.**

Click **OK**.

26. 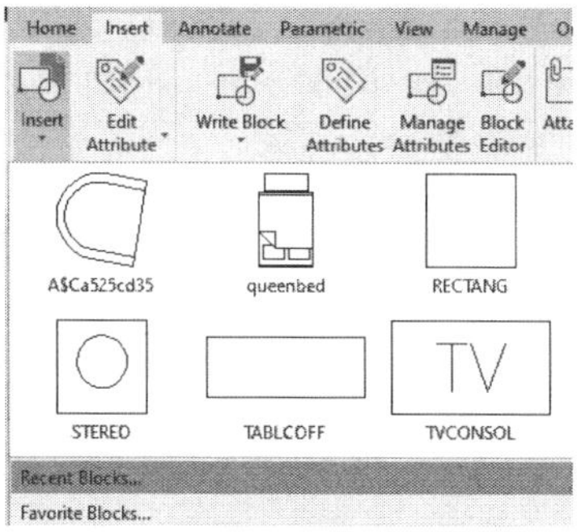

Go to the Insert tool.
When you scroll down, you won't see the mysofa block. That is because you created a global block, not a local block. The block is stored externally so it can be inserted into any drawing.
Click **Recent Blocks**.

27. 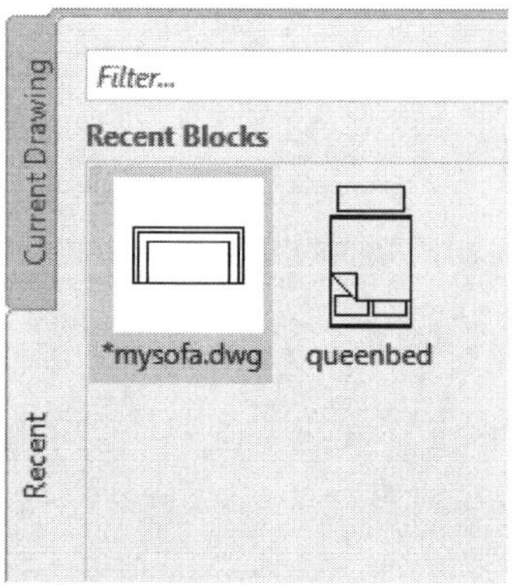

The mysofa block is located on the Recent tab.

Note that the mysofa block has a dwg extension and the queenbed block does not. That's because the mysofa block is in an external drawing file while the queenbed block only resides in this drawing as a local block.

28. 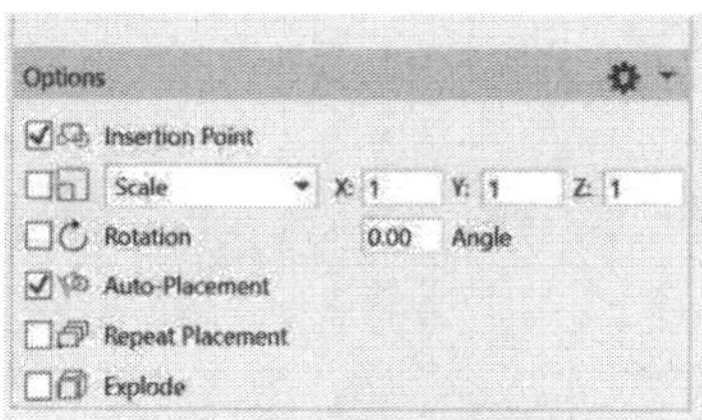

Enable **Insertion Point.**

29. 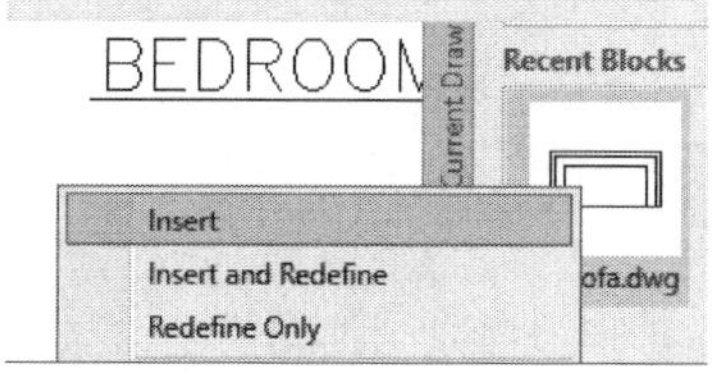

Right click on the mysofa block and select **Insert**.

30. 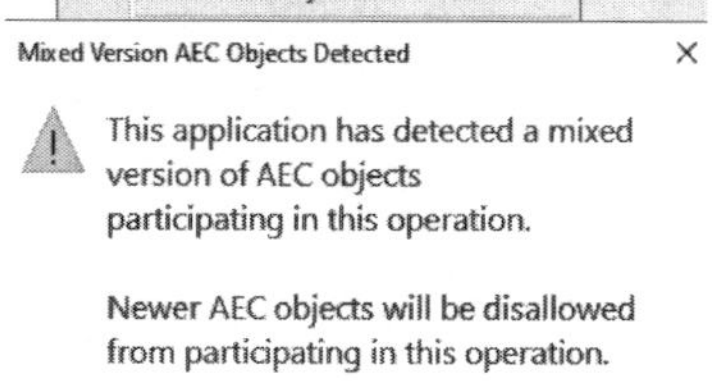

If you see this dialog, click **Close**.

31. 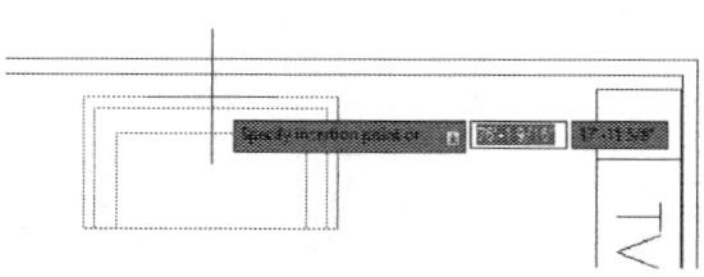

Place the sofa block in a similar location as the room on the left.

32.

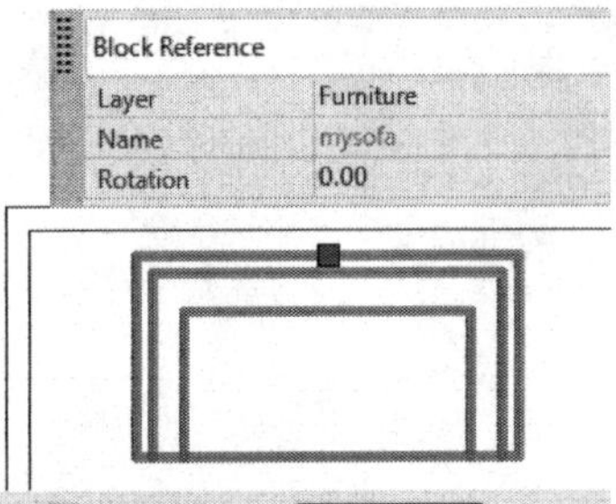

Select the sofa block to inspect the Quick Properties.
Note that the sofa is placed on the layer Furniture—the current layer.
Click **ESC** to release the selection.

33.

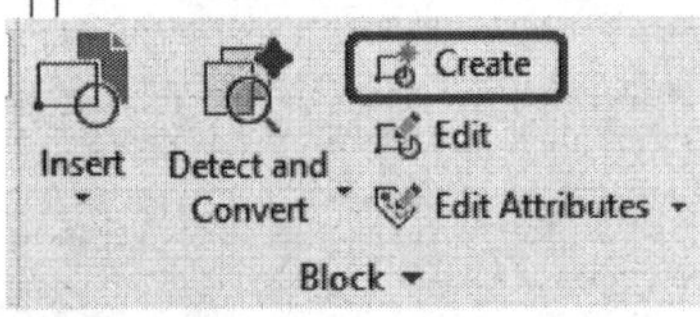

Select **Create Block** from the Home ribbon.

34.

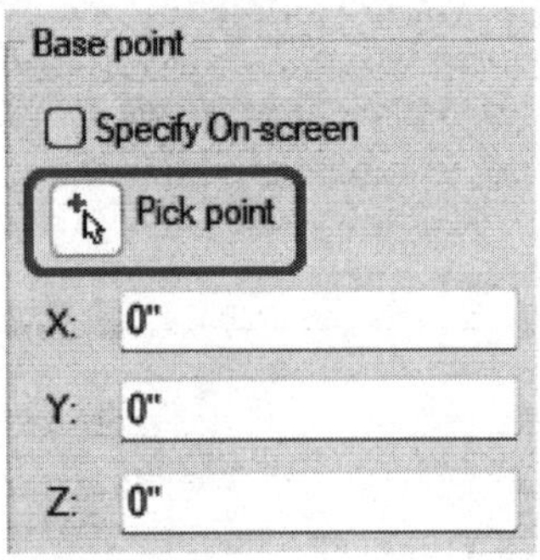

Select **Pick point** to specify the base point for insertion.

35.

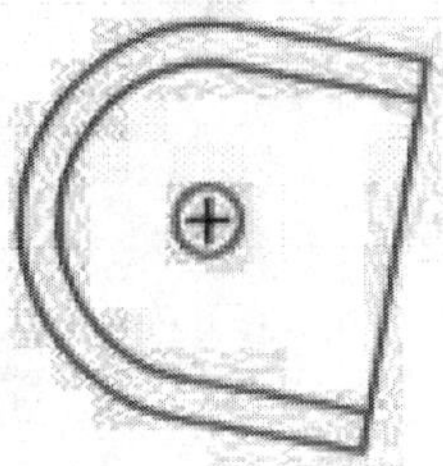

Use the center point of the arc as the Base Point for the block.

36.

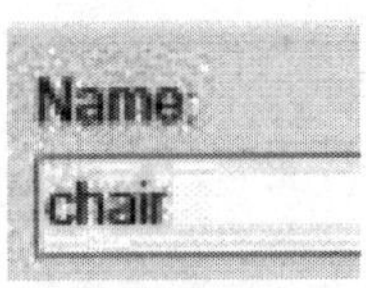

Name the block **chair**.
Type **chair** as the description.

37.

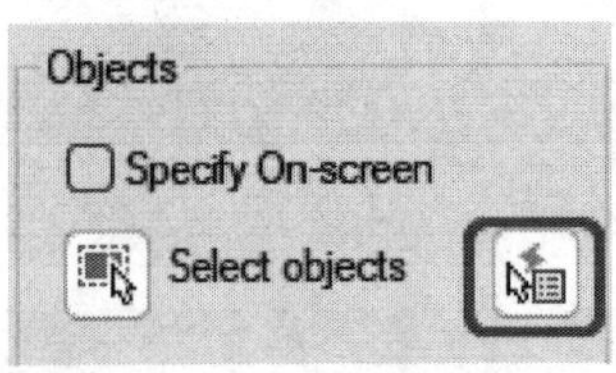

Left click on the **Quick Select** tool.

38.

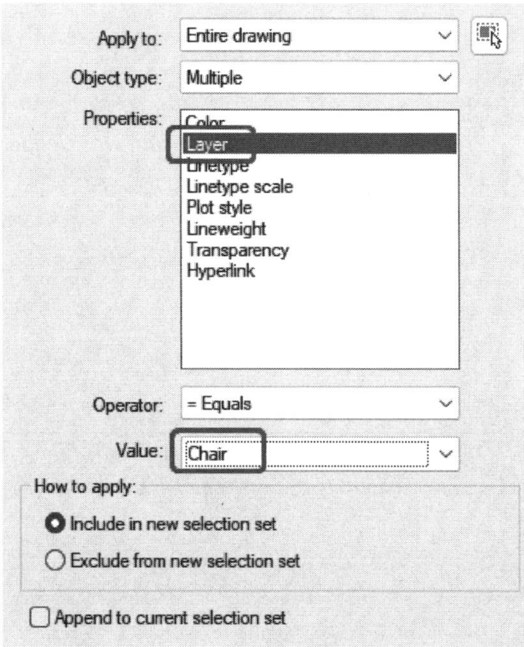

Under Properties:

Select **Layer**.

Under Value:

Select **Chair**.

Click **OK**.

This selects all elements on the Layer Chair.

39.

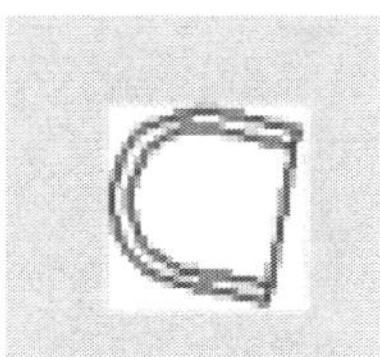

A preview of the selected elements is added to the dialog.

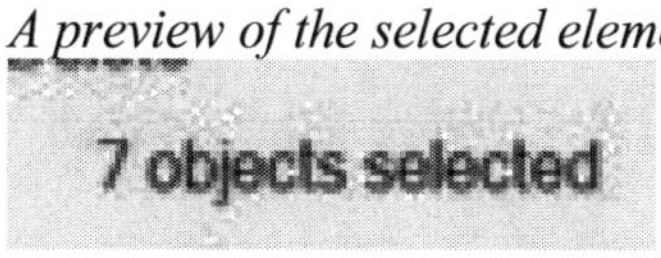

Note 7 objects were selected.

40.

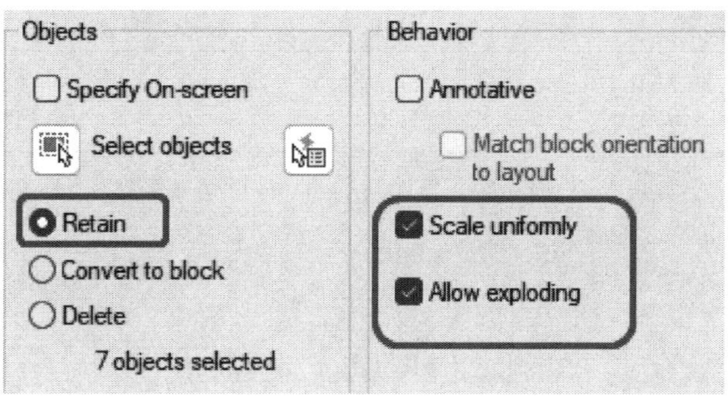

Enable **Retain**.
Disable **Annotative.**
Enable **Scale Uniformly.**
Enable **Allow Exploding**.
Click **OK**.

41.

On the Home ribbon, set the Current Layer to **0.**

42. 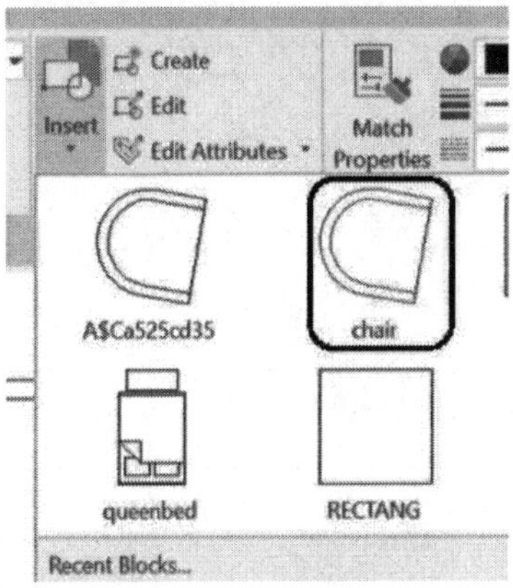

Activate the Home ribbon.
Select **Insert** from the Block panel.

Locate and select the chair block.
Note we see the chair because it was defined as a local block.

43. 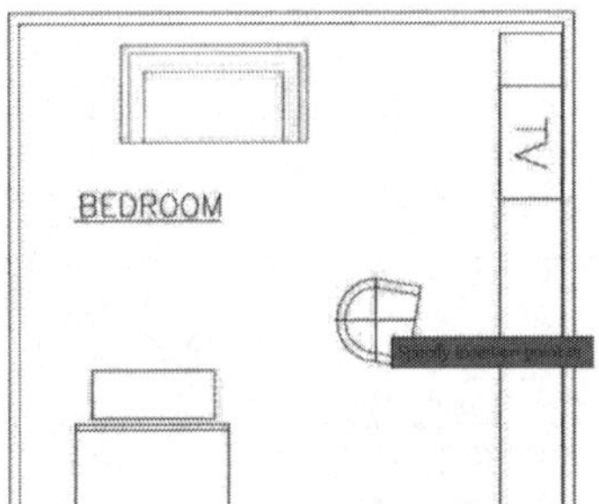

The chair block appears at the end of the cursor.
Place the chair in the room on the right.

44. 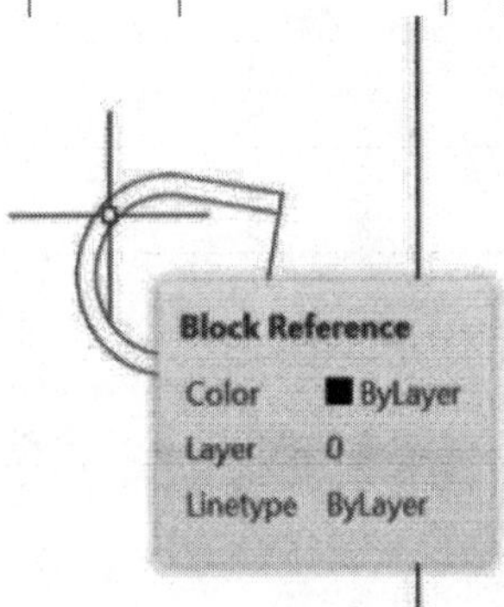

Hover your mouse over the chair.

Notice that the chair is located on the current layer—0 but retains the properties of the chair layer.

45. 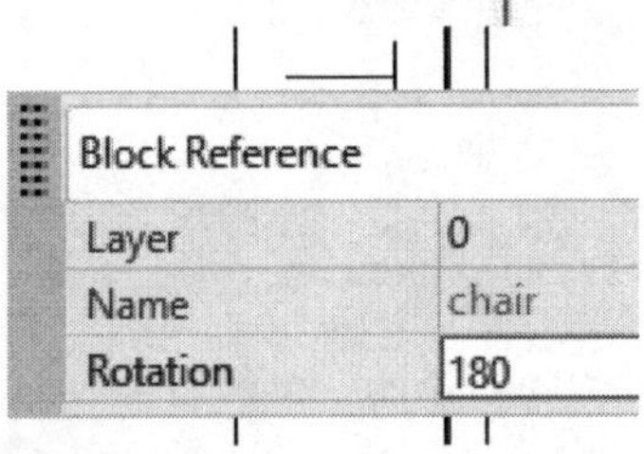

Select the chair.
Using Quick Properties:

Change the Rotation to **180.00°**.
Click **ESC** to release the selection.

Command Exercise

Exercise 11-6 – Create an AEC Block

Drawing Name: **arch-blocks.dwg**
Estimated Time to Completion: 20 Minutes

Scope

Create a block with an attribute.
Use on a floor plan.

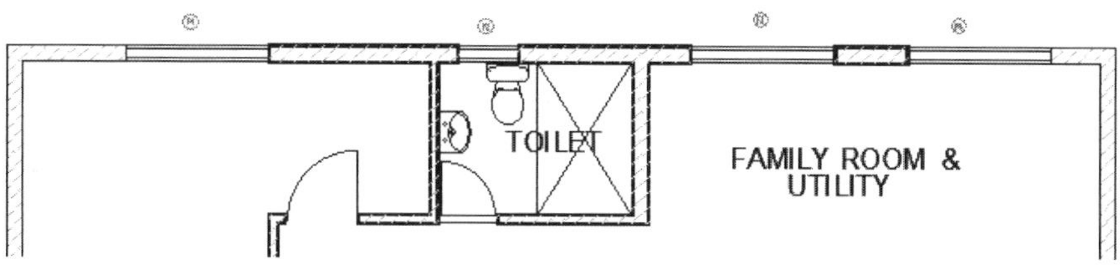

Solution

1. 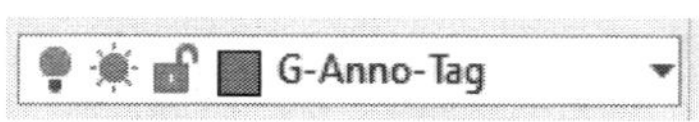

Verify that the current layer is set to **G-Anno-Tag.**

2. 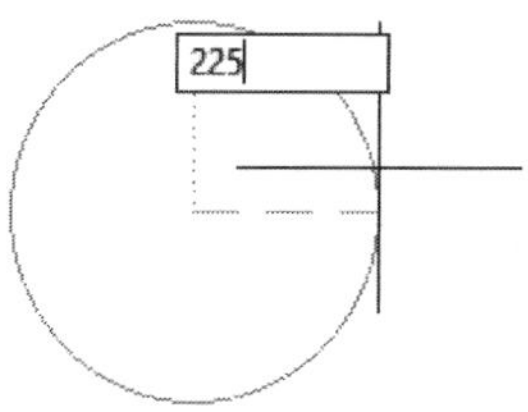

Draw a circle with a radius of 225 units. Place it away from the floor plan.

3. 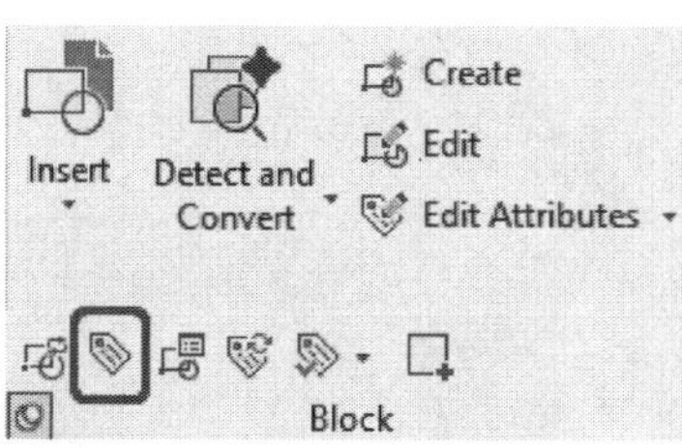

TAtag

On the Home ribbon on the extended Block panel, select **Define Attributes**.

4.

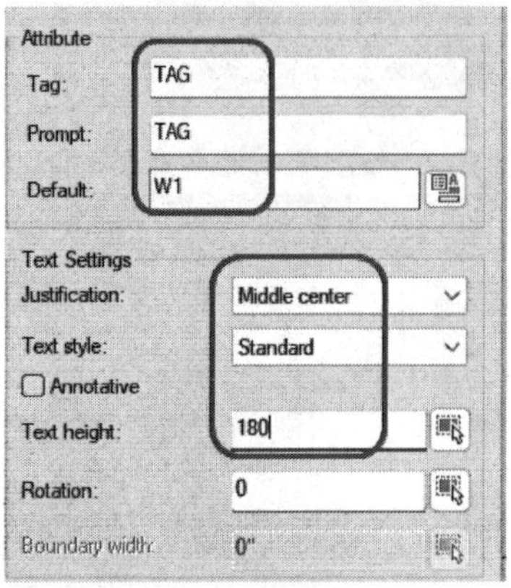

Type **TAG** for the Tag value.

Type **TAG** for the prompt.

Type **W1** in the default field.

Set the justification for **Middle Center**.

Set the Text Style to **Standard**.

Set the Text Height to **180**.

5.

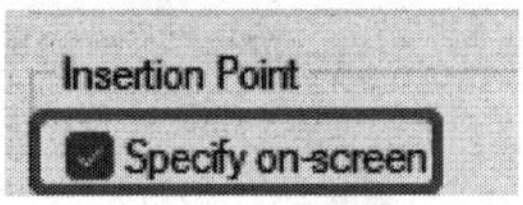

Set the Insertion point to **Specify on –screen.**

Click **OK**.

6.

Select the center of the circle as the insertion point.

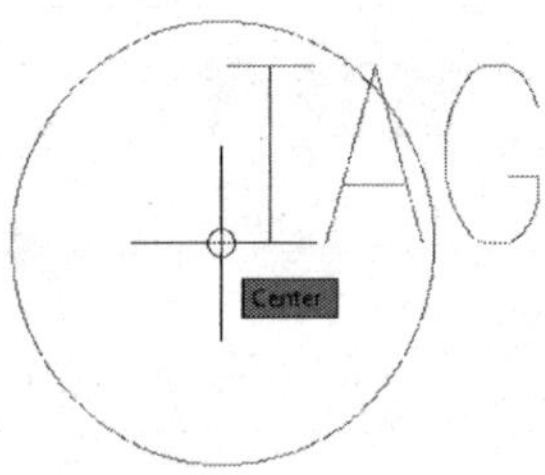

7.

Your block should look like this—a circle with an attribute in the center.

8.

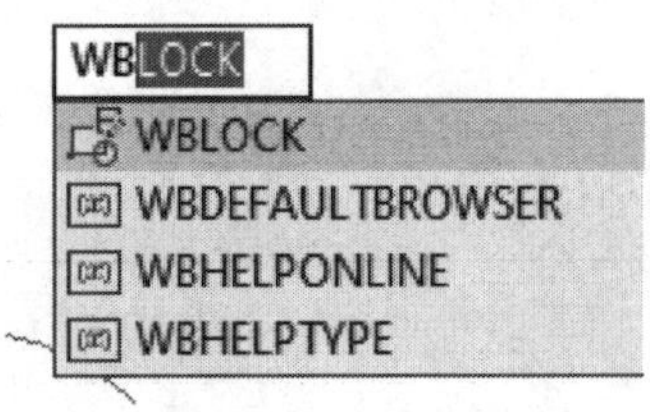

Type **WB** for WBLOCK to create an external block.

9.

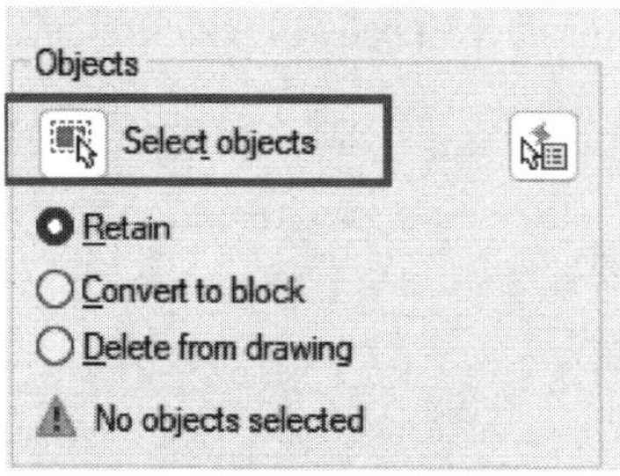

Click **Select objects**.

Select the circle and the attribute.

Click **ENTER** to complete the selection.

10.

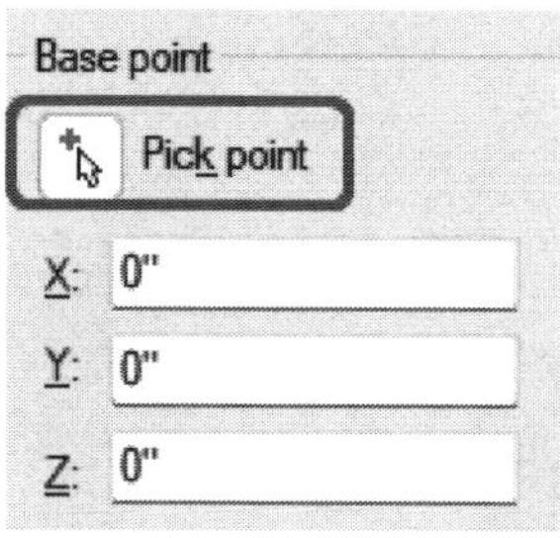

Click **Pick point** for the Base point.

11.

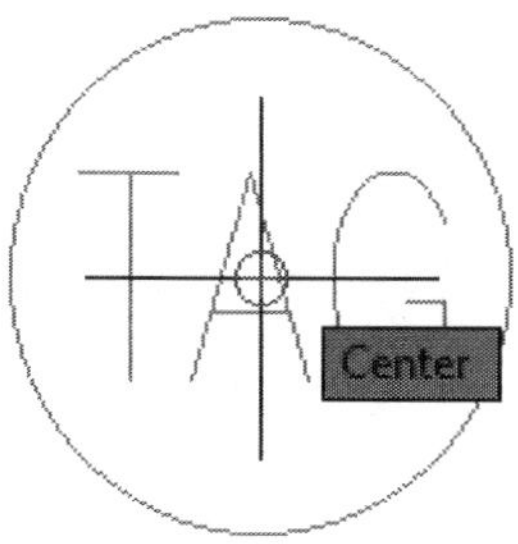

For the base point, select the center of the circle.

Your coordinates will be different from mine depending on where you placed your items in the drawing.

12.

Click the Browse … button next to File name and path.

13.

Save the block in your exercise folder as *tag.dwg*.

14.

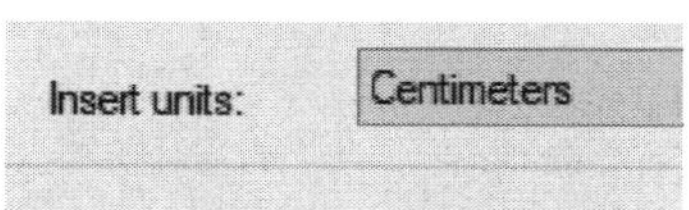

Set the insert units to **Centimeters**.

Click **OK**.

15. 

Select **Insert** and expand to select **Recent Blocks...**

16. 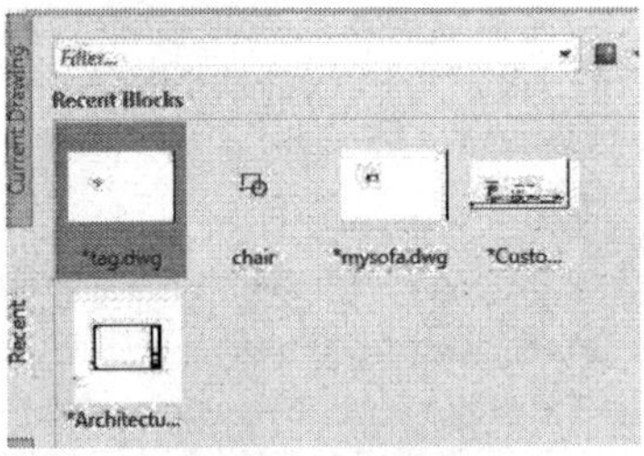

A palette will launch with the Recent tab active.
Locate the tag.dwg block drawing you created.

Highlight that drawing.

17. 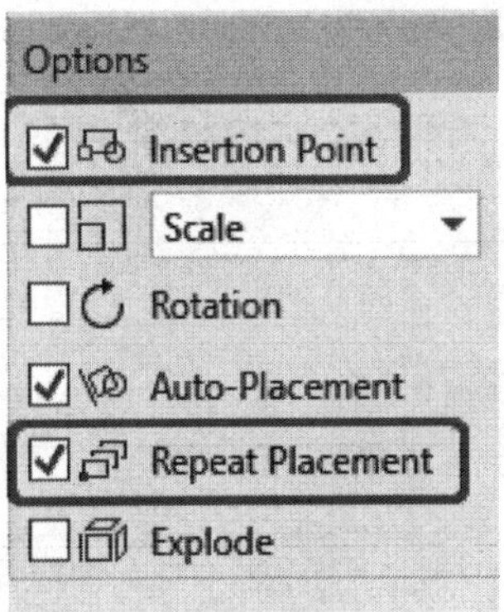

In the bottom of the panel, enable **Insertion Point**.

Accept the default values for Scale and Rotation.

Enable **Repeat Placement**.

Disable **Explode.**

18. 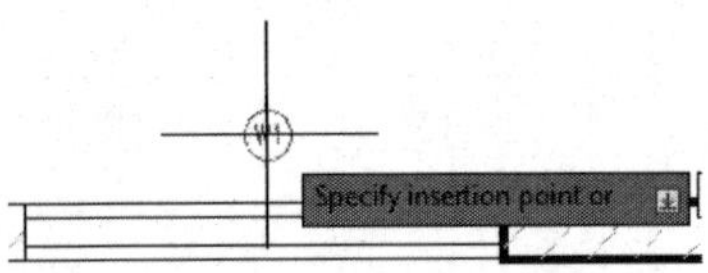

Left click above the window in the upper left corner of the floor plan.

19. 

Type **F4** into the value field for the tag.

20. 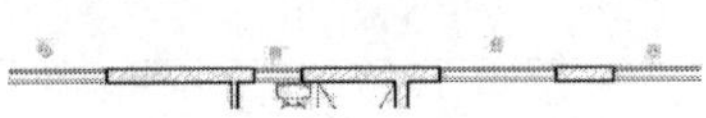

Place tags for the doors and windows as shown.

When completed, Click the **ESC** key or right click and select **CANCEL.**

21.

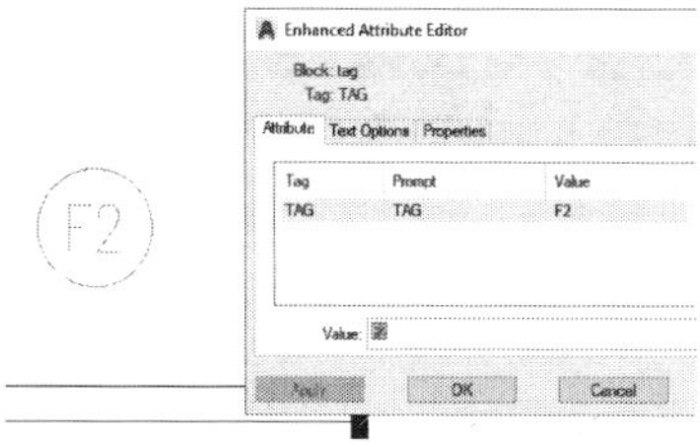

If you need to change the value of one of the attributes, you can double left click on the text to open the dialog box and modify the attribute.

22.

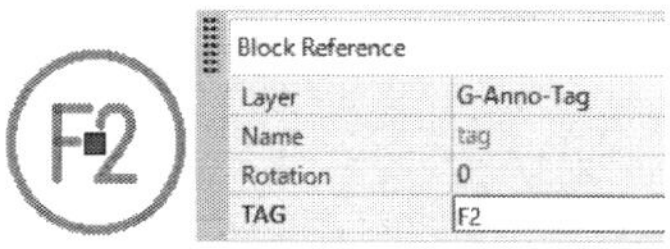

You can also just select the block. If Quick Properties is enabled, the Quick Properties dialog will appear.

You can change the value of the attribute in the Quick Properties dialog.

Auto-Placement

The new Block Placement feature learns from the placement of existing instances of a block in your drawing in order to infer how you may want to place that block again. The tool gives placement suggestions as you move a block you are inserting from the Blocks Palette close to a similar geometry to where you have placed that block before. For example, if you have already placed a chair block close to the corner of a wall, when inserting another instance of that same chair block, the chair will automatically position itself as you move it close to another similar corner. As you move the block, the walls will be highlighted, and the chair block will adjust its position, rotation, and scale to match. You can click to accept the suggestion, press the Tab key to switch to other suggestions, or move the crosshair away to deactivate the current suggestion. You can also use temporary override keys Shift+W or Shift+[(customizable in the CUI dialog) to disable suggestions.

Command Exercise

Exercise 11-7 – Auto-Placement

Drawing Name: **auto-place.dwg**
Estimated Time to Completion: 20 Minutes

Scope

Place a block using the auto-placement tool.

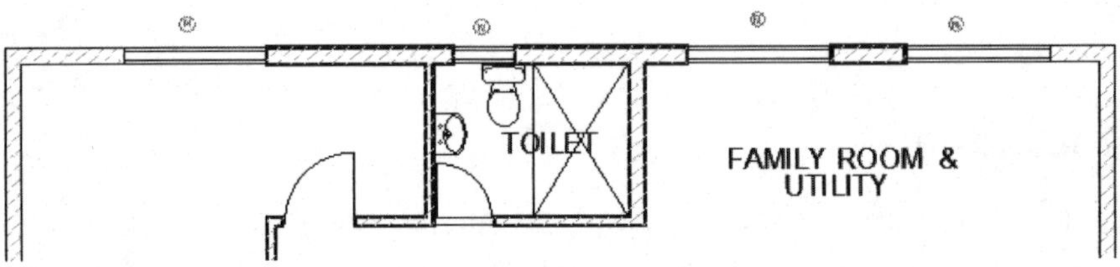

Solution

1. 

Verify that the current layer is set to **FURNITURE.**

2. 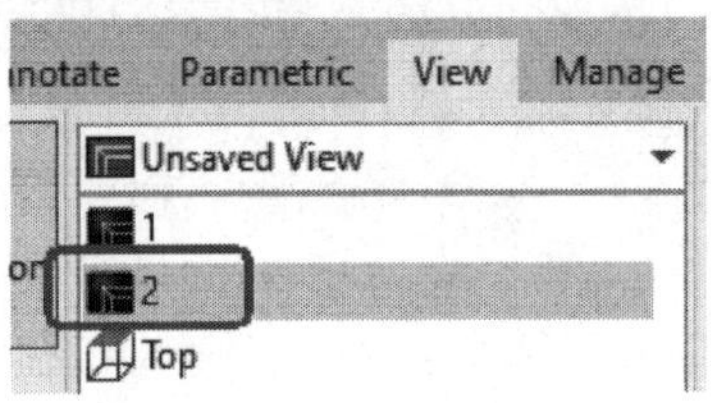

On the View ribbon:

Select the Named View **2**.

3.

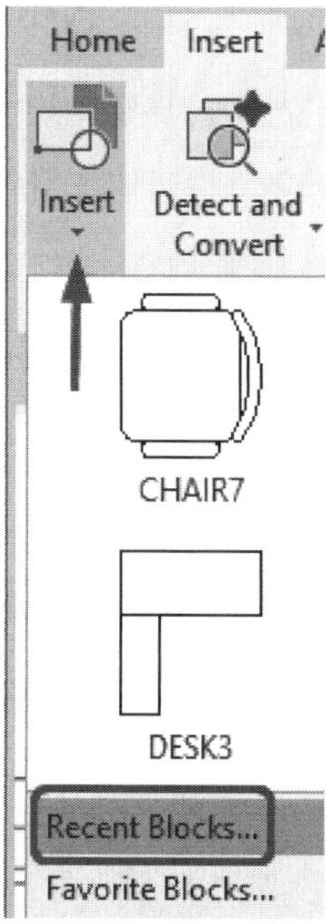

From the Insert ribbon:

Select **Insert→Recent Blocks**.

4.

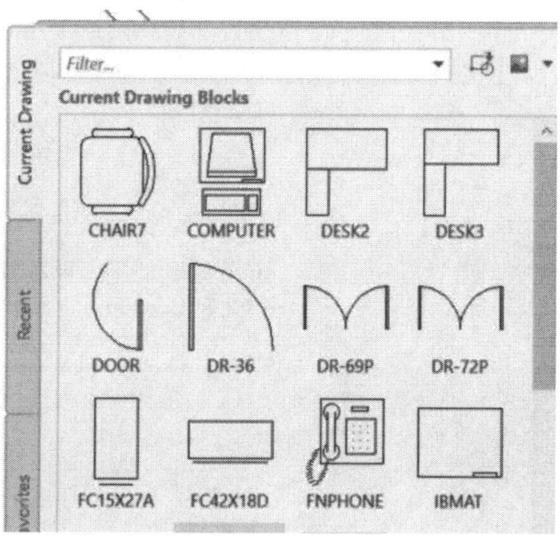

Select the Current Drawing tab.

5.

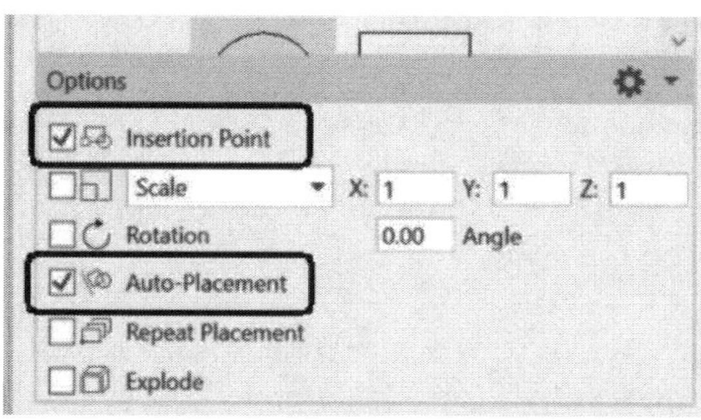

Enable **Insertion Point**.

Disable **Scale**.

Disable **Rotation**.

Enable **Auto-Placement**.

Disable **Repeat Placement**.

Disable **Explode**.

6.

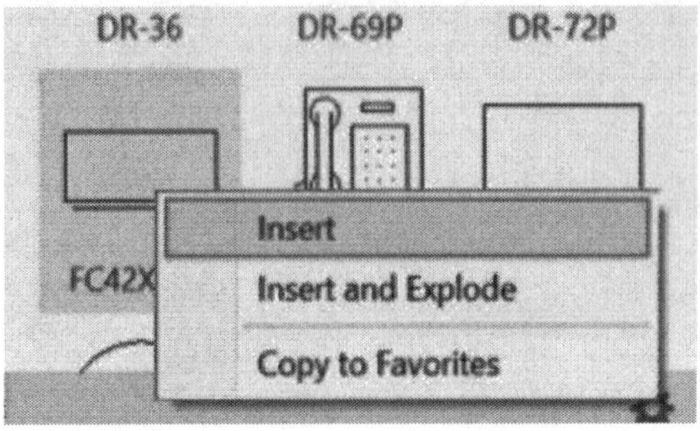

Highlight the **FC42x18D** block.

Right click and select **Insert**.

7.

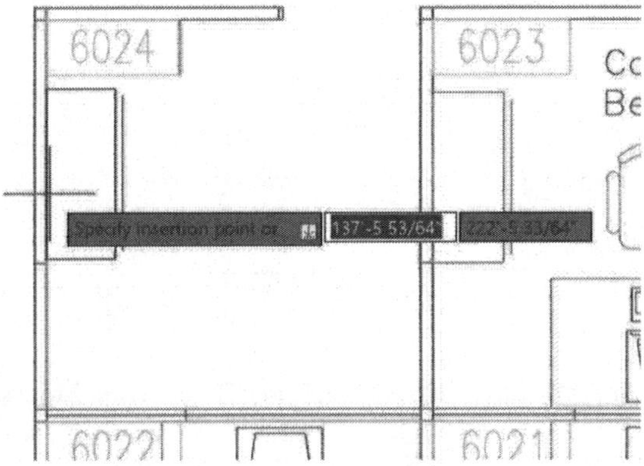

Drag the block into Room 6024.

Note that you have to right click and select Insert before dragging into the drawing or you will not see the auto-rotation.

As you drag close to the left wall, notice the block is oriented similar to the block placement in Room 6023.

Left click to place the block.

8.

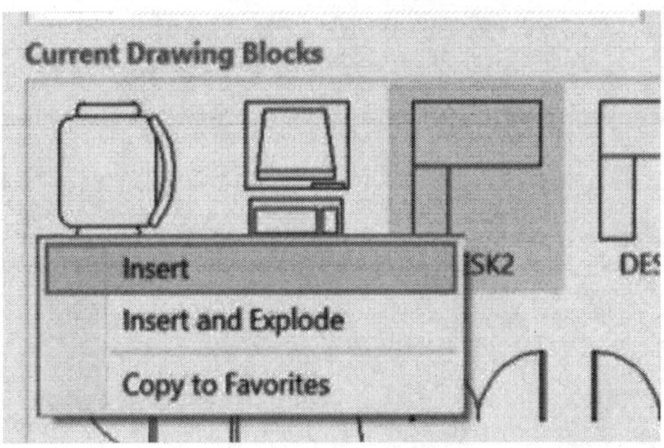

Highlight the **DESK2** block in the BLOCKS palette.

Right click and select **Insert**.

9. Drag the block into Room 6024.

As you drag close to the lower right corner of the room, notice the block is oriented similar to the block placement in Room 6023.

Left click to place the block.

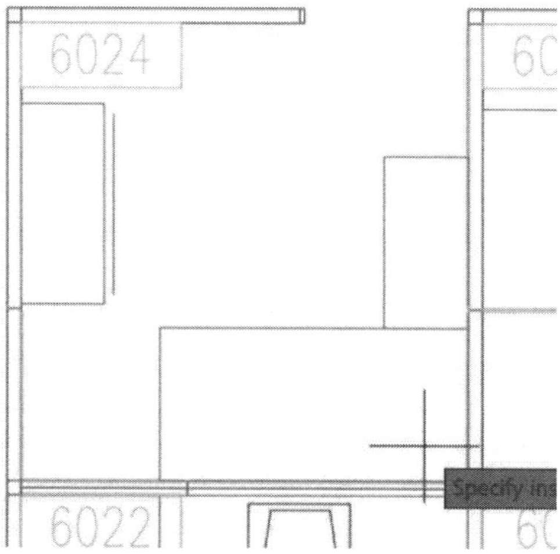

10. Left click on **Make Current** in the Layers panel of the Home ribbon.

11. Select the chair in room 6023.

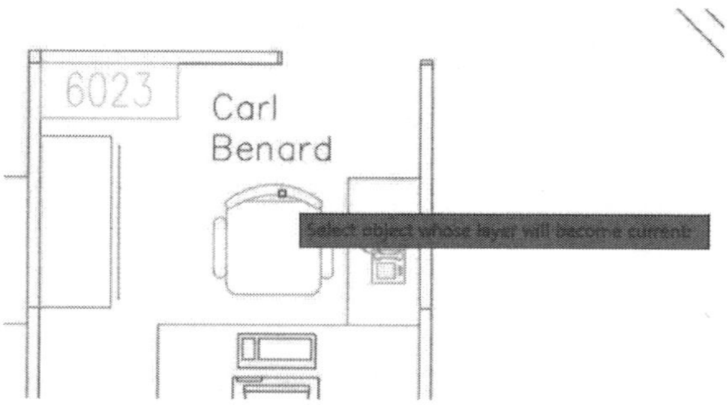

The current layer is now CHAIRS.

12. Highlight the **CHAIR7** block in the BLOCKS palette.

Right click and select **Insert**.

13. 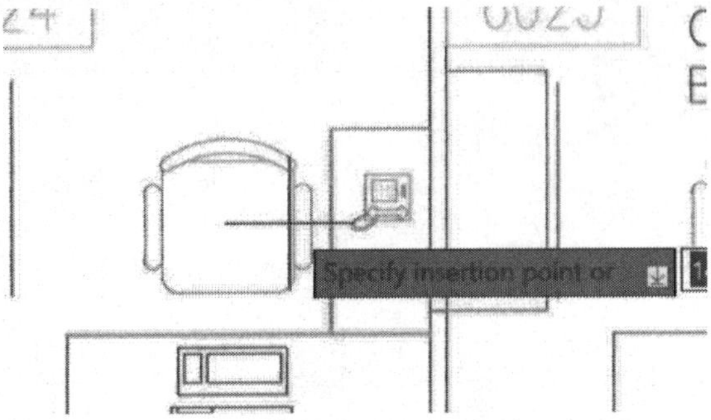

Drag the block into Room 6024.

***Hint:** Look for the inside edges of the desk to highlight.*

Left click to place the block.

14. 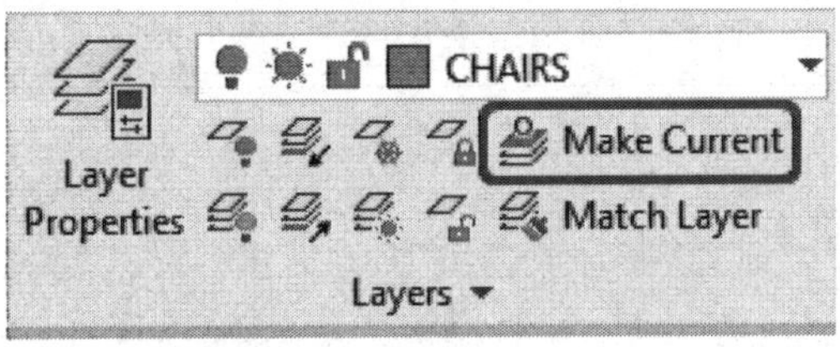

Left click on **Make Current** in the Layers panel of the Home ribbon.

15. 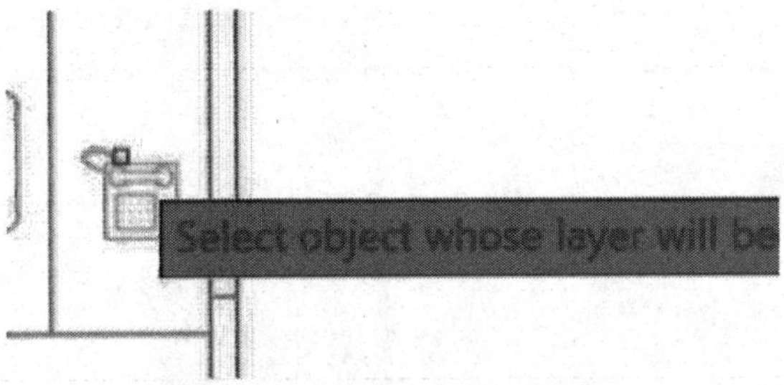

Select the landline in room 6023.

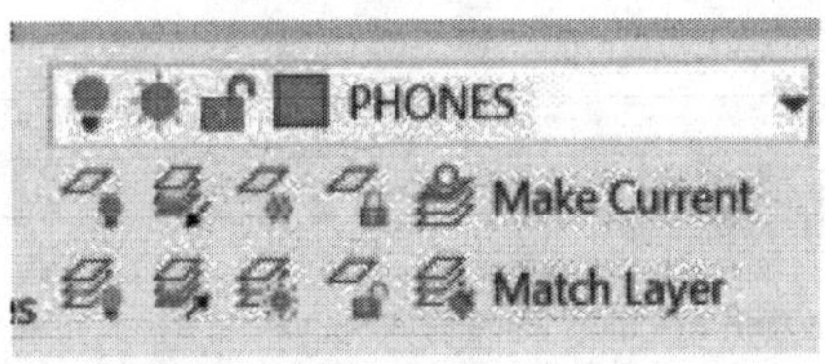

The current layer is now PHONES.

16. 

Highlight the **FNPHONE** block in the BLOCKS palette.

Right click and select **Insert**.

17. 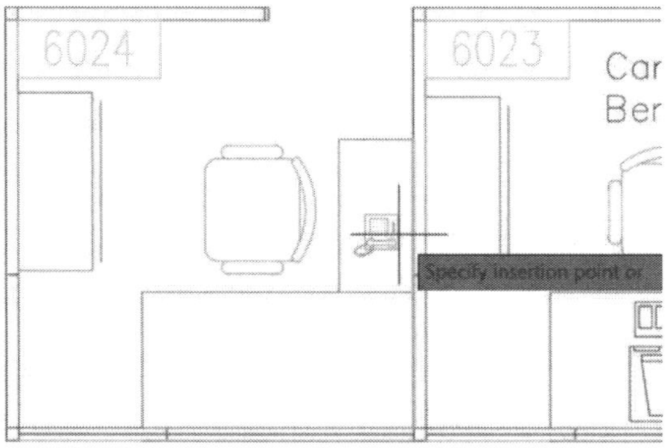

Drag the block into Room 6024.

Left click to place the block.

18. 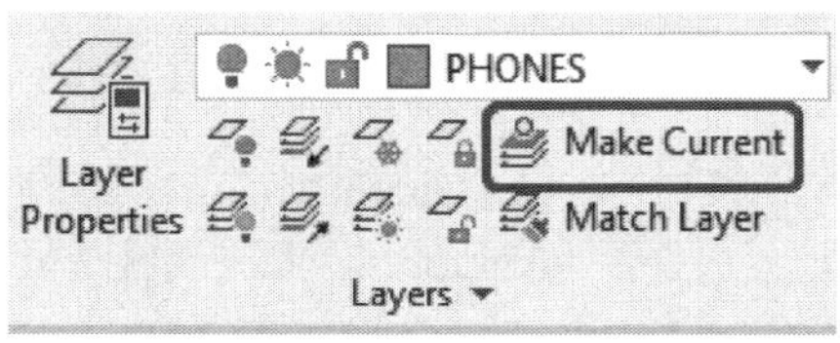

Left click on **Make Current** in the Layers panel of the Home ribbon.

19. 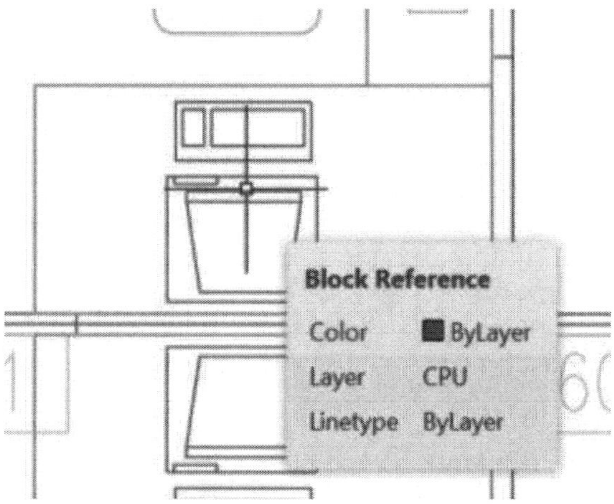

Select the desktop computer in room 6023.

The current layer is now CPU.

20. 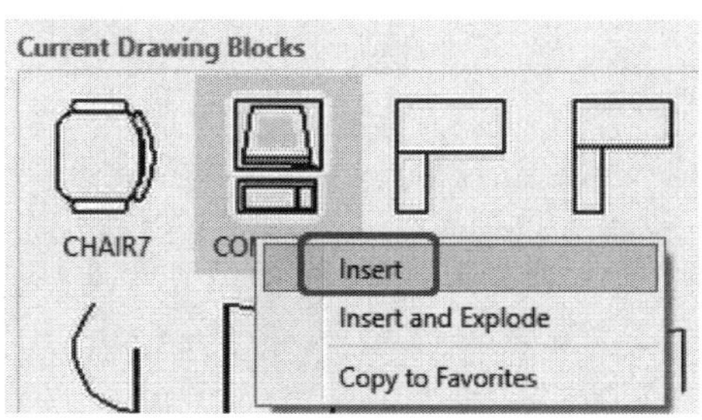

Highlight the **COMPUTER** block in the BLOCKS palette.

Right click and select **Insert**.

21. 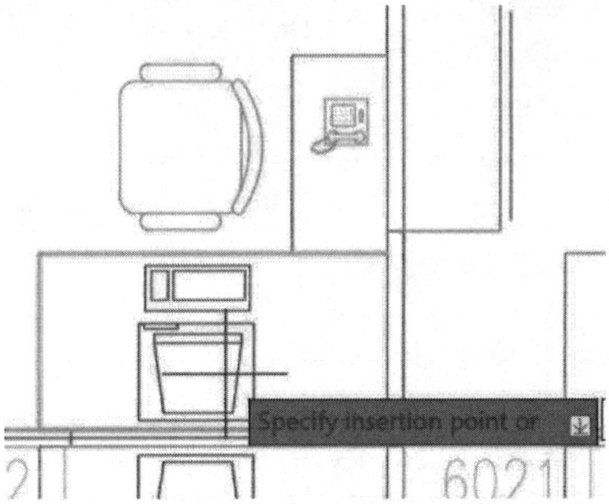

Drag the block into Room 6024.

Left click to place the block.

22. 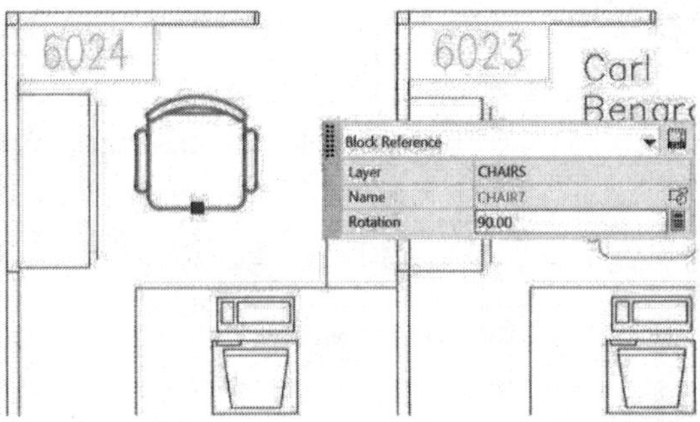

Correct the rotation on any blocks that didn't place properly.

AutoCAD Design Center

Command Locator

Command	ADCENTER
Alias	ADC or DC
Ribbon/View/Palettes	ADCENTER

Command Overview

Organizes access to drawings, blocks, hatches, and other drawing content.

With DesignCenter, you can:

- *Browse for drawing content such as drawings or symbol libraries on your computer, on a networked drive, and on a web page.*
- *View definition tables for blocks and layers in any drawing file and then insert, attach, or copy and paste the definitions into the current drawing.*
- *Update (redefine) a block definition.*
- *Create shortcuts to drawings, folders, and Internet locations that you access frequently.*
- *Add content such as xrefs, blocks, and hatches to a drawing.*
- *Open drawing files in a new window.*
- *Drag drawings, blocks, and hatches to a tool palette for convenient access.*
- *Copy and paste content, such as layer definitions, layouts, and text styles between open drawings.*

General Procedures:

1. Open the AutoCAD Design Center.
2. Browse for the desired content.
3. Drag and drop into the active drawing or copy and paste between open drawings.

To redefine an existing block with an updated version of the block from another drawing, open DesignCenter and navigate to the drawing that hosts the updated block. To access DesignCenter, click the View tab, then select the Palettes panel, and then DesignCenter. Make sure the target drawing (the one you want to update) is the active drawing in AutoCAD. In DesignCenter, navigate to the block category and select the updated block, right click, and select "Redefine Block." All the instances of the block in your target drawing are automatically redefined with the new block definition; no deleting, re-copying, or changing of the block name needed.

Command Exercise

Exercise 11-8 – Creating a Circuit Diagram

Drawing Name: **new drawing**
Estimated Time to Completion: 120 Minutes

Scope

Create circuit diagram symbols with attributes.
Using the Design Center to locate blocks.
Create a Tool Palette.
Place the blocks to create a circuit diagram.
Modify the blocks.
Add donuts for nodes.
Add single line text to label nodes.

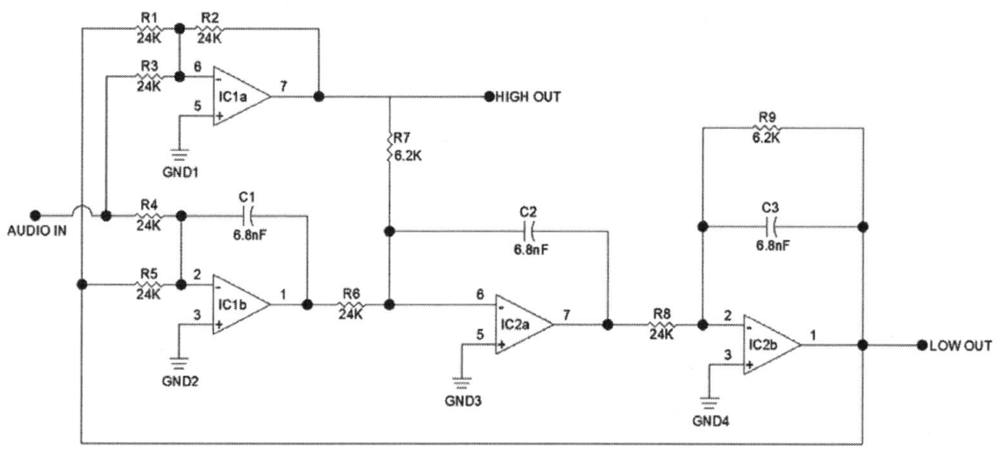

Solution

We need to create four symbols for this circuit diagram—the resistor, the capacitor, ground, and the circuit.

The symbols are available in the Autodesk Design Center (ADC). We can use those symbols and then add attributes to them.

*To launch the ADC, type **ADC** at the command prompt or select Design Center on the View ribbon.*

1. 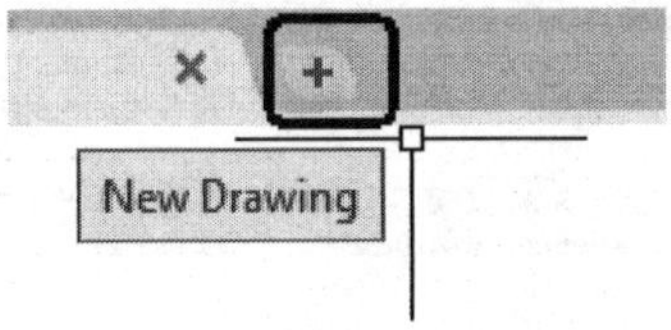

Start a new drawing by clicking on the + tab.

2. 

Click on the **Model** tab.

3. 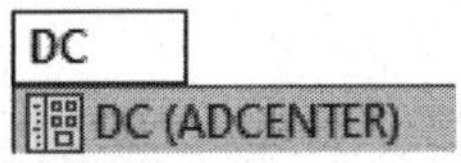

Type **DC** to launch the Design Center.

4. 

Click the **Open File** icon.

5. 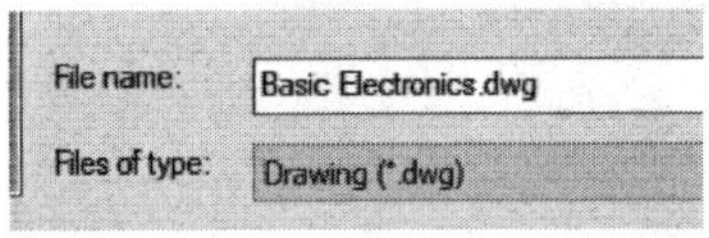

Open the *Basic Electronics.dwg,* located in the publisher's downloaded files.

6. 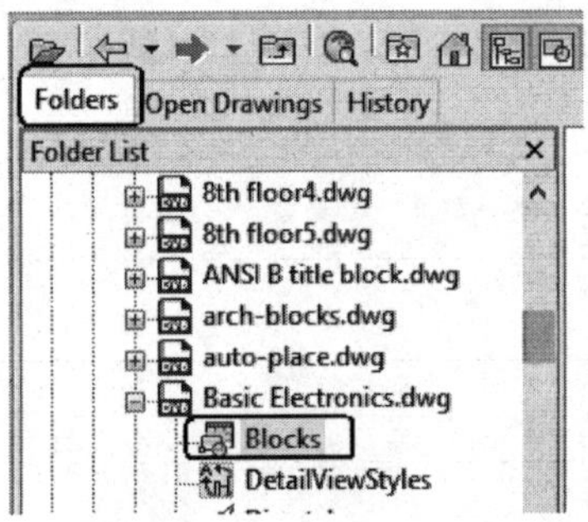

Highlight the Blocks category under the *Basic Electronics.dwg.*

7. 

Right click and select **Create Tool Palette**.

8. 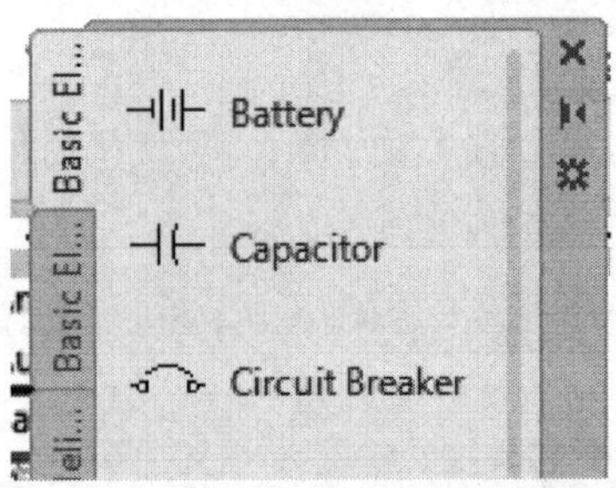

The Tool Palette launches and generates a palette with all the blocks available in the *Basic Electronics.dwg.*

9. 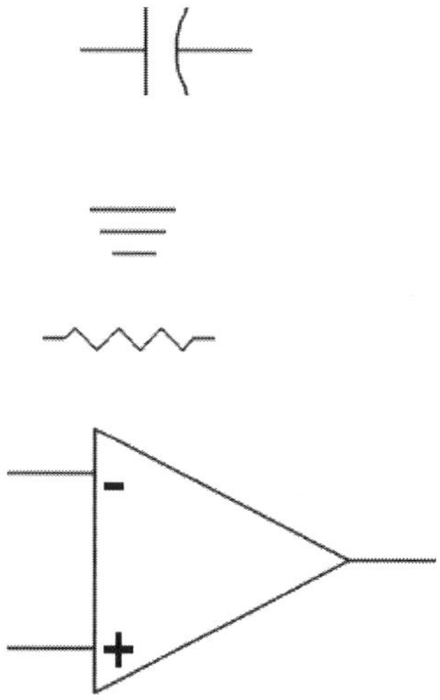

Locate these four symbols and drag them into your drawing.

- Operational Amplifier
- Ground
- Resistor
- Capacitor

Hint: *The blocks are organized alphabetically.*

10. 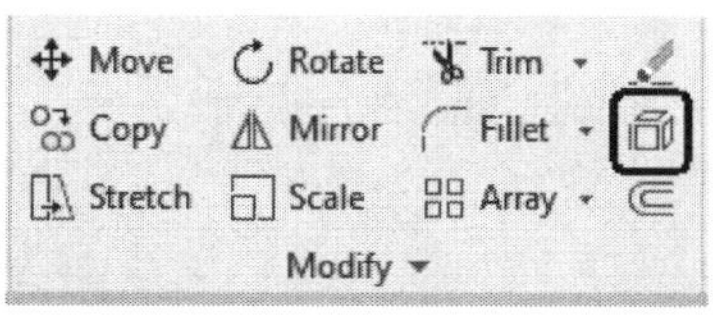

Explode all the blocks.

Exploding a block basically takes it back to the elements as they were before grouped into a block.

11. 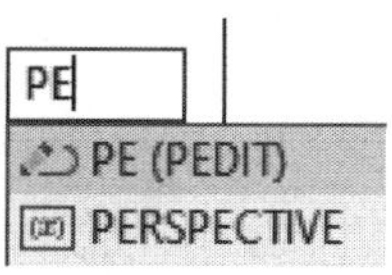

I want to use the geometric center of the triangle to place the designator attribute. In order to do that, I need to connect the three lines composing the triangle to form a polyline.

Type **PE** for polyline edit.

12. 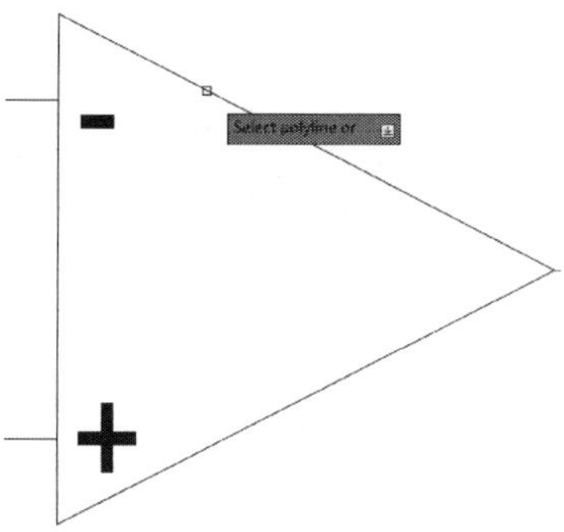

Select one of the lines forming the triangle.

You will be asked if you want to turn the line into a polyline.

Click **ENTER** for Yes.

13.

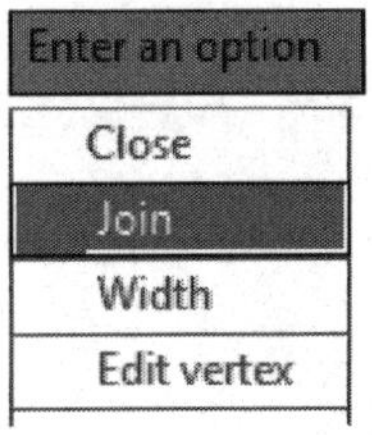

Select **Join** to add the other two lines.

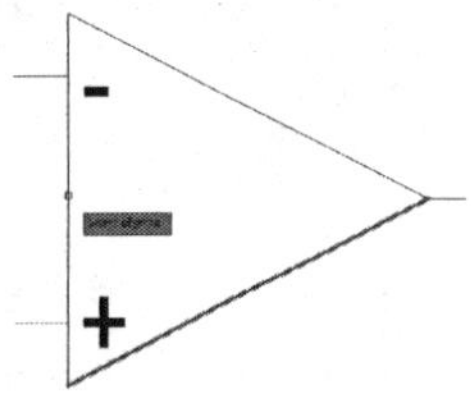

Select the remaining two lines.

Click **ENTER** twice to complete the command.

Click **ESC** to exit the command.

14.

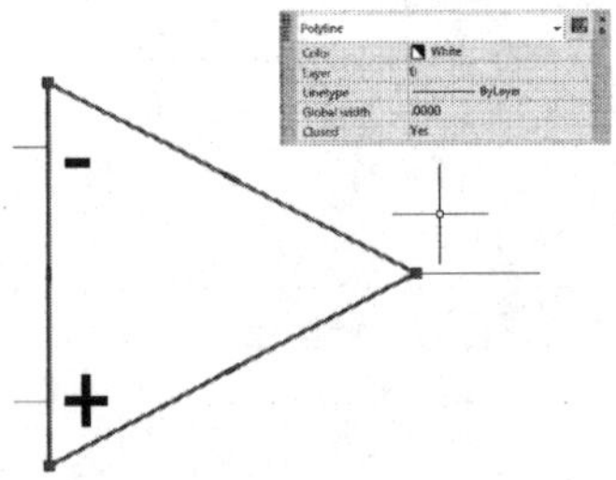

Select the triangle to confirm it is now a polyline and all three lines are joined together.

Click **ESC** to release the selection.

15.

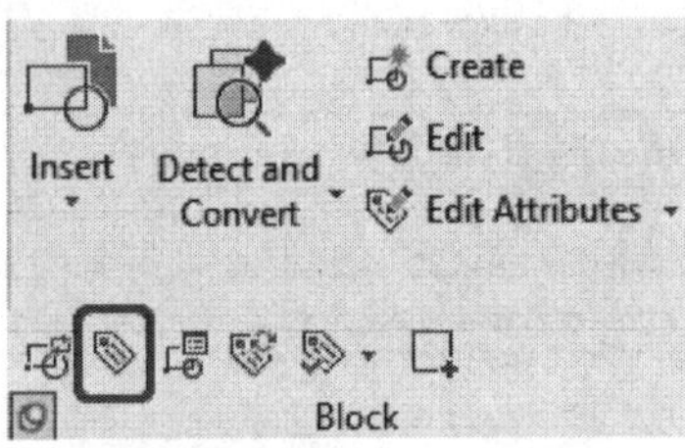

Next we will add attributes to the symbols.

Select **Define Attributes** from the Block panel on the Home ribbon.

16.

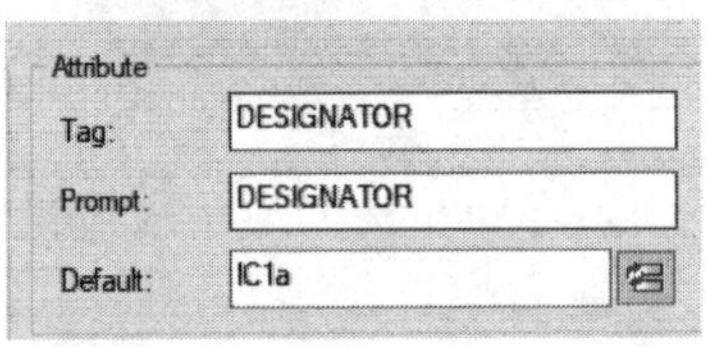

Type **DESIGNATOR** in the Tag field.

Type **DESIGNATOR** in the Prompt field.

Type **IC1a** in the Default field.

I like to put a value in the default field to act as an example of what the user should fill in.

17.

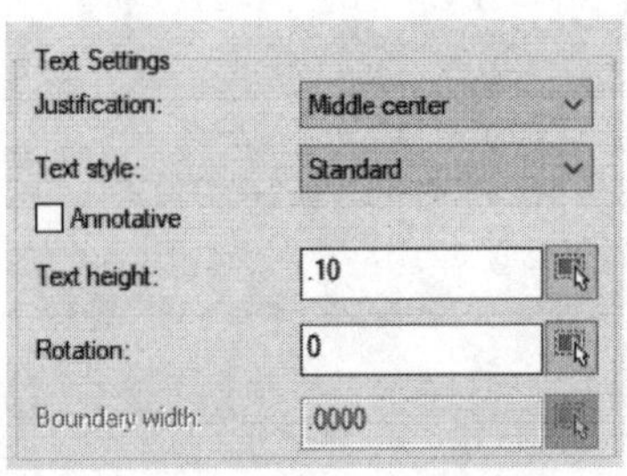

Set the Justification to **Middle Center.**

Set the Text Style to **Standard.**

Set the Text Height to **0.100**.

18. 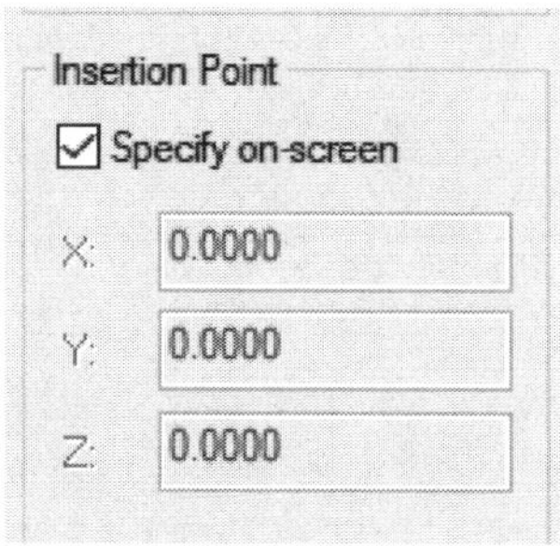

Enable the Insertion Point to **Specify on-screen**.

Click **OK**.

19. 

Select the **Geometric center** of the triangle to place the attribute.

20. 

Left click to place the attribute at the geometric center of the triangle.

Don't worry about the text being too big—remember that's the prompt, not the value.

21. 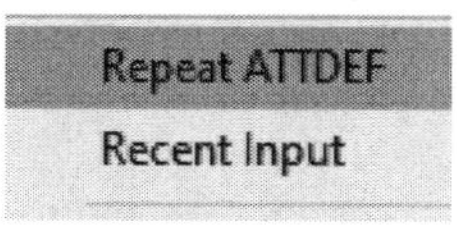

Right click and select **Repeat ATTDEF**.

22. 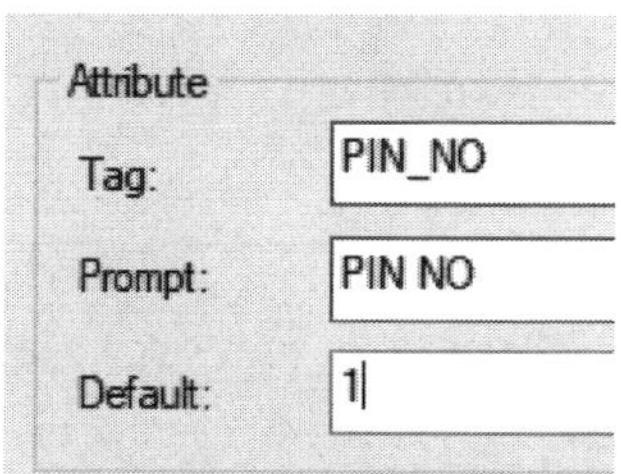

Type **PIN_NO** in the Tag field.

Type **PIN NO** in the Prompt field.

Type **1** in the Default field.

I like to put a value in the default field to act as an example of what the user should fill in.

23. 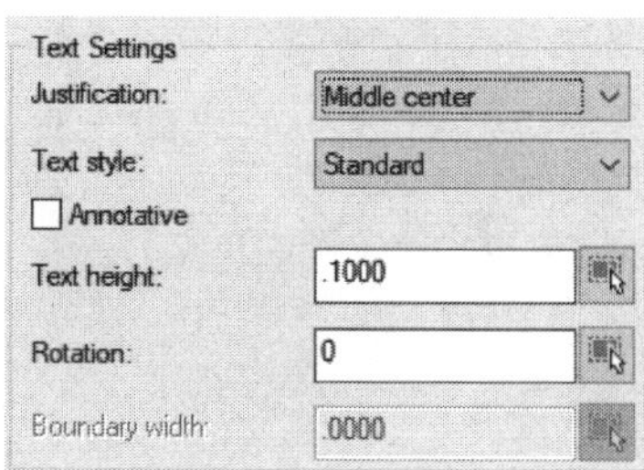

Set the Justification to **Middle Center**.

Set the Text Style to **Standard**.

Set the Text Height to **0.100**.

24. 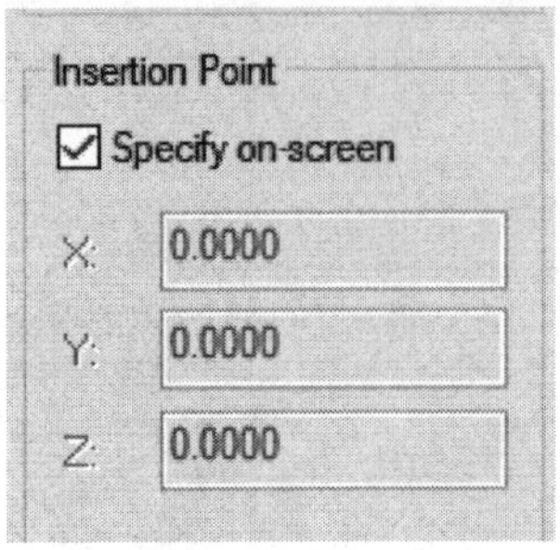

Enable the Insertion Point to **Specify on-screen**.

Click **OK**.

25. 

Place the attribute over the top left wire line.

26. 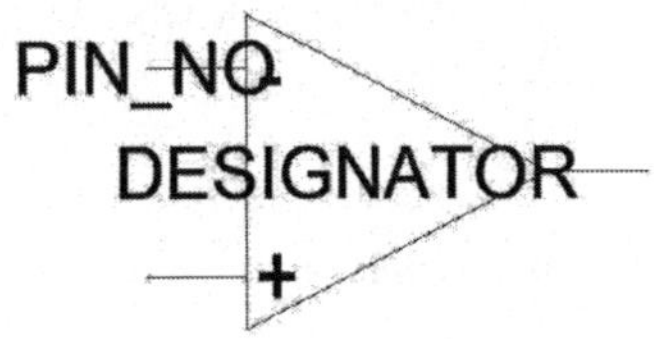

Select the PIN_NO attribute.

Copy to the lower left wire and the right wire.

27. 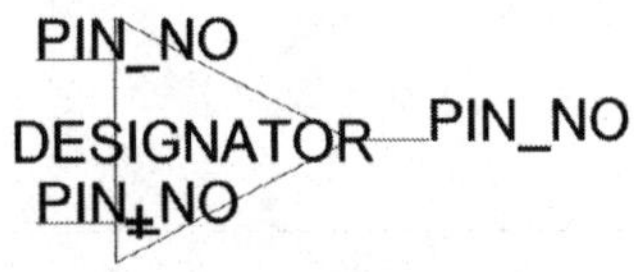

You should have the PIN_NO placed three times.

28. 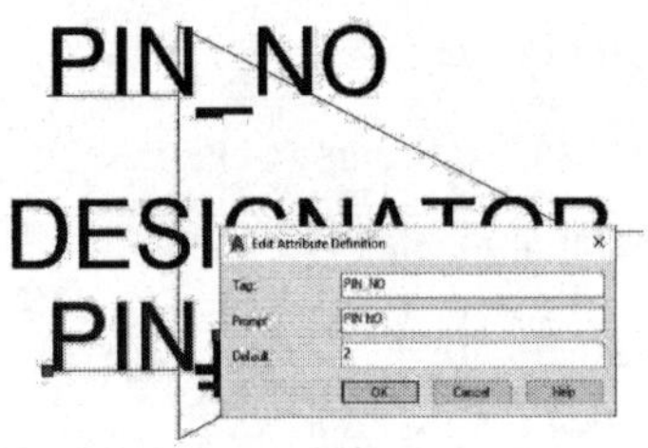

Double click on the lower PIN_NO attribute.

Change the Default value to **2**.

29. 

Double click on the right PIN_NO attribute.

Change the Default value to **3**.

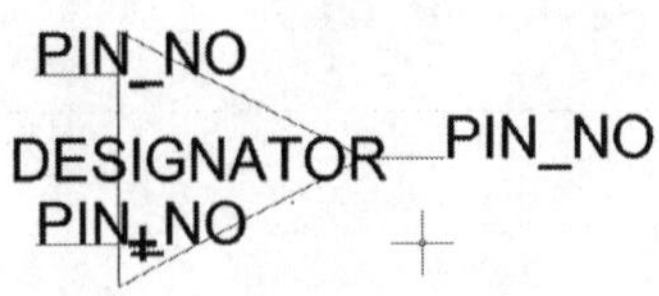

Your IC block should look like this.

30. 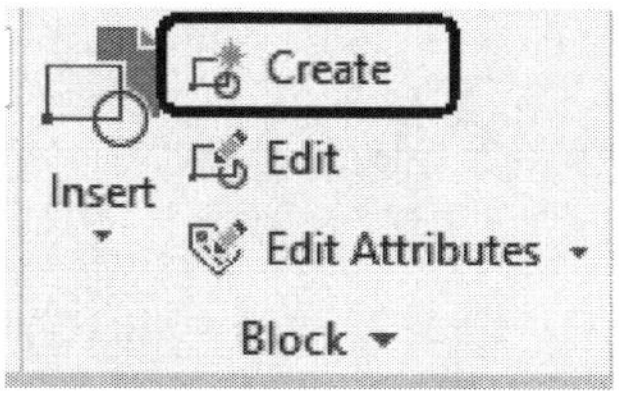

Select **Create Block**.

31. 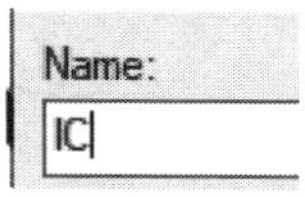

Type **IC** for the Name.

32. 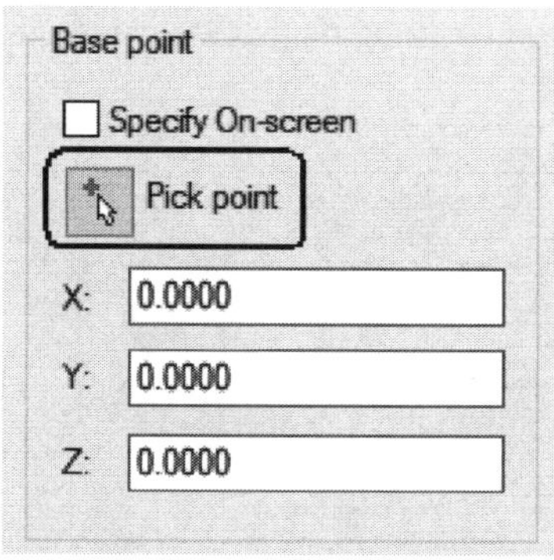

Click **Pick point** under Base point.

33. 

For the insertion point select the endpoint of the right wire line.

34. 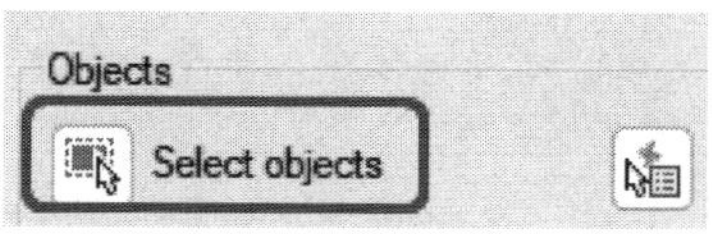

Click **Select objects**.

35. 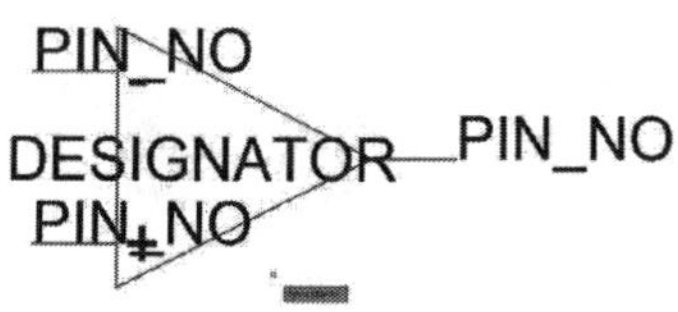

Select the triangle and the wire connectors and the plus and minus symbols.

36. 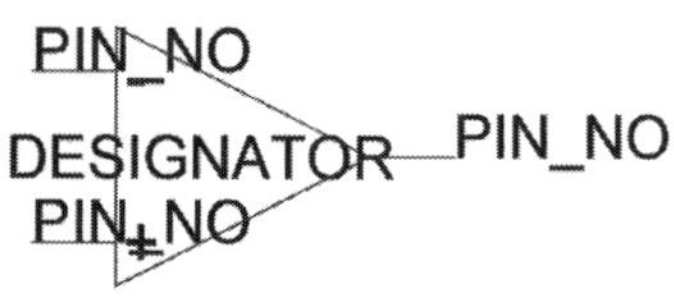

Select the attributes in the order you want to be prompted, so DESIGNATOR, PIN 1, PIN 2, then PIN 3.

Click **ENTER**.

37. 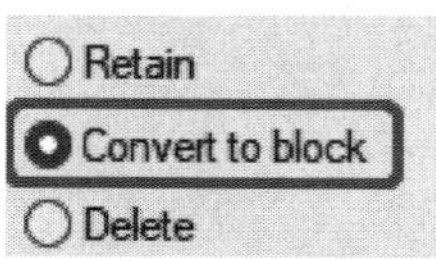

Enable **Convert to Block**.

Click **OK**.

38. 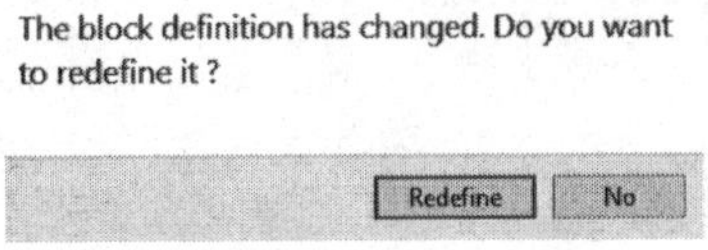

If a dialog appears asking to redefine the block, click **Redefine**.

39. 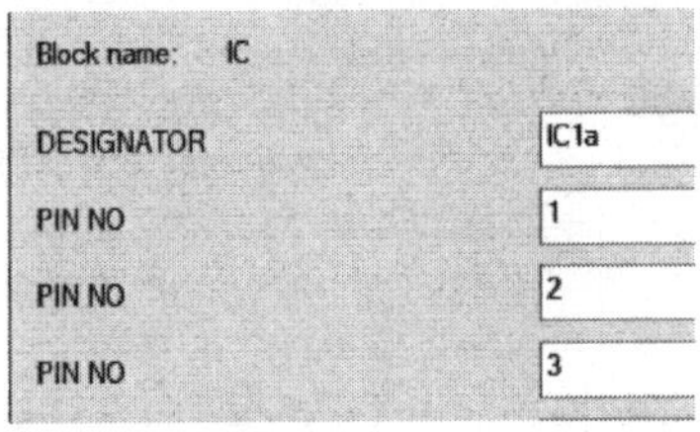

The attribute dialog appears where you can edit the pin values.

Notice that they are in the order attributes were selected.

The block appears with the attribute values.

Click **OK**.

40. 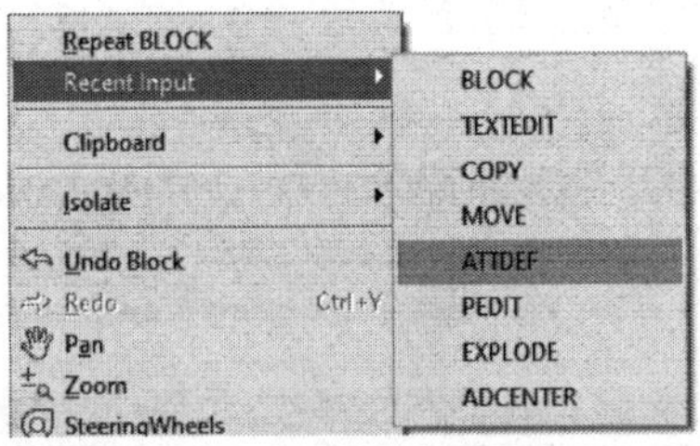

Next, we will add an attribute to the Ground symbol.

Right click and select **Recent Input→ATTDEF.**

41. 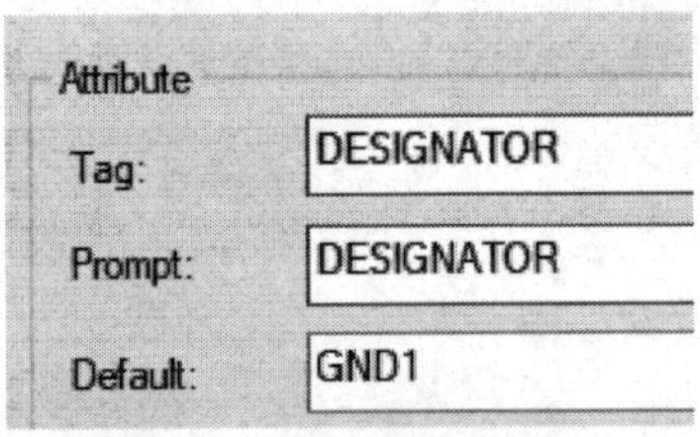

Type **DESIGNATOR** in the Tag field.

Type **DESIGNATOR** in the Prompt field.

Type **GND1** in the Default field.

42. 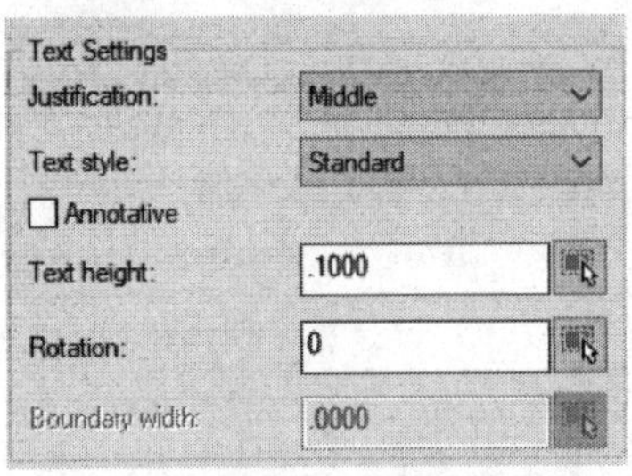

Set the Justification to **Middle.**

Set the Text Style to **Standard.**

Set the Text Height to **0.100**.

43. 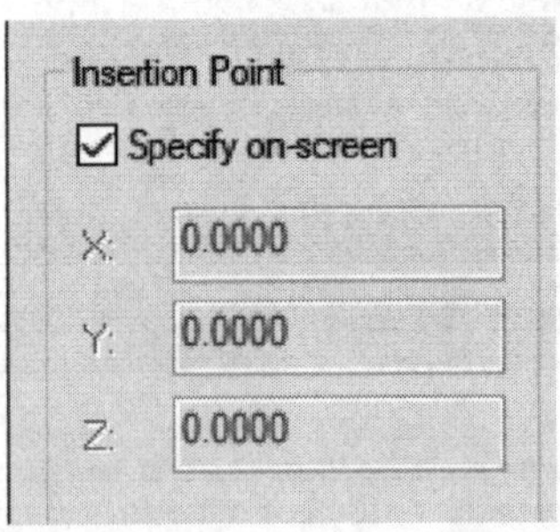

Enable the Insertion Point to **Specify on-screen**.

Click **OK**.

44. 

Place the attribute centered below the ground symbol.

45. 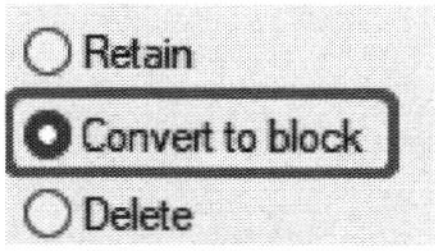

Select **Create Block**.

46. 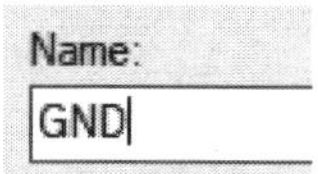

Type **GND** for the Name.

47. 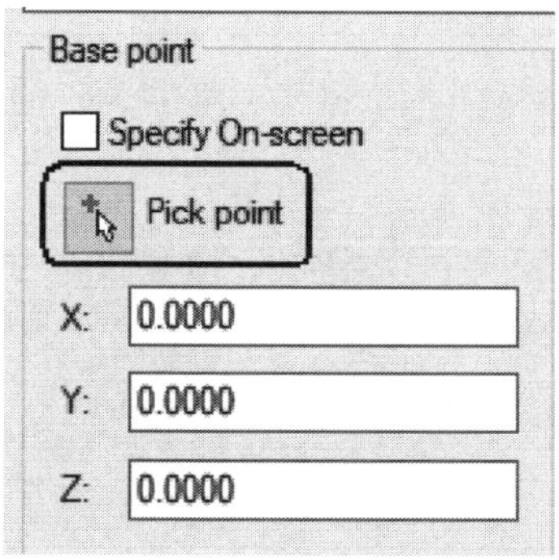

Click **Pick point** under Base point.

48. 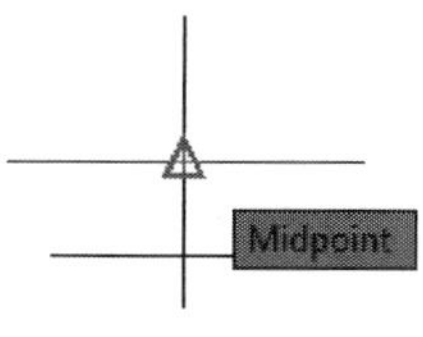

For the insertion point select the midpoint of the top horizontal line.

49. 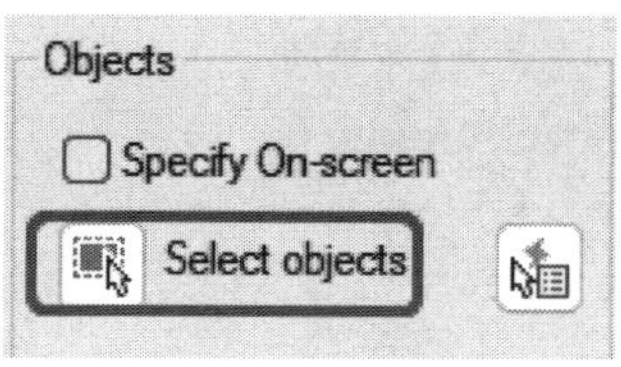

Click **Select objects**.

50. 

Select the lines and the attribute.

Click **ENTER.**

You can window around the elements.

There is only one attribute, so you don't need to worry about the order of selection.

51.

Enable **Convert to Block**.

Enable **Scale uniformly**.

Enable **Allow exploding**.

Click **OK**.

52.

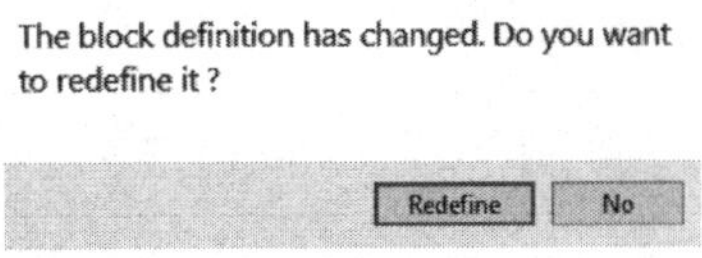

If a dialog appears asking to redefine the block, click **Redefine**.

53.

The attribute dialog appears where you can edit the designator value.

The block appears with the attribute values.

Click **OK**.

54.

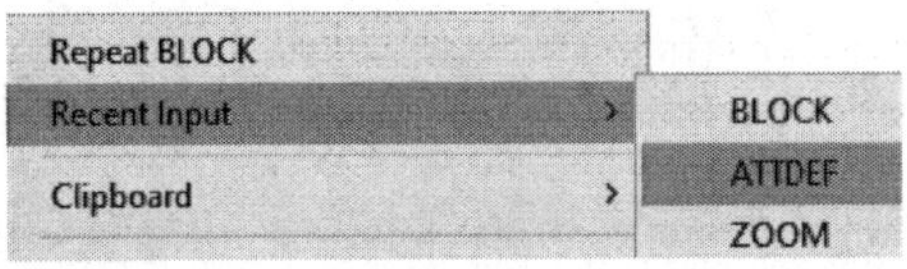

Next, we will add attributes and create the resistor block.

Right click and select **Recent Input→ATTDEF**.

55.

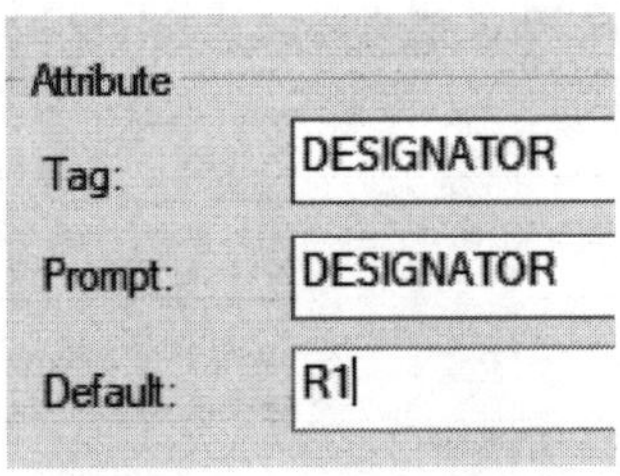

Type **DESIGNATOR** in the Tag field.

Type **DESIGNATOR** in the Prompt field.

Type **R1** in the Default field.

56.

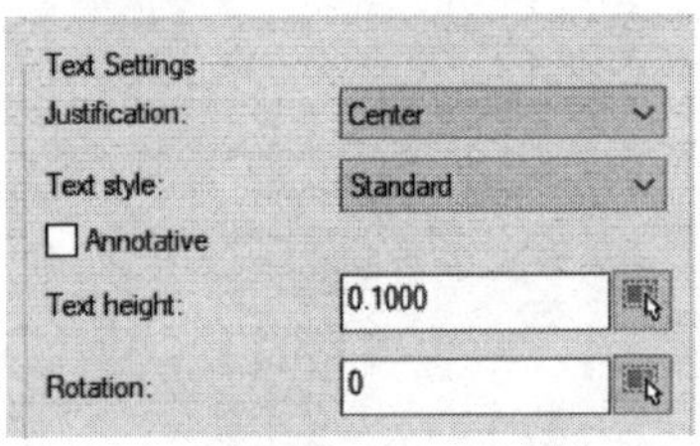

Set the Justification to **Center**.

Set the Text Style to **Standard**.

Set the Text Height to **0.100**.

57.

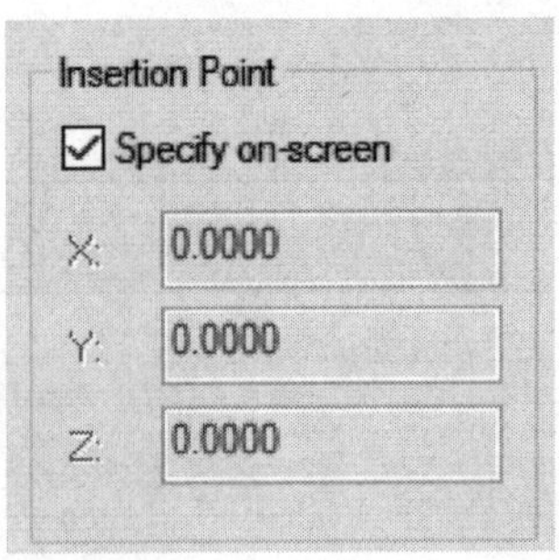

Enable the Insertion Point to **Specify on-screen**.

Click **OK**.

58.

Place the attribute above the jagged lines.

Hint: *Use the bottom center angle to line up the center of the attribute.*

59.

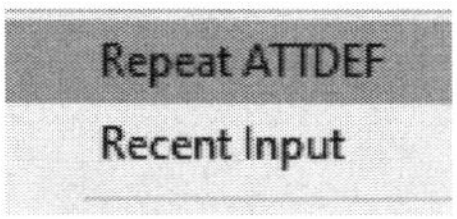

Right click and select **Repeat ATTDEF**.

60.

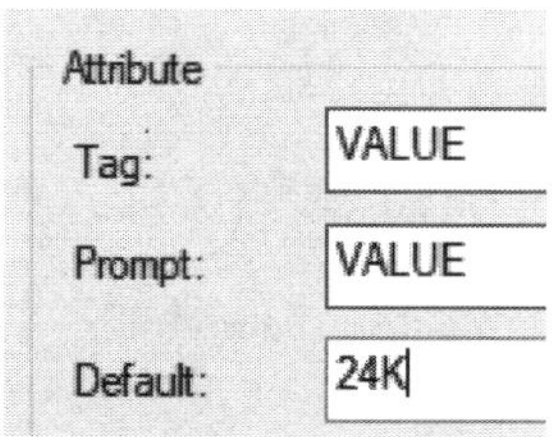

Type **VALUE** in the Tag field.

Type **VALUE** in the Prompt field.

Type **24K** in the Default field.

61.

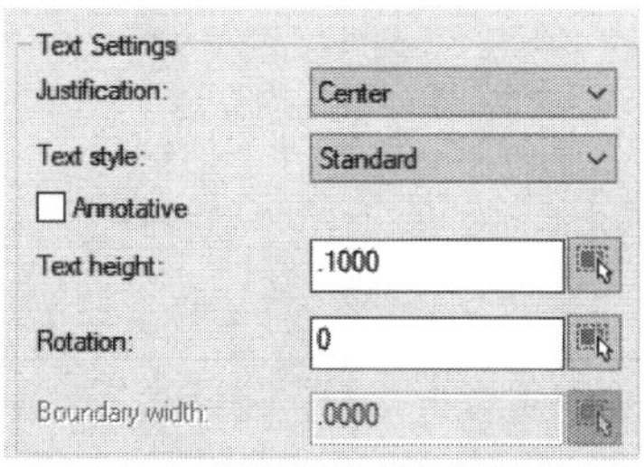

Set the Justification to **Center**.

Set the Text Style to **Standard**.

Set the Text Height to **0.100**.

62.

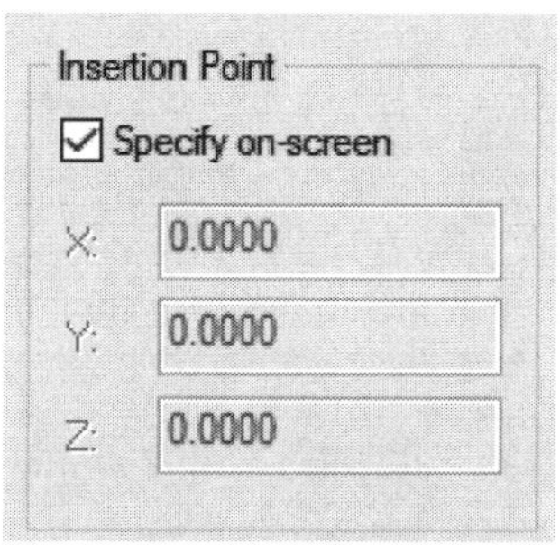

Enable the Insertion Point to **Specify on-screen**.

Click **OK**.

63.

Place the attribute below the jagged lines.

Hint: *Use the bottom center angle to line up the center of the attribute.*

64.

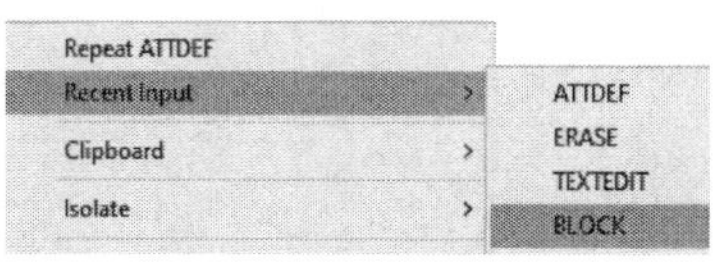

Right click and select **Recent Input→BLOCK**.

65. 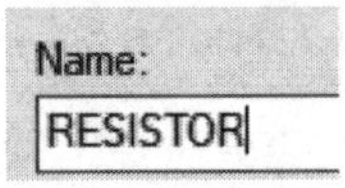

Type **RESISTOR** for the Name.

66. 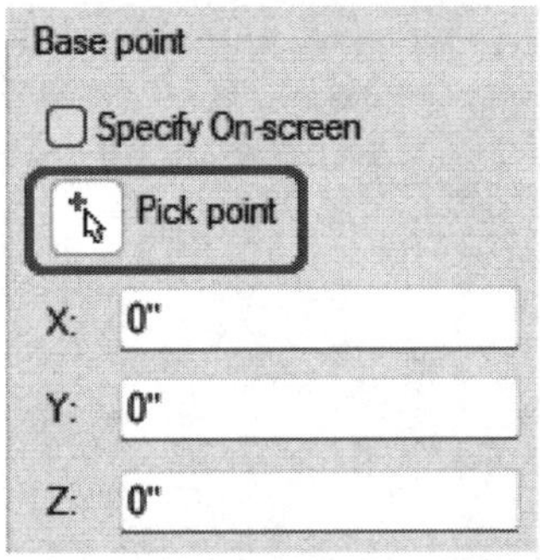

Click **Pick point** under Base point.

67. 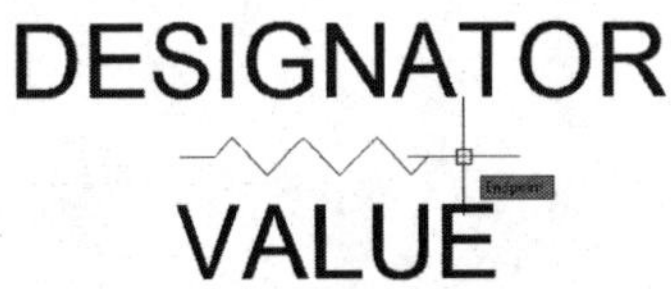

For the insertion point select the endpoint of the right horizontal line.

68. 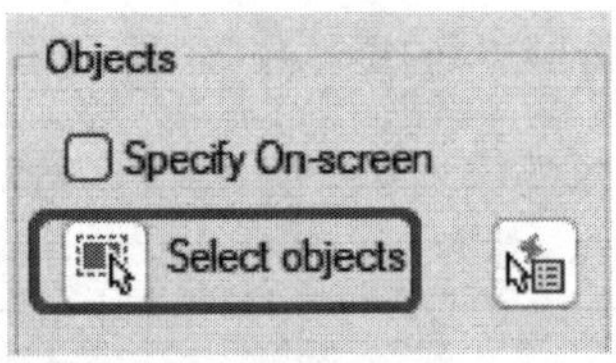

Click **Select objects**.

69. 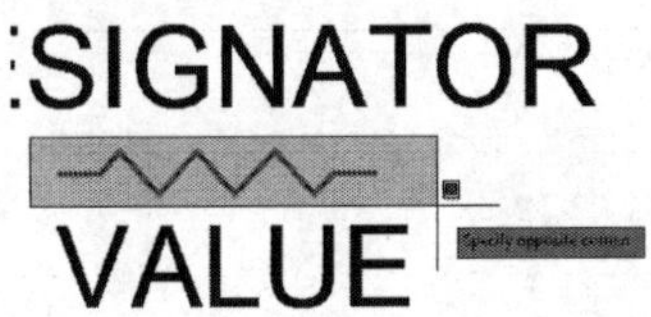

Select the lines.

70. 

Select the Designator attribute and then the Value attribute.

Click **ENTER.**

71. 

Enable **Convert to Block**.

Enable **Scale uniformly**.

Enable **Allow exploding**.

Click **OK**.

72. 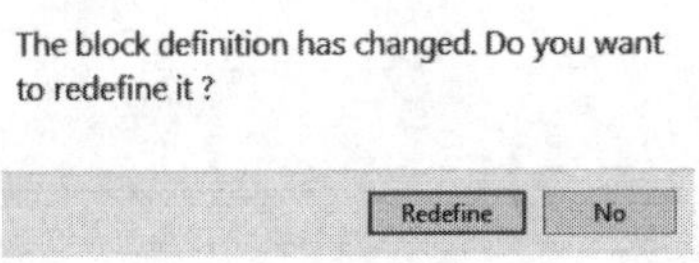

If a dialog appears asking to redefine the block, click **Redefine**.

73.

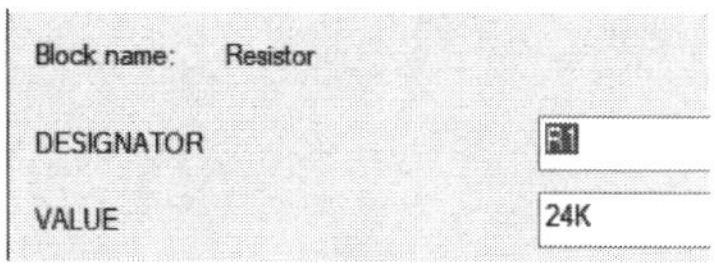

The attribute dialog appears where you can edit the designator value.

The block appears with the attribute values.

Click **OK**.

74.

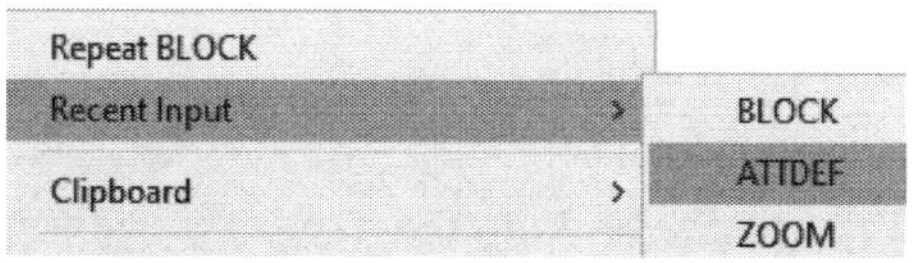

Next, we will add attributes and create the capacitor block.

Right click and select **Recent Input→ATTDEF**.

75.

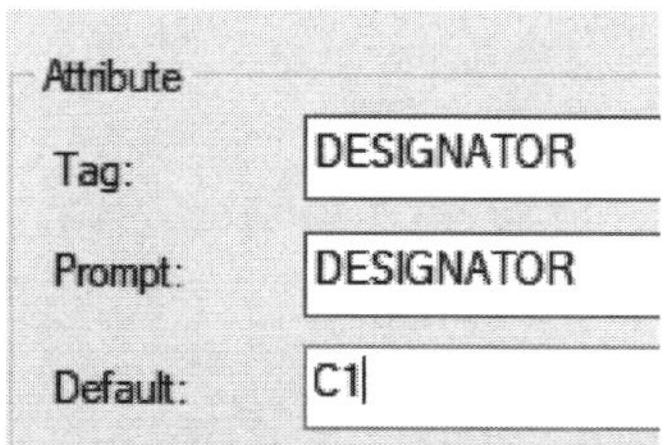

Type **DESIGNATOR** in the Tag field.

Type **DESIGNATOR** in the Prompt field.

Type **C1** in the Default field.

76.

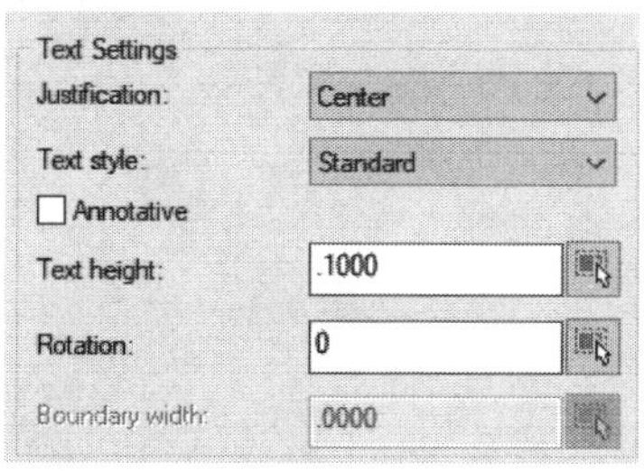

Set the Justification to **Center**.

Set the Text Style to **Standard**.

Set the Text Height to **0.100**.

77.

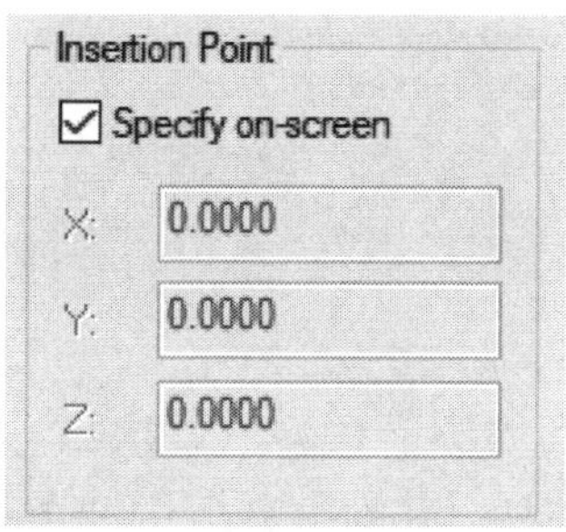

Enable the Insertion Point to **Specify on-screen**.

Click **OK**.

78.

Place the attribute above the capacitor symbol.

79. Right click and select **Repeat ATTDEF**.

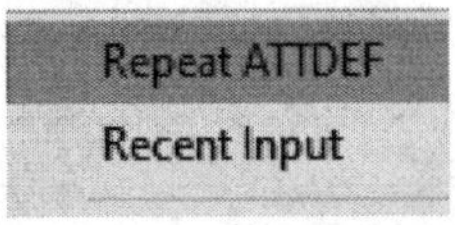

80. Type **VALUE** in the Tag field.

Type **VALUE** in the Prompt field.

Type **6.8nF** in the Default field.

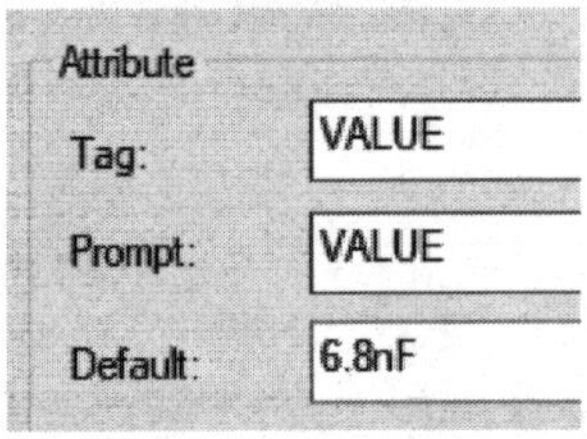

81. Set the Justification to **Center**.

Set the Text Style to **Standard**.

Set the Text Height to **0.100**.

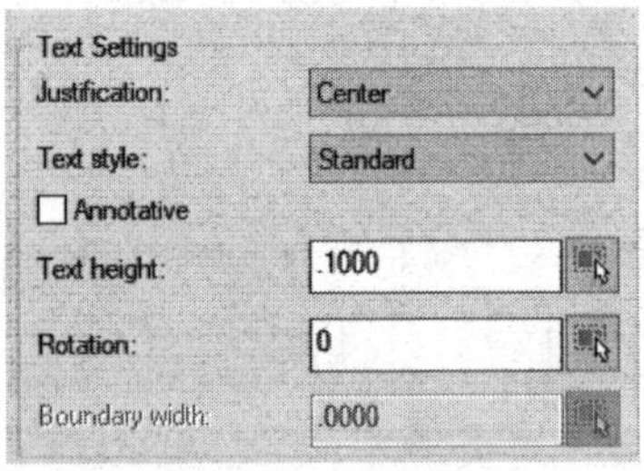

82. Enable the Insertion Point to **Specify on-screen**.

Click **OK**.

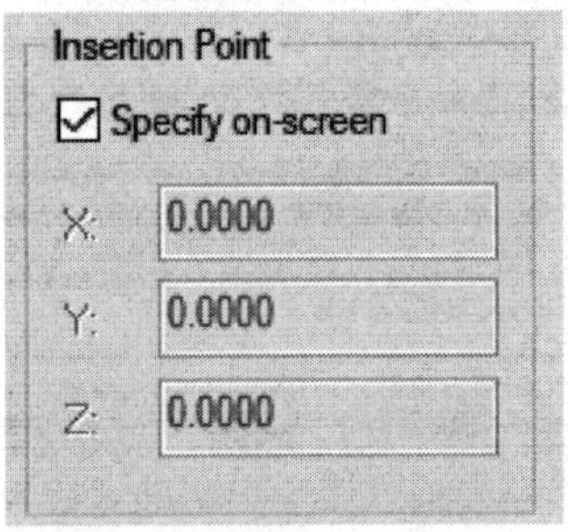

83. Place the attribute below the symbol.

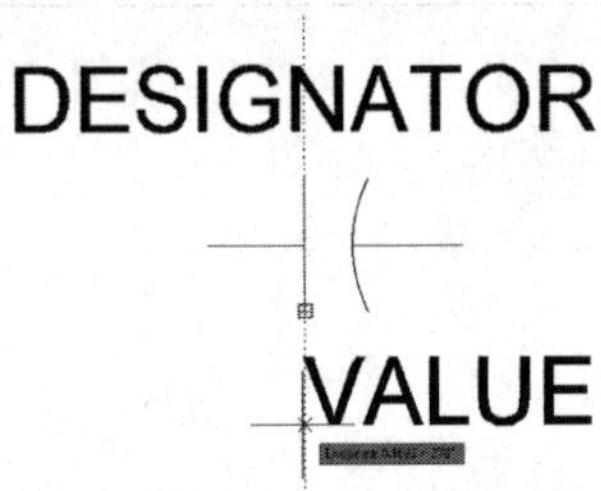

84. Right click and select **Recent Input→BLOCK**.

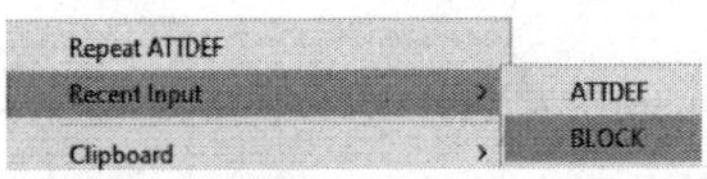

85. Type **CAPACITOR** for the Name.

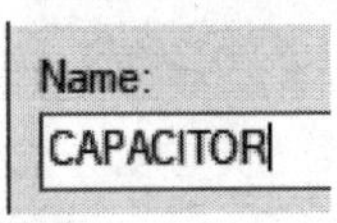

86.

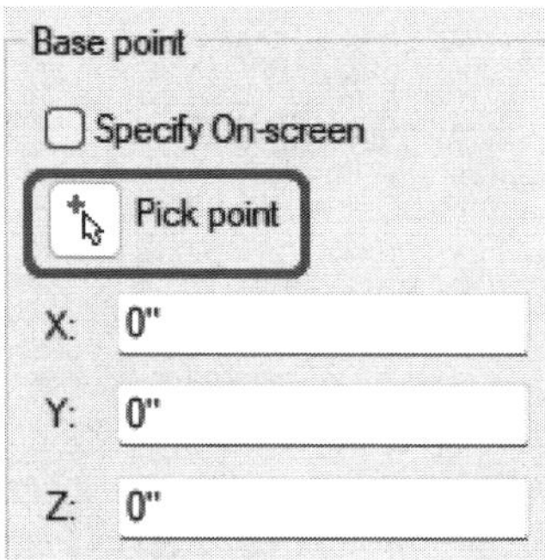

Click **Pick point** under Base point.

87.

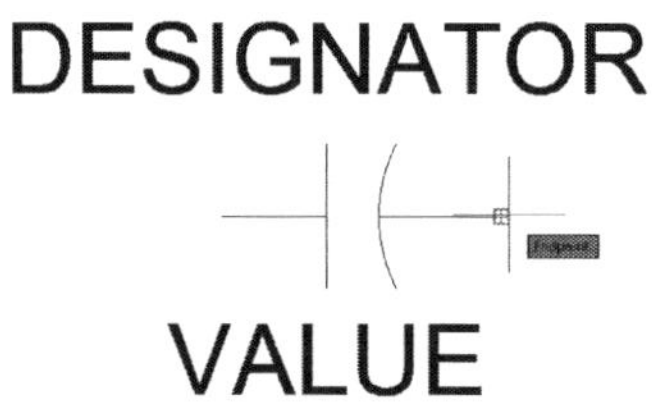

For the insertion point select the endpoint of the right horizontal line.

88.

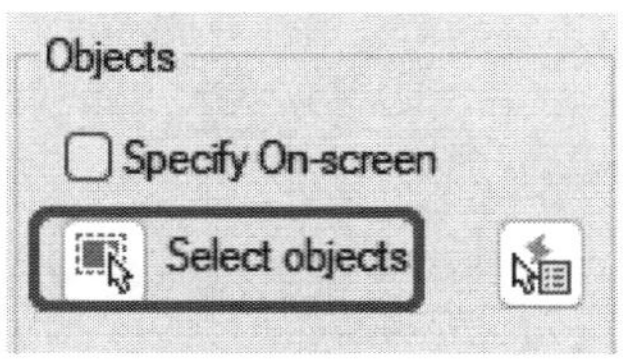

Click **Select objects**.

89.

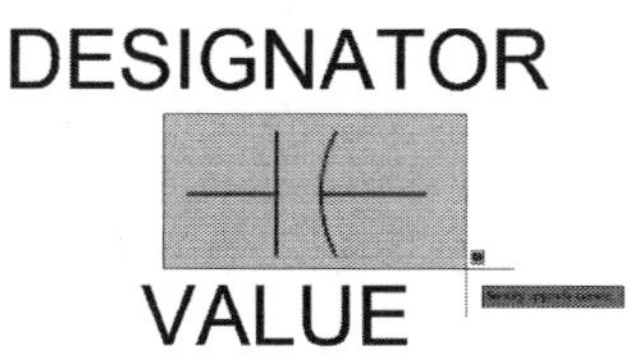

Select the symbol entities (the arc and lines).

Select the Designator attribute and then the Value attribute.

Click **ENTER.**

90.

Enable **Convert to Block**.

Enable **Scale uniformly**.

Enable **Allow exploding**.

Click **OK**.

91.

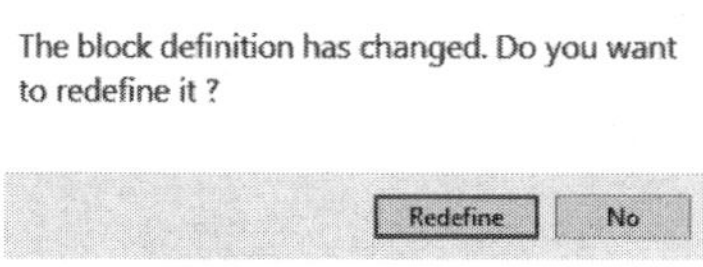

If a dialog appears asking to redefine the block, click **Redefine**.

92.

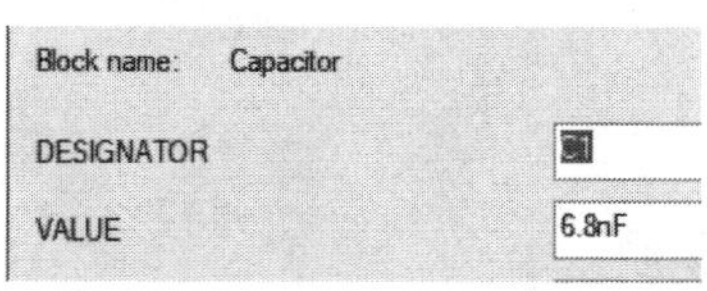

The attribute dialog appears where you can edit the designator and value.

The block appears with the attribute values.

Click **OK**.

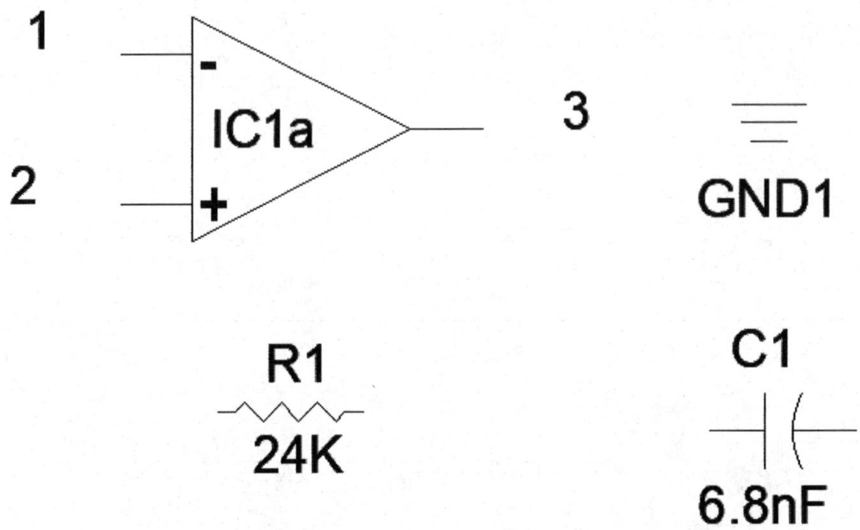

You now have all the tools you need to create the circuit diagram.

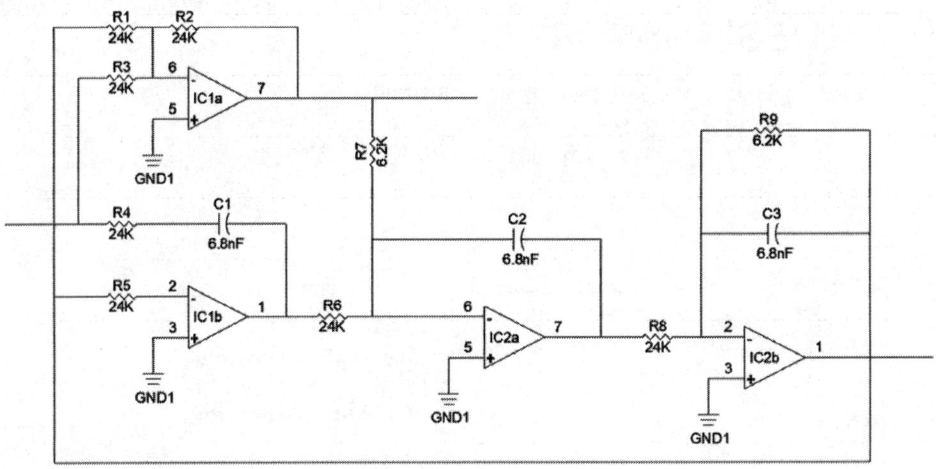

93. Lay out the circuit as shown.

94. *For the R7 resistor:*

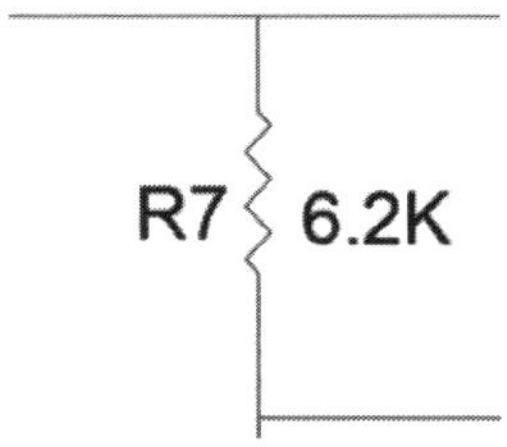

We want to rotate and reposition the attributes for this block.

Type **–ATTEDIT** on the command prompt.

Click **ENTER** until prompted to select the attribute.

Select the R7 attribute.

Select **P** to modify the position.

Place the attribute to the right of the symbol.

Select **A** to modify the rotation angle.

Specify the new rotation angle as **90**.

Use the P option again if you need to reposition.

Click N to exit the command.

Repeat to rotate and position the 6.2K value.

95. Use the Donut command to create the small filled circles which designate junctions or nodes.

Use an inside diameter of 0.

Use an outside diameter of 0.1.

Then just left pick to place the nodes.

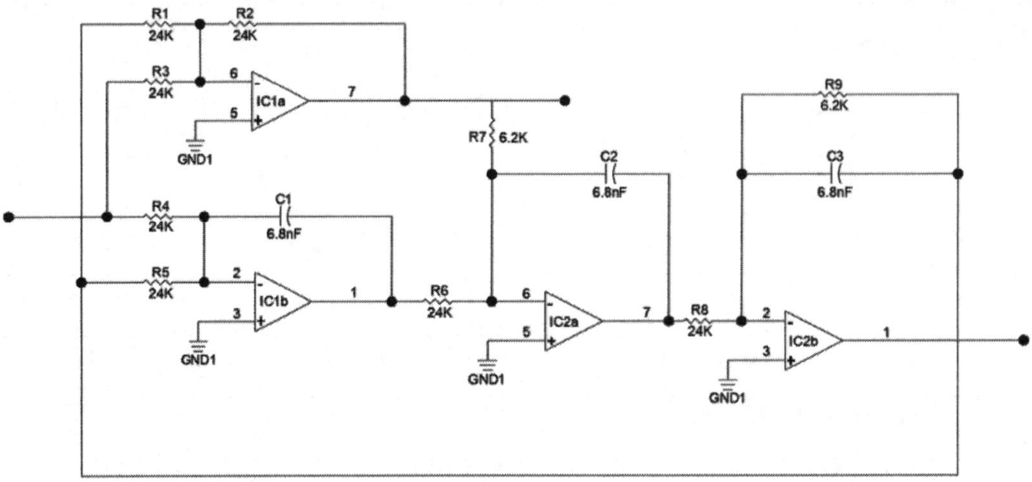

96. 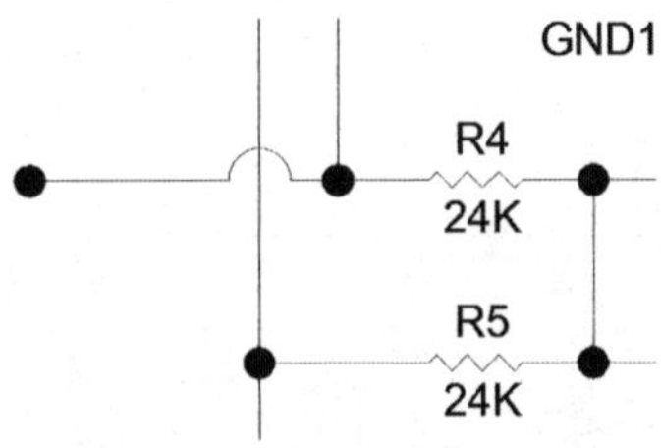

We have two cross over wires.

To create:

Place a circle with 0.1 radius, then trim to make the arc.

97. Complete by placing the final three labels at the nodes using Single Line text.

Verify that all the designators and values are correct.

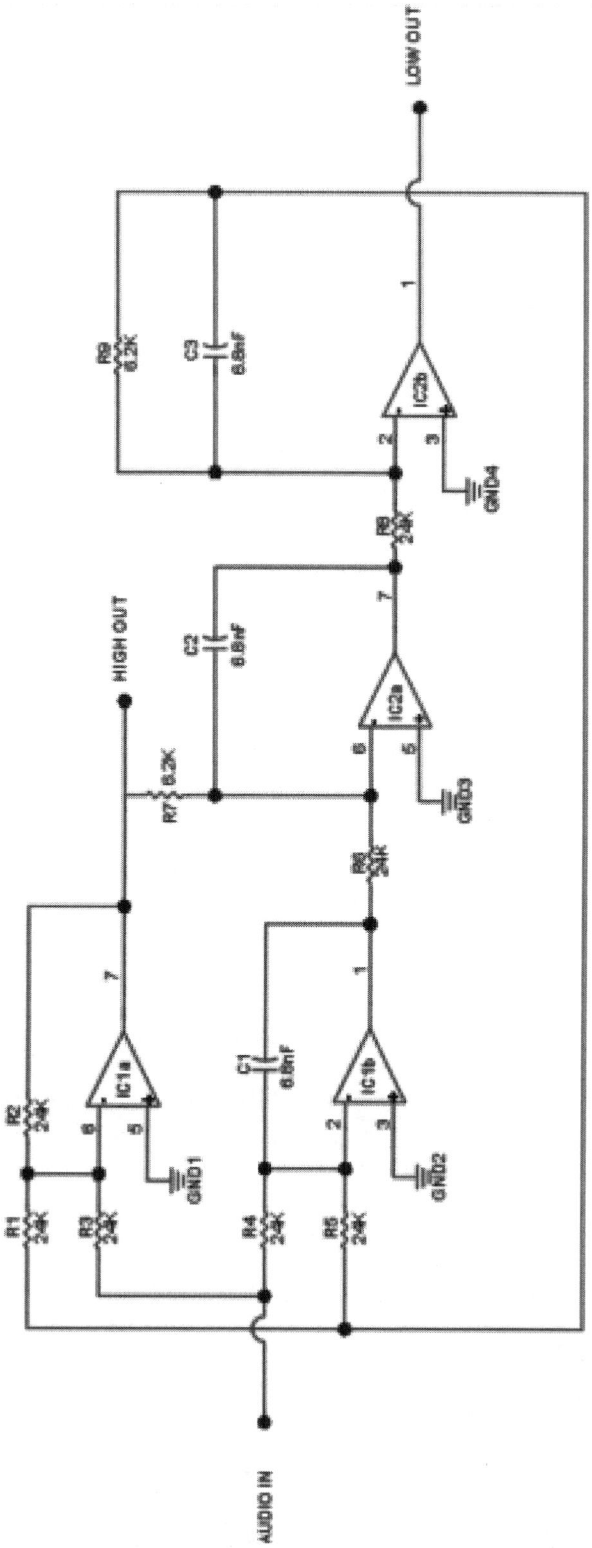
LOW OUT
HIGH OUT
AUDIO IN
GND1
GND2
GND3
GND4

Command Exercise

Exercise 11-9 – Copy Text Styles Using Design Center

Drawing Name: **textstyle1.dwg, textstyle2.dwg**
Estimated Time to Completion: 5 Minutes

Scope

Copy text styles from one drawing to another using the Design Center.

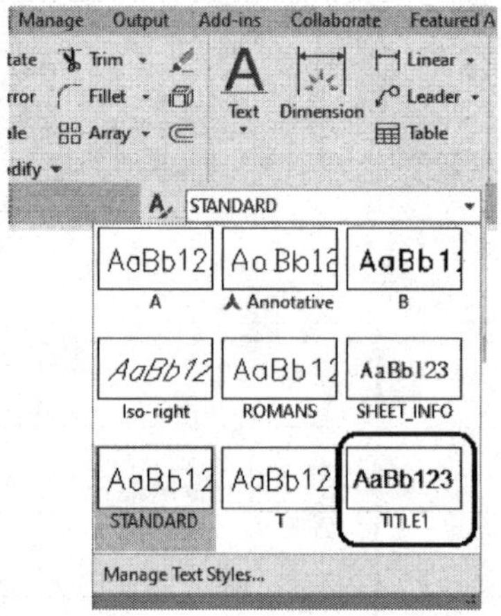

Solution

1. Open *textstyle1.dwg.*

2. 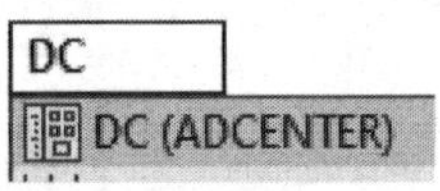

   Type **DC** on the command line to launch the Design Center.

3. 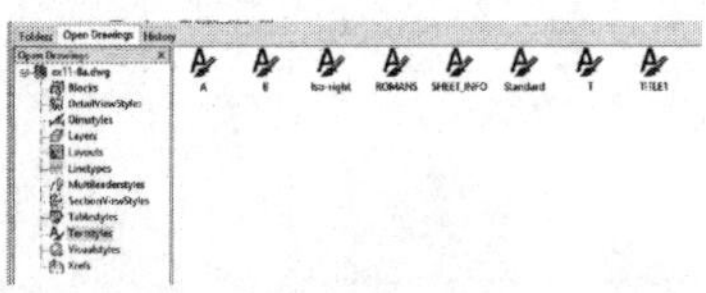

   Select the **Open Drawings** tab on the Design Center.

   Highlight the **Textstyles** category to see what text styles are available inside the drawing.

4. 

   Click on **Open** file.

5. 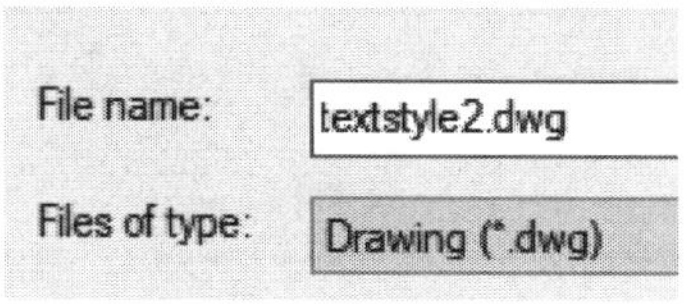

Locate the *textstyle2.dwg* file.

Click **Open**.

6. 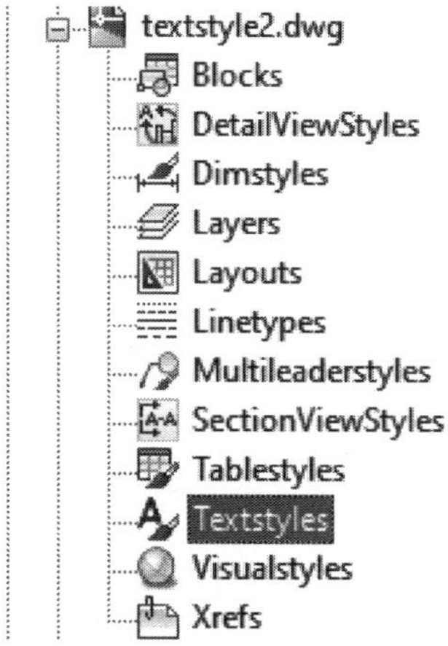

Highlight the **Textstyles** in the textstyle2 drawing.

A list of available textstyles will display.

7. 

Highlight the **TITLE1** textstyle in the Design Center.

8. Drag and drop the **TITLE1** text style into the textstyle1 drawing.

Close the Design Center.

Notice that even though you opened the textstyle2 drawing in the Design Center, only one drawing is open inside of AutoCAD.

9. 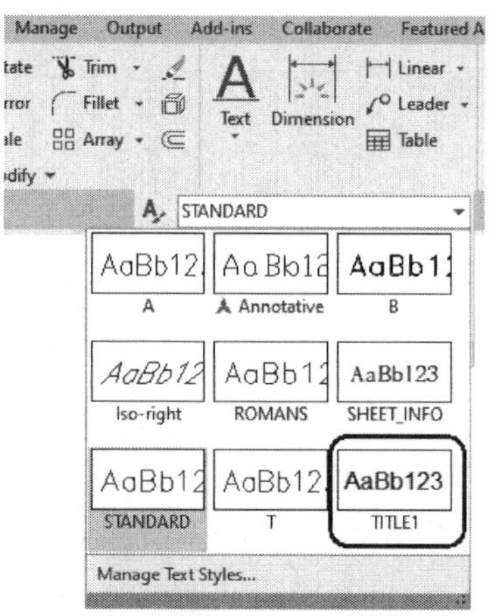

Verify that the text style has been copied over.

Expand the Annotation panel on the Home tab and inspect the text styles listed.

The text style should be listed in the Text Panel.

Command Exercise

Exercise 11-10 – Modify a Block

Drawing Name: **blockedit.dwg**
Estimated Time to Completion: 15 Minutes

Scope

Modify a block.
Modify a hatch.

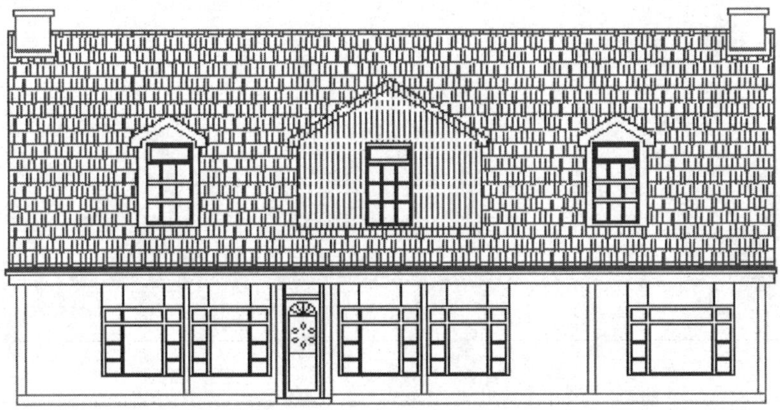

Solution

1. 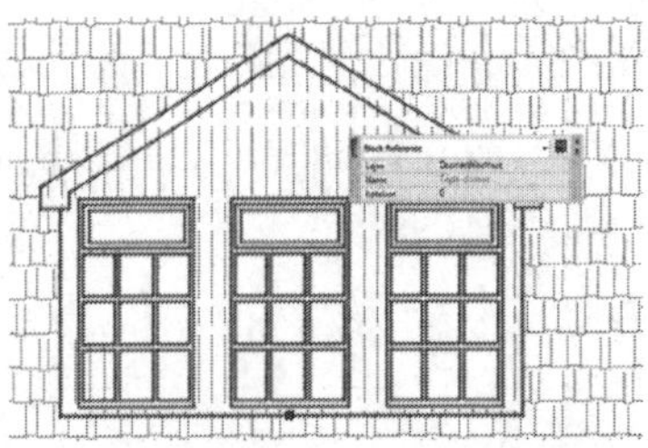

Select the middle Triple-dormer block.

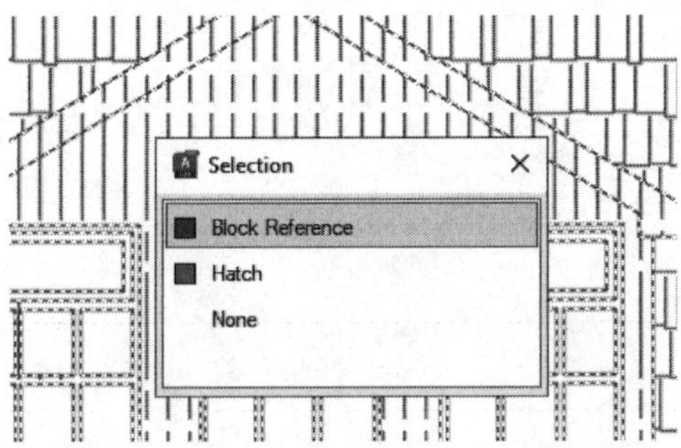

The selection filter dialog can help you select the block.

2. 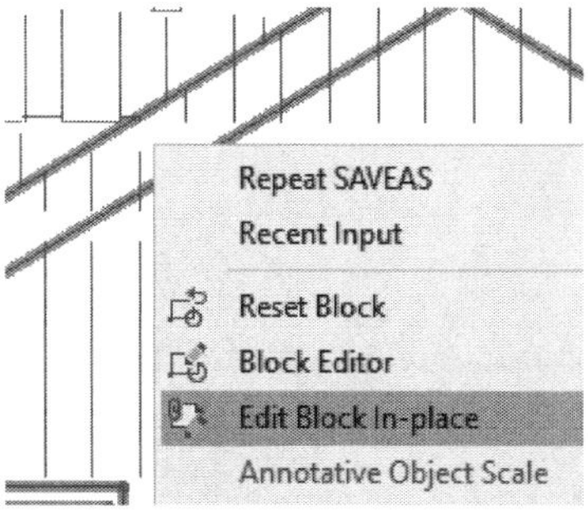

Right click and select **Edit Block In-place**.

3. 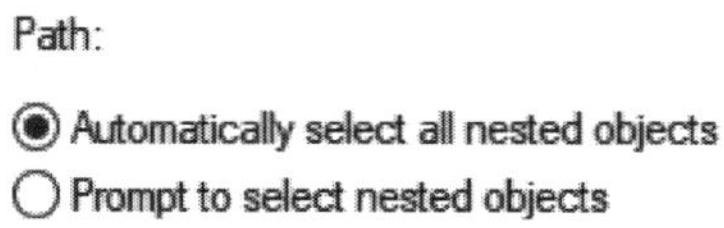

Enable '**Automatically select all nested objects**'.

Click **OK**.

4. 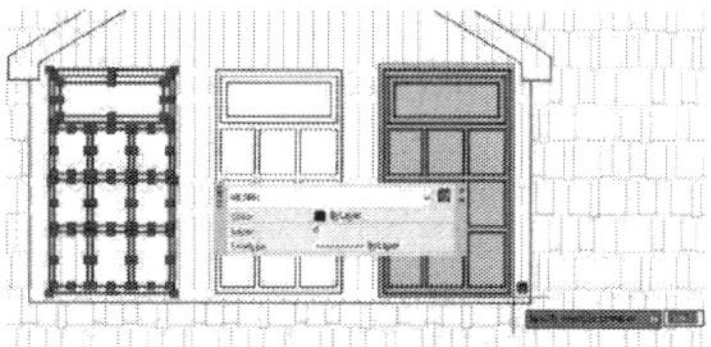
Select the left and right windows.

You can select each individual line or window around each area. Be careful to only select the windows!

5. 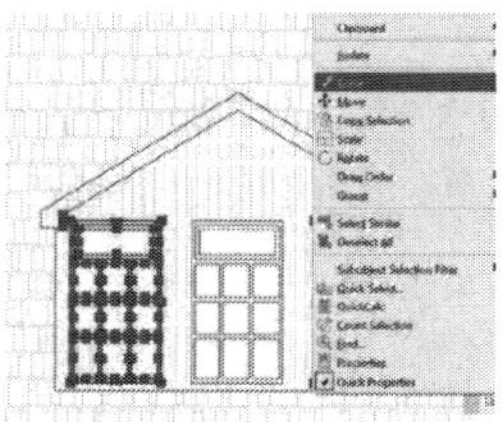
Right click and select **Erase**.

6. 

On the Edit Reference panel on the ribbon, select **Save Changes.**

7. 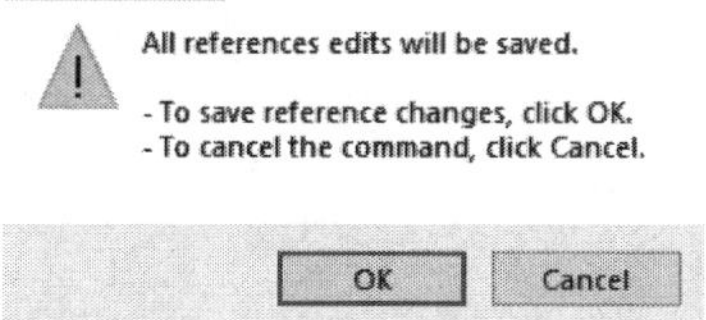

Click **OK.**

8. 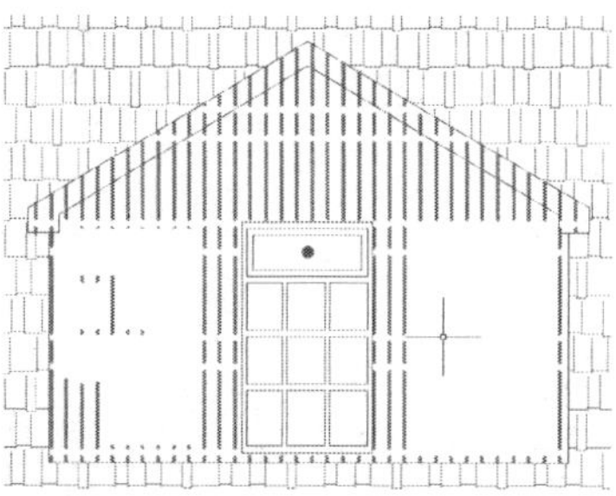
Select the hatch inside the dormer.

9. 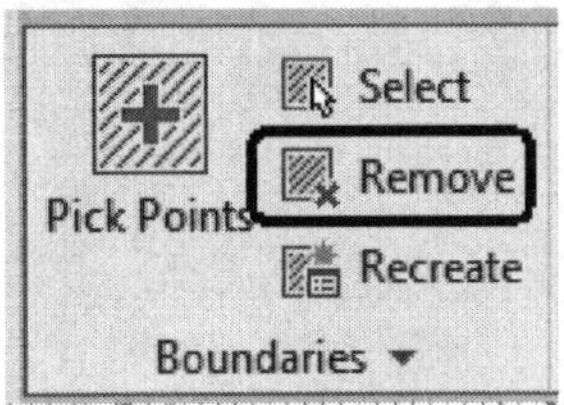

Select **Remove** to delete the boundaries created by the deleted windows.

10. 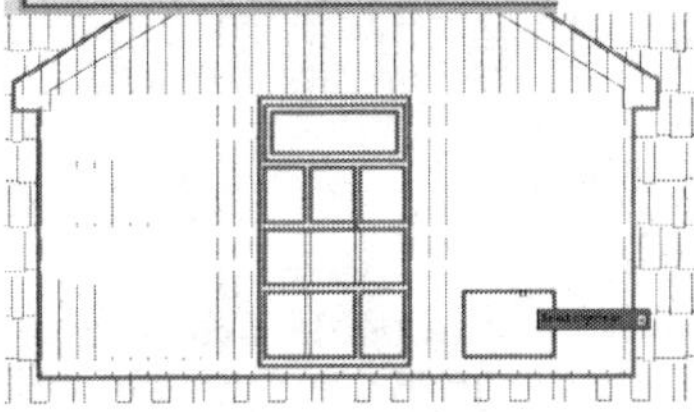

Select the lines and rectangles for the two deleted windows.

Click **ENTER.**

11. 

Select **Close Hatch Editor** on the ribbon.

12. 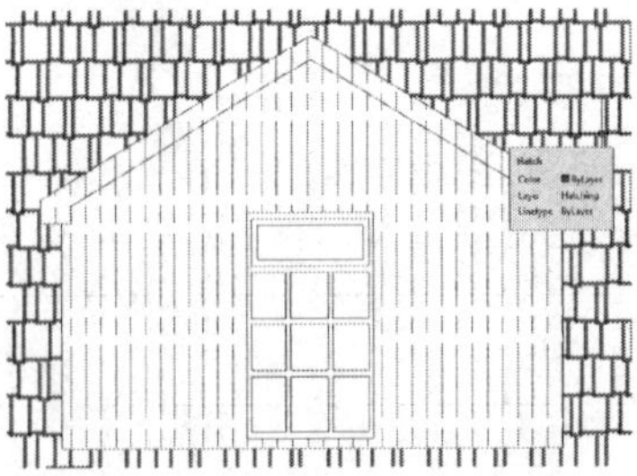

The hatch regenerates to fill the dormer.

If the hatch doesn't regenerate properly, you may have to re-do the exercise to remove the unwanted lines.

Detect and Convert

Command Locator

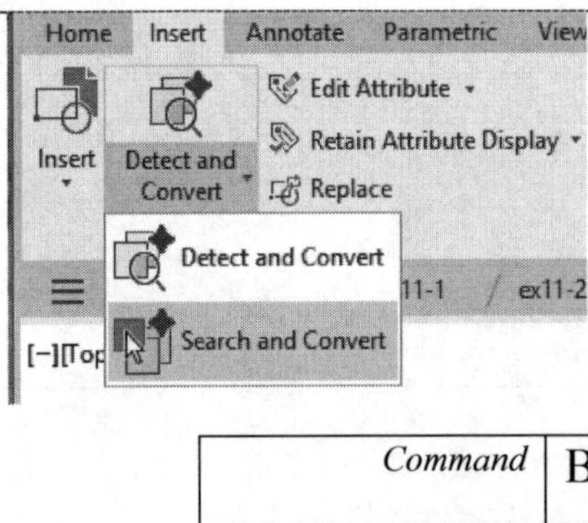

Command	BDETECT
Ribbon/Insert/Block *or* *Home/Block*	**BDETECT**

Command Overview

Detect and Convert analyzes drawings to quickly identify objects that can be converted to blocks. This feature saves time, increases productivity, and reduces errors in the block conversion process.

AutoCAD Detect and Convert uses Autodesk AI to scan your drawing and identify objects that can be converted into blocks.

General Procedures:

1. Launch the BDETECT command.
2. AutoCAD scans the drawing for similar geometry.
3. Identify the geometry you wish to convert to blocks.

Tips & Tricks

If the automatically selected primary instance has a minor drafting error, use the **Change Primary** option on the review toolbar to select a cleaner version of the geometry elsewhere in your drawing before hitting convert.

If text is identified along with geometric elements, it can be converted into attributes.

If your drawing has several potential blocks to be created, convert one asset, save the file, and then proceed to the next set.

Command Exercise

Exercise 11-11 – Detect and Convert

Drawing Name: **detect.dwg**
Estimated Time to Completion: 10 Minutes

Scope

Use BDETECT to convert existing geometry to blocks.
Replace existing geometry with an existing block.
Create new blocks using BDETECT.

1.

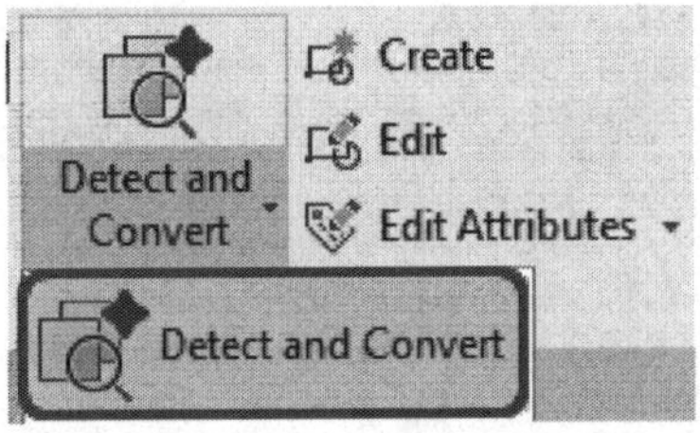

On the Home ribbon:

Select Detect and Convert.

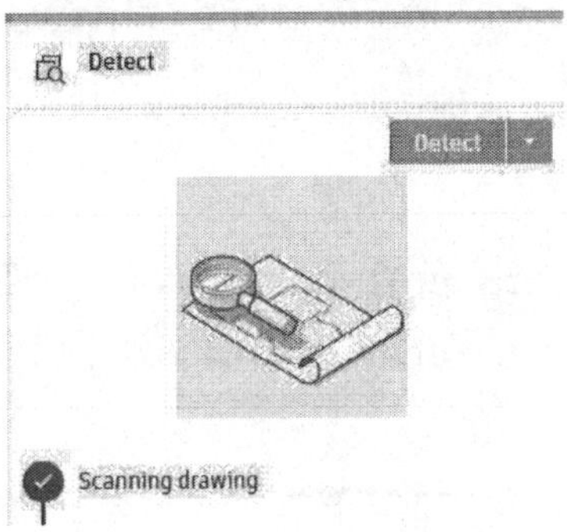

AutoCAD will scan the drawings to locate geometry that can be converted to blocks.

2.

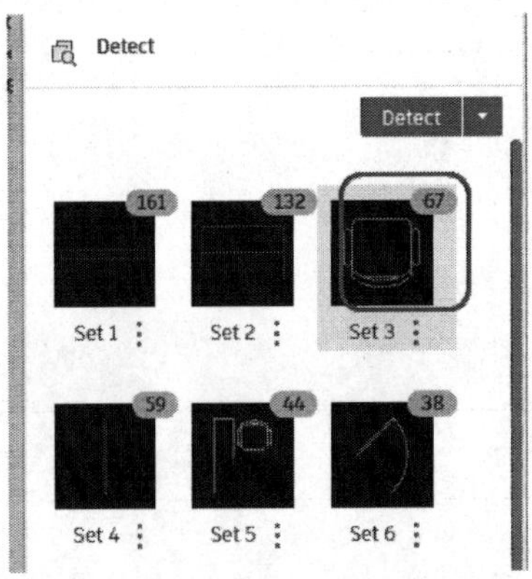

Locate the geometry for the chair.

There are 67 chairs in the drawing.

Click on the chair to select it.

3. 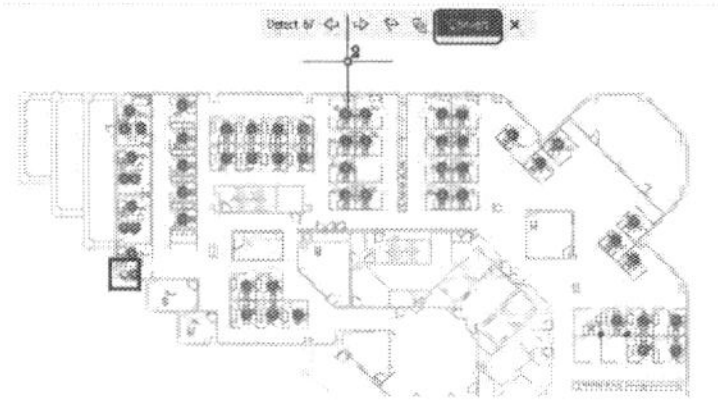

AutoCAD highlights all the geometry that would be converted to a block.

The rectangle identifies the chair that will be used as the primary instance to define the block.

On the small toolbar:

Click **Convert**.

4. 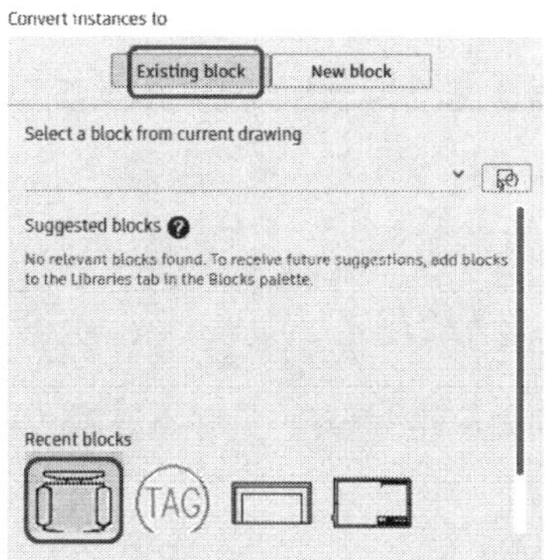

There is another chair block in the drawing.

Enable **Existing block**.

Select the desk chair block.

5. 

Assign the block to layer: **Chairs.**

Click **Convert.**

6. 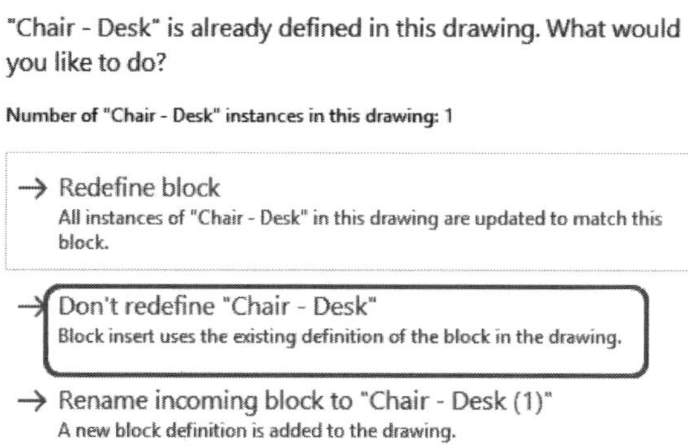

Select **Don't redefine 'Chair-Desk'**

7. 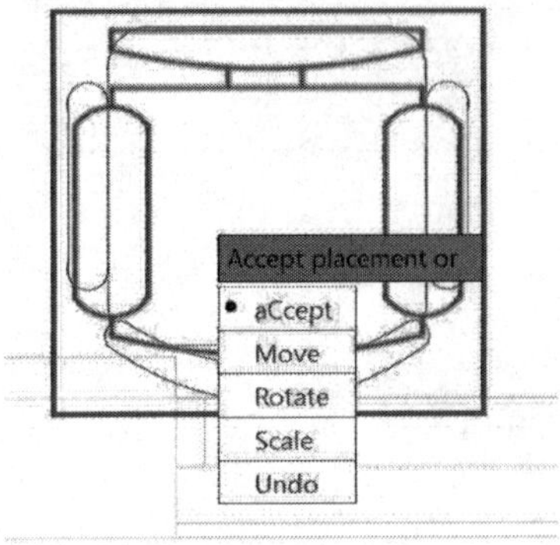

AutoCAD zooms into the primary definition and overlays the new block over the chair.

Use **Rotate** to re-orient the chair so it is facing the correct way.

Select a basepoint.

Rotate the chair 180 degrees.

Click **Accept**.

8. 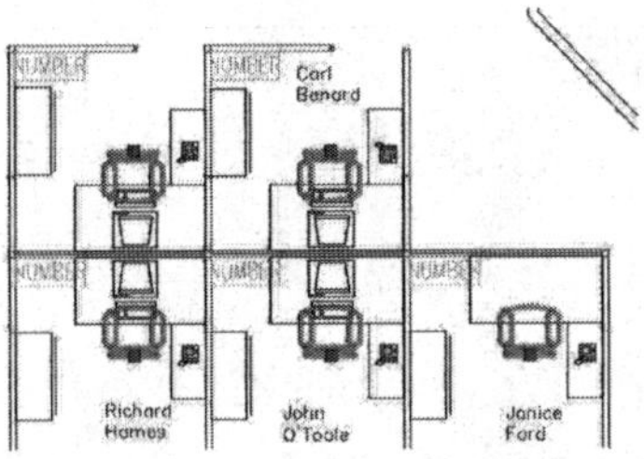

All the chairs are replaced with the new block.

Click **ESC** to release the selection.

9. Save as *ex11-11.dwg*.

Review Questions

1. **T F** If you insert a titleblock into a drawing and then modify the external titleblock drawing, it will automatically update in the drawing(s) where it was inserted.

2. You have a local block with multiple insertions in a drawing. You need to modify the block. You explode one of the block insertions and make the change. You then use BLOCK and select the modified former block. You assign the original block name to the modified block. What happens to the other block insertions in the drawing?

    ❑ They remain unchanged.
    ❑ They are deleted.
    ❑ They update to the new block definition.
    ❑ They become unnamed blocks.

3. **T F** If you do not assign an insertion point to a block, it will by default use the center of the object selected.

4. An insertion point for a block can be defined by:

    ❑ Entering an X, Y, and Z value in the Block Definition dialog box.
    ❑ Selecting a point.
    ❑ Enabling the Align Below Previous Attribute.
    ❑ All of the above.

5. **T F** Blocks can have names up to 255 characters long and include spaces.

6. **T F** When defining a block, you can determine the units or if it will be Unitless. For example, if a block were defined with units of inches and then inserted into a drawing whose base units were millimeters, it would automatically scale by a factor of 25.4.

7. Attributes are created using the _________ command.

    ❑ ATTREQ
    ❑ ATTDIA
    ❑ ATTDISP
    ❑ ATTDEF

8. **T F** When you explode a block, the geometry returns to its original properties.

Review Answers

1. **T F** If you insert a titleblock into a drawing and then modify the external titleblock drawing, it will automatically update in the drawing(s) where it was inserted.

    False

2. You have a local block with multiple insertions in a drawing. You need to modify the block. You explode one of the block insertions and make the change. You then use BMAKE and select the modified former block. You assign the original block name to the modified block. What happens to the other block insertions in the drawing?

    They update to the new block definition.

3. **T F** If you do not assign an insertion point to a block, it will by default use the center of the object selected.

    False

4. An insertion point for a block can be defined by:

    All of the above

5. **T F** Blocks can have names up to 255 characters long and include spaces.

    True

6. **T F** When defining a block, you can determine the units or if it will be Unitless. For example, if a block were defined with units of inches and then inserted into a drawing whose base units were millimeters, it would automatically scale by a factor of 25.4.

    True

7. Attributes are created using the _________ command.

    ATTDEF

8. **T F** When you explode a block, the geometry returns to its original properties.

    True

Lesson 12.0 – Viewports and Layouts

Estimated Class Time: 2.5 Hours

Objectives

This section will cover how to create a drawing Layout from a Model and how to plot a drawing. The general idea is to create the drawing in the Model space window and plot the drawing from the paper space Layout window. Drawings may also be plotted in Model space. There are advantages and disadvantages to using the Model or Layout mode to plot a drawing.

Model Space is the environment in which you create your two–dimensional drawing, or your three–dimensional model. Paper Space (Layout) is the environment where you set up your drawing or model to plot. Although you can plot your drawing in Paper Space or in Model Space, there are certain advantages to setting up your drawing to plot in Paper Space. In Paper Space, you can create multiple views at multiple scales of the same model or drawing. You can also freeze layers in selected paper space view ports. There are a few tricks to working with Paper Space such as controlling line type scales and dimensioning.

Section Objectives:

- **Drawing Layout**

  Create a drawing layout from the drawing Model.

- **Drawing Layout Viewports**

  Insert a title block in the paper space Layout and create drawing views.

- **Adding Viewports**
- **Controlling Viewport Properties**
- **Nonrectangular Viewports**
- **Controlling visibility of layers in viewports**
- **Plotting and Output**
- **Layout Settings**

Option	Model	Layout
Drawing views	In model space, only one view of the drawing may be printed at a time.	In the Layout mode, or paper space, it is possible to plot multiple views of the same drawing. These views can show different parts of the drawing, and views can be zoomed at different scales.
Drawing Layers	In model space, layers are either visible or not since there is only one view port.	In the Layout mode, Layers can be frozen in one view port, but not in the other.
Plot Scale	In model space, the drawing must be plotted to scale. It is therefore important that the drawing limits and title block reflect the drawing scale. Text, Dimension Styles and LTSCALE (linetype scale) must also reflect the plot scale.	Drawings views placed in the Layout Mode must be zoomed to scale (X/XP). Dimensions, notes and the title block are placed in the Layout at a scale of 1. The drawing Layout is plotted at a scale of 1.
Drawing Revisions	In model space, the drawing must be revised in each instance the image is copied in the drawing (for instance if a detail was shown at a scale of 1:1 and 1:10).	In the drawing Layout, each view represents a single drawing. Therefore, if a change is made to the drawing in Model space, the changes will automatically be reflected in the Layout view ports.

Drawing Layout

Command Locator

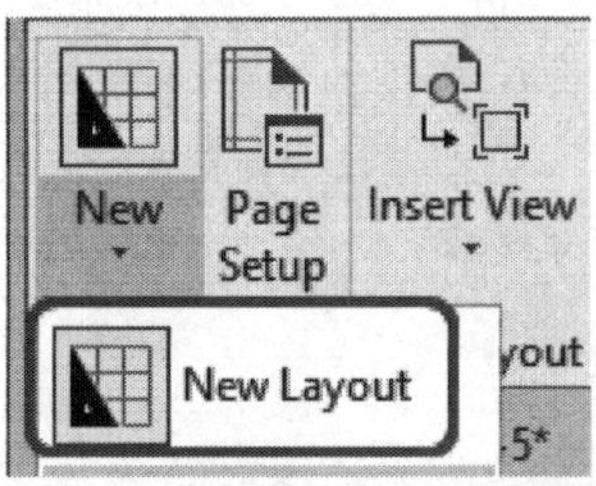

Layout Ribbon	**Layout Panel/New Layout**
Command	**Layout**
Dialog Box	**Page Setup Layout**

Command Overview

The first time the Layout tab is selected, the user will be presented with the Page Setup Layout dialog box. Plot settings for the drawing layout can be chosen here or specified later by invoking the Plot command. If the default settings of the Page Setup Layer dialog box are accepted (Click OK), the Layout will display a single view of the drawing. The dashed line in the drawing layout will represent the plot area of the paper.

The icon in the lower left corner indicates that the user is viewing the drawing Layout or paper space. When the Zoom command is used in the PAPER space mode, the entire drawing layout is affected. When the Zoom command is used with the viewports in the MODEL space mode (see next section), only the active viewport will be zoomed. The Title block should be inserted in the Layout PAPER space mode. The Title block should always be slightly smaller than the paper size, because the plot area will always be less than the paper size, as indicated by the dashed rectangle.

General Procedures:

1. Create the drawing in Model space mode.
2. Select the Layout tab in the Drawing Window.
3. Select OK to accept the Page Setup Layout defaults.
4. Use the Block Insert command to insert a Title Block.

Tips & Tricks

- *The Layout Page Setup can be changed by invoking the Plot command or the Page Setup command.*
- *Select the Model tab in the drawing window to return to Model space.*
- *The Title Block insertion point is typically 0,0. The scale factors should be 1 and the rotation angle should be 0.*
- *Place the viewport on a layer that is set not to plot and you will never have to worry about the viewport border being visible in your plots.*
- *Create as many layouts as needed to show all the views of the drawing necessary.*
- *You may name the layout using up to 255 characters; however, only the first 32 characters will show on the name tab.*
- *You can move your layouts so that they are in a desired order to make it easier to navigate through a drawing set.*
    - *The Layout ribbon will automatically appear when you activate a layout.*

Command Exercise

Exercise 12-1 – Create a New Layout

Drawing Name: **nlayout1.dwg**
Estimated Time to Completion: 5 Minutes

Scope

Create a new layout in the drawing called 'Plan'.

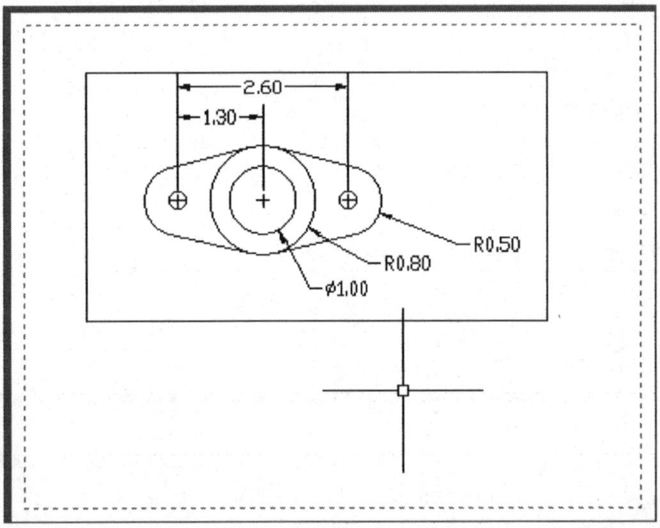

Solution

1. 

Left click on the + tab next to Layout1 to add a layout.

2. 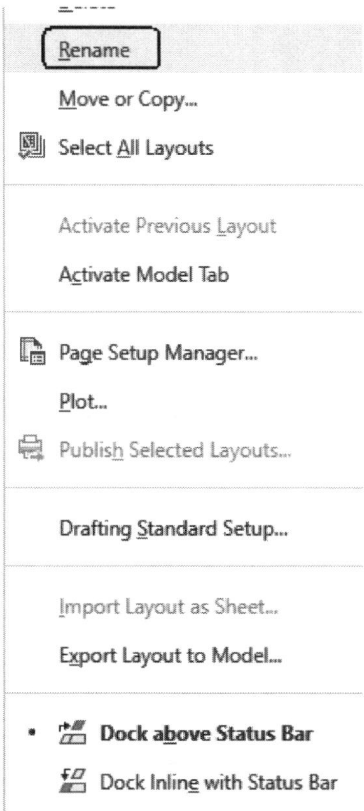

RMB on the new layout tab.

Select **Rename**.

3. 

Type **Plan** to change the layout name.

4. 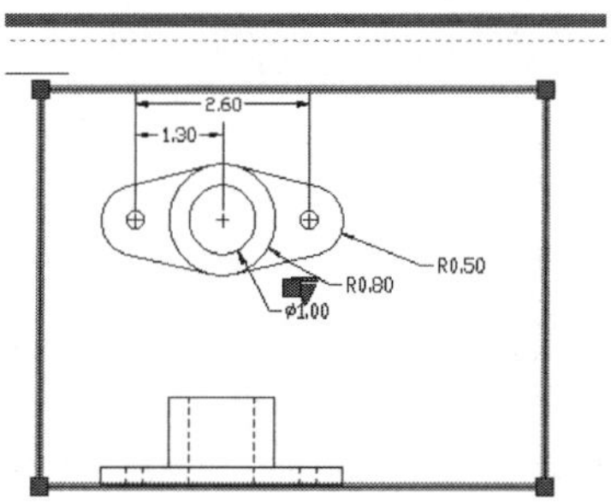

Click on the new **Plan** tab.

Click on the viewport border to activate its grips.

5. 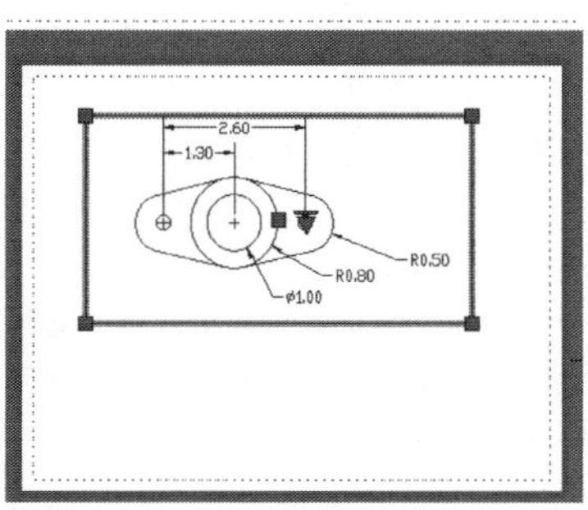

Specify stretch point or [Base point/ Copy/Undo/eXit]:

Stretch the border as shown in the following figure to show only the plan (top) view of the drawing.

Click <**ESC**> to release the grips.

6. 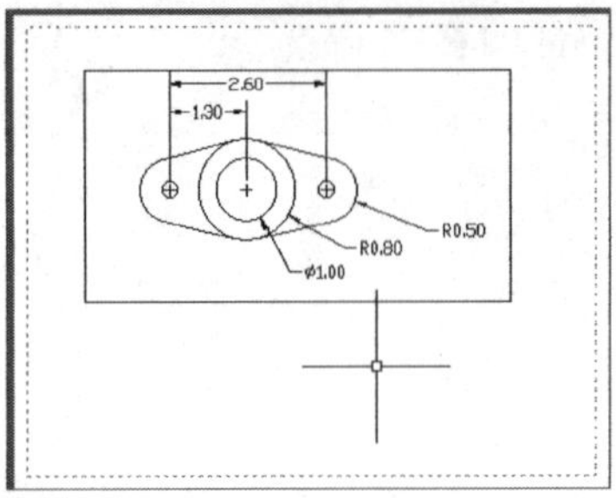

You should only see the top view.

Close without saving.

Viewports

Command Locator

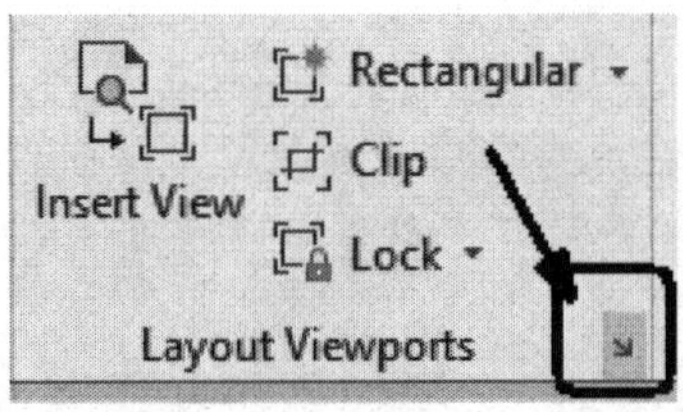

Layout Ribbon	**VIEWPORTS**
Command	**viewports**
Alias	**vports**
RMB Shortcut Menu	**Viewports** *(when New viewports is selected)*

Command Overview

Unlike tiled viewports in the Model space drawing window, viewports in the Layout window can be rectangular or irregular polygon shapes. They can be moved, resized, rotated, and copied using the grip options or the regular Modify commands, and they can be clipped. They can even overlap other viewports. For this reason, they are sometimes referred to as floating viewports. When the drawing is zoomed in the PAPER space mode, the entire Layout is zoomed.

When the Layout viewports are switched from the PAPER space mode to the MODEL space mode from the Status Bar, only the active viewport will be zoomed. Select the viewport to zoom and Zoom All first. Repeat the zoom command by Clicking <ENTER> or by typing Z. Type the scale factor, followed by XP (for times paper space). For example, 1xp would be a scale of 1:1, and 1/2xp would be a scale of 1:2. When all of the viewports have been properly zoomed, switch back to the PAPER space mode by selecting the word MODEL in the Status Bar.

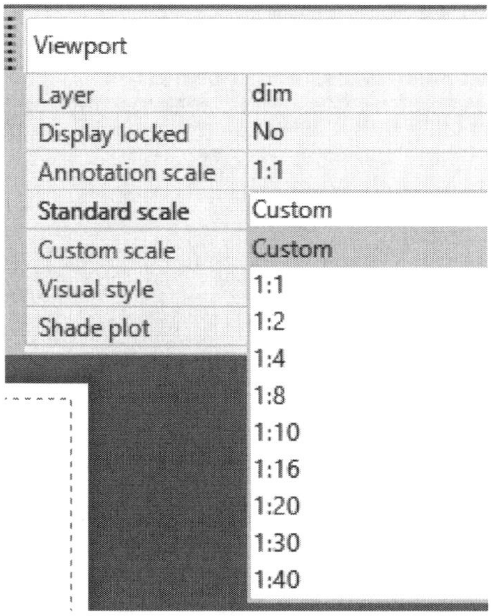

You may also use the Viewport Standard Scale Control. This is a drop-down list of the available scales and is much easier to use than setting the zoom factor correctly. To use this, just select the border of the viewport to scale, then select the scale from the Quick Properties dialog.

The general rule is to create the drawing in the Model space window, and set up the drawing to plot from the Layout tab. Use either the PAPER or MODEL mode to adjust the viewport size and views. Then switch back to PAPER to plot the drawing.

General Procedures:

1. Create the drawing in Model space (the Model tab should be selected).
2. Select the Layout tab in the Drawing Window. Select OK to accept the Page Setup Layout defaults.
3. Use grips to re-size the viewport. Use the Viewports command options to create additional views.
4. Select PAPER in the Status Bar. This will switch the viewport mode to floating MODEL space. Select a viewport and Zoom the drawing view to scale.
5. Select MODEL in the Status Bar to switch the viewport mode back to PAPER space. Add notes, dimensions, etc. and plot the drawing.

- Annotative Scale allows the user to automatically set the scale for dimensions and notes to match the scale of viewports and layouts. You can reset the Annotative Scale on the fly as needed.
- If you elect to use this feature, set up your layouts and viewports before you add any dimensions or text. That way you know what scale you will be using for your views.
- Once you have determined the scale assigned to each viewport, you can set your annotation scale so that it matches and your annotations will automatically scale accordingly.
- You can set the visibility of annotations so only those objects set to the active annotation scale are visible using the Annotation Visibility tool in the Status Bar tray.

Command Exercise

Exercise 12-2 – Add a Viewport

Drawing Name: **nlayout2.dwg**
Estimated Time to Completion: 15 Minutes

Scope

Create a new viewport. Add a scale to the scale list. Set the viewport scale. Lock the viewport display.

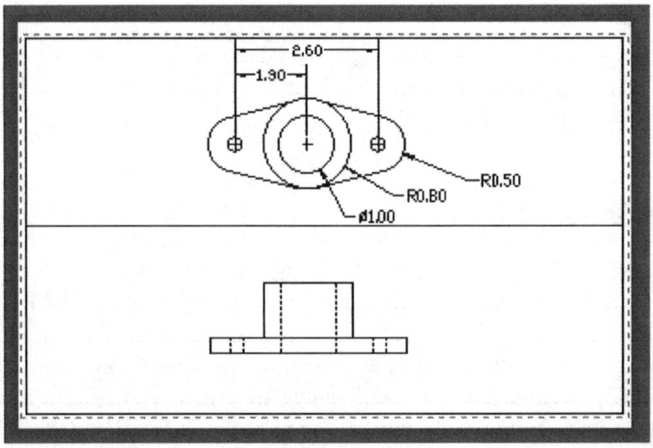

Solution

1. 

Select the Layout 1 tab.

There should not be a viewport on it.
You should see only a blank sheet of paper.

2. 

Set your workspace to **Drafting & Annotation**.

3. 
Verify that Quick Properties is **enabled**.

4. 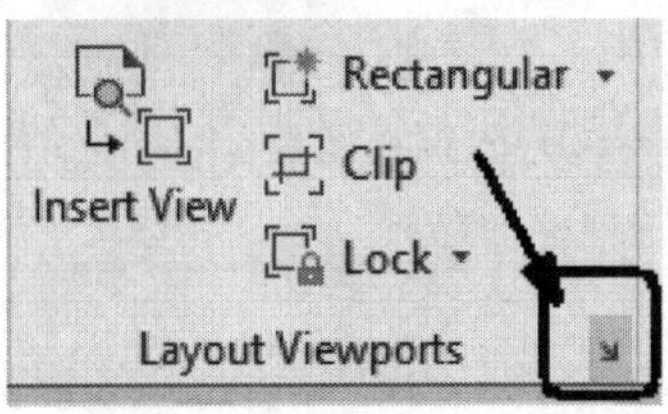

Switch to the **Layout** ribbon.
Select the **Named View** tool on the Layout ribbon
OR
Type **VPORTS** anywhere in the display window.

5. 

Select the **New Viewports** tab.

6. 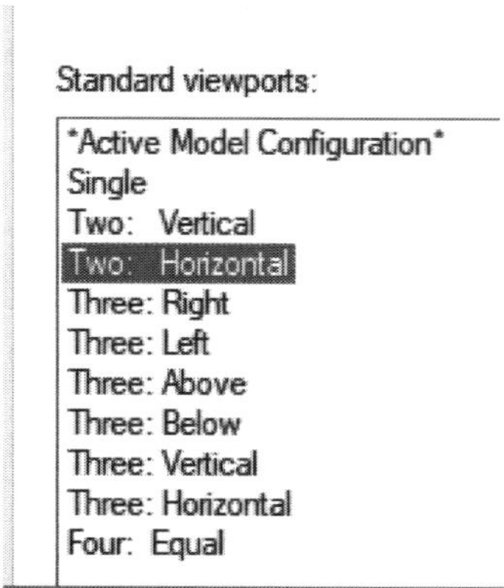

Select the **Two: Horizontal** option.
Click **OK**.

7. 

Select two points (similar to drawing a rectangle).

8. 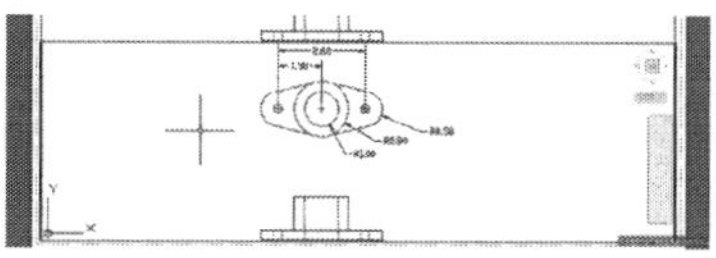

Double click LMB inside the lower viewport to activate MODEL space.

9. 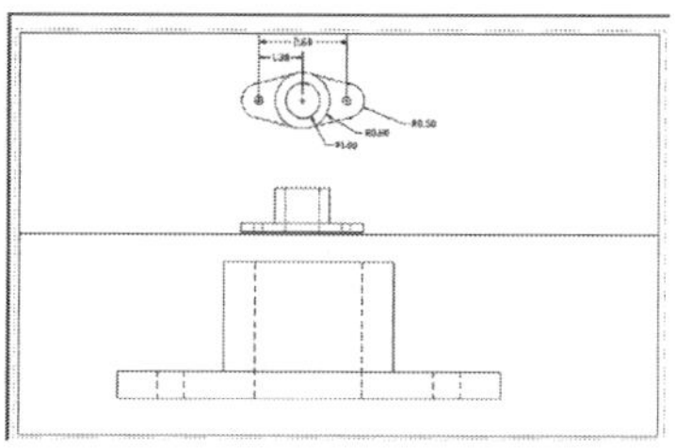

The active viewport's border will appear bold.

You also will see a ViewCube in the upper right corner and the View Controls and Visual Style Controls in the upper left.

Use **Zoom Window** to zoom into the front view of the model.

Click outside of the paper to deactivate the viewport.

10. 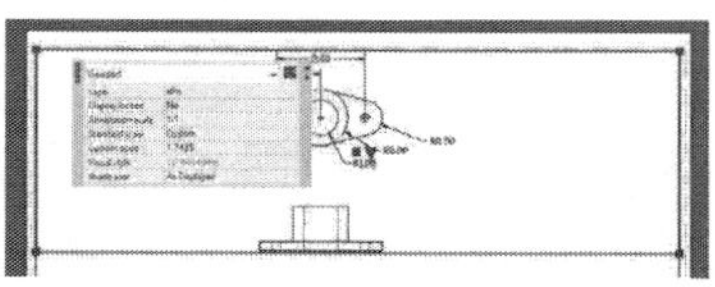

Select the top viewport border so it highlights.

The scale of the viewport is displayed on the Status Bar. Your scale value may be different depending on how you drew your rectangle.

11. 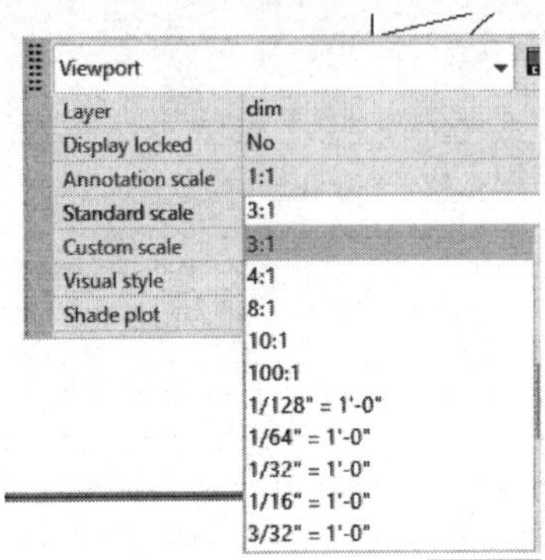

Left click on the viewport scale indicator.

A list of available scales is displayed.

Select the 3:1 scale.

12. 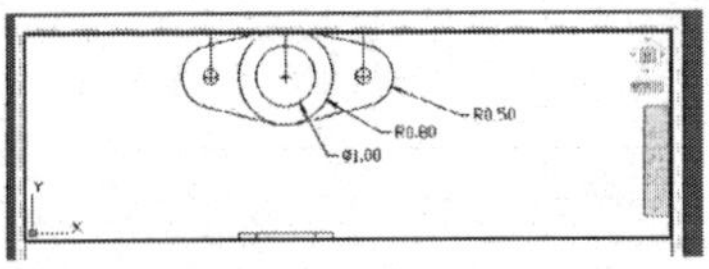

Double click LMB inside the top viewport to activate MODEL space.

The active viewport's border will appear bold.

13. 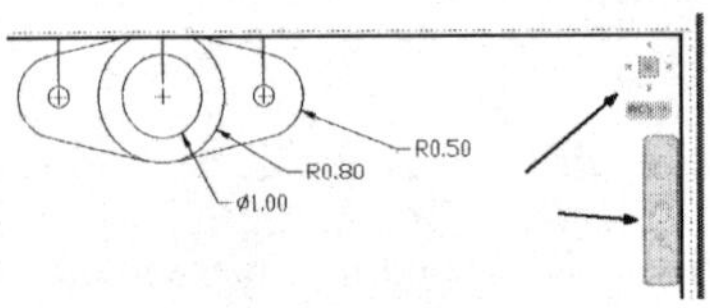

You also will see a ViewCube in the upper right corner.

14. 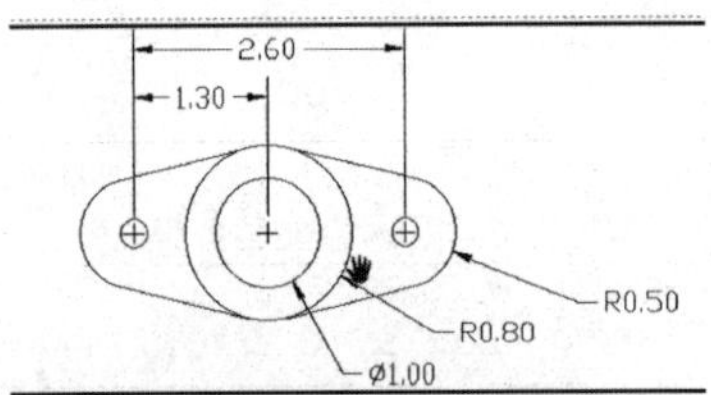

Use **Pan** to position the top view of the model.

Click outside of the paper to deactivate the viewport.

15. 

Select the top viewport border so it highlights.

The scale of the viewport is displayed on the Status Bar.

16. 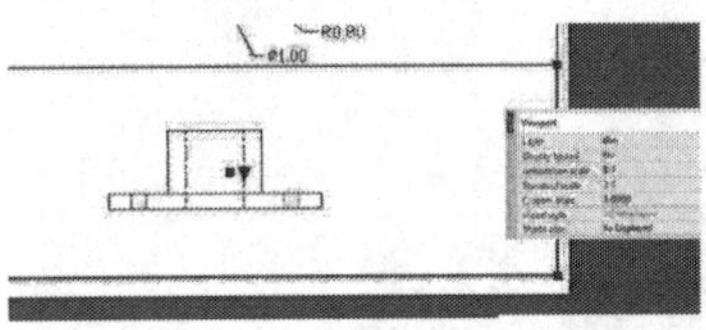

Set the scale for the bottom viewport to **3:1**.

17. 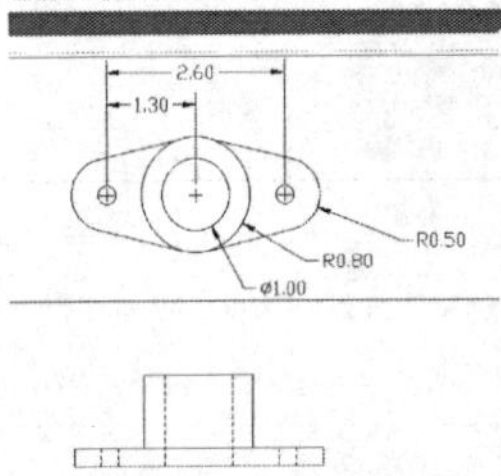

Line up the top and bottom views.

Use PAN to position the views so they are aligned.

18. 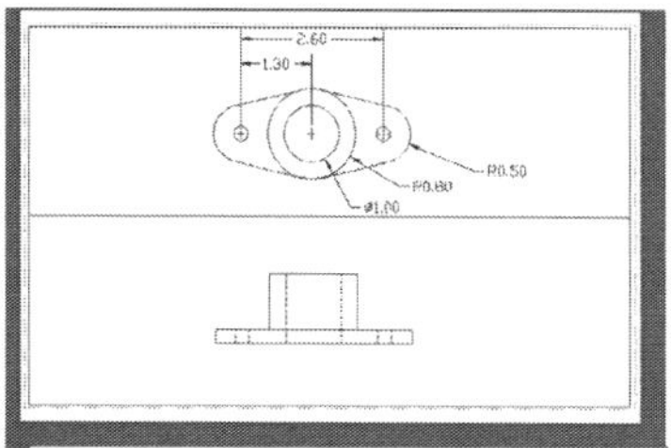

Adjust the sizes of the viewports as needed using grips.

19. 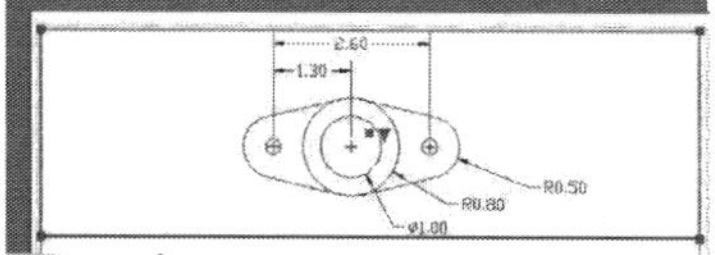

Select the top viewport border so it highlights.

20. 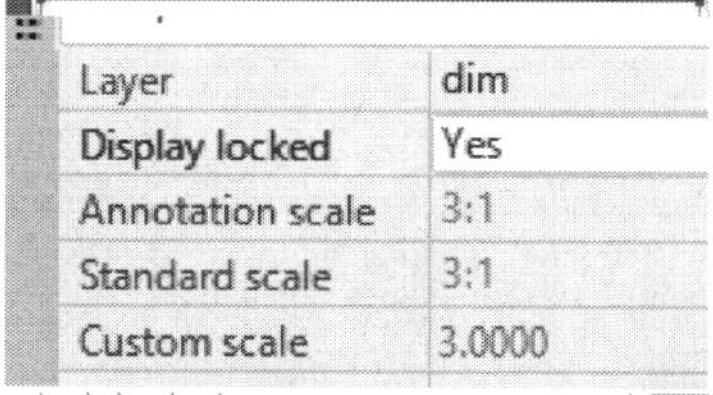

In the Quick Properties dialog:
Set the Annotation scale to **3:1**.
Set Display Locked to **Yes**.

21. 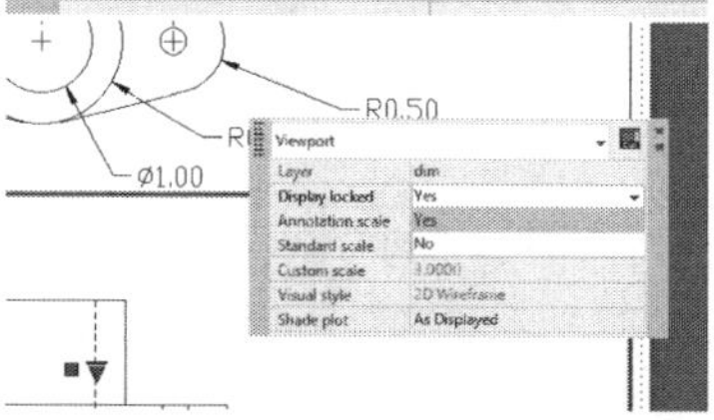

Click **ESC** to release the selection.
Repeat for the bottom viewport.

You can also lock a viewport by selecting the LOCK tool on the ribbon and then selecting the viewport you want to be locked.

22. 

View scale can also be set by selecting the grip on the view inside of model space. This brings up the scale list and allows you to set the view scale.

23. 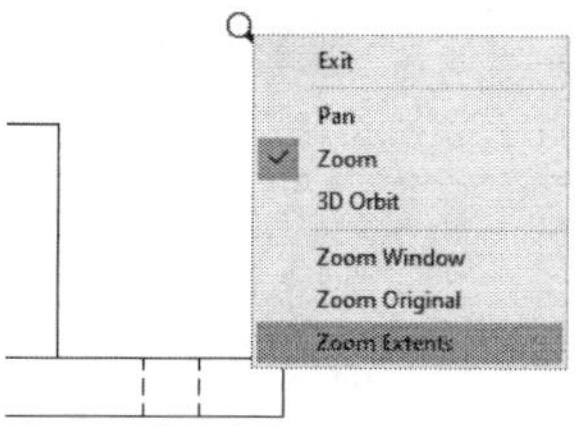

Double click LMB inside the lower viewport to activate MODEL space.

Select **Zoom Extents.**

Note that your display changed, but the view in the viewport did not. That is because you locked the viewport display. It is a good idea to lock your viewport display once you have set up your view to ensure that it does not accidentally get changed as you move about your drawing.

Insert View

Command Locator

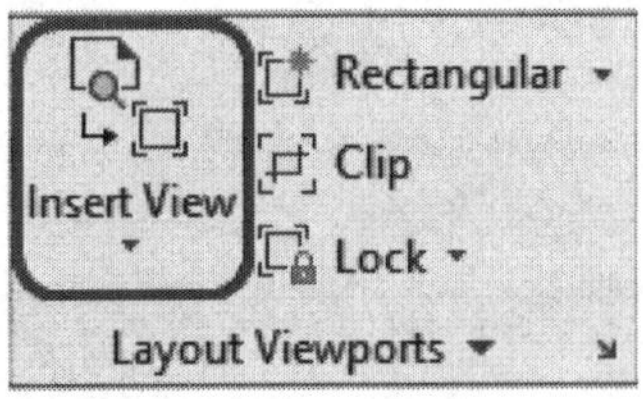

Ribbon/Layout/Layut Viewports	**MVIEW**
Command	**MVIEW**
Alias	**mv**
RMB Shortcut Menu	**ON/OFF/Fit/Shadeplot/Lock/New/Named/Object/Polygonal/Restore/Layer/2/3/4**

Command Overview

Inserts a named view from a palette. If there are no named views, the display will switch to the model tab, and you will be prompted to indicate the view extents. You may also opt to create a desired view 'on the fly'.

General Procedures:

1. Start the **MVIEW** command.
2. If there are named views in the drawing, you will be prompted to select the named view. If there are no named views, you will be asked to define a view.
3. Place the view on the layout.

Tips & Tricks

- *The white area in the layout indicates the actual piece of paper. The paper size is controlled in the Page Setup dialog box.*

Command Exercise

Exercise 12-3 – Insert View

Drawing Name: **insert_view.dwg**
Estimated Time to Completion: 20 Minutes

Scope

Add views to a layout using Insert View and the New View option under Insert View.

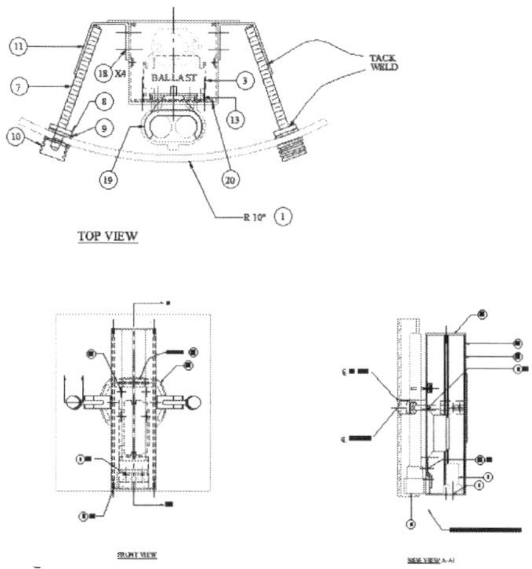

Solution

1. 

Activate the **Layout1** tab.

2. 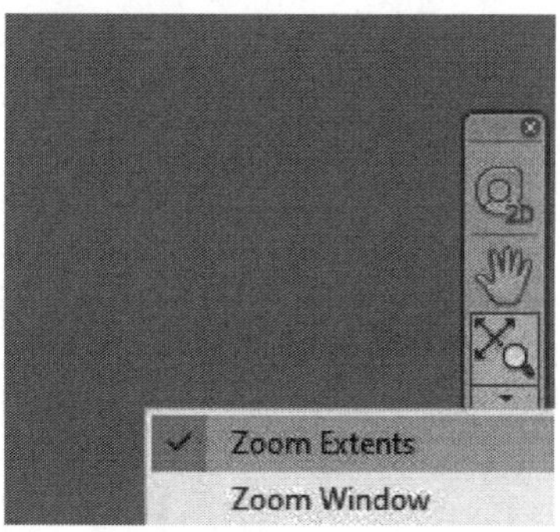

Zoom Extents.

3. 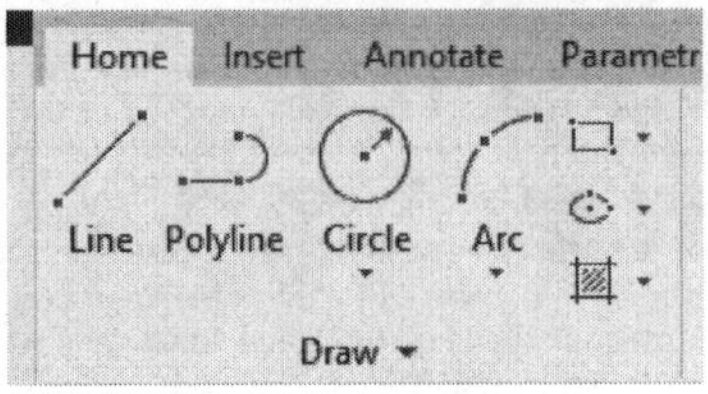

Activate the Home ribbon.

4. 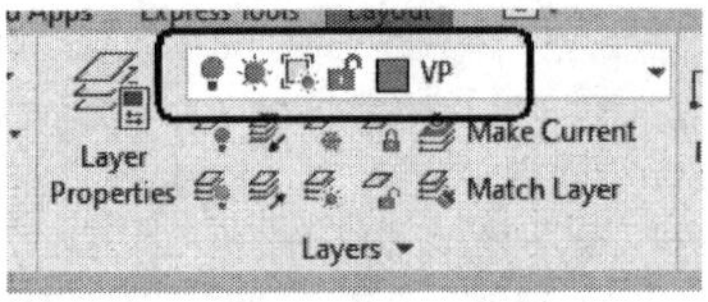

Thaw layer VP and set current.

5. 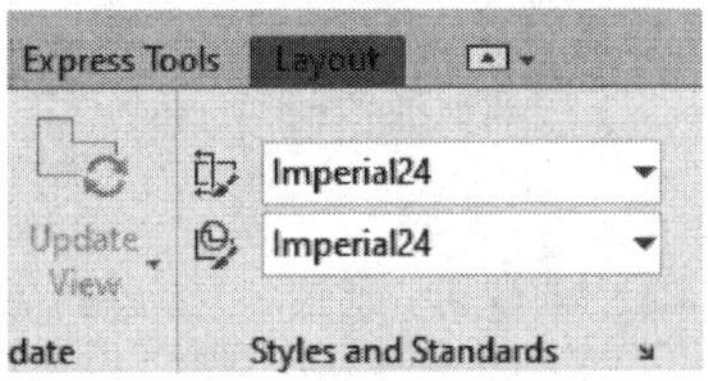

Activate the Layout ribbon.

6. 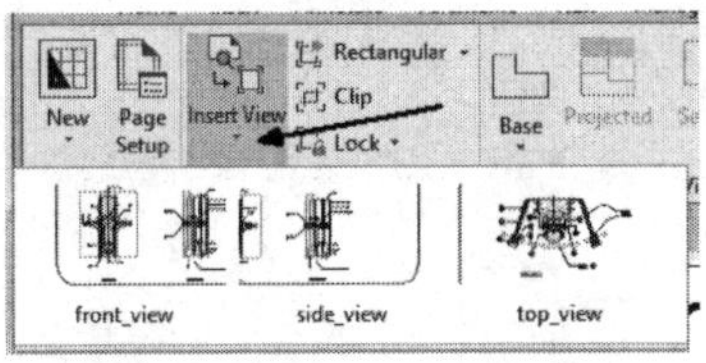

Select the small arrow under **Insert View.**
A preview list of available named views in the drawing will appear.

7. 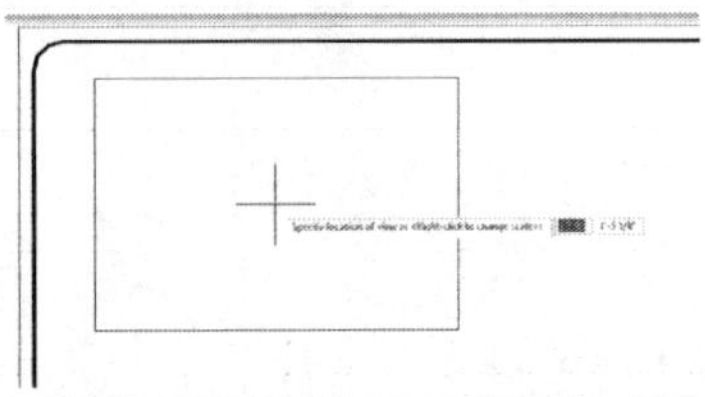

Select the **top_view** and drag onto the layout.

8. 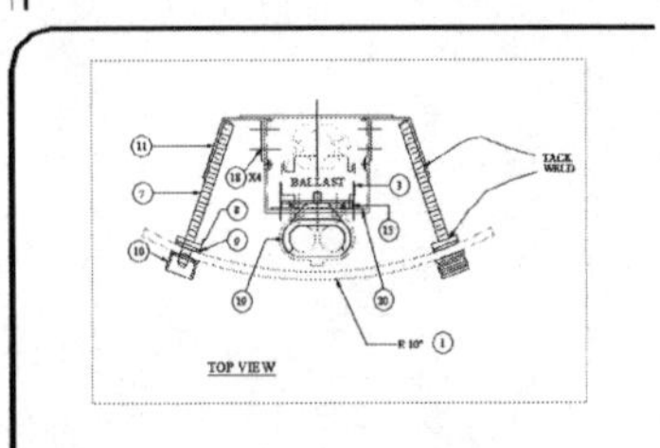

Left click to place the view on the sheet.

9. 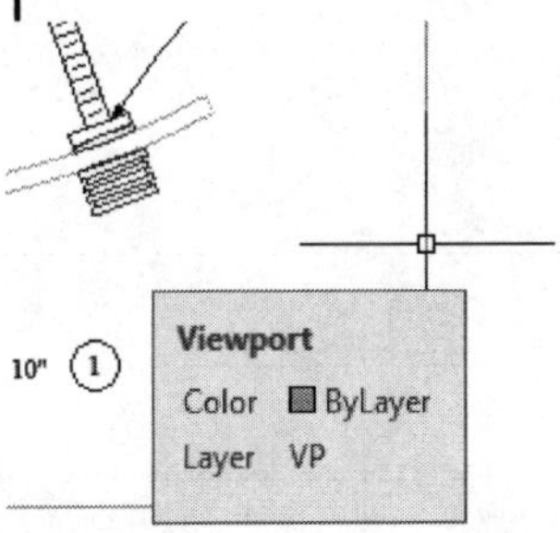

If you hover over the viewport boundary, you will see what layer the viewport was placed on and the view scale.

10. 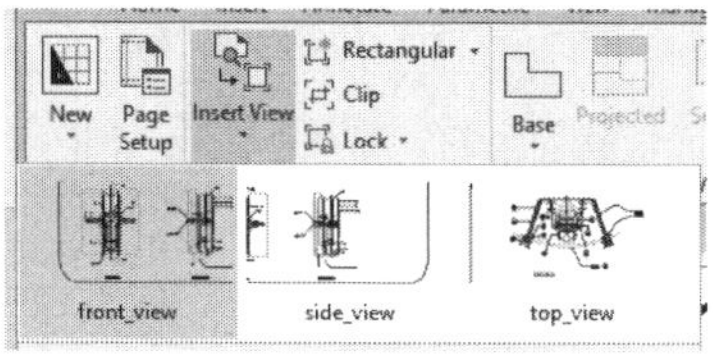

Select **Insert View** on the Layout ribbon.

11. 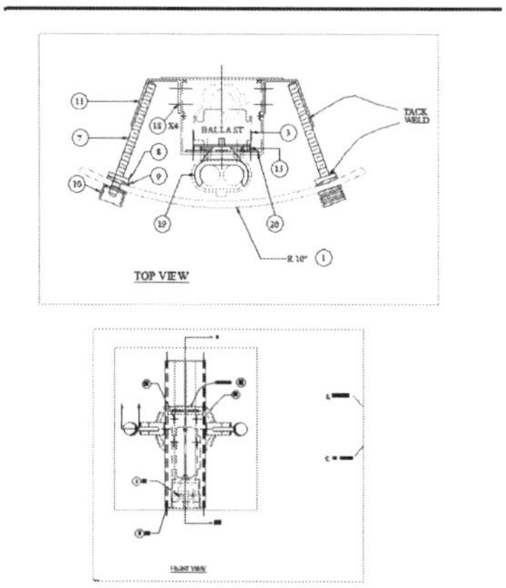

Use the left mouse to drag and drop the front-view on to the sheet.

Place the front_view below the top view.

12. 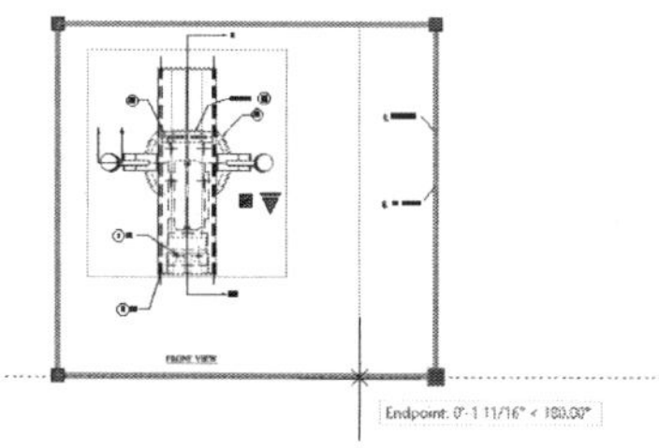

Use the viewport grips to adjust the size of the viewport to only show the front_view.

You can also create a named view on the fly.

13. 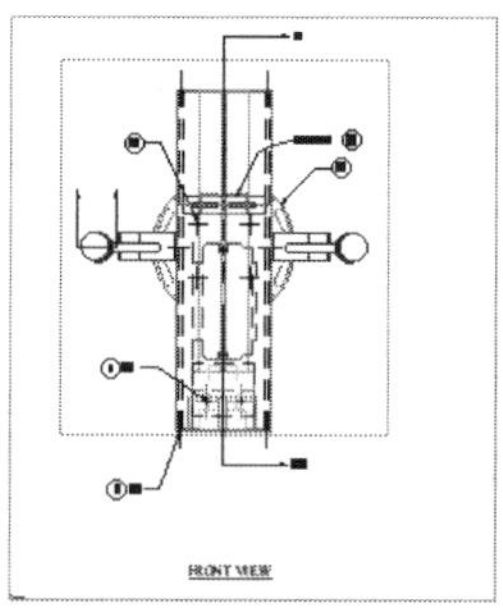

Click **ESC** to release the selection.

14. 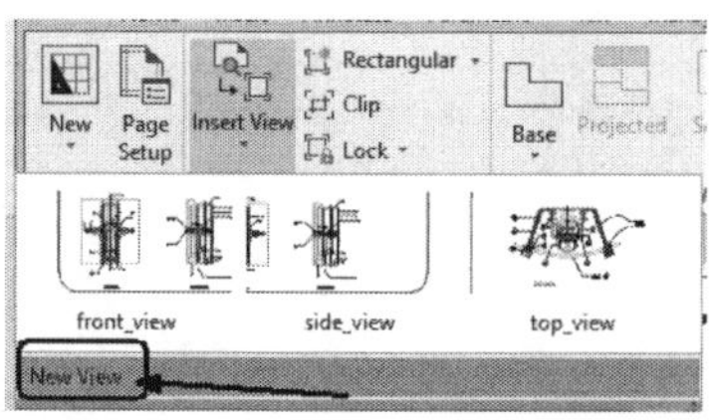

Select **Insert View** on the Layout ribbon.

Select **New View** on the bottom of the drop-down list.

15. 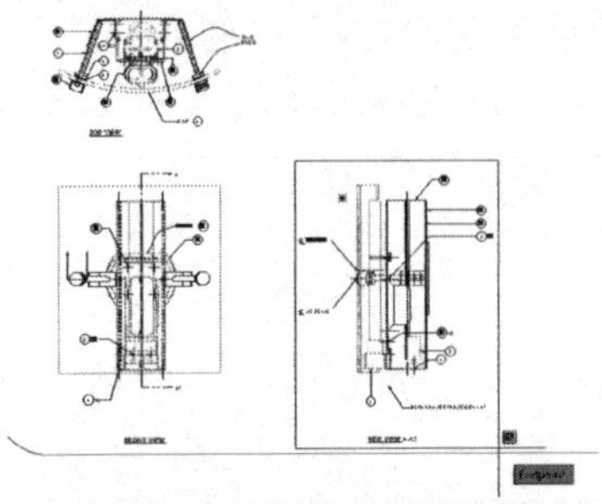

A model space view of the drawing file is opened.

Draw a rectangle/window around the side view.

16. 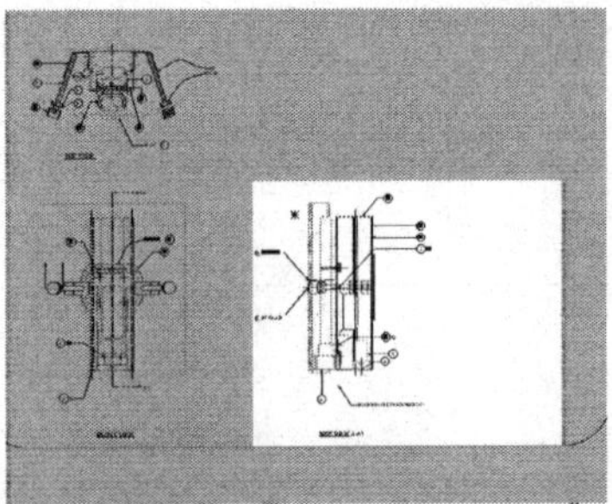

A preview of the selected view will display.

Click **ENTER** to accept the preview.

You will be returned to the layout sheet.

17. 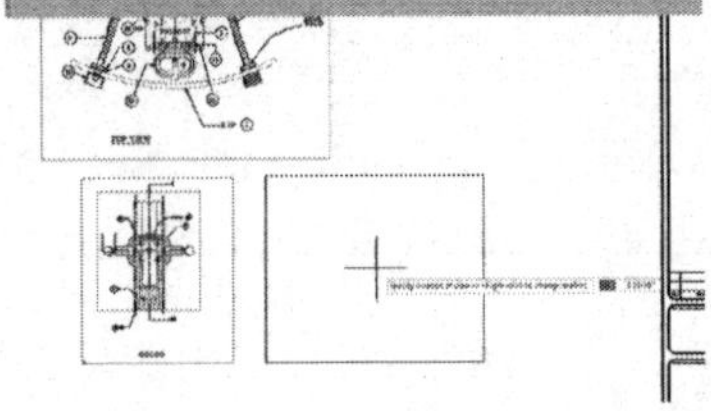

The layout tab will display.

Left click to place the view to the right of the front view.

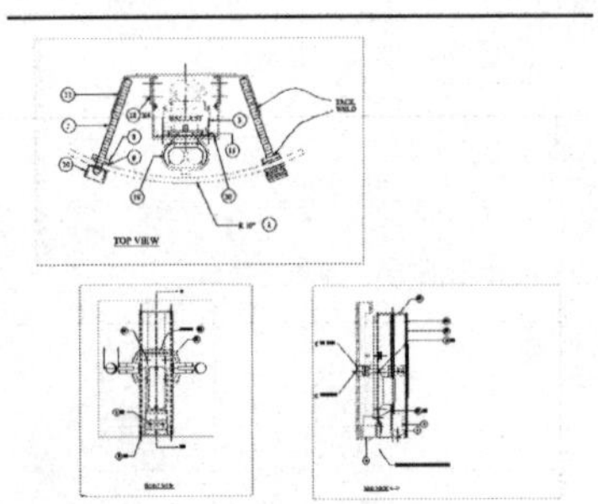

When you create a new view on the fly, it is not saved as a named view.

18. 

Activate the **Home** ribbon.

19. 

Make **Layer 0** the Current layer.

20. 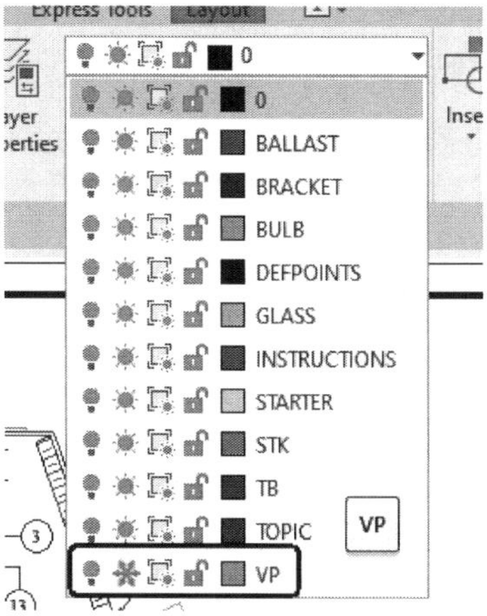

Freeze the **VP** layer to turn off the visibility of the viewports.

21. 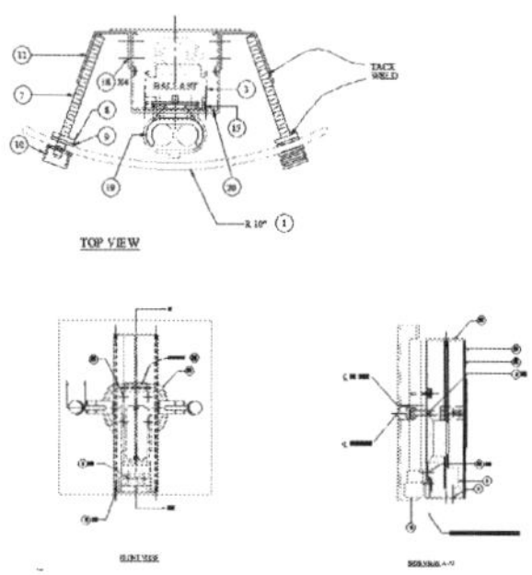

Close without saving.

Command Exercise

Exercise 12-4 – Rotate a Viewport

Drawing Name: **rviewport.dwg**
Estimated Time to Completion: 5 Minutes

Scope

Rotate a viewport.

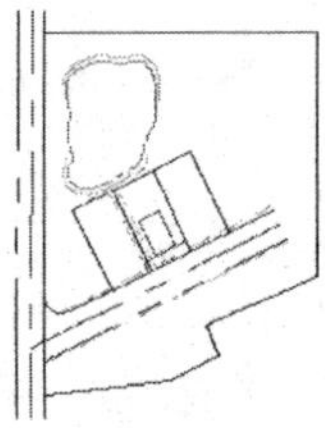

Solution

1. 

Verify that the **Layout1** tab is active.

2. 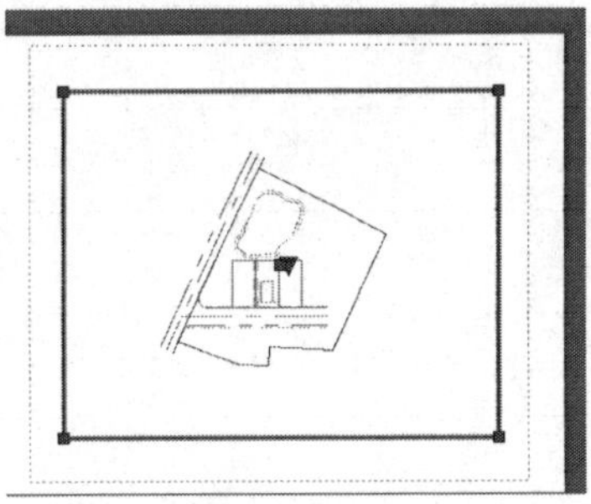

Select the viewport.

3. 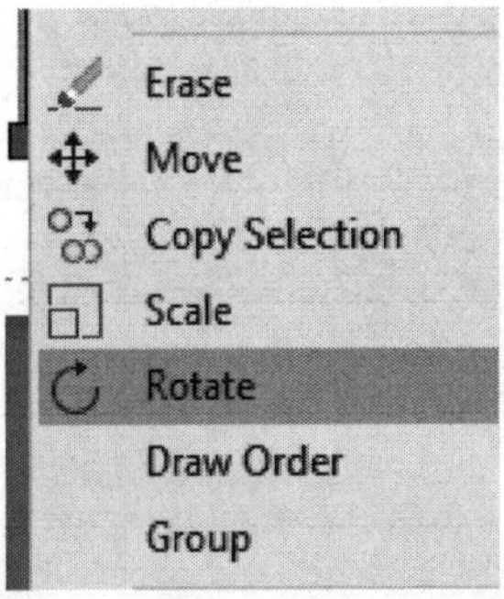

RMB and select **Rotate**.

4.

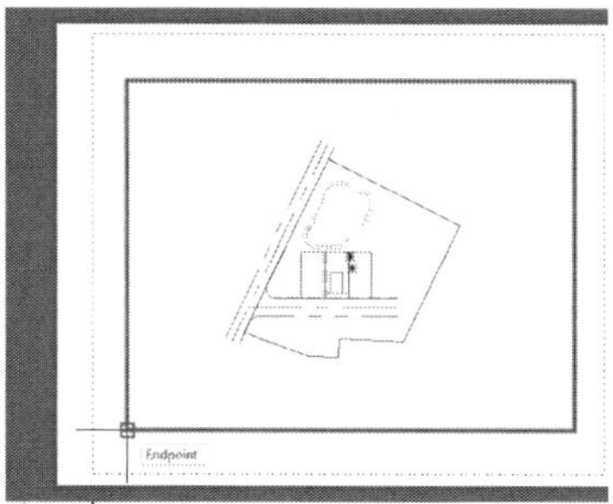

Select the lower left corner of the viewport as the basepoint.

5.

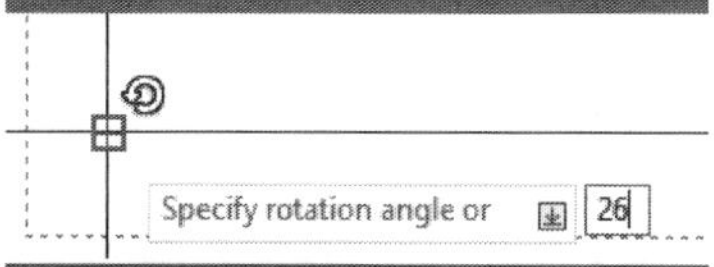

Type **26** for the rotation angle.

Click **ENTER**.

6.

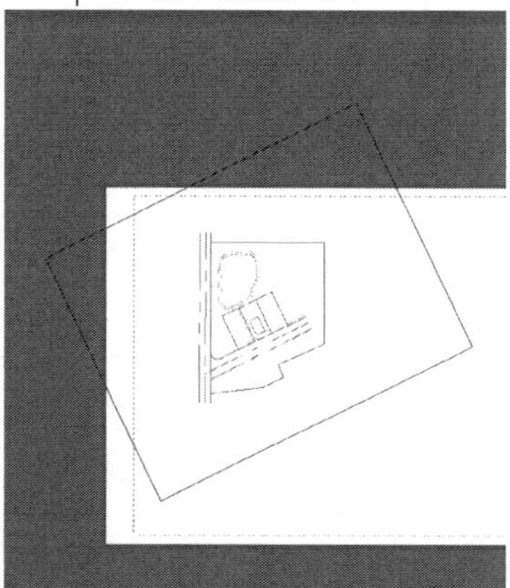

The viewport is rotated.

7.

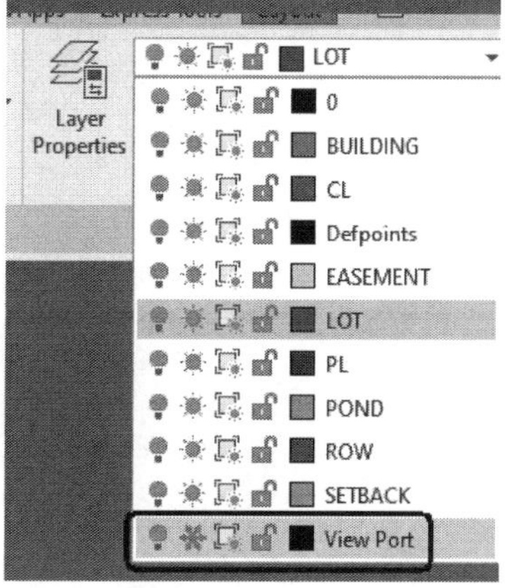

Switch to the **Home** ribbon.

Freeze the viewport layer.

8.

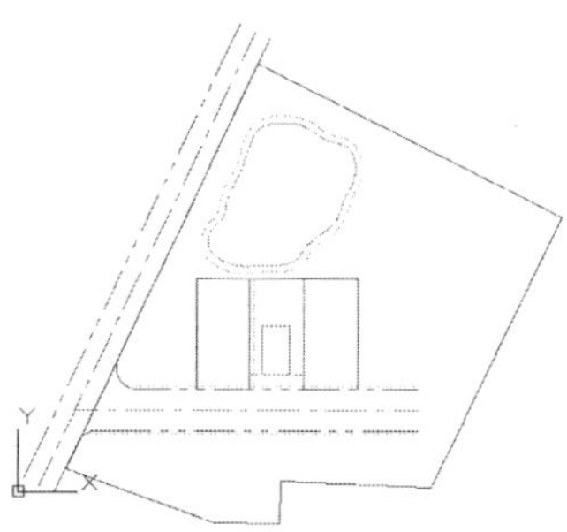

Select the **MODEL** tab.

9. 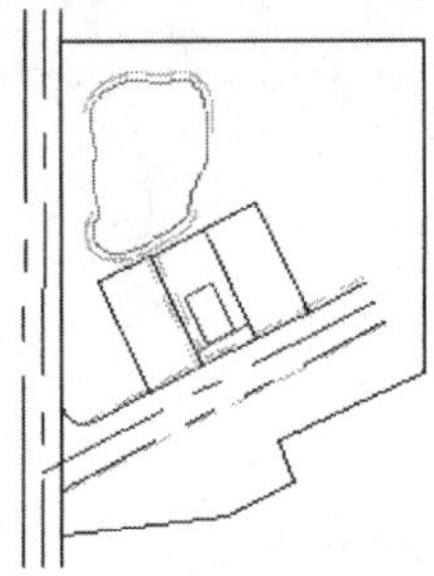

Your rotated view should look like this.

Notice the objects have not rotated in the model tab.

Command Exercise

Exercise 12-5 – Viewport Properties

Drawing Name: **paper1.dwg**
Estimated Time to Completion: 5 Minutes

Scope

Make the floating viewport window frame invisible. Use the Properties Command to set the viewport frame on the VP layer. Freeze the VP layer. Preview the plot.

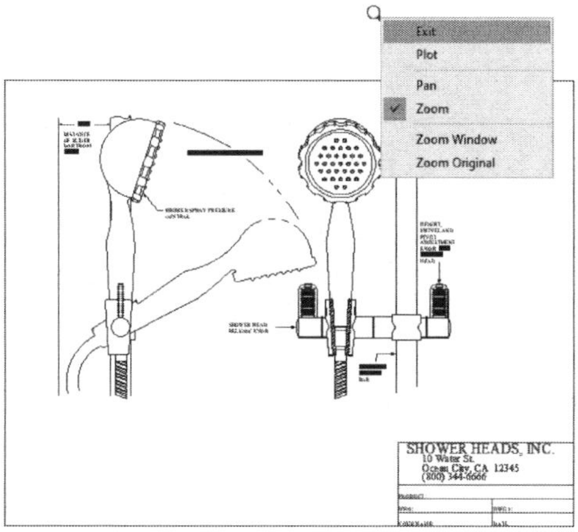

PAPER space must be on!
1.) With the properties command, select the paper space viewport.
2.) Change the layer to VP.
3.) Freeze the VP layer (model space freeze, not paper space).
4.) Zoom to the Title area and type your name and date where indicated.

Solution

1. 

Select the Layout1 tab at the bottom left corner of the drawing window.

2. 

Set your workspace to **Drafting & Annotation**.

3. 

Verify that Paper space is set at the Status bar.

If you don't see the PAPER/MODEL toggle on the status bar, right click on the status bar and enable it.

4.

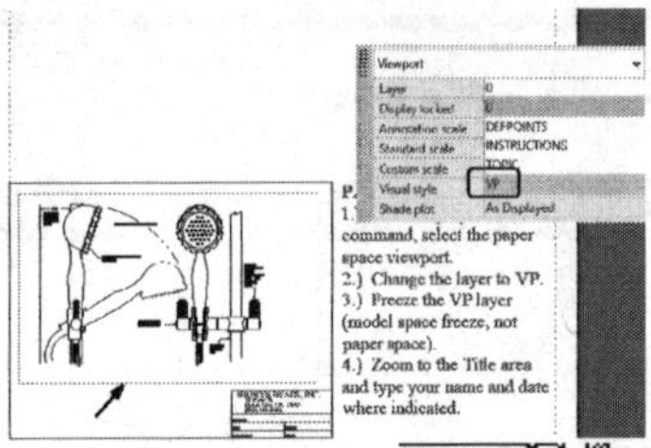

Select the border of the single viewport with the LMB and change the layer to **VP** in the Quick Properties dialog.

Notice that the single viewport window frame changes color. It is now on the VP layer.

5.

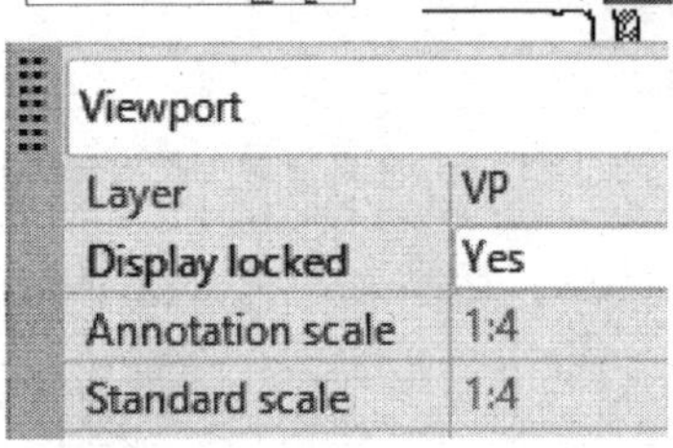

Set the Annotation scale to **1:4**.
Set the Standard scale to **1:4**.
Lock the display.

Deselect the viewport by Clicking **<ESC>**.

6.

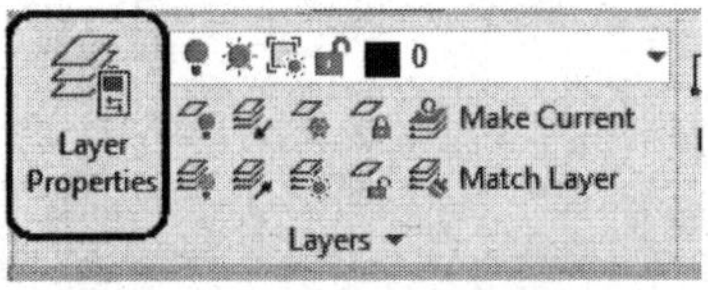

Activate the **Home** ribbon.

Select the **Layer Properties** tool.

7.

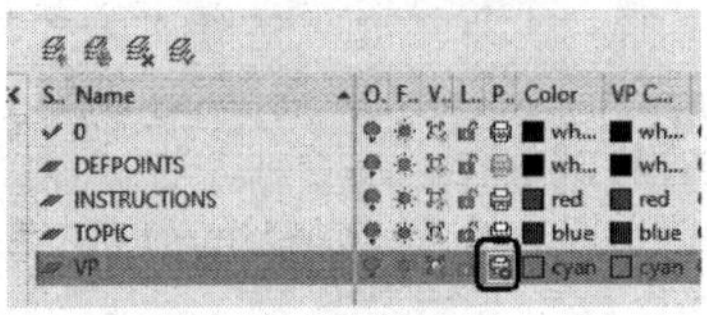

Set the VP layer to **No Plot**.
*When a layer is set to **No Plot**, it can remain visible but won't be printed.*
Close the Layer Properties Manager.

8.

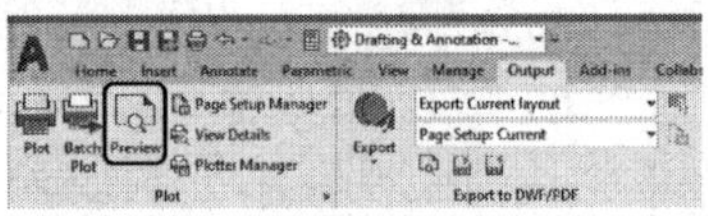

Activate the **Output** ribbon.

Select **Preview**.

The Plot preview shows that the Viewport border is not visible.

9.

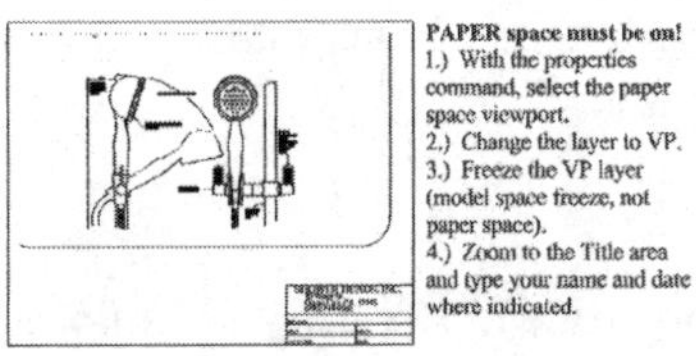

Right click and select **Exit** to exit the preview mode.

Nonrectangular Viewport

Command Locator

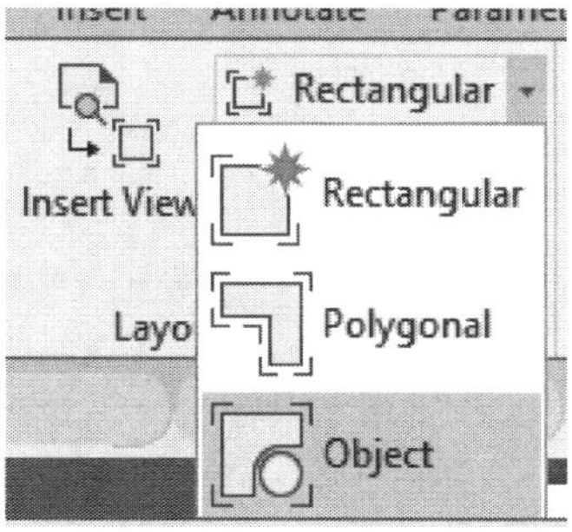

Layout Ribbon	*Layout Viewports/Polygonal or Object*
Command	*-VPORTS*

Command Overview

Non-rectangular viewports can be used to create a cropped view of a very specific area. They also can be used to create a more interesting and visually appealing layout.

General Procedures:

1. Select the Polygonal Viewport tool.
2. Select points to define the polygonal shape.
3. Close the shape and the polygonal viewport will be created and placed.

*To use the **From Object** viewport tool, simply sketch out the desired viewport shape using lines, arcs, and circles. The object must be a closed polygonal shape with no gaps, openings, or intersecting lines.*

Command Exercise

Exercise 12-6 – Nonrectangular Viewport

Drawing Name: **nrview1.dwg**
Estimated Time to Completion: 10 Minutes

Scope

Create a viewport by drawing a hexagon. Then use the object option to create a viewport out of the star shape already in the drawing.

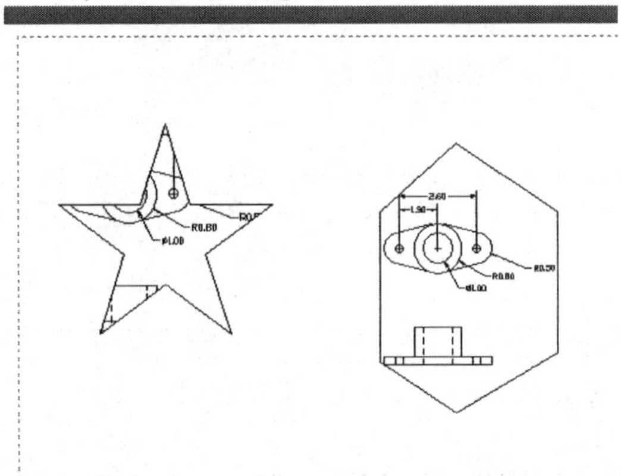

Solution

1. 

Select the Layout1 tab at the bottom left corner of the drawing window.

2. 

Set your workspace to **Drafting & Annotation**.

3. 

Activate the **Layout** ribbon.

4. 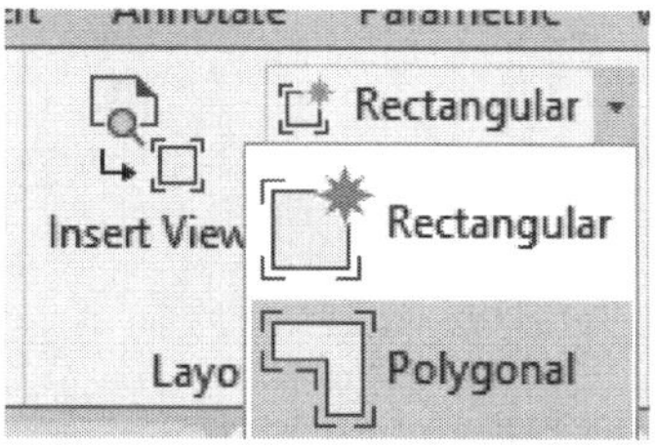

Select **Polygonal** from the Layout viewports panel.

5. 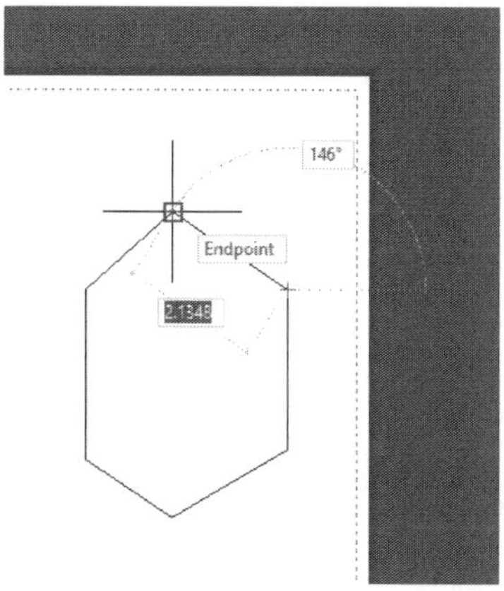

Specify start point:

Draw a closed hexagon shape; do not worry about it being a perfect hexagon.

6. *The viewport is automatically active.*

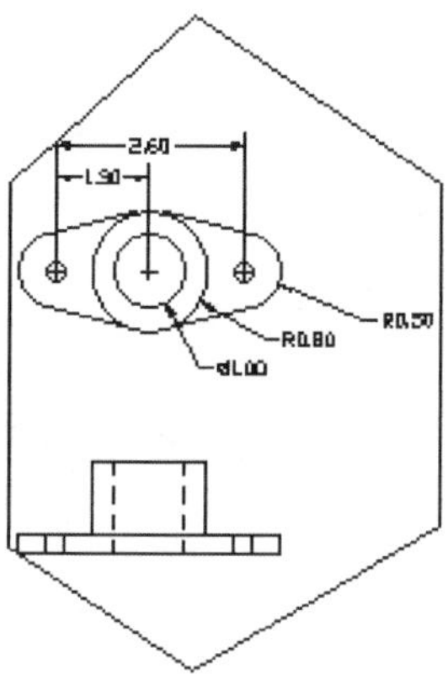

7. 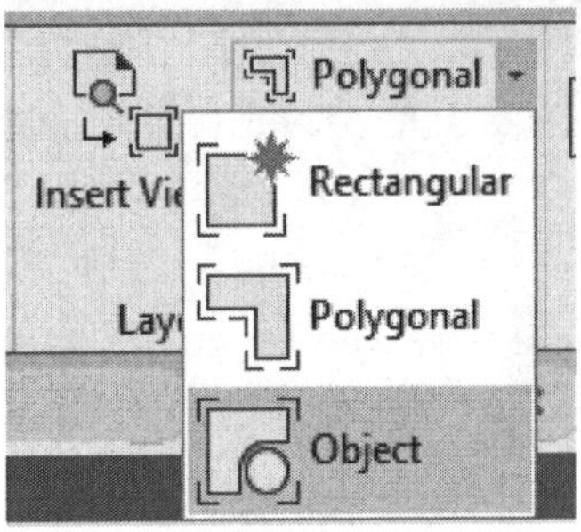

Select **Object** from the Layout Viewports panel.

8. 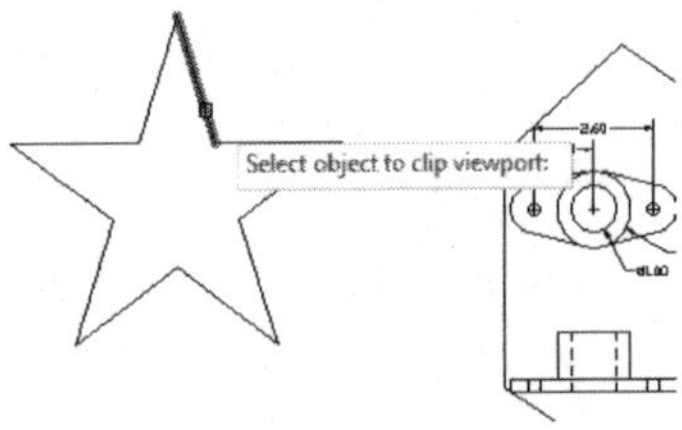

Select object to clip viewport:

Select the star shape.

9. 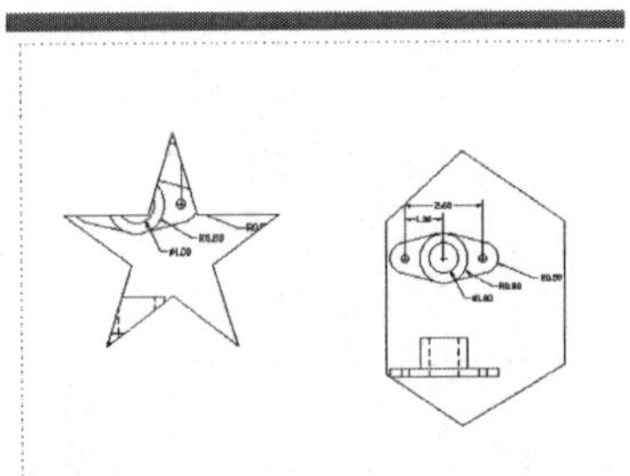

To adjust what is seen in each viewport, activate the viewport, then use Zoom and Pan to position elements inside the viewport.

Extra: *Activate each viewport and get the view to look proper.*

Page Setup

Command Locator

Ribbon/Layout/Layout *or* *Ribbon/Output/Plot*	**Page Setup Manager**
Command	**pagesetup**
RMB Shortcut Menu	**Right-click on the tab of the current layout/Page Setup...**
Dialog Box	**Page Setup**

Command Overview

The Page Setup command is a mixture of the old plot dialog box from earlier releases of AutoCAD and most windows print setup dialog boxes. In this dialog box, you can set up the layout and plotter settings for the current layout. This command is run automatically every time you select a layout tab that has not yet been set up. It is typically run whenever you create a new layout, unless this setting has been turned off by unchecking the 'Display when creating a new layout' checkbox at the bottom of the dialog box. The page setup is saved with its layout, so each layout in a drawing can have a different page setup.

You may edit the name of the layout in the Layout name field. The Page setup name is a drop-down list of available named page setups from which you can select a setup to apply to the current layout. If the setup you want is not in the available list, but is in a different drawing, or if you want to add a named setup, Click the 'Add' button. This will open the User Defined Page Setups dialog box.

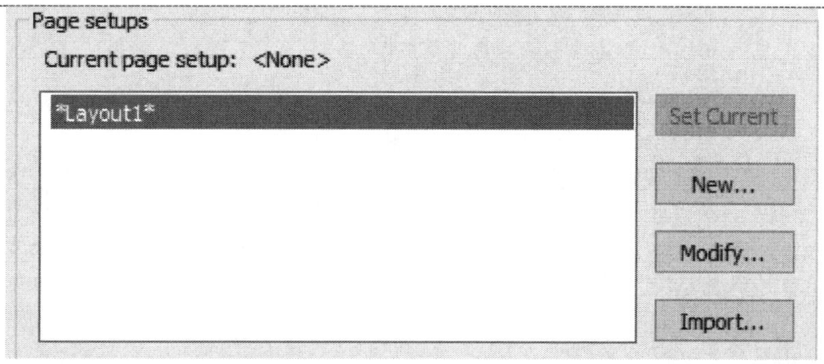

To create a named page setup from the current settings, type in the name in the top field and Click 'OK'. To rename an existing setup, click on the name of the setup to highlight it, Click 'Rename' and type in a new name. To delete an existing setup, click on the name of the setup to highlight it and Click 'Delete'. To import a setup from another file, Click 'Import'. Select the file with the setup in the Select File dialog box and select the setup from the dialog box that opens.

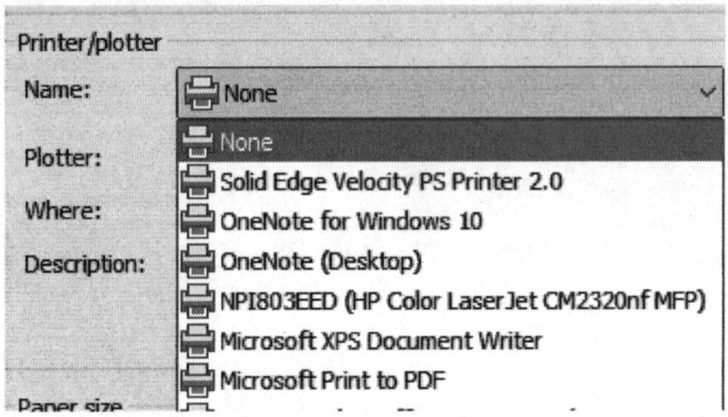

The Plot Device tab of the dialog box allows you to select the plotter to use for the layout, its properties and a plot style table. There is a drop-down list of currently available printer/plotters. You must make sure to set up your printer/plotter in Windows before selecting it here. The 'Properties…' button opens the Plotter Configuration Editor dialog box.

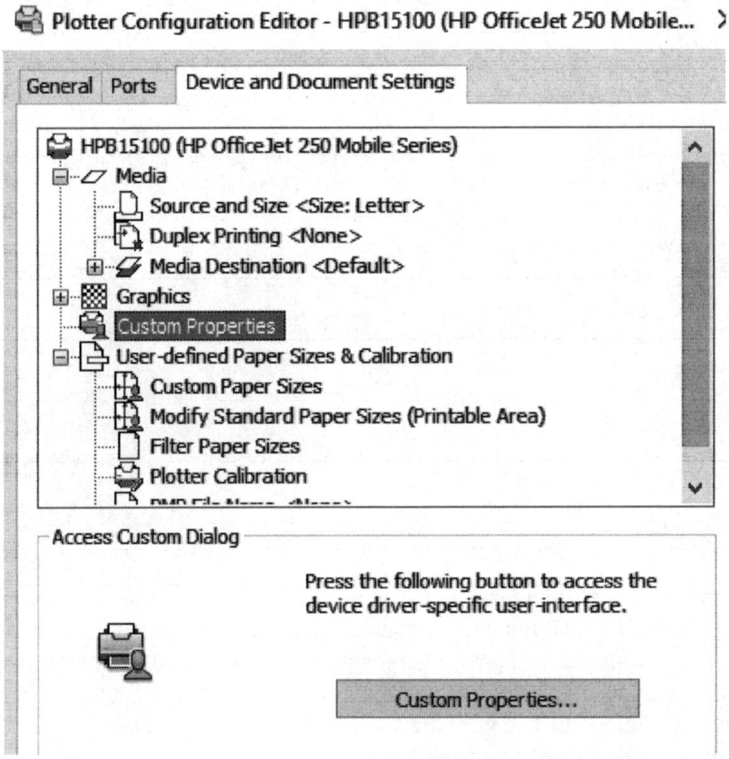

The Properties button for the selected printer brings up the Plotter Configuration dialog box. The General tab displays general information about the drivers for the selected printer/plotter. The Ports tab allows you to set which port to print to, including the ability to print to a file or to a spool. The Device and Document Settings tab has many settings for the media to use, graphic quality, etc. Click on the desired property and the bottom of the dialog box shows available options.

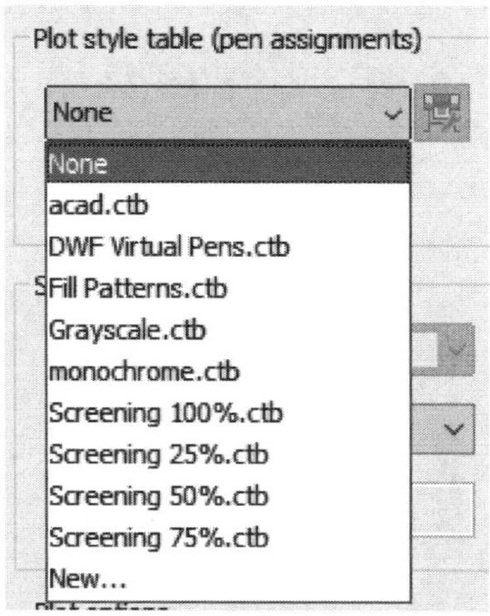

Back in the Plot Device tab of the Page Setup dialog box, you may also select a plot style table to use for the layout. A plot style adjusts the color, lineweight, linetype, fill style, and other settings for plotted output.

General Procedures:

1. Invoke the Page Setup command.
2. Set the plotter configuration and style in the Plot Device tab of the dialog box.
3. Set the rest of the plot settings in the Layout Settings tab of the dialog box.
4. Click 'OK'.

Tips & Tricks

- Use the Layout from Wizard command to create a layout using a step by step interface that is simple to follow.
- The templates linked to the Layout Wizard Dialog are located using the Files Options setting for templates. If you do not see any templates files in the dialog, reset the path for the templates on the Files tab in the Options dialog.

Controlling Layers per Viewport

Command Locator

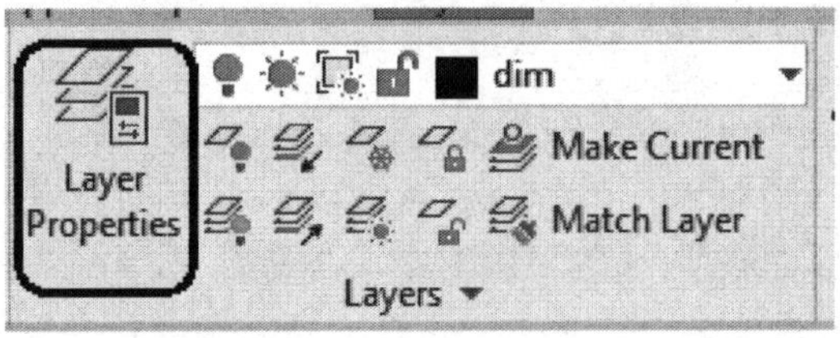

Ribbon/Home/Layers	**Layer Properties**
Command	**Layer**
Alias	**La**
Dialog Box	**Layer Properties Manager**

Command Overview

With TILE mode off and MODEL Space on, layers can be frozen in selected viewports. The Layer Control Dialog has two columns: 'Active VP Freeze' and 'New VP Freeze'.

Options:

Active VP Freeze *– This will freeze a selected layer in the active viewport.*

New VP Freeze *– This will freeze a selected layer in any new viewport created.*

General Procedures:

Freezing Layers in Active Viewport Only:

1. Select a floating model space viewport (TILE should be OFF, MODEL should be ON in the Status Bar).
2. Select the layer from the Layers Dialog Box and select Active VP Freeze.
3. Select OK.

Freezing Layers in New Viewports Only:

1. Invoke the Layer command.
2. Select the layer from the Layers Dialog Box and select New VP Freeze.
3. Select OK.

One method to ensure that all drafters comply with a company's standards is to use a template set up with layers and linetypes. Use of templates is discussed later in this text.

AutoCAD 2004 and above come with a CAD Standards tool to help you ensure that drawings meet company standards.

Command Exercise

Exercise 12-7 – Control Viewport Layer Properties

Drawing Name: **pslayer1.dwg**
Estimated Time to Completion: 15 Minutes

Scope

Switch to Paper Space and freeze (in paper space) the layers in the selected viewports, as indicated in the drawing. Freeze (in model space) the layers VP, which contain the paper space viewport borders and Notes.

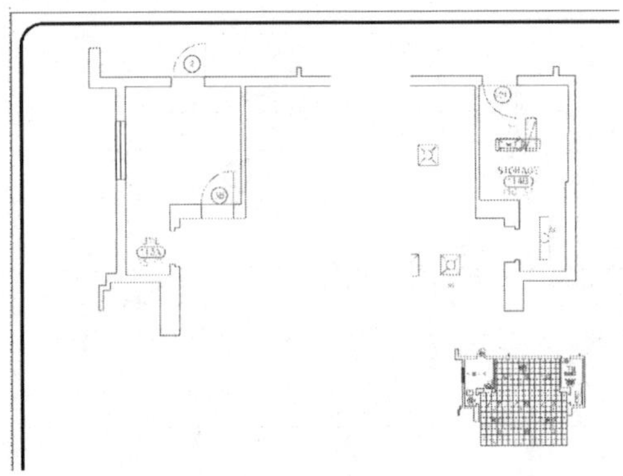

Solution

1. 

Switch to Layout 1 by clicking on its tab at the bottom of the drawing window.

2. 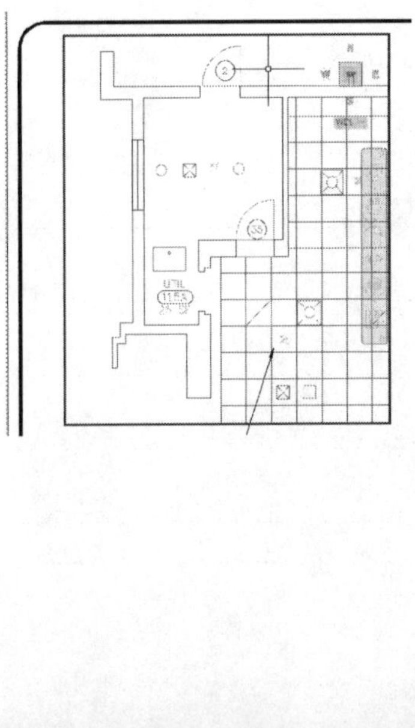

Activate the upper left viewport by double clicking within the viewport area.

Verify that you are in model space by looking on the status bar and the viewport should be bold.

3. 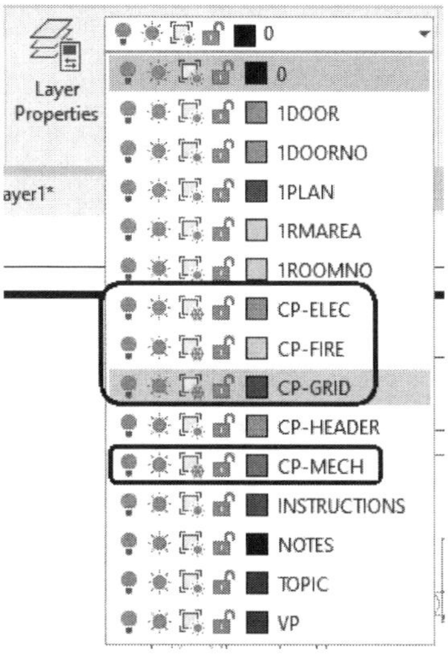

Activate the Home ribbon.

Select the Layers **CP–GRID**, **CP–FIRE**, **CP–ELEC**, and **CP–MECH** in the Layer drop-down and enable the Freeze in Current Viewport option.

Simply left click on the Freeze in Current Viewport icon to enable.

4. 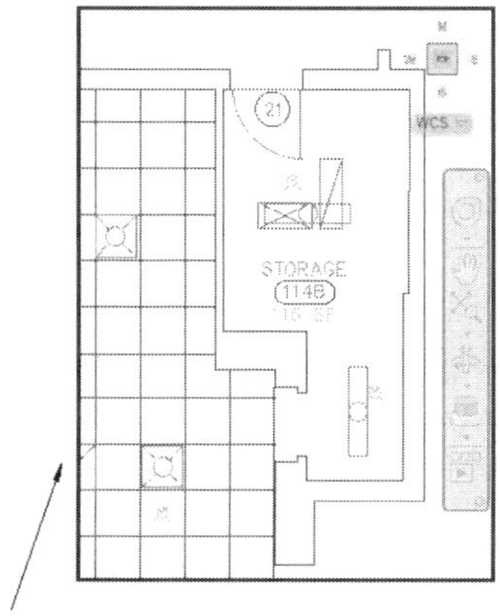

Activate the upper right viewport by clicking within its border.

5. 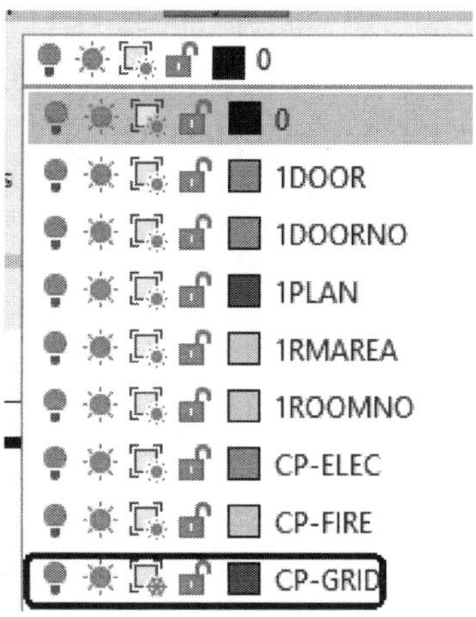

Using the Layer drop-down list freeze the layer **CP–GRID** in that viewport.

6. 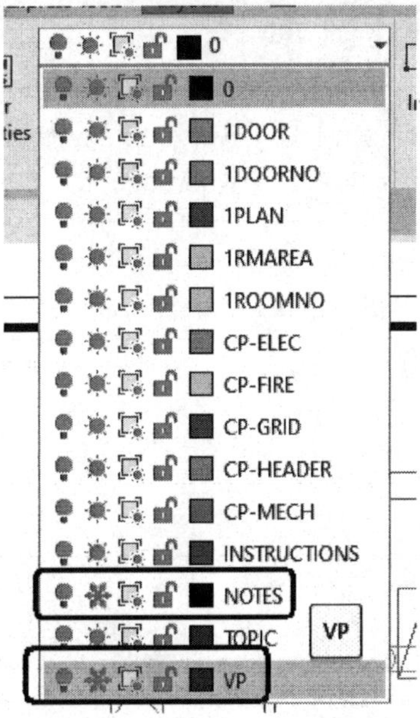

Return to **PAPER** space by clicking outside the viewport.

Freeze the layers named **VP** and **Notes** in all viewports by selecting the Layer Control drop-down list and choosing the **Freeze in ALL viewports** icon for both layers.

7. 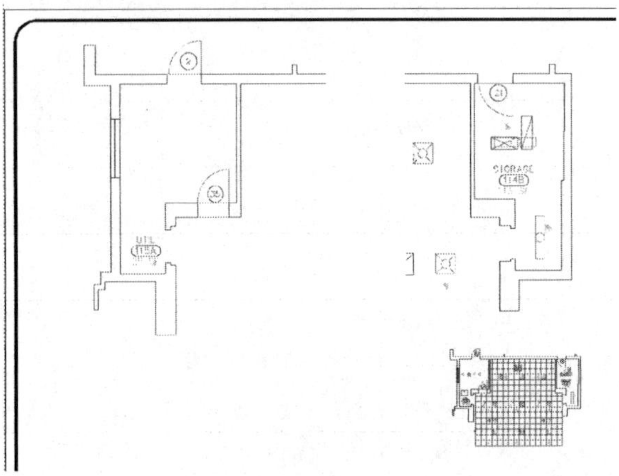

8. *Compare the three viewports.*

Plot

Command Locator

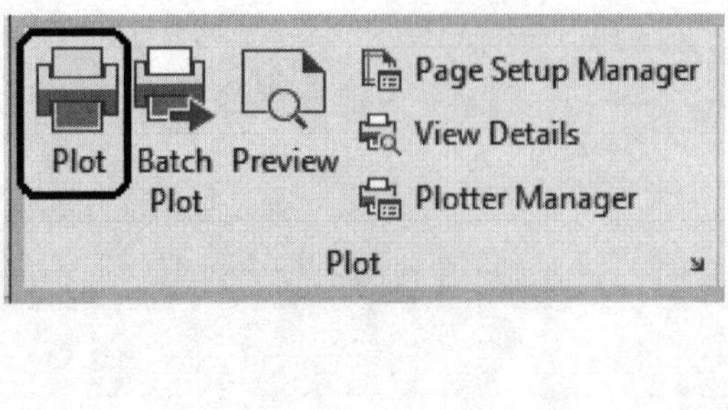

Ribbon/Output/Plot	**Plot**
Command	**Plot**
Alias	**Ctrl+P**
Dialog Box	**Plot**

Command Overview

Drawings may be plotted from the Model tab or the Layout tab. For 2-dimensional drawings, the user may opt to plot either way, though there are certain advantages to plotting from the Layout tab, such as including multiple views of the same drawing. For 3-dimensional drawing, it is necessary to use the Layout tab to print multiple views, such as a top, front and side view, of the 3-D Model on a single page. The Plot command will bring up the Page Setup dialog box. This dialog box includes the Plot Device tab and the Plot Settings tab. Basic options will be covered in this Tutorial. In addition to the plot command is the Preview Plot command, which previews a plot according to the latest plot settings.

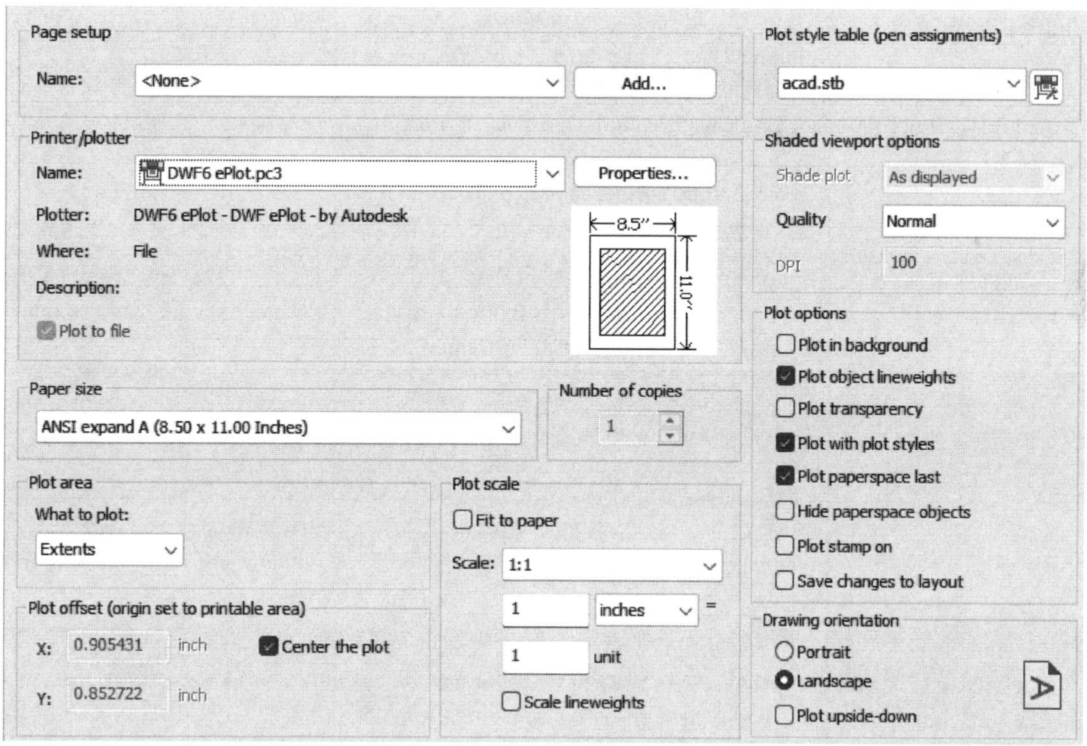

Plot Option	Overview	Typical Options to Choose
Plotter Configuration	Select a Plotting device from the drop-down list if the desired plotter does not appear at the top of this list. Select the	Use the default Plotter. Select a different plotter from the drop-

	Properties button to make changes to the Plotter Settings.	down list.
Plot Style Table **(pen assignments)**	This section allows the user to assign color numbers to pen numbers and set how objects are plotted.	Use the default setting (none)
What to Plot	Allows the user to plot all of the Layout tabs or only the Current tab. Multiple copies can be specified.	Current tab Selected tab All Layout tabs Any number of copies
Plot to File	This section allows the user to create a plot file (.plt) instead of an actual plot. Plot files contain the drawing information with all of the Plot command settings and can be plotted later.	None (leave blank)
Paper size and paper units	The available paper sizes will depend on the plotting device. The printable area will always be less than the paper size because the rollers on the printer need to feed the paper through the machine. The printable area also depends on the printing device. Choose inches or mm, depending on the drawing units.	Select the paper size from the drop-down list.
Drawing orientation	Choose Portrait, Landscape, or Plot upside-down. It is usually necessary to Preview the drawing first, to know which drawing orientation is correct.	Do a Full Preview first, then select Portrait or Landscape as required.
Plot area	The options in this area pertain to the part of the drawing that gets plotted: the drawing Limits, the drawing Extents, the current Display, or choose Window to make a window around the part of the drawing to plot.	Plot Limits *or* Select Window and make a window around the drawing area to plot.
Plot scale	This area controls the Plot scale. It is very easy at first to select "Scale to Fit"; however, eventually the user should learn how to plot to a specified scale.	Select or type a Plot Scale
Plot offset	The default start point for the plot area is 0,0. To change this, type another coordinate or select "Center the plot" (as best as possible).	(Either setting)

Plot options	The miscellaneous options in this section include to Plot with the lineweights that were set in the Layers dialog box, and plot using a pre-set plot style (Hide plot is for 3D drawings).	Plot with lineweights
Full Preview	Select this button for a full Plot preview. Click the RMB (to exit) to preview and return to the Plot dialog box. If there is something wrong with the preview, make adjustments in the Plot dialog box, and Preview again.	Select this option
Partial Preview	This is usually a quicker plot preview, especially if the drawing is large. The paper size, the printable area, the area that will contain the plot and warnings for errors will be listed.	

General Procedures:

Plot a drawing:

1. Invoke the Plot command.
2. Select the Plotter and Paper size.
3. Select the Plot area. Select or type the Plot scale.
4. Select "Full Preview." Right-click in the preview page and Exit to continue. Make any necessary adjustment to the Plot settings. Then Click OK to plot.

Set up a Drawing to Plot the Layout tab:

1. Create the drawing in the Model tab.
2. Select the Layout tab in the Drawing Window. Select OK to accept the Page Setup Layout defaults.
3. Insert a Title Block where the insertion point is 0,0, the x and y scale factors are 0, and the rotation angle is 0.
4. Use grips to re-size the existing viewport, or use the Viewports command options to create additional viewports.
5. Select PAPER in the Status Bar. This will switch the viewport mode to floating MODEL space. Select a viewport and Zoom the drawing view to scale.
6. Select MODEL in the Status Bar to switch the viewport mode back to PAPER space. Add notes, dimensions, etc. and plot the drawing.

Set up a Drawing to Plot the Model tab:

1. Start a New drawing. Set the Drawing Units, and the drawing limits (according to the Drawing Limits / Scale Chart). Zoom All.
2. Insert a Title Block where the insertion point is 0,0, the x and y scale factors are equal to the Plot scale, and the rotation angle is 0.
3. Create the drawing in designated drawing area, then plot the drawing.

- When selecting Plot Extents, be careful that there is not any geometry that may have gotten thrown out into space by accident. This is one reason why it is good to periodically Zoom All, or Zoom Extents to erase errors such as this.
- To add a plotter, open the Plotter Manager from the File pull-down menu. Select "Add a Plotter Wizard."
- Plot settings are saved on the computer and do not automatically go with the drawing. PC2 and PCP files save the plot settings. These are files separate from the drawing file. Plot settings can be saved and used with other drawings. The Batch Plot Utility command contains options that utilize PCP and PC2 files.

Plot Style Table Editor

Command Locator

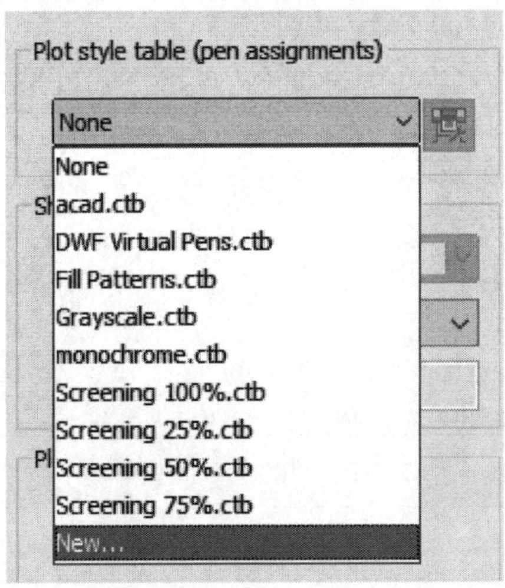

Plot Dialog	Upper right corner
Command	**stylesmanager**
Dialog Box	**Plot Style Table Editor**

Command Overview

The Plot Style Table Editor allows you to edit the plot styles found in a plot style table. Color–dependent plot style tables must have 255 plot styles mapped to 255 colors so you cannot add or delete plot styles in this type of table. However, a named plot style table can have any number of plot styles and the editor will allow you to add and delete styles from this type of table.

The dialog box has three tabs. The first, General, gives general information about the table file. The second and third tabs contain the editable information about the plot styles in two formats, tabular and form. Select the tab of the format you prefer working with; both give the same information.

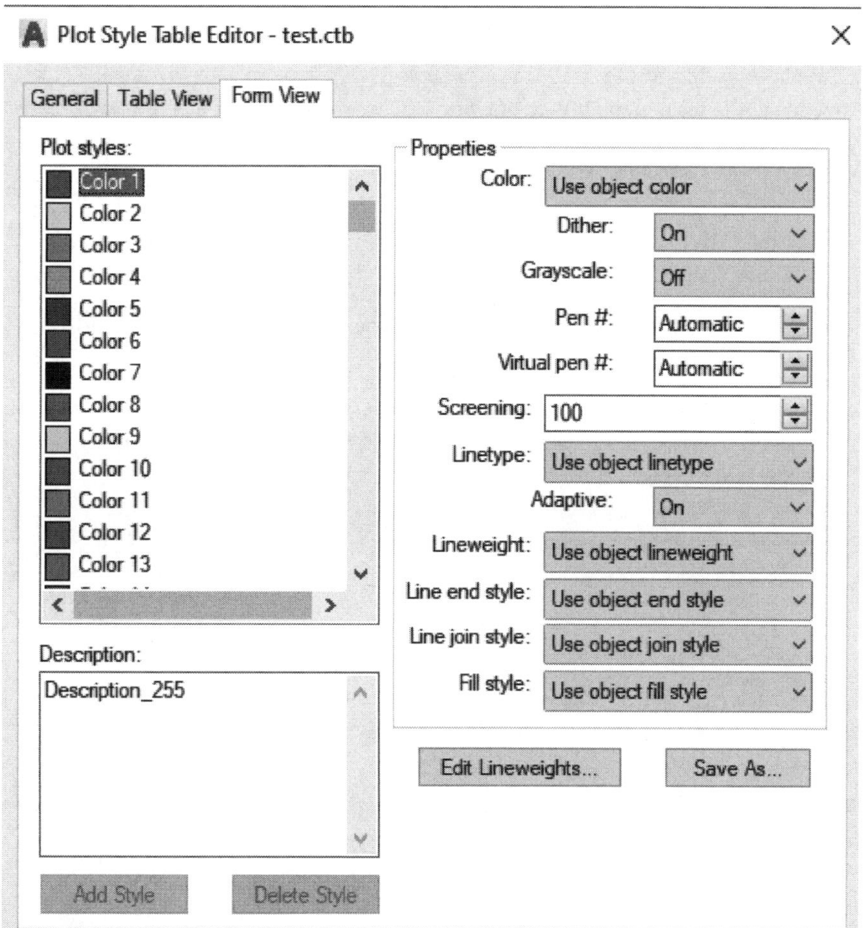

Each plot style has a description and twelve properties.

Color sets the color the object will be plotted with regardless of the color the object was drawn with. The default setting is 'Use object color'.

Dither turns on or off dithering. This is the process of plotting lines as a series of dots in an attempt to create more colors in the plotted output.

Grayscale will convert the color of the object to grayscale.

Pen number sets the number of the pen to use for this style; available numbers are 1 – 32. If you have set the color to 'Use object color' or are using a color–dependent plot style table, you cannot change this setting from 'Automatic' which causes AutoCAD to use the pen with the closest color to that of the Color setting.

Virtual pen is used for non–pen plotters that are set up with virtual pens. Virtual pens can be programmed into many plotters to set up the pen's width, fill pattern, end style and color. If a virtual pen is selected, the other settings for the plot style will be ignored. If the plotter used is a pen plotter or does not have virtual pens set up, this setting is ignored.

Screening sets the intensity of the color to use as a percentage. Setting this to 0 will use no ink and therefore change the color to white, while 100 will set the color to full intensity.

Linetype allows you to set the linetype to use for the style. The default linetype is 'Use object linetype'.

Adaptive adjustment sets the linetype scale of the object to complete the linetype pattern without ending it in the middle. If your drawing looks correct, turn this off; if linetype scaling is not as important as making sure the linetypes show up correctly, turn this on.

Lineweight sets the lineweight of the objects. The default setting is 'Use object lineweight'.

Line end style sets the end style of your lines. The styles available are Butt, Square, Round and Diamond. The default setting is 'Use object end style'.

Line join style sets the style of the joints of lines. The styles available are Miter, Bevel, Round and Diamond. The default setting is 'Use object join style'.

Fill style sets the fill style for the objects. Styles available are Solid, Checkerboard, Crosshatch, Diamonds, Horizontal Bars, Slant Left, Slant Right, Square Dots and Vertical Bar. The default setting is 'Use object fill style'.

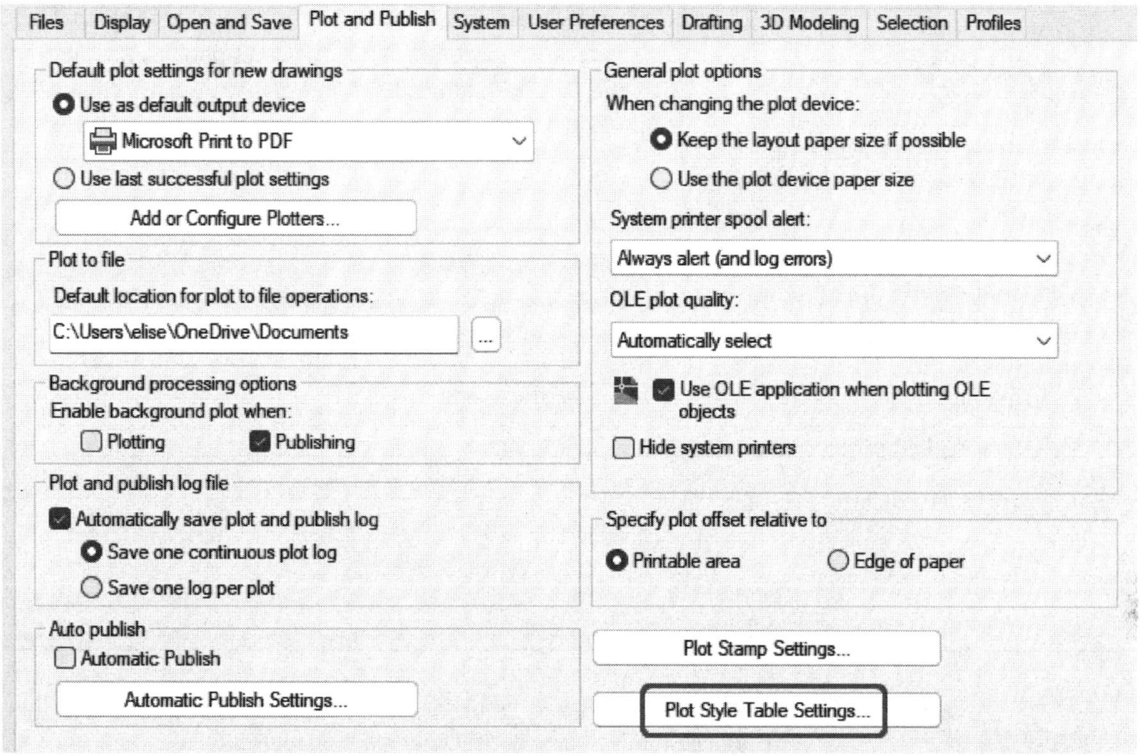

Plot Style Table Settings can also be accessed on the Plot and Publish tab of the Options dialog.

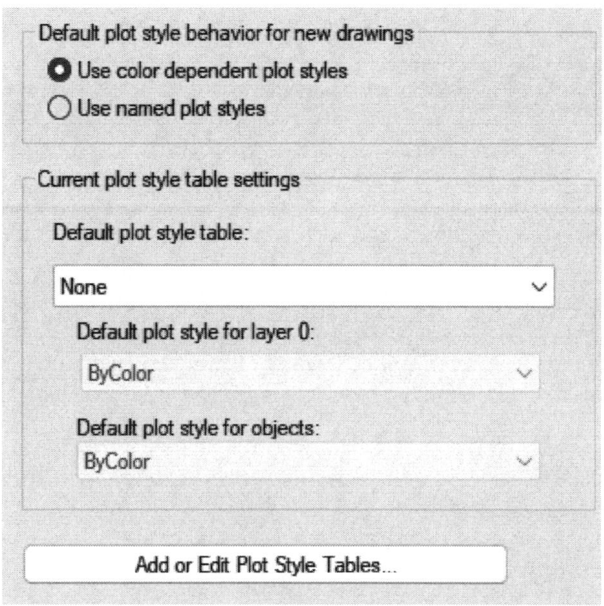

This method takes you to a dialog that walks you through the different plot style table settings.

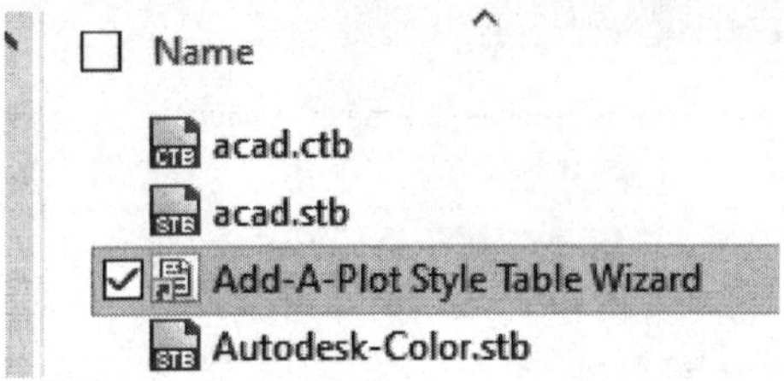

You can also use the **Add-A-Plot Style Table Wizard** to create a plot style table. To access double click on the Autodesk Plotter Manager in the Windows Control Panel.

General Procedures:

1. Invoke the Plot Style Manager command.
2. In the Plot Styles window, double click on the file to edit.
3. Set the desired settings in the dialog box.
4. Click 'Save & Close'.

Another way to get to the Plot Styles window is to double click on the Autodesk Plotter Manager in the Windows Control Panel.

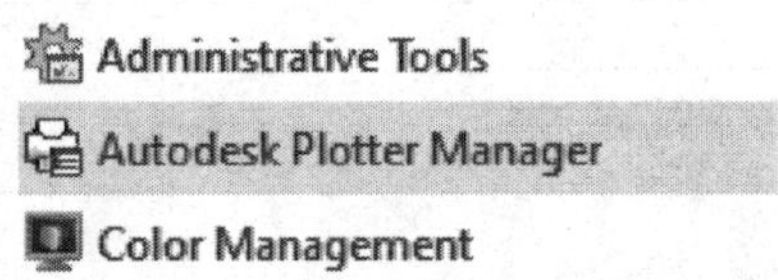

Section Exercise

Exercise 12-8 – Layout Setup

Drawing Name: **Lesson 12 AEC.dwg**
Estimated Time to Completion: 10 Minutes

Scope

Assign a page setup to the layout tab. Create a non-rectangular viewport. Assign a view scale and lock the display. Clip an existing viewport. Insert a title block.

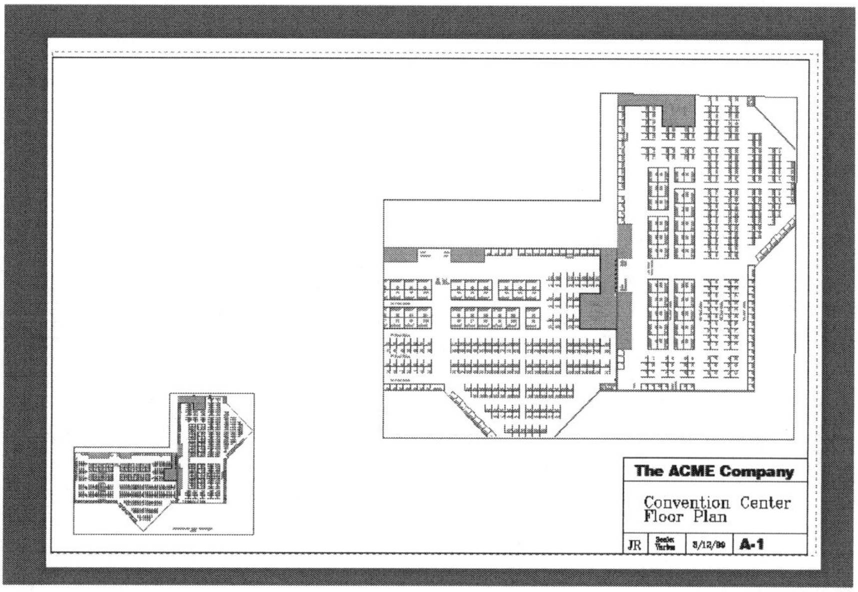

Solution

1. 

Select the **Layout1** tab.

2. 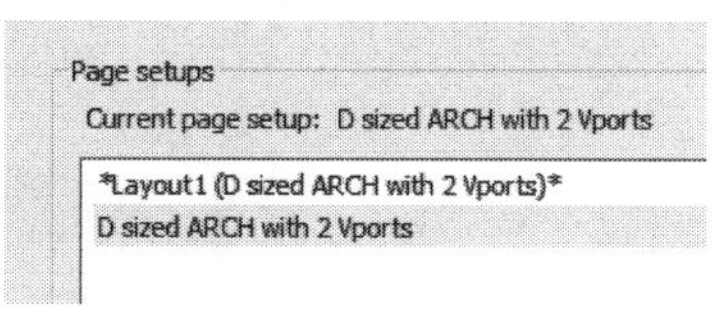

Set the page settings to **D sized ARCH with 2 Vports**.

3. 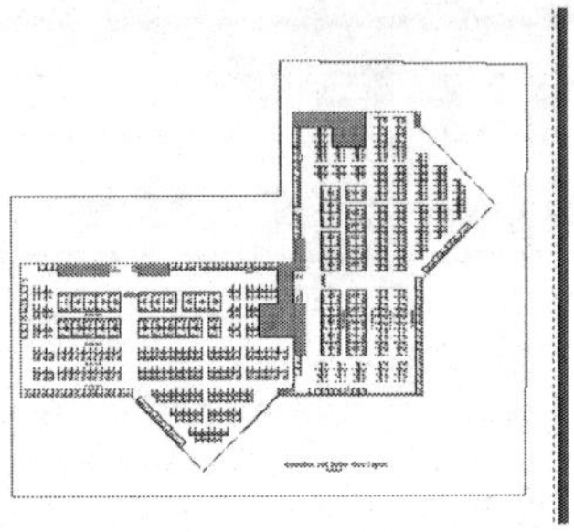

Create a non-rectangular viewport.

4. 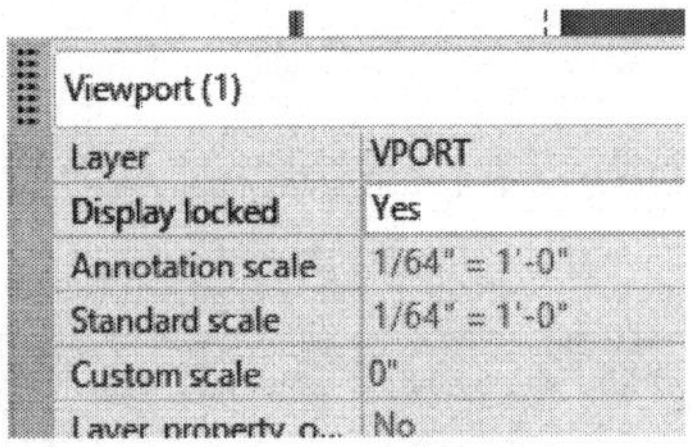

Set the scale of the viewport created.

Lock the display.

5. 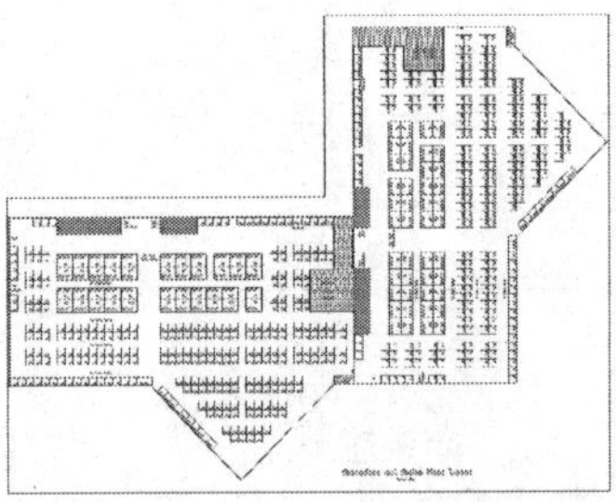

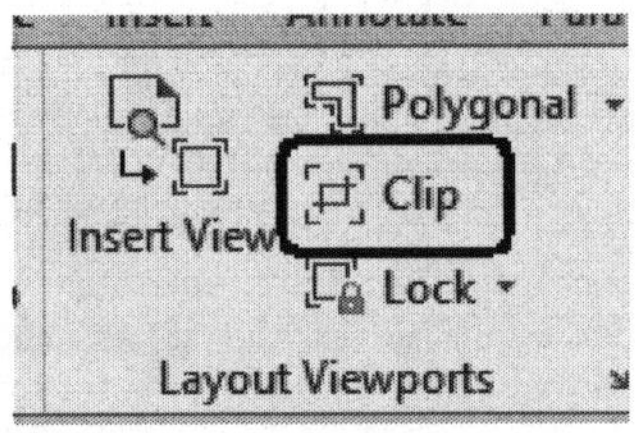

Perform a polygonal clip on the rectangular viewport.

6. 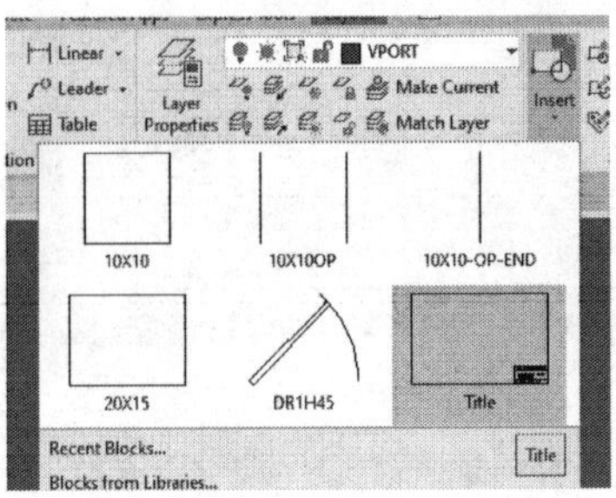

Insert the title block (there is a block pre-loaded in the drawing called Title).

Extra: *Perform a Plot Preview to see what color the yellow entities will be when you plot.*

Section Exercise

Exercise 12-9 – Construction Details

Drawing Name: **details.dwg**
Estimated Time to Completion: 10 Minutes

Scope

Add annotative scales to annotations. Use -ATTEDIT to modify attributes. Create named views. Insert named views onto a layout. Modify the scales of a viewport. Use Properties to modify objects.

1.

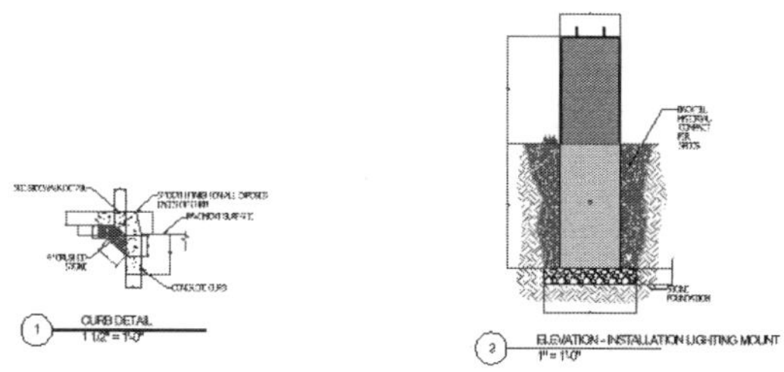

Open the Model tab.

There are two views.

One view will use a scale of 1 ½" = 1'-0".
One view will use a scale of 1" = 1'-0".

2.

Hover the mouse over one of the multileader notes.

You will see one annotative symbol to indicate one annotative scale is applied to the object.

3.

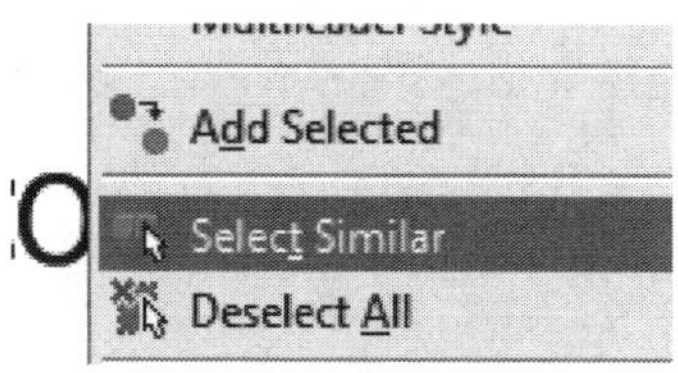

Select the note.
Right click and **Select Similar.**

This will select all the multileader objects.

4.

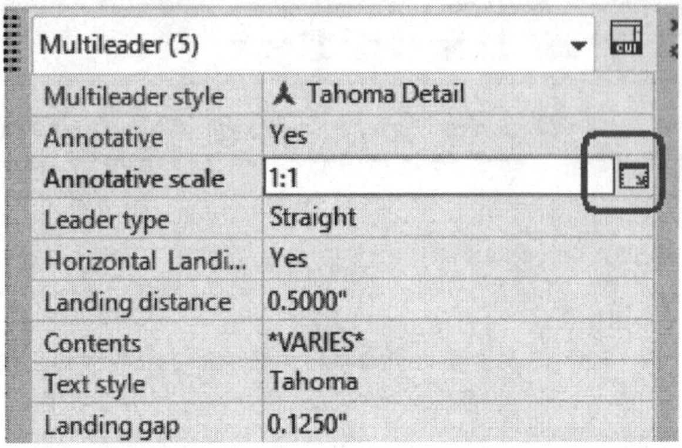

Click the box next to the Annotative scale field.

5.

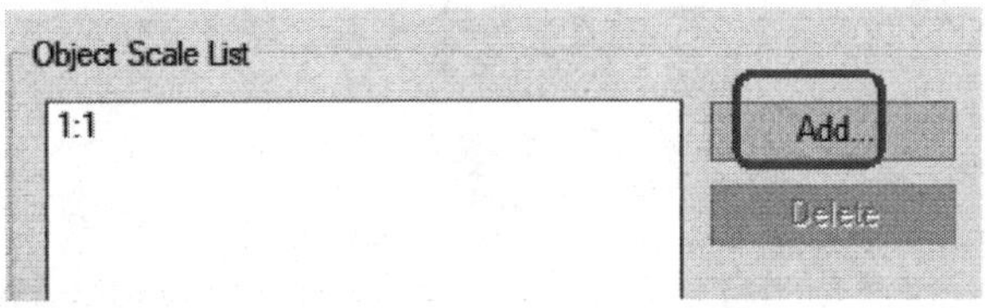

The multileaders currently have a scale of 1:1 applied.

Click **Add**.

6.

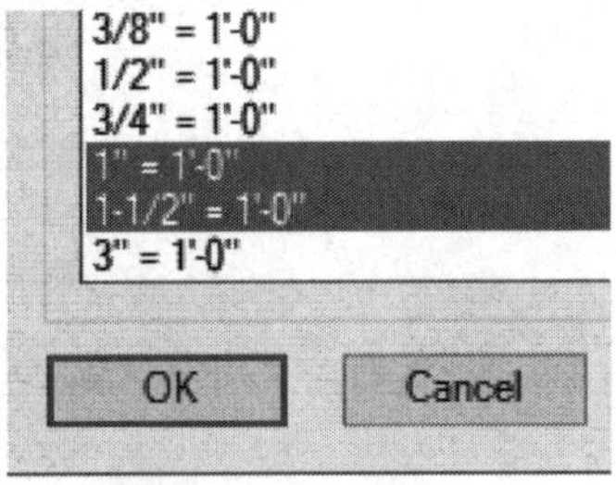

Hold down the CTL key and select 1” = 1’0” and 1-12/” = 1’-0”.

Click **OK**.

7.

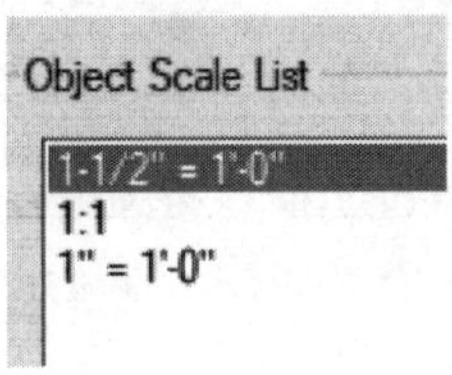

You should see the new scales added.

Click **OK**.

Click **ESC** to release the selection.

8.

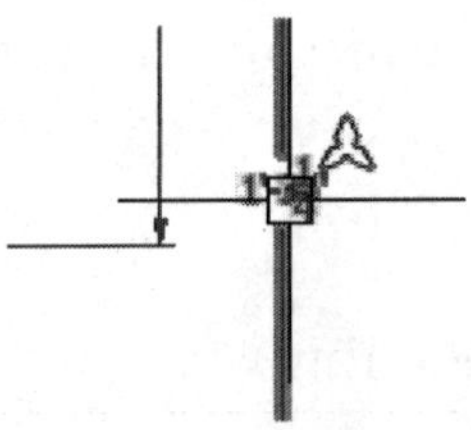

Hover the mouse over one of the dimensions.

You will see one annotative symbol to indicate one annotative scale is applied to the object.

9.

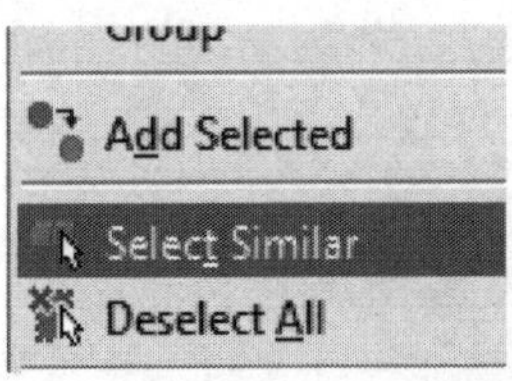

Select the dimension.
Right click and **Select Similar**.

This will select all the dimensions.

10.

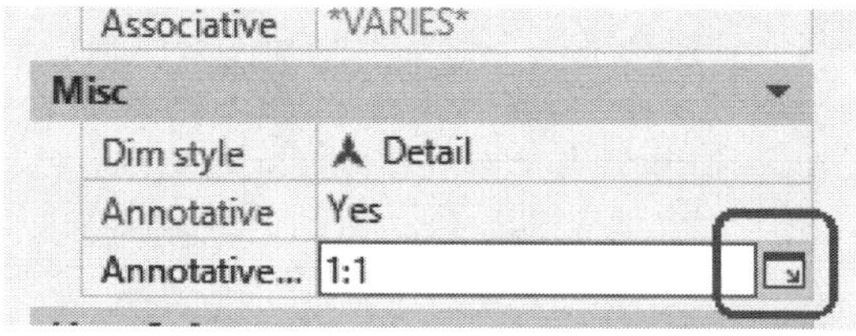

Click the box next to the Annotative scale field.

11.

The dimensions currently have a scale of 1:1 applied.

Click **Add**.

12.

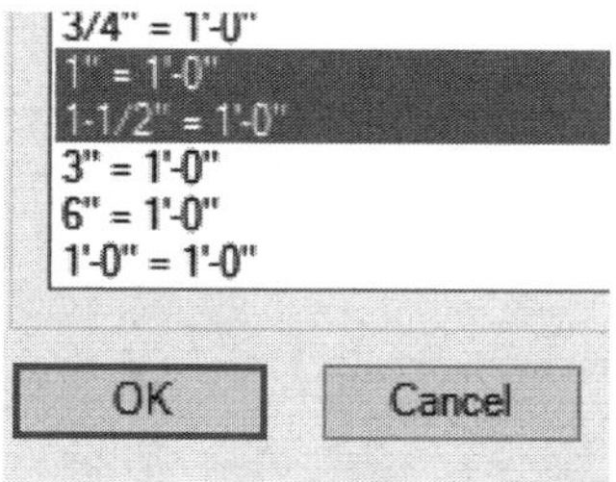

Hold down the CTL key and select 1” = 1’0” and 1-12/” = 1’-0”.

Click **OK**.

13.

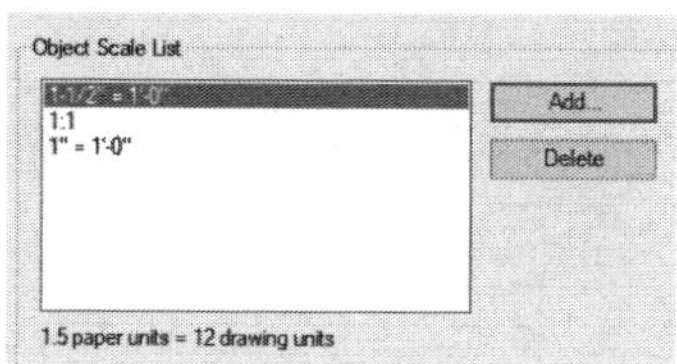

You should see the new scales added.

Click **OK**.

Click **ESC** to release the selection.

14.

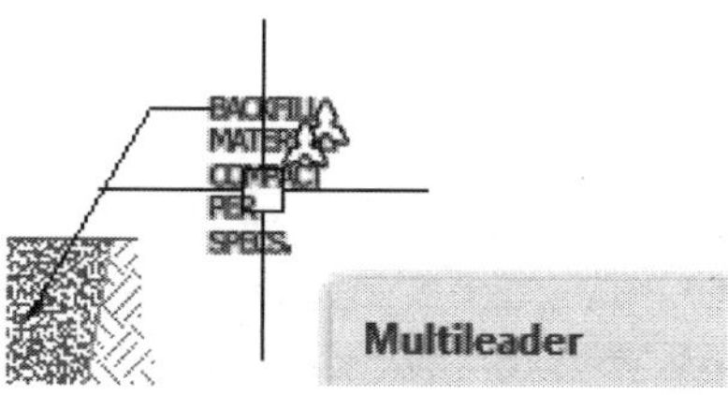

If you hover the mouse over one of the annotations, you will see more than one annotative symbol to indicate that more than one annotative scale is applied.

15. 

Open the View ribbon.

Select the View Manager.

16. 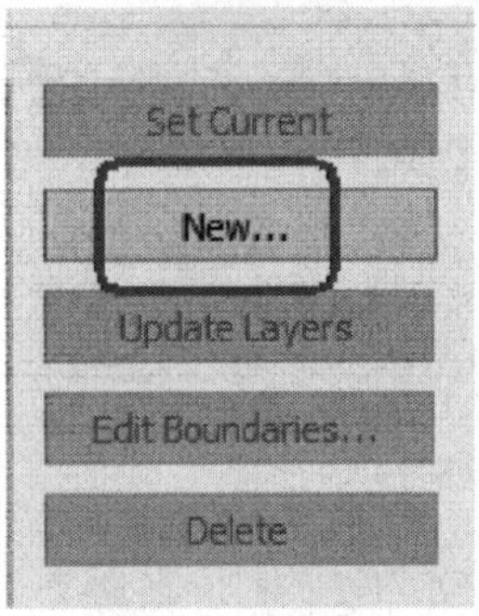

Click **New**.

17. 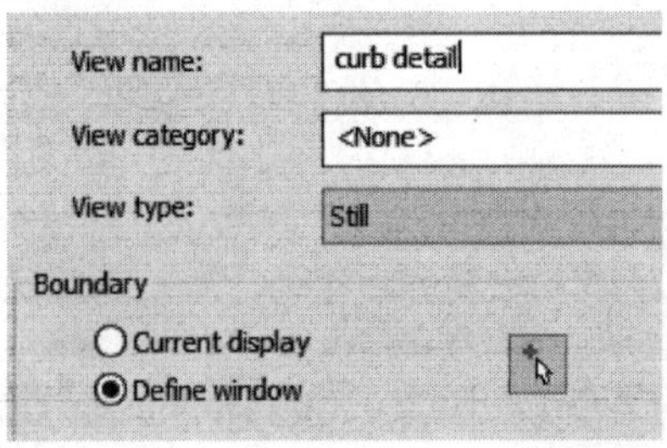

Type **curb detail** for the View name.
Enable **Define window**.

Window around the curb detail on the left.

Click **ENTER**.
Click **OK**.

18. 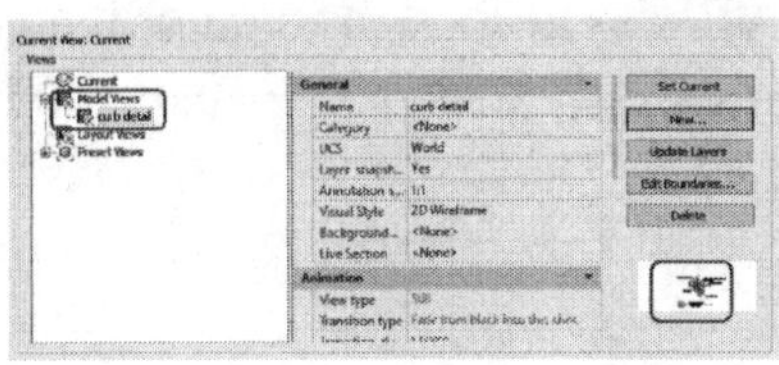

You will see a preview of the view in the lower right corner of the dialog.
You will see the view name listed under Model views.

Repeat to create a named view for the lighting elevation detail.

19. 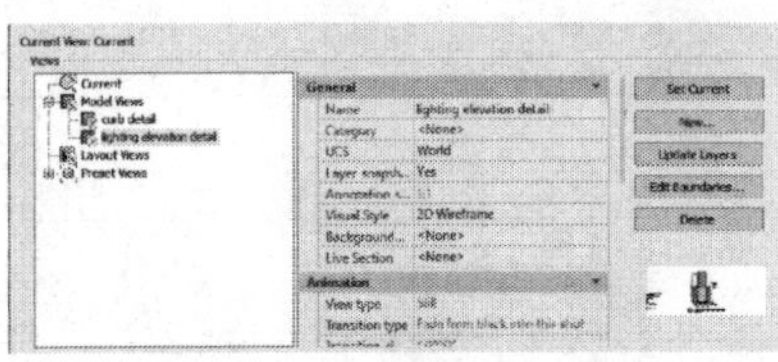

You should see two details listed in the dialog box.

Click **OK**.

20. 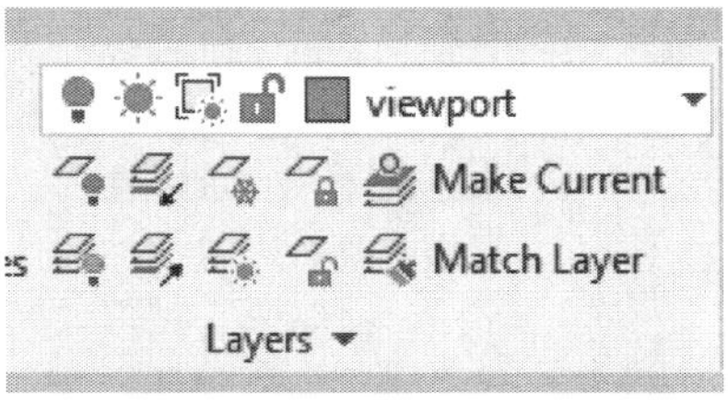

Switch to the Home ribbon.

Set **viewport** as the current layer.

21. 

Switch to the **Layout1** tab.

Open the Layout ribbon.

22. 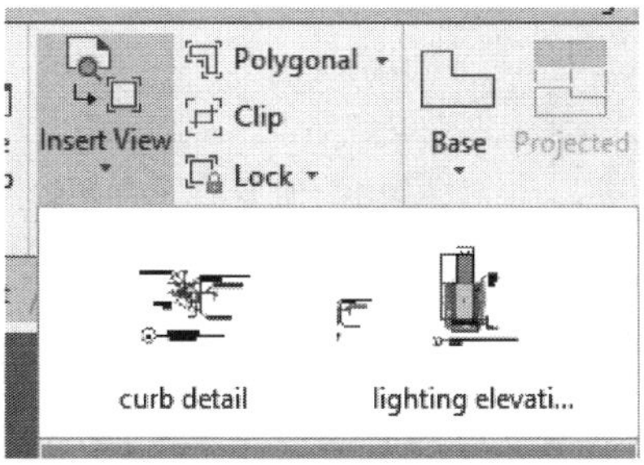

Use Insert View to add the curb detail view and lighting elevation detail view to the sheet.

23. 

Enable **Annotative Objects** on the status bar.

You will not see the annotations unless **Show Annotative Objects** is enabled.

24. 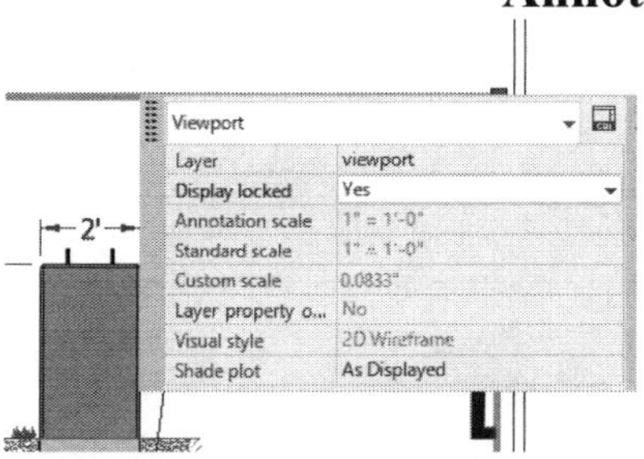

Select each viewport and set it to the Annotation scale and Standard scale indicated by the view label.
Lock the display.

25. 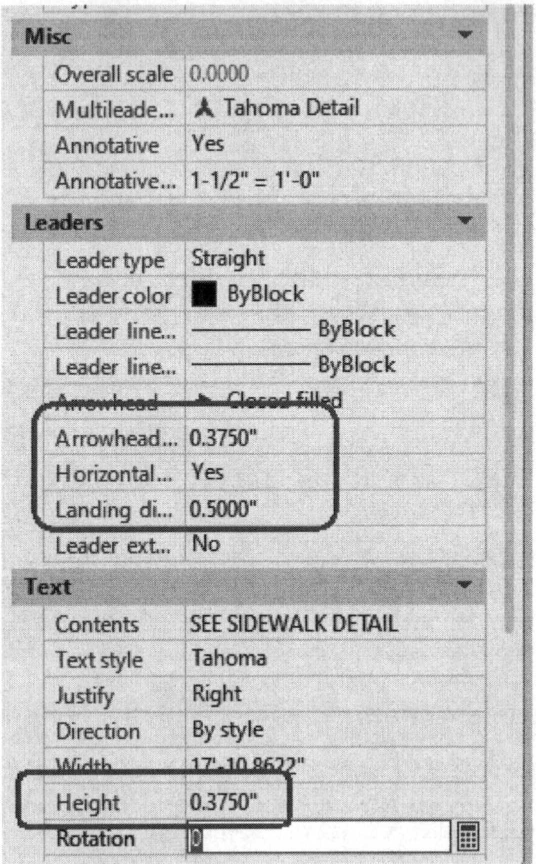

If the text appears to be too large or needs to be adjusted, select the annotation.
Right click and select Properties.

Verify that the correct Annotative scale is applied.

Change the Arrowhead size to .375".

Change the Text Height to .375".

Change the Landing distance to 0.5".

26. 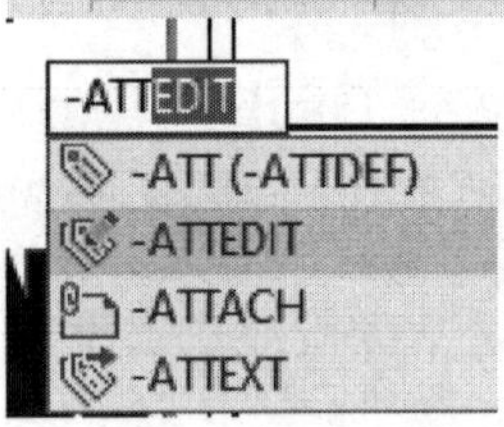

To change the size of the text used in the view labels:
Type **-ATTEDIT**.

27. 

Click ENTER for YES at the prompts until prompted to select an attribute.

28. 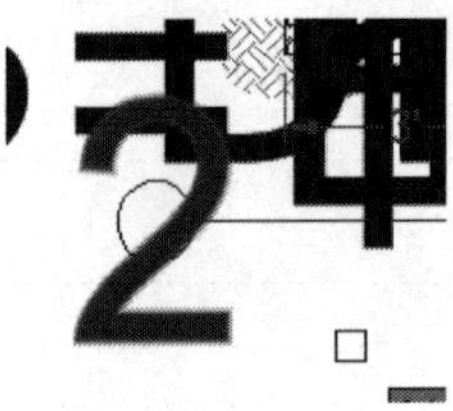

Select the attribute.

Click ENTER.

29. Select Height.

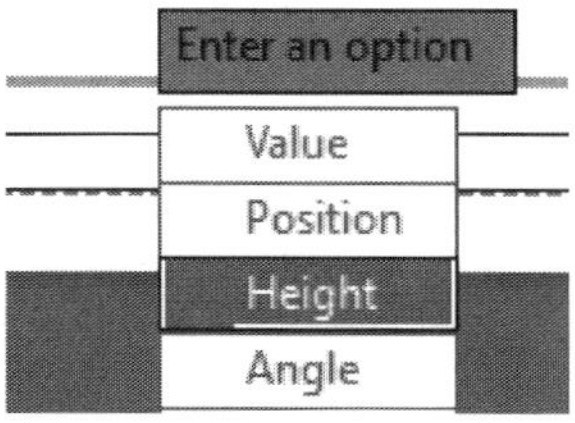

30. 

Adjust the Height.

Click **ENTER**.

Repeat for the remaining attributes.

You can also use POSITION to change the location of an attribute.

31. 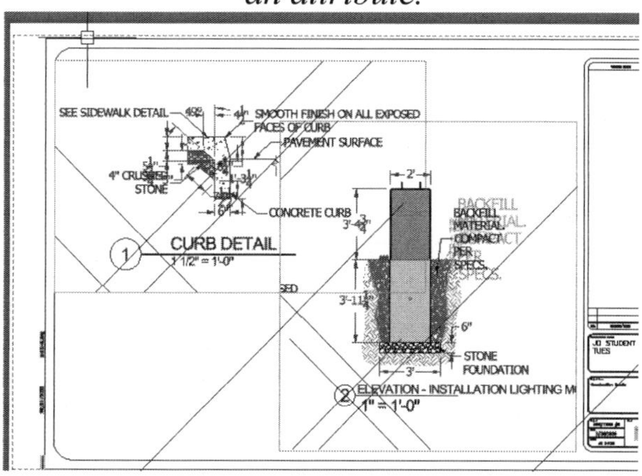

The Xs that are displayed are the insertion points of the attributes.

Save the drawing and close.

Re-open the drawing and you will no longer see the Xs.

32. 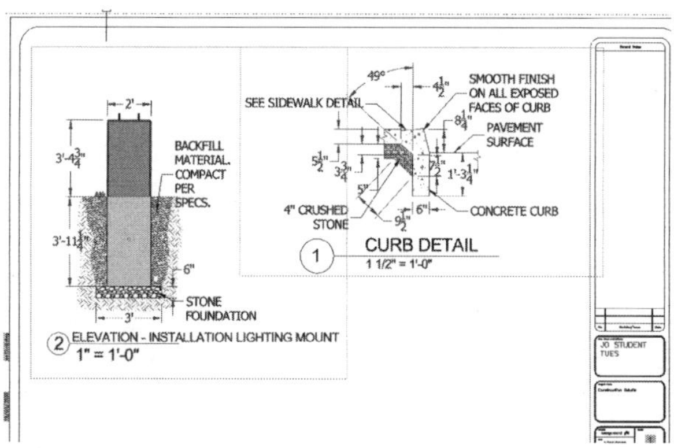

Adjust the annotations so they are not overlapping and are easy to read.

You may need to re-position the viewports so they overlap better.

33. 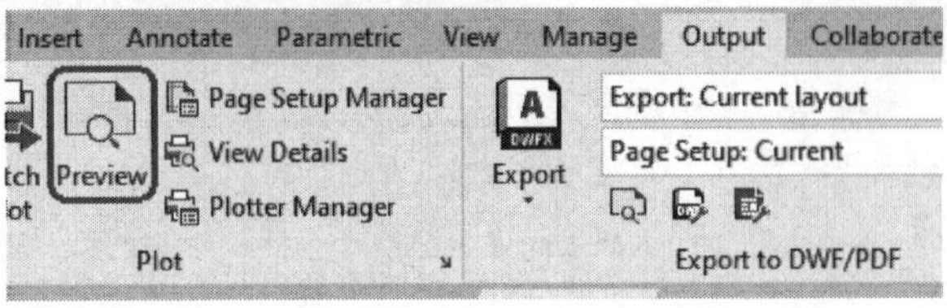

Open the Output ribbon.

Click on Preview to see how your layout looks.

34. 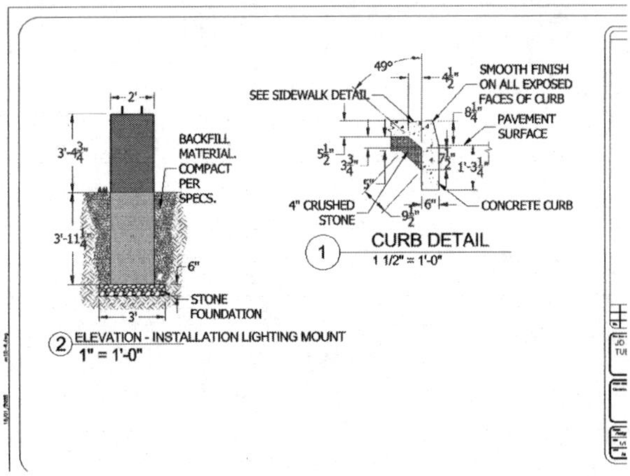

Use the PREVIEW to verify that the views look acceptable.

Save as *ex12-9.dwg.*

Review Questions

1. What does this icon represent?

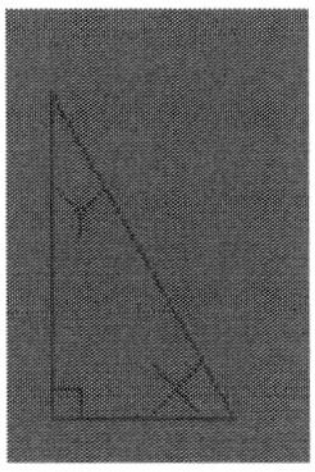

2. **T F** You should create your drawing in Model Space but you can plot your drawing from either the Layout tab (paper space) or the Model tab (model space).

3. **T F** To insert a view, there must already be a named view defined.

False

4. What command does this icon  represent and on which ribbon tab is it located?

5. What command does this icon  represent and where is it located?

6. What toolbars contain the commands for creating drawing Layouts and Viewports?

7. What is the Plot Area and how does this relate to the paper size?

8. **T F** When you plot your drawing in Paper Space, your plot scale is 1=1.

9. What are some advantages to plotting your drawing in Paper Space?

10. With the Model tab selected, what happens when you select the model button 

?

11. With the Layout tab selected, the PAPER button switches to MODEL. What is the difference?

Review Answers

1. What does this icon represent?

   Paper Space

2. **T F** You should create your drawing in Model Space but you can plot your drawing from either the Layout tab (paper space) or the Model tab (model space).

   True

3. **T F** To insert a view, there must already be a named view defined.

   False

4. What command does this icon  represent and which ribbon tab is used to access?

   Plot on the Output tab in the Plot panel

5. What command does this icon  represent and where is it located?

   Plot Preview

6. What toolbars contain the commands for creating drawing Layouts and Viewports?

   Viewports

7. What is the Plot Area and how does this relate to the paper size?

   The Plot Area is the sheet size.

8. **T F** When you plot your drawing in Paper Space, your plot scale is 1=1.

   False...sometimes, but not always.

9. What are some advantages to plotting your drawing in Paper Space?

   You are able to plan how your drawing will look when it is plotted.

10. With the Model tab selected, what happens when you select the model button 

?

    You are in Model Space.

11. With the Layout tab selected, the PAPER button switches to MODEL. What is the difference?

    The Model Space is activated for a viewport or a viewport is made active.

Lesson 13.0 – Utility Commands

Estimated Class Time: 2 Hours

Objectives

This section introduces AutoCAD commands for various utilities, such as calculator, area, quick measure, and distance.

- **Area**
- **Quick Measure**
- **Distance**
- **Find and Replace**
- **Purge**
- **Spell Check**
- **PDF Import**
- **Trace**
- **Count**
- **Transmittal Sets**

Area

Command Locator

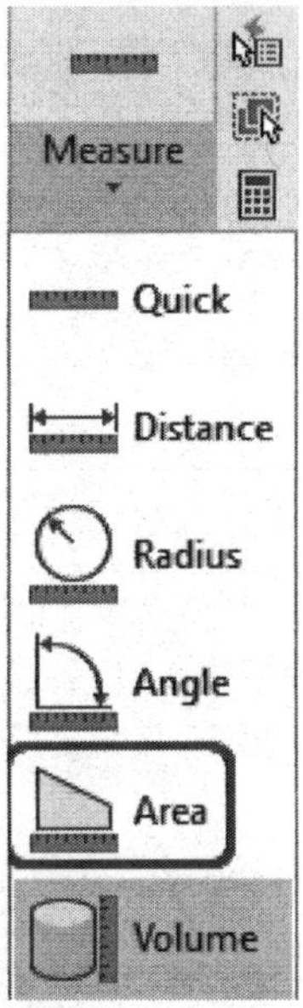

Ribbon/Home/Utilities	**Area**
Command	**Area**

Command Overview

Calculates the area and perimeter of objects. You can use the shortcut menu to add and subtract areas.

Area Option	Overview
Object	Selects a closed polygon or region.
Add	Select one or more objects to include.
Subtract	Select one or more objects to exclude.

Command Exercise

Exercise 13-1 – Area

Drawing Name: **Area.dwg**
Estimated Time to Completion: 30 Minutes

Scope

Calculate the area of a region. Subtract Area L from Area A.

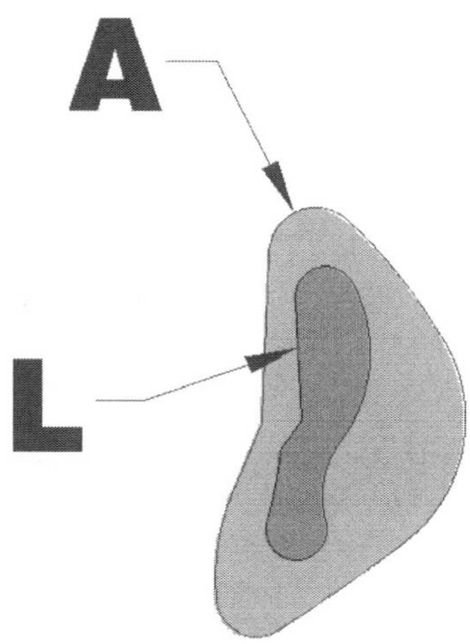

Solution

1.

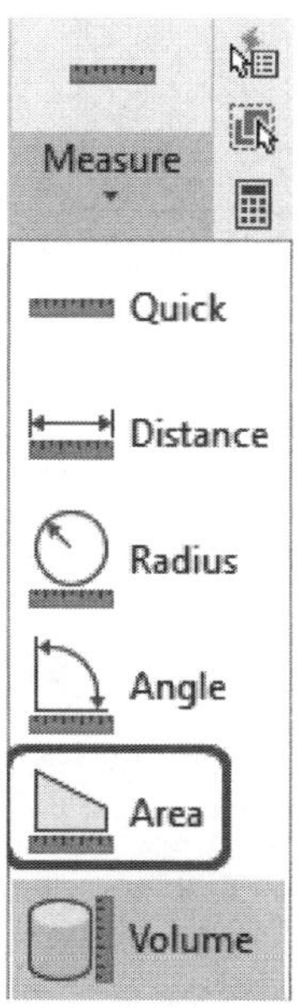

Type **AREA** or select the AREA tool from the Utilities panel on the Home ribbon.

2. 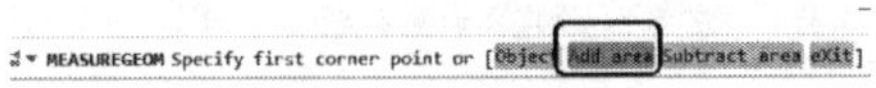

RMB and select **Add area**.

3. 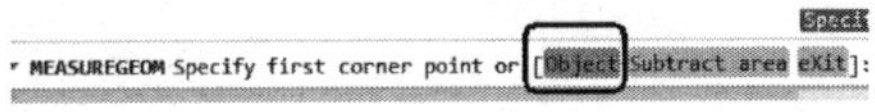

RMB and select **Object**.

4. 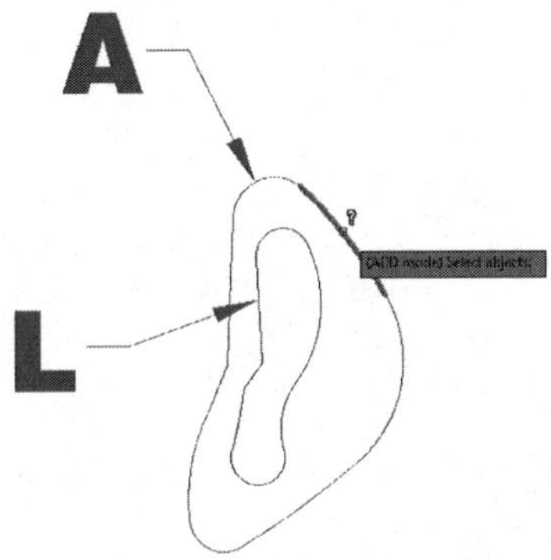

Select polyline A.

Right click to complete the selection being added.

5. 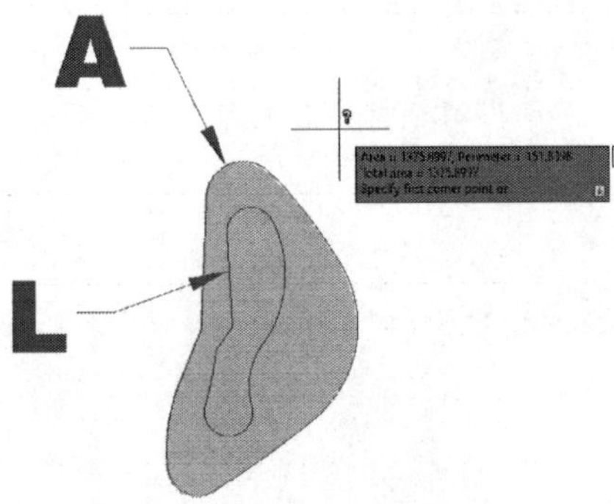

AutoCAD will display the area and perimeter value for polyline A.

6. 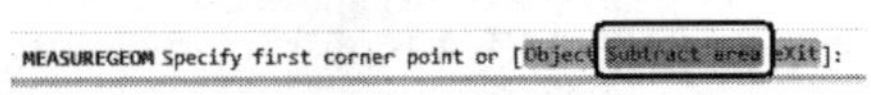

RMB and select **Subtract area**.

7. 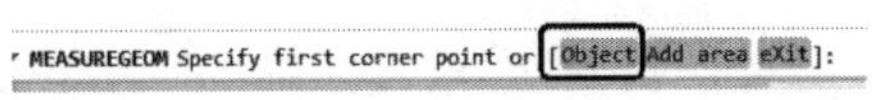

RMB and select **Object**.

8. 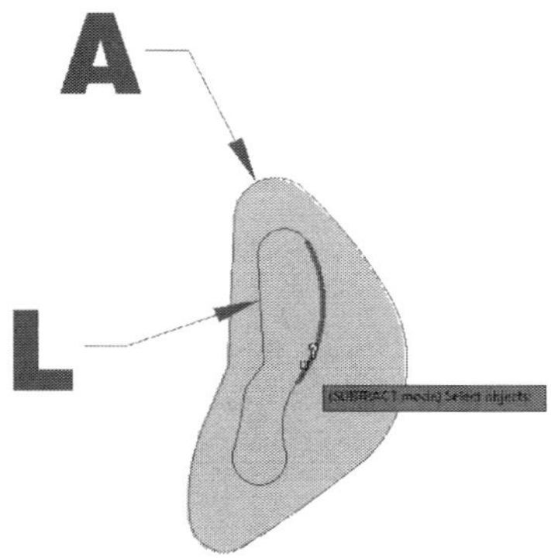

Select polyline L.

Right click to complete selecting objects.

9. 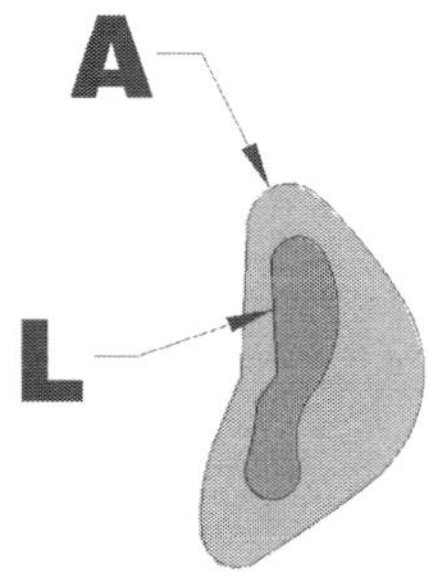

AutoCAD will subtract Area A (1375.8997) from Area L (338.6056) and calculate the total: 1037.2941.

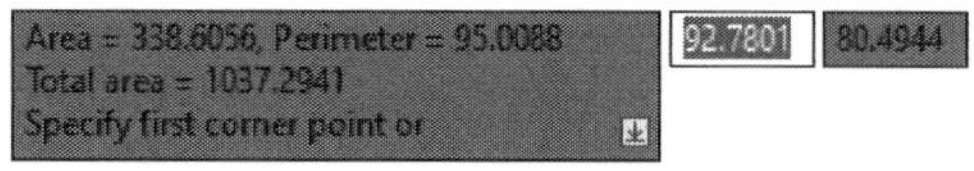

Quick Measure

Command Locator

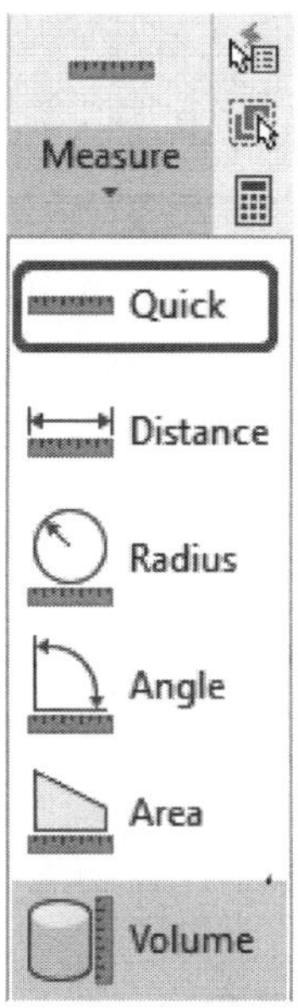

Ribbon/Home/Utilities	Quick
Command	**measuregeom**
Alias	**MEA**
RMB Shortcut Menu	**Distance Radius Angle Area Volume Quick Mode Exit**

Command Overview

The Quick Measure tool displays the measurement of elements by hovering over the object. You can specify which measurement to display by using the options.

To avoid clutter and improve performance, when using the Quick Measure tool, it's best to zoom into complicated areas of your drawing.

Command Exercise

Exercise 13-2 – Quick Measure

Drawing Name: **qm.dwg**
Estimated Time to Completion: 5 Minutes

Scope

Use the Quick Measure tool to determine the size of rooms, wall widths, and the location of elements.

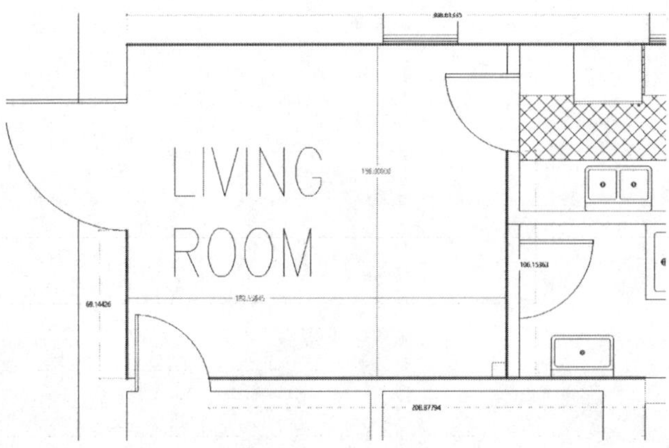

Solution

1.

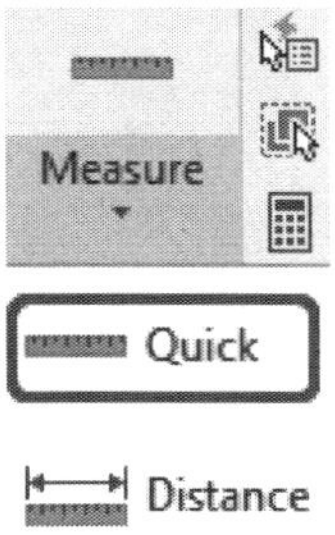

Select the **Quick Measure** tool from the Utilities panel on the Home ribbon.

2.

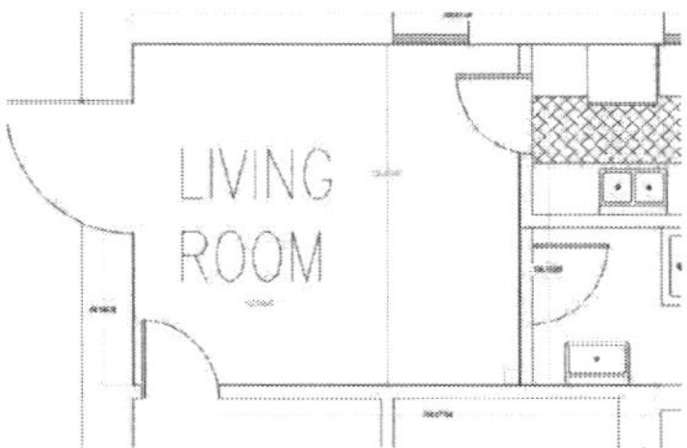

Move the cursor inside the Living Room area.

Note the measurements which display.

3.

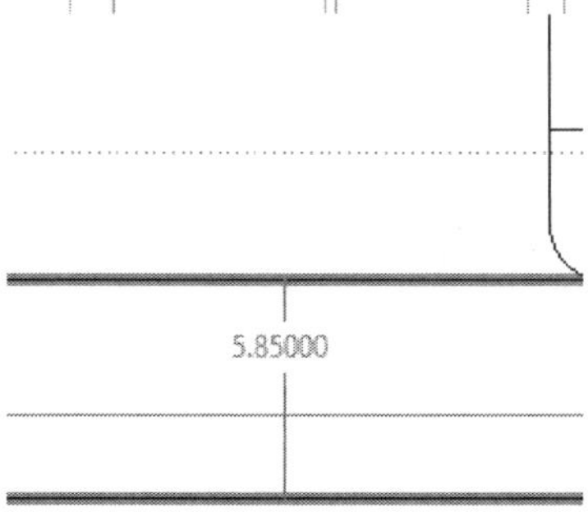

Zoom in and move the cursor between the two horizontal lines designating the wall.

Note that you can now see the wall thickness.

4.

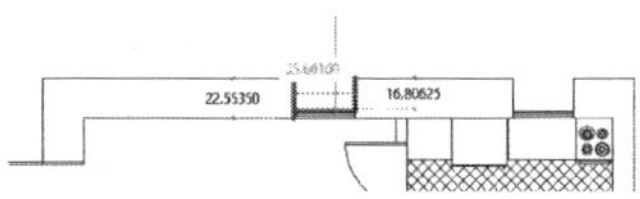

Can you use Quick Measure to determine the width of the window in the living room?

5.

Can you use Quick Measure to determine the distance from the outside wall to the window in the living room?

Distance

Command Locator

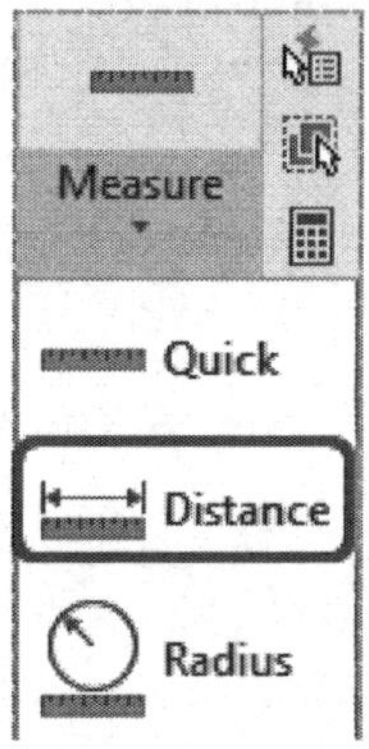

Ribbon/Home/Utilities	**Distance**
Command	**DIST**
Alias	**DI**
RMB Options	**Distance/Radius/Angle/Area/Volume/Quick/Mode**

Command Overview

Displays the distance between elements. You can accumulate distances.

General Procedures:

1. Start the **DISTANCE** command.
2. Select the starting and end points to be measured.
3. To add distances together, select the first point, then right click and select Multiple points.

The optional dimension label always displays the last measured distance. Your start point stays the same throughout.

If you want to change the start point, right-click and select a new start point.

Command Exercise

Exercise 13-3 – Distance

Drawing Name: **dist.dwg**
Estimated Time to Completion: 15 Minutes

Scope

Measure the distance between different elements. Add distances together using the Multiple Points option.

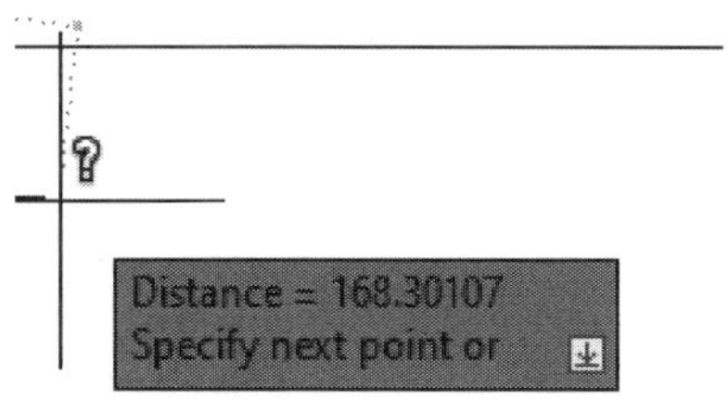

Solution

1. 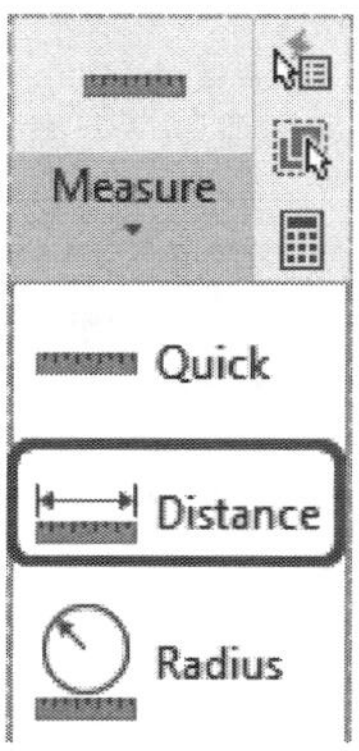

Select the **DISTANCE** tool from the Utilities panel on the Home ribbon.

2. 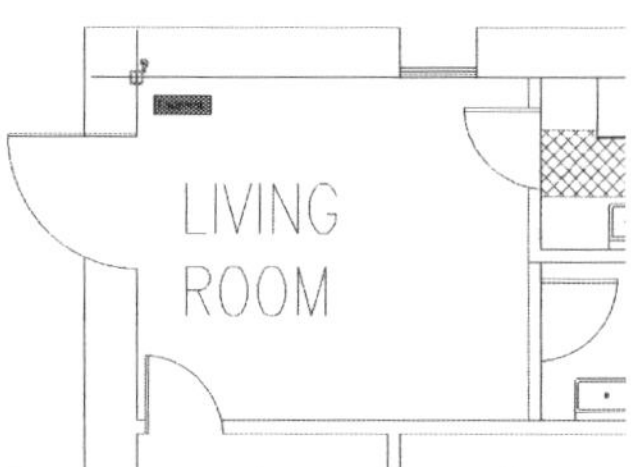

Select the inside face of the west living room wall.

3. 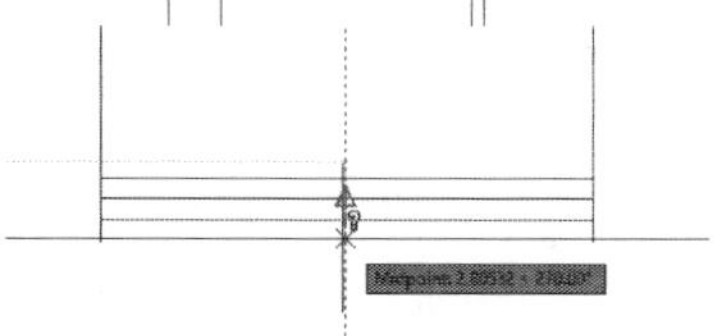

Select the aligned point below the midpoint of the living room window.

4. 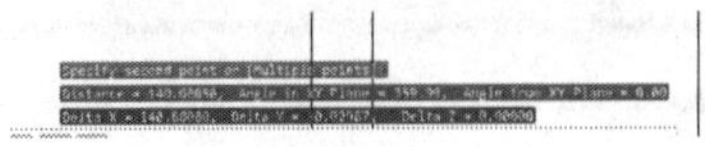

The distance is displayed.

Click **ESC** to exit the command.

5. Right click and select **Repeat MEASUREGEOM**.

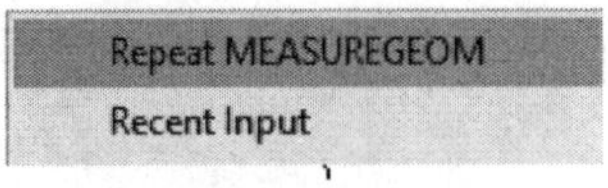

6. 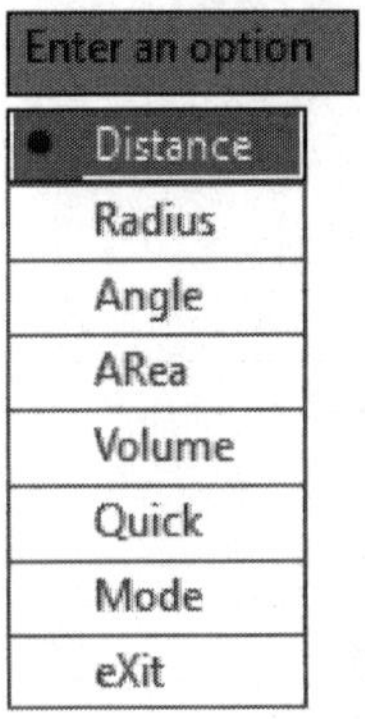

Select the **Distance** option.

7. 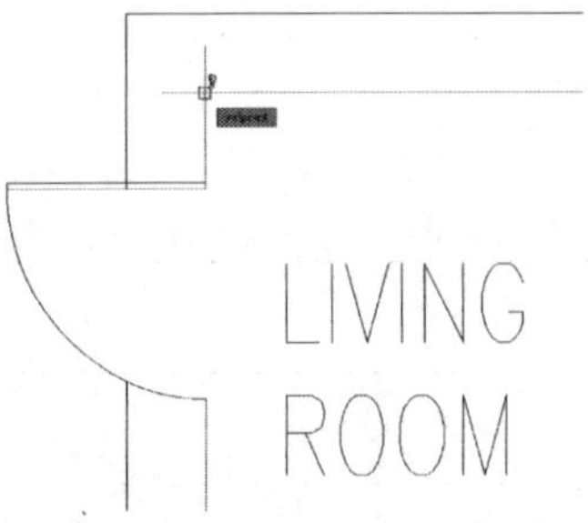

Select the inside top left corner of the living room.

8. 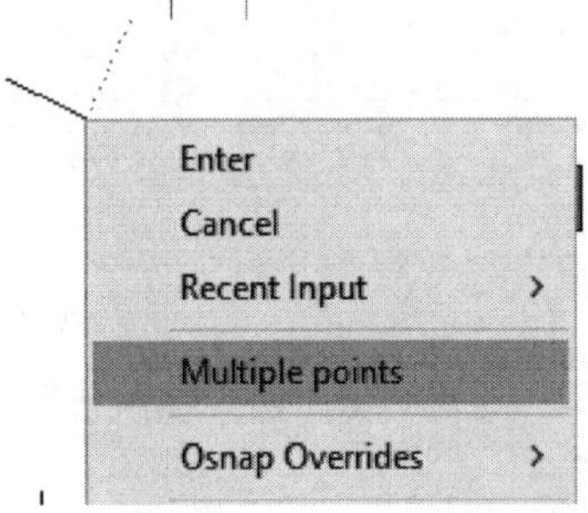

Right click and select **Multiple points**.

9. 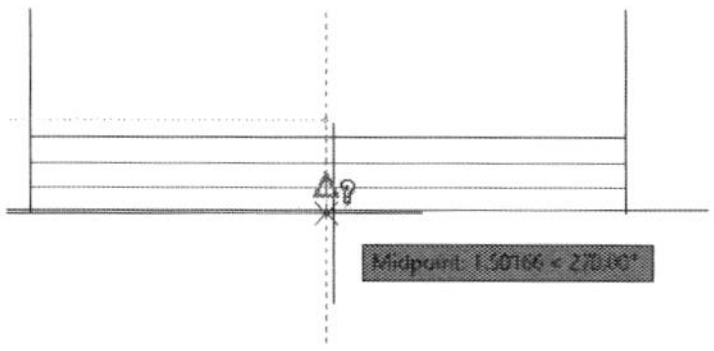

Select the aligned point below the midpoint of the window.

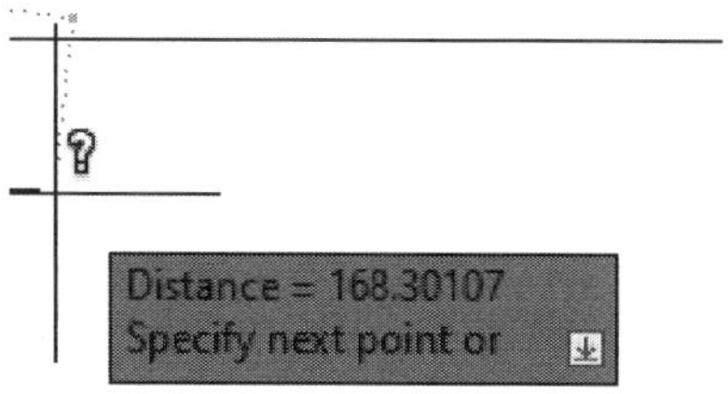

The distance is displayed and you are prompted for the next point.

10. 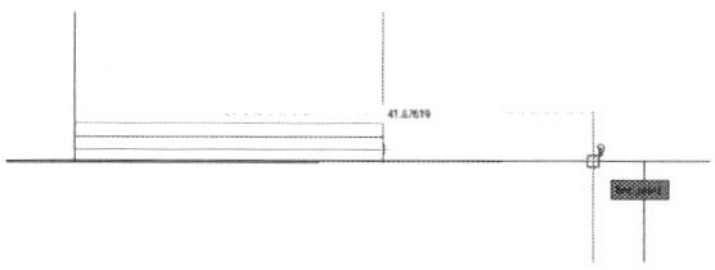

Select the inside top right corner of the living room.

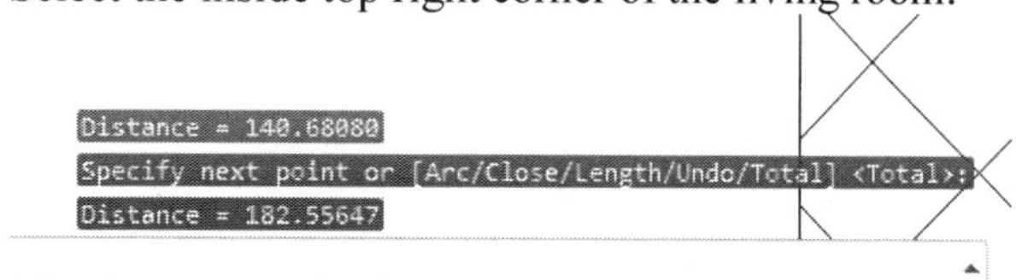

The distance is displayed between the first point and the point that was just selected as well as the total distance.

11. Select **Total.**

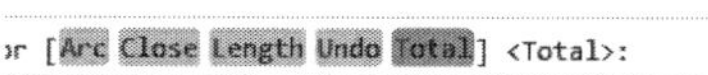

12. 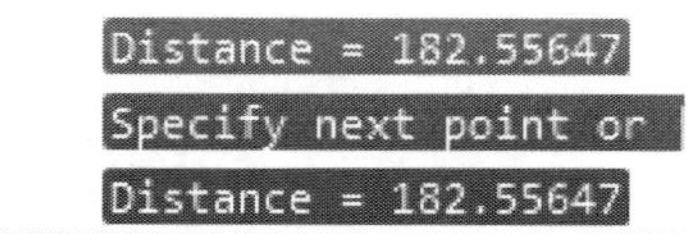

The total distance is displayed.

This is the distance from the first point and the last point selected.

Find and Replace

Command Locator

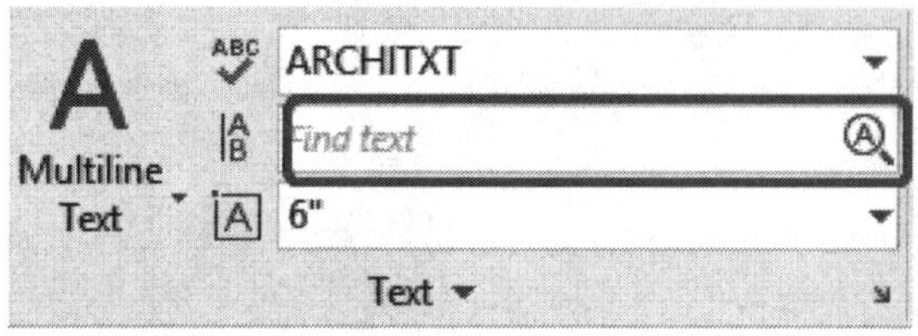

Command	**Find**
RMB Shortcut Menu	**Text Windows in the dialog box**
Dialog Box	**Find and Replace**
Ribbon/Annotate/Text	**Find Text**

Command Overview

The Find and Replace command provides text search with the options to perform a global search or to search selected text. Type in the Text string to find, and type the replacement text.

General Procedures:

1. Invoke the Find and Replace command.
2. Type the text string to Find, and type the replacement text.
3. Select the Find button, then select "Replace All."

Tips & Tricks

- Using this command with selected text is the same as using options in the Find/Replace tab of the Multiline Text dialog box.
- Use the Window option located in the upper right corner to limit the find and replace operation to a specific section of a drawing.

Command Exercise

Exercise 13-4 – Find and Replace

Drawing Name: **findandreplace.dwg**
Estimated Time to Completion: 15 Minutes

Scope

Find and replace text in a drawing.

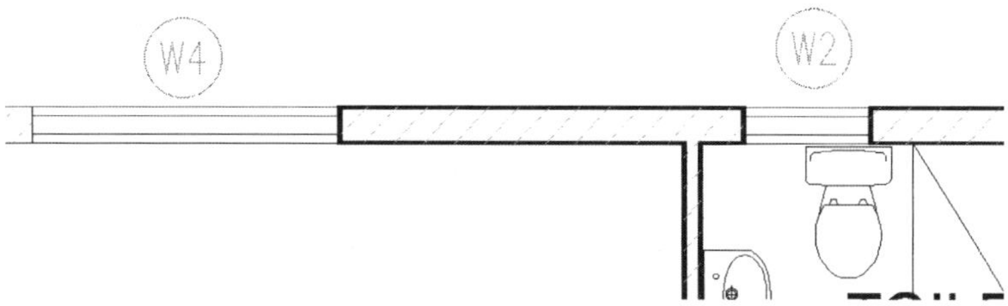

Solution

1. 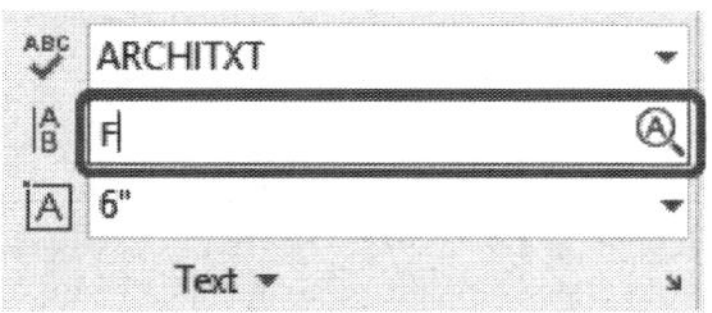

Switch to the **Annotate** ribbon.

Type the letter **F** in the Find and Replace field.

Click on the magnifying glass icon to the right of the field.

2. 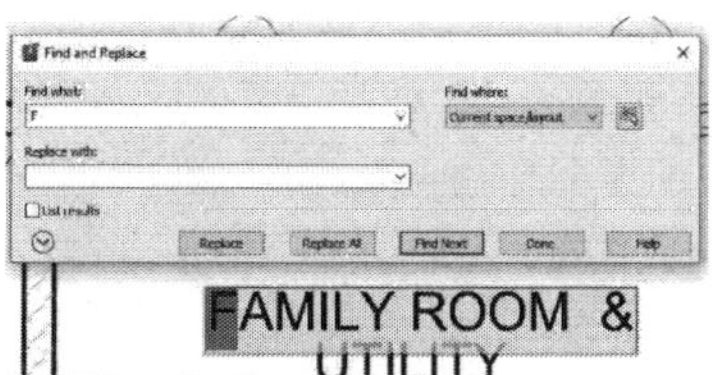

The first word located is family – part of the room label.

Click **Find Next**.

3. 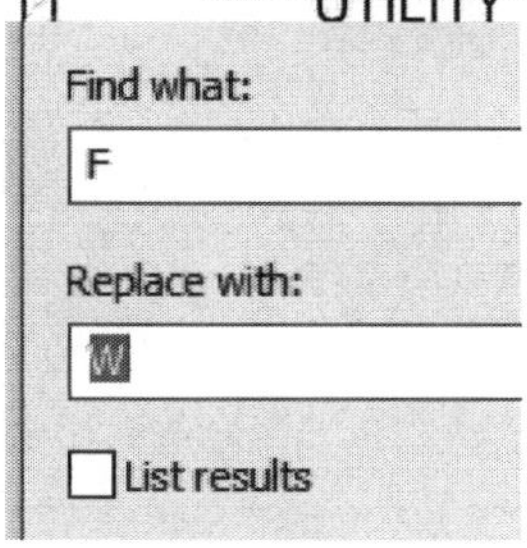

Type **W** in the Replace with field.

Click **Replace**.

4. 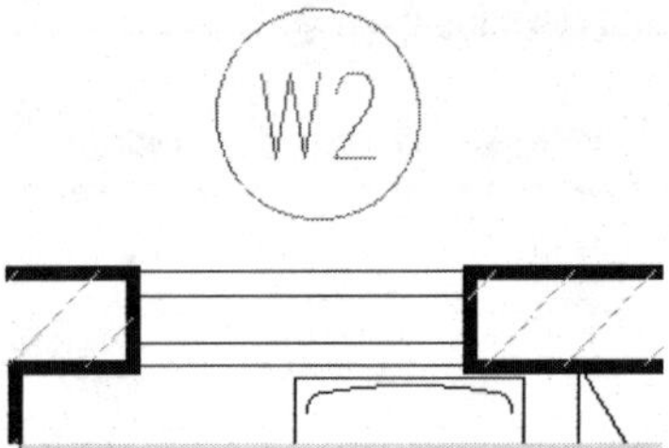

The label is updated.

5. 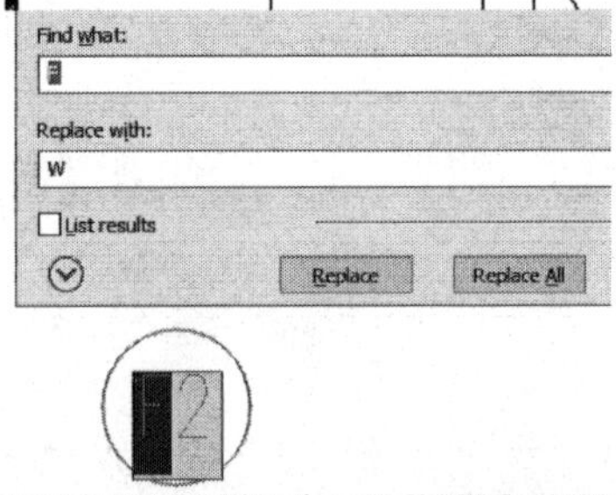

The view updates to the next text.

Click **Replace**.

6. 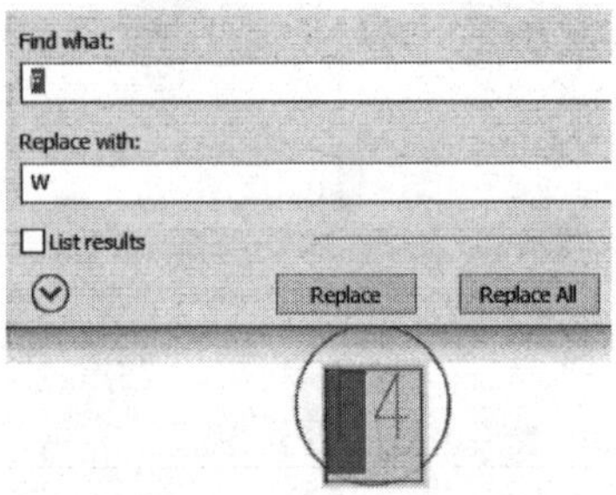

The view updates to the next text.

Click **Replace**.

7. 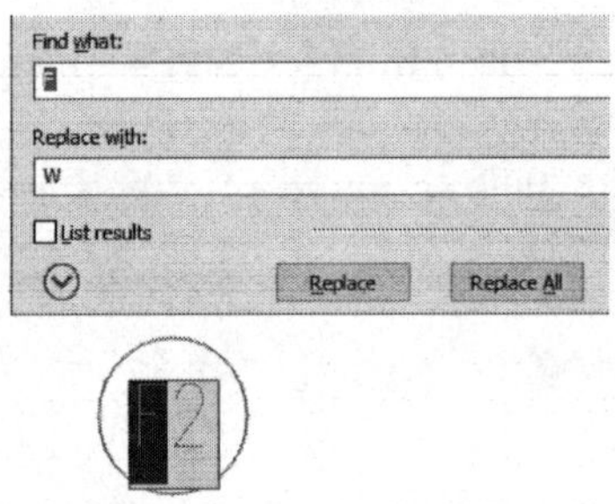

The view updates to the next text.

Click **Replace**.

8. 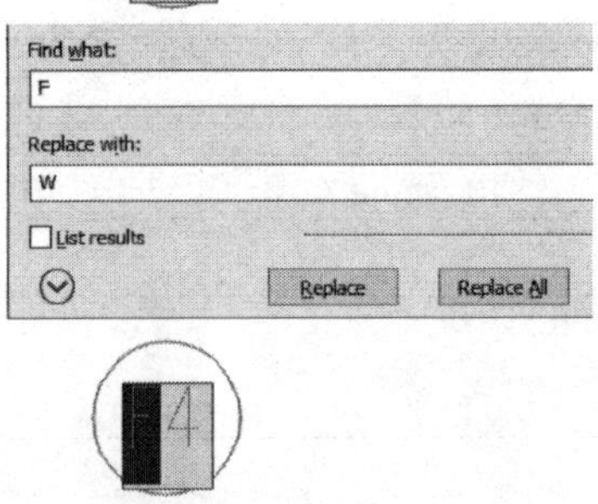

The view updates to the next text.

Click **Replace**.

9. 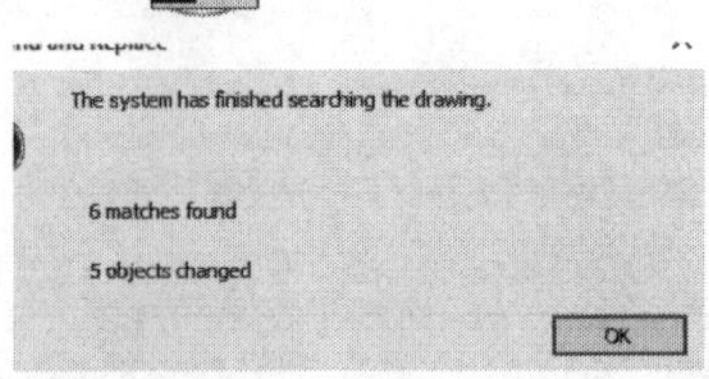

Click **OK**.

Click **Done**.

Spell Check

Command Locator

Ribbon/Annotate/Text	**Spell**
Command	**Spell**
Alias	**SP**
RMB Shortcut Menu	**Text Window of the dialog box**
Dialog Box	**Check Spelling**

Command Overview

Check for spelling errors. Select one line of text or all the text in the drawing. Add words to build a custom dictionary.

Spell Check Option	Overview
Current word	The misspelled word will appear in this area.
Suggestions	Spell check will provide a list of suggested words.
Ignore / Ignore All	Ignore will keep the misspelled word or words as they are.
Change / Change All	This option will substitute the misspelled word or words for a suggested word.
Add	Build a custom dictionary with the Add option.
Lookup	This option will look up more words based on the highlighted suggestion.
Change Dictionary	There are several language dictionaries available with Spell Check, including the custom dictionary.
Context	The sentence context of the misspelled word will appear in this area.

General Procedures:

1. Invoke the Spell command. Select the text to check.
2. Select a suggestion from the list if the current word is incorrect.
3. Select Change, then select OK.

Tips & Tricks

- Building a custom dictionary is useful when abbreviations or technical terms are used frequently in the drawing.

Command Exercise

Exercise 13-5 – Spell Check

Drawing Name: **spell1.dwg**
Estimated Time to Completion: 5 Minutes

Scope

Correct the spelling in the text provided.

Solution

1. 

From the Annotate ribbon, select **Check Spelling**.

2. 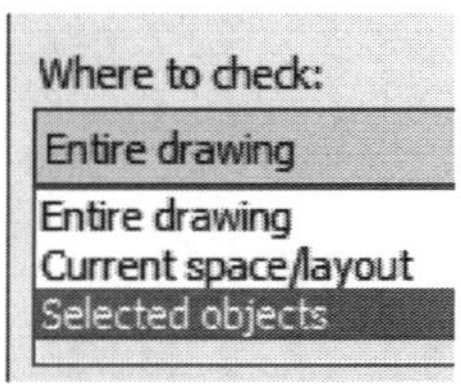

In the Where to check: drop-down, select **Selected objects**.

3. 

Click the **Select** tool to activate the selection mode.

4. 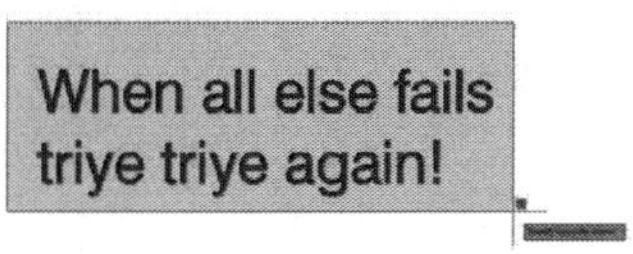

Select objects:
Use the LMB to pick the text to check and click <ENTER> or type **ALL** to check the spelling for the entire drawing.

5. 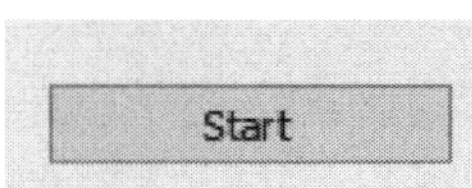

Click **Start**.

6. 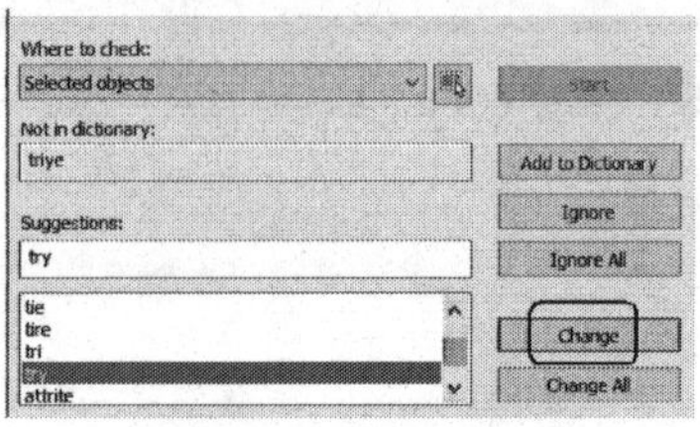

Locate the correct spelling under Suggestions and click **Change**.

7. 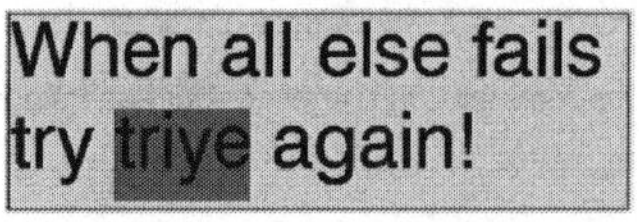

The spell checker will advance to the next misspelled word.
Change that one as well.

8. 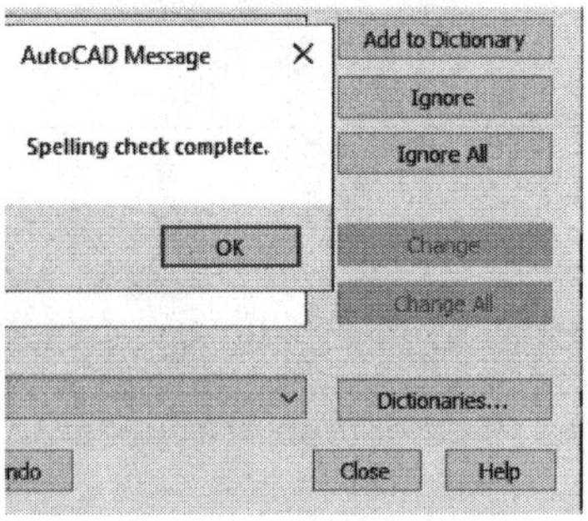

Click **'OK'** when notified that Spell Check is complete to finish the command.

Close the Spell Check dialog.

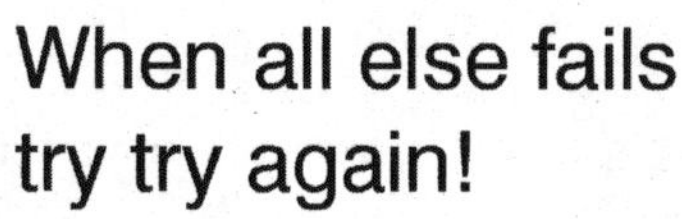

Purge

Command Locator

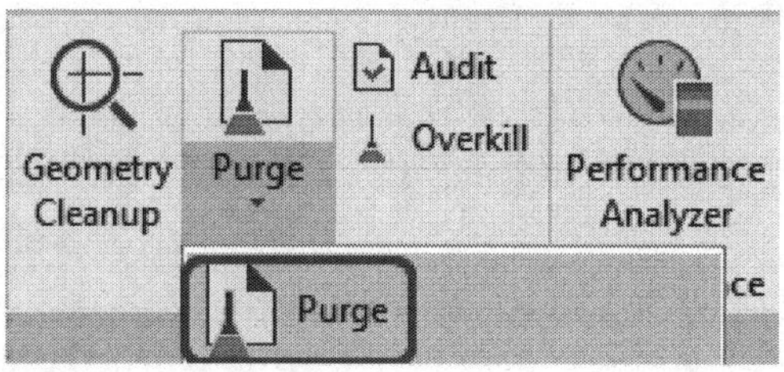

Ribbon/Manage/Cleanup	**Purge**
Command	**Purge**
Alias	**pu**
Dialog Box	**Purge**

Command Overview

Unused named objects can be removed from the current drawing. These include block definitions, dimension styles, groups, layers, linetypes, and text styles. Zero-length geometry, empty text objects, and orphaned DGN linestyle data can also be removed. This reduces the size of the drawing file and also reduces the chances the drawing will become corrupted.

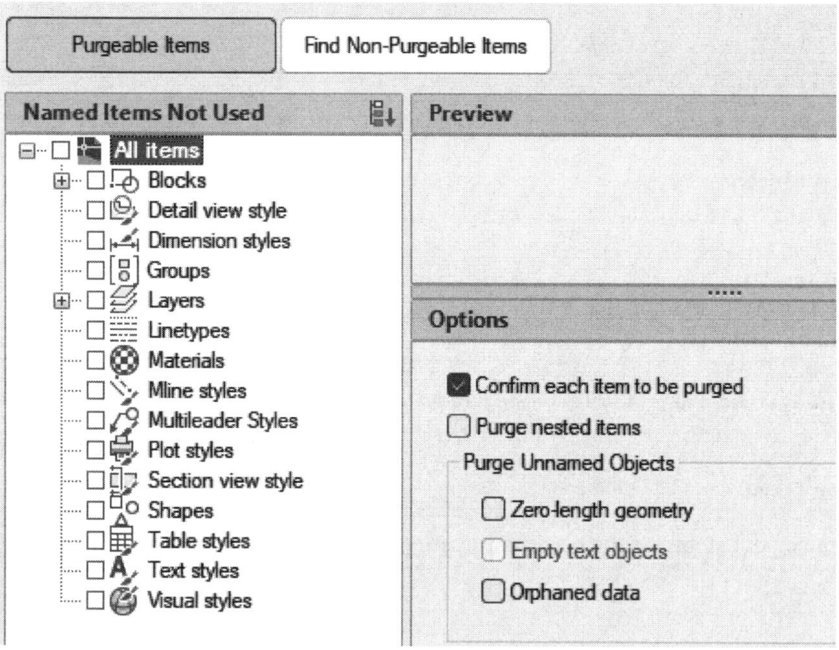

Purgeable Items

Lists the items in your current drawing that you can purge in the tree view pane on the left side. Additional items can be removed from the drawing under the Purge Unnamed Objects pane on the right side of the dialog box.

Named Items Not Used

Lists the named objects that are not used in the current drawing and that are purgeable. You can list the items for any object type by clicking the plus sign or by double-clicking the object type. You can either select an individual item or all the items of that object type.

Purge Nested Items removes items only when you select one of the following options:

- All Items or Blocks in the tree view
- The Purge All button

Preview

Displays a preview of the item you selected in the tree view by clicking on its name.

Options

Confirm Each Item to Be Purged

Displays the Confirm Purge dialog box when you purge an item. This can slow down the process a great deal depending on what you have elected to remove.

Purge Nested Items

Removes all unused named objects from the drawing even if they are contained within or referenced by other unused named objects.

Purge Unnamed Objects

Zero-length geometry
Deletes geometry of zero length, including lines, arcs, circles, and polylines.

Empty text objects
Deletes mtext and text objects that contain only spaces without any text.

Orphaned data
Performs a drawing scan and removes obsolete DGN linestyle data when you open the Purge dialog box.

Note: *The PURGE command will not remove unnamed objects from blocks or locked layers.*

Purge Checked Items

Removes the selected items from the current drawing.

Purge All

Purges all unused items.

Note: *When all purgeable items are removed, various items and options are grayed out and a message displays in the lower-left corner of the dialog box.*

General Procedures:

1. Start the **PURGE** command.
2. Enable the elements to be removed from the drawing.
3. Enable the desired options.
4. Click **Purge All**.

Tips & Tricks

- *You can only purge elements that are not in use.*
- *The Styles toolbar can be used to quickly switch from one text style to another.*

Command Exercise

Exercise 13-6 – Purge Text Styles

Drawing Name: **purge.dwg**
Estimated Time to Completion: 5 Minutes

Scope

Use the Purge command to delete the text style called TEXT2, or delete it from the dialog box.

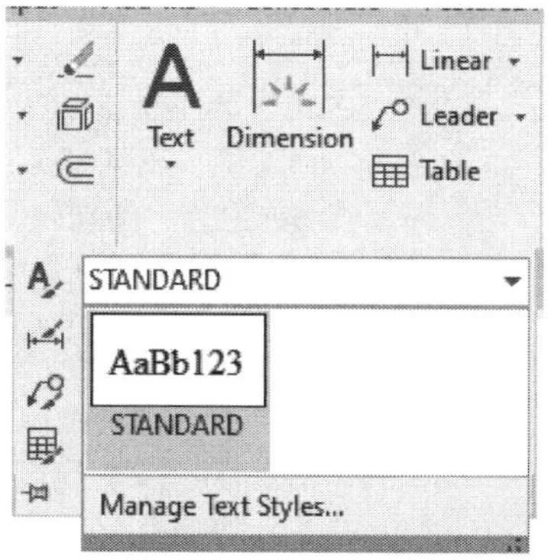

Solution

1.

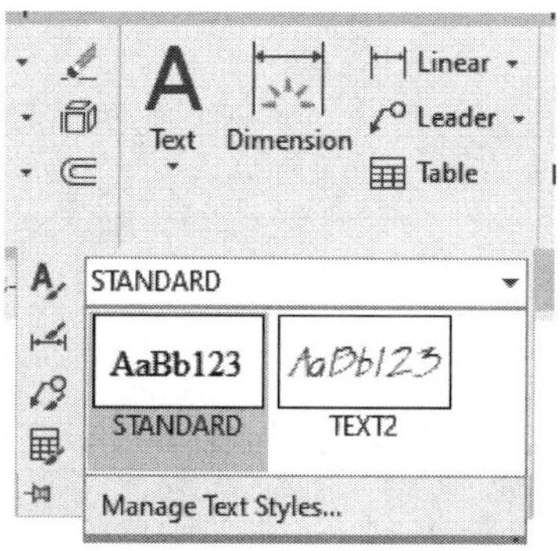

From the Home ribbon, select the **Text Style** tool on the Annotation pull-down.

You can also set the current text style by using the drop-down list next to the Text Style tool.

2.

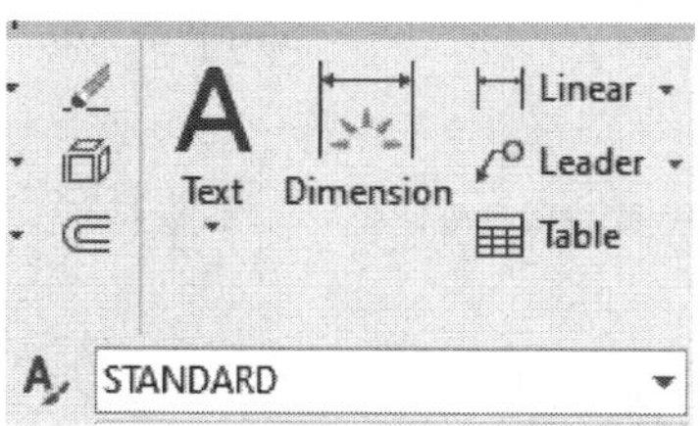

Highlight the **Standard** text style and select to make it current.

Click **Close** to close the Text Style dialog box.

3. 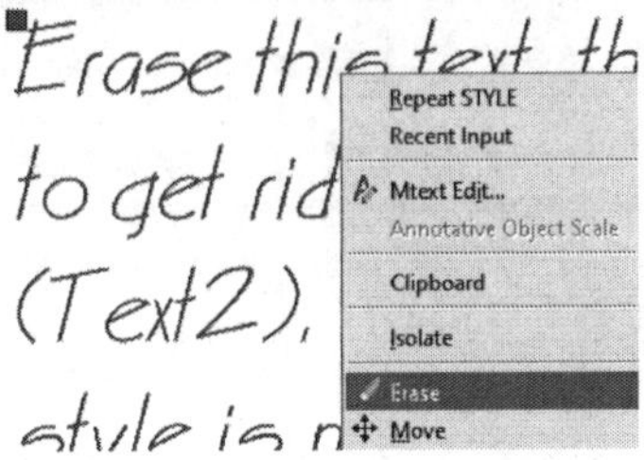

Select the text.

RMB and select **Erase**.

4. 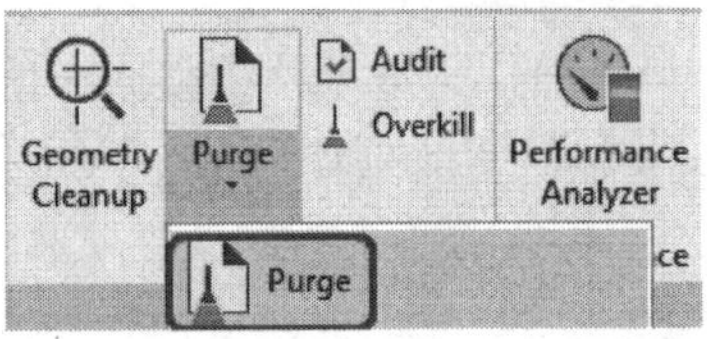

Invoke the Purge command.

Activate the Manage ribbon.

Select the **Purge** tool.

5. 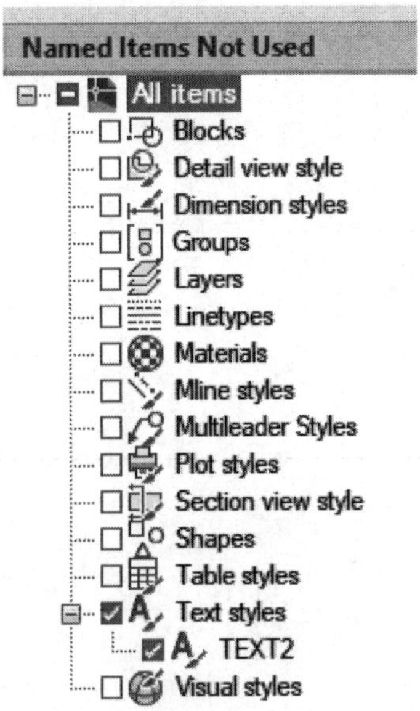

Expand the Text Styles category.
Highlight **TEXT2**.

6. 

Select the **Purge Checked Items** button.

7. 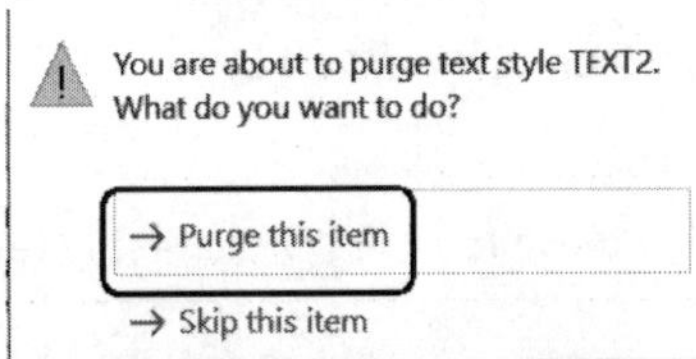

A dialog will pop up to verify that you want to purge the text style.

Select **Purge this item**.

8. 

Click the **Close** button.

*The dialog appeared because **Confirm each item to be purged** is enabled.*

9. 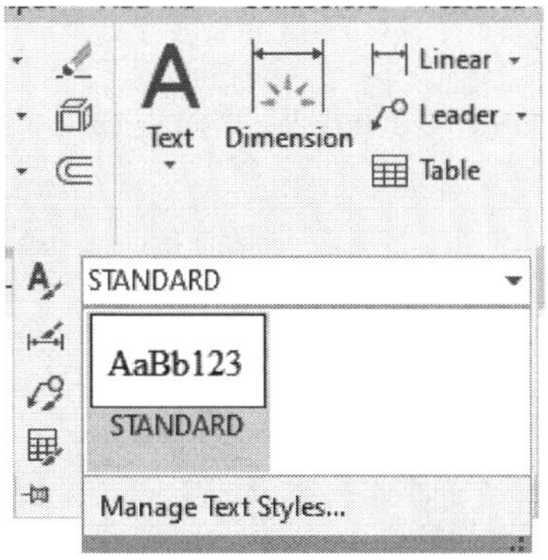

From the Home ribbon, select the Text Style drop-down list pull-down.

The TEXT2 text style is no longer available.

PDF import

Command Locator

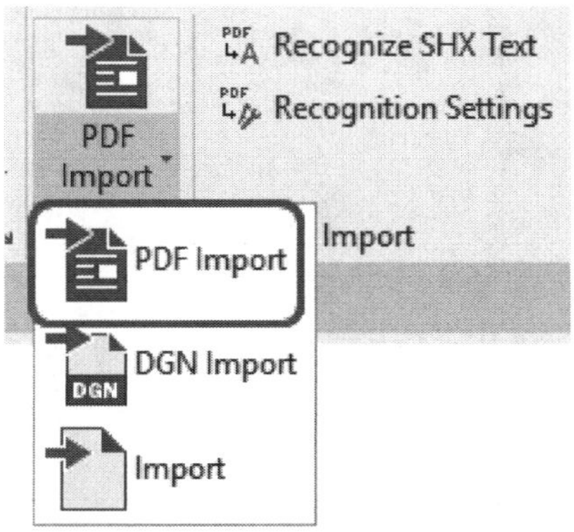

Ribbon/Insert	**PDFIMPORT**
Command	**PDFIMPORT**

Command Overview

Import a pdf drawing and translate the elements to AutoCAD elements, like lines, arcs, and circles.

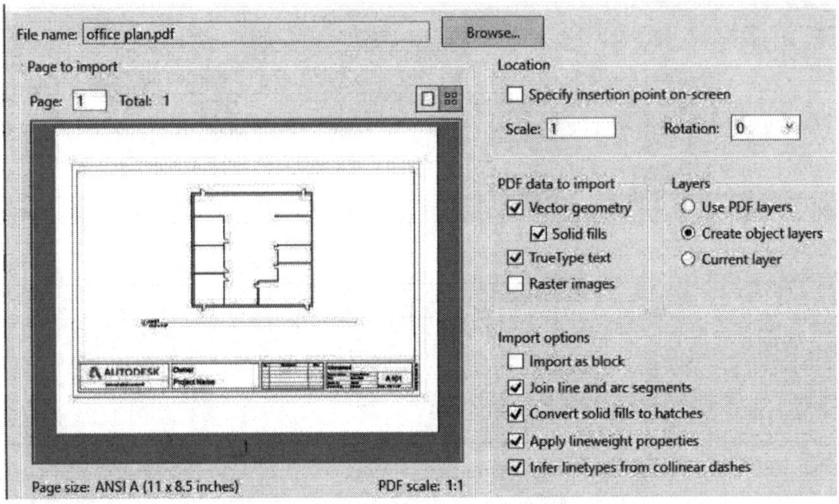

General Procedures:

1. Start the **PDFIMPORT** command.
2. Locate the pdf file to be imported.
3. Select the desired options.
4. Click **OK**.

Tips & Tricks

- *Use the Layer Translator to move PDF layers to the preferred AutoCAD layers.*

Command Exercise

Exercise 13-7 – PDF Import

Drawing Name: **pdfimport.dwg, office plan.pdf**

Estimated Time to Completion: 10 Minutes

Scope

AutoCAD allows users to import PDFs and convert them to AutoCAD drawings. In order for the PDF to convert properly, it must contain vector graphics. If the PDF contains renderings or shading, it is not a vector PDF. It is a raster PDF and would need to be vectorized prior to import.

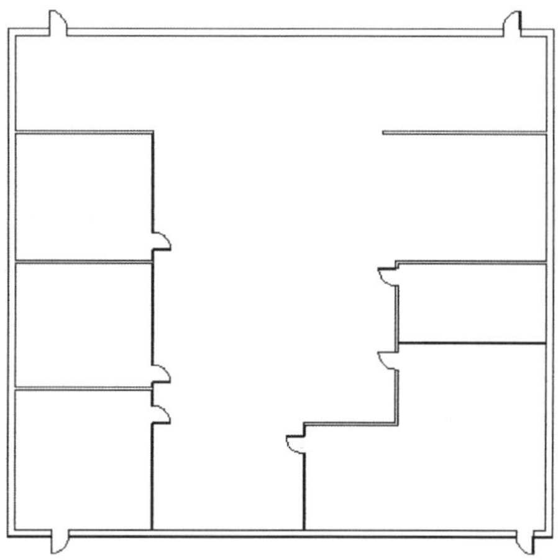

Solution

1. Open *pdfimport.dwg.*
2. Verify that the Model tab is enabled.

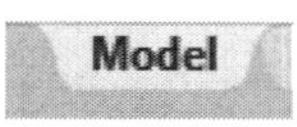

3. Select **PDFImport** on the Insert ribbon.

4. Set Files of type to **PDF**.

5.

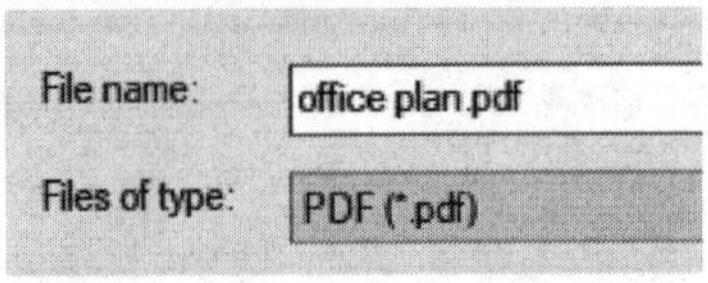

Browse to your exercise folder.
Select *office plan*.
Click **Open**.

6.

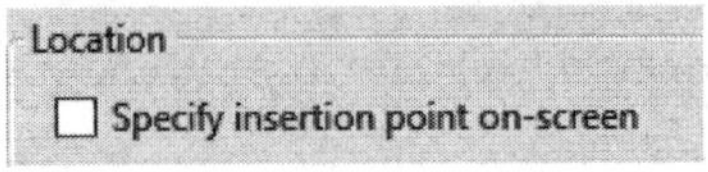

There is only a single page in this pdf.
It is previewed.
Under Location:
Uncheck **Specify insertion point on screen.**
This will automatically insert the PDF at the origin (0,0).

7.

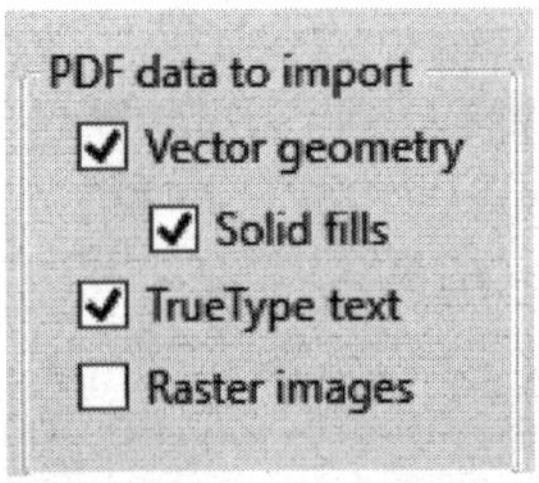

Under PDF data to import:
Enable **Vector geometry**.
Enable **Solid fills.**
Enable **TrueType text**.

8.

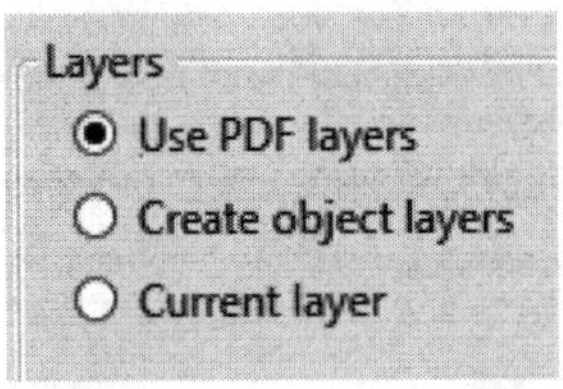

Under Layers:
Enable **Use PDF Layers**.
This will use any PDF layers that have been assigned. If PDF layers exist, they will be listed with a prefix of PDF_. If there are no PDF layers, the Create object layers option will automatically be used. The layers created will be called PDF_Geometry, PDF_Solid Fills, and PDF_Text.
Click **OK**.

9.

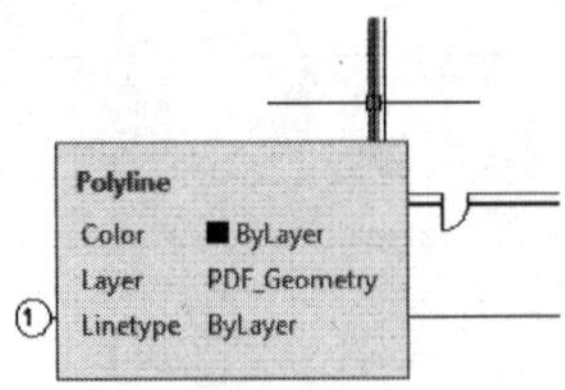

If you mouse over any of the geometry, a dialog will display indicating that it has been imported as an AutoCAD element and the layer it has been placed on.

Trace

Command Locator

Ribbon/Collaborate	**Trace Palette**
Command	**Trace**

Command Overview

Trace provides a safe space to add changes to a drawing in the web and mobile apps without altering the existing drawing. The analogy is of a virtual collaborative tracing paper that is laid over the drawing that allows collaborators to add feedback on the drawing.

Create traces in the web and mobile apps, then send or share the drawing to collaborators so they can view the trace and its contents.

Traces can be viewed in the desktop application but can only be created or edited in the mobile apps.

In order to create a checkout, you need to upload the drawing to the cloud using Forma Data Management.

General Procedures:

1. Open a drawing which has been sent to you by a collaborator.
2. View the traces.

- *Traces are a way to communicate design intentions between collaborators. You can share a drawing with a team member, supervisor or client. They can view it on the free mobile app on their smart phone or tablet and add their comments and return the file to you for review.*

Command Exercise

Exercise 13-8 – Trace

Drawing Name: **trace.dwg**

Estimated Time to Completion: 5 Minutes

Scope

You can share a drawing with a colleague or client and have them add notations for your review using the free mobile app available to smart phones and tablets.

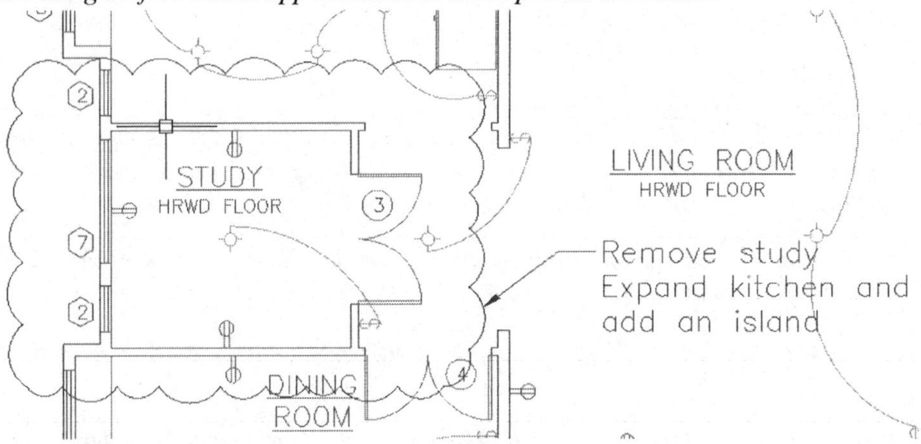

Solution

1.

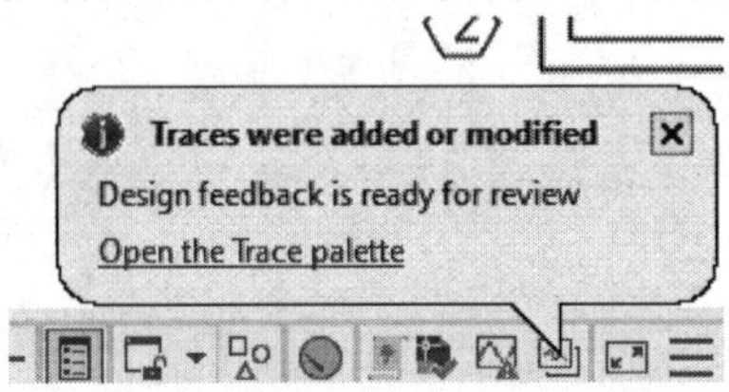

When you open the file, you will see a small notification in the lower right corner that a collaborator has added notes to the drawing.
If you don't see the notification, click on the Traces icon.

Click on the link to **Display the Trace palette**.

2.

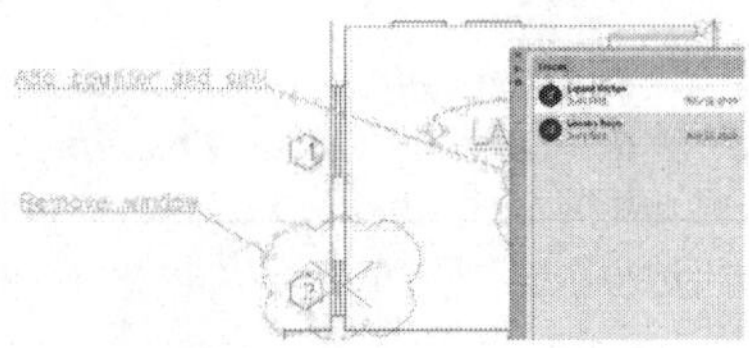

If you click on one of the notes, the drawing will zoom to the area and you will see the notations provided by the collaborator.

3. 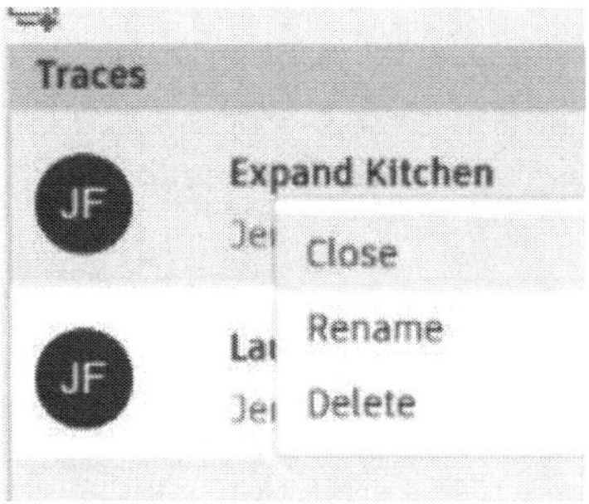

Right click on the trace note.
Select **Close**.

You will no longer see the mark-ups.

Close the Traces palette.

4. 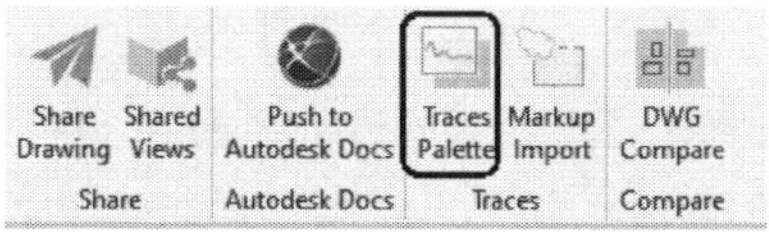

Switch to the **Collaborate** ribbon.

Click on the **Traces Palette**.

5. 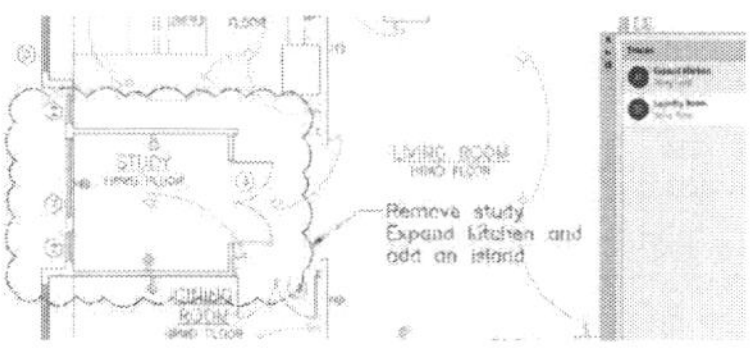

You can review the notes again.

6. Close without saving.

Count

Command Locator

Ribbon/View	**COUNT**
Command	**COUNT**

Command Overview

Counts selected objects and highlights the counted objects in the drawing.

When you are in an active count, the Count toolbar is displayed at the top of the drawing area, and all the instances of the selected object or block are highlighted.

General Procedures:

1. Start the **COUNT** command.
2. Click ENTER to search the entire drawing or select an area of the drawing to search.

➢ COUNT is similar to BATTMAN without the editing functionality.

Command Exercise

Exercise 13-9 – Count

Drawing Name: **count.dwg**

Estimated Time to Completion: 5 Minutes

Scope

Get a quick count of the blocks existing in the drawing.

Solution

1.

Type **COUNT**.

2.

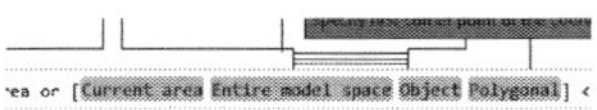

Click on **Entire model space**.
Click **ENTER.**

3.

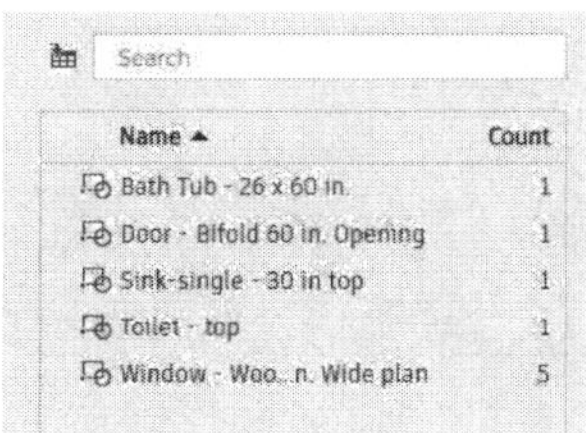

A list of the blocks present in the drawing is displayed.

4.

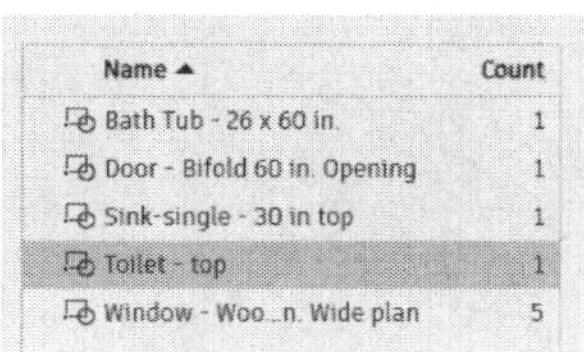

Select **Toilet** in the list.

5.

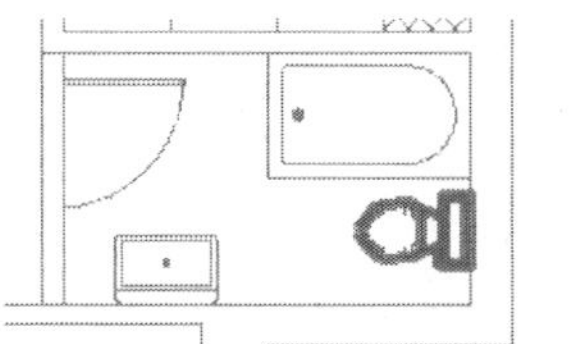

The block is highlighted in the drawing.

6.

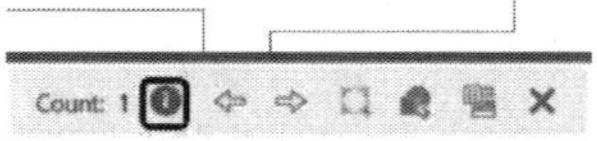

There is a small toolbar displayed.
Click on the info icon.

7. 

Information about the block is displayed.

Close the Count palette.

8. 

Click the X to close the Count toolbar and exit Count mode.

Markup Import

Command Locator

Ribbon/Collaborate	**MARKUPIMPORT**
Command	**MARKUPIMPORT**

Command Overview

Imports an image file or pdf to use as a trace for an existing drawing.

You can convert elements of the trace to AutoCAD elements.

Options		
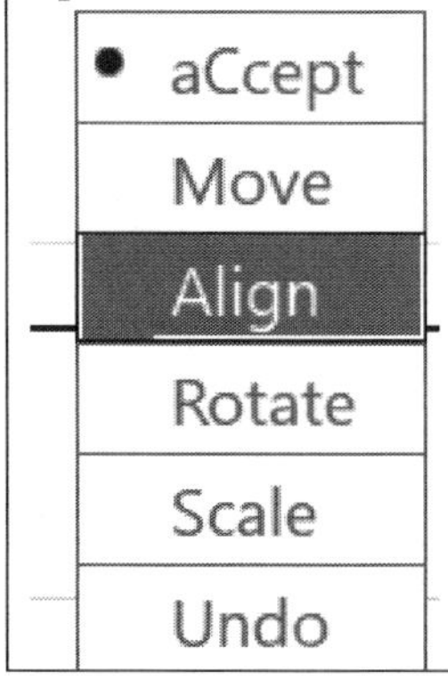	*Accept*	Accepts the position and orientation of the trace.
	Move	Moves the trace to a new position.
	Align	Prompts the user to select a basepoint in the X direction and reference point, then a basepoint in the Y direction and a reference point, then scales and positions the trace to the existing drawing.
	Rotate	Rotates the trace.
	Scale	Scales the trace.

General Procedures:

1. Start the **MARKUPIMPORT** command.
2. Select the pdf or image to import.
3. AutoCAD converts the file to a trace and inserts into the active drawing.
4. User can reposition, scale or rotate the trace to align it with the active drawing.
5. User can convert elements in the trace to AutoCAD elements.

Command Exercise

Exercise 13-10 – Markup Import

Drawing Name: **markupimport.dwg**

Estimated Time to Completion: 15 Minutes

Scope

Import a pdf into a drawing as a mark-up.
Convert the mark ups to AutoCAD elements.

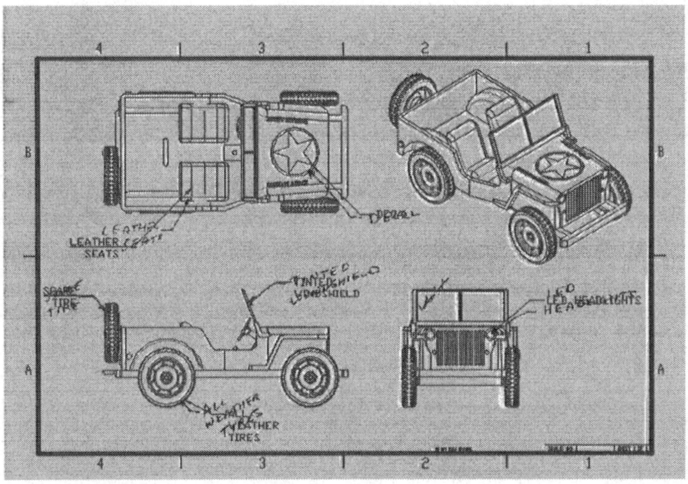

Solution

1.

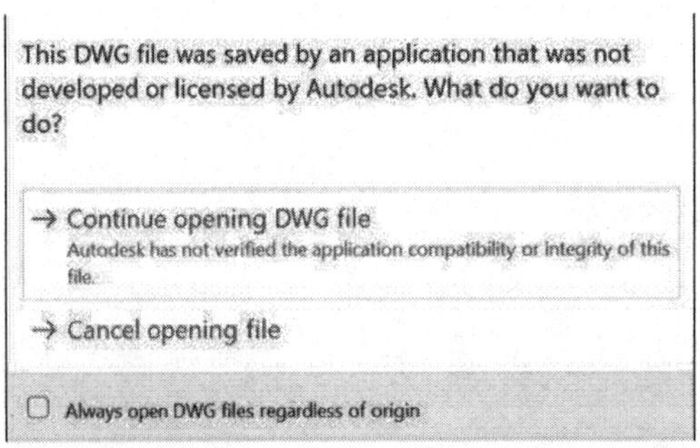

If this dialog appears:

Click **Continue opening DWG file**.

This drawing was created in SOLIDWORKS.

2.

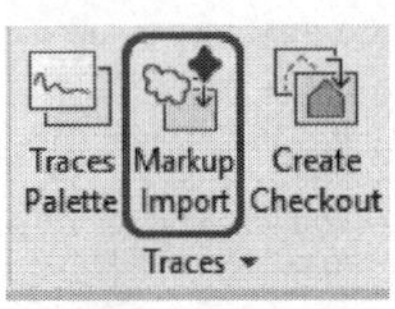

Activate the Collaborate ribbon.

Click **Markup Import**.

3. 

Click **I understand.**

4. 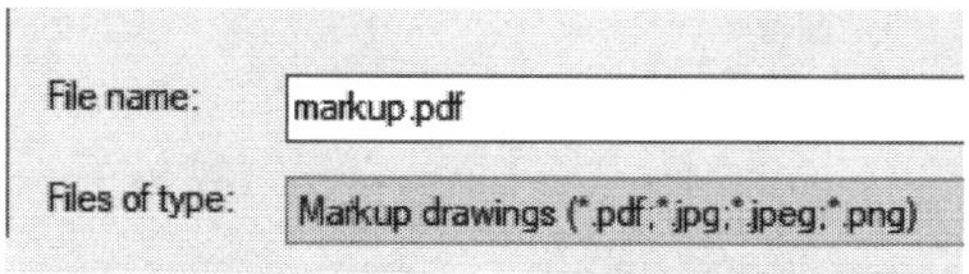

Locate the *markup.pdf* file downloaded from the publisher.

Click **Open.**

5. 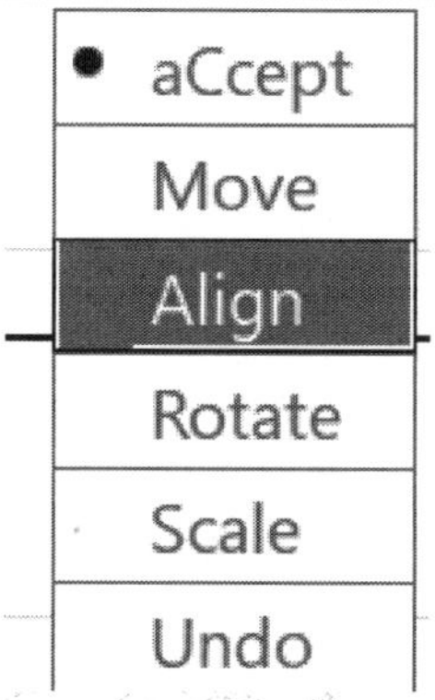

You can adjust the position of the markup so it overlays the existing drawing.

Click **Align**.

6. 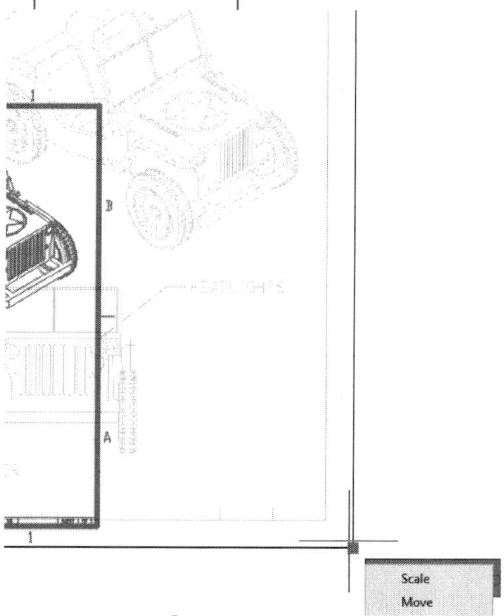

Click the lower right corner of the markup to use as the basepoint.

7. 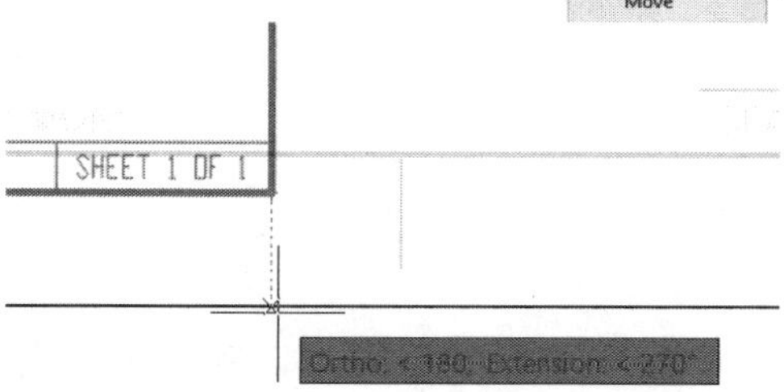

Use the Extension OSNAP to set the X value to scale.

Hint: Enable ORTHO.

8.

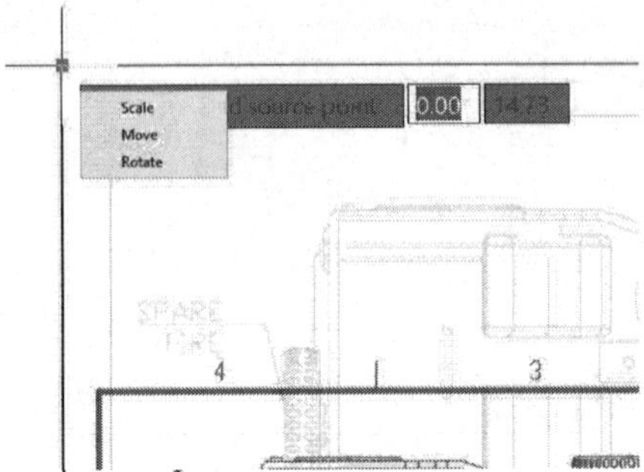

Select the upper left corner of the trace as the second Y basepoint.

9.

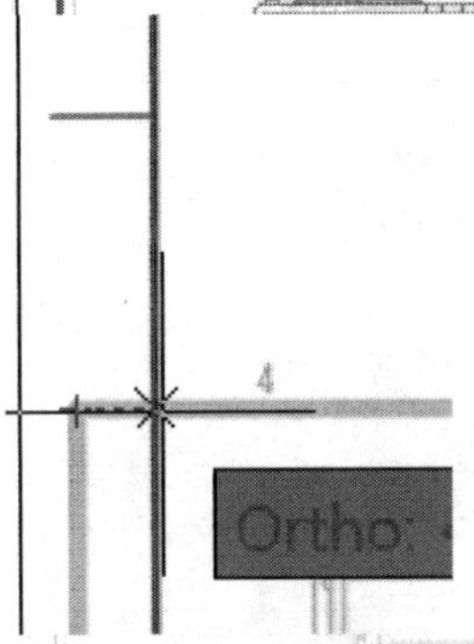

Use the Extension OSNAP to set the Y value to scale.

10.

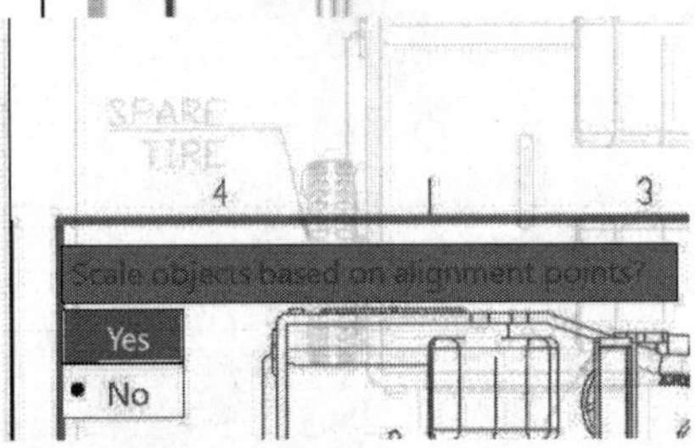

Click **Yes to scale the trace to overlay the drawing.**

11.

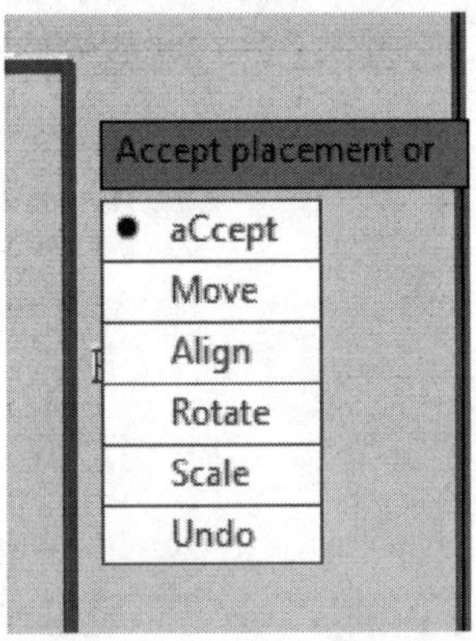

Accept the placement if it looks correct.

If it doesn't look correct, start over by selecting ALIGN.

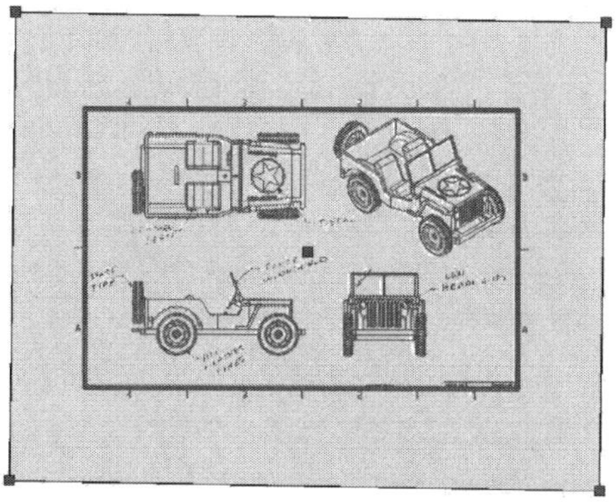

The imported PDF is a trace that is placed on top or below the existing drawing.

When you are done with your adjustments it should look like this.

12.

Highlight the Drawing button.
You should see a little lightning bolt icon. This means MARKUPASSIST mode is activated.

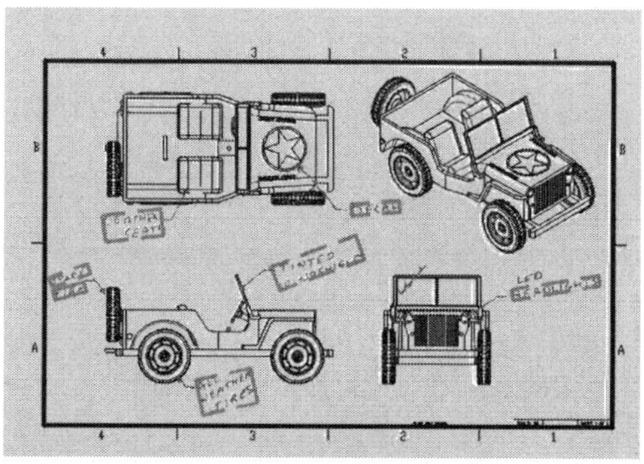

The markups are highlighted.

13.

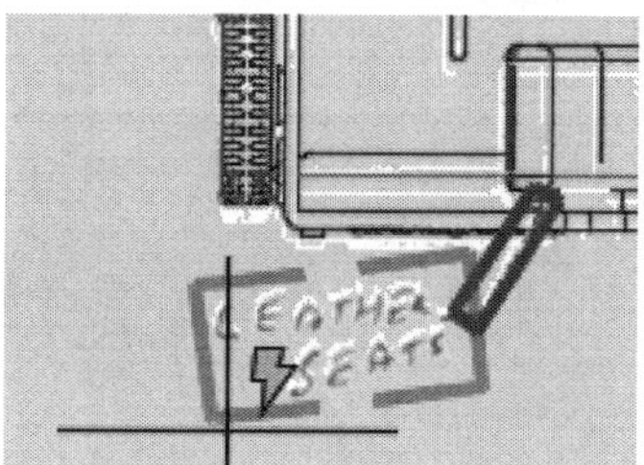

Hover the mouse over one of the blue dashed rectangles.

A small lightning bolt will appear and a small dialog will show the identified text.

Click on the blue rectangle.

14.

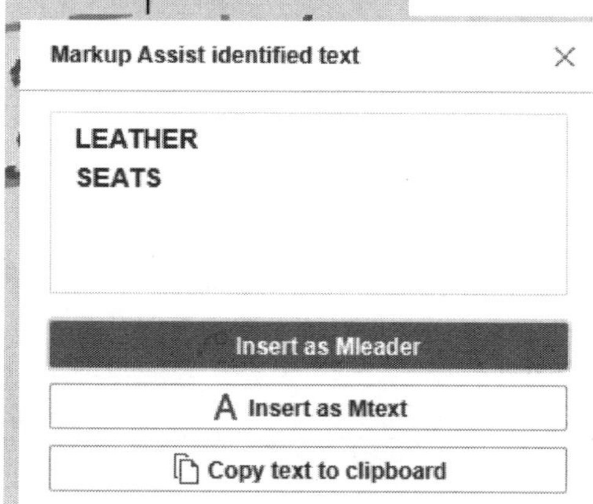

Click **Insert as Mleader**.

15. 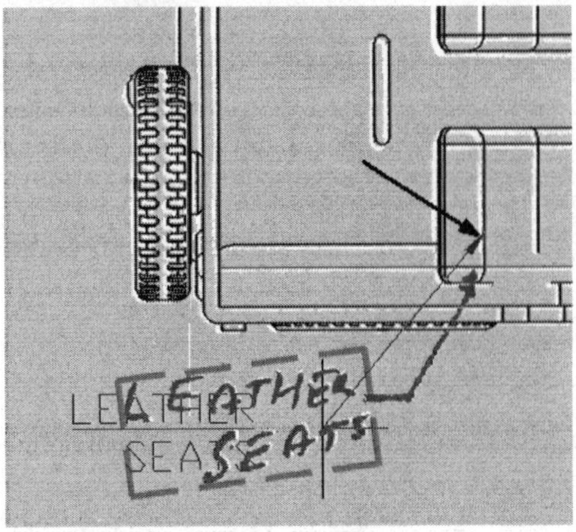

Click to place the arrowhead.

Move the cursor to locate where to place the MTEXT, then click to place the MTEXT.

16. 

Repeat with the remaining markups.

If the MARKASSIST only sees one of the words, you can type in the missing word in the edit box or change the MTEXT to anything you like.

17. 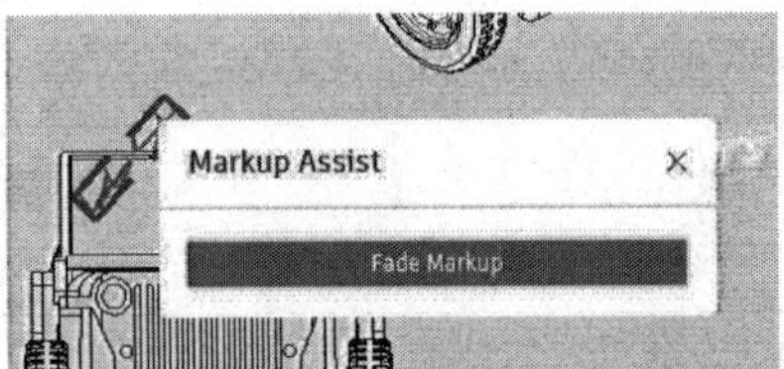

Select the markup on the windshield.
Click **Fade Markup**.

18. 

Toggle the Markup Assist OFF.

19. 

Select the X to close the trace.

20. 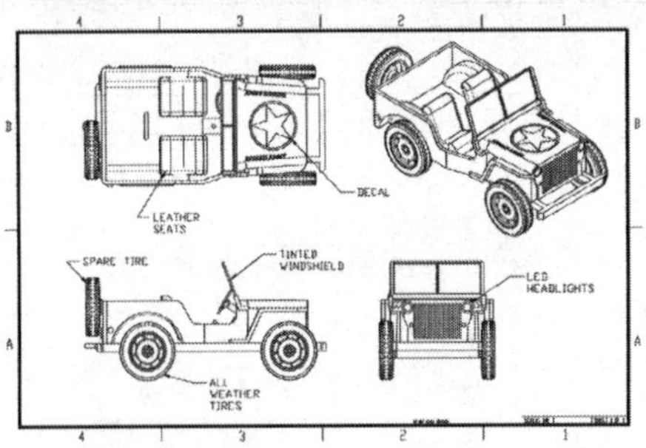

The drawing has been updated.

The imported trace is no longer visible.

21. 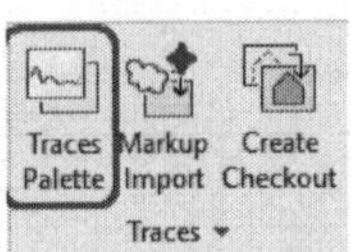

To bring the TRACE up again,
Click on the **Traces Palette**.

22.

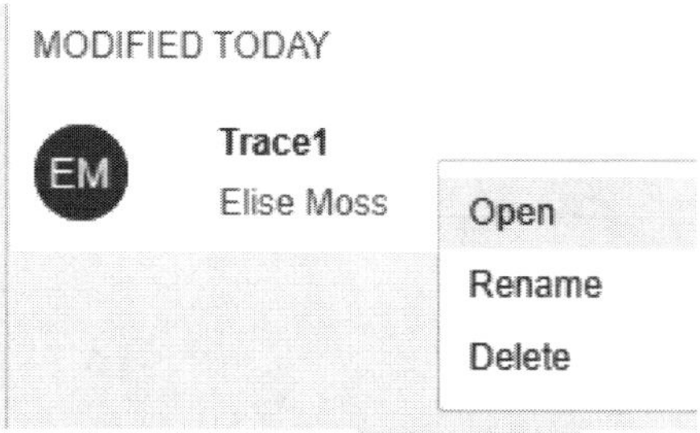

The trace is still in the drawing.

RMB on the Trace file.

Right click and select **Open**.

23.

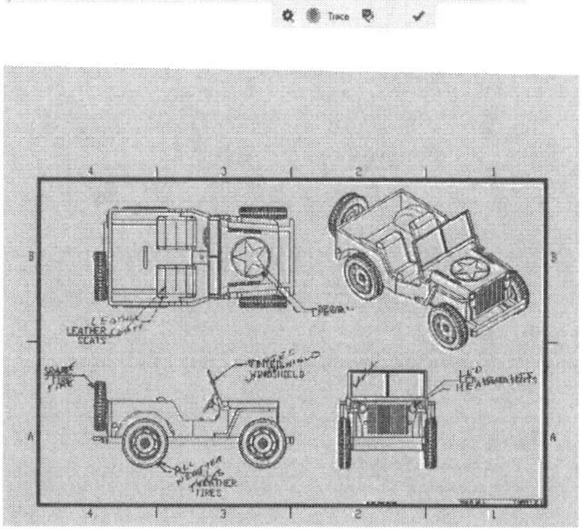

The trace is now visible again.

Use the X to close the trace.

Save and close.

eTransmit

Command Locator

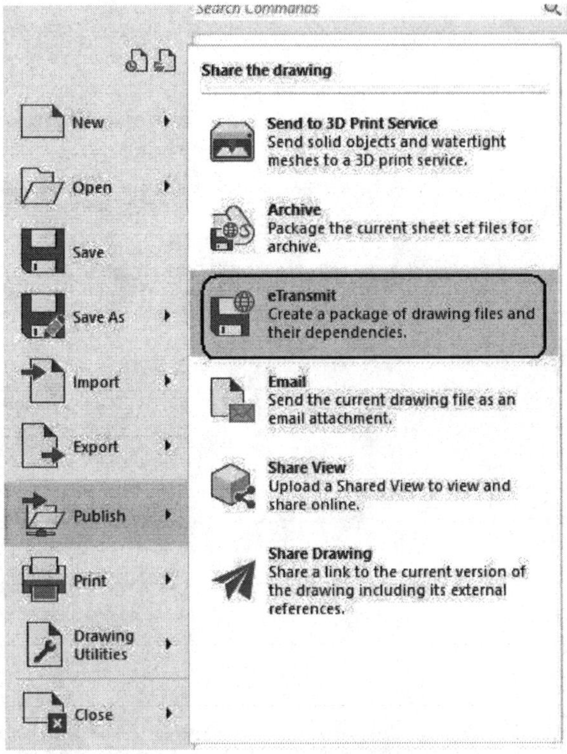

Application Menu/Publish	**eTransmit**
Command	**ETRANSMIT**

Command Overview

eTransmit packages and delivers a set of drawings and supporting files in electronic transmittal packages. The packages can be created as a file folder or a zip (compressed) file.

Many users have found eTransmit useful to create a "snapshot" of their project at different stages so they can maintain a history. For example, when a product is released, the CAD Manager might use eTransmit to bundle up all the current files related to the project and upload the package to a back-up server. You can save the Transmittal Settings to reuse as the project moves forward. eTransmit can also be used to send document sets for submittal to sub-contractors, vendors, or government agencies.

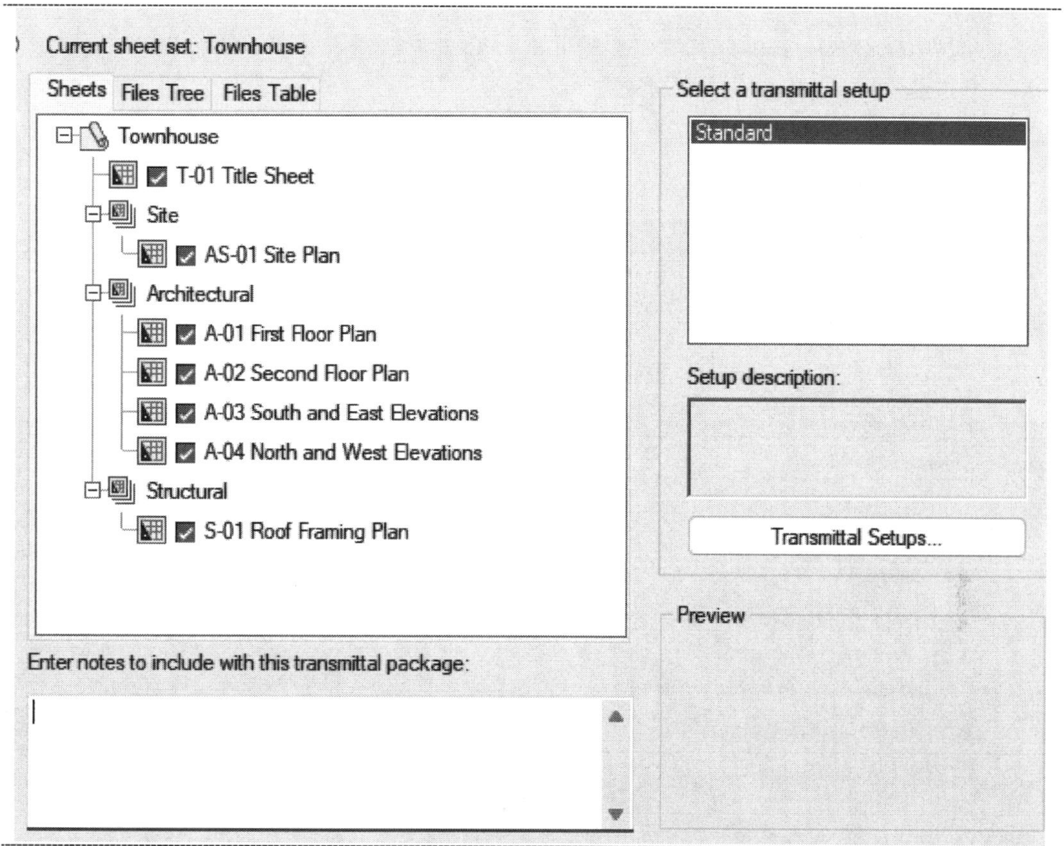

Best practice is to use the Sheet Set Manager to gather the files you want to use for the transmittal package.

If you select the Files Tree Tab: 	You can see how many files are included in the transmittal and add additional files to the transmittal package. This is helpful if you want to include specifications, purchase orders, bills of material, etc. to the document set.

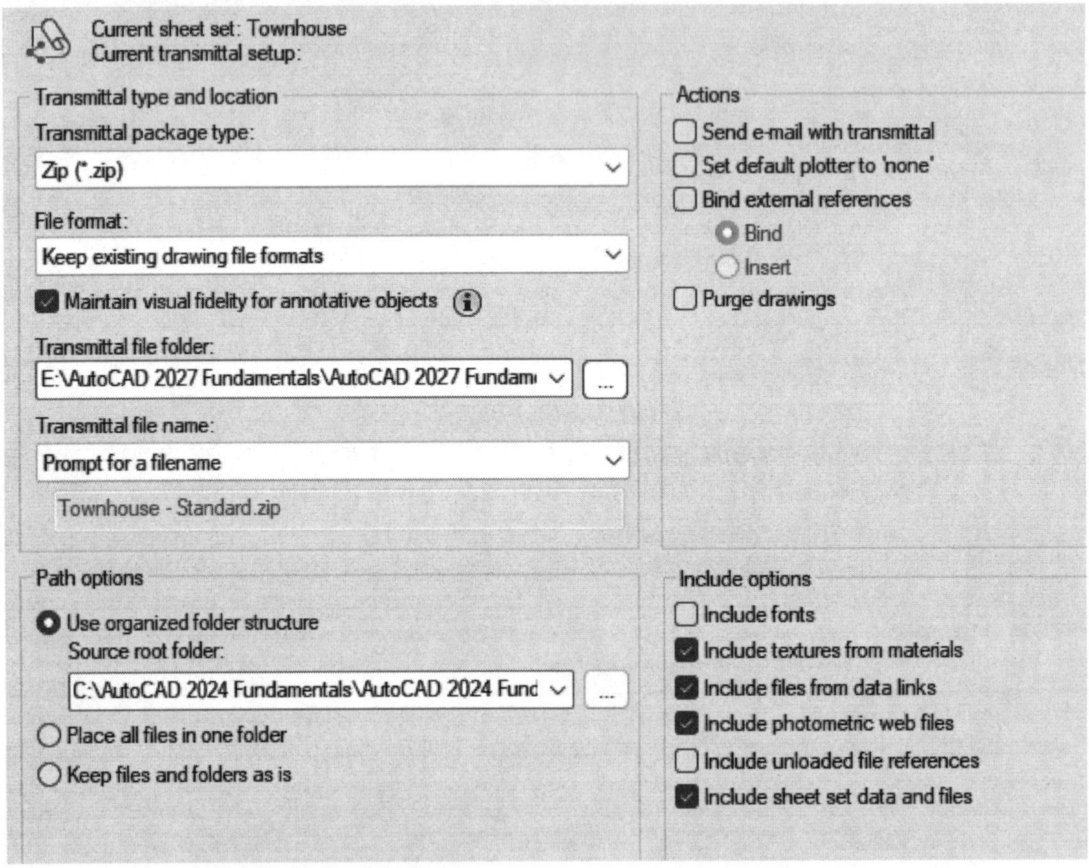

<table>
<tr><td>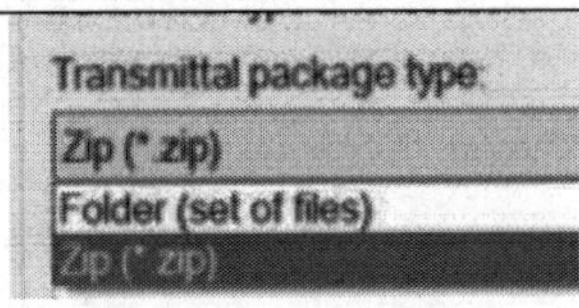
</td><td>Transmittal Package type:
A folder copies all the selected files and references to a folder.
Zip creates a compressed file that can be stored or emailed.</td></tr>
<tr><td>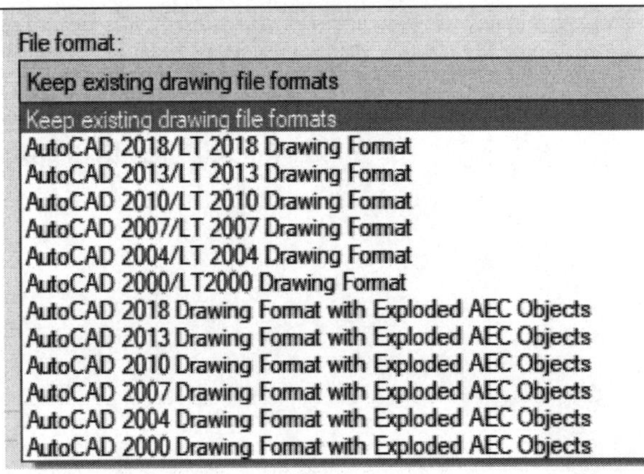
</td><td>File format allows you to save the drawing files to a different AutoCAD version.

This is useful when working with an outside party that is working on an older version of AutoCAD.</td></tr>
</table>

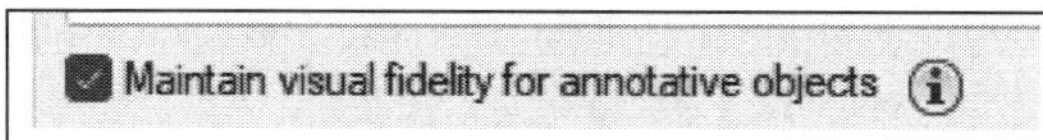	Visual Fidelity allows you to maintain visual fidelity for annotative objects when viewed in earlier releases.
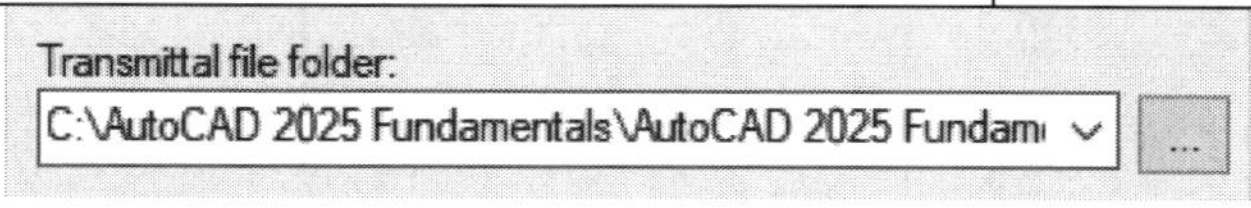	Specify the location to store the eTransmittal file or folder.
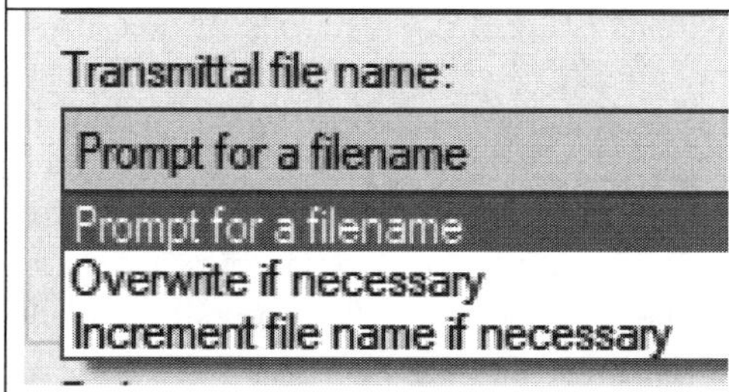	Prompt for a filename allows the user to input a filename. Overwrite if necessary allows AutoCAD to overwrite existing files in the specified folder or an existing zip file. Increment file name if necessary allows AutoCAD to add an identifier so you can track the version of eTransmittal file created.
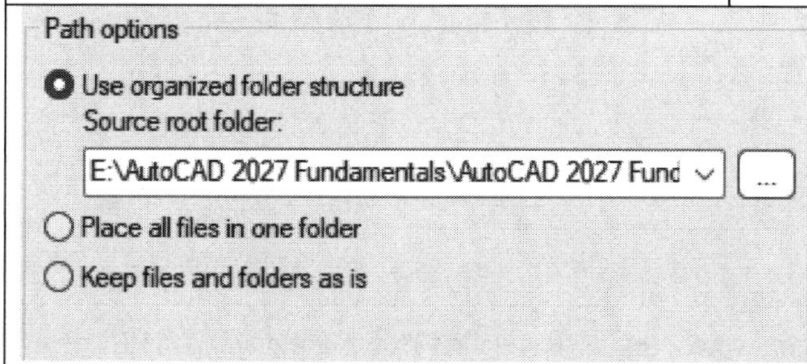	Path options allows you to control how the files are stored. You can "flatten" the file structure or, if you are using sub-folders, you can maintain the file directory structure.
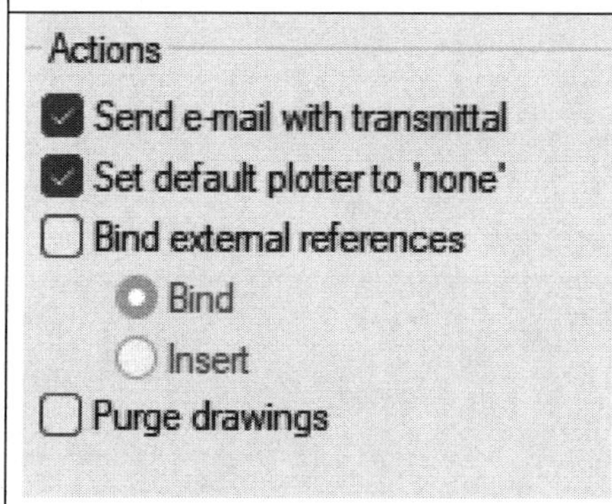	Send e-mail with transmittal will bring up your default email application to allow you to automatically attach the zip file to an email. Set default plotter to 'none' is a good practice as it is unlikely that the recipient of the transmittal package uses the same printer as you do. If you bind external references, they are included in the eTransmittal and exploded. If you insert external references, they are included in the eTransmittal as blocks. If you enable Purge drawings, this removes any unused fonts, layers, blocks, etc., which reduces the file sizes.

<table>
<tr>
<td>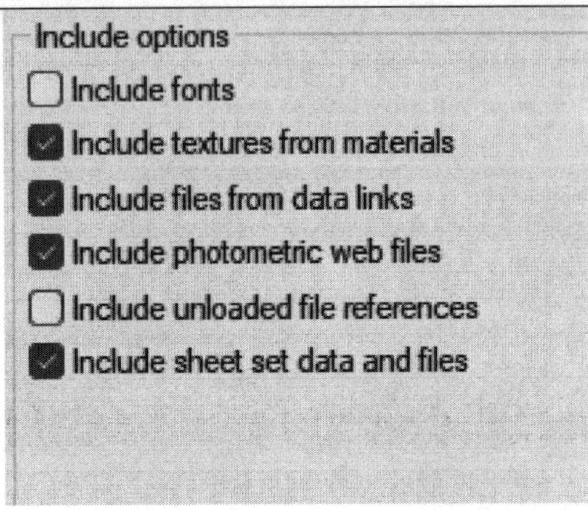
</td>
<td>The include options ensure that the drawings look correct when opened.
Many architectural firms use custom fonts. They don't want outside parties using their fonts. So, this option is disabled by default. AutoCAD will automatically substitute a standard font for any custom fonts.
Include textures from materials ensures any renderings look proper.
Include files from data links would include Excel files used for tables.
Include photometric web files would include lighting information for renderings.
Include unloaded file references would include external references which are not loaded.
Include sheet set data and files would include *.dst files and any files referenced by the sheet set.</td>
</tr>
</table>

General Procedures:

1. Launch the Sheet Set Manager.
2. Select the desired sheet set or create one.
3. Right click on the Sheet Set Name and select the **ETRANSMIT** command.
4. Use an existing transmittal setup or create a new one.

Command Exercise

Exercise 13-11 – eTRANSMIT

Drawing Name: **etransmitdwg**

Estimated Time to Completion: 5 Minutes

Scope

Create a compressed file of drawings and their references.
Use the Sheet Set Manager.

Solution

1. 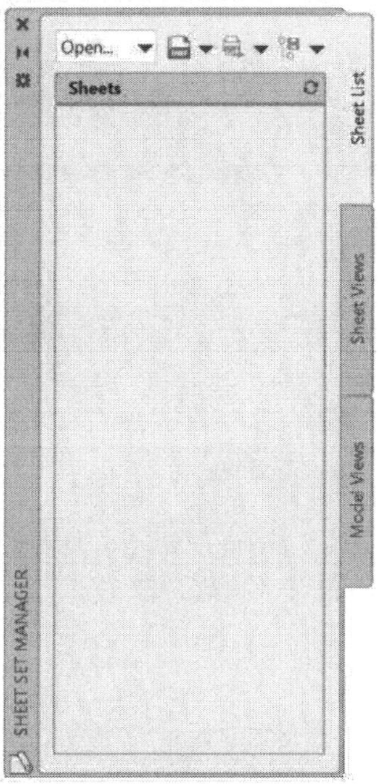

Type **SSM** to launch the Sheet Set Manager.

2. 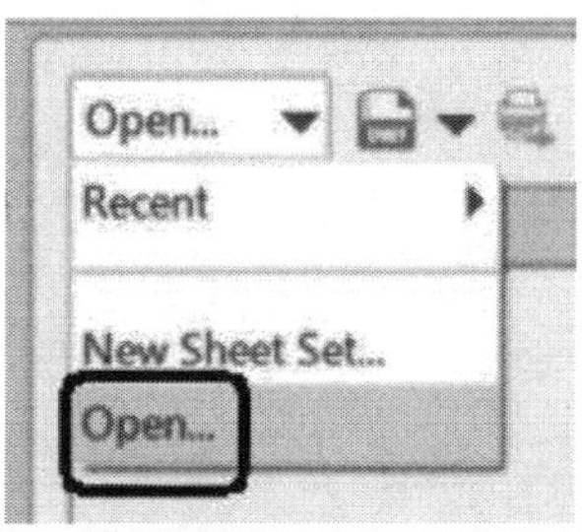

Select **Open** from the drop-down menu to open an existing sheet set.

3. 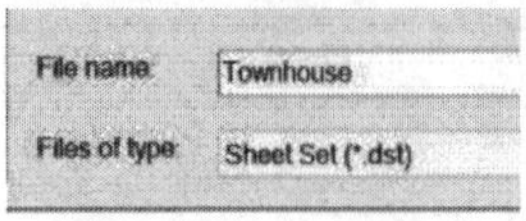

Locate the *Townhouse.dst* file in the files downloaded from the publisher.
Click **Open**.

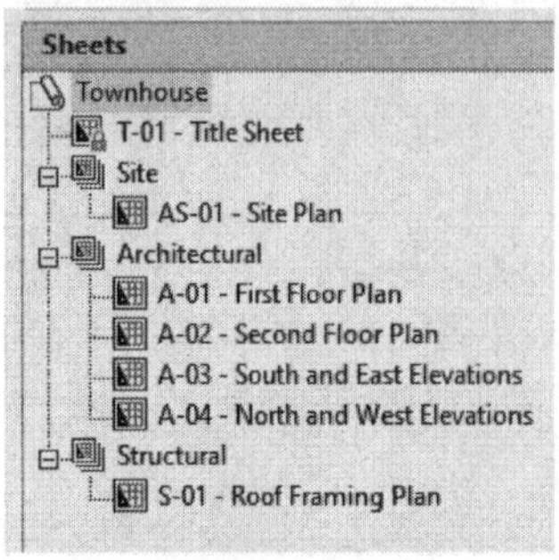

The SSM palette displays the drawings included in the sheet set.

4. 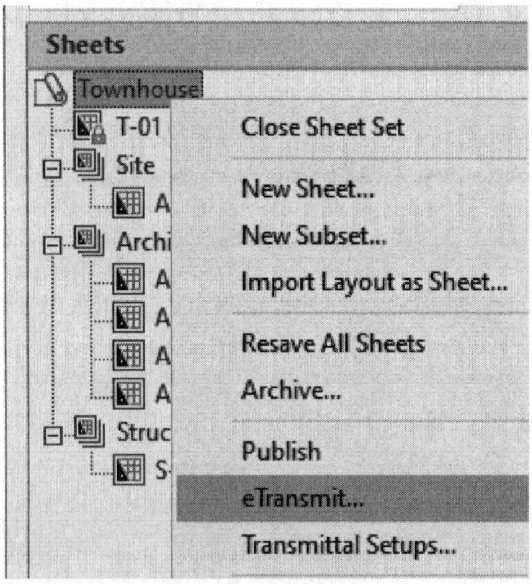

Highlight the Sheet Set Name.
Right click and select **eTransmit**.

5. 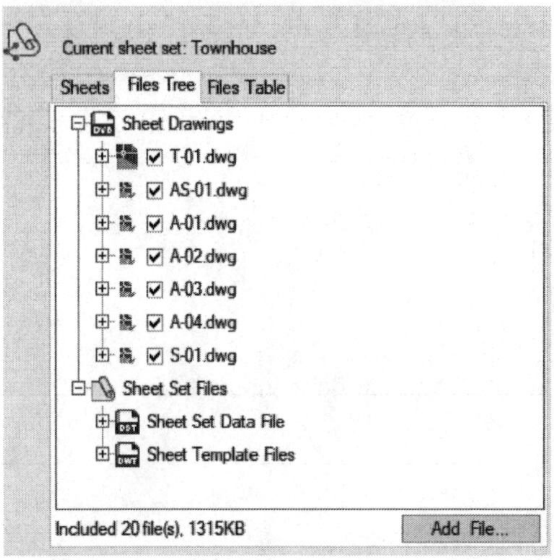

Click the **Files Tree** tab.

Can you determine how many files are included in the transmittal package?

Click **OK**.

6. 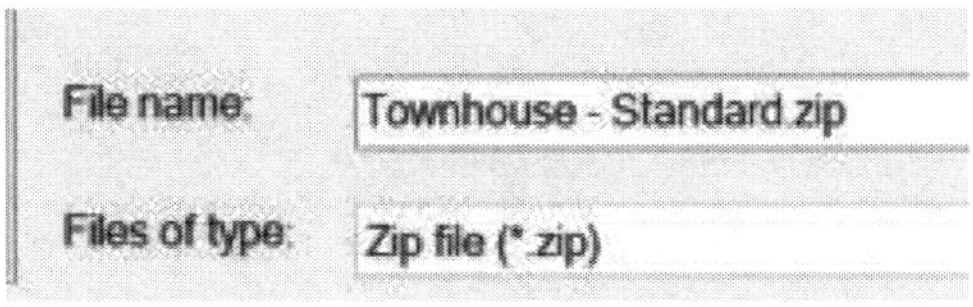

Browse to the folder where you are saving your work.

Click **Save**.

Review Questions

1. To eliminate unused text styles in a drawing, use:
   - ❑ Erase
   - ❑ Purge
   - ❑ Delete
   - ❑ Eliminate

2. **T F** Spell check can be used on fields.

3. **T F** You can only calculate the area of a single object at a time.

4. The PURGE command is located on this ribbon:

   A. Home
   B. Manage
   C. Insert
   D. Collaborate

5. **T F** In order to purge an element, it cannot be in use.

6. **T F** AutoCAD has several language dictionaries available which can be used with SPELLCHECK.

7. **T F** You can add your own jargon words and acronyms to a custom dictionary to be used by SPELLCHECK.

8. **T F** In order to use the DISTANCE command, you must select entire elements, like lines and arcs.

9. **T F** In order to use the QUICKMEASURE tool, you need to select the element to be measured.

Review Answers

1. To eliminate unused text styles in a drawing, use:
   Purge
2. **T F** Spell check can be used on fields.
   False
3. **T F** You can only calculate the area of a single object at a time.
   False
4. The PURGE command is located on this ribbon tab:
   B. Manage
5. **T F** In order to purge an element, it cannot be in use.
   True
6. **T F** AutoCAD has several language dictionaries available which can be used with SPELLCHECK.
   True
7. **T F** You can add your own jargon words and acronyms to a custom dictionary to be used by SPELLCHECK.
   True
8. **T F** In order to use the DISTANCE command, you must select entire elements, like lines and arcs.
   False
9. **T F** In order to use the QUICKMEASURE tool, you need to select the element to be measured.
   False